The Comprehensive Catalogue
of Duet Literature
for Female Voices

Vocal Chamber Duets
with Keyboard Accompaniment
Composed between 1820–1995

Marilyn Stephanie Mercedes Newman

The Scarecrow Press, Inc.
Lanham, Maryland, and London
1999

SCARECROW PRESS, INC.

Published in the United States of America
by Scarecrow Press, Inc.
4720 Boston Way
Lanham, Maryland 20706
http://www.scarecrowpress.com

4 Pleydell Gardens, Folkestone
Kent CT20 2DN, England

British Library Cataloguing in Publication Information Available

Library of Congress Cataloging-in-Publication Data

Newman, Marilyn Stephanie Mercedes, 1954–
    The comprehensive catalogue of duet literature for female voices :
vocal chamber duets with keyboard accompaniment composed between
1820–1995 / Marilyn Stephanie Mercedes Newman.
       p.   cm.
    Includes bibliographical references and index.
    ISBN 0-8108-3647-5 (alk. paper)
    1. Vocal duets with keyboard instrument—19th century—Bibliography.
2. Vocal duets with keyboard instrument—20th century—Bibliography.
I. Title.
ML128.V7N53   1999   99-19510
016.7831'26—dc21   CIP

To Dr. Jack Dane Litten, Professor Emeritus, Southern Connecticut State University, New Haven, CT. A wonderful teacher, friend, and a total musician.

Contents

Tables

Foreword

The joy of singing together has been evidenced throughout the ages by references in plays, depictions in paintings, and a substantial body of notated music that dates back to the Middle Ages. It is an activity that feels necessary to some, like the howling of wolves or the chirping of crickets, and sublime to others, like the sounds of angels or of Romeo and Juliet. It occurs not only in the world of "classical" music, but on street corners in Madagascar, in mountains of Appalachia, and apparently in heaven.

What makes singing together so vital to those of us who are addicted to it? Beyond the general joy of music, it is the feeling of belonging, the challenge of leading, the occasional competitive gesture, the thrill of telling a story, the wonder of how it will all turn out, and the indescribable sensation that takes hold when energies mesh.

Like many others, I have been hooked on singing since childhood. In fact in grade-school, I wanted nothing more than to be accepted into the boys' choir. Choral experiences of the teenage years led to ensemble and solo singing during and since college. I pity those who have not had this interest and these opportunities. And I hope the current volume will break ground toward a renaissance of singing together. It opens our eyes to more than eight thousand pieces in the past two centuries alone. Hopefully it will be the springboard for further research and scavenger hunts. Many of the printed scores prove difficult to find at present, but because of this volume, they may indeed be available once the next few steps have been taken.

Those of us who perform and teach can begin the search. The song recital has been suffering a slow death, but I believe it can be resuscitated by intriguing programming and true chamber settings. Many believe that the *Lied* is indeed the most intimate and expressive form of chamber music. Just one step away is the chamber vocal duet. The listener is intrigued not only by the rich poetry and beautiful music but by the "match," that is, the interaction between the performers.

This interaction is what really interests me. One needs to sharpen aural and rhythmic skills to be sure, but one also must stand ready to lead and follow, to invent musical gestures on the spot, to respond immediately, to anticipate, to interpret. Often singing duets can be the chorister's first experience without a conductor; it demands a new way of listening that is exciting *and* educational. Singing duets should be part of the operatic specialist's diet to ensure that thoughts, images, and feelings can be expressed without theatrical excess. An abundance of solo and duet repertoire appeared in the nineteenth century because lyric poets, inspired to a great extent by their conceptions of folk poetry, wrote from their individual hearts. Composers were drawn to these intimate statements. We as performers and teachers can learn much from the new world they created.

My thanks to Marilyn Newman for providing an entrance into this world.

Richard Lalli
Associate Professor, Yale School of Music
Yale University, New Haven, Connecticut

Introduction

The area of duet literature for female voices is not well known by many musicians, including singers and voice teachers. Although I have accompanied many singers over the years, not many of the works I have performed have been for this medium.

When I learned of Dr. Marilyn Newman's work in this area, I immediately became interested, for there was a body of literature I hardly knew at all and I wanted to know more about this fascinating genre.

Imagine my great surprise when I learned that Dr. Newman had put together a catalogue of over eight thousand duet works that could be used by female voices! This is a staggering accomplishment in itself and she surely must be congratulated to have undertaken this project.

This catalogue is a superb piece of work that makes available information covering a great body of mostly unknown vocal literature. Duet repertoire can be enjoyed by singers, accompanists and the audience. Singing duets can be as much fun as playing duets on the piano or on two pianos. There is frequently less "stage fright" when two are involved, and one is not the soloist, particularly in the case of novice performers.

This information is also of value to historians, who may be surprised at the number of vocal duets composed by many well-known and lesser-known composers.

Singers, voice teachers, coaches, and accompanists should be overjoyed with the contents of this catalogue. Take the time to read carefully the opening chapters; there is a wealth of information here. The catalogue itself is a gold mine. May it help to bring more of this beautiful repertoire to life, not only for singers, teachers, coaches and accompanists, but hopefully to audiences around the world.

Maurice Hinson
Professor of Piano, School of Church Music
Southern Baptist Theological Seminary
Lexington, Kentucky

Preface

Vocal literature consists not only of works for solo voice, but of a great body of ensemble literature, particularly the vocal chamber duet for female voices. Much of this genre includes accompaniment of piano (or organ, harmonium) or is *a cappella*. Most of these duets were composed during the nineteenth and the early part of the twentieth centuries. In addition to providing aesthetic merit, chamber vocal duets are valuable for pedagogical reasons: they can enhance the skills required for vocal training and musicianship, including ensemble and blend that cannot otherwise be accomplished by the exclusive study of solo singing.

Performers and vocal teachers often recognize the value of this vast genre, but a common complaint is that duet literature is difficult to procure. Many vocal catalogues do not specify duet literature, and existing catalogues and appendices addressing duet literature have been limited. A major requirement enabling location is to have knowledge of the composer, the exact title, the opus or piece number, and the publisher. The purpose of this comprehensive catalogue is to provide interested parties with a central source listing composers and titles of works, and including information pertaining to specified voice parts and publishers. Duets are listed that are otherwise unspecified in anthologies, except by examination. Some of the works listed are out of print. However, the information enables one to search in libraries, or to obtain authorized photocopies from publishers. Additionally, many publishers are currently reprinting out of print works. Having this knowledge is the best way to access these works.

This comprehensive catalogue was developed by examining nonspecific catalogues of printed literature from the nineteenth and twentieth centuries, and identifying pertinent duet pieces. Duets are also included from private collections that have not previously appeared in other catalogues or listings.

In this catalogue, works are listed alphabetically by composer, by title of the work, and include opus or piece number, voices specified, accompaniment if other than piano, and comments significant to the work. Appendices list composers, publishers, and the contents of number of pertinent and available anthologies. The appendix also lists cross references that specify voice types, language of work, keyboard accompaniment type, or *a cappella*. An Index of Song Titles provides an alphabetical listing of the music by title, with reference to specific entries in the catalogue.

This catalogue contains eight thousand eight hundred entries representing over two thousand composers. It will provide singers, music students, teachers, and vocal coaches with information that will aid in the procurement of specific chamber duet literature for female voices.

Every attempt has been made to ensure the accuracy of the information in this catalogue. There are aspects of the information, such as the identity of certain composers, that remain unanswerable at the time of this writing. It is the hope of the author that what is known will prove to be of value, and will lead others to seek the complete answers. It is a never-ending process.

Acknowledgments

This book could not be complete without my thanks given to the many people who contributed their assistance in a variety of ways.

The most thanks to my husband Norman Hall, who not only has rehearsed and performed the music, but has followed me on my trail of research. He has carried books and bags to the far corners of the world: from New York to New Haven, from Pennsylvania to London and Vienna.

Special thanks also to the upper voice in the duet partnership *Duetto Cantabile*, Kathryn Thomas, who willingly sings anywhere and anytime. Additional thanks goes to Kathryn for her computer expertise, and her ability to translate program manuals with the greatest of ease.

Thanks and appreciation to my friend Dr. Eileen Hunt, Minister of Music, Greens Farms Church, Westport, CT, who patiently listened to my project designs and helped me get them into a logical order.

Many thanks to the various educators who have influenced me and allowed me to develop my interests: Dr. Lee Pogonowski, Columbia University Teachers College, my doctoral advisor; Mary Mack, Hartt School, University of Hartford, my voice teacher and friend; to Dr. Jack Litten, Professor Emeritus, Southern Connecticut State University, my first voice teacher; Willard Pierce of New York City, my voice teacher for five years; and Dr. Richard Lalli, Yale University, coach, friend, and fellow art song enthusiast.

Thanks and appreciation is given to Dr. Maurice Hinson, Professor of Church Music, Southern Baptist Theological Seminary, Louisville, KY, who listened to my research problems, offered sound advice, and who has provided marvelous models for this type of research.

Special thanks for professional help goes to Glendower Jones, Publisher and Head of Classical Vocal Reprints, who supplied extremely valuable information directly applicable to this research. Additionally, he opened his extensive library to feed my curiosity and interest.

Thanks also to Jay Stevens and Caroline Murphy of Foundry Music Company, New Haven, for their invaluable assistance in locating scores, catalogues, and reference books, and lending me space in their store in which to work.

Many thanks to Dr. Mark Brombaugh, Director of Music, United Church on the Green, New Haven, for additional computer advice and recommendations for creating cross-referencing tables.

Special thanks also to the staff of the following libraries: Yale University Music Library, Allen Music Library of the Hartt School (University of Hartford), Westminster Choir College, and Milbank and Dodge libraries of Columbia University.

To all of the many unnamed people who offered assistance in libraries and music shops, in the transliteration of Russian titles, and who helped with computer advice, many thanks.

M. S. M. N.

Abbreviations

Publisher abbreviations (variable depending on source), definitions, information, and addresses, if known, are listed in appendix F, pages 429-444.

ABBREVIATION	DEFINITION	ABBREVIATION	DEFINITION
A	alto	i.	in (German "in")
acap	a cappella	inst.	instrumental
accomp.	accompaniment	Ice.	Icelandic, Iceland
a.k.a.	also known as	inc.	includes, including
Amer.	American	It.	Italian
Anth.	anthology	Japn.	Japanese
arr.	arranged	Kbd	keyboard
ASR	*Art of the Song Recital*	Lang.	language
		Lat.	Latin
attr.	attributed	med.	medium
Austral.	Australian	MS	mezzo-soprano
avail.	available	MSN	Marilyn S. Newman (personal library)
B	bass		
BBC	*British Broadcasting Corporation*	NATS	*National Association of Teachers of Singing*
Belg.	Belgian	Nor.	Norwegian
Br	baritone	OP #	opus number (or piece number)
Brit.	British		
ca.	circa	opt.	optional
CHAL	*Challier Katalog*	orch.	orchestra(l)
coll.	collection	org	organ
comp.	composed, composer	pf	pianoforte
compi.	compiled	Pol.	Polish
ContraA	Contralto	Polyn.	Polynesian
CVMP	*Classical Vocal Music in Print*	poss.	possibly
		prob.	probably
Czech	Czech	pub.	published
Dan.	Danish	REC	record number
DTS	dates	Russ.	Russian
Dial.	Dialect	S	soprano
Dut.	Dutch	sacr.	sacred
Ed.	edition	Serb.-Croat.	Serbo-Croatian
Eng.	English	Span.	Spanish
et al.	and others	SRC	Source
f.	für (German "for")	SVD	sacred vocal duets
Finn.	Finnish	Swed.	Swedish
fl.	flourished	T	tenor
Fr.	French	tr.	translation
Grmn.	German	translit.	transliteration
harm	harmonium	u.	und (German "and")
Hebr.	Hebrew	Unspec.	unspecified
Hung.	Hungarian	v.	voices

ABBREVIATION	DEFINITION	ABBREVIATION	DEFINITION
Var.	various	vol(s).	volume(s)
VCD	vocal chamber duets	w/	with
VCG	voicing	w/o	without
vln	violin	Welsh	Welsh

CHAPTER 1

The Need for a Comprehensive Duet Catalogue

Duet vocal literature has proved to be one of singing's best-kept secrets. At some point in their performing lives, singers, whether professional or student, voice teachers, accompanists, and coaches will encounter an anthology of vocal duets and pursue a limited study of this genre. Often the results of the collaboration prove to be of great value, not only aesthetically but for pedagogical reasons. Art song literature for the duet vocal ensemble, although widely available as a genre has been largely neglected in comparison to solo vocal literature and vocal ensemble literature from opera. Duets provide many positive aspects. They offer variety both in vocal color and in programming, providing interest for performers and listeners alike. Additionally, they can serve as an appropriate medium for pedagogical study for students of singing, as well as accompanists and coaches who work with singers. Duet vocal literature is a great alternative to either choral or solo singing, and possesses unique properties that should not be neglected.

Voice teachers and singers frequently express a common complaint: that locating information about duet vocal literature is limited and difficult. Common methods of location are by chance and by word of mouth. Few resources are available that give the singer or teacher a reference to finding vocal literature specifically addressing the vocal duet. Those that do make the attempt are far from comprehensive or are not widely known to the general public. Music researchers who wish to acquire knowledge of the total output of specific composers may not find or be aware of vocal duets because of the lack of comprehensive references addressing the genre. This illustrates the need for a resource catalogue that will serve to provide a solution to this problem.

It is necessary to qualify terms at the onset of this work that pertain to classical vocal literature. The term *art song* as defined in *The New Grove Dictionary of Music and Musicians* is: "A song of serious artistic purpose written by a professional composer, as opposed to a folk song. The term is more often applied to solo than to polyphonic songs and embraces the nineteenth-century lied and *mélodie*."[1] An almost identical definition is expressed by Willi Apel.[2] To Ned Rorem the term *art song* typically applies to "a musical setting of a lyric poem for one voice with piano accompaniment. The setting is by a specific composer, as distinct from, say, an aria that is part of a whole; and is distinct from approximately noted so-called popular songs."[3] Rorem expands this term to include duet and terzet literature, which he himself has composed.[4] His nine-movement duet cycle *Gloria* for soprano, mezzo soprano, and piano was composed as "a gift to all singers who bemoan the lack of duets."[5] The term *art song* will be employed to include duet literature in this catalogue.

The term *vocal chamber duet* will be used to define that literature written for two voices, and that is not part of larger oratorio works or opera. In the *Harvard Dictionary of Music,* Apel defines the "vocal duet" as a two-voiced work with accompaniment, and those without accompaniment are called "unaccompanied vocal duets."[6] Taylor and Gatty use the term "vocal duet" to indicate two-voiced music with or without accompaniment.[7] This definition is also shared by Tilmouth.[8] Corre Berry, in her dissertation and later in her publications, uses the term "'vocal chamber duet'...for two voices with or without instrumental accompaniment and intended for performance by a single musician to each part; they are further restricted to works written primarily for performance in a room or chamber."[9] Since Berry's definition is in keeping within the parameters of this research, the term "vocal chamber duet" will be employed here.

THE PRACTICAL PROBLEMS OF PROCUREMENT

This study has focused on duets written for, or potentially usable by, female vocal combinations, although the problems of location of materials and the benefits of study are global for all vocal combinations in this genre and for other vocal chamber ensembles as well. Vocal chamber duet literature, although reasonably prolific, is often difficult to locate. Essentially, one must be aware of it before one can find it. Avey states that delays can occur in ordering or locating any music as the result of having inadequate information when placing an order. "Delays can occur when your dealer or his supplier must research this information."[10] Lack of information and subsequent delays can create difficulties in exploring the literature leading to its neglect.

A discussion with Jay Stevens, Manager, Foundry Music Inc. New Haven, CT, sheds light on the problem of this lack of information: Often the consumer must have very specific knowledge of what is desired before he/she can search for it, and even so, if the output of the composer in this genre is limited, it is extremely difficult to locate. Such knowledge includes exact title (original language), opus numbers, and often a prior knowledge of the publisher.[11]

Glendower Jones, music dealer, publisher and founder of Classical Vocal Reprints, a company that specializes in the location and the republishing[12] of obscure vocal works, has been extremely helpful and encouraging in pursuing practical solutions to this problem. He has provided the author with a number of rare resources. In his view, the problem of procurement and knowledge of vocal chamber duets is widespread. According to Jones, scholarship in this area has mainly been restricted to narrow library study rather than broader research into acquisition or basic knowledge of the works and their availability.[13]

Generally speaking, research up to the present (including dissertations and articles on chamber duets) has focused mainly on analysis and historical reviews of the works, rather than addressing the problems of practical location. Much research has dealt with music earlier than the dates stipulated in this catalogue.

A study and compilation of identifiable volumes of this specific type of vocal literature can offer a valuable resource to the singer, vocal student, teacher, historian, accompanist, and coach by creating a central catalogue that will provide as much information as possible beneficial to identification and to location. This information includes the composer-output in this genre, exact names of works (as they appear in the published form), opus numbers when provided, and publisher names. A number of the works are currently out of print, and many of the nineteenth-century publishers are now out of business. However, access to this kind of detailed information will benefit the interested party in a search for specific copies in libraries, or book handlers that specialize in out of print manuscripts. Additionally, a significant number of publishers prepare and release obscure and formerly unknown copies of works for purchase as an ongoing process.

Specific pedagogical benefits of pursuing the study of duet vocal literature are addressed in detail in chapter 3: Pedagogical Advantages of Studying the Vocal Chamber Duet—Who Can Benefit? (pages 7-9). Briefly, a catalogue of this genre will give the student, teacher, performer, historian, coach, accompanist, and enthusiast access to substantial knowledge of a largely ignored body of literature that can significantly enhance the study of vocal literature, both aesthetically and pedagogically. In addition, it will provide historians with a resource guide to works of composers that may otherwise be overlooked.

PURPOSE AND OBJECTIVES OF THIS STUDY

The purpose of this research is to provide the interested party with a comprehensive list of vocal chamber duet literature for female singers with an accessible accompaniment (mainly piano). Accessible in this sense means accompaniment that is the most feasible for singers to use, the most common collaboration for singers at all levels of proficiency to encounter and employ. Exceptions to this collaboration include works for vocal duet and organ (or harmonium), or unaccompanied works.

This research focuses on duet literature for any combination of female voices. Precise combinations appearing in this study are listed in appendix C: Entries Indexed by Voice Specification (pages 403-412). A partial list includes: soprano and soprano, soprano and alto, soprano and mezzo soprano, alto and alto, two female voices, and vocal combinations unspecified as to gender, such as two high or two low voices.

Several objectives have ensured that the purpose was met. The first objective was to conduct research and collect materials that generated information leading to a compilation of the body of literature. The second objective was to create a catalogue/database that will allow one to obtain knowledge and information about this genre. The third was to examine the pedagogical applications of vocal chamber duet literature, keeping in mind that this repertoire provides benefits for vocal studies as well as for artistic and programming reasons.

There is no way to include all of the published works in the world, although eight thousand eight hundred entries of published works meeting the criteria stipulated in the purpose of this research fulfills the definition of comprehensive. The reference volumes from which the compiled information was drawn are those that document published works. In addition, unlisted published works were located and included. They represent a cross-section of available works worldwide. While there exist a number of works currently unavailable to the global market, every attempt has been made to include a wide cross-section of works. This is identified in terms of published languages (twenty-three in number), the global distribution of publishers,[14] and the representation of the composers (over two thousand).

NOTES

1. "Art Song," *The New Grove Dictionary of Music and Musicians*, vol. 1, Stanley Sadie, ed. (London: Macmillan, 1980), 646.

2. W. Apel, "Art Song," *Harvard Dictionary of Music,* (Cambridge, MA: Harvard University Press, 1972), 60.

3. Ned Rorem, "The American art song: dead or alive?" *Opera News* (August 1996): 15.

4. Ned Rorem, composer, letter to author, 11 July 1996.

5. Ned Rorem, brochure, *Ariel, Gloria, King Midas.* Phoenix label, PHCD 126. 1995. Compact disc.

6. W. Apel, "Vocal Duet," *Harvard Dictionary of Music,* 248.

7. F. Taylor and N. C. Gatty, "Duet," *Grove's Dictionary of Music and Musicians Fifth Edition,* vol. II, Eric Blom, ed. (London: Macmillan, 1955), 792.

8. M. Tilmouth, "Duet," *The New Grove Dictionary of Music and Musicians*, vol. 5, Stanley Sadie, ed. (London: Macmillan, 1980), 673.

9. Corre Ivy Berry, "A Study of the Vocal Chamber Duet Through the Nineteenth Century" (Ph.D. diss., North Texas State University, 1974), 1.

10. D. H. Avey, "Why can't I get the music?" *The NATS Journal,* (September/October 1988): 17.

11. Jay Stevens, Manager, The Foundry Music Company, Audubon Street, New Haven, CT, conversation with author, 15 June 1996.

12. Although a number of publishers, particularly those from the nineteenth century have gone out of business or have become absorbed into other companies, companies that specialize in republication, such as Classical Vocal Reprints (see number 13) can aid in the location of these materials. There are also references that trace the history of music publishers and printers (see bibliography for Krummel, D. W. and Sadie, S.).

13. Glendower Jones, Publisher/Dealer, Classical Vocal Reprints, 3253 Cambridge Avenue 2nd Floor, Riverdale NY, conversation with author, 17 October 1996.

14. Although a number of the publishers no longer exist, companies that specialize in republications can aid in location. Specific references by Krummel and Sadie, and Lenneberg (see bibliography) can assist in tracking the history of extinct publishers. Additionally, publisher availability and distributors may be found in the most up-to-date listings by seeking information on the Internet.

CHAPTER 2

A Brief Overview of the Historical Aspects of the Vocal Chamber Duet

The vocal chamber duet has been prevalent throughout the history of song. A brief discussion about its function, style, and historical metamorphosis will be included here.

Vocal chamber duets have reflected the musical tastes of their times, sharing the musical characteristics of their period as any other music from a specific era. Berry has written extensively on the history of the vocal chamber duet, which was the basis of her dissertation. She details the musical function of the compositions from about the early seventeenth century through the nineteenth century.

The early duets were primarily imitative of instrumental works, often consisting of homophonic and polyphonic sections, and followed the dominating Italian style of the period. Voices were essentially treated instrumentally.[1]

The soprano-alto (or soprano-mezzo soprano) ensemble has been featured throughout the history of Western music as a favored ensemble; this vocal combination appearing more frequently than any other vocal pairing. Many Baroque operas popularized the combination of the treble voices, although initially the vocal duo consisted primarily of *castrati*. This vocal pairing was carried over into the non-operatic world in the sacred and secular cantatas. Composers such as Monteverdi, Purcell, and Handel all wrote for this genre, in both the opera and cantata arenas.

Into the Classical period a number of composers, including Johann Christian Bach, composed for this ensemble. According to Berry the domination of Italian music began to decrease with the increased interest in poetry of other languages. There were still a

number of duets written in the Italian manner, such as those of Johann Christian Bach, but during this period folk-song arrangements for two voices emerged.[2] These are represented in the works by Haydn and Beethoven who set folk poetry and folk songs of the British Isles. Most are designated for male voices and are therefore specifically excluded from this research. Several sacred *a cappella* canons of Haydn are included, and within the collections of Beethoven folk-song settings of applicable duets are to be found.

With the outpouring of poetry in the late Classical-early Romantic periods, in combination with the improvement and exploitation of the piano, there came a substantial interest in the art song, or non-operatic vocal music. During the nineteenth century, Italian domination of vocal musical style declined, and the leading countries in vocal music became France and Germany. The *musicale* or *musical soirée* in the home was becoming more regular and more popular. A number of opera composers also delved into non-operatic composition for these homespun musical offerings, including Rossini, Cherubini, Meyerbeer, and Donizetti.[3]

The art song provided a melding of two great art forms: the expressive poem combined with a musical vehicle to convey the emotion. This was indeed a happy union. Many famous German writers, including Goethe, Herder, Schiller and others, "had a lively and often Romantic interest in music."[4] A number of composers, particularly in Germany and its surrounding countries, took advantage of this new medium, and exploited it greatly. These composers include Schubert, who wrote over six hundred songs, Schumann, Brahms, Dvorak, Wolf, Mahler, and many more. There were parallels in other countries such as France, in song composers including Fauré, Debussy, Berlioz, and others. Many of these composers also wrote a number of art songs for vocal chamber duets, although not always for the female voices. During this period the art song became a substantial and distinct genre from operatic music. In fact, it was considered that "solo song could not become a really important branch of composition until it ceased to be a poor relation of opera, and it is significant that none of the great song-writers of the nineteenth century was particularly successful as a composer for the stage."[5] It became a time when art song literature was finally judged for its own distinction. Whether for solo voice or chamber duet, the art song repertoire expanded greatly in the Romantic era. It provided an abundance of unique literature, and continued to exist as a genre into the twentieth century, although its proliferation has ebbed and flowed throughout the periods.

During the nineteenth century there was a staggering amount of duets written. Many were for pedagogical studies (for example vocalises and exercises for ear training) and a significant number written for use by amateurs, particularly voice students. Berry cites that many of these works were composed by a "fairly large number of voice teachers."[6]

During this period, many pieces that did not strictly reflect folk elements were of strophic or modified strophic form of medium range, and composed

for home entertainment. Many of Felix Mendelssohn's and Robert Schumann's duets fall into this category. Dvořák composed twenty-three duets with piano, combining Czech folk poetry with original music. Several of the duets were commissioned by the family of students for whom he taught piano in Prague.[7]

In the process of documenting this literature, it was found that indeed a decline exists in the number of vocal duets being composed in the twentieth century as compared to the nineteenth century. Perhaps, however, this decline is not as Mr. Rorem indicated, supporting his need to compose his *Gloria* as a gift to those who "bemoan the lack of duets."[8] There is clearly no lack of duets. More precisely, there are less being composed in a traditional sense: that is, they don't always use the more accessible accompaniment of piano (or organ, or *a cappella*). A number of works were excluded from this catalogue because they cited voice requirements outside the specified parameters of this research. Also, many were excluded because they require atypical instrumentation or numerous instrumental ensembles, or else specify other and larger vocal combinations outside of the parameters of this research. The novel effects of these works are unquestionably unique, and indeed provide a special timbre. It is unfortunate, however, that works of this type are often impractical and expensive to produce, and this is not in keeping with the purpose of this catalogue.

NOTES

1. C. I. Berry, "The Italian vocal chamber duets of the Baroque period," *The NATS Bulletin* (September/October 1978): 12.

2. ——. *A Study of the Vocal Chamber Duet Through the Nineteenth Century* (Ph.D. diss., North Texas State University, 1974), 142.

3. ——. "Salon duets by operatic composers," *The NATS Bulletin* (September/October 1980): 15.

4. R. M. Longyear, *Nineteenth-Century Romanticism in Music* (Englewood Cliffs, NJ: Prentice-Hall, Inc. 1973), 8.

5. P. Radcliffe, "Germany and Austria," in *A History of Song*, Denis Stevens, ed. (New York: W. W. Norton & Company, 1970), 235.

6. C. I. Berry, "The Italian vocal chamber duets of the Baroque period," 1978: 10.

7. C. Berry, "Airs from the British Isles and airs from Moravian duets incorporating diverse folk materials," *The NATS Bulletin* (November/December 1979): 9.

8. Ned Rorem, brochure, *Ariel, Gloria, King Midas*. Phoenix label, PHCD 126. 1995. Compact disc.

CHAPTER 3

Pedagogical Advantages of Studying the Vocal Chamber Duet— Who Can Benefit?

Singers, both student and professional, as well as teachers and others who work with vocalists can benefit from the study of the vocal chamber duet. In addition, other performers in a variety of musical situations should also consider the benefits of including the study of vocal chamber duets as part of their perpetual education and practice.

Utilizing vocal duets as a teaching tool can be traced back to the Bel Canto era of the eighteenth century. Giambattista Mancini in his famous *Practical Reflections on Figured Singing* written in 1774 states:

> The study of duets is also necessary to accustom the ear to rule intonation with perfection, and to possess oneself of expression, and finally to render one practiced in graduating the voice, so that it is perfectly united to that of his colleague.[1]

These objectives are as valuable today as they were three hundred years ago.

In a more recent volume, Emmons and Sonntag enthusiastically encourage singers to pursue and explore chamber ensemble singing:

> and Doubtless there will come a time in your singing career when the pleasures of collaboration with another singer will entice you. Our advice is: succumb immediately! Using your voice with another voice or two is truly enjoyable; ensemble between voices as compared to voice with instruments, presents new skills to be explored. . .
> A singer who tastes of this literature cannot help but experience a musical and artistic growth. Most especially a young singer will find duets trios, not to mention larger ensembles, an admirable way of trying his wings before an audience with somewhat less personal responsibility.[2]

Berton Coffin wrote extensively on vocal technique and vocal repertoire. He has emphasized the importance of using multiple voices: "Scarcely a studio exists in this country in which two or more good voices are not available. The added vocal line or lines will highlight the listening pleasure of an audience and give valuable ensemble experience to the singers."[3]

Additionally, repertoire should always be viewed as a resource and tool for teaching and developing technique. Christy mentions the pedagogical method, "The Song Approach,"[4] which he supports as a positive method, and, he says that "Most vocal teachers . . . agree that emphasis in study of singing should be primarily on expression and secondarily on technic [sic]."[5] The students use songs as a method to reinforce the technique they are acquiring, while simultaneously learning and interpreting repertoire. Certainly vocal chamber duet literature would apply to "The Song Approach," by enhancing development of the same skills of expression, and by adding the additional dimensions of cooperation, phrasing, balance between two voices, and rapport between singers, all of which contribute to development of musicianship.

For the singing teacher and the vocal student the vocal duet has certain pedagogical applications that make it distinct from the solo song genre. Berry mentions the existence of a number of chamber duets categorized as "'Pedagogical' duets [that] appeared throughout the seventeenth, eighteenth, and nineteenth centuries, forming a class determined primarily by the use for which they were designed."[6] In a later article, Berry discusses the important implications of pedagogical duets, "Voice teachers often overlook an important source of repertoire which can provide desirable variety for recitals and supply useful material for teaching singers."[7] She points out the historical styles of these compositions, from the sixteenth century to the present. Many, collectively called *bicinia*[8] specifying their two-part structure, make use of canon and contrapuntal techniques to develop ear training. There also exist textless duets that function as vocalises.

As Emmons and Sonntag have stated, there is a psychological benefit to singing in an ensemble, particularly for beginning students. The beginner can gain confidence by working with another singer.[9] Also, there is the benefit of exploring ensemble literature, which helps to develop musicianship skills. This can be applied to various areas of musical study.

Knowles writes of the importance of two-voice polyphony in the training of conductors. She states: "Hearing and performing two-voice polyphony is a basic skill for any music student. It is expected that they will be able to demonstrate how two voices move in a polyphonic texture and to hear whether their groups are performing them correctly."[10] She additionally stresses the importance of this medium in developing sight-singing and solfege skills.

Teachers of singing teach more than just vocal technique; music is a collaborative art. There is the responsibility for developing collaborative skills in students of singing. Wooldridge,[11] Kinsey,[12] Abusamra,[13] and Johnson[14] extol the positive attributes of class voice, citing collaboration, team effort, and peer support as key objectives. Kinsey states: "The prime objective of voice teaching is to establish a feeling for and an ear for tone color, both in terms of one's own voice and the voices of others."[15] She has found that group-learning situations reinforce this objective. These aspects are directly applicable to the study and performance of duet literature because of their collaborative nature. Di Natale and Russell support cooperative learning strategies as a model for teaching music: "One ensemble that benefits from the application of cooperative learning principles is the chamber group…chamber groups offer students the opportunity to be responsible for their own music learning experiences."[16] Furthermore, "musicianship can and will develop individually and collectively."[17]

Besides the support and musical development that are benefits of collaboration, there are ways that collaboration can enhance the immersion and enjoyment of the musical performance. Green and Gallwey have written on methods enabling one to attain a level of immersion in music that is so great that "everything is somehow just right—the program and the performance—and we feel caught up in the joy of a composer who loved and died a century or more before our time."[18] They recommend relaxation and awareness steps to reduce "self-inter-ference…the tension in your body, and even the conflicts that were taking place in your head."[19] They claim that sometimes the best performing experiences occur when one is "barely awake (or very relaxed indeed)."[20] Green refers to the piano playing of his cousin, who describes her playing "in this state as 'relaxed' and 'flowing.'"[21] With regard to ensemble playing, Green and Gallwey state that "As a member of a larger groups, we may feel freer to express our musicianship without self-consciousness than we would if our individual playing was spotlighted."[22] While there are specific musical objectives in ensemble situations, there is also the making of music that has to do with self-trust and the trust of others, self-confidence, flexibility, and awareness.

Csikszentmihalyi supports ensemble music (specifically choral in this article, although there are direct parallels in any collaborative musical experience) as an activity in which one can achieve what he refers to as "The Flow Experience."[23] According to Csikszentmihalyi, "when what they [participants in an ensemble] do becomes worth doing for its own sake—it's so enjoyable that you get caught up in it, you want to keep doing it. I call this state of mind 'Flow Experience.'"[24] The nine components Csikszentmihalyi cites as occurring are that (a) goals are clear, (b) feedback is immediate, (c) skills match challenges, (d) concentration is deep, (e) problems are forgotten, (f) control is possible, (g) self-consciousness disappears, (h) the sense of time is altered, and (i) the experience becomes autotelic. Csikszentmihalyi claims that the choral musician can find these components in rehearsal, performance, and score study.[25] Duet singing is a form of ensemble singing, and its benefits are those shared with choral singing, although with more intimacy.

The latter two references emphasize the importance of collaboration as a means to achieve a state of "flow," where one can become so involved in the music that the music transcends the human failings of fear, tension, and self-interference. Duet singing can certainly serve as a vehicle to assist the young, inexperienced singer in developing this level that enhances musicianship and confidence. Furthermore, it can apply to anyone at any level of expertise in which creating a positive musical experience is the most important objective.

SUMMARY

The vocal chamber duet is a vehicle that strengthens the skills of collaboration. These skills include the development of creating nuances, using blend and phrasing that are essential to the give-and-take of performing with others.

For the singer, the vocal chamber duet is both an alternative and an enhancement to solo repertoire. It is a resource that provides variety in programming.

The development of musical skills can be enhanced in a situation of collaborating in the performance of a duet, as much as in any other chamber ensemble group or choir. The skills derived from this type of study and collaboration can strengthen the techniques required in other aspects of music besides singing technique, such as instrumental performance or conducting.

NOTES

1. Giambattista Mancini, *Practical Reflections on Figured Singing* (1774, 1777), Edward Foreman, ed. (Champaign, IL: Pro Musica Press, 1967), 79.

2. S. Emmons and S. Sonntag, *The Art of the Song Recital* (New York: Schirmer Books, 1979), 256.

3. B. Coffin, *Singer's Repertoire. 2nd ed.: Part II Mezzo Soprano and Contralto* (New York: Scarecrow Press, Inc., 1960), 8.

4. V. A. Christy, *Foundations in Singing*, (Dubuque, IA: Wm. C. Brown Company Publishers, 1978), xv.

5. V. A. Christy, *Foundations in Singing*, xv.

6. C. I. Berry, *A Study of the Vocal Chamber Duet Through the Nineteenth Century*, (Ph. D. diss., North Texas State University, 1974), 10.

7. C. Berry, "Duets for pedagogical use," *The NATS Bulletin* (December 1977): 8.

8. *Bicinia*, the plural of bicinium, is a sixteenth-century name, used mainly in Italy and Germany. A bicinium is defined as a composition for voice or instruments in two parts and unaccompanied (see W. Apel, 1972, p. 94).

9. S. Emmons and S. Sonntag, *The Art of the Song Recital*, 256.

10. R. Knowles, "Basic musicianship for future conductors: hearing and performing two-voice polyphony," *Choral Journal* (April 1982): 23.

11. W. Wooldridge, (1971). "Why not class voice?" *The NATS Bulletin* (December 1971): 20-21.

12. B. Kinsey, "Voice class structure and purpose," *The NATS Bulletin* (December 1973): 18-22.

13. W. Abusamra, "Small group vs. individual instruction in the performance studio," *The NATS Bulletin* (May 1978): 37-38.

14. S. O. Johnson, "Group instruction an alternative for freshman voice students," *The NATS Bulletin* (March/April 1979): 20-21.

15. B. Kinsey, "Voice class structure and purpose," 18.

16. J. Di Natale and G. S. Russell, "Cooperative learning for better performance," *Music Educators Journal,* (September 1995): 26.

17. J. Di Natale and G. S. Russell, "Cooperative learning for better performance," 28.

18. B. Green with W. T. Gallwey, *The Inner Game of Music* (Garden City, NY: Anchor Press/Doubleday, 1986), 2.

19. B. Green with W. T. Gallwey, *The Inner Game of Music*, 13.

20. B. Green with W. T. Gallwey, *The Inner Game of Music*, 21.

21. B. Green with W. T. Gallwey, *The Inner Game of Music*, 21.

22. B. Green with W. T. Gallwey, *The Inner Game of Music*, 191.

23. M. Csikszentmihalyi, "Singing and the self: choral music as 'active leisure,'" *Choral Journal* (February 1995): 14.

24. M. Csikszentmihalyi, "Singing and the self," 14.

25. M. Csikszentmihalyi, "Singing and the self," 14.

CHAPTER 4

Existing Bibliographical Sources for Song Literature: A Survey of Available Resources Serves to Define the Problems under Consideration

A number of literature sources were helpful in providing information in several aspects. They are as follows:

Indices and catalogues tend to focus on solo literature or sporadic listings of duet literature.

1. In general, the song indices are limited in their listing of this literature. The "Bible" of music in print, notably *Classical Vocal Music in Print*[1] only lists duet music by its exact title, including anthologies. For example:

    > DUET ALBUM (Morris; Anderson)
    > high solo & med solo, pno BOOSEY
    > [No listing of contents][2].

2. *The Music Buying Guide II,*[3] which focuses on listings by European publishers, lists vocal music by collections, solo, voice and guitar, and voice and instruments. No reference to vocal chamber duet literature (or other vocal ensemble) is included.

3. Music company catalogues may or may not list duet scores. Frequently they may be contained in anthologies with no specific reference to content. These catalogues are specific to the holdings within the company they represent.

References devoted to the cataloguing of vocal and song literature largely focus on solo vocal music.

1. *Classical Vocal Music in Print* (1976) has been explained. Its supplements published in 1986[4] and 1995[5] reflect the same problems.

2. *Song Index*[6] and its supplement[7] list only solo pieces.

3. *Music for the Voice*[8] focuses only on solo literature.

4. *The Singer's Repertoire Part II Mezzo Soprano and Contralto*[9] does provide a selected list of duet vocal music that is largely partnered with soprano. It lists the works by opera, oratorio, cantata, or by the country of the composer's origin. Additionally, it lists the title frequently translated into English, and publisher. It is limited; a select list.

5. *The Art of the Song Recital*[10] also offers a select list of ensemble vocal music. It includes a section, "Voice with other voices," that is listed alphabetically by composer, and provides the publisher.

Although the last two examples are helpful, they are far from comprehensive, and include many materials not appropriate to the parameters of this topic.

Much of the duet literature represented appears randomly and almost untraceable in anthologies. They are often translated into English (both in title and performing text) from their original language, which can cause difficulties in searching specific works.

Existing guides or bibliographies that address duet literature have limitations.

1. The bibliographies by Corre Berry (later Brusse) *Vocal Chamber Duets An Annotated Bibliography,*

published in 1981,[11] and *Sacred Vocal Duets An Annotated Bibliography*, published in 1987[12] are indeed helpful as they include information on publisher, tessitura, range, etc. These bibliographies include duets for various combinations of voices, and are restricted only to works that she was able to locate as published material, either in or out of print at the time of her research.[13] However, they are not comprehensive enough for the voice-types specified in this research, and include a number of reductions and arrangements from the Baroque and Classical periods that would not be included in the focus of this topic.

2. The BBC (British Broadcasting Corporation) in London, England has published a listing of art song music, including a bulletin of duets entitled: *Duets BBC Listing*.[14] This brief volume lists duets by composer, edition, when available, and publisher. It is divided by voice combination type. It lists a number of works by English composers.

3. The most comprehensive guide to this material ever published to date is Ernst Challier's *Grosser Duetten-Katalog*, published in 1898,[15] with supplements added in 1901,[16] 1906,[17] and 1911.[18] This guide contains some fundamental problems: It is outdated, including barely anything of the twentieth century. Also, the greatest difficulty is that the pieces are listed entirely in alphabetical order *by title*. Unless one is trying to pursue a specific title, there is no way to adequately review the full output of works by the composer.

It should be noted that many of the problems of early catalogues are due to the lack of database resources now available to those in the business. Many of the early catalogues were produced by human compilation. A catalogue of the vastness of the Challier series would doubtless have been more efficient if it could have been prepared with the aid of a database computer program.

Additional annotated bibliographies are published that mainly cater to solo voice repertoire:

1. *American Vocal Chamber Music, 1945-1980.*[19] This volume gives one insight into the literature available for this specific topic. It includes ensemble works listed for various combinations of instruments, and focuses largely on solo-voice literature. There is only one possible duet listing that

would fall into the parameters specified by this research, and, in that, it requires two-piano accompaniment.

2. *A Singer's Guide to The American Art Song 1870-1980.*[20] This work provides a fine comprehensive listing of American composers, both men and women, with good biographical material. It focuses only on solo voice literature, and lists a *select* output of works by the composers.

DISSERTATIONS ADDRESSING DUET MATERIAL

Many dissertations addressing duet literature are concerned with historical or theoretical objectives, and the majority are about works prior to the Late Classical/Romantic era. These include the following:

A survey of dissertations covering duet topics:

1. *Soprano-Tenor Chamber Duets of Steffani.*[21]
2. *The Chamber Duets and Trios of Carissimi.*[22]
3. *The Chamber Duets of Agostino Steffani (1654-1728) With Transcriptions and Catalogue.*[23]
4. *The Sacred Vocal Duets of Heinrich Schütz and J. S. Bach: An Introduction and Annotated Listing.*[24]
5. *Italian Secular Duets and Dialogues c. 1600-1643.*[25]

The dissertation by JoAnn Padley Hunt entitled *Analyses of Music for Solo Voice and Percussion, 1950-1990: An Annotated Catalogue of Representative Repertoire*[26] is an exhaustive work providing the reader with a guide and resource of this specific type of vocal literature. Its bibliography of literature served as a model for this research.

The dissertation written by Corre Berry entitled *A Study of the Vocal Chamber Duet Through the 19th Century*[27] surveys duets written over a number of centuries, and with a variety of accompaniments and vocal combinations. This work, written in 1974, was the basis of her later publications (for NATS) previously discussed. Her dissertation is an overview of evolution of the vocal chamber duet, and omits a number of compositions within the dates stated in the parameters of this catalogue (such as the twentieth century). It is outdated in terms of currently available resources and information.

JOURNAL ARTICLES RELATED TO THIS TOPIC ARE APPLICABLE IN SEVERAL RESPECTS

Pedagogical

Coffin[28] supports the use of multiple voices in the study of repertoire. Boytim[29,30] has written on the encouragement of teaching vocal students sacred solo duets as a way to enhance musical development, gain experience in church music, as well as promoting ensemble singing. Knowles[31] promotes hearing and performing two-voiced polyphony as a valuable pedagogical method to enhance musical development, including sight-singing skills and intonation. Several related articles support the benefits of ensemble singing as cooperative learning, including Di Natale and Russell[32] and Csikszentmihalyi.[33]

Articles discussing related techniques applied in choral ensemble singing are pertinent to the pedagogical aspects of studying vocal chamber duet literature: Miller[34] discusses the solo singer in the choral ensemble. Class voice situations are promoted with positive support, some of which explore collaborative literature: Wooldridge,[35] Kinsey,[36] Abusamra,[37] and Johnson.[38]

History and Repertoire

Coffin,[39] previously cited, has promoted the use of ensemble pieces for inclusion in the study of vocal repertoire. Berry[40-44] and Brusse (née Berry, same person)[45] has written articles pertaining to the history of music in this genre, selected opera composers who have written in this genre, as well as possible insights into the choosing of voices to represent certain texts. Timms[46] has explored vocal duets, dividing those with texts chosen for dialogue between two characters from those when the text represents a single idea sung by both voices. Berry[47] has also addressed this issue. Rorem[48] has written an article in support of the American art song, in which the basic information has application to this topic.

Certain choral directors have considered duet literature as a resource for small choral ensembles, including Shafferman[49] and Wolverton.[50]

Acquisition

Avey[51] wrote an article offering brief suggestions for singers on how to research specifics of a song in order to aid in its acquisition. Its information is extremely limited as applied to this topic. However, it does identify the problem.

SUMMARY

The survey of related literature indicates a void in references that can assist the interested party in the clues necessary to the procurement of vocal chamber duet repertoire for female voices. Current existing references largely concentrate on solo repertoire, and although attempts have been made to address vocal chamber ensemble literature, these are often far less than comprehensive in supplying information necessary for identification and procurement. These references have frequently omitted certain resources that provide a more comprehensive source of information.

Interest in duet literature for scholarly research has primarily concentrated on early works prior to the dates specified in this proposal.

Existing research directly supports chamber vocal ensemble singing as a necessary part of both vocal and non-vocal musical study. Additionally, a number of positive benefits and techniques cited that support choral ensemble singing can easily be applied to the study of chamber vocal duet literature.

The insights gained through this research indicate that there is a clear need for a catalogue of this valuable literature. It is hoped that the information obtained will prove beneficial for singers, both professionals and students, voice teachers, accompanists, coaches, and historians. The fact that there have been so many duets composed over a great span of vocal music history is a testament to its viability as a genre. In both performance and in practice, duets provide both aesthetic and pedagogical benefits.

NOTES

1. T. R. Nardone, ed. *Classical Vocal Music in Print,* (Philadelphia: Musicdata, Inc., 1976).

2. T. R. Nardone, ed. *Classical Vocal Music in Print,* 150.

3. *The Music Buying Guide II.* (Valley Forge, PA: European American Music Distributors Corporation, 1991).

4. G. S. Eslinger and F. M. Daugherty, eds., *Classical Vocal Music in Print 1985 Supplement Music-In-Print Series, vol. 4s.* (Philadelphia: Musicdata, Inc., 1986).

5. F. M. Daugherty, ed., *Classical Vocal Music in Print 1995 Supplement Music-In-Print Series, vol. 4t.* (Philadelphia: Musicdata, Inc., 1995).

6. M. E. Sears, *Song Index An Index to More Than 12000 Songs in 177 Song Collections Comprising 262 Volumes* (New York: The H. W. Wilson Company, 1926).

7. ——. *Song Index Supplement An Index to More Than 7000 Songs in 104 Song Collections Comprising 124 Volumes,* (New York: The H. W. Wilson Company, 1936).

8. S. Kagen, *Music for the Voice* (Bloomington, IN: Indiana University Press, 1968).

9. B. Coffin, *Singer's Repertoire, 2nd ed.: Part II Mezzo Soprano and Contralto* (New York: Scarecrow Press, Inc., 1960).

10. S. Emmons and S. Sonntag, *The Art of the Song Recital* (New York: Schirmer Books, 1979).

11. C. I. Berry, *Vocal Chamber Duets An Annotated Bibliography* (Jacksonville, FL: The National Association of Teachers of Singing, Inc., 1981).

12. C. B. Brusse, *Sacred Vocal Duets An Annotated Bibliography* (Jacksonville, FL: The National Association of Teachers of Singing, Inc., 1987).

13. C. I. Berry, *Vocal Chamber Duets An Annotated Bibliography*, ix.

14. *Duets BBC Listing* (London, England: The British Broadcasting Corporation, 1975).

15. E. Challier, *Grosser Duetten-Katalog* (Giessen: Ernst Challier's Selbstverlag, 1898).

16. ——. *Erster Nachtrag zu Grosser Duetten-Katalog* (Giessen: Ernst Challier's Selbstverlag, 1901).

17. ——. *Zweiter Nachtrag zu Grosser Duetten-Katalog* (Giessen: Ernst Challier's Selbstverlag, 1906).

18. ——. *Dritter Nachtrag zu Grosser Duetten-Katalog* (Giessen: Ernst Challier's Selbstverlag, 1911).

19. P. Lust, *American Vocal Chamber Music, 1945-1980* (Westport, CT: Greenwood Press, 1985).

20. V. E. Villamil, *A Singer's Guide to The American Art Song 1870-1980* (Metuchen, NJ: The Scarecrow Press, Inc., 1993).

21. C. W. Raridon, *Soprano-Tenor Chamber Duets of Steffani* (D.M.A. diss., University of Iowa, 1972).

22. I. M. Buff, *The Chamber Duets and Trios of Carissimi* (Ph.D. diss., University of Rochester, 1973).

23. C. R. Timms, *The Chamber Duets of Agostino Steffani (1654-1728) With Transcriptions and Catalogue* (Ph.D. diss., University of London, England, 1976).

24. L. L. Bailey, *The Sacred Vocal Duets of Heinrich Schütz and J. S. Bach: An Introduction and Annotated Listing* (D.M.A. diss., Southern Baptist Theological Seminary, 1976).

25. E. J. Whenham, *Italian Secular Duets and Dialogues c. 1600-1643* (Ph.D. diss., Oxford University, Oxford, England, 1979).

26. J. P. Hunt, *Analyses of Music for Solo Voice and Percussion, 1950-1990: An Annotated Catalogue of Representative Repertoire* (Ed.D. diss., Teachers College, Columbia University, 1992).

27. C. I. Berry, *A Study of the Vocal Chamber Duet Through the Nineteenth Century* (Ph.D. diss., North Texas State University, 1974).

28. B. Coffin, "Repertoire and the singer," *The Bulletin* (May 15, 1960): 8-9.

29. J. F. Boytim, "Why neglect the sacred solo duet?" *The NATS Bulletin* (February/March 1972): 13-37.

30. ——. "Duet literature for the Christmas season," *The NATS Bulletin* (October 1976): 13-45.

31. R. Knowles, "Basic musicianship for future conductors: hearing and performing two-voice polyphony," *Choral Journal* (April 1982): 23-25.

32. J. Di Natale and G. S. Russell, "Cooperative learning for better performance," *Music Educators Journal* (September 1995): 26-28.

33. M. Csikszentmihalyi, "Singing and the self: choral music as 'active leisure,'" *Choral Journal* (February 1995): 13-19.

34. R. Miller, "The solo singer in the choral ensemble," *Choral Journal* (March 1995): 31-36.

35. W. Wooldridge, "Why not class voice?" *The NATS Bulletin* (December 1971): 20-21.

36. B. Kinsey, "Voice class structure and purpose," *The NATS Bulletin* (December 1973): 18-22.

37. W. Abusamra, "Small group vs individual instruction in the performance studio," *The NATS Bulletin* (May 1978): 37-38.

38. S. O. Johnson, "Group instruction an alternative for freshman voice students," *The NATS Bulletin* (March/April 1979): 20-21.

39. B. Coffin, "Repertoire and the singer," (1960).

40. C. Berry, "Duets for pedagogical use," *The NATS Bulletin* (December 1977): 8-12.

41. ——. "The Italian vocal chamber duets of the Baroque period," *The NATS Bulletin* (September/October 1978): 12-18.

42. ——. "Airs from the British Isles and airs from Moravian duets incorporating diverse folk materials," *The NATS Bulletin* (November/December 1979a): 8-20.

43. ——. "The dialogue duet: 1600-1900," *The Music Review,* XL, no. 4: (1979b): 272-284.

44. ——. "Salon duets by operatic composers," *The NATS Bulletin* (September/October 1980): 15-17.

45. C. B. Brusse, "The relationship between poetic structure and musical structure in selected vocal duets," *The NATS Journal* (March/April 1987): 20-25.

46. C. Timms, "Revisions in Steffani's chamber duets," *Proceedings of the Royal Musical Association*, xcvi no. 119, 1969-70.

47. C. I. Berry, "The dialogue duet: 1600-1900," (1979b).

48. Ned Rorem, "The American art song: dead or alive?" *Opera News* (August 1996): 15-30.

49. J. A. Shafferman, "Music for the small church choir" *Choral Journal* (November 1990): 19-24.

50. V. D. Wolverton, "Repertoire for small vocal ensembles in high schools," *Choral Journal* (October 1990): 33-40.

51. D. H. Avey, "Why can't I get the music?" *The NATS Journal* (September/October 1988): 17-18.

CHAPTER 5

Parameters and Resources of the Catalogue

PARAMETERS ESTABLISHED

This catalogue focuses on published works intended for, or else usable by, female vocal combinations. Exact vocal combinations are specified in the catalogue, if known. If publishers have listed compositions additionally for male voices or female-male combinations, these are included and cited as long as there is also a specific listing for female voices. If there are no gender specifications or reference to vocal ranges, these works will be designated as *unspecified*. Unspecified works typically indicate a decision either by the composer or by the publisher of suitability for either male or female combinations. Unfortunately, an unspecified listing does not provide exact knowledge of vocal range. Therefore it is left to the singer or teacher to make a determination as to the suitability of specific range and the significance of text meaning upon acquisition. Personal observations have demonstrated that unspecified works tend largely to be for medium-ranged voices (meaning an average range of C^4-E^5, and a *tessitura*[1] of about A^4-B^4). Boytim supports this observation, after describing her considerations of pairing voices by similar abilities, strengths, and same basic vocal technique:

> You will notice that I have not mentioned voice types. After reviewing much of the literature, I have discovered that there is some available material for any type of combination. Even though most octavo duet compositions are listed SA, this to me means it is merely in two parts [*sic*].[2]

Only works with piano accompaniment (or organ or *a cappella*) have been considered. The reasons for this choice include to compile a list of repertoire emphasizing this specific collaboration and its particular timbre and to provide a significant repertoire list for an ensemble combination that is most practical and accessible for the performers. This combination of voice and piano was especially popular during the nineteenth century with the improvement and exploitation of the piano. Unaccompanied works are not excluded, nor are works with organ (or harmonium) accompaniment. These works appear infrequently by comparison, and as these ensemble requirements are also accessible to performance and study, they are included.

The works selected are concert literature only, with secular or sacred texts. Some of the works may be intended for, or suitable for, worship. Opera duets and those that are part of larger works such as oratorio are excluded.

The body of literature largely encompasses that written or published between 1820 and 1995, the earlier date approximately indicating the onset of compositions produced for voice and piano.

Only published literature, in or out of print, is included. Out of print works may be available directly from publishers, republishing companies, or from libraries.

As there is an increasing interest in publishing the complete works of previously neglected or less well-known composers, both men and women, there is reason to believe that a work out of print at the moment may become available in the near future. A listing of works by identifiable women composers is also included (see appendix B: List of Identifiable Women Composers, page 401).

A database was created compiling an extensive list of chamber vocal duet literature for two female voices with the previously specified accompaniment. The database addresses any obtainable information on: (a) composer, (b) dates pertaining to composer, (c) title of work, (d) opus or piece number, (e) voice parts listed, (f) publisher, (g) comments, including variations on accompaniment and significant facts of interest, and (h) the source of the piece.

Cross-referenced appendices are provided, including identification lists of vocal combinations, a complete list of all composers appearing in this work, a list of identifiable women composers, and a distribution of composers by languages in which works are published.

SOURCES USED TO OBTAIN INFORMATION FOR THE CATALOGUE

A number of sources provided information included in the compilation of this catalogue. These include the following:

1. *Classical Vocal Music in Print*: designated CVMP (1976),[3] CVMP (1985),[4] and CVMP (1995).[5] The first is the complete volume, the latter two supplements. These volumes provide music handlers with information on the availability of all published works. Duet literature is intermingled with solo, as previously explained.
2. Ernst Challier catalogues: (a) *Grosser Duetten-Katalog*, designated CHAL (1898),[6] (b) *Erster Nachtrag zu Grosser Duetten-Katalog*, designated CHAL (1901),[7] (c) *Zweiter Nachtrag zu Grosser Duetten-Katalog*, designated CHAL (1906),[8] and (d) *Dritter Nachtrag zu Grosser Duetten-Katalog*, designated CHAL (1911).[9] The first is the complete volume, the latter three supplements. These catalogues were produced by Ernst Challier publishers (Berlin), who handled a large amount of the published works produced in Western Europe at the turn of the twentieth century.
3. *Duets British Broadcasting Corporation Listing*: designated BBC.[10] This catalogue, produced in 1975, provides a select list of published duets from all periods and vocal combinations, especially of English works.
4. *Vocal Chamber Duets An Annotated Bibliography* (1981): designated NATS-VCD.[11] This is the catalogue of secular chamber duets published by National Association of Teachers of Singing (NATS).

5. *Sacred Vocal Duets An Annotated Bibliography* (1987): designated NATS-SVD.[12] This is the catalogue of sacred chamber duets published by National Association of Teachers of Singing (NATS).
6. *The Art of the Song Recital* (1979): designated ASR.[13] The appendix of this book provides a select listing of a number of duets from various periods and vocal combinations.
7. Personal library: designated MSN, provided a number of unique published works not included in other references.

The entries that appear in this catalogue are listed alphabetically by *composer*, *dates of the composer*, *title*, *opus or piece number*, *vocal designation*, *publisher*, and include unique *comments*, if applicable, as they are listed in the references from which they come. *Sources* from where the information is previously listed is also included. Duplicate listings of specific works are included as separate entries if they differ in source from where information is obtained, differ in publishers, in title variation, in listed vocal combinations, or possess some other piece of unique information. Each entry is assigned a *record number*.

An Index of Song Titles (pages 463-572) provides a cross-reference of song titles, and may also provide information to those who wish to examine multiple settings of the same text, or seek out a composer of a specific work.

RESEARCH SOURCES

Research sources from which the information was obtained include the following:

1. Libraries: Columbia University Dodge and Butler Libraries and Milbank Memorial Library at Teachers College (New York City), Yale University Music Library (New Haven, CT), Allen Music Library, Hartt School, University of Hartford (West Hartford, CT), Talbott Library, Westminster Choir College, The School of Music of Rider University (Princeton, NJ), Barbican Centre Music Library, City of London Public Libraries, and The British Library (London, England).
2. Music handlers: Foundry Music (New Haven, CT), Joseph Patelson's House of Music (New York City), Zera Musicland (Fairfield, CT), Doblingers Musikhaus (Vienna, Austria), Boosey

and Hawkes, Chappell Music, and Barbican Centre Music Store (London, England), Classical Vocal Reprints (Riverdale, NY).

3. Publishers: music publishers were contacted for information and catalogues of repertoire examined. These include Boosey and Hawkes, Concordia, Carl Fischer, Chappell Music, Classical Vocal Reprints, International, Hildegard Press, Peters, Theodore Presser Co., Recital Publications, E. C. Schirmer, and G. Schirmer.

4. Interviews and correspondence with publishers, music handlers, researchers, and composers: Jay Stevens, Manager, Foundry Music (New Haven, CT), Glendower Jones, Head of Classical Vocal Reprints (Riverdale, NY), Ned Rorem, composer (New York City), Maurice Hinson, music scholar (Louisville, KY).

Additional assistance and information was also given by Caroline Murphy, Assistant Manager, Foundry Music (New Haven, CT), from Frank James Staneck, Editor of Musicdata, Inc. (Philadelphia, PA), and various staff at music handlers and publishers.

NOTES AND BIBLIOGRAPHY OF PUBLISHED CATALOGUES USED IN THIS RESEARCH

1. *Tessitura* refers to the average pitches where the voice tends to "lie" in a vocal composition. It differs from range in that it excludes the isolated highest and lowest pitches that are occasionally sung in the vocal composition (Apel, 1972).

2. J. F. Boytim, "Why neglect the sacred solo duet?" *The NATS Bulletin* (February/March 1972): 32.

3. T. R. Nardone, ed., *Classical Vocal Music in Print* (Philadelphia: Musicdata, Inc., 1976).

4. G. S. Eslinger and F. M. Daugherty, eds., *Classical Vocal Music in Print 1985 Supplement Music-In-Print Series, Vol. 4s.* (Philadelphia: Musicdata, Inc., 1986).

5. F. M. Daugherty, ed. *Classical Vocal Music in Print 1995 Supplement Music-In-Print Series, Vol. 4t.* (Philadelphia: Musicdata, Inc., 1995).

6. E. Challier, *Grosser Duetten-Katalog* (Giessen: Ernst Challier's Selbstverlag, 1898).

7. ——. *Erster Nachtrag zu Grosser Duetten-Katalog* (Giessen: Ernst Challier's Selbstverlag, 1901).

8. ——. *Zweiter Nachtrag zu Grosser Duetten-Katalog* (Giessen: Ernst Challier's Selbstverlag, 1906).

9. ——. *Dritter Nachtrag zu Grosser Duetten-Katalog* (Giessen: Ernst Challier's Selbstverlag, 1911).

10. *Duets BBC Listing* (London, England: The British Broadcasting Corporation, 1975).

11. Corre I. Berry, *Vocal Chamber Duets An Annotated Bibliography* (Jacksonville, FL: The National Association of Teachers of Singing, Inc., 1981).

12. Corre Berry Brusse, *Sacred Vocal Duets An Annotated Bibliography* (Jacksonville, FL: The National Association of Teachers of Singing, Inc., 1987).

13. S. Emmons and S. Sonntag, *The Art of the Song Recital* (New York: Schirmer Books, 1979).

CHAPTER 6

The Research Process—Creating the Catalogue

There were several stages in the research process leading to the development of the catalogue.

STAGE ONE: IDENTIFYING THE LITERATURE, OBTAINING SOURCES AND MATERIALS

Stage one involved seeking out reference sources that would provide information on duet literature. Much of this information lies imbedded in extensive catalogues, frequently unspecified amid solo literature, or requiring specific prior knowledge before location (such as composer or title). Resources used specifically to create this comprehensive catalogue have previously been listed in chapter 5: Parameters and Resources of the Catalogue (pages 17-19). These resources fall into three categories:

1. Common publications such as the *Classical Vocal Music in Print* series provide music handlers with pertinent information on printed music within the last two decades. As is stated in the objectives of the Music-In-Print series, which produces the catalogues on instrumental scores as well as vocal scores, "The goal…is to locate and catalog all printed music throughout the world" [Brochure].[1] They are global, mainly providing information on works from Europe, North and South America, Japan, and Australia. Since there is no topical designation as to duet literature, it was necessary to select the titles out of the vast volume of literature. The other common sources, such as the *Duet BBC*

Listings, the *Art of the Song Recital* appendix, and the two NATS bulletins addressing vocal chamber and sacred duets, were researched for appropriate titles, vocal combinations, and accompaniment that were in keeping with the parameters of this topic.

2. A relatively uncommon resource that was suggested by Glendower Jones, founder of Classical Vocal Reprints, proved to be extremely valuable. This is the Challier series that was first published in 1898, with three supplements published through 1911. It is not widely known. In fact, the writer was apparently the first person ever to request it out of the Yale University Music Library. It provided a vast number of titles, almost five thousand five hundred. The works it lists are presented awkwardly in alphabetical order by title; it has many misspellings, and it includes composers' names only by last name and initials. This led to an extensive scavenger hunt in order to seek out information on the composers in order to make sure that they were appropriate for the time constraints of this research.

3. Since the writer is a performer of much of this genre, there is an extensive personal library. This personal library has provided identifiable published materials that are unique, and were not included in any other published resource. Much of this material has been collected over years from antique book stores, libraries, and music handlers worldwide.

STAGE TWO: ANALYZING THE MATERIALS AND CREATING THE DATABASE

A database file was created using FileMaker Pro 3.0[2] (Claris Corporation) for Macintosh power computers. The computer used was a Macintosh Performa 6218CD. Initially, each resource was independently examined, and information entered into the database from each of the volumes listed. The information was eventually pooled into one large volume. The database files initially included the following fields: (a) composer, (b) dates of composer, (c) title of work, (d) opus number (or piece number) if offered, (e) type of accompaniment listed if different from piano, (f) comments, such as a specific date of the composition, or if the work was part of a collection or anthology, or if the composer was a woman, and (g) source, noting from where the information was taken. In finalized form, record numbers were added.

The database program allows for sorting by using a specific keyword or keywords in any given field name. This sorting technique was used to create several appendixes including appendix A: Complete List of Composers (pages 389-400), appendix B: List of Identifiable Women Composers (page 401), appendix C: Entries Indexed by Voice Specification, a cross-referenced appendix of entries sorted by voice type (pages 403-412), appendix E: Accompaniment Other Than Piano, a cross-referenced appendix of entries sorted by other accompaniment (pages 427-428), and the Index of Song Titles (pages 463-572), an alphabetical listing of the entries by title.

STAGE THREE: ANALYZING THE DATA TO DETERMINE APPROPRIATENESS OF THE LITERATURE

Since there are over two thousand composers, it was necessary to determine if they fell into the time parameters of this study. Several works that slightly precede the initial date of 1820 were included if their works were accompanied by piano or otherwise fit the parameters. The research into the appropriateness of the composers and the identification of women composers involved searching through a number of old lexicons, mainly at the Yale University Music Library (New Haven, CT), and additionally at the Hartt School (University of Hartford, CT) Library. Particular difficulties arose with the Challier catalogues, in which most of the composers were listed only with initials for first names. This made their identification extremely troublesome. Identification proved especially difficult or in some cases impossible if the surnames were common, and if the composers had quickly become obscure. Delving into antiquated resource lexicons provided a number of identifications, although many remain that were unable to be identified. In the context of the catalogue, if there was sufficient reason to believe that a composer was *probably* identified, then the designation [prob] precedes the name. Those that remain to be identified are likely to fall into the parameters largely because the titles seem to indicate poetry written during the period, or because they have opus numbers.

It was found that of the initial number of two thousand and twelve composers (including one category of unknown), largely unidentified at the onset of this research, only eight were eliminated because they were determined to be too early for inclusion based on the date parameters. This indicates that it is likely that those remaining unidentified are from the time period specified. Dr. Maurice Hinson, a well-known scholar in the field of piano repertoire, conveyed that "many of these obscure composers remain so because they were not deemed important enough to be carried in lexicons during their lives. Many times, one may happen upon the dates of the composers only by luck, finding a manuscript that happens to have the dates of the composer on it. Most of the time, one will never be able to know their identification for sure."[3]

An additional problem encountered with the same catalogue series is the high number of misspellings. Occasionally two separate composers turned out to be the same person after further examination.

STAGE FOUR: CREATING THE CATALOGUE

After several editing copies and extensive research into locating the composers, as indicated in the previous section, the final catalogue was printed with the categories of *record number*, *composer*, *dates of composer*, *title of work*, *opus number* (or piece number), *voicing specified*, *publisher, comments,* and *source of work.*

As previously stated, any obvious misspellings have been corrected. Inconsistencies in spellings or composer first initials from sources such as the Challier catalogues are noted. Titles of the pieces are listed as they appear in the original catalogue sources. In the case of publisher listings, abbreviations are presented as they appear in the original source, even if there are variations. This is because of the lack of positive identification of many entries, particularly in the case of the Challier catalogues.

Appendix lists were created for all composers, women composers, and a distribution of languages in which the works are published. Cross references using record numbers are provided as to specific vocal combinations. An additional appendix (appendix G, pages 445-461) was created listing the contents of twenty-one anthologies that were obtained. Works whose titles were listed in other sources as belonging to a named anthology are cited as such within the comments field of the catalogue.

NOTES

1. "The Music In Print Series" (Philadelphia, PA: Musicdata, Inc., 1997), brochure.

2. FileMaker Pro Version 3.0 (Santa Clara, CA: Claris Corporation).

3. Maurice Hinson, telephone conversation, 30 April 1997.

CHAPTER 7

The Comprehensive Catalogue of Vocal Chamber Duet Literature for Female Voices

INTRODUCTION TO THE CATALOGUE

The catalogue is the printout of the database previously discussed in chapter 6: The Research Process—Creating the Catalogue (pages 21-23). It is in alphabetical order by composer, with titles listed in alphabetical order within the category of each composer. Information that was discernible is included with regard to composers' full names, dates, and titles of works as they appear in their original sources from which they are drawn. This also applies to variations in capitalization and slight variation in title. Voicings are as indicated in the sources. Comments contain pertinent facts, points of interest, and mention alternate accompaniment if indicated. The source indicates from where the entry is drawn. Several points are addressed as follows:

1. In the case of composers careful research was conducted as explained previously. If a composer is identified as a specific person, but this identification is not provable beyond a reasonable doubt, then the term [prob] for probably appears along with the name.

2. Spellings of names are standardized, such as in the case of Russian names that are transliterated. If there are published common variations, they are listed along with the names in brackets. For example *Tolstoy* and *[Tolstoi]*. Obvious misspellings

were corrected. If the names are known pseudonyms, or if the composer uses other names, they are listed in the comments column. The same applies to women composers who have published under birth names and married names.

3. Users of this catalogue should be aware that older sources occasionally perpetuate misspellings that may appear in indexes of other sources or in actual scores. For example, a common error or variant appeared with high frequency in the spelling of the German word *Weihnachts*. In the *Challier* sources, *Weihnachts* occurred in many titles as *Weinachts*, the first *h* omitted. The spelling is corrected in this work for consistency.

4. All entries listed are accompanied with piano unless otherwise specified.

5. Publisher abbreviations and their variations are cited in the catalogue as they appeared in the original sources. This is because it was often unclear as to whether variations were accidental, or whether there was actually a difference in publisher name, or the city in which the publisher is located.

For an explanation of the abbreviations, please refer to "Abbreviations" on pages xvii-xviii.

Catalogue of Published Duets for Female Voices, In and Out of Print, from Approximately 1820-1995

REC	COMP	DTS	TITLE	OP #	VCG	PUB	COMMENTS	SRC
1	———		A Kamaraének Mesterei Duettek, tercett és kvartett zongorakísérettel eredeti és Magyar szöveggel		Var.	EMB	Anthology. Compi. & ed. T. Füzesséry. Schubert, Saint-Saëns, Smetana, Kodály, Sugár, et al. Pub. 1996.	MSN
2	———		Album of Great Duets from the Masters Vol. 1		S w/other v.	G. Schirm.	Anthology. Ed. Wilkins. Does not specify periods it encompasses.	ASR
3	———		Album of Great Duets from the Masters Vol. 2		MS w/other v.	G. Schirm.	Anthology. Ed. Wilkins. Does not specify periods it encompasses.	ASR
4	———		Album of Sixteen Sacred Duets		Unspec.	G. Schirm.	Anthology. Does not specify periods it encompasses.	ASR
5	———		Album of Sixteen Sacred Duets for Various Voices		Var.	G. Schirm.	pf or org accomp. Anthology. Abt, Bartlett, J. B. Faure, Gounod, Mendelssohn, Smart, Spohr, Stainer et al. (no date)	MSN
6	———		Album of Sixteen Sacred Duets for Various Voices		Var.	G. Schirm.	Anthology. Pub. 1880.	NATS-SVD
7	———		Album of Vocal Duets		Unspec.	Lengnick	Anthology. Bohm, Brahms, Dvorák, Goetze, Henschel, et al.	CVMP (1985)
8	———		Amazing Grace Duets and Solos		Unspec.	Word	Anthology of sacred duets & solos. Ed. R. Carmichael.	CVMP (1976)
9	———		Choice Sacred Duets		Unspec.	Presser	Anthology. Unspec. comp.	CVMP (1976)
10	———		Choice Sacred Duets		Var.	Ditson	Anthology. Mendelssohn, J. B. Faure, Bartlett, Gounod, Schnecker, G. B. Nevin, Smart, F. Lachner, et al. Pub. 1936.	MSN
11	———		Choice Sacred Duets		Var.	Ditson	Anthology. Pub. 1936.	NATS-SVD
12	———		Choice Vocal Duets		S/A et al.	Ditson	Anthology. Does not specify periods it encompasses.	ASR
13	———		Choix et Arrangements pour 2 Voix et Piano de Mélodies Célèbres de Schumann (Scènes Champêtres)		Unspec.	Schott-Frer	Ed. Nauwelaers. Collection of songs & arr. of works by Robert Schumann.	CVMP (1995)
14	———		Choix et Arrangements pour 2 Voix et Piano de Mélodies Célèbres de Strauss (Gazouillis de Printemps)		Unspec.	Schott-Frer	Ed. Nauwelaers. Collection of songs & arr. of works by Johann Strauss.	CVMP (1995)
15	———		Clayton's Solos and Duets Vol. 2		Unspec.	Word	Anthology. Works by John Peterson et al. Ed. N. Clayton. Works for 1- 2 v. Vol. 1 contains only solos.	CVMP (1976)
16	———		Diller-Page Carol Book, The		Unspec.	G. Schirm.	Anthology of Christmas carols. Ed. A. Diller & K. Stearns Page.	CVMP (1976)

REC	COMP	DTS	TITLE	OP #	VCG	PUB	COMMENTS	SRC
17	———		Ditson Collection of Soprano and Alto Duets		S/A	Ditson	Anthology. Bohm, Brahms, Chaminade, Henschel, Logé, Marzials, Mendelssohn, Reinecke, et al. Pub. 1934.	MSN
18	———		Douze Duos		Unspec.	Durand	Anthology. Does not specify periods it encompasses.	ASR
19	———		Duet Album		Unspec.	Boosey	Anthology. Ed. Morris & Anderson	CVMP (1976)
20	———		Duet Album for High and Medium Voices		high & med. v.	Boosey	Anthology. Compi. & ed. V. Morris & V. Anderson. Brahms, Franck, Keel, Schumann, Somervell, Thiman, et al. Pub. ca. 1944.	ASR
21	———		Duet Book, The		Unspec.	Universe	Anthology of sacred works. Ed. D. Ripplinger. Unspec. pieces.	CVMP (1985)
22	———		Duet Book, The		Unspec.	Jackman	Anthology of sacred works. Ed. D. Ripplinger. Unspec. pieces.	CVMP (1985)
23	———		Duet Book: Twelve Duets for Two Equal Voices		Var.	Jackman	Anthology. Compi. & arr. D. Ripplinger. Pub. 1984.	NATS-SVD
24	———		Duets for Female Voices, Vol. 1: From Carissimi to Beethoven		2 female v.	EMB	Anthology. Ed. Forrai. No specific works mentioned.	CVMP (1985)
25	———		Duets for Female Voices, Vol. 2: From Mendelssohn to Kodaly		2 female v.	EMB	Anthology. Ed. Forrai. Unspec. pieces.	CVMP (1985)
26	———		Duets for the Master		high & med. v.	Beckenhorst	Anthology. Arr. C. Courtney. Ahnfelt, Courtney, Holst, Wyeth, folk melodies. Pub. 1989.	MSN
27	———		Duets for Two Female Voices, Vol. 1 Carissimi to Beethoven		2 female v.	Boosey	Anthology. Ed. Forrai	CVMP (1976)
28	———		Duets for Two Female Voices, Vol. 2 Beethoven to Kodaly		2 female v.	Boosey	Anthology. Original and Hung. texts.	CVMP (1976)
29	———		Duets, Russian		S/MS, MS/B	Mez Kniga	Anthology. Ed. V. Artyomov & M. Ziv	CVMP (1976)
30	———		Duettek Nöi Hangokra, Zongorakísérettel [Duets for Female v. w/ pf acc.]		2 female v.	EMB	Anthology. Compi. Miklós Forrai. Brahms, Franck, Kodály, Liszt, Mendelssohn, Rossini, Schumann. Pub. 1959.	MSN
31	———		Duettenkranz		Unspec.	B. & H., Uni v.-Edit.	Anthology. Duets by Var. unspec. comp.	CHAL (1911)
32	———		Duettenkranz: 18 Weltliche Duette für 2 Frauenstimmen		2 female v.	Peters	Anthology. Ed. Martiensen. Unspec. comp. Pub. 1959.	CVMP (1985)
33	———		Duettenkranz Vol. 1, 18 Secular Duets		S/S, S/A	Peters	Anthology. Does not specify periods it encompasses. Ed. Martiensen	ASR
34	———		Duettenkranz Vol. 2, 14 Secular Duets		S/S et al.	Peters	Anthology. Does not specify periods it encompasses. Ed. Martiensen	ASR

REC	COMP	DTS	TITLE	OP #	VCG	PUB	COMMENTS	SRC
35	———		Duettenkranz Vol. I: Eighteen Secular Duets		S/S, S/A	Peters	Anthology. Ed. Martienssen. Albert, Brahms, Cherubini, Loewe, Marcello, Schumann, et al.	CVMP (1976)
36	———		Echos de France, Vol. I		Unspec.	Durand	Anthology. Dalayrac, Gluck, Piccini, Mehul, Lully et al. For 1-3 v.	CVMP (1976)
37	———		Echos de France, Vol. II		Unspec.	Durand	Anthology. Monsigny, Gretry, Dalayrac, Philodor, Albanese, Martini et al. For 1-3 v.	CVMP (1976)
38	———		Eight Polish Christmas Carols		Unspec.	Marks	Anthology. Does not specify periods it encompasses. Ed. Malin	ASR
39	———		Fjorton Sangduetter Heft 1-2		Unspec.	Lundq.	Anthology. Ed. Lundberg. Haggbom, Berg, Farval, Mendelssohn, Rubinstein, Pacius, Lundberg et al.	CVMP (1976)
40	———		Forty-Eight Duets 17th, 18th, 19th Centuries		2 med. v.	G. Schirm.	acap. Anthology. Ed. Prahl	ASR
41	———		Forty-Eight Duets Seventeenth Through Nineteenth Centuries		2 med. v.	ECS	Anthology. Ed. & arr. V. Prahl. Brahms, Mendelssohn, Rubinstein, et al. Program notes for each piece. Pub. 1941, 1970.	MSN
42	———		Geistliche Sologesange ind Duette, Heft I und Heft II		Unspec.	Hug	pf or org accomp. Anthology. Unspec. comp. for 1-2 v.	CVMP (1976)
43	———		Great Duets From the Masters, Vol. I		S/S et al.	G. Schirm.	Anthology. Ed. Wilkins and Wilkins. Handel, Mendelssohn, Mozart, Schubert et al.	CVMP (1976)
44	———		Great Duets From the Masters, Vol. II		MS/MS et al.	G. Schirm.	Anthology. Ed. Wilkins and Wilkins. Handel, Offenbach, Verdi Mendelssohn et al.	CVMP (1976)
45	———		Hale and Wilder Classic Collection of Sacred Duets		Unspec.	Paragon	Anthology. Ed. O. Young. Unspec. pieces.	CVMP (1985)
46	———		Harmonie-Album		Unspec.	Harmonie i. B.	Anthology of duets by Var. unspec. comp.	CHAL (1906)
47	———		Inspiring Gospel Solos and Duets No. I		Unspec.	Lillenas	Anthology. Ed. H. Lillenas. For 1-2 v.	CVMP (1976)
48	———		Inspiring Gospel Solos and Duets No. II		Unspec.	Lillenas	Anthology. Ed. H. Lillenas. For 1-2 v.	CVMP (1976)
49	———		Izbrannye Duety Russkikh Kompozitorov dlia peniia s fortepiano		Var.	GMI	Translit. title Russ. Only Cyrillic. Anthology "Izbrannye Duety Russkikh Kompozitorov dlia peniia s fortepiano" Pub. 1948.	MSN
50	———		Juden-Album "Volkstümliche Lieder"		Unspec.	Peters	Anthology. Ed. L. Erk & A. Jacob. Pub. 19th C.	CHAL (1898)
51	———		Julduetter		Unspec.	Fazer	Anthology of Christmas duets. Ed. V. Hannikainen.	CVMP (1976)
52	———		Let's Sing Duets No. 1		2 female or 2 male v.	Singspir	Anthology. Unspec. comp.	CVMP (1976)

REC	COMP	DTS	TITLE	OP #	VCG	PUB	COMMENTS	SRC
53	——		Let's Sing Duets No. 2		2 female or 2 male v.	Singspir	Anthology. Unspec. comp.	CVMP (1976)
54	——		Let's Sing Duets No. 3		2 female or 2 male v.	Singspir	Anthology. Unspec. comp.	CVMP (1976)
55	——		Let's Sing Duets No. 4		2 female or 2 male v.	Singspir	Anthology. Unspec. comp.	CVMP (1976)
56	——		Let's Sing Duets No. 5		2 female or 2 male v.	Singspir	Anthology. Unspec. comp.	CVMP (1976)
57	——		Lieder der Weihnacht (100)		Unspec.	Breitkopf	Anthology. 100 duets. Does not specify periods it encompasses.	ASR
58	——		Mendelssohn ja Rubinstein Duettoja		Unspec.	Fazer	Anthology. Mendelssohn and Rubinstein.	CVMP (1976)
59	——		New Sacred Solos and Duets		Unspec.	Lillenas	Anthology. Ed. H. Lillenas. Solos & duets.	CVMP (1976)
60	——		New Sacred Solos and Duets		Unspec.	Lillenas	Anthology. Solos & duets. Does not specify periods it encompasses.	ASR
61	——		Ny Samling Sangduetter, Heft 1		Unspec.	Lundq.	Anthology. Ed. Uppling. Anjou, Mendelssohn, Myrberg, Palm, et al.	CVMP (1976)
62	——		Ny Samling Sangduetter, Heft 2		Unspec.	Lundq.	Anthology. Ed. Uppling. Adam, Bengzon, Haggbom, Lago, Myrberg, et al.	CVMP (1976)
63	——		Old-Time Russian Duets		Unspec.	Mez Kniga	Anthology. Unspec. comp.	CVMP (1985)
64	——		Premier Livre de Chansons à Deux Parties, Band 1		Unspec.	LPME	pf with opt. inst. accomp. Anthology. Works by Adrian Le Roy and Robert Ballard.	CVMP (1985)
65	——		Rodeheaver Gospel Solos and Duets, Vol. 4		Unspec.	Word	Anthology. Ed. Rodeheaver. Solos & duets.	CVMP (1976)
66	——		Romantic Duets Great Performers Edition		Var.	G. Schirm.	Anthology. Compi. E. Lear & T. Stewart. Brahms, Dvořák, Gretchaninov, Schubert, et al. Interpretive suggestions. Pub. 1985.	MSN
67	——		Sacred Duet Masterpieces		Unspec.	C. Fischer	Anthology. Ed. Fredrickson. Var. ranges available. Unspec. comp.	CVMP (1976)
68	——		Sacred Duet Masterpieces		Unspec.	C. Fischer	Anthology. Ed. Fredrickson. Var. ranges available. Unspec. comp.	ASR
69	——		Sacred Duet Masterpieces of the World's Great Composers		2 high v.	R. D. Row	org or pf accomp. Anthology. Compi. & arr. C. Fredrickson. Cornelius, Mendelssohn, Stainer, Sullivan, et al. Pub. 1961.	MSN
70	——		Sacred Duets		Unspec.	Presser	Anthology. Ed. W. Shakespeare. Var. ranges. Unspec. comp.	CVMP (1976)
71	——		Sacred Duets for All Voices		Unspec.	Presser	Anthology. Grmn. lang. Unspec. comp.	CVMP (1976)

REC	COMP	DTS	TITLE	OP #	VCG	PUB	COMMENTS	SRC
72	———		Sacred Duets for all Voices		Unspec.	Presser	Anthology of Grmn. duets. Does not specify periods it encompasses.	ASR
73	———		Sacred Duets for Equal Voices		Unspec.	Ausburg	Anthology. Ed. G. W. Cassler. Does not specify periods it encompasses. Unspec. comp.	CVMP (1976)
74	———		Sacred Duets for Equal Voices		Unspec.	Ausburg	Anthology. Ed. G. W. Cassler. Does not specify periods it encompasses. Unspec. comp.	ASR
75	———		Sacred Duets No. I		Unspec.	Lillenas	Anthology. Unspec. comp.	CVMP (1976)
76	———		Sacred Duets No. II		Unspec.	Lillenas	Anthology. Unspec. comp.	CVMP (1976)
77	———		Sacred Duets No. III		Unspec.	Lillenas	Anthology. Unspec. comp.	CVMP (1976)
78	———		Sacred Duets. Vol. 1		2 high v.	Church	Anthology. Compi. & ed. W. Shakespeare. Pub. 1907.	NATS-SVD
79	———		Sacred Duets. Vol. 2		high & low v.	Church	Anthology. Compi. & ed. W. Shakespeare. Pub. 1907.	NATS-SVD
80	———		Sacred Duets Vol. 3		Unspec.	Lillenas	Anthology. Does not specify periods it encompasses. Unspec. comp.	ASR
81	———		Sacred Songs A Collection of Two-Part Songs by the Best Composers Vol. 1		2 high v.	Church	Anthology. Compi. & ed. W. Shakespeare. Abt, J. B. Faure, Gounod, Spohr, Stainer, Saint-Saëns, et al. Lists ranges. Pub. 1907.	MSN
82	———		Sacred Songs A Collection of Two-Part Songs by the Best Composers Vol. 2		high & low v.	Church	Anthology. Compi. & ed. W. Shakespeare. Works by Adam, Bennet, Gounod, Rubinstein, Smart, Topliff, et al. Lists ranges. Pub. 1907.	MSN
83	———		Sangesfrohe Duettischen "51 Duetten"		Unspec.	C. Rühle i. L.	Anthology. 51 duets by Var. unspec. comp.	CHAL (1901)
84	———		Schäffer-Waldburg-Duette "Sammeltitel"		Unspec.	Fr. Dietrich	Anthology. Unspec. comp.	CHAL (1901)
85	———		Schirmer's Favorite Sacred Duets		Unspec.	G. Schirm.	Anthology. Does not specify periods it encompasses.	ASR
86	———		Schirmer's Favorite Sacred Duets for Various Voices		Unspec.	G. Schirm.	Anthology. Fauré, Gounod, Shelley, Adam, et al.	CVMP (1976)
87	———		Schirmer's Favorite Sacred Duets for Various Voices		Var.	G. Schirm.	pf or org accomp. Anthology. Adam, Bassford, J. B. Faure, Granier, Harker, Malotte, Shelley, peaks, et al. Pub. 1955.	NATS-SVD
88	———		Schirmer's Favorite Secular Duets for Various Voices		Unspec.	G. Schirm.	Anthology. Grieg, Mozart, Offenbach, Schubert, et al. Does not specify periods it encompasses.	CVMP (1976)
89	———		Schirmer's Favorite Secular Duets for Various Voices		Unspec.	G. Schirm.	Anthology. Grieg, Mozart, Offenbach, Schubert, et al. Does not specify periods it encompasses.	ASR

REC	COMP	DTS	TITLE	OP #	VCG	PUB	COMMENTS	SRC
90	——		Sing Noel		Unspec.	Lillenas	Anthology. Christmas music for 1-4 v. Unspec. comp.	CVMP (1985)
91	——		Six Popular Duets		Unspec.	Leonard-Eng	Anthology. Does not specify periods it encompasses.	ASR
92	——		Six Popular Vocal Duets Book I for Soprano & Contralto		S/A	Leonard-Eng	Anthology. Ed. & arr. E. Newton. Newton, Barnaby, Rubinstein, Horn., et al. Pub. ca. 1906.	MSN
93	——		Six Standard English Songs		S/MS, S/A et al.	Ashdown	Anthology of arr. Does not specify periods it encompasses.	ASR
94	——		Sixteen Sacred Duets		Unspec.	G. Schirm.	Anthology. Does not specify periods it encompasses.	ASR
95	——		Solo and Duet Specials, Vol. 1		Unspec.	Hope	Anthology. Works for 1-2 v.	CVMP (1976)
96	——		Solo and Duet Specials, Vol. 2		Unspec.	Hope	Anthology. Works for 1-2 v.	CVMP (1976)
97	——		Songs for Young People		Unspec.	Colombo	Anthology. Solos & duets. Does not specify periods it encompasses.	ASR
98	——		Soprano and Alto Duets		S/A	Ditson	Anthology. Ed. H. Kiehl. Bracken, Brambach, Caracciolo, Chaminade, Delibes, Kjerulf, Lassen, Smart, et al. Pub. 1901.	MSN
99	——		Suomalaisia Kansanlauluduettoja Vol. I		Unspec.	Fazer	Anthology of Finn. duets	CVMP (1976)
100	——		Suomalaisia Kansanlauluduettoja Vol. II		Unspec.	Fazer	Anthology of Finn. duets	CVMP (1976)
101	——		Thirty-Eight Modern Canons		Var. Unspec.	Music Press	Anthology. Ed. Reichenback. Canons for 1-5 v. Does not specify periods it encompasses.	ASR
102	——		Tolv Duetter for Flickskolornas Hogre Sangklasser		Unspec.	Lundq.	Anthology. Ed. Uppling. Pfeil, Myrberg, Hallstrom, Andre, Mendelssohn.	CVMP (1976)
103	——		Top Songs for Duets		Unspec.	Singspir	Anthology of sacred duets. Unspec. comp.	CVMP (1976)
104	——		Twenty Choice Vocal Duets for Various Voices		Unspec.	Ditson	Anthology. Does not specify periods it encompasses.	ASR
105	——		Twenty-Five Duets for Two Women's Voices		2 female v.	Universal	Anthology. Ed. Hauptner. Does not specify periods it encompasses.	ASR
106	——		Two-Part Stylings Vol. I, II		Unspec.	Lillenas	Anthology of sacred duets. Does not specify periods it encompasses.	ASR
107	——		Vocal Duets Collection Vol. 1		Var.	Allans	Anthology. S. Foster, Taylor, Mellish, Rimsky-Korsakov, Westendorf, Bond, Yradier, Nevin, Glover, et al. Pub. 1992.	MSN

REC	COMP	DTS	TITLE	OP #	VCG	PUB	COMMENTS	SRC
108	————		Vocal Duets Collection Vol. 2		Var.	Allans	Anthology. Schubert, Liszt, Brahms, Mendelssohn, Martini, Gounod, Grieg, MacDowell, Chopin, folk songs. Pub. 1992.	MSN
109	————		Volkslieder for Two Voices and Piano		Unspec.	Peters	Anthology. Ed. Becker. Does not specify periods it encompasses.	ASR
110	Aaron, E.		Gebrüder Cohn "Wir sind zwei jüd'sche Handelslait"		Unspec.	O. Dietrich		CHAL (1898)
111	Aaron, E.		Wir sind zwei jüd'sche Handelslait		Unspec.	O. Dietrich		CHAL (1906)
112	Abbott, Jane	fl. 1894	Just for Today		S/A	Willis	Eng. woman comp. Also solo.	CVMP (1976)
113	Abramowitz		Judischen Zeitungsleser "Grüss Sie Gott, Herr Diamant"		Unspec.	Kratochwill		CHAL (1898)
114	Abt, Franz	1819-1885	Abend auf der Alm "Alpen glühn im Abendschein"	Op. 69 No. 2	Unspec.	André		CHAL (1898)
115	Abt, Franz	1819-1885	Abend "Es zieht die Liebes Gottes"	Op. 184 No. 2	Unspec.	André		CHAL (1898)
116	Abt, Franz	1819-1885	Abend "Im Westen ist versunken"	Op. 507 No. 1	Unspec.	Bauer		CHAL (1898)
117	Abt, Franz	1819-1885	Abenddämmerung "Durch's Gefild weht Lenzluft"	Op. 407 No. 2	S/A	André		CHAL (1898)
118	Abt, Franz	1819-1885	Abenddämmerung "Im Dunkel schummern die Thäler"	Op. 576 No. 4	S/A	André		CHAL (1898)
119	Abt, Franz	1819-1885	Abendfrieden "Nun ist der laute Tag verhallt	Op. 576 No. 5	Unspec.	Grüninger		CHAL (1898)
120	Abt, Franz	1819-1885	Abendläuten "Durch des Abends heil'ger Stille"	Op. 64 No. 8	Unspec.	André		CHAL (1898)
121	Abt, Franz	1819-1885	Abendläuten "Immer, wenn es Abend läutet"	Op. 507 No. 6	Unspec.	Bauer		CHAL (1898)
122	Abt, Franz	1819-1885	Abendlied	Op. 62 No. 4	2 high v.	Church	In anthology "Sacred Duets A Collection of Two-Part Songs by the Best Composers" Vol. 1. Compi. & ed. W. Shakespeare. Pub. 1907.	MSN
123	Abt, Franz	1819-1885	Abendlied "Herz und verlangst du nicht Ruhe"	Op. 62 No 4	Unspec.	André		CHAL (1898)
124	Abt, Franz	1819-1885	Abendlied "Nun die Sonne geht zu scheiden"	Op. 409 No. 4	Unspec.	Siegel		CHAL (1898)
125	Abt, Franz	1819-1885	Abendlied "Tag geht nun zu Ende"	Op. 91 No. 4	Unspec.	André		CHAL (1898)
126	Abt, Franz	1819-1885	Abendlied "Tag ist vorüber"	Op. 521 No. 4	MS/A	André		CHAL (1898)
127	Abt, Franz	1819-1885	Abendreigen "Von den Bergen sinkt die Sonne"	Op. 81 No. 5	Unspec.	André		CHAL (1898)
128	Abt, Franz	1819-1885	Abendruhe "Abendglockenklang, tönt die Flur"	Op. 132 No. 2	Unspec.	André		CHAL (1898)
129	Abt, Franz	1819-1885	Abschied "Abendlich schon rauscht der Wald"	Op. 575 No. 5	S/A	Coppenrath		CHAL (1898)
130	Abt, Franz	1819-1885	Abschied "Leb wohl du liebes Vaterhaus"	Op. 316 No. 7	Unspec.	André		CHAL (1898)

REC	COMP	DTS	TITLE	OP #	VCG	PUB	COMMENTS	SRC
131	Abt, Franz	1819-1885	Abschied von den Tyroler Bergen "Von meinen Bergen muss ich scheiden"	Op. 457 No. 9	Unspec.	André		CHAL (1898)
132	Abt, Franz	1819-1885	Aepler "I han es Hüsli"	Op. 80 No. 4	Unspec.	André		CHAL (1898)
133	Abt, Franz	1819-1885	Alpenreigen "Von Alpenhöh zur Abendzeit"	Op. 507 No. 2	Unspec.	Bauer		CHAL (1898)
134	Abt, Franz	1819-1885	Am Waldrand steht ein Tannenbaum		Unspec.	C. Rühle i. L.		CHAL (1901)
135	Abt, Franz	1819-1885	An den Mond "Mondesauge zart und sinnig"	Op. 20 No. 2	Unspec.	André		CHAL (1898)
136	Abt, Franz	1819-1885	Aschenbrödel und das weisse Vöglein "Auf deinem Grabe, pflanzt ich"	Op. 545 No. 2	MS/A	André		CHAL (1898)
137	Abt, Franz	1819-1885	Auf blauer Fluth "Purpurner Himmel"	Op. 457 No. 10	Unspec.	André		CHAL (1898)
138	Abt, Franz	1819-1885	Auf den Schub "Winter wird beklommen"	Op. 409 No. 5	Unspec.	Siegel		CHAL (1898)
139	Abt, Franz	1819-1885	Ave Maria "Abendglocken klingen"	Op. 409 No. 1	Unspec.	Siegel		CHAL (1898)
140	Abt, Franz	1819-1885	Ave Maria "Leise sinkt der Dämmrung Schleier"	Op. 540 No. 2	Unspec.	Siegel		CHAL (1898)
141	Abt, Franz	1819-1885	Bald wird der Tag sich neigen	Op. 299 No. 1	S/A	Heinr.		CHAL (1898)
142	Abt, Franz	1819-1885	Beiden Rosen "Es blüthen zwei Rosen"	Op. 299 No. 2	S/A	Heinr.		CHAL (1898)
143	Abt, Franz	1819-1885	Beim Johreswechsel "Lebe wohl, schönes Jahr"	Op. 64 No. 9	Unspec.	André		CHAL (1898)
144	Abt, Franz	1819-1885	Bergkirchlein "Auf Bergesgipfel ein Kirchlein blaut"	Op. 611 No. 1	S/A	Coppenrath		CHAL (1898)
145	Abt, Franz	1819-1885	Bleiben möcht' ich immer	Op. 459 No. 1	Unspec.	Litolff		CHAL (1898)
146	Abt, Franz	1819-1885	Blümchen du holdes, wie prangst du	Op. 576 No. 2	Unspec.	C. Rühle i. L.		CHAL (1901)
147	Abt, Franz	1819-1885	Blumen wie im Wiesengrund	Op. 473 No. 3	Unspec.	André		CHAL (1898)
148	Abt, Franz	1819-1885	Blumenandacht "Kommt der Morgen"	Op. 64 No. 3	Unspec.	André		CHAL (1898)
149	Abt, Franz	1819-1885	Das macht das dunkelgrüne Laub	Op. 473 No. 1	Unspec.	André		CHAL (1898)
150	Abt, Franz	1819-1885	Der Sonntag	Op. 132	high & low v.	Church	In anthology "Sacred Duets A Collection of Two-Part Songs by the Best Composers" Vol. 2. Compi. & ed. W. Shakespeare. Pub. 1907.	MSN
151	Abt, Franz	1819-1885	Die Schwalben sind gekommen		S/A or S/B	C. Fischer	In catalogue page "Selected Vocal Duets By Favorite Composers" Carl Fischer NY (no date)	MSN
152	Abt, Franz	1819-1885	Dort hinter jenem Fensterlein	III No. 4	Unspec.	C. Rühle i. L.	Arr. Necke	CHAL (1901)
153	Abt, Franz	1819-1885	Du frischer, froher Morgenwind	Op. 305 No. 3	S/A	André		CHAL (1898)
154	Abt, Franz	1819-1885	Erinnerung "Still ist die Nacht"	Op. 540 No. 6	Unspec.	Siegel		CHAL (1898)
155	Abt, Franz	1819-1885	Feldmarschall Frühling "Frühling ist"	Op. 91 No. 10	Unspec.	André		CHAL (1898)

REC	COMP	DTS	TITLE	OP #	VCG	PUB	COMMENTS	SRC
156	Abt, Franz	1819-1885	Fink und Drossel "Zur Drossel sprach der Fink"	Op. 317 No. 2	Unspec.	André		CHAL (1898)
157	Abt, Franz	1819-1885	Fliege, du Vöglein		S/A or S/Br	C. Fischer	In catalogue page "Selected Vocal Duets By Favorite Composers" Carl Fischer NY (no date)	MSN
158	Abt, Franz	1819-1885	Fliege du Vöglein	Op. 176 No. 1	Unspec.	André		CHAL (1898)
159	Abt, Franz	1819-1885	Fly away birdling		S/A	Bayley & Ferguson	Eng. trans. Grmn.	BBC (1975)
160	Abt, Franz	1819-1885	Fly Away, Birdling!		S/A or S/Br	C. Fischer	Eng. trans. Grmn.	MSN
161	Abt, Franz	1819-1885	Frau Nachtigall "Frau Nachtigall, klein's Waldvöglein"	Op. 473 No. 4	Unspec.	André		CHAL (1898)
162	Abt, Franz	1819-1885	Fröhlichen Schiffer "Schiffer schaukelt hin und wieder"	Op. 70 No. 9	Unspc.	André		CHAL (1898)
163	Abt, Franz	1819-1885	Frohsinn "Giebt es Schön'res wohl im Leben"	Op. 91 No. 2	Unspec.	André		CHAL (1898)
164	Abt, Franz	1819-1885	Frühling ist da	Op. 576 No. 11	Unspec.	C. Rühle i. L.		CHAL (1901)
165	Abt, Franz	1819-1885	Frühling ist da "Bächlein zum Bache scwoll"	Op. 174 No. 10	S/A	Bauer		CHAL (1898)
166	Abt, Franz	1819-1885	Frühlingsauferstehung "was ist denn für ein hohes Fest"	Op. 70 No. 1	Unspec.	André		CHAL (1898)
167	Abt, Franz	1819-1885	Frühlingserwachen "Sei gegrüsst o Frühlings-haucht"	Op. 265 No. 1	S/A	Siegel		CHAL (1898)
168	Abt, Franz	1819-1885	Frühlingserwachen "Weite Himmel blaut"	Op. 507 No. 5	Unspec.	Bauer		CHAL (1898)
169	Abt, Franz	1819-1885	Frühlingsfeier "Klar die Berge, grün die Auen"	Op. 507 No. 7	Unspec.	Bauer		CHAL (1898)
170	Abt, Franz	1819-1885	Frühlingsgruss "Es blühet der Dorn"	Op. 457 No. 7	Unspec.	André		CHAL (1898)
171	Abt, Franz	1819-1885	Frühlingsgruss "Nunwehet wieder lind"	Op. 461 No. 1	Unspec.	Kistner		CHAL (1898)
172	Abt, Franz	1819-1885	Frühlingsjubel "Aus grünen Gezweigen"	Op. 547 No. 3	Unspec.	Siegel		CHAL (1898)
173	Abt, Franz	1819-1885	Frühlingsleben "Funkelnde Felder"	Op. 132 No. 9	Unspec.	André		CHAL (1898)
174	Abt, Franz	1819-1885	Frühlingslied "Frühling naht"	Op. 95 No. 3	S/A	André		CHAL (1898)
175	Abt, Franz	1819-1885	Frühlingslust "Zweige flüstern"	Op. 64 No. 2	Unspec.	André		CHAL (1898)
176	Abt, Franz	1819-1885	Frühlingsscene "Schneeglöcken läuten"	Op. 70 No. 7	Unspec.	André		CHAL (1898)
177	Abt, Franz	1819-1885	Frühlingswiederkehr "Wenn der Duft quillt"	Op. 91 No. 3	Unspec.	André		CHAL (1898)
178	Abt, Franz	1819-1885	Frühlingswölkchen "Siehst du Kind die schneeigen Wölkchen"	Op. 265 No. 1	S/A	Siegel		CHAL (1898)
179	Abt, Franz	1819-1885	Frühlingszeit "Frühlings-sonne steigt herauf"	Op. 316 No. 2	Unspec.	André		CHAL (1898)
180	Abt, Franz	1819-1885	Gestillte Sehnsucht "In goldnen Abendschein getaucht"	Op. 69 No. 4	Unspec.	André		CHAL (1898)
181	Abt, Franz	1819-1885	Gleiches Loos "Wie zwei Sterne"	Op. 473 No. 2	Unspec.	André		CHAL (1898)

REC	COMP	DTS	TITLE	OP #	VCG	PUB	COMMENTS	SRC
182	Abt, Franz	1819-1885	Glockengeläute "O Glockengeläute von Bergeshöh'n"	Op. 575 No. 1	S/A	Coppenrath		CHAL (1898)
183	Abt, Franz	1819-1885	Gruss an Maria		2 high v.	Church	In anthology "Sacred Duets A Collection of Two-Part Songs by the Best Composers" Vol. 1. Compi. & ed. W. Shakespeare. Pub. 1907.	MSN
184	Abt, Franz	1819-1885	Gruss an Maria "Nacht entflieht"	Op. 62 No. 5	Unspec.	André		CHAL (1898)
185	Abt, Franz	1819-1885	Grüsse "Wandl' ich Nachts"	Op. 91 No. 1	Unspec.	André		CHAL (1898)
186	Abt, Franz	1819-1885	Gute Nacht du mein herziges Kind "All Abend bevor ich zur Ruhe geh'"	Op. 137 No. 2	T/B or S/A	André		CHAL (1898)
187	Abt, Franz	1819-1885	Gute Nacht "Es sinkt die Nacht zur Erde nieder"	Op. 459 No. 3	Unspec.	Litolff		CHAL (1898)
188	Abt, Franz	1819-1885	Gute Nacht "Schon fängt es an zu dämmern"	Op. 95 No. 4	S/A	André		CHAL (1898)
189	Abt, Franz	1819-1885	Guten Morgen "Nun reibet euch die Aeuglein wach"	Op. 91 No. 8	Unspec.	André		CHAL (1898)
190	Abt, Franz	1819-1885	Harrenden "Stand ein Bäumlein auf der Höh'"	Op. 305 No. 2	S/A	André		CHAL (1898)
191	Abt, Franz	1819-1885	Heimath "Muttererde, heilig Land"	Op. 70 No. 3	Unspec.	André		CHAL (1898)
192	Abt, Franz	1819-1885	Heimweh "Wo auf hohen Tannenspitzen"	Op. 184 No. 9	Unspec.	André		CHAL (1898)
193	Abt, Franz	1819-1885	Herbstlied "Sommers Fäden weben"	Op. 176 No. 4	Unspec.	André		CHAL (1898)
194	Abt, Franz	1819-1885	Hinaus in's Freie "Wie blüht es im Thale"	Op. 91 No. 3	Unspec.	André		CHAL (1898)
195	Abt, Franz	1819-1885	Holder Maientag "O wie ist doch"	Op. 521 No. 1	MS/A	André		CHAL (1898)
196	Abt, Franz	1819-1885	Ich denke dein "Bei jedem Lüftchen"	Op. 95 No. 1	S/A	André		CHAL (1898)
197	Abt, Franz	1819-1885	Ich muss nun einmal singen "Vöglein, Vöglein, was singest du"	Op. 139 No. 1	Unspec.	André		CHAL (1898)
198	Abt, Franz	1819-1885	Im Dunkeln Schlummern die Thäler	Op. 576 No. 4	Unspec.	C. Rühle i. L.		CHAL (1901)
199	Abt, Franz	1819-1885	Im Freien "Bald in dem Busche"	Op. 316 No. 3	Unspec.	André		CHAL (1898)
200	Abt, Franz	1819-1885	Im Spätherbst "Blätter fallen gelb und matt"	Op. 132 No. 5	Unspec.	André		CHAL (1898)
201	Abt, Franz	1819-1885	Im Walde die Amsel	Op. 461 No. 2	Unspec.	Kistner		CHAL (1898)
202	Abt, Franz	1819-1885	Im Walde, im grünen (Wald) Walde	Op. 174 No. 3	S/A	Bauer		CHAL (1898)
203	Abt, Franz	1819-1885	Im Walde, im grünen (Wald) Walde	Op. 457 No. 5	Unspec.	André		CHAL (1898)
204	Abt, Franz	1819-1885	Im Walde "Im Walde, im Walde"	Op. 184 No. 7	Unspec.	André		CHAL (1898)
205	Abt, Franz	1819-1885	In der Ferne "Heilige Sonntagsstille"	Op. 457 No. 4	Unspec.	André		CHAL (1898)

REC	COMP	DTS	TITLE	OP #	VCG	PUB	COMMENTS	SRC
206	Abt, Franz	1819-1885	In der Fremde "Hab' ich doch Tag und Nacht"	Op. 316 No. 4	Unspec.	André		CHAL (1898)
207	Abt, Franz	1819-1885	Jugendlieder, leichte	Op. 70, 184, 316	Unspec.	André	About 10 pieces per opus	CHAL (1898)
208	Abt, Franz	1819-1885	Kahnfahrt "Kein Lüftchen säuselt"	Op. 611 No. 4	S/A	Coppenrath		CHAL (1898)
209	Abt, Franz	1819-1885	Kinderwacht "Wenn fromme Kindlein schlafen geh'n"	Op. 507 No. 3	Unspec.	Bauer		CHAL (1898)
210	Abt, Franz	1819-1885	Kunst und Liebe "Wo sich die Knust ein Hüttchen baut"	Op. 81 No. 2	Unspec.	André		CHAL (1898)
211	Abt, Franz	1819-1885	Lenzestraum "Blüth-enbaum hegt sel'gen Traum"	Op. 461 No. 3	Unspec.	Kistner		CHAL (1898)
212	Abt, Franz	1819-1885	Lerchensang "Wie schweben hoch wohl über'm Feld"	Op. 174 No. 8	S/A	Bauer		CHAL (1898)
213	Abt, Franz	1819-1885	Lied der Nacht "Es singt die Nacht ein leises Lied"	Op. 459 No. 2	Unspec.	Litolff		CHAL (1898)
214	Abt, Franz	1819-1885	Like the Lark		Unspec.	White-Smith	In catalogue page "Vocal Duetts" White-Smith Music Pub. Co. (no date)	MSN
215	Abt, Franz	1819-1885	Mailied "Maien ist gekommen"	Op. 91 No. 6	Unspec.	André		CHAL (1898)
216	Abt, Franz	1819-1885	May song		S/A	Bayley & Ferguson	Eng. trans. Grmn.	BBC (1975)
217	Abt, Franz	1819-1885	Mein Herz thu' dich herauf	Op. 507 No. 4	Unspec.	Bauer		CHAL (1898)
218	Abt, Franz	1819-1885	Mit dir zu sein	Op. 62 No. 6	Unspec.	André		CHAL (1898)
219	Abt, Franz	1819-1885	Mondnacht "Wie schön bist du"	Op. 316 No. 1	Unspec.	André		CHAL (1898)
220	Abt, Franz	1819-1885	Morgenwanderung "Wer recht in Freuden wandern will"	Op. 62 No. 2	Unspec.	André		CHAL (1898)
221	Abt, Franz	1819-1885	Morgonsang		Unspec.	Lundq.	Swed. trans. Grmn.	CVMP (1976)
222	Abt, Franz	1819-1885	Muss Einer von dem Andern	Op. 461 No. 4	Unspec.	Kistner		CHAL (1898)
223	Abt, Franz	1819-1885	Nach der Alpe, wo die süssen	Op. 316 No. a	Unspec.	André		CHAL (1898)
224	Abt, Franz	1819-1885	Nachtigall und Rose "Ach warum sing' ich"	Op. 526 No. 4	S/S	André		CHAL (1898)
225	Abt, Franz	1819-1885	Nicht zu früh "Blühe nicht zu frühe"	Op. 184 No. 10	Unspec.	André		CHAL (1898)
226	Abt, Franz	1819-1885	Nun Blümlein kommt hervor geschwind	Op. 457 No. 1	Unspec.	André		CHAL (1898)
227	Abt, Franz	1819-1885	Nun die Flater wieder scherzen	Op. 576 No. 9	Unspec.	C. Rühle i. L.		CHAL (1901)
228	Abt, Franz	1819-1885	Nun ist der laute Tag verhallt	Op. 576 No. 7	Unspec.	C. Rühle i. L.		CHAL (1901)
229	Abt, Franz	1819-1885	Nun kommt der Frühling wieder	Op. 409 No. 2	Unspec.	Siegel		CHAL (1898)
230	Abt, Franz	1819-1885	O, Hur Underskon ar ej Varens Tid		Unspec.	Lundq.	Swed. trans. Grmn.	CVMP (1976)
231	Abt, Franz	1819-1885	O sag' es noch einmal	Op. 540 No. 3	Unspec.	Siegel		CHAL (1898)
232	Abt, Franz	1819-1885	O Schwarzwald, o Heimath	Op. 465 No. 2	Unspec.	André		CHAL (1898)

REC	COMP	DTS	TITLE	OP #	VCG	PUB	COMMENTS	SRC
233	Abt, Franz	1819-1885	O Welt, wie bist du so schön "Es hebt sich ein Mächtiges Klungen"	Op. 176 No. 3	Unspec.	André		CHAL (1898)
234	Abt, Franz	1819-1885	O wundersel'ge Frühlings-zeit "Wenn der Lenz beginnt"	Op. 540 No. 5	Unspec.	Siegel		CHAL (1898)
235	Abt, Franz	1819-1885	Osterfeier "Wenn die Osterglocken klingen"	Op. 64 No. 1	Unspec.	André		CHAL (1898)
236	Abt, Franz	1819-1885	Over the Stars there is rest		S/A	G. Schirm.	Arr. D. Buck. In anthology "Album of Sixteen Sacred Duets" (no date)	MSN
237	Abt, Franz	1819-1885	Over the stars there is rest		S/A	G. Schirm.	pf or org accomp. Eng. trans. Grmn. In catalogue page "Sacred Vocal Duets" G. Schirmer, Inc. NY (no date)	MSN
238	Abt, Franz	1819-1885	Postillin "Hörst du den lust'gen Postillon"	Op. 64 No. 10	Unspec.	André		CHAL (1898)
239	Abt, Franz	1819-1885	Rauschet ihr Zweige	Op. 576 No. 6	Unspec.	C. Rühle i. L.		CHAL (1901)
240	Abt, Franz	1819-1885	Rose und Nachtigall "Rose lag im Schlummer"	Op. 317 No. 1	Unspec.	André		CHAL (1898)
241	Abt, Franz	1819-1885	Rosentod "Es zittert über die Haide"	Op. 305 No. 1	S/A	André		CHAL (1898)
242	Abt, Franz	1819-1885	Rothkehlchen "Rothkehl-chen singt"	Op. 521 No. 2	MS/A	André		CHAL (1898)
243	Abt, Franz	1819-1885	Sagt an ihr goldenen Sterne	Op. 576 No. 8	Unspec.	C. Rühle i. L.		CHAL (1901)
244	Abt, Franz	1819-1885	Schiffahrt "Über die hellen funkelnden Wellen"	Op. 184 No. 4	Unspec.	André		CHAL (1898)
245	Abt, Franz	1819-1885	Schifferabend "Schifflein in die Weite"	Op. 132 No. 10	Unspec.	André		CHAL (1898)
246	Abt, Franz	1819-1885	Schifferlied "Durch die Fluthen ohne Zagen"	Op. 575 No. 2	S/A	Coppenrath		CHAL (1898)
247	Abt, Franz	1819-1885	Schifferlied "Kommt herbei, frisch und frei"	Op. 62 No. 3	Unspec.	André		CHAL (1898)
248	Abt, Franz	1819-1885	Schifferlied "Schaukle mein Schifflein"	Op. 69 No. 3	Unspec.	André		CHAL (1898)
249	Abt, Franz	1819-1885	Schifferliedchen "Hinauf und hinunter"	Op. 70 No. 8	Unspec.	André		CHAL (1898)
250	Abt, Franz	1819-1885	Schlaf, Dornröschen, schlaf	Op. 409 No. 3	Unspec.	Siegel		CHAL (1898)
251	Abt, Franz	1819-1885	Schlummre auch du [sic]	Op. 457 No. 2	Unspec.	André		CHAL (1898)
252	Abt, Franz	1819-1885	Schönste "Schönste hier auf Erden"	Op. 70 No. 6	Unspec.	André		CHAL (1898)
253	Abt, Franz	1819-1885	Schwalben Scheidergruss "Ade, ade"	Op. 64 No. 6	Unspec.	André		CHAL (1898)
254	Abt, Franz	1819-1885	Sehnsucht nach den Alpen "Wo der Rasen wie Smaragd"	Op. 611 No. 2	S/A	Coppenrath		CHAL (1898)
255	Abt, Franz	1819-1885	Sehnsucht nach den Bergen "Wo den Himmel Berge grenzen"	Op. 174 No. 6	S/A	Bauer		CHAL (1898)
256	Abt, Franz	1819-1885	Sehnsucht nach der Hei-math "Ich höre das frohe Gelispel"	Op. 176 No. 2	Unspec.	André		CHAL (1898)
257	Abt, Franz	1819-1885	Sennenlied "Wenn die Blumen wieder blühen"	Op. 69 No. 1	Unspec.	André		CHAL (1898)

REC	COMP	DTS	TITLE	OP #	VCG	PUB	COMMENTS	SRC
258	Abt, Franz	1819-1885	Siehst du dort die Bergeshöhen	Op. 407 No. 1	S/A	André		CHAL (1898)
259	Abt, Franz	1819-1885	Singt "Vöglein singt, so gut es kann"	Op. 611 No. 5	S/A	Coppenrath		CHAL (1898)
260	Abt, Franz	1819-1885	Sommer kommt mit Rosenduft	Op. 521 No. 2	MS/A	André		CHAL (1898)
261	Abt, Franz	1819-1885	Sommerabend "Schwäne kommen gezogen"	Op. 64 No. 2	Unspec.	André		CHAL (1898)
262	Abt, Franz	1819-1885	Sonntag am Meere "Am Himmelssaum"	Op. 457 No. 6	Unspec.	André		CHAL (1898)
263	Abt, Franz	1819-1885	Sonntag auf dem Meere "Es haucht der Ost"	Op. 184 No. 1	Unspec.	André		CHAL (1898)
264	Abt, Franz	1819-1885	Sonntag ist's	Op. 407 No. 4	Unspec.	André		CHAL (1898)
265	Abt, Franz	1819-1885	Sonntag "Liebe Sonntag ist nun da"	Op. 132 No. 1	Unspec.	André		CHAL (1898)
266	Abt, Franz	1819-1885	Sonntagsfrühe "So still und mild der Tag"	Op. 174 No. 1	S/A	Bauer		CHAL (1898)
267	Abt, Franz	1819-1885	Sonntagsglocken "Sonntagsglocken, Freudenschall"	Op. 70 No. 5	Unspec.	André		CHAL (1898)
268	Abt, Franz	1819-1885	Sonntagsstille "Sonntagsstille in der Weite"	Op. 409 No. 6	Unspec.	Siegel		CHAL (1898)
269	Abt, Franz	1819-1885	Sternlein am Himmel	Op. 316 No. 10	Unspec.	André		CHAL (1898)
270	Abt, Franz	1819-1885	Still is the Night		Unspec.	Leonard-Eng	Eng. trans. Grmn.	CVMP (1976)
271	Abt, Franz	1819-1885	Still ruht der See	Op. 575 No. 3	S/A	Coppenrath		CHAL (1898)
272	Abt, Franz	1819-1885	Stille Wasserrose steigt aus dem blauen See	Op. 540 No. 4	Unspec.	Siegel		CHAL (1898)
273	Abt, Franz	1819-1885	Surre, surre, Käferlein "Maienkäfer summen"	Op. 132 No. 6	Unspec.	André		CHAL (1898)
274	Abt, Franz	1819-1885	Süsses Veilchen	Op. 457 No. 3	Unspec.	André		CHAL (1898)
275	Abt, Franz	1819-1885	Tag verblüht uns in der heil'gen Stille	Op. 576 No. 5	Unspec.	C. Rühle i. L.		CHAL (1901)
276	Abt, Franz	1819-1885	Taubenhaus "Bauer hat ein Taubenhaus"	Op. 91 No. 9	Unspec.	André		CHAL (1898)
277	Abt, Franz	1819-1885	Treue Liebe "Es rauschen die Wasser"	Op. 507 No. 9	Unspec.	Bauer		CHAL (1898)
278	Abt, Franz	1819-1885	Vaterhaus "Vergiss mir nie das Vaterhaus"	Op. 70 No. 10	Unspec.	André		CHAL (1898)
279	Abt, Franz	1819-1885	Veilchen Veilchen "Ich fand ein holdes Veilchen" Veilchen unter Gras versteckt"	Op. 174 No. 7	S/A	Bauer		CHAL (1898)
280	Abt, Franz	1819-1885	Veilchen vom Berg	Op. 407 No. 8	S/A	André		CHAL (1898)
281	Abt, Franz	1819-1885	Viel tausend Vöglein fliegen	Op. 576 No. 3	Unspec.	C. Rühle i. L.		CHAL (1901)
282	Abt, Franz	1819-1885	Vogelsang "Wir siegen uns spielend"	Op. 184 No. 5	Unspec.	André		CHAL (1898)
283	Abt, Franz	1819-1885	Vöglein Abschied "Wer klappert am Dach"	Op. 91 No. 7	Unspec.	André		CHAL (1898)
284	Abt, Franz	1819-1885	Vöglein Dank "Ihr Vöglein leicht"	Op. 132 No. 3	Unspec.	André		CHAL (1898)
285	Abt, Franz	1819-1885	Vöglein im Walde "Lustiges Vöglein im Walde"	Op. 547 No. 1	Unspec.	Siegel		CHAL (1898)
286	Abt, Franz	1819-1885	Vöglein im Walde "Lustiges Vöglein im Walde"	Op. 95 No. 2	S/A	André		CHAL (1898)

REC	COMP	DTS	TITLE	OP #	VCG	PUB	COMMENTS	SRC
287	Abt, Franz	1819-1885	Vöglein, nun hebet an	Op. 575 No. 4	S/A	Coppenrath		CHAL (1898)
288	Abt, Franz	1819-1885	Vöglein, was singst du schon	Op. 299 No. 3	S/A	Heinr.		CHAL (1898)
289	Abt, Franz	1819-1885	Vögleins Frage "Bist du da, ja ja"	Op. 457 No. 8	Unspec.	André		CHAL (1898)
290	Abt, Franz	1819-1885	Volks- und Kinderlieder "Ein und Zweistimmig"	Op. 350	Unspec.	André	Folk songs & children's songs for 1-2 v.	CHAL (1898)
291	Abt, Franz	1819-1885	Waldabend "Wenn die Sonn' zur Ruh'"	Op. 316 No. 8	Unspec.	André		CHAL (1898)
292	Abt, Franz	1819-1885	Waldandacht "Früh-morgens, wenn die Hähne kräh'n"	Op. 540 No. 1	Unspec.	Siegel		CHAL (1898)
293	Abt, Franz	1819-1885	Waldbach "Bächlein mit den blauen Augen"	Op. 611 No. 3	S/A	Coppenrath		CHAL (1898)
294	Abt, Franz	1819-1885	Waldfahrt "Im Wald (im Wald) ist's frisch"	Op. 70 No. 4	Unspec.	André		CHAL (1898)
295	Abt, Franz	1819-1885	Waldfrieden "O wie muss dir sein"	Op. 184 No. 3	Unspec.	André		CHAL (1898)
296	Abt, Franz	1819-1885	Waldkirche "Wenn zum grünen Waldesgrunde"	Op. 606 No. 6	S/A	Coppenrath		CHAL (1898)
297	Abt, Franz	1819-1885	Waldlust "Wie herrlich ist's im Walde"	Op. 64 No. 5	Unspec.	André		CHAL (1898)
298	Abt, Franz	1819-1885	Wanderlied "Liebe Sonne strahlt so rein"	Op. 575 No. 6	S/A	Coppenrath		CHAL (1898)
299	Abt, Franz	1819-1885	Wanderlied "War lange nun bei euch"	Op. 184 No. 6	Unspec.	André		CHAL (1898)
300	Abt, Franz	1819-1885	Wanderlied "Wie scheint mir die Sonne"	Op. 507 No. 10	Unspec.	Bauer		CHAL (1898)
301	Abt, Franz	1819-1885	Wanderlust "Es ziehn nach fernen Landen"	Op. 132 No. 8	Unspec.	André		CHAL (1898)
302	Abt, Franz	1819-1885	Wanderlust "Frühling kommt"	Op. 316 No. 6	Unspec.	André		CHAL (1898)
303	Abt, Franz	1819-1885	Wanderlust "Wanderlust, das ist das höchste Glück"	Op. 174 No. 4	S/A	Bauer		CHAL (1898)
304	Abt, Franz	1819-1885	Was willst du mehr "Nennst du ein Hüttchen dein"	Op. 547 No. 2	Unspec.	Siegel		CHAL (1898)
305	Abt, Franz	1819-1885	Was zwitscherst du lieb Vögelein	Op. 184 No. 8	Unspec.	André		CHAL (1898)
306	Abt, Franz	1819-1885	Weihnachtszauber "Sagt an, ihr golden Sterne"	Op. 576 No. 10	Unspec.	Grüniger		CHAL (1898)
307	Abt, Franz	1819-1885	Weiss ich dich in meiner Nähe		S/A or S/Br	C. Fischer	In catalogue page "Selected Vocal Duets By Favorite Composers" Carl Fischer NY (no date)	MSN
308	Abt, Franz	1819-1885	Wem Gott ein braves Lien bescheert	Op. 212a No. 4	S/A	Schlesinger		CHAL (1898)
309	Abt, Franz	1819-1885	Wenn der Frühling auf die Berge steigt"	Op. 132 No. 4	Unspec.	André		CHAL (1898)
310	Abt, Franz	1819-1885	When I Know That Thou Art Near Me		Unspec.	Brainard's Sons	Eng. trans. Grmn. In anthology "Brainard's Collection of Vocal Duets from Popular Modern and Standard Composers" Pub. 1903.	MSN

REC	COMP	DTS	TITLE	OP #	VCG	PUB	COMMENTS	SRC
311	Abt, Franz	1819-1885	Wie der Lerche "Wie die Lerche möcht ich singen"	Op. 174 No. 2	S/A	Bauer		CHAL (1898)
312	Abt, Franz	1819-1885	Wie ist doch die Erde so schön	Op. 62 No. 1	Unspec.	André		CHAL (1898)
313	Abt, Franz	1819-1885	Wie weich die Lüfte wallen	Op. 576 No. 12	Unspec.	C. Rühle i. L.		CHAL (1901)
314	Abt, Franz	1819-1885	Wiegenlied "Vom Berg hinabgestiegen"	Op. 64 No. 4	Unspec.	André		CHAL (1898)
315	Abt, Franz	1819-1885	Wo den Himmel Berge kränzen	Op. 174 No. 6	S/A	Bauer i. Br.		CHAL (1911)
316	Abt, Franz	1819-1885	Wohin "Vöglein im Walde dort"	Op. 174 No. 5	S/A	Bauer		CHAL (1898)
317	Abt, Franz	1819-1885	Wohl über Nacht "Es hat sich wieder Busch und Baum"	Op. 316 No. 5	Unspec.	André		CHAL (1898)
318	Abt, Franz	1819-1885	Wollt ihr die Engelein hören im Chor		2 high v.	Church	In anthology "Sacred Duets A Collection of Two-Part Songs by the Best Composers" Vol. 1. Compi. & ed. W. Shakespeare. Pub. 1907.	MSN
319	Abt, Franz	1819-1885	Wollt ihr die Engelein hören im Chor	Op. 132 No. 7	Unspec.	André		CHAL (1898)
320	Abt, Franz	1819-1885	Wunsch "Möchte wohl ein Vöglein sein"	Op. 507 No. 8	Unspec.	Bauer		CHAL (1898)
321	Abt, Franz	1819-1885	Zwei welke Rosen träumen im Sande	Op. 576 No. 1	Unspec.	C. Rühle i. L.		CHAL (1901)
322	Achenbach, J.		Mei Bua hat a Sträusserl	Op. 20	2 female v.	Gross i. Insbr.		CHAL (1901)
323	Adam, Adolphe Charles	1803-1856	Cantique de Noël		S/A or Unspec.	G. Schirm., Lundq.	Avail. in assorted languages: Eng., It., Swed., Fr.	CVMP (1976)
324	Adam, Adolphe Charles	1803-1856	Cantique de Noël		S/A	G. Schirm.	In anthology "Schirmer's Favorite Sacred Duets for Various Voices" Pub. 1955.	MSN
325	Adam, Adolphe Charles	1803-1856	Cantique de Noël		S/A	G. Schirm.	pf or org accomp. In catalogue page "Sacred Vocal Duets" G. Schirmer, Inc. NY (no date)	MSN
326	Adam, Adolphe Charles	1803-1856	Letzer Gedanke "Verbannt sei jedes Klagen"		Unspec.	Schott (Weber)		CHAL (1898)
327	Adam, Adolphe Charles	1803-1856	Oh, Holy Night!		high & low v.	Church	Eng. trans. Fr. In anth. "Sacred Duets A Coll. of 2-Part Songs by the Best Comp." Vol. 2. Compi. & ed. W. Shakespeare. Pub. 1907.	MSN
328	Adams, Thomas	1785-1858	Ave Maria "Ave Maria gratia pleni"		S/A	Schott		CHAL (1898)
329	Adant, L.		Florentines		Unspec.	Junne		CHAL (1898)
330	Aerts, Felix	1827-1888	A l'amitié	No. 2	Unspec.	Cranz		CHAL (1898)
331	Aerts, Felix	1827-1888	A une institutrice	No. 18	Unspec.	Cranz		CHAL (1898)
332	Aerts, Felix	1827-1888	Chant d'atelier	No. 4	Unspec.	Cranz		CHAL (1898)
333	Aerts, Felix	1827-1888	Chant de tailleur	No. 16	Unspec.	Cranz		CHAL (1898)

REC	COMP	DTS	TITLE	OP #	VCG	PUB	COMMENTS	SRC
334	Aerts, Felix	1827-1888	Chant du départ	No. 19	Unspec.	Cranz		CHAL (1898)
335	Aerts, Felix	1827-1888	Cloche du soir	No. 5	Unspec.	Cranz		CHAL (1898)
336	Aerts, Felix	1827-1888	Cloches de mon village	No. 13	Unspec.	Cranz		CHAL (1898)
337	Aerts, Felix	1827-1888	Départs de l'hirondelle	No. 9	Unspec.	Cranz		CHAL (1898)
338	Aerts, Felix	1827-1888	Lyre de mon pays	No. 5	Unspec.	Cranz		CHAL (1898)
339	Aerts, Felix	1827-1888	Lys de la vallé [vallée?]	No. 1	Unspec.	Cranz		CHAL (1898)
340	Aerts, Felix	1827-1888	Nuits	No. 12	Unspec.	Cranz		CHAL (1898)
341	Aerts, Felix	1827-1888	Papillon	No. 8	Unspec.	Cranz		CHAL (1898)
342	Aerts, Felix	1827-1888	Patrie du Belge	No. 20	Unspec.	Cranz		CHAL (1898)
343	Aerts, Felix	1827-1888	Pourvoir de l'harmonie	No. 11	Unspec.	Cranz		CHAL (1898)
344	Aerts, Felix	1827-1888	Puissance de l'harmonie	No. 6	Unspec.	Cranz		CHAL (1898)
345	Aerts, Felix	1827-1888	Retour de l'hirondelle	No. 10	Unspec.	Cranz		CHAL (1898)
346	Aerts, Felix	1827-1888	Verbe prier	No. 17	Unspec.	Cranz		CHAL (1898)
347	Ahnfelt, Oscar	fl. 1872	Day by Day and with Each Passing Moment		high & low v.	Becken-horst	Arr. C. Courtney. In anthology "Duets for the Master: Sacred Duets for High and Low Voice and Keyboard" Pub. 1989.	MSN
348	Aiblinger, Johann Kaspar	1779-1867	Christkind "Es weht der Wind und ist so kalt"	No. 2	Unspec.	Werner i. Münch.		CHAL (1898)
349	Aiblinger, Johann Kaspar	1779-1867	Lied bei der Krippe Jesu "Schlaf wohl, du Himmelsknabe"	No. 3	Unspec.	Werner i. Münch.		CHAL (1898)
350	Aiblinger, Johann Kaspar	1779-1867	Weihnachtslieder (3)		Unspec.	Werner i. Münch.	3 Christmas Duets. Unspec.	CHAL (1898)
351	Alberti, G.		Leise zieht durch mein Gemüth	Op. 23 No. 1	Unspec.	Hoffheinz		CHAL (1898)
352	Alberti, G.		Zweigesang "Im Flieder-busch ein Vöglein sass"	Op. 23 No. 2	Unspec.	Hoffheinz		CHAL (1898)
353	Aletter, Wilhelm	1867-1934	Grade beim Hôtel zur Eule		2 med. female v.	Salzer		CHAL (1901)
354	Aletter, Wilhelm	1867-1934	Lebens Pfeffer ist gewiss		Unspec.	Eberle i. Wien		CHAL (1901)
355	Aletter, Wilhelm	1867-1934	Lustigen Schneider "Wir sind drei flotte Schneider"		Unspec.	Bosworth		CHAL (1898)
356	Alexandrov, Anatol	1883-1946	Transbaikal song		Unspec.	Russian State		BBC (1975)
357	Allitsen, Frances	1849-1912	Break, diviner light		Unspec.	Boosey	Eng. woman comp.	BBC (1975)
358	Allitsen, Frances	1849-1912	Break, Diviner Light		Unspec.	Boosey	Eng. woman comp.	CVMP (1976)
359	Allitsen, Frances	1848-1912	Break Diviner Light		2 med. v.	Boosey	Eng. woman comp.	ASR
360	Allitsen, Frances	1849-1912	Lord is my Light (Psalm 27)		Unspec.	Boosey	Eng. woman comp.	CVMP (1976)

REC	COMP	DTS	TITLE	OP #	VCG	PUB	COMMENTS	SRC
361	Allitsen, Frances	1848-1912	Lord is my Light (Psalm 27)		high & med. v.	Boosey	Eng. woman comp.	ASR
362	Altenhofer, C.		Frühjahr "Hell ins Fenster scheint die Sonne"	Op. 31 No. 5	S/A	Hug		CHAL (1898)
363	Altmann, Gustav	1865-1924	Ich lieb' eine Blume	Op. 10 No. 2	2 female v.	Seemann		CHAL (1901)
364	Altmann, Gustav	1865-1924	Schmetterling ist in die Rose verliebt	Op. 10 No. 1	2 female v.	Seemann		CHAL (1901)
365	Altmann, Gustav	1865-1924	Unter'm weissen Raume sitzend	Op. 10 No. 3	2 female v.	Seemann		CHAL (1901)
366	Anderson, Beth	1950-	Torero Piece		Unspec.	ACA	acap. Amer. woman comp.	CVMP (1995)
367	Anderson, Beth	1950-	Torero Piece		2 female v.	ACA	acap. Amer. woman comp.	ASR
368	Anderson, Margaret Tweedie		The crooked bawbee		Unspec.	Bayley & Ferguson	Arr. Mansfield. Eng. woman comp.	BBC (1975)
369	André, Jean Baptiste	1823-1882	Dein Herzlein mild	Op. 47 No. 7	S/A	André		CHAL (1898)
370	André, Jean Baptiste	1823-1882	Guter Rath "Wenn du willst"	Op. 47 No. 3	S/A	André		CHAL (1898)
371	André, Jean Baptiste	1823-1882	Im Grünen "Im Grün erwacht"	Op. 47 No. 6	S/A	André		CHAL (1898)
372	André, Jean Baptiste	1823-1882	Im Walde "Ihr Vöglein in den Zweigen"	Op. 47 No. 4	S/A	André		CHAL (1898)
373	André, Jean Baptiste	1823-1882	In meinem Garten die Nelken	Op. 47 No. 2	S/A	André		CHAL (1898)
374	André, Jean Baptiste	1823-1882	Jägerlied "Zierlich ist des Vogels Tritt"	Op. 47 No. 5	S/A	André		CHAL (1898)
375	André, Jean Baptiste	1823-1882	Sind die Sterne fromme Lämmer	Op. 47 No. 1	S/A	André		CHAL (1898)
376	André, Jean Baptiste	1823-1882	Wanderlied "Wem Gott will rechte Gunst erweisen"	Op. 47 No. 8	S/A	André		CHAL (1898)
377	André, Johann Anton	1775-1842	An die Natur "Süsse heilige Natur"	Op. 51 No. 4	S/A	André		CHAL (1898)
378	André, Johann Anton	1775-1842	An die Tugend "Holde Tugend wohn"	Op. 69 No. 3	S/A	André		CHAL (1898)
379	André, Johann Anton	1775-1842	Aufmunterung "Zum Glück wird alle Welt geboren"	Op. 69 No. 4	S/A	André		CHAL (1898)
380	André, Johann Anton	1775-1842	Blümchen der Freude "Es stürmet so schaurig"	Op. 51 No. 3	S/A	André		CHAL (1898)
381	André, Johann Anton	1775-1842	Freude folgt stets der Tugend	Op. 69 No. 5	S/A	André		CHAL (1898)
382	André, Johann Anton	1775-1842	Freundschaft und Liebe	Op. 69 No. 1	S/A	André		CHAL (1898)
383	André, Johann Anton	1775-1842	Grab "Grab ist tief und stille"	Op. 51 No. 5	S/A	André		CHAL (1898)
384	André, Johann Anton	1775-1842	Jahres letzte Stunde		Unspec.	André	pf or harm	CHAL (1906)
385	André, Johann Anton	1775-1842	Jugend ist das Land der Freunde	Op. 51 No. 2	S/A	André		CHAL (1898)
386	André, Johann Anton	1775-1842	Lebensgenuss "Sie rollen schnell, des Menschen Jahre"	Op. 69 No. 2	S/A	André	Comp. ca. 1840	CHAL (1898)
387	André, Johann Anton	1775-1842	Lebensglück "Wie glücklich lebt, wer Ruh' und Frieden"	Op. 69 No. 6	S/A	André	Comp. ca. 1840	CHAL (1898)
388	André, Johann Anton	1775-1842	Liebe "Wenn nicht mit Göttermacht"	Op. 51 No. 6	S/A	André	Comp. ca. 1828	CHAL (1898)

REC	COMP	DTS	TITLE	OP #	VCG	PUB	COMMENTS	SRC
389	André, Johann Anton	1775-1842	Neujahrslied "Jahres letzte Stunde"		S/S	André		CHAL (1898)
390	André, Johann Anton	1775-1842	Zeit entflieht mit raschen Flügeln	Op. 51 No. 1	S/A	André	Comp. ca. 1828	CHAL (1898)
391	André, L. [prob. Christian Karl André]	1763-1831	A Bleamerl im Mieda	Op. 126 No. 2	Unspec.	André		CHAL (1898)
392	André, L. [prob. Christian Karl André]	1763-1831	Bleamerl vom See "Dort beim See da drunt"	Op. 126 No. 3	Unspec.	André		CHAL (1898)
393	André, L. [prob. Christian Karl André]	1763-1831	Holzknechtlied "Und die Holzknechtbuama"	Op. 126 No. 1	Unspec.	André		CHAL (1898)
394	André, L. [prob. Christian Karl André]	1763-1831	Mirzel magst mit mir auf d' Alma geh'n	Op. 126	Unspec.	André		CHAL (1901)
395	André, L. [prob. Christian Karl André]	1763-1831	Neck "Horch wie der Neck"		S/A	André		CHAL (1898)
396	André, L. [prob. Christian Karl André]	1763-1831	Zwâ Sterndlan "Zwâ Sterndlan am Himmel"	Op. 39 No. 1	2 med. v.	André		CHAL (1898)
397	Andrews, Mark		The radiant Morn hath passed away		2 high v.	Church	In anthology "Sacred Duets A Collection of Two-Part Songs by the Best Composers" Vol. 1. Compi. & ed. W. Shakespeare. Pub. 1907.	MSN
398	Andriessen, Juriaan	1925-	Kerstlied		2 female v.	Donemus	pf or org accomp. Sacred canon.	CVMP (1976)
399	Andriessen, Juriaan	1925-	Kerstlied		2 female v.	Donemus	pf or org accomp.	ASR
400	Androzzo, A. Bazel		If I can help somebody		Unspec.	Boosey	Arr. Carroll	BBC (1975)
401	Anfossi, Pasquale	1727-1797	Non temer, non son più amante		S/S	J. Williams	Ed. Fuller-Maitland	BBC (1975)
402	Angerer, Gottfried	1851-1909	Chum Bueb und lueg dis Ländli	Op. 113	Unspec.	Hug		CHAL (1906)
403	Ansorge, M. [prob. Margarethe]	1872-1944	Auf dem Anger, da gehn die Gänse	Op. 20 No. 7	Unspec.	Becher	Grmn. woman comp.	CHAL (1911)
404	Ansorge, M. [prob. Margarethe]	1872-1944	Aus dem Kinderleben (10)	Op. 20	Unspec.	Becher	10 duets. Grmn. woman comp.	CHAL (1911)
405	Ansorge, M. [prob. Margarethe]	1872-1944	Brause, Regen brause	Op. 20 No. 9	Unspec.	Becher	Grmn. woman comp.	CHAL (1911)
406	Ansorge, M. [prob. Margarethe]	1872-1944	Da liegt im Bett der Hans	Op. 20 No. 2	Unspec.	Becher	Grmn. woman comp.	CHAL (1911)
407	Ansorge, M. [prob. Margarethe]	1872-1944	Entchen, so geh' doch grade	Op. 20 No. 6	Unspec.	Becher	Grmn. woman comp.	CHAL (1911)
408	Ansorge, M. [prob. Margarethe]	1872-1944	Frühling "Was rauscht, was rieselt"		Unspec.	O. Schmidt	Grmn. woman comp.	CHAL (1911)
409	Ansorge, M. [prob. Margarethe]	1872-1944	Habt ihr schon von dem Haus gehört	Op. 20 No. 1	Unspec.	Becher	Grmn. woman comp.	CHAL (1911)

REC	COMP	DTS	TITLE	OP #	VCG	PUB	COMMENTS	SRC
410	Ansorge, M. [prob. Margarethe]	1872-1944	Kleiner, blauer Schmetterling	Op. 20 No. 8	Unspec.	Becher	Grmn. woman comp.	CHAL (1911)
411	Ansorge, M. [prob. Margarethe]	1872-1944	Mutter weint, todkrank ist Hänschen	Op. 20 No. 3	Unspec.	Becher	Grmn. woman comp.	CHAL (1911)
412	Ansorge, M. [prob. Margarethe]	1872-1944	Wann die kleinen Kinder beten	Op. 20 No. 10	Unspec.	Becher	Grmn. woman comp.	CHAL (1911)
413	Ansorge, M. [prob. Margarethe]	1872-1944	Was rauscht, was rieselt	Op. 20 No. 5	Unspec.	Becher	Grmn. woman comp.	CHAL (1911)
414	Ansorge, M. [prob. Margarethe]	1872-1944	Wie stolz er geht	Op. 20 No. 4	Unspec.	Becher	Grmn. woman comp.	CHAL (1911)
415	Apell, Karl	1812-1895	Partenza		Unspec.	Meyer i. Erfurt		CHAL (1898)
416	Arditi, Luigi	1822-1903	Desio		S/A	Ricordi		CHAL (1898)
417	Arditi, Luigi	1822-1903	Il bacio		Unspec.	Ashdown		CHAL (1898)
418	Arditi, Luigi	1822-1903	Trema, o vil		S/A	Ricordi		BBC (1975)
419	Arendt, W.		Ein Küsschen von der Mutter		S/A	Trnfeld i. Gr.-Licht.		CHAL (1901)
420	Arensky, Anton	1861-1906	Alls ruht in der Nacht		S/A	Jurgns.	Grmn. Tr. Russ.	CHAL (1901)
421	Arensky, Anton	1861-1906	Dve Rozï	Op. 45 No. 2	S/A or MS/A	State Mus. Pub. (Moscow)	Translit. of Russ. In collection "Dueti i Kvarteti" works of A. Arensky. Pub. 1967.	NATS-VCD
422	Arensky, Anton	1861-1906	Ein stilles Glück kann nimmer walten	Op. 29 No. 1	S/A	Jurgensen i . M.		CHAL (1906)
423	Arensky, Anton	1861-1906	Es liegen zwei verwelkte Rosen	Op. 45 No. 2	S/A	Jurgns.	Grmn. tr. Russ.	CHAL (1901)
424	Arensky, Anton	1861-1906	Fialka		S/A	GMI	Translit. title of Russ. Only Cyrillic. Anth. "Izbrannye Duety Russkikh Kompozitorov dlia peniia s fortepiano" Pub. 1948.	MSN
425	Arensky, Anton	1861-1906	Fialka	Op. 29 No. 3	S/A or S/MS or MS/A	State Mus. Pub. (Moscow)	Translit. of Russ. In collection "Dueti i Kvarteti" works of A. Arensky. Pub. 1967.	NATS-VCD
426	Arensky, Anton	1861-1906	Gestrige Nacht hat wonnig gelacht	Op. 29 No. 2	S/A	Jurgensen i . M.		CHAL (1906)
427	Arensky, Anton	1861-1906	Minutï Schastya	Op. 29 No. 1	S/A	State Mus. Pub. (Moscow)	Translit. of Russ. In collection "Dueti i Kvarteti" works of A. Arensky. Pub. 1967.	NATS-VCD
428	Arensky, Anton	1861-1906	Minuty schastia [Minutes of Happiness]		S/A	GMI	Translit. title of Russ. Only Cyrillic. Anth. "Izbrannye Duety Russkikh Kompozitorov dlia peniia s fortepiano" Pub. 1948.	MSN
429	Arensky, Anton	1861-1906	Tikho vse sred Choruiushchei Nochi [Everything is quiet in the Enchanting Nights]		S/A	GMI	Translit. title of Russ. Only Cyrillic. Anth. "Izbrannye Duety Russkikh Kompozitorov dlia peniia s fortepiano" Pub. 1948.	MSN

REC	COMP	DTS	TITLE	OP #	VCG	PUB	COMMENTS	SRC
430	Arensky, Anton	1861-1906	Tikho Vsyo Sred Charushchey Nochi	Op. 45 No. 1	S/A or MS/A	State Mus. Pub. (Moscow)	Translit. of Russ. In collection "Duetï i Kvartetï" works of A. Arensky. Pub. 1967.	NATS-VCD
431	Arensky, Anton	1861-1906	Veilchen verbirgt sich vor Strahlen der Sonne	Op. 29 No. 3	S/A	Jürgensen i. M.		CHAL (1906)
432	Arnaud, Etienne	1807-1863	Quand on aime		Unspec.	Schott		CHAL (1898)
433	Arndts, Maria Vespermann	1823-1882	Lass' tief in dir mich lesen	Op. 13	S/S	Goll i. W.	German woman comp. Née Vespermann.	CHAL (1898)
434	Arndts, Maria Vespermann	1823-1882	Lieblich sind die Juninächte		Unspec.	Schöningh.	German woman comp. Née Vespermann.	CHAL (1898)
435	Arndts, Maria Vespermann	1823-1882	Süsser Schlag der Heidelerche		Unspec.	Schöningh.	German woman comp. Née Vespermann.	CHAL (1898)
436	Arndts, Maria Vespermann	1823-1882	Weihnachts "Das ist die rechte Weihnachtszeit"	Op. 14	S/A	Goll i. W.	German woman comp. Née Vespermann.	CHAL (1898)
437	Arndts, Maria Vespermann	1823-1882	"Wonnig ist's in Frühlingstagen"		Unspec.	Schöningh. i. Pad.	German woman comp. Née Vespermann.	CHAL (1898)
438	Ascher		Love's dream is past		S/A	White-Smith	In catalogue page "Vocal Duetts" of White-Smith Music Pub. Co. (no date)	MSN
439	Ascher, E.		Ballfreuden "Sehr amusant auf jeden Fall"		2 female v.	Meissner		CHAL (1898)
440	Ascher, E.		Wie so, ach so, aha, na ja "Jetzt singe ich mal"		Unspec.	Meissner		CHAL (1898)
441	Ascher, E.		Wir auch, wir nicht "Ich bin ein lustig frisches Blut"		Unspec.	Meissner		CHAL (1898)
442	Ascher, Joseph	1829-1869	Alice (Life's Dream is O'er)		high & low v.	Hinds, Hayden & Eldredge	In anthology "The Most Popular Vocal Duets" Ed. Dr. E. J. Biedermann. Pub. 1914.	MSN
443	Ascher, Joseph	1829-1869	Life's Dream is O'er (Alice)		high & low v.	Hinds, Hayden & Eldredge	In anthology "The Most Popular Vocal Duets" Ed. Dr. E. J. Biedermann. Pub. 1914.	MSN
444	Ashford, E. L.		My Task		S/A	Lorenz		CVMP (1976)
445	Attenhofer, Karl	1837-1914	Abendlied "Tagwerk ist vollbracht"	Op. 31 No. 2	S/A	Hug		CHAL (1898)
446	Attenhofer, Karl	1837-1914	Auf die Berge möcht' ich hin	II No. 4	Unspec.	Hug		CHAL (1901)
447	Attenhofer, Karl	1837-1914	Blauer Himmel, klare Lüfte	II No. 3	Unspec.	Hug		CHAL (1901)
448	Attenhofer, Karl	1837-1914	Es zieht ein stiller Engel	II No. 2	Unspec.	Hug		CHAL (1901)
449	Attenhofer, Karl	1837-1914	Für Schule und Haus "16 Mädchenlieder"		Unspec.	Hug	Collection. 16 duets for female v.	CHAL (1901)
450	Attenhofer, Karl	1837-1914	Grasemückchen an dem Brückchen	Op. 31 No. 7	S/A	Hug		CHAL (1898)
451	Attenhofer, Karl	1837-1914	Hell in's Fenster scheindt die Sonne	I No. 5	Unspec.	Hug		CHAL (1901)
452	Attenhofer, Karl	1837-1914	Ich hört' ein Vöglein singen	II No. 5	Unspec.	Hug		CHAL (1901)

REC	COMP	DTS	TITLE	OP #	VCG	PUB	COMMENTS	SRC
453	Attenhofer, Karl	1837-1914	Im Grünen "Willkommen im Grünen"	Op. 31 No. 6	S/A	Hug		CHAL (1898)
454	Attenhofer, Karl	1837-1914	Im Herbste "Bald fällt von diesen Zweigen"	Op. 31 No. 3	S/A	Hug		CHAL (1898)
455	Attenhofer, Karl	1837-1914	Kein Hälmlein wächst auf Erden	I No. 4	Unspec.	Hug		CHAL (1901)
456	Attenhofer, Karl	1837-1914	Kein Hälmlein wächst auf Erden	Op. 31 No. 4	S/A	Hug		CHAL (1898)
457	Attenhofer, Karl	1837-1914	Lerche singt, der Kuckuck schreit	II No. 8	Unspec.	Hug		CHAL (1901)
458	Attenhofer, Karl	1837-1914	Machs wie die Lerche, juble voraus	II No. 6	Unspec.	Hug		CHAL (1901)
459	Attenhofer, Karl	1837-1914	Schweizerische Volks- und Vaterlandslieder (44)		Unspec.	Hug	Collection of 44 Duets, unspec.	CHAL (1898)
460	Attenhofer, Karl	1837-1914	So war's zu aller Frist	II No. 7	Unspec.	Hug		CHAL (1901)
461	Attenhofer, Karl	1837-1914	Steig herauf, Tag des Herrn	Op. 31 No. 1	S/A	Hug		CHAL (1898)
462	Attenhofer, Karl	1837-1914	Steige herauf, Tag des Herrn	I No. 1	Unspec.	Hug		CHAL (1901)
463	Attenhofer, Karl	1837-1914	Tagewerke ist abgethan	I No. 2	Unspec.	Hug		CHAL (1901)
464	Attenhofer, Karl	1837-1914	Waldfrieden "O wie muss dir sein"	Op. 31 No. 8	S/A	Hug		CHAL (1898)
465	Attenhofer, Karl	1837-1914	Willkommen in Grünen	I No. 6	Unspec.	Hug		CHAL (1901)
466	Aue, U.		Gondoliera "O komm zu mir"	Op. 1	S/B or S/MS	Junne		CHAL (1898)
467	August, J.		Anna and Johanna, die Männerfeindinnen "Weib ist der Schöpfung Zier"	Op. 28	2 female v.	Kleine i. P.		CHAL (1898)
468	August, J.		Max und Moritz, die lustigen Brüder "Ha, ha wir sind zwei lust'ge Brüder"	Op. 21	Unspec.	Kleine i. P.		CHAL (1898)
469	Augustin, F. H.		In auer Tramway sitzt a Köchin		S/A	Eberle		CHAL (1906)
470	Ayre, Nat D.		Wonderful girl, wonderful boy		Unspec.	Feldman		BBC (1975)
471	Baader, R.		Fräulein Miezel und Fräulein Striezel "Nein, wie's jetzt die Männer treiben"		2 female v.	O. Dietrich		CHAL (1898)
472	Baader, R.		Wir Evastöchter sind fürwahr		2 female v.	O. Dietrich		CHAL (1901)
473	Babbitt, Milton	1916-	Four Canons		S/A or S/S or MS/A	Rongwen	From Birthday Canons for Carl Engel by Arnold Schoenberg. Pub. 1973.	NATS -VCD
474	Babick, J.		Lass ruhig fliessen		Unspec.	Leiner i. L.		CHAL (1898)
475	Bach, Leonard Emil	1849-1902	Eulenspiegeleien "Wir gingen spazieren"		S/A	Paez		CHAL (1898)
476	Bach, Otto	1833-1893	Am Morgen "Was sollte das zur Nachtzeit sein"	Op. 23	2 female v.	Cranz		CHAL (1898)
477	Bach, Otto	1833-1893	Frühlingsglocken "Schneeglöcken thut läuten"	Op. 15 No. 1	S/S	Schott		CHAL (1898)
478	Bach, Otto	1833-1893	Herbstlied "Feldenwärts flog ein Vögelein"	Op. 15 No. 3	S/S	Schott		CHAL (1898)
479	Bach, Otto	1833-1893	Sternlein "Uüd die Sonne machte den weiten Ritt"	Op. 15 No. 2	S/S	Schott		CHAL (1898)

REC	COMP	DTS	TITLE	OP #	VCG	PUB	COMMENTS	SRC
480	Bachhofer, R.		Blauen Jung's wed'n wir genannt		Unspec.	Jäger i. Berl.		CHAL (1906)
481	Backman, Hjalmar		Matkani Muistot (Fardeminnen)		Unspec.	Fazer		CVMP (1976)
482	Backman, Hjalmar		Sunnuntaiaamuna (Sondagmorgon)		Unspec.	Fazer		CVMP (1976)
483	Bade, Ph.		Wo immer Lieb' und Liebe ruht		S/A	André		CHAL (1911)
484	Bading, P.		Zur Nacht "Gute Nacht, allen Müden seis gebracht"	Op. 3	Unspec.	Rühle i. Berl.		CHAL (1898)
485	Baer, Abel		June night		Unspec.	F. D. & H.	Arr. Pether	BBC (1975)
486	Bailey		In the wildwood		S/A	White-Smith	In catalogue page "Vocal Duetts" of White-Smith Music Pub. Co. (no date)	MSN
487	Bailey		Life's merry morning		S/A	White-Smith	In catalogue page "Vocal Duetts" of White-Smith Music Pub. (no date)	MSN
488	Bailey		Till we meet again		S/A	White-Smith	In catalogue page "Vocal Duetts" of White-Smith Music Pub. Co. (no date)	MSN
489	Baker, Richard		Wonder of God's Love, The		Unspec.	Crespub		CVMP (1976)
490	Balfe, Michael William	1808-1870	Dämm'rungsthau, deckt sanft		S/A	Schott		CHAL (1898)
491	Balfe, Michael William	1808-1870	Excelsior		Unspec.	Bowerman		BBC (1975)
492	Balfe, Michael William	1808-1870	Oh! Boatman, haste!		S/A	Curwen		BBC (1975)
493	Balfe, Michael William	1808-1870	Schöne Kind "Schöne Kind nimmt Abschied"		S/A	Schott	Trans. from Irish	CHAL (1898)
494	Balfe, Michael William	1808-1870	Sie was so gut		S/A	Schott	Trans. from Irish	CHAL (1898)
495	Balfe, Michael William	1808-1870	The sailor sighs		S/A	J. Williams		BBC (1975)
496	Balfe, Michael William	1808-1870	Trust Her Not		Unspec.	Recital		CVMP (1995)
497	Balfe, Michael William	1808-1870	Trust Her Not		Unspec.	Brainard's Sons	In anthology "Brainard's Collection of Vocal Duets from Popular Modern and Standard Composers" Pub. 1903.	MSN
498	Balfe, Michael William	1808-1870	Trust her not		Unspec.	White-Smith	In catalogue page "Vocal Duetts" of White-Smith Music Pub. Co. (no date)	MSN
499	Balfe, Michael William	1808-1870	Trust Her Not		Unspec.	CVR		MSN
500	Ball, Ernest	1878-1927	In the Garden of My Heart		Unspec.	Allans	Also solo	CVMP (1976)
501	Banck, Karl	1809-1889	Abend "Glühend sinkt die Sonne"	Op. 35 No. 5	Unspec.	Hofmeister		CHAL (1898)
502	Banck, Karl	1809-1889	Abfahrt "Stosst ab vom Land"	Op. 35 No. 1	Unspec.	Hofmeister		CHAL (1898)

REC	COMP	DTS	TITLE	OP #	VCG	PUB	COMMENTS	SRC
503	Banck, Karl	1809-1889	Abschiedsliedlein "Liebe lässst von Liebe nicht"	Op. 78 No. 7	Unspec.	Hoffarth		CHAL (1898)
504	Banck, Karl	1809-1889	Auf dem Meere "Sonne taucht empor"	Op. 35 No. 2	Unspec.	Hofmeister		CHAL (1898)
505	Banck, Karl	1809-1889	Bitte "Weil auf mir du dunkles Auge"	Op. 50 No. 2	Unspec.	Sch. & Co.		CHAL (1898)
506	Banck, Karl	1809-1889	Blumen und Schmetterlinge 2 Duette f. 2 S	Op. 11	S/S	Hofmeister	2 Duets, unspec.	CHAL (1898)
507	Banck, Karl	1809-1889	Blumen "Warum weinst du weisse Rose"	Op. 11 No. 2	S/S	Hofmeister		CHAL (1898)
508	Banck, Karl	1809-1889	Dort oben "Dort oben, dort oben zu der"	Op. 78 No. 3	Unspec.	Hoffarth		CHAL (1898)
509	Banck, Karl	1809-1889	Es fällt ein Stern herunter	Op. 50 No. 1	Unspec.	Sch. & Co.		CHAL (1898)
510	Banck, Karl	1809-1889	Frühlingstraum	Op. 26 No. 3	S/S	Cranz		CHAL (1898)
511	Banck, Karl	1809-1889	Gesang der Peris "Wiegt ihn hinüber"	Op. 25 No. 4	S/S	Cranz		CHAL (1898)
512	Banck, Karl	1809-1889	Gestorben, verdorben "Flieg fort du kleines Waldvöglein"	Op. 78 No. 1	Unspec.	Hoffarth		CHAL (1898)
513	Banck, Karl	1809-1889	Knab' im Walde "Es schlief ein Knab' im grünen Wald"	Op. 25 No. 1	S/S	Cranz		CHAL (1898)
514	Banck, Karl	1809-1889	Lebewohl	Op. 26 No. 4	S/S	Cranz		CHAL (1898)
515	Banck, Karl	1809-1889	Liebesabschied "Allerschönster Engel"	Op. 51 No. 2	Unspec.	Sch. & Co.		CHAL (1898)
516	Banck, Karl	1809-1889	Meeresfahrt 6 Duette	Op. 35	Unspec.	Hofmeister	6 Duets, unspec.	CHAL (1898)
517	Banck, Karl	1809-1889	Meeresstille "Sanfte Lüfte tragen Düfte"	Op. 35 No. 4	Unspec.	Hofmeister		CHAL (1898)
518	Banck, Karl	1809-1889	Mi giuri che m'tami	Op. 3 No. 2	S/A	Peters		CHAL (1898)
519	Banck, Karl	1809-1889	Mondesgruss	Op. 26 No. 1	S/S	Cranz		CHAL (1898)
520	Banck, Karl	1809-1889	Nacht "Tiesfes Dunkel ruhet dem Meer"	Op. 35 No. 6	Unspec.	Hofmeister		CHAL (1898)
521	Banck, Karl	1809-1889	Nachtgesang "Leise, leise schallen Lieder"	Op. 25 No. 2	S/S	Cranz		CHAL (1898)
522	Banck, Karl	1809-1889	Nun fangen die Weiden zu blühen an	Op. 78 No. 4	Unspec.	Hoffarth		CHAL (1898)
523	Banck, Karl	1809-1889	Pupille "Pupille tenere del caro"	Op. 3 No. 3	S/A	Peters		CHAL (1898)
524	Banck, Karl	1809-1889	Rasche Fahrt "Vogel gleich im Flug"	Op. 35 No. 3	Unspec.	Hofmeister		CHAL (1898)
525	Banck, Karl	1809-1889	Rheinischer Schifferreigen	Op. 51 No. 1	Unspec.	Sch. & Co.		CHAL (1898)
526	Banck, Karl	1809-1889	Röslein wann blühest du auf "Es wuchs an einem Rosenbaum"	Op. 78 No. 6	Unspec.	Hoffarth		CHAL (1898)
527	Banck, Karl	1809-1889	Ruscello "Mormorando il chiaro	Op. 3 No. 1	S/A	Peters		CHAL (1898)
528	Banck, Karl	1809-1889	Schifferlied	Op. 26 No. 2	S/S	Cranz		CHAL (1898)
529	Banck, Karl	1809-1889	Schmetterlinge "Himmelsbläue, Purpurflügel"	Op. 11 No. 1	S/S	Hofmeister		CHAL (1898)
530	Banck, Karl	1809-1889	Vergissmeinnicht "Blaublümelein spiegelte sich im Bach"	Op. 78 No. 2	Unspec.	Hoffarth		CHAL (1898)

REC	COMP	DTS	TITLE	OP #	VCG	PUB	COMMENTS	SRC
531	Banck, Karl	1809-1889	Vorüber "Blümlein sie blühen im duftugen Wald"	Op. 25 No. 3	S/S	Cranz		CHAL (1898)
532	Banck, Karl	1809-1889	Wegewart "Es wartet ein bleiches Junfräulein"	Op. 78 No. 5	Unspec.	Hoffarth		CHAL (1898)
533	Banck, Karl (G. F. Handel)	1809-1889	In generoso onor		S/A	Kistner	Arr. of Handel duet	CHAL (1898)
534	Banck, Karl (G. F. Handel)	1809-1889	Vado e vivo		S/S	Kistner	Arr. of Handel duet	CHAL (1898)
535	Bandhartinger, B.		Skolie "Mädchen entsiegelten"		Unspec.	Robitschek		CHAL (1898)
536	Bandisch, J.		Eislauf "Zwischen den Tannen im sinnigen Strahl"		S/S	Hoffheinz		CHAL (1898)
537	Bandisch, J.		Klinge, Sichlein, klinge	Op. 118	2 female v.	Hoffheinz		CHAL (1901)
538	Bank, G.		Stille Nacht, heilige Nacht		Unspec.	Fries i. Z.	Arr. of song.	CHAL (1898)
539	Bantock, Granville	1868-1946	China Mandarin, The		Unspec.	Roberton		CVMP (1976)
540	Bantock, Granville	1868-1946	China Mandarin, The		S/S	Curwen		ASR
541	Bärmann, W.		Mensch ist ein Gewohnheitstier "Menschheit schimpft"		Unspec.	Frz. Dietrich		CHAL (1911)
542	Barnby, J.		Sweet and Low. A Lullaby		S/A	Leonard-Eng	Arr. E. Newton. In anthology "Six Popular Vocal Duets Book I for Soprano & Contralto" Ed. & arr. by E. Newton. Pub. 1906.	MSN
543	Bartel, Günther	1833-1911	Süsser die Glocken nie klingen		S/A or T/B	Grüninger	pf or harm	CHAL (1901)
544	Bartlett, Homer Newton	1845-1940	For ever with the Lord		S/A	G. Schirm.	org or pf accomp. In anthology "Album of Sixteen Sacred Duets" (no date)	MSN
545	Bartlett, Homer Newton	1845-1940	O Lord, remember me		S/A	G. Schirm.	pf or org accomp. In catalogue page "Sacred Vocal Duets" of G. Schirmer, Inc. NY (no date)	MSN
546	Bartlett, J. C.		Day is Ended, The (An Evening Hymn)		S/A	Ditson	Also solo with vln obbligato, quartet. In anthology "Choice Sacred Duets for All Voices" Pub. 1936.	MSN
547	Barwolf, L.		Carté, Musique, Amour		Unspec.	Schott i. Br.		CHAL (1898)
548	Baschinsky, P.		Mondnacht is', alles ist still		high & med. v.	Mayer & Dorn		CHAL (1911)
549	Baselt, Friedrich Gustav Otto	1863-1931	Beiden Stadtposaunen "Es ist heraus"	Op. 39	2 female v.	Siegel		CHAL (1898)
550	Baselt, Friedrich Gustav Otto	1863-1931	Frau Beyer und Frau Geyer "Guten Morgen, Frau Geyer"	Op. 65	MS/MS	Siegel		CHAL (1898)
551	Baselt, Friedrich Gustav Otto	1863-1931	Frau Lustig und ihr Zimmermädchen "Ist's möglich, was ich sah"	Op. 71	2 female v.	Robitschek		CHAL (1898)
552	Baselt, Friedrich Gustav Otto	1863-1931	Frühling und Liebe "Im Rosenbusche die Liebe schlief"	Op. 21	2 female v.	André		CHAL (1898)

REC	COMP	DTS	TITLE	OP #	VCG	PUB	COMMENTS	SRC
553	Baselt, Friedrich Gustav Otto	1863-1931	Kathi und Resi "Gott grüss di mei Resi"	Op. 87	MS/MS	Siegel		CHAL (1898)
554	Baselt, Friedrich Gustav Otto	1863-1931	Reingefallen "Nein diese Frauen 's ist ein Scandal"	Op. 92	MS/MS	Siegel		CHAL (1898)
555	Baselt, Friedrich Gustav Otto	1863-1931	Senfteig "Käthchen, Käthe"	Op. 73	2 female v.	P. & M.		CHAL (1898)
556	Baselt, Friedrich Gustav Otto	1863-1931	Was Konkurrenz zu Wege bringt	Op. 101	Unspec.	Kleine i. P.		CHAL (1901)
557	Baselt, Friedrich Gustav Otto	1863-1931	Zwei Mädchen und kein Mann "Wir armen, armen Mädchen"	Op. 40	2 female v.	Siegel		CHAL (1898)
558	Bassford, William Kipp	1839-1902	My Faith Looks Up to Thee		S/A	Waterloo, G. Schirm.		CVMP (1976)
559	Bassford, William Kipp	1839-1902	My Faith Looks Up to Thee		S/A	G. Schirm.	In anthology "Schirmer's Favorite Sacred Duets for Various Voices" 1955.	MSN
560	Bassford, William Kipp	1839-1902	My Faith looks up to Thee		S/A	G. Schirm.	Based on tune by Lachner (doesn't specify). In anthology "Album of Sixteen Sacred Duets" (no date)	MSN
561	Bassford, William Kipp	1839-1902	My Faith Looks Up to Thee		S/A	Waterloo		ASR
562	Bastyr, Hans	1873-1928	Glaubt man's wohl, was mir passirt [passiert?]	Op. 42	2 female v.	Pohl-Wohnlich		CHAL (1906)
563	Bastyr, Hans	1873-1928	Von des Kirchleins Turme tönet	Op. 141	Unspec.	Förster i. Lockw.		CHAL (1911)
564	Bastyr, Hans	1873-1928	Wir sitzen hier am Telephon		2 female v.	Gleissen-berg		CHAL (1906)
565	Bateman, Ronald		Barcarolle at Dawn		Unspec.	Leonard-Eng	Also solo	CVMP (1976)
566	Bateman, Ronald		Dream Minuet		Unspec.	Leonard-Eng	Also solo	CVMP (1976)
567	Batten, Mrs. George		Little Brown Brother		Unspec.	Cramer	Also solo	CVMP (1976)
568	Battmann, Jacques Louis	1818-1886	Demoiselle		Unspec.	Junne		CHAL (1898)
569	Battmann, Jacques Louis	1818-1886	Soeurs des abeilles		Unspec.	Junne		CHAL (1898)
570	Battmann, Jacques Louis	1818-1886	Un jour de Mai		Unspec.	Junne		CHAL (1898)
571	Bauckner, Arthur	1887-	Vater unser, der du bist im Himmel		Unspec.	Böhm & S.	org	CHAL (1911)
572	Bauer, Friedrich	1876-	Am Ort, wo meine Wiege stand	III No. 2	Unspec.	C. Rühle i. L.	Arr. Necke	CHAL (1901)
573	Baum, C.		Mein Hüttchen im Grünen		S/A	Bahn		CHAL (1898)
574	Baum, W.		Hier siehst du es		2 female v.	Hochstein		CHAL (1911)
575	Baum, W.		In den heut'gen Zeiten		2 female v.	Hochstein		CHAL (1911)
576	Baum, W.		Morgen, auch schon auf den Beiden		2 female v.	Hochstein		CHAL (1911)
577	Baum, W.		Unser Wahlspruch ist "Modern"		2 female v.	Hochstein		CHAL (1911)
578	Baum, W.		Wir dienen in der Stadt		2 female v.	Hochstein		CHAL (1911)
579	Baum, W.		Wir ziehen die Kreuz und die Quer		2 female v.	Hochstein		CHAL (1911)

REC	COMP	DTS	TITLE	OP #	VCG	PUB	COMMENTS	SRC
580	Baumann, Alexander	1814-1857	Erwartung am Meere	Op. 4	Unspec.	Cranz		CHAL (1898)
581	Baumann, Alexander	1814-1857	Fischerin Wiegenlied "Dort im Abendschein treibt"	Op. 11	Unspec.	Cranz		CHAL (1898)
582	Baumann, Alexander	1814-1857	Gondoliera "O komm zu mir"	Op. 2	Unspec.	Cranz		CHAL (1898)
583	Baumann, Alexander	1814-1857	Venetianische Mouferrine "Ei, wie so kühl"	Op. 6	Unspec.	Cranz		CHAL (1898)
584	Baumann, Alexander	1814-1857	Vor dem Gitterthore "Glückberauscht unbelauscht"	Op. 17	Unspec.	Cranz		CHAL (1898)
585	Baumann, Alexander	1814-1857	Zitherständchen "Ich schleiche mit der Zither"	Op. 5	Unspec.	Cranz		CHAL (1898)
586	Baumann, Johann	1909-1871	Es klingt vom hohen Himmelsthron	No. 16	Unspec.	Schergens		CHAL (1906)
587	Baumann, Karl Friedrich	1809-1873	Ersten Liedchen "Sammlung"	Op. 36	Unspec.	Höhr. i. Z.		CHAL (1898)
588	Baumann, Karl Friedrich	1809-1873	Lied vom feinen Sepperl "Lieber Freund, sag wohlgemeint"	Op. 12	Unspec.	Böhm & S.		CHAL (1898)
589	Baumfelder, Friedrich	1836-1916	Beiden Ochsen "Zogen einst der Ochsen zwei"	Op. 358 No. 3	S/A	Schott		CHAL (1898)
590	Baumfelder, Friedrich	1836-1916	Liebling "Edelknabe lieb und fromm"	Op. 358 No. 5	S/A	Schott		CHAL (1898)
591	Baumfelder, Friedrich	1836-1916	Morgen "Fliegt der erste Morgenstrahl"	Op. 358 No. 2	S/A	Schott		CHAL (1898)
592	Baumfelder, Friedrich	1836-1916	Sängers Lohn "Es war in die Welt gegangen"	Op. 358 No. 4	S/A	Schott		CHAL (1898)
593	Baumfelder, Friedrich	1836-1916	Spruch "Treue Freunde zu gewinnen"	Op. 358 No. 1	S/A	Schott		CHAL (1898)
594	Baumgart, A.		Kommt, lasst uns fröhlich singen		Unspec.	Lindner	pf or org or harm	CHAL (1906)
595	Baumgartner		I Rosornas Dagar		Unspec.	Lundq.		CVMP (1976)
596	Baumgartner, Wilhelm	1820-1867	Noch ist die blühende, goldene Zeit	II No. 2	Unspec.	C. Rühle i. L.	Arr. Necke	CHAL (1901)
597	Baumgartner, Wilhelm	1820-1867	Noch sind die Tage der Rosen "Noch ist die blühende gold'ne Zeit"	Op. 24 No. 1	Unspec.	Hug		CHAL (1898)
598	Bazzini, Antonio	1818-1897	Anio e il bacio		S/A	Ricordi		CHAL (1898)
599	Beach, Amy	1867-1944	Ah, Love, But a Day!	Op. 44 No. 2	S/A	CVR	Amer. woman comp. Also solo.	CVMP (1995)
600	Beauplan, A. de		Abendglocken "Wenn die Töne der Glocken"		Unspec.	Schott		CHAL (1898)
601	Beauplan, A. de		Schlafe mein Liebchen		Unspec.	Schott		CHAL (1898)
602	Becker, Albert	1834-1899	Weihnachtslied aus dem XVI. Jahrhundert "Zu Bethlehem geboren"		S/A	R. & E.		CHAL (1898)
603	Becker, Albert	1834-1899	Weihnachtslied aus dem XVI. Jahrhundert "Zu Bethlehem geboren"	Op. 71 No. 1	Unspec.	Oppenheimer		CHAL (1898)
604	Becker, Albert	1834-1899	Weihnachtslied "Sel'ge Stunde, frohe Kunde"	Op. 71 No. 4	Unspec.	Oppenheimer		CHAL (1898)
605	Becker, Cl.	1804-1877	Ich möchte schweben über Thal und Hügel		S/Br or S/A	Henkel		CHAL (1898)
606	Becker, Hugo	1864-	Blumenlied "Ein frisches Blümchen bring' ich dir"	Op. 23 No. 1	S/A	Brauer		CHAL (1898)

REC	COMP	DTS	TITLE	OP #	VCG	PUB	COMMENTS	SRC
607	Becker, Hugo	1864-	Du bist wie eine Blume	Op. 23 No. 2	S/A	Brauer		CHAL (1898)
608	Becker, Hugo	1864-	Ständchen	Op. 23 No. 3	S/A	Brauer		CHAL (1898)
609	Becker, Konstantin Julius	1811-1859	An Italien "Wie ein heller, klarer Spiegel"	Op. 40 No. 1	Unspec.	Peters		CHAL (1898)
610	Becker, Konstantin Julius	1811-1859	Drei Sterne "Es blinken drei freundliche Sterne"	Op. 39 No. 1	Unspec.	Kistner		CHAL (1898)
611	Becker, Konstantin Julius	1811-1859	Finken Gruss "Im Fliederbusch ein Finke sass"	Op. 40 No. 2	Unspec.	Peters		CHAL (1898)
612	Becker, Konstantin Julius	1811-1859	Gondellied "Gleite hin, die glänzende Bahn"	Op. 36 No. 1	2 female v.	Klemm		CHAL (1898)
613	Becker, Konstantin Julius	1811-1859	Lied am Quell "Wo sich gatten jene Schatten"	Op. 36 No. 3	2 female v.	Klemm		CHAL (1898)
614	Becker, Konstantin Julius	1811-1859	Mein Liebchen, wir sassen beisammen	Op. 40 No. 1	Unspec.	Peters		CHAL (1898)
615	Becker, Konstantin Julius	1811-1859	Notturno "Durch die laue Frühlingsnacht"	Op. 36 No. 2	2 female v.	Klemm		CHAL (1898)
616	Becker, Konstantin Julius	1811-1859	Waldfee "Jäger ziehet in den Hain"	Op. 39 No. 3	Unspec.	Kistner		CHAL (1898)
617	Becker, Konstantin Julius	1811-1859	Wasserfee "Du schöne Nix da unten"	Op. 39 No. 2	Unspec.	Kistner		CHAL (1898)
618	Becker, Reinhold	1812-1924	Abend "Schweigt frt Menschen laute Lust"	Op. 17 No. 2	2 female v.	Klemm.		CHAL (1898)
619	Becker, Reinhold	1812-1924	Abschied vom Walde "Ade ihr Felsenballen"	Op. 17 No. 3	2 female v.	Klemm		CHAL (1898)
620	Becker, Reinhold	1812-1924	Höchste Glück hat keine Lieder		S/A	Musik-Woche i. L.		CHAL (1901)
621	Becker, Reinhold	1812-1924	Liebe hält Wacht bei Tag und bei Nacht	Op. 108 No. 2	Unspec.	Musick-woche i. L.		CHAL (1901)
622	Becker, Reinhold	1812-1924	Trauungsgesang "Wo du hingehst"	Op. 60	high & low v.	Näumann	org or harm or pf accomp.	CHAL (1898)
623	Becker, Reinhold	1812-1924	Viel Träume "Viel Vögel sind geflogen"	Op.17 No. 1	2 female v.	Klemm		CHAL (1898)
624	Becker, Valentin Eduard	1814-1890	Gott willkommen, liebe Sonne	Op. 100 No. 2	2 female v.	Coppenrath		CHAL (1898)
625	Becker, Valentin Eduard	1814-1890	Nun fangen die Weiden zu blühen an	Op. 100 No. 3	2 female v.	Coppenrath		CHAL (1898)
626	Becker, Valentin Eduard	1814-1890	Rausche, rausche froher Bach	Op. 100 No. 1	2 female v.	Coppenrath		CHAL (1898)
627	Beeson, Jack	1921-	Model Housekeeper, The		1-4 female v.	Boosey	Rounds and canons	ASR
628	Beethoven, Ludwig van	1770-1827	An ä Bergli bin I gesässe		MS/MS	B. & H.	In collection "Neues Volksliederheft" of L. v. Beethoven. Ed. G. Schünemann. Pub. 1940	NATS-VCD

REC	COMP	DTS	TITLE	OP #	VCG	PUB	COMMENTS	SRC
629	Beethoven, Ludwig van	1770-1827	Complete Works		Var. v.	Univ. Mus. Ed.	pf w/ & w/o inst. accomp. Collection. Repr. of Breitkopf ed. of Works by L. v. Beethoven. Contains duets.	ASR
630	Beethoven, Ludwig van	1770-1827	Constancy		Unspec.	ECS	Scottish air. In anthology "48 Duets Seventeenth Through Nineteenth Centuries" Ed. V. Prahl. Pub. 1941, 1970.	MSN
631	Beethoven, Ludwig van	1770-1827	Gesangesmacht "Gesangesmacht du schleichst dich ein" Irisches Lied		S/A	B. & H.	In anth. "Zweistim. Lied. f. Sop. u. Altstimme mit Klavierbegleitung f. den Haus- u. Schulgebrauch v. H. M. Schletterer" 3 vols.	MSN
632	Beethoven, Ludwig van	1770-1827	Gute Nacht "Gut Nacht! Gut Nacht"	Op. 100	S/A	B. & H.	In anth. "Zweistim. Lied. f. Sop. u. Altstimme mit Klavierbegleitung f. den Haus- u. Schulgebrauch v. H. M. Schletterer" 3 vols.	MSN
633	Beethoven, Ludwig van	1770-1827	Hoffmann, Hoffmann, sei ja kein Hoffmann	No. 9	Unspec.	B. & H. et al.	acap.	CHAL (1898)
634	Beethoven, Ludwig van	1770-1827	In Vain to this Desert my Fate I Deplore	No. 261/17 Op. 108	T/Br or S/MS	B. & H.	In "25 Scottish Songs" Op. 108. In collection "Werke" of L. v. Beethoven. Pub. 1864-1890.	NATS-VCD
635	Beethoven, Ludwig van	1770-1827	Irische Lieder		Unspec.	none listed	Assorted works, some applicable duets.	BBC (1975)
636	Beethoven, Ludwig van	1770-1827	Irish Duets from Op. 223, 224, 225	Op. 223, 224, 225	high & low v.	Kalmus	pf w/ & w/o vln, cello accomp. Collection. Repr. of Breitkopf ed. of Works by L. v. Beethoven. Contains duets.	ASR
637	Beethoven, Ludwig van	1770-1827	Le Départ des Pâtres		Unspec.	Durand	Fr. trans. Grmn.	CVMP (1976)
638	Beethoven, Ludwig van	1770-1827	Lebensgenuss "Schnell vergeht im Wechsel der Stunden"	Op. 82 No. 5	Unspec.	B. & H.		CHAL (1898)
639	Beethoven, Ludwig van	1770-1827	Merkenstein		Unspec.	Litolff		BBC (1975)
640	Beethoven, Ludwig van	1770-1827	Merkenstein "Merkenstein, Merkenstein wo ich wandle"	Op. 100	Unspec.	Schlesinger et al.		CHAL (1898)
641	Beethoven, Ludwig van	1770-1827	Monk's of Bangor March, The	No. 263/2	T/Br or S/MS	B. & H.	In "26 Welsh Songs" In collection "Werke" of L. v. Beethoven. Pub. 1864-1890.	NATS-VCD
642	Beethoven, Ludwig van	1770-1827	Odi l'aura		Unspec.	Litolff		BBC (1975)
643	Beethoven, Ludwig van	1770-1827	Oh! Thou Hapless Soldier	No. 262/10	S/MS or S/Br	B. & H.	In "20 Irish Songs" In collection "Werke" of L. v. Beethoven. Pub. 1864-1890.	NATS-VCD
644	Beethoven, Ludwig van	1770-1827	Schottische Lieder (12), Op. 227	Op. 227	high & low v.	Peters	pf w/ & w/o vln, cello accomp. Collection. Works by L. v. Beethoven. Ed. Friedländer. Duets, solos, trios.	ASR

REC	COMP	DTS	TITLE	OP #	VCG	PUB	COMMENTS	SRC
645	Beethoven, Ludwig van	1770-1827	Scottische Lieder		Unspec.	none listed	Collection of assorted works, some applicable duets.	BBC (1975)
646	Beethoven, Ludwig van	1770-1827	Sweet Power of Song		Unspec.	ECS	Scottish air. In anthology "48 Duets Seventeenth Through Nineteenth Centuries" Ed. V. Prahl. Pub. 1941, 1970.	MSN
647	Beethoven, Ludwig van	1770-1827	Traum und Wirklichkeit "Mir träumt ich lag, wo Blumen springen" Irisches Lied		S/A	B. & H.	In anth. "Zweistim. Lied. f. Sop. u. Altstimme mit Klavierbegleitung f. den Haus- u. Schulgebrauch v. H. M. Schletterer" 3 vols.	MSN
648	Beethoven, Ludwig van	1770-1827	Twelve Scottish Songs		Unspec.	Peters	Eng. & Grmn. Solos & duets.	CVMP (1976)
649	Beethoven, Ludwig van	1770-1827	Wallisische Lieder		Unspec.	none listed	Assorted works, some applicable duets.	BBC (1975)
650	Beethoven, Ludwig van	1770-1827	Welsh Duets from Op. 226	Op. 226	high & low v.	Peters	pf w/ & w/o vln, cello accomp. Collection. Works of L. v. Beethoven.	ASR
651	Beethoven, Ludwig van	1770-1827	Where flowers were springing		Unspec.	ECS	Scottish air. In anthology "48 Duets Seventeenth Through Nineteenth Centuries" Ed. V. Prahl. Pub. 1941, 1970.	MSN
652	Behr, Franz	1837-1898	Abendlied "Abend wird es wieder"		Unspec.	Grüninger		CHAL (1898)
653	Behr, Franz	1837-1898	Schiffahrt "Über die hellen funkelnden Wellen"		Unspec.	Grüninger		CHAL (1898)
654	Bellermann, Heinrich	1832-1903	Erste Veilchen "Als ich daserste Veilchen erblickt"	Op. 5 No. 6	Unspec.	Bahn		CHAL (1898)
655	Bellermann, Heinrich	1832-1903	Herbstlied "Es ist nun der Herbst gekommen"	Op. 38 No. 1	S/A	Thiemer		CHAL (1898)
656	Bellermann, Heinrich	1832-1903	O glücklich wer ein Herz gefunden	Op. 38 No. 2	S/A	Thiemer		CHAL (1898)
657	Belzer, P.		Seid uns gegrüsst viel tausendmal	Op. 15	Unspec.	Danner		CHAL (1906)
658	Bemberg, Henri Hermann	1859-1931	Serenade de Pasquin		S/A or T/B	Salabert		CVMP (1985)
659	Benda, A.		Jugendland "Es giebt auf der Erde ein liebliches Land"		S/A	Kott		CHAL (1898)
660	Bendel, Franz	1833-1874	Wie berührt mich wundersam		S/A	R. & E.		CHAL (1898)
661	Bender, Jan	1909-	Do Not Be Amazed		S/A or T/B	Concordia		ASR
662	Bender, Jan	1909-	Fear Not, For Behold I Bring Good Tidings of Great Joy		S/A	Concordia	May be performed chorally.	CVMP (1976)
663	Bender, Jan	1909-	Fear not, for Behold I Bring Good Tidings of Great Joy		high & med. v.	Concordia		ASR
664	Bender, Jan	1909-	Go Into all the World		S/A or T/B	Concordia	May be performed chorally.	CVMP (1976)
665	Bender, Jan	1909-	Go into all the World		S/A or T/B	Concordia		ASR

REC	COMP	DTS	TITLE	OP #	VCG	PUB	COMMENTS	SRC
666	Bender, Jan	1909-	God so Loved the World		S/S	Concordia	May be performed chorally.	CVMP (1976)
667	Bender, Jan	1909-	God so Loved the World		S/S	Concordia		ASR
668	Bender, Jan	1909-	Hosanna to the Son of David		S/A or T/B	Concordia	May be performed chorally.	CVMP (1976)
669	Bender, Jan	1909-	Hosanna to the Son of David		S/A or T/B	Concordia		ASR
670	Bender, Jan	1909-	I am the Good Shepherd		S/A or T/B	Concordia	May be performed chorally.	CVMP (1976)
671	Bender, Jan	1909-	I Am the Good Shepherd		S/A or T/B	Concordia		ASR
672	Bender, Jan	1909-	If You Ask Anything of the Father		S/A or T/B	Concordia	May be performed chorally.	CVMP (1976)
673	Bender, Jan	1909-	If You Ask Anything of the Father		S/A or T/B	Concordia		ASR
674	Bender, Jan	1909-	It is Not Fair		S/A	Concordia	May be performed chorally.	CVMP (1976)
675	Bender, Jan	1909-	It Is Not Fair		S/A	Concordia		ASR
676	Bender, Jan	1909-	Jesus, Son of David, Have Mercy on Me		S/A or T/B	Concordia	May be performed chorally.	CVMP (1976)
677	Bender, Jan	1909-	Jesus, Son of David, Have Mercy on Me		S/A or T/B	Concordia		ASR
678	Bender, Jan	1909-	Sir, Come Down Before my Child Dies		S/A or T/B	Concordia	May be performed chorally.	CVMP (1976)
679	Bender, Jan	1909-	Sir, Come Down before my Child Dies		S/A or T/B	Concordia		ASR
680	Bender, Jan	1909-	Son, Why have You Treated us So?		S/A	Concordia	May be performed chorally.	CVMP (1976)
681	Bender, Jan	1909-	Son, Why Have You Treated Us So?		S/A	Concordia		ASR
682	Bendl, Karel	1838-1897	Prílítlojaro z daleka	Op. 5 No. b	Unspec.	Hoffmann i. Pr.		CHAL (1898)
683	Bendl, Karel	1838-1897	Umlklo stromii suméni	Op. 5 No. a	Unspec.	Hoffmann i. Pr.		CHAL (1898)
684	Benedict, Jules	1804-1885	Im Waldesgrün "Im Waldes grün ist unsere Lust"	Op. 13	Unspec.	Cranz		CHAL (1898)
685	Benedict, Jules	1804-1885	Moon Has Raised Her Lamp Above, The		high & low v.	Hinds, Hayden & Eldredge	Eng. trans. Grmn. In anthology "The Most Popular Vocal Duets" Ed. Dr. E. J. Biedermann. Pub. 1914.	MSN
686	Bennet, William Sterndale	1816-1875	And who is he that will harm you		high & low v.	Church	In anthology "Sacred Duets A Collection of Two-Part Songs by the Best Composers" Vol. 2. Compi. & ed. W. Shakespeare. Pub. 1907.	MSN
687	Bennet, William Sterndale	1816-1875	And Who Is He That Will Harm You		S/A or A/T or S/Br	Church	In anthology "Sacred Duets for High and Low Voices" Vol. 2. Pub. 1907.	NATS-SVD
688	Bennet, William Sterndale	1816-1875	Cast thy bread upon the waters		high & low v.	Church	In anthology "Sacred Duets A Collection of Two-Part Songs by the Best Composers" Vol. 2. Compi. & ed. W. Shakespeare. Pub. 1907.	MSN

REC	COMP	DTS	TITLE	OP #	VCG	PUB	COMMENTS	SRC
689	Bennet, William Sterndale	1816-1875	Let Thy Mind		high & low v.	Church	In anthology "Sacred Duets A Collection of Two-Part Songs by the Best Composers" Vol. 2. Compi. & ed. W. Shakespeare. Pub. 1907.	MSN
690	Bennet, William Sterndale	1816-1875	Let Thy Mind		S/A or A/T or S/Br	Church	In anthology "Sacred Duets A Collection of Two-Part Songs by the Best Composers" Vol. 2. Compi. & ed. W. Shakespeare. Pub. 1907.	NATS-SVD
691	Bennewitz, Fritz	1874-	Glückselige Herde auf Bethlehem Auen	No. 1	Unspec.	Bennewitz i. L.		CHAL (1906)
692	Bennewitz, Fritz	1874-	In der Höhe Gott sei Ehre	No. 3	Unspec.	Bennewitz i. L.		CHAL (1906)
693	Bennewitz, Fritz	1874-	Weihnachts ist kommen	No. 2	Unspec.	Bennewitz i. L.		CHAL (1906)
694	Bennewitz, Fritz	1874-	Weihnachtslieder (3)		Unspec.	Bennewitz i. L.	3 Christmas duets	CHAL (1906)
695	Benoy, A. W.		Two Rounds for Voices		2 treble v.	OUP		ASR
696	Berger, Francesco	1834-1933	Mondnacht "Es war als hätte der Himmel"	Op. 19	Unspec.	B. & H.		CHAL (1898)
697	Berger, G.		Landparthie nach Greifenstein "Land-parthie is für mi"		Unspec.	Robischek		CHAL (1898)
698	Berger, Jean	1909-	A Set of Songs for Equal Voices and Piano Duets		Unspec.	Summy-Birchard Co.	pf-4 hands accomp. Pub. 1970.	MSN
699	Berger, Jean	1909-	A Wise Old Owl		Unspec.	Summy-Birchard Co.	pf-4 hands accomp. In "A Set of Songs for equal voices and piano duet" Pub. 1970.	MSN
700	Berger, Jean	1909-	Camelopard, The		S/MS, S/T, MS/Br or MS/T	Broude Br.	From "Airs and Rounds" set of eight works for Var. v. w/ and w/o pf. For chorus, may be perf. by soloists.	NATS-VCD
701	Berger, Jean	1909-	For the Want of a Horseshoe Nail		Unspec.	Summy-Birchard Co.	pf-4 hands accomp. In "A Set of Songs for equal voices and piano duet" Pub. 1970. Last line only splits to 3 v., 2 upper may be perf.	MSN
702	Berger, Jean	1909-	Good for Nothing		Unspec.	Summy-Birchard Co.	pf-4 hands accomp. In "A Set of Songs for equal voices and piano duet" Pub. 1970.	MSN
703	Berger, Jean	1909-	Morning		Unspec.	Summy-Birchard Co.	pf-4 hands accomp. In "A Set of Songs for equal voices and piano duet" Pub. 1970.	MSN
704	Berger, Jean	1909-	Roses		Unspec.	Summy-Birchard Co.	pf-4 hands accomp. In "A Set of Songs for equal voices and piano duet" Pub. 1970.	MSN
705	Berger, Rodolphe	1864-1916	Amoureuse		2 female v.	Enoch	Also solo	CVMP (1976)
706	Berger, Rodolphe	1864-1916	Bal Blanc		2 female v.	Enoch	Also solo	CVMP (1976)
707	Berger, Rodolphe	1864-1916	Dans les Fleurs		2 female v.	Enoch		CVMP (1976)

REC	COMP	DTS	TITLE	OP #	VCG	PUB	COMMENTS	SRC
708	Berger, Rodolphe	1864-1916	Eternal Printemps		2 female v.	Enoch		CVMP (1976)
709	Berger, Rodolphe	1864-1916	Loin du Pays		2 female v.	Enoch	Also solo	CVMP (1976)
710	Berger, Rodolphe	1864-1916	Nuages Roses		2 female v.	Enoch		CVMP (1976)
711	Berger, Wilhelm	1861-1911	Du, du liegst mir im Herzen		S/A or MS/A	Ditson	Arr. of Grmn. folk song. In anthology "The Ditson Collection of Soprano and Alto Duets" Pub. 1934.	MSN
712	Bergmann, Gustav	1837-1892	Hoffnung "Und dräut der Winter noch so sehr"	Op. 21 No. 2	Unspec.	Rühle i. L.		CHAL (1898)
713	Bergmann, Gustav	1837-1892	Kameruner Schutzmann-schaft "Erste Polizei in Kamerun"	Op. 35	Unspec.	Fr. Dietrich		CHAL (1898)
714	Bergmann, Gustav	1837-1892	Kein' grösser Freud auf Erden ist	Op. 21 No. 3	Unspec.	Rühle i. L.		CHAL (1898)
715	Bergmann, Gustav	1837-1892	Liebessehnen "Wer treulich leibt ist nicht verlassen"	Op. 21 No. 1	Unspec.	Rühle i. L.		CHAL (1898)
716	Bergmann, Josef	1822-	Verceni (Abendlied)	Op. 11	2 female v.	Hoffmann i. Pr.		CHAL (1898)
717	Bergmann, Th.		Abendlied "Abend wird es wieder"	Op. 32	S/S or T/T	Heinr.		CHAL (1898)
718	Bering, Ch.		Morgenwinde, wogt hernieder	No. 2	2 A or A/Br	Hey i. M.		CHAL (1911)
719	Bering, Ch.		Nacht ist wie ein stilles Meer	No. 1	2 A or A/B	Hey i. M.		CHAL (1911)
720	Berlioz, Hector	1803-1869	Bleich irrt im Wald Colette		T/T or S/S	B. & H.		CHAL (1906)
721	Berlioz, Hector	1803-1869	Complete Songs of Berlioz, Vol. 1-10		Var.	Kalmus	Collection of works of Berlioz. Works for solo & duets, Var. ranges.	ASR
722	Berlioz, Hector	1803-1869	Complete Works of Hector Berlioz, Vol. 1-10		Unspec.	Kalmus	Solos & vocal ensemble works	CVMP (1976)
723	Berlioz, Hector	1803-1869	Dahin an dem Bach ging ein Sehnen	Op. 18 No. 2	Unspec.	B. & H.		CHAL (1906)
724	Berlioz, Hector	1803-1869	Fern der Heimath		S/MS	B. & H.	pf or harp	CHAL (1906)
725	Berlioz, Hector	1803-1869	Hector Berlioz Works		Unspec.	Univ. Mus. Ed.	pf et al. accomp. Collection of works for a variety of instruments and vocal comb. From microfiche.	CVMP (1976)
726	Berlioz, Hector	1803-1869	Hector Berlioz Works Vol. 1-20		Var.	Univ. Mus. Ed.	pf w/ & w/o inst. accomp. Collection of works by Berlioz. Ed. Malherbe & Weingartner. Works for Var. v. comb. & inst. comb.	ASR
727	Berlioz, Hector	1803-1869	Hélène	Op. 2 No. 2	S/A, T/Br, S/MS or S/Br	B. & H., et al.	In collection "Werke" of H. Berlioz. Ed. C. Malherbe & F. Weingatner. Pub. 1900-1907, et al.	NATS-VCD
728	Berlioz, Hector	1803-1869	Hinaus zum Walde, streifte Lisette	Op. 13 No. 3	S/A	B. & H.		CHAL (1906)
729	Berlioz, Hector	1803-1869	Höret nie Helene ihr preisen	Op. 2 No. 2	high & low v.	B. & H.		CHAL (1906)
730	Berlioz, Hector	1803-1869	Irländische Lieder (2)	Op. 2	high & low v.	B. & H.	2 Irish duets	CHAL (1906)

REC	COMP	DTS	TITLE	OP #	VCG	PUB	COMMENTS	SRC
731	Berlioz, Hector	1803-1869	La Mort d'Ophelie	Op. 18	S/A	CVR	Comp. 1848.	MSN
732	Berlioz, Hector	1803-1869	Le Montagnard Exilé		S/MS or MS/MS	B. & H., et al.	In collection "Werke" of H. Berlioz. Ed. C. Malherbe & F. Weingatner. Pub. 1900-1907, et al.	NATS-VCD
733	Berlioz, Hector	1803-1869	Le Trébuchet	Op. 13 No. 3	S/A or S/MS	CVR	Comp. 1850.	MSN
734	Berlioz, Hector	1803-1869	Le Trébuchet	Op. 13 No. 3	S/A or S/MS	B. & H., et al.	In collection "Werke" of H. Berlioz. Ed. C. Malherbe & F. Weingatner. Pub. 1900-1907, et al.	NATS-VCD
735	Berlioz, Hector	1803-1869	O Vater, den alle hier preisen		S/A	B. & H.		CHAL (1906)
736	Berlioz, Hector	1803-1869	Pleure, pauvre Colette		S/S or T/T or S/MS	CVR	Comp. 1828.	MSN
737	Berlioz, Hector	1803-1869	Pleure, Pauvre Colette		T/T or S/S	B. & H., et al.	In collection "Werke" of H. Berlioz. Ed. C. Malherbe & F. Weingatner. Pub. 1900-1907, et al.	NATS-VCD
738	Berlioz, Hector	1803-1869	Sara la Baigneuse	Op. 11	S/A or T/Br or S/MS	B. & H., et al.	In collection "Werke" of H. Berlioz. Ed. C. Malherbe & F. Weingatner. Pub. 1900-1907, et al.	NATS-VCD
739	Berlioz, Hector	1803-1869	Sarah im Bade "Sarah wiegt sich träge"	Op. 11	high & low v.	B. & H.		CHAL (1906)
740	Berlioz, Hector	1803-1869	Songs for 2 or 3 Voices, Op. 2, 13.		Var.	Kalmus	Collection of works of Berlioz. For 1-3 v. included.	ASR
741	Berlioz, Hector	1803-1869	Trébuchet "Zaubernetz"		Unspec.	none listed		CHAL (1898)
742	Berlioz, Hector	1803-1869	Zaubernetz "Einen muntern Buschfink zu fangen"	Op. 13	Unspec.	Cranz		CHAL (1898)
743	Berneker, Constanz	1844-1906	Blumengebilde mit farbigem Glanz		S/A	Kramer-Bangert		CHAL (1906)
744	Berneker, Constanz	1844-1906	Leise zieht durch mein Gemüt	No. 1	S/T or S/S	Giessel jun.		CHAL (1911)
745	Berneker, Constanz	1844-1906	Wenn still mit seinen letzten Flammen	No. 2	S/T or S/S	Giessel jun.		CHAL (1911)
746	Bernier, René	1905-1984	Aube fleuria		Unspec.	Cranz		BBC (1975)
747	Berthold, G.	1795-1856	Cat's Duet		Unspec.	White-Smith	Pen name of Robert Pearsall. In catalogue page "Vocal Duetts" of White-Smith Music Pub. Co. (no date)	MSN
748	Berthold, G.	1795-1856	Katzenduett "Miau, miau, miau"		Unspec.	André, Chal., Siegel	Pen name of Robert Pearsall	CHAL (1898)
749	Berton, F.		Pauvre Pierre		Unspec.	Meissonier i. Par.		CHAL (1898)
750	Beschnitt, Johannes	1825-1880	Abschied "Schwebt ihr Töne zu ihr nieder"	Op. 32 No. 2	high & low v.	Simon i. Berl.		CHAL (1898)
751	Beschnitt, Johannes	1825-1880	An die blaue Himmelsdecke	Op. 42 No. 2	high & low v.	Simon i. Berl.		CHAL (1898)
752	Beschnitt, Johannes	1825-1880	Neuer Frühling "Neuer Frühling ist gekommen"	Op. 32 No. 4	high & low v.	Simon i. Berl.		CHAL (1898)
753	Beschnitt, Johannes	1825-1880	O Wald, wie ewig schön bist du	Op. 32 No. 5	Unspec.	Simon i. Berl.		CHAL (1898)

REC	COMP	DTS	TITLE	OP #	VCG	PUB	COMMENTS	SRC
754	Beschnitt, Johannes	1825-1880	Ständchen "Hüttelein still und klein"	Op. 32 No. 3	high & low v.	Simon i. Berl.		CHAL (1898)
755	Beschnitt, Johannes	1825-1880	Wenn der Frühling auf die Berge steigt"	Op. 41 No. 1	high & low v.	Simon i. Berl.		CHAL (1898)
756	Besly, Maurice	1888-1945	Dainty little maiden		Unspec.	Boosey		BBC (1975)
757	Besly, Maurice	1888-1945	Second Minuet		2 med. v.	Boosey		ASR
758	Beyer, H.		Beiden alten Jungfern "Ach wir Mädchen, ach wir armen"	Op. 15	Unspec.	Bosse		CHAL (1898)
759	Beyer, H.		Gemüthliche Ehepaar "Nicht wahr Gustel, so wie wir"	No. 8	Unspec.	Bosse		CHAL (1898)
760	Beyer, J.		Als kleine Jungen schwärmten wir		Unspec.	O. Dietrich		CHAL (1901)
761	Beyer, J.		Denk' ich der guten alten Zeit		Unspec.	O. Dietrich		CHAL (1911)
762	Bial, Rudolph	1834-1881	Und haben gar kee'n Grund "Ha ha ha das ist zum Lachen"		Unspec.	K. & G.		CHAL (1898)
763	Bicknese, E.		Schrumm aus "Kreuz-bomben und Granaten"	Op. 1	Unspec.	Fr. Dietrich		CHAL (1898)
764	Bieber, C. [prob. Karl]	1839-1911	Königslied "Den zum Segen uns gegeben"	Op. 71	Unspec.	Klemm		CHAL (1898)
765	Bieber, C. [prob. Karl]	1839-1911	Schlehenblüth und wilde Rose		2 female v.	Siegel		CHAL (1901)
766	Biehl, A. [prob. Albert]	1835-1899	Bächlein zieht von dannen	Op. 176 No. 2	Unspec.	Scharff		CHAL (1898)
767	Biehl, A. [prob. Albert]	1835-1899	In der Ferne "Will ruhen unter den Bäumen hier"	Op. 176 No. 3	Unspec.	Scharff		CHAL (1898)
768	Biehl, A. [prob. Albert]	1835-1899	Zweigesang "Im Flieder-busch ein Vöglein sass"	Op. 176 No. 1	Unspec.	Scharff		CHAL (1898)
769	Biehl, Ed.		Wenn sich zwei Herzen scheiden	Op. 10 No. 1	S/A or S/MS	Benjamin		CHAL (1898)
770	Bijvanck, Henk	1909-1969	De Stilte		S/S	Donemus	In "Vier Duetten"	CVMP (1976)
771	Bijvanck, Henk	1909-1969	Die Luft ist Blau		S/S	Donemus	In "Vier Duetten"	CVMP (1976)
772	Bijvanck, Henk	1909-1969	Gij Badt Op Eenen Berg Alleen		S/S	Donemus	In "Vier Duetten"	CVMP (1976)
773	Bijvanck, Henk	1909-1969	Liebe, soviel Stern am Himmel Stehen		S/S	Donemus	In "Vier Duetten"	CVMP (1976)
774	Billert, Karl Friedrich August	1821-1875	Liebesgarten "Liebe ist ein Rosenstrauch"	Op. 5 No. a	Unspec.	Chal.		CHAL (1898)
775	Birn, M.		Lebenslust	Op. 10	high & low v.	André	4 duets	CHAL (1911)
776	Birn, M.		Nachtwind hat in den Bäumen	Op. 10 No. 2	high & low v.	André		CHAL (1911)
777	Birn, M.		Wär' ich nie aus euch gegangen	Op. 10 No. 1	high & low v.	André		CHAL (1911)
778	Birn, M.		Wenn die Quellen selbern fliessen	Op. 10 No. 4	high & low v.	André		CHAL (1911)
779	Birn, M.		Wohl blühet jedem Jahre	Op. 10 No. 3	high & low v.	André		CHAL (1911)
780	Bischoff-Ghilionna, Justin	1845-1927	Par la longue route poudreuse		S/MS	Foetisch		CHAL (1906)

REC	COMP	DTS	TITLE	OP #	VCG	PUB	COMMENTS	SRC
781	Bischoff-Ghilionna, Justin	1845-1927	Qu'il est pur		S/MS or T/Br	Foetisch		CHAL (1906)
782	Bischoff, Karl Bernard	1807-1884	Psalm 103 "Barmherzig, gnädig ist der Herr"	Op. 70 No. 5	Unspec.	Hoffheinz		CHAL (1898)
783	Bischoff, Karl Bernard	1807-1884	Psalm 25 "Herr zeige mir deine Wege"	Op. 70 No. 2	Unspec.	Hoffheinz		CHAL (1898)
784	Bischoff, Karl Bernard	1807-1884	Psalm 27 "Herr ist mein Licht"	Op. 70 No. 3	Unspec.	Hoffheinz		CHAL (1898)
785	Bischoff, Karl Bernard	1807-1884	Psalm 39 "Ich will den Herren loben allezeit"	Op. 70 No. 4	Unspec.	Hoffheinz		CHAL (1898)
786	Bischoff, Karl Bernard	1807-1884	Weihnachts "Und es waren Hirten auf dem Felde"	Op. 70 No. 6	Unspec.	Hoffheinz		CHAL (1898)
787	Bischoff, Karl Jacob	1823-1893	Frisch gesungen "Hab' oft im Kreise der Lieben"	Op. 78 No. 2	Unspec.	Hoffheinz		CHAL (1898)
788	Bischoff, Karl Jacob	1823-1893	Frühlingseinzung "Fenster auf, die Herzen auf"	Op. 78 No. 3	Unspec.	Hoffheinz		CHAL (1898)
789	Bischoff, Karl Jacob	1823-1893	Jauchzet dem Herrn all Welt	Op. 74 No. 3	Unspec.	Hoffheinz		CHAL (1901)
790	Bischoff, Karl Jacob	1868-1936	Jauchzet dem Herrn alle Welt	Op. 74 No. 3	Unspec.	Hoffheinz		CHAL (1906)
791	Bischoff, Karl Jacob	1823-1893	Kaiserlied "Heil dem Kaiser, dessen Ahnen"	Op. 73 No. 1	Unspec.	Hoffheinz		CHAL (1898)
792	Bischoff, Karl Jacob	1823-1893	Lobe den Herrn meine Seele	Op. 74 No. 2	Unspec.	Hoffheinz		CHAL (1901)
793	Bischoff, Karl Jacob	1868-1936	Lobe den Herrn meine Seele	Op. 74 No. 2	Unspec.	Hoffheinz		CHAL (1906)
794	Bischoff, Karl Jacob	1823-1893	Psalm 1 "Wohl dem, der nicht Hoffheinz"	Op. 74 No. 1	Unspec.	Hoffheinz	Cited in CHAL as such. Poss. Karl Bernard Bischoff, who composed Psalms.	CHAL (1898)
795	Bischoff, Karl Jacob	1823-1893	Psalm 121 "ich hebe mein Augen auf zu den Bergen"	Op. 73 No. 5	Unspec.	Hoffheinz	Cited in CHAL as such. Poss. Karl Bernard Bischoff, who composed Psalms.	CHAL (1898)
796	Bischoff, Karl Jacob	1823-1893	Psalm 126 "Wenn der Herr die Gefangenen"	Op. 73 No. 4	Unspec.	Hoffheinz	Cited in CHAL as such. Poss. Karl Bernard Bischoff, who composed Psalms.	CHAL (1898)
797	Bischoff, Karl Jacob	1823-1893	Psalm 130	Op. 73 No. 6	Unspec.	Hoffheinz	Cited in CHAL as such. Poss. Karl Bernard Bischoff, who composed Psalms.	CHAL (1898)
798	Bischoff, Karl Jacob	1823-1893	Psalm 84 "Wie lieblich sind deine Wohnungen"	Op. 44	Unspec.	Hoffheinz	Cited in CHAL as such. Poss. Karl Bernard Bischoff, who composed Psalms.	CHAL (1898)
799	Bischoff, Karl Jacob	1823-1893	Salvum fac regem	Op. 73 No. 3	Unspec.	Hoffheinz		CHAL (1898)
800	Bischoff, Karl Jacob	1823-1893	Wiegenlied "Aeren nur noch nicken"	Op. 78 No. 1	Unspec.	Hoffheinz		CHAL (1898)
801	Bishop, Henry Rowley	1786-1855	All in the greenwood shade		S/A	Curwen	Arr. Oakey	BBC (1975)
802	Bishop, Henry Rowley	1786-1855	As it fell upon a day		S/A	Boosey		BBC (1975)
803	Bishop, Henry Rowley	1786-1855	Home, sweet home		Unspec.	Boosey	Arr. Parker	BBC (1975)
804	Bishop, Henry Rowley	1786-1855	Orpheus with his lute		S/A	Lonsdale		BBC (1975)

REC	COMP	DTS	TITLE	OP #	VCG	PUB	COMMENTS	SRC
805	Bisping, A.		Frühlingsgarten "Im Frühlingsgarten welch' ein Blühen"	Op. 5 No. 2	Unspec.	Weber i. Cöln		CHAL (1898)
806	Bisping, A.		Im Thale "Im Thale der silberne Bach"	Op. 5 No. 1	Unspec.	Weber i. Cöln		CHAL (1898)
807	Bisping, A.		Lustige Rheinfahrt "Es fuhren drei junge Gesellen"	Op. 5 No. 3	Unspec.	Weber i. Cöln		CHAL (1898)
808	Björnsson, Arni	1905-	Sönglistin		Unspec.	Iceland		CVMP (1995)
809	Blaesing, Felix	1858-?	Du meiner Seele schönster Traum	Op. 4 No. 3	S/Br or S/MS	Deneke		CHAL (1898)
810	Blaesing, Felix	1858-?	Taubenflug "Tauben im Flug"	Op. 4 No. 2	S/Br or S/MS	Deneke		CHAL (1898)
811	Blake		Flowers of the Springtime		S/A	White-Smith	In catalogue page "Vocal Duetts" of White-Smith Music Pub. Co. (no date)	MSN
812	Blangini, G. M. M. Felice	1781-1841	Amor der Lose (Amor che nasce)	II No. 6	Unspec.	Simrock		CHAL (1898)
813	Blangini, G. M. M. Felice	1781-1841	Da quel sembiante		Unspec.	Cranz		CHAL (1898)
814	Blangini, G. M. M. Felice	1781-1841	Doris sprach heute	II No. 3	Unspec.	Simrock		CHAL (1898)
815	Blangini, G. M. M. Felice	1781-1841	Dornen "Dornen mir zur Liebem spriesset"		Unspec.	Schlesinger		CHAL (1898)
816	Blangini, G. M. M. Felice	1781-1841	Du weisst, wie ich	V No. 6	Unspec.	Simrock		CHAL (1898)
817	Blangini, G. M. M. Felice	1781-1841	Entfernt dich nicht	IV No. 4	Unspec.	Simrock		CHAL (1898)
818	Blangini, G. M. M. Felice	1781-1841	Fern vom schönen	III No. 5	Unspec.	Simrock		CHAL (1898)
819	Blangini, G. M. M. Felice	1781-1841	Fliesset, o meine	II No. 4	Unspec.	Simrock		CHAL (1898)
820	Blangini, G. M. M. Felice	1781-1841	Ich höre	III No. 1	Unspec.	Simrock		CHAL (1898)
821	Blangini, G. M. M. Felice	1781-1841	Ich muss den Kummer bergen	I No. 1	Unspec.	Simrock		CHAL (1898)
822	Blangini, G. M. M. Felice	1781-1841	Ihr seht mich	I No. 4	Unspec.	Simrock		CHAL (1898)
823	Blangini, G. M. M. Felice	1781-1841	Ja, ja ich will	V No. 2	Unspec.	Simrock		CHAL (1898)
824	Blangini, G. M. M. Felice	1781-1841	Ja unter Qual	V No. 3	Unspec.	Simrock		CHAL (1898)
825	Blangini, G. M. M. Felice	1781-1841	Kannst du von mir	II No. 2	Unspec.	Simrock		CHAL (1898)
826	Blangini, G. M. M. Felice	1781-1841	Kennt Freunde	I No. 5	Unspec.	Simrock		CHAL (1898)
827	Blangini, G. M. M. Felice	1781-1841	Liebliche Lüftchen	III No. 2	Unspec.	Simrock		CHAL (1898)
828	Blangini, G. M. M. Felice	1781-1841	Lohnst du liebend	IV No. 2	Unspec.	Simrock		CHAL (1898)
829	Blangini, G. M. M. Felice	1781-1841	Nicht benenn'	III No. 4	Unpsec.	Simrock		CHAL (1898)
830	Blangini, G. M. M. Felice	1781-1841	Nocturne "Come fugace tempo"		Unspec.	Cranz, Junne		CHAL (1898)
831	Blangini, G. M. M. Felice	1781-1841	O fühltest du	I No. 6	Unspec.	Simrock		CHAL (1898)
832	Blangini, G. M. M. Felice	1781-1841	O Nina, "O Nina mein Glück"		S/S	Schlesinger		CHAL (1898)
833	Blangini, G. M. M. Felice	1781-1841	O sagt mir ihr Blumen		S/S or T/T	Schlesinger		CHAL (1898)

REC	COMP	DTS	TITLE	OP #	VCG	PUB	COMMENTS	SRC
834	Blangini, G. M. M. Felice	1781-1841	Oft wenn ich mich	V No. 5	Unspec.	Simrock		CHAL (1898)
835	Blangini, G. M. M. Felice	1781-1841	Oft wenn ich mich	V No. 5	Unspec.	Simrock		CHAL (1898)
836	Blangini, G. M. M. Felice	1781-1841	Ohne den lieblichen	IV No. 5	Unspec.	Simrock		CHAL (1898)
837	Blangini, G. M. M. Felice	1781-1841	Saht ihr Verliebte	II No. 1	Unspec.	Simrock		CHAL (1898)
838	Blangini, G. M. M. Felice	1781-1841	Sieh' Doris	I No. 2	Unspec.	Simrock		CHAL (1898)
839	Blangini, G. M. M. Felice	1781-1841	Speranza al cor mi dice		Unspec.	Junne, Simrock, et al.		CHAL (1898)
840	Blangini, G. M. M. Felice	1781-1841	Stets inniger sinn' ich dir		Unspec.	Schlesinger		CHAL (1898)
841	Blangini, G. M. M. Felice	1781-1841	Trockne die herbe	V No. 4	Unspec.	Simrock		CHAL (1898)
842	Blangini, G. M. M. Felice	1781-1841	Verliebte Seelen	IV No. 3	Unspec.	Simrock		CHAL (1898)
843	Blangini, G. M. M. Felice	1781-1841	Von reinem Triebe	IV No. 6	Unspec.	Simrock		CHAL (1898)
844	Blangini, G. M. M. Felice	1781-1841	Wer zu Cupido	II No. 5	Unspec.	Simrock		CHAL (1898)
845	Blangini, G. M. M. Felice	1781-1841	Wie schön und lieblich	V No. 1	Unspec.	Simrock		CHAL (1898)
846	Blangini, G. M. M. Felice	1781-1841	Wilst du dein Herz	IV No. 1	Unspec.	Simrock		CHAL (1898)
847	Blangini, G. M. M. Felice	1781-1841	Wo sie doch weilet	III No. 6	Unspec.	Simrock		CHAL (1898)
848	Blangini, G. M. M. Felice	1781-1841	Zwischen Furcht	III No. 3	Unspec.	Simrock		CHAL (1898)
849	Blaufus, Chr.		Auf blauer Fluth "Purpurner Himmel"		Unspec.	Fechner		CHAL (1898)
850	Blaufuss, Walter		My Isle of Golden Dreams		S/A or S/Br	Remick (NY)	Arr. William Stickles	MSN
851	Bleibtreu, C.		B'hüt di Gott "Jetzt b'hüt di Gott"	Op. 2 No. 3	Unspec.	R. & E.		CHAL (1898)
852	Bleibtreu, C.		Brautfahrt "Johann, nun spann die Schimmel an"	Op. 2 No. 4	Unspec.	R. & E.		CHAL (1898)
853	Bleibtreu, C.		Mädchens Wunsch "Hätt' ich doch ach Laso"	Op. 2 No. 1	Unspec.	R. & E.		CHAL (1898)
854	Bleibtreu, C.		Wenn die Lerche zieht "Ade, ade, der Sommer geht"	Op. 2 No. 2	Unspec.	R. & E.		CHAL (1898)
855	Blobner, Johann Baptist	1850-1931	Mein Wien "Sei mir gegrüsst mein theures Wien"	Op. 100	Unspec.	Blaha		CHAL (1898)
856	Blockley, John		Floating away		Unspec.	Blockley		BBC (1975)
857	Blockley, John		Listen to the Convent Bells		S/S	Bayley & Ferguson		BBC (1975)
858	Blockley, John		Ring out wild bells		Unspec.	Blockley		BBC (1975)
859	Blower, Maurice		Mamble		S/S	Curwen		ASR
860	Blum, E.		Toggenburg, der alte Narr	Op. 14	Unspec.	O. Dietrich		CHAL (1906)
861	Blum, Karl Ludwig	1786-1844	An Alexis send ich dich	Op. 13 No. 3	S/S	B. & H.		CHAL (1898)

REC	COMP	DTS	TITLE	OP #	VCG	PUB	COMMENTS	SRC
862	Blum, Karl Ludwig	1786-1844	Bitte "Erblühen deine Tritte"	Op. 134 No. 3	S/A	B. & H.		CHAL (1898)
863	Blum, Karl Ludwig	1786-1844	Entschuldiging "Es war so schwül"	Op. 28 No. 1	S/S	B. & H.		CHAL (1898)
864	Blum, Karl Ludwig	1786-1844	Jägers Horn "Hörnerklang, Jägersang, nah und fern"	Op. 13 No. 6	S/S	B. & H.		CHAL (1898)
865	Blum, Karl Ludwig	1786-1844	Leichter Scherz "Ma Mutter und ma Vetterlen"	Op. 28 No. 2	S/S	B. & H.		CHAL (1898)
866	Blum, Karl Ludwig	1786-1844	Mädchen beim Flechten eines Kranzes "Unter Freude und Entzücken"	Op. 28 No. 3	S/S	B. & H.		CHAL (1898)
867	Blum, Karl Ludwig	1786-1844	Meine Mutter warnt mich immer	Op. 13 No. 1	S/S	B. & H.		CHAL (1898)
868	Blum, Karl Ludwig	1786-1844	Notturno "Lieblich schläft auf der Flur"	Op. 134 No. 1	S/A	B. & H.		CHAL (1898)
869	Blum, Karl Ludwig	1786-1844	Schlaf mir zu verschönen	Op. 13 No. 5	S/S	B. & H.		CHAL (1898)
870	Blum, Karl Ludwig	1786-1844	Schwäne kommen gezogen	Op. 13 No. 2	S/A	B. & H.	In anth. "Zweistim. Lied. f. Sop. u. Altstimme mit Klavierbegleitung f. den Haus- u. Schulgebrauch v. H. M. Schletterer" 3 vols.	MSN
871	Blum, Karl Ludwig	1786-1844	Sommerabend "Schwäne kommen gezogen"	Op. 13 No. 2	S/S	B. & H.		CHAL (1898)
872	Blum, Karl Ludwig	1786-1844	Trennt von dir mich die Ferne	Op. 13 No. 4	S/S	B. & H.		CHAL (1898)
873	Blum, Karl Ludwig	1786-1844	Ungetreue "Sieh mit erneutem Glanze"	Op. 134 No. 2n	S/A	B. & H.		CHAL (1898)
874	Blumenthal, Jacob [Jacques]	1829-1908	In Venezia		Unspec.	Cramer		CVMP (1976)
875	Blumenthal, Jacob [Jacques]	1829-1908	Venetian Boat Song		Unspec.	Cramer	Also solo	CVMP (1976)
876	Blumenthal, Jacob [Jacques]	1829-1908	Venetian Boat Song		high & low v.	Hinds, Hayden & Eldredge	Eng. trans. Grmn. In anthology "The Most Popular Vocal Duets" Ed. Dr. E. J. Biedermann. Pub. 1914.	MSN
877	Blumenthal, Jacob [Jacques]	1829-1908	Venetian Boat Song		S/A	Ditson	Eng. trans. Fr. In anthology "Soprano and Alto Duets" Ed. Heinrich Kiehl. Pub. 1901.	MSN
878	Blumenthal, Jacob [Jacques]	1829-1908	Venetian Boat Song		S/A	Ditson	Eng. trans. Fr. In anthology "The Ditson Collection of Soprano and Alto Duets" Pub. 1934.	MSN
879	Blumenthal, Jacob [Jacques]	1829-1908	Venetian Boat Song		S/A	White-Smith	In catalogue page "Vocal Duetts" of White-Smith Music Pub. Co. (no date)	MSN
880	Blumenthal, Paul	1843-1930	Mottetten (6)	Op. 91	S/A	Bratfisch	org or pf. 6 motets for 2 v.	CHAL (1901)
881	Blumner, Martin	1827-1901	Abendfriede "Es starb der Sonne Jetzner Strahl"	Op. 24 No. 1	S/A	Schlesinger		CHAL (1898)
882	Blumner, Martin	1827-1901	Deine Liebe ist mein Himmel	Op. 24 No. 4	S/A	Schlesinger		CHAL (1898)
883	Blumner, Martin	1827-1901	Es ist kein hoher Berg so hoch	Op. 24 No. 3	S/A	Schlesinger		CHAL (1898)

REC	COMP	DTS	TITLE	OP #	VCG	PUB	COMMENTS	SRC
884	Blumner, Martin	1827-1901	Frühlingsanfang "Schnee ist vergangen"	Op. 24 No. 2	S/A	Schlesinger		CHAL (1898)
885	Boch, Fr.		Berg und Thal "Blick so weit das Auge"	Op. 2 No. 1	Unspec.	Bosworth		CHAL (1898)
886	Boch, Fr.		Zweigesang "Im Fliederbusch ein Vöglein sass"	Op. 2 No. 2	Unspec.	Bosworth		CHAL (1898)
887	Bögler, B.		Gensdarm und der Wanderer "Ich komme vom Gebirge her"		Unspec.	R. & E.		CHAL (1898)
888	Bohm		Entreaty		S/A	White-Smith	In catalogue page "Vocal Duetts" of White-Smith Music Pub. Co. (no date)	MSN
889	Bohm, C.		Erinnerung		S/A or T/Br	C. Fischer	In catalogue page "Selected Vocal Duets By Favorite Composers" of Carl Fischer NY (no date)	MSN
890	Bohm, C.		Lenzige Nacht		S/A or T/Br	C. Fischer	In catalogue page "Selected Vocal Duets By Favorite Composers" of Carl Fischer NY (no date)	MSN
891	Böhm, Karl	1844-1920	Es spielen leise die Blüten	Op. 381 No. 2	S/A or T/B	O. Forberg		CHAL (1911)
892	Böhm, Karl	1844-1920	Es spielen leise die Blüthen	No. 3	Unspec.	Simrock		CHAL (1901)
893	Böhm, Karl	1844-1920	Nun hüllt die Nacht, die lenzige Nacht	Op. 381 No. 1	S/A or T/B	O. Forberg		CHAL (1911)
894	Böhm, Karl	1844-1920	Still as the night		Unspec.	Lengnick	Eng. trans. Grmn.	BBC (1975)
895	Böhm, Karl	1844-1920	Still wie die Nacht	Op. 326 No. 27	S/A	Ditson	Arr. L. R. Dressler. In anthology "The Ditson Collection of Soprano and Alto Duets" Pub. 1934.	MSN
896	Böhm, Karl	1844-1920	Still wie die Nacht (Still as the Night)		Unspec.	Allans, Schaur EE		CVMP (1976)
897	Böhm, Karl	1844-1920	Still wie die Nacht, tief wie das Meer	No. 4	Unspec.	Simrock		CHAL (1901)
898	Böhm, Karl	1844-1920	Über's Jahr, liebster Schatz	No. 2	Unspec.	Simrock		CHAL (1901)
899	Böhm, Karl	1844-1920	Weil' auf mir du dunkles Auge	No. 1	Unspec.	Simrock		CHAL (1901)
900	Böhm, Karl	1844-1920	Wir haben nichts dazu gethan	Op. 363	Unspec.	Hainauer		CHAL (1906)
901	Böhm, Karl	1844-1920	Wonnige Frühlingszeit "Nun singt es süss in allen Zweigen"		Unspec.	R. & E.		CHAL (1898)
902	Böhm, R.		Liebe Sehnsucht "Was zieh'n die Wolken am Himmel"		Unspec.	R. & B.		CHAL (1898)
903	Böhm, W.		Hinan	Op. 3 No. 1	Unspec.	Wattenbach i. Gotha.		CHAL (1898)
904	Böhm, W.		Hinunter	Op. 3 No. 2	Unspec.	Wattenbach i. Gotha.		CHAL (1898)
905	Bohrer, S.		O komm zu mir, wenn durch die Nacht	I No. 3	Unspec.	C. Rühle i. L.	Arr. Necke	CHAL (1901)
906	Böie, Heinrich	1825-1879	Heimweh "Es überkommt ein Sehnen"	Op. 8 No. 2	S/S	Cranz		CHAL (1898)
907	Böie, Heinrich	1825-1879	Schuss "Es ist ein Stern gefallen"	Op. 8 No. 4	S/S	Cranz		CHAL (1898)

REC	COMP	DTS	TITLE	OP #	VCG	PUB	COMMENTS	SRC
908	Böie, Heinrich	1825-1879	Traurige Wanderschaft "Wenn's wieder Frühling worden ist"	Op. 8 No. 3	S/S	Cranz		CHAL (1898)
909	Böie, Heinrich	1825-1879	Vom Scheiden "Schlimm-ste Weh auf Erden"	Op. 8 No. 1	S/S	Cranz		CHAL (1898)
910	Boieldieu, François Adrien	1775-1834	Prière et voeu		Unspec.	Schlesinger		CHAL (1898)
911	Boissière, F.		Boulanger et Charbonnier		Unspec.	Junne		CHAL (1898)
912	Boissière, F.		Deux paysannes "Hé! mais c'est toi"		Unspec.	Schott i. Br.		CHAL (1898)
913	Boissière, F.		Friseur et fumeur		Unspec.	Junne		CHAL (1898)
914	Boissière, F.		Muletiers de Castille "Sous le rage ou sous le soleil"		Unspec.	Fürstner Paris		CHAL (1898)
915	Boissière, F.		Patinneuse		Unspec.	Junne		CHAL (1898)
916	Boissière, F.		Petites Dénicheurs "C'est le moment"		Unspec.	Schott i. Br.		CHAL (1898)
917	Boissière, F.		Sur la sellette "A qui ce beau petit bijou"		Unspec.	Schott i. Br.		CHAL (1898)
918	Boito, Arrigo	1842-1918	Give Thanks Unto God		2 high v.	R. D. Row	org or pf accomp. In anth. "Sacred Duet Masterpieces…" Vol. 3. Compi. & ed. C. Fredrickson. Pub. 1961.	MSN
919	Boito, Arrigo	1842-1918	Polacca e la Greca		MS/A	Ricordi		CHAL (1898)
920	Bond, Carrie Jacobs	1862-1946	Just a Wearyin' for You		Unspec.	Allans	Woman comp . In anth. "Vocal Duets Collect-ion" Vol. 1. Pub. 1992.	MSN
921	Bond, Carrie Jacobs	1862-1946	Just A-Wearyin' For You		Unspec.	Allans	Woman comp. Also solo.	CVMP (1976)
922	Bonheur, Theodore	1775-1850	The battle eve		Unspec.	Ashdown		BBC (1975)
923	Bonoldi, Francesco	d. 1873	"Maria d'Inghelterra"		S/A	Ricordi		CHAL (1898)
924	Bonvin, Ludwig	1850-1939	Ave-Maria	Op. 94	S/A	Schwann	harm or org	CHAL (1911)
925	Bonvin, Ludwig	1850-1939	Wonnig ist's in Frühlingstagen	Op. 73	S/A	B. & H.		CHAL (1906)
926	Borchers, Gustav	1865-1913	Vergiss für mich die Rose nicht "Frühling beut die letzte Spende"		high & low v.	R. & B.		CHAL (1898)
927	Bordèse, Luigi	1815-1886	Aidons-nous les uns les autres		Unspec.	Junne		CHAL (1898)
928	Bordèse, Luigi	1815-1886	Almée		S/MS	Schott		CHAL (1898)
929	Bordèse, Luigi	1815-1886	Amazonen "Nur voran kühne Frauen"		S/S	Schott		CHAL (1898)
930	Bordèse, Luigi	1815-1886	Amour de mère		Unspec.	Junne		CHAL (1898)
931	Bordèse, Luigi	1815-1886	Bataille		Unspec.	Junne		CHAL (1898)
932	Bordèse, Luigi	1815-1886	Beiden Müllerinnen "Müh-len zwei, klein doch rein"		S/S	Schott		CHAL (1898)
933	Bordèse, Luigi	1815-1886	Bekenntnisse "O wie ist's so herrlich"		S/A	Schott		CHAL (1898)

REC	COMP	DTS	TITLE	OP #	VCG	PUB	COMMENTS	SRC
934	Bordèse, Luigi	1815-1886	Béniter		Unspec.	Junne		CHAL (1898)
935	Bordèse, Luigi	1815-1886	Berger du Bon Dieu		Unspec.	Junne		CHAL (1898)
936	Bordèse, Luigi	1815-1886	Beste Brod auf Erden "Bursche, Mädchen lasst uns eilen"		S/S	Schott		CHAL (1898)
937	Bordèse, Luigi	1815-1886	Bon voyage		Unspec.	Junne		CHAL (1898)
938	Bordèse, Luigi	1815-1886	Bonheur facile		Unspec.	Junne		CHAL (1898)
939	Bordèse, Luigi	1815-1886	Brasilianerinnen "Frisch zu, eilt nur"		S/MS	Schott		CHAL (1898)
940	Bordèse, Luigi	1815-1886	Bretonnes		2 female v.	Schott		CHAL (1898)
941	Bordèse, Luigi	1815-1886	Brise d'avril		Unspec.	Junne		CHAL (1898)
942	Bordèse, Luigi	1815-1886	Calabraise		2 female v.	Schott		CHAL (1898)
943	Bordèse, Luigi	1815-1886	Chant du soleil		Unspec.	Junne		CHAL (1898)
944	Bordèse, Luigi	1815-1886	Croix des bois		Unspec.	Junne		CHAL (1898)
945	Bordèse, Luigi	1815-1886	Départ, pour les vacances		Unspec.	Junne		CHAL (1898)
946	Bordèse, Luigi	1815-1886	Destin		Unspec.	Junne		CHAL (1898)
947	Bordèse, Luigi	1815-1886	Dieu bénit des grandes familles		Unspec.	Junne		CHAL (1898)
948	Bordèse, Luigi	1815-1886	Distribution des prix		Unspec.	Junne		CHAL (1898)
949	Bordèse, Luigi	1815-1886	Ecole buissonnière		Unspec.	Junne	.	CHAL (1898)
950	Bordèse, Luigi	1815-1886	Epave		Unspec.	Junne		CHAL (1898)
951	Bordèse, Luigi	1815-1886	Farfadets		Unspec.	Junne		CHAL (1898)
952	Bordèse, Luigi	1815-1886	Fête de la maîtresse		Unspec.	Junne		CHAL (1898)
953	Bordèse, Luigi	1815-1886	Fête du pasteur		Unspec.	Junne		CHAL (1898)
954	Bordèse, Luigi	1815-1886	Fêtes des pensionnats "Duettini"		Unspec.	Junne	Collection of 6 brief duets	CHAL (1898)
955	Bordèse, Luigi	1815-1886	Frühling "O gleitet sanft dahin"		S/A	Schott		CHAL (1898)
956	Bordèse, Luigi	1815-1886	Frühling "Seht der Lenz ist wieder da"		S/A	Schott		CHAL (1898)
957	Bordèse, Luigi	1815-1886	Grain de blé		Unspec.	Junne		CHAL (1898)
958	Bordèse, Luigi	1815-1886	Gras ücken "Wenn die Lerchen sich erheben"		S/A	Schott		CHAL (1898)
959	Bordèse, Luigi	1815-1886	Improvisatorinnen "Blum-en in das Haar gewunden"		S/S	Schott		CHAL (1898)
960	Bordèse, Luigi	1815-1886	Indiennes		2 female v.	Schott		CHAL (1898)
961	Bordèse, Luigi	1815-1886	Junges Mädchen und das Echo		S/A	Schott		CHAL (1898)

REC	COMP	DTS	TITLE	OP #	VCG	PUB	COMMENTS	SRC
962	Bordèse, Luigi	1815-1886	Le Carnaval de Venise		S/MS or S/A	G. Schirm.	In catalogue page "Favorite French and Italian Vocal Duets" of G. Schirmer, Inc. NY (no date)	MSN
963	Bordèse, Luigi	1815-1886	Les Brésiliennes		S/MS	G. Schirm.	In catalogue page "Favorite French and Italian Vocal Duets" of G. Schirmer, Inc. NY (no date)	MSN
964	Bordèse, Luigi	1815-1886	Les Chasseresses		S/A	G. Schirm.	In catalogue page "Favorite French and Italian Vocal Duets" of G. Schirmer, Inc. NY (no date)	MSN
965	Bordèse, Luigi	1815-1886	Les Confidences		S/A	G. Schirm.	In catalogue page "Favorite French and Italian Vocal Duets" of G. Schirmer, Inc. NY (no date)	MSN
966	Bordèse, Luigi	1815-1886	Les Fauvettes		S/MS	G. Schirm.	In catalogue page "Favorite French and Italian Vocal Duets" of G. Schirmer, Inc. NY (no date)	MSN
967	Bordèse, Luigi	1815-1886	Les Zingarelles		S/A	G. Schirm.	In catalogue page "Favorite French and Italian Vocal Duets" of G. Schirmer, Inc. NY (no date)	MSN
968	Bordèse, Luigi	1815-1886	Livre du passé		Unspec.	Junne		CHAL (1898)
969	Bordèse, Luigi	1815-1886	Loi du Baron		Unspec.	Junne		CHAL (1898)
970	Bordèse, Luigi	1815-1886	Lyre d'or des pensionnats et communautés religieuses 24 Duettini		Unspec.	Junne	Collection of 24 brief duets	CHAL (1898)
971	Bordèse, Luigi	1815-1886	Madrilenen "Madrid du hochgeehrte"		S/A	Schott		CHAL (1898)
972	Bordèse, Luigi	1815-1886	Messire Ecbert		Unspec.	Junne		CHAL (1898)
973	Bordèse, Luigi	1815-1886	Miroir de la fontaine		Unspec.	Junne		CHAL (1898)
974	Bordèse, Luigi	1815-1886	Moine de Saint-Gildas		Unspec.	Junne		CHAL (1898)
975	Bordèse, Luigi	1815-1886	Nid de bonheur		Unspec.	Junne		CHAL (1898)
976	Bordèse, Luigi	1815-1886	Norvégiennes		2 female v.	Schott		CHAL (1898)
977	Bordèse, Luigi	1815-1886	Quenouille de grand-maman		Unspec.	Junne		CHAL (1898)
978	Bordèse, Luigi	1815-1886	Rameua de buis		Unspec.	Junne		CHAL (1898)
979	Bordèse, Luigi	1815-1886	Refrain des Forgerons		Unspec.	Junne		CHAL (1898)
980	Bordèse, Luigi	1815-1886	Retour à la pension		Unspec.	Junne		CHAL (1898)
981	Bordèse, Luigi	1815-1886	Rivalen "Wie (Wenn) Sie Verehrte mir erlauben"		S/A	Schott		CHAL (1898)
982	Bordèse, Luigi	1815-1886	Rogations		Unspec.	Junne		CHAL (1898)
983	Bordèse, Luigi	1815-1886	Rose mousseuse		Unspec.	Junne		CHAL (1898)
984	Bordèse, Luigi	1815-1886	Rosenfest "Wies' und Gärten, sie erklärten"		S/MS	Schott		CHAL (1898)
985	Bordèse, Luigi	1815-1886	Sahariennes		2 female v.	Schott		CHAL (1898)

REC	COMP	DTS	TITLE	OP #	VCG	PUB	COMMENTS	SRC
986	Bordèse, Luigi	1815-1886	Schwätzerinnen "Sie schmälen uns"		S/S	Schott		CHAL (1898)
987	Bordèse, Luigi	1815-1886	Sorrentinerinnen "Hier in Sorrento"		S/S	Schott		CHAL (1898)
988	Bordèse, Luigi	1815-1886	Sylphen "Wie die Wolken flieh'n"		S/S	Schott		CHAL (1898)
989	Bordèse, Luigi	1815-1886	Töchter des Glocken-thürmers "Klinget Glocken und hallet"		S/S	Schott		CHAL (1898)
990	Bordèse, Luigi	1815-1886	Transtévérines		2 female v.	Schott		CHAL (1898)
991	Bordèse, Luigi	1815-1886	Un Nido d'Usignuoli		S/MS	G. Schirm.	In catalogue page "Favorite French and Italian Vocal Duets" of G. Schirmer, Inc. NY (no date)	MSN
992	Bordèse, Luigi	1815-1886	Un Pèlerinage à Notre-Dame des Bois		Unspec.	Junne		CHAL (1898)
993	Bordèse, Luigi	1815-1886	Vach à Colas		Unspec.	Junne		CHAL (1898)
994	Bordèse, Luigi	1815-1886	Voyageuses "Voya-geuses cosmopolites"		Unspec.	Fürstner Paris		CHAL (1898)
995	Bordèse, Luigi	1815-1886	Waisen des Regiments "Uns die Töchter eines Braven"		S/A	Schott		CHAL (1898)
996	Bordèse, Luigi	1815-1886	Zigeunerinnen "Naht euch, ihr Mädchen"		S/S	Schott		CHAL (1898)
997	Born, C.		Ich hab' was mitgebracht "Ach, welches Glück, endlich zurück"	Op. 105	Unspec.	Peterling		CHAL (1898)
998	Born, C.		O Sancta Lucia "Wir wollen singen"	Op. 48	Unspec.	Klebahn i. Br.		CHAL (1898)
999	Born, C.		Reclame-Couplet "Zeitungslesen thun wir gerne"	Op. 94	Unspec.	Peterling		CHAL (1898)
1000	Born, C.		Was meinen sie bloss, das wär' doch famos "Vieles giebt es hier auf Erden"	Op. 101	Unspec.	Peterling		CHAL (1898)
1001	Born, C.		Weil wir so reiche, noble Leut		Unspec.	O. Dietrich		CHAL (1906)
1002	Born, C.		Wir sagen nichts und machen nur so "Ist irgend wo was Neu's passirt"		Unspec.	Klebahn i. Br.		CHAL (1898)
1003	Born, C.		Wir wollen singen hier	Op. 48	Unspec.	O. Dietrich		CHAL (1911)
1004	Börner, Kurt	1877-	Ich lehn' am Fenster und schau' in's Meer	Op. 4 No. 7	S/A	Spitzner	In Tuscany songs-choral cycle.	CHAL (1911)
1005	Bornet, R.		Couplets giebt es heute verscheiden	Op. 75	Unspec.	P. & M.		CHAL (1901)
1006	Bornhardt, Johann Heinrich Karl	1774-1840	Am Strahle der Freude gedeihet die Blume	No. 4	Unspec.	B. & H.		CHAL (1898)
1007	Bornhardt, Johann Heinrich Karl	1774-1840	Begünstigt dich das Glück	No. 6	Unspec.	B. & H.		CHAL (1898)
1008	Bornhardt, Johann Heinrich Karl	1774-1840	Holde Tugend, leite mich in meiner Jugend	No. 1	Unspec.	B. & H.		CHAL (1898)

REC	COMP	DTS	TITLE	OP #	VCG	PUB	COMMENTS	SRC
1009	Bornhardt, Johann Heinrich Karl	1774-1840	Ich weiss einen sichern Wanderstab	No. 2	Unspec.	B. & H.		CHAL (1898)
1010	Bornhardt, Johann Heinrich Karl	1774-1840	Selig wer die Rosenjahre	No. 3	Unspec.	B. & H.		CHAL (1898)
1011	Bornhardt, Johann Heinrich Karl	1774-1840	Wenn der holde Frühling lachet	No. 5	Unspec.	B. & H.		CHAL (1898)
1012	Bortniantsky, Dimitri Stephanovich	1751-1825	Ich bete an die Macht der Liebe		Unspec.	C. Rühle i. L.		CHAL (1911)
1013	Bortniantsky, Dimitri Stephanovich	1751-1825	Ich bete an die Macht der Liebe		Unspec.	G. Richter i. L.	Ed. Wittenbecher	CHAL (1906)
1014	Bortolini, G.	1875-	Barcarole "Vieni a barca"		Unspec.	Cranz		CHAL (1898)
1015	Boruttau, Alfred J.	1877-	Waren drei Knäblein zart und fein		Unspec.	Callwey		CHAL (1911)
1016	Bosen, Franz		Frühlingsmorgen "Wie reizend, wie wonnig ist Alles umher"		S/A	B. & H.	In anth. "Zweistim. Lied. f. Sop. u. Altstimme mit Klavierbegleitung f. den Haus- u. Schulgebrauch v. H. M. Schletterer" 3 vols.	MSN
1017	Bosen, Franz		Wie reizend, wie wonnig		S/S	B. & H.		CHAL (1898)
1018	Bosmans, Henriette	1895-1952	Copla		high & med. v.	Donemus	Dut. woman comp.	ASR
1019	Böttcher, E.		Zur Ehre Gottes dienen soll	No. 15	Unspec.	Schergens		CHAL (1906)
1020	Böttger, G.		Wenn der Herr ein Kreuze schict	Op. 42	S/A	Grüniger		CHAL (1898)
1021	Bouman, Paul		Create in Me a Clean Heart		S/S or S/A	Concordia	May be perf. chorally.	CVMP (1976)
1022	Bouman, Paul		Create in Me a Clean Heart, o God		S/S or S/A	Concordia		ASR
1023	Boumann, Leonardus Carolus	1852-1919	Lerchen "Es ziehen die Wolken"	Op. 10 No. 3	Unspec.	Kahnt		CHAL (1898)
1024	Boumann, Leonardus Carolus	1852-1919	Lotosblume und Schwan "O Lotosblume Schwan der Blumenwelt"	Op. 10 No. 2	Unspec.	Kahnt		CHAL (1898)
1025	Boumann, Leonardus Carolus	1852-1919	Sterne "Tausend goldne Sterne winken"	Op. 10 No. 1	Unspec.	Kahnt		CHAL (1898)
1026	Bourgault-Ducoudray, Louis	1840-1910	Chanson alternée		Unspec.	Lemoine	Arr. of Fr. folk songs	BBC (1975)
1027	Boyneburgk, Fr. v.		Lied der Elfen "Bunte Schlangen, zweigezüngt"		Unspec.	André		CHAL (1898)
1028	Bracken, Edith A.		If Thou Wilt Ease Thine Heart		S/A	Ditson	Woman comp. In anthology "Soprano and Alto Duets" Ed. H. Kiehl. Pub. 1901.	MSN
1029	Bradsky, Wenzel Theodor	1833-1881	Hast du Jemand weh' gethau	Op. 42 No. 3	Unspec.	Bahn		CHAL (1898)
1030	Bradsky, Wenzel Theodor	1833-1881	Hollunderbaum "Da droben auf jenem Berge"	Op. 42 No. 4	Unspec.	Bahn		CHAL (1898)

REC	COMP	DTS	TITLE	OP #	VCG	PUB	COMMENTS	SRC
1031	Bradsky, Wenzel Theodor	1833-1881	Im Walde "Waldesnacht, du wunderkühle"	Op. 42 No. 2	Unspec.	Bahn		CHAL (1898)
1032	Bradsky, Wenzel Theodor	1833-1881	Immer leiser wird mein schlummer	Op. 42 No. 1	Unspec.	Bahn		CHAL (1898)
1033	Brah-Müller, Karl Friedrich Gustav	1839-1878	Scheiden und Meiden "So soll ich dich nun meiden"	Op. 13 No. 1	Unspec.	Chal.		CHAL (1898)
1034	Brah-Müller, Karl Friedrich Gustav	1839-1878	Traum "Ich hab' die Nacht geträumet"	Op. 13 No. 2	Unspec.	Chal.		CHAL (1898)
1035	Braham, John	1774-1856	All's Well		Unspec.	White-Smith	In catalogue page "Vocal Duetts" of White-Smith Music Pub. Co. (no date)	MSN
1036	Brahe, Mary Hannah	1884-1956	As I went a-roaming		Unspec.	Enoch	Austral. woman comp.	BBC (1975)
1037	Brahe, Mary Hannah	1884-1956	Bless this house		Unspec.	Boosey	Austral. woman comp.	BBC (1975)
1038	Brahe, Mary Hannah	1884-1956	Bless this House		Unspec.	Boosey	Austral. woman comp. Also solo.	CVMP (1976)
1039	Brahe, Mary Hannah	1884-1956	Bless this House		2 med. v.	Boosey	Austral. woman comp.	ASR
1040	Brahe, Mary Hannah	1884-1956	None-so-pretty		Unspec.	Enoch	Austral. woman comp.	BBC (1975)
1041	Brähmig, Bernard	1822-1872	Arion "Sammlung"		Unspec.	Merse.		CHAL (1898)
1042	Brahms, Johannes	1833-1897	Ach, englische Schäferin	No. 8	Unspec.	Simrock	In collection "Deutsche Volkslieder" Heft II	MSN
1043	Brahms, Johannes	1833-1897	Am Strande "Es sprechen und blicken die Wellen"	Op. 66 No. 3	S/A	Simrock		CHAL (1898)
1044	Brahms, Johannes	1833-1897	Am Strande "Es sprechen und blikken die Wellen"	Op. 66 No. 3	S/A	Simrock		MSN
1045	Brahms, Johannes	1833-1897	Bote der Liebe "Wie viel schon der Boten"	Op. 61 No. 4	S/A	Simrock		CHAL (1898)
1046	Brahms, Johannes	1833-1897	Da unten im Tale	No. 6	Unspec.	Simrock	In collection "Deutsche Volkslieder" Heft I	MSN
1047	Brahms, Johannes	1833-1897	Das Meere	Op. 20 No. 3	Unspec.	ECS	In anthology "48 Duets Seventeenth Through Nineteenth Centuries" Ed. V. Prahl. Pub. 1941, 1970.	MSN
1048	Brahms, Johannes	1833-1897	Deutsche Volkslieder Vol. 1, 2		high & med. v.	Schauer	Ed. Zilcher	ASR
1049	Brahms, Johannes	1833-1897	Deutsche Volkslieder, Vol. I		Unspec.	Schaur EE	Ed. Zilcher	CVMP (1976)
1050	Brahms, Johannes	1833-1897	Deutsche Volkslieder, Vol. II		Unspec.	Schaur EE	Ed. Zilcher	CVMP (1976)
1051	Brahms, Johannes	1833-1897	Die Boten der Liebe "Wie viel schon der Boten flogen die Pfade"	Op. 61 No. 4	S/A	Simrock		MSN
1052	Brahms, Johannes	1833-1897	Die Meere "Alle Winde schlafen auf dem Spiegel der Flut"	Op. 20 No. 3	S/A	Simrock		MSN
1053	Brahms, Johannes	1833-1897	Die Schwestern	Op. 61 No. 1	high & med. v.	Boosey	In anthology "Duet Album: Selected and edited by Viola Morris and Victoria Anderson" Pub. 1944.	MSN

REC	COMP	DTS	TITLE	OP #	VCG	PUB	COMMENTS	SRC
1054	Brahms, Johannes	1833-1897	Die Schwestern	Op. 61 No. 1	Unspec.	ECS	In anthology "48 Duets Seventeenth Through Nineteenth Centuries" Ed. V. Prahl. Pub. 1941, 1970.	MSN
1055	Brahms, Johannes	1833-1897	Die Schwestern "Wir Schwestern zwei"	Op. 61 No. 1	S/A	Simrock		CHAL (1898)
1056	Brahms, Johannes	1833-1897	Die Schwestern "Wir Schwestern zwei"	Op. 61 No. 1	S/A	Simrock		MSN
1057	Brahms, Johannes	1833-1897	Die Sonne scheint nicht mehr	No. 5	Unspec.	Simrock	In collection "Deutsche Volkslieder" Heft I	MSN
1058	Brahms, Johannes	1833-1897	Dort in den Weiden steht ein Haus	No. 31	Unspec.	Simrock	In collection "Deutsche Volkslieder" Heft II	MSN
1059	Brahms, Johannes	1833-1879	Drei Duette Op. 20	Op. 20	S/A or S/MS or S/Br	B. & H., et al.	In collection "Sämtliche Werke" of J. Brahms. Ed. H. Gál & E. Mandyczewski. Pub. 1926-1927 et al.	NATS-VCD
1060	Brahms, Johannes	1833-1897	Duets, Vol. I		S/A	Peters	Collection, contains Op. 20, Op. 61, Op. 66, Op. 75	CVMP (1976)
1061	Brahms, Johannes	1833-1897	Duets Vol. I		S/A	Peters	Collection, contains Op. 20, Op. 61, Op. 66, Op. 75	ASR
1062	Brahms, Johannes	1833-1897	Erlaube mir, fein's Mädchen	No. 2	Unspec.	Simrock	In collection "Deutsche Volkslieder" Heft II	MSN
1063	Brahms, Johannes	1833-1897	Feinsliebchen, du sollst	No. 12	Unspec.	Simrock	In collection "Deutsche Volkslieder" Heft I	MSN
1064	Brahms, Johannes	1833-1897	Five Duets	Op. 66	S/A	Simrock		BBC (1975)
1065	Brahms, Johannes	1833-1897	Five Duets Op. 66	Op. 66	S/A	Schaur EE		CVMP (1976)
1066	Brahms, Johannes	1833-1897	Five Duets Op. 66	Op. 66	Unspec.	Lengnick		CVMP (1985)
1067	Brahms, Johannes	1833-1897	Four Duets	Op. 61	S/A	Simrock		BBC (1975)
1068	Brahms, Johannes	1833-1897	Four Duets Op. 61	Op. 61	S/A	Schaur EE		CVMP (1976)
1069	Brahms, Johannes	1833-1897	Four Duets Op. 61	Op. 61	Unspec.	Lengnick		CVMP (1985)
1070	Brahms, Johannes	1833-1897	Four Duets, Op. 61	Op. 61	S/A	Schauer		ASR
1071	Brahms, Johannes	1833-1879	Fünf Duette Op. 66	Op. 66	S/A or S/MS	B. & H., et al.	In collection "Sämtliche Werke" of J. Brahms. Ed. H. Gál & E. Mandyczewski. Pub. 1926-1927 et al.	NATS-VCD
1072	Brahms, Johannes	1833-1897	Guten Abend, gut' Nacht	Op. 49 No. 4	Unspec.	Simrock		CHAL (1911)
1073	Brahms, Johannes	1833-1879	Guter Rat	Op. 75 No. 2	S/A or S/MS	B. & H., et al.	In collection "Sämtliche Werke" of J. Brahms. Ed. H. Gál & E. Mandyczewski. Pub. 1926-1927 et al.	NATS-VCD
1074	Brahms, Johannes	1833-1897	Guter Rath "Ach Mutter, liebe Mutter"	Op. 75 No. 2	S/A	Simrock		CHAL (1898)
1075	Brahms, Johannes	1833-1897	Hüt' du dich "Ich weiß ein Mäd'lein hübsch und fein"	Op. 66 No. 5	S/A	Simrock		MSN
1076	Brahms, Johannes	1833-1897	Hut' du dich "Ich weiss ein Mädchen (Mägdlein)"	Op. 66 No. 5	S/A	Simrock		CHAL (1898)
1077	Brahms, Johannes	1833-1897	In den Beeren "Singe Mädchen hell und klar"	Op. 84 No. 3	Unspec.	Simrock		CHAL (1898)

REC	COMP	DTS	TITLE	OP #	VCG	PUB	COMMENTS	SRC
1078	Brahms, Johannes	1833-1897	In stiller Nacht	No. 42	Unspec.	Simrock	In collection "Deutsche Volkslieder" Heft I	MSN
1079	Brahms, Johannes	1833-1897	Jägerlied "Jäger, was jagst du"	Op. 66 No. 4	S/A	Simrock		CHAL (1898)
1080	Brahms, Johannes	1833-1897	Jungfräulein, soll ich mit euch gehn	No. 11	Unspec.	Simrock	In collection "Deutsche Volkslieder" Heft I	MSN
1081	Brahms, Johannes	1833-1897	Klänge "Aus der Erde quellen Blumen"	Op. 66 No. 1	S/A	Simrock		MSN
1082	Brahms, Johannes	1833-1897	Klänge I		S/A	EMB	In anthology "Duettek nöi Hangokra Zongorakí-sérettel" Vol. II Compi. Miklós Forrai. Pub. 1959.	MSN
1083	Brahms, Johannes	1833-1897	Klänge I "Aus der Erde quellen Blumen"	Op. 66 No. 1	S/A	Simrock		CHAL (1898)
1084	Brahms, Johannes	1833-1897	Klänge II		S/A	EMB	In anthology "Duettek nöi Hangokra Zongora-kísérettel" Vol. II Compi. Miklós Forrai. Pub. 1959.	MSN
1085	Brahms, Johannes	1833-1897	Klänge II "Wenn ein müder Leib begraben"	Op. 66 No. 2	S/A	Simrock		CHAL (1898)
1086	Brahms, Johannes	1833-1897	Klänge "Wenn ein müder Leib begraben"	Op. 66 No. 2	S/A	Simrock		MSN
1087	Brahms, Johannes	1833-1897	Klosterfräulein "Ach ich armes Klosterfräulein"	Op. 61 No. 2	S/A	Simrock		CHAL (1898)
1088	Brahms, Johannes	1833-1897	Kranz "Mutter hilf mir armen Tochter"	Op. 84 No. 2	Unspec.	Simrock		CHAL (1898)
1089	Brahms, Johannes	1833-1897	Maria ging aus wandern	No. 14	Unspec.	Simrock	In collection "Deutsche Volkslieder" Heft II	MSN
1090	Brahms, Johannes	1833-1897	Meere "Alle Winde schlafen"	Op. 20 No. 3	S/A	Simrock		CHAL (1898)
1091	Brahms, Johannes	1833-1897	Mein Mädel hat einen Rosenmund	No. 25	Unspec.	Simrock	In collection "Deutsche Volkslieder" Heft II	MSN
1092	Brahms, Johannes	1833-1897	Mir ist ein schön's braun's Maidelein	No. 24	Unspec.	Simrock	In collection "Deutsche Volkslieder" Heft II	MSN
1093	Brahms, Johannes	1833-1897	Phänomen	Op. 61 No. 3	Unspec.	ECS	In anthology "48 Duets Seventeenth Through Nineteenth Centuries" Ed. V. Prahl. Pub. 1941, 1970.	MSN
1094	Brahms, Johannes	1833-1897	Phänomen "Wenn zu der Regenwand"	Op. 61 No. 3	S/A	Simrock		CHAL (1898)
1095	Brahms, Johannes	1833-1897	Regina Coeli	Op. 37 No. 3	S/A	Carus	org accomp. Ed. Paul Horn	CVMP (1985)
1096	Brahms, Johannes	1833-1897	Sandman, The		Unspec.	Allans	Eng. trans. Grmn. arr. for 2 v. In anthology "Vocal Duets Collection" Vol. 2. Pub. 1992.	MSN
1097	Brahms, Johannes	1833-1897	Schwesterlein	No. 15	Unspec.	Simrock	In collection "Deutsche Volkslieder" Heft I	MSN
1098	Brahms, Johannes	1833-1897	So lass uns wandern	Op. 75 No. 3	Unspec.	ECS	In anthology "48 Duets Seventeenth Through Nineteenth Centuries" Ed. V. Prahl. Pub. 1941, 1970.	MSN
1099	Brahms, Johannes	1833-1897	Sommerabend "Geh' schlafen, Tochter schlafen"	Op. 84 No. 1	Unspec.	Simrock		CHAL (1898)
1100	Brahms, Johannes	1833-1897	Songs and Romances	Op. 84	Unspec.	Breitkopf		BBC (1975)

REC	COMP	DTS	TITLE	OP #	VCG	PUB	COMMENTS	SRC
1101	Brahms, Johannes	1833-1897	Songs for Two Voices and Piano	Op. 20, 28, 61, 75	Var.	Kalmus		ASR
1102	Brahms, Johannes	1833-1897	Spannung "Guten Abend mein tausiger Schatz"	Op. 84 No. 5	Unspec.	Simrock		CHAL (1898)
1103	Brahms, Johannes	1833-1897	Three Duets	Op. 20	S/A	Peters		BBC (1975)
1104	Brahms, Johannes	1833-1897	Three Duets Op. 20	Op. 20	S/A	Schaur EE		CVMP (1976)
1105	Brahms, Johannes	1833-1897	Three Duets Op. 20	Op. 20	Unspec.	Lengnick		CVMP (1985)
1106	Brahms, Johannes	1833-1897	Three Duets, Op. 20	Op. 20	S/A	Schauer, Augener		ASR
1107	Brahms, Johannes	1833-1897	Vergebliches Ständchen "Guten Abend, mein Schatz"	Op. 84 No. 4	Unspec.	Simrock	Not true duet, may be sung by one v.	CHAL (1898)
1108	Brahms, Johannes	1833-1879	Vier Duette Op. 61	Op. 61	S/A or S/MS or S/S	B. & H., et al.	In collection "Sämtliche Werke" of J. Brahms. Ed. H. Gál & E. Mandyczewski. Pub. 1926-1927 et al.	NATS-VCD
1109	Brahms, Johannes	1833-1879	Walpurgisnacht	Op. 75 No. 4	S/S	B. & H., et al.	In collection "Sämtliche Werke" of J. Brahms. Ed. H. Gál & E. Mandyczewski. Pub. 1926-1927 et al.	NATS-VCD
1110	Brahms, Johannes	1833-1897	Walpurgisnacht "Lieb' Mutter heut Nacht"	Op. 75 No. 4	S/S	Simrock		CHAL (1898)
1111	Brahms, Johannes	1833-1897	Weg der Liebe	Op. 20 No. 1	Unspec.	G. Schirm.	In anthology "Romantic Duets—Great Performers Edition" Compi. E. Lear & T. Stewart. 1985.	MSN
1112	Brahms, Johannes	1833-1897	Weg der Liebe "Den gordischen Knoten"	Op. 20 No. 2	S/A	Simrock		MSN
1113	Brahms, Johannes	1833-1897	Weg der Liebe "Gordischen Knoten"	Op. 20 No. 2	S/A	Simrock		CHAL (1898)
1114	Brahms, Johannes	1833-1897	Weg der Liebe "Über die Berge"	Op. 20 No. 1	S/A	Simrock		CHAL (1898)
1115	Brahms, Johannes	1833-1897	Wiegenlied		Unspec.	Allans	Eng. trans. Grmn. Arr. for 2 v. by C. Stanbridge. In anthology "Vocal Duets Collection" Vol. 2. Pub. 1992.	MSN
1116	Brahms, Johannes	1833-1897	Wiegenlied	Op. 49 No. 4	S/A	Ditson	Arr. L. R. Dressler. In anthology "The Ditson Collection of Soprano and Alto Duets" Pub. 1934.	MSN
1117	Brahms, Johannes (G. F. Handel)	1833-1897	Ahi, nelle sorti umane		S/A	Peters	Arr. of Handel duet	MSN
1118	Brahms, Johannes (G. F. Handel)	1833-1897	Amor dir werd ich nie trauen	No. 3	S/A	Peters	Arr. of Handel duet	CHAL (1898)
1119	Brahms, Johannes (G. F. Handel)	1833-1897	Beato in ver chi può		S/A	Peters	Arr. of Handel duet	MSN
1120	Brahms, Johannes (G. F. Handel)	1833-1897	Blume prangt am Morgen	No. 1	S/A	Peters	Arr. of Handel duet	CHAL (1898)
1121	Brahms, Johannes (G. F. Handel)	1833-1897	Fronda leggiera e mobile		S/A	Peters	Arr. of Handel duet	MSN

REC	COMP	DTS	TITLE	OP #	VCG	PUB	COMMENTS	SRC
1122	Brahms, Johannes (G. F. Handel)	1833-1897	Nein ich werde nimmer trauen		S/A	Peters	Arr. of Handel duet	CHAL (1898)
1123	Brahms, Johannes (G. F. Handel)	1833-1897	Nò, di voi non vo' fidarme (1)		S/A	Peters	Arr. of Handel duet. 1st of two duets with same title.	MSN
1124	Brahms, Johannes (G. F. Handel)	1833-1897	Nò, di voi non vo' fidarme (2)		S/A	Peters	Arr. of Handel duets. 2nd of two duets with same title.	MSN
1125	Brahms, Johannes (G. F. Handel)	1833-1897	O glücklich in Wahrheit ist	No. 4	S/A	Peters	Arr. of Handel duet	CHAL (1898)
1126	Brahms, Johannes (G. F. Handel)	1833-1897	O in den Schicksalsbereiche	No. 6	S/A	Peters	Arr. of Handel duet	CHAL (1898)
1127	Brahms, Johannes (G. F. Handel)	1833-1897	Quel fior che all' alba ride		S/A	Peters	Arr. of Handel duet	MSN
1128	Brahms, Johannes (G. F. Handel)	1833-1897	Schwerer als Laub vom Hauch bewegt	No. 5	S/A	Peters	Arr. of Handel duet	CHAL (1898)
1129	Brahms, Johannes (G. F. Handel)	1833-1897	Sechs Duette für Sopran und Alt		S/S, S/A	Peters	Unspec. pieces. Three S/S, three S/A. Arr. J. Brahms of 6 Italian duets by G. F. Handel.	ASR
1130	Brahms-Zilcher		Da unten im Tale läufts Wasser so trüb	No. 2	Unspec.	Simrock		CHAL (1911)
1131	Brahms-Zilcher		Feinsliebchen, du sollst mir nicht barfuss gehn	No. 5	Unpsec.	Simrock		CHAL (1911)
1132	Brahms-Zilcher		In stiller Nacht, zur ersten Wacht	No. 1	Unspec.	Simrock		CHAL (1911)
1133	Brahms-Zilcher		Jungfräulein, soll ich mit euch gehn	No. 6	Unspec.	Simrock		CHAL (1911)
1134	Brahms-Zilcher		Schwesterlein, wann gehn wir nach Haus	No. 3	Unspec.	Simrock		CHAL (1911)
1135	Brahms-Zilcher		Sonne scheint nicht mehr	No. 4	Unspec.	Simrock		CHAL (1911)
1136	Brambach, Kaspar Joseph	1833-1902	Abend thaut herneider	Op. 44 No. 5	S/A	Cohen		CHAL (1898)
1137	Brambach, Kaspar Joseph	1833-1902	Frühlingsregen "Welch' sanfter, milder Regen"	Op. 2 No. 2	S/S	B. & H.		CHAL (1898)
1138	Brambach, Kaspar Joseph	1833-1902	Frühlingswerden	Op. 2 No. 1	S/A	Ditson	In anthology "Soprano and Alto Duets" Ed. Heinrich Kiehl. Pub. 1901.	MSN
1139	Brambach, Kaspar Joseph	1833-1902	Frühlingswerden "Welch' ein Frühlingsrufen"	Op. 2 No. 1	S/S	B. & H.		CHAL (1898)
1140	Brambach, Kaspar Joseph	1833-1902	Frühlingswerden "Welch ein Frühlingsrufen"	Op. 2 No. 1	S/A	B. & H.	In anth. "Zweistim. Lied. f. Sop. u. Altstimme mit Klavierbegleitung f. den Haus- u. Schulgebrauch v. H. M. Schletterer" 3 vols.	MSN
1141	Brambach, Kaspar Joseph	1833-1902	Gebet "Herr gedenk', wie schwach ich bin"	Op. 44 No. 4	S/A	Cohen		CHAL (1898)
1142	Brambach, Kaspar Joseph	1833-1902	Geistliches Lied "In die Höhe führe mich"	Op. 44 No. 1	S/A	Cohen		CHAL (1898)
1143	Brambach, Kaspar Joseph	1833-1902	Heimweh "Sterne, die ihr niederschaut"	Op. 27 No. 3	S/MS or T/Br	Schott		CHAL (1898)

REC	COMP	DTS	TITLE	OP #	VCG	PUB	COMMENTS	SRC
1144	Brambach, Kaspar Joseph	1833-1902	Herbstwanderung "Nebel weicht"	Op. 27 No. 6	S/MS or T/Br	Schott		CHAL (1898)
1145	Brambach, Kaspar Joseph	1833-1902	Im Grünen "Schallt keck von hohen Bäumen"	Op. 44 No. 6	S/A	Cohen		CHAL (1898)
1146	Brambach, Kaspar Joseph	1833-1902	In der Morgenfrühe "Wohl über die Schlucht"	Op. 27 No. 6	S/MS or T/Br	Schott		CHAL (1898)
1147	Brambach, Kaspar Joseph	1833-1902	Lenz fängt an zu Lächeln	Op. 27 No. 1	S/MS or T/Br	Schott		CHAL (1898)
1148	Brambach, Kaspar Joseph	1833-1902	Lindengang "Welch' süsses, leises Klingen"	Op. 27 No. 2	S/MS or T/Br	Schott		CHAL (1898)
1149	Brambach, Kaspar Joseph	1833-1902	Schönste Zeit "Das ist die schönste Zeit"	Op. 27 No. 4	S/MS or T/Br	Schott		CHAL (1898)
1150	Brambach, Kaspar Joseph	1833-1902	Unter der Loreley "Wie kühl der Felsen dunkelt"	Op. 44 No. 3	S/A	Cohen		CHAL (1898)
1151	Brambach, Kaspar Joseph	1833-1902	Vöglein im Walde "Lustiges Vöglein im Walde"	Op. 2 No. 4	S/S	B. & H.		CHAL (1898)
1152	Brambach, Kaspar Joseph	1833-1902	Vöglein im Walde "Lustiges Vöglein im Walde"	Op. 2 No. 4	S/A	B. & H.	In anth. "Zweistim. Lied. f. Sop. u. Altstimme mit Klavierbegleitung f. den Haus- u. Schulgebrauch v. H. M. Schletterer" 3 vols.	MSN
1153	Brambach, Kaspar Joseph	1833-1902	Waldabendschein "Am Waldrand steht ein Tannenbaum"	Op. 44 No. 2	S/A	Cohen		CHAL (1898)
1154	Brambach, Kaspar Joseph	1833-1902	Wie ist so schön "Wohl ist sie schön"	Op. 2 No. 3	S/S	B. & H.		CHAL (1898)
1155	Brandhurst, Elise	19th C.	Dir wie mir "Guten Morgen liebe Grete"	Op. 51	S/S	Eulenburg	Grmn. woman comp.	CHAL (1898)
1156	Brandt, August	1825-1877	Am Ammersee "Es steht eine Weide am Ammersee"		Unspec.	Hoffheinz		CHAL (1898)
1157	Brandt, F. [prob. Fritz]	1880-	Das ist nicht seit gestern, das ist nicht seit heut' "Jüngst fuhren in 'ner Droschke"		Unspec.	K. & G.		CHAL (1898)
1158	Brandt, F. [prob. Fritz]	1880-	Du musst's beniesen "In Kyritz war ich schon"		Unspec.	K. & G.		CHAL (1898)
1159	Brandt, F. [prob. Fritz]	1880-	Nur immer zu, wozu sind wir denu da "Heut'gen Männer glaube mir"		Unspec.	K. & G.		CHAL (1898)
1160	Brandt, F. [prob. Fritz]	1880-	Was wäre unser Leben wohl ohne Liebesglanz "O weh, welch herbes Missgeschick"		Unspec.	K. & G.		CHAL (1898)
1161	Brandt, Hermann	1840-1893	Nach der Heimath lasst mich ziehen	IV No. 4	Unspec.	C. Rühle i. L.		CHAL (1901)
1162	Brandt, Hermann	1840-1893	Rosenliebe "Es war eine knospende Rose"	Op. 241 No. a	2 med. v.	Glas		CHAL (1898)
1163	Brandt, Hermann	1840-1893	Verschiedene Weine "Von Allem was der Herrgott schuf"	Op. 33	Unspec.	Hoffheinz		CHAL (1898)
1164	Brandt, M.		Liebesklänge "Dich nenn' ich stolz mein eigen"	Op. 23	Unspec.	Augustin i. Berl.		CHAL (1898)
1165	Brandt-Caspari, Alfred	1864-1929	An dem reinsten Frühlingsmorgen	Op. 25 No. 22	Unspec.	Hofmeister		CHAL (1906)
1166	Brandt-Caspari, Alfred	1864-1929	Bei dem Glanz der Abendröthe	Op. 25 No. 23	Unspec.	Hofmeister		CHAL (1906)

REC	COMP	DTS	TITLE	OP #	VCG	PUB	COMMENTS	SRC
1167	Brandt-Caspari, Alfred	1864-1929	Da sitzt ein kleiner Vogel	Op. 27 No. 1	S/A	Stahl i. B.		CHAL (1906)
1168	Brandt-Caspari, Alfred	1864-1929	Dreht sich Feinslieb im Tanz	Op. 27 No. 9	S/A	Stahl i. B.		CHAL (1906)
1169	Brandt-Caspari, Alfred	1864-1929	Hier waren grüne Buchen	Op. 27 No. 4	S/A	Stahl i. B.		CHAL (1906)
1170	Brandt-Caspari, Alfred	1864-1929	Im Eimer das Wasser trieb tanzend	Op. 27 No. 8	S/A	Stahl i. B.		CHAL (1906)
1171	Brandt-Caspari, Alfred	1864-1929	Im Walde hallt es wunderbar	Op. 27 No. 7	S/A	Stahl i. B.		CHAL (1906)
1172	Brandt-Caspari, Alfred	1864-1929	Irrlicht "Irrlichtchen fein und klein"	Op. 27 No. 3	S/A	Stahl i. B.		CHAL (1906)
1173	Brandt-Caspari, Alfred	1864-1929	Rose spricht zur Nachtigall	Op. 27 No. 2	S/A	Stahl i. B.		CHAL (1906)
1174	Brandt-Caspari, Alfred	1864-1929	Thal ist wintertraurig rings	Op. 27 No. 5	S/A	Stahl i. B.		CHAL (1906)
1175	Brandt-Caspari, Alfred	1864-1929	Wie oft hab' ich durchgangen	Op. 27 No. 10	S/A	Stahl i. B.		CHAL (1906)
1176	Bratsch, Johann Georg	1817-1887	Barcarole "Still schaukelt über die Wogen"	Op. 18	Unspec.	Schott		CHAL (1898)
1177	Brauer, W.		Auf den Händen laufen mer a "Wie wir jetzt beide komm'n"		Unspec.	O. Teich		CHAL (1898)
1178	Braun, Albert	1808-1883	Unter dem Christbaum "12 neue Weihnachtslieder"		S/A	Coppenrath	Collection, 12 new Christmas duets.	CHAL (1911)
1179	Braun, Clemens	1862-1933	Beim Aussäen der Blumen "Sink' o Körnlein"	Op. 5 No. 3b	S/MS or T	Heinr.	Grmn. trans. Swed.	CHAL (1898)
1180	Braun, Clemens	1862-1933	Haidenröslein "Sah ein Knab' ein Röslein stehn"	Op. 5 No. 5b	S/MS or T	Heinr.	Grmn. trans. Swed.	CHAL (1898)
1181	Braun, Clemens	1862-1933	Ich lehn' an einen Steine	Op. 33	Unspec.	Zumsteeg	Grmn. trans. Swed.	CHAL (1898)
1182	Braun, Clemens	1862-1933	Jubelhymne "Harfe Davids rausche nieder"	Op. 21	Unspec.	Bahn	Grmn. trans. Swed.	CHAL (1898)
1183	Braun, Clemens	1862-1933	Schu-Tswang "Ma-Fo-Pu-Dang, ach Mütterlein"	Op. 20	S/MS	Zumsteeg	Grmn. trans. Swed.	CHAL (1898)
1184	Braun, Clemens	1862-1933	Vögleins Lied "Ein Vöglein kam"	Op. 5 No. 1b	S/MS or S/T	Heinr.	Grmn. trans. Swed.	CHAL (1898)
1185	Brede, Albrecht	1834-1920	Abendruhe "Über den Hügel hin"	Op. 25 No. 2	S/A	R. & E.		CHAL (1898)
1186	Brede, Albrecht	1834-1920	Frühlingsgewissheit "Wolken ziehen schwarz und schwer"	Op. 25 No. 1	S/A	R. & E.		CHAL (1898)
1187	Brede, Albrecht	1834-1920	Lebewohl "Ade, es sei geschieden"	Op. 25 No. 3	S/A	R. & E.		CHAL (1898)
1188	Brede, Albrecht	1834-1920	O ewig schöne Maienzeit "Geschmückt mit Blüthen"	Op. 44 No. 1	S/A	Kuprion		CHAL (1898)
1189	Brede, Albrecht	1834-1920	Reichgesegnet sei die Stunde	Op. 47	Unspec.	none listed	org or harm or pf	CHAL (1906)
1190	Brede, Albrecht	1834-1920	Veilchenduft "Tief drinn im Herzen"	Op. 44 No. 2	S/A	Kuprion		CHAL (1898)

REC	COMP	DTS	TITLE	OP #	VCG	PUB	COMMENTS	SRC
1191	Brede, Albrecht	1834-1920	Wandern im Frühling "Das ist ein frohes Wandern"	Op. 44 No. 4	S/A	Kuprion		CHAL (1898)
1192	Brede, Albrecht	1834-1920	Wonne des Maien "Mit Veilchen blau"	Op. 44 No. 3	S/A	Kuprion		CHAL (1898)
1193	Bredschneider, Willy	1889-	In das Bummeln noch so schön	No. 1	Unspec.	Ed. Bloch.		CHAL (1911)
1194	Breiderhoff, E.		Ein Blatt aus sommerlichen Tagen	Op. 4 No. 2	S/S	R. & B.		CHAL (1901)
1195	Breiderhoff, E.		Liebchen hat zum Eigenthum	Op. 4 No. 3	S/S	R. & B.		CHAL (1901)
1196	Breiderhoff, E.		Wenn die Vöglein sich gepaart	Op. 4 No. 1	S/S	R. & B.		CHAL (1901)
1197	Breiderhoff, E.		Wenn im Morgengrauen des Frühlingstages	Op. 4 No. 4	S/S	R. & B.		CHAL (1901)
1198	Breitung, F.		O du fröhliche, o du selige		Unspec.	Haushahn i. M.		CHAL (1898)
1199	Breitung, F.		Stille Nacht, heilige Nacht		Unspec.	Haushahn i. M.	Arr. of song	CHAL (1898)
1200	Brenner, Friedrich	1815-1898	Abendliedchen "Abend-glocke schallet"	II No. 11	S/A	Jessen i. Dorp.		CHAL (1898)
1201	Brenner, Friedrich	1815-1898	Ein Fichtenbaum steht einsam	I No. 2	S/A	Jessen i. Dorp.		CHAL (1898)
1202	Brenner, Friedrich	1815-1898	Freuet euch des Herrn	I No. 1	S/A	Jessen i. Dorp.		CHAL (1898)
1203	Brenner, Friedrich	1815-1898	Herbstlied "Feldenwärts flog ein Vögelein"	II No. 8	S/A	Jessen i. Dorp.		CHAL (1898)
1204	Brenner, Friedrich	1815-1898	Herbstlied "Näher rückt die trübe Zeit"	I No. 9	S/A	Jessen i. Dorp.		CHAL (1898)
1205	Brenner, Friedrich	1815-1898	Meine Seele ist stille zu Gott	II No. 7	S/A	Jessen i. Dorp.		CHAL (1898)
1206	Brenner, Friedrich	1815-1898	Schöne Traum "Nun steht in frischer Grüne"	I No. 5	S/A	Jessen i. Dorp.		CHAL (1898)
1207	Brenner, Friedrich	1815-1898	Spinnlied "Spinn, (spinn,) Mägdlein, spinn"	II No. 10	S/A	Jessen i. Dorp.		CHAL (1898)
1208	Brenner, Friedrich	1815-1898	Vöglein "Ich liebe wie die Vögelein"	I No. 4	S/A	Jessen i. Dorp.		CHAL (1898)
1209	Brenner, Friedrich	1815-1898	Wanderlied "Ich gehe durch einen grasgrünen Wald"	I No. 3	S/A	Jessen i. Dorp.		CHAL (1898)
1210	Brenner, Friedrich	1815-1898	Wiegenlied "Guten Abend, gute Nacht"	I No. 6	S/A	Jessen i. Dorp.		CHAL (1898)
1211	Brenner, Friedrich	1815-1898	Wiegenlied "Nun schliess die lieben Aeugelein"	II No. 12	S/A	Jessen i. Dorp.		CHAL (1898)
1212	Bretschger, H.		Tanz' mit mir, mein schönes Herrl		Unspec.	Bretscher i. Karlsruhe		CHAL (1911)
1213	Breu, Simon	1858-1933	Abschied von der Puppe "Liebes Herzepüppchen heut"	Op. 19 No. 10	Unspec.	Kistner		CHAL (1898)
1214	Breu, Simon	1858-1933	An das Planderpüppchen "Ach so gieb' doch einmal Ruh'"	Op. 19 No. 9	Unspec.	Kistner		CHAL (1898)
1215	Breu, Simon	1858-1933	Kranke Püppchen "Ticke, tacke, Bäuerchen"	Op. 19 No. 7	Unspec.	Kistner		CHAL (1898)
1216	Breu, Simon	1858-1933	Mein Püppchen beim Kanarienvogel "Komm her du liebes Püppchen"	Op. 19 No. 5	Unspec.	Kistner		CHAL (1898)
1217	Breu, Simon	1858-1933	Puppenlieder (10)	Op. 19	Unspec.	Kistner	10 duets	CHAL (1898)
1218	Breu, Simon	1858-1933	Ringelreihn "Es waren sieben Kinderlein"	Op. 19 No. 4	Unspec.	Kistner		CHAL (1898)
1219	Breu, Simon	1858-1933	Wenn sich zwei Herzen scheiden's Kind mit der Puppe tantz "Eile mein Püppchen"	Op. 19 No. 6	Unspec.	Kistner		CHAL (1898)

REC	COMP	DTS	TITLE	OP #	VCG	PUB	COMMENTS	SRC
1220	Breu, Simon	1858-1933	Wenn's Püppchen darf spazieren gehn "Himmel ist heiter"	Op. 19 No. 8	Unspec.	Kistner		CHAL (1898)
1221	Breu, Simon	1858-1933	Wenn's Püppchen gewaschen wird "Ei was will das"	Op. 19 No. 3	Unspec.	Kistner		CHAL (1898)
1222	Breu, Simon	1858-1933	Wie das Kind die Puppe weckt "Wach auf du herzig Püppchen"	Op. 19 No. 2	Unspec.	Kistner		CHAL (1898)
1223	Breu, Simon	1858-1933	Wie das Kind seine Puppe in Schlaf singt "Eia popeia thu's Aeuglein zu"	Op. 19 No. 1	Unspec.	Kistner		CHAL (1898)
1224	Briem, W.		Abendglocken Klangen	No. 8	S/A	Coppenrath		CHAL (1911)
1225	Briem, W.		Am Arlberg liegt mein Heimatland	No. 9	S/A	Coppenrath		CHAL (1911)
1226	Briem, W.		Grüss Gott, du lieber Frühlingswind	No. 7	S/A	Coppenrath		CHAL (1911)
1227	Briem, W.		Horch, die Trompeten blasen	No. 3	S/A	Coppenrath		CHAL (1911)
1228	Briem, W.		In die Ferne geht mein Sehnen	No. 4	S/A	Coppenrath		CHAL (1911)
1229	Briem, W.		Mir ist so selig um's Gemüt	No. 1	S/A	Coppenrath		CHAL (1911)
1230	Briem, W.		Müde bin ich, geh' zur Ruh'	No. 12	S/A	Coppenrath		CHAL (1911)
1231	Briem, W.		O Arlbergland, am schönen Rhein	No. 10	S/A	Coppenrath		CHAL (1911)
1232	Briem, W.		O Arlbergland, mein Vaterland	No. 11	S/A	Coppenrath		CHAL (1911)
1233	Briem, W.		Vöglein im grünen Wald	No. 2	S/A	Coppenrath		CHAL (1911)
1234	Briem, W.		Wenn ich ein Vöglein wär'	No. 6	S/A	Coppenrath		CHAL (1911)
1235	Briem, W.		Wir sassen im Schatten von Bäumen	No. 5	S/A	Coppenrath		CHAL (1911)
1236	Briggs		Hold Thou my Hand		S/A or S/T	Belwin	Also solo	CVMP (1976)
1237	Briggs, C. S.		Es naht die Nacht		MS/Br, S/T or S/T	Wood		CHAL (1911)
1238	Britten, Benjamin	1913-1976	A Cradle Song: Sleep, Beauty Bright		S/A	Faber		MSN
1239	Britten, Benjamin	1913-1976	Mother Comfort		Unspec.	Boosey		CVMP (1976)
1240	Britten, Benjamin	1913-1976	Mother Comfort		S/MS or S/S	Boosey	Pub. 1937	NATS-VCD
1241	Britten, Benjamin	1913-1976	Mother Comfort	No. 1	Unspec.	Boosey	In "Two Ballads for Two Voices and Pianoforte"	MSN
1242	Britten, Benjamin	1913-1976	Oxen, The		S/A	Baren		ASR
1243	Britten, Benjamin	1913-1976	Two Ballads for Two Sopranos		S/S	Boosey		ASR
1244	Britten, Benjamin	1913-1976	Underneath the Abject Willow		Unspec.	Boosey		CVMP (1976)
1245	Britten, Benjamin	1913-1976	Underneath the Abject Willow		S/MS or S/S	Boosey	Pub. 1937	NATS-VCD
1246	Britten, Benjamin	1913-1976	Underneath the Abject Willow	No. 2	Unspec.	Boosey	In "Two Ballads for Two Voices and Pianoforte"	MSN
1247	Brixner, J.		Trost in Thränen "Wie kommts, dass du so traurig bist"	Op. 22	Unspec.	Brixner i. W.		CHAL (1898)

REC	COMP	DTS	TITLE	OP #	VCG	PUB	COMMENTS	SRC
1248	Brizzi, S.		Arno "In val d'Arno all' ora"		Unspec.	Kistner		CHAL (1898)
1249	Broadwood, Lucy E.	1858-1929	Keys of Heaven		Unspec.	Cramer	Also solo	CVMP (1976)
1250	Broadwood, Lucy E. & J. A. Fuller Maitland	1858-1929, 1856-1936	keys of heaven, The		Unspec.	Cramer	Arr. Newton. Eng. women comp.	BBC (1975)
1251	Brocksch, R.		Hier und dort "O Seele, du verlangst"	Op. 25	Unspec.	Heinr.		CHAL (1898)
1252	Browne		O Daffodils		Unspec.	Allans	For 1-2 v.	CVMP (1976)
1253	Bruch, Max	1838-1920	Altdeutsches Minnedlied "Mir ist leide, dass der Winter"	Op. 4 No. 2	S/A	B. & H.		CHAL (1898)
1254	Bruch, Max	1838-1920	Beim Pfingstreigen "Pfingsten ist kommen"	Op. 6 II No. 3	2 female v.	Siegel		CHAL (1898)
1255	Bruch, Max	1838-1920	Ihr leben Lerchen guten Tag	Op. 4 No. 1	S/A	B. & H.		CHAL (1901)
1256	Bruch, Max	1838-1920	Im Frühling "Blümlein seid gegrüsset"	Op. 6 II No. 1	2 female v.	Siegel		CHAL (1898)
1257	Bruch, Max	1838-1920	Jesus der Morgenstern "Morgenstern der finsteren Nacht"	Op. 6 II No. 2	2 female v.	Siegel		CHAL (1898)
1258	Bruch, Max	1838-1920	Mir ist leide	Op. 4 No. 2	S/A	B. & H.		CHAL (1901)
1259	Bruch, Max	1838-1920	Wald "Zum Wald steht nur mein Sinn"	Op. 4 No. 3	S/A	B. & H.		CHAL (1898)
1260	Bruch, Max	1838-1920	Wanderlied "Ihr lieben Lerchen guten Tag"	Op. 189 No. 9	S/A	B. & H.		CHAL (1898)
1261	Bruch, Max	1838-1920	Zum Wald, zum Wald steht nur mein Sinn	Op. 4 No. 3	S/A	B. & H.		CHAL (1901)
1262	Brüll, J. [Ignaz]	1846-1907	Auf einsamen Wegen	Op. 75 No. 3	S/A	M. Brockhaus		CHAL (1898)
1263	Brüll, J. [Ignaz]	1846-1907	Durch das abendliche Dunkel	Op. 75 No. 1	S/A	M. Brockhaus		CHAL (1898)
1264	Brüll, J. [Ignaz]	1846-1907	In dunkler Nacht da schleichen sacht	Op. 74 No. 2	S/A or S/B	M. Brockhaus		CHAL (1898)
1265	Brüll, J. [Ignaz]	1846-1907	Kleine Welt "Im heimlichen Versteckt"	Op. 75 No. 2	S/A	M. Brockhaus		CHAL (1898)
1266	Brüll, J. [Ignaz]	1846-1907	Täglich wenn der Abend naht	Op. 74 No. 3	S/A or S/B	M. Brockhaus-		CHAL (1898)
1267	Brüll, J. [Ignaz]	1846-1907	Weisst du noch "Jener erst Kuss, weisst du noch"	Op. 74 No. 1	S/A or S/B	M. Brockhaus		CHAL (1898)
1268	Brunner, Christian Traugott	1792-1874	An den Bach "Immer fliesse sanft"	Op. 16 No. 2	S/S or T/T	Klemm		CHAL (1898)
1269	Brunner, Christian Traugott	1792-1874	Geburtstagstagslied "Nimm unsre kleinen Gaben"	Op. 16 No. 3	S/S or T/T	Klemm		CHAL (1898)
1270	Brunner, Christian Traugott	1792-1874	Leichter Sinn "Über Gebirg und Thal"	Op. 16 No. 6	S/S or T/T	Klemm		CHAL (1898)
1271	Brunner, Christian Traugott	1792-1874	Nachtigall "O könnt' ich doch die Nachtigall"	Op. 16 No. 1	S/S or T/T	Klemm		CHAL (1898)
1272	Brunner, Christian Traugott	1792-1874	Sehnsucht "Ich möchte ach so gerne"	Op. 16 No. 4	S/S or T/T	Klemm		CHAL (1898)
1273	Brunner, Christian Traugott	1792-1874	Waldeslust "Lass mich ganz in dich versinken"	Op. 16 No. 5	S/S or T/T	Klemm		CHAL (1898)
1274	Brunner, Ed.		Ach grau ist alle Theorie	Op. 175	2 female v.	Coppenrath		CHAL (1906)

REC	COMP	DTS	TITLE	OP #	VCG	PUB	COMMENTS	SRC
1275	Brunner, Ed.		Aufsitzer "Du Sepperl sag'"	Op. 105	Unspec.	Coppen-rath		CHAL (1898)
1276	Brunner, Ed.		Blüamli, blamli, alls is der-log'n "Ka Mensch kann's glaub'n"	Op. 80	S/A	Coppen-rath		CHAL (1898)
1277	Brunner, Ed.		Erstemal z' Wien "Schön is ja wohl die Weanastadt"	Op. 107	S/A	Coppen-rath		CHAL (1898)
1278	Brunner, Ed.		Holder Frühling ist's	Op. 174	2 female v.	Coppen-rath		CHAL (1906)
1279	Brunner, Ed.		Horch, was hallet so düster	Op. 164	2 female v.	Coppen-rath		CHAL (1901)
1280	Brunner, Ed.		O Vaterland mein schönster Stern	Op. 87	S/A	Coppen-rath		CHAL (1898)
1281	Brunner, Ed.		Requiem m. Libera	Op. 30	S/A	Coppen-rath	org accomp.	CHAL (1898)
1282	Brunner, Ed.		Wanderlust "Nun blüh'n die Rosen im Thal"	Op. 88	S/A	Coppen-rath		CHAL (1898)
1283	Brunner, Ed.		Wieviel Köpfe hat wohl eine Katze	Op. 166	S/A	Coppen-rath		CHAL (1901)
1284	Buchholz, Karl August	19th C.	Nun ist der Tag gescheiden	Op. 7 No. 1	Unspec.	Bahn		CHAL (1898)
1285	Buchholz, Karl August	19th C.	Schneeglöcken "Lenz will kommen, der Winter ist aus"	Op. 7 No. 3	Unspec.	Bahn		CHAL (1898)
1286	Buchholz, Karl August	19th C.	Ständchen "In dem Himmel ruht die Erde"	Op. 7 No. 4	Unspec.	Bahn		CHAL (1898)
1287	Buchholz, Karl August	19th C.	Wie ist doch die Erde so schön	Op. 7 No. 2	Unspec.	Bahn		CHAL (1898)
1288	Bülow, Charlotte von	19th C.	Nenuphar, die weisse Blume "Mondbeglänzt im stillen Walde"	Op. 11	Unspec.	B. & B.	Grmn. woman comp.	CHAL (1898)
1289	Bunakoff, N.		Vergiss sie nicht		Unspec.	F. Schell-enb.	Arr. Bruno	BBC (1975)
1290	Bünte, August	1836-1920	Neig' schöne Knospe dich zu mir		Unspec.	Nagel		CHAL (1898)
1291	Bünte, Wilhelm	1828-1923	Roth Röselein auf brauner Haid	No. 7	S/A	Oertel		CHAL (1901)
1292	Bünte, Wilhelm	1828-1923	Thut auch das bange Herz dir weh	Op. 26 No. 11	S/A	Oertel		CHAL (1901)
1293	Bünte, Wilhelm	1828-1923	Wenn du ein Herz gefunden, das treu	No. 8	S/A	Oertel		CHAL (1901)
1294	Buri, E. v.		Vöglein wohin so schnell		2 med. v.	Schott		CHAL (1906)
1295	Burwig, G.		Froher Sang für Polterabend und Hochzeit "Schmückt das Haus mit frischem Grün"		Unspec.	Junne		CHAL (1898)
1296	Busch, Carl	1862-1943	Wenn hier jetzt, statt wir, der Ochs säng	Op. 31	Unspec.	Jäckel i. Leipzig		CHAL (1901)
1297	Busche, W.		Wir sind zwei nette Männer		Unspec.	Gleissen-berg		CHAL (1906)
1298	Busoni, Ferrucio Benvenuto	1866-1924	Sogno "Ciel si fa sereeno"	Op. 3	S/A	Schmidt i. Wien		CHAL (1898)
1299	Busser, Henri-Paul	1872-1973	Melodies & Duos		Unspec.	Lemoine		CHAL (1898)
1300	Busser, Henri-Paul	1872-1973	Trois Rondes et Chansons		S/MS	Recital	acap? accomp. unspec.	CVMP (1995)

REC	COMP	DTS	TITLE	OP #	VCG	PUB	COMMENTS	SRC
1301	Butté, E. M.		Babí léto	Op. 10 No. 1	2 female v.	Urbánek		CHAL (1898)
1302	Butté, E. M.		Jarní dést	Op. 10 No. 2	2 female v.	Urbánek		CHAL (1898)
1303	Butté, E. M.		Vojáci	Op. 10 No. 3	2 female v.	Urbánek		CHAL (1898)
1304	Buydens-Lemoine		Fête au pensionat		Unspec.	Cranz		CHAL (1898)
1305	Caballero, Manuel Fernandez	1835-1906	Nena Mia "Baila preciosa nina"		Unspec.	Luckhardt	Span. comp. of Zarzuelas	CHAL (1898)
1306	Cage, John	1912-1993	Litany for the Whale		Unspec.	Peters	acap. Vocalise	CVMP (1985)
1307	Cage, John	1912-1993	Sonata for Two Voices		Unspec.	Peters	acap.	CVMP (1985)
1308	Califano, A.		Pfeiferlied "Ich bin bekannt als Jean Filou"		Unspec.	Maass i. W.		CHAL (1898)
1309	Campana, Fabio	1819-1882	Addio		Unspec.	Cranz		CHAL (1898)
1310	Campana, Fabio	1819-1882	Ah, vienni meco		Unspec.	Lucca		CHAL (1898)
1311	Campana, Fabio	1819-1882	Alla capanna andiamo		S/A	Ricordi		CHAL (1898)
1312	Campana, Fabio	1819-1882	Alla capanna andiamo		S/A	G. Schirm.	In catalogue page "Favorite French and Italian Vocal Duets" of G. Schirmer, Inc. NY (no date)	MSN
1313	Campana, Fabio	1819-1882	Caro dal labbro tuo		S/B or S/A	Ricordi		CHAL (1898)
1314	Campana, Fabio	1819-1882	Danza		S/S	Lucca		CHAL (1898)
1315	Campana, Fabio	1819-1882	Dearest, the Moon Before Us		Unspec.	Brainard's Sons	Eng. Trans. In anthology "Brainard's Collection of Vocal Duets from Popular Modern and Standard Composers" Pub. 1903.	MSN
1316	Campana, Fabio	1819-1882	Forest Shadows		S/A	White-Smith	In catalogue page "Vocal Duetts" of White-Smith Music Pub. Co. (no date)	MSN
1317	Campana, Fabio	1819-1882	Giura amor mio		S/S	Schlesinger		CHAL (1898)
1318	Campana, Fabio	1819-1882	Godiamo	No. 5	Unspec.	Lucca		CHAL (1898)
1319	Campana, Fabio	1819-1882	Guarda che bianca luna		S/A	Schlesinger		CHAL (1898)
1320	Campana, Fabio	1819-1882	Guarda che bianca luna		S/A or T/Br	G. Schirm.	In catalogue page "Favorite French and Italian Vocal Duets" of G. Schirmer, Inc. NY (no date)	MSN
1321	Campana, Fabio	1819-1882	I Live and Love Thee		high & low v.	Hinds, Hayden & Eldredge	In anthology "The Most Popular Vocal Duets" Ed. Dr. E. J. Biedermann. Pub. 1914.	MSN
1322	Campana, Fabio	1819-1882	I live and love thee		S/A	White-Smith	In catalogue page "Vocal Duetts" of White-Smith Music Pub. Co. (no date)	MSN
1323	Campana, Fabio	1819-1882	Io vivi e t'amo		S/A or S/B	G. Schirm.		MSN
1324	Campana, Fabio	1819-1882	Maira Och Rizzio		Unspec.	Lundq.	Swed. trans. It.	CVMP (1976)

REC	COMP	DTS	TITLE	OP #	VCG	PUB	COMMENTS	SRC
1325	Campana, Fabio	1819-1882	Quante volte io ti cercal		S/A	Ricordi		CHAL (1898)
1326	Campana, Fabio	1819-1882	Sag' mir, dass du mich liebst		S/S	Schlesinger		CHAL (1898)
1327	Campana, Fabio	1819-1882	See the pale moon		Unspec.	Banes		BBC (1975)
1328	Campana, Fabio	1819-1882	See the Pale Moon		high & low v.	Hinds, Hayden & Eldredge	In anthology "The Most Popular Vocal Duets" Ed. Dr. E. J. Biedermann. Pub. 1914.	MSN
1329	Campana, Fabio	1819-1882	See the pale moon		S/A or T/Br	White-Smith	In catalogue page "Vocal Duetts" of White-Smith Music Pub. Co. (no date)	MSN
1330	Campana, Fabio	1819-1882	Sempre insieme		S/B or S/A	G. Schirm.	In catalogue page "Favorite French and Italian Vocal Duets" of G. Schirmer, Inc. NY (no date)	MSN
1331	Campana, Fabio	1819-1882	Serenata		S/A or S/B	Ricordi		CHAL (1898)
1332	Campana, Fabio	1819-1882	Sweet is the dream		S/A	Boosey	Ed. Randegger	BBC (1975)
1333	Campana, Fabio	1819-1882	Te 'l rammenti	No. 3	Unspec.	Ricordi		CHAL (1898)
1334	Campana, Fabio	1819-1882	Te'l rammenti?		S/T or S/S	G. Schirm.	In catalogue page "Favorite French and Italian Vocal Duets" of G. Schirmer, Inc. NY (no date)	MSN
1335	Campana, Fabio	1819-1882	Ti ricordi		S/MS or T/MS	Ricordi		CHAL (1898)
1336	Campana, Fabio	1819-1882	Tutto passa		S/A or S/B	Ricordi		CHAL (1898)
1337	Campana, Fabio	1819-1882	Vieni a giurarlo all'ara		S/A or S/B	Ricordi		CHAL (1898)
1338	Campana, Fabio	1819-1882	Vieni Meco [Come with me]		S/A or S/B	White-Smith	In catalogue page "Vocal Duetts" of White-Smith Music Pub. Co. (no date)	MSN
1339	Caracciolo, Luigi		Nearest and Dearest		high & low v.	Hinds, Hayden & Eldredge	In anthology "The Most Popular Vocal Duets" Ed. Dr. E. J. Biedermann. Pub. 1914.	MSN
1340	Caracciolo, Luigi		Nearest and Dearest		S/A	Ditson	Tuscan folk song. Eng. trans. It. In anthology "Soprano and Alto Duets" Ed. Heinrich Kiehl. Pub. 1901.	MSN
1341	Caracciolo, Luigi		Nearest and Dearest		S/A	Ditson	Tuscan folk song. Eng. trans. It. In anthology "The Ditson Collection of Soprano and Alto Duets" Pub. 1934.	MSN
1342	Caracciolo, Luigi		Nearest and Dearest, Tuscan folk-song		S/MS	G. Schirm.	In catalogue page "Selected Vocal Duets" of G. Schirmer, Inc. NY (no date)	MSN
1343	Caracciolo, Luigi		Six Tuscan Folk Songs		Unspec.	Ricordi	Collection	BBC (1975)
1344	Carafa, Michel Enrico	1787-1872	Ai nostri gemiti scioglia		S/S	B. & B.		CHAL (1898)
1345	Carafa, Michel Enrico	1787-1872	Immer neu fühl ich dies süsse Regen		Unspec.	Junne		CHAL (1898)

REC	COMP	DTS	TITLE	OP #	VCG	PUB	COMMENTS	SRC
1346	Carafa, Michel Enrico	1787-1872	Sempre più t'amo		S/S	B. & H., Simrock, et al.	Other pub. inc. Cramer, Schirmer, et al.	CHAL (1898)
1347	Carelli, Benjamino A.	1833-1921	Mein Herz ich will dich fragen		S/A	Schmidt		CHAL (1901)
1348	Carelli, Benjamino A.	1833-1921	Ti voglio domander		S/A	(Leede)		CHAL (1898)
1349	Carey, Harry		A reveille		Unspec.	H. Carey		BBC (1975)
1350	Carey, Harry		This is the day		Unspec.	H. Carey		BBC (1975)
1351	Carnicer, Ramon	1789-1855	El Musico y el Poeta		Unspec.	UME	Ed. Subira	CVMP (1976)
1352	Carse, Roland		There's no one in the world like you		Unspec.	F. D. & H.		BBC (1975)
1353	Carter, John		Three Canzonets on Love		S/A	Frank	Also perf. chorally	ASR
1354	Carulli, Gustav	1797-1877	Schlaf wohl		Unspec.	Schott		CHAL (1898)
1355	Caryll, Ivan	1861-1921	Duo des Bonnes Intentions		Unspec.	Enoch	From "Son Altesse Royale" light comedy	CVMP (1976)
1356	Caryll, Ivan	1861-1921	Ping-pong		Unspec.	F. D. & H.		BBC (1975)
1357	Cassler, G. Winston	1906-	Come Holy Ghost, Creator Blest		S/S or T/T	Ausburg	In collection "Sacred Duets for Equal Voices" music of G. W. Cassler. Pub. 1968.	NATS-SVD
1358	Cassler, G. Winston	1906-	Let the Whole Creation Cry		S/S or T/T	Ausburg	In collection "Sacred Duets for Equal Voices" music of G. W. Cassler. Pub. 1968.	NATS-SVD
1359	Cassler, G. Winston	1906-	My Heart is Longing to Praise My Savior		S/S or T/T	Ausburg	In collection "Sacred Duets for Equal Voices" music of G. W. Cassler. Pub. 1968.	NATS-SVD
1360	Cassler, G. Winston	1906-	Praise, My Soul, the King of Heaven		S/S or T/T	Ausburg	In collection "Sacred Duets for Equal Voices" music of G. W. Cassler. Pub. 1968.	NATS-SVD
1361	Cassler, G. Winston	1906-	Praise the Savior		S/S or T/T	Ausburg	In collection "Sacred Duets for Equal Voices" music of G. W. Cassler. Pub. 1968.	NATS-SVD
1362	Cassler, G. Winston	1906-	Sacred Duets for Equal Voices		2 equal v.	Ausburg	Collection of works by G. W. Cassler. Pub. 1968.	NATS-SVD
1363	Catenhusen, Ernst	1833-1918	Johny, mein Johny	Op. 4 No. 2	S/A	Schweers & H.		CHAL (1898)
1364	Catenhusen, Ernst	1833-1918	Und due Sonne schein so warm	Op. 4 No. 1	S/A	Schweers & H.		CHAL (1898)
1365	Catenhusen, Ernst	1833-1918	Woge rauscht so voll und grün	Op. 4 No. 3	S/A	Schweers & H.		CHAL (1898)
1366	Cattaneo, V.		Inno di Elis		Unspec.	Ricordi		CHAL (1898)
1367	Cavallini, Ernesto	1807-1874	Feuille		Unspec.	Ricordi		CHAL (1898)
1368	Cavallini, Ernesto	1807-1874	Rosa "Garzon, non più"		Unspec.	Ricordi		CHAL (1898)
1369	Cavallini, Ernesto	1807-1874	Veux-tu, mon coeur		Unspec.	Ricordi		CHAL (1898)
1370	Chabeaux, P.		Souvenirs "Te souvient-il des jours heureux"		Unspec.	Mackar i. Paris		CHAL (1898)

REC	COMP	DTS	TITLE	OP #	VCG	PUB	COMMENTS	SRC
1371	Chabrier, Emmanuel	1841-1894	Espana		Unspec.	Enoch	Also solo	CVMP (1976)
1372	Chaminade, Cecile	1857-1944	Angelus, The		high & low v.	Hinds, Hayden & Eldredge	Eng. trans. Fr. Fr. woman comp . In anthology "The Most Popular Vocal Duets" Ed. Dr. E. J. Biedermann. Pub. 1914.	MSN
1373	Chaminade, Cecile	1857-1944	Duo d'Etoiles		S/MS	Enoch	Fr. woman comp.	CVMP (1976)
1374	Chaminade, Cecile	1857-1944	Duo d'Etoiles		S/MS	Enoch	Fr. woman comp.	ASR
1375	Chaminade, Cecile	1857-1944	L'Angelus	Op. 69	S/A or MS/A or MS/Br	Ditson	Fr. woman comp . In anthology "Soprano and Alto Duets" Ed. H. Kiehl. Pub. 1901.	MSN
1376	Chaminade, Cecile	1857-1944	L'Angelus	Op. 69	S/A	Ditson	Fr. woman comp. In anthology "The Ditson Collection of Soprano and Alto Duets" Pub. 1934.	MSN
1377	Chaminade, Cecile	1857-1944	Marthe et Marie		S/MS or S/A	Enoch	Fr. woman comp.	CVMP (1976)
1378	Chaminade, Cecile	1857-1944	Marthe et Marie		S/MS or S/A	Enoch	Fr. woman comp.	ASR
1379	Charisius, M.		Weihnachtslied "Du lieber, grüner Tannenbaum"		Unspec.	Bon i. Königsb.		CHAL (1898)
1380	Charles, Ernest	1895-	Let My Song Fill Your Heart		S/A or S/T	G. Schirm.	Also solo	CVMP (1976)
1381	Chausson, Ernest	1855-1899	La Nuit	Op. 11 No. 1	S/MS	Leduc		CVMP (1985)
1382	Chausson, Ernest	1855-1899	La Nuit	Op. 11 No. 1	high & med. v.	CVR		MSN
1383	Chausson, Ernest	1855-1899	La Nuit	Op. 11 No. 1	Unspec.	Hamelle		MSN
1384	Chausson, Ernest	1855-1899	La Nuit	Op. 11 No. 1	S/T or S/MS	Hamelle		NATS-VCD
1385	Chausson, Ernest	1855-1899	Réveil	Op. 11 No. 2	Unspec.	Leduc	Also solo	CVMP (1985)
1386	Chausson, Ernest	1855-1899	Réveil	Op. 11 No. 2	Unspec.	Hamelle		MSN
1387	Chausson, Ernest	1855-1899	Réveil	Op. 11 No. 2	S/MS or S/T	Hamelle		NATS-VCD
1388	Chelard, Hippolyte André	1789-1861	Nocturne "Ein blosses Lächeln"		Unspec.	Schlesinger		CHAL (1898)
1389	Chelard, Hippolyte André	1789-1861	Nocturne "Un seul sourire"		Unspec.	Schlesinger		CHAL (1898)
1390	Chelard, Hippolyte André	1789-1861	Sourire "Un seul sourire"		S/S	Sulzer		CHAL (1898)
1391	Cherubini, Luigi	1760-1842	Ahi, ch'è il suon del rio		S/S or S/MS	Peters	In "Duette für 2 Soprane"	NATS-VCD
1392	Cherubini, Luigi	1760-1842	Ahi, ch'è il suon del rio che frange		S/S	Peters		BBC (1975)
1393	Cherubini, Luigi	1760-1842	Di tua beltà ragio no ne intenerir	No. 4	S/MS or Unspec.	CVR	pf or harp accomp.	MSN
1394	Cherubini, Luigi	1760-1842	Dite Almeno, amiche fronde		S/S or S/MS	Peters	In "Duette für 2 Soprane"	NATS-VCD
1395	Cherubini, Luigi	1760-1842	Dite almeno, amiche fronde	No. 3	Unspec.	Peters		CHAL (1898)

REC	COMP	DTS	TITLE	OP #	VCG	PUB	COMMENTS	SRC
1396	Cherubini, Luigi	1760-1842	Duette		S/S	Peters	Collection, no specific works mentioned	CVMP (1985)
1397	Cherubini, Luigi	1760-1842	Four Duets		S/S	Peters	pf or harp accomp. Unspec. pieces.	CVMP (1976)
1398	Cherubini, Luigi	1760-1842	Four Duets for Two Sopranos		S/S	Peters	pf or harp accomp.	ASR
1399	Cherubini, Luigi	1760-1842	Grazie a gl'inganni tuo	No. 1	S/MS or Unspec.	CVR	pf or harp accomp.	MSN
1400	Cherubini, Luigi	1760-1842	La libertà à Nice		S/A	R. Birchall		BBC (1975)
1401	Cherubini, Luigi	1760-1842	La mia fille		S/S or S/MS	Peters	In "Duette für 2 Soprane"	NATS-VCD
1402	Cherubini, Luigi	1760-1842	Mancò l'antico ardore e fon tranquillo arfegno	No. 2	S/MS or Unspec.	CVR	pf or harp accomp.	MSN
1403	Cherubini, Luigi	1760-1842	Mia fille, il mio bel foco	No. 2	Unspec.	Peters		CHAL (1898)
1404	Cherubini, Luigi	1760-1842	Quel ch'or m'alletta o spiace se lieto o mesto o fono	No. 6	S/MS or Unspec.	CVR	pf or harp accomp.	MSN
1405	Cherubini, Luigi	1760-1842	Six Italian Duets		S/S or S/MS	CVR	pf or harp accomp. Collection of 6 duets. In catalogue "Classical Vocal Reprints Complete Catalog" Pub. 1997.	MSN
1406	Cherubini, Luigi	1760-1842	Sogno, sogno ma te non miro	No. 3	S/MS or Unspec.	CVR	pf or harp accomp.	MSN
1407	Cherubini, Luigi	1760-1842	Solitario bosco ombroso		S/S or S/MS	Peters	In "Duette für 2 Soprane"	NATS-VCD
1408	Cherubini, Luigi	1760-1842	Solitario bosco ombroso	No. 1	Unspec.	Peters		CHAL (1898)
1409	Cherubini, Luigi	1760-1842	Two- and Three-Voice Canons, 24, Vol. 1	Canons I-XII	Unspec.	Recital	acap. For 2-3 v.	CVMP (1985)
1410	Cherubini, Luigi	1760-1842	Two- and Three-Voice Canons, 24, Vol. 2	Canons XIII-XXIV	Unspec.	Recital	acap. For 2-3 v.	CVMP (1985)
1411	Cherubini, Luigi	1760-1842	Volgimi il guardo altero volgimi	No. 5	S/MS or Unspec.	CVR	pf or harp accomp.	MSN
1412	Chevallerie, Ernst A. H.	1848-1908	Da draussen auf der Haide	Op. 5	Unspec.	Chal.		CHAL (1898)
1413	Chisholm, M. A.		Slumber Sea		Unspec.	Brainard's Sons	Arr. D. J. Muir. In anthology "Brainard's Collection of Vocal Duets from Popular Modern and Standard Composers" Pub. 1903.	MSN
1414	Chopin, Frédéric	1810-1849	Roses of Ispahan		Unspec.	Boosey	Arr. Besly	BBC (1975)
1415	Chopin, Frederic	1810-1849	Tristesse		Unspec.	Allans	Eng. words added to melody. In anthology "Vocal Duets Collection" Vol. 2. Pub. 1992.	MSN
1416	Christian-Jollet		Chez Nous		Unspec.	Ouvrieres		CVMP (1976)
1417	Christiani, E.		Gretelein "Sag' an du liebes Gretchen"		2 female v.	Meissner		CHAL (1898)
1418	Christiani, E.		Schnell, es gilt der Liebe		Unspec.	Benjamin		CHAL (1898)
1419	Christiani, E.		Spanisch "Im Lande der Kastanien"		2 female v.	Meissner		CHAL (1898)

REC	COMP	DTS	TITLE	OP #	VCG	PUB	COMMENTS	SRC
1420	Christiani, E.		Stille Liebe "Rose sage, warum blühest du"		2 female v.	Meissner		CHAL (1898)
1421	Christiani, E.		Wein und die Liebe "Wenn alle maine Sinne" [meine?]	Op. 64	Unspec.	Meissner		CHAL (1898)
1422	Chwatal, Franz Xaver	1808-1879	Lang, lang ist's her "Sag mir's Wort"		Unspec.	Heinr.		CHAL (1898)
1423	Chwatal, Franz Xaver	1808-1879	So Herz an Herz "Es ist fürwahr ein hohes Glück"	Op. 241 No. 1	S/A or T/B	Heinr.		CHAL (1898)
1424	Chwatal, Franz Xaver	1808-1879	Zum Geburtstage des Vaters "Was könnten wir dem Feste bringen"	Op. 210	Unspec.	Heinr.		CHAL (1898)
1425	Ciccarelli, Angelo	1806-	Chi vuol l'immagine		Unspec.	Fürstner		CHAL (1898)
1426	Ciccarelli, Angelo	1806-	Messagiero "Perchè mai"		MS/A	Fürstner		CHAL (1898)
1427	Ciccarelli, Angelo	1806-	Notturno "Ah voi dite"		Unspec.	Fürstner		CHAL (1898)
1428	Ciccarelli, Angelo	1806-	Per le selve		Unspec.	Fürstner		CHAL (1898)
1429	Ciccarelli, Angelo	1806-	Selva romita		Unspec.	Fürstner		CHAL (1898)
1430	Clapisson, Antoine Louis	1808-1866	Ballançons-nous		Unspec.	Schott		CHAL (1898)
1431	Clapisson, Antoine Louis	1808-1866	Ménages chinois		Unspec.	Schott		CHAL (1898)
1432	Clapisson, Antoine Louis	1808-1866	Vorposten "Waffenklänge, Lärm, Gedränge"		Unspec.	Schott		CHAL (1898)
1433	Clarke, Emile		Sincerity		Unspec.	Cramer	Also solo	CVMP (1976)
1434	Claudius, A.		O wär' mein Lieb' jen' Röslein roth	Op. 29 No. 1	S/S	Peters		CHAL (1898)
1435	Claudius, A.		Sie weiss es nicht	Op. 29 No. 3	S/S	Peters		CHAL (1898)
1436	Claudius, A.		Was singen und sagen die Lerche	Op. 29 No. 2	S/S	Peters		CHAL (1898)
1437	Claudius, Otto Karl	1795-1877	Ich flüstre deinen Namen	Op. 23 No. 1	S/S	Peters		CHAL (1898)
1438	Claudius, Otto Karl	1795-1877	Klinget Maienglöckchen	Op. 23 No. 2	S/S	Peters		CHAL (1898)
1439	Claudius, Otto Karl	1795-1877	Vergissmeinnicht "Es blüht ein schönes Blümchen"	Op. 23	S/S	Peters		CHAL (1898)
1440	Clement, M.		Ein Bruder und eine Schwester	Op. 16 No. 1	S/A	B. & B.		CHAL (1906)
1441	Clement, M.		Nacht ist's, die Erde träumet	Op. 16 No. 2	S/A	B. & B.		CHAL (1906)
1442	Clement, M.		Unter der Lindem an der Haiden	Op. 16 No. 3	S/A	B. & B.		CHAL (1906)
1443	Clifton, Harry		The happy policeman		Unspec.	Ashdown	Ed. Hobson	BBC (1975)
1444	Clifton, Harry		Very suspicious		Unspec.	Ashdown	Ed. Hobson	BBC (1975)
1445	Cloos, W.		Glockengeläute "An einem sinnigen Morgen"		Unspec.	B. & B.		CHAL (1898)
1446	Cloos, W.		Gruss in die Ferne "Wenn dich die Abendluft"		Unspec.	B. & B.		CHAL (1898)
1447	Coates, Eric	1886-1957	Bird songs at eventide		Unspec.	Chappell	Arr. Stickles	BBC (1975)
1448	Coccia, Carlo	1782-1873	Gemelli in petto		A/T or A/S	Bahn		CHAL (1898)
1449	Coccia, Carlo	1782-1873	Nigella e Fileno		A/T or A/S	Bahn		CHAL (1898)

REC	COMP	DTS	TITLE	OP #	VCG	PUB	COMMENTS	SRC
1450	Coerne, Louis Adolphe	1870-1920	Be thou faithful		S/A	G. Schirm.	pf or org accomp. In catalogue page "Sacred Vocal Duets" of G. Schirmer, Inc. NY (no date)	MSN
1451	Coëtlosquet, M. du		Getrübte Quelle "Eine Quelle silberhelle"		Unspec.	Hug		CHAL (1898)
1452	Colaco Osorio-Swaab, Reine	1889-	Twee Duetten Op Tekst Uit "Het Koningsgraf"		S/A	Donemus		CVMP (1976)
1453	Coleridge-Taylor, Samuel	1875-1912	Fall on me Like a Silent Dew		Unspec.	Roberton		CVMP (1976)
1454	Coleridge-Taylor, Samuel	1875-1912	Fall on Me like a Silent Dew		2 med. v.	Roberton		ASR
1455	Coleridge-Taylor, Samuel	1875-1912	Fall on me like silent dew		Unspec.	Curwen		BBC (1975)
1456	Coleridge-Taylor, Samuel	1875-1912	Oh, the Summer		Unspec.	Roberton		CVMP (1976)
1457	Coleridge-Taylor, Samuel	1875-1912	Oh, the Summer		2 med. v.	Roberton		ASR
1458	Comes		Merry, merry are we		Unspec.	White-Smith	In catalogue page "Vocal Duetts" of White-Smith Music Pub. Co. (no date)	MSN
1459	Concone, F.		Aprile "Al fin ritorna"		Unspec.	Cranz		CHAL (1898)
1460	Concone, Giuseppi	1801-1861	Adoptivmutter "Wohl schirmt uns Gott"		S/S	Schott		CHAL (1898)
1461	Concone, Giuseppi	1801-1861	Am Gestade des Meeres "Wie schön beim Abendschweigen"		S/S	Schott		CHAL (1898)
1462	Concone, Giuseppi	1801-1861	Blumenkampf "Wie ist so stolz"		S/S	Schott		CHAL (1898)
1463	Concone, Giuseppi	1801-1861	Ehrenfräulein "Mit ihr vereint in diesem Lande"		Unspec.	Schott		CHAL (1898)
1464	Concone, Giuseppi	1801-1861	Ein Concert im Freien "Hold strajlt die milde Sonne"		S/S	Schott		CHAL (1898)
1465	Concone, Giuseppi	1801-1861	Frühlingslüftchen "Muntre Lüftchen, dunkle Lieder"		S/S	Schott		CHAL (1898)
1466	Concone, Giuseppi	1801-1861	Geheimnisse des Glückes "Lebensglück, Blüthenzier, die so selten"		2 female v.	Schott		CHAL (1898)
1467	Concone, Giuseppi	1801-1861	Gräfin und das Mägdlein "Edle Gebieterin"		S/S	Schott		CHAL (1898)
1468	Concone, Giuseppi	1801-1861	Granadas Töchter "Granada geehrt vor allen"		Unspec.	Schott		CHAL (1898)
1469	Concone, Giuseppi	1801-1861	Hirtinnen "Schon sinkt der Abend sanft hernieder"		2 female v.	Schott		CHAL (1898)
1470	Concone, Giuseppi	1801-1861	Judin und Christin "Vor endlos langer Reise"		Unspec.	Schott		CHAL (1898)
1471	Concone, Giuseppi	1801-1861	Mädchen und der Page "Ferne von Sorgen"		S/S	Schott		CHAL (1898)
1472	Concone, Giuseppi	1801-1861	Milchschwestern "Ohne Scutz, ohne Brod"		S/S	Schott		CHAL (1898)
1473	Concone, Giuseppi	1801-1861	Müllerinnen "Wie schön Jeanette"		S/S	Schott		CHAL (1898)

REC	COMP	DTS	TITLE	OP #	VCG	PUB	COMMENTS	SRC
1474	Concone, Giuseppi	1801-1861	Nacht vor dem Gefübde "Morgen ist jener Tag"		S/S	Schott		CHAL (1898)
1475	Concone, Giuseppi	1801-1861	Neubekehrten "Heut'ge Tag er endiget"		MS/MS	Schott		CHAL (1898)
1476	Concone, Giuseppi	1801-1861	Pilgerinnen "Heil'ge Jungfrau Maria"		Unspec.	Schott		CHAL (1898)
1477	Concone, Giuseppi	1801-1861	Sanct Domingue en 1804		S/S	Schott		CHAL (1898)
1478	Concone, Giuseppi	1801-1861	Schaukel "Unter diesen Papplein"		2 female v.	Schott		CHAL (1898)
1479	Concone, Giuseppi	1801-1861	Schifferinnen "Sollst tragen du Nachen"		S/S	Schott		CHAL (1898)
1480	Concone, Giuseppi	1801-1861	Stimmen des Trostes "Ihr Alle, die ein hart Geschick"		Unspec.	Schott		CHAL (1898)
1481	Concone, Giuseppi	1801-1861	The spring returning		S/A	Bayley & Ferguson	Eng trans. Grmn. or It.	BBC (1975)
1482	Concone, Giuseppi	1801-1861	Töchter des Wildschützen "Dort hinter jenen Eichen"		Unspec.	Schott		CHAL (1898)
1483	Concone, Giuseppi	1801-1861	Unter den Palmenzweigen		S/S	Schott		CHAL (1898)
1484	Concone, Giuseppi	1801-1861	Wettkampf der Stimmen "Beim Feste diese Abends"		2 female v.	Schott		CHAL (1898)
1485	Coombs, C. Whitney	1859-	The Conquerer (Easter)		high & low v.	G. Schirm.	pf or org accomp. In catalogue page "Sacred Vocal Duets" of G. Schirmer, Inc. NY (no date)	MSN
1486	Coombs, C. Whitney	1859-	The Dawn of Hope (Christmas)		S/A	G. Schirm.	pf or org accomp. In catalogue page "Sacred Vocal Duets" of G. Schirmer, Inc. NY (no date)	MSN
1487	Coquard, Arthur	1846-1910	Four Duets, Op. 96		S/A	Durand	Unspec. pieces, but also avail. separately.	ASR
1488	Coquard, Arthur	1846-1910	L'Hirondelle	Op. 96 No. 2	S/A	Durand		CVMP (1976)
1489	Coquard, Arthur	1846-1910	Le Chanvre	Op. 96 No. 5	S/A	Durand		CVMP (1976)
1490	Coquard, Arthur	1846-1910	Le Renouveau	Op. 96 No. 4	S/A	Durand		CVMP (1976)
1491	Coquard, Arthur	1846-1910	Nocturne	Op. 96 No. 1	S/A	Durand		CVMP (1976)
1492	Coradini, R. & P.		Halloh, nun sind wir da		Unspec.	P. Fischer i. Berl.		CHAL (1901)
1493	Coradini, R. & P.		Reich zu sein ist keine Schande		Unspec.	P. Fischer i. Berl.		CHAL (1901)
1494	Coradini, R. & P.		Wir kenn'n ein hübsches Mädchen		Unspec.	P. Fischer i. Berl.		CHAL (1901)
1495	Corliss		Rose and a Lily, A		S/T or S/A	White-Smith	In catalogue page "Vocal Duetts" of White-Smith Music Pub. Co. (no date)	MSN
1496	Cornelius, Peter	1824-1874	Christ Child, The		2 high v.	R. D. Row	org or pf acc. In anth. "Sacred Duet Masterpieces…" Vol. 3. Compi. & ed. C. Fredrickson. Pub. 1961.	MSN
1497	Cornelius, Peter	1824-1874	Come away, death	Op. 16 No. 3	Unspec.	ECS	In anthology "48 Duets Seventeenth Through Nineteenth Centuries" Ed. V. Prahl. Pub. 1941, 1970.	MSN

REC	COMP	DTS	TITLE	OP #	VCG	PUB	COMMENTS	SRC
1498	Cornelius, Peter	1824-1874	Duet Volume		S/S	CVR	Collection, duet Nos. 8, 9 for 2 S. In catalogue "Classical Vocal Reprints Complete Catalog" Pub. 1997.	MSN
1499	Cornelius, Peter	1824-1874	Eleven Selected Duets		Var.	Peters	Unspec. pieces. Ed. Friedländer. 3 duets for 2 S.	ASR
1500	Cornelius, Peter	1824-1874	I will lift mine eyes		Unspec.	ECS	Eng. trans. Grmn. In anthology "48 Duets Seventeenth Through Nineteenth Centuries" Ed. V. Prahl. Pub. 1941, 1970.	MSN
1501	Cornelius, Peter	1824-1874	Ich muss nun einmal singen "Vöglein, Vöglein, was singest du"	No. 4	Unspec.	B. & H.		CHAL (1898)
1502	Cornelius, Peter	1824-1874	Ich und du		S/Br or S/MS	Peters, et al.	In collection "Duette" of P. Cornelius. Pub. 1952, et al.	NATS-VCD
1503	Cornelius, Peter	1824-1874	Ich und du "Wir träumten voneinander"		S/B or S/A	Peters	In collection "Duette für zwei Singstimmen mit Pianoforte-begleitung von Peter Cornelius" Ed. M. Friedländer.	MSN
1504	Cornelius, Peter	1824-1874	Ich und du "Wir träumten voneinander"	No. 15	S/B or S/A	B & H	In collection "Sämtliche Duette für Gesang mit und ohne Pianofortebegleitung von Peter Cornelius"	MSN
1505	Cornelius, Peter	1824-1874	In Sternennacht		S/S or S/T	Peters	In collection "Duette für zwei Singstimmen mit Pianoforte-begleitung von Peter Cornelius" Ed. M. Friedländer.	MSN
1506	Cornelius, Peter	1824-1874	In Sternennacht		S/S , S/MS or S/T or T/MS	Peters, et al.	In collection "Duette" of P. Cornelius. Pub. 1952, et al.	NATS-VCD
1507	Cornelius, Peter	1824-1874	In Sternennacht	No. 3	S/S or S/T	B & H	In collection "Sämtliche Duette für Gesang mit und ohne Pianofortebegleitung von Peter Cornelius"	MSN
1508	Cornelius, Peter	1824-1874	In Sternennacht, wenn's dämmert sacht	No. 1	Unspec.	B. & H.		CHAL (1898)
1509	Cornelius, Peter	1824-1874	Irisch "O, kennt ihr nicht Emmchen, die Kleine"	No. 8	S/A	B & H	acap. In collection "Sämtliche Duette für Gesang mit und ohne Pianofortebegleitung von Peter Cornelius"	MSN
1510	Cornelius, Peter	1824-1874	Irisch "Was trauern doch die Mägdelein?"	No. 7	S/A	B & H	acap. In collection "Sämtliche Duette für Gesang mit und ohne Pianofortebegleitung von Peter Cornelius"	MSN
1511	Cornelius, Peter	1824-1874	Komm herbei Tod		S/S or S/B or S/A	B. & H.		CHAL (1906)
1512	Cornelius, Peter	1824-1874	Komm herbei, Tod!	No. 4	S/S	B & H	In collection "Sämtliche Duette für Gesang mit und ohne Pianofortebegleitung von Peter Cornelius"	MSN
1513	Cornelius, Peter	1824-1874	Komm herbei, Tod!	No. 5	S/A	B & H	acap. In collection "Sämtliche Duette für Gesang mit und ohne Pianofortebegleitung von Peter Cornelius"	MSN
1514	Cornelius, Peter	1824-1874	Lied des Narren		S/S or S/MS or MS/MS	Peters, et al.	In collection "Duette" of P. Cornelius. Pub. 1952 et al.	NATS-VCD

REC	COMP	DTS	TITLE	OP #	VCG	PUB	COMMENTS	SRC
1515	Cornelius, Peter	1824-1874	Lied des Narren "Komm herbei, komm herbei, Tod!"		S/S	Peters	In collection "Duette für zwei Singstimmen mit Pianofortebe-gleitung von Peter Cornelius" Ed. M. Friedländer.	MSN
1516	Cornelius, Peter	1824-1874	Mainzer Mägdelied "Mei' Herzensallerliebster das is en Bettelmann"	No. 10	S/A	B & H	acap. In collection "Sämtliche Duette für Gesang mit und ohne Pianofortebegleitung von Peter Cornelius"	MSN
1517	Cornelius, Peter	1824-1874	Mei Herzallerliebster das is en Bettelmann		S/A	B. & H.	Ed. Hasse	CHAL (1906)
1518	Cornelius, Peter	1824-1874	Mein Liebchen ist nicht Heliotrop	No. 9	S/A	B & H	acap. In collection "Sämtliche Duette für Gesang mit und ohne Pianofortebegleitung von Peter Cornelius"	MSN
1519	Cornelius, Peter	1824-1874	Nachts wir uns küssten	No. 3	Unspec.	R. & H.		CHAL (1898)
1520	Cornelius, Peter	1824-1874	Peter Cornelius Musical Works		Unspec.	Uni v. Mus. Ed	pf et al. acc. Ed. Hasse & Bauss-ern. Coll. Wks for Var. of instr. & vocal comb. From micro-fiche. Repr. B. & H. eds. 5 vols.	CVMP (1976)
1521	Cornelius, Peter	1824-1874	Scheiden und Meiden "So soll ich dich meiden"	No. 1	S/S or S/T	B & H	In collection "Sämtliche Duette für Gesang mit und ohne Pianofortebegleitung von Peter Cornelius"	MSN
1522	Cornelius, Peter	1824-1874	Selected Duets		S/S, S/Bar, S/B	Peters	Ed. Friedlander	CVMP (1976)
1523	Cornelius, Peter	1824-1874	Shepherds, The		2 high v.	R. D. Row	org or pf acc. In anth. "Sacred Duet Masterpieces…" Vol. 3. Compi. & ed. C. Fredrickson. Pub. 1961.	MSN
1524	Cornelius, Peter	1824-1874	So soll ich dich nun meiden		S/S or S/T	B. & H.	Ed. Hasse	CHAL (1906)
1525	Cornelius, Peter	1824-1874	So weich und warm	No. 6	S/A	B & H	acap. In collection "Sämtliche Duette für Gesang mit und ohne Pianofortebegleitung von Peter Cornelius"	MSN
1526	Cornelius, Peter	1824-1874	So weich und warm hegt dich kein Arm		S/A	B. & H.	Ed. Hasse	CHAL (1906)
1527	Cornelius, Peter	1824-1874	Sweet flowers now are blooming	Op. 16 No. 2	Unspec.	ECS	Eng. trans. Grmn. In anthology "48 Duets Seventeenth Through Nineteenth Centuries" Ed. V. Prahl. Pub. 1941, 1970.	MSN
1528	Cornelius, Peter	1824-1874	Verratene Liebe		S/S , S/T or S/MS	Peters, et al.	In collection "Duette" of P. Cornelius. Pub. 1952, et al.	NATS-VCD
1529	Cornelius, Peter	1824-1874	Verratene Liebe "Da nachts wir uns küßten"		S/S or S/T	Peters	In collection "Duette für zwei Singstimmen mit Pianoforte-begleitung von Peter Cornel-ius" Ed. M. Friedländer.	MSN
1530	Cornelius, Peter	1824-1874	Verratene Liebe "Da nachts wir uns küßten"	No. 2	S/S or S/T	B & H	In collection "Sämtliche Duette für Gesang mit und ohne Pianofortebegleitung von Peter Cornelius"	MSN
1531	Cornelius, Peter	1824-1874	Verrathene Liebe "Da Nachts wir uns küssten"	No. 2	Unspec.	B. & H.		CHAL (1898)
1532	Cornelius, Peter	1824-1874	Zu dem Bergen hebet sich ein Augenpaar		S/A	B. & H.	Ed. Hasse	CHAL (1906)
1533	Coupé, H.		Mon noeu s'est accompli		Unspec.	Junne		CHAL (1898)

REC	COMP	DTS	TITLE	OP #	VCG	PUB	COMMENTS	SRC
1534	Courtney, Craig	20th C.	Be Thou My Vision		high & low v.	Becken-horst	Irish Folk Tune. Arr. C. Courtney. In anth. "Duets for the Master: Sacred Duets for High & Low Voice & Keyboard" Pub. 1989.	MSN
1535	Courtney, Craig	20th C.	Let Us Break Bread Together		high & low v.	Becken-horst	American Folk Tune. Arr. C. Courtney. In anth. "Duets for the Master: Sacred Duets for High & Low Voice & Keyboard" Pub. 1989.	MSN
1536	Courtney, Craig	20th C.	None Other Lamb		high & low v.	Becken-horst	Arr. C. Courtney. In anth. "Duets for the Master: Sacred Duets for High & Low Voice & Keyboard" Pub. 1989.	MSN
1537	Courtney, Craig	20th C.	Praise Him!		high & low v.	Becken-horst	In anthology "Duets for the Master: Sacred Duets for High and Low Voice and Keyboard" Pub. 1989.	MSN
1538	Cowen, Frederic Hymen	1852-1935	Children's Home, The		Unspec.	Leonard-Eng	Also solo	CVMP (1976)
1539	Cowen, Frederic Hymen	1852-1935	The fountains mingle with the river		Unspec.	J. Williams		BBC (1975)
1540	Cramer, C.		Sehnsucht nach der Heimath "Hörst du nicht ein fernes Klingen"		S/S	Bauer		CHAL (1898)
1541	Crampton, Ernest		If We Marry for Love		Unspec.	Cramer		CVMP (1976)
1542	Crane, Helen	1868-	Ich habe getrunken der Sonne allverzehrende Glut	Op. 8 No. 2	S/A	Junne	Amer. woman comp.	CHAL (1911)
1543	Crane, Helen	1868-	Tag entschwand, Sternlein wacht	Op. 8 No. 1	S/A	Junne	Amer. woman comp.	CHAL (1911)
1544	Crelle, August Leopold	1780-1855	Hectors Abschied "Will sich Hector ewig"		Unspec.	Mauer i. Berl.		CHAL (1898)
1545	Crikeltown, G.		Littl Liftboy muss man lernen "Tanz-Duett"		Unspec.	Bärd & Bruder		CHAL (1911)
1546	Crosse, Gordon	1937-	May Song		S/S or A/T or B/B	OUP	acap.	ASR
1547	Cui, César	1835-1918	Poslednye tsvety [The Last Flowers]		S/MS	GMI	Translit. title of Russ. Only Cyrillic. Anth. "Iz-brannye Duety Russkikh Kompozitorov dlia peniia s fortepiano" Pub. 1948.	MSN
1548	Cui, César	1835-1918	Tuchki nebesnyie [The Heavenly Little Clouds]		S/MS	GMI	Translit. title of Russ. Only Cyrillic. Anth. "Iz-brannye Duety Russkikh Kompozitorov dlia peniia s fortepiano" Pub. 1948.	MSN
1549	Curci, Giuseppi	1808-1877	Partenza dei pescatori		Unspec.	Cranz		CHAL (1898)
1550	Curci, Giuseppi	1808-1877	Tramonto della luna "Vieni o Pietro"		T/B or S/A	Cranz		CHAL (1898)

REC	COMP	DTS	TITLE	OP #	VCG	PUB	COMMENTS	SRC
1551	Cursch-Bühren, Franz Theodor	1859-1908	Beiden Eifersüchtigen "Also hier, ist der Platz"	Op. 141	2 female v.	Vormeyer		CHAL (1898)
1552	Cursch-Bühren, Franz Theodor	1859-1908	Frau Winkler und Frau Trinkler "Beiden Eifersüchtige"		Unspec.	none listed		CHAL (1898)
1553	Cursch-Bühren, Franz Theodor	1859-1908	Im Myrthenkranz "Lag einst im Walde auf Gras und Moos"	Op. 12	2 med. v.	Hug		CHAL (1898)
1554	Cursch-Bühren, Franz Theodor	1859-1908	Mei lieber Bua "Wenn am Firmament rother Schein"	Op. 109 No. 1a	Unspec.	Vormeyer		CHAL (1898)
1555	Cursch-Bühren, Franz Theodor	1859-1908	Nein so mich zu betrügen	Op. 71	2 female v.	Luckhardt		CHAL (1901)
1556	Curschmann, Karl Friedrich	1804-1841	Strauss, den ich gepflücket	I No. 6	Unspec.	C. Rühle i. L.	Arr. Necke	CHAL (1901)
1557	Curschmann, Karl Friedrich	1804-1841	Wach auf du goldnes Morgenroth	II No. 3	Unspec.	C. Rühle i. L.	Arr. Necke	CHAL (1901)
1558	Curschmann, Karl Friedrich	1804-1841	Willkommen du Gottes Sonne	IV No. 11	Unspec.	C. Rühle i. L.	Arr. Necke	CHAL (1901)
1559	Curschmann, Karl Friedrich	1805-1841	Willkommen du Gottes Sonne	Op. 3 No. 1	S/A	Schlesinger		CHAL (1898)
1560	Curti, Franz	1854-1898	Ave Maria, gratia plena	Op. 7	S/A	Wernthal	pf or harm or org	CHAL (1906)
1561	Cutler, E.		Ave Maria "Ave Maria gratia pleni"	Op. 24	S/A	R. & E.		CHAL (1898)
1562	Cuvillier, Charles	1877-1955	Aurore		Unspec.	Enoch		CVMP (1976)
1563	Cuvillier, Charles	1877-1955	L'Aurore		Unspec.	Enoch		CVMP (1976)
1564	Cuvillier, Charles	1877-1955	Petit tout Petit		Unspec.	Enoch		CVMP (1976)
1565	Cuvillier, Charles	1877-1955	What is done you can never undo		Unspec.	Stern		BBC (1975)
1566	Czerwinsky, Wilhelm	1837-1893	Abendglöcklein "Wandrer zieht auf fernen Wegen"	Op. 15	S/A	Cranz		CHAL (1898)
1567	Czibilka, Alphons	1842-1894	Aubade à la fiance		Unspec.	Junne		CHAL (1898)
1568	Czonka, Paul	1905-	Tristis est anima mea		S/A or S/MS	Peer	Pub. 1970	NATS-SVD
1569	d'Anduze, W.		Wohl leuchtet aus der Ferne		Unspec.	Lindner	pf or org or harm	CHAL (1906)
1570	d'Yradier, Chevalier		Il Vestito azurro		S/A	G. Schirm.	In catalogue page "Favorite French and Italian Vocal Duets" of G. Schirmer, Inc. NY (no date)	MSN
1571	Dagland, Abbé J.		Come Ye, See the Saviour		med. & low v.	G. Schirm.	pf or org accomp.	ASR
1572	Dagland, Abbé J.		Sing Alleluia Forth		med. & low v.	G. Schirm.	pf or org accomp.	ASR
1573	Dahlgren, Erland		Harlighetens Morgon		Unspec.	Gehrmans	Also solo	CVMP (1976)
1574	Dahms, M.		Champagner-Compagnie "Ach Geschäfte heut' zu mädchen"		Unspec.	Jäger i. Berl.		CHAL (1898)
1575	Dahms, M.		Musikalisches Frikassée "Jüngst kam ein Bauersmann"		Unspec.	Jäger i. Berl.		CHAL (1898)

REC	COMP	DTS	TITLE	OP #	VCG	PUB	COMMENTS	SRC
1576	Daly		Love's no stranger		S/A	White-Smith	In catalogue page "Vocal Duetts" of White-Smith Music Pub. Co. (no date)	MSN
1577	Dammas, Hellmuth Karl	1816-	Allgemeines Wandern "Vom Grund bis zu den Gipfeln"	Op. 9 No. 1	S/A	Bahn	a.k.a. Feódor Steffen, novelist	CHAL (1898)
1578	Dammas, Hellmuth Karl	1816-	Frische Fahrt "Laue Luft kommt blau geflossen"	Op. 9 No. 3	S/A	Bahn	a.k.a. Feódor Steffen, novelist	CHAL (1898)
1579	Dammas, Hellmuth Karl	1816-	Frühlingsglaube "Linden Lüfte sind erwacht"	Op. 9 No. 4	S/A	Bahn	a.k.a. Feódor Steffen, novelist	CHAL (1898)
1580	Dammas, Hellmuth Karl	1816-	Lockung "Hörst du nicht die Bäume rauschen"	Op. 9 No. 2	S/A	Bahn	a.k.a. Feódor Steffen, novelist	CHAL (1898)
1581	Danysz, K.		Nur noch einaml möcht' ich dich sehen"	Op. 5 No. 1	Unspec.	B. & B.		CHAL (1898)
1582	Danysz, K.		O wollest nicht den Rosenstrauch	Op. 5 No. 2	Unspec.	R. & B.		CHAL (1898)
1583	Dargomizhsky, Alexander	1813-1869	Charm of Days Gone By, The		S/S	Mez Kniga	Eng. trans. Russ.	ASR
1584	Dargomizhsky, Alexander	1813-1869	Deva i Roza		MS/MS or S/S	State Mus. Pub. (Moscow)	Translit. of Russ. In collection "Polnoe Sobranie Vokalnïkh Ansambley I Khorov" ed. M. C. Pekelus. Pub. 1950.	NATS-VCD
1585	Dargomizhsky, Alexander	1813-1869	Deva i Roza [The Maiden and the Rose]		S/S	GMI	Translit. title of Russ. Only Cyrillic. Anth. "Izbrannye Duety Russkikh Kompozitorov dlia peniia s fortepiano" Pub. 1948.	MSN
1586	Dargomizhsky, Alexander	1813-1869	Fifteen Duets		high & low v.	Mez Kniga	Pieces unspec.	ASR
1587	Dargomizhsky, Alexander	1813-1869	Lovely Maidens		S/S	Mez Kniga	Eng. trans. Russ.	ASR
1588	David, Ferdinand	1810-1873	Mein Aug' erheb' ich		S/A or A/T or S/Br	Church	In anthology "Sacred Duets for High and low Voices" Vol. 2 Pub. 1907.	NATS-SVD
1589	David, Ferdinand	1810-1873	Mein Aug' erheb' ich	Op. 33	high & low v.	Church	In anthology "Sacred Duets A Collection of Two-Part Songs by the Best Composers" Vol. 2. Compi. & ed. W. Shakespeare. Pub. 1907.	MSN
1590	David, Ferdinand	1810-1873	Partons		Unspec.	Schott		CHAL (1898)
1591	Day, Maude Craske		Arise, O sun		Unspec.	Cramer	Eng. woman comp.	BBC (1975)
1592	Day, Maude Craske		Arise O Sun		Unspec.	Cramer	Eng. woman comp. Also solo.	CVMP (1976)
1593	Debussy, Claude	1862-1918	Noël des Enfants qui n'ont plus de maison		S/S	Durand		ASR
1594	Decker, Constantine	1810-1878	Gondoliera "O komm zu mir"	Op. 15 No. 1	S/A	Heinr.		CHAL (1898)
1595	Decker, Constantine	1810-1878	In einem Garten	Op. 15 No. 2	S/A	Heinr.		CHAL (1898)
1596	Decker, Constantine	1810-1878	Wenn durch die Piazetta	Op. 15 No. 3	S/A	Heinr.		CHAL (1898)
1597	Decker, H.		Ständchen "Ich halte, Edlitam, am Fenster"	Op. 21 No. 3	S/A	Brauer		CHAL (1898)
1598	Decker, Pauline von	1812-	Blauen Frühlingsaugen schaun aus	Op. 5	S/S	B. & H.	Grmn. woman comp.	CHAL (1898)

REC	COMP	DTS	TITLE	OP #	VCG	PUB	COMMENTS	SRC
1599	Decker, Pauline von	1812-	Meine Liebe lebt im Liede	Op. 17 No. 1	S/A	B. & H.	Grmn. woman comp.	CHAL (1898)
1600	Decker, Pauline von	1812-	So viel Stern' am Himmel stehen	Op. 17 No. 2	S/A	B. & H.	Grmn. woman comp.	CHAL (1898)
1601	Decker-Schenck, Johann	1826-1899	Wasserfahrt		Unspec.	Haushahn	Arr. L. Rainer	CHAL (1898)
1602	Degele, Eugen	1834-1886	Schäfers Sonntagslied "Das ist der Tag des Herrn"	Op. 13 No. 1	Unspec.	R. & E.		CHAL (1898)
1603	Degele, Eugen	1834-1886	Wie singt die Lerche so schön	Op. 13 No. 2	Unspec.	R. & E.		CHAL (1898)
1604	Degenhardt, E.		Heil' ge Nacht, auf Engelsschwingen		S/A or S/Br	E. Schel. i. W.		CHAL (1901)
1605	DeKoven, Reginald	1859-1920	Oh promise me		high & low v.	G. Schirm.	Arr. C. Deis. In catalogue page "Selected Vocal Duets" of G. Schirmer, Inc. NY (no date)	MSN
1606	Delbruck, J.		Prière		Unspec.	Enoch		CVMP (1976)
1607	Delcliseur, F.		Eulalia und ihre Schwärmer "Sehen sie Eulalia"	Op. 4	Unspec.	Fr. Dietrich		CHAL (1898)
1608	Delibes, Leo	1836-1891	Les trois oiseaux		S/S or S/MS	CVR	In catalogue "Classical Vocal Reprints Complete Catalog" Pub. 1997.	MSN
1609	Delibes, Léo	1836-1891	Les trois oiseaux		2 female v.	CVR		MSN
1610	Dell'Acqua, Eva	1856-1930	Ah, voyez le joli chemin	No. 5	S/S	Schott i. Br.	It.-Belg. woman comp.	CHAL (1911)
1611	Dell'Acqua, Eva	1856-1930	Ecoutez, mes soeurs	No. 4	S/S	Schott i. Br.	It.-Belg. woman comp.	CHAL (1911)
1612	Dell'Acqua, Eva	1856-1930	Sérénade joyeuse "Voici la brunne"		Unspec.	Schott i. Br.	It.-Belg. woman comp.	CHAL (1898)
1613	Delmet, Paul	1865-1904	Aimons-Nous		Unspec.	Enoch		CVMP (1976)
1614	Delmet, Paul	1865-1904	Duo des Pêcheurs de Bremes		Unspec.	Enoch		CVMP (1976)
1615	Delmet, Paul	1865-1904	Les Femmes de France		Unspec.	Enoch	Also solo	CVMP (1976)
1616	Delson, L.		Katzen-Liebesduett "Mein liebes holdes Kätzchen"		Unspec.	Thiemer		CHAL (1898)
1617	Denecke, H.		Nacht sank leise hernieder		Unspec.	Fritz Bartels		CHAL (1911)
1618	Denefve, J.	1814-1877	Fête de noël		Unspec.	Junne		CHAL (1898)
1619	Densmore, John H.		Starry Night		S/A	Ditson	Also solo	MSN
1620	Denza, Luigi	1846-1922	Adieu		Unspec.	Enoch		CVMP (1976)
1621	Denza, Luigi	1846-1922	Barcarolle		Unspec.	Enoch		CVMP (1976)
1622	Denza, Luigi	1846-1922	Berceuse		Unspec.	Enoch		CVMP (1976)
1623	Denza, Luigi	1846-1922	Dance of the fays "Dance we to-night"		S/A	Schott		CHAL (1911)
1624	Denza, Luigi	1846-1922	Dansons		Unspec.	Enoch		CVMP (1976)
1625	Denza, Luigi	1846-1922	Les Cloches		Unspec.	Enoch		CVMP (1976)

REC	COMP	DTS	TITLE	OP #	VCG	PUB	COMMENTS	SRC
1626	Denza, Luigi	1846-1922	O fliesse kleines Bächlein		Unspec.	André		CHAL (1901)
1627	Denza, Luigi	1846-1922	Or che notte		Unspec. or high & med. v.	CVR		MSN
1628	Denza, Luigi	1846-1922	When we are young		Unspec.	Ashdown		BBC (1975)
1629	Deppen, Jessie L.		In the Garden of To-Morrow		high & low v.	Chappell	Copyright 1925	MSN
1630	Deprosse, Anton	1838-1878	Als hätt' es Rosen heut' Nacht geschneif	Op. 25 No. 3	S/S or S/MS	Sch. j.		CHAL (1898)
1631	Deprosse, Anton	1838-1878	Beim Spinnen nächtlich sitzen"	Op. 20 No. 1	S/A	Sch. j.		CHAL (1898)
1632	Deprosse, Anton	1838-1878	Blume der Ergebung "Ich bin die Blum' im Garten"	Op. 20 No. 3	S/A	Sch. j.		CHAL (1898)
1633	Deprosse, Anton	1838-1878	O trübe die reine Quelle nicht	Op. 16 No. 3	2 female v.	B. & H.		CHAL (1898)
1634	Deprosse, Anton	1838-1878	Schlummerliedchen "Ich hauch' es in die weite Ferne"	Op. 34	MS/MS	Bauer		CHAL (1898)
1635	Deprosse, Anton	1838-1878	Swanhilde "Es hat ein Graf ein Töchterlein"	Op. 16 No. 2	2 female v.	B. & H.		CHAL (1898)
1636	Deprosse, Anton	1838-1878	Und wär' ich ein Vögelein	Op. 16 No. 1	2 female v.	B. & H.		CHAL (1898)
1637	Deprosse, Anton	1838-1878	Wanderlied "Wie gut der Liebe Gott es meint"	Op. 20 No. 2	S/A	Sch. j.		CHAL (1898)
1638	Deprosse, Anton	1838-1878	Wanderlust "O Wander-glück, O Wanderlust"	Op. 25 No. 2	S/S or S/MS	Sch. j.		CHAL (1898)
1639	Deprosse, Anton	1838-1878	Wasserlilien "Wasserlilien im Wald"	Op. 25 No. 1	S/S or S/MS	Sch. j.		CHAL (1898)
1640	Dessauer, Joseph	1798-1876	An den Mond "Füllest wieder"	Op. 57 No. 2	2 female v.	Cranz		CHAL (1898)
1641	Dessauer, Joseph	1798-1876	Du schwebst mir vor in stiller Nacht	Op. 66 No. 1	S/A	Cranz		CHAL (1898)
1642	Dessauer, Joseph	1798-1876	Frühlingseinzung "Fenster auf, die Herzen auf"	Op. 57 No. 3	2 female v.	Cranz		CHAL (1898)
1643	Dessauer, Joseph	1798-1876	Getrennten "Noch einmal möcht ich vor dir stehn"	Op. 47 No. 3	Unspec.	Kratoch-will		CHAL (1898)
1644	Dessauer, Joseph	1798-1876	Ich muss nun einmal singen "Vöglein, Vöglein, was singest du"	Op. 57 No. 1	2 female v.	Cranz		CHAL (1898)
1645	Dessauer, Joseph	1798-1876	Liebeswünche "Auf dieser Welt hab' ich kein' Freud'"	Op. 47 No. 5	Unspec.	Kratoch-will		CHAL (1898)
1646	Dessauer, Joseph	1798-1876	Lied in der Fremde "Ein-sam, nein, das bin ich nicht"	Op. 47 No. 1	Unspec.	Kratoch-will		CHAL (1898)
1647	Dessauer, Joseph	1798-1876	Mag auch heiss das Scheiden brennen	Op. 66 No. 5	S/A	Cranz		CHAL (1898)
1648	Dessauer, Joseph	1798-1876	O Tannenbaum, o Tannen-baum wie grün (treu)	Op. 47 No. 2	Unspec.	Kratoch-will		CHAL (1898)
1649	Dessauer, Joseph	1798-1876	So viel Stern' am Himmel stehen	Op. 47 No. 4	Unspec.	Kratoch-will		CHAL (1898)
1650	Dessauer, Joseph	1798-1876	Verschwundener Stern "Es stand ein Sternlein am Himmel"	Op. 47 No. 6	Unspec.	Kratoch-will		CHAL (1898)
1651	Dessauer, Joseph	1798-1876	Verzagen "Ich sitz' am Strande der rauschenden See"	Op. 66 No. 4	S/A	Cranz		CHAL (1898)
1652	Dessauer, Joseph	1798-1876	Wenn sich zwei Herzen scheiden	Op. 66 No. 2	S/A	Cranz		CHAL (1898)
1653	Dessauer, Joseph	1798-1876	Wenn still mit seinen letzten Flammen	Op. 66 No. 6	S/A	Cranz		CHAL (1898)

REC	COMP	DTS	TITLE	OP #	VCG	PUB	COMMENTS	SRC
1654	Dessauer, Joseph	1798-1876	Wogen, die da jagen	Op. 66 No. 3	S/A	Cranz		CHAL (1898)
1655	Diabelli, Anton	1781-1858	Frühlingslied	Op. 155 No. 2	Unspec.	Cranz		CHAL (1898)
1656	Diabelli, Anton	1781-1858	Lieder der Unschuld "Für Kinderstimmen"	Op. 118	Unspec.	Cranz		CHAL (1898)
1657	Diabelli, Anton	1781-1858	Mailied	Op. 155 No. 1	Unspec.	Cranz		CHAL (1898)
1658	Diabelli, Anton	1781-1858	Wechsel der Jahreszeiten	Op. 155 No. 3	Unspec.	Cranz		CHAL (1898)
1659	Diabelli, Anton	1781-1858	Weihnachtslied "Glocken klingen fern und nah"	Op. 170	Unspec.	Cranz		CHAL (1898)
1660	Diack, J. Michael	1869-1946	Captain Mackintosh and Colonel Anne		Unspec.	Peterson		BBC (1975)
1661	Dickinson, Clarence	1873-1969	O Nightingales Awake		2 med. v.	Gray		ASR
1662	Dickson, Stanley		Thanks be to God		high & med. v.	Boosey		ASR
1663	Diebels, F.		O sanfter süsser Hauch	II No. 4	Unspec.	C. Rühle i. L.	Arr. Necke	CHAL (1901)
1664	Diebold, Johann	1842-1929	Missa "Adoro te devote"	Op. 18	S/A or T/B	Herder i. Freiburg	org accomp.	CHAL (1898)
1665	Diemer, Louis-Joseph	1843-1919	Mei Madla, di bischt dumm	No. 2	Unspec.	Lederer		CHAL (1898)
1666	Diemer, Louis-Joseph	1843-1919	Oachkatz'l "Heur' geibt's koani Nuus'n"	No. 3	Unspec.	Lederer		CHAL (1898)
1667	Diepenbrock, Alphons	1862-1921	Clair de Lune		S/S	Donemus	pf or orch accomp.	CVMP (1976)
1668	Diepenbrock, Alphons	1862-1921	Clair de Lune		S/S	Donemus		ASR
1669	Diepenbrock, Alphons	1862-1921	Ecoutez la Canson bien douce		S/S	Donemus		ASR
1670	Diepenbrock, Alphons	1862-1921	Ecoutez la Chanson bien Douce		S/S	Donemus	pf or orch accomp. Also solo.	CVMP (1976)
1671	Diercks, H.		Abendfeier "Wie ist der Abend so traulich"	Op. 12 No. 1	S/A or T/B	Lehmann i. H.		CHAL (1898)
1672	Diercks, H.		Andacht "Mir ist so wohl in Gottes Haus"	Op. 12 No. 5	S/A or T/B	Lehmann i. H.		CHAL (1898)
1673	Diercks, H.		Erste Strahl von Osten her	Op. 12 No. 3	S/A or T/B	Lehmann i. H.		CHAL (1898)
1674	Diercks, H.		Erste Strahl von Osten her	Op. 12 No. 3	high & med. v.	Benjamin		CHAL (1906)
1675	Diercks, H.		Frühlingsglaube "Linden Lüfte sind erwacht"	Op. 12 No. 2	S/A or T/B	Benjamin		CHAL (1898)
1676	Diercks, H.		Hinaus, hinaus, du junges Blut	Op. 12 No. 6	S/A or T/B	Lehmann i. H.		CHAL (1898)
1677	Diercks, H.		Hinaus, hinaus du junges Blut	Op. 12 No. 6	high & med. v.	Benjamin		CHAL (1906)
1678	Diercks, H.		Linden Lüfte sind erwacht	Op. 12 No. 2	high & med. v.	Benjamin		CHAL (1906)
1679	Diercks, H.		Mir ist so wohl in Gottes Hand	Op. 12 No. 5	high & med. v.	Benjamin		CHAL (1906)
1680	Diercks, H.		Sternennacht, heilige Nacht	Op. 12 No. 4	S/A or T/B	Lehmann i. H.		CHAL (1898)
1681	Diercks, H.		Sternennacht, heilige Nacht	Op. 12 No. 4	high & med. v.	Benjamin		CHAL (1906)
1682	Diercks, H.		Wie ist der Abend so traulich	Op. 12 No. 1	high & med. v.	Benjamin		CHAL (1906)
1683	Dietler, F.		Abschied "Duftenden Kräuter auf den Au"		Unspec.	Schmid i. M.		CHAL (1898)

REC	COMP	DTS	TITLE	OP #	VCG	PUB	COMMENTS	SRC
1684	Dietmann, E.		Zu Salzburg steht, umgeben	Op. 70	S/A	Sch. J.		CHAL (1906)
1685	Dietrich, Amalia	1838-	Der du am Sternenbogen	Op. 8 No. 6	Unspec.	Simrock	Grmn. woman comp.	CHAL (1898)
1686	Dietrich, Amalia	1838-	Frühlingsbilder "Es regnet"	Op. 8 No. 1	Unspec.	Simrock	Grmn. woman comp.	CHAL (1898)
1687	Dietrich, Amalia	1838-	Schneeglöcken "'S was doch wie ein leises"	Op. 8 No. 5	Unspec.	Simrock	Grmn. woman comp.	CHAL (1898)
1688	Dietrich, Amalia	1838-	Wenn sich zwei Herzen recht verstehn	Op. 8 No. 4	Unspec.	Simrock	Grmn. woman comp.	CHAL (1898)
1689	Dietrich, Amalia	1838-	Wie hat die Nacht	Op. 8 No. 2	Unspec.	Simrock	Grmn. woman comp.	CHAL (1898)
1690	Dietrich, Amalia	1838-	Zauberkreis "Was steht denn"	Op. 8 No. 3	Unspec.	Simrock	Grmn. woman comp.	CHAL (1898)
1691	Dijk, Jan van	1918-	Gebedt [poss. Gebed in Dut. or Gebet in Grmn.]		S/A	Donemus	acap. In collection "Drei Duetten"	CVMP (1976)
1692	Dijk, Jan van	1918-	Gebenedijd [misspelled, poss. Gebedetijd]		S/A	Donemus	acap. In collection "Drei Duetten"	CVMP (1976)
1693	Dijk, Jan van	1918-	Nacht-Stilte		S/A	Donemus	acap. In collection "Drei Duetten"	CVMP (1976)
1694	Dinsmore		Night and Song		S/A	White-Smith	In catalogue page "Vocal Duetts" of White-Smith Music Pub. Co. (no date)	MSN
1695	Dix, J. Arlie		Ould Side Car, The		Unspec.	Leonard-Eng	Also solo (Cramer pub.)	CVMP (1976)
1696	Doebber, Johannes	1866-1921	An die Lerche "Vöglein, Vöglein in den Lüften"	Op. 20 No. 2	Unspec.	Siegel		CHAL (1898)
1697	Doebber, Johannes	1866-1921	Frühling im Alter "Singen die Vögel im grünen Wald"	Op. 20 No. 3	Unspec.	Siegel		CHAL (1898)
1698	Doebber, Johannes	1866-1921	Goldne Leiter "Wenn die Sonne hoch und heiter"	Op. 20 No. 5	Unspec.	Siegel		CHAL (1898)
1699	Doebber, Johannes	1866-1921	Sonntag "Sonntag ist gekommen"	Op. 20 No. 1	Unspec.	Siegel		CHAL (1898)
1700	Doebber, Johannes	1866-1921	Wie ist doch die Erde so schön	Op. 20 No. 4	Unspec.	Siegel		CHAL (1898)
1701	Döhler, Theodor	1814-1856	Nuovo Barcarolo	Op. 57 No. 12	Unspec.	Peters		CHAL (1898)
1702	Döhler, Theodor	1814-1856	Un sguardo ed una voce	Op. 57 No. 1	Unspec.	Peters		CHAL (1898)
1703	Dolan		The convent bells		S/A	White-Smith	In catalogue page "Vocal Duetts" of White-Smith Music Pub. Co. (no date)	MSN
1704	Dolmetsch, Arnold	1858-1940	I prethee keep my sheep		Unspec.	Boosey		BBC (1975)
1705	Dolmetsch, Arnold	1858-1940	Why sigh'st thou, shepherd?		Unspec.	Boosey		CHAL (1898)
1706	Donaudy, Stefano	1879-1925	Amor s'apprende		S/S or MS/MS or T/T	Ricordi	In collection "36 Arie di Stile Antico," Vol. 1 Pub. 1918.	NATS-VCD
1707	Donizetti, Gaetano	1797-1848	Addio "Dunque addio mio caro amore"		Unspec.	B. & H.		CHAL (1898)
1708	Donizetti, Gaetano	1797-1848	Aurora		Unspec.			CHAL (1898)
1709	Donizetti, Gaetano	1797-1848	Bote der Geliebten "Lieblich süsse Wohlgerüche"		Unspec.	Schott		CHAL (1898)
1710	Donizetti, Gaetano	1797-1848	Che vuoi di più		Unspec.	Cranz		CHAL (1898)
1711	Donizetti, Gaetano	1797-1848	Ein Blick ein Wort "Ja dein Blick dringt"		S/S	Schott		CHAL (1898)

REC	COMP	DTS	TITLE	OP #	VCG	PUB	COMMENTS	SRC
1712	Donizetti, Gaetano	1797-1848	Inconstanza d'Irene		Unspec.	Cranz		CHAL (1898)
1713	Donizetti, Gaetano	1797-1848	L'Aurora		S/A	G. Schirm.	In catalogue page "Favorite French and Italian Vocal Duets" of G. Schirmer, Inc. NY (no date)	MSN
1714	Donizetti, Gaetano	1797-1848	Le crepuscule		Unspec.	Ricordi		BBC (1975)
1715	Donizetti, Gaetano	1797-1848	Liebe ist ein Himmelswort		S/S	Schott		CHAL (1898)
1716	Donizetti, Gaetano	1797-1848	Morgenröthe "Purpur färbt schon"		Unspec.	Schott		CHAL (1898)
1717	Donizetti, Gaetano	1797-1848	Predest inazione		Unspec.	Ricordi		BBC (1975)
1718	Donizetti, Gaetano	1797-1848	Predestinazione		Unspec.	Cranz		CHAL (1898)
1719	Donizetti, Gaetano	1797-1848	Qui dove merce negasti		Unspec.	Cranz		CHAL (1898)
1720	Donizetti, Gaetano	1797-1848	Rudre muthvoll nach dem Ziel		S/S	Schlesinger		CHAL (1901)
1721	Donizetti, Gaetano	1797-1848	Schwur "Treu wirst du mich stets finden"		S/S	Schott		CHAL (1898)
1722	Dorel, F.		Garden of your Heart		Unspec.	Boosey		CVMP (1976)
1723	Dorel, F.		Garden of Your Heart		2 med. v.	Boosey		ASR
1724	Döring, August	1837-1904	Heiliger Abend "Selige Freude so rein"		Unspec.	Staeglich		CHAL (1898)
1725	Döring, Carl Heinrich	1834-1916	Abendlied des Wanderers "Wie sich Schatten dehnen"	Op. 11	Unspec.	Oertel		CHAL (1898)
1726	Döring, Carl Heinrich	1834-1916	Frühling ist da "Blümlein horch"	Op. 10	Unspec.	Oertel		CHAL (1898)
1727	Döring, Carl Heinrich	1834-1916	Mailied "Kein' schön're (schöner) Zeit auf Erden ist"	Op. 13	Unspec.	Oertel		CHAL (1898)
1728	Döring, Carl Heinrich	1834-1916	Wandersmann und Lerche "Lerche, wie früh' schon"	Op. 4	MS/Br or MS/A	Nagel		CHAL (1898)
1729	Döring, W. [prob. Wilhelm]	1887-	Hoch vom Himmel holde Kunde	Op. 29	Unspec.	H. Augustin		CHAL (1911)
1730	Dorn, Alexander Julius Paul	1833-1901	Ach wenn wir hätten, o Freundchen	II No. 11	Unspec.	C. Rühle i. L.		CHAL (1901)
1731	Dorn, Alexander Julius Paul	1833-1901	Beiden Paudertaschen "Beste Freudin, guten Morgen"	Op. 122	2 female v.	B. & B.		CHAL (1898)
1732	Dorn, Alexander Julius Paul	1833-1901	Dienstbotenwechsel "Sie werden wohl entschul'gen"	Op. 113	2 female v.	B. & B.		CHAL (1898)
1733	Dorn, Alexander Julius Paul	1833-1901	Du Abendgruss, du Glockenklang	Op. 89 No. 2	S/A	Chal.		CHAL (1898)
1734	Dorn, Alexander Julius Paul	1833-1901	Eine Wassermaus und eine Kröte	Op. 106	Unspec.	Sulzbach i. Berl		CHAL (1898)
1735	Dorn, Alexander Julius Paul	1833-1901	Enten Duett "Es gingen einst zwei Enten"	Op. 91	Unspec.	R. & E.		CHAL (1898)
1736	Dorn, Alexander Julius Paul	1833-1901	Hoch Deutschland "Ob drohend die Wolken auch"	Op. 138	2 female v.	Chal.		CHAL (1898)
1737	Dorn, Alexander Julius Paul	1833-1901	Jugenderinnerungen "Wir gingen, weisst du noch"	Op. 114	2 female v.	B. & B.		CHAL (1898)

REC	COMP	DTS	TITLE	OP #	VCG	PUB	COMMENTS	SRC
1738	Dorn, Alexander Julius Paul	1833-1901	Liebesmai "Wo's einmal hat gemaiet"	Op. 89 No. 1	S/A	Chal.		CHAL (1898)
1739	Dorn, Alexander Julius Paul	1833-1901	Vertauschten Herzen "Hans geht traurig hin und her"	Op. 49	Unspec.	Rühlei. L.		CHAL (1898)
1740	Dorn, Alexander Julius Paul	1833-1901	Was sich die Hunde erzähl-en "Ich armer, armer Kettenhund"	Op. 68 No. 1	Unspec.	Weber i. Cöln		CHAL (1898)
1741	Dorn, Alexander Julius Paul	1833-1901	Was sich die Katzen erzähl-en "Ach ich sitze so alleine"	Op. 68 No. 2	Unspec.	Weber i. Cöln		CHAL (1898)
1742	Dorn, Alexander Julius Paul	1833-1901	Weisst du, was das Lieb bedeutet	Op. 89 No. 2	S/A	Chal.		CHAL (1898)
1743	Dorn, Heinrich L. E.	1804-1892	Abend thaut herneider	Op. 78 No. 5	2 female v.	Bahn		CHAL (1898)
1744	Dorn, Heinrich L. E.	1804-1892	Armes Herz "Wenn ein Stern ist aufgegangen"	Op. 78 No. 1	2 female v.	Bahn		CHAL (1898)
1745	Dorn, Heinrich L. E.	1804-1892	Gottes Rath und Scheiden "Es ist bestimmt in Gottes Rath"	Op. 78 No. 3	2 female v.	Bahn		CHAL (1898)
1746	Dorn, Heinrich L. E.	1804-1892	Hoffnung "Wenn die Hoffnung nicht wär'"	Op. 76 No. 2	Unspec.	Kistner		CHAL (1898)
1747	Dorn, Heinrich L. E.	1804-1892	Hündchen und Kätzchen "Liebes Kätzchen glatt und munter"	Op. 75 No. 4	2 female v.	Bahn		CHAL (1898)
1748	Dorn, Heinrich L. E.	1804-1892	Nähe des Geliebten "Ich denke dien, wenn mir der Sonne Schimmer"	Op. 76 No. 3	Unspec.	Kistner		CHAL (1898)
1749	Dorn, Heinrich L. E.	1804-1892	Sprache der Liebe "Das ist der wahren Liebe Macht"	Op. 76 No. 4	Unspec.	Kistner		CHAL (1898)
1750	Dorn, Heinrich L. E.	1804-1892	Tanzliedchen "Ringel, Ringel, Rosenkranz"	Op. 76 No. 1	Unspec.	Kistner		CHAL (1898)
1751	Dorn, Heinrich L. E.	1804-1892	Trost der Trennung "Dass wir jetzt sollen scheiden"	Op. 76 No. 6	Unspec.	Kistner		CHAL (1898)
1752	Dorn, Heinrich L. E.	1804-1892	Was die Thiere alles lernen "Enten lernen schnattern"	Op. 76 No. 5	Unspec.	Kistner		CHAL (1898)
1753	Dorn, Heinrich L. E.	1804-1892	Zur Kirmes "Horch, wie die Eiche tönt"	Op. 78 No. 6	2 female v.	Bahn		CHAL (1898)
1754	Dorn, Otto	1848-1931	Es eilt und wallt		Unspec.	B. & H.		CHAL (1906)
1755	Dorn, Otto	1848-1931	Geistliches Duett "Vertrau' dem Herrn in deinem Leide"	Op. 41	S/A	Steyl & Th.	org or harm accomp.	CHAL (1898)
1756	Dorn, Otto	1848-1931	Gott grüsse dich, kein andrer Gruss	Op. 20 No. 1	S/A	Coppen-rath		CHAL (1898)
1757	Dorn, Otto	1848-1931	Heraus "Ging unter dichten Zweigen"	Op. 20 No. 2	S/A	Coppen-rath		CHAL (1898)
1758	Dorn, Otto	1848-1931	Maiwanderung "Bei dem Klange der Schalmeien"	Op. 20 No. 4	S/A	Coppen-rath		CHAL (1898)
1759	Dorn, Otto	1848-1931	Schwalben "Viel Glück, zur Reise Schwalben"	Op. 20 No. 3	S/A	Coppen-rath		CHAL (1898)
1760	Dorn, Otto	1848-1931	Sterne blitzen am Himmel	Op. 49 No. 2	Unspec.	B. & H.		CHAL (1906)
1761	Dorn, Otto	1848-1931	Waldlieder (3)	Op. 49	Unspec.	B. & H.	3 duets	CHAL (1906)
1762	Dorn, Otto	1848-1931	Weisse Last drückt alle Bäume	Op. 49 No. 1	Unspec.	B. & H.		CHAL (1906)
1763	Dougherty, Celius	1902-1986	Sweet Spring is your Time		S/S or S/T	G. Schirm.		CVMP (1976)

REC	COMP	DTS	TITLE	OP #	VCG	PUB	COMMENTS	SRC
1764	Dougherty, Celius	1902-1986	Sweet Spring is Your Time		S/T or S/S	G. Schirm.		ASR
1765	Doun, Elza		Father in Heaven		2 med. v.	Boosey	Woman comp.	ASR
1766	Drath, Theodor	1828-1920	Frühlingsläuten "Was hör' ich denn da unten läuten"	Op. 21 No. 1	Unspec.	Körner i. L.		CHAL (1898)
1767	Drath, Theodor	1828-1920	Oben "Von oben kommt die Liebe"	Op. 21 No. 2	Unspec.	Körner i. L.		CHAL (1898)
1768	Drath, Theodor	1828-1920	Tanz von Sonst und Jetzt "Grossmütterchen erzähle"	Op. 21 No. 3	Unspec.	Körner i. L.		CHAL (1898)
1769	Dregert, Alfred	1836-1893	Letze Gruss "Ich kam vom Wald hernieder"	Op. 117 No. 1	Unspec.	O. Forberg		CHAL (1898)
1770	Dregert, Alfred	1836-1893	Zieh' hinaus "Zieh' hinaus beim Morgengrau'n"	Op. 98	Unspec.	O. Forberg		CHAL (1898)
1771	Dreher, F.		Da müasst ma in Wean net auf d'Welt kumma sein "Wann uns was genir'n thät"	No. 4	Unspec.	Krämer		CHAL (1898)
1772	Dreher, F.		Mir Zwa von Schottenfeld "Wie no mir Zwa"	No. 3	Unspec.	Krämer		CHAL (1898)
1773	Dreher, F.		Pasch nur zua mein lieber Franz "Sali a harbe Weanerin"	No. 2	Unspec.	Krämer		CHAL (1898)
1774	Dressel, R.		Freudinnen Trost "Klaget nicht, naht auch die Stunde"	Op. 2	S/A	B. & B.		CHAL (1898)
1775	Dressler, Friedrich August	d. 1919	Esthnische Duetten-Lieder (3)	Op. 23	Unspec.	B. & B.		CHAL (1898)
1776	Dressler, Friedrich August	d. 1919	Hochzeitslied "Junges Mädchen, komm o Mädchen"	Op. 23 No. 3	Unspec.	B. & B.		CHAL (1898)
1777	Dressler, Friedrich August	d. 1919	Jörru "Jörru, Jörru darf ich kommen"	Op. 23 No. 1	Unspec.	B. & B.		CHAL (1898)
1778	Dressler, Friedrich August	19th C.	Liebchen "Liebchen, Brüderchen, du sagtest"	Op. 23 No. 2	Unspec.	B. & B.		CHAL (1898)
1779	Drischner, Max		Der Herr ist mein Hirte (Psalm 23)		Unspec.	Schul	pf or org accomp. Sacred concerto	CVMP (1976)
1780	Drischner, Max		Herr Gott, du bist unsere zuflucht (Psalm 90)		Unspec.	Schul	pf or org accomp. Sacred concerto	CVMP (1976)
1781	Drobisch, Karl Ludwig	1803-1854	Bleibe bei uns, es will Abend werden	Op. 66 No. 6	S/S	Schott		CHAL (1898)
1782	Drobisch, Karl Ludwig	1803-1854	Es kommt ein Tag des Herrn "mag auch die Liebe weinen"	Op. 66 No. 2	S/S	Schott		CHAL (1898)
1783	Drobisch, Karl Ludwig	1803-1854	Frühlings Vorgefühl "Bald ist die Winternacht dahin"	Op. 66 No. 4	S/S	Schott		CHAL (1898)
1784	Drobisch, Karl Ludwig	1803-1854	Im Freien "Kann auch Frühling finster blicken"	Op. 66 No. 3	S/S	Schott		CHAL (1898)
1785	Drobisch, Karl Ludwig	1803-1854	O du fröhliche, o du selige	Op. 66 No. 1	S/S	Schott		CHAL (1898)
1786	Drobisch, Karl Ludwig	1803-1854	Wiedersehn "Wiedersehn, Wort des Trostes"	Op. 66 No. 5	S/S	Schott		CHAL (1898)
1787	Dubois, Théodore	1837-1924	Puer Natus est Nobis		S/A	Heugel	org accomp. Sacred motet	CVMP (1976)
1788	Dubois, Théodore	1837-1924	Puer Natus est Nobis		S/A	Heugel	org accomp. Sacred motet	ASR
1789	Dugge, W.		Herzig's Schätzerl, lass' di herzen	Op. 4	Unspec.	Portius		CHAL (1898)
1790	Dugge, W.		Kleeplatz "Dort auf der Alm, da ist ein Kleeplatz"	Op. 33 No. 3	Unspec.	Hug		CHAL (1898)

REC	COMP	DTS	TITLE	OP #	VCG	PUB	COMMENTS	SRC
1791	Dugge, W.		Über'm Bacherl steht a Haus	Op. 33 No. 1	Unspec.	Hug		CHAL (1898)
1792	Dugge, W.		Wasserfahrt	Op. 33 No. 2	Unspec.	Hug		CHAL (1898)
1793	Dumack, Louis	1838-1914	Bitte "Weil auf mir du dunkles Auge"	Op. 12 No. 1	S/A	Simon i. B.		CHAL (1898)
1794	Dumack, Louis	1838-1914	Rose "Dort einsam steht ein Röslein"	Op. 12 No. 2	S/A	Simon i. B.		CHAL (1898)
1795	Dunayevsky, Isaak	1900-1955	Song of the Fatherland		Unspec.	Russian State	Trans. Russ.	BBC (1975)
1796	Dunhill, Thomas Frederick	1877-1946	How Soft Upon the Ev'ning Air		2 med. v.	Curwen	org accomp.	ASR
1797	Dunhill, Thomas Frederick	1877-1946	The sea garden		S/A	Year Book Press		BBC (1975)
1798	Dunlap, Fern Glasgow		Wedding Prayer		S/A or S/Br	G. Schirm.	Woman comp. Also solo.	CVMP (1976)
1799	Dupré, Claude		Snow is falling		S/S	Musical Million	Arr. of song	BBC (1975)
1800	Durbec, L.		Avril revient		Unspec.	Cranz		CHAL (1898)
1801	Dürck, J.		Ein Fichtenbaum steht einsam	Op. 2 No. 2	S/A	B. & B.		CHAL (1898)
1802	Dürck, J.		Frühzeitiger Frühling "Tage der Wonne, kommt ihr"	Op. 2 No. 1	S/A	B. & B.		CHAL (1898)
1803	Dürck, J.		Schnee im Märzen, Schmerz im Herzen	Op. 2 No. 3	S/A	B. & B.		CHAL (1898)
1804	Düringer, Ph. J.		Warum "Himmel ist so leicht und rein"	No. 6	Unspec.	Klemm		CHAL (1898)
1805	Durra, Hermann	1871-1954	Uns fehlt der dritte Mann "Wie schön ist's wenn am Abend"	Op. 32	Unspec.	Portius		CHAL (1898)
1806	Dussek, Johann Ladislaus	1760-1812	Lass' uns der sel'gen	No. 5	S/S	B. & H.		CHAL (1906)
1807	Duval, Edmond	1809-	Beatus vir		Unspec.	Schott	org accomp.	CHAL (1898)
1808	Duvivier, A. D.		Ave Maria "Ave Maria gratia pleni"	Op. 7	S/A	Leuckart		CHAL (1898)
1809	Dvořák, Antonín	1841-1904	A já ti uplynu [Ich schwimm' dir davon]	Op. 32 No. 1	S/A	Simrock, G. Schirm. (no Czech)	In "Strains of Moravia" [Klänge aus Mähren] Op. 32, based on Moravian national poetry.	MSN
1810	Dvořák, Antonín	1841-1904	Abschied "Tanz mit mir mein liebes Mädchen"	Op. 20 No. 2	Unspec.	Simrock	Grmn. trans. Czech	CHAL (1898)
1811	Dvořák, Antonín	1841-1904	Bescheidene "Blühend, wie ein Röschen"	Op. 32 No. 8	S/A	Simrock	Grmn. trans. Czech	CHAL (1898)
1812	Dvořák, Antonín	1841-1904	Bestimmung "Vergeblich klagest di mein Lieber"	Op. 20 No. 1	Unspec.	Simrock	Grmn. trans. Czech	CHAL (1898)
1813	Dvořák, Antonín	1841-1904	Ctyri Dueta, Op. 38	Op. 38	Var. female v.	Simrock, Artia	Four duets	NATS-VCD
1814	Dvořák, Antonín	1841-1904	Dyby byla kosa nabrósená [Wenn die Sense scharf geschliffen wäre]	Op. 32 No. 3	S/A	Simrock, G. Schirm. (no Czech)	In "Strains of Moravia" [Klänge aus Mähren] Op. 32, based on Moravan national poetry.	MSN
1815	Dvořák, Antonín	1841-1904	Echoes from Moravia (13) Vol. 1, 2		S/A	G. Schirm.		ASR
1816	Dvořák, Antonín	1841-1904	Flucht "Ja auf dem Donaufluss"	Op. 32 No. 1	S/A	Simrock	Grmn. trans. Czech	CHAL (1898)

REC	COMP	DTS	TITLE	OP #	VCG	PUB	COMMENTS	SRC
1817	Dvořák, Antonín	1841-1904	Four Duets	Op. 38	S/A	Lengnick		BBC (1975)
1818	Dvořák, Antonín	1841-1904	Four Duets, Op. 20	Op. 20	S/T or S/A	Baren		ASR
1819	Dvořák, Antonín	1841-1904	Four Duets Op. 38	Op. 38	Unspec.	Lengnick		CVMP (1985)
1820	Dvořák, Antonín	1841-1904	Four Moravian Duets, Op. 38	Op. 38	S/A	Schaur EE		CVMP (1976)
1821	Dvořák, Antonín	1841-1904	Four Moravian Duets, Op. 38	Op. 38	S/A	Schaur		ASR
1822	Dvořák, Antonín	1841-1904	From the Bough	Op. 38 No. 4	Unspec.	ECS	Eng. trans. Czech. In anthology "48 Duets Seventeenth Through Nineteenth Centuries" Ed. V. Prahl. Pub. 1941, 1970.	MSN
1823	Dvořák, Antonín	1841-1904	Gefangene "Ging ein Mädchen Gras zu mähen"	Op. 32 No. 11	S/A	Simrock	Grmn. trans. Czech	CHAL (1898)
1824	Dvořák, Antonín	1841-1904	Gruss aus der Ferne "Leuchte freundlich, lieber Stern"	Op. 38 No. 2	Unspec.	Simrock	Grmn. trans. Czech	CHAL (1898)
1825	Dvořák, Antonín	1841-1904	Hear My Prayer		2 high v.	R. D. Row	org/pf acc. Eng. trans. Czech. In anth. "Sacred Duet Masterpieces..." Vol. 3. Compi. & ed. C. Fredrickson. Pub. 1961.	MSN
1826	Dvořák, Antonín	1841-1904	Holub na javore [Die Taube auf dem Ahorn]	Op. 32 No. 6	S/A	Simrock, G. Schirm., (no Czech)	In "Strains of Moravia" [Klänge aus Mähren] Op. 32, based on Moravian national poetry.	MSN
1827	Dvořák, Antonín	1841-1904	Hore [Schmerz]	Op. 38 No. 4	S/A	Simrock	In "Ctyri dvojzpevy" [Four Duets] Op. 38, based on Moravian national poetry.	MSN
1828	Dvořák, Antonín	1841-1904	Jablko [Der Apfel]	Op. 38 No. 2	S/A	Simrock	In "Ctyri dvojzpevy" [Four Duets] Op. 38 based on Moravian national poetry.	MSN
1829	Dvořák, Antonín	1841-1904	Kinderlied für zwei Kinderstimmen		2 treble v. (male or female)	Artia	acap.	ASR
1830	Dvořák, Antonín	1841-1904	Klänge aus Mähren 13 Duette	Op. 32	S/A	Simrock	Grmn. trans. Czech	CHAL (1898)
1831	Dvořák, Antonín	1841-1904	Kranz "Heimwärts geh'n die Schnitter"	Op. 38 No. 3	Unspec.	Simrock	Grmn. trans. Czech	CHAL (1898)
1832	Dvořák, Antonín	1841-1904	Letzte Wunsch "Suhay pflügt das Brachfeld"	Op. 20 No. 4	Unspec.	Simrock	Trans. from Czech	CHAL (1898)
1833	Dvořák, Antonín	1841-1904	Lord is My Shepherd, The		2 high v.	R. D. Row	org/pf acc. Eng. trans. Czech. In anth. "Sacred Duet Masterpieces..." Vol. 3. Compi. & ed. C. Fredrickson. Pub. 1961.	MSN
1834	Dvořák, Antonín	1841-1904	Maravské Dvojzpévy, Op. 32	Op. 32	Var. female v.	Simrock, Artia	13 Moravian Duets	NATS-VCD
1835	Dvořák, Antonín	1841-1904	Moznost	Op. 38	Unspec.	G. Schirm.	In anthology "Romantic Duets—Great Performers Edition" Compi. E. Lear & T. Stewart. Pub. 1985.	MSN

REC	COMP	DTS	TITLE	OP #	VCG	PUB	COMMENTS	SRC
1836	Dvorák, Antonín	1841-1904	Moznost [Möglichkeit]	Op. 38 No. 1	S/A	Simrock	In "Ctyri dvojzpevy" [Four Duets] Op. 38, based on Moravian national poetry.	MSN
1837	Dvorák, Antonín	1841-1904	Na Tej Nasej Strese		S/A or S/MS	Simrock, Artia		NATS-VCD
1838	Dvorák, Antonín	1841-1904	Neveta [Der Trost]	Op. 32 No. 12	S/A	Simrock, G. Schirm., (no Czech)	In "Strains of Moravia" [Klänge aus Mähren] Op. 32, based on Moravian national poetry.	MSN
1839	Dvorák, Antonín	1841-1904	Pfand der Liebe "Siehe dort am Himmel"	Op. 32 No. 5	S/A	Simrock	Trans. from Czech	CHAL (1898)
1840	Dvorák, Antonín	1841-1904	Prsten [Der Ring]	Op. 32 No. 9	S/A	Simrock, G. Schirm., (no Czech)	In "Strains of Moravia" [Klänge aus Mähren] Op. 32, based on Moravian national poetry.	MSN
1841	Dvorák, Antonín	1841-1904	Ring "Tönet soll heut"	Op. 32 No. 9	S/A	Simrock	Trans. from Czech	CHAL (1898)
1842	Dvorák, Antonín	1841-1904	Russiche Lieder		Unspec.	Supraphon		CVMP (1976)
1843	Dvorák, Antonín	1841-1904	Russische Lieder		S/A	Baren	In Russ. & Czech	ASR
1844	Dvorák, Antonín	1841-1904	Scheiden ohne Leiden "Wie wir uns gefunden"	Op. 32 No. 4	S/A	Simrock	Trans. from Czech	CHAL (1898)
1845	Dvorák, Antonín	1841-1904	Schmerz "Als der Apfel reif war"	Op. 38 No. 4	Unspec.	Simrock	Trans. from Czech	CHAL (1898)
1846	Dvorák, Antonín	1841-1904	Seidenband "Sind es holde Nachtigall"	Op. 20 No. 3	Unspec.	Simrock	Trans. from Czech	CHAL (1898)
1847	Dvorák, Antonín	1841-1904	Sípek [Wilde Rose]	Op. 32 No. 13	S/A	Simrock, G. Schirm., (no Czech)	In "Strains of Moravia" [Klänge aus Mähren] Op. 32, based on Moravian national poetry.	MSN
1848	Dvorák, Antonín	1841-1904	Skromná [Die Bescheidene]	Op. 32 No. 8	S/A	Simrock, G. Schirm., (no Czech)	In "Strains of Moravia" [Klänge aus Mähren] Op. 32, based on Moravian national poetry.	MSN
1849	Dvorák, Antonín	1841-1904	Slavíkovsky Polecko Maly	Op. 32 No. 5	Unspec.	G. Schirm.	In anthology "Romantic Duets—Great Performers Edition" Compi. E. Lear & T. Stewart. Pub. 1985.	MSN
1850	Dvorák, Antonín	1841-1904	Slavíkovsky polecko maly [Der kleine Acker]	Op. 32 No. 5	S/A	Simrock, G. Schirm., (no Czech)	In "Strains of Moravia" [Klänge aus Mähren] Op. 32, based on Moravian national poetry.	MSN
1851	Dvorák, Antonín	1841-1904	Songs My Mother Taught Me	Op. 55 No. 4	Unspec.	Lengnick	Arr. of solo. Eng. trans. Czech	CVMP (1985)
1852	Dvorák, Antonín	1841-1904	Strains from Moravia, Book 1, Op. 32a	Op. 32a	Unspec.	Lengnick		CVMP (1985)
1853	Dvorák, Antonín	1841-1904	Strains from Moravia, Book 2, Op. 32b	Op. 32b	Unspec.	Lengnick		CVMP (1985)
1854	Dvorák, Antonín	1841-1904	Thirteen Moravian Duets	Op. 32	S/A	Simrock		BBC (1975)
1855	Dvorák, Antonín	1841-1904	Thräne "Aus dem Wald im Schatten"	Op. 32 No. 2	S/A	Simrock	Trans. from Czech	CHAL (1898)
1856	Dvorák, Antonín	1841-1904	Trennung Wenn die Sichel scharf"	Op. 32 No. 3	S/A	Simrock	Trans. from Czech	CHAL (1898)
1857	Dvorák, Antonín	1841-1904	Trost "Ach du mein schöner Wald"	Op. 32 No. 12	S/A	Simrock	Trans. from Czech	CHAL (1898)
1858	Dvorák, Antonín	1841-1904	V dobrym sme se sesli [Freundlich laß uns scheiden]	Op. 32 No. 4	S/A	Simrock, G. Schirm., (no Czech)	In "Strains of Moravia" [Klänge aus Mähren] Op. 32, based on Moravian national poetry.	MSN

REC	COMP	DTS	TITLE	OP #	VCG	PUB	COMMENTS	SRC
1859	Dvořák, Antonín	1841-1904	Velet', vtácku [Fliege, Vöglein]	Op. 32 No. 2	S/A	Simrock, G. Schirm., (no Czech)	In "Strains of Moravia" [Klänge aus Mähren] Op. 32, based on Moravian national poetry.	MSN
1860	Dvořák, Antonín	1841-1904	Venecek [Kränzlein]	Op. 38 No. 3	S/A	Simrock	In "Ctyri dvojzpevy" [Four Duets] Op. 38, based on Moravian national poetry.	MSN
1861	Dvořák, Antonín	1841-1904	Vergebliches Hoffen "Klagt ein Vogel seine Lieder"	Op. 38 No. 1	Unspec.	Simrock	Trans. from Czech	CHAL (1898)
1862	Dvořák, Antonín	1841-1904	Verlassene "Eine Taube flog"	Op. 32 No. 6	S/A	Simrock	Trans. from Czech	CHAL (1898)
1863	Dvořák, Antonín	1841-1904	Voda a plác [Wasser und Weinen]	Op. 32 No. 7	S/A	Simrock, G. Schirm., (no Czech)	In "Strains of Moravia" [Klänge aus Mähren] Op. 32, based on Moravian national poetry.	MSN
1864	Dvořák, Antonín	1841-1904	Vöglein "Fliege Vöglein, fliege"	Op. 32 No. 2	S/A	Simrock	Trans. from Czech	CHAL (1898)
1865	Dvořák, Antonín	1841-1904	When the Cuckoo sings	Op. 38 No. 1	Unspec.	ECS	Eng. trans. Czech. In anthology "48 Duets Seventeenth Through Nineteenth Centuries" Ed. V. Prahl. Pub. 1941, 1970.	MSN
1866	Dvořák, Antonín	1841-1904	Wilde Rose "Es ging ein Mädchen schön"	Op. 32 No. 13	S/A	Simrock	Trans. from Czech	CHAL (1898)
1867	Dvořák, Antonín	1841-1904	Zajatá [Die Gefangene]	Op. 32 No. 11	S/A	Simrock, G. Schirm., (no Czech)	In "Strains of Moravia" [Klänge aus Mähren] Op. 32, based on Moravian national poetry.	MSN
1868	Dvořák, Antonín	1841-1904	Zelenaj se, zelenaj [Grüne, du Gras!]	Op. 32 No. 10	S/A	Simrock, G. Schirm., (no Czech)	In "Strains of Moravia" [Klänge aus Mähren] Op. 32, based on Moravian national poetry.	MSN
1869	Dvořák, Antonín	1841-1904	Zivot Vojensky		Var. female v.	Simrock, Artia		NATS-VCD
1870	Dvořák, Antonín	1841-1904	Zuversicht "Grüne, grüne liebes Gras"	Op. 32 No. 10	S/A	Simrock	Trans. from Czech	CHAL (1898)
1871	Dyson, George	1883-1964	Sea music		Unspec.	Cramer		BBC (1975)
1872	Dyson, George	1883-1964	Sea Music		Unspec.	Cramer		CVMP (1976)
1873	Dzerzhinsky, Ivan	1909-1978	From border unto border		Unspec.	Russian State	Trans. from Russ.	BBC (1975)
1874	Eben, Petr	1929-	Zehn Poetische Duette auf Worte von Vitezslav Nezval		S/A	Baren	No specific works mentioned. Czech and Grmn. poetry. Optional chorus.	CVMP (1985)
1875	Eberhard, G.		Grosspapa (or Grossmama) zum Geburtstage "Man sagt du seist wie ich ein Kind"		Unspec.	Glas i. Berl.		CHAL (1898)
1876	Eberhardt, Anton	1855-1922	Im Wald "Es ist so still"	Op. 8 No. 3	Unspec.	Kistner		CHAL (1898)
1877	Eberhardt, Anton	1855-1922	Jugendzeit, Morgenherrlichkeit	Op. 8 No. 1	Unspec.	Kistner		CHAL (1898)
1878	Eberhardt, Anton	1855-1922	Lobe dem Hernn meine Seele	Op. 8 No. 2	Unspec.	Kistner		CHAL (1898)
1879	Eberle, Friedrich	1853-1930	Unter dem Lindenbaum "Ein Vöglein sang im Lindenbaum"	Op. 7	Unspec.	Benjamin		CHAL (1898)

REC	COMP	DTS	TITLE	OP #	VCG	PUB	COMMENTS	SRC
1880	Ebner, L.		Abends Purpur ergiesst den Strahl	Op. 37 No. 2	S/A	Boesn.		CHAL (1901)
1881	Ebner, L.		Klar und hell eilender Quell	Op. 37 No. 1	S/A	Boesn.		CHAL (1901)
1882	Edmunds, John	1913-1986	Three Christmas Carols		high & low v.	World	Unspec. pieces	ASR
1883	Edwards, Clara		By the Bend of the River		S/A or S/Br	G. Schirm.	Woman comp. Arr. C. Deis. In catalogue page "Selected Vocal Duets" of G. Schirmer, Inc. NY (no date)	MSN
1884	Edwards, George	1943-	Three Hopkinson Songs		S/S	APNM	2-pf accomp.	CVMP (1995)
1885	Edwards, George	1943-	Three Hopkinson Songs		S/S	ACA	2-pf accomp.	ASR
1886	Egger-Rieser, T.		Gott grüass't di mei Bua	Op. 13	Unspec.	Portius		CHAL (1906)
1887	Eggers, G.		Du bist wie eine stille Sternennacht		Unspec.	Wessel		CHAL (1898)
1888	Ehlert, C. F.		Hör' ich das Liedchen klingen	Op. 11 No. 3	Unspec.	B. & B.		CHAL (1898)
1889	Ehlert, C. F.		Schneeglöcken "Lenz will kommen, der Winter ist aus"	Op. 11 No. 1	Unspec.	B. & B.		CHAL (1898)
1890	Ehlert, C. F.		Traurige Jäger "Zur ewigen Ruh sie sangen"	Op. 11 No. 2	Unspec.	B. & B.		CHAL (1898)
1891	Ehret, Walter		Lord Jesus, the Infant Holy		2 med. v.	Frank	Arr. W. Ehret of Dan. folk song.	ASR
1892	Ehret, Walter		O Lovely is He to Behold		2 med. v.	Frank	Arr. W. Ehret of Span. folk song.	ASR
1893	Ehret, Walter		On Bethlehem's Hill		2 med. v.	Frank	Arr. W. Ehret of Austrian folk song.	ASR
1894	Ehret, Walter		On this Eve in Cold December		2 med. v.	Frank	Arr. W. Ehret of Fr. folk song.	ASR
1895	Ehrlich, Alfred Heinrich	1822-1899	Zwei Reichsfechtmeister vom reinsten Wasser "Wir Beide sind Fechter"		Unspec.	Ehrlich i. Potsdam		CHAL (1898)
1896	Ehrlich, Rudolph	1872-1924	Mein Fräulein wollen Sie es wagen		Unspec.	Pawliska		CHAL (1906)
1897	Eichberg, Oskar	1845-1898	Leichte Fahrt "Lass mich schaukeln"	Op. 3 No. 2	S/A	Schlesinger		CHAL (1898)
1898	Eichberg, Oskar	1845-1898	Nacht "Nacht ist wie ein stilles Meer"	Op. 3 No. 1	S/A	Schlesinger		CHAL (1898)
1899	Eichler, Max	1868-	Juchhe, Juchhe "Hörst du die schöne Weise"	Op. 113	Unspec.	P. Fischer i. Berl.		CHAL (1898)
1900	Eichler, O.		Es lächelt der See er ladet zum Bade	Op. 6	S/A	Wagner i. Dr.		CHAL (1906)
1901	Eichmann, J. C.		Trost in Thränen "Wie kommts, dass du so traurig bist"	Op. 50 No. 1	Unspec.	R. & B.		CHAL (1898)
1902	Einödshofer, Julius	1863-1930	Liebe verwandelt Kummer und Leid		Unspec.	B. & B.		CHAL (1901)
1903	Einödshofer, Julius	1863-1930	Mägdelein von Rasse		Unspec.	H. Augustin		CHAL (1906)
1904	Einödshofer, Julius	1863-1930	Nun geht es fort im Fluge	No. 3	Unspec	H. Augustin		CHAL (1906)
1905	Einödshofer, Julius	1863-1930	Wer der Kunst sich hat verschrieben		Unspec.	Apollo		CHAL (1911)
1906	Einödshofer & Schmidt	19th C.	Hei die Schule ist nun aus		Unspec.	H. Augustin		CHAL (1906)

REC	COMP	DTS	TITLE	OP #	VCG	PUB	COMMENTS	SRC
1907	Eisersdorf, A.		Nichts gleicht auf der Welt	No. 1	Unspec.	Gleissnbg.		CHAL (1901)
1908	Eisersdorf, A.		Schnell ein Couplet	No. 2	Unspec.	Gleissnbg.		CHAL (1901)
1909	Eisersdorf, A.		Strassenbahn, Strassenbahn	No. 3	Unspec.	Gleissnbg.		CHAL (1901)
1910	Eisler, Hans	1898-1962	Lieder und Kantaten Vol. 6		Unspec.	Deutscher	Unspec. pieces	ASR
1911	Eitner, Robert	1832-1905	Liebe sass als Nachtigall	I No. 2	Unspec.	C. Rühle i. L.	Arr. Necke	CHAL (1901)
1912	Elgar, Edward	1857-1934	Doubt Not Thy Father's Care		S/A or S/MS	Novello		NATS-SVD
1913	Elgar, Edward	1857-1934	Oh, you're here, sir		Unspec.	MS		BBC (1975)
1914	Elimar, Herz. v. Old.		Bitte "Weil auf mir du dunkles Auge"		Unspec.	Fürstner		CHAL (1898)
1915	Elimar, Herz. v. Old.		Wir Beide sein verbunden		Unspec.	Fürstner		CHAL (1898)
1916	Ellerton, John Lodge	1901-1873	Tota pulchra		Unspec.	Schott	org or pf accomp.	CHAL (1898)
1917	Elssner, E.		Armes Vöglein	Op. 3 No. 3	Unspec.	Dümmler i. Löbau		CHAL (1898)
1918	Elssner, E.		Blumen	Op. 7 No. 4	Unspec.	Dümmler i. Löbau		CHAL (1898)
1919	Elssner, E.		Frühzeitiger Frühling "Tage der Wonne, kommt ihr"	Op. 7 No. 2	Unspec.	Dümmler i. Löbau		CHAL (1898)
1920	Elssner, E.		Geburtstagslied	Op. 7 No. 5	Unspec.	Dümmler i. Löbau		CHAL (1898)
1921	Elssner, E.		Schlafgesang	Op. 3 No. 4	Unspec.	Dümmler i. Löbau		CHAL (1898)
1922	Elssner, E.		Treue	Op. 7 No. 3	Unspec.	Dümmler i. Löbau		CHAL (1898)
1923	Elssner, E.		Vater im Himmel	Op. 3 No. 2	Unspec.	Dümmler i. Löbau		CHAL (1898)
1924	Elssner, E.		Weihnachtslied	Op. 7 No. 1	Unspec.	Dümmler i. Löbau		CHAL (1898)
1925	Elssner, E.		Weihnachtszeit	Op. 3 No. 1	Unspec.	Dümmler i. Löbau		CHAL (1898)
1926	Emge, A.		Frühlingsnächte sing gefährlich	Op. 10 No. 2	high & med. v.	Gries		CHAL (1901)
1927	Emge, A.		Maienglöckchen läuten	Op. 10 No. 1	high & med. v.	Gries		CHAL (1901)
1928	Emilius, J.		Am Himmel wandelt der Sterne Heer	Op. 2	2 med. v.	Sch. j.		CHAL (1898)
1929	Emmerlich, Robert	1836-1891	Auf dieser Welt	Op. 8 No. 3	S/S	Peters		CHAL (1901)
1930	Emmerlich, Robert	1836-1891	Frühlingslied	Op. 25 No. 1	S/S	Henkel		CHAL (1898)
1931	Emmerlich, Robert	1836-1891	O du süsse Zeit	Op. 25 No. 2	S/S	Sulzer		CHAL (1898)
1932	Emmerlich, Robert	1836-1891	Spazieren wollt' ich reiten	Op. 8 No. 2	S/S	Peters		CHAL (1901)
1933	Emmerlich, Robert	1836-1891	Um die Maienzeit	Op. 8 No. 1	S/S	Peters		CHAL (1901)
1934	Emmerlich, Robert	1836-1891	Und wenn die Primel schneeweiss blickt	Op. 25 No. 1	S/S	Sulzer		CHAL (1898)
1935	Emmerlich, Robert	1836-1891	Zur schönen guten Nacht	Op. 8 No. 4	S/S	Peters		CHAL (1901)
1936	Emmerlich, Robert	1836-1891	Zweigesang der Elfen "Hörst du das Flüstern"	Op. 25 No. 3	S/S	Sulzer		CHAL (1898)

REC	COMP	DTS	TITLE	OP #	VCG	PUB	COMMENTS	SRC
1937	Engel, David Hermann	1816-1877	Abendlied "Verschwunden ist des Tages Licht"	Op. 61	Unspec.	Siegel		CHAL (1898)
1938	Engel, David Hermann	1816-1877	Ach dass die Liebe ewig bliebe	Op. 81 No. 2	Unspec.	Heinr.		CHAL (1898)
1939	Engel, David Hermann	1816-1877	Im Maien "Im Maien zu Zweien ze gehen"	Op. 65	Unspec.	Heinr.		CHAL (1898)
1940	Engel, David Hermann	1816-1877	Kein Graben so breit	Op. 55	S/T or S/S	Kistner		CHAL (1898)
1941	Engel, David Hermann	1816-1877	Waldlied "Wo das Echo schallt"	Op. 81 No. 1	Unspec.	Heinr.		CHAL (1898)
1942	Engel, David Hermann	1816-1877	Waldrose "Im Wald bei grünen Bäumen"	Op. 63	Unspec.	Kistner		CHAL (1898)
1943	Engelhart, Franz Xaver	1861-1924	Silentium für uns Zwoa "Blümchen am Hag"		Unspec.	Coppenrath		CHAL (1898)
1944	Engelsberg, E. S.	1825-1879	Meine Muttersprache		S/A or S/B	C. Fischer	In catalogue page "Selected Vocal Duets By Favorite Composers" of Carl Fischer NY (no date)	MSN
1945	Engelsberg, E. S.	1825-1879	Meine Muttersprache "O Muttersprache schön und weich"		Unspec.	Kratochwill	Pen name of Dr. Eduard Schön	CHAL (1898)
1946	Engelsberg, E. S.	1825-1879	Zur Krippe nach Bethlehem		Unspec.	Wiener Musikver.		CHAL (1901)
1947	Engler, Karl	1877-	An der Quelle im Walde	Op. 2	2 high v.	Kahnt		CHAL (1906)
1948	Erlanger, Gustav	1842-1908	Frau Sonne "Frau Sonne hell, Frau Sonne hoch"	Op. 47 No. 1	Unspec.	Steyl & Th.		CHAL (1898)
1949	Erlanger, Gustav	1842-1908	Im Haselstrauch "Sag' mir du grüner Haselstrauch"	Op. 47 No. 3	Unspec.	Steyl & Th.		CHAL (1898)
1950	Erlanger, Gustav	1842-1908	Liebesahnung "Sprach eine Maid voll Bangigkeit"	Op. 47 No. 2	Unspec.	Steyl & Th.		CHAL (1898)
1951	Erlanger, Gustav	1842-1908	Reh "Es jagt ein Jäger früh am Tag"	Op. 47 No. 4	Unspec.	Steyl & Th.		CHAL (1898)
1952	Erlanger, Gustav	1842-1908	Wie wundersam "Wie wundersam ist das Verlorengeh'n"	Op. 47 No. 6	Unspec.	Steyl & Th.		CHAL (1898)
1953	Erlanger, Gustav	1842-1908	Wohin "Es geht der Felche auf den tiefen Grund"	Op. 47 No. 5	Unspec.	Steyl & Th.		CHAL (1898)
1954	Erlanger, Ludwig	1830-	Erwachen will das junge Laub	Op. 26 No. 3	2 female v.	Hofbauer	Pen name of R. Langer	CHAL (1898)
1955	Erlanger, Ludwig	1830-	Ich möchte gern den ganzen Tag	Op. 26 No. 2	2 female v.	Hofbauer	Pen name of R. Langer	CHAL (1898)
1956	Erlanger, Ludwig	1830-	Meine Puppe hab' ich in den Schlaf gewiegt	Op. 26 No. 1	2 female v.	Hofbauer	Pen name of R. Langer	CHAL (1898)
1957	Erler, Hermann	1844-1918	Bepo und Carmosenella (12)	Op. 26	Unspec.	Seemann	Collection of It. love-songs. 12 songs & duets	CHAL (1901)
1958	Ernemann, E.		Frohe Botschaft "Wenn der Kuckuck wieder schreit"	Op. 24 No. 4	Unspec.	Hainauer		CHAL (1898)
1959	Ernemann, E.		Lenz ist angekommen	Op. 24 No. 1	Unspec.	Hainauer		CHAL (1898)
1960	Ernemann, E.		Waldlied "Im Walde möcht' ich leben"	Op. 24 No. 3	Unspec.	Hainauer		CHAL (1898)
1961	Ernemann, E.		Wandernden Lieder "Fallen im Herbst die Blätter"	Op. 24 No. 2	Unspec.	Hainauer		CHAL (1898)
1962	Ernemann, M.		Abendlied "Müde bin ich, geh' zur Ruh"	Op. 19 No. 6	Unspec.	Leuckart		CHAL (1898)
1963	Ernemann, M.		Frühlingsliedchen "Vög-lein singt im grünen Wald"	Op. 19 No. 7	Unspec.	Leuckart		CHAL (1898)
1964	Ernemann, M.		Frühlingslust "Draussen welche Wonne"	Op. 19 No. 2	Unspec.	Leuckart		CHAL (1898)

REC	COMP	DTS	TITLE	OP #	VCG	PUB	COMMENTS	SRC
1965	Ernemann, M.		Lustgang "Kommt, lasst uns geh'n spazieren"	Op. 19 No. 4	Unspec.	Leuckart		CHAL (1898)
1966	Ernemann, M.		Reiterlied "Hopp, hopp mein Reiterlein"	Op. 19 No. 5	Unspec.	Leuckart		CHAL (1898)
1967	Ernemann, M.		Sommerlied "Vöglein spielen in der Luft"	Op. 19 No. 1	Unspec.	Leuckart		CHAL (1898)
1968	Ernemann, M.		Tanzliedchen "Lasst uns jetztspringen"	Op. 19 No. 3	Unspec.	Leuckart		CHAL (1898)
1969	Ernemann, R.		Kinderheimath 7 Zweist. Lieder	Op. 19	Unspec.	Leuckart		CHAL (1898)
1970	Ernst, A. [prob. Anton]	1869-	Auf zur Sängerwarte "Wie herrlich ist das Leben"		Unspec.	Doblinger		CHAL (1898)
1971	Ernst, A. [prob. Anton]	1869-	Es gibt halt nur a Kaiserstadt		Unspec.	Mück i. W.		CHAL (1911)
1972	Ertl, Dominik	1857-1911	Dos muass a Weana g'wesen sein "Strassen voll Menschen"		Unspec.	Kratoch-will		CHAL (1898)
1973	Ertl, Dominik	1857-1911	Mai anzige Freud is mei Bua "Mirzl a Dirndl"		Unspec.	Fr. Dietrich		CHAL (1898)
1974	Ertl, Dominik	1857-1911	Mei anzige Freud' is mei Bua		MS/A	C. Fischer	In catalogue page "Selected Vocal Duets By Favorite Composers" of Carl Fischer NY (no date)	MSN
1975	Ertl, Dominik	1857-1911	Weaner Aifsitzer "Was mir heut' d'erlebt hab'n"		Unspec.	Kratoch-will		CHAL (1898)
1976	Eschmann, Johann Karl	1826-1882	In die Veilchen "Kommt hinaus, lasst uns geh'n"	Op. 50 No. 8	Unspec.	R. & B.		CHAL (1898)
1977	Eschmann, Johann Karl	1826-1882	Maria "Da droben auf dem Berge"	Op. 50 No. 3	Unspec.	R. & B.		CHAL (1898)
1978	Eschmann, Johann Karl	1826-1882	Morgenlied "Steht auf, ihr lieben Kinderlein"	Op. 50 No. 5	Unspec.	R. & B.		CHAL (1898)
1979	Eschmann, Johann Karl	1826-1882	Reiterliedchen "Hopp, hopp. hopp mein Kindchen"	Op. 50 No. 6	Unspec.	R. & B.		CHAL (1898)
1980	Eschmann, Johann Karl	1826-1882	Tanzliedchen "Ringel, Ringel, Rosenkranz"	Op. 50 No. 7	Unspec.	R. & B.		CHAL (1898)
1981	Eschmann, Johann Karl	1826-1882	Vogels Freude "In dem goldnen Strahl"	Op. 50 No. 4	Unspec.	R. & B.		CHAL (1898)
1982	Eschmann, Johann Karl	1826-1882	Wenn's Mailüfterl weht	Op. 50 No. 2	Unspec.	R. & B.		CHAL (1898)
1983	Esser, Heinrich	1818-1872	Abendglocken läuten	Op. 21 No. 2	Unspec.	B. & B.		CHAL (1898)
1984	Esser, Heinrich	1818-1872	Abendlied "Abend wird es wieder"	Op. 58 No. 3	Unspec.	Cranz		CHAL (1898)
1985	Esser, Heinrich	1818-1872	Abendlied "Nub schlafen die Vöglein"	Op. 74 No. 3	S/A	Schott		CHAL (1898)
1986	Esser, Heinrich	1818-1872	Abendlied "Sonne sank, der Abend naht"	Op. 58 No. 3	S/A	Cranz		CHAL (1898)
1987	Esser, Heinrich	1818-1872	Abschied "Thränen hab' ich viele, viele vergossen"	Op. 58 No. 2	S/A	Cranz		CHAL (1898)
1988	Esser, Heinrich	1818-1872	Am Morgen "Es taget in dem Osten"	Op. 41 No. 1	S/A	Schott		CHAL (1898)
1989	Esser, Heinrich	1818-1872	An den Mond "Wie blickst du hell und rein"	Op. 55 No. 2	S/A	Cranz		CHAL (1898)
1990	Esser, Heinrich	1818-1872	Du meine Seele, du mein Herz	Op. 21 No. 3	Unspec.	B. & B.		CHAL (1898)
1991	Esser, Heinrich	1818-1872	Frühling und Liebe "Im Ros-enbusche die Liebe schlief"	Op. 58 No. 6	S/A	Cranz		CHAL (1898)
1992	Esser, Heinrich	1818-1872	Frühlingsanfang "Schnee ist vergangen"	Op. 74 No. 1	S/A	Schott		CHAL (1898)

REC	COMP	DTS	TITLE	OP #	VCG	PUB	COMMENTS	SRC
1993	Esser, Heinrich	1818-1872	Frühlingslied "Tief im grünen Frühlingshag"	Op. 33 No. 2	S/A	Schott		CHAL (1898)
1994	Esser, Heinrich	1818-1872	Im Walde, im hellen Sonnenschein	Op. 26 No. 6	Unspec.	B. & B.		CHAL (1898)
1995	Esser, Heinrich	1818-1872	Kein Stern wil grüssend feunkeln	Op. 33 No. 1	S/A	Schott		CHAL (1898)
1996	Esser, Heinrich	1818-1872	Leb wohl du schöner Wald "So scheiden wir mit Sang"	Op. 55 No. 5	S/A	Cranz		CHAL (1898)
1997	Esser, Heinrich	1818-1872	Lenz, o Lenz, wie soll das enden	Op. 33 No. 3	S/A	Schott		CHAL (1898)
1998	Esser, Heinrich	1818-1872	Liebesglück	Op. 58 No. 4	S/A	Cranz		CHAL (1898)
1999	Esser, Heinrich	1818-1872	Morgenlied "Sterne sind erblichen"	Op. 58 No. 1	S/A	Cranz		CHAL (1898)
2000	Esser, Heinrich	1818-1872	Morgenstille "Leiser tönt schon"	Op. 74 No. 2	S/A	Schott		CHAL (1898)
2001	Esser, Heinrich	1818-1872	Müden Abendlied "Verglommen ist der Sonne Licht"	Op. 41 No. 3	S/A	Schott		CHAL (1898)
2002	Esser, Heinrich	1818-1872	Naturlieder (4)		S/A	Schott	4 duets	CHAL (1898)
2003	Esser, Heinrich	1818-1872	O Heimath "Wie lange soll ich noch fern"	Op. 55 No. 1	S/A	Cranz		CHAL (1898)
2004	Esser, Heinrich	1818-1872	O wie freu'n wir uns	Op. 48 No. 2	S/A	Schott		CHAL (1898)
2005	Esser, Heinrich	1818-1872	Rausche, rausche froher Bach	Op. 74 No. 4	S/A	Schott		CHAL (1898)
2006	Esser, Heinrich	1818-1872	Schneeglöcken klingen wieder	Op. 58 No. 5	Unspec.	Cranz		CHAL (1898)
2007	Esser, Heinrich	1818-1872	Sei gegrüsst o Frühlingsstunde	Op. 21 No. 1	Unspec.	B. & B.		CHAL (1898)
2008	Esser, Heinrich	1818-1872	Siehe der Frühling währet nicht lang	Op. 48 No. 1	S/A	Schott		CHAL (1898)
2009	Esser, Heinrich	1818-1872	Um Mitternacht "Um Mitternacht in ernster Stunde"	Op. 21 No. 5	Unspec.	B. & B.		CHAL (1898)
2010	Esser, Heinrich	1818-1872	Verlorner Mai "Es blüht der Mai"	Op. 21 No. 4	Unspec.	B. & B.		CHAL (1898)
2011	Esser, Heinrich	1818-1872	Wälder knospen, Wiesen grünen	Op. 55 No. 3	S/A	Cranz		CHAL (1898)
2012	Esser, Heinrich	1818-1872	Wallfahrtslied "Wir wandern über Berg und Thal"	Op. 41 No. 2	S/A	Schott		CHAL (1898)
2013	Esser, Heinrich	1818-1872	Wanderlied "Vögel singen, Blumen blüh'n"	Op. 55 No. 4	S/A	Cranz		CHAL (1898)
2014	Esser, Heinrich	1818-1872	Wie singt die Lerche schön	Op. 48 No. 3	S/A	Schott		CHAL (1898)
2015	Esser, R.		Eh' ich die Augen schliesse	Op. 57 No. 1	Unspec.	Kaun		CHAL (1901)
2016	Esser, R.		Oft geht an schönen Frühlingstagen	Op. 57 No. 2	Unspec.	Kaun		CHAL (1901)
2017	Evers, Karl	1819-1875	Auf ewig dein, auf ewig dein	Op. 30 No. 2	S/A	Schlesinger		CHAL (1898)
2018	Evers, Karl	1819-1875	Ist es Wonne, ist es Schmerz "Warum schlägt so laut mein Herz"	Op. 39 No. 1	S/A or T/A	Kistner		CHAL (1898)
2019	Evers, Karl	1819-1875	Liebesgarten "Liebe ist ein Rosenstrauch"	Op. 39 No. 2	S/A or T/A	Kistner		CHAL (1898)
2020	Evers, Karl	1819-1875	Sehnsucht im Herzen, Qual in der Brust	Op. 30 No. 1	S/A	Schlesinger		CHAL (1898)
2021	Evers, Karl	1819-1875	Wohin "Lüfte des Himmels, wo ziehet ihr hin"	Op. 30 No. 3	S/A	Schlesinger		CHAL (1898)

REC	COMP	DTS	TITLE	OP #	VCG	PUB	COMMENTS	SRC
2022	Evers, Karl	1819-1875	Zweigesang "Im Fliederbusch ein Vöglein sass"	Op. 39 No. 4	S/T or S/A	Kistner		CHAL (1898)
2023	Exner, O.		Auf der Eisbahn "Winterzeit welche Freud"	Op. 33	Unspec.	O. Forberg		CHAL (1898)
2024	Eykens, J.		Serment		Unspec.	Schott		CHAL (1898)
2025	Eyle, E.		Grünen Barone "Schönste Gigerlnpaar"	Op. 3	Unspec.	Grude		CHAL (1898)
2026	Eyle, W.		A,E,I,O,U "Du kennst die fünf Vokale"		Unspec.	R. Forberg		CHAL (1898)
2027	Eyle, W.		Ach Herrjeh "Als wir das Licht der Welt erblict"		Unspec.	Eulenburg		CHAL (1898)
2028	Eyle, W.		Das klingt fast wie ein Mär-chen aus längst vergangner Zeit "Dass man durch eigne Kraft"		Unspec.	Eulenburg		CHAL (1898)
2029	Eyle, W.		Herrgott, Herrgott, wie rührt uns das "Sind uns're Taschen ausgebrannt"		Unspec.	Eulenburg		CHAL (1898)
2030	Eyle, W.		Koschere Jüd "Im fernen Russland"	No. 71	Unspec.	R. Forberg		CHAL (1898)
2031	Eyle, W.		Neueste Zeitungsnachrichten "Guten Morgen, Herr von. Senfteleben"	No. 70	Unspec.	R. Forberg		CHAL (1898)
2032	Eyle, W.		Reiselustigen "Auf, lasst uns reisen nach Berlin"	No. 79	Unspec.	R. Forberg		CHAL (1898)
2033	Eyle, W.		Silberstein und Cohn "Mir Jüden, Gott gerecht"		Unspec.	Eulenburg		CHAL (1898)
2034	Eyle, W.		Spiele aus der Kinderzeit "Be-trachtet man das Kinderspiel"		Unspec.	Heinr.		CHAL (1898)
2035	Eyle, W.		Tombour Knaut und seine Braut "Ich bin vom elften Regiment"	Op. 37	Unspec.	Eulenburg		CHAL (1898)
2036	Eyle, W.		Verschiedene Wünsche "Man hört der Wünsche viele"		Unspec.	R. Forberg		CHAL (1898)
2037	Eymieu, Henry	1860-1931	Weihnachtsfreude "O Weihnachtszeit, leis' vom"	Op. 67	S/MS	B. & H.		CHAL (1898)
2038	Eyser, Eberhard	1932-	Juegos		S/A	STIM		CVMP (1985)
2039	Eysler, Edmund S.	1874-1949	Hopp, hopp, hopp, immer im Galopp		Unspec.	Bosworth		CHAL (1906)
2040	Fabiani, D.		Addio all' Italia		Unspec.	Lucca		CHAL (1898)
2041	Faccio, Franco	1840-1891	Ungherese et l'Italiana		S/S	Ricordi		CHAL (1898)
2042	Fairfield		Only the stars could tell		S/A	White-Smith	In catalogue page "Vocal Duetts" of White-Smith Music Pub. Co. (no date)	MSN
2043	Falkner, H.		Füsilier August Meier beim Herrn Feldwebel "Als Mutter on der Compagnie"	Op. 18	Unspec.	Danner		CHAL (1898)
2044	Falkner, H.		Zwei fidele Schützenbrüder "Mensch hast du Geist"	Op. 19	Unspec.	Danner		CHAL (1898)
2045	Fall, Leo	1873-1925	Lotte hier ist klein und schwach		Unspec.	Bloch		CHAL (1906)
2046	Fanselow, A.		Kaiser Friedrichs Lieblings-blume "Bescheidnen kleinen Veilchen"	Op. 10	Unspec.	Kaun		CHAL (1898)

REC	COMP	DTS	TITLE	OP #	VCG	PUB	COMMENTS	SRC
2047	Fauré, Gabriel	1845-1924	Ave Maria	Op. 93	S/MS	Faber, Heugel	org or pf accomp. In "Fauré & Saint-Saëns Six Motets for Upper Voices" Ed. T. Brown. Choral or solo v. Pub. separately by Heugel	MSN
2048	Fauré, Gabriel	1845-1924	Ave verum	Op. 65 No. 1	S/A or T/Br	CVR	In catalogue "Classical Vocal Reprints Complete Catalog" Pub. 1997.	MSN
2049	Fauré, Gabriel	1845-1924	Ave verum	Op. 65 No. 1	S/A	Faber	org or pf accomp. In "Fauré & Saint-Saëns Six Motets for Upper Voices" Ed. T. Brown. Choral or solo v.	MSN
2050	Fauré, Gabriel	1845-1924	Cantique		S/A	Hamelle		BBC (1975)
2051	Fauré, Gabriel	1845-1924	Cantique de Racine		S/A	Hamelle		ASR
2052	Fauré, Gabriel	1845-1924	Lieder et Duos		2 med. v.	Enoch	Collection of songs & duets, unspec.	ASR
2053	Fauré, Gabriel	1845-1924	Maria Mater Gratiae		S/MS	Leduc		CVMP (1985)
2054	Fauré, Gabriel	1845-1924	Pavane	Op. 50	S/A	Leduc		CVMP (1985)
2055	Fauré, Gabriel	1845-1924	Pavane	Op. 50	S/A	Recital		CVMP (1995)
2056	Fauré, Gabriel	1845-1924	Pavane	Op. 50	S/A	CVR	In catalogue "Classical Vocal Reprints Complete Catalog" Pub. 1997.	MSN
2057	Fauré, Gabriel	1845-1924	Puisqu' ici-bas tout âme	Op. 10	2 high v.	CVR		MSN
2058	Fauré, Gabriel	1845-1924	Puisqu'ice bas toute âme		S/S or S/T	CVR	In catalogue "Classical Vocal Reprints Complete Catalog" Pub. 1997.	MSN
2059	Fauré, Gabriel	1845-1924	Puisqu'ici bas, toute âme		S/S or S/T	Leduc		CVMP (1985)
2060	Fauré, Gabriel	1845-1924	Puisqu'ici-Bas Toute Âme		S/S or S/T	CVR		CVMP (1995)
2061	Fauré, Gabriel	1845-1924	Puisqu'ici-bas toute âme		S/S or S/T or A/Br	Hamelle		ASR
2062	Fauré, Gabriel	1845-1924	Puisqu'ici-bas toute âme	Op. 10 No. 1	S/S or S/T	Hamelle		NATS-VCD
2063	Fauré, Gabriel	1845-1924	Tarentelle		S/S	Leduc		CVMP (1985)
2064	Fauré, Gabriel	1845-1924	Tarentelle		S/S or S/T	CVR		CVMP (1995)
2065	Fauré, Gabriel	1845-1924	Tarentelle		S/S or S/T	Hamelle		ASR
2066	Fauré, Gabriel	1845-1924	Tarentelle		S/S	Hamelle		MSN
2067	Fauré, Gabriel	1845-1924	Tarentelle	Op. 10 No. 2	S/S	Hamelle		NATS-VCD
2068	Faure, Jean Baptiste	1830-1914	Ave verum		2 high v.	Heugel	pf or org accomp.	CVMP (1976)
2069	Faure, Jean Baptiste	1830-1914	Charité		2 high v.	Heugel	pf or org accomp. From "Chants Religieux"	CVMP (1976)
2070	Faure, Jean Baptiste	1830-1914	Crucifix		Unspec.	Heugel		BBC (1975)
2071	Faure, Jean Baptiste	1830-1914	Crucifix		Unspec.	Heugel	pf or org accomp. From "Chants Religieux"	CVMP (1976)
2072	Faure, Jean Baptiste	1830-1914	Crucifix		S/A or T/Br	G. Schirm.	In anthology "Schirmer's Favorite Sacred Duets for Various Voices" Pub. 1955.	MSN

REC	COMP	DTS	TITLE	OP #	VCG	PUB	COMMENTS	SRC
2073	Faure, Jean Baptiste	1830-1914	Crucifix		S/A	Ditson	In anthology "Choice Sacred Duets for All Voices" Pub. 1936.	MSN
2074	Faure, Jean Baptiste	1830-1914	Crucifix		2 high v.	Church	In anthology "Sacred Duets A Collection of Two-Part Songs by the Best Composers" Vol. 1. Compi. & ed. W. Shakespeare. Pub. 1907.	MSN
2075	Faure, Jean Baptiste	1830-1914	Crucifix		S/A or T/Br	G. Schirm.	pf or org accomp. In catalogue page "Sacred Vocal Duets" of G. Schirmer, Inc. NY (no date)	MSN
2076	Faure, Jean Baptiste	1830-1914	Crucifix		S/A or T/B	G. Schirm. et al.	In Anthology "Schirmer's Favorite Sacred Duets for Various Voices" Pub. 1955 et al.	NATS-SVD
2077	Faure, Jean Baptiste	1830-1914	Notre Père		Unspec.	Heugel	pf or org accomp. From "Chants Religieux"	CVMP (1976)
2078	Faure, Jean Baptiste	1830-1914	O Salutaris		Unspec.	Heugel	pf or org accomp. From "Chants Religieux"	CVMP (1976)
2079	Faust, Karl	1825-1892	Vom Maskenball "Ach so ein Maskenball"		2 female v.	Thiemer		CHAL (1898)
2080	Favre, Georges	1905-	Printemps Breton		Unspec.	Durand		CVMP (1976)
2081	Fearis, John Sylvester	1867-	Beautiful Isle of Somewhere		S/A	Lorenz	Also solo	CVMP (1976)
2082	Fehér, Th. J.		Es wechselt die Mode gar oft		Unspec.	Fr. Dietrich		CHAL (1901)
2083	Fehér, Th. J.		Wohnungsnoth hört' üb'rall auf		Unspec.	Fr. Dietrich		CHAL (1901)
2084	Feist, Alwine	1873-1924	Ein Brunnen muss rauschen in stiller Nacht	Op. 9 No. 2	S/A	Beyer & S.	Grmn. woman comp. Married Steinhausen.	CHAL (1906)
2085	Feist, Alwine	1873-1924	Es ist ein Reih'n geschlungen	Op. 9 No. 3	S/A	Beyer & S.	Grmn. woman comp. Married Steinhausen.	CHAL (1906)
2086	Feist, Alwine	1873-1924	Es singt sich gut des Abends	Op. 9 No. 1	S/A	Beyer & S.	Grmn. woman comp. Married Steinhausen.	CHAL (1906)
2087	Feldheim, G.		Frühling, zog in's Land hinein "Im Wald, im Thal"		Unspec.	Thiemer		CHAL (1898)
2088	Feldow, D.		Wenn Sie uns genau anseh'n		Unspec.	O. Dietrich		CHAL (1906)
2089	Feldow, D.		Wir sind fedele Junggesellen		Unspec.	O. Dietrich		CHAL (1906)
2090	Ferber, R.		I Love You Dear		Unspec.	Brainard's Sons	Arr. D. J. Muir. In anthology "Brainard's Collection of Vocal Duets from Popular Modern and Standard Composers." Pub. 1903.	MSN
2091	Ferrari, J. G.	1763-1842	Bist mir zu listig	II No. 6	Unspec.	B. & H.		CHAL (1898)
2092	Feyhl, Johann	1833-1905	O lieb, so lang du leiben kannst	Op. 135 No. 1	T/B or S/A	Vix i. Göpp.		CHAL (1898)
2093	Feyhl, Johann	1833-1905	Spinn, spinn "Mägdlein heilt Tag und Nacht"		Unspec.	Leuckart		CHAL (1898)
2094	Fiby, Heinrich	1834-1917	Diandl am Apfelbaum "A Büaberl schaut"	Op. 24 No. 2	2 female v.	Robitschek		CHAL (1898)
2095	Fiby, Heinrich	1834-1917	Oeferl "Es giebt a liabs Oeferl"	Op. 24 No. 1	2 female v.	Robitschek		CHAL (1898)
2096	Fidelis, J.		Wichtigste, das ist fürwahr die Grenzwacht	Op. 4	Unspec.	Coppenrath		CHAL (1906)

REC	COMP	DTS	TITLE	OP #	VCG	PUB	COMMENTS	SRC
2097	Fiebrich, F. P.		Wann i so in der Fruah aufsteh'	Op. 71	Unspec.	Bosworth		CHAL (1911)
2098	Fielitz, Alexander von	1860-1930	Hütet euch "Ein Stündlein sind sie beisammen gewest"	Op. 32 No. 3	2 female v.	Heinr.		CHAL (1898)
2099	Fielitz, Alexander von	1860-1930	Im Lenz, im Lenz, wenn Veilchen blühn	Op. 32 No. 1	2 female v.	Heinr.		CHAL (1898)
2100	Fielitz, Alexander von	1860-1930	"In der Mondnacht, in der Frühlingsmondnacht"	Op. 32 No. 2	2 female v.	Heinr.		CHAL (1898)
2101	Fink, Christian	1822-1911	Im Mai, im schönen Mai	II No. 1	Unspec.	C. Rühle i. L.		CHAL (1901)
2102	Fink, Christian	1822-1911	Maiblümelein "Im Mai, im schönen Mai"	Op. 46 No. 1	S/A	Rühle i. L.		CHAL (1898)
2103	Fink, Christian	1822-1911	Psalm 84 "Wie lieblich sind deine Wohnungen"	Op. 44	Unspec.	Rühle i. L.		CHAL (1898)
2104	Fink, Christian	1822-1911	Tanzlied der Mücken "Frisch ihr Blumen und Halme"	Op. 44 No. 2	S/A	Rühle i. L.		CHAL (1898)
2105	Fink, Christian	1822-1911	Wie lieblich sind deine Wohnungen	Op. 44	S/A	C. Rühle i. L.	org or harm or pf. Ed. Scholz	CHAL (1911)
2106	Fink, F.		Da liegt was in der Luft "Ganze Welt steckt d'Schädeln z'samm"		Unspec.	Doblinger		CHAL (1898)
2107	Fink, F.		Das kann ma' nur aus Freundschaft thuan "A G'fälligkeit, do thut ma' nöt"		Unspec.	Doblinger		CHAL (1898)
2108	Fink, F.		Das kennt ma' an Weana in d'Aeugerln schon an "Im Herzen von Weana"		Unspec.	Doblinger		CHAL (1898)
2109	Fink, F.		Es hat ein jedes Land gewiss		Unspec.	Blaha		CHAL (1906)
2110	Fink, F.		Pfiat di Gott, es hat da nöt soll'n sein "Kennst du das Lied"		Unspec.	Doblinger		CHAL (1898)
2111	Fink, F.		Seitdem wir a Platzmusik hab'n "Is früher der Weana"		Unspec.	Kratochwill		CHAL (1898)
2112	Fink, Ferd.		Freuderl, der versteht g'rad' so viel, wie des Gasbock von der Petersil "Im Rathhauspark stehn"		Unspec.	Doblinger		CHAL (1898)
2113	Fink, R.		Warum hat mancher Sänger	Op. 61	Unspec.	Glaser		CHAL (1906)
2114	Fioravanti, Vincenzo	1799-1877	Freilich wenn mit süssen Blicken		S/S	B. & H.		CHAL (1898)
2115	Fiori, Ettore	1825-1898	The walk at sunset		S/A	Boosey	Ed. Randegger	BBC (1975)
2116	Fischer, Anton	1778-1808	Eins, zwei, drei "Ein kleines Kind, wenn's reden lernt"		Unspec.	Glas		CHAL (1898)
2117	Fischer, Anton	1778-1808	Ganze Welt eine Försterei	No. 1	Unspec.	Gleissenberg		CHAL (1906)
2118	Fischer, Anton	1778-1808	Immer lustig, flott und frei	No. 3	Unspec.	Gleissenberg		CHAL (1906)
2119	Fischer, Anton	1778-1808	Zuerst da braucht der Mensch zwei Händ'	No. 3	Unspec.	Gleissenberg		CHAL (1906)
2120	Fischer & Blum		Ach Herrjee "Ein junger Beamter möcht heirathen"	No. 3	Unspec.	Fr. Dietrich		CHAL (1898)
2121	Fischer & Blum		Das hat er nicht gewusst "Ein Herr erscheint auf einem Ball"		Unspec.	O. Dietrich		CHAL (1898)
2122	Fischer & Blum		Das sollten wir einmal thun "Eine Luftnummer sich anzuseh'n"		Unspec.	O. Dietrich		CHAL (1898)

REC	COMP	DTS	TITLE	OP #	VCG	PUB	COMMENTS	SRC
2123	Fischer & Blum		Dummheit stirbt nie aus "Herr Lehmann hat ein junges Weib"	No. 2	Unspec.	Fr. Dietrich		CHAL (1898)
2124	Fischer & Blum		Durch die Blume "Ein Beamter der durchaus nicht"	No. 7	Unspec.	Fr. Dietrich		CHAL (1898)
2125	Fischer & Blum		Einbildung "Neulich kommt vom Land ein Bauer"	No. 6	Unspec.	Fr. Dietrich		CHAL (1898)
2126	Fischer & Blum		Eine vergnügte Landparthie "Vater, die Mutter"		Unspec.	O. Dietrich		CHAL (1898)
2127	Fischer & Blum		Es war ein Montag fürchterlich (Parodie)		Unspec.	Fr. Dietrich		CHAL (1898)
2128	Fischer & Blum		Es war ein Sonntag fürchterlich (Parodie)	No. 10	Unspec.	Fr. Dietrich		CHAL (1898)
2129	Fischer & Blum		Gelungene Antworten "Ein junger Mann mit wenig Bart"		Unspec.	O. Dietrich		CHAL (1898)
2130	Fischer & Blum		Menschen sind wir Alle "Ein junger Mann, dumm wie die Nacht"		Unspec.	O. Dietrich		CHAL (1898)
2131	Fischer & Blum		O unschuldiges Vergnügen ""Nem Ehemann, der schon grau"	No. 1	Unspec.	Fr. Dietrich		CHAL (1898)
2132	Fischer & Blum		Pyramidal "Primadonna kommt daher"	No. 5	Unspec.	Fr. Dietrich		CHAL (1898)
2133	Fischer & Blum		Ritter-Ballade "Auf einem Schlosse wohnt"		Unspec.	O. Dietrich		CHAL (1898)
2134	Fischer & Blum		Schöpfung der Frau "als Gott die Welt erschaffen hat"		Unspec.	O. Dietrich		CHAL (1898)
2135	Fischer & Blum		Taritititum "Stets elegant und fein"		Unspec.	Fr. Dietrich		CHAL (1898)
2136	Fischer & Blum		Unmöglich "Dass sich bei uns ein Hund verliert"	No. 8	Unspec.	Fr. Dietrich		CHAL (1898)
2137	Fischer & Blum		Vor und nach der Hochzeit "Herzensschnudel, Turteltäubchen"		Unspec.	O. Dietrich		CHAL (1898)
2138	Fischer, O. [prob. Oskar]	1870-	Alsen unser	Op. 13	S/A	Plahn i. Jauer		CHAL (1898)
2139	Fischer, O. [prob. Oskar]	1870-	Wer hat das erste Lied erdacht	III No. 1	Unspec.	C. Rühle i. L.	Arr. Necke	CHAL (1901)
2140	Fischer, Osw.		Neuer Frühling "Thu' auf die stillen Pforten"	Op. 30	Unspec.	R. & E.		CHAL (1898)
2141	Fischer, Rudolf	1855-1929	Dichterlings Reinfall "O wie so laut"		S/S	Wernthal		CHAL (1898)
2142	Fischer & Wacker		Ring hab'n ma a	No. 3	Unspec.	O. Teich		CHAL (1906)
2143	Fischer & Wacker		Über Berg und Thal rauscht a Wasserfall	No. 1	Unspec.	O. Teich		CHAL (1906)
2144	Fischer & Wacker		Wenn's giebt im Jänner Schnee	No. 2	Unspec.	O. Teich		CHAL (1906)
2145	Fischof, Robert	1856-1918	Klinge, klinge mein Pandero		S/A	Doblinger		CHAL (1898)
2146	Fisher, Howard		Look Down Dear Eyes		Unspec.	Leonard-Eng	Also solo	CVMP (1976)
2147	Fisher, J.		Ein Liebesleben	Op. 5	Unspec.	Doblinger	Cycle for 1 & 2 v.	CHAL (1901)
2148	Fiske, Roger	1910-1987	In Bethlehem Town		2 med. v.	OUP		ASR
2149	Fiske, Roger	1910-1987	Old Adam, the carrion crow		Unspec.	OUP		BBC (1975)
2150	Fiske, Roger	1910-1987	Sweet echo		Unspec.	OUP		BBC (1975)
2151	Fitzenhagen, W. Karl Friedrich	1848-1890	Stille Liebe "Meeresrauschen, sonn'ger Himmel"	Op. 57 No. 1	S/A	Kistner		CHAL (1898)

REC	COMP	DTS	TITLE	OP #	VCG	PUB	COMMENTS	SRC
2152	Fleck, Fritz	1880-1933	Du weisst, wir bleiben einsam	No. 1	high & med. v.	Schott		CHAL (1911)
2153	Fleck, Fritz	1880-1933	Mit den weissen, wandernden Wolken	No. 2	high & med v., med & low v.	Schott		CHAL (1911)
2154	Fleck, Fritz	1880-1933	Welt wird rot	No. 3	high & med v., med & low v.	Schott		CHAL (1911)
2155	Fleck, Fritz	1880-1933	Wie Sturmnacht zog unsre Wonne vorbei	No. 4	high & low v. or med. & low v.	Schott		CHAL (1911)
2156	Fontenailles, H. de		Chanson d'Avril		Unspec.	Durand		CVMP (1976)
2157	Forman, Edmund		Ta-ra-ra, boom-der-é		Unspec.	F. D. & H.		BBC (1975)
2158	Förster, Alban	1849-1916	Andacht "Durch die Welt zieht leise"	Op. 113 No. 1	Unspec.	Rud. Dietrich		CHAL (1898)
2159	Förster, Alban	1849-1916	Es rauscht der Wald noch halb im Traum		Unspec.	Musik-Woche		CHAL (1906)
2160	Förster, Alban	1849-1916	Frühlingsgruss "O Frühlingszeit, o herrliches Träumen"	Op. 113 No. 2	Unspec.	Rud. Dietrich		CHAL (1898)
2161	Förster, Alban	1849-1916	Was singet in dem Rosenbusch	Op. 113 No. 3	Unspec.	Rud. Dietrich		CHAL (1898)
2162	Förster, Rudolf	1864-1894	Du nur allein kannst mir		Unspec.	Kiener i. Stuttg.		CHAL (1898)
2163	Förster, Rudolf	1864-1894	Erste Lied "Wer hat das erste Lied erdacht"	Op. 206	Unspec.	Rühle & H.		CHAL (1898)
2164	Förster, Rudolf	1864-1894	Unser Genius "Was ist's, was alle Glocken klingen"	Op. 23	Unspec.	Thiemer		CHAL (1898)
2165	Forsyth, Josephine		Lord's Prayer, The		S/A	G. Schirm.	pf or org accomp. Woman comp. In catalogue page "Sacred Vocal Duets" of G. Schirmer, Inc. NY (no date)	MSN
2166	Foster, Myles Birket	1851-1922	Eye hath not seen, nor ear heard		high & low v.	Church	In anthology "Sacred Duets A Collection of Two-Part Songs by the Best Composers" Vol. 2. Compi. & ed. W. Shakespeare. Pub. 1907.	MSN
2167	Foster, Myles Birket	1851-1922	If ye then be risen with Christ		high & low v.	Church	In anthology "Sacred Duets A Collection of Two-Part Songs by the Best Composers" Vol. 2. Compi. & ed. W. Shakespeare. Pub. 1907.	MSN
2168	Foster, Myles Birket	1851-1922	Is it nothing to you?		high & low v.	Church	In anthology "Sacred Duets A Collection of Two-Part Songs by the Best Composers" Vol. 2. Compi. & ed. W. Shakespeare. Pub. 1907.	MSN
2169	Foster, Myles Birket	1851-1922	Night is far spent, The		high & low v.	Church	In anthology "Sacred Duets A Collection of Two-Part Songs by the Best Composers" Vol. 2. Compi. & ed. W. Shakespeare. Pub. 1907.	MSN

REC	COMP	DTS	TITLE	OP #	VCG	PUB	COMMENTS	SRC
2170	Foster, Myles Birket	1851-1922	Song Should Breath of Scents and Flowers		S/A	Ditson	In anthology "Soprano and Alto Duets" Ed. H. Kiehl. Pub. 1901.	MSN
2171	Foster, Myles Birket	1851-1922	The three fishers		S/A	Curwen		BBC (1975)
2172	Foster, Myles Birket	1851-1922	There were Shepherds		high & low v.	Church	In anthology "Sacred Duets A Collection of Two-Part Songs by the Best Composers" Vol. 2. Compi. & ed. W. Shakespeare. Pub. 1907.	MSN
2173	Foster, Myles Birket	1851-1922	Why seek ye the living among the dead?		high & low v.	Church	In anthology "Sacred Duets A Collection of Two-Part Songs by the Best Composers" Vol. 2. Compi. & ed. W. Shakespeare. Pub. 1907.	MSN
2174	Foster, Stephen Collins	1826-1864	Beautiful Dreamer		Unspec.	Allans	In anthology "Vocal Duets Collection" Vol. 1. Pub. 1992.	MSN
2175	Foster, Stephen Collins	1826-1864	Old Black Joe		2 med. v.	Century		CVMP (1976)
2176	Foster, Stephen Collins	1826-1864	The old folks at home		Unspec.	Boosey	Arr. Parker	BBC (1975)
2177	Fragerolle, George Auguste	1855-1920	Les Rosiers Blancs		Unspec.	Enoch		CVMP (1976)
2178	Franck, César	1822-1890	Aux Petits Enfants		S/A	Enoch	In "Six Duos" Pub. 1945	CVMP (1976)
2179	Franck, César	1822-1890	Aux Petits Enfants		S/A	EMB	In anthology "Duettek nöi Hangokra Zongorakísérettel" Vol. II Compi. M. Forrai. Pub. 1959.	MSN
2180	Franck, César	1822-1890	Aux Petits Enfants	No. 2	S/A or S/MS or MS/MS	Enoch	In "Six Duos" Pub. 1945	NATS-VCD
2181	Franck, César	1822-1890	L'Ange Gardien		S/A	Enoch	In "Six Duos" Pub. 1945	CVMP (1976)
2182	Franck, César	1822-1890	L'Ange Gardien	No. 1	S/A or S/MS or MS/MS	Enoch	In "Six Duos" Pub. 1945	NATS-VCD
2183	Franck, César	1822-1890	La Chanson du Vannier		S/A	Enoch	In "Six Duos" Pub. 1945	CVMP (1976)
2184	Franck, César	1822-1890	La Chanson du Vannier	No. 6	S/A or S/MS or MS/MS	Enoch	In "Six Duos" Pub. 1945	NATS-VCD
2185	Franck, César	1822-1890	La Vierge à la Creche		S/A	Enoch	In "Six Duos" Pub. 1945	CVMP (1976)
2186	Franck, César	1822-1890	La Vierge à la Crèche		Unspec.	ECS	In anthology "48 Duets Seventeenth Through Nineteenth Centuries" Ed. V. Prahl. Pub. 1941, 1970.	MSN
2187	Franck, César	1822-1890	La Vierge à la Crèche		S/A	G. Schirm.	pf or org accomp. In catalogue page "Sacred Vocal Duets" of G. Schirmer, Inc. NY (no date)	MSN
2188	Franck, César	1822-1890	La Vierge à la crèche		S/A	CVR	In catalogue "Classical Vocal Reprints Complete Catalog" Pub. 1997.	MSN
2189	Franck, César	1822-1890	La Vierge à la Crèche	No. 3	S/A or S/MS or MS/MS	Enoch	In "Six Duos" Pub. 1945	NATS-VCD

REC	COMP	DTS	TITLE	OP #	VCG	PUB	COMMENTS	SRC
2190	Franck, César	1822-1890	Les danses de Lormont		Unspec.	Boosey	Ed. Morris & Anderson	BBC (1975)
2191	Franck, César	1822-1890	Les Danses de Lormont		S/A	Enoch	In "Six Duos" Pub. 1945	CVMP (1976)
2192	Franck, César	1822-1890	Les Danses de Lormont	.	high & med. v.	Boosey	In anthology "Duet Album: Selected and edited by Viola Morris and Victoria Anderson" Pub. 1944.	MSN
2193	Franck, César	1822-1890	Les Danses de Lormont	No. 4	S/A or S/MS or MS/MS	Enoch	In "Six Duos" Pub. 1945	NATS-VCD
2194	Franck, César	1822-1890	O Salutaris		S/T or S/MS	Leduc	org accomp.	CVMP (1985)
2195	Franck, César	1822-1890	Six Duets for Equal Voices		S/A	Enoch	S/A prob. implied. Unspec. pieces.	ASR
2196	Franck, César	1822-1890	Six Duos		S/A	CVR	Collection of 6 duets. In catalogue "Classical Vocal Reprints Complete Catalog" Pub. 1997.	MSN
2197	Franck, César	1822-1890	Soleil		S/A	Enoch	In "Six Duos" Pub. 1945	CVMP (1976)
2198	Franck, César	1822-1890	Soleil	No. 5	S/A or S/MS or MS/MS	Enoch	In "Six Duos" Pub. 1945	NATS-VCD
2199	Franck, César	1822-1890	Two Children's Duets		S/A	Enoch	S/A prob. implied. Unspec. pieces.	ASR
2200	Franck, César	1822-1890	Veni Creator		S/MS	Leduc	org accomp.	CVMP (1985)
2201	Franck, Eduard	1817-1893	Frühlingsahung "Was ist das für ein reger Drang"	Op. 4 No. 6	S/A	B. & H.		CHAL (1898)
2202	Franck, Eduard	1817-1893	"Herz, mein Herz sei nicht beklommen"	Op. 4 No. 2	S/A	B. & H.		CHAL (1898)
2203	Franck, Eduard	1817-1893	In der Ferne "Will ruhen unter den Bäumen hier"	Op. 4 No. 1	S/A	B. & H.		CHAL (1898)
2204	Franck, Eduard	1817-1893	Morgenlied "Noch ahnt man kaum der Sonne Licht"	Op. 4 No. 4	S/A	B. & H.		CHAL (1898)
2205	Franck, Eduard	1817-1893	Ungenannten "Auf eines Berges Gipfel"	Op. 4 No. 5	S/A	B. & H.		CHAL (1898)
2206	Franck, Eduard	1817-1893	Vevey "Blauer Himmel, balue Wogen"	Op. 4 No. 3	S/A	B. & H.		CHAL (1898)
2207	Francke, W.		Na denn man 'rin in's Vergnügen "Zwei Freunde woll'n nach Hause geh'n"		Unspec.	P. Fischer i. Berl.		CHAL (1898)
2208	Francke, W.		Zwei Freunde woll'n nach Hause wandern		Unspec.	P. Fischer i. Berl.		CHAL (1901)
2209	Franco, Johan	1908-1988	Two Children's Duets		S/A	ACA	acap.	ASR
2210	Frank, Chr.		Frau Basen Gespräch "Frau Nachbarin, Frau Nachbarin"		Unspec.	Edm. Stoll		CHAL (1898)

REC	COMP	DTS	TITLE	OP #	VCG	PUB	COMMENTS	SRC
2211	Frank, Ernst	1847-1889	Ave sanctissima		2 female v.	Doblinger		CHAL (1898)
2212	Frank, Ernst	1847-1889	Blond Gretchen hat Lieschen gebeten	Op. 14 No. 9	S/A	Kistner		CHAL (1898)
2213	Frank, Ernst	1847-1889	Blond Gretchen hat Lieschen gebeten	Op. 14 No. 9	S/A	Kistner	In Collection "16 Duettinen aus 'Am Fenster' in Bildern und Versen von Kate Greenaway für Sopran und Alt"	MSN
2214	Frank, Ernst	1847-1889	Der Mai ist gekommen	Op. 14 No. 3	S/A	Kistner	In Collection "16 Duettinen aus 'Am Fenster' in Bildern und Versen von Kate Greenaway für Sopran und Alt"	MSN
2215	Frank, Ernst	1847-1889	Drei Kinderchen aus dem Fenster sehn	Op. 16 No. 1	S/A	Kistner		CHAL (1898)
2216	Frank, Ernst	1847-1889	Drei süsse kleine Dirnen	Op. 14 No. 10	S/A	Kistner		CHAL (1898)
2217	Frank, Ernst	1847-1889	Drei süsse kleine Dirnen sassen auf dem Zaun	Op. 14 No. 10	S/A	Kistner	In Collection "16 Duettinen aus 'Am Fenster' in Bildern und Versen von Kate Greenaway für Sopran und Alt"	MSN
2218	Frank, Ernst	1847-1889	Ein Liedchen von der Fliege "Sum, sum, sum, sum"	Op. 21 No. 3	Unspec.	Kistner		CHAL (1898)
2219	Frank, Ernst	1847-1889	Erst kommt die braune Ursala	Op. 14 No. 5	S/A	Kistner		CHAL (1898)
2220	Frank, Ernst	1847-1889	Erst kommt die braune Ursula	Op. 14 No. 5	S/A	Kistner	In Collection "16 Duettinen aus 'Am Fenster' in Bildern und Versen von Kate Greenaway für Sopran und Alt"	MSN
2221	Frank, Ernst	1847-1889	Fang mein süsses Herzens kindchen	Op. 14 No. 15	S/A	Kistner	In Collection "16 Duettinen aus 'Am Fenster' in Bildern und Versen von Kate Greenaway für Sopran und Alt"	MSN
2222	Frank, Ernst	1847-1889	Fang' mein süsses Herzenskindchen	Op. 14 No. 15	S/A	Kistner		CHAL (1898)
2223	Frank, Ernst	1847-1889	Freibeuter "Mei Haus hatke Thür"	Op. 5 No. 8	2 female v.	Doblinger		CHAL (1898)
2224	Frank, Ernst	1847-1889	Frühlingsahnung "Was ist das für ein reger Drang"	Op. 4 No. 6	S/A	B. & H.	In anth. "Zweistim. Lied. f. Sop. u. Altstimme mit Klavierbegleitung f. den Haus- u. Schulgebrauch v. H. M. Schletterer" 3 vols.	MSN
2225	Frank, Ernst	1847-1889	Gleich und Gleich "Ein Blumenglöckchen vom Boden hervor (empor)"	Op. 5 No. 2	2 female v.	Doblinger		CHAL (1898)
2226	Frank, Ernst	1847-1889	Guten Tag, guten Tag Frau Gevatterin	Op. 14 No. 8	S/A	Kistner		CHAL (1898)
2227	Frank, Ernst	1847-1889	Guten Tag, guten Tag, Frau Gevatterin	Op. 14 No. 8	S/A	Kistner	In Collection "16 Duettinen aus 'Am Fenster' in Bildern und Versen von Kate Greenaway für Sopran und Alt"	MSN
2228	Frank, Ernst	1847-1889	Hänschen ist führwahr zu dumm	Op. 14 No. 11	S/A	Kistner		CHAL (1898)

REC	COMP	DTS	TITLE	OP #	VCG	PUB	COMMENTS	SRC
2229	Frank, Ernst	1847-1889	Hänschen ist fürwahr zu dumm	Op. 14 No. 11	S/A	Kistner	In Collection "16 Duettinen aus 'Am Fenster' in Bildern und Versen von Kate Greenaway für Sopran und Alt"	MSN
2230	Frank, Ernst	1847-1889	Hier ist der Knecht Ruprecht	Op. 14 No. 12	S/A	Kistner		CHAL (1898)
2231	Frank, Ernst	1847-1889	Hier ist der Knecht Ruprecht	Op. 14 No. 12	S/A	Kistner	In Collection "16 Duettinen aus 'Am Fenster' in Bildern und Versen von Kate Greenaway für Sopran und Alt"	MSN
2232	Frank, Ernst	1847-1889	Lieb Kindchen schau' nicht in die Sonne hinein	Op. 14 No. 2	S/A	Kistner	In Collection "16 Duettinen aus 'Am Fenster' in Bildern und Versen von Kate Greenaway für Sopran und Alt"	MSN
2233	Frank, Ernst	1847-1889	Lieb Kindchen shau' nicht	Op. 14 No. 2	S/A	Kistner	Pub. 1879	CHAL (1898)
2234	Frank, Ernst	1847-1889	"Mai ist gekommen, da wollen wir uns freu'n"	Op. 14 No. 3	S/A	Kistner	Pub. 1879	CHAL (1898)
2235	Frank, Ernst	1847-1889	Mariechen sitzt sinnend	Op. 14 No. 16	S/A	Kistner	Pub. 1879	CHAL (1898)
2236	Frank, Ernst	1847-1889	Mariechen sitzt sinnend unter dem Baum	Op. 14 No. 16	S/A	Kistner	In Collection "16 Duettinen aus 'Am Fenster' in Bildern und Versen von Kate Greenaway für Sopran und Alt"	MSN
2237	Frank, Ernst	1847-1889	März "Es ist ein Schnee gefallen"	Op. 5 No. 1	2 female v.	B. & H.	Pub. 1872	CHAL (1898)
2238	Frank, Ernst	1847-1889	Mein Schwesterchen zieh' ich	Op. 14 No. 14	S/A	Kistner	Pub. 1879	CHAL (1898)
2239	Frank, Ernst	1847-1889	Mein Schwesterchen zieh' ich Strass' auf und Strass' ab	Op. 14 No. 14	S/A	Kistner	In Collection "16 Duettinen aus 'Am Fenster' in Bildern und Versen von Kate Greenaway für Sopran und Alt"	MSN
2240	Frank, Ernst	1847-1889	Mitzikatz "Mitzikatz sitzt in der Eck'"	Op. 21 No. 1	Unspec.	Kistner	Pub. 1887	CHAL (1898)
2241	Frank, Ernst	1847-1889	Morgenlied "Noch ahnt man kaum der Sonne Licht"	Op. 4 No. 4	S/A	B. & H.	In anth. "Zweistim. Lied. f. Sop. u. Altstimme mit Klavierbegleitung f. den Haus- u. Schulgebrauch v. H. M. Schletterer" 3 vols.	MSN
2242	Frank, Ernst	1847-1889	Nachtgebet "Nun kommt die Nacht mit leichtem Schritt"	Op. 21 No. 5	Unspec.	Kistner	Pub. 1887	CHAL (1898)
2243	Frank, Ernst	1847-1889	Prinz Sisi und die Frau Mama	Op. 14 No. 7	S/A	Kistner	Pub. 1879	CHAL (1898)
2244	Frank, Ernst	1847-1889	Priz Sisi und die Frau Mama	Op. 14 No. 7	S/A	Kistner	In Collection "16 Duettinen aus 'Am Fenster' in Bildern und Versen von Kate Greenaway für Sopran und Alt"	MSN
2245	Frank, Ernst	1847-1889	Puppe Wiegenlied "Eia popeia mein Püppchen schlaf ein"	Op. 21 No. 7	Unspec.	Kistner	Pub. 1887	CHAL (1898)
2246	Frank, Ernst	1847-1889	Ringelreihe Rosenkranz	Op. 14 No. 13	S/A	Kistner	Pub. 1879	CHAL (1898)
2247	Frank, Ernst	1847-1889	Ringelreihe Rosenkranz	Op. 14 No. 13	S/A	Kistner	In Collection "16 Duettinen aus 'Am Fenster' in Bildern und Versen von Kate Greenaway für Sopran und Alt"	MSN

REC	COMP	DTS	TITLE	OP #	VCG	PUB	COMMENTS	SRC
2248	Frank, Ernst	1847-1889	Schlaget den Reifen	Op. 16 No. 5	S/A	Kistner	Pub. 1882	CHAL (1898)
2249	Frank, Ernst	1847-1889	Schön Tinchen und Melinchen	Op. 16 No. 2	S/A	Kistner	Pub. 1882	CHAL (1898)
2250	Frank, Ernst	1847-1889	Schweizerlied "Uf'm Bergli bin i g'sesse"	Op. 5 No. 7	2 female v.	Doblinger	Pub. 1872	CHAL (1898)
2251	Frank, Ernst	1847-1889	Sol ich singen?	Op. 14 No. 4	S/A	Kistner	In Collection "16 Duettinen aus 'Am Fenster' in Bildern und Versen von Kate Greenaway für Sopran und Alt"	MSN
2252	Frank, Ernst	1847-1889	Soll ich singen	Op. 14 No. 4	S/A	Kistner	Pub. 1879	CHAL (1898)
2253	Frank, Ernst	1847-1889	Trost in Thränen "Wie kommts, dass du so traurig bist"	Op. 5 No. 5	2 female v.	Doblinger	Pub. 1872	CHAL (1898)
2254	Frank, Ernst	1847-1889	Vöglein witt witt	Op. 21 No. 2	Unspec.	Kistner	Pub. 1887	CHAL (1898)
2255	Frank, Ernst	1847-1889	Wach auf, wach auf, mein Kind	Op. 21 No. 6	Unspec.	Kistner	Pub. 1887	CHAL (1898)
2256	Frank, Ernst	1847-1889	Wanderers Nachtlied "Der der von dem Himmel bist"	Op. 5 No. 3	2 female v.	Doblinger	Pub. 1872	CHAL (1898)
2257	Frank, Ernst	1847-1889	Wanderers Nachtlied "Über allen Gipfeln (Wipfeln) ist Ruh"	Op. 5 No. 4	2 female v.	Doblinger	Pub. 1872	CHAL (1898)
2258	Frank, Ernst	1847-1889	Was stehen die Leute dort	Op. 14 No. 6	S/A	Kistner	Pub. 1879	CHAL (1898)
2259	Frank, Ernst	1847-1889	Was stehen die Leute dort all' auf der Lauer	Op. 14 No. 6	S/A	Kistner	In Collection "16 Duettinen aus 'Am Fenster' in Bildern und Versen von Kate Greenaway für Sopran und Alt"	MSN
2260	Frank, Ernst	1847-1889	Was stehst du so lange	Op. 16 No. 4	S/A	Kistner	Pub. 1882	CHAL (1898)
2261	Frank, Ernst	1847-1889	Weh, Winter weh	Op. 16 No. 3	S/A	Kistner	Pub. 1882	CHAL (1898)
2262	Frank, Ernst	1847-1889	Wie der Frühling den bösen Winter verjagt "Didel dum, der schnee fliegt herum"	Op. 21 No. 4	Unspec.	Kistner	Pub. 1887	CHAL (1898)
2263	Frank, Ernst	1847-1889	Wir ziehen mit Jubeln und Singen hinaus"	Op. 14 No. 1	S/A	Kistner	Pub. 1879	CHAL (1898)
2264	Frank, Ernst	1847-1889	Wir ziehen mit Jubeln und Singen hinaus	Op. 14 No. 1	S/A	Kistner	In Collection "16 Duettinen aus 'Am Fenster' in Bildern und Versen von Kate Greenaway für Sopran und Alt"	MSN
2265	Frank, Ernst	1847-1889	Wonne der Wehmuth "Trocknet nicht Thränen"	Op. 5 No. 6	2 female v.	Doblinger	Pub. 1872	CHAL (1898)
2266	Franke, A.		Menagerie-Bilder "Geht man zum lieben Vieh"		Unspec.	Glas		CHAL (1898)
2267	Franke, Hermann	1834-1919	Abendgang "Sonne sank zu guter Ruh"	Op. 70 No. 8	Unspec.	R. & E.		CHAL (1898)
2268	Franke, Hermann	1834-1919	Abendlied "Sonne geht hinunter"	Op. 30 No. 9	Unspec.	R. & E.		CHAL (1898)
2269	Franke, Hermann	1834-1919	Blühende Welt "Es schweben die Wälder"	Op. 30 No. 2	Unspec.	R. & E.		CHAL (1898)
2270	Franke, Hermann	1834-1919	Der du am Sternenbogen	Op. 30 No. 10	Unspec.	R. & E.		CHAL (1898)
2271	Franke, Hermann	1834-1919	Frühlingsahung "Umfängt dein Herz auch banges Weh'"	Op. 30 No. 1	Unspec.	R. & E.		CHAL (1898)

REC	COMP	DTS	TITLE	OP #	VCG	PUB	COMMENTS	SRC
2272	Franke, Hermann	1834-1919	Frühlingsgruss "O holder Sonnenschein"	Op. 70 No. 10	Unspec.	R. & E.		CHAL (1898)
2273	Franke, Hermann	1834-1919	Frühlingslied "Hell strahlt die Frühlingssonne"	Op. 30 No. 4	Unspec.	R. & E.		CHAL (1898)
2274	Franke, Hermann	1834-1919	Gott grüsse dich, kein andrer Gruss	Op. 30 No. 7	Unspec.	R. & E.		CHAL (1898)
2275	Franke, Hermann	1834-1919	Herbstlied "Feldenwärts flog ein Vögelein"	Op. 70 No. 3	Unspec.	R. & E.		CHAL (1898)
2276	Franke, Hermann	1834-1919	Herein "O Vogelsang, o Blumenduft"	Op. 70 No. 2	Unspec.	R. & E.		CHAL (1898)
2277	Franke, Hermann	1834-1919	Kein Hälmlein wächst auf Erden	Op. 70 No. 9	Unspec.	R. & E.		CHAL (1898)
2278	Franke, Hermann	1834-1919	Maiwanderung "Himmel, wie sonnig"	Op. 30 No. 5	Unspec.	R. & E.		CHAL (1898)
2279	Franke, Hermann	1834-1919	Morgenpsalm "Es steigt von blauen Seen"	Op. 30 No. 8	Unspec.	R. & E.		CHAL (1898)
2280	Franke, Hermann	1834-1919	O sei gegrüsst		S/S	Linke i. Sorau		CHAL (1898)
2281	Franke, Hermann	1834-1919	Ostermorgen "Wacht auf und rauscht"	Op. 70 No. 1	Unspec.	R. & E.		CHAL (1898)
2282	Franke, Hermann	1834-1919	Perle des Jahres "Blau ist der Himmel"	Op. 31	Unspec.	R. & E.		CHAL (1898)
2283	Franke, Hermann	1834-1919	Stille Thal "Im schönsten Wiesengrunde"	Op. 70 No. 5	Unspec.	R. & E.		CHAL (1898)
2284	Franke, Hermann	1834-1919	Verzage nicht	Op. 30 No. 3	Unspec.	R. & E.		CHAL (1898)
2285	Franke, Hermann	1834-1919	Von Innen "Wie die Lerche möcht ich sein"	Op. 30 No. 6	Unspec.	R. & E.		CHAL (1898)
2286	Franke, Hermann	1834-1919	Waldesfrieden "Im Wald ist Frieden"	Op. 70 No. 6	Unspec.	R. & E.		CHAL (1898)
2287	Franke, Hermann	1834-1919	Wie schön bist du mein Vaterland "Auf die Höhen möcht' ich steigen"	Op. 70 No. 7	Unspec.	R. & E.		CHAL (1898)
2288	Franke, Hermann	1834-1919	Wohl über Nacht "Holden Vögel sind erwacht"	Op. 70 No. 4	Unspec.	R. & E.		CHAL (1898)
2289	Frankl, A.		Ich tanz' mit dir "Ich möcht's für's ganze Leben"	Op. 98	Unspec.	P. Fischer i. Berl.		CHAL (1898)
2290	Frankl, A.		Naschkätzchen "Ein niedlich, kleines nasch'ges Ding"	Op. 97	Unspec.	P. Fischer i. Berl.		CHAL (1898)
2291	Franz, J. H.	1843-1926	Auf dem Brocken "Heller wird es schon"	Op. 19 No. 3	Unspec.	Fürstner	Pen name of H. H. Hochberg	CHAL (1898)
2292	Franz, J. H.	1843-1926	Minneweise "Wie holde Schwestern blühen"	Op. 19 No. 1	Unspec.	Fürstner	Pen name of H. H. Hochberg	CHAL (1898)
2293	Franz, J. H.	1843-1926	Zauberei der Töne "Thyrsis singt die schöne Lieder"	Op. 19 No. 2	Unspec.	Fürstner	Pen name of H. H. Hochberg	CHAL (1898)
2294	Franz, Robert	1815-1892	Let Not Your Heart Be Troubled		2 high v.	R. D. Row	org/pf acc. Eng. trans. Grmn. In anth. "Sacred Duet Masterpieces…" Vol. 3. Compi. & ed. C. Fredrickson. Pub. 1961.	MSN
2295	Franz, Robert (G. F. Handel)	1815-1892	Caro, riù amabile beltà		S/A	Kistner	Arr. of Handel duet	CHAL (1898)
2296	Franz, Robert (G. F. Handel)	1815-1892	Deh, perdona		S/A	Kistner	Arr. of Handel duet	CHAL (1898)
2297	Franz, Robert (G. F. Handel)	1815-1892	Jo t'abbaccio		S/A	Kistner	Arr. of Handel duet	CHAL (1898)
2298	Franz, Robert (G. F. Handel)	1815-1892	Langue, geme		S/A	Kistner	Arr. of Handel duet	CHAL (1898)
2299	Franz, Robert (G. F. Handel)	1815-1892	Per le porte de tormento		S/A	Kistner	Arr. of Handel duet	CHAL (1898)

REC	COMP	DTS	TITLE	OP #	VCG	PUB	COMMENTS	SRC
2300	Franz, Robert (G. F. Handel)	1815-1892	Ricordati mio ben		S/A	Kistner	Arr. of Handel duet	CHAL (1898)
2301	Franz, Robert (G. F. Handel)	1815-1892	Se teco vive il cor		S/S	Kistner	Arr. of Handel duet	CHAL (1898)
2302	Franz, Robert (G. F. Handel)	1815-1892	Seid gewiss, dass der Herr unser Gott"		Unspec.	Leuckart	Arr. of Handel duet	CHAL (1898)
2303	Franz, Robert (G. F. Handel)	1815-1892	Teneri affetti il cor s'abbandoni		S/A	Kistner	Arr. of Handel duet	CHAL (1898)
2304	Franz, Robert (G. F. Handel)	1815-1892	Va, speme infida, pur		S/S	Kistner	Arr. of Handel duet	CHAL (1898)
2305	Franz, Robert (G. F. Handel)	1815-1892	Vivo in te		S/A	Kistner	Arr. of Handel duet	CHAL (1898)
2306	Franz, W.		Beiden Schnupfer "Schnupf-tabak ist in der Welt"	Op. 159 No. b	Unspec.	Weber i. Cöln		CHAL (1898)
2307	Franz, W.		Zwei Rauscher "Morgens wann ich fröh opstann"		Unspec.	Weber i. Cöln		CHAL (1898)
2308	Fraser		Love will Find a Way		Unspec.	Allans	Also solo	CVMP (1976)
2309	Freisinger, L.		O Dirndle tief drunt im Thal "Schöne alte Kärtnerlied"		Unspec.	Kratochwill		CHAL (1898)
2310	Freisler, C.		Steht man in d' Fruah		Unspec.	Tandler		CHAL (1906)
2311	Freisler, C.		Zum Heurig'n fahr'n ma alle	Op. 15	Unspec.	Robitschek		CHAL (1906)
2312	Frenkel, R.		Wer 'nem Weib in voller Schönheit	Op. 74	Unspec.	O. Teich		CHAL (1901)
2313	Frenkel-Norden, R.		Ach wie rühmt Homer und Horaz	Op. 235	2 female v.	Gust. Richter		CHAL (1911)
2314	Frenkel-Norden, R.		Ein schön'res Paar, wie wir fürwahr		Unspec.	O. Dietrich		CHAL (1906)
2315	Frenkel-Norden, R.		Lustig bummeln wir durch's Leben		Unspec.	O. Dietrich		CHAL (1906)
2316	Frenkel-Norden, R.		Wandern, wandern, immer wandern		2 female v.	G. Richter i. L.		CHAL (1911)
2317	Frenkel-Norden, R.		Wir winden dir den Jung-fernkranz "Humoristisch"	Op. 234	2 female v.	Gust. Rich-ter i. L.		CHAL (1911)
2318	Freudenberg, Wilhelm	1838-1928	Dulde, gedulde dich fein	Op. 24 No. 4	S/A	Kahnt		CHAL (1898)
2319	Freudenberg, Wilhelm	1838-1928	Einladung "Erde orangt als Frühlingsbraut"	Op. 18 No. 1	S/A	R. & P.		CHAL (1898)
2320	Freudenberg, Wilhelm	1838-1928	Geduld du kleine Knospe	Op. 24 No. 1	S/A	Kahnt		CHAL (1898)
2321	Freudenberg, Wilhelm	1838-1928	Glücksvogel "Es singt ein Vogel in dem Hain"	Op. 24 No. 2	S/A	Kahnt		CHAL (1898)
2322	Freudenberg, Wilhelm	1838-1928	In der Heimath "Es ist ein tiefes Thal"	Op. 18 No. 2	S/A	R. & P.		CHAL (1898)
2323	Freudenberg, Wilhelm	1838-1928	Könnt' ich je zu düster sein "Ich schlich umber betrübt"	Op. 24 No. 3	S/A	Kahnt		CHAL (1898)
2324	Freudenberg, Wilhelm	1838-1928	Serenade "Du ruhest unter dem Lindenbach"	Op. 18 No. 3	S/A	R. & P.		CHAL (1898)
2325	Freudenberg, Wilhelm	1838-1928	Wie ist so schön "Wohl ist sie schön"	Op. 32 No. 1	S/A	Luckhardt		CHAL (1898)
2326	Freudenberg, Wilhelm	1838-1928	Zweigesang "Im Flieder-busch ein Vöglein sass"	Op. 32 No. 2	S/A	Leuckart		CHAL (1898)
2327	Frey, Martin	1872-	Dort drunten im Tale läufts Wasser so trüb	Op. 30 No. 2	S/B or S/MS	Steingräber		CHAL (1911)
2328	Frey, Martin	1872-	Du Dirndl, du nett's	Op. 30 No. 5	A/T or A/S	Steingräber		CHAL (1911)
2329	Frey, Martin	1872-	Hudel, die Trudel	Op. 30 No. 3	S/T or S/S	Steingräber		CHAL (1911)

REC	COMP	DTS	TITLE	OP #	VCG	PUB	COMMENTS	SRC
2330	Frey, Martin	1872-	Ich weiss nicht, wie mir's ist	Op. 30 No. 6	S/Br or S/MS	Steingräber		CHAL (1911)
2331	Frey, Martin	1872-	Tanz, Püppchen, tanz	Op. 18	Unspec.	Grünunger		CHAL (1906)
2332	Fricke, Richard	1877-	Abendlich schon rauscht der Wald	Op. 22 No. 1	2 female v.	Bratfisch		CHAL (1911)
2333	Fricke, Richard	1877-	Ein Jäger längs dem Weiher ging	Op. 40 No. 1	Unspec.	Bratfisch		CHAL (1911)
2334	Fricke, Richard	1877-	Es ist ein Reihen geschlungen	Op. 22 No. 3	2 female v.	Bratfisch		CHAL (1911)
2335	Fricke, Richard	1877-	Luut Matten de Has'	Op. 40 No. 2	Unspec.	Bratfisch		CHAL (1911)
2336	Fricke, Richard	1877-	Wie geheimes Flüstern	Op. 22 No. 2	2 female v.	Bratfisch		CHAL (1911)
2337	Friedland, A.		Im frühlingsgrünen Eichenhain	No. 1	S/MS	Leichssen-ring		CHAL (1906)
2338	Friedland, A.		Lieb' um Liebe, Stund' um Stunde	No. 3	S/MS	Leichssen-ring		CHAL (1906)
2339	Friedland, A.		Süss sind die Laute all'	No. 2	S/MS	Leichssen-ring		CHAL (1906)
2340	Friedrich, R.		Aus fernem Land, vom Meeresstrand	Op. 29 No. 2	S/A	Rud. Dietrich		CHAL (1911)
2341	Friedrich, R.		Heil'ge Nacht auf Engelsschwingen	Op. 29 No. 1	S/A	Rud. Dietrich		CHAL (1911)
2342	Friedrich, R.		Kalter Nordwind brauset	Op. 29 No. 3	S/A	Rud. Dietrich		CHAL (1911)
2343	Friml, Rudolf	1879-1972	Indian Love Call		Unspec.	Warner	pf? accomp. unspec.	CVMP (1985)
2344	Fritzsch, Ernst Wilhelm	1840-1902	Bekränzte Thüren winken	Op. 39	S/A or S/T	Bachmann		CHAL (1898)
2345	Fröhlich, C.		Hereinspaziert "Hasen-haide ist wohl doch"	No. 3	Unspec.	Rathke		CHAL (1898)
2346	Fröhlich, C.		Monats-Klender "Am Ersten sah er sie"	No. 1	Unspec.	Rathke		CHAL (1898)
2347	Fröhlich, C.		Wien-Berlin "Jetzt ist ein schönes Land bekannt"	No. 2	Unspec.	Rathke		CHAL (1898)
2348	Fröhlich, Ernst	1852-1910	Gehet in seinen Thoren ein	No. 2	S/A	Chal.		CHAL (1898)
2349	Fröhlich, Ernst	1852-1910	Jauchzet dem Hernn	No. 1	S/A	Chal.		CHAL (1898)
2350	Fromberg, G.		Gurre, gurre im grünen Laube	Op. 4	S/A	Schlesinger		CHAL (1906)
2351	Fromm, Karl Josef	1873-1923	Da san wir scho "Marsch-Duett"		Unspec.	Eberle		CHAL (1901)
2352	Fromm, Karl Josef	1873-1923	Wart', ich zeig' dir's, wilder Mann		Unspec.	Bosworth		CHAL (1906)
2353	Frommel, Otto	d. 1930	Meine Mutter hat's gewollt		S/A or T/Br	Sommer-meyer		CHAL (1911)
2354	Fuchs, L.		In Blumenduft und Blüth-enschnee "wenn dich ein Frühlingsgruss ereilt"	Op. 12	Unspec.	Haushahn		CHAL (1898)
2355	Fuchs, Robert	1847-1927	Aehren nur noch nicken	Op. 73 No. 4	S/A	Robitschek		CHAL (1906)
2356	Fuchs, Robert	1847-1927	Deine süssen, süssen Schauer	Op. 73 No. 1	S/A	Robitschek		CHAL (1906)
2357	Fuchs, Robert	1847-1927	Fechten ist verboten	Op. 73 No. 6	S/A	Robitschek		CHAL (1906)
2358	Fuchs, Robert	1847-1927	Ging unter dichten Zweigen	Op. 73 No. 3	S/A	Robitschek		CHAL (1906)
2359	Fuchs, Robert	1847-1927	Läuten kaum die Maienglocken	Op. 73 No. 5	S/A	Robitschek		CHAL (1906)

REC	COMP	DTS	TITLE	OP #	VCG	PUB	COMMENTS	SRC
2360	Fuchs, Robert	1847-1927	Luft ist still	Op. 73 No. 2	S/A	Robitschek		CHAL (1906)
2361	Fuentes, Laureano	19th C.	Curucucú "Cancion habanera"		Unspec.	Wagner & Levien		CHAL (1898)
2362	Fuhrmeister, Fritz	1862-	Es pirscht im Wald alleine		Unspec.	Kaun		CHAL (1898)
2363	Gabriel, Mary Ann Virginia	1825-1877	O mayst thou dream of me		Unspec.	Boosey	Eng. woman comp.	BBC (1975)
2364	Gabriel, Mary Ann Virginia	1825-1877	Yet once again		Unspec.	Boosey	Eng. woman comp.	BBC (1975)
2365	Gabussi, C. M.		Fisherman, The		high & low v.	Hinds, Hayden & Eldredge	In anthology "The Most Popular Vocal Duets" Ed. Dr. E. J. Biedermann. Pub. 1914.	MSN
2366	Gabussi, Vincent	1800-1846	Bruna Gondoletta		Unspec.	Cranz		CHAL (1898)
2367	Gabussi, Vincent	1800-1846	Calabraise "Seht die Calabraise (Colla laterna)		S/S	Cranz, Schlesinger		CHAL (1898)
2368	Gabussi, Vincent	1800-1846	Chi ha ragine	No. 10	Unspec.	Cranz		CHAL (1898)
2369	Gabussi, Vincent	1800-1846	Colomba	No. 3	Unspec.	Cranz		CHAL (1898)
2370	Gabussi, Vincent	1800-1846	Consiglio	No. 11	Unspec.	Cranz		CHAL (1898)
2371	Gabussi, Vincent	1800-1846	Contadini di Siena	No. 8	Unspec.	Cranz		CHAL (1898)
2372	Gabussi, Vincent	1800-1846	Contrabandiere	No. 9	Unspec.	Cranz		CHAL (1898)
2373	Gabussi, Vincent	1800-1846	Duolo d'amore	No. 2	Unspec.	Cranz		CHAL (1898)
2374	Gabussi, Vincent	1800-1846	Einsiedler und die Pilgerin "Pilgerin mit den blassen Wangen"		S/A	Schott		CHAL (1898)
2375	Gabussi, Vincent	1800-1846	Getilgte Schuld		S/S	Schott		CHAL (1898)
2376	Gabussi, Vincent	1800-1846	Hab' Erbamen, sieh' meine Leiden		S/A	Schott		CHAL (1898)
2377	Gabussi, Vincent	1800-1846	I Pescatori		S/A or T/B	G. Schirm.	In catalogue page "Favorite French and Italian Vocal Duets" of G. Schirmer, Inc. NY (no date)	MSN
2378	Gabussi, Vincent	1800-1846	Kreuzfahrer Frauen "Viel Monden sind vergangen"		S/S	Schott		CHAL (1898)
2379	Gabussi, Vincent	1800-1846	La Calabrese		S/A	G. Schirm.	In catalogue page "Favorite French and Italian Vocal Duets" of G. Schirmer, Inc. NY (no date)	MSN
2380	Gabussi, Vincent	1800-1846	Liebesgöttin "Steige zum Erdenthale"		S/S	Schott		CHAL (1898)
2381	Gabussi, Vincent	1800-1846	Mode "Ihr jungen, schönen Wittwen"	No. 5	Unspec.	Cranz		CHAL (1898)
2382	Gabussi, Vincent	1800-1846	Ninfe misteriosa	No. 7	Unspec.	Cranz		CHAL (1898)
2383	Gabussi, Vincent	1800-1846	O cara immagine		S/A	G. Schirm.	In catalogue page "Favorite French and Italian Vocal Duets" of G. Schirmer, Inc. NY (no date)	MSN
2384	Gabussi, Vincent	1800-1846	Rath "O Mädchen traut den Männern nicht"		Unspec.	Cranz		CHAL (1898)
2385	Gabussi, Vincent	1800-1846	Riverdere	No. 1	Unspec.	Cranz		CHAL (1898)

REC	COMP	DTS	TITLE	OP #	VCG	PUB	COMMENTS	SRC
2386	Gabussi, Vincent	1800-1846	Rizzio "Rizzio hat keine Krone"	No. 12	Unspec.	Cranz		CHAL (1898)
2387	Gabussi, Vincent	1800-1846	Ronde "Sachte, sachte, leise, leise"	No. 6	Unspec.	Cranz		CHAL (1898)
2388	Gabussi, Vincent	1800-1846	The magic lantern		S/S	Boosey	Ed. Randegger. Trans. It.	BBC (1975)
2389	Gabussi, Vincent	1800-1846	Zeit "Sieh, wie die Rose blühet"	No. 4	Unspec.	Cranz		CHAL (1898)
2390	Gabussi, Vincent	1800-1846	Zingare		S/A	Schott		CHAL (1898)
2391	Gade, Niels Wilhelm	1817-1890	Abendreih'n	Op. 9 No. 2	S/S or S/MS or MS/MS	B. & H., G. Schirm.	In "Neun Lieder (im Volks-ton) für zwei Sopranstim-men" pub. 1889. Also pub. G. Schirm., 1889.	NATS-VCD
2392	Gade, Niels Wilhelm	1817-1890	Abendreihn "Guten Abend lieber Mondenschein"	Op. 9 No. 2	S/S	B. & H.		CHAL (1898)
2393	Gade, Niels Wilhelm	1817-1890	Das Zigeunermädchen	Op. 9 No. 8	S/S or S/MS or MS/MS	B. & H., G. Schirm.	In "Neun Lieder (im Volks-ton) für zwei Sopranstim-men" pub. 1889. Also pub. G. Schirm., 1889.	NATS-VCD
2394	Gade, Niels Wilhelm	1817-1890	Die Nachtigall		S/S or S/MS or MS/MS	G. Schirm.	In "Ten Vocal Duets" Works of N. W. Gade. Pub. 1889.	NATS-VCD
2395	Gade, Niels Wilhelm	1817-1890	Frühlingsgruss	Op. 9 No. 1	S/A	B. & H.	In anthology "Zwei-stimmige Lieder für Sopran und Altstimme mit Klaviergleitung für den Haus- und Schulgebrauch"	MSN
2396	Gade, Niels Wilhelm	1817-1890	Frühlingsgruss	Op. 9 No. 1	S/S or S/MS or MS/MS	B. & H., G. Schirm.	In "Neun Lieder (im Volks-ton) für zwei Sopranstim-men" pub. 1889. Also pub. G. Schirm., 1889.	NATS-VCD
2397	Gade, Niels Wilhelm	1817-1890	Frühlingsgruss "Leise zieht durch mein Gemüht"	Op. 9 No. 1	S/A	B. & H.	In anth. "Zweistim. Lied. f. Sop. u. Altstimme mit Klavierbegleitung f. den Haus- u. Schulgebrauch v. H. M. Schletterer" 3 vols.	MSN
2398	Gade, Niels Wilhelm	1817-1890	Haidenröslein "Sah ein Knab' ein Röslein stehn"	Op. 9 No. 6	S/S	B. & H.		CHAL (1898)
2399	Gade, Niels Wilhelm	1817-1890	Heidenröslein	Op. 9 No. 6	S/S or S/MS or MS/MS	B. & H., G. Schirm.	In "Neun Lieder (im Volks-ton) für zwei Sopranstim-men" pub. 1889. Also pub. G. Schirm., 1889.	NATS-VCD
2400	Gade, Niels Wilhelm	1817-1890	Klinge, klinge mein Pandero	Op. 9 No. 8	S/S	B. & H.		CHAL (1898)
2401	Gade, Niels Wilhelm	1817-1890	Leise zieht durch mein Gemüth	Op. 9 No. 1	S/S	B. & H.		CHAL (1898)
2402	Gade, Niels Wilhelm	1817-1890	Maifeier	Op. 9 No. 9	S/S or S/MS or MS/MS	B. & H., G. Schirm.	In "Neun Lieder (im Volks-ton) für zwei Sopranstim-men" pub. 1889. Also pub. G. Schirm., 1889.	NATS-VCD
2403	Gade, Niels Wilhelm	1817-1890	Maifeier "Ein Kuckuck hier, sein Buhle"	Op. 9 No. 9	S/S	B. & H.		CHAL (1898)
2404	Gade, Niels Wilhelm	1817-1890	Mein Herz ist im Hochland	Op. 9 No. 3	S/S	B. & H.		CHAL (1898)
2405	Gade, Niels Wilhelm	1817-1890	Mein Herz ist im Hochland	Op. 9 No. 3	S/A	B. & H.	In anth. "Zweistim. Lied. f. Sop. u. Altstimme mit Klavierbegleitung f. den Haus- u. Schulgebrauch v. H. M. Schletterer" 3 vols.	MSN

REC	COMP	DTS	TITLE	OP #	VCG	PUB	COMMENTS	SRC
2406	Gade, Niels Wilhelm	1817-1890	Mein Herz ist im Hochland	Op. 9 No. 3	S/A	B. & H.	In anthology "Zweistimmige Lieder für Sopran und Altstimme mit Klavierbegleitung für den Haus- und Schulgebrauch"	MSN
2407	Gade, Niels Wilhelm	1817-1890	Mein Herz ist im Hochland	Op. 9 No. 3	S/S or S/MS or MS/MS	B. & H., G. Schirm.	In "Neun Lieder (im Volkston) für zwei Sopranstimmen" pub. 1889. Also pub. G. Schirmer, 1889.	NATS-VCD
2408	Gade, Niels Wilhelm	1817-1890	Nachtigall "Vom fernen Süd' komm' ich"		S/A	Kahnt		CHAL (1898)
2409	Gade, Niels Wilhelm	1817-1890	Nattergalen		S/S	Hansen		CHAL (1898)
2410	Gade, Niels Wilhelm	1817-1890	Nelken wind' ich Jasmin	Op. 9 No. 7	S/S	B. & H.		CHAL (1898)
2411	Gade, Niels Wilhelm	1817-1890	O, hush thee, my baby (Lullaby)		Unspec.	ECS	In anthology "48 Duets Seventeenth Through Nineteenth Centuries" Ed. V. Prahl. Pub. 1941, 1970.	MSN
2412	Gade, Niels Wilhelm	1817-1890	Reiselied	Op. 9 No. 5	S/S or S/MS or MS/MS	B. & H., G. Schirm.	In "Neun Lieder (im Volkston) für zwei Sopranstimmen" pub. 1889. Also pub. G. Schirmer, 1889.	NATS-VCD
2413	Gade, Niels Wilhelm	1817-1890	Reiselied "Durch Feld und Buchenhallen"	Op. 9 No. 5	S/S	B. & H.		CHAL (1898)
2414	Gade, Niels Wilhelm	1817-1890	Reiselied "Durch Feld und Buchenhallen"	Op. 9 No. 5	S/A	B. & H.	In anth. "Zweistim. Lied. f. Sop. u. Altstimme mit Klavierbegleitung f. den Haus- u. Schulgebrauch v. H. M. Schletterer" 3 vols.	MSN
2415	Gade, Niels Wilhelm	1817-1890	Rose-bud in the heather		Unspec.	ECS	Eng. trans Grmn. In anthology "48 Duets Seventeenth Through Nineteenth Centuries" Ed. V. Prahl. Pub. 1941, 1970.	MSN
2416	Gade, Niels Wilhelm	1817-1890	Schottisches Wiegenlied	Op. 9 No. 4	S/S or S/MS or MS/MS	B. & H., G. Schirm.	In "Neun Lieder (im Volkston) für zwei Sopranstimmen" pub. 1889. Also pub. G. Schirmer, 1889.	NATS-VCD
2417	Gade, Niels Wilhelm	1817-1890	Schottisches Wiegenlied "Schlaf Söhnchen, dein Vater"	Op. 9 No. 4	S/S	B. & H.		CHAL (1898)
2418	Gade, Niels Wilhelm	1817-1890	Spanisches Lied	Op. 9 No. 7	S/S or S/MS or MS/MS	B. & H., G. Schirm.	In "Neun Lieder (im Volkston) für zwei Sopranstimmen" pub. 1889. Also pub. G. Schirmer, 1889.	NATS-VCD
2419	Gall, Jan Karol	1856-1912	Lied der Pagen "Ein Liebster und sein Mädel fein"	Op. 2	2 female v.	Leuckart		CHAL (1898)
2420	Galland, E.		Monsieur Printemps		Unspec.	Durand		CVMP (1976)
2421	Galland, E.		Monsieur Printemps		2 equal v.	Durand		ASR
2422	Gallatly, James M.		The wedding at Lavender Farm		Unspec.	A. H. & C.		BBC (1975)
2423	Gallois, Marie	19th C.	La Source		Unspec.	Durand	Fr. woman comp.	CVMP (1976)
2424	Gallois, Marie	19th C.	Les Papillons		Unspec.	Durand	Fr. woman comp.	CVMP (1976)
2425	Gambini, Carlo Andrea	1819-1865	All' Amante lontano		S/S	Ricordi		CHAL (1898)

REC	COMP	DTS	TITLE	OP #	VCG	PUB	COMMENTS	SRC
2426	Ganz, Rudolph	1877-1972	Aus den braunen Schollen springt	No. 2	S/A	Schott i. L.		CHAL (1911)
2427	Ganz, Rudolph	1877-1972	Ich hab' in kalten Wintertagen	Op. 16 No. 1	S/A	Schott		CHAL (1911)
2428	García de la Parra, Benito		Cancionereo Español		Var.	NYP Libe	Unspec. for 1-4 v.	ASR
2429	Garcia, M. [prob. Mansilla Eduardo]	20th C.	El Majo y la Maja		Unspec.	UME	Ed. Subira	CVMP (1976)
2430	Gastinel, Léon-Gustave-Cyprien	1823-1906	Automne		Unspec.	Durand		CVMP (1976)
2431	Gastinel, Léon-Gustave-Cyprien	1823-1906	Le Ruisseau		Unspec.	Durand		CVMP (1976)
2432	Gastinel, Léon-Gustave-Cyprien	1823-1906	Le Village		Unspec.	Durand		CVMP (1976)
2433	Gastinel, Léon-Gustave-Cyprien	1823-1906	Les Deux Colombes		Unspec.	Durand		CVMP (1976)
2434	Gaston-Murray, Blanche		Who's for the fields?		Unspec.	Boosey	Eng. woman comp.	BBC (1975)
2435	Gatty, Alfred Scott	1847-1918	O that we two were maying		Unspec.	Cocks		BBC (1975)
2436	Gatty, Alfred Scott	1847-1918	O That We Two were Maying		Unspec.	Leonard-Eng		CVMP (1976)
2437	Gaul, Alfred Robert	1837-1913	They shall hunger no more		2 high v.	Church	In anthology "Sacred Duets A Collection of Two-Part Songs by the Best Composers" Vol. 1. Compi. & ed. W. Shakespeare. Pub. 1907.	MSN
2438	Gebauer, H.		Deandle, ach wan' net so	Op. 5 No. 2	Unspec.	Kahnt		CHAL (1906)
2439	Gebbardt, E.		Herr bleibe bei uns, denn es will Abend werden	No. 17	Unspec.	Schergens		CHAL (1906)
2440	Geehl, Henry Ernest	1881-	For You Alone		Unspec.	Leonard-Eng	Also solo	CVMP (1976)
2441	Geehl, Henry Ernest	1881-	Island of the Purple Sea		Unspec.	Leonard-Eng		CVMP (1976)
2442	Geehl, Henry Ernest	1881-	May Time		Unspec.	Leonard-Eng		CVMP (1976)
2443	Geibel		New life		S/A	White-Smith	In catalogue page "Vocal Duetts" of White-Smith Music Pub. Co. (no date)	MSN
2444	Gembert, F.		Liebe Glöcklein "Glöcklein tönet herüber"	Op. 66 No. 2	S/MS	André		CHAL (1898)
2445	Genée, Richard Franz Friedrich	1823-1895	Ahnungsvoll beschleichts die Seele	Op. 32 No. 1	Unspec.	André		CHAL (1898)
2446	Genée, Richard Franz Friedrich	1823-1895	Böse Zungen "Kommt da nicht die Karline"	Op. 188	S/S or S/A	R. Forberg		CHAL (1898)
2447	Genée, Richard Franz Friedrich	1823-1895	Davon kann mancher was erzählen "Deutschland ist ein wunderbares Land"	Op. 134 No. 2	Unspec.	R. Forberg		CHAL (1898)
2448	Genée, Richard Franz Friedrich	1823-1895	Kuss-Duett "Es haben die Gelehrten sich"	Op. 197	S/S	Cranz		CHAL (1898)
2449	Genée, Richard Franz Friedrich	1823-1895	Müller und Schulze "2 Duette"	Op. 134	Unspec.	R. Forberg	2 duets	CHAL (1898)
2450	Genée, Richard Franz Friedrich	1823-1895	Ob ich dich jemals wiederseh	Op. 32 No. 2	Unspec.	André		CHAL (1898)
2451	Genée, Richard Franz Friedrich	1823-1895	Optimisten "'S wird schon besser gehn"	Op. 245 No. 2	Unspec.	R. Forberg		CHAL (1898)

REC	COMP	DTS	TITLE	OP #	VCG	PUB	COMMENTS	SRC
2452	Genée, Richard Franz Friedrich	1823-1895	Pessimisten "Wie ist die Zelt doch schlecht"	Op. 245 No. 1	Unspec.	R. Forberg		CHAL (1898)
2453	Genée, Richard Franz Friedrich	1823-1895	Pfui, was für schlechte Menschen "Ach was giebt es doch für schlechte Menschen"	Op. 134 No. 1	Unspec.	R. Forberg		CHAL (1898)
2454	Genée, Richard Franz Friedrich	1823-1895	Zwei Hausfrauen "Ei schönen guten Morgen"	Op. 83	S/S	R. Forberg		CHAL (1898)
2455	Georg, Priz zu Sch.-C.		B'hüt Gott, du grünes Berchtesgadner Land	Op. 2 No. 2	Unspec.	Hainauer		CHAL (1906)
2456	George, C.		Von drauss' vom Walde komm ich her		high & low v.	Bosworth		CHAL (1911)
2457	Gericke, R. v.		Im Garten "Ich poch an deiner Thüre"	Op. 6 No. 1	S/A or T/B	Annecke		CHAL (1898)
2458	Gericke, R. v.		Lied des Mädchens "Lass schlafen mich"	Op. 6 No. 2	S/A or T/B	Annecke		CHAL (1898)
2459	Gerstenberger, A.		Ach bleib bei mir und geh nicht fort	Op. 141	Unspec.	Gerstenberger		CHAL (1898)
2460	Gerstenberger, A.		Beiden Rivalinnen "Wer bist du, ich kenn' dich nicht"	Op. 165	2 female v.	O. Teich		CHAL (1898)
2461	Gerstenberger, A.		Was sich liebt, das neckt sich	Op. 157	Unspec.	Edm. Stoll		CHAL (1898)
2462	Geyer, A.		Gebet für den König "Du Gott gabst"	Op. 6	S/A	Bahn		CHAL (1898)
2463	Ghedini, Giorgio Federico	1892-1965	4 Duetti Sacri		2 female v.	Zerboni	4 sacred duets	ASR
2464	Ghedini, Giorgio Federico	1892-1965	Concerto spirituale		S/S	Zerboni		BBC (1975)
2465	Ghedini, Giorgio Federico	1892-1965	Quattro Duetti su Testi Sacri		2 female v.	Zerboni	4 sacred duets	CVMP (1976)
2466	Giesen, J.		Nein es ist doch zum Entsetzen		2 female v.	O. Dietrich		CHAL (1901)
2467	Gifford, Alexander M.		The dear little shamrock		Unspec.	Augener	Arr. of folksong	BBC (1975)
2468	Gifford, Alexander M.		The meeting of the water		Unspec.	Augener	Arr. of folksong	BBC (1975)
2469	Gilbert		Memories of the Past		S/A	White-Smith	In catalogue page "Vocal Duetts" of White-Smith Music Pub. Co. (no date)	MSN
2470	Gilbert		Petrel's cry		T/Br or S/A	White-Smith	In catalogue page "Vocal Duetts" of White-Smith Music Pub. Co. (no date)	MSN
2471	Gilbert		Rescued		T/Br or S/A	White-Smith	In catalogue page "Vocal Duetts" of White-Smith Music Pub. Co. (no date)	MSN
2472	Gilbert		Smile again my bonnie lassie		S/A	White-Smith	In catalogue page "Vocal Duetts" of White-Smith Music Pub. Co. (no date)	MSN
2473	Gilbert, Jean	1879-1942	Donnerwetter, ich bin (Sie sind) schick		Unspec.	Thalia-Theater-Verlag	Pen name of Max Winterfeld	CHAL (1911)
2474	Gilbert, Jean	1879-1942	Ich bin vom Land ein dralles Kind		Unspec.	Thalia-Theater-Verlag	Pen name of Max Winterfeld	CHAL (1911)
2475	Gilbert, Jean	1879-1942	Kommt man abends müde nach Haus		Unspec.	Thalia-Theater-Verl.	Pen name of Max Winterfeld	CHAL (1911)

REC	COMP	DTS	TITLE	OP #	VCG	PUB	COMMENTS	SRC
2476	Gimeno, P. [prob. Joaquin]	1817-1849	Ave Maria "Ave Maria gratia pleni"		Unspec.	Schott	pf or org accomp.	CHAL (1898)
2477	Girschner, Karl Friedrich Julius	1794-1860	Ave Maria stella	Op. 36 No. 4	S/S or T/T	Schott	org accomp.	CHAL (1898)
2478	Girschner, Karl Friedrich Julius	1794-1860	Stille der Nacht	Op. 28 No. 1	MS/A or T/A	Hof-meister		CHAL (1898)
2479	Girschner, Karl Friedrich Julius	1794-1860	Vergissmeinnicht	Op. 28 No. 2	MS/A or T/A	Hof-meister		CHAL (1898)
2480	Girschner, Karl Friedrich Julius	1794-1860	Wiegenlied	Op. 28 No. 3	MS/A or T/A	Hof-meister		CHAL (1898)
2481	Glaeser, Franz	1798-1869	Menageris in Krähwinkel, Die		Unspec.	Scien		CVMP (1995)
2482	Glaser, J.		Wir Beide sind Matrosen		Unspec.	H. Augustin		CHAL (1906)
2483	Glazunov, Alexander	1865-1936	Ekh tï Pesnya	Op. 80	S/A or S/MS	State Mus. Pub. (Moscow)	Translit. of Russ. In "Iz-brannïe Romansï" Pub. 1950.	NATS-VCD
2484	Glazunov, Alexander	1865-1936	Ekh ty, Pesnia [Oh You, Songs]		S/A	GMI	Translit. title of Russ. Only Cyrillic. Anth. "Izbrannye Duety Russkikh Kompozi-torov dlia peniia s forte-piano" Pub. 1948.	MSN
2485	Gleich, Ferdinand	1816-1898	Lenznacht "Leise zitternde Abdendwind"	Op. 48	Unspec.	Hoffarth		CHAL (1898)
2486	Glimes, Jean Baptiste Jules de	1814-1881	Ensemble		S/A or T/B	Schott		CHAL (1898)
2487	Glimes, Jean Baptiste Jules de	1814-1881	L'Oiseau Bleu		Unspec.	Durand		CVMP (1976)
2488	Glimes, Jean Baptiste Jules de	1814-1881	Meunière et son seigneur		Unspec.	Schott		CHAL (1898)
2489	Glinger, A.		Wir sind zwei Sänger sehr geschickt		Unspec.	Blaha		CHAL (1906)
2490	Gliniewski, W.		Ständchen "Sorgenvolle, wetterschwüle Mädchenstirne"	Op. 36	Unspec.	Riewe & Th.		CHAL (1898)
2491	Glinka, Mikhail Ivanovich	1804-1857	Ausgewählte Duette		high & med. v.	Sikorski	Unspec. pieces, Grmn. trans. Russ. Russ. lang. included.	ASR
2492	Glinka, Mikhail Ivanovich	1804-1857	Complete Works (18 Volumes)		Var.	Univ. Mus. Ed.	pf w/ & w/o inst. accomp. Unspec. pieces.	ASR
2493	Glinka, Mikhail Ivanovich	1804-1857	In my blood burns the flame of desire		Unspec.	F. Schell-enb.	Trans. Russ.	BBC (1975)
2494	Glinka, Mikhail Ivanovich	1804-1857	Lass mich allein "Wenn am Abend die Sonne sich neigt"		Unspec.	Sch. j.	Grmn. trans. Russ.	CHAL (1898)
2495	Glinka, Mikhail Ivanovich	1804-1857	Romances for Two Voices		Unspec.	Mez Kniga		CVMP (1976)
2496	Glinka, Mikhail Ivanovich	1804-1857	Romances for Two Voices		high & med. v.	Mez Kniga	Unspec. pieces	ASR
2497	Glinka, Mikhail Ivanovich	1804-1857	Vy ne pridete vnov [You Aren't Coming Again]		S/S	GMI	Translit. title of Russ. Only Cyrillic. Anth. "Izbrannye Duety Russkikh Kompozi-torov dlia peniia s forte-piano" Pub. 1948.	MSN
2498	Glover, Charles W.	1806-1863	Rose of Tralee, The		Unspec.	Allans	Irish air, arr. for two v. In anthology "Vocal Duets Col-lection" Vol. 1. Pub. 1992.	MSN
2499	Glover, Stephen	1812-1870	Angels are Watching Us		Unspec.	Brain-ard's Sons	In anthology, "Brainard's Collection of Vocal Duets from Popular Modern and Standard Composers" Pub. 1903.	MSN

REC	COMP	DTS	TITLE	OP #	VCG	PUB	COMMENTS	SRC
2500	Glover, Stephen	1812-1870	Beautiful moonlight		Unspec.	White-Smith	In catalogue page "Vocal Duetts" of White-Smith Music Pub. Co. (no date)	MSN
2501	Glover, Stephen	1812-1870	Gipsy Countess		Unspec.	White-Smith	In catalogue page "Vocal Duetts" of White-Smith Music Pub. Co. (no date)	MSN
2502	Glover, Stephen	1812-1870	Gipsy Countess, The		Unspec.	Leonard-Eng		CVMP (1976)
2503	Glover, Stephen	1812-1870	In the Starlight		Unspec.	White-Smith	In catalogue page "Vocal Duetts" of White-Smith Music Pub. Co. (no date)	MSN
2504	Glover, Stephen	1812-1870	Lily and the Rose		Unspec.	Leonard-Eng		CVMP (1976)
2505	Glover, Stephen	1812-1870	Lily and the Rose, The		Unspec.	White-Smith	In catalogue page "Vocal Duetts" of White-Smith Music Pub. Co. (no date)	MSN
2506	Glover, Stephen	1812-1870	Listen, 'Tis the Wood bird's Song		Unspec.	Brainard's Sons	In anthology "Brainard's Collection of Vocal Duets from Popular Modern and Standard Composers" Pub. 1903.	MSN
2507	Glover, Stephen	1812-1870	Murmuring sea, The		Unspec.	Bayley & Ferguson	Arr. Maxfield	BBC (1975)
2508	Glover, Stephen	1812-1870	Music and her Sister Song		Unspec.	Leonard-Eng		CVMP (1976)
2509	Glover, Stephen	1812-1870	Nightingale and the Rose		Unspec.	Leonard-Eng		CVMP (1976)
2510	Glover, Stephen	1812-1870	Slowly and softly the music should flow		Unspec.	White-Smith	In catalogue page "Vocal Duetts" of White-Smith Music Pub. Co. (no date)	MSN
2511	Glover, Stephen	1812-1870	Tell me, where do fairies dwell?		S/A	Bayley & Ferguson		BBC (1975)
2512	Glover, Stephen	1812-1870	Tell me, where is beauty found?		S/S	Bayley & Ferguson		BBC (1975)
2513	Glover, Stephen	1812-1870	Tell us, oh tell us		S/A	Bayley & Ferguson		BBC (1975)
2514	Glover, Stephen	1812-1870	Tell us, Oh Tell us, Where Shall we Find		Unspec.	Leonard-Eng		CVMP (1976)
2515	Glover, Stephen	1812-1870	Two Forest Nymphs, The		Unspec.	none listed		MSN
2516	Glover, Stephen	1812-1870	We are two forest nymphs		S/A	Bayley & Ferguson		BBC (1975)
2517	Glover, Stephen	1812-1870	What are the Wild Waves Saying?		Unspec.	Leonard-Eng		CVMP (1976)
2518	Glover, Stephen	1812-1870	What are the wild waves saying		Unspec.	White-Smith	In catalogue page "Vocal Duetts" of White-Smith Music Pub. Co. (no date)	MSN
2519	Glück, August	1852-1914	Frühlingsahnung "Wenn es wieder will Frühling werden"	Op. 6 No. 1	S/A	B. & H.		CHAL (1898)
2520	Glück, August	1852-1914	Grüss Gott du lieber Frühlingswind	Op. 6 No. 3	S/A	B. & H.		CHAL (1898)
2521	Glück, August	1852-1914	Lilien und Rosen "Lilien weiss und Rosen roth"	Op. 6 No. 5	S/A	B. & H.		CHAL (1898)
2522	Glück, August	1852-1914	Maifeier "Maienglöcklein läuten"	Op. 6 No. 6	S/A	B. & H.		CHAL (1898)
2523	Glück, August	1852-1914	März "Es ist ein Schnee gefallen"	Op. 6 No. 2	S/A	B. & H.		CHAL (1898)
2524	Glück, August	1852-1914	Wanderers Nachtlied "Über allen Gipfeln (Wipfeln) ist Ruh"	Op. 6 No. 4	S/A	B. & H.		CHAL (1898)

REC	COMP	DTS	TITLE	OP #	VCG	PUB	COMMENTS	SRC
2525	Goatley, Alma		Teasing song		Unspec.	Boosey	Eng. woman comp.	BBC (1975)
2526	Gobbaerts, Jean Louis	1835-1886	Cascatelles		Unspec.	Junne	a.k.a. Levi, Ludovic, Streabbog	CHAL (1898)
2527	Gobbaerts, Jean Louis	1835-1886	Soeurs des fauvettes		Unspec.	Junne		CHAL (1898)
2528	Godard, Benjamin	1849-1895	Cueillons les bouquets		Unspec.	Choudens		BBC (1975)
2529	Godard, Benjamin	1849-1895	Nuit d'été		Unspec.	Choudens		BBC (1975)
2530	Godard, Benjamin	1849-1895	O Thou, Who Madest the Heavens		2 high v.	R. D. Row	org or pf acc. In anth. "Sacred Duet Masterpieces…" Vol. 3. Compi. & ed. C. Fredrickson. Pub. 1961.	MSN
2531	Godfrey, Daniel	1868-1939	Chanson de Mai		Unspec.	Junne		CHAL (1898)
2532	Godfrey, Daniel	1868-1939	Souviens-toi		Unspec.	Junne		CHAL (1898)
2533	Goepfart, Karl Eduard	1859-1942	Heinzelmännchen, König und Königen	Op. 91	S/A	Siegel		CHAL (1911)
2534	Goepfart, Karl Eduard	1859-1942	Psalm 117 "Lobet den Herrn alle Heiden"	Op. 32	S/A	Kistner	org accomp.	CHAL (1898)
2535	Goepfart, Karl Eduard	1859-1942	Weine nicht "Weine nicht roth deine lieben Augen"	Op. 69	Unspec.	Leuckart		CHAL (1898)
2536	Goepfert, P.		Ach wie ist's möglich dann	Op. 3 No. 1	Unspec.	Fritzsche		CHAL (1898)
2537	Goës, C.		Deutschland, da kannst du stolz d'rauf sein "Man soll was Neues singen"	Op. 96	Unspec.	Fr. Dietrich		CHAL (1898)
2538	Goetz, W.		Mit wem, o holdes Mägdelein		Unspec.	Platt		CHAL (1911)
2539	Goetze, Karl [Götze]	1836-1887	Calm as the Night		high & low v.	Hinds, Hayden & Eldredge	Eng. trans. Grmn. In anthology "The Most Popular Vocal Duets." Ed. Dr. E. J. Biedermann. Pub. 1914.	MSN
2540	Goetze, Karl [Götze]	1836-1887	Erste Lied "Wer hat das erste Lied erdacht"	Op. 112 No. 2	S/Br or S/A	P. & M.		CHAL (1898)
2541	Goetze, Karl [Götze]	1836-1887	Es grünen und blühen die Bäume	Op. 192 No. 1	S/A	P. & M.		CHAL (1906)
2542	Goetze, Karl [Götze]	1836-1887	Es grünene und blühen die Bäume	Op. 192 No. 1	S/A	P. & M.		CHAL (1898)
2543	Goetze, Karl [Götze]	1836-1887	Gieb dich zur Ruh', du stürment Herz	Op. 192 No. 3	S/A	P. & M.		CHAL (1906)
2544	Goetze, Karl [Götze]	1836-1887	Gieb dich zur Ruh' "Gieb dich zur Ruh, du stürmisch Herz"	Op. 192 No. 3	S/A	P. & M.		CHAL (1898)
2545	Goetze, Karl [Götze]	1836-1887	Lenz auf blumigen Fluren lag	Op. 192 No. 2	S/A	P. & M.		CHAL (1898)
2546	Goetze, Karl [Götze]	1836-1887	Lenz auf blumigen Fluren lag	Op. 192 No. 2	S/A	P. & M.		CHAL (1906)
2547	Goetze, Karl [Götze]	1836-1887	O schöne eit, o sel'ge Zeit "Es war ein Sonntag hell und klar"	Op. 160	Unspec.	Fischer i. Bremen		CHAL (1898)
2548	Goetze, Karl [Götze]	1836-1887	Still wie die Nacht	Op. 112 No. 1	S/Br or S/A	P. & M.		CHAL (1898)
2549	Göhler, Karl Georg	1874-1954	Es waren drei Jungfrauen		S/Br or S/MS or A/Br	Klemm		CHAL (1911)
2550	Göhler, Karl Georg	1874-1954	Mensch hat nichts so eigen		Unspec.	Klemm	org	CHAL (1911)

REC	COMP	DTS	TITLE	OP #	VCG	PUB	COMMENTS	SRC
2551	Goldberg, William		Cricket, The		S/A	Cormorant		CVMP (1995)
2552	Goldberg, William		Evening		S/A or S/MS	Cormorant	Text by Sappho	CVMP (1995)
2553	Goldner, Wilhelm	1839-1907	Lebewohl "Morgen muss ich fort von hier"	Op. 7 No. a2	A/A	Sch. j.		CHAL (1898)
2554	Goldner, Wilhelm	1839-1907	Wehmuth "Ich kann wohl manchmal singen"	Op. 7 No. a1	A/A	Sch. j.		CHAL (1898)
2555	Goldschmidt, Adalbert von	1848-1906	Abschied "Wievel sind wir"	III No. 18	Unspec.	Chal.		CHAL (1898)
2556	Goldschmidt, Adalbert von	1848-1906	Edelknabe und die Müllerin "Wohin, wohin, schöne Müllerin"	Op. 2	Unspec.	Kratochwill		CHAL (1898)
2557	Goldschmidt, Adalbert von	1848-1906	Zweigesang "Im Flieder-busch ein Vöglein sass"		S/A	B. & H.		CHAL (1898)
2558	Göller, A.		An Bord "Wenn Sturm die Nacht durchsaust"		Unspec.	Kratochwill		CHAL (1898)
2559	Göller, A.		Dann g'fallet's uns viel besser auf der Welt "Wenn einmal die ganze Menschheit"		Unspec.	Robitschek		CHAL (1898)
2560	Göller, A.		Flick und Flock "Alles kennt uns, Gross und Klein"		Unspec.	Kratochwill		CHAL (1898)
2561	Göller, A.		Herzens-Feuerwehr "Mit kühnem Muth"		Unspec.	Kratochwill		CHAL (1898)
2562	Göller, A.		Verliebten "Uns schmeckt ka guater Bissen mehr"		Unspec.	Kratochwill		CHAL (1898)
2563	Gollmick, Karl	1796-1866	Abschied vom Dörfchen "Stilles Dorf, wo uns die Freude"	Op. 38 No. 10	Unspec.	André		CHAL (1898)
2564	Gollmick, Karl	1796-1866	An ein geliebtes Bild "Liebes Bild, du hebest"	Op. 38 No. 9	Unspec.	André		CHAL (1898)
2565	Gollmick, Karl	1796-1866	Auf ewig dein, auf ewig dein	Op. 123	S/A or T/Br	Cranz		CHAL (1898)
2566	Gollmick, Karl	1796-1866	Aufmunterung zur Freude "Wer wollte sich mit Grillen plagen"	Op. 38 No. 4	Unspec.	André		CHAL (1898)
2567	Gollmick, Karl	1796-1866	Bei einer feierlichen Geleg-enheit "Dierser Stunde schöne Weihe"	Op. 38 No. 13	Unspec.	André		CHAL (1898)
2568	Gollmick, Karl	1796-1866	Benutzung der Zeit "Brich die Rosen, wenn sie blüh'n"	Op. 38 No. 11	Unspec.	André		CHAL (1898)
2569	Gollmick, Karl	1796-1866	Erntelied "Sichel schallen, Aehren fallen"	Op. 38 No. 3	Unspec.	Andrè		CHAL (1898)
2570	Gollmick, Karl	1796-1866	Frühling "Winter schwand"	Op. 102 No. 4	Unspec.	Henkel		CHAL (1898)
2571	Gollmick, Karl	1796-1866	Mailied "Seht den Himmel wie heiter"	Op. 38 No. 8	Unspec.	André		CHAL (1898)
2572	Gollmick, Karl	1796-1866	Notturno "Bin ich in deiner Nähe"	Op. 102 No. 2	Unspec.	Henkel		CHAL (1898)
2573	Gollmick, Karl	1796-1866	Schamröthe "Was heisst das Roth"	Op. 38 No. 6	Unspec.	André		CHAL (1898)
2574	Gollmick, Karl	1796-1866	Ständchen "Still, sie schläft! nur leise"	Op. 38 No. 5	Unspec.	Andre		CHAL (1898)
2575	Gollmick, Karl	1796-1866	Unschuld "Unschuld ist vom Truge fern"	Op. 38 No. 2	Unspec.	André		CHAL (1898)
2576	Gollmick, Karl	1796-1866	Weinenden Blumen "Im Morgengolde glühten"	Op. 38 No. 1	Unspec.	André		CHAL (1898)
2577	Gollmick, Karl	1796-1866	Wenn ich ein Vöglein wär und auch zwei Flügel hätt'	Op. 102 No. 3	Unspec.	Henkel		CHAL (1898)

REC	COMP	DTS	TITLE	OP #	VCG	PUB	COMMENTS	SRC
2578	Gollmick, Karl	1796-1866	Wiegenlied "Schlaf und träume, liebes Kind"	Op. 38 No. 12	Unspec.	André		CHAL (1898)
2579	Gollmick, Karl	1796-1866	Willst du mit mir gehen	Op. 102 No. 1	Unspec.	Henkel		CHAL (1898)
2580	Goltermann, Georg	1824-1898	Ach, dass ewig hier die Liebe	Op. 18 No. 2	Unspec.	Peters		CHAL (1901)
2581	Goltermann, Georg	1824-1898	Der du von dem Himmel bist	Op. 18 No. 3	Unspec.	Peters		CHAL (1901)
2582	Goltermann, Georg	1824-1898	Frühlingsliebe	Op. 18 No. 4	Unspec.	Nagel		CHAL (1898)
2583	Goltermann, Georg	1824-1898	Herbstlied "Feldenwärts flog ein Vögelein"	Op. 8 No. 3	Unspec.	Peters		CHAL (1898)
2584	Goltermann, Georg	1824-1898	Kinderlied von den grünen Sommervögeln "Es kamen grüne Vögelein"	Op. 82	Unspec.	André		CHAL (1898)
2585	Goltermann, Georg	1824-1898	Komm zum Garten	Op. 18 No. 4	Unspec.	Peters		CHAL (1901)
2586	Goltermann, Georg	1824-1898	Mein Liebchen, wir sassen beisammen	Op. 40 No. 1	Unspec.	Peters		CHAL (1898)
2587	Goltermann, Georg	1824-1898	Nun die Schatten dunkeln	Op. 8 No. 4	Unspec.	Peters		CHAL (1898)
2588	Goltermann, Georg	1824-1898	Nur dich allein	Op. 19 No. 2	Unspec.	Nagel		CHAL (1898)
2589	Goltermann, Georg	1824-1898	Schwere Hand	Op. 19 No. 3	Unspec.	Nagel		CHAL (1898)
2590	Goltermann, Georg	1824-1898	Waldeslied	Op. 19 No. 1	Unspec.	Nagel		CHAL (1898)
2591	Goltermann, Georg	1824-1898	Wanderers Nachtlied	Op. 18 No. 3	Unspec.	Nagel		CHAL (1898)
2592	Goltermann, Georg	1824-1898	Wenn still mit seinen letzten Flammen	Op. 18 No. 1	Unspec.	Nagel		CHAL (1898)
2593	Goltermann, Georg	1824-1898	Wenn still mit seinen letzten Flammen	Op. 18 No. 1	Unspec.	Peters		CHAL (1901)
2594	Goltermann, Georg	1824-1898	Zufriedenen "Ich sass bei jener Linde"	Op. 8 No. 2	Unspec.	Peters		CHAL (1898)
2595	Gooch		Dream Faces		S/A	White-Smith	Arr. Gooch. In catalogue page "Vocal Duetts" of White-Smith Music Pub. Co. (no date)	MSN
2596	Gooch		Reuben and Rachel		Unspec.	White-Smith	In catalogue page "Vocal Duetts" of White-Smith Music Pub. Co. (no date)	MSN
2597	Goodhart, Arthur Murray	1866-	Sweet lavender		Unspec.	Curwen		BBC (1975)
2598	Gordigiani, Luigi	1806-1860	Addie, compagne mie	V No. 5	S/S	Ricordi		CHAL (1898)
2599	Gordigiani, Luigi	1806-1860	Alla selva, al prato		Unspec.	Lucca		CHAL (1898)
2600	Gordigiani, Luigi	1806-1860	Alles kehrt zurück "Was hast du Mädchen"		S/A	Schott		CHAL (1898)
2601	Gordigiani, Luigi	1806-1860	Amor se mi vuoi ben	V No. 3	S/S	Ricordi		CHAL (1898)
2602	Gordigiani, Luigi	1806-1860	Comala	No. 7	S/A	Ricordi		CHAL (1898)
2603	Gordigiani, Luigi	1806-1860	Die mir das Herz gefangen "Prachtvoll erglänzt das Morgenroth"		S/A or S/Br	Schott		CHAL (1898)
2604	Gordigiani, Luigi	1806-1860	Doppo il temporale		S/A	Ricordi		CHAL (1898)

REC	COMP	DTS	TITLE	OP #	VCG	PUB	COMMENTS	SRC
2605	Gordigiani, Luigi	1806-1860	Ein unangenehmer Gedanke "Ja wenn wir jung noch sind"		Unspec.	Schott		CHAL (1898)
2606	Gordigiani, Luigi	1806-1860	Freude "10 Duette"		Unspec.	Schott	Collection of 10 duets	CHAL (1898)
2607	Gordigiani, Luigi	1806-1860	Giovanottino dalla bella vita		S/S	Cranz		CHAL (1898)
2608	Gordigiani, Luigi	1806-1860	Giudizio	No. 7	S/A	Lucca		CHAL (1898)
2609	Gordigiani, Luigi	1806-1860	Gondelfahrt "Nacht ist so labend"		S/A or S/Br	Schott		CHAL (1898)
2610	Gordigiani, Luigi	1806-1860	Hirtenmädchen unbefangen schertz		Unspec.	Schott		CHAL (1898)
2611	Gordigiani, Luigi	1806-1860	Impazienza	No. 6	Unspec.	Ricordi		CHAL (1898)
2612	Gordigiani, Luigi	1806-1860	In Riva all' Arno		Unspec.	Ricordi		CHAL (1898)
2613	Gordigiani, Luigi	1806-1860	Könnt' ich mit Sturmesschnelle		S/A	Schott		CHAL (1898)
2614	Gordigiani, Luigi	1806-1860	Mi basta cosi		S/A	Ricordi		CHAL (1898)
2615	Gordigiani, Luigi	1806-1860	Non ti fidar	V No. 4	S/S	Ricordi		CHAL (1898)
2616	Gordigiani, Luigi	1806-1860	O valorosi che andate alla guerra	V No. 6	S/S	Ricordi		CHAL (1898)
2617	Gordigiani, Luigi	1806-1860	Piangete amori		Unspec.	Ricordi		CHAL (1898)
2618	Gordigiani, Luigi	1806-1860	Primi amori		Unspec.	Ricordi		CHAL (1898)
2619	Gordigiani, Luigi	1806-1860	Rimembranza	No. 3	S/A	Ricordi		CHAL (1898)
2620	Gordigiani, Luigi	1806-1860	Se vuol vedere	V No. 2	S/S	Ricordi		CHAL (1898)
2621	Gordigiani, Luigi	1806-1860	Sempre insieme	No. 5	S/A	Ricordi		CHAL (1898)
2622	Gordigiani, Luigi	1806-1860	Temporale		S/A	Ricordi		CHAL (1898)
2623	Gordigiani, Luigi	1806-1860	The shepherdess		S/S	Boosey	Ed. Randegger. Eng. trans. It.	BBC (1975)
2624	Gordigiani, Luigi	1806-1860	Voglio più bene ate		S/S	Cranz		CHAL (1898)
2625	Gordigiani, Luigi	1806-1860	Wenn dich dich die Sterne nicht sicher leiten		S/A	Schott		CHAL (1898)
2626	Gordigiani, Luigi	1806-1860	When silent night		S/S	Boosey	Ed. Randegger. Eng. trans. It.	BBC (1975)
2627	Gordigiani, Luigi	1806-1860	Zwei Gräber "Ich bin so schwach"		Unspec.	Schott		CHAL (1898)
2628	Gordigiani, Luigi	1806-1860	Zwei Mägdlein "Algiso, der mich liebt"		S/S	Schott		CHAL (1898)
2629	Gordon, Stanley	d. 1919	The jovial blacksmiths		Unspec.	Darvenski	Pen name of A. W. Rawlings	BBC (1975)
2630	Gorzer-Schulz, O. K. F.		Beiden Röschen Freundschaft und Liebe "Es blühen zwei Röslein"	Op. 27 No. 6	S/S	R. & P.		CHAL (1898)
2631	Gorzer-Schulz, O. K. F.		Frühlingserwachen "Was blinzelt hell"	Op. 27 No. 1	S/S	R. & P.		CHAL (1898)
2632	Gorzer-Schulz, O. K. F.		Frühlingsruf "Ich hör' 'ne wunderliche Stimme"	Op. 27 No. 4	S/S	R. & P.		CHAL (1898)
2633	Gorzer-Schulz, O. K. F.		Ich grüsse dich, o Waldesgrün	Op. 27 No. 2	S/S	R. & P.		CHAL (1898)

REC	COMP	DTS	TITLE	OP #	VCG	PUB	COMMENTS	SRC
2634	Gorzer-Schulz, O. K. F.		Lebenstrost "Auf den Schnee"	Op. 27 No. 5	S/S	R. & P.		CHAL (1898)
2635	Gorzer-Schulz, O. K. F.		Vergissmeinnicht und Rose	Op. 27 No. 3	S/S	R. & P.		CHAL (1898)
2636	Goublier, R.		Message aux hirondelles		Unspec.	Junne		CHAL (1898)
2637	Gounod, Charles	1818-1893	20 Mélodies		Var. med. v.	Lemoine	Collection of unspec. pieces. 1-2 v.	ASR
2638	Gounod, Charles	1818-1893	Arithmètique "Art de compter avec exactitude"		Unspec.	Le Beau		CHAL (1898)
2639	Gounod, Charles	1818-1893	Art de compter avec exactitude		Unspec.	Le Beau		CHAL (1901)
2640	Gounod, Charles	1818-1893	Bells That are Pealing		Unspec.	Cramer	Eng. trans. Fr.	CVMP (1976)
2641	Gounod, Charles	1818-1893	Bienheureux le coeur sincère		S/A	Lemoine		BBC (1975)
2642	Gounod, Charles	1818-1893	Chanson de la brise		S/A	Lemoine		BBC (1975)
2643	Gounod, Charles	1818-1893	Chantez noël		S/A	Fürstner Paris		CHAL (1898)
2644	Gounod, Charles	1818-1893	Chantez Noël!		S/MS or S/T	Choudens	In "Quinze Duos pour Chant et Piano" specifying S/T. Pub. 1869. Two of the pieces for unspec. v.	NATS-VCD
2645	Gounod, Charles	1818-1893	Christmas Song		2 high v.	Church	Eng. trans. Fr. In anth. "Sacred Duets A Coll. of 2-Part Songs by the Best Comps" Vol. 1. Compi. & ed. W. Shakespeare. Pub. 1907.	MSN
2646	Gounod, Charles	1818-1893	Christmas Song		S/S or T/T or S/T	Church	Eng. trans. Fr. In anthology "Sacred Duets for Two High Voices" Vol. 1 Pub. 1907	NATS-SVD
2647	Gounod, Charles	1818-1893	D'un coeur qui t'aime		S/A	Lemoine		BBC (1975)
2648	Gounod, Charles	1818-1893	D'un Coeur qui t'aime		S/S	Lemoine		CVMP (1985)
2649	Gounod, Charles	1818-1893	D'un coeur qui t'aime		S/A	G. Schirm.	pf or org accomp. In catalogue page "Sacred Vocal Duets" of G. Schirmer, Inc. NY (no date)	MSN
2650	Gounod, Charles	1818-1893	D'un coeur qui t'aime		S/A or S/MS	CVR	In catalogue "Classical Vocal Reprints Complete Catalog" Pub. 1997.	MSN
2651	Gounod, Charles	1818-1893	Ecriture "Prêtant un corps à la parole"		Unspec.	Le Beau		CHAL (1898)
2652	Gounod, Charles	1818-1893	For ever with the Lord!		S/A	G. Schirm.	Eng. trans. Fr. In anthology "Album of Sixteen Sacred Duets" No date.	MSN
2653	Gounod, Charles	1818-1893	For ever with the Lord		S/A or MS/Br	G. Schirm.	pf or org accomp. Eng. trans. Fr. In catalogue page "Sacred Vocal Duets" of G. Schirmer, Inc. NY (no date)	MSN
2654	Gounod, Charles	1818-1893	Forever with the Lord		S/A	Ditson	Eng. trans. Fr. In anthology "Choice Sacred Duets for All Voices" Pub. 1936.	MSN
2655	Gounod, Charles	1818-1893	Forever with the Lord		high & low v.	Church	Eng. trans. Fr. In anth. "Sacred Duets A Coll. of 2-Part Songs by the Best Composers" Vol. 2. Compi. & ed. W. Shakespeare. Pub. 1907.	MSN

REC	COMP	DTS	TITLE	OP #	VCG	PUB	COMMENTS	SRC
2656	Gounod, Charles	1818-1893	Forever With the Lord		S/A or A/T or S/Br	Church	Eng. trans. Fr. In anthology "Sacred Duets for High and low Voices" Vol. 2 Pub. 1907 et al.	NATS-SVD
2657	Gounod, Charles	1818-1893	Fuyons o ma Compagne!		S/MS or S/Br	Chou-dens	In "Quinze Duos pour Chant et Piano" specifying S/T. Pub. 1869. Two of the pieces for unspec. v.	NATS-VCD
2658	Gounod, Charles	1818-1893	Gentle Holy Saviour		MS/Bar or S/A	Boston	Eng. trans. Fr.	CVMP (1976)
2659	Gounod, Charles	1818-1893	Glory to Thee, My God		Unspec.	Boston	Eng. trans. Fr. Also solo	CVMP (1976)
2660	Gounod, Charles	1818-1893	Glory to Thee, My God		med. & low v.	Cramer	Eng. trans. Fr.	ASR
2661	Gounod, Charles	1818-1893	Glory to Thee, my God, this night		high & low v.	Church	Eng. trans. Fr. In anth. "Sacred Duets A Coll. of 2-Part Songs by the Best Composers" Vol. 2. Compi. & ed. W. Shakespeare. Pub. 1907.	MSN
2662	Gounod, Charles	1818-1893	Glory to Thee. my God, this night		S/A or MS/Br	G. Schirm.	pf or org accomp. Eng. trans. Fr. In catalogue page "Sacred Vocal Duets" of G. Schirmer, Inc. NY (no date)	MSN
2663	Gounod, Charles	1818-1893	Glory to Thee, My God, This Night		S/A or A/T or S/Br	Church	Eng. trans. Fr. In anth. "Sacred Duets A Coll. of 2-Part Songs by the Best Composers" Vol. 1. Compi. & ed. W. Shakespeare. Pub. 1907.	NATS-SVD
2664	Gounod, Charles	1818-1893	L'arithmétique		2 med. v.	CVR	In catalogue "Classical Vocal Reprints Complete Catalog" Pub. 1997.	MSN
2665	Gounod, Charles	1818-1893	L'Arithmétique		S/S	CVR		MSN
2666	Gounod, Charles	1818-1893	O, Divine Redeemer		high & low v.	Church	Eng. trans. Fr. In anth. "Sacred Duets A Coll. of 2-Part Songs by the Best Composers" Vol. 2. Compi. & ed. W. Shakespeare. Pub. 1907.	MSN
2667	Gounod, Charles	1818-1893	O salutaris		Unspec.	Le Beau		CHAL (1898)
2668	Gounod, Charles	1818-1893	O, that we two were maying		Unspec.	A. H. & C.	Arr. Schröter	BBC (1975)
2669	Gounod, Charles	1818-1893	Par une belle Nuit!		S/A	CVR		MSN
2670	Gounod, Charles	1818-1893	Par une belle nuit		S/A	Fürstner Paris		CHAL (1898)
2671	Gounod, Charles	1818-1893	Par une belle nuit!		S/A	CVR	In catalogue "Classical Vocal Reprints Complete Catalog" Pub. 1997.	MSN
2672	Gounod, Charles	1818-1893	Parce, domine		2 high v.	Church	Eng. trans. Fr. In anth. "Sacred Duets A Coll. of 2-Part Songs by the Best Composers" Vol. 1. Compi. & ed. W. Shakespeare. Pub. 1907.	MSN
2673	Gounod, Charles	1818-1893	Prênant un corps à la parole		Unspec.	Le Beau		CHAL (1901)
2674	Gounod, Charles	1818-1893	Repentir		S/A	G. Schirm.	In anthology "Album of Sixteen Sacred Duets" No date.	MSN
2675	Gounod, Charles	1818-1893	Repentir		S/A or MS/Br	G. Schirm.	pf or org accomp. In catalogue page "Sacred Vocal Duets" of G. Schirmer, Inc. NY (no date)	MSN

REC	COMP	DTS	TITLE	OP #	VCG	PUB	COMMENTS	SRC
2676	Gounod, Charles	1818-1893	Repentir		S/A	CVR	Also solo. In catalogue "Classical Vocal Reprints Complete Catalog" Pub. 1997.	MSN
2677	Gounod, Charles	1818-1893	Serenade		Unspec.	Allans	Eng. trans. Fr. In anthology "Vocal Duets Collection" Vol. 2. Pub. 1992.	MSN
2678	Gounod, Charles	1818-1893	Sous le feuillage		high & med. v.	CVR	In catalogue "Classical Vocal Reprints Complete Catalog" Pub. 1997.	MSN
2679	Gounod, Charles	1818-1893	Sous le Feuillage		S/MS or S/Br or S/T	Choudens	In "Quinze Duos pour Chant et Piano" specifying S/T. Pub. 1869. Two of the pieces for unspec. v.	NATS-VCD
2680	Gounod, Charles	1818-1893	Toujours à toi, Seigneur		S/MS or S/A	Leduc		ASR
2681	Gounod, Charles	1818-1893	Until the day breaks		high & low v.	Church	Arr. P. Felix. Eng. trans. Fr. In anth. "Sacr. Duets Coll. of 2-Part Songs by Best Comps" Vol. 2. Compi. & ed. W. Shakespeare. Pub. 1907.	MSN
2682	Gounod, Charles	1818-1893	Until the day breaks		high & low v.	G. Schirm.	pf or org accomp. Eng. trans. Fr. In catalogue page "Sacred Vocal Duets" of G. Schirmer, Inc. NY (no date)	MSN
2683	Gounod, Charles	1818-1893	Until the day breaks I will magnify Thee, O God		S/S or S/T or MS/A	G. Schirm.	pf or org accomp. In catalogue page "Sacred Vocal Duets" of G. Schirmer, Inc. NY (no date)	MSN
2684	Gounod, Charles	1818-1893	What grief can try me, O Lord		2 high v.	Church	Eng. trans. Fr. In anth. "Sacred Duets A Coll. of 2-Part Songs by the Best Composers" Vol. 1. Compi. & ed. W. Shakespeare. Pub. 1907.	MSN
2685	Gounod, Charles	1818-1893	What Grief Can Try Me, O Lord?		S/S or T/T or S/T	Church	Eng. trans. Fr. In anthology "Sacred Duets for Two High Voices" Vol. 1 Pub. 1907.	NATS-SVD
2686	Grabe, F.		Cohn und der Nacht-wächter "Nacht ist rabenschwarz"		Unspec.	Haus-bahn i. L.		CHAL (1898)
2687	Grabe, F.		Geburtstags kuchen "Ei sieh da, Frau Mandatar"	Op. 91	2 female v.	Haus-hahn i. M.		CHAL (1898)
2688	Grabe, F.		Herr Finke und Herr Linke "Guten Tag lieber Linke"		Unspec.	Haus-hahn i. L.		CHAL (1898)
2689	Grabe, F.		Jette und Miene "Komische scen m. Duett"	Op. 92	2 female v.	Haus-hahn i. M.		CHAL (1901)
2690	Graben-Hoffmann Gustav	1820-1900	Abendlied "Nub schlafen die Vöglein"	Op. 90 No. 3	S/A	Chal.		CHAL (1898)
2691	Graben-Hoffmann Gustav	1820-1900	Abendruhe "Über den Hügel hin"	Op. 90 No. 6	S/A	Chal.		CHAL (1898)
2692	Graben-Hoffmann Gustav	1820-1900	Armes Herz schlaf ein	Op. 90 No. 2	S/A	Chal.		CHAL (1898)
2693	Graben-Hoffmann Gustav	1820-1900	Draussen blühn die Veigelein	Op. 57	2 high or 2 low v.	Sch. & Co.		CHAL (1898)

REC	COMP	DTS	TITLE	OP #	VCG	PUB	COMMENTS	SRC
2694	Graben-Hoffmann Gustav	1820-1900	Frühlingsglaube "Linden Lüfte sind erwacht"	Op. 69	2 low v.	Rühle i. L.		CHAL (1898)
2695	Graben-Hoffmann Gustav	1820-1900	Gondellied "Mein Nachen im leichten Scherzen"	Op. 102	high & med or med. & low v.	Kistner		CHAL (1898)
2696	Graben-Hoffmann Gustav	1820-1900	I Feel Thy Angel Spirit		high & low v.	Hinds, Hayden & Eldredge	Eng. trans. Grmn. In anthology "The Most Popular Vocal Duets" Ed. Dr. E. J. Biedermann. Pub. 1914.	MSN
2697	Graben-Hoffmann Gustav	1820-1900	Ich fühle deinen Odem	Op. 39	S/A	Schlesinger		CHAL (1898)
2698	Graben-Hoffmann Gustav	1820-1900	Ich fühle deinen Odem	Op. 39	S/A or S/Br	C. Fischer	In catalogue page "Selected Vocal Duets By Favorite Composers" of Carl Fischer NY (no date)	MSN
2699	Graben-Hoffmann Gustav	1820-1900	Ich fühle deinen Odem	Op. 39	S/Br or S/A	G. Schirm.	In catalogue page "Selected Vocal Duets" of G. Schirmer, Inc. NY (no date)	MSN
2700	Graben-Hoffmann Gustav	1820-1900	Letzer Gruss "Frühlings-Boten send'"	Op. 17 No. 1	S/A or S/S	Heinr.		CHAL (1898)
2701	Graben-Hoffmann Gustav	1820-1900	Linden Lüfte sind erwacht	I No. 10	S/S	C. Rühle i. L.		CHAL (1901)
2702	Graben-Hoffmann Gustav	1820-1900	Lindengang "Welch' süsses, leises Klingen"	Op. 90 No. 1	S/A	Chal.		CHAL (1898)
2703	Graben-Hoffmann Gustav	1820-1900	Pilger der Liebe "Wir sind die Pilger treuer Liebe"	Op. 38	S/A	Schlesinger		CHAL (1898)
2704	Graben-Hoffmann Gustav	1820-1900	Rausche, rausche froher Bach	Op. 90 No. 4	S/A	Chal.		CHAL (1898)
2705	Graben-Hoffmann Gustav	1820-1900	Sommermorgen "Frischer, thauiger Sommermorgen"	Op. 90 No. 5	S/A	Chal.		CHAL (1898)
2706	Grabert, Martin	1868-1951	Drüben geht die Sonne scheiden	Op. 4 No. 2	Unspec.	Sulzbach i. Berl.		CHAL (1898)
2707	Grabert, Martin	1868-1951	Es steht ein' Lind' in jenem Thal	Op. 4 No. 4	Unspec.	Sulzbach i. Berl.		CHAL (1898)
2708	Grabert, Martin	1868-1951	In der Ferne "Siehst du am Abend die Wolken zieh'n"	Op. 35 No. 2	Unspec.	Sulzbach i. Berl.		CHAL (1898)
2709	Grabert, Martin	1868-1951	Röslein wann blühest du auf "Es wuchs an einem Rosenbaum"	Op. 4 No. 1	Unspec.	Sulzbach i. Berl.		CHAL (1898)
2710	Grädener, Karl Georg Peter	1812-1883	Aprillaunen "Nein es ist mit launischen Leuten"	Op. 67 No. 2	S/S	B. & B.		CHAL (1898)
2711	Grädener, Karl Georg Peter	1812-1883	Erde Recht "Lass der Erde ihr altes Recht"	Op. 67 No. 3	S/S	B. & B.		CHAL (1898)
2712	Grädener, Karl Georg Peter	1812-1883	Hebräische Gesänge	Op. 15	2 female v.	B. & H.		CHAL (1898)
2713	Grädener, Karl Georg Peter	1812-1883	Kehraus "Es fideln die Geigen"	Op. 45 No. 3	S/A	Sch. j.		CHAL (1898)

REC	COMP	DTS	TITLE	OP #	VCG	PUB	COMMENTS	SRC
2714	Grädener, Karl Georg Peter	1812-1883	Mariä Sehnsucht "Es ging Maria in den Morgen"	Op. 45 No. 4	S/A	Sch. j.		CHAL (1898)
2715	Grädener, Karl Georg Peter	1812-1883	Mein Geist ist trüb	Op. 15 No. 1	2 female v.	B. & H.		CHAL (1898)
2716	Grädener, Karl Georg Peter	1812-1883	Neuer Frühling "Frühling miss es werden"	Op. 67 No. 1	S/S	B. & B.		CHAL (1898)
2717	Grädener, Karl Georg Peter	1812-1883	O weint um sie	Op. 15 No. 3	Unspec.	B. & H.		CHAL (1898)
2718	Grädener, Karl Georg Peter	1812-1883	Schalk "Läuten kaum die Maienglocken"	Op. 45 No. 5	S/A	Sch. j.		CHAL (1898)
2719	Grädener, Karl Georg Peter	1812-1883	Singe du Vöglein singe "Es ist keine Hütte so arm"	Op. 67 No. 4	S/S	B. & B.		CHAL (1898)
2720	Grädener, Karl Georg Peter	1812-1883	Tambourinschlägerin "Schwirrend Tambourin"	Op. 45 No. 6	Unspec.	Sch. j.		CHAL (1898)
2721	Grädener, Karl Georg Peter	1812-1883	Traurige Jäger "Zur ewigen Ruh sie sangen"	Op. 45 No. 2	S/A	Sch. j.		CHAL (1898)
2722	Grädener, Karl Georg Peter	1812-1883	Wir sassen am Wasser in Thränen	Op. 15 No. 5	Unspec.	B. & H.		CHAL (1898)
2723	Grädener, Karl Georg Peter	1812-1883	Zigeunerinnen "Am Kreuzweg, da lausche ich"	Op. 45 No. 1	S/A	Sch. j.		CHAL (1898)
2724	Graham, Robert		Holy Child, The		2 med. v.	Walton		ASR
2725	Graham, Robert		In Bethlehem		2 med. v.	Art Masters	May be perf. chorally	ASR
2726	Graham, Robert		When Jesus was Born		2 med. v.	Walton		ASR
2727	Grammann, Karl [Gramman]	1844-1897	Friedel und die Nachtigall "Friedel zählte zwanzig kaum"	Op. 55 No. 4	S/A or T/Br	Seemann		CHAL (1901)
2728	Grammann, Karl [Gramman]	1844-1897	Ging ein Mägdlein durch die Au	Op. 55 No. 2	S/A or T/Br	Seemann		CHAL (1901)
2729	Grammann, Karl [Gramman]	1844-1897	Mit Sturnwind und Regen verschied der April	Op. 55 No. 1	S/A or T/Br	Seemann		CHAL (1901)
2730	Grammann, Karl [Gramman]	1844-1897	Mutter Nacht im Mantel grau	Op. 55 No. 3	S/A or T/Br	Seemann		CHAL (1901)
2731	Grammann, Karl [Gramman]	1844-1897	Marienlied "Aus Himmelsruh' schau erdenwärts"	Op. 18 No. 1	S/A	R. & E.		CHAL (1898)
2732	Grammann, Karl [Gramman]	1844-1897	Volkslied "Im Maien, im Maien singen alle Vögelein"	Op. 18 No. 3	S/A	R. & E.		CHAL (1898)
2733	Grammann, Karl [Gramman]	1844-1897	Volkslied "Wenn ich ein klein's Waldvöglein wär"	Op. 18 No. 2	S/A	R. & E.		CHAL (1898)
2734	Granados, Enrique	1867-1916	Las currutacas modestas		Unspec.	UME		BBC (1975)
2735	Granados, Enrique	1867-1916	Las Currutacas Modestas		Unspec.	CVR		MSN
2736	Graner, R.		Gott ist die Liebe "Vöglein was singst du"	Op. 68	Unspec.	Griesbach i. Gera.		CHAL (1898)
2737	Graner, R.		Mailiedchen "Sonne giebt so hellen Schein"	Op. 68	Unspec.	Griesbach i. Gera		CHAL (1898)
2738	Granier, Jules		Hosanna!		S/A	G. Schirm.	In anthology "Schirmer's Favorite Sacred Duets for Various Voices" Pub. 1955.	MSN
2739	Granier, Jules		Hosanna! (Easter)		S/A	G. Schirm.	pf or org accomp. In catalogue page "Sacred Vocal Duets" of G. Schirmer, Inc. NY (no date)	MSN

REC	COMP	DTS	TITLE	OP #	VCG	PUB	COMMENTS	SRC
2740	Grechaninov, Alexander	1864-1956	Ai-Doo-Doo	Op. 31 No. 7	Unspec.	G. Schirm.	Written out in translit. In anthology "Romantic Duets—Great Performers Edition" Compi. E. Lear & T. Stewart. Pub. 1985.	MSN
2741	Grechaninov, Alexander	1864-1956	Du trauter Wald		S/A	Gutheil	Grmn. trans. Russ.	BBC (1975)
2742	Grechaninov, Alexander	1864-1956	Du trauter Wald, du grüner Wald	Op. 41 No. 2	S/A or T/MS	Gutheil i. M.	Grmn. trans. Russ.	CHAL (1911)
2743	Grechaninov, Alexander	1864-1956	Dubravushka [The Little Leafy Grove]		S/A	GMI	Translit. title of Russ. Only Cyrillic. Anth. "Izbrannye Duety Russkikh Kompozitorov dlia peniia s fortepiano" Pub. 1948.	MSN
2744	Grechaninov, Alexander	1864-1956	Kolibelnaya "Bayoo Bai"	Op. 31 No. 5	Unspec.	G. Schirm.	Written out in translit. In anthology "Romantic Duets—Great Performers Edition" Compi. by E. Lear & T. Stewart. Pub. 1985.	MSN
2745	Grechaninov, Alexander	1864-1956	Posle grozy [After the Thunderstorm]		S/A	GMI	Translit. title of Russ. Only Cyrillic. Anth. "Izbrannye Duety Russkikh Kompozitorov dlia peniia s fortepiano" Pub. 1948.	MSN
2746	Grechaninov, Alexander	1864-1956	Six Russian Children's Songs		Unspec.	Gutheil	Trans. Russ.	BBC (1975)
2747	Grechaninov, Alexander	1864-1956	Winde wehen		S/A	Gutheil	Grmn. trans. Russ.	BBC (1975)
2748	Grechaninov, Alexander	1864-1956	Winde when, böse Stürme weh'n	Op. 41 No. 1	S/A or T/MS	Gutheil i. M.		CHAL (1911)
2749	Greenhill, Harold		Silver		Unspec.	Roberton		CVMP (1976)
2750	Gregoir, J.	1817-1876	Dialogue des anges		Unspec.	Schott		CHAL (1898)
2751	Gregor, Cestmir	1926-	Pisnicki Pracovnich Zaloh [Liedchen der Arbeitsreserven]		2 med. v.	Czech		CVMP (1976)
2752	Greith, Karl	1828-1887	Abendglöcklein "Glöcklein, Abendglöcklein"	Op. 31 No. 3	S/A	Aibl		CHAL (1898)
2753	Greith, Karl	1828-1887	Alle Tage sing' und sage Lob	No. 4	2 female v.	Aibl		CHAL (1898)
2754	Greith, Karl	1828-1887	Am Abend "Schon glänzt der goldne Abendstern"	Op. 42 No. 6	S/A	Aibl		CHAL (1898)
2755	Greith, Karl	1828-1887	An den Frühling "Willkommen schöner Jüngling"	Op. 17 No. 4	S/A	Aibl		CHAL (1898)
2756	Greith, Karl	1828-1887	Auf der Wiese "Viel tausend Blumen"	Op. 22 No. 3	S/A	Aibl.		CHAL (1898)
2757	Greith, Karl	1828-1887	Auf hoher Alp wohnt auch der liebe Gott	Op. 42 No. 8	Unspec.	Aibl.		CHAL (1898)
2758	Greith, Karl	1828-1887	Du lieber, frommer, heil'ger Christ	Op. 48 No. 3	Unspec.	Seiling		CHAL (1898)
2759	Greith, Karl	1828-1887	Es regnet "Es regnet, Gott segnet die Erde"	Op. 17 No. 5	S/A	Aibl		CHAL (1898)
2760	Greith, Karl	1828-1887	Frühlingslied "Alle Vögel sind schon da"	Op. 17 No. 6	S/A	Aibl		CHAL (1898)
2761	Greith, Karl	1828-1887	Frühlingsmorgen "Glockenblumen läuten"	Op. 17 No. 2	S/A	Aibl		CHAL (1898)
2762	Greith, Karl	1828-1887	Ge grüsst seist du	No. 6	2 female v.	Aibl		CHAL (1898)

REC	COMP	DTS	TITLE	OP #	VCG	PUB	COMMENTS	SRC
2763	Greith, Karl	1828-1887	Glocke "Glocke du klingst"	Op. 22 No. 2	S/A	Aibl		CHAL (1898)
2764	Greith, Karl	1828-1887	Gottesgruss "Gottesgruss rauscht im Walde"	Op. 31 No. 5	S/A	Aibl		CHAL (1898)
2765	Greith, Karl	1828-1887	Gotteslob "Kein Thierlein ist auf Erden"	Op. 17 No. 7	S/A	Aibl		CHAL (1898)
2766	Greith, Karl	1828-1887	Heil die o Jungfrau	No. 3	2 female v.	Aibl		CHAL (1898)
2767	Greith, Karl	1828-1887	Instrumentalmesse No. 5	Op. 25	S/A	Verlags-Anst i. Regensb.	org accomp.	CHAL (1898)
2768	Greith, Karl	1828-1887	Kind Jesu-Lied		Inspec.	Pustet	org or harm accomp.	CHAL (1898)
2769	Greith, Karl	1828-1887	Leise zieht durch mein Gemüth	Op. 17 No. 8	S/A	Aibl		CHAL (1898)
2770	Greith, Karl	1828-1887	Mach's ebenso "Sonne blickt mit hellem Schein"	Op. 17 No. 3	S/A	Aibl		CHAL (1898)
2771	Greith, Karl	1828-1887	Mai blümchen "Im Walde dort"	Op. 22 No. 1	S/A	Aibl		CHAL (1898)
2772	Greith, Karl	1828-1887	Mai "Komm holder Mai"	Op. 42 No. 5	S/A	Aibl		CHAL (1898)
2773	Greith, Karl	1828-1887	Mailust "Pflücket ein Kränzchen"	Op. 33	S/A	B. & H.		CHAL (1898)
2774	Greith, Karl	1828-1887	Marienlieder		2 female v.	Aibl		CHAL (1898)
2775	Greith, Karl	1828-1887	Morgen "Ein Morgen-schimmer glüht"	Op. 42 No. 1	S/A	Aibl		CHAL (1898)
2776	Greith, Karl	1828-1887	O du fröhliche, o du selige	Op. 48 No. 1	Unspec.	Seiling		CHAL (1898)
2777	Greith, Karl	1828-1887	O du Heilige	No. 5	2 female v.	Aibl		CHAL (1898)
2778	Greith, Karl	1828-1887	O Königin voll Herrlichkeit	No. 1	2 female v.	Aibl		CHAL (1898)
2779	Greith, Karl	1828-1887	Sommerzeit "Geh' aus, mein Herz"	Op. 42 No. 4	S/A	Aibl		CHAL (1898)
2780	Greith, Karl	1828-1887	Sonnenschein "Sonnen-schein, klar und rein"	Op. 17 No. 1	S/A	Aibl		CHAL (1898)
2781	Greith, Karl	1828-1887	Spazieren "Schönste Leben ist im Freien"	Op. 42 No. 7	S/A	Aibl		CHAL (1898)
2782	Greith, Karl	1828-1887	Storchs Ankunft "Sieh' der Storch"	Op. 31 No. 2	S/A	Aibl		CHAL (1898)
2783	Greith, Karl	1828-1887	Über Nacht "Über Nacht fällt ein Thau"	Op. 31 No. 4	S/A	Aibl		CHAL (1898)
2784	Greith, Karl	1828-1887	Vögleins Tod "Mir starb mein holdes Vögelein"	Op. 42 No. 3	S/A	Aibl		CHAL (1898)
2785	Greith, Karl	1828-1887	Waldlust "Wie herrlich ist's im Walde"	Op. 22 No. 4	S/A	Aibl		CHAL (1898)
2786	Greith, Karl	1828-1887	Wanderlied "Wohlauf noch getrunken"	Op. 31 No. 1	S/A	Aibl		CHAL (1898)
2787	Greith, Karl	1828-1887	Weihnachtslieder (4)	Op. 48	Unspec.	Seiling	4 duets	CHAL (1898)
2788	Greith, Karl	1828-1887	Winterlust "Hei Winter, juchhe"	Op. 42 No. 2	S/A	Aibl		CHAL (1898)
2789	Greith, Karl	1828-1887	Wunderschön prächtige	No. 2	2 female v.	Aibl		CHAL (1898)
2790	Grell, Eduard August	1800-1886	Ave Maria "Ave Maria gratia pleni"		Unspec.	Bahn		CHAL (1898)
2791	Grell, Eduard August	1800-1886	Beata mater		Unspec.	Bahnorg		CHAL (1901)

REC	COMP	DTS	TITLE	OP #	VCG	PUB	COMMENTS	SRC
2792	Grell, Eduard August	1800-1886	Bei der Entlassung der Schüler "Wer unter dem Schirm"	Op. 51 No. 2	Unspec.	Bahn		CHAL (1898)
2793	Grell, Eduard August	1800-1886	Ein getreues Herze		S/A	Schlesinger		CHAL (1898)
2794	Grell, Eduard August	1800-1886	Gebet an der Krippe "So lasst uns vor die Krippe treten"		Unspec.	Bahn		CHAL (1898)
2795	Grell, Eduard August	1800-1886	Kindleins Abendgebet "Wenn die Kinder schlafen ein"	Op. 53 No. 5	S/A	Bahn		CHAL (1898)
2796	Grell, Eduard August	1800-1886	Laurel and the Rose, The		high & low v.	Hinds, Hayden & Eldredge	Eng. trans. Grmn. In anthology "The Most Popular Vocal Duets" Ed. Dr. E. J. Biedermann. Pub. 1914.	MSN
2797	Grell, Eduard August	1800-1886	Liebe "Lieb' ist ein warmer Lenzhauch"	Op. 53 No. 2	S/A	Bahn		CHAL (1898)
2798	Grell, Eduard August	1800-1886	Lieder "Lider sind des Herzens Blumen"	Op. 53 No. 3	S/A	Bahn		CHAL (1898)
2799	Grell, Eduard August	1800-1886	Lorbeer und Rose		S/MS or S/A	C. Fischer	In catalogue page "Selected Vocal Duets By Favorite Composers" of Carl Fischer NY (no date)	MSN
2800	Grell, Eduard August	1800-1886	Lorbeer und Rose "Von zarter Lieb der Lorbeer apricht"	Op. 6	S/S or MS/MS or A/A	Bahn		CHAL (1898)
2801	Grell, Eduard August	1800-1886	Psalm 1 "Wohl dem, der nicht Hoffheinz"		Unspec.	Bahn		CHAL (1898)
2802	Grell, Eduard August	1800-1886	Psalm 133 "Siehe wie fein"	Op. 63 No. 1	S/A	Bahn	org or pf accomp.	CHAL (1898)
2803	Grell, Eduard August	1800-1886	Psalm 27 "Herr ist mein Licht"	Op. 63 No. 2	S/A	Bahn	org or pf accomp.	CHAL (1898)
2804	Grell, Eduard August	1800-1886	Regina mundi		Unspec.	Bahn	org	CHAL (1901)
2805	Grell, Eduard August	1800-1886	Sommerabend "O du schöner goldner Abend"	Op. 53 No. 6	S/A	Bahn		CHAL (1898)
2806	Grell, Eduard August	1800-1886	Weihnachtsfeier "Was klingt wie Festgeläute"		Unspec.	Bahn		CHAL (1898)
2807	Grell, Eduard August	1800-1886	Weihnachtslied "Was spricht der Glocke voller Klang"	Op. 53 No. 4	S/A	Bahn		CHAL (1898)
2808	Grell, Eduard August	1800-1886	Wohl dem, der nicht wandelt im Rathe der Gottlosen		Unspec.	Bahn		CHAL (1901)
2809	Grell, Eduard August	1800-1886	Wort und Gesang "Worte such' ich mir vergebens"	Op. 53 No. 1	S/A	Bahn		CHAL (1898)
2810	Grell, Eduard August	1800-1886	Zum Geburtstage des Königs "Herr, der König freuet sich"	Op. 21 No. 1	Unspec.	Bahn		CHAL (1898)
2811	Grell, Eduard August	1800-1886	Zum Reformationsfest "Ich schäme mich"	Op. 51 No. 2	Unspec.	Bahn		CHAL (1898)
2812	Gressler, Franz Albert	1804-1886	Weisse Rosen (Sammlung)		Unspec.	Siegel		CHAL (1898)
2813	Grever, Maria		Mañana por la mañana		high & low v.	G. Schirm.	Woman comp. In catalogue page "Selected Vocal Duets" of G. Schirmer, Inc. NY (no date)	MSN

REC	COMP	DTS	TITLE	OP #	VCG	PUB	COMMENTS	SRC
2814	Grieg, Edvard	1843-1907	Ich liebe dich		S/T or S/Br or S/A	G. Schirm.	Arr. by C. Deis. In catalogue page "Selected Vocal Duets" of G. Schirmer, Inc. NY (no date)	MSN
2815	Griesbacher, Peter	1864-1933	Marienpreis on Liedern	Op. 37	Unspec.	Pustet	org or harm	CHAL (1901)
2816	Grisar, Albert	1808-1869	Fest der Madonna "Auf, auf ihr jungen Mädchen"		Unspec.	Chal.		CHAL (1898)
2817	Grisar, Albert	1808-1869	Fête des Madones		Unspec.	Schott		CHAL (1898)
2818	Grisar, Albert	1808-1869	Rückkehr des Mai "Ha welche Lust"		Unspec.	Schott		CHAL (1898)
2819	Groh, A.		Kaffeeklatsch "Was giebt es Schön'res auf der Welt"	Op. 1	2 female v.	R. Forberg		CHAL (1898)
2820	Gronau, Ed.		Nun ist die liebe Weihnachtszeit	No. 3	Unspec.	Hoffmann i. Pr.		CHAL (1906)
2821	Grøndahl, Agathe Bäcker	1847-1907	Agnes, min deflige Sommerfugl	Op. 2 No. 1	Unspec.	Norsk	Nor. woman comp.	BBC (1975)
2822	Grosheim, Georg Christoph	1764-1847	Hectors Abschied "Will sich Hector ewig"		Unspec.	Schott		CHAL (1898)
2823	Groskopf, A.		Stille, liebe Seele, stille	No. 18	Unspec.	Schergens		CHAL (1906)
2824	Grosse, L.		Ein kleines Lied, ein kleines, hat Gott	Op. 10 No. 3	Unspec.	Näumann		CHAL (1898)
2825	Grosse, L.		Ein kleines Lied, wie geht's nur an	Op. 54 I No. 3	Unspec.	Näumann		CHAL (1898)
2826	Grosse, L.		Friedensboten der heiligen Nacht "Seid willkommen ihr lieblichen Boten"	Op. 54 II No. 2	Unspec.	Näumann		CHAL (1898)
2827	Grosse, L.		Frühling "Hörst du wohl die Glöcklein klingen"	Op. 10 No. 2	Unspec.	Näumann		CHAL (1898)
2828	Grosse, L.		Frühling "Hörst du wohl die Glöcklein klingen"	Op. 54 I No. 2	Unspec.	Näumann		CHAL (1898)
2829	Grosse, L.		Frühlingsahung "O sanfter, süsser Hauch"	Op. 53	Unspec.	Näumann		CHAL (1898)
2830	Grosse, L.		Leb wohl du schöner Wald "So scheiden wir mit Sang"	Op. 10 No. 1	Unspec.	Näumann		CHAL (1898)
2831	Grosse, L.		Leb wohl du schöner Wald "So scheiden wir mit Sang"	Op. 51 I No. 1	Unspec.	Näumann		CHAL (1898)
2832	Grosse, L.		Wiegenlied "Schlaf, mein Kind, schlaf' ein"	Op. 54 I No. 4	Unspec.	Näumann		CHAL (1898)
2833	Grossjohann, F.		Hoffnung und Gott		Unspec.	Volkening i. Minden		CHAL (1898)
2834	Grua, Carlo Luigi Pietro	1753-1833	Lontan dal suo ben		S/A	Bongiavanni	Ed. Vatielli	BBC (1975)
2835	Gruber, L.		Am Land draust a Kirta is	Op. 500	Unspec.	Blaha		CHAL (1906)
2836	Gruber, L.		Wann i auf'n Kalenberg steh'	Op. 1020	Unspec.	Blaha		CHAL (1911)
2837	Gruber, L.		Weil Alles schon secessionistisch is jetzt	Op. 324	Unspec.	Robitschek		CHAL (1901)
2838	Gruber, L.		Weil mir heut so lusti beinander	Op. 394	Unspec.	Blaha		CHAL (1906)
2839	Gruber, L.		Wer schaut denn dem Menschen am ähnlichsten noch		Unspec.	Blaha		CHAL (1911)
2840	Gruber, L.		Wie schön war's doch in früher'n Jahren		Unspec.	Blaha		CHAL (1906)

REC	COMP	DTS	TITLE	OP #	VCG	PUB	COMMENTS	SRC
2841	Grüel, E.		Psalm 41 "Wie der Hirsch schreit"		2 female or children's v.	Klinner	org accomp.	CHAL (1898)
2842	Grünberger, Ludwig	1839-1896	Hirtenreigen "Was kann schöner sein"	Op. 63 No. 2	Unspec.	Junne		CHAL (1898)
2843	Grund, Friedrich Wilhelm	1791-1874	Es fällt ein Stern herunter	Op. 31 No. 2	Unspec.	Sch. j.		CHAL (1898)
2844	Grund, Friedrich Wilhelm	1791-1874	Hör' ich das Liedchen klingen	Op. 31 No. 1	Unspec.	Sch. j.		CHAL (1898)
2845	Grund, Friedrich Wilhelm	1791-1874	Und wüssten's die Blumen, die kleinen	Op. 31 No. 3	Unspec.	Sch. j.		CHAL (1898)
2846	Grund, Friedrich Wilhelm	1791-1874	Wenn Zwei von einander scheiden	Op. 31 No. 2	Unspec.	Sch. j.		CHAL (1898)
2847	Grüner, G.		Apel au bonheur		S/S or A/B	Cranz		CHAL (1898)
2848	Grunholzer, K.		Autour du clocher "Autour du vieux clocher"		Unspec.	Foetisch		CHAL (1906)
2849	Grunholzer, K.		Ein Zug, der mich zum Himmel trägt		Unspec.	Schergens		CHAL (1906)
2850	Grunholzer, K.		Lebet wohl, es ruft die heil'ge Pflicht	No. 22	Unspec.	Schergens		CHAL (1906)
2851	Gscheidel, P.		Ferne läuten Glockenklänge	Op. 12 No. 2	S/A	Sch. J.		CHAL (1911)
2852	Guastavino, Carlos	1912-	Arroyito serrano		Unspec.	Ricordi		BBC (1975)
2853	Guastavino, Carlos	1912-	Cancion de Navidad		2 med. v.	Colombo		ASR
2854	Gudmundsson, Björgvin	1891-1961	Tonhendur, Nytt Safn 2. Hefti		Unspec.	Iceland	Collection. Also available for solo. "Safn 1" for solo	CVMP (1995)
2855	Guercia, Alfonso	1831-1890	Aspettation		S/A or T/B	Ricordi		CHAL (1898)
2856	Guercia, Alfonso	1831-1890	Desio		MS/A or MS/B	Ricordi		CHAL (1898)
2857	Guercia, Alfonso	1831-1890	Dove sei		MS/A or MS/B	Ricordi		CHAL (1898)
2858	Guercia, Alfonso	1831-1890	Giura		S/MS or S/A	Ricordi		CHAL (1898)
2859	Guercia, Alfonso	1831-1890	Nina		T/B or S/A	Ricordi		CHAL (1898)
2860	Guercia, Alfonso	1831-1890	T'intendo		S/A or T/B	Ricordi		CHAL (1898)
2861	Guglielmo, P. D.		Un Mattino d'Amore		S/A	G. Schirm.	In catalogue page "Favorite French and Italian Vocal Duets" of G. Schirmer, Inc. NY (no date)	MSN
2862	Guiselin, P.		O salutaris	Op. 23	Unspec.	Cranz	org accomp.	CHAL (1898)
2863	Gülker, August	1854-	Du bist mein herzig liebes Kind	Op. 36 No. 1	Unspec.	C. Rühle		CHAL (1911)
2864	Gülker, August	1854-	Du Königin im Hasegau	Op. 48	2 med. v.	Schöningh.		CHAL (1911)
2865	Gülker, August	1854-	Flugs Herr Wirt, noch eine Kanne	Op. 37 No. 2	Unspec.	C. Rühle i. L.		CHAL (1911)
2866	Gülker, August	1854-	Ich denke dein am frühen Morgen	Op. 37 No. 1	Unspec.	C. Rühle i. L.		CHAL (1911)

REC	COMP	DTS	TITLE	OP #	VCG	PUB	COMMENTS	SRC
2867	Gülker, August	1854-	Musst nit so heimlich tun	Op. 36 No. 2	Unspec.	C. Rühle i. L.		CHAL (1911)
2868	Gumbert		Cheerfulness		S/A	White-Smith	In catalogue page "Vocal Duetts" of White-Smith Music Pub. Co. (no date)	MSN
2869	Gumbert, Ferdinand	1818-1896	Frohsinn, Walzer-Rondo		S/A or S/Br	C. Fischer	In catalogue page "Selected Vocal Duets By Favorite Composers" of Carl Fischer NY (no date)	MSN
2870	Gumbert, Ferdinand	1818-1896	Gondellied "Welle kommt"	Op. 66 No. 5	S/MS	André		CHAL (1898)
2871	Gumbert, Ferdinand	1818-1896	Grünes Ufer, blaue Wellen	Op. 66 No. 1	S/MS	André		CHAL (1898)
2872	Gumbert, Ferdinand	1818-1896	Grüsse "Möchte mit der Woge"	Op. 45 No. 3	2 med. v.	André		CHAL (1898)
2873	Gumbert, Ferdinand	1818-1896	Gute Nacht mein Lieb'	Op. 45 No. 2	2 med. v.	André		CHAL (1898)
2874	Gumbert, Ferdinand	1818-1896	Guten Engel "Nun lass dir erzählen"	Op. 48 No. 3	Unspec.	André		CHAL (1898)
2875	Gumbert, Ferdinand	1818-1896	Heimwärts zieh'n die muntern Sänger	Op. 29 No. 4	S/A	Schlesinger		CHAL (1898)
2876	Gumbert, Ferdinand	1818-1896	Herdenglocken "Im grüben Thale"	Op. 48 No. 1	Unspec.	André		CHAL (1898)
2877	Gumbert, Ferdinand	1818-1896	Ich sing' für mich hin	Op. 80 No. 1 a	S/A	Schlesinger		CHAL (1898)
2878	Gumbert, Ferdinand	1818-1896	Knaben Lied "Das ist ein frohes, deutsches Lied"	Op. 48 No. 5	Unspec.	André		CHAL (1898)
2879	Gumbert, Ferdinand	1818-1896	Leichter Sinn "Und wie wär es nicht zu tragen"	Op. 48 No. 8	Unspec.	André		CHAL (1898)
2880	Gumbert, Ferdinand	1818-1896	Leise zieht durch mein Gemüth	Op. 48 No. 2	Unspec.	André		CHAL (1898)
2881	Gumbert, Ferdinand	1818-1896	Lied einier Waise "Am Himmel dort die Sternlein"	Op. 48 No. 6	Unspec.	André		CHAL (1898)
2882	Gumbert, Ferdinand	1818-1896	Mein Frühling "Immer treibt der Vogel"	Op. 29 No. 1	S/A	Schlesinger		CHAL (1898)
2883	Gumbert, Ferdinand	1818-1896	Morgenwanderung "Wer recht in Freuden wandern will"	Op. 48 No. 4	Unspec.	André		CHAL (1898)
2884	Gumbert, Ferdinand	1818-1896	Reiters Abschied "Horch, horch die Trompeten blasen"	Op. 48 No. 7	Unspec.	André		CHAL (1898)
2885	Gumbert, Ferdinand	1818-1896	Schwäbisches Lied "Erde braucht Regen"	Op. 45 No. 4	2 med. v.	André		CHAL (1898)
2886	Gülbert, Ferdinand	1818-1896	Steyrisches Lied "Wie tief im Herzen"	Op. 29 No. 2	S/A	Schlesinger		CHAL (1898)
2887	Gumbert, Ferdinand	1818-1896	Tyrolerlied "Und du fragst noch"	Op. 66 No. 3	S/MS	André		CHAL (1898)
2888	Gumbert, Ferdinand	1818-1896	Vöglein im Walde "Lustiges Vöglein im Walde"	Op. 66 No. 4	S/MS	André		CHAL (1898)
2889	Gumbert, Ferdinand	1818-1896	Von dir "Sternlein, die sprachen"	Op. 45 No. 1	2 med. v.	André		CHAL (1898)
2890	Gumbert, Ferdinand	1818-1896	Wenn Alles schläft in stiller Nacht	Op. 29 No. 3	S/A	Schlesinger		CHAL (1898)
2891	Gumbert, Ferdinand	1818-1896	Wer trägt tief im Herzen	Op. 29 No. 2	S/A	Schlesinger		CHAL (1906)
2892	Gundlach, jun. L.		Ha, he, hi, ho, hu	Op. 44	Unspec.	Lyra i. Dresd.		CHAL (1898)
2893	Gundlach, jun. L.		Ha, he, hi, ho, hu "Ha, ha, ha, ein Wirtshaus"		Unspec.	Grude		CHAL (1901)
2894	Günther, O.		Bleibn nur noch a weng do	Op. 20	Unspec.	Gödsche		CHAL (1911)

REC	COMP	DTS	TITLE	OP #	VCG	PUB	COMMENTS	SRC
2895	Günther, O.		Feieromb	Op. 30	Unspec.	Gödsche		CHAL (1911)
2896	Gurlitt, Cornelius	1820-1901	Blumenabschied "Ein Mägdlein ging und weinte"	Op. 27	2 female v.	O. Forberg		CHAL (1898)
2897	Gurlitt, Cornelius	1820-1901	Frühlingsblumen	Op. 5 No. 2	high & low v.	Sch. & Co.		CHAL (1898)
2898	Gurlitt, Cornelius	1820-1901	Ich möchte wohl der Vogel sein	Op. 13 No. 2	S/A	Sch. & Co.		CHAL (1898)
2899	Gurlitt, Cornelius	1820-1901	"Regen und Tränen sind innig verwandt"	Op. 13 No. 1	S/A	Sch. & Co.		CHAL (1898)
2900	Gurlitt, Cornelius	1820-1901	Sommergang in die Heimath "Wie traurig seh'n die Au'n"	Op. 5 No. 3	high & low v.	Sch. & Co.		CHAL (1898)
2901	Gurlitt, Cornelius	1820-1901	Sonnenspiegel "Frühling lacht, der Weiher glänzt"	Op. 13 No. 3	S/A	Sch. & Co.		CHAL (1898)
2902	Gurlitt, Cornelius	1820-1901	Vöglein im Frühling "Vöglein singen"	Op. 5 No. 1	high & low v.	Sch. & Co.		CHAL (1898)
2903	Gus, M.		Ich seh' dir oft in's Antlitz	Op. 44 No. b	Unspec.	F. Schellenb.		CHAL (1911)
2904	Gus, M.		Über Nacht kommt still das Leid	Op. 3 No. b	Unspec.	F. Schellenb.		CHAL. (1911)
2905	Gustav, P.rinz v. Schweden	1827-1852	Im Rosenduft, vom Blütenhain umfangen		S/A or T/Br	Schott	Ed. Vobach	CHAL (1911)
2906	Güth, J. L.		Gott der Gnade, schau' hernieder	Op. 36	2 female v. or S/Br	André	org	CHAL (1911)
2907	Gutheil, Gustav	1868-1914	Hörst du das Flüstern	Op. 13	S/A	Kahnt		CHAL (1906)
2908	Guzmann, Fr.	1827-1885	Rapelle-toi		Unspec.	Schott		CHAL (1898)
2909	Haagh, J.		Litaniae lauretanae	Op. 4	Unspec.	Pustet	org accomp.	CHAL (1898)
2910	Haan, Willem de [De Haan]	1849-1930	Einsamkeit "Hörst du nicht die Quellen gehen"	Op. 6 No. 1	S/A	Simrock		CHAL (1898)
2911	Haan, Willem de [De Haan]	1849-1930	Frühlingsahnung "Ein Windsoss kommt"	Op. 6 No. 2	S/A	Simrock		CHAL (1898)
2912	Haas, Joseph	1879-1960	Das Osterei	Op. 33 No. 7	Unspec.	Leuckart	For 1-2 v. In set called "Rum Bidi Bum"	CVMP (1976)
2913	Haas, Joseph	1879-1960	Der Widerhall	Op. 33 No. 8	Unspec.	Leuckart	For 1-2 v. In set called "Rum Bidi Bum"	CVMP (1976)
2914	Haas, Joseph	1879-1960	Frau Spinne	Op. 33 No. 9	Unspec.	Leuckart	For 1-2 v. In set called "Rum Bidi Bum"	CVMP (1976)
2915	Haas, Joseph	1879-1960	Kinderreigen	Op. 33 No. 1	Unspec.	Leuckart	For 1-2 v. In set called "Rum Bidi Bum"	CVMP (1976)
2916	Haas, Joseph	1879-1960	Nur eine kleine Geige	Op. 33 No. 3	Unspec.	Leuckart	For 1-2 v. In set called "Rum Bidi Bum"	CVMP (1976)
2917	Haas, Joseph	1879-1960	Ob ich mich Wehre	Op. 33 No. 6	Unspec.	Leuckart	For 1-2 v. In set called "Rum Bidi Bum"	CVMP (1976)
2918	Haas, Joseph	1879-1960	Rum Bidi Bum (10) Op. 33	Op. 33	Var.	Leuckart	Collection of 10 unspec. pieces. For 1-2 v. Includes duets.	ASR
2919	Haas, Joseph	1879-1960	Unser Liebes Franzei	Op. 33 No. 5	Unspec.	Leuckart	For 1-2 v. In set called "Rum Bidi Bum"	CVMP (1976)
2920	Haas, Joseph	1879-1960	Wenn ich mein Huhnchen Locke	Op. 33 No. 2	Unspec.	Leuckart	For 1-2 v. In set called "Rum Bidi Bum"	CVMP (1976)
2921	Haas, Joseph	1879-1960	Wiegenlied	Op. 33 No. 4	Unspec.	Leuckart	For 1-2 v. In set called "Rum Bidi Bum"	CVMP (1976)
2922	Haas, Joseph	1879-1960	Zum Erntekranz	Op. 33 No. 10	Unspec.	Leuckart	For 1-2 v. In set called "Rum Bidi Bum"	CVMP (1976)

REC	COMP	DTS	TITLE	OP #	VCG	PUB	COMMENTS	SRC
2923	Haase, Rudolf	1841-1916?	So wandert denn vereint durch's Leben	Op. 15	S/A	Oppen-heimer	org or pf	CHAL (1906)
2924	Hackel, Anton	1779-1846	Beiden Nachtigallen "Zwei Nachtigallen sassen"	Op. 81	MS/A or Br/B	André		CHAL (1898)
2925	Hackel, Anton	1779-1846	Die beiden Nachtigallen		S/A or T/Br	C. Fischer	In catalogue page "Selected Vocal Duets By Favorite Composers" of Carl Fischer NY (no date)	MSN
2926	Hackel, Anton	1779-1846	Finden und Scheiden "So warm wir uns trafen"	Op. 80	Br/B or MS/A	B. & B.		CHAL (1898)
2927	Hackel, Anton	1779-1846	Glockenstimmen "Zwei ferne Glocken klingen"	Op. 45	S/A or T/B	Schlesin-ger		CHAL (1898)
2928	Hackel, Anton	1779-1846	Two Nightingales		Unspec.	Brainard's Sons	Eng. trans. Grmn. In anthology "Brainard's Collection of Vocal Duets from Popular Modern and Standard Composers" Pub. 1903.	MSN
2929	Hackel, Anton	1779-1846	Zwei Nachtigallen sangen in einem Gartenraum	Op. 31 IV No. 9	Unspec.	C. Rühle i. L.		CHAL (1901)
2930	Hackl, J.		Berg und Thal "Mein Hüttchen steht im Thale"	Op. 58	T/B or S/A	Cranz		CHAL (1898)
2931	Hacks, G.		Ange perdu "Un petit ange à face ronde"		Unspec.	B. & H.		CHAL (1898)
2932	Hacks, G.		Bachstelzchen "Bachstelz-chen schmucker Vogel"		Unspec.	B. & H.		CHAL (1898)
2933	Hadeln, E. v.		Guten Tag mein liebes Jettchen		S/S	P. & M.		CHAL (1906)
2934	Haeber-lein, H.		Im wunderschönen Monat Mai	Op. 12 No. 1	Unspec.	Zierfuss		CHAL (1898)
2935	Haggbom		I Skog och Pa Sjo		Unspec.	Lundq.		CVMP (1976)
2936	Hahn, J. Ch. W.		Abendlied "Ich stand auf Bergeshalde"	Op. 14 No. 2	Unspec.	Hof-meister		CHAL (1898)
2937	Hahn, J. Ch. W.		Frühlingstraum "Nachts ist's mir gewesen"	Op. 14 No. 5	Unspec.	Hof-meister		CHAL (1898)
2938	Hahn, J. Ch. W.		Geduld "Es zieht ein stiller Engel"	Op. 14 No. 3	Unspec.	Hof-meister		CHAL (1898)
2939	Hahn, J. Ch. W.		Hohes "Hohe Lilie, keine ist so stolz"	Op. 14 No. 4	Unspec.	Hof-meister		CHAL (1898)
2940	Hahn, J. Ch. W.		Im Walde "O Thäler weit, o Höhen"	Op. 14 No. 6	Unspec.	Hof-meister		CHAL (1898)
2941	Hahn, J. Ch. W.		Morgengebet "O wunder-bares tiefes Schweigen"	Op. 14 No. 1	Unspec.	Hof-meister		CHAL (1898)
2942	Haim, F.		O diese Männer "Man hört es immer sagen"		2 female v.	Fr. Dietrich		CHAL (1898)
2943	Haim, F.		Zehn an jeden Finger "An Männern giebt es keine Noth"		2 female v.	Fr. Dietrich		CHAL (1898)
2944	Haine, C.		Nun lass' mich geh'n mit die durch's Leben	Op. 88	S/A	André	org or harm or pf	CHAL (1911)
2945	Haine, C.		Zwei Hände wollen heute sich	Op. 75	S/A	Steyl & Thomas		CHAL (1901)
2946	Halle, H.		Beiden Verliebten "Ich hab' ein Liebchen süss"		Unspec.	Bandtlow i. Berl.		CHAL (1898)
2947	Halle, H.		Flotten Hobelmanns "Ja der Familie Zier"		Unspec.	Bandtlow i. Berl.		CHAL (1898)
2948	Halle, H.		Gebrüder Schulze "Immer charmant, pyramidal"		Unspec.	Bandtlow i. Berl.		CHAL (1898)

REC	COMP	DTS	TITLE	OP #	VCG	PUB	COMMENTS	SRC
2949	Hallen, Andreas	1846-1925	Norrland	Op. 55	Unspec.	Gehrmans		CVMP (1976)
2950	Hallen, Andreas	1846-1925	Tre Duetter	Op. 27	Unspec.	Gehrmans	Individual pieces not listed	CVMP (1976)
2951	Hallstrom, Ivar	1826-1901	Isola Bella		Unspec.	Lundq.		CVMP (1976)
2952	Hallstrom, Ivar	1826-1901	Kvallstankar		Unspec.	Lundq.	Also solo	CVMP (1976)
2953	Hallstrom, Ivar	1826-1901	Motsatser		Unspec.	Lundq.		CVMP (1976)
2954	Hallstrom, Ivar	1826-1901	Sangen		Unspec.	Lundq.		CVMP (1976)
2955	Haltnorth, A.		Juden-Duett "Scholem lachem Itzigleben"		Unspec.	Kott		CHAL (1898)
2956	Haltnorth, A.		Reisegeschichten "Scholem aleichem Itzig leben"		Unspec.	Henkel		CHAL (1898)
2957	Hamblen, Bernard		Beside Still Waters		2 med. v.	Boosey		ASR
2958	Hamm, Charles		Round		Unspec	Media	acap.	CVMP (1976)
2959	Hamma, Benjamin	1831-	Dumme Hans "Hänschen will ein Tischler werden"	Op. 17 No. 12	Unspec.	Lichtb.		CHAL (1898)
2960	Hamma, Benjamin	1831-	Guten Morgen "Nun reibet euch die Aeuglein wach"	Op. 17 No. 1	Unspec.	Lichtb.		CHAL (1898)
2961	Hamma, Benjamin	1831-	Heraus "Ging unter dichten Zweigen"	Op. 17 No. 4	Unspec.	Lichtb.		CHAL (1898)
2962	Hamma, Benjamin	1831-	Hinaus, hinaus, zur bunten Flur	Op. 17 No. 2	Unspec.	Lichtb.		CHAL (1898)
2963	Hamma, Benjamin	1831-	Im Walde, im hellen Sonnenschein	Op. 17 No. 6	Unspec.	Lichtb.		CHAL (1898)
2964	Hamma, Benjamin	1831-	Lasset uns marschiren	Op. 17 No. 5	Unspec.	Lichtb.		CHAL (1898)
2965	Hamma, Benjamin	1831-	Maiblümelein "Im Mai, im schönen Mai"	Op. 17 No. 8	Unspec.	Lichtb.		CHAL (1898)
2966	Hamma, Benjamin	1831-	Mailied "Da ist er, der liebliche"	Op. 17 No. 7	Unspec.	Lichtb.		CHAL (1898)
2967	Hamma, Benjamin	1831-	Mairegen "Es regnet der Kuckuck wird nass"	Op. 17 No. 10	Unspec.	Lichtb.		CHAL (1898)
2968	Hamma, Benjamin	1831-	Mühle "Es klappert die Mühle"	Op. 17 No. 11	Unspec.	Lichtb.		CHAL (1898)
2969	Hamma, Benjamin	1831-	Sonnenschein "Sonnenschein, klar und rein"	Op. 17 No. 3	Unspec.	Lichtb.		CHAL (1898)
2970	Hamma, Benjamin	1831-	Spinnlied "Spinn, (spinn,) Mägdlein, spinn"	Op. 17 No. 9	Unspec.	Lichtb.		CHAL (1898)
2971	Hammond, William G.		Far from my Heavenly Home		2 high v.	Church	In anthology "Sacred Duets A Collection of Two-Part Songs by the Best Composers" Vol. 1. Compi. & ed. W. Shakespeare. Pub. 1907.	MSN
2972	Hanisch, Joseph	1812-1892	Auferstehungslied	Op. 27	S/A	Seiling	org accomp.	CHAL (1898)
2973	Hanscom, E. W.		How gentle God's commands		S/A	A. P. Schm. i. Leip.		CHAL (1901)
2974	Hanus, Jan	1915-	European Christmas Song		Unspec.	Merse.	pf or org accomp. Collection. 1-2 v. No specific works mentioned	CVMP (1985)
2975	Hape, Ch. F.		Waldhornlied "Wie lieblich schallt durch Busch und Wald"		S/A	B. & B.		CHAL (1898)

REC	COMP	DTS	TITLE	OP #	VCG	PUB	COMMENTS	SRC
2976	Haring, Ch.		Avril		S/A	Enoch		CVMP (1976)
2977	Harker, F. Flaxington	1876-1936	God shall wipe away all tears	Op. 49 No. 2	S/A	G. Schirm.	Arr. W. Riegger	MSN
2978	Harker, F. Flaxington	1876-1936	God shall wipe away all tears	Op. 49 No. 2	S/A	G. Schirm.	pf or org accomp. In catalogue page "Sacred Vocal Duets" of G. Schirmer, Inc. NY (no date)	MSN
2979	Harker, F. Flaxington	1876-1936	How beautiful upon the mountain [sic]		high & low v.	G. Schirm.	pf or org accomp. In catalogue page "Sacred Vocal Duets" of G. Schirmer, Inc. NY (no date)	MSN
2980	Harker, F. Flaxington	1876-1936	How Beautiful Upon the Mountains		high & low v.	G. Schirm.	In anthology "Schirmer's Favorite Sacred Duets for Various Voices" Pub. 1955.	MSN
2981	Harker, F. Flaxington	1876-1936	How Beautiful Upon the Mountains		S/MS or S/Br or T/Br	G. Schirm.	Available in various anthologies	NATS-SVD
2982	Harker, F. Flaxington	1876-1936	I Will Lift up Mine Eyes		S/A	G. Schirm.		ASR
2983	Harker, F. Flaxington	1876-1936	I Will Lift Up Mine Eyes Unto the Hills		S/A	Shawnee		CVMP (1976)
2984	Hart, M. A.		Through the Gates of Gold		Unspec.	Brainard's Sons	In anthology "Brainard's Collection of Vocal Duets from Popular Modern and Standard Composers" Pub. 1903.	MSN
2985	Hartl, Ph.		Zwei ord'ntliche Leut "So zwa wie mir zwa"		Unspec.	Fr. Dietrich		CHAL (1898)
2986	Hartmann, D.	d. 1931	Der muss aus dem Lokal "Wie sie wohl sehn"	Op. 16	Unspec.	Nauss	Pen name of David Lundhardt	CHAL (1898)
2987	Hartmann, D.	d. 1931	Rosenmädchen "Bräutchen fein und züliglich"	Op. 24	Unspec.	Nauss	Pen name of David Lundhardt	CHAL (1898)
2988	Hartmann, Paul Eugen von	1863-1914	Quasi stella matulina		Unspec.	Ricordi	org or harm	CHAL (1906)
2989	Hartmann, Paul Eugen von	1863-1914	Tantum ergo		Unspec.	Ricordi	org or harm	CHAL (1906)
2990	Hartog, Edouard de	1829-1909	Barcarole "Loin des bruite du monde"	No. 2	S/A	Peters		CHAL (1898)
2991	Hartog, Edouard de	1829-1909	Chanson arabe "O nuit sereine et parfumée"	No. 3	S/A	Peters		CHAL (1898)
2992	Hartog, Edouard de	1829-1909	Clair de lune "Oh que la nuit est charmante"	No. 1	S/A	Peters		CHAL (1898)
2993	Hartog, Edouard de	1829-1909	Fern ab von dem Weltgetriebe	No. 2	S/A	Peters		CHAL (1901)
2994	Hartog, Edouard de	1829-1909	O lächle, duftgetränkte Nacht	No. 3	S/A	Peters		CHAL (1901)
2995	Hartog, Edouard de	1829-1909	Wie ist die Nacht	No. 1	S/A	Peters		CHAL (1901)
2996	Häser, C.	1784-1871	Schlummre Liebchen, weil's auf Erden	IV No. 12	Unspec.	C. Rühle i. L.	Grmn. woman comp., soprano, sister of A. F. Häser	CHAL (1901)
2997	Häser, J. [prob. Johann]	1729-1809	Gott hilft zur rechten Zeit "Was seufzest du im Leben"	Op. 23 No. 1	S/A	R. & P.		CHAL (1898)
2998	Häser, J. [prob. Johann]	1729-1809	Gute Nacht "Gute Nacht, gute Nacht, Gottes Auge"	Op. 23 No. 1	S/A	R. & P.		CHAL (1898)
2999	Hasse		Majnatt		Unspec.	Lundq.		CVMP (1976)
3000	Hasse, Gustav	1834-1889	An grüner Linde "Lustige Blut"	Op. 62 No. 2	S/A	Simon i. Berl.		CHAL (1898)

REC	COMP	DTS	TITLE	OP #	VCG	PUB	COMMENTS	SRC
3001	Hasse, Gustav	1834-1889	Aufbruch "Schon leuchet und flammt"	Op. 59 No. 3	Unspec.	Sulzer		CHAL (1898)
3002	Hasse, Gustav	1834-1889	Schlummerlied "Nacht umhüllt mit wehendem Flügel"	Op. 58 No. 1	Unspec.	R. & P.		CHAL (1898)
3003	Hasse, Gustav	1834-1889	Ständchen "Mond tritt aus der Wolkenwand"	Op. 59 No. 1	Unspec.	Sulzer		CHAL (1898)
3004	Hasse, Gustav	1834-1889	Tagesfrüh "Morgen glüht"	Op. 62 No. 1	S/A	Simon i. Berl.		CHAL (1898)
3005	Hasse, Gustav	1834-1889	Waldlied "Im Walde möcht' ich leben"	Op. 58 No. 2	Unspec.	R. & P.		CHAL (1898)
3006	Hasse, Gustav	1834-1889	Zu deinen Füssen will ich ruh'n	Op. 59 No. 2	Unspec.	Sulzer		CHAL (1898)
3007	Hasselhoff, A.		Ich will dir's nimmer sagen		Unspec.	Peterling		CHAL (1901)
3008	Hasselhoff, A.		Ich will dir's nimmer sagen		Unspec.	Fischer i. Bremen		CHAL (1911)
3009	Hászlinger, J. v.		Frühlingsnacht "Überm Garten durch die Lüfte"	No. 3	S/A	Schlesinger		CHAL (1898)
3010	Hászlinger, J. v.		Gleichheit "Es ist kein Blümlein nicht so klein"	No. 1	S/A	Schlesinger		CHAL (1898)
3011	Hászlinger, J. v.		Nachts "Ich wandre durch die stille Nacht"	No. 2	S/A	Schlesinger		CHAL (1898)
3012	Hászlinger, J. v.		Schall der Nacht "Komm trost der Nacht"	No. 6	S/A	Schlesinger		CHAL (1898)
3013	Hászlinger, J. v.		Süsser Tod "Mir ist, nun ich dich habe"	No. 4	S/A	Schlesinger		CHAL (1898)
3014	Hászlinger, J. v.		Süsser Tod "Wer in der Liebsten Auge blickt"	No. 5	S/A	Schlesinger		CHAL (1898)
3015	Hatton, John L.	1808-1886	Simon the cellarer		Unspec.	Enoch	Arr. Newton	BBC (1975)
3016	Hatton, John L.	1808-1886	Song should breathe		S/A	Curwen		BBC (1975)
3017	Hatton, John L.	1808-1886	When evening's twilight		S/A	Curwen		BBC (1975)
3018	Hauer, Karl	1828-1892	Gebrochenes Herz "Rosen und die Nelken und Flieder"	Op. 11	S/A or T/A	Chal.		CHAL (1898)
3019	Haupt, Karl August	1810-1891	Denkst du noch mein Lieb		Unspec.	Eberle		CHAL (1906)
3020	Hauptmann, Moritz	1792-1868	Abschied "Liebchen, mein Liebchen ade"	Op. 46 No. 10	Unspec.	B. & H.		CHAL (1898)
3021	Hauptmann, Moritz	1792-1868	Andenken "Wo ich wandle, wo ich bin"	Op. 46 No. 9	Unspec.	B. & H.		CHAL (1898)
3022	Hauptmann, Moritz	1792-1868	Aus der Jugendzeit klingt ein Lied	Op. 49 No. 6	Unspec.	Hug		CHAL (1901)
3023	Hauptmann, Moritz	1792-1868	Du Herr hast alles wohlgemacht	Op. 49 No. 4	Unspec.	Hug	Arr. Vogel	CHAL (1901)
3024	Hauptmann, Moritz	1792-1868	Freie Natur "In's duft'ge Heu will ich mich legen"	Op. 46 No. 1	Unspec.	B. & H.		CHAL (1898)
3025	Hauptmann, Moritz	1792-1868	Frischer, thauiger Sommermorgen	Op. 55 No. 1	Unspec.	Hug		CHAL (1901)
3026	Hauptmann, Moritz	1792-1868	Frühling "Wie ist mir so wohl"	Op. 46 No. 6	Unspec.	B. & H.		CHAL (1898)
3027	Hauptmann, Moritz	1792-1868	Hell in's Fenster scheindt die Sonne	Op. 47 No. 2	Unspec.	Hug (Vogel)		CHAL (1901)
3028	Hauptmann, Moritz	1792-1868	Ich stand auf Berges Halde	Op. 32 No. 4	Unspec.	Hug (Vogel)		CHAL (1901)
3029	Hauptmann, Moritz	1792-1868	Ich und mein Haus, wir sind bereit	Op. 33 No. 3	high & low v.	Kistner		CHAL (1901)
3030	Hauptmann, Moritz	1792-1868	Kein Graben so breit	Op. 47 No. 4	Unspec.	Hug (Vogel)		CHAL (1901)

REC	COMP	DTS	TITLE	OP #	VCG	PUB	COMMENTS	SRC
3031	Hauptmann, Moritz	1792-1868	Liebesboten "Holder Mond, noch scheide nimmer"	Op. 46 No. 11	Unspec.	B. & H.		CHAL (1898)
3032	Hauptmann, Moritz	1792-1868	Mailied	Op. 46 No. 7	S/A	B. & H.	In anth. "Zweistim. Lied. f. Sop. u. Altstimme mit Klavierbegleitung f. den Haus- u. Schulgebrauch v. H. M. Schletterer" 3 vols.	MSN
3033	Hauptmann, Moritz	1792-1868	Mailied "Willkommen uns, o schöner Mai"	Op. 46 No. 7	Unspec.	B. & H.		CHAL (1898)
3034	Hauptmann, Moritz	1792-1868	Nachtgesang "Es feiert die Flur"	Op. 46 No. 3	Unspec.	B. & H.		CHAL (1898)
3035	Hauptmann, Moritz	1792-1868	Sah ein Knab' ein Röslein stehn	Op. 24 No. 4	Unspec.	Hug (Vogel)		CHAL (1901)
3036	Hauptmann, Moritz	1792-1868	Sehnen	Op. 46 No. 2	S/A	B. & H.	In anth. "Zweistim. Lied. f. Sop. u. Altstimme mit Klavierbegleitung f. den Haus- u. Schulgebrauch v. H. M. Schletterer" 3 vols.	MSN
3037	Hauptmann, Moritz	1792-1868	Sehnen "In die Lüfte möcht' ich steigen"	Op. 46 No. 2	Unspec.	B. & H.		CHAL (1898)
3038	Hauptmann, Moritz	1792-1868	Sehnen "In die Lüfte möcht ich steigen"	Op. 46 No. 2	S/A	B. & H.	In anth. "Zweistim. Lied. f. Sop. u. Altstimme mit Klavierbegleitung f. den Haus- u. Schulgebrauch v. H. M. Schletterer" 3 vols.	MSN
3039	Hauptmann, Moritz	1792-1868	Ständchen "Schläfst Liebchen schon"	Op. 46 No. 8	Unspec.	B. & H.		CHAL (1898)
3040	Hauptmann, Moritz	1792-1868	Über allen Gipfeln ist Ruh	Op. 25 No. 4	Unspec.	Hug (Vogel)		CHAL (1901)
3041	Hauptmann, Moritz	1792-1868	Unter Lindenbäumchen	Op. 46 No. 4	Unspec.	B. & H.		CHAL (1898)
3042	Hauptmann, Moritz	1792-1868	Waldeslust "Auf dem Rasen im Walde"	Op. 46 No. 4	S/A	B. & H.	In anth. "Zweistim. Lied. f. Sop. u. Altstimme mit Klavierbegleitung f. den Haus- u. Schulgebrauch v. H. M. Schletterer" 3 vols.	MSN
3043	Hauptmann, Moritz	1792-1868	Waldeslust "Auf dem Rasen im Walde"	Op. 46 No. 5	Unspec.	B. & H.		CHAL (1898)
3044	Hauptmann, Moritz	1792-1868	Wenn der Frühling kommt und von den Bergen schaut	Op. 32 No. 3	Unspec.	Hug (Vogel)		CHAL (1901)
3045	Hauptmann, Moritz	1792-1868	Willkommen uns, o schöner Mai	Op. 46 No. 7	S/A	B. & H.	In anth. "Zweistim. Lied. f. Sop. u. Altstimme mit Klavierbegleitung f. den Haus- u. Schulgebrauch v. H. M. Schletterer" 3 vols.	MSN
3046	Hauptmann, Moritz	1792-1868	Wogende Wellen wallen empor	Op. 46 No. 11	Unspec.	B. & H.		CHAL (1898)
3047	Hauptmann, Moritz	1792-1868	Wunderbar ist mir geschehen	Op. 49 No. 12	Unspec.	Hug (Vogel)		CHAL (1901)
3048	Hauptmann, R.		Schamster Diener stell'n uns vor		Unspec.	Blaha		CHAL (1901)
3049	Hause, C.		Augen der Nacht "Aus tausend Augen blickt die Nacht"		Unspec.	Kahnt		CHAL (1898)
3050	Hauser, Moritz H.	1826-1857	An den Sonnenschein "O Sonnenschein"	Op. 5 No. 1	Unspec.	Kratochwill		CHAL (1898)
3051	Hauser, Moritz H.	1826-1857	In der Ferne "Will ruhen unter den Bäumen hier"	Op. 5 No. 2	Unspec.	Kratochwill		CHAL (1898)
3052	Hauser, Moritz H.	1826-1857	Lebewohl "Lebewohl, lebewohl mein Lieb"	Op. 6 No. 1	Unspec.	Kratochwill		CHAL (1898)
3053	Hauser, Moritz H.	1826-1857	Stille "Es weiss und räth es doch Keiner"	Op. 6 No. 2	Unspec.	Kratochwill		CHAL (1898)

REC	COMP	DTS	TITLE	OP #	VCG	PUB	COMMENTS	SRC
3054	Hawley, Charles B.	1858-1915	The sweetest flower that blows		Unspec.	Boosey	Arr. Geehl	BBC (1975)
3055	Hawthorne, Alice	1827-1902	Whispering Hope		Unspec.	Century	Pen name of Septimus Winner. Also solo. First published as solo in 1868.	CVMP (1976)
3056	Hawthorne, Alice	1827-1902	Whispering Hope		high & low v.	G. Schirm.	Pen name of Septimus Winner. In catalogue page "Selected Vocal Duets" of G. Schirmer, Inc. NY (no date)	MSN
3057	Hawthorne, Alice	1827-1902	Whispering Hope		S/A	G. Schirm.	Pen name of Septimus Winner	MSN
3058	Haydn, Franz Joseph	1732-1908	Twenty-Four Canons		Unspec.	Peters	Sacred canons for 2-8 v.	CVMP (1976)
3059	Hazlehurst, Cecil	1880-	O Leave Your Sheep		2 med. v.	Boosey		ASR
3060	Hecht, Gustav	1851-1932	Abendläuten "Immer, wenn es Abend läutet"	Op. 37 No. 2	S/A	Oertel		CHAL (1898)
3061	Hecht, Gustav	1851-1932	Ehre sei Gott inder Höhe "Alte u. neue Weihnachts-lieder"		Unspec.	Vieweg i. Qu.	2 Hefte (2 Parts)	CHAL (1898)
3062	Hecht, Gustav	1851-1932	Frühling "Was rauschet, was rieselt"	Op. 37 No. 1	S/A	Oertel		CHAL (1898)
3063	Hecht, Gustav	1851-1932	Musik "Eine Stimme sucht sich die Freude"	No. 7	S/A	R. & E.		CHAL (1898)
3064	Hefner, Otto	1868-	Verzeihen Sie, dass ich so früh schon kumm	Op. 17	Unspec.	Hefner i. Obern.-Bu.		CHAL (1901)
3065	Heidrich, Maximilian	1864-1909	Auf der Hald' viel Röslein stehn	Op. 13 No. 2	Unspec.	Dörfell		CHAL (1898)
3066	Heidrich, Maximilian	1864-1909	Weil wir doch scheiden müssen	Op. 13 No. 3	Unspec.	Dörfell		CHAL (1898)
3067	Heidrich, Maximilian	1864-1909	Zweigesang "Im Flieder-busch ein Vöglein sass"	Op. 13 No. 1	Unspec.	Dörffel		CHAL (1898)
3068	Heidrich, Th.		Unter der blühenden Linden		Unspec.	Chemnitz Selbstverl.		CHAL (1906)
3069	Heidrich, Th.		Unter der blühenden Linden		Unspec.	S. & V.		CHAL (1911)
3070	Heim, A.		O selige Weihnacht, wie bist du so schön	Op. 48	Unspec.	Haushahn i. M.		CHAL (1898)
3071	Heine, C.		Lauf der Welt "An jedem Abend geh' ich aus"	Op. 26	Unspec.	Otto i. Berl.		CHAL (1898)
3072	Heinemann, Wilhelm	1862-	Dort oben auf dem Berge (Blumenhaus)	Op. 8 No. 4	Unspec.	Heinr.		CHAL (1901)
3073	Heinemann, Wilhelm	1862-	Es regnet, es regnet, die Stäudle werden nass	Op. 8 No. 1	Unspec.	Heinr.		CHAL (1901)
3074	Heinemann, Wilhelm	1862-	Hat unser kleiner Stiefelmann	Op. 8 No. 6	Unspec.	Heinr.		CHAL (1901)
3075	Heinemann, Wilhelm	1862-	Kinderlieder (6)	Op. 8	Unspec.	Heinr.	Collection of 6 duets	CHAL (1901)
3076	Heinemann, Wilhelm	1862-	Männlein, Männlein, geig' einmal	Op. 8 No. 3	Unspec.	Heinr.		CHAL (1901)
3077	Heinemann, Wilhelm	1862-	Sum, sum, sum ganz leise der Landmann geht	Op. 8 No. 2	Unspec.	Heinr.		CHAL (1901)
3078	Heinemann, Wilhelm	1862-	Was tanzen so goldige Sternchen	Op. 8 No. 5	Unspec.	Heinr.		CHAL (1901)
3079	Heinlein, A.		Zwei alte Jungfern "Was wir vor zwanzig Jahr'n"	Op. 1	Unspec.	Fr. Dietrich		CHAL (1898)
3080	Heinrich, Anton Philipp	1781-1861	Schlaf wohl, du Himmelsknabe	Op. 16 No. 2	S/MS	Verlag Melodia		CHAL (1911)

REC	COMP	DTS	TITLE	OP #	VCG	PUB	COMMENTS	SRC
3081	Heinrich, Anton Philipp	1781-1861	Wenn die Weihnachtsglocken klingen	Op. 16	S/MS	Verlag Melodia		CHAL (1911)
3082	Heinrich, E.		Keine Hilfe, keine Rettung	Op. 93	2 female v.	Spitzner		CHAL (1901)
3083	Heins, Karl	1859-1923	An jedem Abend geh' ich aus	Op. 26	Unspec.	Wehde		CHAL (1906)
3084	Heinz, P.		Fortschritt der heutigen Zeit ist sehr gross "Kostüm-Duett"		Unspec.	G. Richter i. L.		CHAL (1911)
3085	Heinz, P.		Im Frühling, wenn die Sonn' erweckt		2 female v.	G. Richter i. L.		CHAL (1911)
3086	Heinz, P.		Trara, die Post ist da		Unspec.	Rau & P.		CHAL (1911)
3087	Heinze, Richard	1845-1893	Anna und Martha "Wenn die Woch geht zu Ende"	Op. 148	S/A	O. Forberg		CHAL (1898)
3088	Heinze, Richard	1845-1893	Ein Dienstmädchen des 19 Jahrhunderts "Wie ist die haus frau schlimm daran"	Op. 28	S/A	Glaser		CHAL (1898)
3089	Heinze, Richard	1845-1893	Eine moderne Frau "Ein Brief von meiner Adelheid"	Op. 146	S/A	Glaser		CHAL (1898)
3090	Heinze, Richard	1845-1893	Frau Hitzig und Frau Spitzig "Auch ich war einst Jungfrau"	Op. 137	S/A	O. Forberg		CHAL (1898)
3091	Heinze, Richard	1845-1893	Linchen und Minchen "Ganze Woche freu' ich mich"	Op. 110	S/A	O. Forberg		CHAL (1898)
3092	Heinze, Richard	1845-1893	Poëtischen Bäckerjungen "Meister und die Meisterin"	Op. 89	2 med. v.	Glaser		CHAL (1898)
3093	Heiser, Wilhelm	1816-1897	Es stand eine rothe Rose	Op. 137	Unspec.	Litolff		CHAL (1898)
3094	Heiser, Wilhelm	1816-1897	Mutterherz "Ich höre trauern und klagen"	Op. 80	S/S or T/T	Junne		CHAL (1898)
3095	Heiser, Wilhelm	1816-1897	Siehe der Frühling währet nicht lang'	IV No. 13	Unspec.	C. Rühle i. L.		CHAL (1901)
3096	Heiser, Wilhelm	1816-1897	Weihnachts "Heilige Nacht, du kehrest wieder"	Op. 344	Unspec.	Grüniger		CHAL (1898)
3097	Heiser, Wilhelm	1816-1897	"Wenn der Frühling auf die Berge steigt"	Op. 92	S/S or T/T	Cranz		CHAL (1898)
3098	Heiter, Ernst	1788-1867	Als lust'ge Damengigerl	Op. 10	2 female v.	Glaser	Pen name of Simon Sechter	CHAL (1906)
3099	Heiter, Ernst	1788-1867	Dass wir sehr flott und nett	Op. 6	Unspec.	Glaser	Pen name of Simon Sechter	CHAL (1906)
3100	Heiter, Ernst	1788-1867	Dass wir zwei gar kreuz fidele Wächter sind	Op. 2	2 med. v.	Glaser	Pen name of Simon Sechter	CHAL (1901)
3101	Heiter, Ernst	1788-1867	Mord in der Dämmerstunde	Op. 8	Unspec.	Glaser	Pen name of Simon Sechter	CHAL (1906)
3102	Heiter, Ernst	1788-1867	O je, o je, wir Armen	Op. 1	Unspec.	Glaser	Pen name of Simon Sechter	CHAL (1901)
3103	Heiter, Ernst	1788-1867	So, nun kann Frau Dreyer kommen	Op. 22	2 female v.	Glaser	Pen name of Simon Sechter	CHAL (1906)
3104	Heitmann, M.		Kinderlieder (12)	Op. 20	Unspec.	Ebner	Collection of 12 duets	CHAL (1901)
3105	Heitmann, M.		Kommet ihr Hirten	Op. 20 No. 12	Unspec.	Ebner		CHAL (1901)
3106	Heitmann, M.		Musche, musche Kuh	Op. 20 No. 6	Unspec.	Ebner		CHAL (1901)
3107	Heitmann, M.		O heiliges Kind	Op. 20 No. 11	Unspec.	Ebner		CHAL (1901)
3108	Heitmann, M.		Regenleed "Regen, Regen drus"	Op. 20 No. 9	Unspec.	Ebner		CHAL (1901)
3109	Heitmann, M.		Spatzen und die Kinder	Op. 20 No. 8	Unspec.	Ebner		CHAL (1901)
3110	Heitmann, M.		Wächter mit dem Silberhorn	Op. 20 No. 7	Unspec.	Ebner		CHAL (1901)

REC	COMP	DTS	TITLE	OP #	VCG	PUB	COMMENTS	SRC
3111	Hekking, P. F. R.		Cantica eucharistica	Op. 6	Unspec.	Rörich	org accomp.	CHAL (1898)
3112	Helbig, W.		August und Fritze, die fidelen Schusterjungen "Hum. Duoscene"	Op. 13	Unspec.	O. Teich		CHAL (1901)
3113	Helbig, W.		Wir sind die Hüter in der Nacht	Op. 105	Unspec.	Fr. Dietrich		CHAL (1906)
3114	Helbig, W.		Zwei kreuzfidele Leut "Wenn uns einmal der Kummer drückt"		Unspec.	Seeling		CHAL (1898)
3115	Hellmesberger Jr., Joseph	1855-1907	Ein Jeder sieht, dass wir keine Kuchenbäcker sein		Unspec.	Eberle		CHAL (1906)
3116	Hellmesberger Jr., Joseph	1855-1907	Fünfzig Wochen hat das Jahr		Unspec.	Eberle		CHAL (1906)
3117	Hellwig, Karl Friedrich Ludwig	1773-1838	Am stillen Abend, Friede und Freude dir		S/A	Junne		CHAL (1898)
3118	Hellwig, Karl Friedrich Ludwig	1773-1838	Blümchen Geguld		Unspec.	Junne		CHAL (1898)
3119	Hely-Hutchinson, Victor	1901-1947	Owl and the Pussycat, The		2-3 med. v.	Paterson	acap.	ASR
3120	Hely-Hutchinson, Victor	1901-1947	Table and Chair		2-3 med. v.	Paterson	acap.	ASR
3121	Hemberg, Eskil	1938-	Anlundavisan		2 female v.	None listed	Ed. E. Hemberg. In "Tva Duetter" Dan. folk tune.	CVMP (1985)
3122	Hemberg, Eskil	1938-	Bakvanda Visan		2 female v.	None listed	Ed. E. Hemberg. In "Tva Duetter" Dan. folk tune.	CVMP (1985)
3123	Hemery, Valentine		Soldiers of Fortune		Unspec.	Leonard-Eng		CVMP (1976)
3124	Hempel, F. R.		Frühling in der Heimath "Es kam der Frühling gezogen"	Op.3 No. 2	S/A or T/B	R. & P.		CHAL (1898)
3125	Hempel, F. R.		Frühlingslust "Es irren und schwirren"	Op. 3 No. 1	S/A or T/B	R. & P.		CHAL (1898)
3126	Hennig, C. [prob. Karl Rafael]	1845-1914	O Abendruh', wie süss bist du	Op. 93 No. 4	S/A or T/B	Ed. Stoll		CHAL (1898)
3127	Hennig, C. [prob. Karl Rafael]	1845-1914	Sei gegrüsst Tag des Herrn	Op. 93 No. 5	S/A or T/B	Ed. Stoll		CHAL (1898)
3128	Hennig, C. [prob. Karl Rafael]	1845-1914	Waldlust "Wie herrlich ist's im Walde"	Op. 93 No. 1	S/A or T/B	Ed. Stoll		CHAL (1898)
3129	Henschel, F.		Frei von allen Sorgen	Op. 31	Unspec.	O. Dietrich		CHAL (1901)
3130	Henschel, George	1850-1934	A Christmas song		S/A	Church		BBC (1975)
3131	Henschel, George	1850-1934	An die Nachtigall		S/A	Simrock		BBC (1975)
3132	Henschel, George	1850-1934	An die Nachtigall "Nachtigall sing' nicht so frühe"	Op. 32 No. 3	S/A	Simrock		CHAL (1898)
3133	Henschel, George	1850-1934	Der bezauberte Knabe		S/A	Simrock		BBC (1975)
3134	Henschel, George	1850-1934	Gondoliera		S/S	Church		BBC (1975)
3135	Henschel, George	1850-1934	Gute Lehre "Grad Herz brich nicht"	Op. 4 No. 3	2 low or 2 high v.	Schlesinger		CHAL (1898)

REC	COMP	DTS	TITLE	OP #	VCG	PUB	COMMENTS	SRC
3136	Henschel, George	1850-1934	Heimliche Liebe "Kein Feuer, keine Kohle"	Op. 4 No. 1	2 high or 2 low v.	Schlesinger		CHAL (1898)
3137	Henschel, George	1850-1934	Ich vergonn' es ihm		S/A	Simrock		BBC (1975)
3138	Henschel, George	1850-1934	Ich vergönn' es ihm "Rosen pflückte ab das Mädchen"	Op. 32 No. 7	S/A	Simrock		CHAL (1898)
3139	Henschel, George	1850-1934	If Thou, Lord, shouldst number trangressions		S/S	Church		BBC (1975)
3140	Henschel, George	1850-1934	Kein Feuer, keine Kohle	Op. 4 No. 1	S/A	Ditson	In anthology "The Ditson Collection of Soprano and Alto Duets" Pub. 1934.	MSN
3141	Henschel, George	1850-1934	Kein Graben so breit		S/S	Church		BBC (1975)
3142	Henschel, George	1850-1934	Lass dich nicht gegeur'n der Thränen	Op. 33 No. 1	Unspec.	B. & B.		CHAL (1898)
3143	Henschel, George	1850-1934	No fire, nor hot embers		Unspec.	ECS	In anthology "48 Duets Seventeenth Through Nineteenth Centuries" Ed. V. Prahl. Pub. 1941, 1970.	MSN
3144	Henschel, George	1850-1934	O that we two were maying		S/S	Church		BBC (1975)
3145	Henschel, George	1850-1934	Oh weep for those that wept by Babel's stream		S/A	Church		BBC (1975)
3146	Henschel, George	1850-1934	Schon häufig an die Pforte meines Herzens	Op. 33 No. 2	Unspec.	B. & B.		CHAL (1898)
3147	Henschel, George	1850-1934	Seliger Eingang		S/S	Church		BBC (1975)
3148	Henschel, George	1850-1934	Sieh', das ist es, was auf Erden	Op. 33 No. 3	Unspec.	B. & B.		CHAL (1898)
3149	Henschel, George	1850-1934	Stille "Es weiss und räth es doch Keiner"	Op. 4 No. 2	2 high or 2 low v.	Schlesinger		CHAL (1898)
3150	Henschel, George	1850-1934	Three Duets	Op. 28	S/S	Church		BBC (1975)
3151	Henschel, George	1850-1934	Three Duets	Op. 33	S/A	Simrock		BBC (1975)
3152	Henschel, George	1850-1934	Three Duets	Op. 4	S/S	Church		BBC (1975)
3153	Henschel, George	1850-1934	Über der dunklen Haide	Op. 33 No. 2	Unspec.	B. & B.		CHAL (1898)
3154	Hensel, Fanny Mendelssohn	1805-1847	April		Unspec.	Arts Venture	Grmn. woman comp. Sister of F. Mendelssohn. Autogr. 1836. In "3 Duets on Texts by J. W. v. Goethe" Score provides historical information.	MSN
3155	Hensel, Fanny Mendelssohn	1805-1847	Aus meinen Tränen spriessen	No. II	S/MS	Arts Venture	Grmn. woman comp. Sister of F. Mendelssohn. Autogr. 1836. In "3 Duets on Texts by J. W. v. Goethe" Score provides historical information.	MSN
3156	Hensel, Fanny Mendelssohn	1805-1847	Die Mitternacht was kalt und stumm	No. I	Unspec.	Arts Venture	Grmn. woman comp. Sister of F. Mendelssohn. Autogr. 1836. In "3 Duets on Texts by J. W. v. Goethe" Score provides historical information.	MSN

REC	COMP	DTS	TITLE	OP #	VCG	PUB	COMMENTS	SRC
3157	Hensel, Fanny Mendelssohn	1805-1847	Ich stand gelehnet war kalt und stumm	No. II	Unspec.	Arts Venture	Grmn. woman comp. Sister of F. Mendelssohn. Autogr. 1836. In "3 Duets on Texts by J. W. v. Goethe" Score provides historical information.	MSN
3158	Hensel, Fanny Mendelssohn	1805-1847	Im wunderschönen Monat Mai	No. III	S/MS	Arts Venture	Grmn. woman comp. Sister of F. Mendelssohn. Autogr. 1836. In "3 Duets on Texts by J. W. v. Goethe" Score provides historical information.	MSN
3159	Hensel, Fanny Mendelssohn	1805-1847	Mai		Unspec.	Arts Venture	Grmn. woman comp. Sister of F. Mendelssohn. Autogr. 1836. In "3 Duets on Texts by J. W. v. Goethe" Score provides historical information.	MSN
3160	Hensel, Fanny Mendelssohn	1805-1847	März		Unspec.	Arts Venture	Grmn. woman comp. Sister of F. Mendelssohn. Autogr. 1836. In "3 Duets on Texts by J. W. v. Goethe" Score provides historical information.	MSN
3161	Hensel, Fanny Mendelssohn	1805-1847	Wenn ich in deine Augen sehe	No. I	S/MS	Arts Venture	Grmn. woman comp. Sister of F. Mendelssohn. Autogr. 1836. In "3 Duets on Texts by J. W. v. Goethe" Score provides historical information.	MSN
3162	Henssige, E.		Vater unser, der du bist im Himmel	Op. 4	S/A	Preiser	org	CHAL (1911)
3163	Herbert, Theodor	1822-1891	Im Maien "Nun (Es) bricht aus allen Zweigen"	Op. 25	Unspec.	Hofmann i. Dresd.		CHAL (1898)
3164	Herbert, Victor	1859-1924	Gypsy Love Song		Unspec.	Allans	Also solo	CVMP (1976)
3165	Hering, C. [prob. Karl Eduard]	1807-1897	Ein Fichtenbaum steht einsam	Op. 103 No. 1	S/A	Bahn		CHAL (1898)
3166	Hering, C. [prob. Karl Eduard]	1807-1897	Frühling "Erguss der Himmels, Lenzeszeit"	Op. 103 No. 3	S/A	Bahn		CHAL (1898)
3167	Hering, C. [prob. Karl Eduard]	1807-1897	Herr, erhöre mein Gebet	Op. 104 No. 2	2 female v.	Bahn		CHAL (1898)
3168	Hering, C. [prob. Karl Eduard]	1807-1897	Herr, segne das Beginnen	Op. 104 No.1	2 female v.	Bahn		CHAL (1898)
3169	Hering, C. [prob. Karl Eduard]	1807-1897	O süsse Mutter ich kann nicht spinnen	Op. 103 No. 2	S/A	Bahn		CHAL (1898)
3170	Herman, Reinhold Ludwig	1849-1920	Ein Rosenhag blüht	Op. 38 No. 1	MS/A	A. P. Schmidt i. L.		CHAL (1901)
3171	Herman, Reinhold Ludwig	1849-1920	Vorüber ist die Rosenzeit	Op. 38 No. 2	S/A	A. P. Schm. i. Leip.		CHAL (1901)
3172	Hermann, E. Hans	1870-1931	Abendlied "Nacht ist niedergegangen"	Op. 2 No. 1	S/S	Heinr.		CHAL (1898)
3173	Hermann, E. Hans	1870-1931	Blätterfall "Leise, windverwehte Blätter"	Op. 2 No. 3	S/S	Heinr.		CHAL (1898)
3174	Hermann, E. Hans	1870-1931	Spröde "An dem reinsten Frühlingsmorgen"	Op. 2 No. 2	S/S	Heinr.		CHAL (1898)

REC	COMP	DTS	TITLE	OP #	VCG	PUB	COMMENTS	SRC
3175	Hermann, E. Hans	1870-1931	Wellen "Wer will uns binden"	Op. 2 No. 4	S/S	Heinr.		CHAL (1898)
3176	Hermann, R. L.	1870-1931	Komm, o nacht, und nimm mich hin	Op. 45 No. 1	high & low v.	Heinr.		CHAL (1906)
3177	Hermann, R. L.	1870-1931	Mond steht über dem Berge	Op. 45 No. 2	high & low v.	Heinr.		CHAL (1906)
3178	Hermann, W.		Jocund spring is here again	Op. 3 No. 1	S/A	A. P. Schm. i. Leip.		CHAL (1901)
3179	Hermann, W.		Outside my open window	Op. 3 No. 2	S/A	A. P. Schm. i. Leip.		CHAL (1901)
3180	Hermann, William		Deutsche Volkslieder Book I, II	Op. 143	S/A or S/Br	Schauer	Unspec. pieces.	ASR
3181	Hermann, William		Deutsche Volkslieder, Vol. I	Op. 143	Unspec.	Schaur EE	Collection. Unspec. pieces.	CVMP (1976)
3182	Hermann, William		Deutsche Volkslieder, Vol. II	Op. 143	Unspec.	Schaur EE	Collection. Unspec. pieces.	CVMP (1976)
3183	Hermany, O.		Breslauer Schnadahüpferl		Unspec.	Starke		CHAL (1898)
3184	Hermes, Eduard	1818-1905	Einsame Röslein im Thal "Es liegt ein Weiler fern im Grund"		Unspec.	Leuckart		CHAL (1898)
3185	Herold, E.		Ich muss nun einmal singen "Vöglein, Vöglein, was singest du"	No. 1	S/A	Bahn		CHAL (1898)
3186	Herold, E.		Leise zieht durch mein Gemüth	No. 3	S/A	Bahn		CHAL (1898)
3187	Herold, E.		Willst du mit so komm "Ein Vogel auf dem Zweige singt"	No. 2	S/A	Bahn		CHAL (1898)
3188	Herrmann, Willy	1868-	Breit' aus die Flügel beide	Op. 79 No. 1	S/A	Oppen-heimer	pf or harm or org	CHAL (1911)
3189	Herrmann, Willy	1868-	Gib dich zufrieden und sei stille	Op. 79 No. 2	S/A	Oppen-heimer	pf or harm or org	CHAL (1911)
3190	Herrmann, Willy	1868-	Ich weiss mein Gott, dass all mein Tun	Op. 79 No. 4	S/A	none listed		CHAL (1911)
3191	Herrmann, Willy	1868-	Sprich ja zu meinen Taten	Op. 79 No. 3	S/A	Oppen-heimer	pf or harm or org	CHAL (1911)
3192	Hertz, H.		Eine Sonnenblume	Op. 7 No. 2	Unspec.	Leo. i. Berl.		CHAL (1898)
3193	Hertz, H.		Wo ich dich nicht sehe	Op. 7 No. 1	Unspec.	Leo i. Berl.		CHAL (1898)
3194	Herzog, Max.		Grab der Gefallenen des k. k. Jäger-Bat. auf St. Lucia "Schlaft wohl auf St. Lucia Kirchhof"	Op. 36	Unspec.	Aibl		CHAL (1898)
3195	Herzog, Max		Oesterreicher Gsangln "Wia scheint da Mond"	Op. 35	Unspec.	Aibl		CHAL (1898)
3196	Hess, Karl	1840-1897	Drei Wünsche "O dass wir zwei im Maien"	Op. 21	Unspec.	Hoffarth		CHAL (1898)
3197	Hesselmann, L.		Dir wird gereicht so manche Dankesblume		Unspec.	P. & M.		CHAL (1901)
3198	Heuler, Raimund	1872-1932	Leichte zweistimmige Weihnachtslieder	Op. 18	S/A	Böhm & S.	pf or harm or org	CHAL (1911)
3199	Heuler, Raimund	1872-1932	Weihnachtslieder (2)		S/A	Bucher i. Würzb.	pf or harm or org. 2 duets	CHAL (1906)
3200	Heuschkel, Johann Peter	d. 1853	"Thut es mir gleich so weh"		Unspec.	Schott		CHAL (1898)
3201	Heuser, Ernst	1863-	Einsamkeit "Hörst du nicht die Quellen gehen"	Op. 20 No. 3	Unspec.	Rud. Dietrich		CHAL (1898)

REC	COMP	DTS	TITLE	OP #	VCG	PUB	COMMENTS	SRC
3202	Heuser, Ernst	1863-	Es blühen an den Wegen	Op. 20 No. 2	Unspec.	Rud. Dietrich		CHAL (1898)
3203	Heuser, Ernst	1863-	Weihnachts "Wunderbare heil'ge Nacht"		Unspec.	Grüniger		CHAL (1898)
3204	Heuser, Ernst	1863-	Zur Nacht "Lind wallt die Nacht hernider"	Op. 20 No. 1	Unspec.	Rud. Dietrich		CHAL (1898)
3205	Heussenstamm, George		With Jesus Will I Go		S/A	Concordia	May be perf. chorally	CVMP (1976)
3206	Hey, Julius	1832-1909	Armes eingesperrtes Vöglein	Op. 15 No. 3	S/A	B. & H.		CHAL (1901)
3207	Hey, Julius	1832-1909	Ei du liebe, liebe Zeit	Op. 15 No. 2	S/A	B. & H.		CHAL (1901)
3208	Hey, Julius	1832-1909	F und E in grossen Zügen	Op. 16 No. 2	S/A	B. & H.		CHAL (1901)
3209	Hey, Julius	1832-1909	Hu, hu, wie saust so kalt	Op. 15 No. 1	S/A	B. & H.		CHAL (1901)
3210	Hey, Julius	1832-1909	Rock und Hose frisch gebügelt	Op. 16 No. 1	S/A	B. & H.		CHAL (1901)
3211	Hey, Julius	1832-1909	Wir schmausen so gerne	Op. 15 No. 4	S/A	B. & H.		CHAL (1901)
3212	Hiens, C. [poss. Karl Heins, uncertain. See entry]		Wohlauf in Gottes schöne Welt	Op. 30	Unspec.	Weinholtz		CHAL (1898)
3213	Hildach, Eugen	1849-1924	Abschied der Vögel		high & med. v.	G. Schirm.	In catalogue page "Selected Vocal Duets" of G. Schirmer, Inc. NY (no date)	MSN
3214	Hildach, Eugen	1849-1924	Abschied der Vögel "Ade ihe Felsenhallen"	Op. 14 No. 1	S/B or S/A	Heinr.		CHAL (1898)
3215	Hildach, Eugen	1849-1924	Sperlinge "Altes Haus mit deinen Löchern"	Op. 14 No. 3	S/Br or S/A	Heinr.		CHAL (1898)
3216	Hildach, Eugen	1849-1924	Überall in Flur und Hain	Op. 14 No. 2	S/Br or S/A	Heinr.		CHAL (1898)
3217	Hill, Lady Arthur		In the Gloaming		Unspec.	Leonard-Eng	Also solo. Woman comp.	CVMP (1976)
3218	Hill, Wilhelm	1838-1902	Abendreihn "Guten Abend lieber Mondenschein"	Op. 19 No. 2	Unspec.	André		CHAL (1898)
3219	Hill, Wilhelm	1838-1902	Am Bach "Klinge, rausche kleiner Bach"	Op. 19 No. 1	Unspec.	André		CHAL (1898)
3220	Hill, Wilhelm	1838-1902	Da drüben "Da drüben über'm Walde"	Op. 38 No. 2	2 female v.	Schweers & H.		CHAL (1898)
3221	Hill, Wilhelm	1838-1902	Es war ein alter König	Op. 19 No. 5	Unspec.	André		CHAL (1898)
3222	Hill, Wilhelm	1838-1902	Grüsse "Wandl' ich Nachts"	Op. 19 No. 6	Unspec.	André		CHAL (1898)
3223	Hill, Wilhelm	1838-1902	Herbstlied "Himmel ist grau umzogen"	Op. 38 No. 3	2 female v.	Schweers & H.		CHAL (1898)
3224	Hill, Wilhelm	1838-1902	Im tiefen Wald verborgen	Op. 19 No. 3	Unspec.	André		CHAL (1898)
3225	Hill, Wilhelm	1838-1902	Lenz ist angekommen	Op. 19 No. e	Unspec.	André		CHAL (1898)
3226	Hill, Wilhelm	1838-1902	Nächtlich "Mond umfluthet und umflicht"	Op. 38 No. 1	2 female v.	Schweers & H.		CHAL (1898)
3227	Hill, Wilhelm	1838-1902	Wie ist doch die Erde so schön	Op. 38 No. 4	2 female v.	Schweers & H.		CHAL (1898)
3228	Hiller		Majsang		Unspec.	Lundq.		CVMP (1976)
3229	Hiller, Ferdinand	1811-1885	Abschied "Abendlich schon rauscht der Wald"	Op. 63 No. 1	S/B or S/A	Cranz		CHAL (1898)
3230	Hiller, Ferdinand	1811-1885	Ade "Ade mein liebes Herz"	Op. 177 No. 1	Unspec.	Cranz		CHAL (1898)

Chapter 7

REC	COMP	DTS	TITLE	OP #	VCG	PUB	COMMENTS	SRC
3231	Hiller, Ferdinand	1811-1885	Alles ist ein Traum "Es saust der Baum auf ödem Feld"	Op. 90 No. 4	Unspec.	Schott		CHAL (1898)
3232	Hiller, Ferdinand	1811-1885	Auf dem Berge "O Berg, von deinem Gipfel"	Op. 121 No. 4	2 low v.	Cranz		CHAL (1898)
3233	Hiller, Ferdinand	1811-1885	Daheim "Längst schon flog zu Nest der Vogel"	Op. 90 No. 3	Unspec.	Schott		CHAL (1898)
3234	Hiller, Ferdinand	1811-1885	Drüben "Drüben, wo aus grünem Wald"	Op. 177 No. 2	Unspec.	Cranz		CHAL (1898)
3235	Hiller, Ferdinand	1811-1885	Ein Fichtenbaum steht einsam	Op. 90 No. 9	Unspec.	Schott		CHAL (1898)
3236	Hiller, Ferdinand	1811-1885	Eine Käferhochzeit "Ich will das Eisenhütlein fragen"	Op. 45	2 female v.	Sch. & Co.		CHAL (1898)
3237	Hiller, Ferdinand	1811-1885	Es fiel ein Reif	Op. 61 No. 6	Unspec.	André		CHAL (1898)
3238	Hiller, Ferdinand	1811-1885	Frieden der Nacht "Tag ist längst geschieden"	Op. 121 No. 1	2 low v.	Cranz		CHAL (1898)
3239	Hiller, Ferdinand	1811-1885	Frühling "Nun werden schon die Bäume grün"	Op. 90 No. 7	Unspec.	Schott		CHAL (1898)
3240	Hiller, Ferdinand	1811-1885	Frühlingsglaube "Linden Lüfte sind erwacht"	Op. 20 No. 5	Unspec.	Schott		CHAL (1898)
3241	Hiller, Ferdinand	1811-1885	Frühlingslied "Tief im grünen Frühlingshag"	Op. 92 No. 5	Unspec.	Schott		CHAL (1898)
3242	Hiller, Ferdinand	1811-1885	Gebet "O Herr Gott, gesetzt ist mein Hoffen"	Op. 121 No. 5	2 low v.	Cranz		CHAL (1898)
3243	Hiller, Ferdinand	1811-1885	Gebet "O Herr Gott, gesetzt ist mein Hoffen"	Op. 177 No. 4	Unspec.	Cranz		CHAL (1898)
3244	Hiller, Ferdinand	1811-1885	Gruss "Wenn zu mei'm Schätzerl kommst"	Op. 39 No. 2	S/A	B. & H.		CHAL (1898)
3245	Hiller, Ferdinand	1811-1885	Heimliche Liebe "Kein Feuer, keine Kohle"	Op. 39 No. 3	S/A	B. & H.		CHAL (1898)
3246	Hiller, Ferdinand	1811-1885	Heimliche Liebe "Mein Schatz, der ist auf den Wanderschaft"	Op. 39 No. 1	S/A	B. & H.		CHAL (1898)
3247	Hiller, Ferdinand	1811-1885	Hoffnung "Wenn die Hoffnung nicht wär'"	Op. 61 No. 3	Unspec.	André		CHAL (1898)
3248	Hiller, Ferdinand	1811-1885	Hut' du dich "Ich weiss ein Mädchen (Mägdlein)"	Op. 61 No. 5	Unspec.	André		CHAL (1898)
3249	Hiller, Ferdinand	1811-1885	Hymne "Schwindet Nächte, weichet Wolken"	Op. 121 No. 6	2 low v.	Cranz		CHAL (1898)
3250	Hiller, Ferdinand	1811-1885	Im Walde, im hellen Sonnenschein	Op. 63 No. 2	S/B or S/A	Cranz		CHAL (1898)
3251	Hiller, Ferdinand	1811-1885	In der Nacht "Ungetrübte Ruh' erfühllt mich"	Op. 177 No. 6	Unspec.	Cranz		CHAL (1898)
3252	Hiller, Ferdinand	1811-1885	Kammer-Duette (6)	Op. 121	2 low v.	Cranz		CHAL (1898)
3253	Hiller, Ferdinand	1811-1885	Komm o Nacht und nimm mich hin	Op. 164 No. 5	Unspec.	Siegel		CHAL (1898)
3254	Hiller, Ferdinand	1811-1885	König in Thule "Es war ein König in Thule"	Op. 205 No. 2	2 female v.	Sch. & Co.		CHAL (1898)
3255	Hiller, Ferdinand	1811-1885	Liedchen erklinge, schwing' dich	Op. 92 No. 1	Unspec.	Schott		CHAL (1898)
3256	Hiller, Ferdinand	1811-1885	Loser, leichter, luftger Wind	Op. 121 No. 3	2 low v.	Cranz		CHAL (1898)
3257	Hiller, Ferdinand	1811-1885	März "Es ist ein Schnee gefallen"	Op. 205 No. 4	2 female v.	Sch. & Co.		CHAL (1898)
3258	Hiller, Ferdinand	1811-1885	Mein Herz ist wie das tiefe Meer	Op. 90 No. 6	Unspec.	Schott		CHAL (1898)
3259	Hiller, Ferdinand	1811-1885	Mein Schatzerl "Mein Schatzerl is wandern"	Op. 39 No. 5	S/A	B. & H.		CHAL (1898)

REC	COMP	DTS	TITLE	OP #	VCG	PUB	COMMENTS	SRC
3260	Hiller, Ferdinand	1811-1885	Meine Boten "Grüss ihn, o Morgenröthe"	Op. 92 No. 3	Unspec.	Schott		CHAL (1898)
3261	Hiller, Ferdinand	1811-1885	O wär' ich ein Stern	Op. 177 No. 3	Unspec.	Cranz		CHAL (1898)
3262	Hiller, Ferdinand	1811-1885	Parsenlied "Hin zur Blume rete"	Op. 90 No. 1	Unspec.	Schott		CHAL (1898)
3263	Hiller, Ferdinand	1811-1885	Römisches Ritornell "Wie schön bist du"	Op. 205 No. 1	2 female v.	Sch. & Co.		CHAL (1898)
3264	Hiller, Ferdinand	1811-1885	Schau himmelwärts "Es weht aus Sündem ein warmer Hauch"	Op. 164 No. 6	Unspec.	Siegel		CHAL (1898)
3265	Hiller, Ferdinand	1811-1885	Schönste Blume "Lieb' ist eine Blume"	Op. 90 No. 8	Unspec.	Schott		CHAL (1898)
3266	Hiller, Ferdinand	1811-1885	Schwäble "Schwäble ziehet"	Op. 61 No. 2	Unspec.	André		CHAL (1898)
3267	Hiller, Ferdinand	1811-1885	Schwalbenlied "Aus fernem Land"	Op. 164 No. 2	Unspec.	Siegel		CHAL (1898)
3268	Hiller, Ferdinand	1811-1885	Sehnsucht "Wie hab' ich mir den Lenz ersehnt"	Op. 90 No. 2	Unspec.	Schott		CHAL (1898)
3269	Hiller, Ferdinand	1811-1885.	Sonntag "So hab' ich denn die ganze Woche"	Op. 39 No. 4	S/A	B. & H.		CHAL (1898)
3270	Hiller, Ferdinand	1811-1885	Spruch "Gott mit mir"	Op. 89	Unspec.	Schott		CHAL (1898)
3271	Hiller, Ferdinand	1811-1885	Sternenlied "Wenn dir in's Aug'"	Op. 121 No. 3	2 low v.	Cranz		CHAL (1898)
3272	Hiller, Ferdinand	1811-1885	Tannenwald "Es grüsst mich aus der Ferne"	Op. 164 No. 3	Unspec.	Siegel		CHAL (1898)
3273	Hiller, Ferdinand	1811-1885	Trost "'S isch no nit lang"	Op. 39 No. 6	S/A	B. & H.		CHAL (1898)
3274	Hiller, Ferdinand	1811-1885	Tyrolermädchen "Frühmorgens"	Op. 61 No. 1	Unspec.	André		CHAL (1898)
3275	Hiller, Ferdinand	1811-1885	Volksthümliche Lieder (7)	Op. 39	S/A	B. & H.	7 duets	CHAL (1898)
3276	Hiller, Ferdinand	1811-1885	Vorgefühl "Im Sommer hört' ich singen"	Op. 92 No. 6	Unspec.	Schott		CHAL (1898)
3277	Hiller, Ferdinand	1811-1885	Waldandacht "Frühmorgens, wenn die Hähne kräh'n"	Op. 92 No. 2	Unspec.	Schott		CHAL (1898)
3278	Hiller, Ferdinand	1811-1885	Was der Frühling ist "Frühling ist ein tapfrer"	Op. 90 No. 10	Unspec.	Schott		CHAL (1898)
3279	Hiller, Ferdinand	1811-1885	Weihnachtslied "In fröhlichem Bewegen"	Op. 92 No. 4	Unspec.	Schott		CHAL (1898)
3280	Hiller, Ferdinand	1811-1885	Wenn der Frühling auf die Berge steigt	Op. 164 No. 4	Unspec.	Siegel		CHAL (1898)
3281	Hiller, Ferdinand	1811-1885	Wenn ich ein Vöglein wär und auch zwei Flügel hätt'	Op. 177 No. 5	Unspec.	Cranz		CHAL (1898)
3282	Hiller, Ferdinand	1811-1885	Wiedersehn "Wiedersehn, du schönes"	Op. 177 No. 7	Unspec.	Cranz		CHAL (1898)
3283	Hiller, Ferdinand	1811-1885	Wiegenlied "Draussen weht der Abendwind"	Op. 39 No. 7	S/A	B. & H.		CHAL (1898)
3284	Hiller, Ferdinand	1811-1885	Wiegenlied "Draussen weht der Abendwind!"	Op. 39 No. 7	S/A	B. & H.	In anth. "Zweistim. Lied. f. Sop. u. Altstimme mit Klavierbegleitung f. den Haus- u. Schulgebrauch v. H. M. Schletterer" 3 vols.	MSN
3285	Hiller, Ferdinand	1811-1885	Zwei Rosen "Kein Sternlein blinkt am Himmelszelt"	Op. 164 No. 1	Unspec.	Siegel		CHAL (1898)

REC	COMP	DTS	TITLE	OP #	VCG	PUB	COMMENTS	SRC
3286	Hiller, Ferdinand	1811-1885	Zwei Rosen "Kein Sternlein blinkt am Himmelszelt"	Op. 205 No. 3	2 female v.	Sch. & Co.		CHAL (1898)
3287	Hiller, Ferdinand	1811-1885	Zwei Wasser "Ach Elslein lieb'"	Op.61 No. 4	Unspec.	André		CHAL (1898)
3288	Hiller, Ferdinand (G. F. Handel)	1811-1885	Wer, wer mag zu widerstehen		S/A	Cohen	Arr. of Handel duet	CHAL (1898)
3289	Hiller, Ferdinand (G. F. Handel)	1811-1885	Wir müssen ewig scheiden		S/A	Cohen	Arr. of Handel duet	CHAL (1898)
3290	Hiller, Paul	1850-	Heimath, muss dich nun verlassen	Op. 100 No. 1	S/A	Merse.		CHAL (1906)
3291	Hiller, Paul	1850-	Kornblume, Veilchen, Mai-glöckchen "Kornblümchen spricht, ich bin bereit"	Op. 100 No. 2	S/A	Merse.		CHAL (1906)
3292	Himmel, Fr. G.		Auferstehn "Auferstehn, auferstehn, ja auferstehn wirst du"		S/A	B. & H.	In anth. "Zweistim. Lied. f. Sop. u. Altstimme mit Klavierbegleitung f. den Haus- u. Schulgebrauch v. H. M. Schletterer" 3 vols.	MSN
3293	Himmel, Fr. G.		Der Abend auf de, Wasser "Es tönt das Lied der Nachtigallen"		S/A	B. & H.	In anth. "Zweistim. Lied. f. Sop. u. Altstimme mit Klavierbegleitung f. den Haus- u. Schulgebrauch v. H. M. Schletterer" 3 vols.	MSN
3294	Himmel, Friedrich Heinrich	1765-1814	Herzenswechsel "Du giebst mir also nicht dein Herz"		Unspec.	Junne		CHAL (1898)
3295	Hinrichs, Friedrich	1820-1892	Abschied "Letzter Blick und letzter Gruss"	Op. 6 No. 4	Unspec.	R. & E.		CHAL (1898)
3296	Hinrichs, Friedrich	1820-1892	Alphorn "Ein Alphorn hör' ich schallen"	Op. 6 No. 11	Unspec.	R. & E.		CHAL (1898)
3297	Hinrichs, Friedrich	1820-1892	An die Nacht "Lass dich bekauschen, du stille Nacht"	Op. 6 No. 12	Unspec.	R. & E.		CHAL (1898)
3298	Hinrichs, Friedrich	1820-1892	Fröhliche Fahrt "O glücklich, wer zum Liebchen zieht"	Op. 6 No. 8	Unspec.	R. & E.		CHAL (1898)
3299	Hinrichs, Friedrich	1820-1892	Geweihte Stätte "Wo Zweie sich küssen zum ersten Mal"	Op. 6 No. 7	Unspec.	R. & E.		CHAL (1898)
3300	Hinrichs, Friedrich	1820-1892	Gott Rad		Unspec.	Lundq.		CVMP (1976)
3301	Hinrichs, Friedrich	1820-1892	Guter Rath "An einem Sommermorgen"	Op. 6 No. 1	Unspec.	R. & E.		CHAL (1898)
3302	Hinrichs, Friedrich	1820-1892	Italienisches Lied "Wenn kühl der Abend winkt"	Op. 6 No. 10	Unspec.	R. & E.		CHAL (1898)
3303	Hinrichs, Friedrich	1820-1892	Sommer "Komm Sommer, schwing dich"	Op. 6 No. 2	Unspec.	R. & E.		CHAL (1898)
3304	Hinrichs, Friedrich	1820-1892	Tyrolerlied "Dass su mich lieb hatt'st"	Op. 6 No. 9	Unspec.	R. & E.		CHAL (1898)
3305	Hinrichs, Friedrich	1820-1892	Vergangen "Ich war ein Blatt am grünen Baum"	Op. 6 No. 5	Unspec.	R. & E.		CHAL (1898)
3306	Hinrichs, Friedrich	1820-1892	Volkslied "Morgen früh beim kühlen Thauen"	Op. 61 No. 3	Unspec.	R. & E.		CHAL (1898)
3307	Hinrichs, Friedrich	1820-1892	Wanderers Nachtlied "Über allen Gipfeln (Wipfeln) ist Ruh"	Op. 6 No. 6	Unspec.	R. & E.		CHAL (1898)
3308	Hinze, R.		Zwei Basen "Ei was seh' ich"	Op. 36	2 female v.	Siegel		CHAL (1898)
3309	Hirsch, Karl	1858-1918	Duftet die Lindenblüt	Op. 127	S/A	O. Forberg		CHAL (1901)

REC	COMP	DTS	TITLE	OP #	VCG	PUB	COMMENTS	SRC
3310	Hirsch, Karl	1858-1918	Ein Stündlein sind sie beisammen gewest	Op. 123 No. 2	Unspec.	Beyer & S.		CHAL (1901)
3311	Hirsch, Karl	1858-1918	In der Mondnacht, in der Frühlingsmondnacht	Op. 123 No. 1	Unspec.	Beyer & S.		CHAL (1901)
3312	Hirsch, Karl	1858-1918	O Jesulein zart	No. 12	S/A	Oppen-heimer		CHAL (1911)
3313	Hirsch, Karl	1858-1918	Wiet, weit aus ferner Zeit		high & low v.	Hug		CHAL (1898)
3314	Hirsch, Rudolf	1816-1872	Mit den Lerchen trillern	Op. 25 No. 3	S/A or S/S	Peters		CHAL (1906)
3315	Hirsch, Rudolf	1816-1872	Was sollte das zur Nacht heut sein	Op. 25 No. 2	S/A or S/S	Peters		CHAL (1906)
3316	Hirsche, C.		O Schwarzwald, o Hei-math, wie bist du schön	Op. 78	Unspec.	Heckel		CHAL (1906)
3317	Hirschfeld, L. v.		Dunkel liegt vor meinem Aug'	Op. 19 No. 3	2 female v.	Hahn & Lang		CHAL (1898)
3318	Hirschfeld, L. v.		Ostseelieder "3 Duette für 2 Frauenst."	Op. 19	2 female v.	Hahn & Lang	3 duets	CHAL (1898)
3319	Hirschfeld, L. v.		Sie sagen, die Luft sei lau	Op. 19 No. 2	2 female v.	Hahn & Lang		CHAL (1898)
3320	Hirschfeld, L. v.		Sonne spielt auf den Wellen	Op. 19 No. 1	2 female v.	Hahn & Lang		CHAL (1898)
3321	Hochberg, Hans Heinrich XIV, Bolko Graf v.	1843-1926	Barcarole "Notte tace"		S/A	André	a.k.a. J. H. Franz	CHAL (1898)
3322	Hochberg, Hans Heinrich XIV, Bolko Graf v.	1843-1926	Nachtgesaug "Bei meinem Saitenspiele"		S/A	André	a.k.a. J. H. Franz	CHAL (1898)
3323	Hochberg, Hans Heinrich XIV, Bolko Graf v.	1843-1926	Tagli ab tuo crine		S/A or S/Contra A	André	a.k.a. J. H. Franz	CHAL (1898)
3324	Hochländer, J.		O Weihnachtsbaum mein Kinderstraum		Unspec.	Reinecke		CHAL (1898)
3325	Hodge, Talbot		Cuckoo Song		S/S	Chester		BBC (1975)
3326	Hofer, Toni	1858-1924	Auf der Alm, da is a wahre Freud	No. 2	2 med. v.	André	Pen name of Ludwig André. Arr. of folksong.	CHAL (1901)
3327	Hofer, Toni	1858-1924	Bald i's auf die Alma geh'	No. 10	2 med. v.	André	Pen name of Ludwig André. Arr. of folksong.	CHAL (1901)
3328	Hofer, Toni	1858-1924	Begegn't mir mei Dirndl	No. 6	2 med. v.	André	Pen name of Ludwig André. Arr. of folksong.	CHAL (1901)
3329	Hofer, Toni	1858-1924	Da hat mir mei Herzel	No. 3	2 med. v.	André	Pen name of Ludwig André. Arr. of folksong.	CHAL (1901)
3330	Hofer, Toni	1858-1924	Du flachshorets Dirndel	No. 2	2 med. v.	André	Pen name of Ludwig André. Arr. of folksong.	CHAL (1901)
3331	Hofer, Toni	1858-1924	Eldenrauten "12 Samm-lung Tyrler Alpenlieder"		2 med. v.	André	Pen name of Ludwig André. Collection of 12 Tyrolian Duets.	CHAL (1901)
3332	Hofer, Toni	1858-1924	Es werf'n die Berge ab	No. 5	2 med. v.	André	Pen name of Ludwig André. Arr. of folksong.	CHAL (1901)
3333	Hofer, Toni	1858-1924	Fern vom Tyrolerland	No. 8	2 med. v.	André	Pen name of Ludwig André. Arr. of folksong.	CHAL (1901)
3334	Hofer, Toni	1858-1924	Frei ist des Wildschütz'n Leben	No. 4	2 med. v.	André	Pen name of Ludwig André. Arr. of folksong.	CHAL (1901)
3335	Hofer, Toni	1858-1924	Seit von euch ich fortgezogen	No. 12	2 med. v.	André	Pen name of Ludwig André. Arr. of folksong.	CHAL (1901)
3336	Hofer, Toni	1858-1924	Senn'rin auf der Alm	No. 11	2 med. v.	André	Pen name of Ludwig André. Arr. of folksong.	CHAL (1901)

REC	COMP	DTS	TITLE	OP #	VCG	PUB	COMMENTS	SRC
3337	Hofer, Toni	1858-1924	Über'm Bacheri steht a Hütten	No. 9	2 med. v.	André	Pen name of Ludwig André. Arr. of folksong.	CHAL (1901)
3338	Hoffmann, Emil Adolf	1879-	Herr und Frau Lehmann auf dem Maskenball "Halt, halt mein Kind"	Op. 6	Unspec.	P. & M.		CHAL (1898)
3339	Hoffmann, L. (F. P. Schubert)		Ständchen "Leise flehen mein Lieder"		T/B or S/A	Leuckart	Arr. of Schubert Lied by L. Hoffmann	CHAL (1898)
3340	Hofmann, Heinrich Karl Johann	1842-1902	Ade denn, du stolze blitzaugige Magd	Op. 41 No. 4	S/A or T/B	Hainauer		CHAL (1898)
3341	Hofmann, Heinrich Karl Johann	1842-1902	Ade denn du stolze blitzaugige Magd	Op. 41 No. 4	Unspec.	Hainauer		CHAL (1906)
3342	Hofmann, Heinrich Karl Johann	1842-1902	Ein Schifflein stösst vom Lande	Op. 41 No. 3	Unspec.	Hainauer		CHAL (1906)
3343	Hofmann, Heinrich Karl Johann	1842-1902	Es haucht die Linde	Op. 41 No. 1	Unspec.	Hainauer		CHAL (1901)
3344	Hofmann, Heinrich Karl Johann	1842-1902	Guten Morgen "Nun reibet euch die Aeuglein wach"	Op. 4 No. 1	Unspec.	Fürstner		CHAL (1898)
3345	Hofmann, Heinrich Karl Johann	1842-1902	Liebeslied "Ich hab' mir eins erwählet"	Op. 4 No. 3	Unspec.	Fürstner		CHAL (1898)
3346	Hofmann, Heinrich Karl Johann	1842-1902	Oft geht an schönen Frühlingstagen	Op. 41 No. 2	Unspec.	Hainauer		CHAL (1901)
3347	Hofmann, Heinrich Karl Johann	1842-1902	Scheiden "Ein Schifflein stösst vom Lande"	Op. 41 No. 3	S/A or T/B	Hainauer		CHAL (1898)
3348	Hofmann, Heinrich Karl Johann	1842-1902	Schneeflöckchen "Schnee-flöckchen leicht und leise"	Op. 4 No. 2	Unspec.	Fürstner		CHAL (1898)
3349	Hofmann, Heinrich Karl Johann	1842-1902	Waldesrauschen "Oft geht an schöner Frühlingstagen"	Op. 41 No. 2	S/A or T/B	Hainauer		CHAL (1898)
3350	Hofmann, Heinrich Karl Johann	1842-1902	Wenn auf der See	Op. 4 No. 4	Unspec.	Fürstner		CHAL (1898)
3351	Hofmann, Heinrich Karl Johann	1842-1902	Zum Abend "Es haucht die Linde"	Op. 41 No. 1	S/A or T/B	Hainauer		CHAL (1898)
3352	Hoft, N.		Lenz ist angekommen		Unspec.	München, Selbst-verlag		CHAL (1898)
3353	Hohfeld, C.		Frühlingsahung "O sanfter, süsser Hauch"	No. 1	S/A	Emmer-mann		CHAL (1898)
3354	Hohfeld, C.		Wenn ich ein Vöglein wär und auch zwei Flügel hätt'	No. 2	S/A	Emmer-mann		CHAL (1898)
3355	Hohnerlein, M.		Ach, wie ist's möglich dann	Op. 37	2 med. female v.	Gleichauf		CHAL (1906)
3356	Hoiby, Lee	1926-	Bermudas		Unspec.	G. Schirm.		CVMP (1995)
3357	Hoiby, Lee	1926-	Bermudas	Op. 37	S/MS	G. Schirm.	Also available as med. v. solo. Copyright 1984.	MSN
3358	Hol, Rijk	1825-1904	Abendlied "Sonne sank, der Abend naht"	Op. 15 No. 2	Unspec.	Weygand		CHAL (1898)
3359	Hol, Rijk	1825-1904	Ein Mondenstrahl wandelt so traurig	Op. 15 No. 4	Unspec.	Weygand		CHAL (1898)

REC	COMP	DTS	TITLE	OP #	VCG	PUB	COMMENTS	SRC
3360	Hol, Rijk	1825-1904	Ein schöner Stern	Op. 42 No. 3	S/A	Roothaan		CHAL (1898)
3361	Hol, Rijk	1825-1904	Es fiel ein Reif	Op. 40 No. 2	S/A	Roothaan		CHAL (1898)
3362	Hol, Rijk	1825-1904	Flog ein bunter Flater	Op. 42 No. 2	S/A	Roothaan		CHAL (1898)
3363	Hol, Rijk	1825-1904	Frühling	Op. 40 No. 3	S/A	Roothaan		CHAL (1898)
3364	Hol, Rijk	1825-1904	Glücklich, wer auf Gott vertraut	Op. 15 No. 6	Unspec.	Weygand		CHAL (1898)
3365	Hol, Rijk	1825-1904	In der nacht	Op. 42 No. 1	S/A	Roothaan		CHAL (1898)
3366	Hol, Rijk	1825-1904	Kaum erblüht vom Reif geknickt		Unspec.	Weygand		CHAL (1898)
3367	Hol, Rijk	1825-1904	Lotosblume "Lotosblume ängstigt sich"	Op. 40 No. 1	S/A	Roothaan		CHAL (1898)
3368	Hol, Rijk	1825-1904	Mädchen Frühlingslied	Op. 15 No. 3	Unspec.	Weygand		CHAL (1898)
3369	Hol, Rijk	1825-1904	O wie freu'n wir uns	Op. 15 No. 5	Unspec.	Weygand		CHAL (1898)
3370	Hollaender, Alexis [Holländer]	1840-1924	Abendfrieden "Wie lachst du voller Frieden	Op. 16 No. 3	S/A	Schlesinger		CHAL (1898)
3371	Hollaender, Alexis [Holländer]	1840-1924	Es blühen die Blumen und Bäume	Op. 16 No. 1	S/A	Schlesinger		CHAL (1898)
3372	Hollaender, Alexis [Holländer]	1840-1924	Frühlingsahnung "O sanfter, süsser Hauch"	Op. 10 No. 3	S/A	B. & H.	In anth. "Zweistim. Lied. f. Sop. u. Altstimme mit Klavierbegleitung f. den Haus- u. Schulgebrauch v. H. M. Schletterer" 3 vols.	MSN
3373	Hollaender, Alexis [Holländer]	1840-1924	Frühlingsahung "O sanfter, süsser Hauch"	Op. 10 No. 3	S/A	B. & H.		CHAL (1898)
3374	Hollaender, Alexis [Holländer]	1840-1924	Frühlingsglaube "Linden Lüfte sind erwacht"	Op. 10 No. 4	S/A	B. & H.		CHAL (1898)
3375	Hollaender, Alexis [Holländer]	1840-1924	Frühlingsklage Wölklein ziehen in den Höhen"	Op. 16 No. 2	S/A	Schlesinger		CHAL (1898)
3376	Hollaender, Alexis [Holländer]	1840-1924	Frühlingsruhe "O legt mich nicht in's dunkle (kühle) Grab"	Op. 10 No. 5	S/A	B. & H.		CHAL (1898)
3377	Hollaender, Alexis [Holländer]	1840-1924	Haidenröslein "Sah ein Knab' ein Röslein stehn"	Op. 10 No. 1	S/A	B. & H.		CHAL (1898)
3378	Hollaender, Alexis [Holländer]	1840-1924	In der Ferne "Will ruhen unter den Bäumen hier"	Op. 10 No. 2	S/A	B. & H.		CHAL (1898)
3379	Hollaender, Alexis [Holländer]	1840-1924	Künftiger Frühling "Wohl blühet jedem Jahr"	Op. 10 No. 6	S/A	B. & H.	In anth. "Zweistim. Lied. f. Sop. u. Altstimme mit Klavierbegleitung f. den Haus- u. Schulgebrauch v. H. M. Schletterer" 3 vols.	MSN
3380	Hollaender, Alexis [Holländer]	1840-1924	Psalm 130	Op. 38 No. 2	S/A	Schlesinger		CHAL (1898)
3381	Hollaender, Alexis [Holländer]	1840-1924	Psalm 23 "Herr ist mein Hirt"	Op. 38 No. 1	S/A	Schlesinger		CHAL (1898)

REC	COMP	DTS	TITLE	OP #	VCG	PUB	COMMENTS	SRC
3382	Hollaender, Alexis [Holländer]	1840-1924	Schäfer "Es war ein fauler Schäfer"	Op. 34 No. 3	S/S	Schlesinger		CHAL (1898)
3383	Hollaender, Alexis [Holländer]	1840-1924	Sterne und Blumen "Sterne machte den Himmel gehn"	Op. 34 No. 2	S/S	Schlesinger		CHAL (1898)
3384	Hollaender, Alexis [Holländer]	1840-1924	Still und friedlich ist die Nacht	Op. 57	Unspec.	Chal.		CHAL (1901)
3385	Hollaender, Alexis [Holländer]	1840-1924	Übermuth "Ein' Gems auf dem Stein"	Op. 34 No. 1	S/S	Schlesinger		CHAL (1898)
3386	Hollaender, Gustav	1855-1915	Pantoffelheld "Ist er hier, ja freilich Hanne"	Op. 5	Unspec.	R. Forberg		CHAL (1898)
3387	Hollaender, Viktor	1866-1940	Als ich einst zog auf Fleischbeschau	No. 8	Unspec.	B. & B.		CHAL (1911)
3388	Hollaender, Viktor	1866-1940	Auf dem Rathhaus stehe ich		Unspec.	Harmonie i. B.		CHAL (1906)
3389	Hollaender, Viktor	1866-1940	Auf Kasinoball man sah	No. 12	Unspec.	B. & B.		CHAL (1911)
3390	Hollaender, Viktor	1866-1940	Drollig von dem Fusse bis zur Haartour		Unspec.	B. & B.		CHAL (1906)
3391	Hollaender, Viktor	1866-1940	Du mein süsses Närrchen	No. 10	Unspec.	B. & B.		CHAL (1911)
3392	Hollaender, Viktor	1866-1940	Es hat uns Deutschland jederzeit "Ein tolles Jahr"		Unspec.	Harmonie i. B.		CHAL (1906)
3393	Hollaender, Viktor	1866-1940	Es tut der Mensch sich nich zu viel		Unspec.	B. & B.		CHAL (1911)
3394	Hollaender, Viktor	1866-1940	Fleisseige Frauenhände "Walzer-Duett"		Unspec.	Kahnt		CHAL (1911)
3395	Hollaender, Viktor	1866-1940	Fräulein Börge bin ich		Unspec.	Apollo		CHAL (1911)
3396	Hollaender, Viktor	1866-1940	Fräulein, Frau "Dich theure Heimath grüss' ich"	Op. 117	2 female v.	Benjamin		CHAL (1898)
3397	Hollaender, Viktor	1866-1940	Grossstadtluft "Ach wie schön muss doch das Leben"	Op. 81	2 female v.	Thiemer		CHAL (1898)
3398	Hollaender, Viktor	1866-1940	Hab' als Hahn	No. 7	Unspec.	B. & B.		CHAL (1911)
3399	Hollaender, Viktor	1866-1940	Hans und Grete "I bin halt a Madel"		Unspec.	Oppenheimer		CHAL (1898)
3400	Hollaender, Viktor	1866-1940	Hochzeitsgratulanten "Da wäre ich glücklich zur Stadt"		Unspec.	Oppenheimer		CHAL (1898)
3401	Hollaender, Viktor	1866-1940	I trag' an Strick statt der Kravatten		Unspec.	B. & B.		CHAL (1906)
3402	Hollaender, Viktor	1866-1940	In Berlin fangts Leben an	No. 12	Unspec.	B. & B.		CHAL (1911)
3403	Hollaender, Viktor	1866-1940	Komm mit mir in den grüner Wald		Unspec.	Harmonie i. B.		CHAL (1911)
3404	Hollaender, Viktor	1866-1940	Kravatten koof ich nicht bei Biester		Unspec.	B. & B.		CHAL (1906)
3405	Hollaender, Viktor	1866-1940	Liebe, süsse, holde, kleine Maus		Unspec.	Harmonie i. B.		CHAL (1906)
3406	Hollaender, Viktor	1866-1940	Mein Schatz, wenn wir im Dämmerschein	No. 2	Unspec.	Wernthal		CHAL (1906)
3407	Hollaender, Viktor	1866-1940	Moderne Dienstboten "Nein, das ist wirklich doch zu stark"	Op. 52	2 female v.	Thiemer		CHAL (1898)
3408	Hollaender, Viktor	1866-1940	Mond, du alter Bummelbruder	No. 6	Unspec.	B. & B.		CHAL (1911)
3409	Hollaender, Viktor	1866-1940	O du kleine fixe Donaunixe		Unspec.	Apollo		CHAL (1911)

REC	COMP	DTS	TITLE	OP #	VCG	PUB	COMMENTS	SRC
3410	Hollaender, Viktor	1866-1940	O lassen sie von ihrer Hand		Unspec.	Harmonie i. B.		CHAL (1906)
3411	Hollaender, Viktor	1866-1940	O welch' Tag voll Seligkeit		S/MS	P. & M.	Pen name of Arricha del Tolveno	CHAL (1901)
3412	Hollaender, Viktor	1866-1940	Otte als Messengerboy		Unspec.	B. & B.		CHAL (1911)
3413	Hollaender, Viktor	1866-1940	Schon geraume Zeit spukt rum		Unspec.	B. & B.		CHAL (1906)
3414	Hollaender, Viktor	1866-1940	Schwarzer Mann kam neulich an	No. 10	Unspec.	B. & B.		CHAL (1911)
3415	Hollaender, Viktor	1866-1940	Unter den blühenden Linden	No. 1	Unspec.	Wernthal		CHAL (1906)
3416	Hollaender, Viktor	1866-1940	Was wohl sagen meine Leute	No. 3	Unspec.	Wernthal		CHAL (1906)
3417	Hollaender, Viktor	1866-1940	Welche Seligkeit und Wonne		2 female v.	De. Dietrich		CHAL (1906)
3418	Hollaender, Viktor	1866-1940	Wenn du heirat'st, sagt' ich mir	No. 4	Unspec.	B. & B.		CHAL (1911)
3419	Hollaender, Viktor	1866-1940	Wenn früh die Hähne krähn		Unspec.	Harmonie i. B.		CHAL (1911)
3420	Hollaender, Viktor	1866-1940	Wie klang doch einst naiv und bieder	No. 5	Unspec.	B. & B.		CHAL (1911)
3421	Hollaender, Viktor	1866-1940	Wir sind die schneidigen Kerls von Bonn	No. 8	Unspec.	B. & B.		CHAL (1911)
3422	Hollaender, Viktor	1866-1940	Wir zerstreun das Geld wie Häcksel	No. 14	Unspec.	B. & B.		CHAL (1911)
3423	Hollaender, Viktor	1866-1940	Wo die letzten Häuser stehen		2 female v.	Fr. Dietrich		CHAL (1906)
3424	Hollaender, Viktor	1866-1940	Ziehn als echte Strassensänger		Unspec.	Harmonie i. B.		CHAL (1911)
3425	Holland, G.		Ja wir sind Deutschlands schönste Zier "Wir sind Soldaten, wie sie seh'n"		Unspec.	Danner		CHAL (1898)
3426	Höller, C.		Jägerlied "Im Walde sein den gauzen Tag"	No. 1	Unspec.	Kratoch-will		CHAL (1898)
3427	Höller, C.		Waldlust "Wald, der grüne Wald"	No. 4	Unspec.	Kratoch-will		CHAL (1898)
3428	Höller, C.		Wanderlust "Es ziehn nach fernen Landen"	No. 3	Unspec.	Kratoch-will		CHAL (1898)
3429	Höller, C.		"Wenn der Frühling auf die Berge steigt"	No. 2	Unspec.	Kratoch-will		CHAL (1898)
3430	Holman, Derek		North Wind, The		Unspec.	Waterloo	pf? accomp. unspec.	CVMP (1985)
3431	Holmès, Augusta	1847-1903	Renouveau "Au fond des bois"		Unspec.	Ricordi	a.k.a. Hermann Zenta. Fr.-Irish woman comp.	CHAL (1898)
3432	Holst, Gustav	1874-1934	Dream of Christmas		S/S	Curwen		ASR
3433	Holst, Gustav	1874-1934	Dream of Christmas, A		Unspec.	Roberton	pf or orch accomp. 1-2 v.	CVMP (1976)
3434	Holst, Gustav	1874-1934	In the Bleak Midwinter		high & low v.	Becken-horst	Arr. C. Courtney. In anthology "Duets for the Master: Sacred Duets for High and Low Voice and Keyboard" Pub. 1989.	MSN
3435	Holstein, Franz von	1826-1878	Abendreihn "Guten Abend lieber Mondenschein"	Op. 7 No. 2	S/A	Litolff		CHAL (1898)
3436	Holstein, Franz von	1826-1878	Am Möverstein "In blauer Nacht bei Vollmondschein"	Op. 25 I	2 female v.	Fritzsch		CHAL (1898)
3437	Holstein, Franz von	1826-1878	Aus der Jugendzeit, aus der Jugendzeit klingt ein Lied	Op. 7 No. 1	S/A	Litolff		CHAL (1898)

REC	COMP	DTS	TITLE	OP #	VCG	PUB	COMMENTS	SRC
3438	Holstein, Franz von	1826-1878	Du mit den schwarzen Augen	Op. 25 No. 8	2 female v.	Fritzsch		CHAL (1898)
3439	Holstein, Franz von	1826-1878	Ein Stündlein wohl vor Tag "Derweil ich schlafend lag"	Op. 25 No. 2	2 female v.	Fritzsch		CHAL (1898)
3440	Holstein, Franz von	1826-1878	Lied der Vöglein "Von Zweig zu Zweig zu hüpfen"	Op. 8 No. 2	S/A	Litolff		CHAL (1898)
3441	Holstein, Franz von	1826-1878	Melusine "Es wohnt ein Mädchen wunderhold"	Op. 25 No. 4	2 female v.	Fritzsch		CHAL (1898)
3442	Holstein, Franz von	1826-1878	Nachts "Über'm Lande die Sterne"	Op. 7 No. 3	S/A	Litolff		CHAL (1898)
3443	Holstein, Franz von	1826-1878	Trost der Nacht "Es heilt die Nacht des Tages Wunden"	Op. 8 No. 3	S/A	Litolff		CHAL (1898)
3444	Holstein, Franz von	1826-1878	Vöglein "Ich hatt ein Vöglein, ach wie fein"	Op. 25 No. 1	2 female v.	Fritzsch		CHAL (1898)
3445	Holstein, Franz von	1826-1878	Volkslied aus der Ukraine	Op. 7 No. 4	S/A	Litolff		CHAL (1898)
3446	Holstein, Franz von	1826-1878	Wandervöglein "Wander-vöglein leichtes Blut"	Op. 5 No. 1	S/A	Litolff		CHAL (1898)
3447	Holstein, Franz von	1826-1878	Wiet, weit aus ferner Zeit	Op. 25 No. 5	2 female v.	Fritzsch		CHAL (1898)
3448	Holstein, Jean-Paul	1939-	Duette Op. 15	Op. 15	Unspec.	Peters	Unspec. pieces	CVMP (1995)
3449	Hönle, A.		Ah Servus so		Unspec.	Bauderer		CHAL (1911)
3450	Hope, H. Ashworth		Dreams		Unspec.	Leonard-Eng	Also solo	CVMP (1976)
3451	Hopfe, J.		Und wenn die Primel schneeweiss blickt		Unspec.	Chal.		CHAL (1898)
3452	Hoppe, Paul	1845-1933	Am Weihnachtsabend "Lieder und Gesang"	Op. 11	Unspec.	Beyer & S.		CHAL (1898)
3453	Hoppe, Paul	1845-1933	Lied der Vöglein "Von Zweig zu Zweig zu hüpfen"	Op. 30 No. 1	S/S	Beyer & S.		CHAL (1898)
3454	Hoppe, Paul	1845-1933	Tanzlieder "Cyclus"	Op. 17	Unspec.	Beyer & S.		CHAL (1898)
3455	Horack, C.		Duet-Quodilibet		Unspec.	Aibl		CHAL (1898)
3456	Horn, August	1825-1893	"Es blickt der Frühlingsmond so still"	No. 2	Unspec.	Kistner		CHAL (1898)
3457	Horn, August	1825-1893	Frühlingsaugen "Wenn im Lenz der blaue Himmel"	Op. 32 No. 1	S/A	B. & H.		CHAL (1898)
3458	Horn, August	1825-1893	Frühlingslied "Tief im grünen Frühlingshag"	Op. 32 No. 2	S/A	B. & H.		CHAL (1898)
3459	Horn, August	1825-1893	Im Walde, im grünen (Wald) Walde	Op. 26 No. c	S/A	Kistner		CHAL (1898)
3460	Horn, August	1825-1893	Lindes Rauschen in den Wipfel	Op. 10 No. 2	Unspec.	R. & B.		CHAL (1898)
3461	Horn, August	1825-1893	Morgenlied "Steht auf, ihr lieben Kinderlein"	Op. 10 No. 3	Unspec.	R. & B.		CHAL (1898)
3462	Horn, August	1825-1893	Serenade "Du ruhest unter dem Lindenbach"	No. 1	Unspec.	Kistner		CHAL (1898)
3463	Horn, August	1825-1893	Vöglein in den sinn'gen Tagen	Op. 10 No. 1	Unspec.	R. & B.		CHAL (1898)
3464	Horn, Charles Edward	1786-1849	I know a bank		Unspec.	Curwen	Ed. Hardy	BBC (1975)
3465	Horn, Charles Edward	1786-1849	I Know a Bank		Unspec.	Leonard-Eng		CVMP (1976)

REC	COMP	DTS	TITLE	OP #	VCG	PUB	COMMENTS	SRC
3466	Horn, Charles Edward	1786-1849	I know a bank		S/S	Leonard-Eng	In anthology "Six Popular Vocal Duets Book I for Soprano & Contralto" Ed. & arr. by E. Newton. Pub. 1906.	MSN
3467	Horn, Charles Edward	1786-1849	I know a bank		S/A	White-Smith	In catalogue page "Vocal Duetts" of White-Smith Music Pub. Co. (no date)	MSN
3468	Horn, Charles Edward	1786-1849	I Know a Bank Whereon the Wild Thyme Blows		high & low v.	Hinds, Hayden & Eldredge	In anthology "The Most Pop-ular Vocal Duets" Ed. Dr. E. J. Biedermann. Pub. 1914.	MSN
3469	Horn, Charles Edward	1786-1849	I know a bank whereon the wild thyme blows		MS/T or MS/A	G. Schirm.	In catalogue page "Selected Vocal Duets" of G. Schirmer, Inc. NY (no date)	MSN
3470	Horn, E.		Im Süden "Ist die Luft so rein gestimmt"	No. 1	Unspec.	Cranz		CHAL (1898)
3471	Horn, E.		Thau der Nacht liegt und auf den Wiesen	No. 3	Unspec.	Cranz		CHAL (1898)
3472	Horn, E.		Verklärung "Nicht weinen sollst du"	No. 2	Unspec.	Cranz		CHAL (1898)
3473	Hornig, A.		A Musi deriss'g Mann stark		Unspec.	Blaha		CHAL (1906)
3474	Hornig, J.		Adam schon im Paradies		Unspec.	Blaha		CHAL (1906)
3475	Hornig, J.		Als klane Kinder in der Wiag'n		Unspec.	Blaha		CHAL (1911)
3476	Hornig, J.		Das thuat am wohl	No. 1	Unspec.	Blaha		CHAL (1901)
3477	Hornig, J.		Der hat am Grill'n im Hirn	No. 3	Unspec.	Blaha		CHAL (1901)
3478	Hornig, J.		Sö der beisst	No. 2	Unspec.	Blaha		CHAL (1901)
3479	Hornig, J.		Wie's uns Zwa seg'n		Unspec.	Blaha		CHAL (1901)
3480	Hornstein, Robert von	1833-1890	Auf die Berge muss ich gehen	Op. 20 No. 2	Unspec.	Bosworth		CHAL (1898)
3481	Hornstein, Robert von	1833-1890	Erste Nachtigall "Ich ging süss träumend alleine"	Op. 20 No. 4	Unspec.	Bosworth		CHAL (1898)
3482	Hornstein, Robert von	1833-1890	Mailied "Kein' schön're (schöner) Zeit auf Erden ist"	Op. 33	Unspec.	Kröner		CHAL (1898)
3483	Hornstein, Robert von	1833-1890	Mondscheinlied "Verstohl-en geht der Mond auf"	Op. 20 No. 3	Unspec.	Bosworth		CHAL (1898)
3484	Hornstein, Robert von	1833-1890	Strauch erzittert	Op. 20 No. 5	Unspec.	Bosworth		CHAL (1898)
3485	Hornstein, Robert von	1833-1890	Trüamen und Wachen "Hab' geträumt von Lenz und Liebe"	Op. 20 No. 1	Unspec.	Bosworth		CHAL (1898)
3486	Hornstein, Robert von	1833-1890	Wurmlinger Kapelle "Lust-ig, wie ein leichter Kahn"	Op. 19	Unspec.	Bosworth		CHAL (1898)
3487	Hötzel, C.		Im Hause Gottes Kirchliche Festgesänge f. S. u. A.	Op. 24	S/A	Protze		CHAL (1898)
3488	Hötzel, C.		Weihnachtsgesang "Fürchtet euch nicht"	Op. 28 No. 1	S/A	Protze	org accomp.	CHAL (1898)
3489	Hoven, Johann	1803-1883	Allgemeines Wandern "Vom Grund bis zu den Gipfeln"	Op. 53 No. 6	S/A or T/B	Cranz	Pen name of J. Vesque von Püttlingen	CHAL (1898)
3490	Hoven, Johann	1803-1883	Alpenrose	Op. 53 No. 3	S/A or T/B	Cranz	Pen name of J. Vesque von Püttlingen	CHAL (1898)

REC	COMP	DTS	TITLE	OP #	VCG	PUB	COMMENTS	SRC
3491	Hoven, Johann	1803-1883	Auf dem See	Op. 53 No. 4	S/A or T/B	Cranz	Pen name of J. Vesque von Püttlingen	CHAL (1898)
3492	Hoven, Johann	1803-1883	Auf ein schlummerndes Kind	Op. 53 No. 5	S/A or T/B	Cranz	Pen name of J. Vesque von Püttlingen	CHAL (1898)
3493	Hoven, Johann	1803-1883	Ländeliches Fest "Ich mochte wollen oder nicht"	Op. 53 No. 2	S/A or T/B	Cranz	Pen name of J. Vesque von Püttlingen	CHAL (1898)
3494	Hoven, Johann	1803-1883	Ob wohl der Mond geplaudert hat "Ich hab' in stiller Nacht"	Op. 53 No. 1	S/A or T/B	Cranz	Pen name of J. Vesque von Püttlingen	CHAL (1898)
3495	Huber, Hans	1852-1921	Entschwundene "Es was ein heitres, goldnes Jahr"	Op. 80 No. 2	Unspec.	Siegel		CHAL (1898)
3496	Huber, Hans	1852-1921	Kapelle am Strande "Langsam und kaum vernehmbar"	Op. 80 No. 7	Unspec.	Siegel		CHAL (1898)
3497	Huber, Hans	1852-1921	Liebesflämmchen "Mutter mahnt mich Abends"	Op. 72 No. 7	S/A	Siegel		CHAL (1898)
3498	Huber, Hans	1852-1921	Liebesgruss "Dein Tüchlein bleib"	Op. 80 No. 1	Unspec.	Siegel		CHAL (1898)
3499	Huber, Hans	1852-1921	Meines Kindes Abendgebet "Tag ist um"	Op. 80 No. 3	Unspec.	Siegel		CHAL (1898)
3500	Huber, Hans	1852-1921	Schifferliedchen "Schon hat die Nacht"	Op. 80 No. 4	Unspec.	Siegel		CHAL (1898)
3501	Huber, Hans	1852-1921	Schwüle "Trüb verglomm der schwüle Sommertag"	Op. 80 No. 6	Unspec.	Siegel		CHAL (1898)
3502	Huber, Hans	1852-1921	Wanderrast "Hier ruht sich's gut"	Op. 80 No. 5	Unspec.	Siegel		CHAL (1898)
3503	Hughes		God Spoke to Me Today		S/A	Lorenz		CVMP (1976)
3504	Hughes, Herbert	1882-1937	The dreadful story about Harriet		Unspec.	Metzler		BBC (1975)
3505	Hughes, Herbert	1882-1937	The story of cruel Frederick		Unspec.	Metzler		BBC (1975)
3506	Hughes, Herbert	1882-1937	The story of Fidgety Philip		Unspec.	Metzler		BBC (1975)
3507	Hugo, F.		Grüss Gott, Herr Gockel	Op. 101	Unspec.	Danner		CHAL (1911)
3508	Hugo, F.		Sonne funkelt im goldnen Rhein	Op. 91	2 female v.	Danner	Duet with dance	CHAL (1911)
3509	Huhn, Bruno		High in the heavens		high & low v.	G. Schirm.	pf or org accomp. In catalogue page "Sacred Vocal Duets" of G. Schirmer, Inc. NY (no date)	MSN
3510	Huhn, Bruno		Hunt, The		high & med. v.	G. Schirm.	In catalogue page "Selected Vocal Duets" of G. Schirmer, Inc. NY (no date)	MSN
3511	Huhn, Bruno		Jesus, Lover of my soul		S/A	G. Schirm.	pf or org accomp. In catalogue page "Sacred Vocal Duets" of G. Schirmer, Inc. NY (no date)	MSN
3512	Hullah, John	1812-1884	Far o'er the rolling sea		Unspec.	J. Dean		BBC (1975)
3513	Hullah, John	1812-1884	Gipsy duet		Unspec.	Chappell		BBC (1975)
3514	Hullah, John	1812-1884	O Jesu, passtor bonus		Unspec.	Novello		BBC (1975)
3515	Hullah, John	1812-1884	Serenading		Unspec.	Chappell		BBC (1975)
3516	Hullah, John	1812-1884	The midsummer call		Unspec.	Chappell		BBC (1975)

REC	COMP	DTS	TITLE	OP #	VCG	PUB	COMMENTS	SRC
3517	Hullah, John	1812-1884	The pier head		Unspec.	Chappell		BBC (1975)
3518	Hülle, W.		Guten Abend "Es ist schon dunkel um mich her"	Op. 2 No. 6	Unspec.	Weber i. Cöln		CHAL (1898)
3519	Hülle, W.		Lied der Lerche "O Mutter, lass' uns gehen"	Op. 2 No. 3	Unspec.	Weber i. Cöln		CHAL (1898)
3520	Hülle, W.		O der blaue, blaue Himmel	Op. 2 No. 5	Unspec.	Weber i. Cöln		CHAL (1898)
3521	Hülle, W.		Schäfers Sonntagslied "Das ist der Tag des Herrn"	Op. 2 No. 2	Unspec.	Weber i. Cöln		CHAL (1898)
3522	Hülle, W.		Tanzlied der Mücken "Frisch ihr Blumen und Halme"	Op. 2 No. 4	Unspec.	Weber i. Cöln		CHAL (1898)
3523	Hülle, W.		Wanderschaft "Wandern ist des Müllers Lust"	Op. 2 No. 7	Unspec.	Weber i. Cöln		CHAL (1898)
3524	Hülle, W.		Wie ist doch die Erde so schön	Op. 2 No. 1	Unspec.	Weber i. Cöln		CHAL (1898)
3525	Hullebroeck, Emiel	1878-	Konninginnelied		Unspec.	Alsbach	In collection "Zes Liederen"	CVMP (1976)
3526	Hullebroeck, Emiel	1878-	Moederke Alleen		Unspec.	Alsbach	In collection "Zes Liederen"	CVMP (1976)
3527	Hullebroeck, Emiel	1878-	Op Kerstdag		Unspec.	Alsbach	In collection "Zes Liederen"	CVMP (1976)
3528	Hullebroeck, Emiel	1878-	Speldewerkerslied		Unspec.	Alsbach	In collection "Zes Liederen"	CVMP (1976)
3529	Hullebroeck, Emiel	1878-	Van 'T Schoone Wiedsterke		Unspec.	Alsbach	In collection "Zes Liederen"	CVMP (1976)
3530	Hullebroeck, Emiel	1878-	Voor Het Kanthussen		Unspec.	Alsbach	In collection "Zes Liederen"	CVMP (1976)
3531	Hume, Alexander	1811-1859	Afton water		S/A	Bayley & Ferguson	Arr. Moffat	BBC (1975)
3532	Hummel, Ferdinand	1855-1928	Alleluia!		2 high v.	R. D. Row	org or pf acc. In anth. "Sacred Duet Master-pieces…" Vol. 3. Compi. & ed. C. Fredrickson. Pub. 1961.	MSN
3533	Hummel, Ferdinand	1855-1928	Kopfüber, kopfunter	Op. 84 No. 4	S/A	Eulen-burg		CHAL (1906)
3534	Hummel, Ferdinand	1855-1928	O sei gegrüsst du Holde	Op. 45 No. 4	S/A or S/Br	Siegel		CHAL (1898)
3535	Hummel, Ferdinand	1855-1928	So kommst du wieder	Op. 45 No. 10, 11	S/A or S/Br	Siegel		CHAL (1898)
3536	Hummel, Ferdinand	1855-1928	So lieblich singt die Nachtigall	Op. 84 No. 3	S/A	Eulen-burg		CHAL (1906)
3537	Hummel, Ferdinand	1855-1928	Vogellieder (4)	Op. 84	S/A	Eulen-burg	4 duets	CHAL (1906)
3538	Hummel, Ferdinand	1855-1928	Wallend geht das Aehrenfeld	Op. 84 No. 1	S/A	Eulen-burg		CHAL (1906)
3539	Hummel, Ferdinand	1855-1928	Wie tönt an Frühlingstagen	Op. 84 No. 2	S/A	Eulen-burg		CHAL (1906)
3540	Humperdinck, Engelbert	1853-1921	Es schaukeln die Winde		S/A	M. Brock-haus		CHAL (1906)
3541	Humperdinck, Engelbert	1853-1921	Es schaukeln die Winde		MS/A	M. Brock-haus		CHAL (1911)
3542	Humperdinck, Engelbert	1853-1921	Wiegenlied		Unspec.	Brock-haus		BBC (1975)
3543	Hutchinson, William Marshall	1854-1933	Dream Faces		Unspec.	Leonard-Eng	Also solo	CVMP (1976)

REC	COMP	DTS	TITLE	OP #	VCG	PUB	COMMENTS	SRC
3544	Hutchinson, William Marshall	1854-1933	Pierrot		Unspec.	Leonard-Eng	Also solo	CVMP (1976)
3545	Hutchinson, William Marshall	1854-1933	Silver Rhine		Unspec.	Leonard-Eng		CVMP (1976)
3546	Huth, Louis	1810-1859	Aus Leila "Gleitet hin in milder Schöne"	Op. 21 No. 2	S/S or T/T	Schlesinger		CHAL (1898)
3547	Huth, Louis	1810-1859	Gesang der Schwäne "Im Abendschein, in Purpurgluth"	Op. 21 No. 4	S/S or T/T	Schlesinger		CHAL (1898)
3548	Huth, Louis	1810-1859	Liebesleben "Lustvereint, Liebchens Aug'"	Op. 21 No. 3	S/S or T/T	Schlesinger		CHAL (1898)
3549	Huth, Louis	1810-1859	Schifferlied "Hinaus, hinaus in das spielende wühlende Meer"	Op. 21 No. 1	S/S or T/T	Schlesinger		CHAL (1898)
3550	Ibert, Jacques	1890-1962	Canzone Madrigalescha de Francesco Milani (XVII Siècle)		Unspec.	Heugel	Copyright 1922	MSN
3551	Iradier, Sebastian [Yradier]	1809-1865	El vestido azul		Unspec.	Heugel		BBC (1975)
3552	Iradier, Sebastian [Yradier]	1809-1865	Herzliebe, wie ein holdes Täubchen		Unspec.	O. Forberg		CHAL (1901)
3553	Iradier, Sebastian [Yradier]	1809-1865	Jota de los toreros		Unspec.	Heugel		BBC (1975)
3554	Iradier, Sebastian [Yradier]	1809-1865	La Paloma		Unspec.	Allans	Arr. for 2 v. Eng. trans. Span. In anthology "Vocal Duets Collection" Vol. 1. Pub. 1992.	MSN
3555	Ireland, John	1879-1962	At Early Dawn		Unspec.	Roberton		CVMP (1976)
3556	Ireland, John	1879-1962	At Early Dawn in Summer Woods		S/A	Curwen		ASR
3557	Ireland, John	1879-1962	Full fathom five		Unspec.	Novello	Ed. Kimmins	BBC (1975)
3558	Ireland, John	1879-1962	In Summer Woods		Unspec.	Roberton		CVMP (1976)
3559	Ireland, John	1879-1962	In Summer Woods		S/S	Curwen		ASR
3560	Isaacson, Michael Neil	1946-	Seasons in Time, Vol. 2: Duets for Holiday and Life Cycle		Unspec.	Transcon	kbd accomp. unspec. Jewish pieces, unspec.	CVMP (1995)
3561	Istel, Edgar	1880-1948	Es ist ein Schnee gefallen	Op. 14	S/A	Kahnt		CHAL (1906)
3562	Itoh, Hiroyuki	1963-	Lecture on Nothing		Unspec.	Japan	acap.	CVMP (1995)
3563	Ivanova, Lidia		21 Canti ad ina, due, e tre voci		1-3 equal v.	Santis	acap.? Unspec. accomp. Woman comp. Collection of unspec. pieces. For 1-3 v. includes duets.	ASR
3564	Jacke, Ch.		Dorthin "Ich kann ja hier nicht glücklich sein"		Unspec.	Uppenborn i. Clausthal		CHAL (1898)
3565	Jäckel, A.		O lasset und singen im frohen Verein	Op. 112	Unspec.	Jäckel		CHAL (1901)
3566	Jacobi, M.		Diebstahl "Mädel trug des Wegs daher"	Op. 11 No. 1	S/A	Paez		CHAL (1898)

REC	COMP	DTS	TITLE	OP #	VCG	PUB	COMMENTS	SRC
3567	Jacobi, M.		Lustiger Rath "Vöglein, lieb' Vöglein, was treibt ihr"	Op. 11 No. 2	S/A	Paez		CHAL (1898)
3568	Jacoby, Wilhelm	1855-1925	Im Maien "Nun (Es) bricht aus allen Zweigen"	Op. 11 No. 2	S/A or T/B	Borne-mann		CHAL (1898)
3569	Jadassohn, Salomon	1831-1902	Am Himmel ist kein Stern	Op. 36 No. 1	Unspec.	B. & H.		CHAL (1898)
3570	Jadassohn, Salomon	1831-1902	As the stars in heav'n are blazing		Unspec.	ECS	Arr. Grmn folk song. Eng. trans. Grmn. In anth. "48 Duets 17th Through 19th Centuries" Ed. V. Prahl. Pub. 1941, 1970.	MSN
3571	Jadassohn, Salomon	1831-1902	Einen Brief soll ich schreiben	Op. 72 No. 7	Unspec.	B. & H.		CHAL (1898)
3572	Jadassohn, Salomon	1831-1902	Einklang "Um Mitternacht entstand dies Leid"	Op. 36 No. 7	Unspec.	B. & H.		CHAL (1898)
3573	Jadassohn, Salomon	1831-1902	Frische Fahrt "Laue Luft kommt blau geflossen"	Op. 72 No. 4	Unspec.	B. & H.		CHAL (1898)
3574	Jadassohn, Salomon	1831-1902	Frühlingsglaube "Linden Lüfte sind erwacht"	Op. 72 No. 3	Unspec.	B. & H.		CHAL (1898)
3575	Jadassohn, Salomon	1831-1902	Gode Nacht "Oever de stillen Straten"	Op. 72 No. 8	Unspec.	B. & H.		CHAL (1898)
3576	Jadassohn, Salomon	1831-1902	Gruss "Ich sende einen Gruss"	Op. 36 No. 8	Unspec.	B. & H.		CHAL (1898)
3577	Jadassohn, Salomon	1831-1902	Gute Nacht "Gute Nacht, die ich dir sage"	Op. 36 No. 4	Unspec.	B. & H.		CHAL (1898)
3578	Jadassohn, Salomon	1831-1902	Haidenröslein "Sah ein Knab' ein Röslein stehn"	Op. 72 No. 6	Unspec.	B. & H.		CHAL (1898)
3579	Jadassohn, Salomon	1831-1902	Heimliche Liebe "Kein Feuer, keine Kohle"	Op. 38 No. 1	2 high or 2 low v.	Kistner		CHAL (1898)
3580	Jadassohn, Salomon	1831-1902	Holdseligen sonder Wank	Op. 38 No. 4	2 high v.	Kistner		CHAL (1898)
3581	Jadassohn, Salomon	1831-1902	Ich weiss, dass mich der Himmel liebt	Op. 36 No. 4	Unspec.	B. & H.		CHAL (1898)
3582	Jadassohn, Salomon	1831-1902	Im Volkston	Op. 72 No. 7	S/A	Ditson	In anthology "Soprano and Alto Duets" Ed. H. Kiehl. Pub. 1901.	MSN
3583	Jadassohn, Salomon	1831-1902	Intermezzo "Dein Bildneiss wunderselig"	Op. 36 No. 3	Unspec.	B. & H.		CHAL (1898)
3584	Jadassohn, Salomon	1831-1902	Marienwürmchen setzte dich	Op. 38 No. 2	2 high v.	Kistner		CHAL (1898)
3585	Jadassohn, Salomon	1831-1902	Mein Herze thut mor gar zu weh!	Op. 72 No. 2	S/A	Ditson	In anthology "Soprano and Alto Duets" Ed. H. Kiehl. Pub. 1901.	MSN
3586	Jadassohn, Salomon	1831-1902	Meine Mutter warnte immer	Op. 38 No. 6	2 high v.	Kistner		CHAL (1898)
3587	Jadassohn, Salomon	1831-1902	Psalm 13 "Herr, wie lange willst du mein sogar vergessen"		S/A	Siegel	org or harm or pf accomp.	CHAL (1898)
3588	Jadassohn, Salomon	1831-1902	Psalm 18 "Herr, Herr, wie lange willst du mein"	Op. 41	S/A	Siegel		CHAL (1898)
3589	Jadassohn, Salomon	1831-1902	So viel Stern' am Himmel stehen		Unspec.	B. & H.		CHAL (1898)
3590	Jadassohn, Salomon	1831-1902	Tausend Grüsse, die wir dir senden	Op. 36 No. 2	Unspec.	B. & H.		CHAL (1898)
3591	Jadassohn, Salomon	1831-1902	Treue Liebe "Es rauschen die Wasser"	Op. 36 No. 6	Unspec.	B. & H.		CHAL (1898)
3592	Jadassohn, Salomon	1831-1902	Treue Liebe "Es rauschen die Wasser"	Op. 72 No. 5	Unspec.	B. & H.		CHAL (1898)

REC	COMP	DTS	TITLE	OP #	VCG	PUB	COMMENTS	SRC
3593	Jadassohn, Salomon	1831-1902	Twelve Times		Unspec.	ECS	Eng. trans. Grmn. In anthology "48 Duets Seventeenth Through Nineteenth Centuries" Ed. V. Prahl. Pub. 1941, 1970.	MSN
3594	Jadassohn, Salomon	1831-1902	Vergissmeinnicht "Freundlich glänzt an stiller Quelle"	Op. 38 No. 3	2 high v.	Kistner		CHAL (1898)
3595	Jadassohn, Salomon	1831-1902	Wanderers Nachtlied "Über allen Gipfeln (Wipfeln) ist Ruh"	Op. 38 No. 5	2 high v.	Kistner		CHAL (1898)
3596	Jadassohn, Salomon	1831-1902	Wär' ich ein Vögelein	Op. 72 No. 1	Unspec.	B. & H.		CHAL (1898)
3597	Jadassohn, Salomon	1831-1902	Wär' ich ein Vögelein	Op. 72 No. 1	S/A	Ditson	In anthology "Soprano and Alto Duets" Ed. H. Kiehl. Pub. 1901.	MSN
3598	Jäger, W.		Es ist ein Reihen geschlungen	Op. 1 No. 3	S/A	C. Rühle i. L.		CHAL (1911)
3599	Jäger, W.		Ich weiss ein fein braun's Mägdelein	Op. 1 No. 1	S/A	C. Rühle i. L.		CHAL (1911)
3600	Jäger, W.		Sangen einst zwei Nachtigallen	Op. 1 No. 2	S/A	C. Rühle i. L.		CHAL (1911)
3601	Jahn-Schulze, Hermann	1862-	Einst flogen zwei Elfchen spazieren	Op. 7 No. 3	Unspec.	Chal.		CHAL (1911)
3602	Jahn-Schulze, Hermann	1862-	Kahn schwankt leise	Op. 7 No. 1	Unspec.	Chal.		CHAL (1911)
3603	Jähns, Friedrich Wilhelm	1809-1888	Bilder aus Glienicke 3 Duette	Op. 39	Unspec.	Schlesinger	Anthology. Unspec. pieces.	CHAL (1898)
3604	Jansen, F. Gustav	1831-1910	Im Abendroth "Wir sind durch Noth und Freude gegangen"	Op. 31 No. 4	MS/A	vom Ende		CHAL (1898)
3605	Jansen, F. Gustav	1831-1910	Mailied "Kein' schön're (schöner) Zeit auf Erden ist"	Op. 31 No. 1	Unspec.	vom Ende		CHAL (1898)
3606	Jansen, F. Gustav	1831-1910	Nun kommt der Frühling wieder	Op. 46 No. 1	S/A	Hofmeister		CHAL (1898)
3607	Jansen, F. Gustav	1831-1910	Siehe der Frühling währet nicht lang	Op. 46 No. 2	S/A	Hofmeister		CHAL (1898)
3608	Jansen, F. Gustav	1831-1910	So wahr die Sonne Scheinet	Op. 31 No. 2	MS/A	vom Ende		CHAL (1898)
3609	Jansen, F. Gustav	1831-1910	Warum "Es verwelken die lieblichsten Kränze"	Op. 46 No. 3	S/A	Hofmeister		CHAL (1898)
3610	Jansen, F. Gustav	1831-1910	Wer Gott das Herze giebt	Op. 31 No. 3	MS/A	vom Ende		CHAL (1898)
3611	Jaques-Dalcroze, Emile	1865-1950	Berceuse pour les Agonisants		Unspec.	Henn	Collection. In "Dix Duos, Vol. 2"	CVMP (1985)
3612	Jaques-Dalcroze, Emile	1865-1950	Charmeuses de Peines		Unspec.	Henn	Collection. In "Dix Duos, Vol. 2"	CVMP (1985)
3613	Jaques-Dalcroze, Emile	1865-1950	J'ai des Petites Fleurs Bleues		Unspec.	Henn	Collection. In "Dix Duos, Vol. 1"	CVMP (1985)
3614	Jaques-Dalcroze, Emile	1865-1950	L'Amour		Unspec.	Henn	Collection. In "Dix Duos, Vol. 1"	CVMP (1985)
3615	Jaques-Dalcroze, Emile	1865-1950	La Chanson Fatale		Unspec.	Henn	Collection. In "Dix Duos, Vol. 1"	CVMP (1985)

REC	COMP	DTS	TITLE	OP #	VCG	PUB	COMMENTS	SRC
3616	Jaques-Dalcroze, Emile	1865-1950	La Femme Ermite		Unspec.	Henn	Collection. In "Dix Duos, Vol. 2"	CVMP (1985)
3617	Jaques-Dalcroze, Emile	1865-1950	La Mort Vaincue		Unspec.	Henn	Collection. In "Dix Duos, Vol. 2"	CVMP (1985)
3618	Jaques-Dalcroze, Emile	1865-1950	La Noce		Unspec.	Henn	Collection. In "Dix Duos, Vol. 1"	CVMP (1985)
3619	Jaques-Dalcroze, Emile	1865-1950	La Ronde		Unspec.	Henn	Collection. In "Dix Duos, Vol. 2"	CVMP (1985)
3620	Jaques-Dalcroze, Emile	1865-1950	La Vent		Unspec.	Henn	Collection. In "Dix Duos, Vol. 1"	CVMP (1985)
3621	Jehring, Julius	1874-	Viele Jahre sind verstrichen	Op. 49	Unspec.	O. Dietrich		CHAL (1906)
3622	Jensen, Adolf	1837-1879	Ein Fichtenbaum steht einsam	No. 2	Unspec.	B. & B.		CHAL (1898)
3623	Jensen, Adolf	1837-1879	Lehn' deine Wang' an meine Wang'	Op. 1 No. 1	S/A or T/A	Leuckart		CHAL (1898)
3624	Jensen, Adolf	1837-1889	Press Thy Cheek Against Mine Own		S/A	Ditson	Arr. H. Kiehl. Eng. trans. Grmn. In anthology "The Ditson Collection of Soprano and Alto Duets" Pub. 1934.	MSN
3625	Jensen, Adolf	1837-1879	Vom Berge "Nun steh' ich auf der höchsten Höh'"	No. 1	Unspec.	B. & B.		CHAL (1898)
3626	Jeppesen, Knud	1892-1974	Sì, sì, mio cor		Unspec.	Hansen		BBC (1975)
3627	Jeppesen, Knud	1892-1974	Soccorretemi per pietà		Unspec.	Hansen		BBC (1975)
3628	Jirasek, Ivo	1920-	Zviretnik		2 female v.	Czech		ASR
3629	Jirasek, Ivo	1920-	Zviretnik "Der Tierkreis"		2 female v.	Czech		CVMP (1976)
3630	Joël, K.		Wenn die Noth am grössten ist		Unspec.	Wernthal		CHAL (1906)
3631	John, F.		Du bist ja mein und ich bin nur dein "Ob nah, ob fern"	Op. 207	Unspec.	Vormeyer		CHAL (1898)
3632	Johnson, Noel		Good night, pretty stars		Unspec.	Chappell		BBC (1975)
3633	Jolas, Betsy	1926-	Caprice à Doux Voix		MS/A or MS/Coun-ter T	Heugel	Fr.-Amer. woman comp.	CVMP (1985)
3634	Jones, W. Bradwen		Father's love		Unspec.	Foyle		BBC (1975)
3635	Jordan, Aug.		Frühlingsankunft "mit Blüthenpracht aog über Nacht"		Unspec.	P. & M.		CHAL (1898)
3636	Jouret, Leon	1828-1905	Clochettes bleues		Unspec.	Junne		CHAL (1898)
3637	Jouret, Leon	1828-1905	Etoile du soir		Unspec.	Junne		CHAL (1898)
3638	Jouret, Leon	1828-1905	Fleurs		Unspec.	Junne		CHAL (1898)
3639	Jouret, Leon	1828-1905	Musique, parfums et prière		Unspec.	Junne		CHAL (1898)

REC	COMP	DTS	TITLE	OP #	VCG	PUB	COMMENTS	SRC
3640	Junghähnel, O.		Ausgekernt "Ausgelernt, ausgelernt"		Unspec.	Fr. Dietrich		CHAL (1898)
3641	Junghähnel, O.		Bäcker und Schuster "Eine Frechheit ohne gleichen"	Op. 39	Unspec.	Fr. Dietrich		CHAL (1898)
3642	Junghähnel, O.		Beiden Bierbrauer "Na endlich treffe ich sie"		Unspec.	O. Dietrich		CHAL (1898)
3643	Junghähnel, O.		Beiden Invaliden "Gott grüsse dich, Kam'rad"	Op. 34	Unspec.	Fr. Dietrich		CHAL (1898)
3644	Junghähnel, O.		Beiden Nachtvögel "Wir Beide wir komm'n uns"	Op. 105	Unspec.	Fr. Dietrich		CHAL (1898)
3645	Junghähnel, O.		Beiden Sitzengeliebenen "Glauben Sie, wir möchten Männer"	Op. 82	2 female v.	Fr. Dietrich		CHAL (1898)
3646	Junghähnel, O.		Beiden Waschweiber "Ei Frau Meyer, wie ich sehe"	Op. 80	2 female v.	Fr. Dietrich		CHAL (1898)
3647	Junghähnel, O.		Beiden Wittwer "Wir Beide sind ledig"	Op. 47	Unspec.	Fr. Dietrich		CHAL (1898)
3648	Junghähnel, O.		Beier und Meier "Bin schon leider sechzig Jahre"	Op. 9	Unspec.	Fr. Dietrich		CHAL (1898)
3649	Junghähnel, O.		Bergleute "Wir Bergleute sind aus 'nem einfachen Stand"	Op. 130	Unspec.	Fr. Dietrich		CHAL (1898)
3650	Junghähnel, O.		Betrübten, Rekruten "Wie ich mich nach der Heimath sehn'"	Op. 102	Unspec.	Fr. Dietrich		CHAL (1898)
3651	Junghähnel, O.		Das ist schrecklich heutzutage	Op. 83	2 female v.	Fr. Dietrich		CHAL (1901)
3652	Junghähnel, O.		Eiden Klatschbasen "Ach Herrje Frau Pappelbrinken"	Op. 50	2 female v.	Fr. Dietrich		CHAL (1898)
3653	Junghähnel, O.		Feinen Schneider "Wir Beide sind, vernehmts"	Op. 104	Unspec.	Fr. Dietrich		CHAL (1898)
3654	Junghähnel, O.		Fidele Fechtbrüder "Wir Beide fechten uns"		Unspec.	O. Dietrich		CHAL (1898)
3655	Junghähnel, O.		Heute bunte Fröhlichkeit	Op. 52	2 female v.	Fr. Dietrich		CHAL (1911)
3656	Junghähnel, O.		Lustigen Briefträger "Jetzt komm'n zwei lust'ge"	Op. 45	Unspec.	Fr. Dietrich		CHAL (1898)
3657	Junghähnel, O.		Milchen und Malchen "Ach Malchen, ich muss"	Op. 51	2 female v.	Fr. Dietrich		CHAL (1898)
3658	Junghähnel, O.		O Pa Pa Pa Pa Pa Pa Pauline "Hier sehn sie zwei rasend Verliebte"		Unspec.	O. Dietrich		CHAL (1898)
3659	Junghähnel, O.		Rekrut Dunzels erster Strafrapport "Herrgott schuf Menschen"	Op. 46	Unspec.	Fr. Dietrich		CHAL (1898)
3660	Junghähnel, O.		Rekrut und Reservist "Hurrah, dass nenn' ich Glück"	Op. 35	Unspec.	Fr. Dietrich		CHAL (1898)
3661	Junghähnel, O.		Stadt- und Landmädchen "Herrlich ist's am frühen Morgen"	Op. 81	2 female v.	Fr. Dietrich		CHAL (1898)
3662	Junghähnel, O.		Theatralischen Hausknechte "Stiefel putzen, Kleider bürsten"	Op. 38	Unspec.	Fr. Dietrich		CHAL (1898)
3663	Junghähnel, O.		Tyroler und Berliner "Himmel Sacra, Kruzi"	Op. 258	Unspec.	Glaser		CHAL (1898)
3664	Junghähnel, O.		Wem gehört das Kind "Keinen Abend mehr zu Hause"	Op. 262	2 male or 2 female v.	Glaser		CHAL (1898)
3665	Junghähnel, O.		Wenn Morgens am Himmel die Sonne	Op. 49	Unspec.	Fr. Dietrich		CHAL (1901)
3666	Junghähnel, O.		Wie bin ich eifersüchtig	Op. 72	Unspec.	Fr. Dietrich		CHAL (1901)
3667	Junghähnel, O.		Wir heirathen nicht "Es sagen die Männer"	Op. 120	2 female v.	Fr. Dietrich		CHAL (1898)
3668	Junghähnel, O.		Zwei Fleissige Maurer "Na Lehmann, bist du ooch schon hier"	Op. 30	Unspec.	Fr. Dietrich		CHAL (1898)
3669	Junghans, J.		Letzen zwei Thaler "Wie schön ist das Leben"	Op. 1	Unspec.	Fr. Dietrich		CHAL (1898)

REC	COMP	DTS	TITLE	OP #	VCG	PUB	COMMENTS	SRC
3670	Jungmann, Albert	1824-1892	Laue Lüftchen tragen Klänge	Op. 17	S/S	Bachmann		CHAL (1898)
3671	Jungmann, Albert	1824-1892	Mein stilles Glück	Op. 9	Unspec.	Heinr.		CHAL (1898)
3672	Jüngst, Hugo	1853-1923	Abendstille "Leise, leise, Käferlein"	Op. 27 No. 2	Unspec.	Rud. Dietrich		CHAL (1898)
3673	Jüngst, Hugo	1853-1923	Nesterl "Wennst a Nesterl willst baun"		Unspec.	Robitschek		CHAL (1898)
3674	Jüngst, Hugo	1853-1923	Spinn, spinn "Mägdlein heilt Tag und Nacht"		Unspec.	Robitschek		CHAL (1898)
3675	Jüngst, Hugo	1853-1923	Tik e tik e tok' mein schwarzbraunes Liebchen	Op. 87 No. 2 d	S/A	O. Forberg		CHAL (1906)
3676	Jüngst, Hugo	1853-1923	Wo des Duro Wellen fliessen	Op. 87 No. 16 d	S/A	O. Forberg		CHAL (1911)
3677	Jurek, Wilhem August	1870-1934	Bevor no der Thomerl		Unspec.	Blaha		CHAL (1911)
3678	Jürisch, E.		Überall und jeder Zeit	Op. 12	Unspec.	Favorit i. Berlin		CHAL (1911)
3679	Kaatz, F.		Wenn Sie uns sehen vor sich stehen		Unspec.	Apollo		CHAL (1901)
3680	Kagerer, Marcus Thomas	1878-1932	Fluren tragen ein Feierkleid	No. 3	Unspec.	Böhm & S.		CHAL (1911)
3681	Kagerer, Marcus Thomas	1878-1932	O heil'ge Weihnacht, sel'ge Zeit	No. 1	Unspec.	Böhm & S.		CHAL (1911)
3682	Kagerer, Marcus Thomas	1878-1932	Vor dir, o Makellose	No. 2	Unspec.	Böhm & S.		CHAL (1911)
3683	Kagerer, Marcus Thomas	1878-1932	Weihnachtszeit (4)		Unspec.	Böhm & S.	4 duets	CHAL (1911)
3684	Kahle, Th.		So nimm denn meine Hände		Unspec.	Hoffheinz		CHAL (1906)
3685	Kahn, Robert	1865-1951	Im Maien "Im Maien zu Zweien ze gehen"	Op. 21 No. 2	high & low v.	Leuckart		CHAL (1898)
3686	Kahn, Robert	1865-1951	März "Es ist ein Schnee gefallen"	Op. 21 No. 4	high & low v.	Leuckart		CHAL (1898)
3687	Kahn, Robert	1865-1951	Waldeinsamkeit "Waldeinsamkeit, du grünes Revier"	Op. 21 No. 1	high & low v.	Leuckart		CHAL (1898)
3688	Kahn, Robert	1865-1951	Zweigesang der Elfen "Hörst du das Flüstern"	Op. 21 No. 3	high & low v.	Leuckart		CHAL (1898)
3689	Kainer, C.		Alpen glüh'n im Abendschein		Unspec.	P. & M.	Arr. Knebelsberger	CHAL (1901)
3690	Kainer, C.		O junger Lenz du bist so schön	Op. 26 No. 1	S/A	Siegel		CHAL (1906)
3691	Kainer, C.		Rosenstock, Holderblüth wenn i mei Dirndel sieh		Unspec.	P. & M.		CHAL (1901)
3692	Kainer, C.		Treibt die Sennrin von der Alm		Unspec.	P. & M.		CHAL (1901)
3693	Kainer, C.		Was willst du, Schatz, im Mondenschein		Unspec.	P. & M.		CHAL (1901)
3694	Kainer, C.		Zwâ Sterndlan "Zwâ Sterndlan am Himmel"		Unspec.	P. & M.		CHAL (1898)
3695	Kaiser, Karl	1876-1932	Abendbild	Op. 10	2 male or 2 female v.	P. Fischer i. Berl.		CHAL (1898)
3696	Kaleikoa, Malie		Ka lai opua		Unspec.	C. E. King	Polynesian song, Ed. King	BBC (1975)
3697	Kalla, C.		Felsenhaus		S/S or S/T	Biehl i. H.		CHAL (1898)
3698	Kallenbach, Georg E. G.	d. 1832	Abschied		Unspec.	Hinrichs i. Leipz.	pf-2 hands	CHAL (1898)
3699	Kalliwoda, Johann Wenzel	1801-1866	Ihr Vögelein so zart und fein	Op. 207 No. 1	S/S	Peters		CHAL (1901)

REC	COMP	DTS	TITLE	OP #	VCG	PUB	COMMENTS	SRC
3700	Kalliwoda, Johann Wenzel	1801-1866	In der Wiege	Op. 207 No. 3	S/S	Peters		CHAL (1901)
3701	Kalliwoda, Johann Wenzel	1801-1866	Seht aus des Himmels goldnem Thor	Op. 207 No. 4	S/S	Peters		CHAL (1901)
3702	Kalliwoda, Johann Wenzel	1801-1866	Singt heut' in frohen Chören	Op. 207 No. 2	S/S	Peters		CHAL (1901)
3703	Kammer, R.		Blumengruss "Struass den ich gepflücket"	Op. 10	Unspec.	Kaun		CHAL (1898)
3704	Kammerlander, Karl	1828-1892	Am Abend "Schafe ziehen heim zur Hürde"	Op. 14 No. 3	Unspec.	Schott		CHAL (1898)
3705	Kammerlander, Karl	1828-1892	Glöcklein "Ein Glöcklein klingt so helle"	Op. 88 No. 2	S/A or T/B	Böhm & S.		CHAL (1898)
3706	Kammerlander, Karl	1828-1892	Morgenlied "Erwacht, er-wacht, es schwand die Nacht"	Op. 14 No. 1	Unspec.	Schott		CHAL (1898)
3707	Kammerlander, Karl	1828-1892	Schon wehen laue lüfte	Op. 14 No. 2	Unspec.	Schott		CHAL (1898)
3708	Kammerlander, Karl	1828-1892	Sonn' ist hin	Op. 88 No. 3	S/A or T/B	Böhm & S.		CHAL (1898)
3709	Kanne, Friedrich August	1778-1833	Danza		Unspec.	Melzer i. Leipz.		CHAL (1898)
3710	Kanzler, W.		Als ich an deiner Brust geruht	III No. 11	Unspec.	C. Rühle i. L.		CHAL (1901)
3711	Kanzler, W.		Auf stiller See "West durchweht gelind die Nacht"	Op. 2 No. 1	Unspec.	Rühle i. L.		CHAL (1898)
3712	Kanzler, W.		Entfernte Glocken klangen herauf	I No. 12	Unspec.	C. Rühle i. L.		CHAL (1901)
3713	Kanzler, W.		Heimkehr "Entfernte Glocken klangen herauf"	Op. 2 No. 5	Unspec.	Rühle i. L.		CHAL (1898)
3714	Kanzler, W.		Im Hafen "Als ich an deiner Brust geruht"	Op. 2 No. 2	Unspec.	Rühle i. L.		CHAL (1898)
3715	Kanzler, W.		Seebilder "3 Duette"	Op. 2	Unspec.	Rühle i. L.	3 duets	CHAL (1898)
3716	Kapeller, A.		Abendlied "Sonne sank, der Abend naht"	No. 1	2 female v.	Schlesinger		CHAL (1898)
3717	Kapeller, A.		Brautlied "Welch' ein Scheiden"	No. 3	2 female v.	Schlesinger		CHAL (1898)
3718	Kapeller, A.		Nussbaum "Es grünet ein Nussbaum"	No. 2	2 female v.	Schlesinger		CHAL (1898)
3719	Karg-Elert, Sigfried (G. F. Handel)	1877-1933	Zartes Blätterdach, du trautes		S/A or T/Br	C. Simon i. B.	Arr. Handel aria	CHAL (1911)
3720	Karlsen, Kjell Mork	1947-	Jesu Syv Ord Pa Korset		S/A	Noton		CVMP (1995)
3721	Kasper, M.		Froh ertönen Weihnachtsglocken	Op. 17	Unspec.	Schiefelbein		CHAL (1906)
3722	Kasper, M.		Umrahmt von Wald und Bergen	Op. 14	Unspec.	Hegner i. S.		CHAL (1906)
3723	Katzer, Karl August	1822-1904	Aber halt liab "Hei ist das lustig"	No. 3	Unspec.	Robitschek		CHAL (1898)
3724	Kauffmann-Jassoy, Erich	1877-	Rebhahnruf und Glockenlauf	Op. 12 No. 1	Unspec.	F. Schellenb. i. W.		CHAL (1911)
3725	Kauppi, Emil		Suomalaisiakansanlaulu duettoja Vol 1,2		high & low v.	Fazer	Unspec. pieces. Finnish duets in 2 vols.	ASR
3726	Kayser, Philipp Christoph	1755-1823	Herr! ein mädchen		Unspec.	Goethe Gesellschaft	Ed. Friedländer	BBC (1975)
3727	Kean, Edmund		Sweet Kitty Clover		Unspec.	Augener	Arr. Moffat	BBC (1975)

REC	COMP	DTS	TITLE	OP #	VCG	PUB	COMMENTS	SRC
3728	Keel, James Frederick	1871-1954	Calm after storm		Unspec.	Boosey		BBC (1975)
3729	Keel, James Frederick	1871-1954	Spring		Unspec.	Boosey		BBC (1975)
3730	Keel, James Frederick	1871-1954	You spotted snakes		S/A	Boosey		BBC (1975)
3731	Keel, James Frederick	1871-1954	You Spotted Snakes		high & med. v.	Boosey	In anthology "Duet Album: Selected and edited by Viola Morris and Victoria Anderson" Pub. 1944.	MSN
3732	Keel, James Frederick	1871-1954	You Spotted Snakes		S/MS	Boosey	In anthology "Duet Album for High and Medium Voices" sel. & ed. V. Morris & V. Anderson. Pub. 1944.	NATS-VCD
3733	Kekepuchi		Kuu lei aloha		Unspec.	C. E. King	Polynesian song, Arr. C. E. King	BBC (1975)
3734	Keller, H.		Abendlüfte wehen lind	Op. 38 No. 3	S/S	B. & H.		CHAL (1898)
3735	Keller, H.		Durch duftende Wälder	Op. 38 No. 7	S/S	B. & H.		CHAL (1898)
3736	Keller, H.		Ein neues Leben ist erwacht	Op. 38 No. 4	S/S	B. & H.		CHAL (1898)
3737	Keller, H.		Lena ist längst vorüber	Op. 38 No. 8	S/S	B. & H.		CHAL (1898)
3738	Keller, H.		Selige Tage sind mir entschwunden	Op. 38 No. 5	S/S	B. & H.		CHAL (1898)
3739	Keller, H.		Wiegenlied "Schlafe nur, schlafe"	Op. 38 No. 6	S/S	B. & H.		CHAL (1898)
3740	Keller, Karl	1784-1855	Colonisten "Wenn im ersten Morgenstrahl"	Op. 61	Unspec.	Peters		CHAL (1898)
3741	Keller, Karl	1784-1855	Lieblich wie der gold'ne Morgen	Op. 38 No. 2	S/A	B. & H.	In anth. "Zweistim. Lied. f. Sop. u. Altstimme mit Klavierbegleitung f. den Haus- u. Schulgebrauch v. H. M. Schletterer" 3 vols.	MSN
3742	Keller, Karl	1784-1855	Lieblich wie der goldne Morgen	Op. 38 No. 2	S/S	B. & H.		CHAL (1898)
3743	Keller, Karl	1784-1855	Liebliche Töne, ihr nur dürft sangen	Op. 38 No. 1	S/S	B. & H.		CHAL (1898)
3744	Keller, Ludwig	1847-1930	Schon fängt es an zu dämmern	Op. 49	S/A	vom Ende		CHAL (1901)
3745	Keller, Ludwig	1847-1930	Sonntag auf dem Meere "Meer ist glatt und athmet kaum"	Op. 21 No. 2	Unspec.	Ullrich i. Cöln		CHAL (1898)
3746	Keller, Ludwig	1847-1930	Weisse Rosen, ach wie blüht ihr	Op. 21 No. 1	Unspec.	Ullrich i. Cöln		CHAL (1898)
3747	Kellie, Lawrence	1862-1932	Oh, wondrous joy		Unspec.	Cocks		BBC (1975)
3748	Kennedy		Star of the East		S/A	Lorenz	Also solo pub. Carl Fischer, Century et al.	CVMP (1976)
3749	Kent, Edward		What would you like to be		Unspec.	Reynolds		BBC (1975)
3750	Kerle, J. H. or H. J.		An diesem Tag der Freude	Op. 11	S/A	Coppen-rath		CHAL (1906)
3751	Kerle, J. H. or H. J.		Gar zu eng ist eine Försterei	Op. 8	S/A	Coppen-rath		CHAL (1901)
3752	Keue, C.		Flotte und Trauerkloss "Ach wie ist so trüb"	Op. 8	Unspec.	Danner		CHAL (1898)

REC	COMP	DTS	TITLE	OP #	VCG	PUB	COMMENTS	SRC
3753	Keycher, O.		Blühende Apfelbaum "Nun seht einmal der Apfelbaum"	Op. 15 No. 1	Unspec.	Rich. Thiele		CHAL (1898)
3754	Keycher, O.		Blumen Dank "Verschwunden ist die stille Nacht"	Op. 15 No. 5	Unspec.	Rich. Thiele		CHAL (1898)
3755	Keycher, O.		Frohe Sinn "Fröhlich und wohlgemuth"	Op. 15 No. 2	Unspec.	Rich. Thiele		CHAL (1898)
3756	Keycher, O.		Psalm 84 "Wie lieblich sind deine Wohnungen"	Op. 22	Unspec.	Weinholtz		CHAL (1898)
3757	Keycher, O.		Sandmännchen "Vöglein sie sangen"	Op. 15 No. 3	Unspec.	Rich. Thiele		CHAL (1898)
3758	Keycher, O.		Vögleins Begräbniss "Unter den rothen Blumen"	Op. 15 No. 4	Unspec.	Rich. Thiele		CHAL (1898)
3759	Keycher, O.		Vom Schlaraffenland "Komm wir wollen uns begeben"	Op. 15 No. 6	Unspec.	Rich. Thiele		CHAL (1898)
3760	Kienzl, Wilhelm	1857-1941	Goldiger, sonniger Maientag	Op. 73 No. 5	Unspec.	Kahnt		CHAL (1911)
3761	Kinkel, Johanna	1810-1858	Weh, dass wir scheiden müssen	I No. 4	Unspec.	C. Rühle i. L.	Arr. Necke, Grmn. woman composer. Née Mockel.	CHAL (1901)
3762	Kipper, Hermann	1826-1910	Ach es ist die arme Magd	Op. 55 No. 4	S/MS	André		CHAL (1898)
3763	Kipper, Hermann	1826-1910	Erste Ball "Nach solch' ereignissfroher Kunde"	Op. 110	2 female v.	Andrè		CHAL (1898)
3764	Kipper, Hermann	1826-1910	Geschichte der Liebe "Wollt ihr wissen, wie die Lieb'"	Op. 40 No. a	Unspec.	Rühle i. L.		CHAL (1898)
3765	Kipper, Hermann	1826-1910	Kauft Beseme, kauft Holzwaare	Op. 88	Unspec.	Rühle i. L.		CHAL (1898)
3766	Kipper, Hermann	1826-1910	Milchmädchen "Gnäd'ges Fräulein, Milch bring' ich"	Op. 81	S/S	Cohen		CHAL (1898)
3767	Kipper, Hermann	1826-1910	Mit dem Sonnenschirm "Dunkel ist es und schon spät"	Op. 79	S/MS or S/A	R. Forberg		CHAL (1898)
3768	Kipper, Hermann	1826-1910	O Mutterherz, wie gross ist deine Liebe	Op. 55 No. 3b	S/A	André		CHAL (1898)
3769	Kipper, Hermann	1826-1910	Schönheiten Ausstellung "Hohe Zeit ist's wahrlich jetzt"	Op. 83	S/S	Glaser		CHAL (1898)
3770	Kipper, Hermann	1826-1910	Thusnelda und Elvira "Wie herrlich, wie fein"	Op. 82	S/S	P. & M.		CHAL (1898)
3771	Kipper, Hermann	1826-1910	Tick-tack-Duett "Es ist doch gar nett"	Op. 55 No. 3a	S/MS	André		CHAL (1898)
3772	Kipper, Hermann	1826-1910	Zwei Sterne "Edle Musike, ach wie dumm"	Op. 114	S/S	Siegel		CHAL (1898)
3773	Kirchl, Adolf	1858-	Kaiser Josef-Hymne "Kaiser Josef, elder Kaiser"		Unspec.	Kratochwill		CHAL (1898)
3774	Kirchner, Hermann	1861-1928	Am Schlehdorn, wisst ihr, wo der steht	Op. 49	Unspec.	Pabst i. L.		CHAL (1911)
3775	Kirchner, Hermann	1861-1928	Es steigen die Glöckchen	Op. 42	Unspec.	Pabst i. L.		CHAL (1911)
3776	Kirchner, Hermann	1861-1928	Es war einmal 'ne dralle Maid	No. 5	Unspec.	Pabst i. L.		CHAL (1911)
3777	Kirchner, Hermann	1861-1928	Holderstrauch, der blüthe schön	No. 1	Unspec.	Pabst i. L.		CHAL (1911)
3778	Kirchner, Hermann	1861-1928	In unsres Nachbars Garten	No. 3	Unspec.	Pabst i. L.		CHAL (1911)
3779	Kirchner, Hermann	1861-1928	Mein Kind, nun lass' dich schmücken	No. 2	Unspec.	Pabst i. L.		CHAL (1911)
3780	Kirchner, Hermann	1861-1928	Nur dein liebes Augenpaar	No. 4	Unspec.	Pabst i. L.		CHAL (1911)
3781	Kirchner, Hermann	1861-1928	Sonntagsglocke, du klingst süss	No. 6	Unspec.	Pabst i. L.		CHAL (1911)

REC	COMP	DTS	TITLE	OP #	VCG	PUB	COMMENTS	SRC
3782	Kirchner, Theodor Fürchtegott	1823-1903	Nun spricht die kleine Schwalbe		Unspec.	Grüninger		CHAL (1906)
3783	Kirschhof, G. F.		Es fällt ein Stern herunter	Op. 42 No. 2	Unspec.	Schott		CHAL (1898)
3784	Kirschhof, G. F.		Ich hab' im Traum geweinet	Op. 42 No. 1	Unspec.	Schott		CHAL (1898)
3785	Kittl, Johann Friedrich	1806-1868	Abendlied "Vom stillen Abendhügel"	Op. 35 No. 2	S/A	Hoffmann i. Pr.		CHAL (1898)
3786	Kittl, Johann Friedrich	1806-1868	An die Nachtigall "Süsse Klage"	Op. 53 No. 3	S/A	Kistner		CHAL (1898)
3787	Kittl, Johann Friedrich	1806-1868	Andacht "Mir ist so wohl in Gottes Haus"	Op. 53 No. 5	S/A	Kistner		CHAL (1898)
3788	Kittl, Johann Friedrich	1806-1868	Andenken an den Tod "Wer weiss wie nahe"	Op. 35 No. 4	S/A	Hoffmann i. Pr.		CHAL (1898)
3789	Kittl, Johann Friedrich	1806-1868	Ein geistlich Abendlied "Es ist so still geworden"	Op. 53 No. 2	S/A	Kistner		CHAL (1898)
3790	Kittl, Johann Friedrich	1806-1868	Er ist's "Frühling lässt sein blaues Band"	Op. 53 No. 4	S/A	Kistner		CHAL (1898)
3791	Kittl, Johann Friedrich	1806-1868	Gefunden "Ich ging im Walde so für mich hin"	Op. 35 No. 1	S/A	Hoffmann i. Pr.		CHAL (1898)
3792	Kittl, Johann Friedrich	1806-1868	Mailied "Wie herrlich leuchtet mir die Natur"	Op. 35 No. 6	S/A	Hoffmann i. Pr		CHAL (1898)
3793	Kittl, Johann Friedrich	1806-1868	O der blaue, blaue Himmel	Op. 53 No. 6	S/A	Kistner		CHAL (1898)
3794	Kittl, Johann Friedrich	1806-1868	Sie liebten sich beide	Op. 53 No. 1	S/A	Kistner		CHAL (1898)
3795	Kittl, Johann Friedrich	1806-1868	Vertrauen auf Gott "Hoffe Herz nur mit Geduld"	Op. 35 No. 5	S/A	Hoffmann i. Pr.		CHAL (1898)
3796	Kittl, Johann Friedrich	1806-1868	Zuversicht "Lerche jubelt mit Gesang"	Op. 35 No. 3	S/A	Hoffmann i. Pr.		CHAL (1898)
3797	Kjerulf, Halfdan	1815-1868	Last Night		S/A	Ditson	Arr. H. Kiehl. Eng. trans. Nor. In anthology "Soprano and Alto Duets" Ed. H. Kiehl. Pub. 1901.	MSN
3798	Kjerulf, Halfdan	1815-1868	Last Night		S/A	Ditson	Arr. H. Kiehl. Eng. trans. Nor. In anthology "The Ditson Collection of Soprano and Alto Duets" Pub. 1934.	MSN
3799	Kleffel, Arno	1840-1913	Alte Heimath "In einem dunkeln Thal"	Op. 8 No. 4	high & low v.	Simon i. Berl.		CHAL (1898)
3800	Kleffel, Arno	1840-1913	Am Grabe der Mutter "Wir armen, armen Mädchen"	Op. 8 No. 10	high & low v.	Simon i. Berl.		CHAL (1898)
3801	Kleffel, Arno	1840-1913	Bei Sonnenuntergang "Fahr wohl, du goldne Sonne"	Op. 8 No. 2	high & low v.	Simon i. Berl.		CHAL (1898)
3802	Kleffel, Arno	1840-1913	Dorf-Grete "Grete vom Land"	Op. 43 No. 7	S/A	B. & B.		CHAL (1898)
3803	Kleffel, Arno	1840-1913	Ein Kohlblättchen "Ich will dir mal was lesen"	Op. 43 No. 4	S/A	B. & B.		CHAL (1898)
3804	Kleffel, Arno	1840-1913	Erste Schneeglöckchen "Wir sind die kleinen Glöckchen"	Op. 43 No. 14	S/A	B. & B.		CHAL (1898)
3805	Kleffel, Arno	1840-1913	Frühling ist da "Bächlein zum Bache scwoll"	Op. 8 No. 7	high & low v.	Simon i. Berl.		CHAL (1898)
3806	Kleffel, Arno	1840-1913	Guten Tag Frau Gevatterin	Op. 43 No. 11	S/A	B. & B.		CHAL (1898)
3807	Kleffel, Arno	1840-1913	Haidenröslein "Sah ein Knab' ein Röslein stehn"	Op. 8 No. 6	high & low v.	Simon i. Berl.		CHAL (1898)
3808	Kleffel, Arno	1840-1913	Ich Hirten erwacht	Op. 43 No. 5	Unspec.	B. & B.		CHAL (1901)

REC	COMP	DTS	TITLE	OP #	VCG	PUB	COMMENTS	SRC
3809	Kleffel, Arno	1840-1913	In der Mühle "Rauschet, rauschet Mühlensteine"	Op. 8 No. 9	high & low v.	Simon i. Berl.		CHAL (1898)
3810	Kleffel, Arno	1840-1913	Nun gute Nacht	Op. 43 No. 15	S/A	B. & B.		CHAL (1898)
3811	Kleffel, Arno	1840-1913	Puppen Wiegenlied "Schlaf, Püppchen, schlaf"	Op. 43 No. 10	S/A	B. & B.		CHAL (1898)
3812	Kleffel, Arno	1840-1913	Putthühnchen, wo hast du deinen Mann	Op. 43 No. 3	S/A	B. & B.		CHAL (1898)
3813	Kleffel, Arno	1840-1913	Schneckenlied "Schneck, Schneck, Mäuschen"	Op. 43 No. 6	S/A	B. & B.		CHAL (1898)
3814	Kleffel, Arno	1840-1913	Schwestern Wiegenlied "Schlaf ein du süsses Kind"	Op. 8 No. 1	high & low v.	Simon i. Berl.		CHAL (1898)
3815	Kleffel, Arno	1840-1913	Soll ich singen	Op. 43 No. 8	S/A	B. & B.		CHAL (1898)
3816	Kleffel, Arno	1840-1913	Spinnlied "Spinn, (spinn,) Mägdlein, spinn"	Op. 43 No. 13	S/A	B. & B.		CHAL (1898)
3817	Kleffel, Arno	1840-1913	Traum "Das was ein niedlich Zeiselein"	Op. 43 No. 12	S/A	B. & B.		CHAL (1898)
3818	Kleffel, Arno	1840-1913	Über Nacht "Über Nacht kommt still das Leid"	Op. 8 No. 8	high & low v.	Simon i. Berl.		CHAL (1898)
3819	Kleffel, Arno	1840-1913	Vögleins Reise "Vöglein, Vöglein, schwinget den Fuss"	Op. 43 No. 2	S/A	B. & B.		CHAL (1898)
3820	Kleffel, Arno	1840-1913	Wallfahrtslied "Wir wandern über Berg und Thal"	Op. 8 No. 5	high & low v.	Simon i. Berl.		CHAL (1898)
3821	Kleffel, Arno	1840-1913	Weihnachtslied "Ihr Hirten erwacht"	Op. 43 No. 5	S/A	B. & B.		CHAL (1898)
3822	Kleffel, Arno	1840-1913	Wie ist doch die Erde so schön	Op. 8 No. 3	high &low v.	Simon i. Berl.		CHAL (1898)
3823	Kleffel, Arno	1840-1913	Wiegenlied "Draussen im Garten"	Op. 43 No. 1	S/A	B. & B.		CHAL (1898)
3824	Kleiber, Karl	1838-1902	Katzen-Rendevous "Mai Mitzl steigt öftner's auf's Doch"		S/A or T/A	Cranz		CHAL (1898)
3825	Klein, O.		Kater Hans und Mietze Grethe "O liebes Mietzchen, holde Braut"	Op. 2	Unspec.	Wilh. Dietrich		CHAL (1898)
3826	Kleinecke, W.		Sel'ge Ruh' senkt sich herneider	Op. 42	high &low v.	Kistner		CHAL (1906)
3827	Kleinmichel, Richard	1846-1901	Frühlingsglaube "Linden Lüfte sind erwacht"	Op. 26 No. 3	Unspec.	R. & B.		CHAL (1898)
3828	Kleinmichel, Richard	1846-1901	Gebrochenes Herz "Rosen und die Nelken und Flieder"	Op. 26 No. 2	Unspec.	R. & B.		CHAL (1898)
3829	Kleinmichel, Richard	1846-1901	Ich hör' ein Vöglein locken	Op. 26 No. 4	Unspec.	R. & B.		CHAL (1898)
3830	Kleinmichel, Richard	1846-1901	Noch sind die Tage der Rosen "Noch ist die blühende goldne Zeit"	Op. 26 No. 1	Unspec.	R. & B.		CHAL (1898)
3831	Kleinmichel, Richard	1846-1901	Sandmann "Zwei feine Stieflein hab' ich"	Op. 26 No. 5	Unspec.	R. & B.		CHAL (1898)
3832	Kleinmichel, Richard	1846-1901	Vogelsprache "Was schmettert die Nachtigall"	Op. 26 No. 6	Unspec.	R. & B.		CHAL (1898)
3833	Klengel, Paul	1854-1935	Brautlied "Welch' ein Scheiden"	Op. 3 No. 4	Unspec.	B. & H.		CHAL (1898)
3834	Klengel, Paul	1854-1935	Dein Bild "O könnt ich doch ein Spiegel sein"	Op. 3 No. 2	Unspec.	B. & H.		CHAL (1898)
3835	Klengel, Paul	1854-1935	Du bist so weit, so weit	Op. 3 No. 5	Unspec.	B. & H.		CHAL (1898)
3836	Klengel, Paul	1854-1935	Ergebung "Trag es nur, was überschwänglich"	Op. 3 No. 3	Unspec.	B. & H.		CHAL (1898)

REC	COMP	DTS	TITLE	OP #	VCG	PUB	COMMENTS	SRC
3837	Klengel, Paul	1854-1935	Ich weiss, ja nicht, was kommen wird	Op. 3 No. 1	Unspec.	B. & H.		CHAL (1898)
3838	Klengel, Paul	1854-1935	Treueste Liebe "Ein Bruder und eine Schwester"	Op. 3 No. 6	Unspec.	B. & B.		CHAL (1898)
3839	Klepsch		Beiden Zeitungleser "Was seh' ich, sie studieren"		Unspec.	Neumann i. Berl.		CHAL (1898)
3840	Klinkmüller, F.		Gefunden "Ich ging im Walde so für mich hin"	Op. 50	S/A or T/A	Edm. Stoll		CHAL (1898)
3841	Klinkmüller, F.		Mutterherz "Ich hab' mir erkoren"	Op. 58	S/A or T/A	Edm. Stoll		CHAL (1898)
3842	Klinkmüller, F.		Nicht sorgen "Waldvögelein, wo singst du"	Op. 49	S/A or T/A	Edm. Stoll.		CHAL (1898)
3843	Klinkmüller, F.		Wenn der Herr ein Kreuze schicht	Op. 51	S/A or MS/Br	Edm. Stoll		CHAL (1898)
3844	Klose, Oskar	1859-1924	Friedlich "Friedlich seh'n rings herum"		Unspec.	Sackur		CHAL (1898)
3845	Kloss, H.		Ach wollt bald der Tag erscheinen	Op. 24	2 female v.	Bloch		CHAL (1901)
3846	Kloss, H.		Heirathslustigen Schwestern "Wir sind ein lustiges Schwesternpaar"	Op. 21	Unspec.	P. & M.		CHAL (1898)
3847	Kloss, H.		Tyroler Sepp und sein Mirzl "Grüss God mein liab's Mirzl"	Op. 26	Unspec.	P. & M.		CHAL (1898)
3848	Kmoch, A.		Beiden Bummler "Wir sind zwei fesche Leut'"		Unspec.	Rühle & H.		CHAL (1898)
3849	Knebel-Döberitz, A. v.		Abendreihn "Guten Abend lieber Mondenschein"	No. 2	Unspec.	Bahn		CHAL (1898)
3850	Knebel-Döberitz, A. v.		Nachtlied "Mond kommt still gegangen"	No. 1	Unspec.	Bahn		CHAL (1898)
3851	Knebelsberger L.		Abend auf der Alm "Alpen glühn im Abendschein"		S/A	P. & M.		CHAL (1898)
3852	Kniese, Julius	1848-1905	Ach, dass ewig hier die Liebe	Op. 6 No. 1	2 female v.	Hainauer		CHAL (1898)
3853	Kniese, Julius	1848-1905	Geht es dor auch wie mir	Op. 6 No. 4	2 female v.	Hainauer		CHAL (1898)
3854	Kniese, Julius	1848-1905	Gleich und Gleich "Ein Blumenglöckchen vom Boden hervor (empor)"	Op. 6 No. 2	2 female v.	Hainauer		CHAL (1898)
3855	Kniese, Julius	1848-1905	Ich muss nun einmal singen "Vöglein, Vöglein, was singest du"	Op. 6 No. 7	2 female v.	Hainauer		CHAL (1898)
3856	Kniese, Julius	1848-1905	Kennst du dies Lied	Op. 6 No. 6	2 female v.	Hainauer		CHAL (1898)
3857	Kniese, Julius	1848-1905	März "Es ist ein Schnee gefallen"	Op. 6 No. 5	2 female v.	Hainauer		CHAL (1898)
3858	Kniese, Julius	1848-1905	Rastlose Liebe "Schnee, dem Regen"	Op. 6 No. 8	2 female v.	Hainauer		CHAL (1898)
3859	Kniese, Julius	1848-1905	Schön ist das Fest des Lenzes	Op. 6 No. 3	2 female v.	Hainauer		CHAL (1898)
3860	Knopf, Martin	1876-	In dem Hotel zur goldnen Gaus		Unspec.	Harmonie i. B.		CHAL (1911)
3861	Knopf, Martin	1876-	Wie ein kleines Spatzenpaar		Unspec.	Harmonie i. B.		CHAL (1906)
3862	Knopf, Martin	1876-	Wilhelmche, Wilhelmineken		Unspec.	Phiharm. Ver. i. B.		CHAL (1911)
3863	Knopf, Martin	1876-	Zwei kleine Mädchen mit 'nem Hängezopf		2 female v.	Harmonie i. B.		CHAL (1911)
3864	Knopf, Martin	1876-	Zwei kleine Mädels mit 'nem Hängezopf		2 female v.	Harmonie i. B.		CHAL (1906)
3865	Koch, August	d. 1914	Waldkirchlein "Es steht ein Kirchlein im grünen Wald"	Op. 20 No. 3	Unspec.	Kratoch-will		CHAL (1898)

REC	COMP	DTS	TITLE	OP #	VCG	PUB	COMMENTS	SRC
3866	Koch, Markus	1879-	Wir san da zwoa Steft'n		Unspec.	Bauderer		CHAL (1911)
3867	Kodály, Zoltán	1881-1967	Álom	No. 8	Unspec.	EMB	In "Epigrammák" In anthology "A kamaraének mesterei" Compi. & ed. T. Füzesséry (no date)	MSN
3868	Kodály, Zoltán	1881-1967	Bánat	No. 3	Unspec.	EMB	In "Epigrammák" In anthology "A kamaraének mesterei" Compi. & ed. T. Füzesséry (no date)	MSN
3869	Kodály, Zoltán	1882-1967	Bicinia Hungarica		2 med. v.	Boosey, NYP Libe	acap. Unspec. pieces	ASR
3870	Kodály, Zoltán	1882-1967	Csillagoknak Teremtöje		S/A	EMB	(Bicinia Hung., II. 80, 1958). In anth. "Duettek nöi Hangok-ra Zongorakísérettel" Vol. II Compi. M. Forrai. Pub. 1959.	MSN
3871	Kodály, Zoltán	1882-1967	Csillagoknak Terëmtöje		S/MS	Editio Musica	In anthology "Duettek" in 2 Vols. Ed. M. Forrai. Pub. 1959.	NATS-VCD
3872	Kodály, Zoltán	1881-1967	Felhö	No. 7	Unspec.	EMB	In "Epigrammák" In anthology "A kamaraének mesterei" Compi. & ed. T. Füzesséry (no date)	MSN
3873	Kodály, Zoltán	1881-1967	Gyöngyvirág	No. 4	Unspec.	EMB	In "Epigrammák" In anthology "A kamaraének mesterei" Compi. & ed. T. Füzesséry (no date)	MSN
3874	Kodály, Zoltán	1882-1967	Kiolvasó		S/A	EMB	(Bicinia Hung., II. 80, 1958). In anth. "Duettek nöi Hangok-ra Zongorakísérettel" Vol. II Compi. M. Forrai. Pub. 1959.	MSN
3875	Kodály, Zoltán	1882-1967	Kiolvasó		S/MS	Editio Musica	In anthology "Duettek" in 2 Vols. Ed. M. Forrai. Pub. 1959.	NATS-VCD
3876	Kohl, A.	d. 1914	An einen Boten "Wenn du zu mei'm Schätzel kommst"	Op. 5 No. 1	Unspec.	Eulen-burg		CHAL (1898)
3877	Kohl, A.	d. 1914	Sehnsucht "Mein Schatz ist nicht da"	Op. 5 No. 2	Unspec.	Eulen-burg		CHAL (1898)
3878	Kohl, L.		Da drüben "Da drüben über'm Walde"	Op. 5 No. 4	Unspec.	Eulen-burg		CHAL (1898)
3879	Kohl, L.		Fensterln "Koan Graben sp breit"	Op. 5 No. 7	Unspec.	Eulen-burg		CHAL (1898)
3880	Kohl, L.		Tritt zu "Brünnlein, die da fliessen"	Op. 5 No. 6	Unspec.	Eulen-burg		CHAL (1898)
3881	Kohl, L.		Von alten Liebesliedern "Spazieren wollt ich reiten"	Op. 5 No. 5	Unspec.	Eulen-burg		CHAL (1898)
3882	Kohl, M.		Gang zur Liebsten "Abends kann ich nicht schlafen gehn"	Op. 5 No. 3	Unspec.	Eulen-burg		CHAL (1898)
3883	Köhler, Christian Louis Heinrich	1820-1886	Abends	Op. 11 No. 2	Unspec.	Litolff		CHAL (1898)
3884	Köhler, Christian Louis Heinrich	1820-1886	Abschied	Op. 11 No. 3	Unspec.	Litolff		CHAL (1898)
3885	Köhler, Christian Louis Heinrich	1820-1886	Asyl "Wenn du ein tiefes Leid erfahren"	Op. 11 No. 1	Unspec.	Litolff		CHAL (1898)

REC	COMP	DTS	TITLE	OP #	VCG	PUB	COMMENTS	SRC
3886	Köhler, Christian Louis Heinrich	1820-1886	Haidenröslein "Sah ein Knab' ein Röslein stehn"	Op. 11 No. 4	Unspec.	Litolff		CHAL (1898)
3887	Köhler-Wümbach, Wilhelm	1858-1926	Ein Strauss aus dem Liedergarten	Op. 11	Unspec.	Benjamin		CHAL (1911)
3888	Kölling, Ch.		Es zog von Blume zu Blume		Unspec.	Dieckmann i. Leipz.		CHAL (1898)
3889	Köllner, Eduard	1839-1891	Christnacht "Heil'ge Nacht, auf Engelschwingen"	Op. 32 No. 8	S/A	Siegel		CHAL (1898)
3890	Köllner, Eduard	1839-1891	Frau Nachtigall "Frau Nachtigall, klein's Waldvöglein"	Op. 32 No. 5	S/A	Siegel		CHAL (1898)
3891	Köllner, Eduard	1839-1891	Heimweh "Wo auf hohen Tannenspitzen"	Op. 32 No. 6	S/A	Siegel		CHAL (1898)
3892	Köllner, Eduard	1839-1891	Lieb ist ein Blümelein	Op. 32 No. 2	S/A	Siegel		CHAL (1898)
3893	Köllner, Eduard	1839-1891	Schifferinnen "Sollst tragen du Nachen"	Op. 32 No. 7	S/A	Siegel		CHAL (1898)
3894	Köllner, Eduard	1839-1891	Vergissmeinnicht "Es blüht ein schönes Blümchen"	Op. 32 No. 3	S/A	Siegel		CHAL (1898)
3895	Köllner, Eduard	1839-1891	Vögleins Abschied "Lass mich nur fliegen"	Op. 32 No. 4	S/A	Siegel		CHAL (1898)
3896	Köllner, Eduard	1839-1891	Wanderlust "Lenz beginnt"	Op. 32 No. 1	S/A	Siegel		CHAL (1898)
3897	Kollo, Walter	1878-1940	Komm, stell' dich hier auf dem Hügel		Unspec.	Harmonie i. B.		CHAL (1911)
3898	Könneritz, Nina [Georgine, neé Eschborn]	1828-1911	Dir "Ich sende diese Blume dir"	Op. 96 No. 6	Unspec.	Sulzbach i. Berl.	Grmn. woman comp.	CHAL (1898)
3899	Konneritz, Nina [Georgine, neé Eschborn]	1828-1911	Du herzig's Dirnd'l du		S/A	Sch. j.	Grmn. woman comp.	CHAL (1898)
3900	Könneritz, Nina [Georgine, neé Eschborn]	1828-1911	Herzenwunsch "O wenn ich doch ein Vöglein wär'"	Op. 97 No. 3	Unspec.	Sulzbach i. Berl.	Grmn. woman comp.	CHAL (1898)
3901	Könneritz, Nina [Georgine, neé Eschborn]	1828-1911	Hier oben auf der Alm	Op. 97 No. 2	Unspec.	Sulzbach i. Berl.	Grmn. woman comp.	CHAL (1898)
3902	Könneritz, Nina [Georgine, neé Eschborn]	1828-1911	Mailied "Wie herrlich leuchtet mir die Natur"	Op. 96 No. 3	Unspec.	Sulzbach i. Berl.	Grmn. woman comp.	CHAL (1898)
3903	Könneritz, Nina [Georgine, neé Eschborn]	1828-1911	Mondnacht "Mondenschein, still und rein"	Op. 96 No. 4	Unspec.	Sulzbach i. Berl.	Grmn. woman comp.	CHAL (1898)
3904	Könneritz, Nina [Georgine, neé Eschborn]	1828-1911	Morgenlied "Noch ahnt man kaum der Sonne Licht"	Op. 96 No. 2	Unspec.	Sulzbach i. Berl.	Grmn. woman comp.	CHAL (1898)
3905	Könneritz, Nina [Georgine, neé Eschborn]	1828-1911	Nachts "Wie der Mond so freundlich schaut"	Op. 97 No. 1	Unspec.	Sulzbach i. Berl.	Grmn. woman comp.	CHAL (1898)
3906	Könneritz, Nina [Georgine, neé Eschborn]	1828-1911	Ständchen "Hüttelein still und klein"	Op. 96 No. 1	Unspec.	Sulzbach i. Berl.	Grmn. woman comp.	CHAL (1898)
3907	Könneritz, Nina [Georgine, neé Eschborn]	1828-1911	Vorsatz "Ich will dir's nimmer sagen"	Op. 96 No. 5	Unspec.	Sulzbach i. Berl.	Grmn. woman comp.	CHAL (1898)
3908	Kopelowitz, B.		Mein liebes Hänschen, komm tummle dich		Unspec.	Harmonie i. B.		CHAL (1906)
3909	Korbay, Francis	1846-1913	Hungarian Melodies, Vol. One		Unspec.	Schott	Arr. of Hung. folk songs	BBC (1975)

REC	COMP	DTS	TITLE	OP #	VCG	PUB	COMMENTS	SRC
3910	Korbay, Francis	1846-1913	Magyar Songs		Unspec.	Schott	Arr. of Hung. folk songs	BBC (1975)
3911	Korel, H.		Abendlied froher Landleute "Kühl und labend sinkt der Thau"	Op. 21 No. 4	S/A	Senff		CHAL (1898)
3912	Korel, H.		An die Heimath "Ihr schaut so treu herüber"	Op. 21 No. 1	S/A	Senff		CHAL (1898)
3913	Korel, H.		Ein Sonntag im Mai "Lenz ist da, hinaus"	Op. 21 No. 6	S/A	Senff		CHAL (1898)
3914	Korel, H.		Mühle "Es klappert die Mühle"	Op. 21 No. 2	S/A	Senff		CHAL (1898)
3915	Korel, H.		Psalm "Hebe deine Augen auf zu den Bergen"	Op. 21 No. 5	S/A	Senff		CHAL (1898)
3916	Korel, H.		Weise Benutzung der Jugendzeit "Wer die kurzen Rosentage"	Op. 21 No. 3	S/A	Senff		CHAL (1898)
3917	Kosch, A.		Wie reizend, wie wonnig	Op. 20 No. 2	Unspec.	Kratoch-will		CHAL (1898)
3918	Koschat, Thomas	1845-1914	A Büchsle zum Schiassen	B. II	Unspec.	Leuckart		CHAL (1898)
3919	Koschat, Thomas	1845-1914	A Busserl von Diandlan "Tanzen und singan" [sic]	Op. 2 (H. VI.)	Unspec.	Leuckart		CHAL (1898)
3920	Koschat, Thomas	1845-1914	Abschied "Armes Diandle, thua nit wanen"	Op. 33 No. b	Unspec.	Leuckart		CHAL (1898)
3921	Koschat, Thomas	1845-1914	Am Wörther See "Bua sei g'schiet"	Op. 26	Unspec.	Leuckart		CHAL (1898)
3922	Koschat, Thomas	1845-1914	Beim Fensterin "Diandle, dei Bua is da"	Op. 41 No. 1	Unspec.	Leuckart		CHAL (1898)
3923	Koschat, Thomas	1845-1914	Betrogen "Um a Liab anzufangen"	Op. 19 No. 2	Unspec.	Leuckart		CHAL (1898)
3924	Koschat, Thomas	1845-1914	Bleamerbrocken "Wia Gott die Welt"	Op. 50	Unspec.	Leuckart		CHAL (1898)
3925	Koschat, Thomas	1845-1914	Bleamerl am Grab "Bleamerin sein schön"	Op. 19 No. 3	Unspec.	Leuckart		CHAL (1898)
3926	Koschat, Thomas	1845-1914	Büaberl mirk dir's fein	Op. 22	Unspec.	Leuckart		CHAL (1898)
3927	Koschat, Thomas	1845-1914	Burschen-Klag "Durt draussen im Wald"	Op. 82	Unspec.	Leuckart		CHAL (1898)
3928	Koschat, Thomas	1845-1914	Fopp-Liadl "Geh' Diandle, bist traurig"	Op. 81	Unspec.	Leuckart		CHAL (1898)
3929	Koschat, Thomas	1845-1914	Guate Râth "Wâs zâhnst denn"	Op. 25 No. 2 (H. II.)	Unspec.	Leuckart		CHAL (1898)
3930	Koschat, Thomas	1845-1914	Hamatliab "Bin g'rast umanânder"	Op. 86	Unspec.	Leuckart		CHAL (1898)
3931	Koschat, Thomas	1845-1914	Hamkehr "Hâb di amol blos g'segen"	Op. 25 No. 3 (H. II)	Unspec.	Leuckart		CHAL (1898)
3932	Koschat, Thomas	1845-1914	Herzfensterl "I kenn a Diandle fein"	Op. 74	Unspec.	Leuckart		CHAL (1898)
3933	Koschat, Thomas	1845-1914	Herzlad "Jêde Lerch' findt' an Bam"	Op. 21 (H. IV.)	Unspec.	Leuckart		CHAL (1898)
3934	Koschat, Thomas	1845-1914	Is dâs nit a Nachtigall	Op. 63	Unspec.	André		CHAL (1911)
3935	Koschat, Thomas	1845-1914	Kaiser Josef-Lied		Unspec.	Robit-schek		CHAL (1898)
3936	Koschat, Thomas	1845-1914	Karntner Bua "Mei Muada sagat's gern"	Op. 4 No. 2 (H. III.)	Unspec.	Leuckart		CHAL (1898)
3937	Koschat, Thomas	1845-1914	Karntner G'müath "Du mei flâchhââret's Diandle"	Op. 11 (H. I.)	Unspec.	Leuckart		CHAL (1898)
3938	Koschat, Thomas	1845-1914	Karntner Liab "Mei Diandl hât zwa Aeugerln"	Op. 1	Unspec.	Leuckart		CHAL (1898)

REC	COMP	DTS	TITLE	OP #	VCG	PUB	COMMENTS	SRC
3939	Koschat, Thomas	1845-1914	Mei Diandle is sauber	Op. 3 (H. V.)	Unspec.	Leuckart		CHAL (1898)
3940	Koschat, Thomas	1845-1914	Mein Schâtzerl "Gott Vâter im Himmel"	Op. 29 (H. II.)	Unspec.	Leuckart		CHAL (1898)
3941	Koschat, Thomas	1845-1914	Pâtschthâler "A roth's und eng's Miaderl"	Op. 19 No. 1 (H. I.)	Unspec.	Leuckart		CHAL (1898)
3942	Koschat, Thomas	1845-1914	Schnaberln "O Muater mein i hätt' a Frâg"	Op. 49 (H. V.)	Unspec.	Leuckart		CHAL (1898)
3943	Koschat, Thomas	1845-1914	Senner-Mizzi "Von Berglan hoch droben"	Op. 23 (H. I V.)	Unspec.	Leuckart		CHAL (1898)
3944	Koschat, Thomas	1845-1914	Städterbua und Alnradirn "Es wâr grâd Tânz"	Op. 13 (H. III)	Unspec.	Leuckart		CHAL (1898)
3945	Koschat, Thomas	1845-1914	Täppele "Und der Kerschbaum treibt Popezlan"	Op. 48	Unspec.	Leuckart		CHAL (1898)
3946	Koschat, Thomas	1845-1914	Verlassen bin I		S/A or S/B	C. Fischer	In catalogue page "Selected Vocal Duets By Favorite Composers" of Carl Fischer NY (no date)	MSN
3947	Koschat, Thomas	1845-1914	Verlâssen bin i	Op. 4 No. 1	Unspec.	Leuckart		CHAL (1898)
3948	Koschat, Thomas	1845-1914	Wâs der Stöfel wer'n will "Geh', Stöfel, geh"	Op. 52 (H. VII.)	Unspec.	Leuckart		CHAL (1898)
3949	Koschat, Thomas	1845-1914	Was fahlt dir, liab's Schâtzerle	Op. 20 (H. III.)	Unspec.	Leuckart		CHAL (1898)
3950	Koschat, Thomas	1845-1914	Wâs wohl d'Liab is "Mir ziemt ma sollt manen"	Op. 25 No. 1 (H. II.)	Unspec.	Leuckart		CHAL (1898)
3951	Koschat, Thomas	1845-1914	Wo i geh, wo i steh	Op. 37 (H. I V.)	Unspec.	Leuckart		CHAL (1898)
3952	Kotsch, H.		Will man heut modern sich kleiden		Unspec.	P. Fischer i. Berl.		CHAL (1901)
3953	Kountz, Richard	1896-1950	The sleigh		Unspec.	G. Schirm.		BBC (1975)
3954	Kozeluch, Leopold	1747-1818	Scottish Airs and Welsh Airs		Unspec.	Preston	Ed. Thomson	BBC (1975)
3955	Krall, J.		Ave Maria "Ave Maria gratia pleni"		Unspec.	Robitschek	org accomp.	CHAL (1898)
3956	Kratzel, Karl [Kratzl]	1852-1904	A Vogerl, a klan's fliagt		Unspec.	Robitschek		CHAL (1901)
3957	Kräulig, L. E.		Gang nach Emaus		Unspec.	Bernard i. Pet.		CHAL (1898)
3958	Krause, C.		Sie seh'n in uns ein Freudespaar		Unspec.	Uhse		CHAL (1911)
3959	Krause, Eduard	1837-1892	Da drunten im tiefen Thal	Op. 19	Unspec.	Cranz		CHAL (1898)
3960	Krause, Eduard	1837-1892	Nachtlied "Mond kommt still gegangen"	Op. 88 No. 1	S/A	Steyl & Th.		CHAL (1898)
3961	Krause, Eduard	1837-1892	Weisse Rose "Du brachst vom Strauch mir"	Op. 88 No. 2	S/A	Steyl & Th.		CHAL (1898)
3962	Krause, Eduard	1837-1892	Zweigesänge f. S. u. A.	Op. 88	S/A	Steyl & Th.	2 duets for soprano & alto	CHAL (1898)
3963	Krebs, Karl August	1804-1880?	Am Geburtstage der Mutter "Heut beim frohen Fest's Erneu'n"	Op. 117 No. 3	Unspec.	Sch. & Co.		CHAL (1898)
3964	Krebs, Karl August	1804-1880?	An die Unschuld	Op. 118 No. 2	Unspec.	Sch. & Co.		CHAL (1898)
3965	Krebs, Karl August	1804-1880?	Auf dem grüner Rasen, wo die Veilchen blühn	Op. 118 No. 1	Unspec.	Sch. & Co.		CHAL (1898)
3966	Krebs, Karl August	1804-1880?	Auf dem Wasser "Mit fröhlichem Muth"	Op. 136 No. 1	S/A or T/A	Schlesinger		CHAL (1898)

REC	COMP	DTS	TITLE	OP #	VCG	PUB	COMMENTS	SRC
3967	Krebs, Karl August	1804-1880?	Ewige Liebe "Hauch der Liebe ist das Lüftchen"	Op. 115 No. 1	S/A or T/Br	Sch. & C.		CHAL (1898)
3968	Krebs, Karl August	1804-1880?	Frühling "Erschliesst unds der Frühling"	Op. 116 No. 1	S/A or T/Br	Sch. & Co.		CHAL (1898)
3969	Krebs, Karl August	1804-1880?	Frühling "Erschliesst uns der Frühling"	Op. 116 No. 1	S/A or T/Br	Sch. & Co.		CHAL (1898)
3970	Krebs, Karl August	1804-1880?	Frühlingsmorgen "Heiter lacht vom Himmelsdom"	Op. 137 No. 4	S/A or T/A	Schlesinger		CHAL (1898)
3971	Krebs, Karl August	1804-1880?	Ich möchte wohl der Vogel sein	Op. 136 No. 2	S/A or T/A	Schlesinger		CHAL (1898)
3972	Krebs, Karl August	1804-1880?	Mailied "Da ist er, der liebliche"	Op. 117 No. 1	Unspec.	Sch. & Co.		CHAL (1898)
3973	Krebs, Karl August	1804-1880?	Röslein "Wohl ein einsam Röslein stand"	Op. 117 No. 2	Unspec.	Sch. & Co.		CHAL (1898)
3974	Krebs, Karl August	1804-1880?	Schiffers Abendlied "Gleite Kahn, gleite fröhlich"	Op. 138 No. 5	S/A or T/A	Schlesinger		CHAL (1898)
3975	Krebs, Karl August	1804-1880?	Schuss "Es ist ein Stern gefallen"	Op. 118 No. 3	Unspec.	Sch. & Co.		CHAL (1898)
3976	Krebs, Karl August	1804-1880?	Stern der Liebe "Es zieht am blauen Himmelsbogen"	Op. 137 No. 3	S/A or T/A	Schlesinger		CHAL (1898)
3977	Krebs, Karl August	1804-1880?	Vergissmeinnicht "Freundlich glänzt an stiller Quelle"	Op. 138 No. 6	S/A or T/A	Schlesinger		CHAL (1898)
3978	Krebs, Karl August	1804-1880?	Waldfahrt "Im Wald (im Wald) ist's frisch"	Op. 115 No. 2	S/A or T/Br	Sch. & Co.		CHAL (1898)
3979	Krebs, Karl August	1804-1880?	Zigeunerlied "Wie klingt's durch den Wald"	Op. 116 No. 2	S/A or T/Br	Sch. & Co.		CHAL (1898)
3980	Kreideweiss, R.		O ihr Männer		Unspec.	Glas		CHAL (1898)
3981	Kremling, P. W.		Im feuchten Haar einen funkelnden Kranz	Op. 6 No. 1	MS/A	Pabst i. L.		CHAL (1911)
3982	Kremling, P. W.		Nun reich' mir die Hand	Op. 6 No. 2	MS/A	Pabst i. L.		CHAL (1911)
3983	Kremser, Eduard	1838-1914	Altniederländische Volkslieder (6)		Unspec.	Leuckart	Collection of 6 duets	CHAL (1898)
3984	Krenn, Franz	1816-1897	Aber a Hetz war doch dabei "Wir waren jetzt beim Rennen"		Unspec.	Robit-schek		CHAL (1898)
3985	Kreutzer, Konradin	1780-1849	Andenken "Ich denke dein, wenn durch den Hain"	Op. 75 No. 12	Unspec.	Chal., Cranz		CHAL (1898)
3986	Kreutzer, Konradin	1780-1849	Es fällt ein Stern herunter	Op. 114 No. 2	S/S or S/A	Cranz		CHAL (1898)
3987	Kreutzer, Konradin	1780-1849	Hans und Grete "Guckst du mir denn immer nach"	Op. 60 No. 5	Unspec.	Kistner		CHAL (1898)
3988	Kreutzer, Konradin	1780-1849	Mein Lied "Ach wenn ich dich nur habe"	Op. 114 No. 1	S/S or S/A	Cranz		CHAL (1898)
3989	Kreutzer, Konradin	1780-1849	Rastlose Liebe "Schnee, dem Regen"		S/S or T/Br	Cranz		CHAL (1898)
3990	Kreutzer, Konradin	1780-1849	Sängers Vorüberziehn "Ich schlief am Blüthenhügel"	Op. 41 No. 1	S/S	B. & H.		CHAL (1898)
3991	Kreutzer, Konradin	1780-1849	Sängers Wunsch "Wenn ein kalter Wind"	Op. 41 No. 2	S/S or T/B	B. & H.		CHAL (1898)
3992	Kreutzer, Konradin	1780-1849	Schloss am Meer "Hast du das Schloss gesehen"		S/S or T/Br	Cranz		CHAL (1898)
3993	Kreutzer, Konradin	1780-1849	Sprache der beglückten Liebe "In unseren Herzen wohnt die Liebe"	Op. 101 No. 2	S/S	Schlesinger		CHAL (1898)
3994	Kreutzer, Konradin	1780-1849	Unter dem Fruchtbaum "O Fruchtbaum auf der Aue"	Op. 114 No. 3	S/S or S/A	Cranz		CHAL (1898)
3995	Kreutzer, Konradin	1780-1849	Verständigung "Weisst' Vöglein du warum"	Op. 41 No. 3	S/S or S/T	B. & H.		CHAL (1898)

REC	COMP	DTS	TITLE	OP #	VCG	PUB	COMMENTS	SRC
3996	Kreymann, L.		Beiden Schwiegermütter "Ei guten Tag, es freut mich"	Op. 27	MS/MS	O. Forberg		CHAL (1898)
3997	Kreymann, L.		Das man das Pulver einst erfand	Op. 109	Unspec.	C. Rühle i. L.		CHAL (1901)
3998	Kreymann, L.		Du verdammter Schusterjunge	Op. 87	Unspec.	Glaser		CHAL (1901)
3999	Kreymann, L.		Wenn der Rechte kommt "Guten Tag geliebte Freundin"	Op. 53	2 female v.	R. Forberg		CHAL (1898)
4000	Krigar, C.		Hochzeitslied "Gärtnerin, von allen Vöglein"	Op. 20	S/A	Bahn		CHAL (1898)
4001	Krigar, Hermann	1819-1880	Auf dem See "Auf dem See, dem mondeshellen"	Op. 11 No. 1	A/A or MS/A	B. & B.		CHAL (1898)
4002	Krigar, Hermann	1819-1880	Heraus "Ging unter dichten Zweigen"	Op. 11 No. 3	A/A or MS/A	B. & B.		CHAL (1898)
4003	Krigar, Hermann	1819-1880	Intermezzo "Dein Bildneiss wunderselig"	Op. 12 No. 1	A/A or MS/A	B. & B.		CHAL (1898)
4004	Krigar, Hermann	1819-1880	Lied der Lauenburger Els "Es sang vor langen Jahren"	Op. 12 No. 3	A/A or MS/A	B. & B.		CHAL (1898)
4005	Krigar, Hermann	1819-1880	Serenade "Bunte Vögel, Sommervögel"	Op. 12 No. 2	A/A or MS/A	B. & B.		CHAL (1898)
4006	Krigar, Hermann	1819-1880	Zu deinen Füssen will ich ruh'n	Op. 11 No. 2	A/A or MS/A	B. & B.		CHAL (1898)
4007	Krill, Karl	1847-1927	Abend am Meer "O Meer im Abendstrahle"	Op. 7 No. 1	S/A	Kratoch-will		CHAL (1898)
4008	Krill, Karl	1847-1927	Im Gebirge "Auf diesen blauen Bergen"	Op. 7 No. 3	S/A	Bösendor-fer		CHAL (1898)
4009	Krill, Karl	1847-1927	Nachtgruss "Mond und goldne Sterne glimmen"	Op. 7 No. 4	S/A	Kratoch-will		CHAL (1898)
4010	Krill, Karl	1847-1927	Trost der Nacht "Es heilt die Nacht des Tages Wunden"	Op. 7 No. 2	S/A	Kratoch-will		CHAL (1898)
4011	Krinninger, F.		Ave Maria "Ave Maria gratia pleni"	Op. 8	S/A	Kratoch-will	org or harm accomp.	CHAL (1898)
4012	Krinninger, F.		Bettlerliebe "O lass' mich nur von ferne steh'n"	Op. 6 No. 3	S/A	Kratoch-will		CHAL (1898)
4013	Krinninger, F.		Du bist gemacht zu wandern	Op. 6 No. 1	S/A	Kratoch-will		CHAL (1898)
4014	Krinninger, F.		Frühlingsglaube "Linden Lüfte sind erwacht"	Op. 6 No. 5	S/A	Kratoch-will		CHAL (1898)
4015	Krinninger, F.		Spinnlied "Rädchen eile, schnurr' immer"	Op. 6 No. 4	S/A	Kratoch-will		CHAL (1898)
4016	Krinninger, F.		Waldlied "Im Walde geh' ich wohlgemuth"	Op. 6 No. 2	S/A	Kratoch-will		CHAL (1898)
4017	Kromer, Karl	1865-	Grüsse au die Heimat		S/A or T/Br	C. Fischer	In catalogue page "Selected Vocal Duets By Favorite Composers" of Carl Fischer NY (no date)	MSN
4018	Kromer, Karl	1865-	Nach der Heimath möcht' ich wieder, nach dem theuren Vaterhaus	Op. 10	Unspec.	Zumsteeg		CHAL (1906)
4019	Kron, Louis	1842-1907	Abends wenn acht Uhr es schlägt	Op. 330	2 female v.	Meissner		CHAL (1901)
4020	Kron, Louis	1842-1907	Als Stütze der Hausfrau "Also sie sind die junge Dame"	Op. 235	S/A	Kistner		CHAL (1898)
4021	Kron, Louis	1842-1907	Auf Reserve "O Bruderherz das Glas zur Hand"	Op. 216	Unspec.	O. Teich		CHAL (1898)
4022	Kron, Louis	1842-1907	Dorf und Stadt "Wir siind zum erstn Mai"	Op. 117 No. 5	S/A	Eulenburg		CHAL (1898)

REC	COMP	DTS	TITLE	OP #	VCG	PUB	COMMENTS	SRC
4023	Kron, Louis	1842-1907	Ei da bist du Alwine	Op. 346	2 female v.	Schimmel		CHAL (1901)
4024	Kron, Louis	1842-1907	Ei, da bist du ja Alwine	Op. 346	2 female v.	P. Fischer i. Berl.		CHAL (1906)
4025	Kron, Louis	1842-1907	Ein Blick in die Zukunft "O schön ist doch die Zeit"	Op. 224	S/A	André		CHAL (1898)
4026	Kron, Louis	1842-1907	Emancipirten "Ja emancipirten sind wir"	Op. 117 No. 6	S/A	Eulenburg		CHAL (1898)
4027	Kron, Louis	1842-1907	Fische und Menschen "Fröhlich ust die Fischerei"	Op. 117 No. 10	S/A	Eulenburg		CHAL (1898)
4028	Kron, Louis	1842-1907	Frau Dr. Schmökerfeld und ihre Köchin "Es ist fürwahr ein hartes Loos"	Op. 132	S/A	Hug		CHAL (1898)
4029	Kron, Louis	1842-1907	Frische Blumen "Frische geflückte Blumen bieten wir"	Op. 117 No. 4	S/A	Eulenburg		CHAL (1898)
4030	Kron, Louis	1842-1907	Heirathsannonce "Hier auf diesem stillen Fleck"	Op. 292	S/A	Rob. Forberg		CHAL (1898)
4031	Kron, Louis	1842-1907	Ida ind Frieda, die Ballschwärmerinnen "Wie reizend liebe Frieda"	Op. 233	S/A	Kistner		CHAL (1898)
4032	Kron, Louis	1842-1907	Infanterie und Cavallerie "Verschwistert seht ihr hier"	Op. 117 No. 9	S/A	Eulenburg		CHAL (1898)
4033	Kron, Louis	1842-1907	Leiden einer Modisten "Wie schlimm hat's doch auf Erden"	Op. 117 No. 11	S/A	Eulenburg		CHAL (1898)
4034	Kron, Louis	1842-1907	Liebespost "Weil die Arbeit ist so gross"	Op. 117 No. 12	S/A	Eulenburg		CHAL (1898)
4035	Kron, Louis	1842-1907	Mit der ganzen Malerei ist es wirklich bald vorbei	Op. 398	S/A	Ulbrich i. Berl.		CHAL (1901)
4036	Kron, Louis	1842-1907	Musikalische Backfische "Welche Freude, welch' Gefühl"	Op. 117 No. 1	S/A	Eulenburg		CHAL (1898)
4037	Kron, Louis	1842-1907	O welche müh' und Plag'	Op. 358	2 female v.	Oppenheimer		CHAL (1901)
4038	Kron, Louis	1842-1907	Philosophische Wäscherinnen "Uns Wäscherinnen wird es leicht"	Op. 117 No. 7	S/A	Eulenburg		CHAL (1898)
4039	Kron, Louis	1842-1907	Schicksalsschwestern "'Ne Köchin in der Hauptstadt sein"	Op. 117 No. 3	S/A	Eulenburg		CHAL (1898)
4040	Kron, Louis	1842-1907	Töchter vom Commerzienrath Cohn "Unser Papa ist lang' schon"	Op. 117 No. 8	S/A	Eulenburg		CHAL (1898)
4041	Kron, Louis	1842-1907	Vergangene Zeiten "Ach was giebt es doch für schlechte Leute"	Op. 117 No. 2	S/A	Eulenburg		CHAL (1898)
4042	Kron, Louis	1842-1907	Vor der Damenwahl "Polterabend-Scene"	Op. 388	S/A	Portius		CHAL (1906)
4043	Kron, Louis	1842-1907	Vor der Trauung "O wie selig bin ich heute"	Op. 123	S/A	O. Forberg		CHAL (1898)
4044	Kron, Louis	1842-1907	Wie schön, dass ich dich wieder sehe	Op. 345	2 female v.	P. Fischer i. Berl.		CHAL (1906)
4045	Kron, Louis	1842-1907	Wie schön, dass ich dich wiederseh'	Op. 345	2 female v.	Schimmel		CHAL (1901)
4046	Krone, W.		Ich bin ein schöner rotbrauner Wicht		Unspec.	Stahl i. B.		CHAL (1911)
4047	Kronegger, Rudolf	d. 1929	Im Wienerwald draussen	Op. 112	Unspec.	Blaha		CHAL (1911)
4048	Kronegger, Rudolf	d. 1929	Ja, wie mir zwa mit grossem G'schra	Op.61	Unspec.	Blaha		CHAL (1911)
4049	Kronensohn, J.		Ein Fleischer auf dem Balle stolpert		Unspec.	Dürre & W.		CHAL (1906)
4050	Krug, Arnold	1849-1904	Abendlied "Ringsum nun wird es stille"	Op. 54 No. 2	Unspec.	A. P. Schmidt i. L.		CHAL (1898)
4051	Krug, Arnold	1849-1904	Abendlied "Still und ruhig wird's im Walde"	Op. 45 No. 2	2 female v.	R. Forberg		CHAL (1898)

REC	COMP	DTS	TITLE	OP #	VCG	PUB	COMMENTS	SRC
4052	Krug, Arnold	1849-1904	Edelfalk sein Töchterlein	Op. 45 No. 3	2 female v.	R. Forberg		CHAL (1898)
4053	Krug, Arnold	1849-1904	Poinisches Erntelied "Komm doch Herr und lass dich sehen"	Op. 45 No. 4	2 female v.	R. Forberg		CHAL (1898)
4054	Krug, Arnold	1849-1904	Sommerregen "Wer pocht so leis an's Fensterlein"	Op. 54 No. 1	Unspec.	A. P. Schmidt i. L.		CHAL (1898)
4055	Krug, Arnold	1849-1904	Wiegenlied "Fragst du mit den Aeugelein"	Op. 45 No. 1	2 female v.	R. Forberg		CHAL (1898)
4056	Krug, Diederich	1821-1880	Du bist wie eine Blume	Op. 18 No. 4	Unspec.	Sch. & Co.		CHAL (1898)
4057	Krug, Diederich	1821-1880	Mein Wunsch "Ich wollt' ich könnte sterben"	Op. 18 No. 1	Unspec.	Sch. & Co.		CHAL (1898)
4058	Krug, Diederich	1821-1880	Schlaf süss "Zu beten bin ich gegangen"	Op. 18 No. 2	Unspec.	Sch. & Co.		CHAL (1898)
4059	Krug, Diederich	1821-1880	Treue "Einst an meines Mädchens Herzen"	Op. 18 No. 3	Unspec.	Sch. & Co.		CHAL (1898)
4060	Krüger, Karl	1867-1930	In's Gesicht und hinter'm Rücken "Grüss di Gott, du Herzensbruder"	Op. 2	Unspec.	Fr. Dietrich		CHAL (1898)
4061	Krüger, Karl	1867-1930	Ratitäten-Cabinet "An Studio, der ka Pfeifen hat"	Op. 1	Unspec.	Fr. Dietrich		CHAL (1898)
4062	Kücken, Friedrich Wilhelm	1810-1882	Abendlied "Goldne Abendsonne"	Op. 35 No. 2	MS/A	Schles-inger		CHAL (1898)
4063	Kücken, Friedrich Wilhelm	1810-1882	Abschied der Schwalben		S/A	Scien	In "Drei Duette für zwei Sopran-Stimmen"	CVMP (1995)
4064	Kücken, Friedrich Wilhelm	1810-1882	Abschied der Schwalben		S/A or S/Br	C. Fischer	In catalogue page "Selected Vocal Duets By Favorite Composers" of Carl Fischer NY (no date)	MSN
4065	Kücken, Friedrich Wilhelm	1810-1882	Abschied der Schwalben "Schwalben, ja die Schwalben"	Op. 8 No. 2	S/S	Peters		CHAL (1898)
4066	Kücken, Friedrich Wilhelm	1810-1882	Ach wenn doch mei Schatzi käm'	Op. 26 No. 3	S/A	Schles-inger		CHAL (1898)
4067	Kücken, Friedrich Wilhelm	1810-1882	Ballade "Es fuhr ein Schiffer"	Op. 87 No. 3	S/T, S/A, T/A, T/B	Kirstner		CHAL (1898)
4068	Kücken, Friedrich Wilhelm	1810-1882	Barcarole		S/A or S/Br	C. Fischer	In catalogue page "Selected Vocal Duets By Favorite Composers" of Carl Fischer NY (no date)	MSN
4069	Kücken, Friedrich Wilhelm	1810-1882	Barcarole	Op. 15 No. 2	Var.	F. Whist-ling		NATS-VCD
4070	Kücken, Friedrich Wilhelm	1810-1882	Barcarole "Treibe, treibe Schifflein schnelle"	Op. 15 No. 2	S/S	Peters		CHAL (1898)
4071	Kucken, Friedrich Wilhelm	1810-1882	Belle Etoile		Unspec.	Durand		CVMP (1976)
4072	Kücken, Friedrich Wilhelm	1810-1882	Der Jäger		S/A or S/B	C. Fischer	In catalogue page "Selected Vocal Duets By Favorite Composers" of Carl Fischer NY (no date)	MSN

REC	COMP	DTS	TITLE	OP #	VCG	PUB	COMMENTS	SRC
4073	Kücken, Friedrich Wilhelm	1810-1882	Die Fischer		S/A or S/Br	C. Fischer	In catalogue page "Selected Vocal Duets By Favorite Composers" of Carl Fischer NY (no date)	MSN
4074	Kücken, Friedrich Wilhelm	1810-1882	Drift, My Bark		high & low v.	Hinds, Hayden & Eldredge	English trans. Grmn. In anthology "The Most Popular Vocal Duets." Ed. Dr. E. J. Biedermann. Pub. 1914.	MSN
4075	Kücken, Friedrich Wilhelm	1810-1882	Ebbe und Fluth "Schifflein liegt am Strande"	Op. 65 No. 1	Unspec.	Kistner		CHAL (1898)
4076	Kücken, Friedrich Wilhelm	1810-1882	Es war ein Abend wie heut'	Op. 105 No. 3	Unspec.	Senff		CHAL (1898)
4077	Kücken, Friedrich Wilhelm	1810-1882	Es war ein alter König	Op. 105 No. 1	Unspec.	Senff		CHAL (1898)
4078	Kücken, Friedrich Wilhelm	1810-1882	Fischer "Es wehen vom Ufer die Lüfte"	Op. 8 No. 1	S/S	Peters		CHAL (1898)
4079	Kücken, Friedrich Wilhelm	1810-1882	Fischer "Wer gleichet uns freudigen Fischern"	Op. 835 No. 7	MS/A	Schlesinger		CHAL (1898)
4080	Kücken, Friedrich Wilhelm	1810-1882	Flight of the swallow		Unspec.	Boosey	Ed. Randegger. Eng. trans. Grmn.	BBC (1975)
4081	Kücken, Friedrich Wilhelm	1810-1882	Frühling "Frühling nun gekommen"	Op. 35 No. 4	MS/A	Schlesinger		CHAL (1898)
4082	Kücken, Friedrich Wilhelm	1810-1882	Frühlingsglocken "Schneeglöcken thut läuten"	Op. 26 No. 2	S/A	Schlesinger		CHAL (1898)
4083	Kücken, Friedrich Wilhelm	1810-1882	Gondoliera "O komm zu mir"	Op. 30 No. 1	Unspec.	Peters		CHAL (1898)
4084	Kücken, Friedrich Wilhelm	1810-1882	Heimkehr "Halt' an, mein munter Rösslein"	Op. 21 No. 2	S/B or S/A	Peters		CHAL (1898)
4085	Kücken, Friedrich Wilhelm	1810-1882	I muse on thee		S/A	Boosey	Eng. trans. Grmn.	BBC (1975)
4086	Kücken, Friedrich Wilhelm	1810-1882	Ich denke dein	Op. 15 No. 1	Var.	F. Whistling		NATS-VCD
4087	Kücken, Friedrich Wilhelm	1810-1882	Ich denke dein "Am stillen Hain, im Abendschein"	Op. 15 No. 1	S/A or T/A	Peters		CHAL (1898)
4088	Kücken, Friedrich Wilhelm	1810-1882	In den Thälern laut erschallts	Op. 30 No. 3	Unspec.	Peters		CHAL (1898)
4089	Kücken, Friedrich Wilhelm	1810-1882	Jäger "O wie schön zum Hörnerklang"	Op. 8 No. 3	S/S	Peters		CHAL (1898)
4090	Kücken, Friedrich Wilhelm	1810-1882	Kahnfahrt "Löset vom Strande"	Op. 105 No. 2	Unspec.	Senff		CHAL (1898)
4091	Kucken, Friedrich Wilhelm	1810-1882	L'Hirondelle "Départ et Retour"		Unspec.	Durand		CVMP (1976)
4092	Kücken, Friedrich Wilhelm	1810-1882	Mädchen am Strande "Wild wogen die Wellen"	Op. 21 No. 1	S/S or A/T	Peters		CHAL (1898)

REC	COMP	DTS	TITLE	OP #	VCG	PUB	COMMENTS	SRC
4093	Kücken, Friedrich Wilhelm	1810-1882	Mailied "Kein' schön're (schöner) Zeit auf Erden ist"	Op. 87 No. 2	S/A or T/B or Unspec.	Kistner		CHAL (1898)
4094	Kücken, Friedrich Wilhelm	1810-1882	Mein Herz ist im Hochland	Op. 30 No. 2	Unspec.	Peters		CHAL (1898)
4095	Kücken, Friedrich Wilhelm	1810-1882	Mein Lieb' ist eine rothe Ros'	Op. 54 No. 1	S/A or S/Br	Peters		CHAL (1898)
4096	Kücken, Friedrich Wilhelm	1810-1882	Morgens in der Frühe	Op. 15 No. 3	S/S	Peters		CHAL (1898)
4097	Kücken, Friedrich Wilhelm	1810-1882	Müllerherz "Dort, wo der Wolke Rosensaum"	Op. 15 No. 3	S/S or A/T	Peters		CHAL (1898)
4098	Kücken, Friedrich Wilhelm	1810-1882	O Swallow, Happy Swallow		Unspec.	Brainard's Sons	Eng. trans. Grmn. In anthology "Brainard's Collection of Vocal Duets from Popular Modern and Standard Composers" Pub. 1903.	MSN
4099	Kücken, Friedrich Wilhelm	1810-1882	O swallow, happy swallow		Unspec.	White-Smith	In catalogue page "Vocal Duetts" of White-Smith Music Pub. Co. (no date)	MSN
4100	Kücken, Friedrich Wilhelm	1810-1882	Schönster Stern "Schönster Stern am Himmelszelt"	Op. 87 No. 1	S/A or T/B	Kistner		CHAL (1898)
4101	Kücken, Friedrich Wilhelm	1810-1882	Von dir gescheiden, bin ich bei dir	Op. 26 No. 1	S/A	Schlesinger		CHAL (1898)
4102	Kücken, Friedrich Wilhelm	1810-1882	Zwei Vöglein fliegen von dem Strauch	Op. 54 No. 2	S/A or T/B	Peters		CHAL (1898)
4103	Kügele, Richard	1850-1926	Ich möcht' dir schenken ein Angebind'	Op. 291 No. 2	Unspec.	Bratfisch		CHAL (1911)
4104	Kuhlau, Friedrich	1786-1832	Dein Blick ist nicht mehr so heiter		Unspec.	Cranz		CHAL (1898)
4105	Kuhlau, Friedrich	1786-1832	Unter allen Wipfel ist Ruh		Unspec.	G. Richter i. L.	Ed. Wittenbecher	CHAL (1906)
4106	Kühle, G.		Als ich zur Herzgeliebten	No. 11	S/A	O. Dietrich		CHAL (1911)
4107	Kühle, G.		Auf einem dürren Aste	No. 13	S/A	O. Dietrich		CHAL (1911)
4108	Kühle, G.		Aus der Fremde in die Heimath	Op. 112	S/A	O. Dietrich		CHAL (1906)
4109	Kühle, G.		Es geht an schönen Frühlingstagen	No. 15	S/A	O. Dietrich		CHAL (1911)
4110	Kühle, G.		Hat der wilde Sturm	No. 4	S/A	O. Dietrich		CHAL (1911)
4111	Kühle, G.		Lieb, von deinen rothen Lippen	Op. 110	Unspec.	O. Dietrich		CHAL (1906)
4112	Kühle, G.		Nun ist die Zeit der Rosen	No. 7	S/A	O. Dietrich		CHAL (1911)
4113	Kühle, G.		Nur wenn dein Herz dich triebe	No. 5	S/A	O. Dietrich		CHAL (1911)
4114	Kühle, G.		Nur wenn dein Herz dich triebe	Op. 95	Unspec.	O. Dietrich		CHAL (1906)
4115	Kühle, G.		'S stehn Rosen am Wege	No. 10	S/A	O. Dietrich		CHAL (1911)
4116	Kühle, G.		Sitzt a Vogerl im Bauer	No. 1	S/A	O. Dietrich		CHAL (1911)

REC	COMP	DTS	TITLE	OP #	VCG	PUB	COMMENTS	SRC
4117	Kühle, G.		Veilchen am Bache	No. 8	S/A	O. Dietrich		CHAL (1911)
4118	Kühle, G.		Verwundetes Rehlein	No. 12	S/A	O. Dietrich		CHAL (1911)
4119	Kühle, G.		Wandern bringt wohl die grösste Freud'	No. 9	S/A	O. Dietrich		CHAL (1911)
4120	Kühle, G.		Wie der Abendglocke Klingen	No. 3	S/A	O. Dietrich		CHAL (1911)
4121	Kühle, G.		Wie der Abendglocke Klingen	Op. 126	S/A or T/Br	Monopol i. L.		CHAL (1906)
4122	Kühle, G.		Wo den Himmel Berge kränzen	No. 6	S/A	O. Dietrich		CHAL (1911)
4123	Kühle, G.		Zwoa kohischwarze Täuberl	No. 14	S/A	O. Dietrich		CHAL (1911)
4124	Kühn		Schäfers Klage		Unspec.	Aderholz i. Br.		CHAL (1898)
4125	Kuhn, C. H.		Liebeswerben "Liebchen, theures Mädchen mein"	Op. 28	Unspec.	Schu. i. W.		CHAL (1898)
4126	Kühn, E. [prob. Edmund]	1874-1935	Drei schneidige Commis "Mit eleganz und Schneid"	Op. 13	Unspec.	P. Fischer i. Berl.		CHAL (1898)
4127	Kühn, E. [prob. Edmund]	1874-1935	Ein junger Mann, der bringt des Nachts		Unspec.	O. Dietrich		CHAL (1906)
4128	Kühn, E. [prob. Edmund]	1874-1935	Jugens vom reichen Krause "So elegant und schneidig"	Op. 14	Unspec.	P. Fischer i. Berl.		CHAL (1898)
4129	Kühn, E. [prob. Edmund]	1874-1935	So elegant und scheidig	Op. 14	Unspec.	P. Fischer i. Berl.		CHAL (1901)
4130	Kühn, E. [prob. Edmund]	1874-1935	Wir lieben eine holde Fee		Unspec.	O. Dietrich		CHAL (1906)
4131	Kühn, Karl	1851-1930	Auf dich, o Herr, vertrauet meine Seele	Op. 32 No. 6	Unspec.	Bratfisch	org or harm or pf	CHAL (1901)
4132	Kühn, Karl	1851-1930	Betet an den Herrn	Op. 32 No. 2	Unspec.	Bratfisch	org or harm or pf	CHAL (1901)
4133	Kühn, Karl	1851-1930	Frohlocket ihr Völker	Op. 32 No. 4	Unspec.	Bratfisch	org or harm or pf	CHAL (1901)
4134	Kühn, Karl	1851-1930	Herr ich habe lieb die Stätte	Op. 32 No. 3	Unspec.	Bratfisch	org or harm or pf	CHAL (1901)
4135	Kühn, Karl	1851-1930	Mag auch die Liebe weinen	Op. 64 No. 1	S/S or S/T	Bratfisch		CHAL (1911)
4136	Kühn, Karl	1851-1930	Man singet mit Freuden	Op. 32 No. 5	Unspec.	Bratfisch	org or harm or pf	CHAL (1901)
4137	Kühn, Karl	1851-1930	Mottetten (6)	Op. 32	Unspec.	Bratfisch	org or harm or pf. 6 motets for 2 v.	CHAL (1901)
4138	Kühn, Karl	1851-1930	O du fröhliche, o du selige		Unspec.	Bratfisch	pf or harm or org	CHAL (1911)
4139	Kühn, Karl	1851-1930	Wo du hingehst, da will auch ich hingehn	Op. 32 No. 1	Unspec.	Bratfisch	org or harm or pf	CHAL (1901)
4140	Kühne, C. T.		Sanft spielt der Mond		Unspec.	André		CHAL (1906)
4141	Kühnhold, Karl	1864-1933	Im Freiheitssturm "2- u. 3st. Volkslieder"		Unspec.	Sch. i. L.	Arr. Kühnhold. 2 & 3- part folksongs.	CHAL (1911)
4142	Kuldell, R.		Oberlehrer sei fidel	Op. 23	Unspec.	Hoffmann i. Str.		CHAL (1898)
4143	Kulenkampff, Gustav	1849-1921	Alles Wasser geht zum Meere	Op. 9 No. 1	Unspec.	Meinhardt i. Br.		CHAL (1898)
4144	Kulenkampff, Gustav	1849-1921	Nachtigallen schwingen lustig ihr Gefleder	Op. 9 No. 5	Unspec.	Meinhardt i. Br.		CHAL (1898)
4145	Kulenkampff, Gustav	1849-1921	Welche Oede, welch' ein Bangen	Op. 9 No. 2	Unspec.	Meinhardt i. Br.		CHAL (1898)
4146	Kulenkampff, Gustav	1849-1921	Wenn Alles schläft in stiller Nacht	Op. 9 No. 3	Unspec.	Meinhardt i. Br.		CHAL (1898)

REC	COMP	DTS	TITLE	OP #	VCG	PUB	COMMENTS	SRC
4147	Kulenkampff, Gustav	1849-1921	"Wenn der Frühling auf die Berge steigt"	Op. 4 No. 2	2 high v.	P. & M.		CHAL (1898)
4148	Kulenkampff, Gustav	1849-1921	Zum Frühling sprach ich, welle	Op. 9 No. 4	Unspec.	Meinhardt i. Br.		CHAL (1898)
4149	Kulenkampff, Gustav	1849-1921	Zweigesang "Im Flieder-busch ein Vöglein sass"	Op. 4 No. 1	2 high v.	P. & M.		CHAL (1898)
4150	Kündig, Felix	1824-1899	Da drüben "Da drüben über'm Walde"	No. 3	Unspec.	R. & P.		CHAL (1898)
4151	Kündig, Felix	1824-1899	Vöglein wohin so schnell	No. 4	Unspec.	R. & P.		CHAL (1898)
4152	Kündig, Felix	1824-1899	Wanderer "Mai ist auf dem Wege"	No. 2	Unspec.	R. & P.		CHAL (1898)
4153	Kündig, Felix	1824-1899	Wehmuth "Ich kann wohl manchmal singen"	No. 1	Unspec.	R. & P.		CHAL (1898)
4154	Künstle, E.		O welch ein süsses Freudenwort		Unspec.	Ruckmich	pf or harm or org	CHAL (1906)
4155	Kuntze, Karl	1817-1883	Anna und Emma "Wo nur Ernst bleibt"	Op. 238	S/S	Kahnt		CHAL (1898)
4156	Kuntze, Karl	1817-1883	Beiden Backfischchen "Röschen, weisst du schon"	Op. 161	S/S	Kistner		CHAL (1898)
4157	Kuntze, Karl	1817-1883	Beiden Ehefrauen "Wer klopft, wer kann das sein"	Op. 158	S/S	R. & E.		CHAL (1898)
4158	Kuntze, Karl	1817-1883	Ein Plauderstündchen "Wo nur die Schnabel bleibt"	Op. 202	S/S	Siegel		CHAL (1898)
4159	Kuntze, Karl	1817-1883	Ein Viertelstündchen auf der Liedertafel "Ei seh'n sie doch Frau Muhsten"	Op. 156	S/S or T/T	Heinr.		CHAL (1898)
4160	Kuntze, Karl	1817-1883	Frau Registratorin und Frau calculatorin "Wo nur Frau Calculator'n bleibt"	Op. 290	2 female v.	André		CHAL (1898)
4161	Kuntze, Karl	1817-1883	Frauen vor Gericht "Liebe Dreier, ich beschwöre mich"	Op. 320	S/S	Pabst i. D.		CHAL (1898)
4162	Kuntze, Karl	1817-1883	Theuren Zeiten "Frau Gevatter, Frau Gevatter"	Op. 47	S/MS	Schlesin-ger		CHAL (1898)
4163	Küstler, J. H.		E pena troppo barbara	No. 3	Unspec.	B. & H.		CHAL (1898)
4164	Küstler, J. H.		Eulibio e un pastorello "Sai tu dirmi"	No. 6	Unspec.	B. & H.		CHAL (1898)
4165	Küstler, J. H.		Più non si trovano	No. 4	Unspec.	B. & H.		CHAL (1898)
4166	Küstler, J. H.		Quanto mai felici seite	No. 1	Unspec.	B. & H.		CHAL (1898)
4167	Küstler, J. H.		Quel fiingere affetto	No. 2	Unspec.	B. & H.		CHAL (1898)
4168	Küstler, J. H.		Soria piacer non pena	No. 5	Unspec.	B. & H.		CHAL (1898)
4169	Kuusisto, Taneli	1905-	Armahin Muisto "Det Karaste Minnet"		Unspec.	Fazer		CVMP (1976)
4170	Labarre, Théodore	1805-1870	Meeresnymphen		Unspec.	Schott		CHAL (1898)
4171	Lachner, Franz	1803-1890	Abendfeier "Ein Schein der ew'gen Jugend"	Op. 86 No. 2	S/S	Schott		CHAL (1898)
4172	Lachner, Franz	1803-1890	An den Mai "Habe Dank du lieber Mai"	Op. 106 No. 2	S/A	Schott		CHAL (1898)
4173	Lachner, Franz	1803-1890	Bettler "Armer Mann mit deinem Stabe"	Op. 106 No. 5	S/A	Schott		CHAL (1898)
4174	Lachner, Franz	1803-1890	Fischerkinder "Hast du von den Fischerkindern"	Op. 184 No. 4	2 female v.	B. & H.		CHAL (1898)
4175	Lachner, Franz	1803-1890	Frühlingsruf "Wacht auf, wacht auf, ihr Thäler"	Op. 97 No. 2	S/S	Schott		CHAL (1898)

REC	COMP	DTS	TITLE	OP #	VCG	PUB	COMMENTS	SRC
4176	Lachner, Franz	1803-1890	Frühlingswonne		S/A	B. & H.	In anthology "Zweistimmige Lieder für Sopran und Altstimme mit Klaviergleitung für den Haus- und Schulgebrauch"	MSN
4177	Lachner, Franz	1803-1890	Frühlingswonne "Frühling im Felde"		S/A	B. & H.	In anth. "Zweistim. Lied. f. Sop. u. Altstimme mit Klavierbegleitung f. den Haus- u. Schulgebrauch v. H. M. Schletterer" 3 vols.	MSN
4178	Lachner, Franz	1803-1890	Gespielen "Ihr Lämmer dort am Himmel"	Op. 106 No. 1	S/A	Schott		CHAL (1898)
4179	Lachner, Franz	1803-1890	Gute Nacht "Schon fängt es an zu dämmern"	Op. 97 No. 3	S/S	Schott		CHAL (1898)
4180	Lachner, Franz	1803-1890	Horch, die Abendglocken klingen	Op. 184 No. 1	2 female v.	B. & H.		CHAL (1898)
4181	Lachner, Franz	1803-1890	Ich liebe dich, weil ich dich lieben muss	Op. 86 No. 3	S/S	Schott		CHAL (1898)
4182	Lachner, Franz	1803-1890	Ihr lieben Vöglein singt	Op. 97 No. 6	S/S	Schott		CHAL (1898)
4183	Lachner, Franz	1803-1890	Im Walde "Ihr Nixen, Gnomen, Elfen"	Op. 106 No. 4	S/A	Schott		CHAL (1898)
4184	Lachner, Franz	1803-1890	Im Walde "Tief durch den Wald"	Op. 97 No. 5	S/S	Schott		CHAL (1898)
4185	Lachner, Franz	1803-1890	Kinder an dem Wasser "Es wogen die Wellen"	Op. 97 No. 1	S/S	Schott		CHAL (1898)
4186	Lachner, Franz	1803-1890	Kurze Freude "Muck und die Fliege"	Op. 184 No. 3	2 female v.	B. & H.		CHAL (1898)
4187	Lachner, Franz	1803-1890	Mailied "Du bist doch treu, geliebter Mai"	Op. 97 No. 4	S/S	Schott		CHAL (1898)
4188	Lachner, Franz	1803-1890	My Faith Looks Up to Thee		S/A	Ditson	Eng. trans. Grmn. In anthology "Choice Sacred Duets for All Voices" Pub. 1936.	MSN
4189	Lachner, Franz	1803-1890	Sonntagmorgen		S/A	B. & H.	In anthology "Zweistimmige Lieder für Sopran und Altstimme mit Klaviergleitung für den Haus- und Schulgebrauch"	MSN
4190	Lachner, Franz	1803-1890	Sonntagsmorgen "Sonntag ist's"		S/A	B. & H.	In anth. "Zweistim. Lied. f. Sop. u. Altstimme mit Klavierbegleitung f. den Haus- u. Schulgebrauch v. H. M. Schletterer" 3 vols.	MSN
4191	Lachner, Franz	1803-1890	Tanzlied "Eia, wie flattert der Kranz"	Op. 86 No. 1	S/S	Schott		CHAL (1898)
4192	Lachner, Franz	1803-1890	Vergangenheit "Hesperus der blasse Funken"	Op. 184 No. 2	2 female v.	B. & H.		CHAL (1898)
4193	Lachner, Franz	1803-1890	Vögleins Tod "Du armes, armes Vöglein"	Op. 106 No. 3	S/A	Schott		CHAL (1898)
4194	Lachner, Franz	1803-1890	Weihnachtsfreude "Draussen ist es dunkel"	Op. 106 No. 6	S/A	Schott		CHAL (1898)
4195	Lachner, Franz	1803-1890	Wildröschen "O wildes Rothröschen"		S/A	B. & H.	In anth. "Zweistim. Lied. f. Sop. u. Altstimme mit Klavierbegleitung f. den Haus- u. Schulgebrauch v. H. M. Schletterer" 3 vols.	MSN
4196	Lachner, Vincenz	1811-1893	April "Gott weiss, wie wohl mir jetzt geschah!"		S/A	B. & H.	In anth. "Zweistim. Lied. f. Sop. u. Altstimme mit Klavierbegleitung f. den Haus- u. Schulgebrauch v. H. M. Schletterer" 3 vols.	MSN

REC	COMP	DTS	TITLE	OP #	VCG	PUB	COMMENTS	SRC
4197	Lachner, Vincenz	1811-1893	Die Mädchen "Gespielen und Schwestern"		S/A	B. & H.	In anth. "Zweistim. Lied. f. Sop. u. Altstimme mit Klavierbegleitung f. den Haus- u. Schulgebrauch v. H. M. Schletterer" 3 vols.	MSN
4198	Lachner, Vincenz	1811-1893	Engelküche "Fünf Englein haben gesungen"	Op. 25 III No. 2	S/S	Schott		CHAL (1898)
4199	Lachner, Vincenz	1811-1893	I, i, i, mein Büblein auf die Knie	Op. 25 II No. 3	S/S	Schott		CHAL (1898)
4200	Lachner, Vincenz	1811-1893	Kind beim Erwachen "Mein Büblein in der Wiegen"	Op. 25 III No. 1	S/S	Schott		CHAL (1898)
4201	Lachner, Vincenz	1811-1893	Kind ruht aus ven Spielen	Op. 25 I No. 3	S/S	Schott		CHAL (1898)
4202	Lachner, Vincenz	1811-1893	Koseliedchen "Mein Kindchen ist fein"	Op. 25 I No. 4	S/S	Schott		CHAL (1898)
4203	Lachner, Vincenz	1811-1893	Musterkind "Wem soll mein klein Bübchen"	Op. 25 II No. 4	Unspec.	Schott		CHAL (1898)
4204	Lachner, Vincenz	1811-1893	Pitsche, patsche Kückelchen	Op. 25 I No. 5	S/S	Schott		CHAL (1898)
4205	Lachner, Vincenz	1811-1893	Reitersmann "Ein Reitersmann muss haben"	Op. 25 II No. 1	S/S	Schott		CHAL (1898)
4206	Lachner, Vincenz	1811-1893	Schlaf, Kindlein, schlaf	Op. 25 I No. 1	S/S	Schott		CHAL (1898)
4207	Lachner, Vincenz	1811-1893	Schlaflied "Schlaf Herzenskindchen"	Op. 25 II No. 2	S/S	Schott		CHAL (1898)
4208	Lachner, Vincenz	1811-1893	Schlafliedchen "Horch Kindchen, was klingst"	Op. 25 II No. 5	S/S	Schott		CHAL (1898)
4209	Lachner, Vincenz	1811-1893	Tanzlied "Tanz', Kindlein tanz'"	Op. 25 III No. 3	S/S	Schott		CHAL (1898)
4210	Lachner, Vincenz	1811-1893	Was ich kann "Wacker Mägdlein bin ich ja"	Op. 25 I No. 6	S/S	Schott		CHAL (1898)
4211	Lachner, Vincenz	1811-1893	Wenn die Kindlein klein noch sind	Op. 25 I No. 2	S/S	Schott		CHAL (1898)
4212	Lacome, Paul	1838-1920	Berceuse		Unspec.	Enoch		CVMP (1976)
4213	Lacome, Paul	1838-1920	Czardas		Unspec.	Enoch		CVMP (1976)
4214	Lacome, Paul	1838-1920	Deborah		Unspec.	Enoch	Biblical work	CVMP (1976)
4215	Lacome, Paul	1838-1920	Estudiantina		Unspec.	Enoch	Also solo	CVMP (1976)
4216	Lacome, Paul	1838-1920	L'Arc-en-Ciel		Unspec.	Enoch	Biblical work	CVMP (1976)
4217	Lacome, Paul	1838-1920	La Danse des Epées		Unspec.	Enoch	pf-4 hands or pf accomp.	CVMP (1976)
4218	Lacome, Paul	1838-1920	La Farandole		Unspec.	Enoch		CVMP (1976)
4219	Lacome, Paul	1838-1920	La Fille de Jephte		Unspec.	Enoch	Biblical work, for 2-4 v.	CVMP (1976)
4220	Lacome, Paul	1838-1920	La Ruche		Unspec.	Enoch		CVMP (1976)
4221	Lacome, Paul	1838-1920	Le Captivité de Babylone		Unspec.	Enoch	Biblical work	CVMP (1976)
4222	Lacome, Paul	1838-1920	Le Colombier		Unspec.	Enoch		CVMP (1976)
4223	Lacome, Paul	1838-1920	Le Grillon		Unspec.	Enoch		CVMP (1976)
4224	Lacome, Paul	1838-1920	Le Ruisseau		Unspec.	Enoch		CVMP (1976)

REC	COMP	DTS	TITLE	OP #	VCG	PUB	COMMENTS	SRC
4225	Lacome, Paul	1838-1920	Le Traineau		Unspec.	Enoch		CVMP (1976)
4226	Lacome, Paul	1838-1920	Les Fillettes au Bois		Unspec.	Enoch	pf-4 hands or pf accomp.	CVMP (1976)
4227	Lacome, Paul	1838-1920	Les Patineurs		Unspec.	Enoch	pf-4 hands or pf accomp.	CVMP (1976)
4228	Lacome, Paul	1838-1920	Les Pêcheurs de la Côte		Unspec.	Enoch		CVMP (1976)
4229	Lacome, Paul	1838-1920	Moise		Unspec.	Enoch	Biblical work	CVMP (1976)
4230	Lacome, Paul	1838-1920	Nocturne		Unspec.	Enoch		CVMP (1976)
4231	Lacome, Paul	1838-1920	Noël		Unspec.	Enoch	Also solo	CVMP (1976)
4232	Lacome, Paul	1838-1920	Ruth et Noemie		Unspec.	Enoch	Biblical work	CVMP (1976)
4233	Lacome, Paul	1838-1920	Segoviane		Unspec.	Enoch	pf-4 hands or pf accomp.	CVMP (1976)
4234	Lacome, Paul	1838-1920	Sicilienne		Unspec.	Enoch	pf-4 hands or pf accomp.	CVMP (1976)
4235	Lacome, Paul	1838-1920	Valse d'Automne		Unspec.	Enoch	pf-4 hands or pf accomp.	CVMP (1976)
4236	Ladendorff, O.		Im Maien "Im Maien zu Zweien ze gehen"	Op. 14 No. 1	2 female v.	Paez		CHAL (1898)
4237	Ladendorff, O.		Sangeskunst "Wir üben eine schöne Pflicht"	Op. 14 No. 3	2 female v.	Paez		CHAL (1898)
4238	Ladendorff, O.		Versunken und begraben	Op. 14 No. 2	2 female v.	Paez		CHAL (1898)
4239	Lafont, Charles-Philippe	1781-1839	Du meines Lebens Sonne		Unspec.	Schlesinger		CHAL (1898)
4240	Lagoanère, Oscar de	1853-1918	A Naïs		Unspec.	Schott		CHAL (1898)
4241	Lagoanère, Oscar de	1853-1918	Brigantine		Unspec.	Schott		CHAL (1898)
4242	Lagoanère, Oscar de	1853-1918	Ecossais		Unspec.	Schott		CHAL (1898)
4243	Lagoanère, Oscar de	1853-1918	Kleinen Savoyarden		Unspec.	Schott		CHAL (1898)
4244	Lagoanère, Oscar de	1853-1918	Plus beau jour		Unspec.	Schott		CHAL (1898)
4245	Lagoanère, Oscar de	1853-1918	Scheiden		Unspec.	Schott		CHAL (1898)
4246	Lagoanère, Oscar de	1853-1918	Schiffers Abreise		Unspec.	Schott		CHAL (1898)
4247	Lalo, Edouard	1823-1892	Au fond des balliers		Unspec.	Hamelle		BBC (1975)
4248	Lalo, Edouard	1823-1892	Dansons!		Unspec.	Hamelle		BBC (1975)
4249	Lalo, Edouard	1823-1892	Dansons		S/A	Hamelle	In "Mélodies pour Chant et Piano" Vol. 1	ASR
4250	Lalo, Edouard	1823-1892	Dansons!	Op. 35	S/MS	Hamelle	Pub. 1913	NATS-VCD
4251	Lammers, Julius	1829-1888	An der Wiege "Blümlein alle schlafen"	Op. 38 No. 12	Unspec.	Kahnt		CHAL (1898)
4252	Lammers, Julius	1829-1888	An die Natur "Süsse heilige Natur"	Op. 43 No. 1	Unspec.	Kahnt		CHAL (1898)
4253	Lammers, Julius	1829-1888	Bayrisches Volkslied-chen "Bin ein- und ausgegange"	Op. 38 No. 5	Unspec.	Kahnt		CHAL (1898)

REC	COMP	DTS	TITLE	OP #	VCG	PUB	COMMENTS	SRC
4254	Lammers, Julius	1829-1888	Blümli "Han am em Ort es Blümli g'seh"	Op. 38 No. 6	Unspec.	Kahnt		CHAL (1898)
4255	Lammers, Julius	1829-1888	Es stand ein Stern am Himmel	Op. 38 No. 9	Unspec.	Kahnt		CHAL (1898)
4256	Lammers, Julius	1829-1888	Herbstlied "Laub fällt von den Bäumen"	Op. 38 No. 4	Unspec.	Kahnt		CHAL (1898)
4257	Lammers, Julius	1829-1888	Mein Herzlein thut mir gar zu weh'	Op. 38 No. 2	Unspec.	Kahnt		CHAL (1898)
4258	Lammers, Julius	1829-1888	Mein Schatz "Ich weiss ein' schön' Glocken"	Op. 38 No. 11	Unspec.	Kahnt		CHAL (1898)
4259	Lammers, Julius	1829-1888	O Maidle du bisch mei Morgenstern	Op. 38 No. 3	Unspec.	Kahnt		CHAL (1898)
4260	Lammers, Julius	1829-1888	Schwäbisches Tanzliedchen "Mei Schätzle ist fein"	Op. 38 No. 7	Unspec.	Kahnt		CHAL (1898)
4261	Lammers, Julius	1829-1888	Siehe der Frühling währet nicht lang	Op. 43 No. 2	Unspec.	Kahnt		CHAL (1898)
4262	Lammers, Julius	1829-1888	Volkstümliche (12)	Op. 38	S/A	Kahnt	Collection of 12 duets	CHAL (1911)
4263	Lammers, Julius	1829-1888	Waldlied "Waldnacht Jagdlust"	Op. 43 No. 3	Unspec.	Kahnt		CHAL (1898)
4264	Lammers, Julius	1829-1888	Wär' ich ein Vögelein	Op. 38 No. 1	Unspec.	Kahnt		CHAL (1898)
4265	Lammers, Julius	1829-1888	Zu dir zieht's mi hin	Op. 38 No. 8	Unspec.	Kahnt		CHAL (1898)
4266	Lampard		Calm is the wave o'er the beautiful sea		S/A	White-Smith	In catalogue page "Vocal Duetts" of White-Smith Music Pub. (no date)	MSN
4267	Lamperen, van		Lutins	Op. 22	Unspec.	(Goldmark) Schott		CHAL (1898)
4268	Lander, Josef	1858-1924	Stille Nacht, heilige Nacht		Unspec.	André	Arr. of song. Pen name of Ludwig André.	CHAL (1898)
4269	Lange, C.		Andenken "Ich denke dein, wenn durch den Hain"	Op. 15 No. 4	S/A	Bachmann		CHAL (1898)
4270	Lange, O. H. [prob. Otto]	1815-1879	Sonntags am Rhein "Sonntags in der Morgenstund"	Op. 39	S/A or T/Br	Oertel		CHAL (1898)
4271	Lange, O. H. [prob. Otto]	1815-1879	Sonntags in der Morgenstund	Op. 39	Unspec.	Oertel		CHAL (1901)
4272	Lange, R.		Abschied vom Walde "Ade du liebes Waldesgrün"	Op. 15 No. 2	S/A or T/B	Oehmigke		CHAL (1898)
4273	Lange, R.		Frühlingsahung "O sanfter, süsser Hauch"	Op. 15 No. 4	S/A or T/B	Oehmigke		CHAL (1898)
4274	Lange, R.		Gottes Zucht "Wenn Alles eben käme"	Op. 15 No. 2	S/A or T/B	Oehmigke		CHAL (1898)
4275	Lange, R.		Hoffnung "Wenn die Hoffnung nicht wär'"	Op. 15 No. 5	S/A or T/B	Oehmigke		CHAL (1898)
4276	Lange, R.		Mein Herz ist im Hochland	Op. 15 No. 1	S/A or T/B	Oehmigke		CHAL (1898)
4277	Lange, R.		Reiselied "Durch Feld und Buchenhallen"	Op. 15 No. 6	S/A or T/B	Oehmigke		CHAL (1898)
4278	Langer, G.		Grossmütterchen "Rosig fein dringt herein"	Op. 20	Unspec.	Hoffarth		CHAL (1898)
4279	Langer, G.		Grossväterchen "Ist still es im Stübchen"	Op. 22	Unspec.	Hoffarth		CHAL (1898)
4280	Langert, Johann August Adolf	1836-1920	Erste Liebe "Lieb' ist vor allen Dingen"	Op. 6 No. 2	Unspec.	Heckel		CHAL (1898)
4281	Langert, Johann August Adolf	1836-1920	Im Vorfrühling "Ich steh' auf hohem Berg allein"	Op. 6 No. 1	Unspec.	Heckel		CHAL (1898)

REC	COMP	DTS	TITLE	OP #	VCG	PUB	COMMENTS	SRC
4282	Langert, Johann August Adolf	1836-1920	Rosen fliehen nicht allein	Op. 6 No. 4	Unspec.	Heckel		CHAL (1898)
4283	Lannoy, Eduard	1787-1853	Guarda che bianca luna	Op. 36 No. 2	MS/A	Cranz		CHAL (1898)
4284	Lannoy, Eduard	1787-1853	Immersa nell aureo vapor	Op. 36 No. 3	MS/A	Cranz		CHAL (1898)
4285	Lannoy, Eduard	1787-1853	Non t'accostar all urna	Op. 36 No. 1	MS/A	Cranz		CHAL (1898)
4286	Lansing		Fast falls the Eventide		S/A or T/Br	White-Smith	In catalogue page "Vocal Duetts" of White-Smith Music Pub. Co. (no date)	MSN
4287	Lanz, A.		Frühlingslied "Himmel lacht"		S/A	Schott		CHAL (1898)
4288	Laparra, Raoul	1876-1943	La Chasse au Forêt		S/A or S/MS or S/B	Enoch		ASR
4289	Laparra, Raoul	1876-1943	La Chasse au Forêt		S/MS, S/A or S/Bar or S/B	Enoch		CVMP (1976)
4290	Larsen, M.		Schönste auf der ganzen Welt		Unspec.	Glas		CHAL (1901)
4291	Laserna, Blas de	1751-1816	La Beata		Unspec.	UME	Ed. Subira	CVMP (1976)
4292	Lassel, Rudolf	1861-1918	Über Felder und Wälder	Op. 7 No. 3	Unspec.	Hug		CHAL (1906)
4293	Lassel, Rudolf	1861-1918	Wenn der Maikäfer schwirrt	Op. 7 No. 1	Unspec.	Hug		CHAL (1906)
4294	Lassen, Eduard	1830-1904	Der Dorflinden	No. 3	S/MS or S/A	G. Schirm.	In collection "Duet-Album 12 Duets for Soprano and Mezzo Soprano or Alto"	MSN
4295	Lassen, Eduard	1830-1904	Der Frühling	No. 2	S/MS or S/A	G. Schirm.	In collection "Duet-Album 12 Duets for Soprano and Mezzo Soprano or Alto"	MSN
4296	Lassen, Eduard	1830-1904	Der Frühling und die Liebe	No. 6	S/MS or S/A	G. Schirm.	In collection "Duet-Album 12 Duets for Soprano and Mezzo Soprano or Alto"	MSN
4297	Lassen, Eduard	1830-1904	Der Geist des Herrn	No. 7	S/MS or S/A	G. Schirm.	In collection "Duet-Album 12 Duets for Soprano and Mezzo Soprano or Alto"	MSN
4298	Lassen, Eduard	1830-1904	Dorflinden "Im Dorfe stehn zwei Linden"	Op. 50 No. 3	S/A	R. & E.		CHAL (1898)
4299	Lassen, Eduard	1830-1904	Dulde, gedulde dich fein	Op. 55 No. 6	S/A	Hainauer		CHAL (1898)
4300	Lassen, Eduard	1830-1904	Entfernung		S/A	Ditson	In anthology "Soprano and Alto Duets" Ed. H. Kiehl. Pub. 1901.	MSN
4301	Lassen, Eduard	1830-1904	Entfernung	No. 10	S/MS or S/A	G. Schirm.	In collection "Duet-Album 12 Duets for Soprano and Mezzo Soprano or Alto"	MSN
4302	Lassen, Eduard	1830-1904	Entfernung "Fern von dir"	Op. 55 No. 4	S/A	Hainauer		CHAL (1898)
4303	Lassen, Eduard	1830-1904	Frühling "Frühling klopft mit frischem Strauss"	Op. 50 No. 2	S/A	R. & E.		CHAL (1898)
4304	Lassen, Eduard	1830-1904	Frühling und Liebe "Im Rosenbusche die Liebe schlief"	Op. 46 No. 5	Unspec.	Hainauer		CHAL (1898)
4305	Lassen, Eduard	1830-1904	Frühlingslied	No. 4	S/MS or S/A	G. Schirm.	In collection "Duet-Album 12 Duets for Soprano and Mezzo Soprano or Alto"	MSN

REC	COMP	DTS	TITLE	OP #	VCG	PUB	COMMENTS	SRC
4306	Lassen, Eduard	1830-1904	Frühlingslied "Tief im grünen Frühlingshag"	Op. 46 No. 1	Unspec.	Hainauer		CHAL (1898)
4307	Lassen, Eduard	1830-1904	Geist des Herrn "O lass kein herz dir fremde bleiben"	Op. 55	S/A	Hainauer		CHAL (1898)
4308	Lassen, Eduard	1830-1904	Hoffe nur!	No. 1	S/MS or S/A	G. Schirm.	In collection "Duet-Album 12 Duets for Soprano and Mezzo Soprano or Alto"	MSN
4309	Lassen, Eduard	1830-1904	Hoffe nur "Hoffe nur in stiller Nacht"	Op. 50 No. 11	S/A	R. & E.		CHAL (1898)
4310	Lassen, Eduard	1830-1904	Lerchengesang	No. 12	S/MS or S/A	G. Schirm.	In collection "Duet-Album 12 Duets for Soprano and Mezzo Soprano or Alto"	MSN
4311	Lassen, Eduard	1830-1904	Lerchengesang "Halme tropfen noch"	Op. 55 No. 6	S/A	Hainauer		CHAL (1898)
4312	Lassen, Eduard	1830-1904	Liebesstation "Am kühlen Brunnen"	Op. 55 No. 3	S/A	Hainauer		CHAL (1898)
4313	Lassen, Eduard	1830-1904	Liebesstationen	No. 9	S/MS or S/A	G. Schirm.	In collection "Duet-Album 12 Duets for Soprano and Mezzo Soprano or Alto"	MSN
4314	Lassen, Eduard	1830-1904	Morgenwanderung im Mondschein	No. 8	S/MS or S/A	G. Schirm.	In collection "Duet-Album 12 Duets for Soprano and Mezzo Soprano or Alto"	MSN
4315	Lassen, Eduard	1830-1904	Morgenwanderung im Mondschein "Wenn das Mondenlicht"	Op. 55 No. 2	S/A	Hainauer		CHAL (1898)
4316	Lassen, Eduard	1830-1904	Si vous n'avez rien à me dire	Op. 46 No. 3	Unspec.	Hainauer		CHAL (1898)
4317	Lassen, Eduard	1830-1904	Si vous n'avez rien à me dire	No. 5	S/MS or S/A	G. Schirm.	In collection "Duet-Album 12 Duets for Soprano and Mezzo Soprano or Alto"	MSN
4318	Lassen, Eduard	1830-1904	Spring Song		high & low v.	Hinds, Hayden & Eldredge	Eng. trans. Grmn. In anthology "The Most Popular Vocal Duets," Ed. Dr. E. J. Biedermann. Pub. 1914.	MSN
4319	Lassen, Eduard	1830-1904	Tanzlied der Kinder "O Sommerlust bei Finkenschlag"	Op. 64 No. 2	S/A	Hainauer		CHAL (1898)
4320	Lassen, Eduard	1830-1904	Über ein Stündlein	No. 11	S/MS or S/A	G. Schirm.	In collection "Duet-Album 12 Duets for Soprano and Mezzo Soprano or Alto"	MSN
4321	Lassen, Eduard	1830-1904	Varen och Karleken		Unspec.	Lundq.	Swed. trans. Grmn.	CVMP (1976)
4322	Laszky, A. B. [prob. Bela Latsky]	1867-	Tag schläft ein		Unspec.	Bärd & Bruder		CHAL (1911)
4323	Latour, A. de		Qui va la		Unspec.	Schott		CHAL (1898)
4324	Lawson, Malcolm	1849-	Maiden of Morven		Unspec.	Cramer		BBC (1975)
4325	Lazarus, Gustav	1861-1920	Gute Nacht, mein Herz	No. 3	S/A	Schlesinger		CHAL (1898)
4326	Lazarus, Gustav	1861-1920	In meinem Garten die Nelken	No. 1	S/A	Schlesinger		CHAL (1898)
4327	Lazarus, Gustav	1861-1920	Schwesterchen, der Lenz ist da	Op. 66 No. 3	S/A	Harmonie i. B.		CHAL (1906)
4328	Lazarus, Gustav	1861-1920	Wie schön geht sich's zu Zweien	Op. 127 No. a	Unspec.	Klinner		CHAL (1911)
4329	Lazarus, Gustav	1861-1920	Wohl waren es Tage der Wonne	No. 2	S/A	Schlesinger		CHAL (1898)

REC	COMP	DTS	TITLE	OP #	VCG	PUB	COMMENTS	SRC
4330	Le Beau, Luise Adolpha	1850-1927	Abendlied "Im West ist still versunken"	Op. 6 No. 2	S/S	R. & P.	Grmn. woman comp.	CHAL (1898)
4331	Le Beau, Luise Adolpha	1850-1927	Frühlingsanfang "Schnee ist vergangen"	Op.6 No. 1	S/S	R. & P.	Grmn. woman comp.	CHAL (1898)
4332	Leal, L.		Ein neues Jahr hat angefangen		Unspec.	Fries i. Z.		CHAL (1906)
4333	Lecocq, Charles	1832-1918	La ciel est noir		Unspec.	Jobert		BBC (1975)
4334	Lecocq, Charles	1832-1918	La ronde des paysannes		Unspec.	Gallet		BBC (1975)
4335	Lecocq, Charles	1832-1918	Le Noël des Petits Enfants		2 med. v.	Enoch		ASR
4336	Lecocq, Charles	1832-1918	Two Birds		S/A	Cramer	Eng. trans. Fr.	CVMP (1976)
4337	Lecocq, Charles	1832-1918	Two Birds		S/A	Cramer	Eng. trans. Fr.	ASR
4338	Lederer-Prina, Felix	1880-	So allein mit dir	Op. 4 No. 1	S/Br or S/A	Heinr.		CHAL (1906)
4339	Lederer-Prina, Felix	1880-	Zu eigen geben möcht' ich mich dir	Op. 4 No. 2	S/Br or S/A	Heinr.		CHAL (1906)
4340	Ledermann, Wilhelm	1854-1889	Zur Hochzeit "Auf, Auf, begrüsst den festlich"	Op. 11	2 female v.	Weber i. Cöln		CHAL (1898)
4341	Lee, Ernest Markham	1874-1956	Dream Seller		S/A	Curwen		ASR
4342	Lee, Ernest Markham	1876-1956	Dream Seller, The		Unspec.	Roberton		CVMP (1976)
4343	Lee, Ernest Markham	1876-1956	Go, Lovely Rose		Unspec.	Roberton		CVMP (1976)
4344	Lee, Ernest Markham	1874-1956	Go Lovely Rose		S/A	Curwen		ASR
4345	Legov, M.	1893-	Eine Kochkünstlerin "Duett mit Prosa"	Op. 48	2 female v.	Glaser	Pen name of Max Vogel	CHAL (1898)
4346	Legov, M.	1893-	Immer wieder muss ich lesen	Op. 82	2 female v.	O. Forberg	Pen name of Max Vogel	CHAL (1901)
4347	Legov, M.	1893-	In der Sommerfrische "Hum. Scene"	Op. 60	2 female v.	Danner	Pen name of Max Vogel	CHAL (1901)
4348	Legov, M.	1893-	Liebesbrief "Ach nun hab' ich's gründlich satt"	Op. 5	2 female v.	Glaser	Pen name of Max Vogel	CHAL (1898)
4349	Legov, M.	1893-	Wer hätte wohl von uns gehört noch nicht	Op. 133	Unspec.	Glaser	Pen name of Max Vogel	CHAL (1911)
4350	Lehár, Franz	1870-1948	Yours is My Heart Alone		S/A or S/Br	Harms (NY)	Arr. W. Stickles. Eng. trans. Grmn.	MSN
4351	Lehmann, Johann Traugott	1782-	Wonne der Wehmuth "Trocknet nicht Thränen"		Unspec.	Hofmeister		CHAL (1898)
4352	Lehmann, Liza	1862-1918	Henna		S/A	Boosey	Eng. woman comp.	BBC (1975)
4353	Lehmann, Liza	1862-1918	Lenz und Liebe (7 Lieder und 3 Duette)		Unspec.	Schott	7 songs & 3 duets, prob. Grmn. tr. Eng. Eng. woman comp.	CHAL (1906)
4354	Lehner, F.		Alt Weana-Schneid "Es hab'n stets die Wiener"		Unspec.	Bosworth		CHAL (1898)
4355	Lehnhard, G.		Ist denn Liebe ein Verbrechen "Nein es lässt sich gar nicht sagen"		Unspec.	K. & G.		CHAL (1898)
4356	Leicht, Fritz	1872-	Menschen sind verschieden	Op. 300	Unspec.	Robitschek		CHAL (1906)
4357	Leicht, Fritz	1872-	Mit dreissig Gulden 's is zum lachen	Op. 265	Unspec.	Robitschek		CHAL (1901)
4358	Leitner, Karl August	1837-1904	Missa Seraphica		S/A or T/B	Böhm & S.	org accomp.	CHAL (1898)

REC	COMP	DTS	TITLE	OP #	VCG	PUB	COMMENTS	SRC
4359	Leitner, Karl August	1837-1904	O du fröhliche, o du selige	No. 1	Unspec.	Böhm & S.	pf or harm. Arr. Leitner	CHAL (1906)
4360	Leitner, Karl August	1837-1904	Stille Nacht, heilige Nacht		Unspec.	Böhm & S.	pf or harm. Arr. of melody by Leitner	CHAL (1906)
4361	Lenz, Leopold	1803-1862	Abend "Dort sinket die Sonne"	Op. 44 No. 5	S/A	Aibl		CHAL (1898)
4362	Lenz, Leopold	1803-1862	Am Morgen "Es taget in dem Osten"	Op. 43 No. 2	Unspec.	Schott		CHAL (1898)
4363	Lenz, Leopold	1803-1862	Aufmunterung zum Singen "Lasst die Töne erklingen"	Op. 44 No. 2	S/A	Aibl		CHAL (1898)
4364	Lenz, Leopold	1803-1862	Aufruf zur Freude "Kommt lasst uns fröhlich singen"	Op. 44 No. 8	S/A	Aibl		CHAL (1898)
4365	Lenz, Leopold	1803-1862	Drei Blätter "Von theurer Hand ein zartes Blatt"	Op. 43 No. 3	Unspec.	Schott		CHAL (1898)
4366	Lenz, Leopold	1803-1862	Fremde Blume "Fern von der Heimath Land"	Op. 44 No. 11	S/A	Aibl		CHAL (1898)
4367	Lenz, Leopold	1803-1862	Frühlingsankunft "Da kommt von den blauen Hügeln"	Op. 44 No. 4	S/A	Aibl		CHAL (1898)
4368	Lenz, Leopold	1803-1862	Frühlingsball "Frühling sprach zur Nachtigall"	Op. 44 No. 10	S/A	Aibl		CHAL (1898)
4369	Lenz, Leopold	1803-1862	Gott sorgt für Alle "Weisst di wie viel Sterne"	Op. 44 No. 9	S/A	Aibl		CHAL (1898)
4370	Lenz, Leopold	1803-1862	Lob Gottes "Lobt froh den Herrn"	Op. 44 No. 1	S/A	Aibl		CHAL (1898)
4371	Lenz, Leopold	1803-1862	Nachtigallen und Frösche "Ei, wem sollt' es nicht behangen"	Op. 44 No. 12	S/A	Aibl		CHAL (1898)
4372	Lenz, Leopold	1803-1862	Schön Röslein "Ich sah an deinem Herzen"	Op. 43 No. 1	Unspec.	Schott		CHAL (1898)
4373	Lenz, Leopold	1803-1862	Schützenlied "Mit dem Pfeil und Bogen"	Op. 44 No. 7	S/A	Aibl		CHAL (1898)
4374	Lenz, Leopold	1803-1862	Schweizerlied "Uf'm Bergli bin i g'sesse"		Unspec.	Schott		CHAL (1898)
4375	Lenz, Leopold	1803-1862	Sommerlied "Tralala, der Sommer ist da"	Op. 44 No. 6	S/A	Aibl		CHAL (1898)
4376	Lenz, Leopold	1803-1862	Spätherbst "Er kommt durch das bereifte Gras"	Op. 44 No. 3	S/A	Aibl		CHAL (1898)
4377	Lenz, Leopold	1803-1862	Wie lieb du mir im Herzen bist "Ich möchte dir so gerne sagen"		Unspec.	Schott		CHAL (1898)
4378	Leo, A.		Süsses Begräbniss "Schäferin, o wie"	Op. 3 No. 6	Unspec.	Heinr.		CHAL (1898)
4379	Leonard, Conrad		If I were sure		Unspec.	L. Wright		BBC (1975)
4380	Leonard, R.		Willst du sein mein Herzensweibchen		Unspec.	Walter Schroeder		CHAL (1911)
4381	Leonhard, Julius Emil	1810-1883	Abendlied des Wanderers "Wie sich Schatten dehnen"	Op. 6 No. 3	Unspec.	Brauer		CHAL (1898)
4382	Leonhard, Julius Emil	1810-1883	Ach in Trauern muss ich schlafen gehn	Op. 15 No. 6	Unspec.	Sch. & Co.		CHAL (1898)
4383	Leonhard, Julius Emil	1810-1883	An die Laute	Op. 6 No. 1	Unspec.	Brauer		CHAL (1898)
4384	Leonhard, Julius Emil	1810-1883	Es blinken keine Sterne	Op. 6 No. 2	Unspec.	Brauer		CHAL (1898)
4385	Leonhard, Julius Emil	1810-1883	Frühlingsliebe "Wenn der Frühling kommt"	Op. 15 No. 2	Unspec.	Sch. & Co.		CHAL (1898)
4386	Leonhard, Julius Emil	1810-1883	Gebet	Op. 6 No. 5	Unspec.	Brauer		CHAL (1898)
4387	Leonhard, Julius Emil	1810-1883	Lass rauschen, Lieb', lass rauschen	Op. 15 No. 1	Unspec.	Sch. & Co.		CHAL (1898)

REC	COMP	DTS	TITLE	OP #	VCG	PUB	COMMENTS	SRC
4388	Leonhard, Julius Emil	1810-1883	Sehnsucht "Wenn die Vöglein so minniglich"	Op. 15 No. 4	Unspec.	Sch. & Co.		CHAL (1898)
4389	Leonhard, Julius Emil	1810-1883	Sind wir geschieden	Op. 15 No. 7	Unspec.	Sch. & Co.		CHAL (1898)
4390	Leonhard, Julius Emil	1810-1883	Stille "Es weiss und räth es doch Keiner"	Op. 15 No. 5	Unspec.	Sch. & Co.		CHAL (1898)
4391	Leonhard, Julius Emil	1810-1883	Waldvöglein Sang	Op. 6 No. 4	Unspec.	Brauer		CHAL (1898)
4392	Leonhard, Julius Emil	1810-1883	Wanderlied "Auf schwankem Ast"	Op. 15 No. 3	Unspec.	Sch. & Co.		CHAL (1898)
4393	Leschetitzky, Theodor	1830-1915	Im Walde "Waldesnacht, du wunderkühle"	Op. 27 No. 2	Unspec.	Peters		CHAL (1898)
4394	Leschetitzky, Theodor	1830-1915	Sehnsucht "Tag wird trüb und trüber" In Verbindung mit Chopins F-moll-Etude"		Unspec.	B. & H.	For 1 or 2 pf accomp. Arr. of Chopin's "F minor Etude"	CHAL (1898)
4395	Leschetitzky, Theodor	1830-1915	Serenade "Ihr blauen Augen gute Nacht"	Op. 27 No. 3	Unspec.	Peters		CHAL (1898)
4396	Leschetitzky, Theodor	1830-1915	Siehst du das Meer	Op. 27 No. 1	Unspec.	Peters		CHAL (1898)
4397	Leser, C.		Erinnerung an den Achensee "O Thäler weit und Höh'n"		S/A	Hansen		CHAL (1898)
4398	Leukauf, Richard	d. 1920	Im Weana-Dialekt "Oft da müssen wir Zwa lachen"		Unspec.	Doblinger		CHAL (1898)
4399	Leukauf, Richard	d. 1920	Kagel-, kegel-, kigel-, kogel-, kugelrund "Mit an Schwomma"		Unspec.	Doblinger		CHAL (1898)
4400	Leukauf, Richard	d. 1920	Mutterherz "In des Lebens Erdendunkel"		Unspec.	Robitschek		CHAL (1898)
4401	Leukauf, Richard	d. 1920	Schaun's uns an		Unspec.	Blaha		CHAL (1906)
4402	Leukauf, Richard	d. 1920	Servus, das is a Hamur "Nur net gespannt sein"		Unspec.	Doblinger		CHAL (1898)
4403	Leukauf, Richard	d. 1920	Zwa Vegetarianer "I bitt, schau'ns uns Zwa nur an"		Unspec.	Doblinger		CHAL (1898)
4404	Levigne, Peter		A night in June		Unspec.	Boosey		BBC (1975)
4405	Levigne, Peter		Whisper in your dreams		Unspec.	Boosey		BBC (1975)
4406	Lewalter, Johann	1862-	Frühling kam [unreadable] über Nacht	Op. 49	2 children's or 2 med. v.	R. & E.		CHAL (1911)
4407	Lewalter, Johann	1862-	Kein Feuer, keine Kohle kann brennen so heiss	Op. 35	Unspec.	R. & E.		CHAL (1901)
4408	Lewalter, Johann	1862-	Wenn ich ein Vöglein wär und auch zwei Flügel hätt'	Op. 43 No. 1	2 med. v.	R. & E.		CHAL (1898)
4409	Lewandowski, Louis	1831-1896	Einladung "Geehrteste Frau"		Unspec.	B. & B.		CHAL (1898)
4410	Lewandowski, Louis	1831-1896	Excellenz "O verteufelt, siehe da"	Op. 31	2 female v.	R. & E.		CHAL (1898)
4411	Lewerth		Dina Bla Ogon		Unspec. or MS/Bar	Lundq.		CVMP (1976)
4412	Leydecker, A.		An dem Waldsaum steht ein Häuschen		2 med. v.	Ebling		CHAL (1906)
4413	Leydecker, A.		Dort oben auf dem Berge		Unspec.	Kreisler i. H.		CHAL (1911)
4414	Leydecker, A.		Zwei Pappelkronen neigen sich		2 med. v.	Ebling		CHAL (1911)
4415	Lichner, Heinrich	1829-1898	Abendglöcklein "Glöcklein, Abendglöcklein"	Op. 70 No. 2	S/A	Siegel		CHAL (1898)

REC	COMP	DTS	TITLE	OP #	VCG	PUB	COMMENTS	SRC
4416	Lichner, Heinrich	1829-1898	Auf der Wiese "Viel tausend Blumen"	Op. 70 No. 5	S/A	Siegel		CHAL (1898)
4417	Lichner, Heinrich	1829-1898	Gesang des Vogels über dem Walde "Im goldnen Strahl, über Wald"	Op. 70 No. 3	S/A	Siegel		CHAL (1898)
4418	Lichner, Heinrich	1829-1898	Morgenwanderung "Wer recht in Freuden wandern will"	Op. 70 No. 1	S/A	Siegel		CHAL (1898)
4419	Lichner, Heinrich	1829-1898	Sonnenschein "Sonnen-schein, klar und rein"	Op. 70 No. 4	S/A	Siegel		CHAL (1898)
4420	Lichner, Heinrich	1829-1898	Wiegenlied "Aeren nur noch nicken"	Op. 70 No. 6	S/A	Siegel		CHAL (1898)
4421	Liddle, Samuel	b. ~1868	The rowan tree		Unspec.	Stainer & Bell		BBC (1975)
4422	Lieb, F. X.		Marienblume "Es blüht der Blumen eine"	Op. 6 No. 1	Unspec.	André	org accomp.	CHAL (1898)
4423	Lieb, F. X.		Opfergesang "Wir schmücken die sein goldnes Haar"	Op. 6 No. 2	Unspec.	André	org accomp.	CHAL (1898)
4424	Lieb, F. X.		Spruch "Dein Herz soll wie dei Quelle sein"	Op. 5 No. 3	Unspec.	André		CHAL (1898)
4425	Lieb, F. X.		Sterne "Wenn die Kinder schlafen ein"	Op. 5 No. 1	S/S	André		CHAL (1898)
4426	Lieb, F. X.		Zwei Rosen	Op. 5 No. 2	S/S	André		CHAL (1898)
4427	Liebe, Eduard Ludwig	1819-1900	Engel kamen	Op. 74 No. 1	2 female v.	Coppen-rath		CHAL (1898)
4428	Liebe, Eduard Ludwig	1819-1900	Herbstlied "Feldenwärts flog ein Vögelein"	Op. 143 No. 1	S/A or T/Br	Feuchtin-ger		CHAL (1898)
4429	Liebe, Eduard Ludwig	1819-1900	Hoch vom Himmel droben	IV No. 3	Unspec.	C. Rühle i. L.	Arr. Necke	CHAL (1901)
4430	Liebe, Eduard Ludwig	1819-1900	Ich schrieb dir gerne einen Brief	III No. 3	Unspec.	C. Rühle i. L.	Arr. Necke	CHAL (1901)
4431	Liebe, Eduard Ludwig	1819-1900	Im Maien "Nun (Es) bricht aus allen Zweigen"	Op. 70 No. 1	S/A or Br/B	Coppen-rath		CHAL (1898)
4432	Liebe, Eduard Ludwig	1819-1900	Liebe und Freundschart "O kennst du Herz"	Op. 70 No. 2	S/A or T/Br	Luckhardt		CHAL (1898)
4433	Liebe, Eduard Ludwig	1819-1900	Meine Seele erhebet den Herrn	Op. 76 No. 1	MS/A	Coppen-rath		CHAL (1898)
4434	Liebe, Eduard Ludwig	1819-1900	So wahr die Sonne Scheinet	Op. 143 No. 2	S/A or T/Br	Luckhardt		CHAL (1898)
4435	Liebe, Eduard Ludwig	1819-1900	Sonnenlicht, Sonnenlicht fällt mir	I No. 1	Unspec.	C. Rühle i. L.	Arr. Necke	CHAL (1901)
4436	Liebe, Eduard Ludwig	1819-1900	Waldesruf	Op. 4 No. 2	S/S or T/T	Schott		CHAL (1898)
4437	Liebe, Eduard Ludwig	1819-1900	Waldklänge "3 Duette"	Op. 4	Unspec.	Schott	3 duets	CHAL (1898)
4438	Liebe, Eduard Ludwig	1819-1900	Waldsehnsucht "Blauer Himmel, laue Lüfte"	Op. 4 No. 3	S/S or T/T	Schott		CHAL (1898)
4439	Liebe, Eduard Ludwig	1819-1900	Waldwünsche "In dem Walde möcht'ich leben"	Op. 4 No. 1	S/S or T/T	Schott		CHAL (1898)
4440	Lier, E.		Streik-Couplet "Täglich hört man nur con Streiken"	Op. 85	2 med. v.	Günther		CHAL (1898)
4441	Lier, E.		Wir sind zwei Wohlbekannte		Unspec.	Meissner		CHAL (1901)
4442	Limbert, Frank L.	1866-1938	Abendbilder "Friedlicher Abend senkt sich"	Op. 12 No. 1	Unspec.	Fr. mus. Ver.		CHAL (1898)
4443	Limbert, Frank L.	1866-1938	Es hat die Rose sich beklagt	Op. 2 No. 1	Unspec.	R. Forberg		CHAL (1898)
4444	Limbert, Frank L.	1866-1938	Kosakenlied aus der Ukräne "Grünes Wäldchen, Rosen-wäldchen"	Op. 12 No. 3	Unspec.	Freie mus. Vereinig		CHAL (1898)

REC	COMP	DTS	TITLE	OP #	VCG	PUB	COMMENTS	SRC
4445	Limbert, Frank L.	1866-1938	Mein treu Herzlieb "Nachtigall klaget im Fliederstrauch"	Op. 12 No. 5	Unspec.	Freie mus. Vereinig		CHAL (1898)
4446	Limbert, Frank L.	1866-1938	Still, still, wein' nicht so heiss	Op. 12 No. 4	Unspec.	Freie mus. Vereinig		CHAL (1898)
4447	Limbert, Frank L.	1866-1938	Unter dem Lindenbaum sassen wir Beide	Op. 12 No. 2	Unspec.	Freie mus. Vereinig		CHAL (1898)
4448	Lincke, Paul	1866-1946	Ach, wie glücklich bin ich heut	Op. 134	Unspec.	Meissner		CHAL (1901)
4449	Lincke, Paul	1866-1946	Berliner Leben "Ein Bild woll'n wir hier geben"		Unspec.	P. Fischer i. Berl		CHAL (1898)
4450	Lincke, Paul	1866-1946	Eben aus dem Pensionat "Endlich frei, kaum kann ich's fassen"	Op. 31	2 female v.	Thiemer		CHAL (1898)
4451	Lincke, Paul	1866-1946	Er und Sie "Leise, nur leise, dass Niemand mich hört"		Unspec.	Danner		CHAL (1898)
4452	Lincke, Paul	1866-1946	Fritz und Rieke "Wie, noch nicht da"		Unspec.	Danner		CHAL (1898)
4453	Lincke, Paul	1866-1946	Ja so ein Pärchen, wie Paul und Klärchen "Klärchen und Paul waren"	Op. 145	Unspec.	P. Fischer i. Berl		CHAL (1898)
4454	Lincke, Paul	1866-1946	Klingen los "Wir sind zwei, die's nicht versth'n"		Unspec.	Neumann i. Berl.		CHAL (1898)
4455	Lincke, Paul	1866-1946	Liebesgeständnisse mit Hindernissen "Endlich habe in mich fortgestohlen"	Op. 181	Unspec.	Danner		CHAL (1898)
4456	Lincke, Paul	1866-1946	Malchen und Julchen "Ach wie glücklich bin ich heut"	Op. 134	S/A	Meissner		CHAL (1898)
4457	Lincke, Paul	1866-1946	Vom Erlaub zurück "Zurück heut kehren alle"	Op. 175	Unspec.	Meissner		CHAL (1898)
4458	Lincke, Paul	1866-1946	Was sich der Wald erzählt "Leute höret die Geschichte"		Unspec.	Hoffheinz		CHAL (1898)
4459	Lincke, Paul	1866-1946	Weisst du noch, wie schön es war		Unspec.	Apollo		CHAL (1911)
4460	Lincke, Paul	1866-1946	Wenn der Mond am Himmel steht		Unspec.	Apollo		CHAL (1911)
4461	Lincke, Paul	1866-1946	Will man froh die Welt durchfliegen		Unspec.	Apollo		CHAL (1911)
4462	Linderer, Ed.		Da gehören wir hin "Wir sind zwei riesige Talente"		Unspec.	Ed. Linderer i. Berl		CHAL (1898)
4463	Linderer, Ed.		Froh und lustig leben wir		Unspec.	O. Dietrich		CHAL (1901)
4464	Linderer, Ed.		Mädchen von Berlin "Preist auch die Welt"		Unspec.	Ed. Linderer i. Berl.		CHAL (1898)
4465	Linderer, Ed.		Ne, die verdammte Steuer		2 female v.	O. Dietrich		CHAL (1911)
4466	Linderer, Ed.		Richtige Temperatur "An den Feuerherd ein Soldate"		Unspec.	Ed. Linderer i. Berl.		CHAL (1898)
4467	Linderer, Ed.		Wiener Cafe "Wenn längst kein Mensch mehr wacht"		Unspec.	Ed. Linderer i. Berl.		CHAL (1898)
4468	Lindgren, Olof	1934-	Be, Sok, Bulta		Unspec.	STIM	acap. Collection. In "Fem Sanger for Tva (Lika) Roster." Biblical works	CVMP (1985)
4469	Lindgren, Olof	1934-	Karlekens Bud		Unspec.	STIM	acap. Collection. In "Fem Sanger for Tva (Lika) Roster." Biblical works	CVMP (1985)

REC	COMP	DTS	TITLE	OP #	VCG	PUB	COMMENTS	SRC
4470	Lindgren, Olof	1934-	Om Nagon Vill Ga I Mina Spar		Unspec.	STIM	acap. Collection. In "Fem Sanger for Tva (Lika) Roster." Biblical works	CVMP (1985)
4471	Lindgren, Olof	1934-	Sa Alskade Gud Variden		Unspec.	STIM	acap. Collection. In "Fem Sanger for Tva (Lika) Roster." Biblical works	CVMP (1985)
4472	Lindgren, Olof	1934-	Saliga De Som Hungrar		Unspec.	STIM	acap. Collection. In "Fem Sanger for Tva (Lika) Roster." Biblical works	CVMP (1985)
4473	Lindner, August	1820-1878	Frühlingswonne	Op. 20 No. 1	Unspec.	Nagel		CHAL (1898)
4474	Lindner, August	1820-1878	Glöcklein im Herzen	Op. 20 No. 3	Unspec.	Nagel		CHAL (1898)
4475	Lindner, August	1820-1878	Jubilate-Amen	Op. 20 No. 2	Unspec.	Nagel		CHAL (1898)
4476	Lindner, August	1820-1878	Wenn sich zwei Herzen scheiden	Op. 7	S/S	Bach-mann		CHAL (1898)
4477	Lindner, E. [prob. Ernst Otto T.]	1820-1867	Sanct Niklas bald ist Weihnacht		Unspec.	Brock-haus		CHAL (1906)
4478	Lindsay, Miss M.	19th C.	Far Away		Unspec.	Leonard-Eng	Pen name of Mrs. Worthington Bliss. Eng. woman comp.	CVMP (1976)
4479	Lindsay, Miss M.	19th C.	Far Away		S/S	Leonard-Eng	Pen name of Mrs. Worthington Bliss. Eng. woman comp.	ASR
4480	Lindsay, Miss M.	19th C.	Pulaski's Banner		Unspec.	Leonard-Eng	Pen name of Mrs. Worthington Bliss. Eng. woman comp. Also solo, pub. by Cramer.	CVMP (1976)
4481	Lindsay, Miss M.	19th C.	Tired		Unspec.	Leonard-Eng	Pen name of Mrs. Worthington Bliss. Eng. woman comp. Also solo.	CVMP (1976)
4482	Lingner, H.		Grüsse an die Heimath "Aus den Lüftchen jubelt nieder"	Op. 15	Unspec.	Lorch		CHAL (1898)
4483	Linnala, Eino	1896-1973	Jeesus Sana Elaman "Jesus Livets Helga Ord"		Unspec.	Fazer		CVMP (1976)
4484	Linnala, Eino	1896-1973	Kun Helmin Heijastaapi "Nar Himlens Faste Malar"		Unspec.	Fazer		CVMP (1976)
4485	Linné, S.		Als reicher Leute Kinder		Unspec.	Benja-min		CHAL (1898)
4486	Linné, S.		Damen und die Herren		Unspec.	Benja-min		CHAL (1906)
4487	Linné, S.		Das ist Vollblut, echte Race "Eine Stute hab' gesehen"		Unspec.	Benja-min		CHAL (1898)
4488	Linné, S.		Jüngst hat, so schreibt doe Zeitung		Unspec.	Benja-min		CHAL (1906)
4489	Linné, S.		Mann entschliesst sich langsam		Unspec.	Benja-min		CHAL (1906)
4490	Linné, S.		Mein Fräulein, darf ich Sie beschützen		Unspec.	Benja-min		CHAL (1906)
4491	Linné, S.		Nach Hause geh'n wir nicht "Nur dem Vergnügen zu leben"		Unspec.	Benja-min		CHAL (1898)

REC	COMP	DTS	TITLE	OP #	VCG	PUB	COMMENTS	SRC
4492	Linné, S.		Wir pfeifen darauf "Auf Tenoristen und Steuerlisten"		Unspec.	Benja-min		CHAL (1898)
4493	Lipart, F.		Kinder Floras "Weckt der Frühling die Natur"		Unspec.	O. Dietrich		CHAL (1898)
4494	Lipart, F.		Wiener-Ruder-Gigerl-Marsch "Wir sind zwar keine Männer"		Unspec.	O. Dietrich		CHAL (1898)
4495	Lipp, Alban	1866-1903	Maienkönigen "16 Lieder zur seligesten Jungfrau"		S/A	Böhm & S.	org or harm. Collection of 16 sacred duets.	CHAL (1901)
4496	Liszt, Franz	1811-1886	Abend am Meer "O Meer im Abendstrahle"		S/A	Kahnt		CHAL (1898)
4497	Liszt, Franz	1811-1886	Liebesträume		Unspec.	Allans	Eng. trans. Grmn. In anthology "Vocal Duets Collection" Vol. 2. Pub. 1992.	MSN
4498	Liszt, Franz	1811-1886	O, Meer im Abendstrahl		S/A	EMB	In anthology "Duettek nöi Hangokra Zongora-kísérettel" Vol. II Compi. M. Forrai. Pub. 1959.	MSN
4499	Liszt, Franz	1811-1886	O Meer im Abendstrahl		S/S or S/MS	B. & H.	In collection "Werke" ed. F. Busoni & P. Raabe. Pub. 1907-1936.	NATS-VCD
4500	Littmann, H.		An meine Liebe		Unspec.	Rühle i. L.		CHAL (1898)
4501	Lloyd Webber, Andrew	1948-	Pie Jesu		S/S or MS/MS	Hal Leonard	pf or org accomp. Part of "Requiem" common-ly perf. separately.	NATS-SVD
4502	Lob, Otto	1834-1908	Zu dir "All' meine Gedanken"	Op. 81	2 med. v.	André		CHAL (1898)
4503	Loes, Harry Dixon & George S. Schuler	1892-1965, ?-?	Christmas Spirit, The		Unspec.	Lillenas	1-2 v.	CVMP (1976)
4504	Loewe, Gilbert	d. 1927?	Till Dawn		Unspec.	Leonard-Eng	Also solo. Pen name of Charles A. Rawlings.	CVMP (1976)
4505	Loewe, Karl Gottfried	1796-1869	Als er, Sami, mit dir jüngst	Op. 104 No. 2	2 high v. or 2 low v.	Schlesin-ger		CHAL (1901)
4506	Loewe, Karl Gottfried	1796-1869	An Sami		2 female v.	Peters	In "Duettenkranz" vol. 3. Ed. Martienssen	ASR
4507	Loewe, Karl Gottfried	1796-1869	An Sami	Op. 104 No. 2	S/S or S/MS	B. & H.	In "Duetten-Trifolium" Op. 104. In collection "Werke" Ed. Max Runze. Pub. 1899-1904.	NATS-VCD
4508	Loewe, Karl Gottfried	1796-1869	An Sami "Als er, Sami, mir dir jüngst"	Op. 104 No. 2	S/S or B/B	Bach-mann		CHAL (1898)
4509	Loewe, Karl Gottfried	1796-1869	Blumenelfen "Wenn es in der Dämmerstunde"	Op. 31 No. 2	S/A	Chal.		CHAL (1898)
4510	Loewe, Karl Gottfried	1796-1869	Die Freude		2 female v.	Peters	In "Duettenkranz" vol. 3. Ed. Martienssen	ASR
4511	Loewe, Karl Gottfried	1796-1869	Die Freude	Op. 104 No. 1	S/S or S/MS	B. & H.	In "Duetten-Trifolium" Op. 104. In collection "Werke" Ed. Max Runze. Pub. 1899-1904.	NATS-VCD
4512	Loewe, Karl Gottfried	1796-1869	Freude "Es flattert um die Quelle"	Op. 104 No. 1	S/S or B/B	Bach-mann		CHAL (1898)
4513	Loewe, Karl Gottfried	1796-1869	Glühwürmchen, stecks Laternchen an	Op. 64 No. 1	S/A	B. & H.	Ed. Riemann	CHAL (1906)

REC	COMP	DTS	TITLE	OP #	VCG	PUB	COMMENTS	SRC
4514	Loewe, Karl Gottfried	1796-1869	März	Op. 104 No. 3	S/S or S/MS	B. & H.	In "Duetten-Trifolium" Op. 104. In collection "Werke" Ed. Max Runze. Pub. 1899-1904.	NATS-VCD
4515	Loewe, Karl Gottfried	1796-1869	März "Es ist ein Schnee gefallen"	Op. 104 No. 3	S/S or B/B	Bach-mann	Pub. 1845	CHAL (1898)
4516	Loewe, Karl Gottfried	1796-1869	'S was mal 'ne Katzen-Königin	Op. 64 No. 2	S/A	B. & H.	Ed. Riemann	CHAL (1906)
4517	Loewe, Karl Gottfried	1796-1869	Stimmen der Elfen "3 Duette"	Op. 31	S/A	Chal.	3 duets. Pub. 1833.	CHAL (1898)
4518	Loewe, Karl Gottfried	1796-1869	Thurmelfen "Unter Schleier des Geheimen"	Op. 31 No. 3	S/A	Chal.	Pub. 1833	CHAL (1898)
4519	Loewe, Karl Gottfried	1796-1869	Waldelfen "Es schweigt im stillen Walde"	Op. 31 No. 1	S/A	Chal.	Pub. 1833	CHAL (1898)
4520	Logé, Henri		Across the still Lagoon		S/A	Ditson	In anthology "Soprano and Alto Duets" Ed. H. Kiehl. Pub. 1901.	MSN
4521	Logé, Henri		Across the still Lagoon		S/A	Ditson	In anthology "The Ditson Collection of Soprano and Alto Duets" Pub. 1934.	MSN
4522	Löhr, Hermann [Frederic]	1871-1943	Friends		Unspec.	Morley	Father of Hermann Löhr (1871-1943)	BBC (1975)
4523	Löhr, Hermann [Frederic]	1871-1943	Rose of my heart		Unspec.	Chappell	Son of Frederic Nicholls Löhr	BBC (1975)
4524	Löhr, Hermann [Frederic]	1871-1943	Sing heigh-ho!		Unspec.	Chappell	Son of Frederic Nicholls Löhr	BBC (1975)
4525	Löhr, Hermann [Frederic]	1871-1943	Supposing		Unspec.	Chappell	Son of Frederic Nicholls Löhr	BBC (1975)
4526	Löhr, Hermann [Frederic]	1871-1943	The day is done		Unspec.	Chappell	Son of Frederic Nicholls Löhr	BBC (1975)
4527	Löhr, Hermann [Frederic]	1871-1943	The little sunbonnet		Unspec.	Boosey	Son of Frederic Nicholls Löhr	BBC (1975)
4528	Löhr, Hermann [Frederic]	1871-1943	The magpie is a gipsy bird		Unspec.	Chappell	Son of Frederic Nicholls Löhr	BBC (1975)
4529	Löhr, Hermann [Frederic]	1871-1943	You'd better ask me		Unspec.	Chappell	Son of Frederic Nicholls Löhr	BBC (1975)
4530	Longstaffe, Ernest		Oh Sarah! Oh 'Enery!		Unspec.	Reynolds		BBC (1975)
4531	Longuet		Endymions Schlaf		Unspec.	Böhme i. H.		CHAL (1898)
4532	Longuet		Nachtgesang		Unspec.	Böhme i. H.		CHAL (1898)
4533	Lorens, Karl	1851-1909	Allweil lustig, froh und munter	Op. 5	Unspec.	Fr. Dietrich		CHAL (1901)
4534	Lorens, Karl	1851-1909	Blumzen und die Leber-wurscht "In einmen Selcherladen"		Unspec.	Fr. Dietrich		CHAL (1898)
4535	Lorens, Karl	1851-1909	Cavalleria rusticana "An' Oper wird jetzt aufgeführt"		Unspec.	Robit-schek		CHAL (1898)
4536	Lorens, Karl	1851-1909	Ein Fräulein geht am Ring spazier'n		2 med. v.	Blaha		CHAL (1901)
4537	Lorens, Karl	1851-1909	Es ist jetzt anders auf der Welt	Op. 4	Unspec.	Fr. Dietrich		CHAL (1901)
4538	Lorens, Karl	1851-1909	Es leben die Menschen heut ha ha		Unspec.	Blaha		CHAL (1911)
4539	Lorens, Karl	1851-1909	Kruzitürken bringt's mir geschwindi		Unspec.	Blaha		CHAL (1901)

REC	COMP	DTS	TITLE	OP #	VCG	PUB	COMMENTS	SRC
4540	Lorens, Karl	1851-1909	Liebe Gott, der All's erschaffen	Op. 7	Unspec.	Fr. Dietrich		CHAL (1901)
4541	Lorens, Karl	1851-1909	Man denkt sich allerei "Emilie, die ist blass"		Unspec.	Robit-schek		CHAL (1898)
4542	Lorens, Karl	1851-1909	Menschen san mir ja Alle "Es ist amal schon Brauch"		Unspec.	Maas i. W.		CHAL (1898)
4543	Lorens, Karl	1851-1909	Mir san Landsleut, weanarische Buam "Welt ist ganz bucklich"		Unspec.	Blahn		CHAL (1898)
4544	Lorens, Karl	1851-1909	Müller und sein Kind "Es kennt wohl Jedermann"		Unspec.	Robit-schek		CHAL (1898)
4545	Lorens, Karl	1851-1909	Schönste Fleck auf Gottes Erd "Welt ist gross, die Welt ist schön"	Op. 50	Unspec.	Robit-schek		CHAL (1898)
4546	Lorens, Karl	1851-1909	Sehr viel Wasser, grosses Fass		2 med. v.	Blaha		CHAL (1901)
4547	Lorens, Karl	1851-1909	Singen woll'n wor jetzt ein Lied	Op. 6	Unspec.	Fr. Dietrich		CHAL (1901)
4548	Lorens, Karl	1851-1909	So müssen d'Weanaleut sein "Beim Heurigen draussen"		Unspec.	Blahn		CHAL (1898)
4549	Lorens, Karl	1851-1909	So was kennst der Weana glei "Sehr viel Wasser"		Unspec.	Blaha		CHAL (1898)
4550	Lorens, Karl	1851-1909	Tschin bum "Grüss Gott, alter Spezi"		Unspec.	Robit-schek		CHAL (1898)
4551	Lorens, Karl	1851-1909	Um zwölf Uhr bei Nacht "Grosse Häuser welche Pracht"		Unspec.	Blaha		CHAL (1898)
4552	Lorens, Karl	1851-1909	Verehrtes Publikim, hör' was ich singe		2 med. v.	Blaha		CHAL (1901)
4553	Lorens, Karl	1851-1909	Wann ma nach Mitternacht		Unspec.	Blaha		CHAL (1906)
4554	Lorens, Karl	1851-1909	Weana is erfindungsreich		2 med. v.	Blaha		CHAL (1901)
4555	Lorens, Karl	1851-1909	Wiener Schnapper-Marsch	Op. 41	Unspec.	Robit-schek		CHAL (1898)
4556	Lorens, Karl	1851-1909	Wir thun so gern tratschen		Unspec.	Blaha		CHAL (1901)
4557	Lorens, Karl	1851-1909	Wissen's, was d' Frau Blaschke sagt		Unspec.	Maass		CHAL (1898)
4558	Lorens, Karl	1851-1909	Zehn kleine Negerlein die thaten einmal sein		Unspec.	Robit-schek		CHAL (1898)
4559	Lorenz, Alfred Ottokar	1868-1939	Ave Maria "Wenn der Tag sich neiget"	Op. 13 No. 1	S/A	Bahn		CHAL (1898)
4560	Lorenz, Alfred Ottokar	1868-1939	Frühlingsahung "O sanfter, süsser Hauch"	Op. 4 No. 1	S/S	Bahn		CHAL (1898)
4561	Lorenz, Alfred Ottokar	1868-1939	Frühlingsglaube "Linden Lüfte sind erwacht"	Op. 4 No. 2	S/S	Bahn		CHAL (1898)
4562	Lorenz, Alfred Ottokar	1868-1939	Klein Minnetraum "Im Walde, von dem Laub der Buchen"	Op. 13 No. 2	S/A	Bahn		CHAL (1898)
4563	Lorenz, Alfred Ottokar	1868-1939	So warst du nie vergessen	Op. 84	S/A or S/MS	Oppen-heimer		CHAL (1911)
4564	Lorenz, Alfred Ottokar	1868-1939	Wir kommen gezogen selbander	Op. 36 No. 2	Unspec.	Siegel		CHAL (1901)
4565	Lorleberg, F.		Entdeckt "Es flattern die willden Tauben"	Op. 52 No. 3	S/S or T/T	Tonger		CHAL (1898)
4566	Lorleberg, F.		Mädel, Mädel, komm und küsse	Op. 52 No. 2	S/S or T/T	Tonger		CHAL (1898)
4567	Lorleberg, F.		Sucht Veilchen "Durch Berge und Klüfte"	Op. 52 No. 1	S/S or T/T	Tonger		CHAL (1898)

REC	COMP	DTS	TITLE	OP #	VCG	PUB	COMMENTS	SRC
4568	Lothar, Mark	1902-	Jahresringe Heft I: Bergengruen-Duette	Op. 44	S/A	Ries	Unspec. pieces	CVMP (1976)
4569	Lothar, Mark	1902-	Jahresringe Heft II: Morgenstern-Duette	Op. 45	S/A	Ries	Unspec. pieces	CVMP (1976)
4570	Lötti, J.		Beim Regen auf durchnässten Wegen	Op. 53	Unspec.	Robit-schek		CHAL (1911)
4571	Lötti, J.		Was ich dich jetzt noch fragen will		Unspec.	Bärd & Bruder		CHAL (1906)
4572	Lovelace, Austin C.	1919-	Wedding Benediction, A		S/A	G. Schirm.	Also solo	CVMP (1976)
4573	Lover, Samuel	1797-1868	What will you do?		Unspec.	Kerr	Arr. Baptie	BBC (1975)
4574	Lowthian, Caroline	1860-1943	Bittersweet		Unspec.	Cramer	Pen name of Mrs. Cyril Prescott. Eng. woman comp.	CVMP (1976)
4575	Lowthian, Caroline	1860-1943	Reign of the Roses		Unspec.	Cramer	Pen name of Mrs. Cyril Prescott. Eng. woman comp. Also solo.	CVMP (1976)
4576	Lubrich, O.		Grüss die Gott o Landesmutter	Op. 66	Unspec.	Hoffmann i. Str.		CHAL (1901)
4577	Lucantoni, Giovanni	1825-1902	Alla Sera		S/A	G. Schirm.	In catalogue page "Favorite French and Italian Vocal Duets" of G. Schirmer, Inc. NY (no date)	MSN
4578	Lucantoni, Giovanni	1825-1902	Bacio "Ridente come tiride"		S/S	Cranz		CHAL (1898)
4579	Lucantoni, Giovanni	1825-1902	Il Bacio		S/S	G. Schirm.	In catalogue page "Favorite French and Italian Vocal Duets" of G. Schirmer, Inc. NY (no date)	MSN
4580	Lucantoni, Giovanni	1825-1902	La Reconciliation		S/Br or S/A	G. Schirm.	In catalogue page "Favorite French and Italian Vocal Duets" of G. Schirmer, Inc. NY (no date)	MSN
4581	Lucantoni, Giovanni	1825-1902	Night in Venice		Unspec.	Cramer	Eng. tr. It.	CVMP (1976)
4582	Lucantoni, Giovanni	1825-1902	Night in Venice, A		Unspec.	Brain-ard's Sons	Eng. tr. It. In anthology "Brainard's Collection of Vocal Duets from Popular Modern and Standard Composers" Pub. 1903.	MSN
4583	Lucantoni, Giovanni	1825-1902	Primavera d'Amore		S/MS	G. Schirm.	In catalogue page "Favorite French and Italian Vocal Duets" of G. Schirmer, Inc. NY (no date)	MSN
4584	Lucantoni, Giovanni	1825-1902	Una notte a Venezia		Unspec.	Ricordi		BBC (1975)
4585	Lucotte		Bienfaits de la nuit "O nuit que ta lumière"		Unspec.	Bahn		CHAL (1898)
4586	Lüdecke, L.		Es fiel ein Stern herunter	Op. 36 No. 1	Unspec.	Cranz		CHAL (1898)
4587	Lüdecke, L.		Was will die einsame Thräne	Op. 36 No. 2	Unspec.	Cranz		CHAL (1898)
4588	Ludwig, August	1865-1946	Fischerln im Bach	Op. 45 No. 23	Unspec.	Ludwig i. Lichterf.		CHAL (1901)
4589	Ludwig, August	1865-1946	Gar sehr lieblich kommt der Maien	Op. 200 No. 1	Unspec.	Ludwig i. Dresden.		CHAL (1906)
4590	Ludwig, August	1865-1946	Holdes Fräulein zart und jung	Op. 200 No. 3	Unspec.	Ludwig i. Dresden		CHAL (1906)

REC	COMP	DTS	TITLE	OP #	VCG	PUB	COMMENTS	SRC
4591	Ludwig, August	1865-1946	Ich hasse das müssig verdriessliche Sitzen	Op. 200 No. 2	Unspec.	Ludwig i. Dresden		CHAL (1906)
4592	Ludwig, August	1865-1946	Im Fliederbusch ein Vöglein sass	Op. 45 No. 20	Unspec.	Ludwig i. Lichterf.		CHAL (1901)
4593	Ludwig, August	1865-1946	Kleine Geiglein, die da klingen	Op. 200 No. 2	Unspec.	Ludwig i. Lichterf.		CHAL (1906)
4594	Ludwig, August	1865-1946	Sing-Tanz-Duett (4)	Op. 200	Unspec.	Ludwig i. Dresden	Collection of 4 duets.	CHAL (1906)
4595	Ludwig, C.	19th C.	Bruder Studio "Hurrah, da sind wir"		Unspec.	F. R. Müller i. Leipz.	Pen name of Jul. E. Gottlöber	CHAL (1898)
4596	Ludwig, C.	19th C.	Fidelen Chinesen "Wer sein denn das"		Unspec.	F. R. Müller i. Leipz.	Pen name of Jul. E. Gottlöber	CHAL (1898)
4597	Ludwig, C.	19th C.	G'brüder Stern "Originale sind wir beid'"		Unspec.	F. R. Müller i. Leipz.	Pen name of Jul. E. Gottlöber	CHAL (1898)
4598	Ludwig, C.	19th C.	Heinze und Janke "Nu was mein'se"		Unspec.	F. R. Müller i. Leipz.	Pen name of Jul. E. Gottlöber	CHAL (1898)
4599	Ludwig, C.	19th C.	Infantrist und Stadtsoldat "Ach welche Lust, Soldat zu sein"		Unspec.	F. R. Müller i. Leipz.	Pen name of Jul. E. Gottlöber	CHAL (1898)
4600	Ludwig, C.	19th C.	Mylord von Höhne und sein Sohn Ferdinand "Oho, was wälzt sich dort"		Unspec.	Müller i. Leipzig	Pen name of Jul. E. Gottlöber	CHAL (1898)
4601	Ludwig, C.	19th C.	Na muss es denn gleich sinn "Als wir noch kleine Jungens"		Unspec.	F. R. Müller i. Leipz.	Pen name of Jul. E. Gottlöber	CHAL (1898)
4602	Ludwig, C.	19th C.	Rentier Mäuschen und sein Gärtnerbursche "Ach es ist eine Wonne"		Unspec.	F. R. Müller i. Leipz.	Pen name of Jul. E. Gottlöber	CHAL (1898)
4603	Luedecke, Raymond	1944-	Whispers of Heavenly Death		S/S	Am. Comp. Al.		CVMP (1995)
4604	Lührsz, Karl	1824-1882	Abendgesang "Schöne Tag o Freundin"	Op. 4 No. 2	S/A	Cranz		CHAL (1898)
4605	Lührsz, Karl	1824-1882	Maienlied "Nun schmückert sich die Wiese grün"	Op. 4 No. 3	S/A	Cranz		CHAL (1898)
4606	Lührsz, Karl	1824-1882	Wenn es Frühling wird	Op. 4 No. 1	S/A	Cranz		CHAL (1898)
4607	Lustig, Gebr.		Jung gefreit, hat niemand gereut "In der Bibel steht zu lesen"		Unspec.	Simon i. Berl.		CHAL (1898)
4608	Lutgen, L.		Voile blanche		Unspec.	Junne		CHAL (1898)
4609	Lyra, Justus Wilhelm	1822-1882	Berge in der blauen Ferne	IV No. 1	Unspec.	B. & H.	Ed. Weigel	CHAL (1906)
4610	Lyra, Justus Wilhelm	1822-1882	Deutsche Weisen "Gesang für 2 u. 3 Singst."		Unspec.	B. & H.	Vol. 4 songs for 2-3 v.	CHAL (1898)
4611	Lyra, Justus Wilhelm	1822-1882	Rose liebte die Lilie	IV No. 5	Unspec.	B. & H.	Ed. Weigel	CHAL (1906)
4612	Maas, Louis	1852-1889	Gendamerie von Rummelsberg "Kom. Duoscene"	Op. 60	Unspec.	Meissner		CHAL (1901)
4613	Maas, Louis	1852-1889	Grete, liebe Grete	Op. 140	Unspec.	Portius		CHAL (1906)
4614	Maas, Louis	1852-1889	Wir sind zwei Turner froh	Op. 38	Unspec.	Meissner		CHAL (1901)
4615	Maase, Wilhelm	d. 1932	Im Fliederbusch ein Vöglein sass	Op. 24 No. 3	Unspec.	Salzer		CHAL (1901)

REC	COMP	DTS	TITLE	OP #	VCG	PUB	COMMENTS	SRC
4616	Maase, Wilhelm	d. 1932	O kirchenstille Waldesruh	Op. 24 No. 2	high & low v.	Salzer		CHAL (1901)
4617	Maase, Wilhelm	d. 1932	Wo teif versteckt im Grunde	Op. 24 No. 1	high & low v.	Salzer		CHAL (1901)
4618	MacDowell, Edward	1860-1908	To A Wild Rose	Op. 5	Unspec.	Allans	In anthology "Vocal Duets Collection" Vol. 2. Pub. 1992.	MSN
4619	Macfarlane, Elsa		Memory treet		Unspec.	F. D. & H.	Eng. woman comp.	BBC (1975)
4620	MacFarlane, William Charles	1870-	O Love divine		S/A	G. Schirm.	pf or org accomp. In catalogue page "Sacred Vocal Duets" of G. Schirmer, Inc. NY (no date)	MSN
4621	Mächtig, Karl	1836-1881	Zweigesang der Elfen "Hörst du das Flüstern"		Unspec.	Leuckart		CHAL (1898)
4622	Mackrot, G. W.		Gute Nacht, mein Herz	Op. 7 No. 3	S/S	Fürstner		CHAL (1898)
4623	Mackrot, G. W.		In meinem Garten die Nelken	Op. 7 No. 1	S/S	Fürstner		CHAL (1898)
4624	Mackrot, G. W.		Mädchenlieder (3)	Op. 7	S/S	Fürstner	3 duets, unspec.	CHAL (1898)
4625	Mackrot, G. W.		Wohl waren es Tage der Wonne	Op. 7 No. 2	S/S	Fürstner		CHAL (1898)
4626	MacLeod, Peter	1797-1859	Oh! Why left I my hame?		Unspec.	Bayley & Ferguson	Arr. Maxfield	BBC (1975)
4627	Mahlberg, C.		Ein geistlich Abendlied "Es ist so still geworden"	Op. 44 No. 3	Unspec.	Riebe i. Br.		CHAL (1898)
4628	Mahlberg, C.		Herbstlied "Sommers Fäden weben"	Op. 44 No. 1	Unspec.	Riebe i. Br.		CHAL (1898)
4629	Mahlberg, C.		Umrauschen auch Freuden und Glanz	No. 2	Unspec.	Offhaus		CHAL (1901)
4630	Mahlberg, C.		Wanderlust "Wanderlust, das ist das höchste Glück"	Op. 44 No. 6	Unspec.	Riebe i. Br.		CHAL (1898)
4631	Mahlberg, C.		Wenn der Frühling auf die Berge steigt	No. 1	Unspec.	Offhaus		CHAL (1901)
4632	Mahlberg, C.		Wie der Lerche "Wie die Lerche möcht ich singen"	Op. 44 No. 5	Unspec.	Riebe i. Br.		CHAL (1898)
4633	Mahlberg, C.		Wo sind alle die Blumen hin	Op. 44 No. 2	Unspec.	Riebe i. Br.		CHAL (1898)
4634	Mahlberg, C.		Wohin "Vöglein im Walde dort"	Op. 44 No. 4	Unspec.	Riebe i. Br.		CHAL (1898)
4635	Mahnecke, R.		Es lässt in einem Lied sich		Unspec.	Urse		CHAL (1901)
4636	Maier, Amanda	1853-1894	Kinder Weihnachten in Sang und Klang		Unspec.	Beyer & Söhne	a.k.a. Amanda Röygen (married name). Grmn. woman comp.	CHAL (1898)
4637	Maikowski, M.		Zwei Commis "Immer fein nach neu'ster Mode"		Unspec.	Danner		CHAL (1898)
4638	Malek, W.		Capital-Gecken "Uns Gecken kennt man überall"		Unspec.	Grude		CHAL (1898)
4639	Malek, W.		Der ist verrückt "Wer in der Früh' statt Kaffee"		Unspec.	O. Dietrich		CHAL (1898)
4640	Malibran, Alexander	1823-1867	Batelièr		Unspec.	Schlesinger		CHAL (1898)

REC	COMP	DTS	TITLE	OP #	VCG	PUB	COMMENTS	SRC
4641	Malibran, Alexander	1823-1867	Belle viens à moi "Entends tu les gondoles"		Unspec.	Schlesinger		CHAL (1898)
4642	Malibran, Alexander	1823-1867	Lutin "Notre grand mère, et si vieille"		Unspec.	Schlesinger		CHAL (1898)
4643	Malibran, Alexander	1823-1867	Rendez-vous "Déja la nuit sombre"		Unspec.	Schlesinger		CHAL (1898)
4644	Malin, Don		Eight Polish Christmas Carols		2 med. v.	Marks	acap. Unspec. pieces. May be perf. chorally.	ASR
4645	Malling, Jorgen	1836-1905	Weihnachten "10 Lieder des Kindes schönstes Fest"		Unspec.	Cranz	10 duets	CHAL (1898)
4646	Malotte, Albert Hay	1895-1964	Lord's Prayer, The		S/A	G. Schirm.	In anthology "Schirmer's Favorite Sacred Duets for Various Voices" Pub. 1955.	MSN
4647	Mangold, Karl Ludwig Armand	1813-1889	Abschied "Was soll ich erst kaufen"	Op. 39 No. 3	Unspec.	B. & H.		CHAL (1898)
4648	Mangold, Karl Ludwig Armand	1813-1889	Ausforderung "Eine hohe Hahnenfeder"	Op. 39 No. 5	Unspec.	B. & H.		CHAL (1898)
4649	Mangold, Karl Ludwig Armand	1813-1889	Berghirt "Wenn auf den höchsten"	Op. 39 No. 2	Unspec.	B. & H.		CHAL (1898)
4650	Mangold, Karl Ludwig Armand	1813-1889	Ergebung "Bin gefahren auf dem Wasser"	Op. 39 No. 6	Unspec.	B. & H.		CHAL (1898)
4651	Mangold, Karl Ludwig Armand	1813-1889	Erlösung "Vor meines Mädchens Fenster"	Op. 39 No. 4	Unspec.	B. & H.		CHAL (1898)
4652	Mangold, Karl Ludwig Armand	1813-1889	Höhen und Thäler "Mein Mädchen wohnt"	Op. 39 No. 1	Unspec.	B. & H.		CHAL (1898)
4653	Mannfred, Heinrich	1866-	Guten Tag, Baby		2 young female v.	Bloch		CHAL (1911)
4654	Manning, Kathleen Lockhart		In the Luxembourg Gardens		S/A or T/Br	G. Schirm.	Woman comp. In catalogue page "Selected Vocal Duets" of G. Schirmer, Inc. NY (no date)	MSN
4655	Manookin, Robert P.		Blessed Be the Name of Our God		2 high v.	Sonos		CVMP (1985)
4656	Mansfeldt, H.		Am Himmelsgrund schiessen so lustig die Sterne	No. 2	S/A	Schott		CHAL (1901)
4657	Mansfeldt, H.		Castagnetten lustig schwingen	No. 1	S/A	Schott		CHAL (1901)
4658	Mansfeldt, H.		Gedichte (Drei) als Duette "Sammeltitel"		S/A	Schott	2 duets	CHAL (1901)
4659	Mansfeldt, H.		Möcht wissen was sie schlagen	No. 3	S/A	Schott		CHAL (1901)
4660	Manziarly, Marcelle de	1899-	La Naine		Unspec.	Salabert	Fr. woman comp.	CVMP (1985)
4661	Manziarly, Marcelle de	1899-	Le Rhume		Unspec.	Salabert	Fr. woman comp.	CVMP (1985)
4662	Marais, Josef		Berg op Zoom		Unspec.	G. Schirm.		BBC (1975)
4663	Marais, Josef		Chow Willy		Unspec.	G. Schirm.		BBC (1975)
4664	Marais, Josef		Mother Mary is rocking her child		Unspec.	G. Schirm.		BBC (1975)

REC	COMP	DTS	TITLE	OP #	VCG	PUB	COMMENTS	SRC
4665	Marais, Josef		The dilly song		Unspec.	G. Schirm.		BBC (1975)
4666	Marais, Josef		The messenger of love		Unspec.	G. Schirm.		BBC (1975)
4667	Marais, Josef		The rumble-drum		Unspec.	G. Schirm.		BBC (1975)
4668	Marais, Josef		The silver fleet		Unspec.	G. Schirm.		BBC (1975)
4669	Marchesi de Castrone, Mathilde [neé Graumann]	1826-1913	Canto siciliano "Spezzar mi sento"	Op. 18	Unspec.	Doblinger	Grmn. woman comp.	CHAL (1898)
4670	Marchesi de Castrone, Salvatore	1822-1908	Am Abend		Unspec.	R. & E.		CHAL (1898)
4671	Marchesi de Castrone, Salvatore	1822-1908	Am Morgen		Unspec.	R. & E.		CHAL (1898)
4672	Marchetti, Filippo	1831-1902	Morremo "Morremo e sciolti di quaggiù"		MS/A	Ricordi		CHAL (1898)
4673	Margot, T.		Ei sieh' da, die liebe Schillern		2 female v.	Bloch		CHAL (1911)
4674	Mariz, C. J.		Wienacht, hochgepries'ne Nacht	Op. 3	Unspec.	Vetter		CHAL (1911)
4675	Marschner, Adolf Eduard	1819-1853	An die Frühlingswolken "Ihr Segler dort oben"	Op. 41 No. 1	S/S	Klemm		CHAL (1898)
4676	Marschner, Adolf Eduard	1819-1853	Gruss an Madonna "Ist mein Seele bang"	Op. 14 No. 2	S/S	Klemm		CHAL (1898)
4677	Marschner, Adolf Eduard	1819-1853	Wasserfahrt "Auf des See's sanften Wellen"	Op. 14 No. 3	S/S	Klemm		CHAL (1898)
4678	Marschner, Heinrich August	1795-1861	Abend am Meer "O flieh, der Abendhimmel"	Op. 157 No. 1	S/A	Hofmeister		CHAL (1898)
4679	Marschner, Heinrich August	1795-1861	Im Herbst "Es rauschen die Winde'"	Op. 145 No. 2	S/S	Kistner		CHAL (1898)
4680	Marschner, Heinrich August	1795-1861	Kindesauge "O wie mir unergründlich"	Op. 157 No. 4	S/A	Hofmeister		CHAL (1898)
4681	Marschner, Heinrich August	1795-1861	O du lieber Schatz wir müssen scheiden	II No. 6	Unspec.	C. Rühle i. L.		CHAL (1901)
4682	Marschner, Heinrich August	1795-1861	Schalk "Läuten kaum die Maienglocken"	Op. 157 No. 3	S/A	Hofmeister		CHAL (1898)
4683	Marschner, Heinrich August	1795-1861	Tanzenden Mädchen "O Tanz, du Lieblicher"	Op. 145 No. 3	S/S	Kistner		CHAL (1898)
4684	Marschner, Heinrich August	1795-1861	Wenn kühl der Abend sinkt	Op. 145 No. 1	S/S	Kistner		CHAL (1898)
4685	Marschner, Heinrich August	1795-1861	Wiedersehn "O weine nicht, wenn aus"	Op. 157 No. 2	S/A	Hofmeister		CHAL (1898)
4686	Marti, E.		De notre beau pays l'Espagne		Unspec.	Schott		CHAL (1901)
4687	Martin, Easthope	1882-1925	Come to the Fair		2 med. v.	Boosey		ASR
4688	Martin, Easthope	1882-1925	Hatfield bells		Unspec.	Enoch		BBC (1975)
4689	Martin, Easthope	1882-1925	Holy Child		2 med. v.	Boosey		ASR
4690	Martin, Easthope	1882-1925	Who goes a-walking?		Unspec.	Enoch		BBC (1975)
4691	Martini, F. v.		Im schönen Mai "3 Tanzliedchen"		Unspec.	Hug	3 dance-duets	CHAL (1911)
4692	Martini, F. v.		Kommt, lasst uns tanzen	No. 1	Unspec.	Hug		CHAL (1911)

REC	COMP	DTS	TITLE	OP #	VCG	PUB	COMMENTS	SRC
4693	Martini, F. v.		Liebchen, der Lenz ist da	No. 2	Unspec.	Hug		CHAL (1911)
4694	Martini, F. v.		Mein Fried'l komm und tanz' mit mir	No. 3	Unspec.	Hug		CHAL (1911)
4695	Martini, Hugo	1857-	Seltnes Fest der Silber-(gold'nen) Hochzeit	Op. 87	S/A	André		CHAL (1906)
4696	Martini, Jean Paul Egide	1741-1816	Bergerette		Unspec.	Durand		CVMP (1976)
4697	Martini, Jean Paul Egide	1741-1816	Plaisie d'Amour		Unspec.	Allans	Eng. trans. Fr. Arr. for 2 v. In anthology "Vocal Duets Collection" Vol. 2. Pub. 1992.	MSN
4698	Martinu, Bohuslav	1890-1959	Petrklic		S/A	Panton	pf or inst accomp.	CVMP (1976)
4699	Martinu, Bohuslav	1890-1959	Petrklic		S/A	Artia	pf or inst accomp.	ASR
4700	Marvia, Einari	1915-	Kuoleman Tantu "Dodsfornimmelsen"	Op. 6 No. 1	Unspec.	Fazer		CVMP (1976)
4701	Marx, Adolf Bernard	1795?-1866	Rêverie au bord du lac "O nuit divine"		Unspec.	Schott		CHAL (1898)
4702	Marx, Adolf Bernard	1795?-1866	Zigeunerinnen "Zur Kirmes drunten bin ich"		S/A	Hof-meister		CHAL (1898)
4703	Marx, Joseph	1882-1964	Mehrstimmige Gesänge		var	Peters	Unspec. pieces. Solos & duets.	ASR
4704	Marx, Karl	1897-1985	Reifende Frucht	Op. 23	S/A	Baren		CVMP (1976)
4705	Marx, Karl	1897-1985	Reifende Frucht, Op. 23	Op. 23	S/A	Baren		ASR
4706	Marzials, Théodor	1850-	Eight Vocal Duets		Unspec.	Cramer	Collection. Unspec. pieces.	CVMP (1976)
4707	Marzials, Théodor	1850-	Friendship		S/A	Ditson		BBC (1975)
4708	Marzials, Théodor	1850-	Friendship		Unspec.	Cramer		CVMP (1976)
4709	Marzials, Théodor	1850-	Friendship		S/A	Ditson	Eng. trans. Grmn. In anthology "The Ditson Collection of Soprano and Alto Duets" Pub. 1934.	MSN
4710	Marzials, Théodor	1850-	Go pretty rose		Unspec.	Boosey		BBC (1975)
4711	Marzials, Théodor	1850-	Go, Pretty Rose		2 med. v.	G. Schirm.	Canon for 2 v. In catalogue page "Selected Vocal Duets" of G. Schirmer, Inc. NY (no date)	MSN
4712	Marzials, Théodor	1850-	Of You I Dream		Unspec.	Cramer		CVMP (1976)
4713	Marzials, Théodor	1850-	Sing Lullaby for the Year		Unspec.	Cramer		CVMP (1976)
4714	Marzials, Théodor	1850-	Such Merry Folk are We		Unspec.	Cramer		CVMP (1976)
4715	Mascheroni, Angelo	1855-1905	For all eternity		S/A	Leonard-Eng		BBC (1975)
4716	Mascheroni, Angelo	1856-1905	For All Eternity		Unspec.	Leonard-Eng	pf with opt. vln accomp. Also solo.	CVMP (1976)
4717	Masini, A. [prob. Angelo]	1845-1926	Neapel "Seht nun den Lenz erwaschen"		Unspec.	Schlesinger		CHAL (1898)
4718	Masini, Francesco	1804-1863	Au rivage, bon ménage		Unspec.	Schott		CHAL (1898)
4719	Masini, Francesco	1804-1863	Belles nuits d'été "Soleil a grandi"		Unspec.	Schott		CHAL (1898)

REC	COMP	DTS	TITLE	OP #	VCG	PUB	COMMENTS	SRC
4720	Masini, Francesco	1804-1863	Genfer See "Schiffen wir zwei"		Unspec.	Schott		CHAL (1898)
4721	Masini, Francesco	1804-1863	Land of the Swallows		Unspec.	Brainard's Sons	In anthology "Brainard's Collection of Vocal Duets from Popular Modern and Standard Composers" Pub. 1903.	MSN
4722	Masini, Francesco	1804-1863	Patrie des hirondelles "Hirondelles légères"		Unspec.	Schott		CHAL (1898)
4723	Masini, Francesco	1804-1863	The land of the swallows		Unspec.	Bayley & Ferguson	Arr. Moffat. Eng. trans. Grmn.	BBC (1975)
4724	Masini, Francesco	1804-1863	Un même soir		Unspec.	Schott		CHAL (1898)
4725	Masini, Francesco	1804-1863	Unter blühenden Mandelbäumen		Unspec.	Schott		CHAL (1898)
4726	Masini, Francesco	1804-1863	Wie kurz ist doch der Winter		Unspec.	Schott		CHAL (1898)
4727	Mason, Gerry		Say a little prayer		Unspec.	A. H. & C.	Arr. Noble	BBC (1975)
4728	Massenet, Jules	1842-1912	A la Zuecca		S/MS or S/A	Heugel		ASR
4729	Massenet, Jules	1842-1912	Aux Etoiles		2 equal v.	Heugel		ASR
4730	Massenet, Jules	1842-1912	Bois de pins "Ombre descend de leurs rameaux"	Op. 2 No. 2	Unspec.	Durand		CHAL (1898)
4731	Massenet, Jules	1842-1912	Bonne nuit "Terre dort au ciel pur"	Op. 2 No. 1	Unspec.	Durand		CHAL (1898)
4732	Massenet, Jules	1842-1912	Chansons des Bois d'Amaranthe		Unspec.	CVR	Collection for 1-4 v.	CVMP (1995)
4733	Massenet, Jules	1842-1912	Horace et Lydie		Unspec.	Heugel		BBC (1975)
4734	Massenet, Jules	1842-1912	Immortalité		Unspec.	Bardic	acap. Canon for 2 v.	CVMP (1995)
4735	Massenet, Jules	1842-1912	Joie		S/S	Durand		BBC (1975)
4736	Massenet, Jules	1842-1912	Joie		Unspec.	Durand	In "Trois Melodies, Deux Duos et un Trio"	CVMP (1976)
4737	Massenet, Jules	1842-1912	Joie "Un oiselet sautille et chante"	Op. 2 No. 5	S/S	Durand		CHAL (1898)
4738	Massenet, Jules	1842-1912	Le poète et le fantôme		2 med. v.	CVR	In catalogue "Classical Vocal Reprints Complete Catalog" Pub. 1997.	MSN
4739	Massenet, Jules	1842-1912	Marine		Unspec.	Durand	In "Trois Melodies, Deux Duos et un Trio"	CVMP (1976)
4740	Massenet, Jules	1842-1912	Marine "Viens la voile matine"	Op. 2 No. 4	Unspec.	Durand		CHAL (1898)
4741	Massenet, Jules	1842-1912	Poëme d'Amour		Unspec.	Bardic	acap. 6 pieces, includes 1 duet.	CVMP (1995)
4742	Massenet, Jules	1842-1912	Salut, printemps		2 equal v.	Heugel		ASR
4743	Massenet, Jules	1842-1912	Verger "Oh combien j'aime le verger"	Op. 2 No. 3	Unspec.	Durand		CHAL (1898)
4744	Massini		Land of swallows, The		S/A	White-Smith	In catalogue page "Vocal Duetts" of White-Smith Music Pub. Co. (no date)	MSN

REC	COMP	DTS	TITLE	OP #	VCG	PUB	COMMENTS	SRC
4745	Matthes, J.		Ständchen "Was wecken aus dem Schlummer mich"	No. 2	S/A	Annecke		CHAL (1898)
4746	Matthiae, E.		Frühlingsglaube "Linden Lüfte sind erwacht"	Op. 15	Unspec.	Hug		CHAL (1898)
4747	Matthias, W.		Gott was for'n Stuss "Wir sind beliebt in alle Welt"		Unspec.	Hoffheinz		CHAL (1898)
4748	Matthieux, Johanna	1810-1858	Aus meinen Thränen spriessen	Op. 11 No. 1	S/A	Bahn	Grmn. woman comp. Neé Mockel, divorced Matthieux, later married Kinkel.	CHAL (1898)
4749	Matthieux, Johanna	1810-1858	Fischerkinder "Hast du von den Fischerkindern"	Op. 12 No. 1	2 female v.	Bahn	Grmn. woman comp. Neé Mockel, divorced Matthieux, later married Kinkel.	CHAL (1898)
4750	Matthieux, Johanna	1810-1858	Frühling und Liebe "Im Rosenbusche die Liebe schlief"	No. 1	S/A	Annecke	Grmn. woman comp. Neé Mockel, divorced Matthieux, later married Kinkel.	CHAL (1898)
4751	Matthieux, Johanna	1810-1858	Mein Liebchen, wir sassen beisammen	Op. 11 No. 2	S/A	Bahn	Grmn woman comp. Neé Mockel, divorced Matthieux, later married Kinkel.	CHAL (1898)
4752	Matthieux, Johanna	1810-1858	Nachtgesang "O gieb vom weichen Pfühle"	Op. 12 No. 3	2 female v.	Bahn	Grmn. woman comp. Neé Mockel, divorced Matthieux, later married Kinkel.	CHAL (1898)
4753	Matthieux, Johanna	1810-1858	Seejungfern Gesang "Mond ist aufgegangen"	Op. 11 No. 3	S/A	Bahn	Grmn woman comp. Neé Mockel, divorced Matthieux, later married Kinkel.	CHAL (1898)
4754	Matthieux, Johanna	1810-1858	Sommerabend "Sommerabend schauet"	Op. 12 No. 2	2 female v.	Bahn	Grmn. woman comp. Neé Mockel, divorced Matthieux, later married Kinkel.	CHAL (1898)
4755	Mauri, J.		Porqué Iloras, Madre mia		Unspec.	Hofmeister		CHAL (1901)
4756	Mauri, J.		Todo Congo tiene fortuna		Unspec.	Hofmeister		CHAL (1901)
4757	Mauss, A.		Psalm "Wohl dem der den Herrn fürchtet"		S/A	Henkel		CHAL (1898)
4758	Maxfield, Henry W.		The auld Scotch sangs		Unspec.	Bayley & Ferguson	Scottish folk songs. Ed. Maxfield	BBC (1975)
4759	May, Siegfried	1880-	Heil dir, du junges Paar	Op. 19	Unspec. or choir	Schlesinger		CHAL (1911)
4760	Mayer, Joseph Anton	1855-1936	Sie und Er "Was schimmert so lieblich"	No. 1	Unspec.	Hofmeister		CHAL (1898)
4761	Mayer, Joseph Anton	1855-1936	Süssesten Gaben der Götter "Wie duften so süss"		Unspec.	Hofmeister		CHAL (1898)
4762	Mayer, Martin		Das Weihnachtsevangelium		S/A	Nagel	Ed. Koschinsky	BBC (1975)
4763	Mayer, William	1925-	Barbara, What Have you Done?		S/S	C. Fischer		ASR
4764	Mayerhoff, Fritz	1864-	Abend kommt so abend kühl	Op. 22 No. 3	high & med. v.	Kistner		CHAL (1906)
4765	Mayerhoff, Fritz	1864-	In einer sommerwarmen Herbstnacht	Op. 22 No. 1	high & med. v.	Kistner		CHAL (1906)

REC	COMP	DTS	TITLE	OP #	VCG	PUB	COMMENTS	SRC
4766	Mayerhoff, Fritz	1864-	Wenn die Sonne in ein andres Land hinüber träumt	Op. 22 No. 2	high & med. v.	Kistner		CHAL (1906)
4767	McEwen, John	1868-1948	To daffodils		Unspec.	Stainer & Bell		BBC (1975)
4768	Meienreis, R.		Kätzchen klein, Kätzchen fein		Unspec.	Oppen-heimer		CHAL (1911)
4769	Meier, K.		Das kann kein gutes Zeichen sein "Wenn heutzutage was passiert"		Unspec.	Fr. Dietrich		CHAL (1898)
4770	Meijroos, Heinrich Arnoldus [Meyroos]	1830-1900	Bächlein	Op. 16 No. 2	Unspec.	Weygand		CHAL (1898)
4771	Meijroos, Heinrich Arnoldus [Meyroos]	1830-1900	Kapelle	Op. 16 No. 1	Unspec.	Weygand		CHAL (1898)
4772	Meijroos, Heinrich Arnoldus [Meyroos]	1830-1900	Mond "In stillem heiter'm Glanz"	Op. 4 No. 3	Unspec.	Meijroos & K. i. Arnh.		CHAL (1898)
4773	Meijroos, Heinrich Arnoldus [Meyroos]	1830-1900	Morgenlied "Morgen erwacht"	Op. 4 No. 1	Unspec.	Meijroos & K. i. Arnh.		CHAL (1898)
4774	Meijroos, Heinrich Arnoldus [Meyroos]	1830-1900	Nähe des Herrn	Op. 16 No. 3	Unspec.	Weygand		CHAL (1898)
4775	Meijroos, Heinrich Arnoldus [Meyroos]	1830-1900	Zufriedenheit "Was frag ich viel nach Geld und Gut"	Op. 4 No. 2	Unspec.	Meijroos & K. i. Arnh.		CHAL (1898)
4776	Meinardus, Ludwig	1827-1896	Abendlied "Siehe, es will Abend werden"	Op. 15 II No. 1	Unspec.	B. & H.		CHAL (1898)
4777	Meinardus, Ludwig	1827-1896	Abendstern "Du lieblicher Stern"	Op. 39 No. 5	Unspec.	O. Forberg		CHAL (1898)
4778	Meinardus, Ludwig	1827-1896	Ein getreues Herze	Op. 15 No. I1	Unspec.	B. & H.		CHAL (1898)
4779	Meinardus, Ludwig	1827-1896	Es schimmert von der Zweigen	Op. 21 No. 1	Unspec.	vom Ende		CHAL (1898)
4780	Meinardus, Ludwig	1827-1896	Gute Nacht "Im tiefsten Innern"	Op. 21 No. 7	Unspec.	vom Ende		CHAL (1898)
4781	Meinardus, Ludwig	1827-1896	Kikriki "Kikriki weckt der Hahn"	Op. 39 No. 4	Unspec.	O. Forberg		CHAL (1898)
4782	Meinardus, Ludwig	1827-1896	Kleine Lieder für 2 Kinderstimmen (6)	Op. 39	Unspec.	O. Forberg	Collection of 6 brief duets for 2 children's v.	CHAL (1898)
4783	Meinardus, Ludwig	1827-1896	Lebe Wohl "Wann sich Seelen recht erkennen"	Op. 15 No. 4	S/A	B. & H.	In anth. "Zweistim. Lied. f. Sop. u. Alt-stimme mit Klavier-begleitung f. den Haus- u. Schulge-brauch v. H. M. Schletterer" 3 vols.	MSN
4784	Meinardus, Ludwig	1827-1896	Lebewohl "Lebewohl, lebewohl mein Lieb"	Op. 21 No. 3	Unspec.	vom Ende		CHAL (1898)

REC	COMP	DTS	TITLE	OP #	VCG	PUB	COMMENTS	SRC
4785	Meinardus, Ludwig	1827-1896	Lebewohl "Wann sich Seelen recht erkennen"	Op. 15 I No. 4	Unspec.	B. & H.		CHAL (1898)
4786	Meinardus, Ludwig	1827-1896	Liebe bleibt wie Rosen immer neu	Op. 21 No. 6	Unspec.	vom Ende		CHAL (1898)
4787	Meinardus, Ludwig	1827-1896	Nach Canaan "Wie so wunderlich und schmerz-lich"	Op. 15 II No. 2	Unspec.	B. & H.		CHAL (1898)
4788	Meinardus, Ludwig	1827-1896	Nach Canaan "Wie so wunderlich und schmerz-lich"	Op. 15 No. 2	S/A	B. & H.	In anth. "Zweistim. Lied. f. Sop. u. Altstimme mit Klavierbegleitung f. den Haus- u. Schulgebrauch v. H. M. Schletterer" 3 vols.	MSN
4789	Meinardus, Ludwig	1827-1896	Regenlied "Was ist das für ein Wetter heut"	Op. 39 No. 3	Unspec.	O. Forberg		CHAL (1898)
4790	Meinardus, Ludwig	1827-1896	Ringel, Ringel, Rosen-kranz "Lenz erwacht"	Op. 39 No. 6	Unspec.	O. Forberg		CHAL (1898)
4791	Meinardus, Ludwig	1827-1896	Scheiden und Meiden "So soll ich dich nun meiden"	Op. 29 No. 4	Unspec.	vom Ende		CHAL (1898)
4792	Meinardus, Ludwig	1827-1896	Singe holde Philomele	Op. 21 No. 2	Unspec.	vom Ende		CHAL (1898)
4793	Meinardus, Ludwig	1827-1896	Waldconcert "Concert ist heute angesagt"	Op. 39 No. 2	Unspec.	O. Forberg		CHAL (1898)
4794	Meinardus, Ludwig	1827-1896	Wärst du mein "So wie die liebe Sonne"	Op. 21 No. 5	Unspec.	vom Ende		CHAL (1898)
4795	Meinardus, Ludwig	1827-1896	Weil ich dich liebe	I No. 3	Unspec.	B. & H.		CHAL (1898)
4796	Meinardus, Ludwig	1827-1896	Welt ist gross und weit	Op. 15 I No. 2	Unspec.	B. & H.		CHAL (1898)
4797	Meinardus, Ludwig	1827-1896	Wenn Püppchen nicht schlafen will "Schlafe, mein Kindelein"	Op. 39 No. 1	Unspec.	O. Forberg		CHAL (1898)
4798	Meinhold, P.		Spiesezettel-Duett "Kleine Mädchen in Pension"		Unspec.	Thiemer		CHAL (1898)
4799	Meister, Casimir	1869-	Silbern erglänzt der Mond	Op. 50	T/B or S/A or MS/T	Foetisch		CHAL (1911)
4800	Melchert, J.		Abend thaut herneider	Op. 48 No. 2	S/A	Rühle i. Berl.		CHAL (1898)
4801	Melchert, J.		Es rauscht der Wald ein stolzes Lied	Op. 48 No. 1	S/A	Rühle i. Berl.		CHAL (1898)
4802	Melchert, J.		Flüsterndes Silber		S/A or S/Br	C. Fischer	In catalogue page "Se-lected Vocal Duets By Favorite Composers" of Carl Fischer NY (no date)	MSN
4803	Melchert, J.		Ich wollt', meine Liebe		S/A or S/B	C. Fischer	In catalogue page "Se-lected Vocal Duets By Favorite Composers" of Carl Fischer NY (no date)	MSN
4804	Melchert, J.		O säh' ich auf der Haide dort		S/A or S/B	C. Fischer	In catalogue page "Se-lected Vocal Duets By Favorite Composers" of Carl Fischer NY (no date)	MSN
4805	Mellish, Colonel (attr.)		Drink to me Only		Unspec.	Allans	In anthology "Vocal Duets Collection" Vol. 1. Pub. 1992.	MSN

REC	COMP	DTS	TITLE	OP #	VCG	PUB	COMMENTS	SRC
4806	Mello, Alfred	1872-1934	Wer seinen Gott und Herrn vertraut		S/A	Musik-Woche		CHAL (1906)
4807	Melvin, Ernest		Saint Paul on Ludgate Hill		Unspec.	Chappell		BBC (1975)
4808	Membrée, Edmond	1820-1882	Quitter la ville		S/A or T/Br	Heugel		CHAL (1898)
4809	Mendel, Hermann	1834-1876	Es schneit, es schneit		Unspec.	Kromp-holz		CHAL (1906)
4810	Mendelssohn, Felix	1809-1847	Abendlied		Unspec.	G. Schirm.	In anthology "Romantic Duets—Great Performers Edition" Compi. E. Lear & T. Stewart. Pub. 1985.	MSN
4811	Mendelssohn, Felix	1809-1847	Abendlied		Unspec.	ECS	In anthology "48 Duets Seventeenth Through Nineteenth Centuries" Ed. V. Prahl. Pub. 1941, 1970.	MSN
4812	Mendelssohn, Felix	1809-1847	Abendlied		Var.	Peters, et al.	In "Drie Volkslieder" but only the first two apply to female v. In collection "Duette" of F. Mendels-sohn-Bartholdy et al.	NATS-VCD
4813	Mendelssohn, Felix	1809-1847	Abendlied "Wenn ich auf dem Lager liege"		Unspec.	Schlesin-ger et al.		CHAL (1898)
4814	Mendelssohn, Felix	1809-1847	Abendlied "Wenn ich auf dem Lager liege"		Unspec.	Peters	In collection of "Men-delssohn Duette für zwei Singstimmen" Ed. M. Friedländer.	MSN
4815	Mendelssohn, Felix	1809-1847	Abschied der Zugvögel "Wie was so schön doch"	Op. 63 No. 2	Unspec.	Kistner et al.		CHAL (1898)
4816	Mendelssohn, Felix	1809-1847	Abschiedslied der Zugvögel		S/A	EMB	In anthology "Duettek nöi Hangokra Zongorakísér-ettel" Vol. II Compi. M. Forrai. Pub. 1959.	MSN
4817	Mendelssohn, Felix	1809-1847	Abschiedslied der Zugvögel "Wie war so schön"	Op. 63 No. 2	Unspec.	Peters	In collection of "Men-delssohn Duette für zwei Singstimmen" Ed. M. Friedländer.	MSN
4818	Mendelssohn, Felix	1809-1847	Abschiedslied der Zugvögel "Wie war so schön doch Wald und Feld"	Op. 63 No. 2	S/A	B. & H.	In anth. "Zweistim. Lied. f. Sop. u. Altstimme mit Klavierbegleitung f. den Haus- u. Schulgebrauch v. H. M. Schletterer" 3 vols.	MSN
4819	Mendelssohn, Felix	1809-1847	Adieu Gentilles Hirondelles		Unspec.	Enoch	Fr. trans. Grmn.	CVMP (1976)
4820	Mendelssohn, Felix	1809-1847	Aehrenfeld "Ein Leben war's im Aerenfeld"	Op. 77 No. 2	Unspec.	Kistner et al.		CHAL (1898)
4821	Mendelssohn, Felix	1809-1847	An des lustgen Brunnens Rand	IV No. 5	Unspec.	C. Rühle i. L.		CHAL (1901)
4822	Mendelssohn, Felix	1809-1847	Auf flügeln des gesanges		S/A	Ditson	Arr. H. Kiehl. In anth-ology "Soprano and Alto Duets" Ed. Heinrich Kiehl. Pub. 1901.	MSN
4823	Mendelssohn, Felix	1809-1847	Auf flügeln des gesanges		S/A	Ditson	Arr. H. Kiehl. In anth-ology "The Ditson Collection of Soprano and Alto Duets" Pub. 1934.	MSN
4824	Mendelssohn, Felix	1809-1847	Aus dem "Lobgesang"	Op. 52	S/S	Peters	In collection of "Mendelssohn Duette für zwei Singstimmen" Ed. M. Friedländer.	MSN

REC	COMP	DTS	TITLE	OP #	VCG	PUB	COMMENTS	SRC
4825	Mendelssohn, Felix	1809-1847	Aus Psalm 95	Op. 46	S/S	Peters	In collection of "Mendelssohn Duette für zwei Singstimmen" Ed. M. Friedländer.	MSN
4826	Mendelssohn, Felix	1809-1847	Barcarolle		Unspec.	Enoch	Fr. trans Grmn.	CVMP (1976)
4827	Mendelssohn, Felix	1809-1847	Comme ils ont fui		Unspec.	Enoch	Fr. trans Grmn.	CVMP (1976)
4828	Mendelssohn, Felix	1809-1847	Complete Songs, Vol. 1-4		Var.	Kalmus	Solos & duets.	ASR
4829	Mendelssohn, Felix	1809-1847	Das Aehrenfeld "Ein Leben war's im Aehrenfeld"	Op. 77 No. 2	S/A	B. & H.	In anth. "Zweistim. Lied. f. Sop. u. Altstimme mit Klavierbegleitung f. den Haus- u. Schulgebrauch v. H. M. Schletterer" 3 vols.	MSN
4830	Mendelssohn, Felix	1809-1847	Das Ährenfeld		S/A	EMB	In anthology "Duettek nöi Hangokra Zongorakísérettel" Vol. II Compi. M. Forrai. Pub. 1959.	MSN
4831	Mendelssohn, Felix	1809-1847	Das Ährenfeld	Op. 77 No. 2	Unspec.	Peters	In collection of "Mendelssohn Duette für zwei Singstimmen" Ed. M. Friedländer.	MSN
4832	Mendelssohn, Felix	1809-1847	Das ist der Tag des Herrn	I No. 9	Unspec.	C. Rühle i. L.		CHAL (1901)
4833	Mendelssohn, Felix	1809-1847	Denn in seine Hand ist	Op. 46 No. 3	Unspec.	B. & H.		CHAL (1898)
4834	Mendelssohn, Felix	1809-1847	Denn in seiner (Psalm 95)		2 high v.	Church	In anthology "Sacred Duets A Collection of Two-Part Songs by the Best Composers" Vol. 1. Compi. & ed. W. Shakespeare. Pub. 1907.	MSN
4835	Mendelssohn, Felix	1809-1847	Drei Lieder, Op. 77	Op. 77	Var.	Gregg	Solos & duets. Series 18 #130.	ASR
4836	Mendelssohn, Felix	1809-1847	Drei Lieder, Op. 77	Op. 77	S/S or MS/MS or S/MS	Peters, et al.	Three duets, but only the first two apply to female v. In collection "Duette" of F. Mendelssohn-Bartholdy.	NATS-VCD
4837	Mendelssohn, Felix	1809-1847	Drei Volkslieder		high & low v.	Gregg	Solos & duets. Series 18 #139.	ASR
4838	Mendelssohn, Felix	1809-1847	Drei Zweistimmige Lieder, Op. 77	Op. 77	Unspec.	Scien		CVMP (1995)
4839	Mendelssohn, Felix	1809-1847	Duette		Var.	Peters	Collection of works by F. Mendelssohn.	NATS-SVD
4840	Mendelssohn, Felix	1809-1847	Duodici Canti a due voci		Unspec.	Ricordi-Eng	Collection. It. texts.	CVMP (1976)
4841	Mendelssohn, Felix	1809-1847	Eighteen Duets		S/MS	Hansen-Den	Collection	CVMP (1976)
4842	Mendelssohn, Felix	1809-1847	Eighteen Duets		S/A	Hansen		ASR
4843	Mendelssohn, Felix	1809-1847	Fleurs de Mai		Unspec.	Enoch	Fr. trans Grmn.	CVMP (1976)
4844	Mendelssohn, Felix	1809-1847	Gruss		S/A	EMB	In anthology "Duettek nöi Hangokra Zongorakísérettel" Vol. II Compi. M. Forrai. Pub. 1959.	MSN
4845	Mendelssohn, Felix	1809-1847	Gruss	Op. 63 No. 3	S/A	Ditson	In anthology "Soprano and Alto Duets" Ed. H. Kiehl. Pub. 1901.	MSN

REC	COMP	DTS	TITLE	OP #	VCG	PUB	COMMENTS	SRC
4846	Mendelssohn, Felix	1809-1847	Gruss	Op. 63 No. 3	S/A	Ditson	In anthology "The Ditson Collection of Soprano and Alto Duets" Pub. 1934.	MSN
4847	Mendelssohn, Felix	1809-1847	Gruss "Wohin ich geh' und schaue"	Op. 63 No. 3	Unspec.	Kistner et al.		CHAL (1898)
4848	Mendelssohn, Felix	1809-1847	Gruß "Wohin ich geh' und schaue in Feld und Wald und Thal"	Op. 63 No. 3	Unspec.	Peters	In collection of "Mendelssohn Duette für zwei Singstimmen" Ed. M. Friedländer.	MSN
4849	Mendelssohn, Felix	1809-1847	Heilige Nacht "Heilige Nacht des Herrn"	Op. 77 No. 1	Unspec.	Zum-steeg		CHAL (1898)
4850	Mendelssohn, Felix	1809-1847	Herbstlied		S/A	EMB	In anthology "Duettek nöi Hangokra Zongorakísérettel" Vol. II Compi. M. Forrai. Pub. 1959.	MSN
4851	Mendelssohn, Felix	1809-1847	Herbstlied	Op. 63 No. 4	S/A or S/S	Ditson	In anthology "Soprano and Alto Duets" Ed. H. Kiehl. Pub. 1901.	MSN
4852	Mendelssohn, Felix	1809-1847	Herbstlied "Ach, wie so bald"	Op. 63 No. 4	S/A	B. & H.	In anth. "Zweistim. Lied. f. Sop. u. Altstimme mit Klavier-begleitung f. den Haus- u. Schulgebrauch v. H. M. Schletterer" 3 vols.	MSN
4853	Mendelssohn, Felix	1809-1847	Herbstlied "Ach, wie so bald verhallet"	Op. 63 No. 4	Unspec.	Peters	In collection of "Mendelssohn Duette für zwei Singstimmen" Ed. M. Friedländer.	MSN
4854	Mendelssohn, Felix	1809-1847	Herbstlied "Ach wie so bald verhal-let der Reigen"	Op. 63 No. 4	Unspec.	Kistner et al.		CHAL (1898)
4855	Mendelssohn, Felix	1809-1847	I Waited for the Lord		S/MS	G. Schirm.		ASR
4856	Mendelssohn, Felix	1809-1847	I waited for the Lord		S/A	CVR	In catalogue "Classical Vocal Reprints Complete Catalog" Pub. 1997.	MSN
4857	Mendelssohn, Felix	1809-1847	I Would That My Love		high & low v.	Hinds, Hayden & Eld-redge	Eng. trans. Grmn. In anthology "The Most Popular Vocal Duets" Ed. Dr. E. J. Biedermann. Pub. 1914.	MSN
4858	Mendelssohn, Felix	1809-1847	I would that my love		S/A	White-Smith	Eng. trans. Grmn. In catalogue page "Vocal Duetts" of White-Smith Music Pub. Co. (no date)	MSN
4859	Mendelssohn, Felix	1809-1847	Ich harrete des Hernn	Op. 52 No. 5	Unspec.	Schles-inger et al.		CHAL (1898)
4860	Mendelssohn, Felix	1809-1847	Ich harrete des Herrn		2 high v.	Church	In anthology "Sacred Duets A Collection of Two-Part Songs by the Best Composers" Vol. 1. Compi. & ed. W. Shakespeare. Pub. 1907.	MSN
4861	Mendelssohn, Felix	1809-1847	Ich harrete des Herrn		S/MS	G. Schirm.	In anthology "Album of Six-teen Sacred Duets" (no date)	MSN
4862	Mendelssohn, Felix	1809-1847	Ich harrete des Herrn	II No. 3	Unspec.	C. Rühle i. L.		CHAL (1901)
4863	Mendelssohn, Felix	1809-1847	Ich Harrete des Herrn	Op. 52 No. 5	S/MS	Ditson	In anthology "Choice Sacred Duets for All Voices" Pub. 1936.	MSN
4864	Mendelssohn, Felix	1809-1847	Ich harrete des Herrn	Op. 52 No. 5	S/S	Univ.-Biblio-thek		CHAL (1911)

REC	COMP	DTS	TITLE	OP #	VCG	PUB	COMMENTS	SRC
4865	Mendelssohn, Felix	1809-1847	Ich stand gelehnet an den Mast	III No. 6	Unspec.	C. Rühle i. L.		CHAL (1901)
4866	Mendelssohn, Felix	1809-1847	Ich wollt' mein Lieb' ergösse sich		S/A	EMB	In anthology "Duettek nöi Hangokra Zongorakísér-ettel" Vol. II Compi. M. Forrai. Pub. 1959.	MSN
4867	Mendelssohn, Felix	1809-1847	Ich wollt' mein Liebe ergösse sich	III No. 2	Unspec.	C. Rühle i. L.		CHAL (1901)
4868	Mendelssohn, Felix	1809-1847	Ich wollt' meine Lieb		S/A	G. Schirm.	In catalogue page "Selected Vocal Duets" of G. Schirmer, Inc. NY (no date)	MSN
4869	Mendelssohn, Felix	1809-1847	Ich wollt' meine Lieb' ergösse sich	Op. 63 No. 1	S/S	Kistner et al.		CHAL (1898)
4870	Mendelssohn, Felix	1809-1847	Ich wollt, meine Lieb ergösse sich	Op. 63 No. 1	S/S	Peters	In collection of "Mendels-sohn Duette für zwei Singstimmen" Ed. M. Friedländer.	MSN
4871	Mendelssohn, Felix	1809-1847	Ich wollt', meine Liebe ergösse sich	Op. 63 No. 1	Unspec.	Benja-min		CHAL (1911)
4872	Mendelssohn, Felix	1809-1847	King of Love my Shepherd Is, The		2 high v.	R. D. Row	org or pf acc. Eng. words to "Auf den flügeln" In anth. "Sacred Duet Master-pieces…" Vol. 3. ed. C. Fredrickson. Pub. 1961.	MSN
4873	Mendelssohn, Felix	1809-1847	L'Automne		Unspec.	Durand	Fr. trans. Grmn. In "Douze Duos"	CVMP (1976)
4874	Mendelssohn, Felix	1809-1847	Le Bal des Fleurs		Unspec.	Durand	Fr. trans. Grmn. In "Douze Duos"	CVMP (1976)
4875	Mendelssohn, Felix	1809-1847	Le Bal des Fleurs	Op. 63 No. 6	high & low v.	Durand	Fr. trans. Grmn. In Fr. & Grmn.	ASR
4876	Mendelssohn, Felix	1809-1847	Le retour		Unspec.	Chou-dens		BBC (1975)
4877	Mendelssohn, Felix	1809-1847	Les Bles		Unspec.	Durand	Fr. trans. Grmn. In "Douze Duos"	CVMP (1976)
4878	Mendelssohn, Felix	1809-1847	Les Oiseaux Voyageurs		Unspec.	Durand	Fr. trans. Grmn. In "Douze Duos"	CVMP (1976)
4879	Mendelssohn, Felix	1809-1847	Lied aus Ruy Blas	Op. 77 No. 3	Unspec.	Peters	In collection of "Mendels-sohn Duette für zwei Singstimmen" Ed. M. Friedländer.	MSN
4880	Mendelssohn, Felix	1809-1847	Lied aus Ruy Blas "Wo-zu der Vöglein Chöre"	Op. 77 No. 3	Unspec.	Kistner et al.		CHAL (1898)
4881	Mendelssohn, Felix	1809-1847	Madrigal		Unspec.	Enoch		CVMP (1976)
4882	Mendelssohn, Felix	1809-1847	Maiglöckchen läutet in dem Thal	IV No. 6	Unspec.	C. Rühle i. L.		CHAL (1901)
4883	Mendelssohn, Felix	1809-1847	Maiglöckchen und die Blümelein		S/A	EMB	In anthology "Duettek nöi Hangokra Zongorakísér-ettel" Vol. II Compi. M. Forrai. Pub. 1959.	MSN
4884	Mendelssohn, Felix	1809-1847	Maiglockchen und die Blümelein	Op. 63 No. 6	Unspec.	G. Schirm.	In anthology "Romantic Duets—Great Performers Edition" Compi. E. Lear & T. Stewart. Pub. 1985.	MSN
4885	Mendelssohn, Felix	1809-1847	Maiglöckchen und die Blümelein	Op. 63 No. 6	Unspec.	Peters	In collection of "Mendels-sohn Duette für zwei Singstimmen" Ed. M. Friedländer.	MSN
4886	Mendelssohn, Felix	1809-1847	Maiglöckchen und die Blümelein "Maiglöck-chen läutet in dem Thal"	Op. 63 No. 6	Unspec.	Kistner et al.		CHAL (1898)

REC	COMP	DTS	TITLE	OP #	VCG	PUB	COMMENTS	SRC
4887	Mendelssohn, Felix	1809-1847	Maiglöcken und die Blümelein "Maiglock-en läutet in dem Thal"	Op. 63 No. 6	S/A	B. & H.	In anth. "Zweistim. Lied. f. Sop. u. Altstimme mit Klavierbegleitung f. den Haus- u. Schulgebrauch v. H. M. Schletterer" 3 vols.	MSN
4888	Mendelssohn, Felix	1809-1847	My song shall be alway		2 high v.	Church	Eng. trans. Grmn. In anth. "Sacred Duets A Coll. of 2-Part Songs by the Best Comps." Vol. 1. Compi. & ed. W. Shakespeare. Pub. 1907.	MSN
4889	Mendelssohn, Felix	1809-1847	Nineteen Duets		Unspec.	Peters	Collection. Ed. Friedlander	CVMP (1976)
4890	Mendelssohn, Felix	1809-1847	Nineteen Duets		2 high v. or high & med. v.	Peters	Collection.	ASR
4891	Mendelssohn, Felix	1809-1847	O säh ich auf der Haide		S/MS or S/A	G. Schirm.	In catalogue page "Selected Vocal Duets" of G. Schirmer, Inc. NY (no date)	MSN
4892	Mendelssohn, Felix	1809-1847	O säh ich auf der Haide	Op. 63 No. 5	S/A	Ditson	In anthology "Soprano and Alto Duets" Ed. Heinrich Kiehl. 1901.	MSN
4893	Mendelssohn, Felix	1809-1847	O säh ich auf der Haide	Op. 63 No. 5	S/A	Ditson	In anthology "The Ditson Collection of Soprano and Alto Duets" 1934.	MSN
4894	Mendelssohn, Felix	1809-1847	O säh ich auf der Haide dort	I No. 8	Unspec.	C. Rühle i. L.		CHAL (1901)
4895	Mendelssohn, Felix	1809-1847	O säh' ich auf der Heide dort	Op. 63 No. 5	Unspec.	Benjamin		CHAL (1911)
4896	Mendelssohn, Felix	1809-1847	O, Wert Thou in the Cauld Blast		high & low v.	Hinds, Hayden & Eldredge	Eng. trans. Grmn. In anthology "The Most Popular Vocal Duets" Ed. Dr. E. J. Biedermann. Pub. 1914.	MSN
4897	Mendelssohn, Felix	1809-1847	O wie selig ist das Kind		2 high v.	Church	In anthology "Sacred Duets A Collection of Two-Part Songs by the Best Composers" Vol. 1. Compi. & ed. W. Shakespeare. Pub. 1907.	MSN
4898	Mendelssohn, Felix	1809-1847	O wie Selig ist das Kind		S/T or S/S	Peters	In collection "Duette" music of F. Mendelssohn-Bartholdy	NATS-SVD
4899	Mendelssohn, Felix	1809-1847	O wie selig ist das Kind (from Athalia)		Unspec.	Litolff, Peters, et al.		CHAL (1898)
4900	Mendelssohn, Felix	1809-1847	On Wings of Song		Unspec.	Allans	Eng. trans. Grmn. Arr. for 2 v. In anthology "Vocal Duets Collection" Vol. 2. Pub. 1992.	MSN
4901	Mendelssohn, Felix	1809-1847	Pres de Toi		Unspec.	Enoch	Fr. trans. Grmn.	CVMP (1976)
4902	Mendelssohn, Felix	1809-1847	Schäfers Sonntagslied "Das ist der Tag des Herrn"	Op. 77 No. 1	S/S	Kistner et al.		CHAL (1898)
4903	Mendelssohn, Felix	1809-1847	Sechs Lieder, Op. 63	Op. 63	S/S	Gregg	Series 18 #137	ASR
4904	Mendelssohn, Felix	1809-1847	Sechs Lieder, Op. 63	Op. 63	S/S or MS/MS or S/MS	Peters, et al.	Six duets. In collection "Duette" of F. Mendelssohn-Bartholdy et al.	NATS-VCD

REC	COMP	DTS	TITLE	OP #	VCG	PUB	COMMENTS	SRC
4905	Mendelssohn, Felix	1809-1847	Secret Place, The		2 high v.	R. D. Row	org/pf acc. Eng. trans. Grmn. In anth. "Sacred Duet Master-pieces..." Vol. 3. ed. C. Fredrickson. Pub. 1961.	MSN
4906	Mendelssohn, Felix	1809-1847	Sixteen Part-Songs		Unspec.	G. Schirm.	Collection.	ASR
4907	Mendelssohn, Felix	1809-1847	Sonntagsmorgen		high & low v.	Church	In anthology "Sacred Duets A Collection of Two-Part Songs by the Best Composers" Vol. 2. Compi. & ed. W. Shakespeare. Pub. 1907.	MSN
4908	Mendelssohn, Felix	1809-1847	Sonntagsmorgen	Op. 77 No. 1	Unspec.	Peters	In Collection of "Mendelssohn Duette für zwei Singstimmen" Ed. M. Friedländer.	MSN
4909	Mendelssohn, Felix	1809-1847	Sonntagsmorgen "Das ist der Tag des Herrn"	Op. 77 No. 1	S/A	B. & H.	In anth. "Zweistim. Lied. f. Sop. u. Altstimme mit Klavier-begleitung f. den Haus- u. Schulgebrauch v. H. M. Schletterer" 3 vols.	MSN
4910	Mendelssohn, Felix	1809-1847	Suleika und Hatem		Unspec.	Peters	Arr. Dörffel	BBC (1975)
4911	Mendelssohn, Felix	1809-1847	Suleika und Hatem "An des lust'gen Brunnens Rand"		Unspec.	Schlesin-ger et al.		CHAL (1898)
4912	Mendelssohn, Felix	1809-1847	Tulerunt Dominum meum		Unspec.	ECS	In anthology "48 Duets Sev-enteenth Through Nineteenth Centuries" Ed. V. Prahl. Pub. 1941, 1970.	MSN
4913	Mendelssohn, Felix	1809-1847	Tulerunt Dominum meum		S/S	G. Schirm.	org accomp. In Collection of "16 Two-Part Songs"	MSN
4914	Mendelssohn, Felix	1809-1847	Tulerunt Dominum meum	Op. 39	S/S	Peters	Arr. Dörffel	BBC (1975)
4915	Mendelssohn, Felix	1809-1847	Vogue, leger Zephir		Unspec.	Enoch	Fr. trans. Grmn.	CVMP (1976)
4916	Mendelssohn, Felix	1809-1847	Volkslied "O säh' ich auf der Haide dort"	Op. 63 No. 5	Unspec.	Kistner et al.		CHAL (1898)
4917	Mendelssohn, Felix	1809-1847	Volkslied "O säh ich auf der Heide dort"	Op. 63 No. 5	Unspec.	Peters	In collection of "Mendelssohn Duette für zwei Singstimmen" Ed. M. Friedländer.	MSN
4918	Mendelssohn, Felix	1809-1847	Wasserfahrt "Ich stand gelehnet and em Mast"		Unspec.	Schles-inger et al.		CHAL (1898)
4919	Mendelssohn, Felix	1809-1847	Wasserfahrt "Ich stand gelehret an den Mast"		Unspec.	Peters	In collection of "Mendelssohn Duette für zwei Singstimmen" Ed. M. Friedländer.	MSN
4920	Mendelssohn, Felix	1809-1847	Wie kann ich froh und lustig sein		Unspec.	Schlesin-ger et al.		CHAL (1898)
4921	Mendelssohn, Felix	1809-1847	Wie kann ich froh und lustig sein?		Unspec.	Peters	In collection of "Mendelssohn Duette für zwei Singstimmen" Ed. M. Friedländer.	MSN
4922	Mendelssohn, Felix	1809-1847	Wie kann ich froh und lustig sein?		Unspec.	G. Schirm.	In collection of "16 Two-Part Songs"	MSN
4923	Mendelssohn, Felix	1809-1847	Wie kann ich froh und lustig sein		S/S or MS/MS or S/MS	Peters, et al.	In "Drie Volkslieder" but only the first two apply to female v. In collection "Duette" of F. Mendelssohn-Bartholdy et al.	NATS-VCD

REC	COMP	DTS	TITLE	OP #	VCG	PUB	COMMENTS	SRC
4924	Mendelssohn, Felix	1809-1847	Wohin habt ihr ihn getragen		2 high v.	Church	In anthology "Sacred Duets A Collection of Two-Part Songs by the Best Composers" Vol. 1. Compi. & ed. W. Shakespeare. Pub. 1907.	MSN
4925	Mendelssohn, Felix	1809-1847	Wohin habt ihr ihn getragen	Op. 39 No. 3	S/S	Simrock et al.		CHAL (1898)
4926	Mendelssohn, Felix	1809-1847	Wohin ich geh' und schaue	IV No. 7	Unspec.	C. Rühle i. L.		CHAL (1901)
4927	Mendelssohn, Felix	1809-1847	Wohin ich geh' und schaue	Op. 63 No. 3	Unspec.	Benjamin		CHAL (1911)
4928	Mendelssohn, Felix	1809-1847	Zion strecht ihre Hände aus		Unspec.	Peters	Arr. Dörffel	BBC (1975)
4929	Menzel, J.		Wenn im Mai die Knospen springne		Unspec.	Glaser		CHAL (1906)
4930	Mercadante, Saverio	1895-1870	Che bella vita		S/A	Bahn		CHAL (1898)
4931	Mercier, Ch.		Ce que j'aime		Unspec.	Schott		CHAL (1898)
4932	Mercier, Ch.		Souvenir d'Italie		Unspec.	Junne		CHAL (1898)
4933	Merikanto, Oskar	1868-1924	Onnelliset		Unspec.	Fazer		CVMP (1976)
4934	Merker, R.		Zeiten sind jetzt wirklich schlecht	Op. 50	Unspec.	Gleissenberg		CHAL (1906)
4935	Mertens, H. de.		Ave Maria "Ave Maria gratia pleni"		Unspec.	Cranz	org accomp.	CHAL (1898)
4936	Messager, Andre	1853-1929	Le Credo de la Victoire		Unspec.	Enoch	Also solo	CVMP (1976)
4937	Messer, F.		Frische Fahrt "Laue Luft kommt blau geflossen"	Op. 3 No. 3	S/A	André		CHAL (1898)
4938	Messer, F.		Ich will meine Seele tauschen	Op. 3 No. 1	S/A	André		CHAL (1898)
4939	Messer, F.		Wenn Alles schläft in stiller Nacht	Op. 3 No. 2	S/A	André		CHAL (1898)
4940	Mestrozzi, Paul	d. 1928	O Jugendzeit du Inbegriff von Seligkeit		Unspec.	Blaha		CHAL (1906)
4941	Metcalf, John W.	1856-	Absent		Unspec.	Boosey		BBC (1975)
4942	Methfessel, Albert Gottlieb	1785-1869	Abendlied "Schlaft wohl, ihr Sonnenstrahlen"		S/A	B. & H.	In anth. "Zweistim. Lied. f. Sop. u. Altstimme mit Klavierbegleitung f. den Haus- u. Schulgebrauch v. H. M. Schletterer" 3 vols.	MSN
4943	Methfessel, Albert Gottlieb	1785-1869	Zweigesang "Im Fliederbusch ein Vöglein sass"	Op. 111 No. 3	S/S	Weinholtz		CHAL (1898)
4944	Methfessel, C.		Morgenlied "Werde heiter, mein Gemüthe"	Op. 101 No. 2	S/S	Cranz		CHAL (1898)
4945	Methfessel, Ernst	1811-1886	Abendstern "Du lieblicher Stern"	Op. 101 No. 5	S/S	Cranz		CHAL (1898)
4946	Methfessel, Ernst	1811-1886	Frühlingsliedchen "Frühling hat sich eingestellt"	Op. 101 No. 6	S/S	Cranz		CHAL (1898)
4947	Methfessel, Ernst	1811-1886	Jugendlust "20 Gesangsduettinen"	Op. 40	Unspec.	Cranz	Collection of 20 duets	CHAL (1898)
4948	Methfessel, Ernst	1811-1886	Kindheit "Schön, wie's Lied der Nachtigallen"	Op. 101 No. 1	S/S	Cranz		CHAL (1898)

REC	COMP	DTS	TITLE	OP #	VCG	PUB	COMMENTS	SRC
4949	Methfessel, Ernst	1811-1886	Schiffahrt "Über die hellen funkelnden Wellen"	Op. 101 No. 3	S/S	Cranz		CHAL (1898)
4950	Methfessel, Ernst	1811-1886	Vergissmeinnicht "Es blüht ein schönes Blümchen"	Op. 101 No. 4	S/S	Cranz		CHAL (1898)
4951	Meves, Wilhelm	1808-1871	Alpensängerlied "Auf den Bergen"	I No. 26	Unspec.	B. & H.		CHAL (1898)
4952	Meves, Wilhelm	1808-1871	An die Unschuld "O Unschuld"	I No. 6	Unspec.	B. & H.		CHAL (1898)
4953	Meves, Wilhelm	1808-1871	Auf dem grüner Rasen, wo die Veilchen blühn	I No. 22	Unspec.	B. & H.		CHAL (1898)
4954	Meves, Wilhelm	1808-1871	Barcarole "Wiege, Schifflein wiege"	II No. 16	Unspec.	B. & H.		CHAL (1898)
4955	Meves, Wilhelm	1808-1871	Der Vöglein Wiegenlied "Schlafet, schlafet ein"		S/A	B. & H.	In anth. "Zweistim. Lied. f. Sop. u. Altstimme mit Klavierbegleitung f. den Haus- u. Schulgebrauch v. H. M. Schletterer" 3 vols.	MSN
4956	Meves, Wilhelm	1808-1871	Freude im Mai "La, la, der Mai ist da"	II No. 10	Unspec.	B. & H.		CHAL (1898)
4957	Meves, Wilhelm	1808-1871	Frühling "Hört ihr's, das sind"	II No. 14	Unspec.	B. & H.		CHAL (1898)
4958	Meves, Wilhelm	1808-1871	Gebet "Gott deine Kinder treten"	No. 1	Unspec.	B. & H.		CHAL (1898)
4959	Meves, Wilhelm	1808-1871	Gegensätze "Eins, zwei drei"	No. 10	Unspec.	B. & H.		CHAL (1898)
4960	Meves, Wilhelm	1808-1871	Im Walde "Im Wald, im schönen"	II No. 18	Unspec.	B. & H.		CHAL (1898)
4961	Meves, Wilhelm	1808-1871	Jäger "Fahret hin, Grillem"	I No. 9	Unspec.	B. & H.		CHAL (1898)
4962	Meves, Wilhelm	1808-1871	Jägers Lust "Hei, das ist wahre"	I No. 32	Unspec.	B. & H.		CHAL (1898)
4963	Meves, Wilhelm	1808-1871	Jugendlieder (40) 1 u. 2 St.		Unspec.	B. & H.	For 1-2 voices	CHAL (1898)
4964	Meves, Wilhelm	1808-1871	Mailied "Da ist er, der liebliche"	I No. 12	Unspec.	B. & H.		CHAL (1898)
4965	Meves, Wilhelm	1808-1871	Morgen "Schon die trüben Schatten"	I No. 31	Unspec.	B. & H.		CHAL (1898)
4966	Meves, Wilhelm	1808-1871	Morgenlied "Ich bin vom süssen"	I No. 23	Unspec.	B. & H.		CHAL (1898)
4967	Meves, Wilhelm	1808-1871	Polka "Polka lasst uns singen"	II No. 3	Unspec.	B. & H.		CHAL (1898)
4968	Meves, Wilhelm	1808-1871	Röslein "Wohl ein einsam Röslein stand"	I No. 17	Unspec.	B. & H.		CHAL (1898)
4969	Meves, Wilhelm	1808-1871	Ruf am Morgen im Walde "Wacht auf, ihr Vöglein"	II No. 6	Unspec.	B. & H.		CHAL (1898)
4970	Meves, Wilhelm	1808-1871	Ruf am Morgen im Walde "Wacht auf, wacht auf, ihr Vögelien"		S/A	B. & H.	In anth. "Zweistim. Lied. f. Sop. u. Altstimme mit Klavierbegleitung f. den Haus- u. Schulgebrauch v. H. M. Schletterer" 3 vols.	MSN
4971	Meves, Wilhelm	1808-1871	Schuss "Es ist ein Stern gefallen"	I No. 13	Unspec.	B. & H.		CHAL (1898)
4972	Meves, Wilhelm	1808-1871	Vöglein im Frühling "Vöglein singen"	I No. 4	Unspec.	B. & H.		CHAL (1898)
4973	Meves, Wilhelm	1808-1871	Vögleins Wiegenlied "Schlafet ein"	II No. 1	Unspec.	B. & H.		CHAL (1898)
4974	Meves, Wilhelm	1808-1871	Wahre Freude "Stille sanfte Freude"	I No. 21	Unspec.	B. & H.		CHAL (1898)

REC	COMP	DTS	TITLE	OP #	VCG	PUB	COMMENTS	SRC
4975	Meves, Wilhelm	1808-1871	Winter ade, Scheiden thut weh	I No. 20	Unspec.	B. & H.		CHAL (1898)
4976	Meves, Wilhelm	1808-1871	Winter "Wie rauh, wie scharf"	I No. 15	Unspec.	B. & H.		CHAL (1898)
4977	Meves, Wilhelm	1808-1871	Winterlied "Juchhe willkommen"	I No.3	Unspec.	B. & H.		CHAL (1898)
4978	Meyer, Wilhelm	1845-1917	Abschied "Nun ade, Keinen kümmerts"	Op. 23	Unspec.	Michaël-is i. N.		CHAL (1898)
4979	Meyer, Wilhelm	1808-1871	Mutter, Mutter, liebe Mutter	Op. 43	Unspec.	Michaël-is i. N.		CHAL (1906)
4980	Meyer-Helmund, Erik	1861-1932	Dies und das "Wie traurig sind wir Mädchen d'rau"	No. 1	S/A	Bosworth		CHAL (1898)
4981	Meyer-Helmund, Erik	1861-1932	Was klappert im Hause so laut		S/A	Bosworth		CHAL (1898)
4982	Meyer-Stolzenau, Wilhelm	1868-	Aennchen von Tharau ist's, die mir gefällt	Op. 73 No. 2	Unspec.	Simrock		CHAL (1911)
4983	Meyer-Stolzenau, Wilhelm	1868-	Im schönsten Wiesengrunde	Op. 73 No. 3	Unspec.	Simrock		CHAL (1911)
4984	Meyerbeer, Giacomo	1791-1864	Appenzeller Kuhreigen "Sonn' will untergehen"		S/S	Schlesinger		CHAL (1898)
4985	Meyerbeer, Giacomo	1791-1864	Grossmutter "Herein mein Kind, es kommt ein Wetter"		S/A	Schlesinger		CHAL (1898)
4986	Meyerbeer, Giacomo	1791-1864	Le Ranz-des-vaches d'Appenzell		S/A or S/MS	Brandus	In collection "40 Mélodies à une et à plusieurs voix" Pub. 1849	NATS-VCD
4987	Meyerbeer, Giacomo	1791-1864	Mère Grand		S/A or S/MS	Brandus	In collection "40 Mélodies à une et à plusieurs voix" Pub. 1849	NATS-VCD
4988	Meysel, E.		Heute, da will ich meine Lieder "Duo-Scene"		Unspec	Gleissenberg		CHAL (1911)
4989	Michaelis, Ad. Alfred	1854-	Fröhlich soll mein Herz	Op. 31 No. 4	S/A	Hofmeister		CHAL (1898)
4990	Michaelis, Ad. Alfred	1854-	Stille Nacht, heilige Nacht	Op. 31 No. 2	S/A	Hofmeister	Arr. of song.	CHAL (1898)
4991	Michaelis, Ad. Alfred	1854-	Vom Himmel Hoch	Op. 31 No. 3	S/A	Hofmeister		CHAL (1898)
4992	Michaelis, Ad. Alfred	1854-	Weihnachtslied "Es ist ein' Ros' entsprungen"	Op. 31 No. 1	S/A	Hofmeister		CHAL (1898)
4993	Michaelis, Gustav	1828-1887	Das ist die Posse von Berlin "Wer um sich schaut mit klarem Blick"		Unspec.	Bahn		CHAL (1898)
4994	Michaelis, Gustav	1828-1887	Puppem-Duett "Betrachtet man die Menschengruppen"		Unspec.	K. & G.		CHAL (1898)
4995	Michielsen, A.		De Spin		S/A	Broekmans	Also solo	CVMP (1976)
4996	Migot, Georges	1891-	Cygne Blanc		S/MS	Leduc	pf or inst accomp. In "Trois Chansons de Margot"	CVMP (1976)
4997	Migot, Georges	1891-	Douceur		S/MS	Leduc	pf or inst accomp. In "Trois Chansons de Margot"	CVMP (1976)
4998	Migot, Georges	1891-	Nenni-da		S/MS	Leduc	pf or inst accomp. In "Trois Chansons de Margot"	CVMP (1976)
4999	Milhaud, Darius	1892-1974	Chanson du Capitaine		Unspec.	Salabert		CVMP (1985)

REC	COMP	DTS	TITLE	OP #	VCG	PUB	COMMENTS	SRC
5000	Mililotti, Leopoldo	1835-	Nacht "Wie ist der Abend heiter"		S/S or S/T	B. & B.		CHAL (1898)
5001	Millard, H.		Vieni al mio sen!		S/T or S/S	G. Schirm.	In catalogue page "Favorite French and Italian Vocal Duets" of G. Schirmer, Inc. NY (no date)	MSN
5002	Millard, Harrison	1829-1895	Pilot Brave		Unspec.	Cramer	Also solo	CVMP (1976)
5003	Millard, Harrison	1829-1895	Such Merry Maids are We		Unspec.	Cramer		CVMP (1976)
5004	Millard, Harrison	1829-1895	Trip, Trip, Trip		Unspec.	Cramer	Canon	CVMP (1976)
5005	Miller, Henry Colin		The bonnie banks of Loch Lomond		Unspec.	Kerr	Arr. of Scottish folksong	BBC (1975)
5006	Millöcker, Karl	1842-1899	Flüster-Duett "Nun kommen sie, mein Herr"		Unspec.	Cranz		CHAL (1898)
5007	Millöcker, Karl	1842-1899	G'stanz'ln "So a Weana, a echta"		Unspec.	Cranz		CHAL (1898)
5008	Millöcker, Karl	1842-1899	Ha es klopft, wer mag deas sein		Unspec.	Cranz		CHAL (1898)
5009	Millöcker, Karl	1842-1899	Müller und sein Kind "Es giebt in Wien noch unglückselge Leut"		Unspec.	Cranz		CHAL (1898)
5010	Millöcker, Karl	1842-1899	O, du himmelblauer See!		S/A or S/Br	C. Fischer	In catalogue page "Selected Vocal Duets By Favorite Composers" of Carl Fischer NY (no date)	MSN
5011	Millöcker, Karl	1842-1899	O du himmelblauer See "Zwischen Felsen die voll Schnee"		Unspec.	Cranz		CHAL (1898)
5012	Miltitz, Carl Borromäus von	1781-1841	Anime inamorate	No. 3	Unspec.	B. & H.		CHAL (1898)
5013	Miltitz, Carl Borromäus von	1781-1841	Bella pastorella sen và	No. 2	Unspec.	B. & H.		CHAL (1898)
5014	Miltitz, Carl Borromäus von	1781-1841	Voi che'l mio cor sapete	No. 1	Unspec.	B. & H.		CHAL (1898)
5015	Minkwitz, Bruno	1874-	Ein Geheimnis woll'n wir hier enthüllen		Unspec.	O. Dietrich		CHAL (1911)
5016	Minkwitz, Bruno	1874-	Fidele Bauern-Duette		Unspec.	O. Dietrich		CHAL (1911)
5017	Minkwitz, Bruno	1874-	Hab'ns im Leben schon Bauern g'sehn		Unspec.	O. Dietrich		CHAL (1911)
5018	Minkwitz, Bruno	1874-	Mir kemma heut' in Sunntagsg'wand		Unspec.	O. Dietrich		CHAL (1911)
5019	Mittmann, Paul	1868-1920	In meine Heimath kam ich wieder	Op. 27 No. b	Unspec.	Hoffmann i. Str.		CHAL (1901)
5020	Mittmann, Paul	1868-1920	Is der Frühling do	Op. 63 No. 4	Unspec.	Hoffmann i. Str.		CHAL (1901)
5021	Mittmann, Paul	1868-1920	Vom Berg herabgestiegen	Op. 119	2 female v.	Hoffmann i. Str.		CHAL (1901)
5022	Mjöen, J. A.		Wenn Zwei sich lieben von ganzem Herzen		MS/A or MS/Br	Schmid i. M.		CHAL (1898)
5023	Moffat, Alfred	1856-1950	bonnie Earl o' Moray, The		S/A	Bayley & Ferguson	Arr. of Eng. folksong	BBC (1975)
5024	Moffat, Alfred	1856-1950	Feeding time		Unspec.	Novello	Arr. of Eng. folksong	BBC (1975)

REC	COMP	DTS	TITLE	OP #	VCG	PUB	COMMENTS	SRC
5025	Moffat, Alfred	1856-1950	Fiddle and drum		Unspec.	Novello	Arr. of Eng. folksong	BBC (1975)
5026	Moffat, Alfred	1856-1950	keel row, The		S/A	Bayley & Ferguson	Arr. of Eng. folksong	BBC (1975)
5027	Moffat, Alfred	1856-1950	My love is like a red rose		Unspec.	Bayley & Ferguson	Arr. of Eng. folksong	BBC (1975)
5028	Moffat, Alfred	1856-1950	rownan tree, The		S/A	Bayley & Ferguson	Arr. of Eng. folksong	BBC (1975)
5029	Moffat, Alfred	1856-1950	Sweet babe, a golden cradle		S/A	Bayley & Ferguson	Arr. of Eng. folksong	BBC (1975)
5030	Moffat, Alfred	1856-1950	Sweet kitty clover		S/A	Augener	Arr. of Eng. folksong	BBC (1975)
5031	Moffat, Alfred	1856-1950	Turn ye to me		S/A	Bayley & Ferguson	Arr. of Eng. folksong	BBC (1975)
5032	Moffat, Alfred	1856-1950	Ye banks and braes		S/A	Bayley & Ferguson	Arr. of Eng. folksong	BBC (1975)
5033	Mögling, G. Fr.		Fürchtet euch nicht		S/A	Hey		CHAL (1911)
5034	Möhring, Ferdinand	1816-1887	Abschied "Da draussen auf jenem Berge"	Op. 68 No. 6	S/A	Oehmigke		CHAL (1898)
5035	Möhring, Ferdinand	1816-1887	Alte Heimath "In einem dunkeln Thal"	Op. 19 No. 5	Unspec.	André		CHAL (1898)
5036	Möhring, Ferdinand	1816-1887	Am Bodensee "Schwelle die Segel"	Op. 19 No. 4	Unspec.	André		CHAL (1898)
5037	Möhring, Ferdinand	1816-1887	Aus dem Alpenthal "Auf öder Alpe stand ich"	Op. 19 No. 1	Unspec.	André		CHAL (1898)
5038	Möhring, Ferdinand	1816-1887	Bitte "Weil auf mir du dunkles Auge"	Op. 68 No. 2	S/A	Oehmigke		CHAL (1898)
5039	Möhring, Ferdinand	1816-1887	Frohe Lieder willl ich singen	Op. 14 No. 4	S/A	Bahn		CHAL (1898)
5040	Möhring, Ferdinand	1816-1887	Frühlingslied "Gekommen ist der Mai"	Op. 14 No. 2	S/A	Bahn		CHAL (1898)
5041	Möhring, Ferdinand	1816-1887	Herz "Es schlägt so bang und warm"	Op. 68 No. 5	S/A	Oehmigke		CHAL (1898)
5042	Möhring, Ferdinand	1816-1887	Im Walde "Im Walde, da weht es so linde"	Op. 68 No. 3	S/A	Oehmigke		CHAL (1898)
5043	Möhring, Ferdinand	1816-1887	In der Fremde "Es steht ein Baum im Odenwald"	Op. 14 No. 1	S/A	Kahnt		CHAL (1898)
5044	Möhring, Ferdinand	1816-1887	Kindergebetlein "Lieber Heiland, mach' mich fromm"	Op. 68 No. 1	S/A	Oehmigke		CHAL (1898)
5045	Möhring, Ferdinand	1816-1887	Lebewohl "Lebewohl, lebewohl mein Lieb"	Op. 14 No. 3	S/A	Bahn		CHAL (1898)
5046	Möhring, Ferdinand	1816-1887	Schifferlied "Dort in den Weiden steht ein Haus"	Op. 68 No. 4	S/A	Oehmigke		CHAL (1898)
5047	Möhring, Ferdinand	1816-1887	Und wenn die Primel schneeweiss blickt	Op. 19 No. 2	Unspec.	André		CHAL (1898)
5048	Möhring, Ferdinand	1816-1887	Winter "Nun weht auf der Haide"	Op. 19 No. 3	Unspec.	André		CHAL (1898)
5049	Moir, Frank Lewis	1852-1902	Echoes		S/S	White-Smith	In catalogue page "Vocal Duetts" of White-Smith Music Pub. Co. (no date)	MSN
5050	Molbe, Heinrich	1835-1915	Offertorium		S/A	Röhrich	org accomp. Pen name of Heinrich Freiherr von Bach.	CHAL (1898)

REC	COMP	DTS	TITLE	OP #	VCG	PUB	COMMENTS	SRC
5051	Molbe, Heinrich	1835-1915	Vor den Fenstern lasst euch warnen	Op. 12	Unspec.	Röhrich	Pen name of Heinrich Freiherr von Bach	CHAL (1898)
5052	Molique, Wilhelm Bernhard	1802-1869	Die Jahreszeiten		2 high v.	Church	In anthology "Sacred Duets A Collection of Two-Part Songs by the Best Composers" Vol. 1. Compi. & ed. W. Shakespeare. Pub. 1907.	MSN
5053	Molique, Wilhelm Bernhard	1802-1869	Du bist, o Gott		2 high v.	Church	In anthology "Sacred Duets A Collection of Two-Part Songs by the Best Composers" Vol. 1. Compi. & ed. W. Shakespeare. Pub. 1907.	MSN
5054	Molique, Wilhelm Bernhard	1802-1869	Du bist, o Gott, des Lebens Licht	Op. 49 No. 1	Unspec.	Hofmeister		CHAL (1898)
5055	Molique, Wilhelm Bernhard	1802-1869	Gottes Vorsehung "Siehe die Lilien auf dem Felde"	Op. 49 No. 2	Unspec.	Hofmeister		CHAL (1898)
5056	Molique, Wilhelm Bernhard	1802-1869	It is of the Lord's great mercies		2 high v.	Church	Eng. trans. Grmn. In anth. "Sacred Duets A Coll. of 2-Part Songs by the Best Comps." Vol. 1. Compi. & ed. W. Shakespeare. Pub. 1907.	MSN
5057	Molique, Wilhelm Bernhard	1802-1869	Jahreszeiten "Wie freundlich ist der Herr"	Op. 49 No. 4	Unspec.	Hofmeister		CHAL (1898)
5058	Molique, Wilhelm Bernhard	1802-1869	Rose "Wie schön ist die Rose"	Op. 49 No. 5	Unspec.	Hofmeister		CHAL (1898)
5059	Molique, Wilhelm Bernhard	1802-1869	Seine Macht ist unerforschlich		2 high v.	Church	In anthology "Sacred Duets A Collection of Two-Part Songs by the Best Composers" Vol. 1. Compi. & ed. W. Shakespeare. Pub. 1907.	MSN
5060	Molique, Wilhelm Bernhard	1802-1869	Seine Macht ist unerforschlich	Op. 49 No. 6	Unspec.	Hofmeister		CHAL (1898)
5061	Molique, Wilhelm Bernhard	1802-1869	Weint, Kinder von Israel!		2 high v.	Church	In anthology "Sacred Duets A Collection of Two-Part Songs by the Best Composers" Vol. 1. Compi. & ed. W. Shakespeare. Pub. 1907.	MSN
5062	Molique, Wilhelm Bernhard	1802-1869	Weint Kinder von Israel	Op. 49 No. 3	Unspec.	Hofmeister		CHAL (1898)
5063	Molloy, James Lyman	1837-1909	Kerry Dance		Unspec.	Boosey	Also solo	CVMP (1976)
5064	Molloy, James Lyman	1837-1909	Love's Old Sweet Song		Unspec.	Boosey	Also solo	CVMP (1976)
5065	Molloy, James Lyman	1837-1909	Love's sweet old song		S/A	Boosey		BBC (1975)
5066	Monche, L.		An die Jungfrau "Ich sehe dich in tausend Bildern"	No. 2	Unspec.	Cranz		CHAL (1898)
5067	Monche, L.		Tristan und Isolde "Siehst mich an mit Lächeln"	No. 1	Unspec.	Cranz		CHAL (1898)

REC	COMP	DTS	TITLE	OP #	VCG	PUB	COMMENTS	SRC
5068	Moniuszko, Stanislaw	1819-1872	Cracoviak		Unspec.	Durand		BBC (1975)
5069	Moniuszko, Stanislaw	1819-1872	Cracoviak		2 med. v.	Durand		ASR
5070	Moniuszko, Stanislaw	1819-1872	Idylle		Unspec.	Durand		BBC (1975)
5071	Moniuszko, Stanislaw	1819-1872	La fête pascale		Unspec.	Durand		BBC (1975)
5072	Moniuszko, Stanislaw	1819-1872	La fuite		Unspec.	Durand		BBC (1975)
5073	Moolenaar, S. [prob. Frieso]	1881-	Alles still in süsser Ruh	Op. 11 No. 2	Unspec.	Wage-naar		CHAL (1911)
5074	Moolenaar, S. [prob. Frieso]	1881-	Wenn einst auf deinem Pfade	Op. 11 No. 1	Unspec.	Wage-naar		CHAL (1911)
5075	Moór, Emanuel	1863-1931	Als der Ruf der Trommel erklang	No. 3	S/A	Schmid i. M.		CHAL (1906)
5076	Moór, Emanuel	1863-1931	Oed' und leer, grau und schwer	No. 1	S/A	Schmid i. M.		CHAL (1906)
5077	Moór, Emanuel	1863-1931	Seliges Wiedersehn, Liebe, wie bist du so schön	No. 2	S/A	Schmid i. M.		CHAL (1906)
5078	Moore, Dorothy Rudd	1940-	Lullaby		S/A	ACA	Amer. woman comp.	CVMP (1995)
5079	Morgan, Robert Orlando	1865-	Flower fairies		S/A	Augener		BBC (1975)
5080	Moritz		Erster Streich "Mancher giebt sich viele Müh'"	Op. 7	Unspec.	Schles-inger		CHAL (1898)
5081	Moritz		Fünfter Streich "Wer im Dorfe oder Stadt"	Op. 11	Unspec.	Schles-inger		CHAL (1898)
5082	Moritz		Klapphorn "Zwei Knaben gingen durch das Korn"	Op. 9	Unspec.	Schles-inger		CHAL (1898)
5083	Moritz		Sechtster Streich "Max und Moritz wehe euch"	Op. 11	Unspec.	Schles-inger		CHAL (1898)
5084	Moritz		Zweiter Streich "Jedermann im Dorfe kannte"	Op. 7 No. 2	Unspec.	Schles-inger		CHAL (1898)
5085	Moritz, Franz	1872-	Weihnachtsglocken hör' ich klingen		Unspec.	Schir-mer i. L.		CHAL (1911)
5086	Moroni, L.		E dolce l'alito d'anvetta estiva		S/S	Ricordi		CHAL (1898)
5087	Morris, C. H.		Stranger of Galilee, The		S/A	Boston	Also solo	CVMP (1976)
5088	Morse, Th. F.		Meine Lotte schaut mich nicht mehr an		Unspec.	Benja-min		CHAL (1911)
5089	Mortari, Virgilio	1902-	Stabat Mater		2 female v.	Carisch		CVMP (1985)
5090	Moscheles, Ignaz	1794-1870	Am Bach "Kleiner Bach nimm diese Rosen"	Op. 132 No. 2	S/A	Kistner		CHAL (1898)
5091	Moscheles, Ignaz	1794-1870	Lilienmädchens Wiegen-lied "Schlafe Kindlein"	Op. 132 No. 1	S/A	Kistner	Pub. after 1850	CHAL (1898)
5092	Moscheles, Ignaz	1794-1870	Unter den Bäumen "Lenz hat wieder sein grünes Zelt"	Op. 132 No. 4	S/A	Kistner	Pub. after 1850	CHAL (1898)
5093	Moscheles, Ignaz	1794-1870	Winter und Frühling "Dein Herz ist wie der weisse Schnee"	Op. 132 No. 3	S/A	Kistner	Pub. after 1850	CHAL (1898)
5094	Mosenthal, Joseph	1834-1896	I will magnify Thee, O God		S/S	G. Schirm.	In anthology "Album of Sixteen Sacred Duets" (no date)	MSN

REC	COMP	DTS	TITLE	OP #	VCG	PUB	COMMENTS	SRC
5095	Mosenthal, Joseph	1834-1896	I Will Magnify Thee, O God		S/S or S/T	G. Schirm.	Also in anthology "Album of Sixteen Sacred Duets for Various Voices" (Schirmer) Pub. 1880.	NATS-SVD
5096	Mücke, Franz	1819-1863	Gott grüsse dich, kein andrer Gruss		Unspec.	Chal.		CHAL (1898)
5097	Mücke, Franz	1819-1863	Gott grüsse dich, kein andrer Gruss		Unspec.	Walter Schröder	Arr. Rich. Thiele	CHAL (1906)
5098	Mühling, August	1786-1847	Hoffnung "Sonne sinkt der Abend blinkt"	Op. 32 No. 9	S/S	Klemm		CHAL (1898)
5099	Mühling, August	1786-1847	Sommernacht "Heiter an des Himmels Bogen"	Op. 32 No. 1	S/A or T/B	Klemm		CHAL (1898)
5100	Mulder-Fabri, Rich.		Grosses Walzer-Duo "Welch ein Glück"	Op. 48	Unspec.	André		CHAL (1898)
5101	Müller, Donat	1804-	Jugendlieder aud Chr. Schmidt's Blüthen f. 1 od. 2 Singst. m. Org. od Pfte. od. V.		Unspec.	Böhm i. A.	Collection, org or pf (or vln) accomp.	CHAL (1898)
5102	Müller, Franz	1806-1876	Wir suchen in der Kindheit Träumen	Op. 84	S/A or S/S	Hofmeister		CHAL (1898)
5103	Müller, Heinrich Fidelis	1827-1905	Volksthümliche Kinderlieder (30)	Op. 23	Unspec.	Maier i. Fulda	Collection, 30 songs for 1 or 2 v.	CHAL (1901)
5104	Müller, J. [prob. Johann]	d. 1924	Seg'ns, so hat's der Weana gern "A jedes echte Weana Kind"	Op. 22	Unspec.	Robitschek		CHAL (1898)
5105	Müller, L. S.		Gekommen ist der Maie		S/A	Schott		CHAL (1906)
5106	Müller, M.		Christkindchen "Christkindchen kommt vom Himmel geflogen"		Unspec.	Giessel jun.		CHAL (1901)
5107	Müller, Richard	1830-1904	Kaferlied "Es war'n einmal drei Käferknab'n"		2 female v.	Kahnt		CHAL (1898)
5108	Müller, Sr., Adolf	1801-1886	Frau Hinze und Frau Kuntze "Frau Nachbar, haben sie gelesen"	Op. 6	MS/MS	O. Forberg		CHAL (1898)
5109	Müller, Sr., Adolf	1801-1886	Nanny und Fanny "Was ich oft im Traume sah"	Op. 7	S/A	O. Forberg		CHAL (1898)
5110	Müller, Sr., Adolf	1801-1886	Vertrau dem Herrn "Haben böse Mächte"		S/A	Heinr.		CHAL (1898)
5111	Müller, Sr., Adolf	1801-1886	Waldkappele "Am Waldessaum im grünen Raum"	Op. 93	S/S	Cranz		CHAL (1898)
5112	Müller, Sr., Adolf	1801-1886	Wenn Frauen auseinandergeh'n, dann bleiben sie noch lange stehn "Ach liebe Schmidt"	Op. 4	MS/MS	O. Forberg		CHAL (1898)
5113	Müller-Hartman, Robert	1884-1950	Where love is		S/A	Hinrichsen		BBC (1975)
5114	Munkelt, F.		Allerfeinsten Gigerln "Wir sind bekannt fast"		Unspec.	O. Dietrich		CHAL (1898)
5115	Munkelt, T.		Ach du lieber guter Bruder "Wenn ich mal sehe"		Unspec.	O. Teich		CHAL (1898)
5116	Munkelt, T.		Beiden Schnapsbrüder "Hum. Duoscene"		Unspec.	O. Dietrich		CHAL (1901)
5117	Munkelt, T.		Fidelen Reservisten "Heut' uns're zwei Jahre"		Unspec.	O. Dietrich		CHAL (1898)
5118	Munkelt, T.		Mann und Frau "Hum. Duoscene"		Unspec.	O. Dietrich		CHAL (1901)

REC	COMP	DTS	TITLE	OP #	VCG	PUB	COMMENTS	SRC
5119	Munkelt, T.		Schorschels erste Schiess-übung "Hum. Duoscene"		Unspec.	O. Dietrich		CHAL (1901)
5120	Munkelt, T.		Wenn Lieb' erfühllt das Menschherz "Es sehnt der Mensch auf dieser Welt"		Unspec.	O. Dietrich		CHAL (1898)
5121	Münz, C.		Beiden Schacherer "Als wir auf die Welt gekommen"		Unspec.	Eulenberg		CHAL (1898)
5122	Músiol, Robert Paul Johann	1846-1903	Über's Jahr mein Schatz, über's Jahr	IV No. 8	Unspec.	C. Rühle i. L.	Arr. Necke	CHAL (1901)
5123	Myrberg, August Melcher	1825-1917	Aftonklockan		Unspec.	Lundq.		CVMP (1976)
5124	Myrberg, August Melcher	1825-1917	Aftonstamning		Unspec.	Lundq.		CVMP (1976)
5125	Myrberg, August Melcher	1825-1917	Aftonstjarnan		Unspec.	Lundq.		CVMP (1976)
5126	Myrberg, August Melcher	1825-1917	Fagelsang		Unspec.	Lundq.		CVMP (1976)
5127	Myrberg, August Melcher	1825-1917	Fem Sanger For Tvenne Roster		Unspec.	Lundq.		CVMP (1976)
5128	Myrberg, August Melcher	1825-1917	Fjarran Toner		Unspec.	Lundq.		CVMP (1976)
5129	Myrberg, August Melcher	1825-1917	Hostvisa		Unspec.	Lundq.		CVMP (1976)
5130	Myrberg, August Melcher	1825-1917	Nar Jag Fran Dig Far		Unspec.	Lundq.		CVMP (1976)
5131	Myrberg, August Melcher	1825-1917	Pa Lagunen		Unspec.	Lundq.		CVMP (1976)
5132	Myrberg, August Melcher	1825-1917	Vad Viskade Du?		Unspec.	Lundq.		CVMP (1976)
5133	Myrberg, August Melcher	1825-1917	Vinden Somnat I Den Stilla Kvall		Unspec.	Lundq.		CVMP (1976)
5134	Nagiller, Matthäus	1815-1874	Sänger und die Hirten "Du pflückest so schöne Blumen"	Op. 3	Unspec.	Gross i. Insbr.		CHAL (1898)
5135	Nagler, Franziskus	1873-	Bleibe bei uns Herr, denn es will Abend werden	Op. 58 No. 4	Unspec.	Kistner	org	CHAL (1911)
5136	Nagler, Franziskus	1873-	Hirten Wiegenlied "Schlafe, o schlafe lieb Christkindlein"	No. 5	Unspec.	Klemm		CHAL (1898)
5137	Nápravník, Eduard	1839-1916	Abendroth zieht müde Kreise	Op. 70 No. 2	high & low v.	Jurgns.		CHAL (1901)
5138	Nápravník, Eduard	1839-1916	Hoffnungswalzer lockt und klingt	Op. 70 No. 4	high & low v.	Jurgns.		CHAL (1901)
5139	Nápravník, Eduard	1839-1916	Vater unser höre, den Ruf	Op. 70 No. 1	high &low v.	Jurgns.		CHAL (1901)
5140	Nater, Johann	1826-1906	Daheim, o süsses trautes Wort	No. 4	Unspec.	Hug		CHAL (1906)
5141	Nater, Johann	1826-1906	Es wurde grosse Stille	No. 5	Unspec.	Hug		CHAL (1906)
5142	Nater, Johann	1826-1906	Im Namen Gottes lege ich zur Ruhe	No. 2	Unspec.	Hug		CHAL (1906)
5143	Nater, Johann	1826-1906	Im Namen Gottes steh' ich auf	No. 1	Unspec.	Hug		CHAL (1906)
5144	Nater, Johann	1826-1906	Lieber Nicolaus, komm' in unser Haus	No. 6	Unspec.	Hug		CHAL (1906)
5145	Nater, Johann	1826-1906	Schliess die Aeuglein zu	No. 3	Unspec.	Hug		CHAL (1906)
5146	Nater, Johann	1826-1906	Was der Jugend frommt (6)		Unspec.	Hug	Collection of 6 duets	CHAL (1906)
5147	Naubert, Friedrich August	1839-1897	Auswanderer "Winter ist kommen"	Op. 27 No. 2	Unspec.	R. & E.		CHAL (1898)
5148	Naubert, Friedrich August	1839-1897	Dudeldumdel, nun haben wir den Mai	Op. 33 No. 1	Unspec.	R. & E.		CHAL (1898)

REC	COMP	DTS	TITLE	OP #	VCG	PUB	COMMENTS	SRC
5149	Naubert, Friedrich August	1839-1897	Erste Schneeglöckchen "Wir sind die kleinen Glöckchen"	Op. 33 No. 3	Unspec.	R. & E.		CHAL (1898)
5150	Naubert, Friedrich August	1839-1897	Frühlingsruf "Ein Vogel, ein Vogel, o hört"	Op. 42 No. 1	S/A	Schlesinger		CHAL (1898)
5151	Naubert, Friedrich August	1839-1897	Im Lenze "Hinaus zum grünen Walde"	Op. 42 No. 2	S/A	Schlesinger		CHAL (1898)
5152	Naubert, Friedrich August	1839-1897	Mausekätzchen "Mauskätzchen, wo bleibst du"	Op. 27 No. 6	Unspec.	R. & E.		CHAL (1898)
5153	Naubert, Friedrich August	1839-1897	Miez ist krank	Op. 27 No. 4	Unspec.	R. & E.		CHAL (1898)
5154	Naubert, Friedrich August	1839-1897	Nach dem Spaziergange "Mein Reh mit flinken Füssen"	Op. 27 No. 3	Unspec.	R. & E.		CHAL (1898)
5155	Naubert, Friedrich August	1839-1897	Puppe "O allerschönste Puppe mein"	Op. 27 No. 5	Unspec.	R. & E.		CHAL (1898)
5156	Naubert, Friedrich August	1839-1897	Putthühnchen, wo hast du deinen Mann	Op. 33 No. 5	Unspec.	R. & E.		CHAL (1898)
5157	Naubert, Friedrich August	1839-1897	Schneckenliedchen "Schneck, Schneck, Mäuschen"	Op. 33 No. 6	Unspec.	R. & E.		CHAL (1898)
5158	Naubert, Friedrich August	1839-1897	Strampelchen "Still, wie still, 's ist Mitternacht"	Op. 33 No. 4	Unspec.	R. & E.		CHAL (1898)
5159	Naubert, Friedrich August	1839-1897	Vögleins Frage "Bist du da, ja ja"	Op. 27 No. 1	Unspec.	R. & E.		CHAL (1898)
5160	Naubert, Friedrich August	1839-1897	Zeisleins Traum "Es war ein niedlich Zeiselein"	Op. 33 No. 2	Unspec.	R. & E.		CHAL (1898)
5161	Nauwerk, E.		Himmelsthräne "Himmel hat ein Thräne geweint"	Op. 3 No. 1	S/A	Chal.		CHAL (1898)
5162	Nauwerk, E.		Ständchen "Morgens als Lerche möcht' ich"	Op. 3 No. 2	S/A	Chal.		CHAL (1898)
5163	Nauwerk, E.		Wanderers Nachtlied "Der der von dem Himmel bist"	Op. 15 No. 2	Unspec.	Chal.		CHAL (1898)
5164	Nauwerk, E.		Wär' ich. Geliebte, der Blumen Wonne	Op. 15 No. 1	Unspec.	Chal.		CHAL (1898)
5165	Nauwerk, E.		Wiegenlied "Aeren nur noch nicken"	Op. 15 No. 3	Unspec.	Chal.		CHAL (1898)
5166	Necke, Hermann	1850-1912	Ein Vöglein sang im Lindenbaum	I No. 5	Unspec.	C. Rühle i. L.		CHAL (1901)
5167	Neckheim, H.		Beim Bachlein steaht a Hütt'n	No. 2	S/A	Leon. sen.		CHAL (1898)
5168	Neckheim, H.		Mei Dierndle is jung und schean	No. 5	S/A	Leon sen.		CHAL (1898)
5169	Neckheim, H.		Mei Schatz hat zwa Aeuglan	No. 4	S/A	Leon sen.		CHAL (1898)
5170	Neckheim, H.		Sun geaht schon niedar	No. 1	S/A	Leon sen.		CHAL (1898)
5171	Neckheim, H.		Won s'Glöggle hell klingt	No. 3	S/A	Leon sen.		CHAL (1898)
5172	Neibig, G.		Nette Ehen "Ehe schliesst so manches Paar"	Op. 91	Unspec.	Haushahn i. L.		CHAL (1898)
5173	Neidhardt, August	1867-	Zwa von Nummero vier "I und du von Numme vier"	Op. 34	Unspec.	Blaha		CHAL (1898)
5174	Neidlinger, William Harold	1863-1924	Birthday of a King, The		S/A	G. Schirm.	Christmas piece	CVMP (1976)
5175	Neidlinger, William Harold	1863-1924	Birthday of a King, The		S/A	G. Schirm.	In anthology "Schirmer's Favorite Sacred Duets for Various Voices" Pub. 1955.	MSN

REC	COMP	DTS	TITLE	OP #	VCG	PUB	COMMENTS	SRC
5176	Neidlinger, William Harold	1863-1924	O Love divine Thy peace, O Lord		S/A or S/Br	G. Schirm.	pf or org accomp. In catalogue page "Sacred Vocal Duets" of G. Schirmer, Inc. NY (no date)	MSN
5177	Nekes, Franz	1844-1914	Missa in honorem St. Aloysii Gorzagae	Op. 21	Unspec.	Coppen-rath		CHAL (1898)
5178	Nelson, Rudolph	1878-	Kommt die Sommernacht		Unspec.	Fritz Bartels		CHAL (1911)
5179	Nelson, Rudolph	1878-	Mädel, braun wie Schokolade		Unspec.	Harmonie i. B.		CHAL (1911)
5180	Nemours, A.		Comtesse und Marquis "Comtess'chen ich bitt'"	Op. 10	Unspec.	Eisoldt & R. Schles.		CHAL (1906)
5181	Nesmüller, F.		Polka-Tanz-Duett "Ja das Leben gleicht dem Tanze"		Unspec.	Hof-meister		CHAL (1898)
5182	Nessler, Victor E.	1841-1890	Blume Tod "Lieb' Blüm-lein du blickst so fromm"	Op. 68 No. 1	Unspec.	R. Forberg		CHAL (1898)
5183	Nessler, Victor E.	1841-1890	Gebrochene Herz "Ich sah mal a Blümle"	Op. 68 No. 2	Unspec.	R. Forberg		CHAL (1898)
5184	Nessler, Victor E.	1841-1890	Ich hör' ein Vöglein locken	Op. 58 No. 3	Unspec.	Siegel		CHAL (1898)
5185	Nessler, Victor E.	1841-1890	Mitgefühl "Ein Vogel auf dem Baume"	Op. 68 No. 3	Unspec.	R. Forberg		CHAL (1898)
5186	Nessler, Victor E.	1841-1890	Nachtigall und Sänger "Nachtigall singt in den Wald hinein"	Op. 58 No. 2	Unspec.	Siegel		CHAL (1898)
5187	Nessler, Victor E.	1841-1890	Waldlied "Wenn ich geh' im grünen Walde"	Op. 58 No. 1	Unspec.	Siegel		CHAL (1898)
5188	Nessler, Victor E.	1841-1890	Wandertreue "Wenn Schneeglöckchen läuten"	Op. 58 No. 4	Unspec.	Siegel		CHAL (1898)
5189	Netzer, Joseph	1808-1864	Ringlein "Auf der Liebsten fünften Finger"	Op. 26	S/A or T/Br	Peters		CHAL (1898)
5190	Neubner, Ottomar	1843-1913	Geheimniss "Heckenrös-lein über Nacht"	Op. 26	MS/A	Tonger		CHAL (1898)
5191	Neugebauer, J.		Maien-Briefe "Frohe Bot-schaft ist uns kommen"	Op. 54 No. 1	2 female v.	R. & E.		CHAL (1898)
5192	Neugebauer, J.		Trotzige "Nun sag' uns doch Liesel"	Op. 52	Unspec.	R. & E.		CHAL (1898)
5193	Neugebauer, J.		Volkslied "In der Früh' im Morgenroth"	Op. 54 No. 2	2 female v.	R. & E.		CHAL (1898)
5194	Neukomm, Sigismund	1778-1858	An mein Schifflein "Frag mich Schifflein leise"		S/A	Junne, Schott		CHAL (1898)
5195	Neukomm, Sigismund	1778-1858	Es zieht herauf	II No. 9	S/S	Kistner		CHAL (1898)
5196	Neukomm, Sigismund	1778-1858	Freundschaft "Freundschaft ist"	II No. 12	S/S	Kistner		CHAL (1898)
5197	Neukomm, Sigismund	1778-1858	Gebet "Du, den ich tief"	I No. 2	S/S	Kistner		CHAL (1898)
5198	Neukomm, Sigismund	1778-1858	Glaube, Hoffnung, Liebe "Einst wird der Glaub'"	I No. 5	S/S	Kistner		CHAL (1898)
5199	Neukomm, Sigismund	1778-1858	Herbstlied "Feldenwärts flog ein Vögelein"	I No. 1	S/S	Kistner		CHAL (1898)
5200	Neukomm, Sigismund	1778-1858	Mit dem Bäumen spielt der Wind	II No. 8	S/S	Kistner		CHAL (1898)
5201	Neukomm, Sigismund	1778-1858	Rastlose Liebe "Schnee, dem Regen"	I No. 3	S/S	Kistner		CHAL (1898)
5202	Neukomm, Sigismund	1778-1858	Soldatenbraut "Ach wenn's nur der König"	II No. 11	S/S	Kistner		CHAL (1898)
5203	Neukomm, Sigismund	1778-1858	Ständchen "In dem Himmel ruht die Erde"	II No. 10	S/S	Kistner		CHAL (1898)

REC	COMP	DTS	TITLE	OP #	VCG	PUB	COMMENTS	SRC
5204	Neukomm, Sigismund	1778-1858	Was ist das für ein Ahnen	II No. 7	S/S	Kistner		CHAL (1898)
5205	Neukomm, Sigismund	1778-1858	Wiegenlied "Am dunkeln Himmel"	I No. 6	S/S	Kistner		CHAL (1898)
5206	Neukomm, Sigismund	1778-1858	Zweigesang "Im Flieder-busch ein Vöglein sass"	I No. 4	S/S	Kistner		CHAL (1898)
5207	Neuland, W.		Schöpfer lasst uns danken		MS/A	Braun-Peretti		CHAL (1898)
5208	Neumann, Emil	1836-1922	A Bisserl Lieb' und a Bisserl Treu' "Was man auch betrachten möge"		Unspec.	Neumann i. Berl.		CHAL (1898)
5209	Neumann, Emil	1836-1922	Aber wie, aber wo, aber was, aber wann "Clavier hört spielen man"		Unspec.	Neumann i. Berl.		CHAL (1898)
5210	Neumann, Emil	1836-1922	Ach du lieber guter Bruder "Ein Herr jüngst auf 'nem Esel ritt"		Unspec.	Neumann i. Berl		CHAL (1898)
5211	Neumann, Emil	1836-1922	Berlin und Dresden "Dres-dener ist 'ne lust'ge Seel'"	Op. 67	Unspec.	R. Forberg		CHAL (1898)
5212	Neumann, Emil	1836-1922	Berlin und Leipzig "In Berlin muss man fein"		Unspec.	Neumann i. Berl.		CHAL (1898)
5213	Neumann, Emil	1836-1922	Dunnemals un heide		Unspec.	Starcke		CHAL (1898)
5214	Neumann, Emil	1836-1922	Es hat geschnappt "Lassen wir uns Beide seh'n"		Unspec.	Neumann i. Berl.		CHAL (1898)
5215	Neumann, Emil	1836-1922	Fesche Geister "Schon Schiller sagt, O Königin"	No. 68	Unspec.	R. Forberg		CHAL (1898)
5216	Neumann, Emil	1836-1922	Herrgott, sind wir vergnügt "In meinen Taschen ist es leer"	No. 66	Unspec.	R. Forberg		CHAL (1898)
5217	Neumann, Emil	1836-1922	Noth gehorchend, nicht dem eignen Triebe "Man hat als Freier"		Unspec.	Neumann i. Berl.		CHAL (1898)
5218	Neumann, Emil	1836-1922	Wir sein froh, dass wir nicht dabei gewesen sein "Es kommen zwei Bummler"		Unspec.	Neumann i. Berl.		CHAL (1898)
5219	Neumann, Emil	1836-1922	Wir sind wir und schreib'n uns vor "Wir sind allemal noch wir"		Unspec.	Neumann i. Berl.		CHAL (1898)
5220	Neumann, H.		Ein Jeder wieht's im Saale		Unspec.	Fredebaeul & K.		CHAL (1906)
5221	Neumann, H.		Heute haben wir die Ehre		Unspec.	Kleine i. P.		CHAL (1901)
5222	Neumann, H.		Hopla, hopla, hopsasa		Unspec.	Fredebeul & K.		CHAL (1906)
5223	Neumann, H.		Ja ihr Leute, lasst euch sagen		Unspec.	Kleine i. P.		CHAL (1901)
5224	Nevin, Ethelbert Woodbridge	1862-1901	A Song of Love	No. IV	S/A	Boston	In collection "Six Duets for Soprano and Alto, arranged from Songs of Ethelbert Nevin by Carl Engel"	MSN
5225	Nevin, Ethelbert Woodbridge	1862-1901	Deep in a Rose's Glowing Heart	No. II	S/A	Boston	In collection "Six Duets for Soprano and Alto, arranged from Songs of Ethelbert Nevin by Carl Engel"	MSN

REC	COMP	DTS	TITLE	OP #	VCG	PUB	COMMENTS	SRC
5226	Nevin, Ethelbert Woodbridge	1862-1901	Ev'ry Night	No. V	S/A	Boston	In collection "Six Duets for Soprano and Alto, arranged from Songs of Ethelbert Nevin by Carl Engel"	MSN
5227	Nevin, Ethelbert Woodbridge	1862-1901	In a Bower	No. III	S/A	Boston	In collection "Six Duets for Soprano and Alto, arranged from Songs of Ethelbert Nevin by Carl Engel"	MSN
5228	Nevin, Ethelbert Woodbridge	1862-1901	O, dass wir Mailust hieten		S/A or S/Br	Schott	Ed. Schneider. Poss. Grmn. tr. Eng., but Nevin studied & lived in Germany.	CHAL (1906)
5229	Nevin, Ethelbert Woodbridge	1862-1901	Rosary, The		Unspec.	Allans	Also solo. Pub. Allans, Boston, Ashley.	CVMP (1976)
5230	Nevin, Ethelbert Woodbridge	1862-1901	Rosary, The		Unspec.	Allans	In anthology "Vocal Duets Collection" Vol. 1. Pub. 1992	MSN
5231	Nevin, Ethelbert Woodbridge	1862-1901	Slumber Song	No. VI	S/A	Boston	In collection "Six Duets for Soprano and Alto, arranged from Songs of Ethelbert Nevin by Carl Engel"	MSN
5232	Nevin, Ethelbert Woodbridge	1862-1901	The Merry, Merry Lark	No. I	S/A	Boston	In collection "Six Duets for Soprano and Alto, arranged from Songs of Ethelbert Nevin by Carl Engel"	MSN
5233	Nevin, Ethelbert Woodbridge	1862-1901	The Nightingale's Song		high & med. v.	Church	Arr. C. G. Spross	MSN
5234	Nevin, George Balch	1859-1933	Jesu, Word of God Incarnate		S/A	Ditson	In anthology "Choice Sacred Duets for All Voices" Pub. 1936	MSN
5235	Nevin, George Balch	1859-1933	Jesu, Word of God Incarnate		S/A or S/MS	Ditson	In anthology "Choice Sacred Duets" Pub. 1936	NATS-SVD
5236	Newton, Ernest	20th C.	A madrigal in May		S/A	Boosey		BBC (1975)
5237	Newton, Ernest	20th C.	A-hunting we will go		Unspec.	Enoch	Arr. Eng. folksong	BBC (1975)
5238	Newton, Ernest	20th C.	Bill and Jack		Unspec.	Leonard-Eng		CVMP (1976)
5239	Newton, Ernest	20th C.	Down the Flowing Stream		Unspec.	Cramer		CVMP (1976)
5240	Newton, Ernest	20th C.	Drink to me only with thine eyes		Unspec.	Enoch	Arr. of Eng. folksong	BBC (1975)
5241	Newton, Ernest	20th C.	Golden Slumbers		S/A	Leonard-Eng	Arr. E. Newton of 17th C. tune. In anth. "Six Popular Vocal Duets Book I for Soprano & Contralto" Ed. & arr. E. Newton. Pub. 1906	MSN
5242	Newton, Ernest	20th C.	Here's to the maiden of bashful fifteen		Unspec.	Enoch	Arr. of Eng. folksong	BBC (1975)
5243	Newton, Ernest	20th C.	Irish Slumber Song		Unspec.	Leonard-Eng	Also solo	CVMP (1976)
5244	Newton, Ernest	20th C.	Irish Slumber Song		S/A or med. & low v.	Leonard-Eng		ASR
5245	Newton, Ernest	20th C.	It was a lover and his lass		Unspec.	Enoch	Arr. Eng. folksong	BBC (1975)
5246	Newton, Ernest	20th C.	It was a lover and his lass		S/A	Leonard-Eng	Arr. E. Newton of tune by T. Morley. In anth. "6 Popular Vocal Duets Bk. I for Sop. & Contralto" Ed. & arr. E. Newton. Pub. 1906	MSN

REC	COMP	DTS	TITLE	OP #	VCG	PUB	COMMENTS	SRC
5247	Newton, Ernest	20th C.	Laugh, Little River		Unspec.	Leonard-Eng		CVMP (1976)
5248	Newton, Ernest	20th C.	Now is the Month of Maying		S/A	Leonard-Eng	In anthology "Six Popular Vocal Duets Book I for Soprano & Contralto" Ed. & arr. E. Newton. Pub. 1906.	MSN
5249	Newton, Ernest	20th C.	Oh, dear! oh, dear!		Unspec.	Enoch	Arr. Eng. folksong	BBC (1975)
5250	Newton, Ernest	20th C.	Polly Oliver		Unspec.	Enoch	Arr. Eng. folksong	BBC (1975)
5251	Newton, Ernest	20th C.	Simon the cellarer		Unspec.	Enoch	Arr. Eng. folksong	BBC (1975)
5252	Newton, Ernest	20th C.	Six Popular Vocal Duets, Book I		Unspec.	Leonard-Eng	Collection. Works by E. Newton. Unspec. pieces.	CVMP (1976)
5253	Newton, Ernest	20th C.	The girl and the duck		Unspec.	Enoch	Arr. Eng. folksong	BBC (1975)
5254	Newton, Ernest	20th C.	Underneath the trees		Unspec.	Enoch	Arr. Eng. folksong	BBC (1975)
5255	Newton, Ernest	20th C.	When Love was Young		Unspec.	Cramer		CVMP (1976)
5256	Newton, Ernest	20th C.	Where the chestnuts bloom		S/A	Leonard-Eng		BBC (1975)
5257	Newton, Ernest	20th C.	Where the Chestnuts Bloom		Unspec.	Leonard-Eng	Also solo	CVMP (1976)
5258	Newton, Ernest	20th C.	Where the Chestnuts Bloom		S/A or high & med. v.	Leonard-Eng		ASR
5259	Nicolai, Otto	1810-1849	Ein Wort "O spricht es aus der Liebe Wort"		Unspec.	Cranz		CHAL (1898)
5260	Nicolai, Otto	1810-1849	Wenn sanft der Abend	Op. 2	S/A or S/B	Heinr.		CHAL (1898)
5261	Nicolai, Otto	1810-1849	Wie der Tag mir schleicht	Op. 15 No. 1	Unspec.	S. & B., Bahn		CHAL (1898)
5262	Nicolai, Wilhelm Frederik Gerard	1829-1896	Frühling "Saaten-grün, Lerchenwirbel"	Op. 11 No. 3	S/A	B. & H.	In anth. "Zweistim. Lied. f. Sop. u. Altstimme mit Klavierbegleitung f. den Haus- u. Schulgebrauch v. H. M. Schletterer" 3 vols.	MSN
5263	Nicolai, Wilhelm Frederik Gerard	1829-1896	Frühling "Saaten-grün, Veilchenduft"	Op. 11 No. 3	S/A	B. & H.		CHAL (1898)
5264	Nicolai, Wilhelm Frederik Gerard	1829-1896	Frühlingsglaube "Linden Lüfte sind erwacht"	Op. 11 No. 2	S/A	B. & H.		CHAL (1898)
5265	Nicolai, Wilhelm Frederik Gerard	1829-1896	Halt recht im Gemüthe	Op. 11 No. 1	S/A	B. & H.		CHAL (1898)
5266	Niedermayer, Louis	1802-1861	Pena troppo barbara		S/S	Schlesinger		CHAL (1898)
5267	Niedermayer, Louis	1802-1861	S'il vous souvient du mal d'amour		S/S	Schlesinger		CHAL (1898)
5268	Niedermayer, Louis	1802-1861	Vois d'aurore (Sieh die Morgenröthe)		S/S or S/T	Schlesinger		CHAL (1898)
5269	Nieland, H.		Het Looze Moolenatinnetje		Unspec.	Alsbach	In "Drie Werkjes"	CVMP (1976)
5270	Nieland, H.		Sneeuwklokjes		Unspec.	Alsbach	In "Drie Werkjes"	CVMP (1976)

REC	COMP	DTS	TITLE	OP #	VCG	PUB	COMMENTS	SRC
5271	Nieland, H.		Zondagmorgen		Unspec.	Alsbach	In "Drie Werkjes"	CVMP (1976)
5272	Niemann, Gustav	1841-1881	Ihr Kinderlein kommt	Op. 9 No. 1	Unspec.	Bauer		CHAL (1898)
5273	Niemann, Gustav	1841-1881	O du fröhliche, o du selige	Op. 9 No. 2	Unspec.	Bauer		CHAL (1898)
5274	Niemann, Gustav	1841-1881	O du fröhliche, Weihnachtszeit	No. 9	Unspec.	Bauer		CHAL (1898)
5275	Niemann, Gustav	1841-1881	O Tannenbaum, o Tannenbaum wie grün (treu)	Op. 9 No. 3	Unspec.	Bauer		CHAL (1898)
5276	Niemann, Gustav	1841-1881	Stille Nacht, heilige Nacht	Op. 9 No. 1	Unspec.	Bauer	Arr. of song.	CHAL (1898)
5277	Niese, E.		Maiglöckchen "Glöcklein des Mai"	Op. 2 No. 1	Unspec.	Dienemann i. Potsd.		CHAL (1898)
5278	Niese, Th.		Am Meer "Es kommt ein tiefer, voller Klang"	Op. 2 No. 3	Unspec.	Dienemann i. Potsd.		CHAL (1898)
5279	Niese, Th.		Sonntagsfrühe "Aus den Thälern hör' ich schallen"		Unspec.	Dienemann i. Potsd.		CHAL (1898)
5280	Nikel, Emil	1851-1921	Missa quarta	Op. 15	S/A	Kothe i. Loebschütz	org accomp.	CHAL (1898)
5281	Nikisch, Arthur	1855-1922	So ein Fussel		Unspec.	Harmonie i. B.		CHAL (1911)
5282	Nohé, S.		Wir haben die Mittel "Heute ein Couplet zu singen"		Unspec.	O. Dietrich		CHAL (1898)
5283	Noland, Gary	1957-	My God, Why hast Thou Forsaken Me?	Op. 9	S/A or T/B	Freepub	acap.	CVMP (1995)
5284	Nolopp, Werner	1835-1903	Neue Referendar "Ist's erlaubt, darf ich stören"	Op. 74	2 female v.	Fritzsche		CHAL (1898)
5285	Nolopp, Werner	1835-1903	Weihnachtslied "Sei tausendmal willkommen"	Op. 35	Unspec.	Haushahn i. L.		CHAL (1898)
5286	Norbert, R.		Peng, peng, kommen wir so still daher	Op. 58	Unspec.	Hoffmann i. Str.		CHAL (1901)
5287	Norman, Fredrik Vilhelm Ludvig	1831-1885	Duo ur Drottning Lovisas Begrafningskantat "Höldig Drottning"	Op. 17 No. 5	S/S	Elkan & Sch.		CHAL (1898)
5288	Norman, Fredrik Vilhelm Ludvig	1831-1885	Herbstgedanken "Vöglein hat sich heiser gesungen"	Op. 17 No. 2	S/S	Elkan & Sch.		CHAL (1898)
5289	Norman, Fredrik Vilhelm Ludvig	1831-1885	Wenn du nicht weisst, was die Bächlein sagen	Op. 17 No. 1	S/S	Elkan & Sch.	Grmn. trans. Swed.	CHAL (1898)
5290	Norman, Fredrik Vilhelm Ludvig	1831-1885	Zeislein "Zeislein, wo ist dein Hauslein"	Op. 17 No. 3	S/S	Elkan & Sch.	Grmn. trans. Swed.	CHAL (1898)
5291	Nöroth, J.		Juchhei Moselwein "Juchhei, juchhei, schafft Wein herbei"	No. 13	Unspec.	Hoenes		CHAL (1901)
5292	Nöroth, J.		Moselblümchen, Mädchen, Männer "Moselblümchen, o wie duftig"	No. 3	Unspec.	Hoenes		CHAL (1901)
5293	Nöroth, J.		O Moselland, mein Heimathland	No. 11	Unspec.	Hoenes		CHAL (1901)
5294	Nöroth, J.		Was duftet da für Duft	No. 7	Unspec.	Hoenes		CHAL (1901)
5295	Nöroth, J.		Was macht so fröhlich	No. 8	Unspec.	Hoenes		CHAL (1901)
5296	Nöroth, J.		Wer jemals der Nixe der Mosel gelauscht	No. 16	Unspec.	Hoenes		CHAL (1901)
5297	Nöroth, J.		Wo der klare Moselstrom	No. 2	Unspec.	Hoenes		CHAL (1901)
5298	North, Michael		Such Lovely Things		Unspec.	Boosey	Also solo	CVMP (1976)
5299	Norton, Caroline E. S.	1808-1877	Juanita		S/A	Bayley & Ferguson	Eng. woman comp. Comp. 1853.	BBC (1975)

REC	COMP	DTS	TITLE	OP #	VCG	PUB	COMMENTS	SRC
5300	Norton, Caroline E. S.	1808-1877	Juanita		Unspec.	Brain-ard's Sons	Eng. woman comp. In anthology "Brainard's Collection of Vocal Duets from Popular Modern and Standard Composers" Pub. 1903.	MSN
5301	Norton, Caroline E. S.	1808-1877	Juanita		S/A	White-Smith	Eng. woman comp. In catalogue page "Vocal Duetts" of White-Smith Music Pub. Co. (no date)	MSN
5302	Noskowski, Zygmund	1846-1909	Gdy wczystem polu "Idyllisches Minnelied"		Unspec.	none listed		CHAL (1898)
5303	Noskowski, Zygmund	1846-1909	Idyllisches Minnelied "Wenn über Wiessen"	Op. 10 No. 3	2 female v.	Kistner		CHAL (1898)
5304	Noskowski, Zygmund	1846-1909	Taube "Pflegt ein artig' schönes Mädchen"	Op. 10 No. 1	2 female v.	Kistner		CHAL (1898)
5305	Noskowski, Zygmund	1846-1909	Treues Mädchen "Dort im grünen Walde"	Op. 10 No. 2	2 female v.	Kistner		CHAL (1898)
5306	Novaro, Michele	1822-1885	Inno di Mameli		Unspec.	Carisch		CVMP (1985)
5307	Nuhn, Fr.		Ich stehe in Waldes-schatten		S/A	B. & H.		CHAL (1898)
5308	Nus, B.		Frühling kommt "Thut auch das bange Herz die weh'"	Op. 3 No. 1	S/S	Deubner		CHAL (1898)
5309	Nus, B.		Siehst du am Weg ein Blümlein blühn "Viel tau-send Blümlein auf der Au"	Op. 3 No. 2	S/S	Deubner		CHAL (1898)
5310	Nus, B.		Wenn du ein Herz gefunden	Op. 3 No. 3	S/S	Deubner		CHAL (1898)
5311	O'Hara, Geoffrey	1882-1867	I Walked Today Where Jesus Walked		S/A or S/T or A/Bar	G. Schirm.	Also solo	CVMP (1976)
5312	Oberhoffer, Heinrich	1824-1885	Katzenduett "Miau, miau, miau"	Op. 19	Unspec.	Br. & B.		CHAL (1898)
5313	Oberstoetter, H. E.	1824-1885	Du nur allein kannst mir		Unspec.	Kiener i. Stuttg.		CHAL (1898)
5314	Oberthür, Karl	1819-1895	Ade "Wir wandern aus dem Vaterland"		Unspec.	Litolff		CHAL (1898)
5315	Ochs, Siegfried	1858-1929	Es geht die Mühl' im Thale	Op. 7 No. 3	2 female v.	R. & P.		CHAL (1898)
5316	Ochs, Siegfried	1858-1929	Hexenlied "Aus felsinger Kluft"	Op. 7 No. 1	2 female v.	R. & P.		CHAL (1898)
5317	Ochs, Siegfried	1858-1929	Im Mondenglanze ruht das Meer	Op. 7 No. 2	2 female v.	R. & P.		CHAL (1898)
5318	Oddone, Elisabetta	1878-1972	Ben Arrivata		Unspec.	Bongio-vanni	It. woman comp. Used pen name Eliodd. In "Rispetti e Stornelli della Lucchesia"	CVMP (1976)
5319	Oddone, Elisabetta	1878-1972	Che C-Cosa e Stato?		Unspec.	Bongio-vanni	It. woman comp. Used pen name Eliodd. In "Rispetti e Stornelli della Lucchesia"	CVMP (1976)
5320	Oddone, Elisabetta	1878-1972	I Canti dei Campi		Unspec.	Bongio-vanni	It. woman compo. Used pen name Eliodd.	CVMP (1976)
5321	Oddone, Elisabetta	1878-1972	Rispetti e Stornelli della Luccheria (6)		high & med. v.	Bongio-vanni	It. woman comp. Used pen name Eliodd. Six unspec. duets	ASR
5322	Oddone, Elisabetta	1878-1972	Sento in Fischietto Venire di Lontano		Unspec.	Bongio-vanni	It. woman comp. Used pen name Eliodd. In "Rispetti e Stornelli della Lucchesia"	CVMP (1976)

REC	COMP	DTS	TITLE	OP #	VCG	PUB	COMMENTS	SRC
5323	Oddone, Elisabetta	1878-1972	Si da Principio a questa Serenata		Unspec.	Bongio-vanni	It. woman comp. Used pen name Eliodd. In "Rispetti e Stornelli della Lucchesia"	CVMP (1976)
5324	Oddone, Elisabetta	1878-1972	Stornelli		Unspec.	Bongio-vanni	It. woman comp. Used pen name Eliodd. In "Rispetti e Stornelli della Lucchesia"	CVMP (1976)
5325	Oddone, Elisabetta	1878-1972	Vedo un Cavallin		Unspec.	Bongio-vanni	It. woman comp. Used pen name Eliodd. In "Rispetti e Stornelli della Lucchesia"	CVMP (1976)
5326	Odersky, A.		Bin ich hinausgegangen	Op. 4	Unspec.	Glaser		CHAL (1906)
5327	Oehmler, L.		Lord, Hear My Prayer		Unspec.	Brain-ard's Sons	Arr. D. J. Muir. In anthology "Brainard's Collection of Vocal Duets from Popular Modern and Standard Composers" Pub. 1903.	MSN
5328	Oelschläger, Friedrich	1798-1858	Harmonie "Ein Engel waltet über alles Leben"	Op. 9 No. 2	Unspec.	Simon i. Berl.		CHAL (1898)
5329	Offenbach, Jacques	1819-1880	Gendarmes		Unspec.	Allans, Boosey		CVMP (1976)
5330	Ogarew, M.		Emanuel Geibel's Scheidelied "Leb wohl, du grüne Wildniss"	Op. 63	S/A	Lichtb.		CHAL (1898)
5331	Olson, Daniel	1898-	Nu Loser Solen Sitt Blonda Harr		Unspec.	Gehr-mans	In "Tva Duetter"	CVMP (1976)
5332	Olson, Daniel	1898-	Psalmodikon		Unspec.	Gehr-mans	In "Tva Duetter"	CVMP (1976)
5333	Opel, R.		Es ist ein Reihen geschlungen	Op. 4 No. 1	S/A	R. & E.		CHAL (1906)
5334	Opel, R.		Kein Graben so breit	Op. 4 No. 3	S/A	R. & E.		CHAL (1906)
5335	Opel, R.		Wenn sich Liebes von dir lösen will	Op. 4 No. 2	S/A	R. & E.		CHAL (1906)
5336	Operti		We've gone through life together		S/A	White-Smith	In catalogue page "Vocal Duetts" of White-Smith Music Pub. Co. (no date)	MSN
5337	Opladen, Adolf	1837-	Heimathrosen		S/A or T/Br	C. Fischer	In catalogue page "Selected Vocal Duets By Favorite Composers" of Carl Fischer NY (no date)	MSN
5338	Orr, Buxton	1924-	anyone lived in a pretty how town	No. 1	S/A or S/MS	Anglo-Continental	In "many kinds of yes" reproduced from manuscript. Pub. 1913.	NATS-VCD
5339	Orr, Buxton	1924-	love is more thicker than forget	No. 4	S/A or S/MS	Anglo-Continental	In "many kinds of yes" reproduced from manuscript. Pub. 1913.	NATS-VCD
5340	Orr, Buxton	1924-	maggie and milly and molly and may	No. 3	S/A or S/MS	Anglo-Continental	In "many kinds of yes" reproduced from manuscript. Pub. 1913.	NATS-VCD
5341	Orr, Buxton	1924-	many kinds of yes		S/A	Kunzel	Song cycle	CVMP (1995)
5342	Orr, Buxton	1924-	many kinds of yes		S/A	Eulenburg	Unspec. pieces within set	ASR
5343	Orr, Buxton	1924-	sitting in a tree	No. 2	S/A or S/MS	Anglo-Continental	In "many kinds of yes" reproduced from manuscript. Pub. 1913.	NATS-VCD
5344	Orr, Buxton	1924-	sweet spring is your time	No. 5	S/A or S/MS	Anglo-Continental	In "many kinds of yes" reproduced from manuscript. Pub. 1913.	NATS-VCD
5345	Ortner, A.		Ade "Wie schienen die Sternlein"	No. 3	S/A	Aibl		CHAL (1898)

REC	COMP	DTS	TITLE	OP #	VCG	PUB	COMMENTS	SRC
5346	Ortner, A.		Im Walde "Im Walde lasst uns weilen"	No. 2	S/A	Aibl		CHAL (1898)
5347	Ortner, A.		Winterseufzer "Himmel ist so hell"	No. 1	S/A	Aibl		CHAL (1898)
5348	Orton, Irv		Just One Day at a Time		S/A or S/Bar or S/T	G. Schirm.		CVMP (1976)
5349	Otto, A.		Schlaf nun sanft und selig ein		Unspec.	Bauer i. Br.		CHAL (1906)
5350	Otto, Ernst Julius	1804-1877	Angra Pequenta "Herrlich-es Schiff, auf schäumen-den Wogen"		Unspec.	Renner i. Dr.		CHAL (1898)
5351	Otto, Franz Joseph	1809-1842	Wonne der Wehmuth "Trocknet nicht Thränen"	Op. 11 No. 6	S/S	Klemm		CHAL (1898)
5352	Overeem, M. v.		Eté, lorsque le jour a fui		S/S	Cranz		CHAL (1906)
5353	Owen, Anita		Farewell, Dear Heart		Unspec.	Brainard's Sons	Woman comp. In anthology "Brainard's Collection of Vocal Duets from Popular Modern and Standard Composers" Pub. 1903.	MSN
5354	Paasch, W.		Ich lob' mir das schmucke Militär	Op. 152	S/A	Danner		CHAL (1911)
5355	Pache, Joseph	1861-1926	Abendglocken "Abend-glocken rufen müde nun"	Op. 170 No. 2	Unspec.	Hug		CHAL (1898)
5356	Pache, Joseph	1861-1926	Abendlied "Tag neigt sich zu Ende"	Op. 170 No. 4	Unspec.	Hug		CHAL (1898)
5357	Pache, Joseph	1861-1926	Am Abend "Wie ist der Abend stille"	Op. 59 No. 3	Unspec.	Robol-sky		CHAL (1898)
5358	Pache, Joseph	1861-1926	Andacht "Mir ist so wohl in Gottes Haus"		S/A	Robol-sky		CHAL (1898)
5359	Pache, Joseph	1861-1926	Blätter und Blüthen 6 Mädchenlieder	Op. 170	Unspec.	Hug	Duet collection	CHAL (1898)
5360	Pache, Joseph	1861-1926	Frühlingseinzung "Wie es in den Lüfften flimmert"	Op. 170 No. 3	Unspec.	Hug		CHAL (1898)
5361	Pache, Joseph	1861-1926	Komm hernieder stille Nacht "Komm hernieder stille, bleiche"	Op. 141 No. 4	Unspec.	Rud. Dietrich		CHAL (1898)
5362	Pache, Joseph	1861-1926	Lenz ist da "Es klingt wie Festgeläute"	Op. 59 No. 2	Unspec.	Robol-sky		CHAL (1898)
5363	Pache, Joseph	1861-1926	Maiennacht "Das war ein buntes Gewimmel"	Op. 170 No. 1	Unspec.	Hug		CHAL (1898)
5364	Pache, Joseph	1861-1926	Morgenlust "Duftiges Gewölk im Blauen"	Op. 59 No. 1	Unspec.	Robol-sky		CHAL (1898)
5365	Pache, Joseph	1861-1926	Nun ruh' ich und bin stille		S/A	Robol-sky		CHAL (1898)
5366	Pache, Joseph	1861-1926	Nun winkt's und flüstert's aus den Bächen	Op. 170 No. 6	Unspec.	Hug		CHAL (1898)
5367	Pache, Joseph	1861-1926	Schlummerlied "Schlafe, schlaf mein Kindelein"	Op. 16	2 female v.	Grude		CHAL (1898)
5368	Pache, Joseph	1861-1926	Spinnerlied "Hurtig, wie die Mägdelein"	Op. 170 No. 5	Unspec.	Hug		CHAL (1898)
5369	Pache, Joseph	1861-1926	Trauungsgesang "Wo du hingehst"		S/A	Hug	org or pf	CHAL (1898)
5370	Pache, Joseph	1861-1926	Vor deinem Bild in einer Stunde	Op. 141 No. 2	Unspec.	Rud. Dietrich		CHAL (1898)
5371	Pache, Joseph	1861-1926	Weisst du noch, wie ich am Felsen	Op. 141 No. 1	Unspec.	Rud. Dietrich		CHAL (1898)
5372	Pache, Joseph	1861-1926	Wir sassen im duftenden Garten	Op. 141 No. 3	Unspec.	Rud. Dietrich		CHAL (1898)

REC	COMP	DTS	TITLE	OP #	VCG	PUB	COMMENTS	SRC
5373	Pachkov, N. J.		Die zwei Zigeunerinnen		Unspec.	F. Schellenb.	Arr. Bruno	BBC (1975)
5374	Packenius, J.		Jugenderinnerungen "Nun liebe Tante"		S/A	Tonger		CHAL (1898)
5375	Packenius, J.		Mimmi und Lilli "Guten Morgen, liebe Mimmi"		2 female or 2 male v.	Tonger		CHAL (1898)
5376	Paër, Ferdinando [Paer]	1771-1839	Hectors Abschied "Will sich Hector ewig"		Unspec.	Schlesinger		CHAL (1898)
5377	Paër, Ferdinando [Paer]	1771-1839	Vezzosa mia Nice		Unspec.	Bosworth		CHAL (1898)
5378	Page, Nathanael Clifford	1866-	All Through the Night		S/A	Ditson	Welsh melody. Arr. N. C. Page. Eng. trans. Welsh. In anthology "The Ditson Collection of Soprano and Alto Duets" Pub. 1934.	MSN
5379	Paisiello, Giovanni	1740-1816	Nun fühl' ich auf's Neue		S/S	Leuckart	Grmn. trans. It.	CHAL (1898)
5380	Palloni, Gaetano	1831-1892	L'Ora conventuna		S/MS	G. Schirm.	In catalogue page "Favorite French and Italian Vocal Duets" of G. Schirmer, Inc. NY (no date)	MSN
5381	Palloni, Gaetano	1831-1892	Una Sera in Mare		S/T or S/S	G. Schirm.	In catalogue page "Favorite French and Italian Vocal Duets" of G. Schirmer, Inc. NY (no date)	MSN
5382	Palme, Rudolf	1834-1909	Christnacht und Weihnachten 6 Weihnachtslieder	Op. 64	Unspec.	Heinr.	Collection of 6 Christmas duets	CHAL (1898)
5383	Palme, Rudolf	1834-1909	Engel und Hirten "Kommet ihr Hirten"	Op. 64 No. 2	Unspec.	Heinr.		CHAL (1898)
5384	Palme, Rudolf	1834-1909	Fröhliche Weihnacht überall	Op. 64 No. 5	Unspec.	Heinr.		CHAL (1898)
5385	Palme, Rudolf	1834-1909	O du fröhliche, o du selige	Op. 64 No. 4	Unspec.	Heinr.		CHAL (1898)
5386	Palme, Rudolf	1834-1909	Weihnachts "Wir wollen ihm die Krippe schücken"	Op. 64 No. 1	Unspec.	Heinr.		CHAL (1898)
5387	Palme, Rudolf	1834-1909	Weihnachtsgesang "Ehre sei Gott in der Höhe"	Op. 64 No. 6	Unspec.	Heinr.		CHAL (1898)
5388	Palme, Rudolf	1834-1909	Weihnachtslied "Wo zünden wir den Christbaum an"	Op. 64 No. 3	Unspec.	Heinr.		CHAL (1898)
5389	Panofka, Heinrich	1807-1887	On the blue wave		S/S	White-Smith	In catalogue page "Vocal Duets" of White-Smith Music Pub. Co. (no date)	MSN
5390	Panseron, Auguste	1796-1859	Adoremus		S/S	Schott	org accomp.	CHAL (1898)
5391	Panseron, Auguste	1796-1859	Am einsamen See	No. 8	Unspec.	B. & H.		CHAL (1898)
5392	Panseron, Auguste	1796-1859	Ave Maria stella		S/S	Schott	org accomp.	CHAL (1898)
5393	Panseron, Auguste	1796-1859	Coeur sacré		S/S	Schott	org accomp.	CHAL (1898)
5394	Panseron, Auguste	1796-1859	Es ertöne ein muntrer Gesang		Unspec.	Schott		CHAL (1898)
5395	Panseron, Auguste	1796-1859	Es tönt der Morgenchor	No. 4	Unspec.	B. & H.		CHAL (1898)

REC	COMP	DTS	TITLE	OP #	VCG	PUB	COMMENTS	SRC
5396	Panseron, Auguste	1796-1859	Es tönt der Morgenchor "Die dunklen Schleier fallen"		S/A	B. & H.	In anth. "Zweistim. Lied. f. Sop. u. Altstimme mit Klavierbegleitung f. den Haus- u. Schulgebrauch v. H. M. Schletterer" 3 vols.	MSN
5397	Panseron, Auguste	1796-1859	Gondelfahrt "Rasch hinaus, auf die Wogen"	No. 12	Unspec.	B. & H.		CHAL (1898)
5398	Panseron, Auguste	1796-1859	Ma nacelle "Sur une onde tranquille"		Unspec.	Schlesinger		CHAL (1898)
5399	Panseron, Auguste	1796-1859	O salutaris		S/S	Schott	org accomp.	CHAL (1898)
5400	Panseron, Auguste	1796-1859	Tag erwacht		Unspec.	Schlesinger		CHAL (1898)
5401	Panseron, Auguste	1796-1859	Vierge modeste		S/S	Schott	org accomp.	CHAL (1898)
5402	Pardow, J. H.		Liebesgedanken "Ein Blümchen kenn' ich auf der Welt"	Op. 45	Unspec.	Weiss Nachf. i. Berl.		CHAL (1898)
5403	Pargolesi, Coronato	d. 1900	Eco del Friuli "50 Villote"		Unspec.	Schmidl	Pen name of Stefano Persoglia	CHAL (1898)
5404	Parker, Alice	1925-	A Garland of Carols		S/A	G. Schirm.	Amer. woman comp. Unspec. pieces.	ASR
5405	Parker, Henry	1842-	Hark to the Mandoline		Unspec.	Cramer		CVMP (1976)
5406	Parker, Henry	1842-	Hark to the Mandoline		Unspec.	Cramer		ASR
5407	Parker, Henry	1842-	In the Dusk of the Twilight		Unspec.	Cramer		CVMP (1976)
5408	Parker, Henry	1842-	In the Dusk of Twilight		Unspec.	Cramer		ASR
5409	Parker, Henry	1842-	Our Mountain Home		Unspec.	Cramer		CVMP (1976)
5410	Parker, Henry	1842-	Our Mountain Home		Unspec.	Cramer		ASR
5411	Parker, Henry	1842-	Sea Maidens		Unspec.	Cramer		CVMP (1976)
5412	Parker, Henry	1842-	See Maidens		Unspec.	Cramer		ASR
5413	Parker, Henry	1842-	Spirit of the Wood		Unspec.	Cramer		CVMP (1976)
5414	Parker, Henry	1842-	Spirit of the Wood		Unspec.	Cramer		ASR
5415	Parlow, Edmund	1855-	Liebes, leichtes, luft'ges Ding	Op. 63 No. 1	S/A	Beyer & S.		CHAL (1906)
5416	Parlow, Edmund	1855-	Wie so still, nur der Wipfel sanftes Rauschen	Op. 62 No. 2	S/A	Beyer & S.		CHAL (1906)
5417	Pastory, A.		Ich bin der Hans		Unspec.	Uhse		CHAL (1906)
5418	Patat, J.		Wenn wir da hier recht munter		Unspec.	Klöckner		CHAL (1901)
5419	Pavesi, Stefano	1779-1850	Ah, tu non sie più mio		Unspec.	Cranz		CHAL (1898)
5420	Pavesi, Stefano	1779-1850	Bist du mir noch Vater		Unspec.	Schott		CHAL (1898)
5421	Paxon, Charles W.		We come to thee, Savot		Unspec.	Bayley & Ferguson	Arr. Maxfield	BBC (1975)
5422	Pearsall, Robert Lucas de	1795-1856	Duet for Two Cats		S/A	Schott	Attr. to Rossini	ASR

REC	COMP	DTS	TITLE	OP #	VCG	PUB	COMMENTS	SRC
5423	Pearsall, Robert Lucas de	1795-1856	Duet for Two Cats		MS/MS	Schott	Attr. to Rossini ("Duet-to Buffo di due Gatti"). Pearsall a.k.a. G. Berthold. Pub. 1959.	NATS-VCD
5424	Peellaert, Augustin de	1793-1876	Prière à la Vierge		Unspec.	Junne		CHAL (1898)
5425	Pelissier, H. G.		Awake		Unspec.	Leonard-Eng	Also solo	CVMP (1976)
5426	Pelissier, H. G.		Awake		Unspec.	Leonard-Eng		ASR
5427	Pembaur, Karl	1876-1936	Lied zum Aloysius "In des Himmels heil'gen Hallen"		S/A or T/B	Gross i. Insbr.	org or harm accomp.	CHAL (1898)
5428	Pembaur, Karl	1876-1936	Vor der Krippe "O Kind, in deine Hände"		S/A	Gross i. Insbr.		CHAL (1898)
5429	Pembaur, Karl	1876-1936	Vor einem Marienbild "Jungfrau, zu deinen Füssen"		Unspec.	Gross i. Insbr.	org accomp.	CHAL (1898)
5430	Pembaur, Sr., Joseph	1848-1923	Knabe aus Tyrol "Du kommst so frisch und frölich"	Op. 42	Unspec.	Siegel		CHAL (1898)
5431	Pentenrieder, Franz Xaver	1813-1867	Am Bodensee "Schwelle die Segel"	Op. 30 No. 1	Unspec.	André		CHAL (1898)
5432	Pentenrieder, Franz Xaver	1813-1867	Frühmorgens "Ich weiss nicht säuselt in den Bäumen"	Op. 30 No. 2	S/A	André		CHAL (1898)
5433	Perger, Richard von	1854-1911	Es liebten sich beide	No. 1	S/A	Bos-worth		CHAL (1911)
5434	Perger, Richard von	1854-1911	Ich sass im Grünen	No. 2	S/A	Bos-worth		CHAL (1911)
5435	Perger, Richard von	1854-1911	Warum duften die Levkojen	No. 3	S/A	Bos-worth		CHAL (1911)
5436	Perpignan, F.		Duo Turc		Unspec.	Enoch		CVMP (1976)
5437	Perpignan, F.		Les Emboîteurs		Unspec.	Enoch		CVMP (1976)
5438	Perpignan, F.		Sur le Bateau Mouche		Unspec.	Enoch		CVMP (1976)
5439	Persichetti, Vincent	1915-1987	a politician	Op. 129 No. V	Unspec.	Elkan-Vogel	In "glad and very, five cummings choruses." Intended for chorus, may be perf. as duet. Copyright 1976.	MSN
5440	Persichetti, Vincent	1915-1987	dominic has a doll	Op. 98, No. 1	Unspec.	Elkan-Vogel	In "four cummings choruses." Intended for chorus, may be perf. as duet. Copyright 1966.	MSN
5441	Persichetti, Vincent	1915-1987	four cummings choruses	Op. 98	Unspec.	Elkan-Vogel	Set intended for chorus, may be perf. as duet. Copyright 1966.	MSN
5442	Persichetti, Vincent	1915-1987	glad and very	Op. 129	Unspec.	Elkan-Vogel	Set intended for chorus, may be perf. as duet. Copyright 1976.	MSN
5443	Persichetti, Vincent	1915-1987	i am so glad and very	Op. 129 No. II	Unspec.	Elkan-Vogel	In "glad and very, five cummings choruses." Intended for chorus, may be perf. as duet. Copyright 1976.	MSN
5444	Persichetti, Vincent	1915-1987	jake hates all the girls	Op. 129 No. IV	Unspec.	Elkan-Vogel	In "glad and very, five cummings choruses." Intended for chorus, may be perf. as duet Copyright 1976.	MSN

REC	COMP	DTS	TITLE	OP #	VCG	PUB	COMMENTS	SRC
5445	Persichetti, Vincent	1915-1987	little man	Op. 129 No. I	Unspec.	Elkan-Vogel	In "glad and very, five cummings choruses." Intended for chorus, may be perf. as duet. Copyright 1976.	MSN
5446	Persichetti, Vincent	1915-1987	maggie and milly and molly and may	Op. 98, No. 3	Unspec.	Elkan-Vogel	In "four cummings choruses." Intended for chorus, may be perf. as duet. Copyright 1966.	MSN
5447	Persichetti, Vincent	1915-1987	maybe god	Op. 129 No. III	Unspec.	Elkan-Vogel	In "glad and very, five cummings choruses." Intended for chorus, may be perf. as duet Copyright 1976.	MSN
5448	Persichetti, Vincent	1915-1987	nouns to nouns	Op. 98, No. 2	Unspec.	Elkan-Vogel	In "four cummings choruses." Intended for chorus, may be perf. as duet. Copyright 1966.	MSN
5449	Persichetti, Vincent	1915-1987	uncles	Op. 98, No. 4	Unspec.	Elkan-Vogel	In "four cummings choruses." Intended for chorus, may be perf. as duet. Copyright 1966.	MSN
5450	Peter, G.		Dein denk' ich immer		Unspec.	Hochstein		CHAL (1911)
5451	Peter, G.		Eins, zwei, drei, ei, ei, ei		Unspec.	Hochstein		CHAL (1911)
5452	Peter, G.		Grüss dich. Line, ei wie fein		2 female v.	Hochstein		CHAL (1906)
5453	Peter, G.		Ihr Damen und Herren merket auf		Unspec.	Hochstein		CHAL (1906)
5454	Peter, G.		Im Sonnengold, im Abendroth		2 female v.	Hochstein		CHAL (1906)
5455	Peter, G.		Keine Ruh bei Tag und Nacht		2 female v.	Hochstein		CHAL (1911)
5456	Peter, G.		Musiker vor Gericht "Duo-Scene"		Unspec.	Hochstein		CHAL (1906)
5457	Peter, G.		Noch klingt mir von Hause		2 female v.	Hochstein i. H.		CHAL (1906)
5458	Peter, G.		Wir sind vakante Mädchen		2 female v.	Hochstein		CHAL (1911)
5459	Peter, G.		Zwei steinalte Jungfern		2 female v.	Hochstein		CHAL (1911)
5460	Peterkin, Norman	1886-	Soontree		Unspec.	OUP		BBC (1975)
5461	Peuschel, Moritz	1838-1892	Beiden Nachbarinnen "Wo nur mein liebes Männchen"	Op. 33 No. 1	S/S	P. & M.		CHAL (1898)
5462	Peuschel, Moritz	1838-1892	Beiden Wittwen "Ha, es ist fürwahr zum lachen"	Op. 25	S/S	P. & M.		CHAL (1898)
5463	Peuschel, Moritz	1838-1892	Flieg' aus, du einsam' Vögelein "Ein Pärchen hat sein Nest gefunden"	Op. 56 No. 1	S/A	Eulenburg		CHAL (1898)
5464	Peuschel, Moritz	1838-1892	Frau Professorin und Frau Assessorin "Ei guten Morgen"		S/S	Cranz		CHAL (1898)
5465	Peuschel, Moritz	1838-1892	Glückliche Stunden "Ei wie hell die Kerzen glänzen"	Op. 63 No. 4	Unspec.	Strauch		CHAL (1898)
5466	Peuschel, Moritz	1838-1892	Im Schatten der Linde	Op. 59	S/A	Hug		CHAL (1898)
5467	Peuschel, Moritz	1838-1892	Julia und Selika "Ei liebe Julia, da sind Sie ja"	Op. 36	S/S	P. & M.		CHAL (1898)

REC	COMP	DTS	TITLE	OP #	VCG	PUB	COMMENTS	SRC
5468	Peuschel, Moritz	1838-1892	Klage Frau Professorin "Darf ich meinen Augen trau'n"	Op. 20	S/S	P. & M.		CHAL (1898)
5469	Peuschel, Moritz	1838-1892	Lockung "Hörst du nicht die Bäume rauschen"	Op. 56 No. 2	S/A	Eulenburg		CHAL (1898)
5470	Peuschel, Moritz	1838-1892	Unterm schimmernden Weihnachtsbaum "Ihr theuren Eltern mein"	Op. 36 No. 1	Unspec.	Strauch		CHAL (1898)
5471	Peuschel, Moritz	1838-1892	Wachtelschlag "Wie frisch erquick"	Op. 56 No. 3	S/A	Eulenburg		CHAL (1898)
5472	Peuschel, Moritz	1838-1892	Zum frohen Weihnachtsfeste "Sammlung"	Op. 63	Unspec.	Strauch		CHAL (1898)
5473	Pfannschmidt, A.		Nun klingt es allerwegen	Op. 11 No. d	Unspec.	Plothow	pf or org	CHAL (1906)
5474	Pfannschmidt, Heinrich	1863-	Über deinem Haupte schwebe	Op. 19	S/A	Schlesinger		CHAL (1911)
5475	Pfeil, Heinrich	1835-1899	Aus fernen längst vergangenen Tagen	Op. 19	Unspec.	Salzer		CHAL (1901)
5476	Pfeil, Heinrich	1835-1899	Still ruht der See	Op. 10 No. 1	Unspec.	Siegel		CHAL (1898)
5477	Pfennig, R. A.		Aus alten Märchen winkt es	II No. 2	S/A	B. & H.		CHAL (1906)
5478	Pflueger		Faithful forevermore		Unspec.	White-Smith	In catalogue page "Vocal Duetts" of White-Smith Music Pub. Co. (no date)	MSN
5479	Philipp, A.		Ob dir, ob dich		Unspec.	H. Augustin		CHAL (1911)
5480	Philipp, Bernard Edward	1803-1850	Begräbnisslieder (12)	Op. 12	S/A or T/B	Leuckart	Collection of 12 duets.	CHAL (1898)
5481	Philipp, J.		Brüder Springinsfeld "Brüder Springinsfeld heissen wir"	Op. 71	2 med. v.	O. Teich		CHAL (1898)
5482	Phillips, Montegue Fawcett	1885-1969	Beyond the meadow gate		Unspec.	Chappell		BBC (1975)
5483	Piel, Peter	1835-1904	Antiphona "O sacrum convivium"		Unspec.	Feuchtinger & G.	org accomp.	CHAL (1898)
5484	Piel, Peter	1835-1904	Cor dulce, cor amabile		2 female v.	Feuchtinger & G.	org accomp.	CHAL (1898)
5485	Piel, Peter	1835-1904	Gnädig hast du uns geboren		S/A	Schwann	harm	CHAL (1901)
5486	Piel, Peter	1835-1904	Juravit, Dominus		2 female v.	Feuchtinger & G.	org accomp.	CHAL (1898)
5487	Piel, Peter	1835-1904	O pulchritudo		Unspec.	Feuchtinger & G.	org accomp.	CHAL (1898)
5488	Piel, Peter	1835-1904	Offertorium "Justus ut palma"		Unspec.	Feuchtinger & G.	org accomp.	CHAL (1898)
5489	Piel, Peter	1835-1904	Pie Pelicane, Jesu Domine		Unspec.	Feuchtinger & G.	org accomp.	CHAL (1898)
5490	Pierson, Henry Hugh	1815-1873	Frühling im Herbst "Schon ist der letzte Blüthenstern"	Op. 89 No. 2	Unspec.	Sch. & Co.		CHAL (1898)
5491	Pierson, Henry Hugh	1815-1873	Wanderers Nachtlied "Über allen Gipfeln (Wipfeln) ist Ruh"	Op. 89 No. 1	Unspec.	Sch. & Co.		CHAL (1898)
5492	Pinkham, Daniel	1923-	Litany, A		S/A	AMP	pf or org accomp.	CVMP (1976)
5493	Pinsuti, Ciro	1829-1888	Bygone days		Unspec.	Novello		BBC (1975)
5494	Pinsuti, Ciro	1829-1888	Due Perle "Non siamo sorelle"	No. 2	S/A	Fürstner		CHAL (1898)

REC	COMP	DTS	TITLE	OP #	VCG	PUB	COMMENTS	SRC
5495	Pinsuti, Ciro	1829-1888	False love and true love		Unspec.	Novello		BBC (1975)
5496	Pinsuti, Ciro	1829-1888	Life is passing away		high & low v.	Church	In anthology "Sacred Duets A Collection of Two-Part Songs by the Best Composers" Vol. 2. Compi. & ed. W. Shakespeare. Pub. 1907.	MSN
5497	Pinsuti, Ciro	1829-1888	Love and friendship		Unspec.	Novello		BBC (1975)
5498	Pinsuti, Ciro	1829-1888	Nightless land, The		S/A	White-Smith	In catalogue page "Vocal Duetts" of White-Smith Music Pub. Co. (no date)	MSN
5499	Pinsuti, Ciro	1829-1888	Sunrise		Unspec.	Brain-ard's Sons	In anthology "Brainard's Collection of Vocal Duets from Popular Modern and Standard Composers" Pub. 1903.	MSN
5500	Pinsuti, Ciro	1829-1888	The magicians		Unspec.	Novello		BBC (1975)
5501	Pinsuti, Ciro	1829-1888	The mermaids		Unspec.	Novello		BBC (1975)
5502	Pinsuti, Ciro	1829-1888	There is a Reaper		2 high v.	Church	In anthology "Sacred Duets A Collection of Two-Part Songs by the Best Composers" Vol. 1. Compi. & ed. W. Shakespeare. Pub. 1907.	MSN
5503	Pinsuti, Ciro	1829-1888	There is a Reaper		high & low v.	Church	In anthology "Sacred Duets A Collection of Two-Part Songs by the Best Composers" Vol. 2. Compi. & ed. W. Shakespeare. Pub. 1907.	MSN
5504	Pinsuti, Ciro	1829-1888	Under the stars		Unspec.	Novello		BBC (1975)
5505	Pinsuti, Ciro	1829-1888	Venezia "Vieni la notto"	No. 6	A/T or S/A	Fürstner		CHAL (1898)
5506	Pinsuti, Ciro	1829-1888	When life is brightest		S/A	Curwen		BBC (1975)
5507	Pirani, Eugenio	1852-1939	Glockenklang "Weisst du noch, mein liebes Kind"	Op. 56 No. 1	Unspec.	Schlesin-ger		CHAL (1898)
5508	Pirani, Eugenio	1852-1939	O lieb' anch du "Es flüstern die Wellen"	Op. 56 No. 1	Unspec.	Schlesin-ger		CHAL (1898)
5509	Pircher, J.		Mir Zwoa san verlassen	Op. 34	S/A	Potius		CHAL (1906)
5510	Pivoda, F.	1824-1898	Dar nejneznejsi "Zná-te dárek nejmilejsí"	Op. 37	Unspec.	Hofmann i. Pr.		CHAL (1898)
5511	Pivoda, F.	1824-1898	Verceni (Abendlied)	Op. 47	2 female v.	Hoffmann i. Pr.		CHAL (1898)
5512	Pivoda, F.	1824-1898	Waldlied "Wo Büsche steh'n und Bäume"	Op. 20	Unspec.	Leuckart		CHAL (1898)
5513	Pivoda, F.	1824-1898	Wanderers Abendlied "Die ihr mit dem Oden"	Op. 18	Unspec.	Leuckart		CHAL (1898)
5514	Pla, M.		El Soldado		Unspec.	UME	Ed. Subira	CVMP (1976)
5515	Plag, Johann	1863-1921	Ein froher Festtag kehret wieder	Op. 20 No. 1	Unspec.	Bayr-hoffer		CHAL (1898)
5516	Plag, Johann	1863-1921	Ein Lied will ich dir weihen	Op. 20 No. 2	Unspec.	Bayr-hoffer		CHAL (1898)
5517	Plag, Johann	1863-1921	Gratulanten "5 Dichtungen"	Op. 20	Unspec.	Bayr-hoffer	5 duets	CHAL (1898)

REC	COMP	DTS	TITLE	OP #	VCG	PUB	COMMENTS	SRC
5518	Plag, Johann	1863-1921	Heute bringe ich auf's Neue	Op. 20 No. 3	Unspec.	Bayrhoffer		CHAL (1898)
5519	Plag, Johann	1863-1921	Missa in honorem St. Aloysii	Op. 17	Unspec.	Schwann	org accomp.	CHAL (1898)
5520	Plag, Johann	1863-1921	Missa in honorem St. Francisi Xaverii	Op. 15	Unspec.	Schwann	org accomp.	CHAL (1898)
5521	Plag, Johann	1863-1921	O die Freude, die uns heute	Op. 20 No. 5	Unspec.	Bayrhoffer		CHAL (1898)
5522	Plag, Johann	1863-1921	Wir erscheiden dich zu grüssen	Op. 20 No. 4	Unspec.	Bayrhoffer		CHAL (1898)
5523	Plantade, Charles Henri	1764-1839	Ad te Domine clamabo		Unspec.	Schott	pf and org accomp.	CHAL (1898)
5524	Plantade, Charles Henri	1764-1839	Exaudiat	No. 22	Unspec.	Schott	pf and org accomp.	CHAL (1898)
5525	Plantade, Charles Henri	1764-1839	Mater misericordiae	No. 20	Unspec.	Schott	pf and org accomp.	CHAL (1898)
5526	Plantade, Charles Henri	1764-1839	Scene d'Esther	No. 5	Unspec.	Schott	pf and org accomp.	CHAL (1898)
5527	Plengorth, Friedrich	1828-1896	Wanderlust "O Wander-glück, O Wanderlust"	Op. 26	Unspec.	Tonger		CHAL (1898)
5528	Plengorth, Friedrich	1828-1896	Im Maien "Nun (Es) bricht aus allen Zweigen"	Op. 12	Unspec.	Hartmann i. Elberf.		CHAL (1898)
5529	Pleskow, Raoul	1931-	Six Brief Verses		S/A	Am. Comp. Al.		CVMP (1995)
5530	Pleyel, Ianos [Ignaz Josef]	1757-1831	Scottish Airs		Unspec.	Preston	Ed. Thomson. Arr. of Scot. Airs. Originally appeared ~1792.	BBC (1975)
5531	Pocci, Franz von	1807-1876	Mein Wunsch "Ich möchte mit dem Strome rauschen"	Op. 8 No. 2	S/A	B. & H.		CHAL (1898)
5532	Pocci, Franz von	1807-1876	Nachtgesang im Walde "Vöglein schlummern"	Op. 8 No. 1	S/A	B. & H.		CHAL (1898)
5533	Pocci, Franz von	1807-1876	Voga, voga, il vento face	Op. 8 No. 3	S/A	B. & H.		CHAL (1898)
5534	Pogge, H.		Dies ist der Herbst	Op. 2 No. 3	S/A	Leichssen-ring		CHAL (1901)
5535	Pogge, H.		Es geht ein Wandrer durch die Nacht	Op. 2 No. 1	S/A	Leichssen-ring		CHAL (1901)
5536	Pogge, H.		Unter Rosen und Ranken	Op. 2 No. 2	Unspec.	Leichssen-ring		CHAL (1901)
5537	Pohl, Max	1869-1928	O Herr, erleuchte sie durch deinen Geist	Op. 45	Unspec.	Kaun	org	CHAL (1911)
5538	Pommer, Josef	1845-1918	Turracher-Lieder "35 Volks-lieder von der steyrisch-kärtnerischen Grenze"		Unspec.	Robits-chek	Arr. Pommer. Anthol-ogy. Arr. of 35 folk-duets.	CHAL (1911)
5539	Ponflick, F.		Frühling "So wundersam ist doch der Morgen"	No. 1	Unspec.	R. & E.		CHAL (1898)
5540	Ponflick, F.		Herbst "Bedächt' ger, doch mit frischem Sinn"	No. 3	Unspec.	R. & E.		CHAL (1898)
5541	Ponflick, F.		Jahreszeiten 4 Duette		Unspec.	R. & E.	4 duets	CHAL (1898)
5542	Ponflick, F.		Sommer "In tiefer stiller Sommernacht"	No. 2	Unspec.	R. & E.		CHAL (1898)
5543	Ponflick, F.		Winter "Rastlos prasselnd tobt schnöder Ost"	No. 4	Unspec.	R. & E.		CHAL (1898)
5544	Pontet, Henry	1835-1902	Broken Pitcher, The		Unspec.	Leonard-Eng	Also solo	CVMP (1976)
5545	Pontet, Henry	1835-1902	I'd rather not		Unspec.	Sheard		BBC (1975)
5546	Ponvet, A. M.		Yo quiero unbesito "Ven a mi lado"		Unspec.	Wagner & Levien		CHAL (1898)

REC	COMP	DTS	TITLE	OP #	VCG	PUB	COMMENTS	SRC
5547	Popp, Wilhelm	1828-1903	Ein Schwalbenlied "Du liebe, süsse Schwalbenfrau"	Op. 464 No. 1	Unspec.	Benjamin		CHAL (1898)
5548	Popp, Wilhelm	1828-1903	Guter Fang "Ging ein muntrer Vogelsteller"	Op. 464 No. 5	Unspec.	Benjamin		CHAL (1898)
5549	Popp, Wilhelm	1828-1903	Im Thüringer Wald "In dem Thüringer Wald, wo die Erbeeren blühn"	Op. 464 No. 2	Unspec.	Benjamin		CHAL (1898)
5550	Popp, Wilhelm	1828-1903	Mädchenlied "Ich bin so arm und niedrig"	Op. 464 No. 3	Unspec.	Benjamin		CHAL (1898)
5551	Popp, Wilhelm	1828-1903	Rosenlied "O goldne Zeit der Rosen"	Op. 464 No. 6	Unspec.	Benjamin		CHAL (1898)
5552	Popp, Wilhelm	1828-1903	Schätzlein und Kätzlein "Ich hatt' ein liebes Schätzchen"	Op. 464 No. 4	Unspec.	Benjamin		CHAL (1898)
5553	Por, C.		In Grinzing und Sievring da is'		Unspec.	Winklmn i W.		CHAL (1901)
5554	Porepp, Georg	1895-	Christkind kam in den Winterwald	Op. 13	Unspec.	Virgilius-Verlag	a.k.a. Gregor Popper	CHAL (1911)
5555	Porepp, Georg	1895-	Silberflocken, leicht und leise	Op. 24	Unspec.	Eisoldt & R. Schles.	a.k.a. Gregor Popper	CHAL (1911)
5556	Pourny, Ch.		Jeune marchande d'images "Achetez moi"		Unspec.	Cranz		CHAL (1898)
5557	Pourny, Ch.		Soleil et la lune "Car j'aime á voir"		Unspec.	Cranz		CHAL (1898)
5558	Praeger, Heinrich Aloys	1783-1854	Liebes-Katechimus "Schaterl, wann liabst mi"		Unspec.	Kistner		CHAL (1898)
5559	Prechtl, Ludwig	1865-1930	O lieber Schatz, ich denke dein "In zahloser Reihe die Sterne"	Op. 2	Unspec.	Robit-schek		CHAL (1898)
5560	Prechtl, Ludwig	1865-1930	Treueutsches Niederösterreich "Flotte Geister Weanakinder"	Op. 8	Unspec.	Rörich		CHAL (1898)
5561	Preil, Paul	1879-	Wir sind fidele Brüder	No. 5	Unspec.	Danner	a.k.a. J. B. Lupton and Erich Seifert	CHAL (1911)
5562	Preitz, Franz	1856-1916	Wo du hingehst, da will auch ich hingehen	Op. 19	S/A or S/Br	Haushahn	org or pf	CHAL (1906)
5563	Pressel, Gustav Adolf	1827-1890	Hier hab' ich so manches liebe Mal		Unspec.	Simrock	Ed. Himmel	CHAL (1911)
5564	Pressel, Gustav Adolf	1827-1890	Trommlers Tagewacht "Morgens zwischen drei'n und vieren"		Unspec.	Simrock	Conducted exhaustive research on Mozart "Requiem"	CHAL (1898)
5565	Preyer, Gottfried von	1807-1901	Nacht und Träume "Heil'ge Nacht, du sinkest"	Op. 51	2 female v.	Cranz		CHAL (1898)
5566	Prior-Lipart, A.		Ja wir sind lustig und fidel		Unspec.	O. Dietrich		CHAL (1906)
5567	Proch, Heinrich	1809-1878	Es hat in stiller Nacht	Op. 19	med. & high v.	Rühle i. L.		CHAL (1911)
5568	Proch, Heinrich	1809-1878	Frühlingswonne "Hoch in den grünen Zweigen"	Op. 227 No. 3	2 female v.	Cranz		CHAL (1898)
5569	Proch, Heinrich	1809-1878	Glaube, Hoffe, Liebe "Glaube, spricht die innre Stimme"	Op. 227 No. 2	2 female v.	Cranz		CHAL (1898)
5570	Proch, Heinrich	1809-1878	O lasse Lieb' nicht von dir geh'n "Eine Hand, die in der deinen liegt"	Op. 227 No. 1	2 female v.	Cranz		CHAL (1898)
5571	Proch, Heinrich	1809-1878	Zwei Träume	Op. 19	Unspec.	Cranz		CHAL (1898)
5572	Procházka, J.		Dobrou noc	Op. 22 No. 1	2 female v.	Urbánek		CHAL (1898)
5573	Procházka, J.		Jede mily na konicku	Op. 22 No. 3	2 female v.	Urbánek		CHAL (1898)

REC	COMP	DTS	TITLE	OP #	VCG	PUB	COMMENTS	SRC
5574	Procházka, J.		Logika lásky	Op. 22 No. 2	2 female v.	Urbânek		CHAL (1898)
5575	Procházka, Ludwig	1837-1888	Sternennacht "Golden winkt die Sonne"	No. 3	Unspec.	Simrock		CHAL (1898)
5576	Procházka, Ludwig	1837-1888	Verrath "Mägdlein! nicht verrathe"	No. 2	Unspec.	Simrock		CHAL (1898)
5577	Procházka, Ludwig	1837-1888	Wildente "Wildentlein seewärts flog"	No. 1	Unspec.	Simrock		CHAL (1898)
5578	Prochazka, Rudolf	1864-1936	Ein Vöglein hat gesungen	Op. 1 No. 6	MS/A	Luckhardt		CHAL (1898)
5579	Prochazka, Rudolf	1864-1936	O komm zu mir, wenn flüsternd der Wind	Op. 1 No. 7	S/A	Luckhardt		CHAL (1898)
5580	Prokofiev, Serge	1891-1953	Prokoviev Vocal Works	Vol II	Unspec.	Mez Kniga	Collection. Works for 1-2 v.	CVMP (1976)
5581	Prokofiev, Serge	1891-1953	Vocal Works, Vol. II		Var.	Mez Kniga	Unspec. pieces for 1-2 v. Includes duets.	ASR
5582	Proschel, G. (Johann Strauss Jr.)		Wiener Blut "Quando schiudi il tuo labro"		Unspec.	Cranz	Arr. of Strauss waltz by G. Proschel	CHAL (1898)
5583	Puchat, Max	1859-1919	Aus den Bergen 2 Duetten f. S. u. A.	Op. 19	S/A	Bisping i. M.	Duet collection	CHAL (1898)
5584	Puchat, Max	1859-1919	Rauber, Mei Schatz is a Rauber"	Op. 19 No. 2	S/A	Bisping		CHAL (1898)
5585	Puchat, Max	1859-1919	Volkslied "Wozu, wozu mir sein sollte"	Op. 19 No. 1	S/A	Bisping i. M.		CHAL (1898)
5586	Pucitta, Vincenzo	d. 1925	Un palpiti mi sento		S/S or S/T	Cranz, Junne, Heinr.		CHAL (1898)
5587	Puget, Louise-Françoise	1810-1889	Singende Nachtigall		Unspec.	Schott	Fr. woman comp.	CHAL (1898)
5588	Queling, Theodor	1856-	Luise Hensel-Album "Ein- u. Mehrst."		Unspec.	Junfermann	Collection, for 1 v., 2 v. to many v.	CHAL (1911)
5589	Quilter, Roger	1877-1953	Cradle in Bethlehem, The		Unspec.	Roberton		CVMP (1976)
5590	Quilter, Roger	1877-1953	Cradle in Bethlehem, The		S/S	Curwen	pf or inst accomp.	ASR
5591	Quilter, Roger	1877-1953	Summer sunset		S/A	A. H. & C.		BBC (1975)
5592	Quilter, Roger	1877-1953	Windy nights		S/A	A. H. & C.		BBC (1975)
5593	Quiquerez, Hermann	d. 1925	Das wär' ein' Idee "Mein Fräulein darf ich bitten"	Op. 44	Unspec.	Robitschek		CHAL (1898)
5594	Quiquerez, Hermann	d. 1925	Jetzt möcht' ich nur wissen warum "In aller Fruah hört man"	No. 47	Unspec.	Robitschek		CHAL (1898)
5595	Quiquerez, Hermann	d. 1925	Orpheum-Speise-Karte "Hier im Saal hat er's gedicht'"	Op. 45	Unspec.	Robitschek		CHAL (1898)
5596	Rachmaninov, Sergei	1873-1943	Two partings		Unspec.	Gutheil	Tr. from Russ.?	BBC (1975)
5597	Rachmaninov, Sergei	1873-1943	We shall have peace		Unspec.	Gutheil	Tr. from Russ.?	BBC (1975)
5598	Radecke, Robert	1830-1911	Aus der Jugendzeit, aus der Jugendzeit klingt ein Lied	Op. 22 No. 1	Unspec.	Bahn		CHAL (1898)
5599	Radecke, Robert	1830-1911	Aus der Tiefe rufe ich	Op. 31 No. 1	S/A	Bahn		CHAL (1901)
5600	Radecke, Robert	1830-1911	Ich bin gekommen	Op. 31 No. 2	S/A	Bahn		CHAL (1901)
5601	Radecke, Robert	1830-1911	In der Nacht "Leben ist draussen verrauschet"	Op. 14 No. 2	S/A	Bahn		CHAL (1898)

REC	COMP	DTS	TITLE	OP #	VCG	PUB	COMMENTS	SRC
5602	Radecke, Robert	1830-1911	O der blaue, blaue Himmel	Op. 47 No. 3	S/A	B. & B.		CHAL (1898)
5603	Radecke, Robert	1830-1911	Schlaf ein mein Herz	Op. 14 No. 3	S/A	Bahn		CHAL (1898)
5604	Radecke, Robert	1830-1911	Stille "Wiege mich ein, du Mutter alles Trostes"	Op. 47 No. 1	S/A	B. & B.		CHAL (1898)
5605	Radecke, Robert	1830-1911	Winterlied "Lautlos steht der ernste Wald"	Op. 47 No. 2	Unspec.	B. & B.		CHAL (1898)
5606	Radecke, Robert	1830-1911	Zweigesang der Elfen "Hörst du das Flüstern"	Op. 16	S/S	Schlesinger		CHAL (1898)
5607	Radecke, Robert	1830-1911	Zweigesang "Im Fliederbusch ein Vöglein sass"	Op. 14 No. 1	S/A	Bahn		CHAL (1898)
5608	Radecke, Rudolph	1829-1893	Singvöglein und Sommervöglein "Singvöglein schwingt hoch sie"	Op. 8	2 female v.	Bahn		CHAL (1898)
5609	Raff, Joseph	1822-1882	Frühlingsmorgen "Wenn die Lämmer wieder springen"	Op. 114 No. 2	Unspec.	R. Forberg		CHAL (1898)
5610	Raff, Joseph	1822-1882	Glücklich, wer auf Gott vertraut	Op. 114 No. 3	Unspec.	R. Forberg		CHAL (1898)
5611	Raff, Joseph	1822-1882	Kapelle "Droben stehet die Kapelle"	Op. 114 No. 1	Unspec.	R. Forberg		CHAL (1898)
5612	Raff, Joseph	1822-1882	Liebesreim "Ich bin dein, du bist mein"	Op. 114 No. 5	Unspec.	R. Forberg		CHAL (1898)
5613	Raff, Joseph	1822-1882	Nach diesen trüben Tagen	Op. 114 No. 6	Unspec.	R. Forberg		CHAL (1898)
5614	Raff, Joseph	1822-1882	Rosenlied "Rose blüht"	Op. 114 No. 7	Unspec.	R. Forberg		CHAL (1898)
5615	Raff, Joseph	1822-1882	Ständchen "In dem Himmel ruht die Erde"	Op. 114 No. 4	Unspec.	R. Forberg		CHAL (1898)
5616	Raff, Joseph	1822-1882	Vergissmeinnicht "Es blüht ein schönes Blümchen"	Op. 114 No. 8	Unspec.	R. Forberg		CHAL (1898)
5617	Raff, Joseph	1822-1882	Vögleins Frage "Bist du da, ja ja"	Op. 114 No. 9	Unspec.	R. Forberg		CHAL (1898)
5618	Raff, Joseph	1822-1882	Wallfahrtslied "Wir wandern über Berg und Thal"	Op. 114 No. 10	Unspec.	R. Forberg		CHAL (1898)
5619	Raff, Joseph	1822-1882	Was singt die Lerche so schön	Op. 114 No. 11	Unspec.	R. Forberg		CHAL (1898)
5620	Raff, Joseph	1822-1882	Zum neuen Jahr "Wie heimlicher Weise"	Op. 114 No. 12	Unspec.	R. Forberg		CHAL (1898)
5621	Raida, Karl Alexander	1852-1923	Flatter-Duett "Nach dem klaten Land der Reussen"		Unspec.	K. & G.		CHAL (1898)
5622	Raillard, Theodor	1864-1929	Nun gute Nacht du lieber Gottessohn		Unspec.	Rud. Dietrich		CHAL (1906)
5623	Raillard, Theodor	1864-1929	Nur du "Rings ist die Nacht"	Op. 4 No. 2	S/A	Zschocher		CHAL (1898)
5624	Raillard, Theodor	1864-1929	O glücklich wer ein Herz gefunden	Op. 4 No. 2	S/A	Zschocher		CHAL (1898)
5625	Raillard, Theodor	1864-1929	Schlaf, Jesulein, schlafe und träume		Unspec.	Rud. Dietrich		CHAL (1901)
5626	Ramann, Bruno	1832-1887	Abendfieier in Venedig "Ave Maria, Meer und Himmel"	Op. 36 No. 1	Unspec.	Hoffarth		CHAL (1898)
5627	Ramann, Bruno	1832-1887	Ade "Es pflegt sich der Saft"	Op. 57 No. 10	Unspec.	Siegel		CHAL (1898)
5628	Ramann, Bruno	1832-1887	Auf dem See "Kaum haben wir verlassen"	Op. 52 No. 6	Unspec.	R. & E.		CHAL (1898)
5629	Ramann, Bruno	1832-1887	Ave Maria, Meer und Himmel ruh'n	Op. 36 No. 1	Unspec.	Hoffarth		CHAL (1901)
5630	Ramann, Bruno	1832-1887	Da drüben "Da drüben über'm Walde"	Op. 57 No. 9	Unspec.	Siegel		CHAL (1898)
5631	Ramann, Bruno	1832-1887	Du Krone der Welt "Zwei Äuglein so hold"	Op. 57 No. 8	Unspec.	Siegel		CHAL (1898)

REC	COMP	DTS	TITLE	OP #	VCG	PUB	COMMENTS	SRC
5632	Ramann, Bruno	1832-1887	Einien Brief soll ich schreiben	Op. 57 No. 4	Unspec.	Siegel		CHAL (1898)
5633	Ramann, Bruno	1832-1887	Erwartung "Vom grünen Wald ein Posthorn schallt"	Op. 57 No. 6	Unspec.	Siegel		CHAL (1898)
5634	Ramann, Bruno	1832-1887	Es steigt aus blauen Seen	Op. 36 No. 2	Unspec.	Hoffarth		CHAL (1898)
5635	Ramann, Bruno	1832-1887	Es steigt von blauen Seen	Op. 36 No. 2	Unspec.	Hoffarth		CHAL (1901)
5636	Ramann, Bruno	1832-1887	Herbstlied "Nun wird so braun so falbe"	Op. 52 No. 8	Unspec.	R. & E.		CHAL (1898)
5637	Ramann, Bruno	1832-1887	In der Fremde "Wind, o lass dein scharfes Weh'n"	Op. 57 No. 12	Unspec.	Siegel		CHAL (1898)
5638	Ramann, Bruno	1832-1887	In meinem Garten die Nelken	Op. 36 No. 3	Unspec.	Hoffarth		CHAL (1898)
5639	Ramann, Bruno	1832-1887	In meinem Garten die Nelken	Op. 36 No. 3	Unspec.	Hoffarth		CHAL (1901)
5640	Ramann, Bruno	1832-1887	Kein Graben so breit	Op. 36 No. 4	Unspec.	Hoffarth		CHAL (1898)
5641	Ramann, Bruno	1832-1887	Kein Graben so breit	Op. 36 No. 4	Unspec.	Hoffarth		CHAL (1901)
5642	Ramann, Bruno	1832-1887	Kein' schön're Zeit auf Erden ist	Op. 36 No. 6	Unspec.	Hoffarth		CHAL (1901)
5643	Ramann, Bruno	1832-1887	Libellentanz "Wir Libellen hüpfen"	Op. 52 No. 2	Unspec.	R. & E.		CHAL (1898)
5644	Ramann, Bruno	1832-1887	Liebeswonne "Welt, die weite Gotteswelt"	Op. 57 No. 1	Unspec.	Siegel		CHAL (1898)
5645	Ramann, Bruno	1832-1887	Mailied "Kein' schön're (schöner) Zeit auf Erden ist"	Op. 36 No. 6	Unspec.	Hoffarth		CHAL (1898)
5646	Ramann, Bruno	1832-1887	Robin Adair "Willkommen am Strand die denn"	Op. 57 No. 11	Unspec.	Siegel		CHAL (1898)
5647	Ramann, Bruno	1832-1887	Schiffer stösst vom Strande	Op. 57 No. 2	Unspec.	Siegel		CHAL (1898)
5648	Ramann, Bruno	1832-1887	Schöne Traum "Nun steht in frischer Grüne"	Op. 52 No. 3	Unspec.	R. & E.		CHAL (1898)
5649	Ramann, Bruno	1832-1887	Sel'ge Zeit "Mein Herz ist wie der Himmel weit"	Op. 17 No. 4	Unspec.	B. & B.		CHAL (1898)
5650	Ramann, Bruno	1832-1887	Seliges Ende "In einem grünen Wald"	Op. 57 No. 7	Unspec.	Siegel		CHAL (1898)
5651	Ramann, Bruno	1832-1887	Sommermorgen "Wie herrlich strahlt im Morgenthau"	Op. 52 No. 4	Unspec.	R. & E.		CHAL (1898)
5652	Ramann, Bruno	1832-1887	Unter den Bäumen "Leise rauschen die Blätter"	Op. 52 No. 5	Unspec.	R. & E.		CHAL (1898)
5653	Ramann, Bruno	1832-1887	Vöglein im Walde "Lust-iges Vöglein im Walde"	Op. 52 No. 1	Unspec.	R. & E.		CHAL (1898)
5654	Ramann, Bruno	1832-1887	Vögleins Dank "Hört ich nicht ein Vöglein singen"	Op. 52 No. 9	Unspec.	R. & E.		CHAL (1898)
5655	Ramann, Bruno	1832-1887	Wald und Wiese "Blumen des Waldes"	Op. 52 No. 7	Unspec.	R. & E.		CHAL (1898)
5656	Ramann, Bruno	1832-1887	Wegewart "Es wartet ein bleiches Junfräulein"	Op. 57 No. 5	Unspec.	Siegel		CHAL (1898)
5657	Ramann, Bruno	1832-1887	Wenn Zwei sich lieben von ganzem Herzen	Op. 57 No. 3	Unspec.	Siegel		CHAL (1898)
5658	Ramann, Bruno	1832-1887	Winterlied "In Schnee und Eis starrt"	Op. 52 No. 10	Unspec.	R. & E.		CHAL (1898)
5659	Ramann, Bruno	1832-1887	Wir sassen auf hohem Felsgestein	Op. 36 No. 5	Unspec.	Hoffarth		CHAL (1898)
5660	Ramann, Bruno	1832-1887	Wir sassen auf hohem Felsgestein	Op. 36 No. 5	Unspec.	Hoffarth		CHAL (1901)
5661	Ramshorst, J. D. von		Wij Zijn Jong		Unspec.	Alsbach	Works for 1-3 v.	CVMP (1976)

REC	COMP	DTS	TITLE	OP #	VCG	PUB	COMMENTS	SRC
5662	Randhartinger, Benedict	1802-1893	Waldliebe "Fort, nur fort"		Unspec.	Robit-schek		CHAL (1898)
5663	Raphael, Georg	19th C.	Christkindlein kommt von Gottes Thron		S/A	Oppen-heimer		CHAL (1901)
5664	Raphael, Gunther	1903-1960	Herr Christ, hilf uns		S/A	Hanssler	org accomp.	CVMP (1976)
5665	Raphael, Gunther	1903-1960	Herr Christ, hilf uns		S/A	Hanssler	org accomp.	ASR
5666	Rasbach, Oscar		Trees		S/A or T/Br	G. Schirm.	Arr. C. Deis. In catalogue page "Selected Vocal Duets" of G. Schirmer, Inc. NY (no date)	MSN
5667	Rathgeber, Georg	1869-	Missa in honorem St. Agathae	Op. 6	Unspec.	Feuchtin-ger	org or harm accomp.	CHAL (1898)
5668	Ray, Lilian		The Sunshine of Your Smile		high & low v.	Harms (NY)	Woman comp.	MSN
5669	Recli, Giulia	1890-	La Sorellina Dorme		S/A	Bongio-vanni	It. woman comp.	ASR
5670	Reger, Max	1873-1916	Abendgang	Op. 111a No. 3	S/A or S/MS or S/Br	B. & H.	In "Drei Duette für Sopran und Alt" Op. 111a, although v. vary. In collection "Sämtliche Werke" Pub. 1954.	NATS-VCD
5671	Reger, Max	1873-1916	Abendlied	Op. 14 No. 2	S/S	Schotts	In "Funf Duette für Sopran und Alt"	CVMP (1976)
5672	Reger, Max	1873-1916	Abendlied	Op. 14 No. 2	S/A or S/MS or S/Br	B. & H.	In "Fünf Duette für Sopran und Alt" Op. 14, although v. vary. In collection "Sämtliche Werke" Pub. 1954.	NATS-VCD
5673	Reger, Max	1873-1916	Abendlied "Über allen Gipfeln ist Ruh"	Op. 14 No. 2	S/A	Schott	In "Fünf Duette für Sopran und Alt"	MSN
5674	Reger, Max	1873-1916	Aus scimmernden Zweigen	Op. 111a No. 3	S/A	B. & B.		CHAL (1911)
5675	Reger, Max	1873-1916	Five Duets, Op. 14	Op. 14	S/A	Schott	Unspec. pieces	ASR
5676	Reger, Max	1873-1916	Frühlingsfeier	Op. 111a No. 2	S/A or S/MS or S/Br	B. & H.	In "Drei Duette für Sopran und Alt" Op. 111a, although v. vary. In collection "Sämtliche Werke" Pub. 1954.	NATS-VCD
5677	Reger, Max	1873-1916	Gäb's ein einzig Brünnelein	Op. 14 No. 4	S/A	Augener		CHAL (1898)
5678	Reger, Max	1873-1916	Gab's ein einzig Brunnelein	Op. 14 No. 4	S/S	Schotts	In "Funf Duette für Sopran und Alt"	CVMP (1976)
5679	Reger, Max	1873-1916	Gäb's ein einzig Brünnelein	Op. 14 No. 4	S/A	Schott	In "Fünf Duette für Sopran und Alt"	MSN
5680	Reger, Max	1873-1916	Gäb's ein einzig Brünnelein!	Op. 14 No. 4	S/A or S/MS or S/Br	B. & H.	In "Fünf Duette für Sopran und Alt" Op. 14, although v. vary. In collection "Sämtliche Werke" Pub. 1954.	NATS-VCD
5681	Reger, Max	1873-1916	Marias Wiegenlied		S/S	Bote		ASR
5682	Reger, Max	1873-1916	Nachts	Op. 14 No. 1	S/S	Schotts	In "Funf Duette für Sopran und Alt"	CVMP (1976)
5683	Reger, Max	1873-1916	Nachts	Op. 14 No. 1	S/A or S/MS or S/Br	B. & H.	In "Fünf Duette für Sopran und Alt" Op. 14, although v. vary. In collection "Sämtliche Werke" Pub. 1954.	NATS-VCD

REC	COMP	DTS	TITLE	OP #	VCG	PUB	COMMENTS	SRC
5684	Reger, Max	1873-1916	Nachts "Ich wandre durch die stille Nacht"	Op. 14 No. 1	S/A	Augener		CHAL (1898)
5685	Reger, Max	1873-1916	Nachts "Ich wandre durch die stille, stille Nacht"	Op. 14 No. 1	S/A	Schott	In "Fünf Duette für Sopran und Alt"	MSN
5686	Reger, Max	1873-1916	O frage Nicht	Op. 14 No. 5	S/S	Schotts	In "Funf Duette für Sopran und Alt"	CVMP (1976)
5687	Reger, Max	1873-1916	O frage Nicht!	Op. 14 No. 5	S/A or S/MS or S/Br	B. & H.	In "Fünf Duette für Sopran und Alt" Op. 14, although v. vary. In collection "Sämtliche Werke" Pub. 1954.	NATS-VCD
5688	Reger, Max	1873-1916	O frage nicht in bitt'rem Harm	Op. 14 No. 5	S/A	Augener		CHAL (1898)
5689	Reger, Max	1873-1916	O fragt nicht	Op. 14 No. 5	S/A	Schotts	In "Fünf Duette für Sopran und Alt"	MSN
5690	Reger, Max	1873-1916	Sämliche Werke		Unspec.	B. & H.	Collection of works by M. Reger. Pub. 1954.	NATS-SVD
5691	Reger, Max	1873-1916	Sommernacht	Op. 14 No. 3	S/S	Schotts	In "Funf Duette für Sopran und Alt"	CVMP (1976)
5692	Reger, Max	1873-1916	Sommernacht	Op. 14 No. 3	S/A or S/MS or S/Br	B. & H.	In "Fünf Duette für Sopran und Alt" Op. 14, although v. vary. In collection "Sämtliche Werke" Pub. 1954.	NATS-VCD
5693	Reger, Max	1873-1916	Sommernacht "Tausend goldne Sterne glänzen"	Op. 14 No. 3	S/A	Augener		CHAL (1898)
5694	Reger, Max	1873-1916	Sommernacht "Tausend goldne Sterne glänzen and des Abend himmels Pracht"	Op. 14 No. 3	S/A	Schott	In "Fünf Duette für Sopran und Alt"	MSN
5695	Reger, Max	1873-1916	Sonntag und Frühlingsmorgen	Op. 111 No. a 2	S/A	B. & B.		CHAL (1911)
5696	Reger, Max	1873-1916	Tantum ergo No. 1	Op. 61B No. 1	S/A or T/B	B. & H.	In "Vier 'Tantum ergo'" In collection "Sämtliche Werke" Vol. 30. Works of M. Reger. Pub. 1954.	NATS-SVD
5697	Reger, Max	1873-1916	Tantum ergo No. 2	Op. 61B No. 2	S/A or T/B	B. & H.	In "Vier 'Tantum ergo'" In collection "Sämtliche Werke" Vol. 30. Works of M. Reger. Pub. 1954.	NATS-SVD
5698	Reger, Max	1873-1916	Tantum ergo No. 3	Op. 61B No. 3	S/A or T/B	B. & H.	In "Vier 'Tantum ergo'" In collection "Sämtliche Werke" Vol. 30. Works of M. Reger. Pub. 1954.	NATS-SVD
5699	Reger, Max	1873-1916	Tantum ergo No. 4	Op. 61B No. 4	S/A or T/Br	B. & H.	In "Vier 'Tantum ergo'" In collection "Sämtliche Werke" Vol. 30. Works of M. Reger. Pub. 1954.	NATS-SVD
5700	Reger, Max	1873-1916	Three Duets		S/A	Universal	Unspec. pieces	ASR
5701	Reger, Max	1873-1916	Und haben auch im grünen Wald	Op. 111 No. a 1	S/A	B. & B.		CHAL (1911)
5702	Reger, Max	1873-1916	Waldesstille	Op. 111a No. 1	S/A or S/MS or S/Br	B. & H.	In "Drei Duette für Sopran und Alt" Op. 111a, although v. vary. In collection "Sämtliche Werke" Pub. 1954.	NATS-VCD
5703	Reger, Max	1873-1916	Wanderers Nachtlied "Über allen Gipfeln (Wipfeln) ist Ruh"	Op. 14 No. 2	S/A	Augener		CHAL (1898)

REC	COMP	DTS	TITLE	OP #	VCG	PUB	COMMENTS	SRC
5704	Reh, H.		Ohne Weiber sind wir seelen-lose Leiber "Ohne Weiber giebts kein Leben"		Unspec.	Heinr.		CHAL (1898)
5705	Reh, H.		Sorgenlosen "Heiter ist uns die Welt"		Unspec.	Heinr.		CHAL (1898)
5706	Reich, Reinhold	1842-1900	Abschied vom Walde "Ade du liebes Waldesgrün"	Op. 37 No. 5	Unspec.	Beyer & S.		CHAL (1898)
5707	Reich, Reinhold	1842-1900	Christbaum am Himmel "Da droben muss Christtag sein"	No. 1	Unspec.	Beyer & S.		CHAL (1898)
5708	Reich, Reinhold	1842-1900	Christkindlein kommt 3 kleine Lieder		Unspec.	Beyer & S.	Three small songs (duets)	CHAL (1898)
5709	Reich, Reinhold	1842-1900	Engel am Christabend "Über den beschneiten Rüstern"		Unspec.	Beyer & S.		CHAL (1898)
5710	Reich, Reinhold	1842-1900	Frühlingslied "Der du kamst von lichten Höhen"	Op. 37 No. 1	Unspec.	Beyer & S.		CHAL (1898)
5711	Reich, Reinhold	1842-1900	Frühlingssonntag "Das muss vom Sonntag kommen"	Op. 37 No. 2	Unspec.	Beyer & S.		CHAL (1898)
5712	Reich, Reinhold	1842-1900	Für Haus "Kleine Lieder (10)"	Op. 37	Unspec.	Beyer & S.	Collection of 10 brief songs (duets)	CHAL (1898)
5713	Reich, Reinhold	1842-1900	Herbstlied "Feldenwärts flog ein Vögelein"	Op. 37 No. 7	Unspec.	Beyer & S.		CHAL (1898)
5714	Reich, Reinhold	1842-1900	Mach' voller Einfalt mich	Op. 37 No. 10	Unspec.	Beyer & S.		CHAL (1898)
5715	Reich, Reinhold	1842-1900	Nachtied "Milde dort oben"	Op. 37 No. 6	Unspec.	Beyer & S.		CHAL (1898)
5716	Reich, Reinhold	1842-1900	Schäfers Sonntagslied "Das ist der Tag des Herrn"	Op. 37 No. 8	Unspec.	Beyer & S.		CHAL (1898)
5717	Reich, Reinhold	1842-1900	Waldconcert "Concert ist heute angesagt"	Op. 37 No. 4	Unspec.	Beyer & S.		CHAL (1898)
5718	Reich, Reinhold	1842-1900	Wanderlied "Lerche singt ihr Morgenlied"	Op. 37 No. 3	Unspec.	Beyer & S.		CHAL (1898)
5719	Reich, Reinhold	1842-1900	Weihnachten "Ein Engel stiegt hernieder"		Unspec.	Beyer & S.		CHAL (1898)
5720	Reich, Reinhold	1842-1900	Weihnachtslied "Ich schau' das Lied von Bethlehem"	Op. 37 No. 9	Unspec.	Beyer & S.		CHAL (1898)
5721	Reichardt, Gustav	1797-1884	Chi dice mal d'amore		S/S	Steinmetz i. Hamb.		CHAL (1898)
5722	Reichardt, Johann Friedrich	1752-1814	Danza		Unspec.	Melzer i. Leipz.		CHAL (1898)
5723	Reichardt, Johann Friedrich	1752-1814	Das Veilchen "Ein Veilchen auf der Wiese stand"		S/A	B. & H.	In anth. "Zweistim. Lied. f. Sop. u. Alt-stimme mit Klavierbe-gleitung f. den Haus- u. Schulgebrauch v. H. M. Schletterer" 3 vols.	MSN
5724	Reichardt, Johann Friedrich	1752-1814	In dem stillen Mondenscheine		Unspec.	Goethe-Gesell-schaft		BBC (1975)
5725	Reichardt, Johann Friedrich	1752-1814	Jäger "es ritt ein Jägersmann über die Flur"		Unspec.	Junne		CHAL (1898)
5726	Reiche, V.		Nun steht die Welt so voll Blühen		Unspec.	Leichs-seuring		CHAL (1911)
5727	Reichel, Adolf Heinrich Johann	1820-1896	Lieb ist wie ein Vögelein "Lieb' Mütterlein, lieb' Mütterlein"	Op. 73 No. 2	S/A	Leuckart		CHAL (1898)

REC	COMP	DTS	TITLE	OP #	VCG	PUB	COMMENTS	SRC
5728	Reichel, Adolf Heinrich Johann	1820-1896	Liebesgruss "Ich schlaf, ich wach"	Op. 73 No. 1	S/A	Leuckart		CHAL (1898)
5729	Reichel, Adolf Heinrich Johann	1820-1896	Schnee zerrinnt	Op. 73 No. 3	S/A	Leuckart		CHAL (1898)
5730	Reid, Alwyn		Mad midsummer days		Unspec.	Cavendish		BBC (1975)
5731	Reifner, Vincenz	1878-1922	Unterm Schirm zu zwel'n	Op. 3	Unspec.	Eulenberg		CHAL (1911)
5732	Reilly, Myles [Attr.]		Farewell to Lochaber		Unspec.	Bayley & Ferguson	Arr. Moffat	BBC (1975)
5733	Reim, Edmund	1859-1928	Frühling erwacht, Maiglöckchen lacht		Unspec.	Doblinger		CHAL (1911)
5734	Reimann, Heinrich	1850-1906	Der du am Sternenbogen	Op. 2 No. 1	2 female v.	Hainauer		CHAL (1898)
5735	Reimann, Heinrich	1850-1906	Der du am Sternenbogen	Op. 2 No. 1	2 female v.	Hainauer		CHAL (1906)
5736	Reimann, Heinrich	1850-1906	Frau Nachtigall "Frau Nachtigall, ich hör' dich singen"	Op. 2 No. 2	2 female v.	Hainauer		CHAL (1898)
5737	Reimann, Heinrich	1850-1906	Frühlingstaumel "Blätter wogen rings umher"	Op. 2 No. 4	2 female v.	Hainauer		CHAL (1898)
5738	Reimann, Heinrich	1850-1906	Nachtigall ich hör' dich singen	Op. 2 No. 2	2 female v.	Hainauer		CHAL (1906)
5739	Reimann, Heinrich	1850-1906	Schlaf wohl, du Hirtenknabe		Unspec.	Simrock	Ed. Himmel	CHAL (1911)
5740	Reimann, Heinrich	1850-1906	Und ob der holde Tag vergangen	Op. 2 No. 3	2 female v.	Hainauer	Pub. 1880	CHAL (1898)
5741	Reimann, Heinrich	1850-1906	Und ob der holde Tag vergangen	Op. 2 No. 3	2 female v.	Hainauer		CHAL (1906)
5742	Reinberger, J.		Knabe, dich gab uns Bethlehem	Op. 118 No. 6	Unspec.	R. Forberg	org accomp.	CHAL (1898)
5743	Reinecke, Carl	1824-1910	A bird sat on a hawthorne tree		Unspec.	Augener	Eng. trans. Grmn.	BBC (1975)
5744	Reinecke, Carl	1824-1910	Abendfriede "Aller Jubel ist verklungen"	Op. 109 No 4	2 female v.	B. & H.		CHAL (1898)
5745	Reinecke, Carl	1824-1910	Abendlied "Mond ist aufgegangen"	Op. 217 No. 1	S/S	Augener		CHAL (1898)
5746	Reinecke, Carl	1824-1910	Abendlied "Nun hüllen graue Nebel"	Op. 232 No. 4	Unspec.	Hug		CHAL (1898)
5747	Reinecke, Carl	1824-1910	Abschied von der Heimath "Lebe wohl du schöne Stunde"	Op. 217 No. 4	S/S	Augener		CHAL (1898)
5748	Reinecke, Carl	1824-1910	Am Bache Bachstelzchen heugt zierlich	Op. 270 No. 6	Unspec.	B. & H.		CHAL (1906)
5749	Reinecke, Carl	1824-1910	Am Geburtstage der Mutter "Einst an diesem Tage"	Op. 91 No. 2	Unspec.	B. & H.		CHAL (1898)
5750	Reinecke, Carl	1824-1910	Am Geburtstage der Mutter "Glück und Segen allerwegen"	Op. 91 No. 3	Unspec.	B. & H.		CHAL (1898)
5751	Reinecke, Carl	1824-1910	Aus jungen Tagen 6 Mädchenlieder	Op. 232	Unspec.	Hug	Collection of duets for female v.	CHAL (1898)
5752	Reinecke, Carl	1824-1910	Bescheidenes Veilchen	Op. 163 No. 10	2 female v.	R. Forberg		CHAL (1898)
5753	Reinecke, Carl	1824-1910	Bitten "Vater kröne du mit Segen"		Unspec.	Ausgb. C. Reinecke		CHAL (1898)
5754	Reinecke, Carl	1824-1910	Brautlied "Welch' ein Scheiden"	Op. 64 No. 2	S/A	Hainauer		CHAL (1898)
5755	Reinecke, Carl	1824-1910	Buntblümlein hat die Haide	Op. 189 No. 12	Unspec.	B. & H.		CHAL (1898)

REC	COMP	DTS	TITLE	OP #	VCG	PUB	COMMENTS	SRC
5756	Reinecke, Carl	1824-1910	Das Veilchen "Wie der Himmel klar und blau"	Op. 12 No. 4	S/A	B. & H.	In anth. "Zweistim. Lied. f. Sop. u. Altstimme mit Klavierbegleitung f. den Haus- u. Schulgebrauch v. H. M. Schletterer" 3 vols.	MSN
5757	Reinecke, Carl	1824-1910	Der du am Sternenbogen	Op. 64 No. 4	S/A	Hainauer		CHAL (1898)
5758	Reinecke, Carl	1824-1910	Die Roggenmohme "Lass stehn die Blume"	Op. 91 No. 5	S/A	B. & H.	In anth. "Zweistim. Lied. f. Sop. u. Altstimme mit Klavierbegleitung f. den Haus- u. Schulgebrauch v. H. M. Schletterer" 3 vols.	MSN
5759	Reinecke, Carl	1824-1910	Du flinker Gesell im rothbraunen Fell	Op. 270 No. 3	Unspec.	B. & H.		CHAL (1906)
5760	Reinecke, Carl	1824-1910	Du Himmel so blau	Op.109 No. 5	2 female v.	B. & H.		CHAL (1898)
5761	Reinecke, Carl	1824-1910	Du lieber, frommer, heil'ger Christ	Op. 91 No. 7	Unspec.	B. & H.		CHAL (1898)
5762	Reinecke, Carl	1824-1910	Duften nicht Jasminenlauben	Op. 109 No. 1	2 female v.	B. & H.		CHAL (1898)
5763	Reinecke, Carl	1824-1910	Ein Leben ohne Liebe	Op. 163 No. 1	2 female v.	R. Forberg		CHAL (1898)
5764	Reinecke, Carl	1824-1910	Elfe "Bleib' bei uns"	Op. 32 No. 2	S/S	Simrock		CHAL (1898)
5765	Reinecke, Carl	1824-1910	Fröhliche Armuth "So ein-er hat kein Zweigespann"	Op. 189 No. 7	Unspec.	B. & H.		CHAL (1898)
5766	Reinecke, Carl	1824-1910	Frühling "Und wenn die Lerche hell anstimmt"	Op. 32 No. 1	S/S	Simrock		CHAL (1898)
5767	Reinecke, Carl	1824-1910	Frühlingsblumen	Op. 26	S/A	Ditson	In anthology "The Ditson Collection of Soprano and Alto Duets" Pub. 1934.	MSN
5768	Reinecke, Carl	1824-1910	Frühlingsblumen "Nun glänzen im Lenzen"	Op. 4 No. 4	S/S	Annecke		CHAL (1898)
5769	Reinecke, Carl	1824-1910	Frühlingsglocken		S/A	F. Schel-lenb.		CVMP (1995)
5770	Reinecke, Carl	1824-1910	Gebet auf den Wassern "Nacht ist her"	Op. 163 No. 11	2 female v.	R. Forberg		CHAL (1898)
5771	Reinecke, Carl	1824-1910	Gebrochenes Herz "Rosen und die Nelken und Flieder"	Op. 32 No. 5	S/S	Simrock		CHAL (1898)
5772	Reinecke, Carl	1824-1910	Geistliches Lied "So nimm denn meine Hände"	Op. 217 No. 11	S/S	Augener		CHAL (1898)
5773	Reinecke, Carl	1824-1910	Grüss Gott du goldengrüner Hain	Op. 109 No. 6	2 female v.	B. & H.		CHAL (1898)
5774	Reinecke, Carl	1824-1910	Grüss Gott, du goldengrüner Hain	Op. 109 No. 6	S/A	B. & H.	In anth. "Zweistim. Lied. f. Sop. u. Altstimme mit Klavierbegleitung f. den Haus- u. Schulgebrauch v. H. M. Schletterer" 3 vols.	MSN
5775	Reinecke, Carl	1824-1910	Gut' Nacht "Gut' Nacht rauscht's in den Linden"	Op. 189 No. 10	Unspec.	B. & H.		CHAL (1898)
5776	Reinecke, Carl	1824-1910	Guter Rath "Willst du armer Musikant"	Op. 232 No. 5	Unspec.	Hug		CHAL (1898)
5777	Reinecke, Carl	1824-1910	Hell ist ein Lied erklungen	Op. 217 No. 5	S/S	Augener		CHAL (1898)
5778	Reinecke, Carl	1824-1910	Im Wald "Im Wald, im Wald ist Lust und Fried"	Op. 12 No. 3	S/A	B. & H.	In anth. "Zweistim. Lied. f. Sop. u. Altstimme mit Klavierbegleitung f. den Haus- u. Schulgebrauch v. H. M. Schletterer" 3 vols.	MSN
5779	Reinecke, Carl	1824-1910	Im Wald "Im Wald ist Lust und Fried'"	Op. 12 No. 3	S/S	B. & H.		CHAL (1898)

REC	COMP	DTS	TITLE	OP #	VCG	PUB	COMMENTS	SRC
5780	Reinecke, Carl	1824-1910	In dem Walde sah'n wir heut	Op. 270 No. 5	Unspec.	B. & H.		CHAL (1906)
5781	Reinecke, Carl	1824-1910	Intermezzo "Wann der Hahn kräht"	Op. 32 No. 3	S/S	Simrock		CHAL (1898)
5782	Reinecke, Carl	1824-1910	Iss die Frucht und gieb den Kern	Op. 163 No. 5	2 female v.	R. Forberg		CHAL (1898)
5783	Reinecke, Carl	1824-1910	Kind am Grabe der Mutter "Schläftest sanft in deinem Kämmerlein"	Op. 189 No. 2	Unspec.	B. & H.		CHAL (1898)
5784	Reinecke, Carl	1824-1910	Kinderlieder (8)	Op. 270	Unspec.	B. & H.	Collection of 8 children's duets.	CHAL (1906)
5785	Reinecke, Carl	1824-1910	Kirchlein im Dorfe	Op. 270 No. 4	Unspec.	B. & H.		CHAL (1906)
5786	Reinecke, Carl	1824-1910	Kleinen goldnen Sterne	Op. 270 No. 2	Unspec.	B. & H.		CHAL (1906)
5787	Reinecke, Carl	1824-1910	Lasset uns marschiren	Op. 91 No. 4	Unspec.	B. & H.		CHAL (1898)
5788	Reinecke, Carl	1824-1910	Leben ohne Liebe	Op. 163 I No. 1	2 female v.	R. Forberg		CHAL (1898)
5789	Reinecke, Carl	1824-1910	Lenz ist da "Turih, tarah, der Lenz ist da"	Op. 217 No. 3	S/S	Augener		CHAL (1898)
5790	Reinecke, Carl	1824-1910	Lob der Musika "O Musika mein's Herzenlust"	Op. 189 No. 3	Unspec.	B. & H.		CHAL (1898)
5791	Reinecke, Carl	1824-1910	Mondscheinlied "Verstohlen geht der Mond auf"	Op. 189 No. 4	Unspec.	B. & H.		CHAL (1898)
5792	Reinecke, Carl	1824-1910	Morgengebet "Morgen ist erglommen"	Op. 217 No. 7	S/S	Augenauer		CHAL (1898)
5793	Reinecke, Carl	1824-1910	Morgenlied "Kein Stimmlein noch schallt"	Op. 32 No. 6	S/A	Simrock		CHAL (1898)
5794	Reinecke, Carl	1824-1910	Mühle "Es klappert die Mühle"	Op. 91 No. 1	Unspec.	B. & H.		CHAL (1898)
5795	Reinecke, Carl	1824-1910	Mühle im Thale "Mühle, Mühle im lieblichen Thal"	Op. 109 No. 8	2 female v.	B. & H.		CHAL (1898)
5796	Reinecke, Carl	1824-1910	Nacht ist schwarz	Op. 208 No. 4	S/S	Reinecke		CHAL (1898)
5797	Reinecke, Carl	1824-1910	Nun gute Nacht	Op. 163 No. 4	2 female v.	R. Forberg		CHAL (1898)
5798	Reinecke, Carl	1824-1910	O blick zum ewigen Himmel auf	Op. 136 No. 7	2 female v.	R. Forberg		CHAL (1898)
5799	Reinecke, Carl	1824-1910	Roggenmuhme "Lass stehn die Blume"	Op. 91 No. 5	Unspec.	B. & H.		CHAL (1898)
5800	Reinecke, Carl	1824-1910	Rose prangt als Königin der Düfte	Op. 163 No. 2	2 female v.	R. Forberg		CHAL (1898)
5801	Reinecke, Carl	1824-1910	Rosen und Lieder "Ist unser Häuschen auch noch so klein"	Op. 232 No. 1	Unspec.	Hug		CHAL (1898)
5802	Reinecke, Carl	1824-1910	Röslein wann blühest du auf "Es wuchs an einem Rosenbaum"	Op. 217 No. 18	S/S	Augener		CHAL (1898)
5803	Reinecke, Carl	1824-1910	Schmetterling und Biene "Wie hat mich Gott so schön"	Op. 217 No. 6	S/S	Augener		CHAL (1898)
5804	Reinecke, Carl	1824-1910	Schmetterling und das Kind "Mögt gern mit Gott so schön"	Op. 38 No. 7	Unspec.	André		CHAL (1898)
5805	Reinecke, Carl	1824-1910	Schneeweisschen, du bist allzu jung	Op. 208 No. 7	S/S	Reinecke		CHAL (1898)
5806	Reinecke, Carl	1824-1910	Schwesterlein, heut woll'n wir Rosen streu'n	Op. 270 No. 1	Unspec.	B. & H.		CHAL (1906)
5807	Reinecke, Carl	1824-1910	So nimm denn meine Hände	Op. 217 No. 11	S/S	Augener		CHAL (1911)
5808	Reinecke, Carl	1824-1910	Sternlein "Uüd die Sonne machte den weiten Ritt"	Op. 32 No. 4	S/S	Simrock		CHAL (1898)
5809	Reinecke, Carl	1824-1910	Stolzer Schwan, wie ziehst du leise	Op. 270 No. 7	Unspec.	B. & H.		CHAL (1906)

REC	COMP	DTS	TITLE	OP #	VCG	PUB	COMMENTS	SRC
5810	Reinecke, Carl	1824-1910	Tanzlied der Fliegen "Summ summ summ"	Op. 139 No. 1	S/A	Siegel		CHAL (1898)
5811	Reinecke, Carl	1824-1910	Tanzlied "Es tanzet die helle krystalle Welle"	Op. 232 No. 3	Unspec.	Hug		CHAL (1898)
5812	Reinecke, Carl	1824-1910	Tanzlied "Schmückt euch, ihr Mädchen"	Op. 163 No. 12	2 female v.	R. Forberg		CHAL (1898)
5813	Reinecke, Carl	1824-1910	Thautropfen "Morgen lächelt in seliger Ruh"	Op. 4 No. 2	S/S	Annecke		CHAL (1898)
5814	Reinecke, Carl	1824-1910	Traue Nicht "Und wenn am schönsten die Rose erblüht"	Op. 189 No. 8	Unspec.	B. & H.		CHAL (1898)
5815	Reinecke, Carl	1824-1910	Treueste Liebe "Ein Bruder und eine Schwester"	Op. 64 No. 1	S/A	Hainauer		CHAL (1898)
5816	Reinecke, Carl	1824-1910	Veilchen "Wie der Himmel klar"	Op. 12 No. 4	S/S	B. & H.		CHAL (1898)
5817	Reinecke, Carl	1824-1910	Volkslied "Ich weiss nicht, wie kommt es"	Op. 109 No. 2	2 female v.	B. & H.		CHAL (1898)
5818	Reinecke, Carl	1824-1910	Wachtelruf "Glockenklang über'm Wald"	Op. 232 No. 2	Unspec.	Hug		CHAL (1898)
5819	Reinecke, Carl	1824-1910	Waldconcert "Concertsaal ist der Wald"	Op. 217 No. 8	S/S	Augener		CHAL (1898)
5820	Reinecke, Carl	1824-1910	Waldconcert "Herr Frühling giebt jetzt ein Concert"	Op. 91 No. 6	Unspec.	B. & H.		CHAL (1898)
5821	Reinecke, Carl	1824-1910	Wanderlied "Vögel singen, Blumen blüh'n"	Op. 64 No. 3	S/A	Hainauer		CHAL (1898)
5822	Reinecke, Carl	1824-1910	Was kletterst du, da Papagei	Op. 270 No. 8	Unspec.	B. & H.		CHAL (1906)
5823	Reinecke, Carl	1824-1910	Wecke nicht den Schlafenden	Op. 163 No. 3	2 female v.	R. Forberg		CHAL (1898)
5824	Reinecke, Carl	1824-1910	Wehe dem, der zu sterben geht	Op. 163 No. 6	2 female v.	R. Forberg		CHAL (1898)
5825	Reinecke, Carl	1824-1910	Weil die lieben Engelein selber Musikanten sein "Wer sich die Musik erkies"	Op. 189 No. 6	Unspec.	B. & H.		CHAL (1898)
5826	Reinecke, Carl	1824-1910	Weihnachts "Heilige Nacht, du kehrest wieder"	Op. 232 No. 6	Unspec.	Hug		CHAL (1898)
5827	Reinecke, Carl	1824-1910	Weihnachtslied "Als das Christkind ward zur Welt gebracht"	Op. 163 No. 9	2 female v.	R. Forberg		CHAL (1898)
5828	Reinecke, Carl	1824-1910	Wenn der Vogel naschen will "Amsel in dem schwarzen Kleid"	Op. 189 No. 1	Unspec.	B. & H.		CHAL (1898)
5829	Reinecke, Carl	1824-1910	Wenn Zwei von einander scheiden	Op. 12 No. 2	S/S	B. & H.		CHAL (1898)
5830	Reinecke, Carl	1824-1910	Wenn's Christkind kommt "Christkindchen kommy zu uns"	Op. 217 No. 2	S/S	Augener		CHAL (1898)
5831	Reinecke, Carl	1824-1910	Wie es in der Mühle aussicht "Eins, zwei, drei, bicke, backe, bei"		S/A	B. & H.	In anth. "Zweistim. Lied. f. Sop. u. Alt-stimme mit Klavier-begleitung f. den Haus- u. Schulgebrauch v. H. M. Schletterer" 3 vols.	MSN
5832	Reinecke, Carl	1824-1910	Wie es in der Mühle aussieht "eins, zwei, drei"	Op. 91 No. 8	Unspec.	B. & H.		CHAL (1898)
5833	Reinecke, Carl	1824-1910	Wie ist doch die Erde so schön	Op. 217 No. 9	S/S	Augener		CHAL (1898)
5834	Reinecke, Carl	1824-1910	Wiedersehn "Das i gar nix mehr gehört hab"	Op. 189 No. 5	Unspec.	B. & H.		CHAL (1898)
5835	Reinecke, Carl	1824-1910	Winter "Erde steht verschwiegen"	Op. 12 No. 1	S/S	B. & H.		CHAL (1898)

REC	COMP	DTS	TITLE	OP #	VCG	PUB	COMMENTS	SRC
5836	Reinecke, Carl	1824-1910	Wohl ist das Glück ein gar flüchtiges Ding	Op. 136 No. 8	2 female v.	R. Forberg		CHAL (1898)
5837	Reinecke, Carl	1824-1910	Zauber der Frühlingsnacht "Lass deinen Zauber trinken"	Op. 207 No. 10	S/S	Augener		CHAL (1898)
5838	Reinecke, Karl Ludwig	1774-1820	Air suisse "Encens des fleurs"		Unspec.	Annecke		CHAL (1898)
5839	Reinhardt, F.		Bayrische Farben "Blau scheint das Hochland"		S/A	Näumann		CHAL (1898)
5840	Reinhardt, Heinrich	1865-1922	Adventlied		Unspec.	Krenn	org accomp.	CVMP (1985)
5841	Reinthaler, Karl Martin	1822-1896	Märchen "Man sagt durch's Zimmer walle"	Op. 28 No. 2	S/A	P. & M.		CHAL (1898)
5842	Reinthaler, Karl Martin	1822-1896	Psalm 23 "Gott ist mein Hirt"	Op. 34	S/A	Kistner		CHAL (1898)
5843	Reinthaler, Karl Martin	1822-1896	Sternennacht "Es lächeln und nicken in's Dunkel"	Op. 28 No. 3	S/A	P. & M.		CHAL (1898)
5844	Reinthaler, Karl Martin	1822-1896	Veilchenduft "Was weckt aus den Tiefen"	Op. 28 No. 4	S/A	P. & M.		CHAL (1898)
5845	Reinthaler, Karl Martin	1822-1896	"Wenn der Frühling auf die Berge steigt"	Op. 28 No. 1	S/A	P. & M.		CHAL (1898)
5846	Reissiger, Friedrich August	1809-1883	Abendstern "Du lieblicher Stern"	Op. 27 No. 3	S/S	Klemm		CHAL (1898)
5847	Reissiger, Friedrich August	1809-1883	An die heilige Jungfrau "Maria süsse Königin"	Op. 24 No. 3	S/MS	Chal.		CHAL (1898)
5848	Reissiger, Friedrich August	1809-1883	Du bist wie eine Blume		S/A	Warmuth		CHAL (1898)
5849	Reissiger, Friedrich August	1809-1883	Frühlingseinzung "Fenster auf, die Herzen auf"	Op. 27 No. 1	S/S	Klemm		CHAL (1898)
5850	Reissiger, Friedrich August	1809-1883	Jägers Horn "Hörnerklang, Jägersang, nah und fern"	Op. 34 No. 4	Unspec.	B. & B.		CHAL (1898)
5851	Reissiger, Friedrich August	1809-1883	Lenzes Wiederkehr "Wenn's wieder Lenz geworden"	Op. 24 No. 1	S/MS	Chal.		CHAL (1898)
5852	Reissiger, Friedrich August	1809-1883	Meeresstille "Leise wogt die weiche Welle"	Op. 30 No. 4	S/S	Klemm		CHAL (1898)
5853	Reissiger, Friedrich August	1809-1883	Meine Heimath "So viel Wolken droben"	Op. 30 No. 2	S/S	Klemm		CHAL (1898)
5854	Reissiger, Friedrich August	1809-1883	Morgenstern "Du blüh'nder Stern"	Op. 27 No. 2	S/S	Klemm		CHAL (1898)
5855	Reissiger, Friedrich August	1809-1883	Schwabenlied "So herzig, wie die Schwaben"	Op. 34 No. 2	Unspec.	B. & B.		CHAL (1898)
5856	Reissiger, Friedrich August	1809-1883	Sonnenschein "Wenn auf der spiegelklaren"	Op. 30 No. 1	S/S	Klemm		CHAL (1898)
5857	Reissiger, Friedrich August	1809-1883	Sonnenuntergang in die Heimath "Wie traurig stehn die Auen"	Op. 34 No. 1	Unspec.	B. & B.		CHAL (1898)
5858	Reissiger, Friedrich August	1809-1883	Wie ist doch die Erde so schön	Op. 34 No. 3	Unspec.	B. & B.		CHAL (1898)
5859	Reissiger, Friedrich August	1809-1883	Winsamkeit und Freudesnähe "Noch glüht mir deines Lichtes Schein"	Op. 24 No. 2	S/MS	Chal.		CHAL (1898)

REC	COMP	DTS	TITLE	OP #	VCG	PUB	COMMENTS	SRC
5860	Reissiger, Karl Gottlieb	1798-1859	Al bosco caccia borigia	Op. 112 II No. 4	S/S	Bahn		CHAL (1898)
5861	Reissiger, Karl Gottlieb	1798-1859	Aus Ruy Blas "Wozu soll ich länger belauschen"	Op. 148 No. 2	S/S	Peters		CHAL (1898)
5862	Reissiger, Karl Gottlieb	1798-1859	Blauen Frühlingsaugen schaun aus	Op. 109 No. 4	S/MS	Schlesinger		CHAL (1898)
5863	Reissiger, Karl Gottlieb	1798-1859	Come il candore	Op. 112 II No. 2	S/S	Bahn		CHAL (1898)
5864	Reissiger, Karl Gottlieb	1798-1859	Digli ch'io don fidele	Op. 43 No. 1	S/MS	Hofmeister		CHAL (1898)
5865	Reissiger, Karl Gottlieb	1798-1859	Dir muss ich immer singen	Op. 136 No. 1	S/S	Peters		CHAL (1898)
5866	Reissiger, Karl Gottlieb	1798-1859	Er ist's "Frühling lässt sein blaues Band"	Op. 204 No. 1	S/S	B. & B.		CHAL (1898)
5867	Reissiger, Karl Gottlieb	1798-1859	Erstes Begegne "Mir ist, als kennt' ich"	Op. 109 No. 3	S/MS	Schlesinger		CHAL (1898)
5868	Reissiger, Karl Gottlieb	1798-1859	Frühlingslied "Lämmlein hüpfen auf Rasen grün"	Op. 160 No. 7	Unspec.	Schlesinger		CHAL (1898)
5869	Reissiger, Karl Gottlieb	1798-1859	Frühlingswiederkehr "Wenn der Duft quillt"	Op. 136 No. 2	S/S	Peters		CHAL (1898)
5870	Reissiger, Karl Gottlieb	1798-1859	Frühlingszeit "Frühlingszeit, schönste Zeit"	Op. 160 No. 2	Unspec.	Schlesinger		CHAL (1898)
5871	Reissiger, Karl Gottlieb	1798-1859	Gott schützt die Kinder "Aus dem Himmel ferne"	Op. 160 No. 3	Unspec.	Schlesinger		CHAL (1898)
5872	Reissiger, Karl Gottlieb	1798-1859	Ihr "Seid meines Herzens stille Vertraute"	Op. 166 No. 2	S/S or S/T	Sch. & Co.		CHAL (1898)
5873	Reissiger, Karl Gottlieb	1798-1859	Im grünen Laub, so dicht	Op. 148 No. 3	S/S	Peters		CHAL (1906)
5874	Reissiger, Karl Gottlieb	1798-1859	In der Ferne "Will ruhen unter den Bäumen hier"	Op. 194 No. a2	S/S or S/A	B. & H.		CHAL (1898)
5875	Reissiger, Karl Gottlieb	1798-1859	Keine Rosen ohne Dornen "Auf den schimmernden Lagunen"	Op. 204 No. 2	Unspec.	B. & B.		CHAL (1898)
5876	Reissiger, Karl Gottlieb	1798-1859	Lebens Mai "Süsser als Abendruh'"	Op. 109 No. 1	S/MS	Schlesinger		CHAL (1898)
5877	Reissiger, Karl Gottlieb	1798-1859	Libertà del care	Op. 43 No. 5	S/MS	Hofmeister		CHAL (1898)
5878	Reissiger, Karl Gottlieb	1798-1859	Liebeszauber "Kann's tiefern Zauber geben"	Op. 136 No. 2	S/S	Peters		CHAL (1898)
5879	Reissiger, Karl Gottlieb	1798-1859	Liedes Macht "Wenn sich Wunsch und Hoffnung regen"	Op. 166 No. 1	S/S or S/T	Sch. & Co.		CHAL (1898)
5880	Reissiger, Karl Gottlieb	1798-1859	Mi guère	Op. 112 II No. 1	S/S	Bahn		CHAL (1898)
5881	Reissiger, Karl Gottlieb	1798-1859	Mio ben ricordati	Op. 43 No. 2	S/MS	Hofmeister		CHAL (1898)
5882	Reissiger, Karl Gottlieb	1798-1859	Morgenlied		S/S	Brauer		CHAL (1898)
5883	Reissiger, Karl Gottlieb	1798-1859	Morgenlied "Dunklen Schatten fliehen"		S/S	Peters		CHAL (1898)
5884	Reissiger, Karl Gottlieb	1798-1859	Nachbarin "Mein Stübchen ist mir lieber"		S/S	Peters		CHAL (1898)
5885	Reissiger, Karl Gottlieb	1798-1859	Nascesti alle pene mie	Op. 43 No. 3	S/MS	Hofmeister		CHAL (1898)
5886	Reissiger, Karl Gottlieb	1798-1859	O schöner, sel'ger Gottesfriede	Op. 148 No. 1	S/S	Peters		CHAL (1906)
5887	Reissiger, Karl Gottlieb	1798-1859	Perchè, perchè mi fuggio Nice	Op. 112 II No. 3	S/S	Bahn		CHAL (1898)
5888	Reissiger, Karl Gottlieb	1798-1859	Reiterlied "Hopp, hopp mein Reiterlein"	Op. 160 No. 5	Unspec.	Schlesinger		CHAL (1898)
5889	Reissiger, Karl Gottlieb	1798-1859	Scheiden, Meiden "Ja müsst die Liebe nicht scheiden"	Op. 204 No. 3	Unspec.	B. & B.		CHAL (1898)

REC	COMP	DTS	TITLE	OP #	VCG	PUB	COMMENTS	SRC
5890	Reissiger, Karl Gottlieb	1798-1859	Se viver non poss'io	Op. 43 No. 4	S/MS	Hof-meister		CHAL (1898)
5891	Reissiger, Karl Gottlieb	1798-1859	Sehnsucht "Ich bat das Leben"	Op. 109 No. 2	S/MS	Schlesin-ger		CHAL (1898)
5892	Reissiger, Karl Gottlieb	1798-1859	Sie weiss es nicht	Op. 194 No. a3	S/S or S/A	Senff		CHAL (1898)
5893	Reissiger, Karl Gottlieb	1798-1859	Soldatenlied "Ein scheckiges Pferd, ein blankes Gewehr"	Op. 160 No. 1	Unspec.	Schlesin-ger		CHAL (1898)
5894	Reissiger, Karl Gottlieb	1798-1859	Thu' nichts Böses, thu' es nicht	Op. 160 No. 4	Unspec.	Schlesin-ger		CHAL (1898)
5895	Reissiger, Karl Gottlieb	1798-1859	Vöglein "Vöglein in hohem Baum"	Op. 160 No. 6	Unspec.	Schlesin-ger		CHAL (1898)
5896	Reissiger, Karl Gottlieb	1798-1859	Voi che'l mio cor sapete	Op. 112 II No. 5	Unspec.	Bahn		CHAL (1898)
5897	Reissiger, Karl Gottlieb	1798-1859	Vorgefühl "O schöner, sel'ger Gottesfriede"	Op. 148 No. 1	S/S	Peters		CHAL (1898)
5898	Reissiger, Karl Gottlieb	1798-1859	Waldlied "In den Wald, in den stillen, grünen Wald"	Op. 166 No. 3	S/S or S/T	Sch. & Co.		CHAL (1898)
5899	Reissiger, Karl Gottlieb	1798-1859	Waldvöglein Sang "Im grünen Laub so dicht und traut"	Op. 148 No. 3	Unspec.	Peters		CHAL (1898)
5900	Reissiger, Karl Gottlieb	1798-1859	Wer's nur verstünde "Was ist gescheh'n"	Op. 194 No. 9, 1	S/S or S/A	Senff		CHAL (1898)
5901	Reissiger, Karl Gottlieb	1798-1859	Wiedersehn, Wiederfinden "Wiedersehn, Herzensglaube"		S/S	Peters		CHAL (1898)
5902	Reissiger, Karl Gottlieb	1798-1859	Wohin "Lüfte des Himmels, wo ziehet ihr hin"	Op. 109 No. 5	S/MS	Schlesin-ger		CHAL (1898)
5903	Reissiger, Karl Gottlieb	1798-1859	Wozu soll ich länger belauschen	Op. 148 No. 2	S/S	Peters		CHAL (1906)
5904	Reissmann, August	1825-1903	Abend "Sehet es kehret der Abend"	Op. 39 No. 5	high & low v.	Simon i. Berl.		CHAL (1898)
5905	Reissmann, August	1825-1903	Abendfeier "Wie ist der Abend so traulich"	Op. 12 No. 4	S/S	Kahnt		CHAL (1898)
5906	Reissmann, August	1825-1903	Bittenden Vöglein "Bitte, stillet unsre Noth"	Op. 39 No. 4	high & low v.	Simon i. Berl.		CHAL (1898)
5907	Reissmann, August	1825-1903	Durch die Felder musst du schweifen	Op. 39 No. 6	high & low v.	Simon i. Berl.		CHAL (1898)
5908	Reissmann, August	1825-1903	Erwachte Rose "Rose träumte"	Op. 39 No. 3	high & low v.	Simon i. Berl.		CHAL (1898)
5909	Reissmann, August	1825-1903	In der Morgenfrühe "Herr, der du vom schweigenden Himmel"	Op. 12 No. 2	S/S	Kahnt		CHAL (1898)
5910	Reissmann, August	1825-1903	Libellentanz "Wir Libellen hüpfen"	Op. 39 No. 2	high & low v.	Simon i. Berl.		CHAL (1898)
5911	Reissmann, August	1825-1903	Maiklänge "Blüthen alle"	Op. 39 No. 1	high & low v.	Simon i. Berl.		CHAL (1898)
5912	Reissmann, August	1825-1903	Marsch auf Schub "Winter wird beklommen"	Op. 60 No. 4	Unspec.	Kahnt		CHAL (1898)
5913	Reissmann, August	1825-1903	Osterlied "Glocken läuten das Ostern ein"	Op. 12 No. 1	S/S	Kahnt		CHAL (1898)
5914	Reissmann, August	1825-1903	Sommer und Winter "So komm doch heraus"	Op. 12 No. 3	S/S	Kahnt		CHAL (1898)
5915	Reissmann, August	1825-1903	Zeit geht schnell	Op. 12 No. 5	S/S	Kahnt		CHAL (1898)
5916	Reissmann, H.		Horch mein Schätzchen, wie das Spätzchen	Op. 5 II No. 6	Unspec.	Kahnt		CHAL (1898)
5917	Reissmann, H.		Unbewusst "Ich habe dich lieb gewonnen"	Op. 2 No. 3	2 female v.	Hainauer		CHAL (1898)
5918	Reiter, Ernst	1814-1875	Wiet, weit aus ferner Zeit	Op. 15 No. 1	Unspec.	Hug		CHAL (1898)
5919	Renardy, A.		Jeunes Batelières		Unspec.	Junne		CHAL (1898)

REC	COMP	DTS	TITLE	OP #	VCG	PUB	COMMENTS	SRC
5920	Renaud, Albert	1855-	Au Bord de la Mer		Unspec.	Durand	In "Douze Duos"	CVMP (1976)
5921	Renaud, Albert	1855-	Deux lapins		2 female v.	Schott		CHAL (1898)
5922	Renaud, Albert	1855-	Habenera		Unspec.	Durand	In "Douze Duos"	CVMP (1976)
5923	Renker, Felix	1867-1935	Baron Borg und sein Diener Storch "Aehm ich reise durch die Welt"		Unspec.	Kleine i. P.		CHAL (1898)
5924	Renker, Felix	1867-1935	Ein Kandidat zwar reich an Wissen		Unspec.	O. Dietrich		CHAL (1901)
5925	Renker, Felix	1867-1935	Rentier Bärnestiel in Afrika "Endlich wäre ich nun da"	Op. 61	Unspec.	O. Teich		CHAL (1898)
5926	Renker, Felix	1867-1935	So der Kaffee wäre fertig		2 female v.	O. Dietrich		CHAL (1901)
5927	Renker, Felix	1867-1935	So mancherlei passiert im Leben		Unspec.	O. Dietrich		CHAL (1901)
5928	Renker, Felix	1867-1935	Wir springen gackfidel durch's Leben		Unspec.	O. Dietrich		CHAL (1901)
5929	Renner, Josef	1868-1934	Missa in honorem St. Petri Apostoli		Unspec.	Pustet	org accomp.	CHAL (1898)
5930	Renner, M.		Der weil ich schlafend lag	Op. 2 No. 2	S/A	Cranz		CHAL (1901)
5931	Renner, M.		Es war ein alter König	Op. 2 No. 1	S/A	Cranz		CHAL (1898)
5932	Renner, M.		Es war ein alter König	Op. 2 No. 1	S/A	Cranz		CHAL (1901)
5933	Renner, M.		Schnee zerrinnt	Op. 2 No. 3	S/A	Cranz		CHAL (1898)
5934	Renner, M.		Schnee zerrinnt, der Mai beginnt		S/A	Cranz		CHAL (1901)
5935	Rennes, Catharina van	1858-1940	Abendfrieden "Dämmrung Schleier auf Wald"	Op. 5 No. 3	Unspec.	v. Wahberg	Dut. woman comp.	CHAL (1898)
5936	Rennes, Catharina van	1858-1940	Angelus läutet von ferne	Op. 5 No. 1	Unspec.	v. Wahlberg	Dut. woman comp.	CHAL (1898)
5937	Rennes, Catharina van	1858-1940	Angelus läutet von ferne	Op. 5 No. 1	Unspec.	Siegel	Dut. woman comp.	CHAL (1906)
5938	Rennes, Catharina van	1858-1940	Dämmrung Schleier auf Wald und Feld	Op. 5 No. 3	Unspec.	Siegel	Dut. woman comp.	CHAL (1906)
5939	Rennes, Catharina van	1858-1940	Frühling "Wer winket uns droben"	Op. 5 No. 4	Unspec.	v. Wahlberg	Dut. woman comp.	CHAL (1898)
5940	Rennes, Catharina van	1858-1940	Frühlingszauber "5 zweist. Lieder"	Op. 5	Unspec.	v. Wahlberg	5 duets. Dut. woman comp.	CHAL (1898)
5941	Rennes, Catharina van	1858-1940	Frühlingszauber "5 zweist. Lieder"	Op. 5	Unspec.	Siegel	5 duets. Dut. woman comp.	CHAL (1906)
5942	Rennes, Catharina van	1858-1940	Gleich und Gleich "Ein Blumen-glöckchen vom Boden hervor (empor)"	Op. 13 No. 1	S/A	Steyl & Th.	Dut. woman comp.	CHAL (1898)
5943	Rennes, Catharina van	1858-1940	Het Angelus Klept in de Verte		Unspec.	Alsbach	Dut. woman comp. Also solo	CVMP (1976)
5944	Rennes, Catharina van	1858-1940	Ich fand ein holdes Vielchen	Op. 5 No. 2	Unspec.	Siegel	Dut. woman comp.	CHAL (1906)

REC	COMP	DTS	TITLE	OP #	VCG	PUB	COMMENTS	SRC
5945	Rennes, Catharina van	1858-1940	Im Freien 8 Duette f. S. u. A.	Op. 13	S/A	Steyl & Th.	Collection of 8 duets. Dut. woman comp.	CHAL (1898)
5946	Rennes, Catharina van	1858-1940	Im Walde, im hellen Sonnenschein	Op. 13 No. 8	S/A	Steyl & Th.	Dut. woman comp.	CHAL (1898)
5947	Rennes, Catharina van	1858-1940	In's Freie "Wer geht mit mir in's freie Feld"	Op. 15 No. 4	Unspec.	B. & H.	Dut. woman comp.	CHAL (1898)
5948	Rennes, Catharina van	1858-1940	Jägerliedchen "Es war ein Jäger wohl keck und kühn"	Op. 13 No. 6	S/A	Steyl & Th.	Dut. woman comp.	CHAL (1898)
5949	Rennes, Catharina van	1858-1940	Kinderwacht "Wenn fromme Kindlein schlafen geh'n"	Op. 15 No. 3	Unspec.	B. & H.	Dut. woman comp.	CHAL (1898)
5950	Rennes, Catharina van	1858-1940	Knabe mit dem Wunderhorn "Ich bin ein lustiger Geselle"	Op. 13 No. 2	S/A	Steyl & Th.	Dut. woman comp.	CHAL (1898)
5951	Rennes, Catharina van	1858-1940	Lebenslust 6 zweist. Kinderlieder	Op. 15	Unspec.	B. & H.	6 children's duets, Dut. woman comp.	CHAL (1898)
5952	Rennes, Catharina van	1858-1940	Lebewohl "Lebewohl, lebewohl mein Lieb"	Op. 13 No. 7	S/A	Steyl & Th.	Dut. woman comp.	CHAL (1898)
5953	Rennes, Catharina van	1858-1940	Maimorgen "Heda, ihr Blümlein"	Op. 15 No. 1	Unspec.	B. & H.	Dut. woman comp.	CHAL (1898)
5954	Rennes, Catharina van	1858-1940	Schlummre sacht	Op. 5 No. 4	Unspec.	Siegel	Dut. woman comp.	CHAL (1906)
5955	Rennes, Catharina van	1858-1940	Schnee kommt eisig geflogen	Op. 13 No. 4	S/A	Steyl & Th.	Dut. woman comp.	CHAL (1898)
5956	Rennes, Catharina van	1858-1940	Sei gegrüsst du schöne Frühlingszeit "Wenn der Winter flieht"	Op. 15 No. 5	Unspec.	B. & H.	Dut. woman comp.	CHAL (1898)
5957	Rennes, Catharina van	1858-1940	Singen "Von selbst, wie der Vogel"	Op. 15 No. 2	Unspec.	B. & H.	Dut. woman comp.	CHAL (1898)
5958	Rennes, Catharina van	1858-1940	Sternlein "Uüd die Sonne machte den weiten Ritt"	Op. 13 No. 3	S/A	Steyl & Th.	Dut. woman comp.	CHAL (1898)
5959	Rennes, Catharina van	1858-1940	Sylvesterabend "Wieder ist ein Jahr verronene"	Op. 15 No. 6	Unspec.	B. & H.	Dut. woman comp.	CHAL (1898)
5960	Rennes, Catharina van	1858-1940	Veilchen "Ich fand ein holdes Veilchen"	Op. 5 No. 2	Unspec.	v. Wahlberg	Dut. woman comp.	CHAL (1898)
5961	Rennes, Catharina van	1858-1940	Vöglein wohin so schnell	Op. 13 No. 5	S/A	Steyl & Th.	Dut. woman comp.	CHAL (1898)
5962	Rennes, Catharina van	1858-1940	Wer winket uns droben	Op. 5 No. 5	Unspec.	Siegel	Dut. woman comp.	CHAL (1906)
5963	Reuss, August	1871-1935	Das ist des Abends Segen	Op. 24 No. 1	S/A	Kistner		CHAL (1911)
5964	Reuss, August	1871-1935	Es blühen die Blumen em bunten Schein	Op. 24 No. 4	S/A	Kistner		CHAL (1911)
5965	Reuss, August	1871-1935	Knospen tragen alle Bäume	Op. 24 No. 3	S/A	Kistner		CHAL (1911)
5966	Reuss, August	1871-1935	Lichte Abendwolken wandern	Op. 24 No. 2	S/A	Kistner		CHAL (1911)

REC	COMP	DTS	TITLE	OP #	VCG	PUB	COMMENTS	SRC
5967	Reutter, Hermann	1900-	Spanische Totentanz		2 med. v.	Schott	pf or inst accomp.	ASR
5968	Reutter, Hermann	1900-	Spanischen Totentanz		2 med. v.	Schotts	pf or orch accomp.	CVMP (1976)
5969	Reutter, Otto	1870-1931	So ziehen wir Beide stets Hand in Hand	No. 120	Unspec.	O. Teich		CHAL (1906)
5970	Reynolds, Alfred		She loves me, she loves me not		Unspec.	Elkin		BBC (1975)
5971	Rheinberger, Josef	1839-1901	Alma redemptoris	Op. 171 No. 2	S/A	Leuckart		CHAL (1898)
5972	Rheinberger, Josef	1839-1901	Ave maris stella	Op. 118 No. 5	Unspec.	R. Forberg	org accomp.	CHAL (1898)
5973	Rheinberger, Josef	1839-1901	Ave maris stella	Op. 171 No. 4	S/A	Leuckart	org or pf accomp.	CHAL (1898)
5974	Rheinberger, Josef	1839-1901	Neige o Ewiger	Op. 118 No. 4	Unspec.	R. Forberg	org accomp.	CHAL (1898)
5975	Rheinberger, Josef	1839-1901	O sei eingedenk	Op. 118 No. 2	Unspec.	R. Forberg	org accomp.	CHAL (1898)
5976	Rheinberger, Josef	1839-1901	O wie so wunderbar	Op. 118 No. 3	Unspec.	R. Forberg	org accomp.	CHAL (1898)
5977	Rheinberger, Josef	1839-1901	Sei uns gegrüsst	Op. 118 No. 1	Unspec.	R. Forberg	org accomp.	CHAL (1898)
5978	Rheineck, S.		Volksthümliche Jugendlieder (52)		Unspec.	Böhm & S.	Collection of 52 duets	CHAL (1901)
5979	Ricci, Federico	1809-1877	Mezza notte		Unspec.	Cranz		CHAL (1898)
5980	Ricci, Luigi	1805-1859	Liebe Angst "Horch wie ängstlich die Lüftchen"		S/S	Schott		CHAL (1898)
5981	Ricci, Luigi	1805-1859	Schweige, wenn du beglückest		S/S	Schott		CHAL (1898)
5982	Ricci, Luigi	1805-1859	Weisst du noch jene Mondnacht		S/S	Schott		CHAL (1898)
5983	Riccius, August Ferdinand	1819-1886	Abends "Drüben steht im Duft"	Op. 15 No. 1	S/A	Heinr.		CHAL (1898)
5984	Riccius, August Ferdinand	1819-1886	Glück "Wie zauberherrlich des Himmelsblau"	Op. 46 No. 5	S/A	Cranz		CHAL (1898)
5985	Riccius, August Ferdinand	1819-1886	Herbst "Sommer entschwand"	Op. 46 No. 3	S/A	Cranz		CHAL (1898)
5986	Riccius, August Ferdinand	1819-1886	Julottesang		Unspec.	Lundq.	Swed. trans. Grmn.	CVMP (1976)
5987	Riccius, August Ferdinand	1819-1886	Muntrer Bach, was rausch'st du so	Op. 46 No. 4	S/A	Cranz		CHAL (1898)
5988	Riccius, August Ferdinand	1819-1886	O wie welt liegt die goldne Zeit	Op. 46 No. 1	S/A	Cranz		CHAL (1898)
5989	Riccius, August Ferdinand	1819-1886	Seufzer "Dein Liebesfeuer ach Herr"	Op. 15 No. 3	S/A	Heinr.		CHAL (1898)
5990	Riccius, August Ferdinand	1819-1886	Vorgefühl "Schon fegen die Winde"	Op. 46 No. 2	S/A	Cranz		CHAL (1898)
5991	Riccius, August Ferdinand	1819-1886	Weihnachtslied "Glockentöne schallen"	Op. 15 No. 2	S/A	Heinr.		CHAL (1898)
5992	Richard, T.		Wir sind in unsrer Compagnie		Unspec.	Uhse		CHAL (1901)
5993	Richards, Brinley	1817-1885	How Beautiful is Night		Unspec.	Brainard's Sons	In anthology "Brainard's Collection of Vocal Duets from Popular Modern and Standard Composers." Pub. 1903.	MSN

REC	COMP	DTS	TITLE	OP #	VCG	PUB	COMMENTS	SRC
5994	Richardy, J.		Nein, was hat man heutzutage	Op. 60	2 female v.	Glaser		CHAL (1911)
5995	Richardy, Johann	1878-	Es ist ein Ros' entsprungen	Op. 58	Unspec.	Glaser	Pen name of Johann Richter	CHAL (1906)
5996	Richstaetter, M. or W.		Gar viel vergass ich bald	Op. 23 No. 2	S/A	Junfermann		CHAL (1906)
5997	Richstaetter, M. or W.		In meinen Gedanken lebst du	Op. 23 No. 3	S/A	Junfermann		CHAL (1906)
5998	Richstaetter, M. or W.		Tagtäglich klang in den Zweigen	Op. 23 No. 4	Unspec.	Junfermann		CHAL (1906)
5999	Richstaetter, M. or W.		Wenn ich ein einzig Wörtchen sing'	Op. 23 No. 1	S/A	Junfermann		CHAL (1906)
6000	Richter, Alfred	1846-1919	Wir beide sind fürwahr		Unspec.	Berlin Selbstverl.		CHAL (1901)
6001	Richter, Ernst Friedrich	1808-1879	Abschied "Es treibt dich fort"	Op. 13 No. 5	S/S	Kistner		CHAL (1898)
6002	Richter, Ernst Friedrich	1808-1879	Botschaft "Mondenschein, stiller Mondenschein"	Op. 13 No. 2	S/S	Kistner		CHAL (1898)
6003	Richter, Ernst Friedrich	1808-1879	Dein "Wohl kenn' ich eine Sprache"		high & low v.	Leuckart		CHAL (1898)
6004	Richter, Ernst Friedrich	1808-1879	Frühlingsglaube "Die linden Lüfte sind erwacht"	Op. 35	S/A	B. & H.	In anth. "Zweistim. Lied. f. Sop. u. Altstimme mit Klavierbegleitung f. den Haus- u. Schulgebrauch v. H. M. Schletterer" 3 vols.	MSN
6005	Richter, Ernst Friedrich	1808-1879	Frühlingslied "Kommt heraus, lasst uns gehn"	Op. 13 No. 3	S/S	Kistner		CHAL (1898)
6006	Richter, Ernst Friedrich	1808-1879	Gondoliera "O komm zu mir"	Op. 13 No. 1	S/S	Kistner		CHAL (1898)
6007	Richter, Ernst Friedrich	1808-1879	Schäfchen am Himmel "Was treibt ihr dort in ferner Höh'"	Op. 13 No. 4	S/S	Kistner		CHAL (1898)
6008	Richter, Ernst Friedrich	1808-1879	Und wenn die Primel schneeweiss blickt	Op. 13 No. 6	S/S	Kistner		CHAL (1898)
6009	Riedel, August	1855-1929	Macht der Töne "Tragt mich hinauf zum Himmelsraume"	Op. 5 No. 1	2 female v.	Siegel		CHAL (1898)
6010	Riedel, August	1855-1929	Tanzlied im Mai "Zum Reigen herbei"	Op. 5 No. 3	2 female v.	Siegel		CHAL (1898)
6011	Riedel, August	1855-1929	Wiegenlied "Alles still in süsser Ruh"	Op. 5 No. 2	2 female v.	Siegel		CHAL (1898)
6012	Riem, Friedrich Wilhelm	1779-1857	Blumengruss "Struass den ich gepflücket"		S/S	Hampe i. Br.		CHAL (1898)
6013	Riemenschneider, Georg	1848-1913	Wie Gott mich führt, so will ich geh'n	Op. 38	S/A	Steingräber	org	CHAL (1906)
6014	Ries, Ferdinand	1784-1838	Durch die wolkige Maiennacht	Op. 24 No. 1	Unspec.	R. & E.		CHAL (1898)
6015	Ries, Ferdinand	1784-1838	Heraus "Ging unter dichten Zweigen"	Op. 24 No. 2	Unspec.	R. & E.		CHAL (1898)
6016	Ries, Ferdinand	1784-1838	Lied des Mädchens "Lass schlafen mich"	Op. 14 No. 3	S/MS	Sulzer		CHAL (1898)
6017	Ries, Ferdinand	1784-1838	Neue Liebe, neues Leben "Herz mein Herz, was soll das geben"	Op. 14 No. 2	S/MS	Sulzer		CHAL (1898)
6018	Ries, Ferdinand	1784-1838	Neuer Frühling "Neuer Frühling ist gekommen"	Op. 24 No. 4	Unspec.	R. & E.		CHAL (1898)

REC	COMP	DTS	TITLE	OP #	VCG	PUB	COMMENTS	SRC
6019	Ries, Ferdinand	1784-1838	Schöne Tag sind gewesen	Op. 24 No. 3	Unspec.	R. & E.		CHAL (1898)
6020	Ries, Ferdinand	1784-1838	Ständchen "Schliesse deine holden Augen"	Op. 14 No. 1	S/MS	Sulzer		CHAL (1898)
6021	Rieter, E.		Nun die Schatten dunkeln	Op. 15 No. 2	S/A	Hug		CHAL (1898)
6022	Rietz, J. August Wilhelm	1812-1877	Ave Maria "Ave Maria gratia pleni"	Op. 9 No. 3	S/A	Hofmeister		CHAL (1898)
6023	Rietz, J. August Wilhelm	1812-1877	Benedicam Dominum	Op. 9 No. 2	S/A	Hofmeister		CHAL (1898)
6024	Rietz, J. August Wilhelm	1802-1832	O salutaris hostia	Op. 9 No. 1	S/A	Hofmeister		CHAL (1898)
6025	Riga, Frantz	1831-1892	Ave Maria "Ave Maria gratia pleni"	Op. 30	Unspec.	Schott i. Br.	org accomp.	CHAL (1898)
6026	Righini, Vincenzo	1756-1812	Echo "O Geliebte du mein Entzücken"		Unspec.	Junne		CHAL (1898)
6027	Righini, Vincenzo	1756-1812	Lasst uns dem Höchstein Opfer bringen		T/T or S/S	Heinr.	org accomp.	CHAL (1898)
6028	Righini, Vincenzo	1756-1812	Tauben		Unspec.	Sch. j.		CHAL (1898)
6029	Righini, Vincenzo	1756-1812	Veilchen		Unspec.	Sch. j.		CHAL (1898)
6030	Rijken, Georg	1863-	Im Walde, im hellen Sonnenschein	Op. 3	Unspec.	Lichtenauer		CHAL (1898)
6031	Rilvas, C. de		Gondoliera "Bello è il cielo"		Unspec.	Fürstner		CHAL (1898)
6032	Rimsky-Korsakov, Nicolai	1844-1908	A Song of India [Chanson du marchand Hindou]		S/A	Ditson	Arr. C. F. Manney. Eng. & Fr. trans. Russ. In anthology "The Ditson Collection of Soprano and Alto Duets" Pub. 1934.	MSN
6033	Rimsky-Korsakov, Nicolai	1844-1908	Angel i Demon	Op. 52 No. 2	S/Br or T/MS [also S/MS]	State Mus. Pub. (Moscow)	Other eds. list v. as S/MS in add. to male-fem. v. In coll. "Polnoe Sobranie Sochineny" works of Rimsky-Korsakov. Pub. 1948.	NATS-VCD
6034	Rimsky-Korsakov, Nicolai	1844-1908	Angel i demon [Angel and Demon]	Op. 52 No. 2	S/MS or T/Br	Belwin	Translit. title of Russ. In Cyrillic and Eng.	MSN
6035	Rimsky-Korsakov, Nicolai	1844-1908	Gornïy Kluch	Op. 52 No. 1	S/MS or T/Br	State Mus. Pub. (Moscow)	In collection "Polnoe Sobranie Sochineny" works of N. Rimsky-Korsakov. Pub. 1948-	NATS-VCD
6036	Rimsky-Korsakov, Nicolai	1844-1908	Gornyi Kliuch [Mountain Spring]	Op. 52 No. 1	S/MS or T/Br	Belwin	Translit. title of Russ. In Cyrillic and Eng.	MSN
6037	Rimsky-Korsakov, Nicolai	1844-1908	Hindoo Song		S/A	Allans	Eng. trans. Russ. In anthology "Vocal Duets Collection" Vol. 1. Pub. 1992.	MSN
6038	Rimsky-Korsakov, Nicolai	1844-1908	Mountain Spring	Op. 52 No. 1	S/MS or T/Br	Belwin	Autograph dated 1897. Russ. (Eng. trans).	MSN
6039	Rimsky-Korsakov, Nicolai	1844-1908	The Angel and the Demon	Op. 52 No. 2	S/MS or T/Br	Belwin	Autograph dated 1897. Russ. (Eng. trans).	MSN

REC	COMP	DTS	TITLE	OP #	VCG	PUB	COMMENTS	SRC
6040	Rimsky-Korsakov, Nicolai	1844-1908	Two Vocal Works	Op. 52 and Op. 53 [trio]	S/MS or T/Bar [also female trio]	Kalmus	Collection. Includes "Dragonflies" Op. 53 (female trio) and Op. 52 "Two Duets"	CVMP (1995)
6041	Rinck, Johann Christian Heinrich	1770-1846	Abend "Stillen Abendstunden"	Op. 83 No. 1	Unspec.	Simrock		CHAL (1898)
6042	Rinck, Johann Christian Heinrich	1770-1846	Du bist's, der uns zum Guten treibt	Op. 83 No. 5	Unspec.	Simrock		CHAL (1898)
6043	Rinck, Johann Christian Heinrich	1770-1846	Empor Kalender es hück "Barbier in der Klemme"	Op. 86 No. 12	Unspec.	Simrock		CHAL (1898)
6044	Rinck, Johann Christian Heinrich	1770-1846	Es wohnet schon hienieden	Op. 83 No. 4	Unspec.	Simrock		CHAL (1898)
6045	Rinck, Johann Christian Heinrich	1770-1846	Ew'ge Liebe, die zum Bilde	Op. 86 No. 7	Unspec.	Simrock		CHAL (1898)
6046	Rinck, Johann Christian Heinrich	1770-1846	Glaube "Holder Glaube"	Op. 86 No. 10	Unspec.	Simrock		CHAL (1898)
6047	Rinck, Johann Christian Heinrich	1770-1846	Gott gab uns	Op. 86 No. 8	Unspec.	Simrock		CHAL (1898)
6048	Rinck, Johann Christian Heinrich	1770-1846	Immer bleibst du Herr	Op. 83 No. 2	Unspec.	Simrock		CHAL (1898)
6049	Rinck, Johann Christian Heinrich	1770-1846	Leben des Menschen	Op. 83 No. 6	Unspec.	Simrock		CHAL (1898)
6050	Rinck, Johann Christian Heinrich	1770-1846	O du, des ew'gen Vaters Sohn	Op. 86 No. 9	Unspec.	Simrock		CHAL (1898)
6051	Rinck, Johann Christian Heinrich	1770-1846	Urquell aller Seeligkeit	Op. 86 No. 11	Unspec.	Simrock		CHAL (1898)
6052	Rinck, Johann Christian Heinrich	1770-1846	Zum Glück von zwei Welten	Op. 83 No. 3	Unspec.	Simrock		CHAL (1898)
6053	Ringer, A.		Da kriegt man gleich den Schnupfen "Kein Geld in meiner Tasche"	Op. 46 No. a	Unspec.	O. Dietrich		CHAL (1898)
6054	Rinnow, P.		Firma is jut "Kaufmann im Dalles"		Unspec.	Haushahn i. M.		CHAL (1898)
6055	Rischbieter, Wilhelm Albert	1834-1910	Abschied "Wie wird mir denn so weh"	Op. 32 No. 3	S/A	Näumann		CHAL (1898)
6056	Rischbieter, Wilhelm Albert	1834-1910	Es ist ein Schnee gefallen	Op. 32 No. 2	Unspec.	Wernthal		CHAL (1906)
6057	Rischbieter, Wilhelm Albert	1834-1910	Frühling währt nicht immer	Op. 32 No. 1	Unspec.	Wernthal		CHAL (1906)
6058	Rischbieter, Wilhelm Albert	1834-1910	Kurze-Frühling "Frühling währt nicht immer"	Op. 32 No. 1	S/A	Näumann		CHAL (1898)
6059	Rischbieter, Wilhelm Albert	1834-1910	Mailied "Wie herrlich leuchtet mir die Natur"	Op. 29	Unspec.	André		CHAL (1898)
6060	Rischbieter, Wilhelm Albert	1834-1910	März "Es ist ein Schnee gefallen"	Op. 32 No. 2	S/A	Näumann		CHAL (1898)
6061	Rischbieter, Wilhelm Albert	1834-1910	Über die Berge, über die Wellen	Op. 32 No. 4	Unspec.	Wernthal		CHAL (1906)
6062	Rischbieter, Wilhelm Albert	1834-1910	Weg der Liebe "Über die Berge"	Op. 32 No. 4	S/A	Näumann		CHAL (1898)

REC	COMP	DTS	TITLE	OP #	VCG	PUB	COMMENTS	SRC
6063	Rischbieter, Wilhelm Albert	1834-1910	Wie wird mir denn so weh	Op. 32 No. 3	Unspec.	Wernthal		CHAL (1906)
6064	Risinger, Karel	1920-	Tri Zenske Dvojzpevy		S/A	Czech		CVMP (1976)
6065	Rittau, Bj.		Weihnachtsalbum		Unspec.	Gaertner i. Königs-bütte	Anthology. Christmas duets & trios.	CHAL (1911)
6066	Ritter, Hermann	1849-1926	Will ruhen unter den Bäumen hier	III No. 5	Unspec.	C. Rühle i. L.	Arr. Necke	CHAL (1901)
6067	Roberton, Hugh Stevenson	1874-1952	All in the April Evening		S/A	Roberton		ASR
6068	Roberton, Hugh Stevenson	1874-1952	White Waves on the Water		Unspec.	Roberton		CVMP (1976)
6069	Roberton, Hugh Stevenson	1874-1952	White Waves on the Water		S/A	Roberton		ASR
6070	Roberton, Hugh Stevenson	1874-1952	Yno Yn Hwyrddydd Ebrill [All in the April Evening]		Unspec.	Roberton	Also solo, trio. Welsh/Eng.	CVMP (1976)
6071	Robricht, P.		Hoch drob'n auf steller Bergeshöh'	Op. 32	S/A	Portius		CHAL (1906)
6072	Rocca, Lodovico	1895-	Lo Sposo Thio alla sua Atti e la Risposta della Sposa		Unspec.	Bongio-vanni		CVMP (1976)
6073	Röder, Ewald	1863-1914	Am Charfreitage "An deinem Kreuzesstamme"	Op. 28	S/A	Klinner	org accomp.	CHAL (1898)
6074	Rödger, Emil	1870-	'Nen Traum hab' i heint Nacht gehabt	Op. 5 No. 2	S/A	Sch. J.		CHAL (1906)
6075	Rödger, Emil	1870-	Wie ist doch die Welt so schön	Op. 5 No. 1	S/A	Sch. J.		CHAL (1906)
6076	Roeder, Martin [Röder]	1851-1895	Das ist der schöne Frühling	Op. 6 No. 2	S/A	B. & H.		CHAL (1906)
6077	Roeder, Martin [Röder]	1851-1895	Dort überm Wolkenmeere	Op. 6 No. 1	Unspec.	B. & H.		CHAL (1906)
6078	Roeder, Martin [Röder]	1851-1895	Liebesfrage "Geschwind fliesst die Welle"	Op. 53 No. 1	S/A or S/Br	B. & H.	a.k.a. Raro Meindtner	CHAL (1898)
6079	Roeder, Martin [Röder]	1851-1895	Nachtgesang "O Mond-licht zart und milde"	Op. 53 No. 3	S/A or S/Br	B. & H.	a.k.a. Raro Meindtner	CHAL (1898)
6080	Roeder, Martin [Röder]	1851-1895	O letzter Hoffnungs-strahl	Op. 53 No. 2	S/A or S/Br	B. & H.	a.k.a. Raro Meindtner	CHAL (1898)
6081	Roes, Carol Lasater		E Kuu Lei [To You My Love]		Unspec.	Mele Loke	Woman comp. Polynesian song.	CVMP (1985)
6082	Roessel, J. or L.		Trauungsgesang "Herr du bist, von dem der Segen"	Op. 30	S/A	Schlesin-ger	org or pf accomp.	CHAL (1898)
6083	Roessel, J. or L.		Trauungsgesang "Wo du hingehst"	Op. 21	S/A	Junne	org accomp.	CHAL (1898)
6084	Roff, Joseph		Bless, O Lord, these Rings		Unspec.	GIA	org accomp. Also solo.	CVMP (1976)
6085	Roger, J.		Au printemps tout fleurit		Unspec.	Bahn		CHAL (1898)
6086	Rogers, James H.		At Parting		S/A	G. Schirm.	In catalogue page "Se-lected Vocal Duets" of G. Schirmer, Inc. NY (no date)	MSN
6087	Rogers, James H.		Julia's Garden		S/A	G. Schirm.	In catalogue page "Se-lected Vocal Duets" of G. Schirmer, Inc. NY (no date)	MSN
6088	Röhde, A.		Gefangene Sänger "Vög-lein einsam in dem Bauer"	No. 2	high & low v.	Hug		CHAL (1898)

REC	COMP	DTS	TITLE	OP #	VCG	PUB	COMMENTS	SRC
6089	Röhde, A.		Zweigesang "Im Fliederbusch ein Vöglein sass"	No. 1	high & low v.	Hug		CHAL (1898)
6090	Rohde, Eduard	1828-1883	Aus der Jugendzeit, aus der Jugendzeit klingt ein Lied	Op. 59 No. 2	Unspec.	R. & E.		CHAL (1898)
6091	Rohde, Eduard	1828-1883	Frühlingsabend "O wie so freundlich grüssest du"	Op. 40 No. 3	Unspec.	R. & E.		CHAL (1898)
6092	Rohde, Eduard	1828-1883	Frühlingsglaube "Linden Lüfte sind erwacht"	Op. 59 No. 4	Unspec.	R. & E.		CHAL (1898)
6093	Rohde, Eduard	1828-1883	Frühlingsmorgen "Morgen ist erstanden"	Op. 40 No. 2	Unspec.	R. & E.		CHAL (1898)
6094	Rohde, Eduard	1828-1883	Frühlingssehnsucht "Zu knospen freu'n sich"	Op. 40 No. 1	Unspec.	R. & E.		CHAL (1898)
6095	Rohde, Eduard	1828-1883	Gute Nacht "Schon fängt es an zu dämmern"	Op. 59 No. 10	Unspec.	R. & E.		CHAL (1898)
6096	Rohde, Eduard	1828-1883	Heimweh "Wo auf hohen Tannenspitzen"	Op. 59 No. 1	Unspec.	R. & E.		CHAL (1898)
6097	Rohde, Eduard	1828-1883	Herbst "Rothen Blätter fallen"	Op. 40 No. 8	Unspec.	R. & E.		CHAL (1898)
6098	Rohde, Eduard	1828-1883	Hinaus "Nun hinaus in das freie Feld"	Op. 40 No. 6	Unspec.	R. & E.		CHAL (1898)
6099	Rohde, Eduard	1828-1883	Im Maien "Nun (Es) bricht aus allen Zweigen"	Op. 59 No. 7	Unspec.	R. & E.		CHAL (1898)
6100	Rohde, Eduard	1828-1883	Im Spätherbst "Wie schön willst du dich schmücken"	Op. 59 No. 5	Unspec.	R. & E.		CHAL (1898)
6101	Rohde, Eduard	1828-1883	Jahreszeiten "O Frühlingszeit, o Frühlingszeit"	Op. 59 No. 3	Unspec.	R. & E.		CHAL (1898)
6102	Rohde, Eduard	1828-1883	Sonntag "Sonntag ist da"	Op. 59 No. 8	Unspec.	R. & E.		CHAL (1898)
6103	Rohde, Eduard	1828-1883	Sonntagsfrühe "Aus den Thälern hör' ich schallen"	Op. 40 No. 7	Unspec.	R. & E.		CHAL (1898)
6104	Rohde, Eduard	1828-1883	Stumme trauer "Todtenstille, tiefstes Schweigen"	Op. 40 No. 9	Unspec.	R. & E.		CHAL (1898)
6105	Rohde, Eduard	1828-1883	Wald "O Wald, grünwogig Meer"	Op. 59 No. 6	Unspec.	R. & E.		CHAL (1898)
6106	Rohde, Eduard	1828-1883	Waldvöglein "Vöglein hat ein schönes Loos"	Op. 40 No. 5	Unspec.	R. & E.		CHAL (1898)
6107	Rohde, Eduard	1828-1883	Wasserfahrt im Frühling "Gleite sanft dahin"	Op. 40 No. 4	Unspec.	R. & E.		CHAL (1898)
6108	Rohde, Eduard	1828-1883	Winter "Tief entschlummert sind die Bäume"	Op. 40 No. 10	Unspec.	R. & E.		CHAL (1898)
6109	Rohde, Eduard	1828-1883	Wohin "Lüfte des Himmels, wo ziehet ihr hin"	Op. 59 No. 9	Unspec.	R. & E.		CHAL (1898)
6110	Rohde, H.		Hallelujah, auferstanden ist der Herr	Op. 18	2 female v. or children's v.	Oppenheimer	org or pf	CHAL (1901)
6111	Röhricht, Paul	1867-1925	Abschied von den Tyroler Bergen "Von meinen Bergen muss ich scheiden"		S/A	Portius		CHAL (1898)
6112	Röhricht, Paul	1867-1925	Glüht die Sonne, brennt das Land	Op. 71	S/A	Portius		CHAL (1911)
6113	Röhricht, Paul	1867-1925	Heimkehr "Holdrio, juchhe"		S/A	Portius		CHAL (1898)
6114	Röhricht, Paul	1867-1925	Ja, die Liab ist ein Glöckerl	Op. 26	S/A	Portius		CHAL (1901)
6115	Röhricht, Paul	1867-1925	Kreuz am See "Hoch drob'n in Herrgotts Nähe"	Op. 16	S/A	Portius		CHAL (1898)
6116	Röhricht, Paul	1867-1925	Nein, nein, das wird mir faktisch endlich doch zu bunt	Op. 41	2 female v.	Portius		CHAL (1906)
6117	Röhricht, Paul	1867-1925	Nun stellt der Abend leis' sich ein	Op. 42	2 female v.	Portius		CHAL (1906)

REC	COMP	DTS	TITLE	OP #	VCG	PUB	COMMENTS	SRC
6118	Röhricht, Paul	1867-1925	Sennerin Sehnsucht nach der Alm "Almenrausch und Edelweiss"		S/A	Portius		CHAL (1898)
6119	Röhricht, Paul	1867-1925	Tyroler Duett-Album "36 ausgewählte Lieder"		Unspec.	Portius	Collection of 36 duets.	CHAL (1911)
6120	Röhricht, Paul	1867-1925	Über die Pusta weht eisig der Wind	Op. 72	S/A	Portius		CHAL (1911)
6121	Röhricht, Paul	1867-1925	Zwei Busserln "Bäurin guckt vom Thorweg aus"	Op. 18 No. 6	S/A	Portius		CHAL (1898)
6122	Rolla, Ch.		Wir stützen uns in den Strudel 'nein "In Toilette schneidig"	Op. 195	Unspec.	Thiemer		CHAL (1898)
6123	Romberg, A. [prob. Andreas]	1767-1841	Lehrstunde "Lenz ist, Aedi gekommen"		Unspec.	Cranz		CHAL (1898)
6124	Ronald, Landon	1873-1938	Birthday Morn, The		Unspec.	Leonard-Eng	Also solo	CVMP (1976)
6125	Ronconi [prob. Felice]	1811-1875	Amicizia		MS/A	Bernard i. Pet.		CHAL (1898)
6126	Röntgen, Julius	1855-1932	Ach dürft' ich doch mit dir	Op. 9 No. 4	S/A	B. & H.		CHAL (1898)
6127	Roose, H.		Lasset uns singen (12)	Op. 4	Unspec.	Kober i. B.	Collection of 12 duets.	CHAL (1911)
6128	Rorem, Ned	1923-	Four Dialogues		Unspec.	Boosey	2-pf accomp. Calls for high voices, generally performed by man and woman, but may be performed by 2 v. of either gender.	CVMP (1976)
6129	Rorem, Ned	1923-	Gloria		S/MS	Boosey	Nine movements following Gloria of mass. Includes two solo sections, one for each v. Comp. 1970.	CVMP (1976)
6130	Rorem, Ned	1923-	Gloria		S/MS	Boosey	Nine movements following Gloria of mass. Includes two solo sections, one for each v. Comp. 1970.	ASR
6131	Rorem, Ned	1923-	Gloria		S/MS	Boosey	Nine movements following Gloria of mass. Includes two solo sections, one for each v. Comp. 1970.	NATS-SVD
6132	Roscher, Josef	1860-1932	Es sprach zum Hänschen Gretchen	Op. 128 No. 5	2 female v.	Wiener Musikver.		CHAL (1901)
6133	Roscher, Josef	1860-1932	Heckenröslein über Nacht	Op. 128 No. 2	2 female v.	Wiener Musikver.		CHAL (1901)
6134	Roscher, Josef	1860-1932	Holder Mond jetzt strahlst du	Op. 128 No. 4	2 female v.	Wiener Musikver.		CHAL (1901)
6135	Roscher, Josef	1860-1932	Maienblüthen zart und fein	Op. 128 No. 1	2 female v.	Wiener Musikver.		CHAL (1901)
6136	Roscher, Josef	1860-1932	Tausend Sternlein in der Nacht	Op. 128 No. 3	2 female v.	Wiener Musikver.		CHAL (1901)
6137	Roscher, Josef	1860-1932	Und ist ihr Gärtchen noch so klein	Op. 128 No. 6	2 female v.	Wiener Musikver.		CHAL (1901)
6138	Rosenberg, Wilhelm [Vilhelm]	1862-	Bitte "Weil auf mir du dunkles Auge"	Op. 1 No. 4	S/A	Hansen		CHAL (1898)
6139	Rosenberg, Wilhelm [Vilhelm]	1862-	Frühlingseinzung "Fenster auf, die Herzen auf"	Op. 1 No. 1	S/A	Hansen		CHAL (1898)

REC	COMP	DTS	TITLE	OP #	VCG	PUB	COMMENTS	SRC
6140	Rosenberg, Wilhelm [Vilhelm]	1862-	Ich sah den Wald sich färben	Op. 3 No. 1	S/A	Hansen		CHAL (1898)
6141	Rosenberg, Wilhelm [Vilhelm]	1862-	Veilchen "Ein Veilchen auf der Wiese stand"	Op. 1 No. 5	S/A	Hansen		CHAL (1898)
6142	Rosenberg, Wilhelm [Vilhelm]	1862-	Waldlied "Nachtwind hat in den Bäumen"	Op. 1 No. 2	S/A	Hansen		CHAL (1898)
6143	Rosenfeld, J.		Im Herbste "Seid gegrüsst mit Frühlingswonne"	Op. 4	Unspec.	Chal.		CHAL (1898)
6144	Rosenfeld, J.		Reinheit "Auf dem Dach die Flügelein"	Op. 30	Unspec.	Chal.		CHAL (1898)
6145	Rosenfeld, Leopold	1850-1909	Am Abend "Leise rauschend durch Ruinen"	Op. 33 No. 3	S/A	Hansen		CHAL (1898)
6146	Rosenfeld, Leopold	1850-1909	Du mit den schwarzen Augen	Op. 13 No. 1	Unspec.	O. Forberg		CHAL (1898)
6147	Rosenfeld, Leopold	1850-1909	Hochsommer "Im Föhrenwald wie schwüle"	Op. 33 No. 1	S/A	Hansen		CHAL (1898)
6148	Rosenfeld, Leopold	1850-1909	Schwebe Mond im tiefen Blau	Op. 33 No. 1	S/A	Hansen		CHAL (1898)
6149	Rosenfeld, Leopold	1850-1909	Wenn alle Vögel schlagen "In lichten Frühlingstagen"	Op. 33 No. 2	S/A	Hansen		CHAL (1898)
6150	Rosenfeld, Leopold	1850-1909	Wenn ich an dich gedenke	Op. 13 No. 2	Unspec.	O. Forberg		CHAL (1898)
6151	Rosenfeld, Leopold	1850-1909	Wiet, weit aus ferner Zeit	Op. 13 No. 3	Unspec.	O. Forberg		CHAL (1898)
6152	Rosenfeld & Thiele		Chanukka Hymne		S/A	Philipp & S.		CHAL (1898)
6153	Rosenhain, Jacob	1813-1894	Im Walde, im hellen Sonnenschein	Op. 60 No. 3	Unspec.	Schott		CHAL (1898)
6154	Rosenhain, Jacob	1813-1894	Neapolitanisches Lied "Gross ist das Königreich"	Op. 60 No. 4	Unspec.	Schott		CHAL (1898)
6155	Rosenhain, Jacob	1813-1894	Nun ist die Tag geschwunden	Op. 60 No. 2	Unspec.	Schott		CHAL (1898)
6156	Rosenhain, Jacob	1813-1894	So viel Stern' am Himmel stehen	Op. 60 No. 5	Unspec.	Schott		CHAL (1898)
6157	Rosenhain, Jacob	1813-1894	Ständchen "Hüttelein still und klein"	Op. 60 No. 6	Unspec.	Schott		CHAL (1898)
6158	Rosenhain, Jacob	1813-1894	Und wenn die Primel schneeweiss blickt	Op. 60 No. 1	Unspec.	Schott		CHAL (1898)
6159	Rosenhain, Jacob	1813-1894	Wasserfahrt "Ich stand gelehnet und em Mast"		S/S	B. & H.		CHAL (1898)
6160	Rosenmeyer, H.		Abschied "Frühling kommt den Andern"	No. 1	Unspec.	Zierfuss		CHAL (1898)
6161	Rosensweig, H.		Es ust due Elektricität		Unspec.	Blaha		CHAL (1901)
6162	Rosenthal, Manuel	1904-	3 Chants de Femmes Berbères		S/A	Jobert	Unspec. pieces. Three duets	ASR
6163	Rosenthal, Manuel	1904-	Allègez le pas	No. III	S/A	Jobert	In "Trois Chants de Femmes Berbères" Autograph 1972.	MSN
6164	Rosenthal, Manuel	1904-	Rehala	No. II	S/A	Jobert	In "Trois Chants de Femmes Berbères" Autograph 1972.	MSN
6165	Rosenthal, Manuel	1904-	Repos	No. I	S/A	Jobert	In "Trois Chants de Femmes Berbères" Autograph 1972.	MSN
6166	Rosenthal, Manuel	1904-	Trois Chants de Femmes Berbères		S/A	Jobert		CVMP (1976)

REC	COMP	DTS	TITLE	OP #	VCG	PUB	COMMENTS	SRC
6167	Rosenzweig, Wilhelm	d. 1899	Da waht ganz a andere Luft "A Böhmin drei Jahr alt"		Unspec.	Doblinger		CHAL (1898)
6168	Rosenzweig, Wilhelm	d. 1899	Echo der Liebe "Leben zu verschönern uns"	No. 1	Unspec.	Maass i. W.		CHAL (1898)
6169	Rosenzweig, Wilhelm	d. 1899	Fortsetzung folgt "A Geck schwärmt an Maderl vor"		Unspec.	Kratoch-will		CHAL (1898)
6170	Rosenzweig, Wilhelm	d. 1899	Gemüathlichen "Gemäth-lichen seg'ns"		Unspec.	Kratoch-will		CHAL (1898)
6171	Rosenzweig, Wilhelm	d. 1899	Herzens-Echo "Wenn ich ein Vögerl' singen hör'"	No. 2	Unspec.	Maass i. W.		CHAL (1898)
6172	Rosenzweig, Wilhelm	d. 1899	Segn's, so heiter is das Leb'n in Wien "Recht harbe, flotte G'stangl'n"		Unspec.	Doblinger		CHAL (1898)
6173	Rosenzweig, Wilhelm	d. 1899	Widiwumpas, Katumpas "In Wien hab'n ma Alles"		Unspec.	Doblinger		CHAL (1898)
6174	Rosenzweig, Wilhelm	d. 1899	Zelten werd'n schlimmer "A Maderl wie Mili"		Unspec.	Doblinger		CHAL (1898)
6175	Rosenzweig, Wilhelm	d. 1899	Zwa Lugenschippeln "Du hörst mei lieber Freund"		Unspec.	Doblinger		CHAL (1898)
6176	Rossi, E.		Amore in mare "Qui sul mio cor"		S/Br or MS/A	Carisch & J. i. Mailand		CHAL (1898)
6177	Rossini, Gioacchino	1792-1868	Abreise "Nun lass uns scheiden		S/A	Hof-meister	Grmn. trans. It.	CHAL (1898)
6178	Rossini, Gioacchino	1792-1868	Abschied "Ach Italien blühend Gefilde"		S/A	Hof-meister	Grmn. trans. It.	CHAL (1898)
6179	Rossini, Gioacchino	1792-1868	Abschied von Italien		S/A	Hof-meister	2 Duets for S/A. Grmn. trans. It.	CHAL (1898)
6180	Rossini, Gioacchino	1792-1868	Duetto Buffo di due Gatti		high & low v.	Peters, Doblinger	Attr. to R. Pearsall	ASR
6181	Rossini, Gioacchino	1792-1868	Fischfang "Langsam kommt die Nacht"		S/S	Schott	Grmn. trans. It.	CHAL (1898)
6182	Rossini, Gioacchino	1792-1868	I marinari		Unspec.	Ricordi		BBC (1975)
6183	Rossini, Gioacchino	1792-1868	La pesca		S/A	Boosey	From "Soirées Musi-cales" [Serate Musicali]	BBC (1975)
6184	Rossini, Gioacchino	1792-1868	La Pesca		S/S	Ricordi	Contained in "Serate Musicali, Vol. II"	CVMP (1976)
6185	Rossini, Gioacchino	1792-1868	La Pesca	No. 2	S/S	Kalmus	In "Serate Musicali" Part II, 4 Duetti (contains other duets for S/T and T/B).	MSN
6186	Rossini, Gioacchino	1792-1868	La Regata Veneziana		S/S	Ricordi	Contained in "Serate Musicali, Vol. II"	CVMP (1976)
6187	Rossini, Gioacchino	1792-1868	La Regata Veneziana		S/S	CVR	In catalogue "Class-ical Vocal Reprints Complete Catalog" Pub. 1997.	MSN
6188	Rossini, Gioacchino	1792-1868	La Regata Veneziana	No. 1	S/S	Kalmus	In "Serate Musicali" Part II, 4 Duetti (contains other duets for S/T and T/B).	MSN
6189	Rossini, Gioacchino	1792-1868	La serenata		Unspec.	Ricordi		BBC (1975)
6190	Rossini, Gioacchino	1792-1868	Le départ		Unspec.	Aulagnier	Fr. trans. It.	BBC (1975)
6191	Rossini, Gioacchino	1792-1868	Regata Veneziana "Nottorno a due voci"		S/S	CVR	In Serrate Musicali.	CVMP (1995)
6192	Rossini, Gioacchino	1792-1868	Regatta Veneziana "Rudre muthvoll nach dem Ziel"		S/MS	Schott	Grmn. trans. It.	CHAL (1898)

REC	COMP	DTS	TITLE	OP #	VCG	PUB	COMMENTS	SRC
6193	Rossini, Gioacchino	1792-1868	Rudre muthvoll nach dem Ziel	III No. 8	Unspec.	C. Rühle i. L.	Grmn. tr. It.	CHAL (1901)
6194	Rossini, Gioacchino	1792-1868	Serate Musicali Vol II		S/S	Ricordi	Includes 2 duets, "La Regata Veneziana" & "La Pesca" for female v.	ASR
6195	Rossini, Gioacchino	1792-1868	"Soirées Musicales" ["Serrati Musicale"]		S/A	Boosey	Ed. Randegger	BBC (1975)
6196	Rossini, Gioacchino [attr.]	1792-1868	Duetto Buffo di due Gatti		2 female v. or Unspec.	Peters, Doblinger, Ricordi, et al.	Attr. to Rossini, pub. as such. Actually by Robert Pearsall (1795-1856). Voicing specified as "primo and secondo gatti"	CVMP (1976)
6197	Rossini, Gioacchino [attr.]	1792-1868	Duetto Buffo di due Gatti		S/A	EMB	Actually by R. Pearsall (1795-1856). In anth. "Duettek nöi Hangokra Zongorakísérettel" Vol. II Compi. M. Forrai. Pub. 1959.	MSN
6198	Rossini, Gioacchino [attr.]	1792-1868	Duetto Buffo di due Gatti	No. 2	Unspec.	Peters	Actually by R. Pearsall (1795-1856). Voicing specified as "primo and secondo gatti"	MSN
6199	Rossini, Gioaccino	1792-1868	La Pesca		MS/MS	Ricordi, Belwin	In "Soirées Musicales" Vol. 2	NATS-VCD
6200	Rossini, Gioaccino	1792-1868	La Regata Veneziana		MS/MS	Ricordi, Belwin	In "Soirées Musicales" Vol. 2	NATS-VCD
6201	Rossini, Gioaccino [attr.]	1792-1868	Duetto Buffo di due Gatti		MS/MS	Benjamin, et al.	Attr. to Rossini, pub. as such. Actually by Robert Pearsall (1795-1856). Voicing specified as "primo and secondo gatti"	NATS-VCD
6202	Rössler, Richard	1880-	An jedem Morgen freu' ich mich	No. 1	Unspec.	R. & P. Verl.		CHAL (1906)
6203	Rössler, Richard	1880-	Ein Vogel singt gottlobesam	No. 2	Unspec.	R. & P. Verl.		CHAL (1906)
6204	Rössler, Richard	1880-	Wo tief versteckt im Grunde		S/A	Simrock		CHAL (1906)
6205	Roth, Bertrand	1855-1938	Nacht ist nieder gangen	Op. 15 No. 1	high & med. v.	Klemm		CHAL (1911)
6206	Roth, Bertrand	1855-1938	Sorglosen Lächelns die Lippen geschürzt	Op. 15 No. 2	high & med. v.	Klemm		CHAL (1911)
6207	Roth, Franz	1837-1907	A Köchin kauft Aepfeln ein	Op. 434	Unspec.	Maass		CHAL (1901)
6208	Roth, Franz	1837-1907	Ach, wenn ich mein Ideal	Op. 433	Unspec.	Maass		CHAL (1901)
6209	Roth, Franz	1837-1907	Nett'l die wascht sich	Op. 431	Unspec.	Maass		CHAL (1901)
6210	Rothlauf, B.		Auf dem Berge da wehet der Wind	Op. 3 No. 11	Unspec.	Coppenrath		CHAL (1906)
6211	Rothlauf, B.		Habt ihr ihn noch nicht vernommen	Op. 3 No. 4	Unspec.	Coppenrath		CHAL (1906)
6212	Rothlauf, B.		Jedes Spätzchen hat sein Plätzchen	Op. 3 No. 6	Unspec.	Coppenrath		CHAL (1906)
6213	Rothlauf, B.		Müde bin ich, geh' zur Ruh'	Op. 3 No. 14	Unspec.	Coppenrath		CHAL (1906)
6214	Rothlauf, B.		So schlaf in Ruh'	Op. 3 No. 13	Unspec.	Coppenrath		CHAL (1906)
6215	Rothlauf, B.		Steht auf ihr lieben Kinderlein	Op. 3 No. 1	Unspec.	Coppenrath		CHAL (1906)
6216	Rothlauf, B.		Weihnachtsglocken läuten	Op. 3 No. 10	Unspec.	Coppenrath		CHAL (1906)

REC	COMP	DTS	TITLE	OP #	VCG	PUB	COMMENTS	SRC
6217	Rothlauf, B.		Wir sind noch jung	Op. 3 No. 5	Unspec.	Coppen-rath		CHAL (1906)
6218	Rothlauf, B.		Wo der Schnee geschmolzen ist	Op. 3 No. 3	Unspec.	Coppen-rath		CHAL (1906)
6219	Rothstein, James	1871-	Komm, mein nettes Schmollemäulchen	Op. 72	Unspec.	Harmonie i. B.		CHAL (1906)
6220	Rotschy, J. B.		Recueil de chant pour la famille		Unspec.	Hug		CHAL (1898)
6221	Rott, Carl Maria	1858-1884	Das is ka Caféhaus for mir "Ein Sprachwort ist hier sehr bekannt"		Unspec.	Maas		CHAL (1898)
6222	Roussel, L.		Um Mitternacht		Unspec.	Schott		CHAL (1898)
6223	Rubbra, Edmund	1901-1986	Dear Eliza		Unspec.	Curwen		BBC (1975)
6224	Rubini, Giovanni Battista	1794-1854	Andenken		Unspec.	Schott		CHAL (1898)
6225	Rubinstein, Anton	1829-1894	Aller Berge Gipfel ruh'n	Op. 48 No. 2	Unspec.	Senff		CHAL (1901)
6226	Rubinstein, Anton	1829-1894	Am Abend	Op. 48 No. 11	S/MS or S/Br or T/Br	G. Schirm., Peters	Grmn. trans. of Russ. In collection "18 Two-Part Songs" Pub. 1901. Also "Zweistimmige Lieder"	NATS-VCD
6227	Rubinstein, Anton	1829-1894	Am Abend "Der drück-emd schwüle Tag hat ausgeglüht"	Op. 48 No. 11	Unspec.	Senff, G. Schirm.	In coll. "Zweistimmige Lieder mit Begleitung des Pianoforte compon-irt von A. Rubinstein" Also "Rubinstein: 18 2-Part Songs" (Schirm).	MSN
6228	Rubinstein, Anton	1829-1894	Beim Scheiden	Op. 48 No. 6	S/A or S/MS	Ditson	In anthology "Soprano and Alto Duets" Ed. H. Kiehl. Pub. 1901.	MSN
6229	Rubinstein, Anton	1829-1894	Beim Scheiden	Op. 48 No. 6	S/MS or S/Br or T/Br	G. Schirm., Peters	Grmn. trans. of Russ. In collection "18 Two-Part Songs" Pub. 1901 and "Zweistimmige Lieder"	NATS-VCD
6230	Rubinstein, Anton	1829-1894	Beim Scheiden "Beredt war die Zunge"	Op. 48 No. 6	Unspec.	Senff		CHAL (1898)
6231	Rubinstein, Anton	1829-1894	Beim Scheiden "Beredt war die Zunge"	Op. 48 No. 6	Unspec.	Senff, G. Schirm.	In coll. "Zweistimmige Lieder mit Begleitung des Pianoforte compon-irt von A. Rubinstein" Also "Rubinstein: 18 2-Part Songs" (Schirm).	MSN
6232	Rubinstein, Anton	1829-1894	Das Vögelien	Op. 48 No. 9	S/MS or S/Br or T/Br	G. Schirm., Peters	Grmn. trans. of Russ. In collection "18 Two-Part Songs" Pub. 1901 and "Zweistimmige Lieder"	NATS-VCD
6233	Rubinstein, Anton	1829-1894	Das Vöglein "Glücklich lebt vor Noth geborgen"	Op. 48 No. 9	Unspec.	Senff, G. Schirm.	In coll. "Zweistimmige Lieder mit Begleitung des Pianoforte compon-irt von A. Rubinstein" Also "Rubinstein: 18 2-Part Songs" (Schirm).	MSN
6234	Rubinstein, Anton	1829-1894	Der Engel		high & low v.	Church	In anthology "Sacred Duets A Collection of Two-Part Songs by the Best Composers" Vol. 2. Compi. & ed. W. Shakespeare. Pub. 1907.	MSN

REC	COMP	DTS	TITLE	OP #	VCG	PUB	COMMENTS	SRC
6235	Rubinstein, Anton	1829-1894	Der Engel		S/A or S/B	C. Fischer	In catalogue page "Selected Vocal Duets By Favorite Composers" of Carl Fischer NY (no date)	MSN
6236	Rubinstein, Anton	1829-1894	Der Engel		S/A or S/Br	G. Schirm.	In catalogue page "Selected Vocal Duets" of G. Schirmer, Inc. NY (no date)	MSN
6237	Rubinstein, Anton	1829-1894	Der Engel	Op. 48 No. 1	S/A	Ditson	In anthology "Soprano and Alto Duets" Ed. H. Kiehl. Pub. 1901.	MSN
6238	Rubinstein, Anton	1829-1894	Der Engel	Op. 48 No. 1	S/A	Ditson	In anthology "The Ditson Collection of Soprano and Alto Duets" Pub. 1934.	MSN
6239	Rubinstein, Anton	1829-1894	Der Engel	Op. 48 No. 1	S/MS or S/Br or T/Br	G. Schirm., Peters	Grmn. trans. of Russ. In collection "18 Two-Part Songs" Pub. 1901 and "Zweistimmige Lieder"	NATS-VCD
6240	Rubinstein, Anton	1829-1894	Der Engel "Es schwebt ein Engel dem Himmel entlang"	Op. 48 No. 1	Unspec.	Senff		CHAL (1898)
6241	Rubinstein, Anton	1829-1894	Der Engel "Es schwebte ein Engel den Himmel entlang"	Op. 48 No. 1	Unspec. or S/MS	Senff, G. Schirm.	In coll. "Zweistimmige Lieder mit Begleitung des Piano-forte componirt von A. Rubinstein" Also "Rubinstein: 18 2-Part Songs" (Schirm).	MSN
6242	Rubinstein, Anton	1829-1894	Die Nacht	Op. 48 No. 7	S/MS or S/Br or T/Br	G. Schirm., Peters	Grmn. trans. of Russ. In collection "18 Two-Part Songs" Pub. 1901 and "Zweistimmige Lieder"	NATS-VCD
6243	Rubinstein, Anton	1829-1894	Die Nacht "Des Tages letztes Glühen"	Op. 48 No. 7	Unspec.	Senff, G. Schirm.	In coll. "Zweistimmige Lieder mit Begleitung des Piano-forte componirt von A. Rubinstein" Also "Rubinstein: 18 2-Part Songs" (Schirm).	MSN
6244	Rubinstein, Anton	1829-1894	Die Turteltaube und der Wanderer	Op. 48 No. 10	S/MS or S/Br or T/Br	G. Schirm., Peters	Grmn. trans. of Russ. In collection "18 Two-Part Songs" Pub. 1901 and "Zweistimmige Lieder"	NATS-VCD
6245	Rubinstein, Anton	1829-1894	Die Turteltaube und der Wanderer "Sprich, warum sitzest du dort auf dem Zweige"	Op. 48 No. 10	Unspec.	Senff, G. Schirm.	In coll. "Zweistimmige Lieder mit Begleitung des Piano-forte componirt von A. Rubinstein" Also "Rubinstein: 18 2-Part Songs" (Schirm).	MSN
6246	Rubinstein, Anton	1829-1894	Die Wolke	Op. 48 No. 8	S/MS or S/Br or T/Br	G. Schirm., Peters	Grmn. trans. of Russ. In collection "18 Two-Part Songs" Pub. 1901 and "Zweistimmige Lieder"	NATS-VCD
6247	Rubinstein, Anton	1829-1894	Die Wolke "Vorbei ist der Sturm"	Op. 48 No. 8	Unspec.	Senff, G. Schirm.	In coll. "Zweistimmige Lieder mit Begleitung des Piano-forte componirt von A. Rubinstein" Also "Rubinstein: 18 2-Part Songs" (Schirm).	MSN
6248	Rubinstein, Anton	1829-1894	Eighteen Vocal Duets	Op. 48 Op. 67	S/A	Peters	Grmn. lang.	ASR
6249	Rubinstein, Anton	1829-1894	Es schwebt ein Engel	Op. 48 No. 1	Unspec.	Senff		CHAL (1901)
6250	Rubinstein, Anton	1829-1894	Frühlingsglaube	Op. 67 No. 3	S/MS or S/Br or T/Br	G. Schirm., Peters	Grmn. trans. of Russ. In collection "18 Two-Part Songs" Pub. 1901 and "Zweistimmige Lieder"	NATS-VCD

REC	COMP	DTS	TITLE	OP #	VCG	PUB	COMMENTS	SRC
6251	Rubinstein, Anton	1829-1894	Frühlingsglaube "Die linden Lüfte sind erwacht"	Op. 67 No. 3	Unspec.	Senff, G. Schirm.	In coll. "Zweistimmige Lieder mit Begleitung des Pianoforte componirt von A. Rubinstein" Also "Rubinstein: 18 2-Part Songs" (Schirm).	MSN
6252	Rubinstein, Anton	1829-1894	Frühlingsglaube "Linden Lüfte sind erwacht"	Op. 67 No. 3	Unspec.	Senff		CHAL (1898)
6253	Rubinstein, Anton	1829-1894	Gornye vershiny [Mountain Heights]		S/MS	GMI	Translit. title of Russ. Only Cyrillic. Anth. "Izbrannye Duety Russkikh Kompozitorov dlia peniia s fortepiano" Pub. 1948.	MSN
6254	Rubinstein, Anton	1830-1894	Huntsman, The		Unspec.	ECS	Eng. trans. Russ. In anthology "48 Duets Seventeenth Through Nineteenth Centuries" Ed. V. Prahl. Pub. 1941, 1970.	MSN
6255	Rubinstein, Anton	1829-1894	Im heimischen Land	Op. 48 No. 3	S/MS or S/Br or T/Br	G. Schirm., Peters	Grmn. trans. of Russ. In collection "18 Two-Part Songs" Pub. 1901 and "Zweistimmige Lieder"	NATS-VCD
6256	Rubinstein, Anton	1829-1894	Im heimischen Land "Im heimlischen Land steht ein friedlicher Hain"	Op. 48 No. 3	Unspec.	Senff, G. Schirm.	In coll. "Zweistimmige Lieder mit Begleitung des Pianoforte componirt von A. Rubinstein" Also "Rubinstein: 18 2-Part Songs" (Schirm).	MSN
6257	Rubinstein, Anton	1829-1894	Im heimlichen Land steht ein friedlicher Hain"	Op. 48 No. 3	Unspec.	Senff		CHAL (1898)
6258	Rubinstein, Anton	1829-1894	Lied	Op. 67 No. 6	S/MS or S/Br or T/Br	G. Schirm., Peters	Grmn. trans. of Russ. In collection "18 Two-Part Songs" Pub. 1901 and "Zweistimmige Lieder"	NATS-VCD
6259	Rubinstein, Anton	1829-1894	Lied der Vögelein	Op. 67 No. 1	S/MS or S/Br or T/Br	G. Schirm., Peters	Grmn. trans. of Russ. In collection "18 Two-Part Songs" Pub. 1901 and "Zweistimmige Lieder"	NATS-VCD
6260	Rubinstein, Anton	1829-1894	Lied der Vögelein "Von Zweig zu Zweige"	Op. 67 No. 1	Unspec.	Senff, G. Schirm.	In coll. "Zweistimmige Lieder mit Begleitung des Pianoforte componirt von A. Rubinstein" Also "Rubinstein: 18 2-Part Songs" (Schirm).	MSN
6261	Rubinstein, Anton	1829-1894	Lied der Vöglein		S/A	Peters	From "Duettenkranz" Vol III. Ed. Martienssen	ASR
6262	Rubinstein, Anton	1829-1894	Lied "Die Lotosblume ängstigt sich"	Op. 67 No. 6	Unspec.	Senff, G. Schirm.	In coll. "Zweistimmige Lieder mit Begleitung des Pianoforte componirt von A. Rubinstein" Also "Rubinstein: 18 2-Part Songs" (Schirm).	MSN
6263	Rubinstein, Anton	1829-1894	Lotosblume "Lotosblume ängstigt sich"	Op. 67 No. 6	Unspec.	Senff	Pub. 1864	CHAL (1898)
6264	Rubinstein, Anton	1829-1894	Lotosflower, The		high & low v.	Hinds, Hayden & Eldredge	Eng. trans. Grmn. In anthology "The Most Popular Vocal Duets" Ed. Dr. E. J. Biedermann. Pub. 1914.	MSN
6265	Rubinstein, Anton	1830-1894	Lotus-Flower, The		Unspec.	ECS	Eng. trans. Grmn. In anthology "48 Duets Seventeenth Through Nineteenth Centuries" Ed. V. Prahl. Pub. 1941, 1970.	MSN

REC	COMP	DTS	TITLE	OP #	VCG	PUB	COMMENTS	SRC
6266	Rubinstein, Anton	1829-1894	Meeresabend	Op. 67 No. 5	S/MS or S/Br or T/Br	G. Schirm., Peters	Grmn. trans. of Russ. In collection "18 Two-Part Songs" Pub. 1901 and "Zweistimmige Lieder"	NATS-VCD
6267	Rubinstein, Anton	1829-1894	Meeresabend "Sie hat den ganzen Tag getobt"	Op. 67 No. 5	Unspec.	Senff	Pub. 1864	CHAL (1898)
6268	Rubinstein, Anton	1829-1894	Meeresabend "Sie hat den ganzen Tag getobt"	Op. 67 No. 5	Unspec.	Senff, G. Schirm.	In coll. "Zweistimmige Lieder mit Begleitung des Pianoforte compon-irt von A. Rubinstein" Also "Rubinstein: 18 2-Part Songs" (Schirm).	MSN
6269	Rubinstein, Anton	1829-1894	Nacht "Tages letztes Glüthen"	Op. 48 No. 7	Unspec.	Senff	Pub. 1852	CHAL (1898)
6270	Rubinstein, Anton	1829-1894	Nattvandrarens Sang		Unspec.	Fazer	Finn. trans. of Grmn.	CVMP (1976)
6271	Rubinstein, Anton	1830-1894	O Weary Soul		Unspec.	ECS	Eng. trans. Russ. In anthology "48 Duets Seventeenth Through Nineteenth Centuries" Ed. V. Prahl. Pub. 1941, 1970.	MSN
6272	Rubinstein, Anton	1829-1894	Op. 48		Unspec.	Boosey	Ed. Eisoldt	BBC (1975)
6273	Rubinstein, Anton	1829-1894	Op. 67		Unspec.	Boosey	Ed. Eisoldt	BBC (1975)
6274	Rubinstein, Anton	1829-1894	Sang das Vöglein "Sang wohl, sang das Vöglein"	Op. 48 No. 2	Unspec.	Senff	Pub. 1852	CHAL (1898)
6275	Rubinstein, Anton	1829-1894	Sang das Vöglein "Sang wohl, sang das Vöglein"	Op. 48 No. 2	Unspec.	Senff, G. Schirm.	In coll. "Zweistimmige Lieder mit Begleitung des Pianoforte compon-irt von A. Rubinstein" Also "Rubinstein: 18 2-Part Songs" (Schirm).	MSN
6276	Rubinstein, Anton	1829-1894	Sang der Vöglein		S/A	Peters	From "Duettenkranz" Vol III. Ed. Martienssen	ASR
6277	Rubinstein, Anton	1829-1894	Sang des Vögelein	Op. 48 No. 2	S/MS or S/Br or T/Br	G. Schirm., Peters	Grmn. trans. of Russ. In collection "18 Two-Part Songs" Pub. 1901 and "Zweistimmige Lieder"	NATS-VCD
6278	Rubinstein, Anton	1829-1894	The Angel		S/A	White-Smith	Eng. trans. Grmn. In catalogue page "Vocal Duetts" of White-Smith Music Pub. Co. (no date)	MSN
6279	Rubinstein, Anton	1829-1894	Turteltaube und der Wan-derer "Sprich warum sitzest du"	Op. 48 No. 10	Unspec.	Senff	Pub. 1852	CHAL (1898)
6280	Rubinstein, Anton	1829-1894	Twelve Duets	Op. 48	S/A	Hansen-Den	Collection. Unspec. pieces.	CVMP (1976)
6281	Rubinstein, Anton	1829-1894	Twelve Duets Op. 48	Op. 48	S/A	Hansen	Unspec. pieces	ASR
6282	Rubinstein, Anton	1829-1894	Vid Nattetid		Unspec.	Lundq.	Swed. trans. Grmn.	CVMP (1976)
6283	Rubinstein, Anton	1829-1894	Vöglein "Glücklich lebt vor Noth geborgen"	Op. 48 No. 9	Unspec.	Senff	Pub. 1852	CHAL (1898)
6284	Rubinstein, Anton	1829-1894	Volkslied	Op. 48 No. 12	S/MS or S/Br or T/Br	G. Schirm., Peters	Grmn. trans. of Russ. In collection "18 Two-Part Songs" Pub. 1901 and "Zweistimmige Lieder"	NATS-VCD

REC	COMP	DTS	TITLE	OP #	VCG	PUB	COMMENTS	SRC
6285	Rubinstein, Anton	1829-1894	Volkslied	Op. 48 No. 4	S/MS or S/Br or T/Br	G. Schirm., Peters	Grmn. trans. of Russ. In collection "18 Two-Part Songs" Pub. 1901 and "Zweistimmige Lieder"	NATS-VCD
6286	Rubinstein, Anton	1829-1894	Volkslied "Mägdlein auf die Wiese gingen"	Op. 48 No. 4	Unspec.	Senff	Pub. 1852	CHAL (1898)
6287	Rubinstein, Anton	1829-1894	Volkslied "Mägdlein auf die Wiese gingen"	Op. 48 No. 4	Unspec.	Senff, G. Schirm.	In coll. "Zweistimmige Lieder mit Begleitung des Pianoforte componirt von A. Rubinstein" Also "Rubinstein: 18 2-Part Songs" (Schirm).	MSN
6288	Rubinstein, Anton	1829-1894	Volkslied "Sonne scheint noch"	Op. 48 No. 12	Unspec.	Senff, G. Schirm.	In coll. "Zweistimmige Lieder mit Begleitung des Pianoforte componirt von A. Rubinstein" Also "Rubinstein: 18 2-Part Songs" (Schirm).	MSN
6289	Rubinstein, Anton	1829-1894	Vorüber	Op. 67 No. 4	S/MS or S/Br or T/Br	G. Schirm., Peters	Grmn. trans. of Russ. In collection "18 Two-Part Songs" Pub. 1901 and "Zweistimmige Lieder"	NATS-VCD
6290	Rubinstein, Anton	1829-1894	Vorüber "Vorüber, wo die lichte Rose"	Op. 67 No. 4	Unspec.	Senff	Pub. 1864	CHAL (1898)
6291	Rubinstein, Anton	1829-1894	Vorüber "Vorüber, wo die lichte Rose"	Op. 67 No. 4	Unspec.	Senff, G. Schirm.	In coll. "Zweistimmige Lieder mit Begleitung des Pianoforte componirt von A. Rubinstein" Also "Rubinstein: 18 2-Part Songs" (Schirm).	MSN
6292	Rubinstein, Anton	1829-1894	Waldlied	Op. 67 No. 2	S/MS or S/Br or T/Br	G. Schirm., Peters	Grmn. trans. of Russ. In collection "18 Two-Part Songs" Pub. 1901 and "Zweistimmige Lieder"	NATS-VCD
6293	Rubinstein, Anton	1829-1894	Waldlied "Der Nachtwind hat in den Bäumen"	Op. 67 No. 2	Unspec.	Senff, G. Schirm.	In coll. "Zweistimmige Lieder mit Begleitung des Pianoforte componirt von A. Rubinstein" Also "Rubinstein: 18 2-Part Songs" (Schirm).	MSN
6294	Rubinstein, Anton	1829-1894	Wanderer's Evensong, The		S/A	Leonard-Eng	Eng. trans. Grmn. Arr. E. Newton. In anth. "6 Popular Vocal Duets Book I for Sop. & Contr." Ed. & arr. by E. Newton. Pub. 1906.	MSN
6295	Rubinstein, Anton	1829-1894	Wanderer's Nachtlied		S/A or S/Br	C. Fischer	In catalogue page "Selected Vocal Duets By Favorite Composers" of Carl Fischer NY (no date)	MSN
6296	Rubinstein, Anton	1829-1894	Wanderer's Night Song		high & low v.	Hinds, Hayden & Eldredge	Eng. trans. Grmn. In anthology "The Most Popular Vocal Duets" Ed. Dr. E. J. Biedermann. Pub. 1914.	MSN
6297	Rubinstein, Anton	1829-1894	Wanderer's night song		S/A	White-Smith	Eng. trans. Grmn. In catalogue page "Vocal Duetts" of White-Smith Music Pub. Co. (no date)	MSN
6298	Rubinstein, Anton	1829-1894	Wanderer's Night Song [Wanderers Nachtlied]	Op. 48 No. 5	S/A	Ditson	Eng. trans. Grmn. In anthology "The Ditson Collection of Soprano and Alto Duets" Pub. 1934.	MSN
6299	Rubinstein, Anton	1829-1894	Wanderers Nachtlied		S/A or S/Br	G. Schirm.	In catalogue page "Selected Vocal Duets" of G. Schirmer, Inc. NY (no date)	MSN
6300	Rubinstein, Anton	1829-1894	Wanderers Nachtlied	Op. 48 No. 5	S/A	Ditson	In anthology "Soprano and Alto Duets" Ed. H. Kiehl. Pub. 1901.	MSN

REC	COMP	DTS	TITLE	OP #	VCG	PUB	COMMENTS	SRC
6301	Rubinstein, Anton	1829-1894	Wanderers Nachtlied	Op. 48 No. 5	S/MS or S/Br or T/Br	G. Schirm., Peters	Grmn. trans. of Russ. In collection "18 Two-Part Songs" Pub. 1901 and "Zweistimmige Lieder"	NATS-VCD
6302	Rubinstein, Anton	1829-1894	Wanderers Nachtlied "Aller Berge Gipfel ruhn"	Op. 48 No. 5	Unspec.	Senff	Pub. 1852	CHAL (1898)
6303	Rubinstein, Anton	1829-1894	Wanderers Nachtlied "Aller Berge Gipfel ruhn"	Op. 48 No. 5	Unspec.	Senff, G. Schirm.	In coll. "Zweistimmige Lieder mit Begleitung des Pianoforte componirt von A. Rubinstein" Also "Rubinstein: 18 2-Part Songs" (Schirm).	MSN
6304	Rubinstein, Anton	1829-1894	Wolke "Vorbei ist der Sturm"	Op. 48 No. 8	Unspec.	Senff	Pub.1852	CHAL (1898)
6305	Rubinstein, Nicolai	1835-1881	Am Abend "Drückend schwüle Tag hat ausgeglüht"	Op. 48 No. 11	Unspec.	Senff	Brother of Anton Rubinstein	CHAL (1898)
6306	Rubinstein, Nicolai	1835-1881	Lied der Vöglein "Von Zweig zu Zweig zu hüpfen"	Op. 67 No. 1	Unspec.	Senff	Brother of Anton Rubinstein	CHAL (1898)
6307	Rubinstein, Nicolai	1835-1881	Volkslied "Sonne scheinet noch"	Op. 48 No. 12	Unspec.	Senff	Brother of Anton Rubinstein	CHAL (1898)
6308	Rubinstein, Nicolai	1835-1881	Waldlied "Nachtwind hat in den Bäumen"	Op. 67 No. 2	Unspec.	Senff	Brother of Anton Rubinstein	CHAL (1898)
6309	Rübner, Cornelius [Rybner]	1855-1903	Vöglein wohin so schnell	Op. 14	2 female v.	Sommer-meyer	Head of Columbia Univ. Music Department, 1904-1919	CHAL (1898)
6310	Ruch, Hannes	1867-1928?	Frau Wirtin, musst dich eilen		Unspec.	Schar-frichter-Verlag	Pen name of Hans Richard Weinhöppel	CHAL (1911)
6311	Ruch, Hannes	1867-1928?	Tag ist wohl entschwunden		Unspec.	Schar-frichter-Verlag	Pen name of Hans Richard Weinhöppel	CHAL (1911)
6312	Rückauf, Anton	1855-1903	Deine kecken Liebesscherze	Op. 11 No. 4	S/A	Kistner		CHAL (1898)
6313	Rückauf, Anton	1855-1903	Guter rath "Ach Mutter, liebe Mutter"	Op. 11 No. 3	S/A	Kistner		CHAL (1898)
6314	Rückauf, Anton	1855-1903	Tröstung "Wer über meinem Haupte"	Op. 11 No. 1	S/A	Kistner		CHAL (1898)
6315	Rücker, August	1871-	Nun prangt in allen Enden	II No. 1	Unspec.	Verlag d. Trakta-hauses		CHAL (1906)
6316	Rücker, August	1871-	O Weihnachtszeit, wir jubeln die entgegen	II No. 4	Unspec.	Verlag d. Trakta-hauses		CHAL (1906)
6317	Rücker, August	1871-	Trage di Schifflein des Lebens mich fort	II No. 2	Unspec.	Verlag d. Trakta-hauses		CHAL (1906)
6318	Rücker, August	1871-	Wach' auf mein Herz	II No. 3	Unspec.	Verlag d. Trakta-hauses		CHAL (1906)
6319	Rücker, August	1871-	Zu Gott empor "4 Duette"	II	Unspec.	Verlag d. Trakta-hauses	Set of 4 duets.	CHAL (1906)
6320	Rückert, Theodor	1859-	Du Bächlein, silberhell und klar	Op. 21	MS/A	Kaun		CHAL (1911)
6321	Rudnick, Wilhelm	1850-1927	Also hat Gott die Welt geliebet		S/A	Feuchtin-ger	org or harm	CHAL (1906)
6322	Rudnick, Wilhelm	1850-1927	Aufwärts "Dass es Licht im Herzen werde"	Op. 29 No. 2	S/S	Schmidt i. Heilbr.	org accomp.	CHAL (1898)

REC	COMP	DTS	TITLE	OP #	VCG	PUB	COMMENTS	SRC
6323	Rudnick, Wilhelm	1850-1927	Christ ist erstanden von den Todten		S/A	Feuchtinger	org or pf	CHAL (1906)
6324	Rudnick, Wilhelm	1850-1927	Die auf den Herrn hoffen		S/A	Feuchtinger		CHAL (1906)
6325	Rudnick, Wilhelm	1850-1927	Du Friedenszeit voll reichem Segen		S/A	Feuchtinger		CHAL (1906)
6326	Rudnick, Wilhelm	1850-1927	Ein Himmelshauch weht uns entgegen		S/A	Feuchtinger		CHAL (1906)
6327	Rudnick, Wilhelm	1850-1927	Herr, dieses Paar ist vor dich getreten		S/A	Feuchtinger	org or harm	CHAL (1906)
6328	Rudnick, Wilhelm	1850-1927	Ich harre des Herrn		S/A	Feuchtinger	org or harm	CHAL (1906)
6329	Rudnick, Wilhelm	1850-1927	Kommt Kinder, kommt zur Krippe		S/A	Feuchtinger		CHAL (1906)
6330	Rudnick, Wilhelm	1850-1927	Lobe den Herrn mein Seele, Herr mein Gott		S/A	Feuchtinger	pf or harm	CHAL (1906)
6331	Rudnick, Wilhelm	1850-1927	Nun weiss ich, was die Liebe ist		S/A	Feuchtinger	org or harm	CHAL (1906)
6332	Rudnick, Wilhelm	1850-1927	O wüsste es die ganze Welt		S/A	Feuchtinger	org or harm	CHAL (1906)
6333	Rudnick, Wilhelm	1850-1927	So soll es sein	Op. 74 No. 1	Unspec.	Preiser	org	CHAL (1906)
6334	Rudnick, Wilhelm	1850-1927	Und du Bethlehem bist mit nichten		S/A	Feuchtinger	org or pf	CHAL (1906)
6335	Rudnick, Wilhelm	1850-1927	Vertrauen auf Gott "Was willst du sorgen"		S/S	Schmidt i. Heilbr.	org	CHAL (1898)
6336	Rudnick, Wilhelm	1850-1927	Wacht auf und rauscht durch's Thal		S/A	Feuchtinger		CHAL (1906)
6337	Rudnick, Wilhelm	1850-1927	Wenn ich in Todesängsten bin	Op. 74 No. 3	Unspec.	Preiser	org	CHAL (1906)
6338	Rudnick, Wilhelm	1850-1927	Wenn ich nur dich habe		S/A	Feuchtinger	org or harm	CHAL (1906)
6339	Rudnick, Wilhelm	1850-1927	Wenn Trauer mir das Herz beschwert	Op. 74 No. 2	Unspec.	Preiser	org	CHAL (1906)
6340	Rudorff, E. [Friedrich Karl]	1840-1916	Am Staubbach "Rauschet Fluthen, rauschet nieder"	Op. 35 No. 1	2 female v.	Schlesinger		CHAL (1898)
6341	Rudorff, E. [Friedrich Karl]	1840-1916	Auf dem Gebirg, da gehen zu Zwein	Op. 35 No. 2	2 female v.	Schlesinger		CHAL (1898)
6342	Rudorff, E. [Friedrich Karl]	1840-1916	Glocken "Aus dem fernen Thal"	Op. 34 No.1	2 female v.	Schlesinger		CHAL (1898)
6343	Rudorff, E. [Friedrich Karl]	1840-1916	Goldne Brücken seien alle Lieder mir	Op. 34 No. 3	2 female v.	Schlesinger		CHAL (1898)
6344	Rudorff, E. [Friedrich Karl]	1840-1916	Heimath "Ich weiss ein theuerwethes Land"	Op. 35 No. 3	2 female v.	Schlesinger		CHAL (1898)
6345	Rudorff, E. [Friedrich Karl]	1840-1816	Schifferinnen "Bin zur Welt gekommen einst"	Op. 34 No. 2	2 female v.	Schlesinger		CHAL (1898)
6346	Rügamer, F.		O diese Don Juans "Ach, wie heiter ind wie fröhlich"	Op. 31	2 female v.	O. Teich		CHAL (1898)
6347	Rühl, Friedrich Wilhelm	1817-1874	Abendläuten		S/A	Hedler i. Frankf.		CHAL (1898)
6348	Rühl, Friedrich Wilhelm	1817-1874	Es ist der Wald	Op. 8 No. 1	S/A	Schott		CHAL (1898)

REC	COMP	DTS	TITLE	OP #	VCG	PUB	COMMENTS	SRC
6349	Rühl, Friedrich Wilhelm	1817-1874	Zu Gott erhebt sich meine Seele	Op. 8 No. 2	S/A	Schott		CHAL (1898)
6350	Rühricht, P.		Lustige Leute, allwell voll Freud'	Op. 70	S/A	Portius		CHAL (1911)
6351	Rungenhagen, Karl Friedrich	1778-1851	An den Herbst "Ach entblättert sinkt"	Op. 3 No. 1	S/S	Sch. & Co.		CHAL (1898)
6352	Rungenhagen, Karl Friedrich	1778-1851	Erguss "Klage, klage"	No. 1	S/S	Bahn		CHAL (1898)
6353	Rungenhagen, Karl Friedrich	1778-1851	Ermahnung "Ihr Ritter und ihr Frauen zart"	No. 3	S/S	Bahn		CHAL (1898)
6354	Rungenhagen, Karl Friedrich	1778-1851	Frühlingsempfindung "Horch, wie so hell"		S/S	Bahn		CHAL (1898)
6355	Rungenhagen, Karl Friedrich	1778-1851	Frühlingssehnsucht "Frühling komm' hervor"	Op. 27 No. 3	S/S	Sch. & Co.		CHAL (1898)
6356	Rungenhagen, Karl Friedrich	1778-1851	Geist der Harmonie "Von fernen Fluren weht ein Geist"	Op. 8 No. 1	S/S	Sch. & Co.		CHAL (1898)
6357	Rungenhagen, Karl Friedrich	1778-1851	Italischer Himmel "Welch' süsser Athem"	No. 2	S/S	Bahn		CHAL (1898)
6358	Rungenhagen, Karl Friedrich	1778-1851	Klage im Walde "Laue Lüfte spielen lind"	Op. 31 No. 1	S/S	Sch. & Co.		CHAL (1898)
6359	Rungenhagen, Karl Friedrich	1778-1851	Lied an die Wolken "Wie schwimmt ihr, ihr Wolken"	Op. 34 No. 1	A/A	Sch. & Co.		CHAL (1898)
6360	Rungenhagen, Karl Friedrich	1778-1851	Lied aus Albano "Es flüstert still in dunkler Nacht"	Op. 34 No. 2	A/A	Sch. & Co.		CHAL (1898)
6361	Rungenhagen, Karl Friedrich	1778-1851	Lied der Wasserfee "Auf Wogen gezogen"	Op. 31 No. 3	S/S	Sch. & Co.		CHAL (1898)
6362	Rungenhagen, Karl Friedrich	1778-1851	Lorbeerkranz "Für die süsse zarte Liebe"	Op. 31 No. 2	S/S	Sch. & Co.		CHAL (1898)
6363	Rungenhagen, Karl Friedrich	1778-1851	Nacht "Süsse Ahnungs-schauer gleiten"	Op. 8 No. 3	S/S	Sch. & Co.		CHAL (1898)
6364	Rungenhagen, Karl Friedrich	1778-1851	Rausche Fluss das Thal entlang	Op. 27 No. 1	S/S	Sch. & Co.		CHAL (1898)
6365	Rungenhagen, Karl Friedrich	1778-1851	Sinnblüthe "Sinkt die Sonn' am Abend"	Op. 27 No. 2	S/S	Sch. & Co.		CHAL (1898)
6366	Rungenhagen, Karl Friedrich	1778-1851	Sterne "Wie freundlich strahlt ihr Sterne"	Op. 34 No. 3	A/A	Sch. & Co.		CHAL (1898)
6367	Rungenhagen, Karl Friedrich	1778-1851	Töne "Liebe denkt in süssen Tönen"	Op. 8 No. 2	S/S	Sch. & Co.		CHAL (1898)
6368	Rungenhagen, Karl Friedrich	1778-1851	Vögel "Wie lieblich, wie fröhlich"	Op. 3 No. 3	S/S	Sch. & Co.		CHAL (1898)
6369	Rungenhagen, Karl Friedrich	1778-1851	Wanderers Nachtlied "Über allen Gipfeln (Wipfeln) ist Ruh"	Op. 3 No. 2	S/S	Sch. & Co.		CHAL (1898)
6370	Russell, Armand		Ballad with Epitaphs		2 med. v.	Seesaw		ASR
6371	Russell, Kennedy	1883-	I was thinking of you		Unspec.	P. Maurice		BBC (1975)
6372	Rust, Wilhelm Karl	1822-1892	Ave Maria "Ave Maria gratia pleni"	Op. 1 No. 1	S/A	B. & H.	org or pf accomp.	CHAL (1898)
6373	Rust, Wilhelm Karl	1822-1892	Du bleicher Mondenschein "Herz mit seinem Hoffen"	Op. 23 No. 1	S/MS	Schles-inger		CHAL (1898)
6374	Rust, Wilhelm Karl	1822-1892	Frühlingslied "Was regt sich so mächtig"	Op. 23 No. 3	S/MS	Schles-inger		CHAL (1898)
6375	Rust, Wilhelm Karl	1822-1892	Gedankenflug "Wenn Gedanken sichtbar wären"	Op. 23 No. 2	S/MS	Schles-inger		CHAL (1898)
6376	Ruta, Michele	1827-1896	Barcarole	No. 2	Unspec.	Ricordi		CHAL (1898)

REC	COMP	DTS	TITLE	OP #	VCG	PUB	COMMENTS	SRC
6377	Ruta, Michele	1827-1896	Dichiarazione	No. 1	Unspec.	Ricordi		CHAL (1898)
6378	Ruta, Michele	1827-1896	Letizia e amore	No. 3	Unspec.	Ricordi		CHAL (1898)
6379	S. G. P.		Life's Dream is O'er		Unspec.	Brainard's Sons	In anthology "Brainard's Collection of Vocal Duets from Popular Modern and Standard Composers" Pub. 1903.	MSN
6380	Saar, L. V. [Franz]	1868-1937	Frau Nachtigall, ich hör' dich singen	Op. 49 No. 4	S/MS	Simrock		CHAL (1911)
6381	Saar, L. V. [Franz]	1868-1937	Was schimmern die Sternlein so hell	Op. 49 No. 1	S/A	Simrock		CHAL (1911)
6382	Sachs, Johann Melchior Ernst	1843-1917	Beharre "Scheide, ach scheide doch von der Liebe nicht"	Op. 108 No. 1	S/A	Fischer i. Bremen		CHAL (1898)
6383	Sachs, Johann Melchior Ernst	1843-1917	Frühlingslied "Frühling schwang den Zauberstab"	Op. 108 No. 2	S/A	Fischer i. Bremen		CHAL (1898)
6384	Sachs, Johann Melchior Ernst	1843-1917	Im Lenze "Hinaus zum grünen Walde"	Op. 108 No. 4	S/A	Fischer i. Bremen		CHAL (1898)
6385	Sachs, Johann Melchior Ernst	1843-1917	Immer leiser wird mein schlummer	Op. 108 No. 3	S/A	Fischer i. Bremen		CHAL (1898)
6386	Sachs, Johann Melchior Ernst	1843-1917	Liebeslied "Hoch überm Walde"	Op. 33 No. 2	Unspec.	Rühle i. L.		CHAL (1898)
6387	Sachs, Johann Melchior Ernst	1843-1917	Schifferlied "Es gleitet ein Schifflein"	Op. 33 No. 1	Unspec.	Rühle i. L.		CHAL (1898)
6388	Sacks, Woldemar	1868-	Es ist kein grösser Freud'	Op. 24 No. 2	S/A or S/Br	Edm. Stoll		CHAL (1911)
6389	Sackur, C.		Ringkampf "Zum Kampfspiel treten Beide wir"	Op. 85	Unspec.	Sackur		CHAL (1898)
6390	Saint Quentin, Edward		The night attack		Unspec.	Marshalls		BBC (1975)
6391	Saint-Saëns, Camille	1835-1921	12 Duos		Unspec.	Durand	pf or inst accomp. Collection of 12 unspec. pieces.	ASR
6392	Saint-Saëns, Camille	1835-1921	Aime! Eros		S/A	Durand	pf or inst accomp.	ASR
6393	Saint-Saëns, Camille	1835-1921	Aux Conquerants de l'Air		Unspec.	Durand	In "Douze Duos"	CVMP (1976)
6394	Saint-Saëns, Camille	1835-1921	Ave Maria		Unspec.	Durand	pf or org accomp. Also solo	CVMP (1985)
6395	Saint-Saëns, Camille	1839-1921	Ave Maria		S/MS or T/Br	EMB	org or pf accomp. In anthology "A kamaraének mesterei" Compi. & ed. T. Füzesséry (no date)	MSN
6396	Saint-Saëns, Camille	1839-1921	Ave Maria		high & low v.	Church	In anthology "Sacred Duets A Collection of Two-Part Songs by the Best Composers" Vol. 2. Compi. & ed. W. Shakespeare. Pub. 1907.	MSN
6397	Saint-Saëns, Camille	1835-1921	Ave Maria		S/A	Faber	org or pf accomp. In "Fauré & Saint-Saëns Six Motets for Upper Voices" Ed. T. Brown. Choral or for solo v.	MSN

REC	COMP	DTS	TITLE	OP #	VCG	PUB	COMMENTS	SRC
6398	Saint-Saëns, Camille	1835-1921	Ave Maria		A/A or T/T or S/T	Church	In anthology "Sacred Duets for Two High Voices" Vol. 1 and "Sacred Duets for High and Low Voices" Vol. 2. Pub. 1907.	NATS-SVD
6399	Saint-Saëns, Camille	1835-1921	Ave verum		Unspec.	Durand	pf or org accomp.	CVMP (1985)
6400	Saint-Saëns, Camille	1835-1921	Ave verum		S/A	Faber	org or pf accomp. In "Fauré & Saint-Saëns Six Motets for Upper Voices" Ed. T. Brown. Choral or for solo v.	MSN
6401	Saint-Saëns, Camille	1839-1921	Ave Maria		2 high v.	Church	In anthology "Sacred Duets A Collection of Two-Part Songs by the Best Composers" Vol. 1. Compi. & ed. W. Shakespeare. Pub. 1907.	MSN
6402	Saint-Saëns, Camille	1835-1921	El Deschidado		S/S	Durand		BBC (1975)
6403	Saint-Saëns, Camille	1835-1921	El Desdichado		S/A	Durand	pf or orch accomp. In "Douze Duos"	CVMP (1976)
6404	Saint-Saëns, Camille	1835-1921	El Desdichado		S/A or S/MS or S/T	CVR		CVMP (1995)
6405	Saint-Saëns, Camille	1835-1921	El Desdichado		S/S	CVR		MSN
6406	Saint-Saëns, Camille	1835-1921	El Desdichado (Bolero)		S/S	Durand		ASR
6407	Saint-Saëns, Camille	1835-1921	El desdichado "Peu m'importe que fleurisse"		Unspec.	Durand		CHAL (1898)
6408	Saint-Saëns, Camille	1835-1921	La cloche		Unspec.	Durand		BBC (1975)
6409	Saint-Saëns, Camille	1835-1921	Pastorale		Unspec.	Durand		BBC (1975)
6410	Saint-Saëns, Camille	1835-1921	Pastorale		Unspec.	ECS	In anthology "48 Duets Seventeenth Through Nineteenth Centuries" Ed. V. Prahl. Pub. 1941, 1970.	MSN
6411	Saint-Saëns, Camille	1835-1921	Tout dort dans la nuit lourde		S/MS	Durand	pf or inst accomp.	ASR
6412	Saint-Saëns, Camille	1835-1921	Viens!		Unspec.	Durand		BBC (1975)
6413	Saint-Saëns, Camille	1835-1921	Vingt Melodies et Dous, Vol. I		Unspec.	Durand	pf or inst accomp. Collection for 1-2 v.	CVMP (1976)
6414	Saint-Saëns, Camille	1835-1921	Vingt Melodies et Dous, Vol. II		Unspec.	Durand	pf or inst accomp. Collection for 1-2 v.	CVMP (1976)
6415	Saint-Saëns, Camille	1835-1921	Zehn Lieder und Duette		Unspec.	Durand	Collection of songs and duets	CVMP (1976)
6416	Salinger, J.		Abendlied "Ich stand auf Bergeshalde"	No. 8	S/A	S. & V.		CHAL (1898)
6417	Salinger, J.		Frisch gesungen "Hab' oft im Kreise der Lieben"	No. 4	S/A	S. & V.		CHAL (1898)
6418	Salinger, J.		Frühlingswanderung "Laue Lüfte fühl' ich wehen"	No. 7	S/A	S. & V.		CHAL (1898)
6419	Salinger, J.		Hoffnung "Und dräut der Winter noch so sehr"	No. 9	S/A	S. & V.		CHAL (1898)

REC	COMP	DTS	TITLE	OP #	VCG	PUB	COMMENTS	SRC
6420	Salinger, J.		Neuer Frühling "Neuer Frühling ist gekommen"	No. 3	S/A	S. & V.		CHAL (1898)
6421	Salinger, J.		Nun kommt der Frühling wieder	No. 6	S/A	S. & V.		CHAL (1898)
6422	Salinger, J.		Singen und wandern "Nun ist die schöne Frühlingszeit"	No. 10	S/A	S. & V.		CHAL (1898)
6423	Salinger, J.		Waldleben "Wer recht in Freiheit leben will"	No. 5	S/A	S. & V.		CHAL (1898)
6424	Salis, P.		Asyl "Wenn du ein tiefes Leid erfahren"	Op. 11 No. 6	Unspec.	R. & E.		CHAL (1898)
6425	Salis, P.		Auftrag an den Frühling "Kein Zweiglein giebts"	Op. 11 No. 10	Unspec.	R. & E.		CHAL (1898)
6426	Salis, P.		Frühlingslied "Frühling ist gekommen"	Op. 3 No. 1	Unspec.	R. & E.		CHAL (1898)
6427	Salis, P.		Gruss an den Wald "Winde heben die Flügel"	Op. 11 No. 4	Unspec.	R. & E.		CHAL (1898)
6428	Salis, P.		Grüss Gott, Herr März "Schneeglöckein läutet in Sturm"	Op. 11 No. 7	Unspec.	R. & E.		CHAL (1898)
6429	Salis, P.		Heimkehr "In meine Heimath kam ich"	Op. 11 No. 1	Unspec.	R. & E.		CHAL (1898)
6430	Salis, P.		Heraus "Ging unter dichten Zweigen"	Op. 11 No. 9	Unspec.	R. & E.		CHAL (1898)
6431	Salis, P.		Herbstlied "Durch die Wälder streif ich munter"	Op. 11 No. 2	Unspec.	R. & E.		CHAL (1898)
6432	Salis, P.		Holden Rosen sind dahin "Nicht klag' ich um den Schmuck"	Op. 3 No. 7	Unspec.	R. & E.		CHAL (1898)
6433	Salis, P.		Im Grunde "Mein Herz du musst dich fügen"	Op. 3 No. 6	Unspec.	R. & E.		CHAL (1898)
6434	Salis, P.		Im Walde "Hinaus, hinaus in's Freie"	Op. 3 No. 5	Unspec.	R. & E.		CHAL (1898)
6435	Salis, P.		Lindengang "Welch' süsses, leises Klingen"	Op. 3 No. 8	Unspec.	R. & E.		CHAL (1898)
6436	Salis, P.		Morgenwanderung "Wie blitz so hell"	Op. 3 No. 4	Unspec.	R. & E.		CHAL (1898)
6437	Salis, P.		Schlummersehnsucht "Stern' am Himmel singen"	Op. 3 No. 10	Unspec.	R. & E.		CHAL (1898)
6438	Salis, P.		Sommernacht "Laute Tag ist fortgezogen"	Op. 11 No. 5	Unspec.	R. & E.		CHAL (1898)
6439	Salis, P.		Sternlein am Himmel	Op. 11 No. 3	Unspec.	R. & E.		CHAL (1898)
6440	Salis, P.		Und die Sonne scheint so golden	Op. 11 No. 8	Unspec.	R. & E.		CHAL (1898)
6441	Salis, P.		Verblüht "Sagt, wo sind die Veilchen hin"	Op. 3 No. 9	Unspec.	R. & E.		CHAL (1898)
6442	Salis, P.		Vom Berg ergeht ein Rufen	Op. 3 No. 3	Unspec.	R. & E.		CHAL (1898)
6443	Salis, P.		Wenn der Frühling auf die Berge steigt"	Op. 3 No. 2	Unspec.	R. & E.		CHAL (1898)
6444	Sallneuve, C.		Erinnerung "Ich weiss ein stilles Häuschen"	Op. 15 No. 3	S/S	Chal.		CHAL (1898)
6445	Sallneuve, E.		Absence	Op. 31 No. 1	Unspec.	Chal.		CHAL (1898)
6446	Sallneuve, E.		Ahnung des Göttlichen "Ich ahne dich Alliebender"	Op. 15 No. 1	S/S	Chal.		CHAL (1898)

REC	COMP	DTS	TITLE	OP #	VCG	PUB	COMMENTS	SRC
6447	Sallneuve, E.		Angelus	Op. 31 No. 3	Unspec.	Chal.		CHAL (1898)
6448	Sallneuve, E.		Berge "Auf den Bergen froh und heiter"	Op. 15 No. 2	S/S	Chal.		CHAL (1898)
6449	Sallneuve, E.		Frühlingsempfindung "Junge Keime, frisches Leben"	Op. 15 No. 4	S/S	Chal.		CHAL (1898)
6450	Sallneuve, E.		Heimliche Liebe "Kein Feuer, keine Kohle"	Op. 19 No. 4	S/S	Chal.		CHAL (1898)
6451	Sallneuve, E.		Liebe Macht "Liebe sie eilet mit flüchtigem Flug"	Op. 31 No. 3	Unspec.	Chal.		CHAL (1898)
6452	Sallneuve, E.		Liebe "Mir ist so wohl in deiner Nähe"	Op. 19 No. 1	S/S	Chal.		CHAL (1898)
6453	Sallneuve, E.		Matelots et les bergères	Op. 31 No. 2	Unspec.	Chal.		CHAL (1898)
6454	Sallneuve, E.		Zweigesang "Im Fliederbusch ein Vöglein sass"	Op. 31 No. 2	Unspec.	Chal.		CHAL (1898)
6455	Salvi, Matteo	1816-1887	Serenata		Unspec.	Cranz		CHAL (1898)
6456	Samson, L.		Aufblühende "Im Kinderkreis die Knospe steht"	Op. 49 No. 3	S/A	Löbel		CHAL (1898)
6457	Samson, L.		Eros Abkunft "Wundert ihr euch"	Op. 37 No. 11	S/A	Löbel		CHAL (1898)
6458	Samson, L.		Es muss ein Wunderbares sein	Op. 44 No. 4	S/A	Löbel		CHAL (1898)
6459	Samson, L.		Frühling und Liebe "Lass den heitern Frühlingsschein"	Op. 44 No. 2	S/A	Löbel		CHAL (1898)
6460	Samson, L.		Frühlingslied "Es trägt des Windes Schwingen"	Op. 42 No. 1	S/A	Hoffarth		CHAL (1898)
6461	Samson, L.		Geflügelte Amor "Amor kam, wie andere Knaben"	Op. 37 No. 6	S/A	Löbel		CHAL (1898)
6462	Samson, L.		Glaube, Liebe, Hoffnung "Wo bist du hin"	Op. 37 No. 13	S/A	Löbel		CHAL (1898)
6463	Samson, L.		Herrliche Nacht "O herrliche Nacht"	Op. 37 No. 5	S/A	Löbel		CHAL (1898)
6464	Samson, L.		Hüte dich "Wenn die Reb' im Safte schwillt"	Op. 44 No. 1	S/A	Löbel		CHAL (1898)
6465	Samson, L.		Klage "Fliesse Klage aus der Seele"	Op. 42 No. 2	S/A	Hoffarth		CHAL (1898)
6466	Samson, L.		Lachen "Lachen was heimathlos"	Op. 37 No. 9	S/A	Löbel		CHAL (1898)
6467	Samson, L.		Mailied "Kein' schön're (schöner) Zeit auf Erden ist"	Op. 37 No. 4	S/A	Löbel		CHAL (1898)
6468	Samson, L.		Marie "Marie am Fenster sitzest du"	Op. 37 No. 12	S/A	Löbel		CHAL (1898)
6469	Samson, L.		Morgenroth "Schau', das Morgenroth glüht"	Op. 49 No. 5	S/A	Löbel		CHAL (1898)
6470	Samson, L.		Neig' schöne Knospe dich zu mir	Op. 42 No. 3	S/A	Hoffarth		CHAL (1898)
6471	Samson, L.		O glücklich wer ein Herz gefunden	Op. 49 No. 2	S/A	Löbel		CHAL (1898)
6472	Samson, L.		Pilger "Auf dürrer Haide geht"	Op. 37 No. 1	S/A	Löbel		CHAL (1898)
6473	Samson, L.		Rastlose Liebe "Schnee, dem Regen"	Op. 42 No. 4	S/A	Hoffarth		CHAL (1898)
6474	Samson, L.		Ständchen "Schummerlos rauschen die Saiten"	Op. 37 No. 8	S/A	Löbel		CHAL (1898)
6475	Samson, L.		Süsses Finden "Süss, wie dem durstenden Wanderer"	Op. 37 No. 2	S/A	Löbel		CHAL (1898)

REC	COMP	DTS	TITLE	OP #	VCG	PUB	COMMENTS	SRC
6476	Samson, L.		Todte Soldat "Auf ferner, fremder Aue"	Op. 44 No. 3	S/A	Löbel		CHAL (1898)
6477	Samson, L.		Treu' Lied, liebt treue Brust "Ach, wem ein rechtes Gedenken blüht"	Op. 37 No. 10	S/A	Löbel		CHAL (1898)
6478	Samson, L.		Verlassen "Knabe, dir gefiel die duft'gen Rose"	Op. 37 No. 3	S/A	Löbel		CHAL (1898)
6479	Samson, L.		Vertröstung "Frühling und Liebestraum"	Op. 37 No. 7	S/A	Löbel		CHAL (1898)
6480	Samson, L.		Vorbei "Das ist der alte Baum nicht mehr"	Op. 44 No. 5	S/A	Löbel		CHAL (1898)
6481	Samson, L.		Wolken "Wolken ihr himmlischen"	Op. 49 No. 1	S/A	Löbel		CHAL (1898)
6482	Samuel-Rosseau, Marcel	1882-1955	Ecce Panis		Unspec.	Heugel	pf or org accomp.	CVMP (1976)
6483	Samuel-Rosseau, Marcel	1882-1955	Pater Noster		Unspec.	Heugel	pf or org accomp.	CVMP (1976)
6484	Sanderson, Wilfred	1878-	The voyagers		Unspec.	Boosey		BBC (1975)
6485	Sanderson, Wilfred	1878-	Until		Unspec.	Boosey	Also solo	CVMP (1976)
6486	Sans-Souci, Gertrude		When song is sweet		S/A	Harris	Eng. woman comp.	BBC (1975)
6487	Santi, G.		Caro l'estremo addio		Unspec.	Lucca		CHAL (1898)
6488	Santner, Karl	1819-1885	Abschiedslied "lebe wohl und denk' an mich"		Unspec.	Oertel		CHAL (1898)
6489	Santner, Karl	1819-1885	Alles mit Gott "Mit deam Herrn fang' Alles an"	No. 1	S/A or Br/B	Coppen-rath		CHAL (1898)
6490	Santner, Karl	1819-1885	Auswanderer "Leb wohl du deutsche Erde"		Unspec.	Cranz		CHAL (1898)
6491	Santner, Karl	1819-1885	Christabend "Nie vermag zu klingen"	No. 1	Unspec.	Coppen-rath		CHAL (1898)
6492	Santner, Karl	1819-1885	Freundschaft "Lieblich strahlt der Abendthau"	No. 6	S/A or Br/B	Coppen-rath		CHAL (1898)
6493	Santner, Karl	1819-1885	Gärtnerlied "Gedeihe, liebe Blume"	No. 3	S/A or Br/B	Coppen-rath		CHAL (1898)
6494	Santner, Karl	1819-1885	Herbstklang "Schon ist die von dem höchsten Ast"	No. 6	Unspec.	Coppen-rath		CHAL (1898)
6495	Santner, Karl	1819-1885	Kinder Wanderlied "Hoch wandelt die Sonne"	No. 4	Unspec.	Coppen-rath		CHAL (1898)
6496	Santner, Karl	1819-1885	Lebenspuls "Wenn hoch am fernen Himmelsbogen"	No. 5	S/A or Br/B	Coppen-rath		CHAL (1898)
6497	Santner, Karl	1819-1885	Maikäfer-Walzer "Sagt, haben wir lustigen Käfer nicht"	No. 3	Unspec.	Coppen-rath		CHAL (1898)
6498	Santner, Karl	1819-1885	Perle des Jahres "Blau ist der Himmel"		Unspec.	Oertel		CHAL (1898)
6499	Santner, Karl	1819-1885	Postillon Frühling "Frühling ist ein Postillon"	No. 2	Unspec.	Coppen-rath		CHAL (1898)
6500	Santner, Karl	1819-1885	Rosen-Schicksal "Zwei welke Rosen lagen"		Unspec.	Oertel		CHAL (1898)
6501	Santner, Karl	1819-1885	Schutzgeist "O Mutter, sag, wer ist es"		Unspec.	Oertel		CHAL (1898)
6502	Santner, Karl	1819-1885	Sommerabend "Heim kehrt die Turteltaub"	No. 5	Unspec.	Coppen-rath		CHAL (1898)
6503	Santner, Karl	1819-1885	Süsses Klingen, hold Geläute		Unspec.	Oertel		CHAL (1898)

REC	COMP	DTS	TITLE	OP #	VCG	PUB	COMMENTS	SRC
6617	Schindler, J.		Es grassirt heut' a Krankheit		Unspec.	Fr. Dietrich		CHAL (1901)
6618	Schindler, J.		Für mcih leucht' ka Sterndl am Himmel		MS/A	C. Fischer	In catalogue page "Selected Vocal Duets By Favorite Composers" of Carl Fischer NY (no date)	MSN
6619	Schindler, J.		Für mich leutcht' ka Sterndl am Himmel "Da wo man tanzt"		Unspec.	O. Dietrich		CHAL (1898)
6620	Schindler, J.		Gretchen im Walde "Gretchen ist ein Bauermädchen"		Unspec.	O. Dietrich		CHAL (1898)
6621	Schindler, J.		Josef und Protiphar "Ach mir zitteern alle Glieder"		Unspec.	O. Dietrich		CHAL (1898)
6622	Schindler, J.		Schwache Stunden "Schlauheit ist des Weibes Waffe"		Unspec.	O. Dietrich		CHAL (1898)
6623	Schindler, J.		Sehr ein bürgerlicher Schuster		Unspec.	Fr. Dietrich		CHAL (1901)
6624	Schindler, J.		Vielleicht in Temeswar, in Szegedin giebt's so was nöt "Vier Spreizen san in Keller"		Unspec.	Kratochwill		CHAL (1898)
6625	Schindler, J.		Was klingt in der Tasche so lieblich und laut		Unspec.	Fr. Dietrich		CHAL (1901)
6626	Schindler, J.		Wett'n aber nöt schwörn "Es kömmt sehr häufig vor"		Unspec.	Doblinger		CHAL (1898)
6627	Schirmer, A.		Telephon "Wenn man heutzutage"		Unspec.	Thiemer		CHAL (1898)
6628	Schläger, Hans	1820-1885	Bitte "Weil auf mir du dunkles Auge"	Op. 10 No. 3	2 female v.	Cranz		CHAL (1898)
6629	Schläger, Hans	1820-1885	Da kommen sie und jagen	Op. 33 No. 3	2 female v.	Schlesinger		CHAL (1898)
6630	Schläger, Hans	1820-1885	Fernsicht "Mein Dach sind grüne Linden"	Op. 23 No. 2	2 female v.	Kratochwill		CHAL (1898)
6631	Schläger, Hans	1820-1885	Hollunderbaum "Da droben auf jenem Berge"	Op. 33 No. 4	2 female v.	Schlesinger		CHAL (1898)
6632	Schläger, Hans	1820-1885	Ich hör' ein Vöglein locken	Op. 23 No. 1	2 female v.	Kratochwill		CHAL (1898)
6633	Schläger, Hans	1820-1885	Im Walde, im hellen Sonnenschein	Op. 33 No. 1	2 female v.	Schlesinger		CHAL (1898)
6634	Schläger, Hans	1820-1885	Lied der Vöglein "Von Zweig zu Zweig zu hüpfen"	Op. 10 No. 2	2 female v.	Cranz		CHAL (1898)
6635	Schläger, Hans	1820-1885	Stille "Es weiss und räth es doch Keiner"	Op. 10 No. 1	2 female v.	Cranz		CHAL (1898)
6636	Schläger, Hans	1820-1885	Sympathie "Es schwebt in liebendem Umfangen"	Op. 33 No. 2	2 female v.	Schlesinger		CHAL (1898)
6637	Schläger, Hans	1820-1885	Wanderlust "Biene, der Käfer, der Schmetterling"	Op. 23 No. 3	2 female v.	Kratochwill		CHAL (1898)
6638	Schleidt, Wilhelm	1840-1912	Lied der Sennerinnen "Blitz noch so schimmernd"	Op. 22	S/A	Hug		CHAL (1898)
6639	Schleidt, Wilhelm	1840-1912	Maienfahrt "Mai bricht in den Wald herein"	Op. 21	S/A	Hug		CHAL (1898)
6640	Schleiffarth, G.		Mit der Guitarr' zieh' lustig ich		Unspec.	Hinz	Ed. Grau.	CHAL (1906)
6641	Schlesinger		Ich bete an die Macht der Liebe "Altruss. Kirchenlied"		Unspec.	Zumsteeg		CHAL (1898)
6642	Schletterer, Hans Michel	1824-1893	Abendgebet "O lieber Gott im Himmel"	Op. 29 No. 4	S/A	Kistner		CHAL (1898)
6643	Schletterer, Hans Michel	1824-1893	Abendwonne "Wie hold und lieblich"	Op. 41 No. 8	S/A	Kistner		CHAL (1898)

REC	COMP	DTS	TITLE	OP #	VCG	PUB	COMMENTS	SRC
6531	Schäffer, August	1814-1879	Frau von Dreissig "Ja, ja die Doctor Eitelwein"	Op. 105	Unspec.	Kistner		CHAL (1898)
6532	Schäffer, August	1814-1879	Frauenbund "Frau Schwarz, als Sprecherin"	Op. 95	Unspec.	Kistner		CHAL (1898)
6533	Schäffer, August	1814-1879	Fröhlich und Wohlgemuth "Sieh' da, mein lieber Wohlgemuth"	Op. 109	Unspec.	Simrock		CHAL (1898)
6534	Schäffer, August	1814-1879	Gardinenpredigt "Liebe Duster ja ich bin empört"	Op. 81	2 female v.	Bahn		CHAL (1898)
6535	Schäffer, August	1814-1879	Gekränkte Mutterherz "Schönsten Gruss, verzeit"	Op. 134	Unspec.	Kistner		CHAL (1898)
6536	Schäffer, August	1814-1879	Hausschlüssel "Was, das hat der Hasenfuss gesagt"	Op. 85	Unspec.	Leuckart		CHAL (1898)
6537	Schäffer, August	1814-1879	Ideal "Meine liebe Registratorin"	Op. 71	2 female v.	Leuckart		CHAL (1898)
6538	Schäffer, August	1814-1879	Jenseits "Sie Liebes. gutes Tantchen fragen"	Op. 110	Unspec.	Kistner		CHAL (1898)
6539	Schäffer, August	1814-1879	Kluge Hausfrau "Wie Madam Meier, sie sind krank"	Op. 44	S/MS	Schlesinger		CHAL (1898)
6540	Schäffer, August	1814-1879	Lesekränzchen "Wohin so eilig Madam Füller"	Op. 43	S/MS	Schlesinger		CHAL (1898)
6541	Schäffer, August	1814-1879	Madam Dankelmann und Madam Wankelmann "Diensboten"		Unspec.	none listed		CHAL (1898)
6542	Schäffer, August	1814-1879	Madam Runkel und Madam Kunkel "Zufriedenen"		Unspec.	none listed		CHAL (1898)
6543	Schäffer, August	1814-1879	Mariechen Schlau "Scherz in 2 Scenen"	Op. 124	Unspec.	Kistner		CHAL (1898)
6544	Schäffer, August	1814-1879	Rose und Kuss "Was bin ich heut vergnügt"	Op. 139	Unspec.	Leuckart		CHAL (1898)
6545	Schäffer, August	1814-1879	Stockfisch "Grüss Gott, Frau Hein"	Op. 115	2 female v.	Chal.		CHAL (1898)
6546	Schäffer, August	1814-1879	Tante Räthin "Mus. Scherz in 3 Scenen"	Op. 82	Unspec.	Kistner		CHAL (1898)
6547	Schäffer, August	1814-1879	Theorie und Praxis "Mein lieber Gevatter Bullerich"	Op. 72	Unspec.	Siegel		CHAL (1898)
6548	Schäffer, August	1814-1879	Tückische Schauspieler "Madam Stempel, hab'n sie meinen Sohn gesehn"	Op. 63	2 female v.	Bahn		CHAL (1898)
6549	Schäffer, August	1814-1879	Witterung "Guten Morgen, Herr Amtmann"	Op. 65	Unspec.	Leuckart		CHAL (1898)
6550	Schäffer, August	1814-1879	Zufriedenen "Ja liebe Madam Runkel"	Op. 51	Unspec.	Leuckart		CHAL (1898)
6551	Schäffer, August	1814-1879	Zwei Wahlmänner "Herr Flink, ich grüsse schön"	Op. 98	Unspec.	Leuckart		CHAL (1898)
6552	Schäffer, Heinrich	1808-1874	Fischermädchen "Hörst de die Wellen rauschen"	No. 1	high & low v.	Sch. j.		CHAL (1898)
6553	Schäffer, Heinrich	1808-1874	Schiffer "Fröhlich vergnügt auf silberner Bahn"	No. 2	high & low v.	Sch. j.		CHAL (1898)
6554	Schäffer, Theodor [Schäfer]	1872-	Zweigesang "Im Fliederbusch ein Vöglein sass"	Op. 28 No. 11	S/A	Junne		CHAL (1898)
6555	Schaper, Gustav	1845-1906	Christnacht 2 Lieder	Op. 32	Unspec.	Heinr.	2 duets	CHAL (1898)
6556	Schaper, Gustav	1845-1906	Christnacht "Heil'ge Nacht, auf Engelschwingen"	Op. 32 No. 1	Unspec.	Heinr.		CHAL (1898)
6557	Schaper, Gustav	1845-1906	Frühlingsglaube "Linden Lüfte sind erwacht"	Op. 8	Unspec.	Heinr.		CHAL (1898)

REC	COMP	DTS	TITLE	OP #	VCG	PUB	COMMENTS	SRC
6558	Schaper, Gustav	1845-1906	O du fröhliche, o du selige	Op. 32 No. 2	Unspec.	Heinr.		CHAL (1898)
6559	Schaper, Gustav	1845-1906	Sedansfestlied "Auf, auf, ihr deutschen Brüder"		Unspec.	Heinr.		CHAL (1898)
6560	Schaper, O.		O herrliches Deutschland	Op. 19 No. 3	Unspec.	Neumann i. Magdeb.		CHAL (1898)
6561	Schärf, P.		Mach' freie Bahn dem heil'gen Christ	Op. 4	S/A	Oppen- heimer	org or pf	CHAL (1906)
6562	Schauer, H.		Vom Himmel in die tiefsten Klüfte	Op. 10	S/A	Pabst i. D.		CHAL (1911)
6563	Schenk, A.		O, ich hab' die Ehre, liebe Frau von Meier		S/A	Bosworth		CHAL (1911)
6564	Schenk, A.		Sei gegrüsst, herzliebste Mitzi		S/A	Danner		CHAL (1911)
6565	Schetana, M.		Neue Unterschiedscouplet "Solch echter Wiener Gogerl"		Unspec.	O. Dietrich		CHAL (1898)
6566	Schiedel, P.		Wie herrlich ist's im Maien	Op. 12 No. 1	S/A	Sch. J.		CHAL (1911)
6567	Schiemer, Georg	d. 1914	O wie ist die Welt verdorben		Unspec.	Blaha		CHAL (1901)
6568	Schierbeck, Poul	1888-	Galm	Op. 28 No. 2	Unspec.	FOG III	In "Tre Italienske Duetter" Op. 28	CVMP (1976)
6569	Schierbeck, Poul	1888-	Morgen i Napoli	Op. 28 No. 1	Unspec.	FOG III	In "Tre Italienske Duetter" Op. 28	CVMP (1976)
6570	Schierbeck, Poul	1888-	Solnedgang	Op. 28 No. 3	Unspec.	FOG III	In "Tre Italienske Duetter" Op. 28	CVMP (1976)
6571	Schifferl, F.		Dorischen "Wia schaut's denn jetzt"		Unspec.	Krämer i. W.		CHAL (1898)
6572	Schifferl, F.		Jeder Mensch hat sein Vergnügen		Unspec.	Blaha		CHAL (1906)
6573	Schild, Theodor	d. 1929	Ach mein Fräulein, seit 'ner Stunde	III No. 12	Unspec.	C. Rühle i. L.		CHAL (1901)
6574	Schild, Theodor	d. 1929	Büaberl, Büaberl, nimm di z'samm "'S kriegt der Schuastermacher"		Unspec.	Robit- schek		CHAL (1898)
6575	Schild, Theodor	d. 1929	Carl und die Caroline, sie war so hübsch	II No. 7	Unspec.	C. Rühle i. L.		CHAL (1901)
6576	Schild, Theodor	d. 1929	Cav'lier-Marsch	Op. 496	Unspec.	Robit- schek		CHAL (1898)
6577	Schild, Theodor	d. 1929	Culinato pfutschiaro maledetto	I No. 1	Unspec.	C. Rühle i. L.		CHAL (1901)
6578	Schild, Theodor	d. 1929	Das g'hört nach Eipeldau		Unspec.	F. Hofbauer		CHAL (1898)
6579	Schild, Theodor	d. 1929	Das is dick unddas ist dünn		Unspec.	Hofbauer		CHAL (1898)
6580	Schild, Theodor	d. 1929	Das is'n Weuna sein Schan	Op. 241	Unspec.	Robit- schek		CHAL (1898)
6581	Schild, Theodor	d. 1929	Das wer'n ma bei uns net erleb'n		Unspec.	Hofbauer		CHAL (1898)
6582	Schild, Theodor	d. 1929	Dös san lauter altdeutsche Sachen		Unspec.	Cranz		CHAL (1898)
6583	Schild, Theodor	d. 1929	Echte Weanblut	Op. 21	Unspec.	Robit- schek		CHAL (1898)
6584	Schild, Theodor	d. 1929	Einbruch bei ein'n Goldarbeiter	II No. 3	Unspec.	C. Rühle i. L.		CHAL (1901)
6585	Schild, Theodor	d. 1929	Eine lebzeltene Ballade "Bei einem Kirchtag stand"		Unspec.	Robit- schek		CHAL (1898)
6586	Schild, Theodor	d. 1929	Er lacht, sie lacht "No Schatzerl, wenn's d'magst"	Op. 651	Unspec.	Robit- schek		CHAL (1898)

REC	COMP	DTS	TITLE	OP #	VCG	PUB	COMMENTS	SRC
6702	Schlottmann, Louis	1826-1905	Mailied "Mai kommt nun herbei"	Op. 12 No. 1	S/S	B. & H.		CHAL (1898)
6703	Schlottmann, Louis	1826-1905	Wenn sich zwei Herzen scheiden	Op. 12 No. 2	S/S	B. & H.		CHAL (1898)
6704	Schlözer, K. [prob. Karl]	1830-1913	Aufmunterung zur Freude "Wer wollte sich mit Grillen plagen"	Op. 8	Unspec.	Cranz		CHAL (1898)
6705	Schlözer, K. [prob. Karl]	1830-1913	Gondolierlied "Abends führt' ich in dem Nachen"		Unspec.	Cranz		CHAL (1898)
6706	Schmeidler, K. [prob. Karl]	1859-	Gott zum Gruss am Weihnachtsfeste	Op. 7	S/A	Schweers & H.		CHAL (1911)
6707	Schmeidler, K. [prob. Karl]	1859-	Himmelglanz der Ostertag	Op. 4	S/A	Plothow	pf or org or harm	CHAL (1906)
6708	Schmid, Heinrich Kaspar	1874-1953	Komm, gieb mir die Hand	Op. 9 No. 5	Unspec.	Lewy i. München		CHAL (1906)
6709	Schmid, Joseph	1868-	Geh', liaba Schatz		Unspec.	Blaha		CHAL (1911)
6710	Schmid, Joseph	1868-	Geh, liaba Schatz, gieb ma an Schmatz		Unspec.	Pawliska		CHAL (1906)
6711	Schmid, Joseph	1868-	Liab' is a Vorg'schmack vom Himmel "Liab ist das höchste"		Unspec.	Blaha		CHAL (1898)
6712	Schmid, Joseph	1868-	Steffel geht zum Dirndl spät	Op. 52	Unspec.	Pawliska		CHAL (1906)
6713	Schmid, Th.		Zipfel Zapfel	No. 9	Unspec.	Blaha		CHAL (1901)
6714	Schmidt, A.	1801-1886	Danklied nach der esten heil "Communion der Kinder"		S/A	Böhm & S.	org accomp. a.k.a. Adolf Müller	CHAL (1898)
6715	Schmidt, A.	1801-1886	Trennung "Ein freundlich milder, zaubergleicher Schimmer"		Unspec.	Schott	a.k.a. Adolf Müller	CHAL (1898)
6716	Schmidt, Gustav	1816-1882	Stille		S/S	Hampe i. Br.		CHAL (1898)
6717	Schmidt, Hans	1854-1923	Kornblume "Glaub' mir Blümchen"	Op. 6 No. 1	MS/A	B. & H.		CHAL (1898)
6718	Schmidt, Hans	1854-1923	Kranz "Mutter hilf mir armen Tochter"	Op. 6 No. 8	MS/A	B. & H.		CHAL (1898)
6719	Schmidt, Hans	1854-1923	Linde "Warum rauscht du denn"	Op. 6 No. 2	MS/A	B. & H.		CHAL (1898)
6720	Schmidt, Hans	1854-1923	Sense "Lasst uns nach der Sense schauen"	Op. 6 No. 4	MS/A	B. & H.		CHAL (1898)
6721	Schmidt, M.		Beim Theater war mein Vater		2 female v.	Danner		CHAL (1911)
6722	Schmidt, M.		Bin Sennerin, da liegt was d'rin "Jodel-Duett aus 'Hochtourist'"	No. 4	Unspec.	H. Augustin		CHAL (1906)
6723	Schmidt, M.		Wenn am Horizont es dunkelt		Unspec.	Apollo		CHAL (1911)
6724	Schmidt, M.		Wenn azurblau der Himmel		2 female v.	Danner		CHAL (1911)
6725	Schmidt, M. H.		An die Madonna	Op. 3 No. 4	Unspec.	Hampe i. Br.		CHAL (1898)
6726	Schmidt, M. H.		Brasilianisches Liedchen	Op. 3 No. 2	Unspec.	Hampe i. Br.		CHAL (1898)
6727	Schmidt, M. H.		Komm, komm und fort auf die Bergeshöh'	Op. 3 No. 1	Unspec.	Hampe i. Br.		CHAL (1898)
6728	Schmidt, M. H.		Maimorgenlied	Op. 3 No. 3	Unspec.	Hampe i. Br.		CHAL (1898)
6729	Schmidt, O.		Abendlied "Nub schlafen die Vöglein"	Op. 32 No. 3	S/A	Chal.		CHAL (1898)
6730	Schmidt, O.		Es ist kein Bächlein so verborgen	Op. 40 No. 5	S/A	Leuckart		CHAL (1911)

REC	COMP	DTS	TITLE	OP #	VCG	PUB	COMMENTS	SRC
6504	Santner, Karl	1819-1885	Waldconcert "Herr Frühling giebt jetzt ein Concert"	No. 2	S/A or Br/B	Coppen-rath		CHAL (1898)
6505	Santner, Karl	1819-1885	Wohin "Bächlein, wohin so schnell"		Unspec.	Oertel		CHAL (1898)
6506	Santner, Karl	1819-1885	Wolken "Als treue Begleiter"	No. 4	S/A or Br/B	Coppen-rath		CHAL (1898)
6507	Santner, Karl	1819-1885	Zecher "Flasche, was blickst du"	Op. 85	Unspec.	Cranz		CHAL (1898)
6508	Sarjeant, J.		Sylvia		Unspec.	Boosey		BBC (1975)
6509	Sarjeant, J.		Watchman! What of the Night?		Unspec.	Boosey		ASR
6510	Sarjeant, J.		Watchman! What of the night?		Unspec.	Boosey		BBC (1975)
6511	Sarjeant, J.		Watchman! What of the Night		Unspec.	Boosey		CVMP (1976)
6512	Sarti, Giuseppe	1729-1802	Geh' nun empfang' die Krone		S/S	Leuckart		CHAL (1898)
6513	Sarti, Giuseppe	1729-1802	Vanne a regnar		S/S	Leuckart		CHAL (1898)
6514	Säuberlich, C.		Zwei ord'ntliche Leut "So zwa wie mir zwa"		Unspec.	Bloch		CHAL (1898)
6515	Sauer, L. & G.		Heut' thu i mi putzen		2 female v.	Danner		CHAL (1906)
6516	Sauer, L. & G.		Net um Gold und Edelstein		2 female v.	O. Dietrich		CHAL (1911)
6517	Sauerbrey, J. W. C. C.		Hoffnung "Hoffnung endet alle Schmerzen"	Op. 6 No. 2	Unspec.	Cranz		CHAL (1898)
6518	Sawyer		arrow and the song, The		Unspec.	White-Smith	In catalogue page "Vocal Duetts" of White-Smith Music Pub. Co. (no date)	MSN
6519	Schachner, J. B.		Abendhymne "Lasst uns den Abendlüften lauschen"		S/T or S/S	Steyl & Th.		CHAL (1898)
6520	Schäfer, P.		Auf grüner Wiesenmatte	Op. 16 No. 1	S/A	Gleich-auf		CHAL (1911)
6521	Schäfer, P.		Hast du Kummer, hast du Sorgen	Op. 16 No. 2	S/A	Gleich-auf		CHAL (1911)
6522	Schäfer, P.		Nun schlummre wohl zur guten Nacht	Op. 8	S/A	Gleich-auf		CHAL (1906)
6523	Schäfer, P.		Still ruht der Wald, ein heilig Schweigen	Op. 16 No. 3	S/A	Gleich-auf		CHAL (1911)
6524	Schäffer, August	1814-1879	Barometer "Guten Tag, Guten Tag liebe Anna"	Op. 102	Unspec.	Kistner		CHAL (1898)
6525	Schäffer, August	1814-1879	Beiden Gevatterinnen "Ach schon zwölf und noch kein Brautpaar"	Op. 26	Unspec.	Kistner		CHAL (1898)
6526	Schäffer, August	1814-1879	Die da "Es haben vier geistreiche Damen"	Op. 79 No. c	Unspec.	Leuckart		CHAL (1898)
6527	Schäffer, August	1814-1879	Dienstboten "Ja meine liebe Madam Dankelmann"	Op. 68	Unspec.	Kistner		CHAL (1898)
6528	Schäffer, August	1814-1879	Ein Mädchenbund "Es klopft, ja ja"	Op. 119	Unspec.	Leuckart		CHAL (1898)
6529	Schäffer, August	1814-1879	Erste April "Ja heut' Abend hier im Garten"	Op. 58	Unspec.	Kistner		CHAL (1898)
6530	Schäffer, August	1814-1879	Frau Directorin und Frau Inspec-torin "Noch ein Tässchen, Frau Inspectern"	Op. 34	Unspec.	Kistner		CHAL (1898)

REC	COMP	DTS	TITLE	OP #	VCG	PUB	COMMENTS	SRC
6644	Schletterer, Hans Michel	1824-1893	Als Vater zu lange ausblieb "Habe Blumen gepflügket"	Op. 29 No. 2	S/A	Kistner		CHAL (1898)
6645	Schletterer, Hans Michel	1824-1893	Am Geissbach "O wie schön aus der Tannen Nacht"	Op. 41 No. 9	S/A	Kistner		CHAL (1898)
6646	Schletterer, Hans Michel	1824-1893	An den Nordwind "Du rauher Nordwind"	Op. 37 No. 10	S/A	Kistner		CHAL (1898)
6647	Schletterer, Hans Michel	1824-1893	Blumen Dank "Verschwunden ist die stille Nacht"	Op. 29 No. 1	S/A	Kistner		CHAL (1898)
6648	Schletterer, Hans Michel	1824-1893	Blümlein Antwort "In unsers Vaters Garten"	Op. 41 No. 4	S/A	Kistner		CHAL (1898)
6649	Schletterer, Hans Michel	1824-1893	Ein Tag ist wieder hin	Op. 60 No. 2	S/A	Kistner		CHAL (1906)
6650	Schletterer, Hans Michel	1824-1893	Er ist's "Frühling lässt sein blaues Band"	Op. 37 No. 6	S/A	Kistner		CHAL (1898)
6651	Schletterer, Hans Michel	1824-1893	Fischlein im Wasser "Auf dem Wasser welch' ein Leben"	Op. 29 No. 9	S/A	Kistner		CHAL (1898)
6652	Schletterer, Hans Michel	1824-1893	Flücht' hinaus	Op. 53 No. 6	S/A	Kistner		CHAL (1898)
6653	Schletterer, Hans Michel	1824-1893	Frühling "Frühling kommt"	Op. 37 No. 8	S/A	Kistner		CHAL (1898)
6654	Schletterer, Hans Michel	1824-1893	Frühling ist nah'	Op. 37 No. 4	S/A	Kistner		CHAL (1898)
6655	Schletterer, Hans Michel	1824-1893	Frühlingsfeier "Klar die Berge, grün die Auen"	Op. 29 No. 6	S/A	Kistner		CHAL (1898)
6656	Schletterer, Hans Michel	1824-1893	Frühlingsjubel "Nach des Winters trüben Tagen"	Op. 53 No. 5	S/A	Kistner		CHAL (1898)
6657	Schletterer, Hans Michel	1824-1893	Frühlingsmorgen "Glockenblumen läuten"	Op. 37 No. 3	S/A	Kistner		CHAL (1898)
6658	Schletterer, Hans Michel	1824-1893	Geh' mit Gott, vergiss mein nicht	Op. 38 No. 1	S/S	Bos-worth		CHAL (1898)
6659	Schletterer, Hans Michel	1824-1893	Goldkäfer "Goldkäferlein du stolzer Mann"	Op. 60 No. 7	S/A	Kistner		CHAL (1906)
6660	Schletterer, Hans Michel	1824-1893	Grüss Gott, ihr lauen Weste	Op. 60 No. 9	S/A	Kistner		CHAL (1906)
6661	Schletterer, Hans Michel	1824-1893	Gute Hausfrau "Hausfrau sollte, merket fein"	Op. 53 No. 7	S/A	Kistner		CHAL (1898)
6662	Schletterer, Hans Michel	1824-1893	Herbstabend "Wolken kommen schwarz gezogen"	Op. 53 No. 8	S/A	Kistner		CHAL (1898)
6663	Schletterer, Hans Michel	1824-1893	Hinaus, hinaus zum grünen Wald	Op. 60 No. 5	S/A	Kistner		CHAL (1906)
6664	Schletterer, Hans Michel	1824-1893	Ich hab' in dienem Auge	Op. 35 No. 1	S/S	Kistner		CHAL (1898)
6665	Schletterer, Hans Michel	1824-1893	Im März "Mit seinen Veilchen kommt der März"	Op. 37 No. 5	S/A	Kistner		CHAL (1898)
6666	Schletterer, Hans Michel	1824-1893	In der dunkeln weiten Himmelsferne	Op. 60 No. 10	S/A	Kistner		CHAL (1906)
6667	Schletterer, Hans Michel	1824-1893	Kleine Weihnachtscantate "Wach' auf, liebe Christenheit"	Op. 53 No. 1	S/A	Kistner		CHAL (1898)
6668	Schletterer, Hans Michel	1824-1893	Knabe und Maikäfer "Maikäferm summ, summ, summ"	Op. 37 No. 7	S/A	Kistner		CHAL (1898)
6669	Schletterer, Hans Michel	1824-1893	Kuckuck's Ruf "Kuckuck hat gerufen"	Op. 29 No. 5	S/A	Kistner		CHAL (1898)
6670	Schletterer, Hans Michel	1824-1893	Leise rauschen die Blätter im Wald	Op. 60 No. 8	S/A	Kistner		CHAL (1906)
6671	Schletterer, Hans Michel	1824-1893	Lilien auf dem Felde "Nicht was gekleidet Salome"	Op. 37 No. 2	S/A	Kistner		CHAL (1898)
6672	Schletterer, Hans Michel	1824-1893	Mach's wie die Lerche	Op. 60 No. 3	S/A	Kistner		CHAL (1906)
6673	Schletterer, Hans Michel	1824-1893	Maienwonne "Wollt ihr schauen, was im Maien"	Op. 38 No. 4	S/S	Bos-worth		CHAL (1898)

REC	COMP	DTS	TITLE	OP #	VCG	PUB	COMMENTS	SRC
6674	Schletterer, Hans Michel	1824-1893	Morgenfrühe "Vorüber ist die dunkle Nacht"	Op. 29 No. 3	S/A	Kistner		CHAL (1898)
6675	Schletterer, Hans Michel	1824-1893	Morgenwanderung "Wie blitz so hell"	Op. 41 No. 10	S/A	Kistner		CHAL (1898)
6676	Schletterer, Hans Michel	1824-1893	Mutterglück "Linder Frühlingsregen"	Op. 41 No. 7	S/A	Kistner		CHAL (1898)
6677	Schletterer, Hans Michel	1824-1893	O glücklich wer ein Herz gefunden	Op. 38 No. 3	S/S	Bos-worth		CHAL (1898)
6678	Schletterer, Hans Michel	1824-1893	O wie freu'n wir uns	Op. 60 No. 6	S/A	Kistner		CHAL (1906)
6679	Schletterer, Hans Michel	1824-1893	Oster-Antiphonie "Ost erglühet"	Op. 53 No. 2	S/A	Kistner		CHAL (1898)
6680	Schletterer, Hans Michel	1824-1893	Pfingstlied "Du aller Gläub'gen Sehnsucht"	Op. 53 No. 3	S/A	Kistner		CHAL (1898)
6681	Schletterer, Hans Michel	1824-1893	Schmetterling "In den Lüften so lau"	Op. 37 No. 9	S/A	Kistner		CHAL (1898)
6682	Schletterer, Hans Michel	1824-1893	Schöne Traum "Nun steht in frischer Grüne"	Op. 37 No. 1	S/A	Kistner		CHAL (1898)
6683	Schletterer, Hans Michel	1824-1893	Seh' ich Aepfel möcht' ich sie haben	Op. 60 No. 4	S/A	Kistner		CHAL (1906)
6684	Schletterer, Hans Michel	1824-1893	So wahr die Sonne Scheinet	Op. 35 No. 2	S/S	Kistner		CHAL (1898)
6685	Schletterer, Hans Michel	1824-1893	Sonne blicket wieder	Op. 60 No. 1	S/A	Kistner		CHAL (1906)
6686	Schletterer, Hans Michel	1824-1893	Spätsommer "Marienfäden weisse"	Op. 29 No. 8	S/A	Kistner		CHAL (1898)
6687	Schletterer, Hans Michel	1824-1893	Stilles Glück "Unter den Aehren"	Op. 41 No. 3	S/A	Kistner		CHAL (1898)
6688	Schletterer, Hans Michel	1824-1893	Trost im Winter "Hüben noch Eis und Schnee"	Op. 41 No. 1	S/A	Kistner		CHAL (1898)
6689	Schletterer, Hans Michel	1824-1893	Trostlied "Tröster der Betrübten"	Op. 53 No. 4	S/A	Kistner		CHAL (1898)
6690	Schletterer, Hans Michel	1824-1893	Verlassene Liebe "In Liebe gehn, ist aller Schmerzen Tod"	Op. 38 No. 2	S/S	Bos-worth		CHAL (1898)
6691	Schletterer, Hans Michel	1824-1893	Vöglein, nun hebet an	Op. 53 No. 10	S/A	Kistner		CHAL (1898)
6692	Schletterer, Hans Michel	1824-1893	Waldeinsamkeit "Es ist so süss zu träumen"	Op. 41 No. 2	S/A	Kistner		CHAL (1898)
6693	Schletterer, Hans Michel	1824-1893	Waldkappele "Wo tief im Tannengründe"	Op. 29 No. 7	S/A	Kistner		CHAL (1898)
6694	Schletterer, Hans Michel	1824-1893	Waldmorgen "Es ist so still die Maiennacht"	Op. 41 No. 5	S/A	Kistner		CHAL (1898)
6695	Schletterer, Hans Michel	1824-1893	Wanderlust "Heraus, heraus, der Vögel Chor"	Op. 41 No. 6	S/A	Kistner		CHAL (1898)
6696	Schletterer, Hans Michel	1824-1893	Wie könnt' ich dein vergessen!		S/A	B. & H.	In anth. "Zweistim. Lied. f. Sop. u. Altstimme mit Klavierbegleitung f. den Haus- u. Schulgebrauch v. H. M. Schletterer" 3 vols.	MSN
6697	Schletterer, Hans Michel	1824-1893	Winterlust "Was schimmern die Bäume"	Op. 53 No. 9	S/A	Kistner		CHAL (1898)
6698	Schlosser, Paul		Chant de Noël		Unspec.	Durand		CVMP (1976)
6699	Schlosser, Paul		Chant de Noël		2 med. v.	Durand		ASR
6700	Schlosser, Paul		Pour la Fête des Mères		high & low v.	Durand	Contains one duet, unspec.	ASR
6701	Schlottmann, Louis	1826-1905	Frühlingsglaube "Lin-den Lüfte sind erwacht"	Op. 12 No. 3	S/S	B. & H.		CHAL (1898)

REC	COMP	DTS	TITLE	OP #	VCG	PUB	COMMENTS	SRC
6587	Schild, Theodor	d. 1929	Fiaker-Duett "Weil mer echte Weana san"		Unspec.	Robit-schek		CHAL (1898)
6588	Schild, Theodor	d. 1929	Für uns giebt's auf dieser Erden	II No. 11	Unspec.	C. Rühle i. L.		CHAL (1901)
6589	Schild, Theodor	d. 1929	Halloh, i hob' an Terno g'macht	Op. 326	Unspec.	Robit-schek		CHAL (1898)
6590	Schild, Theodor	d. 1929	Harbe Poldi	Op. 240	Unspec.	Robit-schek		CHAL (1898)
6591	Schild, Theodor	d. 1929	Höchste Leb'n in Grinzing "Mei Weanastadt, mei Vaterstadt"		Unspec.	Blaha		CHAL (1898)
6592	Schild, Theodor	d. 1929	Hörst du den Sang der Nachtigall	II No. 9	Unspec.	C. Rühle i. L.		CHAL (1901)
6593	Schild, Theodor	d. 1929	Hurrah, jetzt fangt die Musik an	Op. 296	Unspec.	Robit-schek		CHAL (1898)
6594	Schild, Theodor	d. 1929	I drah auf und i drah zua		Unspec.	Hofbauer		CHAL (1898)
6595	Schild, Theodor	d. 1929	Mi san gebor'n am Podiebrad		Unspec.	Lorenz i. Trautenau		CHAL (1901)
6596	Schild, Theodor	d. 1929	Mir hab'n a Reschen "Mir san zwa fesche Spezi"		Unspec.	Robit-schek		CHAL (1898)
6597	Schild, Theodor	d. 1929	Ob Sommer oder Winter		Unspec.	Blaha		CHAL (1901)
6598	Schild, Theodor	d. 1929	Rudi-Marsch	Op. 298	Unspec.	Robit-schek		CHAL (1898)
6599	Schild, Theodor	d. 1929	'S kommt der magere Zipfel Zapfel		Unspec.	Blaha		CHAL (1901)
6600	Schild, Theodor	d. 1929	Sag Bruderherz, wo fürst mich hin	I No. 2	Unspec.	C. Rühle i. L.		CHAL (1901)
6601	Schild, Theodor	d. 1929	Schau'n mir in den Guckkasten h'nein		Unspec.	Hofbauer		CHAL (1898)
6602	Schild, Theodor	d. 1929	Schwarz auf Weiss steht hier	I No. 10	Unspec.	C. Rühle i. L.		CHAL (1901)
6603	Schild, Theodor	d. 1929	Sport über Sport ist die Losung der Zeit	I No. 4	Unspec.	C. Rühle i. L.		CHAL (1901)
6604	Schild, Theodor	d. 1929	Unsere Veteranen	Op. 28	Unspec.	Robit-schek		CHAL (1898)
6605	Schild, Theodor	d. 1929	Unverwüstlichen "Allweil listi, fesch und munter"		Unspec.	Wernthal		CHAL (1898)
6606	Schild, Theodor	d. 1929	Wann der Auerhahn baltz "Wann der Mondschein schön scheint"		Unspec.	Robit-schek		CHAL (1898)
6607	Schild, Theodor	d. 1929	Wann wir den alten Steffel sehn	Op. 85	Unspec.	Robit-schek		CHAL (1898)
6608	Schild, Theodor	d. 1929	Was ist das "Ein Ehmann, der vom Weiberl sich"		Unspec.	Robit-schek		CHAL (1898)
6609	Schild, Theodor	d. 1929	Weil mir auf dö Pflanz nöt mehr flieg'n		Unspec.	Hofbauer		CHAL (1898)
6610	Schild, Theodor	d. 1929	Wie's uns Zwa da anschau'n	I No. 6	Unspec.	C. Rühle i. L.		CHAL (1901)
6611	Schild, Theodor	d. 1929	Wo denn heunt mei Büaberl bleibt	I No. 8	Unspec.	C. Rühle i. L.		CHAL (1901)
6612	Schilling, Ferdinand	1849-	Zweigesang der Elfen "Hörst du das Flüstern"	Op. 35	MS/A	Steyl & Th.		CHAL (1898)
6613	Schindler, J.		A Maderl, so schön wie a Eugel		Unspec.	Fr. Dietrich		CHAL (1906)
6614	Schindler, J.		Alter Herr, schwach schon sehr		Unspec.	Fr. Dietrich		CHAL (1901)
6615	Schindler, J.		Baron und Baronin "Von Lakeien stets umgeben"		Unspec.	O. Teich		CHAL (1898)
6616	Schindler, J.		Ein Liebesdrama "Vorhang hebt sich in die Höh"		Unspec.	O. Dietrich		CHAL (1898)

REC	COMP	DTS	TITLE	OP #	VCG	PUB	COMMENTS	SRC
6731	Schmidt, O.		Herziges Schätzle	Op. 40 No. 4	S/A	Leuckart		CHAL (1911)
6732	Schmidt, O.		Kränze "Von Kränzen die gewunden"	Op. 32 No. 1	S/A	Chal.		CHAL (1898)
6733	Schmidt, O.		Mädchen ging im Feld allein	Op. 40 No. 6	S/A	Leuckart		CHAL (1911)
6734	Schmidt, O.		Vom Berg zum Tal das Waldhorn klang	Op. 40 No. 1	S/A	Leuckart		CHAL (1911)
6735	Schmidt, O.		Was rieselt, was rauscht	Op. 40 No. 2	S/A	Leuckart		CHAL (1911)
6736	Schmidt, O.		Weisse Rose, träumerisch neigst du	Op. 40 No. 3	S/A	Leuckart		CHAL (1911)
6737	Schmidt, O.		Zum Reien "Es grünet die Haide"	Op. 32 No. 2	S/A	Chal.		CHAL (1898)
6738	Schmitt, Aloys	1788-1866	Pilgertrost "Eine ernste Deutung hat das Leben"		Unspec.	Schott		CHAL (1898)
6739	Schmitt, Cornelius	1874-	An dem dünnsten Silberseil	II No. 10	Unspec.	Banger		CHAL (1906)
6740	Schmitt, Cornelius	1874-	Es hüpft und schlüpft ein Bürschlein flink	II No. 7	Unspec.	Banger		CHAL (1906)
6741	Schmitt, Cornelius	1874-	Heide, die rote	III No. 9	Unspec.	Banger		CHAL (1911)
6742	Schmitt, Cornelius	1874-	Kindchen tazt "Kindchen soll tanzen gehn"	III No. 4	Unspec.	Banger		CHAL (1911)
6743	Schmitt, Cornelius	1874-	Kinderlieder (10)		Unspec.	Banger	Collection of 10 children's duets	CHAL (1911)
6744	Schmitt, Cornelius	1874-	Lenz ist da	I No. 4	Unspec.	Banger		CHAL (1906)
6745	Schmitt, Cornelius	1874-	Sobald am Baum die Kirsche reift	III No. 6	Unspec.	Banger		CHAL (1911)
6746	Schmitt, Florent	1870-1958	3 Duos, Op. 136	Op. 136	high & med. v.	Durand	3 unspec. duets.	ASR
6747	Schmitt, Florent	1870-1958	Ballade pour la Paix	Op. 136 No. 2	Unspec.	Durand	pf? accomp. unspec. In "Trois Duos" Op. 136.	CVMP (1976)
6748	Schmitt, Florent	1870-1958	Eloge des Chapons	Op. 136 No. 3	Unspec.	Durand	pf? accomp. unspec. In "Trois Duos" Op. 136.	CVMP (1976)
6749	Schmitt, Florent	1870-1958	L'Escarpolette	Op. 136 No. 1	Unspec.	Durand	pf? accomp. unspec. In "Trois Duos" Op. 136.	CVMP (1976)
6750	Schmitt, Georg Aloys	1827-1902	Wälze weiter deine Wogen	No. 12	2 med. v.	Tonger		CHAL (1901)
6751	Schmitter, C.		Wann ma dö net hätt'n "Wann a Weana stirbt"		Unspec.	Kratochwill		CHAL (1898)
6752	Schmutz & Katzer		A do legst di nieder "Mir zwa haben erst neulich"		Unspec.	Kratochwill		CHAL (1898)
6753	Schnabel, Josef Ignaz	1767-1831	Abendgesang "Wenn der Abend kühl und labend		Unspec.	Leuckart		CHAL (1898)
6754	Schnabel, Karl	1809-1881	Frisch-Engagement "Qua, qua"	Op. 58	Unspec.	Leuckart		CHAL (1898)
6755	Schnabel, Karl	1809-1881	Kranke Mädchen "Es geht ein krankes Mädchen"	Op. 25 No. 2	S/A	Leuckart		CHAL (1898)
6756	Schnabel, Karl	1809-1881	Sterne und Blumen "Sterne machte den Himmel gehn"	Op. 25 No. 1	S/A	Leuckart		CHAL (1898)
6757	Schnaubelt, Heinrich	1814-1871	An Emma "Weit in nebelgrauer Ferne"	Op. 23 No. 1	Unspec.	B. & H.		CHAL (1898)
6758	Schnaubelt, W.		Am Neckar, am Rhein "O wär' ich am Neckar"	Op. 23 No. 4	Unspec.	B. & H.		CHAL (1898)
6759	Schnaubelt, W.		Lerche und Nachtigall "Wie nur jauchzen rings"	Op. 23 No. 2	Unspec.	B. & H.		CHAL (1898)
6760	Schnaubelt, W.		Morgens im Thaue	Op. 23 No. 3	Unspec.	B. & H.		CHAL (1898)

REC	COMP	DTS	TITLE	OP #	VCG	PUB	COMMENTS	SRC
6761	Schnecker, P. A.		In his hands are all the corners of the earth		S/A	G. Schirm.	In anthology "Album of Sixteen Sacred Duets" (no date)	MSN
6762	Schnecker, P. A.		In His hands are all the corners of the earth		S/A	G. Schirm.	pf or org accomp. In catalogue page "Sacred Vocal Duets" of G. Schirmer, Inc. NY (no date)	MSN
6763	Schnecker, P. A.		Jesus, the Very Thought of Thee		S/A	Ditson	In anthology "Choice Sacred Duets for All Voices" Pub. 1936.	MSN
6764	Schneeberger, Ferdinand	1843-1906	Mignon "Kennst du das Land"	Op. 70	Unspec.	Schneeberger i. Biel.	pf and harm	CHAL (1898)
6765	Schneeberger, Ferdinand	1843-1906	Wie ist's auf Bergen doch so schön	Op. 154	Unspec.	Schneeberger i. Biel.		CHAL (1906)
6766	Schneeberger, Ferdinand	1843-1906	Wiedersehn "Gott grüsse dich"	Op. 10	Unspec.	Schneeberger i. Biel.		CHAL (1898)
6767	Schneider, Bernhard	1861-	Ei Frau Schwalbe, guten Morgen	Op. 22 No. 2	S/A	Steingräber	Née Bjarnat Krawe	CHAL (1911)
6768	Schneider, Bernhard	1861-	Grete, Lene, Franz und Anneliese	Op. 22 No. 8	S/A	Steingräber	Née Bjarnat Krawe	CHAL (1911)
6769	Schneider, Bernhard	1861-	Helle Kerzenlichter zittern	Op. 22 No. 3	S/A	Steingräber	Née Bjarnat Krawe	CHAL (1911)
6770	Schneider, Bernhard	1861-	Ich bin ein Mädchen fein und jung	Op. 22 No. 4	S/A	Steingräber	Née Bjarnat Krawe	CHAL (1911)
6771	Schneider, Bernhard	1861-	Ich stand am Gartenzaun	Op. 22 No. 6	S/A	Steingräber	Née Bjarnat Krawe	CHAL (1911)
6772	Schneider, Bernhard	1861-	Nachtigall, warum tönt nicht mehr	Op. 22 No. 7	S/A	Steingräber	Née Bjarnat Krawe	CHAL (1911)
6773	Schneider, Bernhard	1861-	Und bild' dir nur im Traum nichts ein	Op. 22 No. 1	S/A	Steingräber	Née Bjarnat Krawe	CHAL (1911)
6774	Schneider, J. [prob. Johann Gottlob II]	1789-1864	Abendlied "Wenn der Abendstern"	Op. 23 No. 1	S/A	Bahn		CHAL (1898)
6775	Schneider, J. [prob. Johann Gottlob II]	1789-1864	Ade "Ade, ade, mir ist so weh"	Op. 23 No. 3	S/A	Bahn		CHAL (1898)
6776	Schneider, J. [prob. Johann Gottlob II]	1789-1864	Maienblümlein "Maienblümlein so schön"	Op. 23 No. 2	S/A	Bahn		CHAL (1898)
6777	Schneider, J. [prob. Johann Gottlob II]	1789-1864	Seufzer "Sollt ich dich missen"	Op. 23 No. 4	S/A	Bahn		CHAL (1898)
6778	Schnippering, W.		Abend wölkchen glühen		Unspec.	Tormann		CHAL (1906)
6779	Schöbe, C.		Hase "Seht mir einer den Hasen an"	Op. 5 No. 4	Unspec.	vom Ende		CHAL (1898)
6780	Schöbe, C.		Hirsch "Was das nicht des Jagdhorns Ton"	Op. 5 No. 5	Unspec.	vom Ende		CHAL (1898)
6781	Schöbe, C.		Knabe und Schmetterling "Schmetterling, kleines Ding"	Op. 5 No. 3	Unspec.	vom Ende		CHAL (1898)
6782	Schöbe, C.		Pferd und Sperling "Pferdchen, du hast die Krippe voll"	Op. 5 No. 2	Unspec.	vom Ende		CHAL (1898)
6783	Schöbe, C.		Rabe "Was ist das für ein Bettelmann"	Op. 5 No. 1	Unspec.	vom Ende		CHAL (1898)
6784	Schöbe, C.		Schneemann "Seht den Mann, o grosse Noth"	Op. 5 No. 8	Unspec.	vom Ende		CHAL (1898)
6785	Schöbe, C.		Störche "Ihr lieben Störche"	Op. 5 No. 6	Unspec.	vom Ende		CHAL (1898)

REC	COMP	DTS	TITLE	OP #	VCG	PUB	COMMENTS	SRC
6786	Schöbe, C.		Vogel am Fenster "An das Fenster klopft es"	Op. 5 No. 9	Unspec.	vom Ende		CHAL (1898)
6787	Schöbe, C.		Vögel vor der Sceuer "Im Felde draussen"	Op. 5 No. 7	Unspec.	vom Ende		CHAL (1898)
6788	Schöbe, C.		Wandersmann und Lerche "Lerche, wie früh' schon"	Op. 5 No. 10	Unspec.	vom Ende		CHAL (1898)
6789	Schoeck, Othmar	1886-1957	Drei Lieder		Unspec.	Hug	For 1-2 v. Unspec. pieces.	CVMP (1976)
6790	Schofield, Joe		He is My Redeemer		Unspec.	Jackman	pf? accomp. unspec. Ed. Greg Jackson.	CVMP (1995)
6791	Scholz, Bernard	1835-1916	Abendlied "Mond ist aufgegangen"	Op. 67 No. 3	S/A	Firnberg		CHAL (1898)
6792	Scholz, Bernard	1835-1916	Blick' in den Strom "Sahst du ein Glück vorübergehn"	Op. 11 No. 6	Unspec.	R. & B.		CHAL (1898)
6793	Scholz, Bernard	1835-1916	Frühlingsglocken "Schnee-glöcken thut läuten"	Op. 11 No. 2	Unspec.	R. & B.		CHAL (1898)
6794	Scholz, Bernard	1835-1916	Kurze-Frühling "Frühling währt nicht immer"	Op. 64 No. 1	S/A	Firnberg		CHAL (1898)
6795	Scholz, Bernard	1835-1916	Liebessänger "Wenn du willst im Menschenherzen"	Op. 11 No. 4	Unspec.	R. & B.		CHAL (1898)
6796	Scholz, Bernard	1835-1916	Liederfrühling "Lenz ist da"	Op. 67 No. 2	S/A	Firnberg		CHAL (1898)
6797	Scholz, Bernard	1835-1916	Nachtigall "Kuckuck hat sich zu Tode gefallen"	Op. 64 No. 2	S/A	Firnberg		CHAL (1898)
6798	Scholz, Bernard	1835-1916	Nachtlied "Vergangen ist der lichte Tag"	Op. 11 No. 1	Unspec.	R. & B.		CHAL (1898)
6799	Scholz, Bernard	1835-1916	Spinnerin "Spinn, spinn meine liebe Tochter"	Op. 64 No. 4	S/A	Firnberg		CHAL (1898)
6800	Scholz, Bernard	1835-1916	Trost "Wenn die auch Leid und Gram"	Op. 64 No. 3	S/A	Firnberg		CHAL (1898)
6801	Scholz, Bernard	1835-1916	Weihnachtslied "Es ist ein' Ros' entsprungen"	Op. 11 No. 3	Unspec.	R. & B.		CHAL (1898)
6802	Scholz, Bernard	1835-1916	Wettermacher "Wenn sich das Wetter"	Op. 67 No. 1	S/A	Firnberg		CHAL (1898)
6803	Scholz, Bernard	1835-1916	Wiegenlied "Aeren nur noch nicken"	Op. 11 No. 5	Unspec.	R. & B.		CHAL (1898)
6804	Scholz, Bernard	1835-1916	Zwei Reigen "Ein Cherub schritt das Thal empor"	Op. 67 No. 4	Unspec.	Firnberg		CHAL (1898)
6805	Schonberg, Stig Gustav	1933-	Kristi Ord Befriar Bonen; Koralkantat		Unspec.	STIM	org & opt. vln accomp.	CVMP (1985)
6806	Schorcht, H.		Wenn die Flocken Fallen auf den Schirm "Mein schönes Kind"		Unspec.	Benja-min		CHAL (1898)
6807	Schorsch, L.		Frühlingsruhe "O legt mich nicht in's dunkle (kühle) Grab"	No. 2	Unspec.	Bayr-hoffer		CHAL (1898)
6808	Schorsch, L.		"Wenn der Frühling auf die Berge steigt"	No. 1	Unspec.	Bayr-hoffer		CHAL (1898)
6809	Schorsch, L.		Zigeunerleben "Im Schatten des Waldes"	No. 3	Unspec.	Bayr-hoffer		CHAL (1898)
6810	Schotte, Karl	1864-1917?	Es liegt eine schillernde Perle		Unspec.	Uhse		CHAL (1898)
6811	Schouwman, Hans	1902-1967	4 Samenzangen		S/A	Wage-naar	Unspec. pieces	ASR
6812	Schouwman, Hans	1902-1967	Het Verwaend Kwezeltje	Op. 15b No. 4	S/A	Wage-naar	In "Vier Samensangen" Op. 15b	CVMP (1976)
6813	Schouwman, Hans	1902-1967	Loflied	Op. 15b No. 3	S/A	Wage-naar	In "Vier Samensangen" Op. 15b	CVMP (1976)
6814	Schouwman, Hans	1902-1967	Maria Coninghinne	Op. 15b No. 2	S/A	Wage-naar	In "Vier Samensangen" Op. 15b	CVMP (1976)

REC	COMP	DTS	TITLE	OP #	VCG	PUB	COMMENTS	SRC
6815	Schouwman, Hans	1902-1967	Meylied	Op. 15b No. 1	S/A	Wagenaar	In "Vier Samensangen" Op. 15b	CVMP (1976)
6816	Schouwman, Hans	1902-1967	Nieuw Kerstlied	Op. 71b	S/A	Donemus		CVMP (1976)
6817	Schouwman, Hans	1902-1967	Nieuw Kerstlied	Op. 71b	S/A	Donemus		ASR
6818	Schrammel, Johann	1850-1893	Gemüthliche Weanerin "'S geht a fesch Maderl"		Unspec.	Cranz		CHAL (1898)
6819	Schrammel, Johann	1850-1893	Herz von an echten Weana "All' weil hamurisch munter"		Unspec.	André		CHAL (1898)
6820	Schrammel, Johann	1850-1893	Mir san ja in Wien a Herz und a Sinn "Mir san zwa Weana"		Unspec.	Kratochwill		CHAL (1898)
6821	Schrammel, Johann	1850-1893	Muck'n und Elefanten "In uns'rer Weanastadt"	Op. 129	Unspec.	Cranz		CHAL (1898)
6822	Schrammel, Johann	1850-1893	Unser Nachwuchs "Unsre Schulbub'n, Donnerwetter"	Op. 122	Unspec.	Cranz		CHAL (1898)
6823	Schreck, Gustav	1849-1918	Primula veris "Liebliche Blume, bist du so früh schon"	Op. 3 No. 4	S/A	Kistner		CHAL (1898)
6824	Schreck, Gustav	1849-1918	Primula veris "Liebliche Blume, Primula veris"	Op. 3 No. 5	S/A	Kistner		CHAL (1898)
6825	Schreck, Gustav	1849-1918	Vorüber "Es lodert die Flamme im Herde"	Op. 3 No. 2	S/A	Kistner		CHAL (1898)
6826	Schreck, Gustav	1849-1918	Zweigesang der Elfen "Hörst du das Flüstern"	Op. 3 No. 3	S/A	Kistner		CHAL (1898)
6827	Schreck, Gustav	1849-1918	Zweigesang "Im Fliederbusch ein Vöglein sass"	Op. 3 No. 1	S/A	Kistner		CHAL (1898)
6828	Schröder, M. [prob. Max]	1880-	Als Lieschen eben siebzehn Jahr	Op. 212	Unspec.	Meissner	With dance	CHAL (1911)
6829	Schröder, M. [prob. Max]	1880-	Auf ihr Fraun, 's gibt ein Vergnügen	Op. 220	2 female v.	Danner		CHAL (1911)
6830	Schroeder, Hermann	1904-	Es wird schon gleich dunkel		S/MS or S/S	Schott	In "Sechs Weihnachtslieder" Pub. 1947	NATS-VCD
6831	Schroeder, Hermann	1904-	Kindelein zart		S/MS or S/S	Schott	In "Sechs Weihnachtslieder" Pub. 1947	NATS-VCD
6832	Schroeder, Hermann	1904-	Komm, Nachtigall mein!		S/MS or S/S	Schott	In "Sechs Weihnachtslieder" Pub. 1947	NATS-VCD
6833	Schroeder, Hermann	1904-	Lieb Nachtigall, wach auf!		S/MS or S/S	Schott	In "Sechs Weihnachtslieder" Pub. 1947	NATS-VCD
6834	Schroeder, Hermann	1904-	O Schlafe lieblicher		S/MS or S/S	Schott	In "Sechs Weihnachtslieder" Pub. 1947	NATS-VCD
6835	Schroeder, Hermann	1904-	Sechs Weihnachtslieder		2 med. v. or 2 female v.	Schotts	pf or org accomp. 6 Christmas duets. Unspec. pieces.	CVMP (1976)
6836	Schroeder, Hermann	1904-	Six Christmas Songs for Two Medium Voices		2 med. v.	Schott	Collection of 6 unspec. pieces	ASR
6837	Schroeder, Hermann	1904-	Susani		S/MS or S/S	Schott	In "Sechs Weihnachtslieder" Pub. 1947	NATS-VCD
6838	Schröter, L.		Liebessehnsucht "Wohl viele tausend Vögelein"	Op. 11	S/A	Heinr.		CHAL (1898)
6839	Schubert, Franz Ludwig	1794-1859	Abendlied "Tag geht nun zu Ende"	Op. 45 II No. 8	Unspec.	Cranz		CHAL (1898)
6840	Schubert, Franz Ludwig	1794-1859	Frohsinn "Giebt es Schön'res wohl im Leben"	Op. 45 I No. 5	Unspec.	Cranz		CHAL (1898)
6841	Schubert, Franz Ludwig	1794-1859	Guten Abend "Es ist schon dunkel um mich her"	Op. 45 No. 4	Unspec.	Cranz		CHAL (1898)
6842	Schubert, Franz Ludwig	1794-1859	Herbstlust "Spatzen und die Kinder"	Op. 45 I No. 6	Unspec.	Cranz		CHAL (1898)

REC	COMP	DTS	TITLE	OP #	VCG	PUB	COMMENTS	SRC
6843	Schubert, Franz Ludwig	1794-1859	Herbstlust "Trauben reifen, es ist eine Pracht"	Op. 45 II No. 9	Unspec.	Cranz		CHAL (1898)
6844	Schubert, Franz Ludwig	1794-1859	Monat März "Im März, im März, sei froh mein Herz"	Op. 45 No. 15	Unspec.	Böhme		CHAL (1898)
6845	Schubert, Franz Ludwig	1794-1859	Morgenlied "Steht auf, ihr lieben Kinderlein"	Op. 45 No. 3	Unspec.	Cranz		CHAL (1898)
6846	Schubert, Franz Ludwig	1794-1859	Reiterlied auf den Knieen "Ritt, ritt, ritt, Anfangs nur"	Op. 45 I No. 2	Unspec.	Cranz		CHAL (1898)
6847	Schubert, Franz Ludwig	1794-1859	Täublein "Dort oben auf dem Berfe, da steht ein hohes Haus"	Op. 45 I No. 1	Unspec.	Cranz		CHAL (1898)
6848	Schubert, Franz Ludwig	1794-1859	Vöglein Abschied "Wer klappert am Dach"	Op. 45 II No. 10	Unspec.	Cranz		CHAL (1898)
6849	Schubert, Franz Ludwig	1794-1859	Was die Thiere alles lernen "Enten lernen schnattern"	Op. 45 II No. 11	Unspec.	Cranz		CHAL (1898)
6850	Schubert, Franz Ludwig	1794-1859	Wohl zu speisen "Mutter fliegt nach Futter aus"	Op. 45 II No. 7	Unspec.	Cranz		CHAL (1898)
6851	Schubert, Franz Peter	1797-1828	Auf dem Wassern wohnt mein stilles Leben	No. 10	Unspec.	B. & H.	Ed. Mandyczewski	CHAL (1906)
6852	Schubert, Franz Peter	1797-1828	Auf der Berge freien Höhen	No. 3	Unspec.	B. & H.	Ed. Mandyczewski	CHAL (1906)
6853	Schubert, Franz Peter	1797-1828	Auf seinem goldnen Throne	No. 11	Unspec.	B. & H.	Ed. Mandyczewski	CHAL (1906)
6854	Schubert, Franz Peter	1797-1828	Cronnan		Unspec.	Breitkopf		BBC (1975)
6855	Schubert, Franz Peter	1797-1828	Dein Schwert, wie ist es von Blut so roth	No. 18	Unspec.	B. & H.	Ed. Mandyczewski	CHAL (1906)
6856	Schubert, Franz Peter	1797-1828	Der Tod Oscars		Unspec.	Breitkopf		BBC (1975)
6857	Schubert, Franz Peter	1797-1828	Der Tod und das Mädchen		Unspec.	Breitkopf		BBC (1975)
6858	Schubert, Franz Peter	1797-1828	Du bist die Ruh', du Frieden mild	No. 6	Unspec.	Leuckart	Ed. van Eyken	CHAL (1911)
6859	Schubert, Franz Peter	1797-1828	Er ist's o welch Entzücken	No. 3	Unspec.	Peters	Ed. Friedländer	CHAL (1906)
6860	Schubert, Franz Peter	1797-1828	Grüner wird die Au		Unspec.	Peters, Friedländer	Ed. Friedländer	CHAL (1906)
6861	Schubert, Franz Peter	1797-1828	Ha, dort kömmt er	No. 7	Unspec.	B. & H.	Ed. Mandyczewski	CHAL (1906)
6862	Schubert, Franz Peter	1797-1828	Heil'ge Nacht du sinkest	No. 5	Unspec.	Leuckart	Ed. van Eyken	CHAL (1911)
6863	Schubert, Franz Peter	1797-1828	Ich muss sie finden	No. 4	Unspec.	Peters	Ed. Friedländer	CHAL (1906)
6864	Schubert, Franz Peter	1797-1828	Ich rühme mir mein Dörfchen	Op. 11 No. 1	Unspec.	B. & H.	Ed. Böthig	CHAL (1906)
6865	Schubert, Franz Peter	1797-1828	Ich sitz' an der moosigten Quelle	No. 9	Unspec.	B. & H.	Ed. Mandyczewski	CHAL (1906)
6866	Schubert, Franz Peter	1797-1828	Ihr hohen Himmlischen	No. 15	Unspec.	B. & H.	Ed. Mandyczewski	CHAL (1906)
6867	Schubert, Franz Peter	1797-1828	Liebe ist ein süsses Licht	No. 12	Unspec.	B. & H.	Ed. Mandyczewski	CHAL (1906)
6868	Schubert, Franz Peter	1797-1828	Liebe ist ein süsses Licht	No. 2	Unspec.	Peters	Ed. Friedländer	CHAL (1906)
6869	Schubert, Franz Peter	1797-1828	Linden Lüfte sind erwacht	No. 2	Unspec.	Leuckart	Ed. van Eycken	CHAL (1911)
6870	Schubert, Franz Peter	1797-1828	Mailied		Unspec.	Breitkopf		BBC (1975)
6871	Schubert, Franz Peter	1797-1828	Mailied "Grün wird die Au"		Unspec.	Cranz et al.	Comp. 1816	CHAL (1898)
6872	Schubert, Franz Peter	1797-1828	Mein Geliebter ist ein Sohn des Hügels	No. 5	Unspec.	B. & H.	Ed. Mandyczewski	CHAL (1906)

REC	COMP	DTS	TITLE	OP #	VCG	PUB	COMMENTS	SRC
6873	Schubert, Franz Peter	1797-1828	Mignon und der Harfner "Nur Wer die Sehnsucht Kennt"	Op. 62 No. 1	Unspec.	G. Schirm.	In anthology "Romantic Duets—Great Performers Edition" Compi. E. Lear & T. Stewart. Pub. 1985.	MSN
6874	Schubert, Franz Peter	1797-1828	Mitten im Schimmer der spiegelnden Wellen	No. 3	Unspec.	Leuckart	Ed. van Eycken	CHAL (1911)
6875	Schubert, Franz Peter	1797-1828	Nacht ist dumpfig und finster	No. 14	Unspec.	B. & H.	Ed. Mandyczewski	CHAL (1906)
6876	Schubert, Franz Peter	1797-1828	Nun wer die Sehnsucht kennt	No. 1	Unspec.	Peters	Ed. Friedländer	CHAL (1906)
6877	Schubert, Franz Peter	1797-1828	Nun wer die Sehnsucht kennt	No. 17	Unspec.	B. & H.	Ed. Mandyczewski	CHAL (1906)
6878	Schubert, Franz Peter	1797-1828	Nur dir will ich gehören	No. 6	Unspec.	Peters	Ed. Friedländer	CHAL (1906)
6879	Schubert, Franz Peter	1797-1828	Nur wer die Sehnsucht kennt	Op. 62 No. 1	Unspec.	Cranz et al.		CHAL (1898)
6880	Schubert, Franz Peter	1797-1828	Ruh'n in Frieden alle Seelen	No. 1	Unspec.	Leuckart	Ed. van Eycken	CHAL (1911)
6881	Schubert, Franz Peter	1797-1828	Sah' ein Knab' ein Röslein stehn	No. 4	Unspec.	Leuckart	Ed. van Eycken	CHAL (1911)
6882	Schubert, Franz Peter	1797-1828	Schlacht du brichst an	No. 2	Unspec.	B. & H.	Ed. Mandyczewski	CHAL (1906)
6883	Schubert, Franz Peter	1797-1828	Schnee zerrinnt		Unspec.	none listed		CHAL (1898)
6884	Schubert, Franz Peter	1797-1828	Schnee zerrinnt, der Mai beginnt	No. 8	Unspec.	Peters	Ed. Friedländer	CHAL (1906)
6885	Schubert, Franz Peter	1797-1828	Serenade		high & low v.	Hinds, Hayden & Eldredge	Eng. trans. Grmn. In anthology "The Most Popular Vocal Duets" Ed. Dr. E. J. Biedermann. Pub. 1914.	MSN
6886	Schubert, Franz Peter	1797-1828	Shilrik und Vinvela		Unspec.	Breit-kopf		BBC (1975)
6887	Schubert, Franz Peter	1797-1928	Singübungen		S/S or T/T	B. & H.	In "Werke" of F. Schubert, ed. J. Brahms. Pub. 1888-1897.	NATS-VCD
6888	Schubert, Franz Peter	1797-1828	Songs and Cantatas for Two or Three Voices		Unspec.	Dover	Collection of unspec. pieces, duets, and trios. Ed. Gansbacher & Mandyczewski. Repr. of Boosey ed.	ASR
6889	Schubert, Franz Peter	1797-1828	Sonne sinkt, o könnt' ich mit ihr scheiden	No. 16	Unspec.	B. & H.	Ed. Mandyczewski	CHAL (1906)
6890	Schubert, Franz Peter	1797-1828	Ständchen		S/T or S/A	G. Schirm.	In catalogue page "Selected Vocal Duets" of G. Schirmer, Inc. NY (no date)	MSN
6891	Schubert, Franz Peter	1797-1828	Ständchen "Leise flehen"		S/A or T/Br	C. Fischer	In catalogue page "Selected Vocal Duets By Favorite Composers" of Carl Fischer NY (no date)	MSN
6892	Schubert, Franz Peter	1797-1828	Ständchen [Serenade]		high & med. v.	CVR	Arr. P. Rondinella. In catalogue "Classical Vocal Reprints Complete Catalog" Pub. 1997.	MSN
6893	Schubert, Franz Peter	1797-1828	Tod und das Mädchen "Vorüber, ach vorüber geh"	Op. 7 No. 3	Unspec.	Cranz		CHAL (1898)
6894	Schubert, Franz Peter	1797-1828	Vor dem Busen möge blühen	No. 5	Unspec.	Peters	Ed. Friedländer	CHAL (1906)
6895	Schubert, Franz Peter	1797-1828	Vorüber, ach vorüber geh'	No. 13	Unspec.	B. & H.	Ed. Mandyczewski	CHAL (1906)
6896	Schubert, Franz Peter	1797-1828	Warum öffnet du wieder	No. 8	Unspec.	B. & H.	Ed. Mandyczewski	CHAL (1906)
6897	Schubert, Franz Peter	1797-1828	Weine du nicht	No. 4	Unspec.	B. & H.	Ed. Mandyczewski	CHAL (1906)

REC	COMP	DTS	TITLE	OP #	VCG	PUB	COMMENTS	SRC
6898	Schubert, Franz Peter	1797-1828	Wie anders Gretchen was dir's	No. 1	Unspec.	B. & H.	Ed. Mandyczewski	CHAL (1906)
6899	Schubert, Franz Peter	1797-1828	Wiegenlied		Unspec.	Allans	Eng. trans. Grmn. Arr. for 2 v. by C. Stanbridge. In anth. "Vocal Duets Collection" Vol. 2. Pub. 1992.	MSN
6900	Schubert, Franz Peter	1797-1828	Will soch Hektor ewig von mir wenden	No. 6	Unspec.	B. & H.	Ed. Mandyczewski	CHAL (1906)
6901	Schubert, Georgine	1840-1878	Ave Maria "Ave Maria Mater Deo"	II No. 3	Unspec.	Hoffarth	Grmn. woman comp. Daughter of F. L. Schubert.	CHAL (1898)
6902	Schubert, Georgine	1840-1878	Barcarole "Voli l'agile barchetta"	II No. 1	Unspec.	Hoffarth	Grmn. woman comp. Daughter of F. L. Schubert.	CHAL (1898)
6903	Schubert, Georgine	1840-1878	Ich möcht' ein Lied dir singen		Unspec.	Hoffarth	Grmn. woman comp. Daughter of F. L. Schubert.	CHAL (1898)
6904	Schubert, Georgine	1840-1878	Träumende See "See ruht tief im blauen Traum"	II No. 2	Unspec.	Hoffarth	Grmn. woman comp. Daughter of F. L. Schubert.	CHAL (1898)
6905	Schubert, Louis	1828-1884	Dämmerung "Sanft und mild auf's Gefild"	Op. 26 No. 3	Unspec.	Hoffarth		CHAL (1898)
6906	Schubert, Louis	1828-1884	Im Frühling "Wie bist du Frühling gut und treu"	Op. 26 No. 1	Unspec.	Hoffarth		CHAL (1898)
6907	Schubert, Louis	1828-1884	Im Herbst "O Waldesluft, wie gehst du bang"	Op. 26 No. 2	Unspec.	Hoffarth		CHAL (1898)
6908	Schubert, Louis	1828-1884	In meinem Garten die Nelken	Op. 17 No. 2	S/S	Schlesinger		CHAL (1898)
6909	Schubert, Louis	1828-1884	Vögleins Liebesreise "Fliege, stilles Vöglein du"	Op. 17 No. 1	S/S	Schlesinger		CHAL (1898)
6910	Schubert, Louis	1828-1884	Waldgesang "Unter dies Grünlaubdach"	Op. 17 No. 3	S/S	Schlesinger		CHAL (1898)
6911	Schuh, H.		O lieber heil'ger Josef		S/A or T/B	Lentner i. Mün.	org or harm	CHAL (1901)
6912	Schuh, J.		Gelobt sie Christus		S/A	Böhm & S.	org	CHAL (1911)
6913	Schuh, J.		Gelobt sie Jesus Christus		S/A	Böhm & S.	org. Sacred cycle.	CHAL (1911)
6914	Schultz, C.		Zweigesang der Elfen "Hörst du das Flüstern"	Op. 2	S/S	Luckhardt		CHAL (1898)
6915	Schultz, Edwin	1827-1907	A welcome to the sweet springtime	Op. 245 No. 3	Unspec.	A. P. Schm. i. Leip.	Eng. tr. Grmn.?	CHAL (1906)
6916	Schultz, Edwin	1827-1907	Abendstille "Wer kann den Klang mir deuten"	Op. 75 No. 2	Unspec.	Bahn		CHAL (1898)
6917	Schultz, Edwin	1827-1907	Ave Maria "Laute Tag ist nun verhallt"	Op. 181 No. 3	MS/MS or Br/Br	Wernthal		CHAL (1898)
6918	Schultz, Edwin	1827-1907	Bienchen und Liebchen "Warum im dift'gen Revier"	Op. 201 No. 1	MS/MS or Br/Br	Wernthal		CHAL (1898)
6919	Schultz, Edwin	1827-1907	Call fairest flowers	Op. 245 No. 1	Unspec.	A. P. Schm. i. Leip.	Eng. tr. Grmn.?	CHAL (1906)
6920	Schultz, Edwin	1827-1907	Frühling, Herbst "Als der Frühling die Kränze"	Op. 20 No. 2	Unspec.	Leuckart		CHAL (1898)
6921	Schultz, Edwin	1827-1907	Frühlingszeit "Frühlingssonne steigt herauf"	Op. 161 No. 3	Unspec.	Rühle & H.		CHAL (1898)
6922	Schultz, Edwin	1827-1907	Heimkehr "Entfernte Glocken klangen herauf"	Op. 186 No. 2	MS/MS or Br/Br	Wernthal		CHAL (1898)
6923	Schultz, Edwin	1827-1907	Ich will dich hegen und pflegen	Op. 20 No. 1	Unspec.	Leuckart		CHAL (1898)
6924	Schultz, Edwin	1827-1907	Im Maien, im Maien ist's lieblich und schön	Op. 232 No. 1	Unspec.	Luckhardt		CHAL (1901)

REC	COMP	DTS	TITLE	OP #	VCG	PUB	COMMENTS	SRC
6925	Schultz, Edwin	1827-1907	Inneges Verständniss "Es wiegt sich auf den Zweigen"	Op. 201 No. 2	MS/MS or Br/Br	Wern-thal		CHAL (1898)
6926	Schultz, Edwin	1827-1907	Leise zieht durch mein Gemüth	Op. 71	Unspec.	Bahn		CHAL (1898)
6927	Schultz, Edwin	1827-1907	Nun bricht aus allen Zweigen	Op. 176	Unspec.	B. & B.		CHAL (1911)
6928	Schultz, Edwin	1827-1907	O du lieber Schatz wir müssen scheiden	Op. 232 No. 2	Unspec.	Luck-hardt		CHAL (1901)
6929	Schultz, Edwin	1827-1907	O fair evening star	Op. 245 No. 2	Unspec.	A. P. Schm. i. Leip.	Eng. tr. Grmn.?	CHAL (1906)
6930	Schultz, Edwin	1827-1907	Roth Röselein "Ich weiss im Thal ein Röselein"	Op. 126 No. 1	Unspec.	B. & B.		CHAL (1898)
6931	Schultz, Edwin	1827-1907	Schwere Abend "Dunklen Wolken hingen"	Op. 20 No. 3	Unspec.	Leuck-art		CHAL (1898)
6932	Schultz, Edwin	1827-1907	Singe kleines Vögelein	Op. 232 No. 3	Unspec.	Luck-hardt		CHAL (1901)
6933	Schultz, Edwin	1827-1907	Singe kleines Vögelein	Op. 232 No. 3	Unspec.	Wern-thal		CHAL (1906)
6934	Schultz, Edwin	1827-1907	Sommernacht "O träum'-risch süsse, wundersel'ge Nacht"	Op. 181 No. 1	MS/MS or Br/Br	Wern-thal		CHAL (1898)
6935	Schultz, Edwin	1827-1907	Überall in Flur und Hain	Op. 181 No. 2	MS/MS or Br/Br	Wern-thal		CHAL (1898)
6936	Schultz, Edwin	1827-1907	Vergissmeinnicht "Blau-blümelein spiegelte sich im Bach"	Op. 201 No. 3	MS/MS or Br/Br	Wern-thal		CHAL (1898)
6937	Schultz, Edwin	1827-1907	Vom Berg ergeht ein Rufen	Op. 31	Unspec.	Bahn		CHAL (1898)
6938	Schultz, Edwin	1827-1907	Waldelnsamkeit "Deine süssen, süssen Schauer"	Op. 186 No. 1	MS/MS or Br/Br	Wern-thal		CHAL (1898)
6939	Schultz, Edwin	1827-1907	Weihnachtsfeier "Was klingt wie Festgeläute"	Op. 161 No. 2	Unspec.	Rühle & H.		CHAL (1898)
6940	Schultz, Edwin	1827-1907	Wenn still mit seinen letzten Flammen	Op. 75 No. 1	Unspec.	Bahn		CHAL (1898)
6941	Schulz, August	1837-1909	Blatt im Buche "Ich hab' eine alte Muhme"	Op. 33 No. 1	Unspec.	Litolff		CHAL (1898)
6942	Schulz, August	1837-1909	Frühlingsglaube "Linden Lüfte sind erwacht"	Op. 33 No. 2	Unspec.	Litolff		CHAL (1898)
6943	Schulz, Chr.		Die Schwalbe "Es fliegen zwei Schwalben" Vertrauen "Nicht den Sternen sollst du trauen"		S/A	B. & H.	In anth. "Zweistim. Lied. f. Sop. u. Altstimme mit Klavierbegleitung f. den Haus- u. Schulgebrauch v. H. M. Schletterer" 3 vols.	MSN
6944	Schulz, R.		Bergauf, bergab, durch Feld und Wald		Unspec.	Toubié		CHAL (1906)
6945	Schumacher, Heinrich Vollrat	1861-1919	Jetzt sind wir Mann und Frau		Unspec.	Bloch		CHAL (1911)
6946	Schumacher, Richard	1860-1932	Abendlied "Im Abendroth erglüh'n		2 high or 2 low v.	Sulz-bach i. Berl.		CHAL (1898)
6947	Schumacher, Richard	1860-1932	Abends, wenn die Sonne sinkt	Op. 48	high & low v.	Sulz-bach i. Berl.		CHAL (1901)
6948	Schumacher, Richard	1860-1932	Durch die wolkige Maiennacht	Op. 48	high & low v.	Sulz-bach i. Berl.		CHAL (1901)
6949	Schumacher, Richard	1860-1932	Herzliebe, süsse Weihnachtszeit	Op. 44	high & low v.	Sulz-bach i. Berl.		CHAL (1901)

REC	COMP	DTS	TITLE	OP #	VCG	PUB	COMMENTS	SRC
6950	Schumacher, Richard	1860-1932	Meinem Blümelein "Lieben Abendwinde"	Op. 35	2 female v.	Sulzbach i. Berl.		CHAL (1898)
6951	Schumacher, Richard	1860-1932	Müde Sommertag vergluhtet	Op. 40	high & low v.	Sulzbach i. Berl.		CHAL (1901)
6952	Schumann, Clara Wieck	1819-1896	Herr von dein Antlitz treten Zwei		S/A	P. & M.	Grmn woman comp.	CHAL (1901)
6953	Schumann, Georg Alfred	1866-1952	Was tönt so wundersamer Klang	Op. 3 No. 1	S/A	Siegel		CHAL (1898)
6954	Schumann, Georg Alfred	1866-1952	Weihnachts "Heilige Nacht, du kehrest wieder"	Op. 3 No. 2	S/A	Siegel		CHAL (1898)
6955	Schumann, Georg Alfred	1866-1952	Weihnachtslieder (2)	Op. 3	S/A	Siegel	2 Christmas duets	CHAL (1898)
6956	Schumann, Robert	1810-1856	12 Duos		2 equal v.	Durand	pf w/ & w/o inst accomp. Collection of 12 duets.	ASR
6957	Schumann, Robert	1810-1856	34 Duets		Var.	Peters	Unspec. pieces. Ed. Friedländer. Collection of 34 duets for Var. v. comb.	ASR
6958	Schumann, Robert	1810-1856	Abendschlummer umarmt die Flur	Op. 112 No. 17	S/A	Kistner et al.		CHAL (1898)
6959	Schumann, Robert	1810-1856	An den Abendstern		S/A	CVR		MSN
6960	Schumann, Robert	1810-1856	An den Abendstern	Op. 103 No. 4	Unspec.	Durand	In "Douze Duos"	CVMP (1976)
6961	Schumann, Robert	1810-1856	An den Abendstern	Op. 103 No. 4	high & med. v.	Boosey	In anthology "Duet Album: Selected and edited by Viola Morris and Victoria Anderson" Pub. 1944.	MSN
6962	Schumann, Robert	1810-1856	An den Abendstern	Op. 103 No. 4	S/S or S/MS	B. & H.	In "Mädchenlied von E. Kulmann" Op. 103. In "Werke" of R. Schumann, ed. Clara Schumann. Pub. 1881-1893.	NATS-VCD
6963	Schumann, Robert	1810-1856	An den Abendstern "Schweb' empor am Himmel"	Op. 103 No. 4	S/S or S/A	Kistner et al.		CHAL (1898)
6964	Schumann, Robert	1810-1856	An den Abendstern "Schweb empor am Himmel"	Op. 103 No. 4	S/A	Peters	In collection of "Schumann Duette" Ed. M. Friedländer.	MSN
6965	Schumann, Robert	1810-1856	An die Nachtigall	Op. 103 No. 3	Unspec.	Durand	In "Douze Duos"	CVMP (1976)
6966	Schumann, Robert	1810-1856	An die Nachtigall	Op. 103 No. 3	S/S or S/MS	B. & H.	Collection. In "Mädchenlied von E. Kulmann" Op. 103. In "Werke" of R. Schumann, ed. Clara Schumann. Pub. 1881-1893.	NATS-VCD
6967	Schumann, Robert	1810-1856	An die Nachtigall "Bleibe hier und singe"	Op. 103 No. 3	S/A	Kistner et al.		CHAL (1898)
6968	Schumann, Robert	1810-1856	An die Nachtigall "Bleibe hier und singe"	Op. 103 No. 3	S/A	Peters	In collection of "Schumann Duette" Ed. M. Friedländer.	MSN
6969	Schumann, Robert	1810-1856	Auf ihrem Grab		Unspec.	Peters	Ed. Dörffel	BBC (1975)
6970	Schumann, Robert	1810-1856	Awaken, my Darling		Unspec.	ECS	Eng. trans. Grmn. In anthology "48 Duets Seventeenth Through Nineteenth Centuries" Ed. V. Prahl. Pub. 1941, 1970.	MSN
6971	Schumann, Robert	1810-1856	Bedeckt mich mit Blumen	Op. 138 No. 4	S/A	R. & B. et al.		CHAL (1898)

REC	COMP	DTS	TITLE	OP #	VCG	PUB	COMMENTS	SRC
6972	Schumann, Robert	1810-1856	Bedeckt mich mit Blumen	Op. 138 No. 4	S/A	Peters	In collection of "Schumann Duette" Ed. M. Friedländer.	MSN
6973	Schumann, Robert	1810-1856	Bedeckt mich mit Blumen	Op. 138 No. 4	S/A or S/MS	B. & H.	Collection. In "Werke" of R. Schumann, ed. Clara Schumann. Pub. 1881-1893.	NATS-VCD
6974	Schumann, Robert	1810-1856	Botschaft	Op. 74 No. 8	S/A or S/MS	B. & H.	Collection. In "Werke" of R. Schumann, ed. Clara Schumann. Pub. 1881-1893.	NATS-VCD
6975	Schumann, Robert	1810-1856	Botschaft "Nelken wind' ich und Jasmin"	Op. 74 No. 8	S/A	Peters	In collection of "Schumann Duette" Ed. M. Friedländer.	MSN
6976	Schumann, Robert	1810-1856	Das Glück		S/S	Peters	Ed. Dörffel	BBC (1975)
6977	Schumann, Robert	1810-1856	Das Glück		S/A	EMB	In anthology "Duettek nöi Hangokra Zongorakísérettel" Vol. II Compi. M. Forrai. Pub. 1959.	MSN
6978	Schumann, Robert	1810-1856	Das Glück	Op. 79 No. 16	S/S	B. & H.	In "Werke" of R. Schumann, ed. Clara Schumann. Pub. 1881-1893.	NATS-VCD
6979	Schumann, Robert	1810-1856	Das Glück "Vöglein vom Zweig"	Op. 79 No. 16	S/S	Peters	In collection of "Schumann Duette" Ed. M. Friedländer.	MSN
6980	Schumann, Robert	1810-1856	Das Glück "Vöglein vom Zweig lustig sogleich"	Op. 79 No. 16	S/A	B. & H.	In anth. "Zweistim. Lied. f. Sop. u. Altstimme mit Klavierbegleitung f. den Haus- u. Schulgebrauch v. H. M. Schletterer" 3 vols.	MSN
6981	Schumann, Robert	1810-1856	Der Abenschlummer umarmt die Flur		S/A	CVR		MSN
6982	Schumann, Robert	1810-1856	Die Schwalbe "Es fliegen zwei Schwalben"	Op. 79 No. 27	S/A	B. & H.	In anth. "Zweistim. Lied. f. Sop. u. Altstimme mit Klavierbegleitung f. den Haus- u. Schulgebrauch v. H. M. Schletterer" 3 vols.	MSN
6983	Schumann, Robert	1810-1856	Die Schwalben		S/S	Breitkopf		BBC (1975)
6984	Schumann, Robert	1810-1856	Die Schwalben	Op. 79 No. 21	S/S or S/MS	B. & H.	Collection. In "Werke" of R. Schumann, ed. Clara Schumann. Pub. 1881-1893.	NATS-VCD
6985	Schumann, Robert	1810-1856	Die Schwalben "Es fliegen zwei Schwalben"	Op. 79 No. 21	S/S	Peters	In collection of "Schumann Duette" Ed. M. Friedländer.	MSN
6986	Schumann, Robert	1810-1856	Ei Mühle, liebe Mühle		S/A	Peters	Ed. Dörffel	BBC (1975)
6987	Schumann, Robert	1810-1856	Ei Mühle, liebe Mühle	Op. 112 No. 20	S/A	Kistner et al.		CHAL (1898)
6988	Schumann, Robert	1810-1856	Ei Mühle, liebe Mühle	Op. 112 No. 20	S/A	Peters	In collection of "Schumann Duette" Ed. M. Friedländer.	MSN
6989	Schumann, Robert	1810-1856	Ei Mühle, liebe Mühle	Op. 112 No. 20	S/A or S/MS	Peters	Collection. In "Duette" of R. Schumann, ed. M. Friedländer. Pub. 1899?	NATS-VCD
6990	Schumann, Robert	1810-1856	Ei Mühle, liebe Mühle	Op. 112 No. 20	S/A	B. & H.		CHAL (1906)
6991	Schumann, Robert	1810-1856	Erste Begegnung	Op. 74 No. 1	S/A or S/MS	B. & H.	Collection. In "Werke" of R. Schumann, ed. Clara Schumann. Pub. 1881-1893.	NATS-VCD
6992	Schumann, Robert	1810-1856	Erste Begegnung "Von dem Rosenbusch, o Mutter"	Op. 74 No. 1	S/A	Kistner et al.		CHAL (1898)
6993	Schumann, Robert	1810-1856	Erste Begegnung "Von dem Rosenbusch, o Mutter"	Op. 74 No. 1	S/A	Peters	In collection of "Schumann Duette" Ed. M. Friedländer.	MSN

REC	COMP	DTS	TITLE	OP #	VCG	PUB	COMMENTS	SRC
6994	Schumann, Robert	1810-1856	Frühlingsglocken "Schneeglöcken thut läuten"	Op. 33e No. 1	Unspec.	Sch. & Co.		CHAL (1898)
6995	Schumann, Robert	1810-1856	Frühlingslied		S/S	Peters	Ed. Dörffel	BBC (1975)
6996	Schumann, Robert	1810-1856	Frühlingslied	Op. 103 No. 2	Unspec.	Durand	In collection "Douze Duos"	CVMP (1976)
6997	Schumann, Robert	1810-1856	Frühlingslied	Op. 103 No. 2	S/S or S/MS	B. & H.	Collection. In "Mädchenlied von E. Kulmann" Op. 103. In "Werke" of R. Schumann, ed. Clara Schumann. Pub. 1881-1893.	NATS-VCD
6998	Schumann, Robert	1810-1856	Frühlingslied	Op. 79 No. 19	S/S or S/MS	B. & H.	Collection. In "Werke" of R. Schumann, ed. Clara Schumann. Pub. 1881-1893.	NATS-VCD
6999	Schumann, Robert	1810-1856	Frühlingslied "Der Frühling kehret wieder"	Op. 103 No. 2	S/A	Peters	In collection of "Schumann Duette" Ed. M. Friedländer.	MSN
7000	Schumann, Robert	1810-1856	Frühlingslied "Frühling kehret wieder"	Op. 103 No. 2	S/S or S/A	Kistner et al.		CHAL (1898)
7001	Schumann, Robert	1810-1856	Frühlingslied "Schneeglöcken klingen wieder"	Op. 79 No. 19	S/S	Peters	In collection of "Schumann Duette" Ed. M. Friedländer.	MSN
7002	Schumann, Robert	1810-1856	Glück "Vöglein vom Zweig"	Op. 79 No. 15	S/S	B. & H. et al.		CHAL (1898)
7003	Schumann, Robert	1810-1856	Herbstlied		S/A	Peters	Ed. Friedländer	BBC (1975)
7004	Schumann, Robert	1810-1856	Herbstlied	Op. 43 No. 2	Var.	B. & H.	Collection, Drei Duette für zwei Singstimmen, Op. 43. In "Werke" of R. Schumann, ed. Clara Schumann. Pub. 1881-1893.	NATS-VCD
7005	Schumann, Robert	1810-1856	Herbstlied "Das Laub fällt von den Bäumen"	Op. 43 No. 2	S/A	Peters	In collection of "Schumann Duette" Ed. M. Friedländer.	MSN
7006	Schumann, Robert	1810-1856	Herbstlied "Laub fällt von den Bäumen"	Op. 43 No. 2	S/A	Simrock et al.		CHAL (1898)
7007	Schumann, Robert	1810-1856	In der Nacht "Alle gingen Herz zur Ruh'"	Op. 74 No. 4	S/A	Kistner et al.		CHAL (1898)
7008	Schumann, Robert	1810-1856	Ländliches Lied		S/S	Peters	Ed. Dörffel	BBC (1975)
7009	Schumann, Robert	1810-1856	Landliches Lied	Op. 29 No. 1	Unspec.	Durand	In collection "Douze Duos"	CVMP (1976)
7010	Schumann, Robert	1810-1856	Ländliches Lied	Op. 29 No. 1	Var.	B. & H.	In "Werke" of R. Schumann, ed. Clara Schumann. Pub. 1881-1893.	NATS-VCD
7011	Schumann, Robert	1810-1856	Ländliches Lied "Und wenn die Primel"	Op. 29 No. 1	S/S	Peters	In collection of "Schumann Duette" Ed. M. Friedländer.	MSN
7012	Schumann, Robert	1810-1856	Libesgram "Dereinst, dereinst, o Gedanke mein"	Op. 74 No. 3	S/A	Peters	In collection of "Schumann Duette" Ed. M. Friedländer.	MSN
7013	Schumann, Robert	1810-1856	Liebesgram	Op. 74 No. 3	S/A or S/MS or MS/MS	B. & H.	Collection. In "Werke" of R. Schumann, ed. Clara Schumann. Pub. 1881-1893.	NATS-VCD
7014	Schumann, Robert	1810-1856	Liebesgram "Dereinst, dereinst, o Gedanke mein"	Op. 74 No. 3	S/A	Kistner et al.		CHAL (1898)
7015	Schumann, Robert	1810-1856	Liebste, was kann denn uns schreiden?		Unspec.	Peters	Ed. Dörffel	BBC (1975)
7016	Schumann, Robert	1810-1856	Lotosblume "Lotosblume ängstigt sich"	Op. 33 No. c2	Unspec.	Sch. & Co. et al.		CHAL (1898)

REC	COMP	DTS	TITLE	OP #	VCG	PUB	COMMENTS	SRC
7017	Schumann, Robert	1810-1856	Mädchenlieder		Unspec.	Augener		BBC (1975)
7018	Schumann, Robert	1810-1856	Mädchenlieder (4)	Op. 103	S/S or S/A	Kistner et al.	Set of 4 duets	CHAL (1898)
7019	Schumann, Robert	1810-1856	Mailied	Op. 103 No. 1	Unspec.	Durand	In collection "Douze Duos"	CVMP (1976)
7020	Schumann, Robert	1810-1856	Mailied	Op. 103 No. 1	S/S or S/MS	B. & H.	Collection. In "Mädchen lied von E. Kulmann" Op. 103. In "Werke" of R. Schumann, ed. Clara Schumann. Pub. 1881-1893.	NATS-VCD
7021	Schumann, Robert	1810-1856	Mailied	Op. 79 No. 10	S/A or S/MS	B. & H.	Collection. In "Werke" of R. Schumann, ed. Clara Schumann. Pub. 1881-1893.	NATS-VCD
7022	Schumann, Robert	1810-1856	Mailied "Komm, lieber Mai"	Op. 79 No. 10	S/S	Peters	In collection of "Schumann Duette" Ed. M. Friedländer.	MSN
7023	Schumann, Robert	1810-1856	Mailied "Komm lieber Mai und mache die Bäume wieder grün"	Op. 79 No. 10	S/A	B. & H.	In anth. "Zweistim. Lied. f. Sop. u. Altstimme mit Klavierbegleitung f. den Haus- u. Schulgebrauch v. H. M. Schletterer" 3 vols.	MSN
7024	Schumann, Robert	1810-1856	Mailied "Pflücket Rosen"	Op. 103 No. 1	S/A	Peters	In collection of "Schumann Duette" Ed. M. Friedländer.	MSN
7025	Schumann, Robert	1810-1856	Mailied "Pflücket Rosen, um das Haar"	Op. 103 No. 1	S/S or S/A	Kistner		CHAL (1898)
7026	Schumann, Robert	1810-1856	Nelken wind' ich Jasmin	Op. 78 No. 4	S/A	Kistner		CHAL (1898)
7027	Schumann, Robert	1810-1856	Romanze		Unspec.	Litolff		BBC (1975)
7028	Schumann, Robert	1810-1856	Rose stand im Thau		S/A	Stürtz i. W.		CHAL (1906)
7029	Schumann, Robert	1810-1856	Schneeglöcken klingen wieder	Op. 79 No. 18	S/A	B. & H.		CHAL (1898)
7030	Schumann, Robert	1810-1856	Schön Blümelein		S/A	Peters	Ed. Dörffel	BBC (1975)
7031	Schumann, Robert	1810-1856	Schön Blümelein	Op. 43 No. 3	Unspec.	G. Schirm.	In anthology "Romantic Duets—Great Performers Edition" Compi. E. Lear & T. Stewart. Pub. 1985.	MSN
7032	Schumann, Robert	1810-1856	Schön Blümelein	Op. 43 No. 3	Var.	B. & H.	Collection "Drei Duette für zwei Singstimmen Op. 43. In "Werke" of R. Schumann, ed. Clara Schumann. Pub. 1881-1893.	NATS-VCD
7033	Schumann, Robert	1810-1856	Schön Blümelein "Ich bin hinausgegangen"	Op. 43 No. 3	S/A	Simrock et al.		CHAL (1898)
7034	Schumann, Robert	1810-1856	Schön Blümelein "Ich bin hinausgegangen"	Op. 43 No. 3	S/A	Peters	In collection of "Schumann Duette" Ed. M. Friedländer.	MSN
7035	Schumann, Robert	1810-1856	Schön ist das Fest des Lenzes	III No. 9	Unspec.	C. Rühle i. L.		CHAL (1901)
7036	Schumann, Robert	1810-1856	Schön ist das Fest des Lenzes	Op. 37 No. 7	2 high v.	B. & H.		CHAL (1898)
7037	Schumann, Robert	1810-1856	Schumann Duette Pieces		Unspec.	Ongaku	Collection. Ed. Masaru Adachi. Unspec. pieces.	CVMP (1995)
7038	Schumann, Robert	1810-1856	Schumann Duos		Unspec.	Ricordi-Arg BA	Collection. Grmn./Span. lang. Selected works. Includes wks from Op. 103, 79, 138, 43.	CVMP (1976)

REC	COMP	DTS	TITLE	OP #	VCG	PUB	COMMENTS	SRC
7039	Schumann, Robert	1810-1856	Schumann Thirty-Four Duets		S/S, S/A, S/T, S/Br, A/B, T/B	Peters	Collection. Ed. Friedlander. Unspec. pieces.	CVMP (1976)
7040	Schumann, Robert	1810-1856	Schwalben "Es fliegen zwei Schwalben"	Op. 79 No. 20	S/A	B. & H. et al.		CHAL (1898)
7041	Schumann, Robert	1810-1856	So wahr die Sonne scheinet		Unspec.	ECS	In anthology "48 Duets Seventeenth Through Nineteenth Centuries" Ed. V. Prahl. Pub. 1941, 1970.	MSN
7042	Schumann, Robert	1810-1856	So wahr die Sonne scheinet	I No. 2	Unspec.	C. Rühle i. L.	Arr. Necke	CHAL (1901)
7043	Schumann, Robert	1810-1856	So Wahr die Sonne Scheinet	Op. 37 No. 12	Unspec.	G. Schirm.	In anthology "Romantic Duets—Great Performers Edition" Compi. E. Lear & T. Stewart. Pub. 1985.	MSN
7044	Schumann, Robert	1810-1856	Sommerruh		Unspec.	Peters	Ed. Friedländer	BBC (1975)
7045	Schumann, Robert	1810-1856	Sommerruh		S/A	EMB	In anthology "Duettek nöi Hangokra Zongorakíséerettel" Vol. II Compi. M. Forrai. Pub. 1959.	MSN
7046	Schumann, Robert	1810-1856	Sommerruh "Sommer-ruh, wie schön bist du"		Unspec.	Fritzsch		CHAL (1898)
7047	Schumann, Robert	1810-1856	Sommerruh', "Sommer-ruh', wie schön bist du"		S/A	Peters	In collection of "Schumann Duette" Ed. M. Friedländer.	MSN
7048	Schumann, Robert	1810-1856	Sommeruh		S/A or S/MS	B. & H.	Collection. In "Werke" of R. Schumann, ed. Clara Schumann. Pub. 1881-1893.	NATS-VCD
7049	Schumann, Robert	1810-1856	Spanische Liebeslieder		S/A	R. & B.	Includes applicable duets	BBC (1975)
7050	Schumann, Robert	1810-1856	Spanisches Liederspiel		S/A	Peters	Includes applicable duets	BBC (1975)
7051	Schumann, Robert	1810-1856	Spanisches Liederspiel Op. 74	Op. 74	S/S or S/A	Peters	Unspec. pieces. Contains 2 duets for 2 S and 3 duets for S/A	ASR
7052	Schumann, Robert	1810-1856	Spinnelied	Op. 79 No. 24	Unspec.	Durand	In collection "Douze Duos"	CVMP (1976)
7053	Schumann, Robert	1810-1856	To an Evening Star		Unspec.	ECS	Eng. trans. Grmn. In anthology "48 Duets Seventeenth Through Nineteenth Centuries" Ed. V. Prahl. Pub. 1941, 1970.	MSN
7054	Schumann, Robert	1810-1856	To the Nightingale		Unspec.	ECS	Eng. trans. Grmn. In anthology "48 Duets Seventeenth Through Nineteenth Centuries" Ed. V. Prahl. Pub. 1941, 1970.	MSN
7055	Schumann, Robert	1810-1856	Tragödie "Entflieh mit mir" (Auf ihrem Grab)	Op. 64 No. 3	Unspec.	Peters et al.		CHAL (1898)
7056	Schumann, Robert	1810-1856	Und wenn die Primel schneeweiss blickt	Op. 29 No. 1	S/A or T/Br	B. & H. et al.		CHAL (1898)
7057	Schumann, Robert	1810-1856	Vocal Duets		Unspec.	G. Schirm.	Collection of unspec. pieces. Unspec. vocal comb.	ASR
7058	Schumann, Robert	1810-1856	Wenn ich ein Vöglein	Op. 43 No. 1	Var.	B. & H.	Collection "Drei Duette für zwei Singstimmen Op. 43. In "Werke" of R. Schumann, ed. Clara Schumann. Pub. 1881-1893.	NATS-VCD
7059	Schumann, Robert	1810-1856	Wenn ich ein Vöglein wär		S/A	Peters	Ed. Dörffel	BBC (1975)

REC	COMP	DTS	TITLE	OP #	VCG	PUB	COMMENTS	SRC
7060	Schumann, Robert	1810-1856	Wenn ich ein Vöglein wär		S/A	EMB	In anthology "Duettek nöi Hangokra Zongorakísérettel" Vol. II Compi. M. Forrai. Pub. 1959.	MSN
7061	Schumann, Robert	1810-1856	Wenn ich ein Vöglein wär'	IV No. 10	Unspec.	C. Rühle i. L.		CHAL (1901)
7062	Schumann, Robert	1810-1856	Wenn ich ein Vöglein wär	Op. 43 No. 1	S/A	Peters	In collection of "Schumann Duette" Ed. M. Friedländer.	MSN
7063	Schumann, Robert	1810-1856	Wenn ich ein Vöglein wär und auch zwei Flügel hätt'	Op. 43 No. 1	S/A	Klemm et al.		CHAL (1898)
7064	Schumann, Robert	1810-1856	Wo bleib die Frühjahrspracht		Unspec.	Jurgensen i. M.	Ed. Bredow	CHAL (1906)
7065	Schumann, Robert	1810-1856	Zelcher als Doctrinair "Was quälte dir dein banges Herz"	Op. 33 No. c3	Unspec.	Sch. & Co. et al.		CHAL (1898)
7066	Schumann, Robert	1810-1856	Zigeunerleben	Op. 29 No. 3	Unspec.	Durand	In collection "Douze Duos"	CVMP (1976)
7067	Schumann, Robert	1810-1856	Zwischen grünen Bäumen		Unspec.	Augener		BBC (1975)
7068	Schumann, Robert	1810-1856	Zwischen grünen Bäumen		S/A	CVR		MSN
7069	Schumann, Robert	1810-1856	Zwischen grünen Bäumen	Op. 112 No. 12	S/A	Kistner et al.		CHAL (1898)
7070	Schütky, Franz Josef	1817-1893	Willkommen "Willkommen im traulichen Kreise"	Op. 14	2 female v.	Bosworth		CHAL (1898)
7071	Schütky, Franz Josef	1817-1893	Woche Lied "Wenn's emol Samstig isch"	Op. 37 No. b	Unspec.	Zumsteeg		CHAL (1898)
7072	Schwartz, Alexander	1874-	Vergiss es nicht, das alte Heck	Op. 15	S/A	Junne	a.k.a. Sascha Landry	CHAL (1911)
7073	Schwarz, C.		Patentfatzken "Wir sind von der Grand hautvolée"	Op. 1	Unspec.	Fr. Dietrich		CHAL (1898)
7074	Schwarz, N.		Rosenkranz und Güldenstern "Meine Herren, meine Damen"		Unspec.	Thiemer		CHAL (1898)
7075	Schwarzlose, Otto	1858-	Abend ist gekommen	No. 3	Unspec.	Beyer & S.		CHAL (1906)
7076	Schwarzlose, Otto	1858-	Armes Bäumchen dauert mich	No. 2	Unspec.	Beyer & S.		CHAL (1906)
7077	Schwarzlose, Otto	1858-	Kinderlieder (4)		Unspec.	Beyer & S.	Set of 4 duets	CHAL (1906)
7078	Schwarzlose, Otto	1858-	Lenz will kommen	No. 1	Unspec.	Beyer & S.		CHAL (1906)
7079	Schwarzlose, Otto	1858-	Sonntags am Rhein "Sonntags in der Morgenstund'"	No. 4	Unspec.	Beyer & S.		CHAL (1906)
7080	Schweiger, J.		Weihnachtslied nach einer alten Volksweise aus Kärnten		Unspec.	Bosworth		CHAL (1906)
7081	Schwertzell, Wilhelmine von	19th C.	Abschied "Was singst und klinget die Strasse herauf"		Unspec.	Kistner	Grmn. woman comp.	CHAL (1898)
7082	Schwertzell, Wilhelmine von	19th C.	Jägerlied "Es lohnet ich heute"		Unspec.	Kistner	Grmn. woman comp.	CHAL (1898)
7083	Schwick, J.		Abendlied "Schon an der Berge Gipfel"	No. 2	Unspec.	Rühle i. L.		CHAL (1898)

REC	COMP	DTS	TITLE	OP #	VCG	PUB	COMMENTS	SRC
7084	Schwick, J.		Am abend "Auf Waldes-wipfeln funkelt"	No. 1	Unspec.	Rühle i. L.		CHAL (1898)
7085	Schwick, J.		Auf die Berge "Auf die Berge zieht mich immer"	No. 3	Unspec.	Rühle i. L.		CHAL (1898)
7086	Schwick, J.		Auf due Berge, auf die Berg ziehts mich immer	I No. 14	Unspec.	C. Rühle i. L.		CHAL (1901)
7087	Schwick, J.		Auf Waldeswipfel funkelt	IV No. 14	Unspec.	C. Rühle i. L.		CHAL (1901)
7088	Schwick, J.		Ein alter Spruch "Lass, o lass die Sorgen geh'n"	No. 5	Unspec.	Rühle i. L.		CHAL (1898)
7089	Schwick, J.		Es stürmt da draussen gar so sehr	II No. 10	Unspec.	C. Rühle i. L.		CHAL (1901)
7090	Schwick, J.		Es stürmt da draussen gar so sehr	No. 4	Unspec.	Rühle i. L.		CHAL (1898)
7091	Schwick, J.		Fahr wohl, fahr wohl auf immerdar	I No. 13	Unspec.	C. Rühle i. L.		CHAL (1901)
7092	Schwick, J.		Lass o lass die Sorgen geh'n	II No. 9	Unspec.	C. Rühle i. L.		CHAL (1901)
7093	Schwick, J.		Scheiden "Fahr wohl auf immerdar"	No. 6	Unspec.	Rühle i. L.		CHAL (1898)
7094	Schwick, J.		Schon an der Berge Gipfel	III No. 10	Unspec.	C. Rühle i. L.		CHAL (1901)
7095	Seestädt, J.		Morgenwanderung "Wer recht in Freuden wandern will"	Op. 12 No. 1	Unspec.	Portius		CHAL (1898)
7096	Seestädt, J.		Vogelsprache "Was schmettert die Nachtigall"	Op. 12 No. 3	Unspec.	Portius		CHAL (1898)
7097	Seestädt, J.		Wiegenlied "Aeren nur noch nicken"	Op. 12 No. 2	Unspec.	Portius		CHAL (1898)
7098	Seidel, O.		O Weihnachtszeit du hast die schönsten Bäume		Unspec.	Michaëlis i. N.		CHAL (1906)
7099	Seifert, Uso	1852-1912	Wo du hingehst, da will auch ich hingehen	Op. 22 No. d	2 high v. or 2 med. v.	Hoffarth		CHAL (1911)
7100	Seiffert, Alexander	1850-1916	Abendfeier	Op. 9 No. 1	Unspec.	Weygand		CHAL (1898)
7101	Seiffert, Alexander	1850-1916	Im Frühling	Op. 9 No. 2	Unspec.	Weygand		CHAL (1898)
7102	Seiffert, Alexander	1850-1916	Im Walde	Op. 9 No. 3	Unspec.	Weygand		CHAL (1898)
7103	Seiffert, Alexander	1850-1916	Vertrauen	Op. 9 No. 4	Unspec.	Weygand		CHAL (1898)
7104	Seiffert, Karl	1856-1929	Es ist so still geworden	Op. 18	Unspec.	Schweers & H.	org or harm or pf	CHAL (1906)
7105	Seiffert, Karl	1856-1929	Lob der Freundschaft "Mensch hat nichts so eigen"	Op. 3 No. 6	Unspec.	Schweers & H.		CHAL (1898)
7106	Seiffert, Karl	1856-1929	Nun fangen die Weiden zu blühen an	Op. 3 No. 3	Unspec.	Schweers & H.		CHAL (1898)
7107	Seiffert, Karl	1856-1929	Spinnlied "Spinn, (spinn,) Mägdlein, spinn"	Op. 3 No. 1	Unspec.	Schweers & H.		CHAL (1898)
7108	Seiffert, Karl	1856-1929	Vogelgesang "Was singst du in den Zweigen"	Op. 3 No. 2	Unspec.	Schweers & H.		CHAL (1898)
7109	Seiffert, Karl	1856-1929	Waldeinsamkeit "Es ist so süss zu träumen"	Op. 3 No. 4	Unspec.	Schweers & H.		CHAL (1898)
7110	Seiffert, Karl	1856-1929	Was ist das für ein Ahnen	Op. 3 No. 5	Unspec.	Schweers & H.		CHAL (1898)
7111	Seitz, F. [prob. Friedrich]	1848-1918	Du bist wie eine Blume	Op. 1 No. 1	S/A	Läuterer		CHAL (1898)
7112	Seitz, F. [prob. Friedrich]	1848-1918	Du bist wie eine Blume	Op. 1 No. 1	S/A	Wester-mair		CHAL (1906)

REC	COMP	DTS	TITLE	OP #	VCG	PUB	COMMENTS	SRC
7113	Seitz, F. [prob. Friedrich]	1848-1918	Ein kleines Lied, wie geht's nur an	Op. 1 No. 3	S/A	Läuterer		CHAL (1898)
7114	Seitz, F. [prob. Friedrich]	1848-1918	Ein kleines Lied, wie geht's nur an	Op. 1 No. 3	S/A	Westermair		CHAL (1906)
7115	Seitz, F. [prob. Friedrich]	1848-1918	O lieb, so lang du leiben kannst	Op. 1 No. 2	S/A	Läutnerer		CHAL (1898)
7116	Seitz, F. [prob. Friedrich]	1848-1918	O lieb, so lange du lieben kannst	Op. 1 No. 2	S/A	Westermair		CHAL (1906)
7117	Selmer, Johan Peter	1844-1910	Freiheit und die Liebe	Op. 47 No. 4	Unspec.	Siegel	Prob. Grmn. tr. Nor.	CHAL (1906)
7118	Selmer, Johan Peter	1844-1910	Lichte Töne "4 Duette"	Op. 46	Unspec.	Siegel	4 duets. Prob. Grmn. tr. Nor.	CHAL (1906)
7119	Selmer, Johan Peter	1844-1910	Nun kleidet die Lenzmaid sich an	Op. 46 No. 2	Unspec.	Siegel	Prob. Grmn. tr. Nor.	CHAL (1906)
7120	Selmer, Johan Peter	1844-1910	Rothe Schwäne leise hinschweben		Unspec.	Siegel	Prob. Grmn. tr. Nor.	CHAL (1906)
7121	Selmer, Johan Peter	1844-1910	Schau' um dich im Kreis	Op. 46 No. 1	Unspec.	Siegel	Prob. Grmn. tr. Nor.	CHAL (1906)
7122	Selmer, Johan Peter	1844-1910	Still, stille, nachtumwoben schläft der Gletscher	Op. 46 No. 3	Unspec.	Siegel	Prob. Grmn. tr. Nor.	CHAL (1906)
7123	Selmer, Johan Peter	1844-1910	Wie eine Mutter lieb' ich dich		Unspec.	Siegel	Prob. Grmn. tr. Nor.	CHAL (1906)
7124	Sennes, H.		Ave Maria		S/A	Bohm	org or pf accomp.	CVMP (1976)
7125	Sennes, H.		Ave Maria		S/A	Bohm	org or pf accomp.	ASR
7126	Sering, Friedrich Wilhelm	1822-1901	Am Waldteich "O trate, traute Stelle"	Op. 64	Unspec.	B. & B.		CHAL (1898)
7127	Sering, Friedrich Wilhelm	1822-1901	Herr, erhöre mein Gebet	Op. 3 No. 2	S/A	Chal.		CHAL (1898)
7128	Sering, Friedrich Wilhelm	1822-1901	Morgenstille "Leiser tönt schon"	Op. 63	Unspec.	B. & B.		CHAL (1898)
7129	Sering, Friedrich Wilhelm	1822-1901	Wie lieblich o Herr	Op. 3 No. 1	S/A	Chal.		CHAL (1898)
7130	Serradell, N.		La Golondrina		Unspec.	Allans	Eng. trans It. In anthology "Vocal Duets Collection" Vol. 1. Pub. 1992.	MSN
7131	Sessi, M. [prob. Marianne]	1776-1847	Notturno "Gia la notte s'avvicina"		Unspec.	B. & H.	It. woman comp.	CHAL (1898)
7132	Seyffardt, Ernst Hermann	1859-1942	Herr, unser Herrscher, wie herrlich	Op. 14 No. 3	Unspec.	Siegel		CHAL (1898)
7133	Seyffardt, Ernst Hermann	1859-1942	Herr, wenn ich dich nur habe	Op. 14 No. 1	Unspec.	Siegel		CHAL (1898)
7134	Seyffardt, Ernst Hermann	1859-1942	Im Pfarrhaus "Hallo, mein Pfarrherr"	Op. 2 No. 4	MS/A	B. & H.		CHAL (1898)
7135	Seyffardt, Ernst Hermann	1859-1942	Im Walde "Was flüstern im Walde"	Op. 2 No. 9	MS/A	B. & H.		CHAL (1898)
7136	Seyffardt, Ernst Hermann	1859-1942	Psalm 103 "Barmherzig, gnädig ist der Herr"	Op. 14 No. 2	Unspec.	Siegel		CHAL (1898)
7137	Seyffardt, Ernst Hermann	1859-1942	Psalm 121 "Ich hebe mein Augen auf zu den Bergen"	Op. 13 No. 2	Unspec.	R. & E.		CHAL (1898)
7138	Seyffardt, Ernst Hermann	1859-1942	Psalm 139 "Herr du erforschest mich"	Op. 13 No. 1	Unspec.	R. & E.		CHAL (1898)
7139	Seyffardt, Ernst Hermann	1859-1942	Psalm 33 "Danket dem Herrn mit Harfen"	Op. 13 No. 3	Unspec.	R. & E.		CHAL (1898)
7140	Sharman, Cecil		Orpheus with his lute		Unspec.	Boosey		CHAL (1898)

REC	COMP	DTS	TITLE	OP #	VCG	PUB	COMMENTS	SRC
7141	Sharpe, Evelyn		One Little Hour		Unspec.	Cramer	Also solo	CVMP (1976)
7142	Sharpe, Evelyn		The thrush		Unspec.	Cramer		BBC (1975)
7143	Sharpe, Evelyn		Tulips		Unspec.	Cramer		BBC (1975)
7144	Shaw, Martin	1875-1958	I Know a Bank		Unspec.	Cramer	Also solo	CVMP (1976)
7145	Shaw, Martin	1875-1958	Matthew, Mark, Luke and John		S/S	Curwen		ASR
7146	Shelley, Harry Rowe	1858-1947	Alleluia, Amen! (Easter)		high & low v.	G. Schirm.	pf or org accomp. In catalogue page "Sacred Vocal Duets" of G. Schirmer, Inc. NY (no date)	MSN
7147	Shelley, Harry Rowe	1858-1947	Christ, The		high & low v.	G. Schirm.	pf or org accomp. In catalogue page "Sacred Vocal Duets" of G. Schirmer, Inc. NY (no date)	MSN
7148	Shelley, Harry Rowe	1858-1947	Christian, the Morn breaks sweetly o'er thee		high & low v.	G. Schirm.	In anthology "Schirmer's Favorite Sacred Duets for Various Voices" Pub. 1955.	MSN
7149	Shelley, Harry Rowe	1858-1947	Christian, the morn breaks sweetly o'er thee		high & low v.	G. Schirm.	pf or org accomp. In catalogue page "Sacred Vocal Duets" of G. Schirmer, Inc. NY (no date)	MSN
7150	Shelley, Harry Rowe	1858-1947	Christian, the Morn Breaks Sweetly O'er Thee		S/MS or S/Br or T/Br	G. Schirm.	In Anthology "Schirmer's Favorite Sacred Duets for Various Voices" Pub. 1955.	NATS-SVD
7151	Shelley, Harry Rowe	1858-1947	Christmas		high & low v.	G. Schirm.	pf or org accomp. In catalogue page "Sacred Vocal Duets" of G. Schirmer, Inc. NY (no date)	MSN
7152	Shelley, Harry Rowe	1858-1947	Easter Vespers		high & low v.	G. Schirm.	pf or org accomp. In catalogue page "Sacred Vocal Duets" of G. Schirmer, Inc. NY (no date)	MSN
7153	Shelley, Harry Rowe	1858-1947	God is Love		high & low v.	G. Schirm.	pf or org accomp. In catalogue page "Sacred Vocal Duets" of G. Schirmer, Inc. NY (no date)	MSN
7154	Shelley, Harry Rowe	1858-1947	Hark! Hark, My Soul		S/A	G. Schirm.		CVMP (1976)
7155	Shelley, Harry Rowe	1858-1947	Hark! hark, my Soul		S/A	G. Schirm.	In anthology "Schirmer's Favorite Sacred Duets for Various Voices" Pub. 1955.	MSN
7156	Shelley, Harry Rowe		Hark! hark my soul!		S/A	G. Schirm.	pf or org accomp. In catalogue page "Sacred Vocal Duets" of G. Schirmer, Inc. NY (no date)	MSN
7157	Shelley, Harry Rowe	1858-1947	Hark! hark my Soul!		S/A or S/MS	G. Schirm.	In anthology "Schirmer's Favorite Sacred Duets for Various Voices" Pub. 1955.	NATS-SVD
7158	Shelley, Harry Rowe	1858-1947	King of Love my Shepherd is		high & low v.	G. Schirm.	In anthology "Schirmer's Favorite Sacred Duets for Various Voices" Pub. 1955.	MSN
7159	Shelley, Harry Rowe	1858-1947	King of Love My Shepherd Is, The		S/MS or S/Br or T/Br	G. Schirm.	Pub. sep. Also in anthology "Album of Sixteen Sacred Duets for Various Voices" (Schirmer). Pub. 1880 et al.	NATS-SVD
7160	Shelley, Harry Rowe	1858-1947	Noël of the Bells (Christmas Chimes)		high & low v.	G. Schirm.	pf or org accomp. In catalogue page "Sacred Vocal Duets" of G. Schirmer, Inc. NY (no date)	MSN

REC	COMP	DTS	TITLE	OP #	VCG	PUB	COMMENTS	SRC
7161	Shelley, Harry Rowe	1858-1947	Saviour, when night involves the skies		high & low v.	G. Schirm.	pf or org accomp. In catalogue page "Sacred Vocal Duets" of G. Schirmer, Inc. NY (no date)	MSN
7162	Shelley, Harry Rowe	1858-1947	Songs of praise the angels sang		high & low v.	G. Schirm.	pf or org accomp. In catalogue page "Sacred Vocal Duets" of G. Schirmer, Inc. NY (no date)	MSN
7163	Shelley, Harry Rowe	1858-1947	The King of love my shepherd is		high & low v.	G. Schirm.	pf or org accomp. In catalogue page "Sacred Vocal Duets" of G. Schirmer, Inc. NY (no date)	MSN
7164	Shelley, Harry Rowe	1858-1947	The King of Love My Shepherd Is		high & low v.	G. Schirm.	org accomp. Copyright 1886	MSN
7165	Shelley, Harry Rowe	1858-1947	Vesper Hour		S/A or T/A	G. Schirm.	pf or org accomp. In catalogue page "Sacred Vocal Duets" of G. Schirmer, Inc. NY (no date)	MSN
7166	Shield, William	1748-1829	You're a man (woman)		Unspec.	Longman & Broderlip		BBC (1975)
7167	Shiomi, Mieko	1938-	In the Afternoon or Structure of the Dream		Unspec., narrators	Academ	For 1-2 v. narrators	CVMP (1985)
7168	Shostakovich, Dmitri	1906-1975	Anxious mama and aunt		S/A	R. S. M.	Trans. Russ.	BBC (1975)
7169	Shostakovich, Dmitri	1906-1975	Die fürsirgliche Mutter zur Kindes		S/A	Peters	Grmn. trans. Russ.	BBC (1975)
7170	Shostakovich, Dmitri	1906-1975	Iz Evreiskoi Narodnoi Noezii [From Yiddish Folk-Poetry] Op. 79	Op. 79	S/A et al.	Sikorski	Translit. title of Russ. Cyrillic & Grmn. Song cycle includes two duets (No. 1,2) for S/A. Composed 1948. Pub. 1982.	MSN
7171	Shostakovich, Dmitri	1906-1975	Klage über dem Tod eines kleinen Kindes		S/A	Peters	Grmn. trans. Russ.	BBC (1975)
7172	Shostakovich, Dmitri	1906-1975	Lament over the Death of a Small Child	Op. 79 No. 1	S/A	Sikorski	pf or orch accomp. In song cycle, "From Yiddish Folk-Poetry" Eng. & Russ. Russ. tr. Yiddish. Solos & trios also. Comp. 1948.	MSN
7173	Shostakovich, Dmitri	1906-1975	Ploch ob umershem mlodentse [Lament over the Death of a Small Child]	Op. 79 No. 1	S/A et al.	Sikorski	In "Iz Evreiskoi Narodnoi Noezii" Translit. title of Russ. Cyrillic & Grmn. Comp. 1948.	MSN
7174	Shostakovich, Dmitri	1906-1975	Song Cycle of Jewish Folk Poetry Op. 79		S/A	Peters	Grmn. trans. Russ. Duets for S/A, and other vocal solos and comb.	ASR
7175	Shostakovich, Dmitri	1906-1975	Songs After Jewish Folk Poems Op. 79	Op. 79	S, A, T, S/A, S/T, A/T, S/A/T	Peters	Contains 11 movements for various combinations. Contains S/A duet.	CVMP (1976)
7176	Shostakovich, Dmitri	1906-1975	The Loving Mother	Op. 79 No. 2	S/A	Sikorski	pf or orch accomp. In song cycle, "From Yiddish Folk-Poetry" Eng. & Russ. Russ. tr. Yiddish. Solos & trios also. Comp. 1948.	MSN
7177	Shostakovich, Dmitri	1906-1975	Zabotlivye mama i tetia [The Loving Mother]	Op. 79 No. 2	S/A et al.	Sikorski	In "Iz Evreiskoi Narodnoi Noezii" Translit. title of Russ. Cyrillic & Grmn. Comp. 1948.	MSN
7178	Sieber, Ferdinand	1822-1895	Abendlied "Sonne geht hinunter"	Op. 101 No. 2	S/A	R. & B.		CHAL (1898)

REC	COMP	DTS	TITLE	OP #	VCG	PUB	COMMENTS	SRC
7179	Sieber, Ferdinand	1822-1895	Blühende Welt "Es schweben die Wälder"	Op. 101 No. 1	S/A	R. & B.		CHAL (1898)
7180	Sieber, Ferdinand	1822-1895	Costanza "Più non si trovano"	Op. 65 No. 2	S/A	R. & B.		CHAL (1898)
7181	Sieber, Ferdinand	1822-1895	Es giebt ja keine zwei Berge	Op. 61 No. 3	S/A	Schmid i. M.		CHAL (1898)
7182	Sieber, Ferdinand	1822-1895	Frühroth leuchtet in's Thal hinein	Op. 61 No. 1	S/A	Schmid i. M.		CHAL (1898)
7183	Sieber, Ferdinand	1822-1895	Gleich und Gleich "Ein Blumenglöckchen vom Boden hervor (empor)"	Op. 25 No. 1	Unspec.	Peters		CHAL (1898)
7184	Sieber, Ferdinand	1822-1895	Gubener Stunden 5 Duette	Op. 125	Unspec.	Heinr.	5 duets	CHAL (1898)
7185	Sieber, Ferdinand	1822-1895	Gute Nacht "Schon fängt es an zu dämmern"	Op. 25 No. 3	S/A	Peters		CHAL (1898)
7186	Sieber, Ferdinand	1822-1895	Im Mai "Musst nicht allein im Freien"	Op. 61 No. 2	S/A	Schmid i. M.		CHAL (1898)
7187	Sieber, Ferdinand	1822-1895	In Riva al Lago di Como	Op. 65	Unspec.	R. & B.		CHAL (1898)
7188	Sieber, Ferdinand	1822-1895	Lied der Vöglein "Von Zweig zu Zweig zu hüpfen"	Op. 51	S/A	Heinr.		CHAL (1898)
7189	Sieber, Ferdinand	1822-1895	Liedchen erklinge, schwing' dich	Op. 10 No. 2	S/A	Heinr.		CHAL (1898)
7190	Sieber, Ferdinand	1822-1895	März "Es ist ein Schnee gefallen"	Op. 10 No. 1	S/A	Heinr.		CHAL (1898)
7191	Sieber, Ferdinand	1822-1895	Nachtlied "Erde ruht, der Himmel wacht"	Op. 100 No. 1	S/A	R. & B.		CHAL (1898)
7192	Sieber, Ferdinand	1822-1895	Spurlos "Schneeflocken schweben"	Op. 100 No. 2	S/A	R. & B.		CHAL (1898)
7193	Sieber, Ferdinand	1822-1895	Waldesstimmung "Es rauscht der Wald"	Op. 101 No. 3	S/A	R. & B.		CHAL (1898)
7194	Sieber, Ferdinand	1822-1895	Waldnacht "Schnurre, schnurre Miesekätzchen"	Op. 100 No. 3	S/A	R. & B.		CHAL (1898)
7195	Sieber, Ferdinand	1822-1895	Zage nicht "Zage nicht, wenn die Blumen auch verblühn"	Op. 25 No. 2	S/A	Peters		CHAL (1898)
7196	Sieber, Ferdinand	1822-1895	Zweigesang "Im Fliederbusch ein Vöglein sass"	Op. 109	S/A	Simon i. Berl.		CHAL (1898)
7197	Siebmann, F.		Frühlingslied "Nun weht gelind der Frühlingswind"	Op. 54 No. 5	S/A	R. & E.		CHAL (1898)
7198	Siebmann, F.		Leise zieht durch mein Gemüth	Op. 54 No. 1	S/A	R. & E.		CHAL (1898)
7199	Siebmann, F.		Mich zieht es nach dem Dörfchen hin	Op. 54 No. 3	S/A	R. & E.		CHAL (1898)
7200	Siebmann, F.		Mit Myrthen, Tausend-schönchen	Op. 54 No. 6	S/A	R. & E.		CHAL (1898)
7201	Siebmann, F.		Tambourinschlägerin "Schwirrend Tambourin"	Op. 54 No. 4	S/A	R. & E.		CHAL (1898)
7202	Siebmann, F.		Wiet, weit "Wie kann ich froh und munter sein"	Op. 54 No. 2	S/A	R. & E.		CHAL (1898)
7203	Silber, Philip	1876-	Ist so ein fader Tag endlich zu End'		Unspec.	Pawliska		CHAL (1906)
7204	Silber, Philip	1876-	Ist so ein fader Tag endlich zu End' "Wiener Duett"		Unspec.	Blaha		CHAL (1911)
7205	Silcher, Friedrich	1789-1860	Ausländische Volksmelodien		Unspec.	Auer i. St.		CHAL (1906)
7206	Simon, Ernst	1850-1916	A Büchsal auf'n Rück'n	Op. 329 No. 18	Unspec.	P. & M.		CHAL (1898)
7207	Simon, Ernst	1850-1916	Abend auf der Alm "Alpen glühn im Abendschein"	Op. 329 No. 16	Unspec.	P. & M.		CHAL (1898)
7208	Simon, Ernst	1850-1916	Abschied von den Tyroler Bergen "Von meinen Bergen muss ich scheiden"	Op. 329 No. 6	Unspec.	P. & M.		CHAL (1898)

REC	COMP	DTS	TITLE	OP #	VCG	PUB	COMMENTS	SRC
7209	Simon, Ernst	1850-1916	Alpenrosen 27 Tyrolerduette	Op. 329	Unspec.	P. & M.		CHAL (1898)
7210	Simon, Ernst	1850-1916	Auf der Alm da giebts doa Sünd "Von der Alpe ragt ein Haus"	Op. 329 No. 17	Unspec.	P. & M.		CHAL (1898)
7211	Simon, Ernst	1850-1916	Auf der Alm ist koa Bleib'n	Op. 329 No. 13	Unspec.	P. & M.		CHAL (1898)
7212	Simon, Ernst	1850-1916	Auf der Alm ist's schön "wann hoch auf der Alma"	Op. 329 No. 7	Unspec.	P. & M.		CHAL (1898)
7213	Simon, Ernst	1850-1916	Aufgeklärte Missverständniss "Es spricht die Welt"		2 med. v.	Wernthal		CHAL (1898)
7214	Simon, Ernst	1850-1916	Aus des Herzens tiefstem Grunde	Op. 564	2 med. v.	Glaser		CHAL (1911)
7215	Simon, Ernst	1850-1916	Das kann ein Blinder mit dem Krückstock fühlen "So manch-mal bringt man"		Unspec.	Nagel		CHAL (1898)
7216	Simon, Ernst	1850-1916	Dirnd'l wie ist mir so wohl "Schaut der Jäger in das Thal"	Op. 329 No. 4	Unspec.	P. & M.		CHAL (1898)
7217	Simon, Ernst	1850-1916	Dornröschens Herzelied "Dorn-röschen steht am Waldesrand"	Op. 517	Unspec.	Glaser		CHAL (1906)
7218	Simon, Ernst	1850-1916	E. D. Sohn und sein Phonograph "Fast jeder, der was erfand"	Op. 217	2 med. v.	Glaser		CHAL (1898)
7219	Simon, Ernst	1850-1916	Edelweiss "Wer nennt mir jene Blume"	Op. 329 No. 22	Unspec.	P. & M. (Peuschel)		CHAL (1898)
7220	Simon, Ernst	1850-1916	Ei, was seh' ich, liebste Lilly	Op. 518	S/S	Hainauer		CHAL (1906)
7221	Simon, Ernst	1850-1916	Ein Gruss der Sänger aus Tyrol		2 med. v.	Gross i. Insbr.	Yodeling piece	CHAL (1906)
7222	Simon, Ernst	1850-1916	Ein Tauber wollte freien	Op. 506	Unspec.	Glaser		CHAL (1906)
7223	Simon, Ernst	1850-1916	Emancipirten "Guten Morgen liebe Rath"	Op. 269	MS/MS	Vormeyer		CHAL (1898)
7224	Simon, Ernst	1850-1916	Frische Madl' im Thal "Bin i nit a frisch's Madel"	Op. 329 No. 8	Unspec.	P. & M.		CHAL (1898)
7225	Simon, Ernst	1850-1916	Frühlingszeit "Jetzt kommt kie schöne Frühlingseit"	Op. 329 No. 9	Unspec.	P. & M.		CHAL (1898)
7226	Simon, Ernst	1850-1916	Heimweh "Nur einmal noch in meinem Leben"	Op. 329 No. 27	Unspec.	P. & M.		CHAL (1898)
7227	Simon, Ernst	1850-1916	Hochzeit auf der Alm "Sag' mir du saggrisch Bua"	Op. 329 No. 1	Unspec.	P. & M.		CHAL (1898)
7228	Simon, Ernst	1850-1916	Hütterl am Rain "Auf der Alm, da steht allein"	Op. 329 No. 21	Unspec.	P. & M.		CHAL (1898)
7229	Simon, Ernst	1850-1916	Ideal "Taschen-Musikalbum"		Unspec.	Glaser	Duet anthology. 2 vols.	CHAL (1911)
7230	Simon, Ernst	1850-1916	Im Land Tyrol "In dem schönen Land Tyrol"	Op. 129 No. 25	Unspec.	P. & M. (Peuschel)		CHAL (1898)
7231	Simon, Ernst	1850-1916	Im Theaterbureau "Wenn man nur ein Mittel hätte"	Op. 224	2 med. v.	Siegel		CHAL (1898)
7232	Simon, Ernst	1850-1916	In den Sternen stet's geschrieben	Op. 374	2 female v.	Heinr.		CHAL (1901)
7233	Simon, Ernst	1850-1916	Jodelplatz "Z'nächst bin i halt gegang"	Op. 329 No. 11	Unspec.	P. & M.		CHAL (1898)
7234	Simon, Ernst	1850-1916	Kappler Alm "Von der Kappler Alm, da hab' i."	Op. 329 No. 19	Unspec.	P. & M.		CHAL (1898)
7235	Simon, Ernst	1850-1916	Lustigen Tyroler "Tyroler sind lustig, sind munter"	Op. 329 No. 2	Unspec.	P. & M.		CHAL (1898)
7236	Simon, Ernst	1850-1916	Mailüfterl "Schneller als die flücht'ge Möve"	Op. 229	2 med. v.	Heinr.		CHAL (1898)
7237	Simon, Ernst	1850-1916	Mein Turteltäubchen "Liebes Dirndel erhöre mein Flehen"	Op. 329 No. 26	Unspec.	P. & M. (Peuschel)		CHAL (1898)
7238	Simon, Ernst	1850-1916	Mir klingt im Ohr ein leises Rauschen	Op. 519	S/S	Hainauer		CHAL (1906)

REC	COMP	DTS	TITLE	OP #	VCG	PUB	COMMENTS	SRC
7239	Simon, Ernst	1850-1916	O Sonnenstrahl aus schöner Zeit "Hast jemals du geliebt im Leben"	Op. 354	Unspec.	Heinr.		CHAL (1898)
7240	Simon, Ernst	1850-1916	Rechnung ohne Wirth "Rechtsgelehrter jetzt zu werden"	Op. 206 No. 1	2 med. v.	Siegel		CHAL (1898)
7241	Simon, Ernst	1850-1916	Rekrut Jürgens auf Urlaub "Lesen und das Schreiben"	Op. 352 T. I. II.	Unspec.	André		CHAL (1898)
7242	Simon, Ernst	1850-1916	Rivalen "Liebchen höre meine Lieder"	Op. 309 T. I. II. (Br.)	Unspec.	Glaser		CHAL (1898)
7243	Simon, Ernst	1850-1916	Schnadahüpf'l "Alle Hähne krähen, nur die"	Op. 329 No. 20	Unspec.	P. & M.		CHAL (1898)
7244	Simon, Ernst	1850-1916	Sehnsucht nach der Schweiz "Gern in das Schweizerland"	Op. 329 No. 23	Unspec.	P. & M.		CHAL (1898)
7245	Simon, Ernst	1850-1916	Sennerin auf der Alm "Alm der Alm is a Freud'"	Op. 329 No. 10	Unspec.	P. & M.		CHAL (1898)
7246	Simon, Ernst	1850-1916	Tanzstunden-Erinnerungen "Hum. Duoscene"	Op. 397	S/S	Heinr.		CHAL (1901)
7247	Simon, Ernst	1850-1916	Traum "Nee is det en Hundeleben"	Op. 206 No. 2	2 med. v.	Siegel		CHAL (1898)
7248	Simon, Ernst	1850-1916	Tyroler Bue "Bin a frischer Tyroler Bue"	Op. 329 No. 3	Unspec.	P. & M.		CHAL (1898)
7249	Simon, Ernst	1850-1916	Tyroler Jäger "Was gleicht wohl an Jaga"	Op. 329 No. 12	Unspec.	P. & M.		CHAL (1898)
7250	Simon, Ernst	1850-1916	Vom bayrischen Hochlande "Schaut's aussi, wie's regnet"	Op. 329 No. 24	Unspec.	P. & M.		CHAL (1898)
7251	Simon, Ernst	1850-1916	Vor dem Polterabend "So für circa zwanzig Tassen"	Op. 238	2 med. v.	Heinr.		CHAL (1898)
7252	Simon, Ernst	1850-1916	Wasserfahrt	Op. 329 No. 14	Unspec.	P. & M.		CHAL (1898)
7253	Simon, Ernst	1850-1916	Welch' ein Poltern hier im Haus	Op. 563	2 med. v.	Glaser		CHAL (1911)
7254	Simon, Ernst	1850-1916	Wenn der erste Sonnenstrahl	Op. 561	2 med. v.	Glaser		CHAL (1911)
7255	Simon, Ernst	1850-1916	Wenn die Blümlein mit dem ersten Grün	Op. 469	Unspec.	Glaser		CHAL (1906)
7256	Simon, Ernst	1850-1916	Wenn die Linden blüh'n	Op. 467	Unspec.	Glaser		CHAL (1906)
7257	Simon, Ernst	1850-1916	Wenn die Rosen wieder blüh'n	Op. 505	Unspec.	Glaser		CHAL (1906)
7258	Simon, Ernst	1850-1916	Wenn i Morgens früh aufsteh	Op. 329 No. 5	Unspec.	P. & M.		CHAL (1898)
7259	Simon, Ernst	1850-1916	Wenn im Morgenstrahl	Op. 521	Unspec.	Glaser		CHAL (1906)
7260	Simon, Ernst	1850-1916	Wenn je ein grenzenloser Schmerz	Op. 351	Unspec.	André		CHAL (1901)
7261	Simon, Ernst	1850-1916	Wie Lerchenjubel und Finkenschlag	Op. 494	high & low v.	Simon i. M.		CHAL (1906)
7262	Simon, Ernst	1850-1916	Wie süsse Märchenweisen	Op. 562	2 med. v.	Glaser		CHAL (1911)
7263	Simon, Ernst	1850-1916	Wir kommen zu grüssen	Op. 422	2 med. v.	André		CHAL (1906)
7264	Simon, Ernst	1850-1916	Wo im bleichen Mondenschimmer	Op. 516	Unspec.	Glaser		CHAL (1906)
7265	Simon, Ernst	1850-1916	Zillerthal, du bist mei Freud	Op. 329 No. 15	Unspec.	P. & M.		CHAL (1898)
7266	Simon, O.		Musik-Enthusiasten "Musik-Enthusiasten sind wir"		Unspec.	O. Dietrich		CHAL (1898)
7267	Singer, Jeanne		Winter Identity		S/S	AMC	Woman comp.	ASR

REC	COMP	DTS	TITLE	OP #	VCG	PUB	COMMENTS	SRC
7268	Sinico, Giuseppe	1836-1907	Adieu à Nice		S/A	Ricordi		CHAL (1898)
7269	Sinigaglia, Leone	1868-1944	Abendständchen "Schlafe Liebchen weil's auf Erden"	No. 2	2 female v.	Simrock		CHAL (1898)
7270	Sinigaglia, Leone	1868-1944	Mägdleins Begräbniss "Blümlein alle schwanken"	No. 1	2 female v.	Simrock	Pub. 1896	CHAL (1898)
7271	Sinigaglia, Leone	1868-1944	Schlummerlied "Still ist's im Stübchen"	No. 3	2 female v.	Simrock	Pub. 1896	CHAL (1898)
7272	Sinnhold, R.		I weiss a kleins Häusle		2 high v. or 2 low v.	none listed		CHAL (1911)
7273	Sint-Lubin, Léon de	1805-1850	Al chiaro della Luna	Op. 50	Unspec.	B. & B.		CHAL (1898)
7274	Sioly, Johann	1843-1911	A altes Kindersprüchel "Woa, ir no' klane Fratzen"	No. 73	Unspec.	Krämer		CHAL (1898)
7275	Sioly, Johann	1843-1911	A paar Weana Vorstadt-Kinder "Wir trag'n das gleiche G'wand"	No. 138	Unspec.	Krämer		CHAL (1898)
7276	Sioly, Johann	1843-1911	Acht Vers' auf ein' Reim "Weil mir Zwa in die Duetten	No. 74	Unspec.	Krämer		CHAL (1898)
7277	Sioly, Johann	1843-1911	Allerhand Zeitwörter "Schmink' di, putz di"	No. 134	Unspec.	Krämer		CHAL (1898)
7278	Sioly, Johann	1843-1911	Alte Theaterzetteln "Hermin' is' kokett"	No. 160	Unspec.	Krämer		CHAL (1898)
7279	Sioly, Johann	1843-1911	Am Fensterbrtt'l "In Heine sin' Gedicht" [sic]	No. 14	Unspec.	Hofbauer		CHAL (1898)
7280	Sioly, Johann	1843-1911	Am Land sein's halt no nöt voraus "Bei uns thut's gehn"	No. 21	Unspec.	Hofbauer		CHAL (1898)
7281	Sioly, Johann	1843-1911	Anmal der, anmal i "Saprament und kein End"	No. 152	Unspec.	Krämer		CHAL (1898)
7282	Sioly, Johann	1843-1911	Anzige Punkt "Es tanzt auf ein' Ball"	No. 16	Unspec.	Hofbauer		CHAL (1898)
7283	Sioly, Johann	1843-1911	Automat "Mein Spezi nöt gern reden thuat"	No. 150	Unspec.	Krämer		CHAL (1898)
7284	Sioly, Johann	1843-1911	Bim, Bam, Bom, Bum "Höchste zu jeder Zeit"	No. 172	Unspec.	Krämer		CHAL (1898)
7285	Sioly, Johann	1843-1911	Blüaht nur anmal "Verstorbene Klesheim"	No. 179	Unspec.	Krämer		CHAL (1898)
7286	Sioly, Johann	1843-1911	Bum "Gesang ist herrlich"	No. 164	Unspec.	Krämer		CHAL (1898)
7287	Sioly, Johann	1843-1911	Chineser und a Frauenzopf		Unspec.	Blaha		CHAL (1901)
7288	Sioly, Johann	1843-1911	Da braucht ma' gar kan Papa dazu "Zwa Gigerin dö vor d' Leut'"	No. 163	Unspec.	Krämer		CHAL (1898)
7289	Sioly, Johann	1843-1911	Dann hat er's überstanden "Ein' Bauern thuat unbändi weh"	No. 17	Unspec.	Hofbauer		CHAL (1898)
7290	Sioly, Johann	1843-1911	Den g'fallt's, mir g'fallt's "Mir kennen a jungs Wesen"	No. 162	Unspec.	Krämer		CHAL (1898)
7291	Sioly, Johann	1843-1911	Der gift 'si nöt "'S is jetzt bei meiner Ehr'"	No. 148	Unspec.	Krämer		CHAL (1898)
7292	Sioly, Johann	1843-1911	Dichtung und Wahrheit "Wie schön beschreibt uns"	No. 153	Unspec.	Krämer		CHAL (1898)
7293	Sioly, Johann	1843-1911	Dort, wo der Kuckuck schreit "Verliabten Leut' hab'n nie a Freud'"		Unspec.	Blaha		CHAL (1898)
7294	Sioly, Johann	1843-1911	Dulli ulli ulli histahö	No. 76	Unspec.	Krämer		CHAL (1898)
7295	Sioly, Johann	1843-1911	Ein Zeichen der Zeit ist's		Unspec.	Blaha		CHAL (1901)

REC	COMP	DTS	TITLE	OP #	VCG	PUB	COMMENTS	SRC
7296	Sioly, Johann	1843-1911	Eine Parthie Piquet "A Wittfrau gut erhalten no"	No. 139	Unspec.	Krämer		CHAL (1898)
7297	Sioly, Johann	1843-1911	Einigucken, zucharucken, andrucken "A Bekanntschaft machen"	No. 137	Unspec.	Krämer		CHAL (1898)
7298	Sioly, Johann	1843-1911	Es giebt heut' noch mitunter		Unspec.	Blaha		CHAL (1901)
7299	Sioly, Johann	1843-1911	Es is' nöt so pressant "Wir werd'n kriegen eine Stadtbahn"	No. 178	Unspec.	Krämer		CHAL (1898)
7300	Sioly, Johann	1843-1911	Es thuat a Jeder, was er kann "Rauchfangkehrer geht jahraus, jahrein"	No. 158	Unspec.	Krämer		CHAL (1898)
7301	Sioly, Johann	1843-1911	Für alles Andre bürgt die Firma "Stellen vor sich zwei Claquere"	No. 147	Unspec.	Krämer		CHAL (1898)
7302	Sioly, Johann	1843-1911	Gedankenleser "Gedanken zu lesen ist jetzt modern"	No. 141	Unspec.	Krämer		CHAL (1898)
7303	Sioly, Johann	1843-1911	Grädeste vom Graden "Kommen zu Stellung h'nein"	No. 180	Unspec.	Krämer		CHAL (1898)
7304	Sioly, Johann	1843-1911	I kriag an Zron jed'smal		Unspec.	Blaha		CHAL (1906)
7305	Sioly, Johann	1843-1911	In der Früh' z'Mittag und auf d'Nacht "Es lasst si' wer a Haus"	No. 75	Unspec.	Krämer		CHAL (1898)
7306	Sioly, Johann	1843-1911	In der Woll' "Ein Professor, der belehrt uns"	No. 72	Unspec.	Krämer		CHAL (1898)
7307	Sioly, Johann	1843-1911	In Wien da lebt man billig "'S ist nöt wahr"	No. 161	Unspec.	Krämer		CHAL (1898)
7308	Sioly, Johann	1843-1911	Ja wann si' dö das g'fallen lassen "Mir kennen a paar Ehemänner"	No. 135	Unspec.	Krämer		CHAL (1898)
7309	Sioly, Johann	1843-1911	Jedes Häferl hat sein Deckerl	No. 22	Unspec.	Hof-bauer		CHAL (1898)
7310	Sioly, Johann	1843-1911	Jessa na', san mir erschrocken "Unlängst tramt uns allen Beiden"	No. 11	Unspec.	Hof-bauer		CHAL (1898)
7311	Sioly, Johann	1843-1911	Jessas nan, das bricht ihm's Gnack "Geliebte hat zur Maid"	No. 171	Unspec.	Krämer		CHAL (1898)
7312	Sioly, Johann	1843-1911	Jetzt geh'n ma in a ander's Haus "A Brautschau hab'n zwei Freund"	No. 143	Unspec.	Krämer		CHAL (1898)
7313	Sioly, Johann	1843-1911	Klassisch und Weanerisch "Was in der Sprach' der Dichterwelt"	No. 151	Unspec.	Krämer		CHAL (1898)
7314	Sioly, Johann	1843-1911	Kleine Romanze "Er hat etwas Stroh im Kopf"	No. 20	Unspec.	Hof-bauer		CHAL (1898)
7315	Sioly, Johann	1843-1911	Leichtsinnigen "Weil mir g'rad im Sommer"	No. 77	Unspec.	Krämer		CHAL (1898)
7316	Sioly, Johann	1843-1911	Mariahilfer Schwosser "Fesche Bindeln, ein' fein' Cylinder"	No. 131	Unspec.	Krämer		CHAL (1898)
7317	Sioly, Johann	1843-1911	Mir alten Weaner, mir sterb'n aus "Wenn a Weanakind von früher"	No. 159	Unspec.	Krämer		CHAL (1898)
7318	Sioly, Johann	1843-1911	Mir san aus'm Wasser "Zwei Damen, schön aufgeputzt"	No. 167	Unspec.	Krämer		CHAL (1898)
7319	Sioly, Johann	1843-1911	Mir san so viel zerstreut "So Zerstretue, wie wir Zwa"	No. 17-4	Unspec.	Krämer		CHAL (1898)
7320	Sioly, Johann	1843-1911	Mir san überall dabei "Zwa so Nasen wia dö unser'n"	No. 136	Unspec.	Krämer		CHAL (1898)
7321	Sioly, Johann	1843-1911	Mondscheinbrüder "Für uns gibt's nur a Beleuchtung"	No. 80	Unspec.	Krämer		CHAL (1898)
7322	Sioly, Johann	1843-1911	Nöt um an' Preis der Welt "Mir Zwa, mir sein sehr starke Männer"	No. 144	Unspec.	Krämer		CHAL (1898)
7323	Sioly, Johann	1843-1911	Pardon mein Fräulein, pardon mein Herr "Als Domino schwebt sie"	No. 12	Unspec.	Hof-bauer		CHAL (1898)
7324	Sioly, Johann	1843-1911	Pomali, pomali "Geg'ntheil von flott"	No. 149	Unspec.	Krämer		CHAL (1898)
7325	Sioly, Johann	1843-1911	Pschütt "Es hat nöt nur der Weaner"	No. 156	Unspec.	Krämer		CHAL (1898)

REC	COMP	DTS	TITLE	OP #	VCG	PUB	COMMENTS	SRC
7326	Sioly, Johann	1843-1911	Rauchlose Pulver "Im Jenseits der Schwarz"	No. 166	Unspec.	Krämer		CHAL (1898)
7327	Sioly, Johann	1843-1911	'S bleibt Alles, wia's war "Sonn' wird heuer grad"	No. 132	Unspec.	Krämer		CHAL (1898)
7328	Sioly, Johann	1843-1911	'S giebt fruchtbare Dichter		Unspec.	Blaha		CHAL (1901)
7329	Sioly, Johann	1843-1911	Schottenfelder Sonntagskinder "Am Schottenfeld drent"	No. 79	Unspec.	Krämer		CHAL (1898)
7330	Sioly, Johann	1843-1911	Sieben Fetten und die sieben Magern "Es ist doch aus der Bibel"	No. 173	Unspec.	Krämer		CHAL (1898)
7331	Sioly, Johann	1843-1911	Siegst es, so machst "Wann mir amal"	No. 133	Unspec.	Krämer		CHAL (1898)
7332	Sioly, Johann	1843-1911	So guat is's Geschäft no gar nia g'angen "Selcher fahrt mit'n Würstelwag'n"	No. 155	Unspec.	Krämer		CHAL (1898)
7333	Sioly, Johann	1843-1911	Stimmen aus dem Publikum "Es ist die Gasbeleuchtung"	Op. 71	Unspec.	Krämer		CHAL (1898)
7334	Sioly, Johann	1843-1911	Uns kommt's ja nöt drauf an "Mir san immer echte"	No. 177	Unspec.	Krämer		CHAL (1898)
7335	Sioly, Johann	1843-1911	Variationen über ein bekanntes Gestanzeln "'S was Alles schon da"	No. 157	Unspec.	Krämer		CHAL (1898)
7336	Sioly, Johann	1843-1911	Wann a and'rer Mensch a Unglück hat, wie kann ma denn da lachen "Es fahrt der magre Bräutigam"	No. 175	Unspec.	Krämer		CHAL (1898)
7337	Sioly, Johann	1843-1911	Was an fleissiger Mann an Vormittag alles ausrichten kann "Tischler X, der hat arbeit fast nie"	No. 165	Unspec.	Krämer		CHAL (1898)
7338	Sioly, Johann	1843-1911	Was hat er g'sagt, wia hat er g'sagt "'S stenn vor der Lotterie"	No. 169	Unspec.	Krämer		CHAL (1898)
7339	Sioly, Johann	1843-1911	Weil das a fein're Gattung is "Wann Aner auf der Strassen"	No. 13	Unspec.	Hofbauer		CHAL (1898)
7340	Sioly, Johann	1843-1911	Weni' Fleisch und viel Ban' "Wer ma' san, was ma' san"	No. 78	Unspec.	Krämer		CHAL (1898)
7341	Sioly, Johann	1843-1911	Werkelmann "An Eck dort steht a Werkelmann"	No. 140	Unspec.	Krämer		CHAL (1898)
7342	Sioly, Johann	1843-1911	Wia müasst' denn das sein "Wenn die Plunzen a Fell hätt'"	No. 146	Unspec.	Krämer		CHAL (1898)
7343	Sioly, Johann	1843-1911	Wiener Tratschereien "Neu'ste, sagt Frau Blaschke"		Unspec.	Krämer		CHAL (1898)
7344	Sioly, Johann	1843-1911	Woher nehman und nöt stehl'n "Neuche Liader"	No. 154	Unspec.	Krämer		CHAL (1898)
7345	Sioly, Johann	1843-1911	Zu Fuss und zu Pferd "Wenn Pane Schneider"	No. 15	Unspec.	Hofbauer		CHAL (1898)
7346	Sioly, Johann	1843-1911	Zuag'schnitten is's schon, jetzt darf's nur no g'naht werd'n "Duette zu bringen"	No. 142	Unspec.	Krämer		CHAL (1898)
7347	Sioly, Johann	1843-1911	Zum Nachtmahl is's uns z'weni, zu der Zausen is's uns z'viel "A recht a keckes Wecken"	No. 176	Unspec.	Krämer		CHAL (1898)
7348	Sioly, Johann	1843-1911	Zwa Weaner Pflastertreter "Weil für zwa Wiener Kinder"	No. 170	Unspec.	Krämer		CHAL (1898)
7349	Sioly-Weisberg		Da ziag'n ma die Uhr auf "Wenn wir in der Zeitung"	No. 2	Unspec.	Hofbauer		CHAL (1898)
7350	Sioly-Weisberg		Gemischte Gesellschaft aus der Theaterwelt "Hamlet, Prinz von Dänemark"	No. 5	Unspec.	Hofbauer		CHAL (1898)
7351	Sioly-Weisberg		Gute Gedanken und hinkende Ross "Rindfleisch jetzt allerweil"	No. 4	Unspec.	Hofbauer		CHAL (1898)
7352	Sioly-Weisberg		Hab'n ma erst gestern drahlt, drah'n ma heut a "Mir san zwa Solche"	No. 6	Unspec.	Hofbauer		CHAL (1898)
7353	Sioly-Weisberg		Hausierer und Zeitungsleser "So schau dass d'amal"	No. 3	Unspec.	Hofbauer		CHAL (1898)

REC	COMP	DTS	TITLE	OP #	VCG	PUB	COMMENTS	SRC
7354	Sioly-Weisberg		Im Fluge durch die Welt "Herr von Pumpus hat"	No. 8	Unspec.	Hof-bauer		CHAL (1898)
7355	Sioly-Weisberg		Jetzt geht's am stärksten "A Wahl, die war"	No. 7	Unspec.	Hof-bauer		CHAL (1898)
7356	Sioly-Weisberg		Unter der Kanon "Z'erst ist die Marianka"	No. 10	Unspec.	Hof-bauer		CHAL (1898)
7357	Sioly-Weisberg		Wart i sag's mein grosser Bruader "Wann die Buam"	No. 1	Unspec.	Hof-bauer		CHAL (1898)
7358	Sioly-Weisberg		Weg'n an anzigen Wort "Wann man zum Altar tritt"	No. 9	Unspec.	Hof-bauer		CHAL (1898)
7359	Sirsch, R.		Herz mein Herz sei nicht beklommen	Op. 25 No. 1	S/A or S/S	Peters		CHAL (1906)
7360	Sjogren, Emil	1853-1918	O, Kom Med Mig I Stjarneglans!		Unspec.	Lundq.		CVMP (1976)
7361	Skerjanc, Lucijan Marija	1900-	Sest Mladinskih Pesmi		Unspec.	Drzavna	Serbo-Croatian woman comp. For 1-2 v. Unspec. pieces.	CVMP (1976)
7362	Skop, V. E.		Messe zu Ehren der seligsten Jungfrau	Op. 9	S/A	Böhm & S.	org accomp.	CHAL (1898)
7363	Slunicko, Jan	1852-1923	Blumen thun die Augen auf	Op. 39 No. 2	Unspec.	Böhm & S.		CHAL (1901)
7364	Slunicko, Jan	1852-1923	Du frischer, heller Frühlingswind	Op. 39 No. 5	Unspec.	Böhm & S.		CHAL (1901)
7365	Slunicko, Jan	1852-1923	Einer letzten Glocke Klang	Op. 39 No. 4	Unspec.	Böhm & S.		CHAL (1901)
7366	Slunicko, Jan	1852-1923	Im Hag nah bei des Bächleins Lauf	Op. 39 No. 3	Unspec.	Böhm & S.		CHAL (1901)
7367	Slunicko, Jan	1852-1923	O singe Kind, aus voller Brust	Op. 39 No. 1	Unspec.	Böhm & S.		CHAL (1901)
7368	Slunicko, Jan	1852-1923	Vom Land Litalien komm ich her	Op. 39 No. 6	Unspec.	Böhm & S.		CHAL (1901)
7369	Smart, Henry	1813-1879	Come sail, my barque is waiting for thee		Unspec.	Curwen		BBC (1975)
7370	Smart, Henry	1813-1879	Evening		2 high v.	Church	In anthology "Sacred Duets A Collection of Two-Part Songs by the Best Com-posers" Vol. 1. Compi. & ed. W. Shakespeare. Pub. 1907.	MSN
7371	Smart, Henry	1813-1879	Evening		high & low v.	Church	In anthology "Sacred Duets A Collection of Two-Part Songs by the Best Com-posers" Vol. 2. Compi. & ed. W. Shakespeare. Pub. 1907.	MSN
7372	Smart, Henry	1813-1879	Faint not, fear not, God is near thee		high & low v.	Church	In anthology "Sacred Duets A Collection of Two-Part Songs by the Best Com-posers" Vol. 2. Compi. & ed. W. Shakespeare. Pub. 1907.	MSN
7373	Smart, Henry	1813-1879	Faint Not, Fear Not, God is Near Thee		S/A or A/T or S/Br	Church	In anthology "Sacred Duets for High and low Voices" Vol. 2 Pub. 1907.	NATS-SVD
7374	Smart, Henry	1813-1879	Hark! The goat-bells are ringing		Unspec.	Curwen		BBC (1975)
7375	Smart, Henry	1813-1879	How sighs the gale of morning		Unspec.	Curwen		BBC (1975)
7376	Smart, Henry	1813-1879	In the greenwood		Unspec.	Curwen		BBC (1975)
7377	Smart, Henry	1813-1879	Lord is my Shepherd		S/A	G. Schirm.	In anthology "Album of Six-teen Sacred Duets" (no date)	MSN
7378	Smart, Henry	1813-1879	Lord is My Shepherd, The		S/A	Ditson	In anthology "Choice Sacred Duets for All Voices" Pub. 1936.	MSN

REC	COMP	DTS	TITLE	OP #	VCG	PUB	COMMENTS	SRC
7379	Smart, Henry	1813-1879	Lord is my Shepherd, The		2 high v.	Church	In anthology "Sacred Duets A Collection of Two-Part Songs by the Best Composers" Vol. 1. Compi. & ed. W. Shakespeare. Pub. 1907.	MSN
7380	Smart, Henry	1813-1879	Lord is my Shepherd, The		high & low v.	Church	In anthology "Sacred Duets A Collection of Two-Part Songs by the Best Composers" Vol. 2. Compi. & ed. W. Shakespeare. Pub. 1907.	MSN
7381	Smart, Henry	1813-1879	Lord is My Shepherd, The		S/A	G. Schirm.		ASR
7382	Smart, Henry	1813-1879	Lord is my Shepherd, The		S/A	White-Smith	In catalogue page "Vocal Duetts" of White-Smith Music Pub. Co. (no date)	MSN
7383	Smart, Henry	1813-1879	Lord is my Shepherd, The		S/A	G. Schirm.	pf or org accomp. In catalogue page "Sacred Vocal Duets" of G. Schirmer, Inc. NY (no date)	MSN
7384	Smart, Henry	1813-1879	Lord is My Shepherd, The		S/A or S/MS	G. Schirm.	Also in anthology "Album of Sixteen Sacred Duets for Various Voices" (Schirmer). Pub. 1880 et al.	NATS-SVD
7385	Smart, Henry	1813-1879	My Boat is Waiting Here for Thee		high & low v.	Hinds, Hayden & Eldredge	In anthology "The Most Popular Vocal Duets" Ed. Dr. E. J. Biedermann. Pub. 1914.	MSN
7386	Smart, Henry	1813-1879	Sabbath Bell, The		high & low v.	Church	In anthology "Sacred Duets A Collection of Two-Part Songs by the Best Composers" Vol. 2. Compi. & ed. W. Shakespeare. Pub. 1907.	MSN
7387	Smart, Henry	1813-1879	Sailing Away		S/A	Ditson	In anthology "Soprano and Alto Duets" Ed. H. Kiehl. Pub. 1901.	MSN
7388	Smart, Henry	1778-1823	The Lord is My Shepherd		S/A	G. Schirm.		MSN
7389	Smart, Henry	1813-1879	There was joy in Heaven		high & low v.	Church	In anthology "Sacred Duets A Collection of Two-Part Songs by the Best Composers" Vol. 2. Compi. & ed. W. Shakespeare. Pub. 1907.	MSN
7390	Smart, Henry	1813-1879	Vox Matutina		high & low v.	Church	In anthology "Sacred Duets A Collection of Two-Part Songs by the Best Composers" Vol. 2. Compi. & ed. W. Shakespeare. Pub. 1907.	MSN
7391	Smart, Henry	1813-1879	Vox Matutina		S/A or A/T or S/Br	Church	In anthology "Sacred Duets for High and low Voices" Vol. 2. Pub. 1907.	NATS-SVD
7392	Smart, Henry	1813-1879	When brighter suns and milder skies		high & low v.	Church	In anthology "Sacred Duets A Collection of Two-Part Songs by the Best Composers" Vol. 2. Compi. & ed. W. Shakespeare. Pub. 1907.	MSN
7393	Smart, Henry	1813-1879	When Brighter Suns and Milder Skies		S/A or A/T or S/Br	Church	In anthology "Sacred Duets for High and low Voices" Vol. 2. Pub. 1907	NATS-SVD
7394	Smart, Henry	1813-1879	When the Shadow is Passing		S/A	Ditson	In anthology "Soprano and Alto Duets" Ed. H. Kiehl. Pub. 1901.	MSN
7395	Smart, Henry	1813-1879	When the wind blows in from the sea		Unspec.	Davison		BBC (1975)

REC	COMP	DTS	TITLE	OP #	VCG	PUB	COMMENTS	SRC
7396	Smart, Henry	1813-1879	Where the Weary are at Rest		high & low v.	Church	In anthology "Sacred Duets A Collection of Two-Part Songs by the Best Composers" Vol. 2. Compi. & ed. W. Shakespeare. Pub. 1907.	MSN
7397	Smit, Leo	1921-	La Mort (3)		S/A	Donemus	3 duets	ASR
7398	Smit, Leo	1921-	La Mort des Amants		S/A	Donemus	In "La Mort"	CVMP (1976)
7399	Smit, Leo	1921-	La Mort des Artistes		S/A	Donemus	In "La Mort"	CVMP (1976)
7400	Smit, Leo	1921-	La Mort des Pauvres		S/A	Donemus	In "La Mort"	CVMP (1976)
7401	Smith, Alice Mary	1839-1884	Maying		S/A	Bayley & Ferguson	Eng. woman comp.	BBC (1975)
7402	Smith, Alice Mary	1839-1884	O That We Two Were Maying		Unspec.	Brainard's Sons	Eng. woman comp . In anthology "Brainard's Collection of Vocal Duets from Popular Modern and Standard Composers" Pub. 1903.	MSN
7403	Smith, H. Arnold		The pitcher		Unspec.	Boosey		BBC (1975)
7404	Smith, Lilian		The cloud house		Unspec.	Cramer	Eng. woman comp.	BBC (1975)
7405	Smith, Seymour		Where are you going to, my pretty maid?		Unspec.	Pitman Hart		BBC (1975)
7406	Söchting, Emil	1858-	Kommst du wieder schönster aller Tage		Unspec.	Simon i. Berl.		CHAL (1906)
7407	Södermann, Johan August	1832-1876	Bröllops-Marsch "Vom Himmel leuchtet	Op. 13 No. c	high & low v.	Simon i. Berl.		CHAL (1898)
7408	Sodermann, Johan August	1832-1876	Brollopsmarsch		Unspec.	Lundq.		CVMP (1976)
7409	Sodermann, Johan August	1832-1876	Fjarran Ovan Stjarnor Alla		S/MS	Gehrmans		CVMP (1976)
7410	Solbrück, C.		Abschied "Was soll ich erst kaufen"	Op. 10 No. 5	Unspec.	Weinholtz		CHAL (1898)
7411	Solbrück, C.		Erlösung "Vor meines Mädchens Fenster"	Op. 10 No. 6	Unspec.	Niemeyer		CHAL (1898)
7412	Solbrück, C.		Es fliegt manch' Vöglein in der Nacht	Op. 10 No. 2	S/S	Weinholtz		CHAL (1898)
7413	Solbrück, C.		Gekommen ist der Maie	Op. 10 No. 3	S/S	Weinholtz		CHAL (1898)
7414	Solbrück, C.		Höhen und Thäler "Mein Mädchen wohnt"	Op. 10 No. 4	Unspec.	Weinholtz		CHAL (1898)
7415	Solbrück, C.		Wundert's dich "Wenn die Bäume grünen"	Op. 10 No. 1	S/S	Weinholtz		CHAL (1898)
7416	Soler, Joseph	1935-	Stunden Buch, Das		S/S	Biol		CVMP (1995)
7417	Söllner, E.		Wir Rastelbinder sind bekannt		Unspec.	Danner		CHAL (1911)
7418	Solomon, John	1856-	After the honeymoon		Unspec.	F. D. & H.		BBC (1975)
7419	Somervell, Arthur	1863-1937	Two doves on the self same branch		S/A	Boosey		BBC (1975)
7420	Somervell, Arthur	1863-1937	Under the greenwood tree		Unspec.	Boosey	In anthology "Duet Album for High and Medium Voices" sel. & ed. V. Morris & V. Anderson. Pub. 1944.	BBC (1975)

REC	COMP	DTS	TITLE	OP #	VCG	PUB	COMMENTS	SRC
7421	Somervell, Arthur	1863-1937	Under the Greenwood Tree		S/S or S/MS	Boosey	In anthology "Duet Album for High and Medium Voices" sel. & ed. V. Morris & V. Anderson. Pub. 1944	NATS-VCD
7422	Sor, Fernando [Sors]	1778-1839	Alla stagion novella	No. 3	Unspec.	Peters		CHAL (1901)
7423	Sor, Fernando [Sors]	1778-1839	Con vanto menzognero	No. 1	Unspec.	Peters		CHAL (1901)
7424	Sor, Fernando [Sors]	1778-1839	O che felici pianti	No. 2	Unspec.	Peters		CHAL (1901)
7425	Sowerby, Leo	1895-1968	Snow Lay on the Ground, The		high & low v.	Gray	acap.? accomp. unspec. May be perf. chorally	ASR
7426	Sowinsky, A. Wojcieh [Albert]	1805?-1880	Noch ist Polen nicht verlorn		Unspec.	Schott		CHAL (1898)
7427	Spahn, Adolf	1878-	Als frischgebackne junge Eheleut		Unspec.	Fr. Dietrich		CHAL (1911)
7428	Spahn, Adolf	1878-	Als Hausfrau heisst es immer	Op. 78	2 female v.	Fr. Dietrich		CHAL (1906)
7429	Spahn, Adolf	1878-	Fräulein Adelheid, ich bitt' se		2 female v.	Frz. Dietrich		CHAL (1911)
7430	Spahn, Adolf	1878-	Sag' mir Cousinchen, was du liest "Spiel-Duett"		Unspec.	Fr. Dietrich		CHAL (1911)
7431	Spahn, Adolf	1878-	Verehrtes Publikum, Sie werden entschuld'gen	No. 1	Unspec.	André		CHAL (1901)
7432	Spahn, Adolf	1878-	Wir zwei, wir leben in der Welt	No. 1	Unspec.	Fr. Dietrich		CHAL (1901)
7433	Spahn, Adolf	1878-	Wo nur meine gute Schulzen wieder bleibt		2 female v.	Frz. Dietrich		CHAL (1911)
7434	Spahn, Adolf	1878-	Zwei strenge Wächter des Gesetzes		Unspec.	Frz. Dietrich		CHAL (1911)
7435	Sparhakel, A.		Dass wir halt echte Weaner san		Unspec.	Eberle i. Wien		CHAL (1901)
7436	Speaks, Oley	1874-1948	Morning		S/Br or S/A	G. Schirm.	Arr. C. Deis. In catalogue page "Selected Vocal Duets" of G. Schirmer, Inc. NY (no date)	MSN
7437	Speaks, Oley	1874-1948	Prayer Perfect, The		Unspec.	Allans	Also solo	CVMP (1976)
7438	Speaks, Oley	1874-1948	Prayer Perfect, The		S/Br or S/A	G. Schirm.	In anthology "Schirmer's Favorite Sacred Duets for Various Voices" Pub. 1955	MSN
7439	Speaks, Oley	1874-1948	Prayer, Perfect, The		S/Br or S/A	G. Schirm.	pf or org accomp. In catalogue page "Sacred Vocal Duets" of G. Schirmer, Inc. NY (no date)	MSN
7440	Speaks, Oley	1874-1948	Sylvia		S/Br or S/A	G. Schirm.	Arr. C. Deis. In catalogue page "Selected Vocal Duets" of G. Schirmer, Inc. NY (no date)	MSN
7441	Speiser, Wilhelm	1873-	Nein, es ist nicht zu ertragen	Op. 122	2 female v.	G. Richter i. L.		CHAL (1911)
7442	Spengler, Ludwig	1840-1909	Hand in Hand mit heil'gem Beten		S/A	Oppenheimer	org or pf or harm	CHAL (1911)
7443	Spielter, Hermann	1860-1925	Hüte dich "Nachtigall hüte dich"	Op. 39 No. 2	S/A or S/Br	Luckhardt		CHAL (1898)

REC	COMP	DTS	TITLE	OP #	VCG	PUB	COMMENTS	SRC
7444	Spielter, Hermann	1860-1925	Mit dem Bäumen spielt der Wind	Op. 39 No. 3	S/A or S/Br	Luckhardt		CHAL (1898)
7445	Spielter, Hermann	1860-1925	Nachtigall singt überall	Op. 39 No. 1	S/A or S/Br	Luckhardt		CHAL (1898)
7446	Spohr, Louis	1784-1859	Abendlied	Op. 108 No. 1	S/S or S/MS or MS/MS	Simrock	In "Drei Duetten für zwei Sopran" Op. 108. Pub. 1840.	NATS-VCD
7447	Spohr, Louis	1784-1859	Abendlied "Stille Nacht"	Op. 108 No. 1	S/S	Simrock		CHAL (1898)
7448	Spohr, Louis	1784-1859	Children, pray this love to cherish		2 high v.	Church	Eng. trans. Grmn. In anth. "Sacred Duets A Coll. of 2-Part Songs by the Best Comps." Vol. 1. Compi. & ed. W. Shakespeare. Pub. 1907.	MSN
7449	Spohr, Louis	1784-1859	Das Herz	Op. 108 No. 2	S/S or S/MS or MS/MS	Simrock	In "Drei Duetten für zwei Sopran" Op. 108. Pub. 1840.	NATS-VCD
7450	Spohr, Louis	1784-1859	Forsake me not		2 high v.	Church	Eng. trans. Grmn. In anth. "Sacred Duets A Coll. of 2-Part Songs by the Best Comps." Vol. 1. Compi. & ed. W. Shakespeare. Pub. 1907.	MSN
7451	Spohr, Louis	1784-1859	Herz "Es sehnt sich das Herz"	Op. 108 No. 2	S/S	Simrock		CHAL (1898)
7452	Spohr, Louis	1784-1859	Mein Heimathland "Wo reiner Liebe gold'ne Strahlen"		Unspec.	B. & B.		CHAL (1898)
7453	Spohr, Louis	1784-1859	Mein Heimathland "Wo reiner Liebe gold'ne Strahlen"		S/A	B. & H.	In anth. "Zweistim. Lied. f. Sop. u. Altstimme mit Klavierbegleitung f. den Haus- u. Schulgebrauch v. H. M. Schletterer" 3 vols.	MSN
7454	Spohr, Louis	1784-1859	Ruhe	Op. 108 No. 3	S/S or S/MS or MS/MS	Simrock	In "Drei Duetten für zwei Sopran" Op. 108. Pub. 1840.	NATS-VCD
7455	Spohr, Louis	1784-1859	Ruhe "Wenn im letzten Dämm'rungsstrahle"	Op. 108 No. 3	S/S	Simrock	Pub. 1839	CHAL (1898)
7456	Sponholtz, Adolf Heinrich	1803-1852	Wenn still mit seinen letzten Flammen	Op. 38	MS/MS	Sch. & Co.		CHAL (1898)
7457	Spontini, Gasparo	1774-1851	Abschied "Thränen, ach Thränen"	No. 2	Unspec.	B. & B.		CHAL (1898)
7458	Spontini, Gasparo	1774-1851	Borussia "Wo ist das Volk, das kühn von That"		Unspec.	Schlesinger		CHAL (1898)
7459	Spontini, Gasparo	1774-1851	Herzenssprache "Ende, ende, ich hab' errathen"	No. 3	Unspec.	B. & B.		CHAL (1898)
7460	Spontini, Gasparo	1774-1851	Liebesqual "Von all' meinen Leiden"	No. 1	Unspec.	B. & B.		CHAL (1898)
7461	Spontini, Gasparo	1774-1851	Nocturni (3) f. 2 Singstimmen		Unspec.	B. & B.	3 duets	CHAL (1898)
7462	Springer, Max	1877-1954	Meer liegt glatt	Op. 12 No. 7	Unspec.	Coppenrath	pf or harm	CHAL (1911)
7463	Squire, William Henry	1871-1963	Mountain Lovers		Unspec.	Boosey	Also solo	CVMP (1976)
7464	Squire, William Henry	1871-1963	My prayer		Unspec.	Boosey		BBC (1975)
7465	Squire, William Henry	1871-1963	Singing Lesson		Unspec.	Boosey		CVMP (1976)

REC	COMP	DTS	TITLE	OP #	VCG	PUB	COMMENTS	SRC
7466	Squire, William Henry	1871-1963	The harbour lights		Unspec.	Boosey		BBC (1975)
7467	Squire, William Henry	1871-1963	The singing lesson		Unspec.	Boosey		BBC (1975)
7468	Stacey, Gilbert		Down in the gardens at Kew		Unspec.	A. H. & C.		BBC (1975)
7469	Stafford, C. Lloyd		Watchman, what of the night?		Unspec.	Bayley & Ferguson		BBC (1975)
7470	Stainer, John	1840-1901	God So Loved the World		2 high v.	R. D. Row	org or pf acc. In anth. "Sacred Duet Masterpieces..." Vol. 3. Compi. & ed. C. Fredrickson. Pub. 1961.	MSN
7471	Stainer, John	1840-1901	Love Divine! all love excelling		2 high v.	Church	In anthology "Sacred Duets A Collection of Two-Part Songs by the Best Composers" Vol. 1. Compi. & ed. W. Shakespeare. Pub. 1907.	MSN
7472	Stainlein, Louis von	1819-1867	Frühlingsgesänge (2)	Op. 17	2 female v.	Werner i. Münch.	2 duets	CHAL (1898)
7473	Stainlein, Louis von	1819-1867	Im April	Op. 17 No. 1	2 female v.	Werner i. Münch.		CHAL (1898)
7474	Stainlein, Louis von	1819-1867	Morgenwanderung	Op. 17 No. 2	2 female v.	Werner i. Münch.		CHAL (1898)
7475	Standke, Otto	1832-1885	Am Geburtstage der Mutter "Welche Freude, welche Wonne"	Op. 20 No. 2	Unspec.	Standke i. Bonn		CHAL (1898)
7476	Standke, Otto	1832-1885	Am Geburtstage des Vaters "Sei o Tag uns gegrüsst"	Op. 20 No. 1	Unspec.	Standke i. Bonn		CHAL (1898)
7477	Standke, Otto	1832-1885	Geburtstagslieder (2)	Op. 20	Unspec.	Standke i. Bonn	2 birthday duets	CHAL (1898)
7478	Stanford, Charles Villiers	1852-1924	A carol of bells		Unspec.	Enoch		BBC (1975)
7479	Stanford, Charles Villiers	1852-1924	Lark's Grave, The		Unspec.	Roberton	pf or orch accomp.	CVMP (1976)
7480	Stanford, Charles Villiers	1852-1924	Larks's Grave		Unspec.	Roberton	pf or orch accomp.	ASR
7481	Stange, Max	1856-1932	Abend so schön	Op. 19 No. 3	Unspec.	Wernthal		CHAL (1906)
7482	Stange, Max	1856-1932	Abendroth säumte mit Purpur	Op. 91 No. 1	Unspec.	Wernthal		CHAL (1906)
7483	Stange, Max	1856-1932	Aus grünenden Hecken schallt süsser Gesang	Op. 84 No. 5	MS/A	Rahter		CHAL (1901)
7484	Stange, Max	1856-1932	Das ist ein frohes Wandern	Op. 84 No. 2	MS/A	Rahter		CHAL (1901)
7485	Stange, Max	1856-1932	Ein Bächlein spricht zum andern	Op. 84 No. 4	MS/A	Rahter		CHAL (1901)
7486	Stange, Max	1856-1932	In der Fremde "Heil'ge Sonntagsstille"	Op. 49 No. 1	S/A	R. & P.		CHAL (1898)
7487	Stange, Max	1856-1932	Leise, leise durch die Wipfel	Op. 84 No. 3	MS/A	Rahter		CHAL (1901)
7488	Stange, Max	1856-1932	Maiklänge "Blätterspitzen im dunklen Hain"	Op. 49 No. 2	S/A	R. & P.		CHAL (1898)
7489	Stange, Max	1856-1932	Noch rauschen die Quellen	Op. 19 No. 5	Unspec.	Wernthal		CHAL (1906)
7490	Stange, Max	1856-1932	Nun ist es Abend worden	Op. 84 No. 1	MS/A	Rahter		CHAL (1901)

REC	COMP	DTS	TITLE	OP #	VCG	PUB	COMMENTS	SRC
7491	Stange, Max	1856-1932	Nun nimm die Pracht	Op. 19 No. 2	Unspec.	Wern-thal		CHAL (1906)
7492	Stange, Max	1856-1932	Über stillen Wassern glänzt des Mondes Pracht	Op. 19 No. 4	Unspec.	Wern-thal		CHAL (1906)
7493	Stange, Max	1856-1932	Verwundet "Bitt' ihn o Mutter"	Op. 49 No. 3	S/A	R. & P.		CHAL (1898)
7494	Stange, Max	1856-1932	Voglein im Walde	Op. 54 No. 3	S/A	Ditson	In anthology "Sopra-no and Alto Duets" Ed. H. Kiehl. Pub. 1901.	MSN
7495	Stange, Max	1856-1932	Vöglein im Walde "Lustiges Vöglein im Walde"	Op. 54 No. 3	S/A	R. & P.		CHAL (1898)
7496	Stange, Max	1856-1932	Wer sagt wohl, dass dem Vögelein	Op. 54 No. 2	S/A	R. & P.		CHAL (1898)
7497	Stange, Max	1856-1932	Zweifach Leiden "Ach wie ein zweifach bittres Leid"	Op. 54 No. 1	S/A	R. & P.		CHAL (1898)
7498	Stanislas, A.		Es sitzen zwei Engelein Hand in Hand	Op. 27	2 female v.	Harmon-ie i. B.		CHAL (1906)
7499	Starck, L.		Du isch gar a herzig Wörtle	IV No. 1	Unspec.	C. Rühle i. L.	Arr. Necke	CHAL (1901)
7500	Starck, L.		Mädele guck raus, guck raus	IV No. 2	Unspec.	C. Rühle i. L.	Arr. Necke	CHAL (1901)
7501	Starck, W.		Nun breitet ihre dunklen Flügel	Op. 6 No. 1	S/A or S/Br	Stahl		CHAL (1901)
7502	Stark, Ludwig	1831-1884	Am Morgen "Es taget in dem Osten"	Op. 52 No. 1	S/A	Aibl		CHAL (1898)
7503	Stark, Ludwig	1831-1884	An die Welle "Gehab' dich wohl, du kleine Welle"	Op. 52 No. 4	S/A	Aibl		CHAL (1898)
7504	Stark, Ludwig	1831-1884	Denkspruch "Lass den Grabgesang tönen"	Op. 52 No. 2	S/A	Aibl		CHAL (1898)
7505	Stark, Ludwig	1831-1884	Frühlingsfeier "Blätter und Blüthen hauchen so warm"		S/S	Bos-worth		CHAL (1898)
7506	Stark, Ludwig	1831-1884	Sängers Trost "Weint auch einst kein Liebchen"	Op. 52 No. 3	S/A	Aibl		CHAL (1898)
7507	Starke, Gustav	1862-1931	Schnurrige Begebenheit "Vor dem Thore steh'n die Mädchen"		S/A	Kahnt		CHAL (1898)
7508	Starke, H.		Gigerl Geck und Schneider Meck "Ach so ein Gigerl sein"	Op. 500	Unspec.	Starke i. Bresl.		CHAL (1898)
7509	Starke, J.		So hab' ich doch die ganze Woche	Op. 27	Unspec.	P. Fisch-er i. F.		CHAL (1906)
7510	Steffens, Gustav	1842-1912	Das war für die Leut' eine goldne Zeit "Wie sich der alte Deutsche noch"		Unspec.	K. & G.		CHAL (1898)
7511	Steffens, Gustav	1842-1912	Rätschel-Duett "Am Dönhofsplatz prangt stolz"		Unspec.	K. & G.		CHAL (1898)
7512	Steffens, Gustav	1842-1912	Wir Wesen vom zarten Ge-schlecht "Wenn wir die Männer"		2 female v.	K. & G.		CHAL (1898)
7513	Stehle, J. Gustav Eduard	1839-1915	Altes Weihnachtslied "In dulci jubilo"	Op. 53 No. 2	Unspec.	Schwend-imann		CHAL (1898)
7514	Stehle, J. Gustav Eduard	1839-1915	Weihnachts "Über Wald und Strom"	Op. 53 No. 1	Unspec.	Schwend-imann		CHAL (1898)
7515	Steiber, P.		Weit ist die Emancipation des Weibes vorgeschritten	Op. 32	2 female v.	Oppen-heimer		CHAL (1906)
7516	Steidl, F.		Hatschi, Prosit "Beim Hindernissrennen haben wir"		Unspec.	Haushahn i. L.		CHAL (1898)
7517	Steidl-Duette		Influenza-Couplet "Vom Westen bis zum Osten"	No. 4	Unspec.	Fr. Dietrich		CHAL (1898)
7518	Stein, C. [prob. Karl]	1824-1902	Du Kindlein an der Krippe		Unspec.	Michael-is i. N.	Ed. Seidel	CHAL (1906)

REC	COMP	DTS	TITLE	OP #	VCG	PUB	COMMENTS	SRC
7519	Stein, C. [prob. Karl]	1824-1902	Heimathlied	Op. 5 No. 1	S/A	Stein i. Potsd.		CHAL (1898)
7520	Stein, C. [prob. Karl]	1824-1902	Herr, deine Güte reicht so weit	No. 14	Unspec.	Schergens		CHAL (1906)
7521	Stein, C. [prob. Karl]	1824-1902	In diesen bangen Tagen	Op. 5 No. 2	S/A	Stein i. Potsd.		CHAL (1898)
7522	Stein, C. [prob. Karl]	1824-1902	Wohin wir immer wallen	No. 19	Unspec.	Schergens		CHAL (1906)
7523	Stein, Josef	1845-1915	Missa in honorem St. Ignatii	Op. 55	S/A	Coppenrath	org accomp.	CHAL (1898)
7524	Stein, V.		Ach kehr' zurück		Unspec.	B. & B.		CHAL (1898)
7525	Steinecke, A.		Als armes 25 Pfg.-Stückl		Unspec.	Mignon-Verlag		CHAL (1911)
7526	Steinhart, W. W.		Liebesqual "Sie lehnt traurig an dem Fenster"	Op. 34	S/A	Bosworth		CHAL (1898)
7527	Steinhart, W. W.		Trinklied "Wirth, der hat ein Fässlein"	Op. 29	Unspec.	Bosworth		CHAL (1898)
7528	Steinitzer, M. [prob. Max]	1864-	Liebes Mägdelein sieh doch freundlich drein	No. 2	Unspec.	Schmid i. M.		CHAL (1906)
7529	Steinkühler, Emil	1824-1872	Glockentöne		S/A	Beyer i. Düsseld.		CHAL (1898)
7530	Steizhammer		Flöckerl "Mein Bua had a Fel"		Unspec.	Schlesinger		CHAL (1898)
7531	Steizhammer		Närrisch Liab "I hán di liebá"		Unspec.	Schlesinger		CHAL (1898)
7532	Stekel, W.		Das war ein niedliches Zeiselein	No. 6	S/A	Bosworth		CHAL (1911)
7533	Stekel, W.		Grosse Kinderlieder und Kinderduette (10)		Unspec.	Bosworth	Collection of 10 children's songs & duets	CHAL (1911)
7534	Stekel, W.		Grosse Loch, wie kam es doch	No. 8	S/A	Bosworth		CHAL (1911)
7535	Stekel, W.		Ich bin der kleine Zeisig	No. 10	S/A	Bosworth		CHAL (1911)
7536	Sterkel, Johann F. X.	1750-1817	Graf und die Bäuerin "Komm Dirne mit"		Unspec.	B. & H.		CHAL (1898)
7537	Sterkel, Johann F. X.	1750-1817	Gräfin und der Hirt "Verschmähter Hirtenjunge"		Unspec.	B. & H.		CHAL (1898)
7538	Stern, Hermann	1901-	Hinunter ist der Sonnen schein		S/A or S/M	Hänssler-Verlag	Pub. 1963	NATS-SVD
7539	Stern, Julius	1820-1883	Altitalienisches Lied "Warum eillst du andre"	Op. 15 No. 3a	high & low v.	Heinr.		CHAL (1898)
7540	Stern, Julius	1820-1883	Botschaft "Mein Gruss, er kömmt gezogen"	Op. 15 No. 2a	high & low v.	Heinr.		CHAL (1898)
7541	Stern, Julius	1820-1883	Ehe ist ein schöner Stand "Frauerl, das er heimgeführt"		Unspec.	Robitschek		CHAL (1898)
7542	Stern, Julius	1820-1883	Soldaten-Abschied "Morgen marschiren wir"	Op. 15 I No. a	high & low v.	Heinr.		CHAL (1898)
7543	Stern, S.		Waldvöglein "Vöglein hat ein schönes Loos"	Op. 16	S/A	B. & B.		CHAL (1898)
7544	Steven, G.		Unsre neuen Frauen "Ei guten Abend Dora"	Op. 13	MS/A	Zweifel & Weber		CHAL (1898)
7545	Stieber, P.		Ach, wir armen Schwiegermütter	Op. 14	S/A	Siegel		CHAL (1906)
7546	Stieber, P.		Ein Mädchen ging zum grünnen Wald		Unspec.	Siegel		CHAL (1906)
7547	Stieber, P.		Friederike und Ulrike, die beiden Kaffeeschwestern "Ein Hochzeitsvortrag"	Op. 42	2 female v.	Oppenheimer		CHAL (1906)

REC	COMP	DTS	TITLE	OP #	VCG	PUB	COMMENTS	SRC
7548	Stieber, P.		Frühling ist es wieder	Op. 25 No. 8	Unspec.	Siegel		CHAL (1906)
7549	Stieber, P.		Im Walde möcht' ich leben	Op. 25 No. 4	Unspec.	Siegel		CHAL (1906)
7550	Stieber, P.		Im Walde zieh' ich wohlgemuth	Op. 25 No. 3	Unspec.	Siegel		CHAL (1906)
7551	Stieber, P.		Liebchen komm, tanz mit mir	Op. 25 No. 2	Unspec.	Siegel		CHAL (1906)
7552	Stieber, P.		So lieblich lacht am Morgen	Op. 25 No. 5	Unspec.	Siegel		CHAL (1906)
7553	Stieber, P.		Wie ist der Abend so traulich	Op. 25 No. 6	Unspec.	Siegel		CHAL (1906)
7554	Stieber, P.		Wie ist der Himmel doch so blau	Op. 25 No. 1	Unspec.	Siegel		CHAL (1906)
7555	Stiegmann, Eduard	1880-	Wenn die Sonne traut	I No. 11	Unspec.	C. Rühle i. L.		CHAL (1901)
7556	Stiehl, Karl	1826-1911	Es ist der Wald aus seinen Träumen erwacht"	Op. 3 No. 2n	Unspec.	Cranz		CHAL (1898)
7557	Stiehl, Karl	1826-1911	Wanderlied "Vögel singen, Blumen blüh'n"	Op. 3 No. 1	Unspec.	Cranz		CHAL (1898)
7558	Stiehl, Karl	1826-1911	Winter ade, Scheiden thut weh	Op. 3 No. 3	Unspec.	Cranz		CHAL (1898)
7559	Stöbe, Paul	1863-	Zweigesang "Im Fliederbusch ein Vöglein sass"		Unspec.	Protze		CHAL (1898)
7560	Stock, Ed.		Wenn das Geschäft man schliesst		Unspec.	P. Fischer i. Berl.		CHAL (1901)
7561	Stockhausen, Karlheinz	1928-	Im Himmel Wandre Ich…		Unspec.	Stockhaus	acap.	CVMP (1985)
7562	Stockhausen, Karlheinz	1928-	Im Himmel wandre ich… (Indianerlieder)	Op. 36 1/2	Unspec.	Stockhausen-Verlag	acap. Based on Native American poetry. Uses contemporary notation. Edition contains explanation of work.	MSN
7563	Stöger, A.		Salon-Schnadahüpf'l "Schö' langsam, schö' langsam"		Unspec.	Attenkofer i. Landsh.		CHAL (1898)
7564	Stöger, A.		Salon-Schnadahüpf'l "Solchi, die mer a vor Damen"		Unspec.	Attenkofer i. Landsh.		CHAL (1898)
7565	Stokhausen, E. v.		Irische Volkslieder		Unspec.	B. & H.		CHAL (1901)
7566	Stolberg-Stolberg, L.		Du zarte Ros' im Morgenthau		Unspec.	Klemm		CHAL (1898)
7567	Storch, Anton M.	1813-1888	Auf dem grüner Rasen, wo die Veilchen blühn	Op. 136 No. 3	Unspec.	Cranz		CHAL (1898)
7568	Storch, Anton M.	1813-1888	Frohsinn "Wenn ich ein Vöglein seh"	Op. 136 No. 6	Unspec.	Cranz		CHAL (1898)
7569	Storch, Anton M.	1813-1888	Frühling "Heraus, heraus ihr Kinder"	Op. 136 No. 1	Unspec.	Cranz		CHAL (1898)
7570	Storch, Anton M.	1813-1888	Frühlingsbotschaft "Kuckuck, Kuckuck ruft aus dem Wald"	Op. 136 No. 2	Unspec.	Cranz		CHAL (1898)
7571	Storch, Anton M.	1813-1888	Kleinen Soldaten "Auf, auf, ihr Knaben"	Op. 136 No. 4	Unspec.	Cranz		CHAL (1898)
7572	Storch, Anton M.	1813-1888	Macht Gottes "Meer ist tief, das Meer ist weit"	Op. 136 No. 5	Unspec.	Cranz		CHAL (1898)
7573	Storch, Anton M.	1813-1888	Mühle "Es klappert die Mühle"	Op. 136 No. 7	Unspec.	Cranz		CHAL (1898)
7574	Storch, Anton M.	1813-1888	Postillon "Postillon ist ein glücklicher Mann"	Op. 136 No. 8	Unspec.	Cranz		CHAL (1898)

REC	COMP	DTS	TITLE	OP #	VCG	PUB	COMMENTS	SRC
7575	Storch, Anton M.	1813-1888	Renouveau "Hiver fuit la plaine"		S/A	Cranz		CHAL (1898)
7576	Storch, Anton M.	1813-1888	Schiffer	Op. 112	Unspec.	Cranz		CHAL (1898)
7577	Strand, Tor		Julesang		S/A	Noton	pf or org accomp.	CVMP (1995)
7578	Strauch, Fr.		O grüsset sie	Op. 12	S/S	Linke i. Sorau		CHAL (1898)
7579	Straus, Oscar	1870-1954	Aus leuchtenden Parketten	Op. 80	S/S	Harmonie i. B.		CHAL (1906)
7580	Straus, Oscar	1870-1954	Ringelringelrosenkranz ich tanz' mit meiner Frau	Op. 61	Unspec.	Bloch		CHAL (1901)
7581	Straus, Oscar	1870-1954	Wir Schwestern zwei, wir holden	Op. 57	S/S	Harmonie i. B.		CHAL (1901)
7582	Strauss, Jr. Johann	1825-1899	An der schönen blauen Donau "Donau so blau"	Op. 314	Unspec.	Cranz		CHAL (1898)
7583	Strauss, Jr. Johann	1825-1899	Brüssler Spitzen "O kommt und kauft euch"		Unspec.	Schott		CHAL (1898)
7584	Strauss, Jr. Johann	1825-1899	Philomele "Philomele stimmt die Kehle"		Unspec.	Schott		CHAL (1898)
7585	Streabbog, L.	1835-1886	Heureuse enfance	No. 1	Unspec.	Cranz	Pen name of J. L. Gobbaerts, a.k.a. Levi, Ludovic.	CHAL (1898)
7586	Streabbog, L.	1835-1886	Humbles novices	No. 2	Unspec.	Cranz	Pen name of J. L. Gobbaerts, a.k.a. Levi, Ludovic.	CHAL (1898)
7587	Streabbog, L.	1835-1886	Jours de printemps	No. 3	Unspec.	Cranz	Pen name of J. L. Gobbaerts, a.k.a. Levi, Ludovic.	CHAL (1898)
7588	Strimer, Joseph	1881-	Lorsque nous Avions Trios Dindons		Unspec.	Durand	For 1-2 v. Unspec. pieces.	CVMP (1976)
7589	Strino, S. A.		Voici la nuit	No. 8	Unspec.	Schmidl		CHAL (1901)
7590	Strubel, J.		In der Christnacht "Kommt ihr Christen fröhlich"	Op. 35 No. 1	Unspec.	Böhm & S.		CHAL (1898)
7591	Strubel, J.		In dulci jubilo "Mit süssem Freudenschall"	Op. 35 No. 2	Unspec.	Böhm & S.		CHAL (1898)
7592	Strubel, J.		Weihnachtslieder (2)	Op. 35	Unspec.	Böhm & S.	2 duets	CHAL (1898)
7593	Stuckenschmidt, H.		Bergreihen "Gar herzlich thut mich erfreuen"	Op. 4 No. 2	Unspec.	Schott		CHAL (1898)
7594	Stuckenschmidt, H.		In meinem Garten die Nelken	Op. 4 No. 1	Unspec.	Schott		CHAL (1898)
7595	Stuckenschmidt, J. H.		Frühlingsahung "Wenn es wieder will Frühling werden"	Op. 8 No. 1	Unspec.	Leuckardt		CHAL (1898)
7596	Stuckenschmidt, J. H.		Schnadahüpfeln "Diendl, wie freust mi Du"		Unspec.	Aibl		CHAL (1898)
7597	Stuckenschmidt, J. H.		Traum "Ich hab' die Nacht geträumet"	Op. 8 No. 2	Unspec.	Leuckart		CHAL (1898)
7598	Succo, Franz Adolf	1801-1879	Frühlingslied "Es duftet der Frühling"	Op. 4	S/A or T/B	B. & B.		CHAL (1898)
7599	Succo, Reinhold	1837-1897	Himmelfahrt "Wie prangt im Frühlingskleide"	Op. 19 No. 1	S/S	Schlesinger		CHAL (1898)
7600	Succo, Reinhold	1837-1897	Siehe, schon harret er dein	Op. 19 No. 2	S/A	Bornemann		CHAL (1898)
7601	Sugár, Rezsö	1919-1988	Elmúlt a Vész		S/A or S/MS	EMB	In anthology "A kamaraének mesterei" Compi. & ed. T. Füzesséry (no date)	

REC	COMP	DTS	TITLE	OP #	VCG	PUB	COMMENTS	SRC
7602	Sugiura, Masayoshi	1921-	Seki Butsu Sho		Unspec.	Japan	Translit. of Japanese	CVMP (1985)
7603	Suhy, K.		Perle ist mein Wien "Blaue Donaustrom durchfliesst"		Unspec.	Doblinger		CHAL (1898)
7604	Sullivan, Arthur	1842-1900	Coming home		Unspec.	Boosey	Ed. Randegger	BBC (1975)
7605	Sullivan, Arthur	1842-1900	Honour, riches, marriage		Unspec.	Novello		BBC (1975)
7606	Sullivan, Arthur	1842-1900	Lord Has Risen, The		2 high v.	R. D. Row	org or pf acc. In anth. "Sacred Duet Master-pieces..." Vol. 3. Compi. & ed. C. Fredrickson. Pub. 1961.	MSN
7607	Sullivan, Arthur	1842-1900	The sisters		Unspec.	Lucas, Weber		BBC (1975)
7608	Sulzbach, Emil	1855-1932	Abendstille "Nun ruht die Welt in Schweigen"	Op. 27 No. 1	high & low v.	Steyl & Th.		CHAL (1898)
7609	Sulzbach, Emil	1855-1932	Bin ich wirklich auf dem Wege	Op. 27 No. 4	high & low v.	Firnberg		CHAL (1906)
7610	Sulzbach, Emil	1855-1932	Grauer Vogel über der Haide	Op. 27 No. 3	high & low v.	Steyl & Th.		CHAL (1898)
7611	Sulzbach, Emil	1855-1932	Grauer Vogel über der Haide	Op. 27 No. 3	high & low v.	Firnberg		CHAL (1906)
7612	Sulzbach, Emil	1855-1932	Nächtlich wandern all Flüsse	Op. 27 No. 2	high & low v.	Firnberg		CHAL (1906)
7613	Sulzbach, Emil	1855-1932	Nun ruht die Welt in Schweigen	Op. 27 No. 1	high & low v.	Firnberg		CHAL (1906)
7614	Sulzbach, Emil	1855-1932	Stimmen der Nacht "Nächtlich wandern alle Flüsse"	Op. 27 No. 2	high & low v.	Steyl & Th.		CHAL (1898)
7615	Suppé, Franz von	1819-1895	Abschied von Tyrol "Wia die Stellung war"		Unspec.	Cranz		CHAL (1898)
7616	Suppé, Franz von	1819-1895	Glöckchen-Duettino "Wenn draussen so der Morgen"		S/S	Siegel		CHAL (1898)
7617	Suppé, Franz von	1819-1895	Invitation à la danse "Venez, venez accourez au signal"		Unspec.	Cranz		CHAL (1898)
7618	Suppé, Franz von	1819-1895	Rauschend auf dem Pflaster seidne Roben		S/S or S/T	Siegel		CHAL (1898)
7619	Suppé, Franz von	1819-1895	Savoyardenlied "O reicht ein Almosen mir"		S/S or S/T	Siegel		CHAL (1898)
7620	Suppé, Franz von	1819-1895	Version des Duettes Ab-schied von Tyrol "Zwoa aus'm Weanerwalde"		Unspec.	Cranz		CHAL (1898)
7621	Sutherland, Margaret	1897-	Break of Day		S/A	L'Oiseau	Brit.-Austral. woman comp.	CVMP (1976)
7622	Sutherland, Margaret	1897-	Green Singer, The		S/A	L'Oiseau	Brit.-Austral. woman comp.	CVMP (1976)
7623	Suzuki, Hideaki	1938-	Okin No Hanakanzashi		S/MS	Japan	Translit. of Japanese	CVMP (1985)
7624	Suzuki, Hideaki	1938-	Yuki-Musume		S/MS	Japan	Translit. of Japanese	CVMP (1985)
7625	Svara, Danilo	1902-1981	Deset Narodnih [1]		Unspec.	Drustvo		CVMP (1985)
7626	Svara, Danilo	1902-1981	Deset Narodnih [2]		Unspec.	Drustvo		CVMP (1985)
7627	Svara, Danilo	1902-	Deset Narodnoh, Vol. I		Unspec.	Drzavna	Collection. Includes pieces for 1-2 v.	CVMP (1976)

REC	COMP	DTS	TITLE	OP #	VCG	PUB	COMMENTS	SRC
7628	Svara, Danilo	1902-	Deset Narodnoh, Vol. II		Unspec.	Drzavna	Collection. Includes pieces for 1 v.-2 v.	CVMP (1976)
7629	Sveinbjörnsson, Sveinbjörn	1847-1927	Now is the Month of Maying		Unspec.	Iceland		CVMP (1995)
7630	Swann, Donald	1923-1994	Jubilate Domino		high & med. v.	Galaxy		ASR
7631	Szymanowski, Karol Maciej	1882-1937	Durch den Wald, das Feld, die Heide		Unspec.	Neumann i. Dresden	Grmn. tr. Pol.	CHAL (1911)
7632	Szymanowski, Karol Maciej	1882-1937	Heute geht es auf den Bummel		Unspec.	Neumann i. Dresden	Grmn. tr. Pol.	CHAL (1911)
7633	Szymanowski, Karol Maciej	1882-1937	Nieder sinkt das Abenddunkel		Unspec.	Neumann i. Dresden	Grmn. tr. Pol.	CHAL (1911)
7634	Szymanowski, Karol Maciej	1882-1937	Wir Künstler, wir leben sehr heiter		Unspec.	Neumann i. Dresden	Grmn. tr. Pol.	CHAL (1911)
7635	Szymanowski, Karol Maciej	1882-1937	Wir sind die Banditen		Unspec.	Neumann i. Dresden	Grmn. tr. Pol.	CHAL (1911)
7636	Talma, Louise	1906-	Carmina Mariana		S/S	Libe C	Woman comp.	ASR
7637	Tancioni, E.		E mio quel cor		S/MS or A/T	Lucca		CHAL (1898)
7638	Tate, James W.	1875-1922	Collaboration		Unspec.	F. D. & H.		BBC (1975)
7639	Tate, Phyllis	1911-	Victorian Garland		Unspec.	OUP	pf or inst or orch accomp. Brit. woman comp.	CVMP (1976)
7640	Taubert, Ernst Eduard	1838-1934	Du liebes, kleines Mägdelein	Op. 26 No. 4	2 female v.	Siegel		CHAL (1898)
7641	Taubert, Ernst Eduard	1838-1934	Lied und Blüthe "Wind im weissen Blüthenbaum"	Op. 26 No. 1	2 female v.	Siegel		CHAL (1898)
7642	Taubert, Ernst Eduard	1838-1934	Schlafe nur Herz	Op. 26 No. 8	2 female v.	Siegel		CHAL (1898)
7643	Taubert, Ernst Eduard	1838-1934	Über Nacht "Über Nacht kommt still das Leid"	Op. 26 No. 2	2 female v.	Siegel		CHAL (1898)
7644	Taubert, H.		In die Veilchen "Kommt hinaus, lasst uns geh'n"	Op. 77 No. 2	S/S	B. & B.		CHAL (1898)
7645	Taubert, Otto	1833-1903	Christnacht "Heil'ge Nacht, auf Engelschwingen"	Op. 13	Unspec.	Junne		CHAL (1898)
7646	Taubert, Otto	1833-1903	Weihnachtsgebet "Wo der Stern ist aufgegangen"		Unspec.	Junne		CHAL (1898)
7647	Taubert, Wilhelm	1811-1891	Abendfieier in Venedig "Ave Maria, Meer und Himmel"	Op. 43 No. 1	S/S or S/T	Hof-meister		CHAL (1898)
7648	Taubert, Wilhelm	1811-1891	Abendgeläut "Aus dem Dörfleini da drüben"	Op. 94 No. 1	S/S	Bahn		CHAL (1898)
7649	Taubert, Wilhelm	1811-1891	Abendlied "Bald ist es wieder Nacht"	Op. 78 No. 3	Unspec.	B. & B.		CHAL (1898)
7650	Taubert, Wilhelm	1811-1891	Doppelleben "Am See am Teich, wie schaukeln"	Op. 43 No. 2	S/S or S/T	Hof-meister		CHAL (1898)
7651	Taubert, Wilhelm	1811-1891	Dornröschen "Und sie kam zur Hexe"	Op. 78 No. 1	Unspec.	B. & B.		CHAL (1898)
7652	Taubert, Wilhelm	1811-1891	Einladung "Musst nicht vor dem Tage fliehen"	Op. 43 No. 3	S/S or S/T	Hof-meister		CHAL (1898)
7653	Taubert, Wilhelm	1811-1891	Finken Gruss "Im Flieder-busch ein Finke sass"	Op. 94 No. 5	S/S	Bahn		CHAL (1898)
7654	Taubert, Wilhelm	1811-1891	Freude, holde Freude "Hüpft ein Vöglein"	Op. 178 No. 5	Unspec.	Chal.		CHAL (1898)
7655	Taubert, Wilhelm	1811-1891	Gott grüsse dich, kein andrer Gruss	Op. 140 No. 1	Unspec.	Kistner		CHAL (1898)
7656	Taubert, Wilhelm	1811-1891	Kuckuck "Im lieblichen Mai, tönt Vogelgeschrei"	Op. 94 No. 4	S/S	Bahn		CHAL (1898)

REC	COMP	DTS	TITLE	OP #	VCG	PUB	COMMENTS	SRC
7657	Taubert, Wilhelm	1811-1891	Liedergarten f. d. weibliche Jugend (6 Duette)	Op. 140	Unspec.	Kistner	6 Duets	CHAL (1898)
7658	Taubert, Wilhelm	1811-1891	Mägdlein Schmuck "Es wächst ein Blümlein Bescheidenheit"	Op. 140 No. 6	Unspec.	Kistner		CHAL (1898)
7659	Taubert, Wilhelm	1811-1891	Marienwürmchen setzte dich	Op. 94 No. 3	S/S	Bahn		CHAL (1898)
7660	Taubert, Wilhelm	1811-1891	Mond "Wie ist doch über Wald und Feld"	Op. 140 No. 5	Unspec.	Kistner		CHAL (1898)
7661	Taubert, Wilhelm	1811-1891	Mondliedchen "Wie der Mond so schön scheint"	Op. 94 No. 2	S/S	Bahn		CHAL (1898)
7662	Taubert, Wilhelm	1811-1891	Mondscheinlied "Verstohlen geht der Mond auf"	Op. 77 No. 3	S/S	B. & B.		CHAL (1898)
7663	Taubert, Wilhelm	1811-1891	Morgenlied im Freien "Meeresfluth mit Purpurgluth"	Op. 140 No. 2	Unspec.	Kistner		CHAL (1898)
7664	Taubert, Wilhelm	1811-1891	Nachts "Ich wandre durch die stille Nacht"	Op. 77 No. 1	S/S	B. & B.		CHAL (1898)
7665	Taubert, Wilhelm	1811-1891	Schnadahüpferl "Dass im Wald finsta is"		Unspec.	Bahn		CHAL (1898)
7666	Taubert, Wilhelm	1811-1891	Sehnsucht "Ich blick' in mein Herz"	Op. 178 No. 1	Unspec.	Chal.		CHAL (1898)
7667	Taubert, Wilhelm	1811-1891	Sommertag "Blümlein blühen"	Op. 178 No. 2	Unspec.	Chal.		CHAL (1898)
7668	Taubert, Wilhelm	1811-1891	Spaziergang "Ich wollt einmal recht früh aufstehn"	Op. 78 No. 5	Unspec.	B. & B.		CHAL (1898)
7669	Taubert, Wilhelm	1811-1891	Veilchen "Ein Veilchen auf der Wiese stand"	Op. 78 No. 4	Unspec.	B. & B.		CHAL (1898)
7670	Taubert, Wilhelm	1811-1891	Veilchen "Veilchen verkünden die holdeste Zeit"	Op. 140 No. 4	Unspec.	Kistner		CHAL (1898)
7671	Taubert, Wilhelm	1811-1891	Vöglein im Walde "Vöglein singt im Walde"	Op. 78 No. 2	Unspec.	B. & B.		CHAL (1898)
7672	Taubert, Wilhelm	1811-1891	Vom Wald bin i füra	Op. 43 No. 4	S/S or S/T	Hof-meister		CHAL (1898)
7673	Taubert, Wilhelm	1811-1891	Waldlied "Im Walde möcht' ich leben"	Op. 77 No. 4	S/S	B. & B.		CHAL (1898)
7674	Taubert, Wilhelm	1811-1891	Wenn ich ein Vöglein wär und auch zwei Flügel hätt'	Op. 178 No. 4	Unspec.	Chal.		CHAL (1898)
7675	Taubert, Wilhelm	1811-1891	Wenn ich zwei Flügel hätt' "Da drüben auf dem Berge"	Op. 140 No. 3	Unspec.	Kistner		CHAL (1898)
7676	Taubert, Wilhelm	1811-1891	Witt, witt, kommt mit "Es singt ein Vögelein"	Op. 178 No. 3	Unspec.	Chal.		CHAL (1898)
7677	Tauwitz, Eduard	1812-1894	An des Waldes Herz "Mit dem Gram"	Op. 77 No. 3	Unspec.	Wetzler i. Pr.		CHAL (1898)
7678	Tauwitz, Eduard	1812-1894	Du frischer, froher Morgenwind	Op. 77 No. 4	Unspec.	Wetzler i. Pr.		CHAL (1898)
7679	Tauwitz, Eduard	1812-1894	Frühlingstrost "Nun zieh'n sie wieder, Jung und Alt"	Op. 112 No. 2	S/A	Simon i. Berl.		CHAL (1898)
7680	Tauwitz, Eduard	1812-1894	Hinauf, hinab "Wie schön recht weit"	Op. 77 No. 2	Unspec.	Wetzler i. Pr.		CHAL (1898)
7681	Tauwitz, Eduard	1812-1894	Hüben und drüben "Hüben ein Thal"	Op. 99 No. 3	Unspec.	Litolff		CHAL (1898)
7682	Tauwitz, Eduard	1812-1894	In stiller Nacht "Stille, stille ist die Nacht"	Op. 112 No. 3	S/A	Simon i. Berl.		CHAL (1898)
7683	Tauwitz, Eduard	1812-1894	Singe mit "Horch, wie singet das Vögelein"	Op. 99 No. 1	Unspec.	Litolff		CHAL (1898)
7684	Tauwitz, Eduard	1812-1894	Wanderlust "Heraus, heraus, der Vögel Chor"	Op. 112 No. 1	S/A	Simon i. Berl.		CHAL (1898)
7685	Tauwitz, Eduard	1812-1894	Wiegenlied achte will's dämmern"	Op. 77 No. 1	Unspec.	Wetzler i. Pr.		CHAL (1898)
7686	Taylor, T.		Down By the Old Mill Stream		Unspec.	Allans	In anthology "Vocal Duets Collection" Vol. 1. Pub. 1992.	MSN

REC	COMP	DTS	TITLE	OP #	VCG	PUB	COMMENTS	SRC
7687	Tchaikovsky, Peter Ilyich	1840-1893	Abend	Op. 46 No. 1	S/MS	Carus	In "Sechs Duette" All but No. 2 for S/MS. (No. 2 for S/Br). Grmn. trans. Russ. Cyrillic included.	MSN
7688	Tchaikovsky, Peter Ilyich	1840-1893	Abend "Nieder sinkt die Sonne"	Op. 46 No. 1	S/MS	Rahter	Grmn. ed.	CHAL (1898)
7689	Tchaikovsky, Peter Ilyich	1840-1893	Dawn	Op. 46 No. 6	S/MS	CVR	Eng. trans. Russ. In catalogue "Classical Vocal Reprints Complete Catalog" Pub. 1997.	MSN
7690	Tchaikovsky, Peter Ilyich	1840-1893	Evening	Op. 46 No. 1	S/MS	CVR	Eng. trans. Russ. In catalogue "Classical Vocal Reprints Complete Catalog" Pub. 1997.	MSN
7691	Tchaikovsky, Peter Ilyich	1840-1893	Im Garten	Op. 46 No. 4	S/MS	Carus	In "Sechs Duette" All but No. 2 for S/MS. (No. 2 for S/Br). Grmn. trans. Russ. Cyrillic included.	MSN
7692	Tchaikovsky, Peter Ilyich	1840-1893	In dem Garten am Flusse	Op. 46 No. 4	S/MS	Rahter	Grmn. trans. Russ.	CHAL (1898)
7693	Tchaikovsky, Peter Ilyich	1840-1893	In the Garden near the River	Op. 46 No. 4	S/MS	CVR	In catalogue "Classical Vocal Reprints Complete Catalog" Pub. 1997.	MSN
7694	Tchaikovsky, Peter Ilyich	1840-1893	Minula Strast	Op. 46 No. 5	S/MS	Kalmus	In Six Duets, Op. 46. Translit. of Russ. Kalmus Miniature Score 6760. All but No. 2 for S/MS. (No. 2 for S/Br).	NATS-VCD
7695	Tchaikovsky, Peter Ilyich	1840-1893	Minula Strast [Lost Passion]	Op. 46 No. 5	S/MS et al.	Carlus-Verlag	In "Shest Duetov" Translit. title of Russ. Cyrillic & Grmn.	MSN
7696	Tchaikovsky, Peter Ilyich	1840-1893	Morgendämmerung	Op. 46 No. 6	S/MS	Carus	In "Sechs Duette" All but No. 2 for S/MS. (No. 2 for S/Br). Grmn. trans. Russ. Cyrillic included.	MSN
7697	Tchaikovsky, Peter Ilyich	1840-1893	Morgenroth "Schau', das Morgenroth glüht"	Op. 46 No. 6	S/MS	Rahter	Grmn. trans. Russ.	CHAL (1898)
7698	Tchaikovsky, Peter Ilyich	1840-1893	Nicht Leidenschaft mit zügellosem Wagen	Op. 46 No. 5	S/T or S/A	Rahter	For S/A. Grmn. trans. Russ.	CHAL (1898)
7699	Tchaikovsky, Peter Ilyich	1840-1893	Op. 46	Op. 46	Unspec.	none listed	These spec. elsewhere, Nos. 1, 3-6 S/MS	BBC (1975)
7700	Tchaikovsky, Peter Ilyich	1840-1893	Passion spent	Op. 46 No. 5	S/MS	CVR	In catalogue "Classical Vocal Reprints Complete Catalog" Pub. 1997.	MSN
7701	Tchaikovsky, Peter Ilyich	1840-1893	Rassved [The Dawn]		S/MS	GMI	Translit. title of Russ. Only Cyrillic. Anth. "Izbrannye Duety Russkikh Kompozitorov dlia peniia s fortepiano" Pub. 1948.	MSN
7702	Tchaikovsky, Peter Ilyich	1840-1893	Rassved [The Dawn]	Op. 46 No. 6	S/MS et al.	Carlus-Verlag	In "Shest Duetov" Translit. title of Russ. Cyrillic & Grmn.	MSN
7703	Tchaikovsky, Peter Ilyich	1840-1893	Rassved [The Dawn]	Op. 46 No. 6	S/MS	Kalmus	In Six Duets, Op. 46. Translit. of Russ. Kalmus Miniature Score 6760. All but No. 2 for S/MS. (No. 2 for S/Br).	NATS-VCD
7704	Tchaikovsky, Peter Ilyich	1840-1893	Schottische Ballade "Wess' Blut hat dein Schwert"	Op. 46 No. 2	S/MS	Rahter	Grmn. trans. Russ.	CHAL (1898)
7705	Tchaikovsky, Peter Ilyich	1840-1893	Sechs Duette Op. 42	Op. 46	S/MS	Carus	Nos. 1, 3-6 comp. for S/MS. All but No. 2 for S/MS. (No. 2 for S/Br). Grmn. trans. Russ. Cyrillic included.	CVMP (1985)
7706	Tchaikovsky, Peter Ilyich	1840-1893	Shest Duetov [Six Duets], Op. 46	Op. 46	S/MS et al.	Carlus-Verlag	Translit. title of Russ. Cyrillic & Grmn. Six duets. All but No. 2 for S/MS. (No. 2 for S/Br).	MSN
7707	Tchaikovsky, Peter Ilyich	1840-1893	Shest Duetov [Six Duets], Op. 46	Op. 46	S/MS et al.	Carlus-Verlag	Translit. title of Russ. Cyrillic & Grmn. Six duets. All but No. 2 for S/MS. (No. 2 for S/Br).	MSN

REC	COMP	DTS	TITLE	OP #	VCG	PUB	COMMENTS	SRC
7708	Tchaikovsky, Peter Ilyich	1840-1893	Slezy [Tears]	Op. 46 No. 3	S/MS et al.	Carlus-Verlag	In "Shest Duetov" Translit. title of Russ. Cyrillic & Grmn.	MSN
7709	Tchaikovsky, Peter Ilyich	1840-1893	Slyozï	Op. 46 No. 3	S/MS	Kalmus	In Six Duets, Op. 46. Translit. of Russ. Kalmus Miniature Score 6760. All but No. 2 for S/MS. (No. 2 for S/Br).	NATS-VCD
7710	Tchaikovsky, Peter Ilyich	1840-1893	Tears	Op. 46 No. 3	S/MS	CVR	Eng. trans. Russ. In catalogue "Classical Vocal Reprints Complete Catalog" Pub. 1997.	MSN
7711	Tchaikovsky, Peter Ilyich	1840-1893	Thränen "Thränen der Menscheit"	Op. 46 No. 3	S/MS	Rahter	Grmn. trans. Russ.	CHAL (1898)
7712	Tchaikovsky, Peter Ilyich	1840-1893	Tränen	Op. 46 No. 3	S/MS	Carus	In "Sechs Duette" All but No. 2 for S/MS. (No. 2 for S/Br). Grmn. trans. Russ. Russ. lang. included.	MSN
7713	Tchaikovsky, Peter Ilyich	1840-1893	V Ogorod vozle Brodu [In the Vegetable Garden by the Ford]		S/MS	GMI	Translit. title of Russ. Only Cyrillic. Anth. "Izbrannye Duety Russkikh Kompozitorov dlia peniia s fortepiano" Pub. 1948.	MSN
7714	Tchaikovsky, Peter Ilyich	1840-1893	V Ogorode, Bozle Brodu [In the Vegetable Patch]	Op. 46 No. 4	S/MS et al.	Carlus-Verlag	In "Shest Duetov" Translit. title of Russ. Cyrillic & Grmn.	MSN
7715	Tchaikovsky, Peter Ilyich	1840-1893	V Ogorode, Bozle Brodu [In the Vegetable Patch]	Op. 46 No. 4	S/MS	Kalmus	In Six Duets, Op. 46. Translit. of Russ. Kalmus Miniature Score 6760. All but No. 2 for S/MS. (No. 2 for S/Br).	NATS-VCD
7716	Tchaikovsky, Peter Ilyich	1840-1893	Vecher	Op. 46 No. 1	S/MS	Kalmus	In Six Duets, Op. 46. Translit. of Russ. Kalmus Miniature Score 6760. All but No. 2 for S/MS. (No. 2 for S/Br).	NATS-VCD
7717	Tchaikovsky, Peter Ilyich	1840-1893	Vecher [Evening]	Op. 46 No. 1	S/MS et al.	Carlus-Verlag	In "Shest Duetov" Translit. title of Russ. Cyrillic & Grmn.	MSN
7718	Tchaikovsky, Peter Ilyich	1840-1893	Vergangene Leidenschaft	Op. 46 No. 5	S/MS	Carus	In "Sechs Duette" All but No. 2 for S/MS. (No. 2 for S/Br). Grmn. trans. Russ. Russ. lang. included.	MSN
7719	Teich, Otto	1866-1935	Ach schrecklich ist's und eine Plage	Op. 357	2 female v.	O. Teich		CHAL (1906)
7720	Teich, Otto	1866-1935	Ach, wie bin ich glücklich heute	Op. 373	2 female v.	O. Teich		CHAL (1906)
7721	Teich, Otto	1866-1935	Alles ist heut' ausgeflogen	Op. 405	2 female v.	O. Teich		CHAL (1906)
7722	Teich, Otto	1866-1935	Als ich hier diesen Brief erhalten	Op. 481	2 female v.	O. Teich		CHAL (1911)
7723	Teich, Otto	1866-1935	Als lustige Pieretten	Op. 509	Unspec.	O. Teich		CHAL (1911)
7724	Teich, Otto	1866-1935	Annette und Babette, die beiden Dorfschönen "Es giebt im Dorf kein schönres Paar"	Op. 217	Unspec.	O. Teich		CHAL (1898)
7725	Teich, Otto	1866-1935	Backfischstreiche "Endlich bin ich ausgekniffen"	Op. 97	2 female v.	O. Teich		CHAL (1898)
7726	Teich, Otto	1866-1935	Baron von Klix und Herr von Stix "Ich stell' mich vor"	Op. 179	Unspec.	O. Teich		CHAL (1898)
7727	Teich, Otto	1866-1935	Bei ins auf den Bergen	Op. 397	2 female v.	O. Teich		CHAL (1906)

REC	COMP	DTS	TITLE	OP #	VCG	PUB	COMMENTS	SRC
7728	Teich, Otto	1866-1935	Beiden Commis von Meyerstein "Wir sind die zwei Commis"	Op. 146	Unspec.	O. Teich		CHAL (1898)
7729	Teich, Otto	1866-1935	Comtesschen im Pensionat	Op. 260	2 female v.	O. Teich		CHAL (1901)
7730	Teich, Otto	1866-1935	Dusel und Tute, die veiden Nachtwächter "O hört ihr Damen"	Op. 155	Unspec.	O. Teich		CHAL (1898)
7731	Teich, Otto	1866-1935	Eine Liebeserklärung auf dem Lande "Hans und Grethe"		Unspec.	none listed		CHAL (1898)
7732	Teich, Otto	1866-1935	Einjähriger Nasewitz und sein Putzer "Hum. Duoscene"	Op. 255	Unspec.	O. Teich		CHAL (1901)
7733	Teich, Otto	1866-1935	Fidel und voll Humor	Op. 482	2 female v.	O. Teich		CHAL (1911)
7734	Teich, Otto	1866-1935	Fips und Faps, die vergnügten Schneider "Wir sind zwei Nadelhelden"	Op. 151	Unspec.	O. Teich		CHAL (1898)
7735	Teich, Otto	1866-1935	Flick und Flock, die lustigen Junggesellen "Wir sind zwei Junggesellen"	Op. 145	Unspec.	O. Teich		CHAL (1898)
7736	Teich, Otto	1866-1935	Florian und Baldrian, das beliebte Zwillingspaar "Wir Beide sind ein Zwillingspaar"	Op. 137	Unspec.	O. Teich		CHAL (1898)
7737	Teich, Otto	1866-1935	Flucht aus der Pension "Ach es ist nicht zu entragen"	Op. 121	2 female v.	O. Teich		CHAL (1898)
7738	Teich, Otto	1866-1935	Friedel und Christel "Es sind zwei Wochen"	Op. 173	Unspec.	O. Teich		CHAL (1898)
7739	Teich, Otto	1866-1935	Guten Morgen, Vielliebchen "Hum. Duoscene"	Op. 284	2 female v.	O. Teich		CHAL (1901)
7740	Teich, Otto	1866-1935	Hans und Peter, die Don Juans vom Lande "Mein Trine ich beschwör' es"	Op. 156	Unspec.	O. Teich		CHAL (1898)
7741	Teich, Otto	1866-1935	Heisa, lustig und fidel	Op. 434	2 female v.	O. Teich		CHAL (1911)
7742	Teich, Otto	1866-1935	Herren von Strahl "Wir Zwei gehör'n zur feinen Welt"	Op. 134	Unspec.	O. Teich		CHAL (1898)
7743	Teich, Otto	1866-1935	Hipp, hipp hurra, das ist der Gruss	Op. 306	Unspec.	O. Teich		CHAL (1901)
7744	Teich, Otto	1866-1935	Ich bin im Glück geboren	Op. 415	Unspec.	O. Teich		CHAL (1906)
7745	Teich, Otto	1866-1935	Ich und mein Bruder Theobald	Op. 282	Unspec.	O. Teich		CHAL (1901)
7746	Teich, Otto	1866-1935	Irma und Elsa die beiden Maikätzchen "Hum. Duoscene"	Op. 283	2 female v.	O. Teich		CHAL (1901)
7747	Teich, Otto	1866-1935	Jubel und Strubel, die beiden Strohwittwer "Hum. Duoscene"	Op. 258	Unspec.	O. Teich		CHAL (1901)
7748	Teich, Otto	1866-1935	Jungens von Banquier Meyer "Wir geben uns die Ehre"	Op. 119	Unspec.	O. Teich		CHAL (1898)
7749	Teich, Otto	1866-1935	Kieslack und Dämlack, die betrüb-ten Rekruten "Dass wir zwei Rekruten sind"	Op. 135	Unspec.	Fr. Dietrich		CHAL (1898)
7750	Teich, Otto	1866-1935	Klitsch und Klatsch, die fleisigen Maurer	Op. 270	Unspec.	O. Teich		CHAL (1901)
7751	Teich, Otto	1866-1935	Klops und Mops, die fidelen Köche	Op. 271	Unspec.	O. Teich		CHAL (1901)
7752	Teich, Otto	1866-1935	Kuhmagd und Gouvernante "Aus dem dumpfen Stadtgewühl"	Op. 137	2 female v.	O. Teich		CHAL (1898)
7753	Teich, Otto	1866-1935	Lumpen, Lumpen, wer hat Lumpen	Op. 442	Unspec.	O. Teich		CHAL (1911)
7754	Teich, Otto	1866-1935	Lustig an die Arbeit gehts		2 female v.	O. Teich		CHAL (1901)
7755	Teich, Otto	1866-1935	Lustig klingt's Zigeunerliedel	Op. 406	2 female v.	O. Teich		CHAL (1906)

REC	COMP	DTS	TITLE	OP #	VCG	PUB	COMMENTS	SRC
7756	Teich, Otto	1866-1935	Marie und Amanda "Wir sind zwei Schwestern"	Op. 149	2 female v.	O. Teich		CHAL (1898)
7757	Teich, Otto	1866-1935	Max und Woldemar, das Brüderpaar "Wir sind ein nettes Brüderpaar"	Op. 89	Unspec.	O. Teich		CHAL (1898)
7758	Teich, Otto	1866-1935	Mit Riesenschritten naht heran	Op. 294	2 female v.	O. Teich		CHAL (1901)
7759	Teich, Otto	1866-1935	Morgen kommt mein Männchen wieder	Op. 503	2 female v.	O. Teich		CHAL (1911)
7760	Teich, Otto	1866-1935	Nein, das ist nicht zu ertragen	Op. 365	2 female v.	O. Teich		CHAL (1906)
7761	Teich, Otto	1866-1935	Neue Diener "Ohne Diener schon drei Tage"	Op. 184	Unspec.	O. Teich		CHAL (1898)
7762	Teich, Otto	1866-1935	O wie glücklich, o wie selig		2 female v.	O. Teich		CHAL (1911)
7763	Teich, Otto	1866-1935	Pauline und Auguste die beiden Köchinnen "Jesses so zwei von der Kochkunst"	Op. 193	2 female v.	O. Teich		CHAL (1898)
7764	Teich, Otto	1866-1935	Polle und Knolle, zwei fidele Handwerksburschen "Hum. Duoscene"	Op. 254	Unspec.	O. Teich		CHAL (1901)
7765	Teich, Otto	1866-1935	Radsort Gigerl "Wir Radler, wir Radler"	Op. 212	Unspec.	O. Teich		CHAL (1898)
7766	Teich, Otto	1866-1935	Rittmeister Schnabel und sein Bursche Zabel "Schwadron zurück vom Exercir'n"	Op. 218	Unspec.	O. Dietrich		CHAL (1898)
7767	Teich, Otto	1866-1935	Röschen auf dem Lande "Hum. Duoscene"	Op. 319	2 female v.	O. Teich		CHAL (1901)
7768	Teich, Otto	1866-1935	Schainsten Länder auf der Welt	Op. 305	Unspec.	O. Teich		CHAL (1901)
7769	Teich, Otto	1866-1935	Schusterkarl und Bäckernante, zwei intelligente Lehrjungen "Wahrhaf'g 's nicht"	Op. 232	Unspec.	O. Teich		CHAL (1898)
7770	Teich, Otto	1866-1935	Sergeant Knaster und Rekrut Pleps "Himmelschwerenoth potz Donner"	Op. 211	Unspec.	O. Teich		CHAL (1898)
7771	Teich, Otto	1866-1935	Sie schauen in uns beiden	Op. 441	Unspec.	O. Teich		CHAL (1911)
7772	Teich, Otto	1866-1935	Um mitternächtliche Stunde "Kostüm-Duett"	Op. 466	Unspec.	O. Teich		CHAL (1911)
7773	Teich, Otto	1866-1935	Volontaire Carl und Fritz "Sagen Sie, verehrte Dam'n"	Op. 178	Unspec.	O. Teich		CHAL (1898)
7774	Teich, Otto	1866-1935	Wachmeister Stramm und Rekrut Dämel "Hum. Duoscene"	Op. 276	Unspec.	O. Teich		CHAL (1901)
7775	Teich, Otto	1866-1935	Washalb, wieso, warum "Im Wirthshaus flucht ein Herr"	Op. 49	Unspec.	O. Teich		CHAL (1898)
7776	Teich, Otto	1866-1935	Weaner Wäschermadeln "Es merkt gewiss ein Jeder"	Op. 56	2 female v.	O. Teich		CHAL (1898)
7777	Teich, Otto	1866-1935	Welches Glück, Sie hier zu treffen	Op. 461	2 female v.	O. Teich		CHAL (1911)
7778	Teich, Otto	1866-1935	Wenn draussen auf dem Felde	Op. 193	2 female v.	O. Teich		CHAL (1901)
7779	Teich, Otto	1866-1935	Wie plagt der Mensch sich heute doch	Op. 307	Unspec.	O. Teich		CHAL (1901)
7780	Teich, Otto	1866-1935	Wir sehen schon, wie Alles lacht	Op. 285	Unspec.	O. Teich		CHAL (1901)
7781	Teich, Otto	1866-1935	Wir sind die beiden Pikkolos	Op. 443	Unspec.	O. Teich		CHAL (1911)
7782	Teich, Otto	1866-1935	Wir sind die Schmiedegesellen	Op. 286	Unspec.	O. Teich		CHAL (1901)
7783	Teich, Otto	1866-1935	Wir sind lust'ge Seekadotten	Op. 417	Unspec.	O. Teich		CHAL (1906)
7784	Teich, Otto	1866-1935	Wir sind zwei fesche Weiber	Op. 526 No. a	2 female v.	O. Teich		CHAL (1911)

REC	COMP	DTS	TITLE	OP #	VCG	PUB	COMMENTS	SRC
7785	Teich, Otto	1866-1935	Wir sind zwei flotte Leutenants	Op. 444	Unspec.	O. Teich		CHAL (1911)
7786	Teich, Otto	1866-1935	Wir sind zwei lust'ge Babies	Op. 438	Unspec.	O. Teich		CHAL (1911)
7787	Teich, Otto	1866-1935	Zwei fidele Frösche "Uns Frösche kennt ein jeder Mann"	Op. 8	2 med. v.	O. Teich		CHAL (1898)
7788	Teich, Otto	1866-1935	Zwei Mode-Fexen "Als wir die Welt erblickten"	Op. 17	Unspec.	O. Teich		CHAL (1898)
7789	Teich, Otto	1866-1935	Zwei philosophische Schust-erjungen "Ach wie ist das Leben schön"	Op. 127	Unspec.	O. Teich		CHAL (1898)
7790	Teichmann, A. or O.		Barcarole "E la notte, più s'imbruna"		S/S	Cranz		CHAL (1898)
7791	Teichmann, A. or O.		E la notte, più s'imbruna "Barcarola"		Unspec.	none listed		CHAL (1898)
7792	Teichmann, A. or O.		Strahlend im Schmucke des Lenzes "Passegiata"		Unspec.	none listed		CHAL (1898)
7793	Terriss, Ellaline		If ever you're in trouble		Unspec.	F. D. & H.	Eng. woman comp.	BBC (1975)
7794	Teschner, Gustav Wilhelm	1800-1883	Illa se un moto impenetrabile		Unspec.	Bahn	Based on theme of Tenaglia (17th C.)	CHAL (1898)
7795	Teschner, Gustav Wilhelm	1800-1883	Musica scelta "Auswahl von Gesängen altitalienischer Meister"		Unspec.	Bahn		CHAL (1898)
7796	Teschner, Wilhelm (A. Caldara)	1868-	Casa nea vere est cibus		S/MS	Bahn	Arr. Teschner of A. Caldara aria (1670-1736)	CHAL (1901)
7797	Thaler, J. B.		Messe zu Ehren des heiligen Johannes Baptista		S/A or T/B	Coppen-rath	org accomp.	CHAL (1898)
7798	Thamm, P.		List gegen List "Ach welche Noth, welch' grosse Pein"	Op. 7	Unspec.	Pabst i. D.		CHAL (1898)
7799	Thiel, Carl	1862-1939	Das ist des Lenzes belebender Hauch	Op. 1	S/S	Sulzbach i. Berl.		CHAL (1906)
7800	Thiele, Eduard	1812-1895	An die Entfernte "Glock-entöne hör' ich klingen"	Op. 13 No. 2	Unspec.	B. & B.		CHAL (1898)
7801	Thiele, Eduard	1812-1895	Im Walde "O Thäler weit, o Höhen"	Op. 13 No. 1	Unspec.	B. & B.		CHAL (1898)
7802	Thiele, Eduard	1812-1895	Weihnachtsgesang "Ehre sei Gott in der Höhe"	Op. 13 No. 4	Unspec.	B. & B.		CHAL (1898)
7803	Thiele, Eduard	1812-1895	Zuversicht "Wohlauf, es ruft der Sonnenschein"	Op. 13 No. 3	Unspec.	B. & B.		CHAL (1898)
7804	Thiele, Louis	1816-1848	An dir allein o Gott	Op. 1	S/A	Peschke		CHAL (1901)
7805	Thiele, Richard	1847-1903	Colonisations-Duett "Heute den Europamüden"		Unspec.	K. & G.		CHAL (1898)
7806	Thiele, Richard	1847-1903	Ein Jahr in die Zukunft geschaut "Mensch ist unzufrieden"		Unspec.	K. & G.		CHAL (1898)
7807	Thiele, Richard	1847-1903	Jockey's "Wir lust'gen Jockey's sind nun da"		Unspec.	Neumann i. Berl.		CHAL (1898)
7808	Thiele, Richard	1847-1903	Liebe Freundin sei nicht böse		S/A	Bloch		CHAL (1901)
7809	Thiele, Richard	1847-1903	Lina und Minna "Nein, das ist nicht zu entragen"	Op. 204	S/A	O. Forberg		CHAL (1898)
7810	Thiele, Richard	1847-1903	O ihr Frauenzimmer, wäret ihr micht so reitzend "Frauen nennt im Allgemeinen"		Unspec.	K. & G.		CHAL (1898)
7811	Thiele, Richard	1847-1903	Wer da klopft, dem wird aufgethan "Wir sind zwei Mädchen"		Unspec.	K. & G.		CHAL (1898)

REC	COMP	DTS	TITLE	OP #	VCG	PUB	COMMENTS	SRC
7812	Thiele, Richard	1847-1903	Wir bleiben ledig "Ade ihr Gespielen"	Op. 30	MS/MS	Thiemer		CHAL (1898)
7813	Thiele, Richard	1847-1903	Zum Geburtstage "Sieh' da, ei das trifft soch schön"	Op. 46	MS/MS	Schlesinger		CHAL (1898)
7814	Thiele, Richard	1847-1903	Zwei von der sel'gen Bürgerwehr "Duett-Scene"		Unspec.	Bloch		CHAL (1901)
7815	Thiele, Rudolf	1866-	Falsche Waldemar "Guten Morgen liebes Minchen"	Op. 44	MS/MS	Schlesinger		CHAL (1898)
7816	Thiele, Rudolf	1866-	Frau Nachbarin, Frau Nachbarin, was ist das für'n Rumor	Op. 47	2 female v.	Danner		CHAL (1901)
7817	Thiele, Rudolf	1866-	Wir beide greifen an das Recht der Herr'n		2 med. female v.	Rud. Dietrich		CHAL (1911)
7818	Thiele, Th.		Miau, miau, miau "Ein jüngling Lieb' entbrannt"		Unspec.	Wehde		CHAL (1898)
7819	Thielen, P. H.		Du reine, makellose	Op. 157	S/A	Coppenrath		CHAL (1906)
7820	Thielen, P. H.		Ein Kindelein so löbelich	Op. 116 No. 3	S/A	Coppenrath	org or harm	CHAL (1906)
7821	Thielen, P. H.		In süssem Jubelschall	Op. 116 No. 6	S/A	Coppenrath	org or harm	CHAL (1906)
7822	Thielen, P. H.		Lasst uns zum Kindlein eilen	Op. 116 No. 1	S/A	Coppenrath	org or harm	CHAL (1906)
7823	Thielen, P. H.		Mein Herz will ich dir schenken	Op. 116 No. 4	S/A	Coppenrath	org or harm	CHAL (1906)
7824	Thielen, P. H.		O du liebes Jesukind	Op. 116 No. 5	S/A	Coppenrath	org or harm	CHAL (1906)
7825	Thielen, P. H.		Zu Bethlehem geboren	Op. 116 No. 2	S/A	Coppenrath	org or harm	CHAL (1906)
7826	Thierfelder, Albert Wilhelm	1846-1924	Fortrostan		Unspec.	Lundq.	Swed. trans. Grmn.	CVMP (1976)
7827	Thierfelder, Albert Wilhelm	1846-1924	Heimlichen Gruss "Mond ist schlafen gangen"	Op. 2 No. 4	S/A	Hofmeister		CHAL (1898)
7828	Thierfelder, Albert Wilhelm	1846-1924	Im Mai "Musst nicht allein im Freien"	Op. 2 No. 6	S/A	Hofmeister		CHAL (1898)
7829	Thierfelder, Albert Wilhelm	1846-1924	Nachgefühl "Wenn die Reben wieder blühend"	Op. 2 No. 1	S/A	Hofmeister		CHAL (1898)
7830	Thierfelder, Albert Wilhelm	1846-1924	Sind wir auch feld geschieden	Op. 2 No. 2	S/A	Hofmeister		CHAL (1898)
7831	Thierfelder, Albert Wilhelm	1846-1924	Vaxelsang		Unspec.	Lundq.	Swed. trans. Grmn.	CVMP (1976)
7832	Thierfelder, Albert Wilhelm	1846-1924	Wehmuth "Ihr verblühet süsse Rosen"	Op. 2 No. 5	S/A	Hofmeister		CHAL (1898)
7833	Thierfelder, Albert Wilhelm	1846-1924	Zweigesang "Im Fliederbusch ein Vöglein sass"	Op. 2 No. 3	S/A	Hofmeister		CHAL (1898)
7834	Thieriot, Ferdinand	1838-1919	Durchsüsset, geblümet sind die reinen Frauen	Op. 33 No. 1	2 female v.	B. & H.		CHAL (1898)
7835	Thieriot, Ferdinand	1838-1919	Geh' ich im grünen Wald		S/A	R. & B.		CHAL (1906)
7836	Thieriot, Ferdinand	1838-1919	In dem grünen Klee sah ich die Holde	Op. 33 No. 3	2 female v.	B. & H.		CHAL (1898)
7837	Thieriot, Ferdinand	1838-1919	Wiegenlied "In der Wiege liegt das Kind"	Op. 33 No. 2	2 female v.	B. & H.		CHAL (1898)
7838	Thiman, Eric Harding	1900-1975	Morning Song		Unspec.	Roberton		CVMP (1976)
7839	Thiman, Eric Harding	1900-1975	Morning Song		S/A	Curwen	May be perf. chorally	ASR
7840	Thiman, Eric Harding	1900-1975	Song at Evening		Unspec.	Roberton		CVMP (1976)

REC	COMP	DTS	TITLE	OP #	VCG	PUB	COMMENTS	SRC
7841	Thiman, Eric Harding	1900-1975	Spring Wind		high & med. v.	Boosey	In anthology "Duet Album: Selected and edited by Viola Morris and Victoria Anderson" Pub. 1944.	MSN
7842	Thiman, Eric Harding	1900-1975	Spring Wind		S/MS	Boosey	In anthology "Duet Album: Selected and edited by Viola Morris and Victoria Anderson" Pub. 1944.	NATS-VCD
7843	Thiman, Eric Harding	1900-1975	Wee Road from Cushendall, The		Unspec.	Roberton		CVMP (1976)
7844	Thiman, Eric Harding	1900-1975	Wee Road from Cushendall, The		S/S	Curwen		ASR
7845	Thoma, Rudolf	1829-1908	Abendglocken läuten	Op. 22 No. 8	Unspec.	R. & E.		CHAL (1898)
7846	Thoma, Rudolf	1829-1908	Abendlied "Sonne geht hinunter"	Op. 37 No. 2	S/A	Siegel		CHAL (1898)
7847	Thoma, Rudolf	1829-1908	Am süssesten duften die Blumen im Wald	Op. 37 No. 6	S/A	Siegel		CHAL (1898)
7848	Thoma, Rudolf	1829-1908	An mein Schifflein "Frag mich Schifflein leise"	Op. 22 No. 7	Unspec.	R. & E.		CHAL (1898)
7849	Thoma, Rudolf	1829-1908	Bächlein "Du Bächlein silberhell und klar"	Op. 22 No. 4	Unspec.	R. & E.		CHAL (1898)
7850	Thoma, Rudolf	1829-1908	Daheim "Längst schon flog zu Nest der Vogel"	Op. 22 No. 9	Unspec.	R. & E.		CHAL (1898)
7851	Thoma, Rudolf	1829-1908	Frühlingsankunft "Bald, bald erblüht die Welt"	Op. 22 No. 3	Unspec.	R. & E.		CHAL (1898)
7852	Thoma, Rudolf	1829-1908	Frühlingsglaube "Linden Lüfte sind erwacht"	Op. 37 No. 5	S/A	Siegel		CHAL (1898)
7853	Thoma, Rudolf	1829-1908	Frühlingsjubel "Frühling, Frühling wonnige Zeit"	Op. 37 No. 1	S/A	Siegel		CHAL (1898)
7854	Thoma, Rudolf	1829-1908	Hut' du dich "Ich weiss ein Mädchen (Mägdlein)"	Op. 24 No. 2	Unspec.	R. & E.		CHAL (1898)
7855	Thoma, Rudolf	1829-1908	Lebewohl "Morgen muss ich fort von hier"	Op. 24 No. 1	Unspec.	R. & E.		CHAL (1898)
7856	Thoma, Rudolf	1829-1908	Lied der Lieder "Es giebt ein Lied der Lieder"	Op. 22 No. 6	Unspec.	R. & E.		CHAL (1898)
7857	Thoma, Rudolf	1829-1908	Liedestrost "Wenn stilles Weh dein Herz bedrückt"	Op. 22 No. 10	Unspec.	R. & E.		CHAL (1898)
7858	Thoma, Rudolf	1829-1908	Morgenlied "Noch ahnt man kaum der Sonne Licht"	Op. 22 No. 1	Unspec.	R. & E.		CHAL (1898)
7859	Thoma, Rudolf	1829-1908	Schlummre auch du	Op. 37 No. 7	S/A	Siegel		CHAL (1898)
7860	Thoma, Rudolf	1829-1908	Sehnsucht nach dem Frühling "Frühling kehret wieder"	Op. 22 No. 2	Unspec.	R. & E.		CHAL (1898)
7861	Thoma, Rudolf	1829-1908	Tanzliedchen "Lasst uns tanzen, lasst uns springen"	Op. 37 No. 3	S/A	Siegel		CHAL (1898)
7862	Thoma, Rudolf	1829-1908	Waldvögelein "Wie lieblich ist's im Wald"	Op. 37 No. 8	S/A	Siegel		CHAL (1898)
7863	Thoma, Rudolf	1829-1908	Wär' Alles nur ein Traum "Wenn man so sitzt"	Op. 37 No. 4	S/A	Siegel		CHAL (1898)
7864	Thoma, Rudolf	1829-1908	Welden ist der Schöpfung Zier "Anna und Johanna die Männerfeindinnen"	Op. 22 No. 5	Unspec.	R. & E.		CHAL (1898)
7865	Thomas, Arthur Goring	1851-1892	Contentment		Unspec.	ECS	In anthology "48 Duets Seventeenth Through Nineteenth Centuries" Ed. V. Prahl. Pub. 1941, 1970.	MSN
7866	Thomas, Arthur Goring	1850-1892	Sous les Etoiles ['Neath the Stars]		Unspec.	Cramer, G. Schirm.		CVMP (1976)

REC	COMP	DTS	TITLE	OP #	VCG	PUB	COMMENTS	SRC
7867	Thomas, Arthur Goring	1850-1892	Sunset		Unspec.	Cramer		CVMP (1976)
7868	Thomas, Arthur Goring	1851-1892	Sunset		S/A	Ditson	In anthology "Soprano and Alto Duets" Ed. H. Kiehl. Pub. 1901.	MSN
7869	Thomas, N.		Auf der Pferdebahn "Auf der grossen Pferdebahn"		Unspec.	Jäger i. Berl.		CHAL (1898)
7870	Thomas, N.		Das weiss nur ein echt Berliner Kind "Da schreibt wohl in der ganzen Welt"		Unspec.	Jägeri. Berl.		CHAL (1898)
7871	Thomas, N.		Ich bin von dieser Zunkunftsfrau		Unspec.	Jäger i. Berl.		CHAL (1901)
7872	Thomas, N.		Sprichwörter-Duett "Es giebt im deutschen Vaterland"		Unspec.	Jäger i. Berl.		CHAL (1898)
7873	Thomas, N.		Strassenbilder, Ponoroma von Berlin		Unspec.	P. Fischer i. Berl.		CHAL (1901)
7874	Thooft, Willem Frans	1829-1900	An den Frühling "Willkommen schöner Jüngling"	Op. 5 No. 5	S/A	Peters		CHAL (1898)
7875	Thooft, Willem Frans	1829-1900	Herbstgefühl "O wär es blos der Wange Pracht"	Op. 1 No. 1	S/A	Peters		CHAL (1898)
7876	Thooft, Willem Frans	1829-1900	Vöglein im Walde "Lustiges Vöglein im Walde"	Op. 5 No. 4	S/A	Peters		CHAL (1898)
7877	Thooft, Willem Frans	1829-1900	Wiegenlied "Schlaf Kindlein, schlafe sanft"	Op. 5 No. 3	S/A	Peters		CHAL (1898)
7878	Thooft, Willem Frans	1829-1900	Wohin "Lüfte des Himmels, wo ziehet ihr hin"	Op. 5 No. 2	S/A	Peters		CHAL (1898)
7879	Thorn, C.		Freies Singvöglein "Komm lieb Vögelein"	Op. 42	Unspec.	Roz i. B.		CHAL (1898)
7880	Thudichum, Gustav	1866-	Allein mit dir "Hier ganz allein mit dir"	Op. 4 No. 3	Unspec.	Schmid i. M.		CHAL (1898)
7881	Thudichum, Gustav	1866-	Nebel "Ich leide, müd und schwer"	Op. 4 No. 2	Unspec.	Schmid i. M.		CHAL (1898)
7882	Thudichum, Gustav	1866-	Schneefall "Es fällt aus luft'ger Höh'"	Op. 4 No. 1	Unspec.	Schmid i. M.		CHAL (1898)
7883	Tichy, Rudolf	d. 1926	Wem macht der Wald die grösste Freud'		Unspec.	Blaha		CHAL (1911)
7884	Tiehsen, Otto	1817-1849	Auf geheimen Waldespfade	Op. 25 No. 5	Unspec.	B. & B.		CHAL (1898)
7885	Tiehsen, Otto	1817-1849	Heimliche Liebe "Kein Feuer, keine Kohle"	Op. 16 No. 1	S/MS	B. & B.		CHAL (1898)
7886	Tiehsen, Otto	1817-1849	Kuckuck "Im lieblichen Mai, tönt Vogelgeschrei"	Op. 25 No. 2	Unspec.	B. & B.		CHAL (1898)
7887	Tiehsen, Otto	1817-1849	Leise zieht durch mein Gemüth	Op. 16 No. 2	S/MS	B. & B.		CHAL (1898)
7888	Tiehsen, Otto	1817-1849	Müller und der Bach "Wo ein treues Herz"	Op. 25 No. 3	Unspec.	B. & B.		CHAL (1898)
7889	Tiehsen, Otto	1817-1849	Nacht "Süsse Ahnungsschauer gleiten"	Op. 16 No. 4	S/MS	B. & B.		CHAL (1898)
7890	Tiehsen, Otto	1817-1849	Notturno "Tu sei quel dolce"	Op. 30 No. 4	Unspec.	Bahn		CHAL (1898)
7891	Tiehsen, Otto	1817-1849	Schlummerlied "Wie so leis die Blätter"	Op. 25 No. 1	Unspec.	B. & B.		CHAL (1898)
7892	Tiehsen, Otto	1817-1849	Sonntag "Sonntag ist gekommen"	Op. 30 No. 2	Unspec.	Bahn		CHAL (1898)
7893	Tiehsen, Otto	1817-1849	Tannenbaum, "O Tannenbaum, du edles Reis"	Op. 30 No. 3	Unspec.	Bahn		CHAL (1898)
7894	Tiehsen, Otto	1817-1849	Was rauschen die Wogen	Op. 30 No. 1	Unspec.	Bahn		CHAL (1898)
7895	Tiehsen, Otto	1817-1849	Wassermann "Es war in des Maien"	Op. 25 No. 4	Unspec.	B. & B.		CHAL (1898)

REC	COMP	DTS	TITLE	OP #	VCG	PUB	COMMENTS	SRC
7896	Tiehsen, Otto	1817-1849	Wehmuth "Ich kann wohl manchmal singen"	Op. 16 No. 3	S/MS	B. & B.		CHAL (1898)
7897	Tinel, Edgar Pierre Joseph	1854-1912	Assisi sah ein Kind geboren		one v. w/ choir or 2 unspec. v.	B. & H.		CHAL (1911)
7898	Tolstoy, Alexei [Tolstoi]	1817-1875	Im Frühling "12 Kinderlieder"		Unspec.	Neldner	12 children's duets.	CHAL (1901)
7899	Tolstoy, Alexei [Tolstoi]	1817-1875	Kinderlieder (34)		Unspec.	Neldner	34 children's duets.	CHAL (1901)
7900	Tomaschek, Johann Wenzel	1774-1850	Edelknabe und die Müller-in "Wohin, wohin, schöne Müllerin"	Op. 60 No. 1	Unspec.	Hoffmann i. Pr.		CHAL (1898)
7901	Tomaschek, Johann Wenzel	1774-1850	Junhhesell und der Mühl-bach "Wo willst du klares Bächlein hin"	Op. 60 No. 3	Unspec.	Hoffmann i. Pr.		CHAL (1898)
7902	Tomaschek, Johann Wenzel	1774-1850	Vorschlag zur Güte "Du gefällst mir so wohl"	Op. 60 No. 2	Unspec.	Hoffmann i. Pr.		CHAL (1898)
7903	Topliff, Robert		Consider the Lilies		high & low v.	Church	In anthology "Sacred Duets A Collection of Two-Part Songs by the Best Composers" Vol. 2. Compi. & ed. W. Shakespeare. Pub. 1907.	MSN
7904	Toselli, Enrico	1883-1926	Serenata		Unspec.	Allans, Boston	Also solo	CVMP (1976)
7905	Tosti, Francesco Paolo	1846-1916	Because of you		Unspec.	Ricordi	Arr. Harriss	BBC (1975)
7906	Tosti, Francesco Paolo	1846-1916	Good-Bye		high & low v.	Hinds, Hayden & Eldredge	In anthology "The Most Popular Vocal Duets" Ed. Dr. E. J. Biedermann. Pub. 1914.	MSN
7907	Tosti, Francesco Paolo	1846-1916	Venetian Song		Unspec.	Chappell	Unspec. v. but dedicated to 2 women.	MSN
7908	Tourbié, Richard	1867-	Ach, wie ist's im Ehestand		2 female v.	Meissner	a.k.a. Richard Berndt and Rolf Wieland.	CHAL (1906)
7909	Tourbié, Richard	1867-	Hei, wir sind die Künstlerschar	Op. 280	Unspec.	O. Teich	a.k.a. Richard Berndt and Rolf Wieland.	CHAL (1901)
7910	Tourbié, Richard	1867-	Nein, nein, ich leiste d'rauf Verzicht		Unspec.	Meissner	a.k.a. Richard Berndt and Rolf Wieland.	CHAL (1901)
7911	Tourbié, Richard	1867-	Noble Manieren lernt' ich sehr leicht		Unspec.	Meissner	a.k.a. Richard Berndt and Rolf Wieland.	CHAL (1901)
7912	Tränkner, M.		Ach was ist wohl die schönste Zeit	Op. 41	2 female v.	Weissbach		CHAL (1911)
7913	Tränkner, M.		Aus stiller Bergeshöh	Op. 43	2 female v.	Weissbach		CHAL (1911)
7914	Traunfels, H.		'S giebt viele Humoristen		Unspec.	Kleine i. P.		CHAL (1901)
7915	Traventi		Amor to solo, to solo amai		S/A	Schott		CHAL (1901)
7916	Triest, Heinrich	1808-1885	Abendlied "Herz und verlangst du nicht Ruhe"	Op. 6 No. 4	Unspec.	Chal.		CHAL (1898)
7917	Triest, Heinrich	1808-1885	Frühlingstreiben "Alles Leben"	Op. 6 No. 3	Unspec.	Chal.		CHAL (1898)
7918	Triest, Heinrich	1808-1885	Horch, horch wie über's Wasser	Op. 6 No. 1	Unspec.	Chal.		CHAL (1898)

REC	COMP	DTS	TITLE	OP #	VCG	PUB	COMMENTS	SRC
7919	Triest, Heinrich	1808-1885	Primula veris "Liebliche Blume, bist du so früh schon"	Op. 10 No. 1	Unspec.	Chal.		CHAL (1898)
7920	Triest, Heinrich	1808-1885	Primula veris "Liebliche Blume, Primula veris"	Op. 10 No. 2	Unspec.	Chal.		CHAL (1898)
7921	Triest, Heinrich	1808-1885	Was singen die Cicaden	Op. 6 No. 2	Unspec.	Chal.		CHAL (1898)
7922	Triest, Heinrich	1808-1885	Weg der Liebe "Über die Berge"	Op. 10 No. 3	Unspec.	Chal.		CHAL (1898)
7923	Tritto, Giacomo	1733-1824	Da te mio ben dipendo "Hallt mir von deiner Flöte"		Unspec.	none listed		CHAL (1898)
7924	Troschel, Wilhelm Troszel	1823-1887	Walzer "Vien m'abbraccia"		S/A	Sennewald		CHAL (1898)
7925	Trotere, Henry	1855-1912	I Did Not Know		Unspec.	Leonard-Eng	Also solo	CVMP (1976)
7926	Trotere, Henry	1855-1912	I Don't Suppose		Unspec.	Cramer	Also solo	CVMP (1976)
7927	Trotere, Henry	1855-1912	In Your Dear Eyes		Unspec.	Cramer	Also solo	CVMP (1976)
7928	Trubel, Gerhard		Jesu, meine Freude		S/S or T/T	Hänssler-Verlag		NATS-SVD
7929	Truhn, Friedrich Heironymus	1811-1886	Es fällt ein Stern herunter	Op. 71 No. 2	Unspec.	Bahn		CHAL (1898)
7930	Truhn, Friedrich Heironymus	1811-1886	Festa "Fra nappie profumi"	Op. 72 No. 3	Unspec.	B. & B.		CHAL (1898)
7931	Truhn, Friedrich Heironymus	1811-1886	Mein Liebchen, wir sassen beisammen	Op. 71 No. 1	Unspec.	Bahn		CHAL (1898)
7932	Truhn, Friedrich Heironymus	1811-1886	Passeggiata "Orchi di fiori adorno"	Op. 72 No. 1	S/S	B. & B.		CHAL (1898)
7933	Truhn, Friedrich Heironymus	1811-1886	Tornate sereni	Op. 31	S/S	Peters		CHAL (1898)
7934	Tschiderer, E.		Alphorn "Es waren sich zwei so nahe"	No. 1	Unspec.	Gross i. Insbr.		CHAL (1898)
7935	Tschiderer, E.		Holdseliges Mädchen, dich hab' ich so gern "Ich sag' es den Sternen"	No. 4	Unspec.	Gross i. Insbr.		CHAL (1898)
7936	Tschiderer, E.		Mütterlein "Sieh' Kind am Waldesrand"	No. 2	Unspec.	Gross i. Insbr.		CHAL (1898)
7937	Tschiderer, E.		Tyroler in der Fremde "Horch auf einem Hügelrande"	No. 3	Unspec.	Gross i. Insbr.		CHAL (1898)
7938	Tschirch, Rudolf	1825-1872	Borussia, Britannia "Als König Friedrich wollte frein"		Unspec.	Bahn		CHAL (1898)
7939	Tschirch, Wilhelm	1818-1892	Ach wer das Scheiden uns gebracht	Op. 23	S/S	Kahnt		CHAL (1898)
7940	Tschirch, Wilhelm	1818-1892	An die Musik "Du holde Kunst"		S/A	B. & B.		CHAL (1898)
7941	Tschirch, Wilhelm	1818-1892	Ich bau' auf Gott	Op. 96	S/A	Leuckart		CHAL (1898)
7942	Tschirch, Wilhelm	1818-1892	Still wie die Nacht	Op. 35	S/A	Heinr.		CHAL (1898)
7943	Tuch, Heinrich Agatius Gottlob	1766-1821	Graf und die Tyrolerin "Kom. Wechselgesang"		Unspec.	Kollmann i. Leipz.		CHAL (1898)
7944	Tuma, A.		Abendfeier "Wie ist der Abend so traulich"	Set I No. 1	S/A	Cranz		CHAL (1898)
7945	Tuma, A.		Abschied vom Walde "Lebe wohl du grüner Hain"	II No. 4	S/A	Cranz		CHAL (1898)
7946	Tuma, A.		Herbstlied "Es schleicht um Busch und Halde"	II No. 6	S/A	Cranz		CHAL (1898)
7947	Tuma, A.		Morgenlied "Kein Stimmlein noch schallt"	II No. 5	S/A	Cranz		CHAL (1898)
7948	Tuma, A.		Vergissmeinnicht "Es blüht ein schönes Blümchen"	I No. 2	S/A	Cranz		CHAL (1898)

REC	COMP	DTS	TITLE	OP #	VCG	PUB	COMMENTS	SRC
7949	Tuma, A.		Wanderlied "Vögel singen, Blumen blüh'n"	I No. 3	S/A	Cranz		CHAL (1898)
7950	Tussenbroek, Hendrika von	1854-1935	Meidoorn		Unspec.	Alsbach	Dutch woman comp.	CVMP (1976)
7951	Tuuri, Jaako		Ole Luonani Silloin	Op. 12 No. 2	Unspec.	Fazer		CVMP (1976)
7952	Tuuri, Jaako		Tule, Lykkaamme Laineille Purren	Op. 12 No. 1	Unspec.	Fazer		CVMP (1976)
7953	Tuuri, Jaako		Unten Vienot Viljapellot	Op. 4	Unspec.	Fazer		CVMP (1976)
7954	Uber, Christian Friedrich Hermann	1781-1822	Lob des Gesanges "Gesang verschönt das Leben"		Unspec.	B. & H.		CHAL (1898)
7955	Umlauft, Paul	1853-1934	Auf dem Berge und in dem Thal	Op. 25 No. 5	S/A	R. Forberg		CHAL (1898)
7956	Umlauft, Paul	1853-1934	Ich will Trauern, Trauern schwinden sehn	Op. 25 No. 1	S/A	R. Forberg		CHAL (1898)
7957	Umlauft, Paul	1853-1934	Nun freuet euch, Junge und Alte	Op. 25 No. 4	S/A	R. Forberg		CHAL (1898)
7958	Umlauft, Paul	1853-1934	Nun ist der kühle Winter	Op. 25 No. 2	S/A	R. Forberg		CHAL (1898)
7959	Umlauft, Paul	1853-1934	Tanzweisen in Länderform (5)		S/A	R. Forberg	Collection of 5 unspec. duets, prob. Op. 25	CHAL (1898)
7960	Umlauft, Paul	1853-1934	Weine Herze, weinet Augen	Op. 25 No. 3	S/A	R. Forberg		CHAL (1898)
7961	Unger, A.		Ein Täubchen flog vom Himmelsrand	No. 1	Unspec.	Heins i. B.		CHAL (1911)
7962	Unger, A.		Es blüht ein schönes Blümchen	No. 6	Unspec.	Heins		CHAL (1911)
7963	Unger, A.		Jetzt fröhlich gemut	No. 2	Unspec.	Heins		CHAL (1911)
7964	Unger, A.		Kinderlieder (6)		Unspec.	Heins i. B.	6 children's duets	CHAL (1911)
7965	Unger, A.		O Schmetterling, sprich	No. 5	Unspec.	Heins		CHAL (1911)
7966	Unger, A.		So schlaf' in Ruh'	No. 4	Unspec.	Heins		CHAL (1911)
7967	Unger, A.		Wart', Vögelin, wärt'	No. 3	Unspec.	Heins		CHAL (1911)
7968	Unknown composer or arranger		All Through the Night		Unspec.	Allans	Welsh air. Eng. trans Welsh. Arr. for 2 v. In anthology "Vocal Duets Collection" Vol. 1. Pub. 1992.	MSN
7969	Unknown composer or arranger		Believe Me, If All Those Endearing Young Charms		Unspec.	Allans	Irish air. Arr. for 2 v. In anthology "Vocal Duets Collection" Vol. 1. Pub. 1992.	MSN
7970	Unknown composer or arranger		Dark Eyes		Unspec.	Allans	Russ. gypsy air. Eng. trans. Russ. Arr. for 2 v. In anthology "Vocal Duets Collection" Vol. 1. Pub. 1992.	MSN
7971	Unknown composer or arranger		Lark in the Clear Air, The		Unspec.	Allans	Irish air. Arr. for 2 v. In anthology "Vocal Duets Collection" Vol. 1. Pub. 1992.	MSN
7972	Unknown composer or arranger		Le Poète et le Fantôme		Unspec.	CVR	No comp. listed	MSN

REC	COMP	DTS	TITLE	OP #	VCG	PUB	COMMENTS	SRC
7973	Unknown composer or arranger		Londonderry Air		Unspec.	Allans	Irish air, arr. for 2 v. In anthology "Vocal Duets Collection" Vol. 1. Pub. 1992.	MSN
7974	Unknown composer or arranger		Santa Lucia		Unspec.	Allans	Neapolitan folk song. Eng. trans. It. Arr. for 2 v. In anthology "Vocal Duets Collection" Vol. 1. 1992.	MSN
7975	Unknown composer or arranger		Tiritomba		Unspec.	Allans	Neapolitan folk song. Eng. trans of It. Arr. for 2 v. In anthology "Vocal Duets Collection" Vol. 1. 1992.	MSN
7976	Uray, Ernst Ludwig	1906-	Styri Dvojspevy		S/A	Slov. Hud. Fond.		CVMP (1976)
7977	Urban, Friedrich Julius	1838-1918	Macht der Liebe "Wenn mir hell auf allen Wegen"	Op. 14 No. 1	2 low v.	Bahn		CHAL (1898)
7978	Urban, Friedrich Julius	1838-1918	Mein Liebchen, wir sassen beisammen	Op. 17 No. 1	2 low v.	Bahn		CHAL (1898)
7979	Urban, Friedrich Julius	1838-1918	Rothe Rose "Röslein roth im Walde"	Op. 17 No. 2	2 low v.	Bahn		CHAL (1898)
7980	Urban, Friedrich Julius	1838-1918	Unsterbliche Liebe "Sage nicht, ich sei dein Leben"	Op. 14 No. 2	2 low v.	Bahn		CHAL (1898)
7981	Urlaub, A.		Ein quietschvergnügtes Duo Sie	Op. 49	Unspec.	Uhse		CHAL (1901)
7982	Vadtor, Thomas		Sweet Suffolk owl		Unspec.	Stainer & Bell		BBC (1975)
7983	Van Buskirk, Carl		Song of Yellow		S/A	IMC		CVMP (1985)
7984	Van Cromphout, L.		Hirondelles		S/S	Junne		CHAL (1898)
7985	Vangele, V.		Noël "Voici donc l'heure"		Unspec.	Betram i. Br.		CHAL (1898)
7986	Vater, F. A.		Regina coeli		Unspec.	Grund i. Schön-linde	org or harm accomp.	CHAL (1898)
7987	Vaughan Williams, Ralph	1872-1958	Dirge for Fidele		S/S	Ash-down		BBC (1975)
7988	Vaughan Williams, Ralph	1872-1958	It Was a Lover and His Lass		Unspec.	Rober-ton	pf or orch accomp.	CVMP (1976)
7989	Vaughan Williams, Ralph	1872-1958	Song of the Leaves of Life and the Water of Life, The		S/S	OUP	From "Pilgrims' Progress"	BBC (1975)
7990	Vaughan Williams, Ralph	1872-1958	Song of the Leaves of Life and the Water of Life, The		S/S or S/A	OUP		ASR
7991	Vaughan Williams, Ralph	1872-1958	Songs of the Leaves of Life and the Water of Life, The		S/S or S/A	OUP		CVMP (1976)
7992	Veit, Václav Jindrich [Wenzel Heinrich]	1806-1864	Ave Maria "Leise sinkt der Dämmrung Schleier"	I No. 1	Unspec.	Leuckart		CHAL (1898)
7993	Veit, Václav Jindrich [Wenzel Heinrich]	1806-1864	Gruss an Maria "Nacht entflieht"	I No. 3	Unspec.	Leuckart		CHAL (1898)
7994	Veit, Václav Jindrich [Wenzel Heinrich]	1806-1864	Maria, die Gnaden-sonne "Sei gegrüsst, du Gnadensonne"	II No. 4	Unspec.	Leuckart		CHAL (1898)

REC	COMP	DTS	TITLE	OP #	VCG	PUB	COMMENTS	SRC
7995	Veit, Václav Jindrich [Wenzel Heinrich]	1806-1864	Maria Engelkönigen "Wir grüssen dich heut"	II No. 3	Unspec.	Leuckart		CHAL (1898)
7996	Veit, Václav Jindrich [Wenzel Heinrich]	1806-1864	Maria, Zufluckt der Sünder "Viel süsse Namen schmücken dich"	II No. 5	Unspec.	Leuckart		CHAL (1898)
7997	Veit, Václav Jindrich [Wenzel Heinrich]	1806-1864	Marias Wiegenlied "Die ihr dort wallet"	II No. 2	Unspec.	Leuckart		CHAL (1898)
7998	Veit, Václav Jindrich [Wenzel Heinrich]	1806-1864	Marienlieder		Unspec.	Leuckart		CHAL (1898)
7999	Veit, Václav Jindrich [Wenzel Heinrich]	1806-1864	Pilgerlied "Süsse Maria, bitte für uns"	I No. 4	Unspec.	Leuckart		CHAL (1898)
8000	Veit, Václav Jindrich [Wenzel Heinrich]	1806-1864	Weihelied zum Maisegen Mai ist gekommen"	II No. 1	Unspec.	Leuckart		CHAL (1898)
8001	Veit, Václav Jindrich [Wenzel Heinrich]	1806-1864	Zweigesang der Elfen "Hörst du das Flüstern"	Op. 35	S/A	B. & H.		CHAL (1898)
8002	Verbroek, C. J. J.		Herz, mein Herz sei nicht beklommen"		S/A	Eulenburg		CHAL (1898)
8003	Verelst, P. F.		Alma redemptoris	No. 12	Unspec.	Schott	org accomp.	CHAL (1898)
8004	Verelst, P. F.		Ave Maria "Ave Maria gratia pleni"	No. 10	Unspec.	Schott	org accomp.	CHAL (1898)
8005	Verelst, P. F.		Ave Regina	No. 13	Unspec.	Schott	org accomp.	CHAL (1898)
8006	Verelst, P. F.		Ecce panis	No. 1	Unspec.	Roothaan	org accomp.	CHAL (1898)
8007	Verelst, P. F.		Missa "Adoro te devote"	No. 2	Unspec.	Schott	org accomp.	CHAL (1898)
8008	Verelst, P. F.		Modulamina "Recueil de morceaux religieux"		Unspec.	Schott	org accomp.	CHAL (1898)
8009	Verelst, P. F.		O dulcis amor	No. 5	Unspec.	Schott	org accomp.	CHAL (1898)
8010	Verelst, P. F.		O esca viatorum	No. 8	Unspec.	Schott	org accomp.	CHAL (1898)
8011	Verelst, P. F.		O fidelis anima	No. 9	Unspec.	Schott	org accomp.	CHAL (1898)
8012	Verelst, P. F.		O quam suavis est	No. 4	Unspec.	Schott	org accomp.	CHAL (1898)
8013	Verelst, P. F.		O sacrum convivium	No. 3	Unspec.	Schott	org accomp.	CHAL (1898)
8014	Verelst, P. F.		O salutaris	No. 7	Unspec.	Schott	org accomp.	CHAL (1898)
8015	Verelst, P. F.		Panis angelicus	No. 6	Unspec.	Schott	org accomp.	CHAL (1898)
8016	Verelst, P. F.		Regina coeli	No. 14	Unspec.	Schott	org accomp.	CHAL (1898)
8017	Verelst, P. F.		Salve regina	No. 11	Unspec.	Schott	org accomp.	CHAL (1898)
8018	Verelst, P. F.		Tantum ergo	No. 10	Unspec.	Schott	org accomp.	CHAL (1898)

REC	COMP	DTS	TITLE	OP #	VCG	PUB	COMMENTS	SRC
8019	Verner, H. C.		Love's Awakening		Unspec.	Brain-ard's Sons	In anthology "Brainard's Collection of Vocal Duets from Popular Modern and Standard Composers" Pub. 1903.	MSN
8020	Verner, H. C.		Pride of the Ball		Unspec.	Brain-ard's Sons	In anthology "Brainard's Collection of Vocal Duets from Popular Modern and Standard Composers" Pub. 1903.	MSN
8021	Viardot-Garcia, Pauline	1821-1910	Zigeunerlied "Wir leben nur von heut auf morgen"		Unspec.	Sim-rock	Fr. woman comp. Arr. of Brahms song.	CHAL (1898)
8022	Viardot-Garcia, Pauline (F. Chopin)	1821-1910	La Beauté		Unspec.	poss. Hamelle	Fr. woman comp. Transcription of Chopin "Mazurka" for piano.	
8023	Viardot-Garcia, Pauline (J. Brahms)	1821-1910	Les Bohémiennes		S/MS	G. Schirm.	Fr. woman comp. Arr. of Brahms song. In catalogue page "Selected Vocal Duets" of G. Schirmer, Inc. NY (no date)	MSN
8024	Viardot-Garcia, Pauline (J. Brahms)	1821-1910	Wir leben nur von heut auf morgen		Unspec.	Sim-rock	Fr. woman comp. Arr. P. Viardot-Garcia of Brahms' song	CHAL (1911)
8025	Vierling, Georg	1820-1901	Gretchens Beichte "Wieder ist es lange zehn"	Op. 20	S/A	Leuck-art		CHAL (1898)
8026	Vierling, Georg	1820-1901	Guter rath "Ach Mutter, liebe Mutter"	Op. 45	2 female v.	Chal.		CHAL (1898)
8027	Vierling, Georg	1820-1901	Hunderttausend Lerchen jubeln	Op. 71 No. 3	Unspec.	Schott		CHAL (1898)
8028	Vierling, Georg	1820-1901	Rheinfahrt "Im Maien auf dem Rhein"	Op. 71 No. 1	Unspec.	Schott		CHAL (1898)
8029	Vierling, Georg	1820-1901	Ständchen "In dem Himmel ruht die Erde"	Op. 71 No. 2	Unspec.	Schott		CHAL (1898)
8030	Vincent, Heinrich Joseph	1819-1901	Alte Spielmann "Durch die Mondnacht klingt es klagend"		Unspec.	Schott		CHAL (1898)
8031	Viol, Willy	1848-	Lang, lang ist's her "Sag mirs Wort"		2 high or 2 low v.	R. & E.		CHAL (1898)
8032	Visconti, E.		La Festa alla Marina		S/A	G. Schirm.	In catalogue page "Favorite French and Italian Vocal Duets" of G. Schirmer, Inc. NY (no date)	MSN
8033	Vogel, Bernhardt	1847-1898	Bächleins Lust und Lied "Ein klares Bächlein floss"	Op. 27 No. 3	Unspec.	Kahnt		CHAL (1898)
8034	Vogel, Bernhardt	1847-1898	Blumendanken "Blümchen im lieben mag"	Op. 27 No. 5	Unspec.	Kahnt		CHAL (1898)
8035	Vogel, Bernhardt	1847-1898	Blumensegen "Blumen lieb und Blumen traut"	Op. 27 No. 4	Unspec.	Kahnt		CHAL (1898)
8036	Vogel, Bernhardt	1847-1898	Feldblumen "7 zweist. Lieder"	Op. 27	Unspec.	Kahnt	7 duets	CHAL (1898)
8037	Vogel, Bernhardt	1847-1898	Fröhliche Fink "Fink schlüpft in den Baum"	Op. 27 No. 6	Unspec.	Kahnt		CHAL (1898)
8038	Vogel, Bernhardt	1847-1898	Grösseres Glück "O wie glücklich deine Hand"	Op. 27 No. 2	Unspec.	Kahnt		CHAL (1898)
8039	Vogel, Bernhardt	1847-1898	Heimweh "Du sagtest mir. einst"	Op. 27 No. 7	Unspec.	Kahnt		CHAL (1898)
8040	Vogel, Bernhardt	1847-1898	Winterlicher Frühlingsbote "Kleine Blume sei gegrüsst"	Op. 27 No. 1	Unspec.	Kahnt		CHAL (1898)

REC	COMP	DTS	TITLE	OP #	VCG	PUB	COMMENTS	SRC
8041	Vogel, Hans	1867-	Der du am Sternenbogen	No. 2	2 female v.	R. & B.		CHAL (1898)
8042	Vogel, Hans	1867-	Frühlingsabend "Du feuchter Frühlingsabend"	No. 1	2 female v.	R. & B.		CHAL (1898)
8043	Vogel, M. [prob. Martin]	1863-1930	Auf dem Teich, dem regungslosen	Op. 15 No. 2	2 low v.	Kahnt		CHAL (1898)
8044	Vogel, M. [prob. Martin]	1863-1930	Auf geheimen Waldespfade	Op. 15 No. 1	2 low v.	Kahnt		CHAL (1898)
8045	Vogel, M. [prob. Martin]	1863-1930	Bitten "Vater kröne du mit Segen"	Op. 62 No. 2	Unspec.	Junne		CHAL (1898)
8046	Vogel, M. [prob. Martin]	1863-1930	Festgesang "Schallet laut, ihr Jubelklänge"	Op. 62 No. 1	Unspec.	Junne		CHAL (1898)
8047	Vogel, M. [prob. Martin]	1863-1930	Mädchenlieder		Unspec.	Hug		CHAL (1898)
8048	Vogel, M. [prob. Martin]	1863-1930	Steh' auf und öffne das Fenster	Op. 21 No. 1	Unspec.	R. & E.		CHAL (1898)
8049	Vogel, M. [prob. Martin]	1863-1930	Waldgang "Nun bin ich froh und freue mich"	Op. 21 No. 4	Unspec.	R. & E.		CHAL (1898)
8050	Vogel, M. [prob. Martin]	1863-1930	Wir haben und Beide verstanden	Op. 21 No. 3	Unspec.	R. & E.		CHAL (1898)
8051	Vogel, M. [prob. Martin]	1863-1930	Zum Gedächtniss Kaiser Wilhelmus I "Es ist's in deinen Liedern"	Op. 62 No. 3	Unspec.	Junne		CHAL (1898)
8052	Vogel, M. [prob. Martin]	1863-1930	Zur Nacht "Gute Nacht, allen Müden seis gebracht"	Op. 21 No. 2	Unspec.	R. & E.		CHAL (1898)
8053	Voigt, F.		Martl und Gretl, das lieb-liche Schwesternpaar "Kaum sind der Pension entronnen"	Op. 20	2 female v.	Glaser		CHAL (1898)
8054	Voigt, Henriette	1877-	Heimat, du süsse, du Dörfchen klein	Op. 113	Unspec.	R. & P. Verl.	Grmn. woman comp.	CHAL (1911)
8055	Voigt, Henriette	1877-	Mien Deutschland "Gott segne dich, mein Deutschland"		Unspec.	Kistner	Grmn. woman comp.	CHAL (1898)
8056	Voigt, Henriette	1877-	Mutterliebe "In der Erinn'rung traumverloren"	Op. 148	2 high or 2 low v.	R. & P.	Grmn. woman comp.	CHAL (1898)
8057	Voigt, Hermann	1851-	Mutterliebe		MS/A or MS/B	C. Fischer	In catalogue page "Selected Vocal Duets By Favorite Com-posers" of Carl Fischer NY (no date)	MSN
8058	Voigt-Kudlik, Th.		Scheppern muass' "Uns-'re flotten Weanliader"		Unspec.	Rörich		CHAL (1898)
8059	Volckmar, Wilhelm	1812-1887	An die Hoffnung "Die du gleich der Morgenstunde"	Op. 7 No. 4	S/S	Schott		CHAL (1898)
8060	Volckmar, Wilhelm	1812-1887	Schwarz, Roth und Gold		Unspec.	Schott		CHAL (1898)
8061	Volkmann, W.		Haideblume "Haidebleme, niedich kleine"	Op. 70 No. 3	Unspec.	Peter-ling		CHAL (1898)
8062	Volkmann, W.		Haideblume niedlich kleine	No. 3	S/A	Gerdes i. Cöln		CHAL (1906)
8063	Volkmann, W.		Ich hab' die Nacht geträumet	No. 2	S/A	Gerdes i. Cöln		CHAL (1906)
8064	Volkmann, W.		Ich sah ein Röslein blühen	No. 4	S/A	Gerdes i. Cöln		CHAL (1906)
8065	Volkmann, W.		Kinderlieder (20)		Unspec.	Böhm & S.	20 children's duets	CHAL (1911)
8066	Volkmann, W.		Schlafe Kindlein hold und weiss	No. 1	S/A	Gerdes i. Cöln		CHAL (1906)

REC	COMP	DTS	TITLE	OP #	VCG	PUB	COMMENTS	SRC
8067	Volkmann, W.		Traum "Ich hab' die Nacht geträumet"	Op. 70 No. 2	Unspec.	Peterling		CHAL (1898)
8068	Volkmann, W.		Wiegenlied "Schlafe Kindlein, hold und wiess"	Op. 70 No. 1	Unspec.	Peterling		CHAL (1898)
8069	Volle, Bjarne	1943-	Alles Oyne		S/A	Noton		CVMP (1995)
8070	Volle, Bjarne	1943-	Du Ska Itte Tro I Graset		S/A	Noton	Also solo	CVMP (1995)
8071	Volle, Bjarne	1943-	Liten Vise, En		S/A	Noton	Also solo	CVMP (1995)
8072	Vollstedt, Robert	1854-1919	Mit dir allein in Dämmerschein "Dämmerung schon deckt die Flur"	Op. 66	Unspec.	Thiemer		CHAL (1898)
8073	Voullaire, Waldemar	1825-1902	Weihnachtslied "Licht ist dein Kleid"		S/A	Heinr.	org accomp.	CHAL (1898)
8074	Voutz, H.		Muttersprache, Mutterlaut	Op. 4 No. 1	Unspec.	Kalb		CHAL (1911)
8075	Voutz, H.		Wir wandern und wallen	Op. 10	Unspec.	Kalb		CHAL (1911)
8076	Wachsmann, Johann Joachim	1787-1853	Gleich und Gleich "Ein Blumenglöckchen vom Boden hervor (empor)"	Op. 10 No. 3	Unspec.	Heinr.		CHAL (1898)
8077	Wachsmann, Johann Joachim	1787-1853	Mein Lieb "Wo ist mein Lieb"	Op. 10 No. 2	Unspec.	Heinr.		CHAL (1898)
8078	Wachsmann, Johann Joachim	1787-1853	Sangeslust "Vöglein singt"	Op. 10 No. 1	Unspec.	Heinr.		CHAL (1898)
8079	Wade, Joseph Augustine	1801-1845	I've wandered in dreams		Unspec.	Chappell		BBC (1975)
8080	Wagenblass, W.		Uns arme Mädchen wird Niemand beneiden	Op. 66	Unspec.	Glaser		CHAL (1901)
8081	Wagenbrenner Josef	1873-	Lieder-Album für Schule und Haus		Unspec.	Banger	Anthology. For 1 & 2 v.	CHAL (1911)
8082	Wagenbrenner Josef	1873-	Was eilst du so	I No. 10	Unspec.	Banger		CHAL (1911)
8083	Wagenbrenner Josef	1873-	Was ist das für ein schwarzer Mann	I No. 6	Unspec.	Banger		CHAL (1911)
8084	Wagener, Paul	1870-	Heute ist der erste Maskenball	Op. 76	Unspec.	Bloch	Pen name of Paul Bendix	CHAL (1906)
8085	Wagner, C. [prob. Karl Jakob]	1772-1822	Echo "Du wallst durch die Fluren"		Unspec.	Schott		CHAL (1898)
8086	Wagner, Ernst David	1806-1883	Ihr Kinderlein kommt		Unspec.	Schlesinger		CHAL (1898)
8087	Wagner, Ernst David	1806-1883	O du fröhliche, o du selige		Unspec.	Schlesinger		CHAL (1898)
8088	Wagner, Ernst David	1806-1883	Stille Nacht, heilige Nacht		Unspec.	Schlesinger	Arr. of song	CHAL (1898)
8089	Wagner, Ernst David	1806-1883	Weihnachtsalbum (21)		Unspec.	Schlesinger	Ed. Michael. Collection of 21 Christmas solos & duets.	CHAL (1911)
8090	Wagner, Franz	1870-	Du lieber heil'gen frommer Christ	Op. 57 No. 2	Unspec.	Oppenheimer	org	CHAL (1906)
8091	Wagner, Josef Franz	1856-1908	Unter dem Doppeladler	Op. 159	Unspec.	Robitschek		CHAL (1898)
8092	Wagner, Josef Franz	1856-1908	Wenn i am Wörthersee	Op. 410	Unspec.	Robitschek		CHAL (1911)
8093	Wagner, Paul Emil	1846-	Dass wir schneid'ge Kerle sind		Unspec.	Kleine i. P.		CHAL (1901)
8094	Wakefield, Augusta Mary	1853-1910	The rushbearing		Unspec.	Curwen	Eng. woman comp. Ed. Graham	BBC (1975)
8095	Walden, Otto von	1871-1924	Hörst du, wie die Glocken läuten	Op. 127	Unspec.	O. Forberg	Pen name of Fritz Schindler	CHAL (1901)

REC	COMP	DTS	TITLE	OP #	VCG	PUB	COMMENTS	SRC
8096	Walden, Otto von	1871-1924	Wenn dich Lied bedrängt	Op. 122	Unspec.	O. Forberg	Pen name of Fritz Schindler	CHAL (1901)
8097	Walden, Otto von	1871-1924	Wenn nach langer Winternacht	Op. 112	Unspec.	O. Forberg	Pen name of Fritz Schindler	CHAL (1901)
8098	Waldmann v. d. Aue		Liedergarten "100 alte und neue Gesänge"		Unspec.	Strassburger Druckerei	Anthology of 100 old & new songs. Unspec. comp.	CHAL (1906)
8099	Wallace		Holy Father, guide		S/A	White-Smith	In catalogue page "Vocal Duetts" of White-Smith Music Pub. Co. (no date)	MSN
8100	Wallach Crane, Joelle	20th C.	Five-Fold Amen		S/A	Am. Comp. Al.	acap. Amer. woman comp.	CVMP (1995)
8101	Wallach Crane, Joelle	20th C.	Five-Fold Amen		high & low v.	ACA	acap. Amer. woman comp. Also listed under Wallach.	ASR
8102	Wallach Crane, Joelle	20th C.	V'erastich Li L'olam		S/A	Am. Comp. Al.	acap. Amer. woman comp.	CVMP (1995)
8103	Wallbach, Ludwig	d. 1914	Das ist die liebe Stelle	Op. 36	S/S	Weinholtz		CHAL (1901)
8104	Wallbach, Ludwig	d. 1914	Schön Rohtraut "Wie heisst König Ringangs Töchterlein"	Op. 22	Unspec.	Bosworth		CHAL (1898)
8105	Wallnöfer, Adolf	1854-1946	Das ist die schönste Zeit		S/A	Musik-Woche		CHAL (1906)
8106	Wallnöfer, Adolf	1854-1946	Erste Liebe "Ich fragte leise"	Op. 17 No. 4	med. & low v.	B. & H.		CHAL (1898)
8107	Wallnöfer, Adolf	1854-1946	Frühling "Frühling, wie mit Zauberschwingen"	Op. 17 No. 2	med. & low v.	B. & H.		CHAL (1898)
8108	Wallnöfer, Adolf	1854-1946	Glaubt nicht, es sei mein Angesicht	Op. 13 No. 3	med. & low v.	B. & H.		CHAL (1898)
8109	Wallnöfer, Adolf	1854-1946	Ist's Leben oder Tod "Hell ist mein Geist"	Op. 17 No. 1	med. & low v.	B. & H.		CHAL (1898)
8110	Walter-Kiesel, M.		Steyrer Bua "I bin a Steyrer Bua"		2 med. v.	Blaha		CHAL (1898)
8111	Wandelt, Amadeus	1860-1927	Hör' mal schwarzer Domino		Unspec.	Harmonie i. B.		CHAL (1906)
8112	Wandow, L.		Einladung "Geehrteste Frau"		Unspec.	B. & B.		CHAL (1898)
8113	Waniek, Alois	d. 1919	Wiener Bildeln "I trau mir z'wetten"		Unspec.	Kratochwill		CHAL (1898)
8114	Wannthaler, Gustav	d. 1913	Mama, Papa "Wer bringt das kleine Kind"		Unspec.	Tonger		CHAL (1898)
8115	Wanthaler, Gustav	d. 1913	A Gigerl steigt ein Madel nach		2 med. v.	Blaha		CHAL (1901)
8116	Wanthaler, Gustav	d. 1913	Es sitzen in an Nachtcaffée		Unspec.	Blaha		CHAL (1906)
8117	Wanthaler, Gustav	d. 1913	Herr Schmalzerl, sehr ein alter Herr		2 med. v.	Blaha		CHAL (1901)
8118	Wanthaler, Gustav	d. 1913	Holz und Licht, sowie die Kohl'n		Unspec.	Eberle i. Wien		CHAL (1901)
8119	Wanthaler, Gustav	d. 1913	Ja wer da nöt aufdraht kann ka Weana nöt sein "Es hat g'wiss a Jeder"		Unspec.	Bösendorfer		CHAL (1898)
8120	Wanthaler, Gustav	d. 1913	Lerchenfelder "Mir san von Lerchenfeld"		Unspec.	Kratochwill		CHAL (1898)
8121	Wanthaler, Gustav	d. 1913	Liab hat der Herrgott	Op. 101	Unspec.	Blaha		CHAL (1906)
8122	Wanthaler, Gustav	d. 1913	Pudel ist ein treues Thier		2 med. v.	Blaha		CHAL (1901)

REC	COMP	DTS	TITLE	OP #	VCG	PUB	COMMENTS	SRC
8123	Wanthaler, Gustav	d. 1913	Weana Schwossa "Mir san zwa Scwossa"		Unspec.	Kratoch-will		CHAL (1898)
8124	Wanthaler, Gustav	d. 1913	Weil mir zwa Hallodri san "Wie mir noch klane Buam"		Unspec.	Kratoch-will		CHAL (1898)
8125	Wany, W. J.		Kunstnovize "Schlür-fend braunen Mokka-trank"	Op. 16	S/A	Siegel		CHAL (1898)
8126	Wappaus, Karl	1872-	Ha, was seh' ich, theure Ida		2 female v.	Danner		CHAL (1906)
8127	Wappaus, Karl	1872-	Was tut der Mensch nicht alles	Op. 556	Unspec.	Danner		CHAL (1911)
8128	Wardini, Gebr.		Wie ist doch hier auf Erden		Unspec.	O. Teich		CHAL (1901)
8129	Warren, Betsy		Pussy Cat Duets		Unspec.	United Mus		CVMP (1995)
8130	Watelle, Ch.		Aubade "Voici que l'aub"		Unspec.	Schott		CHAL (1898)
8131	Weatherly, F. E.		Danny Boy		Unspec.	Boosey	Also solo	CVMP (1976)
8132	Weber, A. [prob. Bernhard Anselm]	1766-1821	Weihnachtsgebet "Vom Himmel steigst du Herr"		Unspec.	Vieweg i. Qu.		CHAL (1898)
8133	Weber, Carl Maria von	1786-1826	Abschied "O Berlin ich muss"	Op. 54 No. 4	Unspec.	Schles-inger		CHAL (1898)
8134	Weber, Carl Maria von	1786-1826	Bald ist der Frühling da!		S/A	B. & H.	In anth. "Zweistim. Lied. f. Sop. u. Altstimme mit Klavierbegleitung f. den Haus- u. Schulgebrauch v. H. M. Schletterer" 3 vols.	MSN
8135	Weber, Carl Maria von	1786-1926	Bald ist der Frühling da!		S/A	B. & H.	In anthology "Zweistim-mige Lieder für Sopran und Altstimme mit Klav-iergleitung für den Haus- und Schulgebrauch"	MSN
8136	Weber, Carl Maria von	1786-1826	Dich an dies Herz zu drücken		S/S	Schles-inger		CHAL (1898)
8137	Weber, Carl Maria von	1786-1826	Immer wieder schwur ich Liebe	Op. 31 No. 1	S/S	Schles-inger		CHAL (1898)
8138	Weber, Carl Maria von	1786-1826	Immer wieder süsses Leben	Op. 31	S/A	Simrock et al.		CHAL (1898)
8139	Weber, Carl Maria von	1786-1826	Judäa hochgelobtes Land	Op. 80 No. 2	S/A	Schles-inger	Arr. Hollaender	CHAL (1901)
8140	Weber, Carl Maria von	1786-1826	Mailied "Trarira, der Sommer der ist da"	Op. 64 No. 2	S/S	Schles-inger		CHAL (1898)
8141	Weber, Carl Maria von	1786-1826	Mille Volte	Op. 30 No. 1	S/S or S/MS	Schles-inger	In "Tre Duetti" Op. 30	NATS-VCD
8142	Weber, Carl Maria von	1786-1826	Mille volte mio tesoro		S/S	J. Ewer		BBC (1975)
8143	Weber, Carl Maria von	1786-1826	Quodlibet "So geht es"	Op. 54 No. 2	Unspec.	Schles-inger		CHAL (1898)
8144	Weber, Carl Maria von	1786-1826	Se il mio ben		S/S	J. Ewer		BBC (1975)
8145	Weber, Carl Maria von	1786-1826	Se il mio ben	Op. 30 No. 3	S/S or S/MS	Schles-inger	In "Tre Duetti" Op. 30	NATS-VCD
8146	Weber, Carl Maria von	1786-1826	Trage Geliebter das Scheiden	Op. 31 No. 2	S/S	Schles-inger		CHAL (1898)
8147	Weber, Carl Maria von	1786-1826	Trage Geliebter das Scheiden	Op. 31 No. 2	S/A	Simrock		CHAL (1898)

REC	COMP	DTS	TITLE	OP #	VCG	PUB	COMMENTS	SRC
8148	Weber, Carl Maria von	1786-1826	Va ti consola addio		S/S	J. Ewer		BBC (1975)
8149	Weber, Carl Maria von	1786-1826	Va ti consola addio	Op. 30 No. 2	S/S or S/MS	Schlesinger	In "Tre Duetti" Op. 30	NATS-VCD
8150	Weber, Carl Maria von	1786-1826	Wenn mein Herz	Op. 31 No. 3	S/S	Schlesinger et al.		CHAL (1898)
8151	Weber, Franz	1805-1876	Auf dem Wasser "Es murmeln die Quellen"	I No. 4	Unspec.	Weber i. Cöln	Father of C. M. v. Weber	CHAL (1898)
8152	Weber, Franz	1805-1876	Lied des Trostes "Was grämst du dich"	II No. 5	Unspec.	Weber i. Cöln	Father of C. M. v. Weber	CHAL (1898)
8153	Weber, Franz	1805-1876	Mailied "Da ist er, der liebliche"	I No. 3	Unspec.	Weber i. Cöln	Father of C. M. v. Weber	CHAL (1898)
8154	Weber, Franz	1805-1876	Nachtlied "Erde ruht, der Himmel wacht"	I No. 2	Unspec.	Weber i. Cöln	Father of C. M. v. Weber	CHAL (1898)
8155	Weber, Franz	1805-1876	O du fröhliche, o du selige	I No. 1	Unspec.	Weber i. Cöln	Father of C. M. v. Weber	CHAL (1898)
8156	Weber, Franz	1805-1876	Schäfers Sonntagslied "Das ist der Tag des Herrn"	II No. 6	Unspec.	Weber i. Cöln	Father of C. M. v. Weber	CHAL (1898)
8157	Weber, Franz	1805-1876	Schiffahrt "Über die hellen funkelnden Wellen"	II No. 8	Unspec.	Weber i. Cöln	Father of C. M. v. Weber	CHAL (1898)
8158	Weber, Franz	1805-1876	Wie ist doch die Erde so schön	II No. 7	Unspec.	Weber i. Cöln	Father of C. M. v. Weber	CHAL (1898)
8159	Weber, Gottfried	1779-1839	Alexandria	Op. 43	Unspec.	Kahnt		CHAL (1898)
8160	Weber, Gustav	1845-1887	Aschenputtels Täubchen "Rucke di gu"	No. 5	Unspec.	Hug		CHAL (1898)
8161	Weber, Gustav	1845-1887	Dornröschen "Schliess' mir schöne Blume"	No. 6	Unspec.	Hug		CHAL (1898)
8162	Weber, Gustav	1845-1887	Duettino "Ob Leiden Lieben sei"		Unspec.	Kahnt		CHAL (1898)
8163	Weber, Gustav	1845-1887	Herbstklage "Holder Lenz du bist dahin"	Op. 2 No. 3	S/A	Hofmeister		CHAL (1898)
8164	Weber, Gustav	1845-1887	Jägerlied "frisch auf, ihr Jäger"	Op. 21 No. 5	Unspec.	Simrock		CHAL (1898)
8165	Weber, Gustav	1845-1887	Jorinde singt "Mein Vöglein mit dem Ringlein"	No. 7	Unspec.	Hug		CHAL (1898)
8166	Weber, Gustav	1845-1887	Lied der Zwerge "Tigg und tagg ging es froh"	No. 1	Unspec.	Hug		CHAL (1898)
8167	Weber, Gustav	1845-1887	Märchen-Lieder		Unspec.	Hug		CHAL (1898)
8168	Weber, Gustav	1845-1887	Nicht sorgen "Waldvögelein, wo singst du"	Op. 2 No. 2	S/A	Hofmeister		CHAL (1898)
8169	Weber, Gustav	1845-1887	Osterlied "Glocken läuten das Ostern ein"	Op. 2 No. 4	S/A	Hofmeister		CHAL (1898)
8170	Weber, Gustav	1845-1887	Reiters Morgengesang "Sei gegrüsst Frau Sonne"		Unspec.	Schott		CHAL (1898)
8171	Weber, Gustav	1845-1887	Schlummerlied der Zwerge an Schneewittchens Bettchen "Schlafe, still ruhn die Bäume"	No. 2	Unspec.	Hug		CHAL (1898)
8172	Weber, Gustav	1845-1887	Schneewittchens Morgengesang "Gott grüss dich, du lieber Sonnenschein"	No. 3	Unspec.	Hug		CHAL (1898)
8173	Weber, Gustav	1845-1887	Schneewittchens Tod "Schneewittchen ist todt"	No. 4	Unspec.	Hug		CHAL (1898)
8174	Weber, Gustav	1845-1887	Tod und Trennung "Gottes Milde möcht' es flugen"	Op. 2 No. 1	S/A	Hofmeister		CHAL (1898)
8175	Weber, Gustav	1845-1887	Zu Hernn Kerbes "Nehmt euch wohl Acht"	No. 8	Unspec.	Hug		CHAL (1898)
8176	Weckerlin, Jean Baptiste	1821-1910	Colinette		Unspec.	Heugel		BBC (1975)

REC	COMP	DTS	TITLE	OP #	VCG	PUB	COMMENTS	SRC
8177	Weckerlin, Jean Baptiste	1821-1910	Je vous aime bien		Unspec.	Durand		CHAL (1898)
8178	Wegeler, C.		Blüthenhauch ist alles Leben		S/A	Simrock		CHAL (1898)
8179	Wehner, A.		Ach ich sehne mich nach Tränen	Op. 6 No. 2	S/S	Litolff		CHAL (1898)
8180	Wehner, A.		Aus dem Frühlingskranz "O kühler Wald wo rauschest du"	Op. 6 No. 5	S/S	Litolff		CHAL (1898)
8181	Wehner, A.		Lob des Mais "Liebholder Mai in Hoffnung gehüllt"	Op. 6 No. 6	S/S	Litolff		CHAL (1898)
8182	Wehner, A.		Schwalbe "O dass ich eine Schwalbe"	Op. 3 No. 4	S/S	B. & H.		CHAL (1898)
8183	Wehner, A.		Selbander in der Morgenfrüh "Sonne steigt mit Prangen"	Op. 6 No. 4	S/S	Litolff		CHAL (1898)
8184	Wehner, A.		Überall dein "Schon wieder bin ich"	Op. 3 No. 2	S/S	B. & H.		CHAL (1898)
8185	Wehner, A.		Verlassenheit "Ach wär' ich doch"	Op. 3 No. 3	S/S	B. & H.		CHAL (1898)
8186	Wehner, A.		Verlassenheit "Ach wär' ich doch ein Röslein auch"	Op. 3 No. 3	S/A	B. & H.	In anth. "Zweistim. Lied. f. Sop. u. Alt-stimme mit Klavier-begleitung f. den Haus- u. Schulge-brauch v. H. M. Schletterer" 3 vols.	MSN
8187	Wehner, A.		Vöglein "Glücklich lebt vor Noth geborgen"	Op. 6 No. 1	S/S	Litolff		CHAL (1898)
8188	Wehner, A.		Wenn Zwei von einander scheiden	Op. 3 No. 1	S/S	B. & H.		CHAL (1898)
8189	Wehner, A.		Wiet, weit über Thal fliehen die Wolken	Op. 6 No. 3	S/S	Litolff		CHAL (1898)
8190	Weidt, Heinrich	1828-1901	Begräbniss der Rose "In Blumen und Zweigen begraben"	Op. 58	MS/A or Br/B	R. & P.		CHAL (1898)
8191	Weidt, Heinrich	1828-1901	Fahrwohl "Letzen Becher bring' ich dir"	Op. 7 No. 2	S/A	Cranz		CHAL (1898)
8192	Weidt, Heinrich	1828-1901	Nachtlied "Mond kommt still gegangen"	Op. 7 No. 1	S/A	Cranz		CHAL (1898)
8193	Weidt, Heinrich	1828-1901	Spielmann und sein Kind "Sturmwind braust"	Op. 43	high & med. v.	Sch. j.		CHAL (1898)
8194	Weigel, H.		Banditenstreiche "In des Waldes finstern Gründen"		Unspec.	Haushahn i. L.		CHAL (1898)
8195	Weigel, H.		Sonntagsjäger "Wir sind als kühne Jäger"	Op. 210	Unspec.	O. Dietrich		CHAL (1898)
8196	Weigel, H.		Unangenehme Gesellschaft "Ich frage sie, was thut der Mensch"		Unspec.	Haushahn i. L.		CHAL (1898)
8197	Weil, T.		Viel kleine Lämmer zieh'n aus dem Garten	No. 1	MS/A	B. & H.		CHAL (1901)
8198	Weinberger, Karl Friedrich	1853-1908	Aprilregen "Schnee ist zerronnen"	No. 6	Unspec.	Böhm & S.		CHAL (1898)
8199	Weinberger, Karl Friedrich	1853-1908	Christabend "Nie vermag zu klingen"	No. 10	Unspec.	Böhm & S.		CHAL (1898)
8200	Weinberger, Karl Friedrich	1853-1908	Da sind vier Vöglein dem Nest entflohn	No. 12	Unspec.	Böhm & S.		CHAL (1898)
8201	Weinberger, Karl Friedrich	1853-1908	Druten vor dem Dorfe	No 9	Unspec.	Böhm & S.		CHAL (1898)
8202	Weinberger, Karl Friedrich	1853-1908	Ein Dorf und zwei Nacht-wächter "Nachwächter Veit nimmt"	No. 1a	Unspec.	Böhm & S.		CHAL (1898)

REC	COMP	DTS	TITLE	OP #	VCG	PUB	COMMENTS	SRC
8203	Weinberger, Karl Friedrich	1853-1908	Frühling an das kranke Kind "Nun sind die Wege trocken"	No. 3	Unspec.	Böhm & S.		CHAL (1898)
8204	Weinberger, Karl Friedrich	1853-1908	Frühlingsgruss "Beim murmelnden Bächlein"	No. 5	Unspec.	Böhm & S.		CHAL (1898)
8205	Weinberger, Karl Friedrich	1853-1908	Maikäfer-Walzer "Sagt, haben wir lustigen Käfer nicht"	No. 8	Unspec.	Böhm & S.		CHAL (1898)
8206	Weinberger, Karl Friedrich	1853-1908	Patient "A B C D E, der Kopf thut mir weh"	No. 4a	Unspec.	Böhm & S.		CHAL (1898)
8207	Weinberger, Karl Friedrich	1853-1908	Postillon Frühling "Frühling ist ein Postillon"	No. 4	Unspec.	Böhm & S.		CHAL (1898)
8208	Weinberger, Karl Friedrich	1853-1908	Prinzessin Liesel "Wie klein Liesel vornehm ist"	No. 3	Unspec.	Böhm & S.		CHAL (1898)
8209	Weinberger, Karl Friedrich	1853-1908	Schwäblein im Nest	No. 1	Unspec.	Böhm & S.		CHAL (1898)
8210	Weinberger, Karl Friedrich	1853-1908	Sommerabend "Heim kehrt die Turteltaub"	No. 2a	Unspec.	Böhm & S.		CHAL (1898)
8211	Weinberger, Karl Friedrich	1853-1908	Vorfrühling "Unter welken Blättern"	No. 2	Unspec.	Böhm & S.		CHAL (1898)
8212	Weinberger, Karl Friedrich	1853-1908	Wie ein Junker deutsch reden lernte "Kam aus Frankreich jüngst"	No. 11	Unspec.	Böhm & S.		CHAL (1898)
8213	Weinhardt, F.		Weihnachtslieder (60)		Unspec.	Ensslin & L.	60 Christmas duets.	CHAL (1906)
8214	Weinhardt, F.		Weihnachtslieder "neue, 30"		Unspec.	Ensslin & L.	30 new Christmas duets.	CHAL (1906)
8215	Weinstabl, Karl	1872-	In der reschen, wiffen, feschen		Unspec.	Eberle i. Wien		CHAL (1901)
8216	Weinwurm, Rudolf	1835-1911	Alpenstimmen aus Oesterreich		Unspec.	Kratoch-will		CHAL (1898)
8217	Weinwurm, Rudolf	1835-1911	Darf i's Diarndel lieb'n "I bin jüngst verwichen"	No. 7	S/A	Kratoch-will		CHAL (1898)
8218	Weinwurm, Rudolf	1835-1911	Droben auf der Alm	No. 1	S/A	Kratoch-will		CHAL (1898)
8219	Weinwurm, Rudolf	1835-1911	Du flachshaarets Dianderl	No. 4	S/A	Kratoch-will		CHAL (1898)
8220	Weinwurm, Rudolf	1835-1911	Freude schöner Götterfunken		S/A	Bos-worth	pf or harm	CHAL (1906)
8221	Weinwurm, Rudolf	1835-1911	Ganz und gar nit "Halb und halb hast mi gern"	No. 3	S/A	Kratoch-will		CHAL (1898)
8222	Weinwurm, Rudolf	1835-1911	Ruf zum Dianderl "Du schwarzaugets Dianderl"	No. 2	S/A	Kratoch-will		CHAL (1898)
8223	Weinwurm, Rudolf	1835-1911	Undankbare "Dianderl is harn auf mi"	No. 5	S/A	Kratoch-will		CHAL (1898)
8224	Weinwurm, Rudolf	1835-1911	Verlassen "I thu' wohl als wann nix war"	No. 6	S/A	Kratoch-will		CHAL (1898)
8225	Weischer, Th.		Abendhymne "Horch, horch die Abendhymne"	Op. 20 No. 4	S/A	Weber i. Cöln		CHAL (1898)
8226	Weischer, Th.		Abends um die stile Zeit	Op. 20 No. 1	S/A	Weber i. Cöln		CHAL (1898)
8227	Weischer, Th.		Bergeswehen "Der Hauch der Berge stark und frei"	Op. 20 No. 3	S/A	Weber i. Cöln		CHAL (1898)
8228	Weischer, Th.		Wanderlust "O Wanderlust, o Wanderlust"	Op. 20 No. 2	S/A	Weber i. Cöln		CHAL (1898)
8229	Weismann, Julius	1879-1950	Will ich in mein Gärtlein gehn		S/Br or S/A	Wunder-horn-Verl. i. M.		CHAL (1911)
8230	Weismann, Wilhelm	1900-	Hymne an die Gottin Eos		S/A	Peters		CVMP (1976)
8231	Weiss, J.	1853-	Es wohnten zwei Schwäne im See		S/A	Philipp & S.		CHAL (1901)

REC	COMP	DTS	TITLE	OP #	VCG	PUB	COMMENTS	SRC
8232	Weiss, Laurenz	1810-1884	Canon a due "Siehe, das ist Gottes Lamm"	Op. 44 No. 8	S/A	Cranz		CHAL (1898)
8233	Weiss, Laurenz	1810-1884	Danklied "Danket dem Herrn, denn er"	Op. 43 No. 2	Unspec.	Cranz		CHAL (1898)
8234	Weiss, Laurenz	1810-1884	Gedanken an Gott "Denk' ich an dich"	Op. 44 No. 6	S/A	Cranz		CHAL (1898)
8235	Weiss, Laurenz	1810-1884	Gesänge für die Jugend (8)	Op. 43	Unspec.	Cranz	Collection of 8 duets for the young.	CHAL (1898)
8236	Weiss, Laurenz	1810-1884	Glöcklein "Abendglöcklein läute"	Op. 44 No. 4	S/A	Cranz		CHAL (1898)
8237	Weiss, Laurenz	1810-1884	Guten Morgen "Nun reibet euch die Aeuglein wach"	Op. 44 No. 2	S/A	Cranz		CHAL (1898)
8238	Weiss, Laurenz	1810-1884	Mahnung "Hütet eure Zungen"	Op. 44 No. 3	S/A	Cranz		CHAL (1898)
8239	Weiss, Laurenz	1810-1884	Morgengebet "Lieber Vater hoch in Himmel"	Op. 43 No. 1	Unspec.	Cranz		CHAL (1898)
8240	Weiss, Laurenz	1810-1884	Morgenlied "Morgenwinde weh'n frisch"	Op. 43 No. 3	Unspec.	Cranz		CHAL (1898)
8241	Weiss, Laurenz	1810-1884	Mücke "Sonne kommt, die Mück' erwacht"	Op. 43 No. 8	Unspec.	Cranz		CHAL (1898)
8242	Weiss, Laurenz	1810-1884	Nacht entfleucht	Op. 44 No. 1	S/A	Cranz		CHAL (1898)
8243	Weiss, Laurenz	1810-1884	Stille Thal "Im schönsten Wiesengrunde"	Op. 43 No. 7	Unspec.	Cranz		CHAL (1898)
8244	Weiss, Laurenz	1810-1884	Strickerinnen "Euch zur Arbeit auszuschicken"	Op. 44 No. 7	S/A	Cranz		CHAL (1898)
8245	Weiss, Laurenz	1810-1884	Was ich habe "Zwei Augen hab' ich klar und hell"	Op. 44 No. 5	S/A	Cranz		CHAL (1898)
8246	Weiss, Laurenz	1810-1884	Wen ich liebe fragst du mich	Op. 43 No. 5	Unspec.	Cranz		CHAL (1898)
8247	Weiss, Laurenz	1810-1884	Wenn das Kind aufwacht "Guten Morgen lieber Sonnen"	Op. 43 No. 6	Unspec.	Cranz		CHAL (1898)
8248	Weissbach, M. L.		Ach die schlechten Zeiten "Man hört an allen Orten"	Op. 70	Unspec.	Weissbach i. Burgst.		CHAL (1898)
8249	Weissbach, M. L.		Ach ein Walzer "Als grosser Componist bekannt"		Unspec.	O. Dietrich		CHAL (1898)
8250	Weissbach, M. L.		Das geniert nicht, denn nur so was ist modern "Nimmt man 'ne Zeitung"	Op. 1	Unspec.	O. Dietrich		CHAL (1898)
8251	Weissbach, M. L.		Einsam durch das Leben gehen	Op. 109	2 female v.	Weissbach		CHAL (1911)
8252	Weissbach, M. L.		Frühmorgens, wenn die Sonn' aufgeht	Op. 112	2 female v.	Weissbach		CHAL (1911)
8253	Weissbach, M. L.		G'scheid-Dumm "Ein junger Stutzer elegant"		Unspec.	O. Dietrich		CHAL (1898)
8254	Weissbach, M. L.		Gebrüder Weiss-Marsch "Es sieht wohl jeder gleich"	Op. 51	Unspec.	Weissbach i. Burgst.		CHAL (1898)
8255	Weissbach, M. L.		Gemein, fein "Wir wollen es einmal probiren"	Op. 48	Unspec.	Weissbach i. Burgst.		CHAL (1898)
8256	Weissbach, M. L.		Mitzi und Litzi, die schneidigen Verkäuferinnen im Warenhaus von Abrahamsohn "Hum. Duett"	Op. 84	Unspec.	Weissbach i. Burgst.		CHAL (1911)
8257	Weissbach, M. L.		O jeh, es ist doch gar zu schwer	Op. 104	2 female v.	Weissbach i. Burgst.		CHAL (1911)
8258	Weissbach, M. L.		Sei ruhig "Man hat im Leb'n ganz ungenirt"	Op. 72	Unspec.	Weissbach i. Burgst.		CHAL (1898)

REC	COMP	DTS	TITLE	OP #	VCG	PUB	COMMENTS	SRC
8259	Weissbach, M. L.		Wie geschmiert "Es ist ein eignes Ding"	Op. 71	Unspec.	Weissbach i. Burgst.		CHAL (1898)
8260	Weissbach, M. L.		Wir sind vom Damen-Turnverein	Op. 116	2 female v.	Weissbach i. Burgst.		CHAL (1911)
8261	Weissbach, M. L.		Zwei Original-Negel-Gigerl "Zwei elegante Bengel"	Op. 64	Unspec.	Weissbach i. Burgst.		CHAL (1898)
8262	Wellings, Milton		Some day		Unspec.	Enoch	Arr. Jackson	BBC (1975)
8263	Wendland, Waldemar	1873-1947	Schon als kleine Kinder hatten er und sie		Unspec.	Benjamin		CHAL (1906)
8264	Wendland, Waldemar	1873-1947	Was thut Wilhelminje von früh bis spät "Tanz-Duett"		Unspec.	Harmonie i. B.		CHAL (1906)
8265	Wendt, Ernst	1806-1850	An ein kleines Mädchen "Pflück' die Blumen"	Op. 2 No. 15	S/S	Heinr.		CHAL (1898)
8266	Wennerburg, Gunnar	1817-1901	Musikdel		Unspec.	Gehrmans		CVMP (1976)
8267	Wenzel, Eduard	1805-1884	Frühlingswonne "Frühling strahlt durch Feld und Au"	Op. 31 No. 4	S/A or T/Br	Bachmann		CHAL (1898)
8268	Wenzel, Eduard	1805-1884	Geist des Abends "Geist des Abends ziehet"	Op. 31 No. 3	S/A or T/Br	Bachmann		CHAL (1898)
8269	Wenzel, Eduard	1805-1884	Glocken "Aus dem fernen Thal"	Op. 31 No. 2	S/A or T/Br	Bachmann		CHAL (1898)
8270	Wenzel, Eduard	1805-1884	Verlorene Glück "Durch des Himmels Sternenpracht"	Op. 31 No. 1	S/A or T/Br	Bachmann		CHAL (1898)
8271	Wenzel, H.		Auf der Alm hab' ich gesessen	Op. 154 No. 1	S/A	Portius		CHAL (1906)
8272	Wenzel, H.		Erinnerung an Tyrol "Auf der Alm hab' ich gesessen"	Op. 154	S/A	Portius		CHAL (1898)
8273	Wenzel, H.		In dem Land Tyrol ist es mir so wohl	Op. 154 No. 2	S/A	Portius		CHAL (1906)
8274	Wenzel, H.		Kaum ist der Sonne Strahl erwacht	Op. 154 No. 3	S/A	Portius		CHAL (1906)
8275	Wenzel, H.		Mutterliebe "Es strahlt ein heller Stern durch's Land"	Op. 151	A/A	Portius		CHAL (1898)
8276	Wenzel, H.		Reich, gesegnet sei die Stunde	Op. 190 No. 1	S/A	none listed	org	CHAL (1911)
8277	Wenzel, H.		So nimm denn meine Hände	Op. 190 No. 2	S/A	none listed	org	CHAL (1911)
8278	Wenzel, H.		Von Bergen schallt's Hali	Op. 154 No. 4	S/A	Portius		CHAL (1906)
8279	Wenzel, H.		Wanderers Abschiedslied am Abend "Traute Heimath ich muss scheiden"	Op. 150	A/A	Wenzel		CHAL (1898)
8280	Wermann, Friedrich Oskar	1840-1906	Alle Wälder schweigen	Op. 48 No. 3	Unspec.	Kahnt		CHAL (1898)
8281	Wermann, Friedrich Oskar	1840-1906	Duett der Vögel "Ein jedes kleine Lied von mir"	Op. 80 No. 1	Unspec.	Löbel		CHAL (1898)
8282	Wermann, Friedrich Oskar	1840-1906	Fliegt aus dem Nest ein Vöglein	Op. 48 No. 6	Unspec.	Kahnt		CHAL (1898)
8283	Wermann, Friedrich Oskar	1840-1906	Frühlingslied "Wenn Vöglein ihre Nester bauen"	Op. 48 No. 1	Unspec.	Kahnt		CHAL (1898)
8284	Wermann, Friedrich Oskar	1840-1906	Herbströslein "Ein Röslein blühte am Waldesrand"	Op. 80 No. 4	Unspec.	Löbel		CHAL (1898)
8285	Wermann, Friedrich Oskar	1840-1906	Lenzes Sieg "Nun ist er doch gekommen"	Op. 80 No. 2	Unspec.	Löbel		CHAL (1898)
8286	Wermann, Friedrich Oskar	1840-1906	Lieb ist erwacht	Op. 48 No. 5	Unspec.	Kahnt		CHAL (1898)
8287	Wermann, Friedrich Oskar	1840-1906	So leicht ist Liebe	Op. 48 No. 7	Unspec.	Kahnt		CHAL (1898)

REC	COMP	DTS	TITLE	OP #	VCG	PUB	COMMENTS	SRC
8288	Wermann, Friedrich Oskar	1840-1906	Ver gänglischkeit und Ewigkeit "Gleich wie vom goldenen Becher"	Op. 80 No. 3	Unspec.	Löbel		CHAL (1898)
8289	Wermann, Friedrich Oskar	1840-1906	Wasserfahrt "Sanfte Wellen kräuselt"	Op. 48 No. 2	Unspec.	Kahnt		CHAL (1898)
8290	Wermann, Friedrich Oskar	1840-1906	Wenn Zwei von Herzen lieb sich haben "Wie jagt das Herz nach tausend Dingen"	Op. 48 No. 4	Unspec.	Kahnt		CHAL (1898)
8291	Wermann, Friedrich Oskar	1840-1906	Wiegenlied "Vom Berg hinabgestiegen"	Op. 48 No. 8	Unspec.	Kahnt		CHAL (1898)
8292	Werner, Erich	1901-	Rabbi Akiba		Unspec.	Sac. Mus. Pr.	org or pf accomp. For 1-2 v. Sacred Jewish.	CVMP (1976)
8293	Werner, Erich	1901-	Rabbi Shimon		Unspec.	Sac. Mus. Pr.	org or pf accomp. For 1-2 v. Sacred Jewish.	CVMP (1976)
8294	Werner, Erich	1901-	Rabbi Tarphon		Unspec.	Sac. Mus. Pr.	org or pf accomp. For 1-2 v. Sacred Jewish.	CVMP (1976)
8295	Werner, Otto	19th C.	Beiden Köche "Hum. Duoscene"	Op. 35	Unspec.	Glaser	Pen name of Gustav Krenkel	CHAL (1901)
8296	Werner, Otto	19th C.	Geputzt, geschmückt, nett und charmant	Op. 37	2 female v.	Glaser	Pen name of Gustav Krenkel	CHAL (1901)
8297	Werner, Otto	19th C.	Ich bin die Mirzel, wohlbekannt	Op. 12	2 female v.	Glaser	Pen name of Gustav Krenkel	CHAL (1901)
8298	Werner, Otto	19th C.	Ja so zwa, wie wir zwa sind	Op. 41	2 female v.	Glaser	pf or zither. Pen name of Gustav Krenkel	CHAL (1901)
8299	Werner, Otto	19th C.	Wir kamen als Madeln daher	Op. 13	2 female v.	Glaser		CHAL (1901)
8300	Werth, Joseph	1873-	Jetzo heisst es ausmarschieret	No. 3	S/A	Eulenburg		CHAL (1911)
8301	Werth, Joseph	1873-	Kinderlieder (3)		S/A	Eulenburg	3 children's duets.	CHAL (1911)
8302	Werth, Joseph	1873-	Lieber Heiland mach' mich fromm	No. 1	S/A	Eulenberg		CHAL (1911)
8303	Werth, Joseph	1873-	Schneeglöcken läutet den Frühling ein	No. 2	S/A	Eulenburg		CHAL (1911)
8304	Westendorf, T. P.		I'll Take You Home Again Kathleen		Unspec.	Allans	In anthology "Vocal Duets Collection" Vol. 1. Pub. 1992.	MSN
8305	Westermair, Johann B.	1890-	Wo den Himmel Berge kränzen		Unspec.	Westermair		CHAL (1906)
8306	Westmeyer, Wilhelm	1832-1880	Beim Tanzen "Kommt herbei, kommt nun geschwind"		Unspec.	Hoffarth		CHAL (1898)
8307	Weston, R. P. & B. Lee		How time flies		Unspec.	F. D. & H.		BBC (1975)
8308	Weyts, H.		Déjà la nuit étend ses voiles		2 female v.	Cranz		CHAL (1901)
8309	White		Come join the dance		Unspec.	White-Smith	In catalogue page "Vocal Duetts" of White-Smith Music Pub. Co. (no date)	MSN
8310	White		Come, merry birds of Spring		S/A	White-Smith	In catalogue page "Vocal Duetts" of White-Smith Music Pub. Co. (no date)	MSN
8311	White		Come where the rosebuds sleep		S/A	White-Smith	In catalogue page "Vocal Duetts" of White-Smith Music Pub. Co. (no date)	MSN

REC	COMP	DTS	TITLE	OP #	VCG	PUB	COMMENTS	SRC
8312	White		Hope beyond		T/B or S/A	White-Smith	In catalogue page "Vocal Duetts" of White-Smith Music Pub. Co. (no date)	MSN
8313	White		Our Saviour		S/A	White-Smith	In catalogue page "Vocal Duetts" of White-Smith Music Pub. Co. (no date)	MSN
8314	White		Reconciliation		S/A	White-Smith	In catalogue page "Vocal Duetts" of White-Smith Music Pub. Co. (no date)	MSN
8315	White		Softly the night breeze is sighing		Unspec.	White-Smith	In catalogue page "Vocal Duetts" of White-Smith Music Pub. Co. (no date)	MSN
8316	White		Tell us merry birds		S/A	White-Smith	In catalogue page "Vocal Duetts" of White-Smith Music Pub. Co. (no date)	MSN
8317	White, Maude Valerie	1855-1937	It Is Na, Jean, Thy Bonnie Face		Unspec.	Cramer	Brit. woman comp. Also solo.	CVMP (1976)
8318	Whitehead, Percy Algernon	1874-	Boating Song of the Yo Eh		Unspec.	Cramer		CVMP (1976)
8319	Wibergh, Johann Olof	1890-	Kvallen		Unspec.	Lundq.		CVMP (1976)
8320	Wibergh, Johann Olof	1890-	Pa Sangens Jublande Vingar		Unspec.	Lundq.		CVMP (1976)
8321	Wicher, Alb.		Gretchen-Gavotte "Gretchen ist so hold"		Unspec.	Glas.		CHAL (1898)
8322	Wichern, Karoline	1836-1906	Alpenhirt "Dort hoch auf der Alpe"	Op. 43 No. 1	Unspec.	Cranz	Grmn. woman comp.	CHAL (1898)
8323	Wichern, Karoline	1836-1906	Alte Dessauer "Ich will ein Lied euch singen"	Op. 43 No. 4	Unspec.	Cranz	Grmn. woman comp.	CHAL (1898)
8324	Wichern, Karoline	1836-1906	Am Geburtstage "Liebe Mama, wach' auf"	Op. 43 No. 9	Unspec.	Cranz	Grmn. woman comp.	CHAL (1898)
8325	Wichern, Karoline	1836-1906	Distelstöckchen "Alles was ich vorgedeutet"	Op. 43 No. 21	Unspec.	Cranz	Grmn. woman comp.	CHAL (1898)
8326	Wichern, Karoline	1836-1906	Frieden der Nacht "Tag ist längst geschieden"	Op. 43 No. 12	Unspec.	Cranz	Grmn. woman comp.	CHAL (1898)
8327	Wichern, Karoline	1836-1906	Frühlingsglaube "Linden Lüfte sind erwacht"	Op. 43 No. 16	Unspec.	Cranz	Grmn. woman comp.	CHAL (1898)
8328	Wichern, Karoline	1836-1906	Junge General "Stillgestanden, Grenadiere"	Op. 43 No. 6	Unspec.	Cranz	Grmn. woman comp.	CHAL (1898)
8329	Wichern, Karoline	1836-1906	Kindergrablied "Du bist ein Schatten am Tage"	Op. 43 No. 15	Unspec.	Cranz	Grmn. woman comp.	CHAL (1898)
8330	Wichern, Karoline	1836-1906	Matten Has' "Lütt Matten de Has'"	Op. 43 No. 23	Unspec.	Cranz	Grmn. woman comp.	CHAL (1898)
8331	Wichern, Karoline	1836-1906	Mein Vaterland "Vaterland, wo meine Wiege stand"	Op. 43 No. 5	Unspec.	Cranz	Grmn. woman comp.	CHAL (1898)
8332	Wichern, Karoline	1836-1906	Morgenlied "Vorüber ist die dunkle Nacht"	Op. 43 No. 10	Unspec.	Cranz	Grmn. woman comp.	CHAL (1898)
8333	Wichern, Karoline	1836-1906	Osterhäschen "Flinkes Häschen, willst du Morgen"	Op. 43 No. 20	Unspec.	Cranz	Grmn. woman comp.	CHAL (1898)
8334	Wichern, Karoline	1836-1906	Postillon "Postillon ist ein glücklicher Mann"	Op. 43 No. 7	Unspec.	Cranz	Grmn. woman comp.	CHAL (1898)
8335	Wichern, Karoline	1836-1906	Rab', Rab" "Rab', Rab', grämme dich"	Op. 43 No. 2	Unspec.	Cranz	Grmn. woman comp.	CHAL (1898)
8336	Wichern, Karoline	1836-1906	Rattenfänger von Hameln "Da hinter dem Berg"	Op. 23 No. 24	Unspec.	Cranz	Grmn. woman comp.	CHAL (1898)
8337	Wichern, Karoline	1836-1906	Schaue mir in's Angesicht	Op. 43 No. 14	Unspec.	Cranz	Grmn. woman comp.	CHAL (1898)

REC	COMP	DTS	TITLE	OP #	VCG	PUB	COMMENTS	SRC
8338	Wichern, Karoline	1836-1906	Schaukelpferd "Ha, ha, ha, seht das Pferdchen"	Op. 43 No. 8	Unspec.	Cranz	Grmn. woman comp.	CHAL (1898)
8339	Wichern, Karoline	1836-1906	Sperling "Wer weckt mich aus dem Schlummer"	Op. 43 No. 17	Unspec.	Cranz	Grmn. woman comp.	CHAL (1898)
8340	Wichern, Karoline	1836-1906	Vögleins Begräbniss "Unter den rothen Blumen"	Op. 43 No. 18	Unspec.	Cranz	Grmn. woman comp.	CHAL (1898)
8341	Wichern, Karoline	1836-1906	Wandeln Glocke "Es war ein Kind, das wollte nicht"	Op. 43 No. 10	Unspec.	Cranz	Grmn. woman comp.	CHAL (1898)
8342	Wichern, Karoline	1836-1906	Weegenleed "Still min Hanne"	Op. 43 No. 11	Unspec.	Cranz	Grmn. woman comp.	CHAL (1898)
8343	Wichern, Karoline	1836-1906	Weihnachtslied "Weihnachts, Weihnachts kehret wieder"	Op. 43 No. 13	Unspec.	Cranz	Grmn. woman comp.	CHAL (1898)
8344	Wichern, Karoline	1836-1906	Wenn mancher Mann wüss-te, wer mancher Mann wär'"	Op. 43 No. 3	Unspec.	Cranz	Grmn. woman comp.	CHAL (1898)
8345	Wichern, Karoline	1836-1906	Zu schwer "Ich kann nicht, ich kann wirklich nicht"	Op. 43 No. 25	Unspec.	Cranz	Grmn. woman comp.	CHAL (1898)
8346	Wichmann, Hermann	1824-1905	Aus meinen Thränen spriessen	Op. 4 No. 1	Unspec.	Bahn		CHAL (1898)
8347	Wichmann, Hermann	1824-1905	Du schönes Fischermädchen	Op. 4 No. 5	Unspec.	Bahn		CHAL (1898)
8348	Wichmann, Hermann	1824-1905	Lotosblume "Lotosblume ängstigt sich"	Op. 4 No. 3	Unspec.	Bahn		CHAL (1898)
8349	Wichmann, Hermann	1824-1905	Warum sind die Rosen so blass	Op. 4 No. 4	Unspec.	Bahn		CHAL (1898)
8350	Wichmann, Hermann	1824-1905	Wasserfahrt "Ich stand gelehnet and em Mast"	Op. 4 No. 2	Unspec.	Bahn		CHAL (1898)
8351	Wickede, Friedrich von	1834-1904	Schloss am Meer "Hast du das Schloss gesehen"	Op. 37	high & low v.	Junne		CHAL (1898)
8352	Wickenhauser, Richard	1867-1936	Bei der Guzla Tönen	Op. 61 No. 6	Unspec.	Kistner		CHAL (1911)
8353	Wickenhauser, Richard	1867-1936	Dass mein Liebster treulos war	Op. 61 No. 2	S/A	Kistner		CHAL (1911)
8354	Wickenhauser, Richard	1867-1936	Dich, o Mädchen, kleines Mädchen	Op. 61 No. 5	Unspec.	Kistner		CHAL (1911)
8355	Wickenhauser, Richard	1867-1936	Lazar, o du Herr der Wiese	Op. 61 No. 3	S/A	Kistner		CHAL (1911)
8356	Wickenhauser, Richard	1867-1936	Ruhig mit des Eimers Wucht	Op. 61 No. 4	Unspec.	Kistner		CHAL (1911)
8357	Wickenhauser, Richard	1867-1936	Täubchen "Täubchen mein, o Täubchen klein"	Op. 61 No. 1	S/A	Kistner		CHAL (1911)
8358	Widmann, Benedikt	1820-1910	Auf dürrem Ast ein Finke sass	Op. 11 No. 4	S/A	Merse.		CHAL (1898)
8359	Widmann, Benedikt	1820-1910	Erster April, lache wer will	Op. 11 No. 7	S/A	Merse.		CHAL (1898)
8360	Widmann, Benedikt	1820-1910	Frisches Bächlein	Op. 11 No. 5	S/A	Merse.		CHAL (1898)
8361	Widmann, Benedikt	1820-1910	Frühling ist kommen	Op. 11 No. 1	S/A	Merse.		CHAL (1898)
8362	Widmann, Benedikt	1820-1910	Hoch wandern die Vögel	Op. 11 No. 12	S/A	Merse.		CHAL (1898)
8363	Widmann, Benedikt	1820-1910	Lass mich in dich versinken	Op. 11 No. 3	S/A	Merse.		CHAL (1898)
8364	Widmann, Benedikt	1820-1910	Lass' sie rauschen	Op. 11 No. 6	S/A	Merse.		CHAL (1898)
8365	Widmann, Benedikt	1820-1910	Lasset uns schligen den Frühling	Op. 11 No. 8	S/A	Merse.		CHAL (1898)
8366	Widmann, Benedikt	1820-1910	O könnt' ich sein wie die Vögelein	Op. 11 No. 2	S/A	Merse.		CHAL (1898)
8367	Widmann, Benedikt	1820-1910	Stille Abendroth so weit und breit	Op. 11 No. 10	S/A	Merse.		CHAL (1898)

REC	COMP	DTS	TITLE	OP #	VCG	PUB	COMMENTS	SRC
8368	Widmann, Benedikt	1820-1910	Wer, wer spannt den Bogen	Op. 11 No. 11	S/A	Merse.		CHAL (1898)
8369	Widmann, Benedikt	1820-1910	Wie azurblau der Himmel	Op. 11 No. 3	S/A	Merse.		CHAL (1898)
8370	Wiedecke, Adolph	d. 1901	Feuerwehr kommt "Was jagt so schnell daher"		Unspec.	Meissner		CHAL (1898)
8371	Wiedemann, Max	1875-1932	Am Weihnachtsbaum die Lichter brennen	Op. 6 No. 10	Unspec.	Kaun		CHAL (1911)
8372	Wiedemann, Max	1875-1932	Dies ist der Tag, den Gott gemacht	Op. 6 No. 9	Unspec.	Kaun		CHAL (1911)
8373	Wiedemann, Max	1875-1932	Drei Könige wandern aus Morgenland	Op. 6 No. 15	Unspec.	Kaun		CHAL (1911)
8374	Wiedemann, Max	1875-1932	Ein neues, andächtiges Kindelwiegen	Op. 6 No. 4	Unspec.	Kaun		CHAL (1911)
8375	Wiedemann, Max	1875-1932	Es ist ein Ros' entsprungen	Op. 6 No. 13	Unspec.	Kaun		CHAL (1911)
8376	Wiedemann, Max	1875-1932	Jäger (der) geistlich	Op. 6 No. 12	Unspec.	Kaun		CHAL (1911)
8377	Wiedemann, Max	1875-1932	Kommet, ihr hirten	Op. 6 No. 2	Unspec.	Kaun		CHAL (1911)
8378	Wiedemann, Max	1875-1932	Kommt und lasst uns Christum ehren	Op. 6 No. 7	Unspec.	Kaun		CHAL (1911)
8379	Wiedemann, Max	1875-1932	Nun singet und seid froh	Op. 6 No. 8	Unspec.	Kaun		CHAL (1911)
8380	Wiedemann, Max	1875-1932	O du fröhliche, o du selige	Op. 6 No. 5	Unspec.	Kaun		CHAL (1911)
8381	Wiedemann, Max	1875-1932	O Jesulein süss	Op. 6 No. 14	Unspec.	Kaun		CHAL (1911)
8382	Wiedemann, Max	1875-1932	Schlaf, mein Kindelein	Op. 6 No. 3	Unspec.	Kaun		CHAL (1911)
8383	Wiedemann, Max	1875-1932	Stille Nacht, heilige Nacht	Op. 6 No. 5	Unspec.	Kaun		CHAL (1911)
8384	Wiedemann, Max	1875-1932	Tochter Zion, freue dich	Op. 6 No. 11	Unspec.	Kaun		CHAL (1911)
8385	Wiedemann, Max	1875-1932	Zu Bethlehem geboren	Op. 6 No. 1	Unspec.	Kaun		CHAL (1911)
8386	Wiel, Taddeo	1849-1920	Haar fliegt und wallet	No. 3	S/A	B. & H.		CHAL (1901)
8387	Wiel, Taddeo	1849-1920	Rings ist nun Dämmerung heraufgekommen	No. 2	MS/A	B. & H.		CHAL (1901)
8388	Wielhorski, Mikhail	1788-1856	Du bist wie eine Blume	No. 2	S/S	B. & B.		CHAL (1898)
8389	Wielhorski, Mikhail	1788-1856	Ein Fichtenbaum steht einsam	No. 1	S/S	B. & B.		CHAL (1898)
8390	Wielhorski, Mikhail	1788-1856	"Herz, mein Herz sei nicht beklommen"	No. 4	S/S	B. & B.		CHAL (1898)
8391	Wielhorski, Mikhail	1788-1856	Leise zieht durch mein Gemüth	No. 3	S/S	B. & B.		CHAL (1898)
8392	Wielhorski, Mikhail	1788-1856	Mag da draussen Schnee sich thürmen	No. 5	S/S	B. & B.		CHAL (1898)
8393	Wielhorski, Mikhail	1788-1856	Nacht liegt auf fremden Wegen	No. 4	S/S	B. & B.		CHAL (1898)
8394	Wienand, V.		Abschied vom Walde "Ade du liebes Waldesgrün"	Op. 18 No. 10	Unspec.	Kahnt		CHAL (1898)
8395	Wienand, V.		Ave Maria "Madonna santa höre mich"	Op. 16 No. 2	Unspec.	Kahnt		CHAL (1898)
8396	Wienand, V.		Bach im haine "Am Bache im Haine"	Op. 18 No. 3	Unspec.	Kahnt		CHAL (1898)
8397	Wienand, V.		Bleib bei uns "Ach bleib bei uns"	Op. 18 No. 2	Unspec.	Kahnt		CHAL (1898)

REC	COMP	DTS	TITLE	OP #	VCG	PUB	COMMENTS	SRC
8398	Wienand, V.		Entflohener Sommer "Ach der Sommer ist entflogen"	Op. 16 No. 10	Unspec.	Kahnt		CHAL (1898)
8399	Wienand, V.		Frommer Glaube "Zu heil'gen Kirchenhallen"	Op. 18 No. 4	Unspec.	Kahnt		CHAL (1898)
8400	Wienand, V.		Gebet "Vater hör' mein Flehen"	Op. 17 No. 1	Unspec.	Kahnt		CHAL (1898)
8401	Wienand, V.		Harre des Herrn "Harre meine Seele"	Op. 18 No. 8	Unspec.	Kahnt		CHAL (1898)
8402	Wienand, V.		Lied der Vöglein "Von Zweig zu Zweig zu hüpfen"	Op. 18 No. 7	Unspec.	Kahnt		CHAL (1898)
8403	Wienand, V.		Lied im Sommer "Hinaus in's Feld"	Op. 16 No. 4	Unspec.	Kahnt		CHAL (1898)
8404	Wienand, V.		Lied von den Sommervögeln "Es kamen viele Vögelein"	Op. 17 No. 9	Unspec.	Kahnt		CHAL (1898)
8405	Wienand, V.		Nacht entfleucht	Op. 17 No. 1	Unspec.	Kahnt		CHAL (1898)
8406	Wienand, V.		Postknecht "Ein Postknecht [unreadable] ich werden"	Op. 17 No. 3	Unspec.	Kahnt		CHAL (1898)
8407	Wienand, V.		Reiterlied "Ist die Nacht doch hell und heiter"	Op. 17 No. 8	Unspec.	Kahnt		CHAL (1898)
8408	Wienand, V.		Schlummerlied "Alles schläft in süsser Ruh"	Op. 16 No. 5	Unspec.	Kahnt		CHAL (1898)
8409	Wienand, V.		Sonne des Lebens "Schauet den Morgen"	Op. 16 No. 8	Unspec.	Kahnt		CHAL (1898)
8410	Wienand, V.		Stille Stunden "Wo kann der Geist sich heben"	Op. 16 No. 3	Unspec.	Kahnt		CHAL (1898)
8411	Wienand, V.		Tanzlied im Mai "Zum Reigen herbei"	Op. 16 No. 1	Unspec.	Kahnt		CHAL (1898)
8412	Wienand, V.		Turners Wanderlied "Auf ihr Turner frisch und frei"	Op. 17 No. 4	Unspec.	Kahnt		CHAL (1898)
8413	Wienand, V.		Vaterlandslied "Heil dem deutschen Vaterland"	Op. 18 No. 1	Unspec.	Kahnt		CHAL (1898)
8414	Wienand, V.		Vergissmeinnicht "Es blüht ein schönes Blümchen"	Op. 16 No. 7	Unspec.	Kahnt		CHAL (1898)
8415	Wienand, V.		Vom armen Finken "Sass ein Fink in dunkler Hecke"	Op. 18 No. 5	Unspec.	Kahnt		CHAL (1898)
8416	Wienand, V.		Vom Blumensämlein "Ins Herz hinein, recht tief hinein"	Op. 18 No. 9	Unspec.	Kahnt		CHAL (1898)
8417	Wienand, V.		Waldlied "Im Walde möcht' ich leben"	Op. 16 No. 6	Unspec.	Kahnt		CHAL (1898)
8418	Wienand, V.		Wanderer in der Sägemühle "Dort unten in der Mühle"	Op. 17 No. 2	Unspec.	Kahnt		CHAL (1898)
8419	Wienand, V.		Was willst du mehr "Herz hüte dich zu wünschen viel"	Op. 16 No. 9	Unspec.	Kahnt		CHAL (1898)
8420	Wienand, V.		Wie ist doch die Erde so schön	Op. 17 No. 5	Unspec.	Kahnt		CHAL (1898)
8421	Wienand, V.		Winterabend "Nichts Besser's giebt es weit und breit"	Op. 17 No. 10	Unspec.	Kahnt		CHAL (1898)
8422	Wienand, V.		Wohin und wodurch "Durch Nacht zum Licht"	Op. 18 No. 6	Unspec.	Kahnt		CHAL (1898)
8423	Wieniawski, Joseph	1837-1912	Mailied "Wie herrlich leuchtet mir die Natur"	Op. 47 No. 4	Unspec.	R. & E.		CHAL (1898)
8424	Wieniawski, Joseph	1837-1912	Omar der Khalif "Einst hab' ich die Kameele"	Op. 47 No. 2	Unspec.	R. & E.		CHAL (1898)
8425	Wieniawski, Joseph	1837-1912	Spinnerin "Role liebe Spindel"	Op. 47 No. 3	Unspec.	R. & E.		CHAL (1898)
8426	Wieniawski, Joseph	1837-1912	Viel Träume "Viel Vögel sind geflogen"	Op. 47 No. 4	Unspec.	R. & E.		CHAL (1898)
8427	Wieniawski, Joseph	1837-1912	Wach auf, o Herz	Op. 47	Unspec.	R. & E.		CHAL (1898)

REC	COMP	DTS	TITLE	OP #	VCG	PUB	COMMENTS	SRC
8428	Wieniawski, Joseph	1837-1912	Wanderers Nachtlied "Über allen Gipfeln (Wipfeln) ist Ruh"	Op. 47 No. 6	Unspec.	R. & E.		CHAL (1898)
8429	Wiesomowil-uki, R.		Eduard und Kunigunde "Schauerballade"		Unspec.	Danner		CHAL (1906)
8430	Wiesomowil-uki, R.		Lieschen, pst.		Unspec.	Danner		CHAL (1906)
8431	Wilhelm, Karl Friedrich	1815-1873	Abendlied "Abend wird es wieder"	No. 44	Unspec.	B. & H.		CHAL (1898)
8432	Wilhelm, Karl Friedrich	1815-1873	Abendlied "Mond ist aufgegangen"	No. 28	Unspec.	B. & H.		CHAL (1898)
8433	Wilhelm, Karl Friedrich	1815-1873	Abschied der Schwalben "Schwalben, ja die Schwalben"	No. 43	Unspec.	B. & H.		CHAL (1898)
8434	Wilhelm, Karl Friedrich	1815-1873	Am Geburtstage des Vaters "In dieser heil'gen Stille"	No. 55	Unspec.	B. & H.		CHAL (1898)
8435	Wilhelm, Karl Friedrich	1815-1873	Auf dem Spaziergang "Singend gehn wir durch die Fluren"	No. 30	Unspec.	B. & H.		CHAL (1898)
8436	Wilhelm, Karl Friedrich	1815-1873	Auf hoher Alp wohnt auch der liebe Gott	No. 19	Unspec.	B. & H.		CHAL (1898)
8437	Wilhelm, Karl Friedrich	1815-1873	Aufmunterung zum Singen "Lasst die Töne erklingen"	No. 18	Unspec.	B. & H.		CHAL (1898)
8438	Wilhelm, Karl Friedrich	1815-1873	Bach im haine "Am Bache im Haine"	No. 49	Unspec.	B. & H.		CHAL (1898)
8439	Wilhelm, Karl Friedrich	1815-1873	Bauernknabe am Abend "Schön ost es, wenn das Abendroth"	No. 57	Unspec.	B. & H.		CHAL (1898)
8440	Wilhelm, Karl Friedrich	1815-1873	Blümchen am Felsen "Wie der Fels auch glühet"	No. 61	Unspec.	B. & H.		CHAL (1898)
8441	Wilhelm, Karl Friedrich	1815-1873	Ein Bäumchen trug schon jung und zart	No. 22	Unspec.	B. & H.		CHAL (1898)
8442	Wilhelm, Karl Friedrich	1815-1873	Frühlingsliedchen "Frühling hat sich eingestellt"	No. 34	Unspec.	B. & H.		CHAL (1898)
8443	Wilhelm, Karl Friedrich	1815-1873	Gesellschaftslied für Kinder "Ei seht mir doch die muntre Welt"	No. 41	Unspec.	B. & H.		CHAL (1898)
8444	Wilhelm, Karl Friedrich	1815-1873	Hirtenknabe "Ich bin vom Berg der Hirtenknab'"	No. 21	Unspec.	B. & H.		CHAL (1898)
8445	Wilhelm, Karl Friedrich	1815-1873	Hüttchen "Ich hab' ein kleines Hüttchen nur"	No. 51	Unspec.	B. & B.		CHAL (1898)
8446	Wilhelm, Karl Friedrich	1815-1873	Im Wald "Im Wald, im frischen grünen Wald"	No. 31	Unspec.	B. & H.		CHAL (1898)
8447	Wilhelm, Karl Friedrich	1815-1873	Käfer "Bist so nackt und klein"	No. 33	Unspec.	B. & H.		CHAL (1898)
8448	Wilhelm, Karl Friedrich	1815-1873	Lass die Tön' erklingen	No. 19	Unspec.	B. & H.		CHAL (1898)
8449	Wilhelm, Karl Friedrich	1815-1873	Lerche "Frische Lenz lag auf der Au"	No. 42	Unspec.	B. & H.		CHAL (1898)
8450	Wilhelm, Karl Friedrich	1815-1873	Lerche "Lerche in den Lüften schwebt"	No. 24	Unspec.	B. & H.		CHAL (1898)
8451	Wilhelm, Karl Friedrich	1815-1873	Lieben Sternelein "Seht wie blinken"	No. 50	Unspec.	B. & H.		CHAL (1898)
8452	Wilhelm, Karl Friedrich	1815-1873	Lilie "Schöne Silberblüthe"	No. 37	Unspec.	B. & H.		CHAL (1898)
8453	Wilhelm, Karl Friedrich	1815-1873	Lob des Singens "Singens ist ein köstlich Ding"	No. 54	Unspec.	B. & H.		CHAL (1898)
8454	Wilhelm, Karl Friedrich	1815-1873	Lobgesang "Lobt den Hernn"	No. 48	Unspec.	B. & H.		CHAL (1898)
8455	Wilhelm, Karl Friedrich	1815-1873	Mägdleins Fleiss "Trag ich gleich kein Kleid"	No. 32	Unspec.	B. & H.		CHAL (1898)
8456	Wilhelm, Karl Friedrich	1815-1873	Mailied "Da ist er, der liebliche"	No. 53	Unspec.	B. & H.		CHAL (1898)
8457	Wilhelm, Karl Friedrich	1815-1873	Mond "In stillem heiter'm Glanz"	No. 45	Unspec.	B. & H.		CHAL (1898)

REC	COMP	DTS	TITLE	OP #	VCG	PUB	COMMENTS	SRC
8458	Wilhelm, Karl Friedrich	1815-1873	Neinchen "Liebe kleine Bienchen"	No. 35	Unspec.	B. & H.		CHAL (1898)
8459	Wilhelm, Karl Friedrich	1815-1873	O du fröhliche, o du selige	No. 20	Unspec.	B. & B.		CHAL (1898)
8460	Wilhelm, Karl Friedrich	1815-1873	O Nachtigall dein heller Schall	No. 36	Unspec.	B. & H.		CHAL (1898)
8461	Wilhelm, Karl Friedrich	1815-1873	Sehnsucht nach dem Frühling "O wie ist es kalt geworden"	No. 26	Unspec.	B. & H.		CHAL (1898)
8462	Wilhelm, Karl Friedrich	1815-1873	Thräne und Lied "Thräne perlt aus weichem Herzen"	No. 52	Unspec.	B. & H.		CHAL (1898)
8463	Wilhelm, Karl Friedrich	1815-1873	Vaterlandslied "Ich bin ein deutsches Mädchen"	No. 56	Unspec.	B. & H.		CHAL (1898)
8464	Wilhelm, Karl Friedrich	1815-1873	Veilchen "Es blühet dicht an Erd'"	No. 58	Unspec.	B. & H.		CHAL (1898)
8465	Wilhelm, Karl Friedrich	1815-1873	Veilchen "Veilchen, wie so schweigend"	No. 40	Unspec.	B. & H.		CHAL (1898)
8466	Wilhelm, Karl Friedrich	1815-1873	Vergissmeinnicht an der Quelle "In der klaren, stillen Quelle"		S/A	B. & H.	In anth. "Zweistim. Lied. f. Sop. u. Altstimme mit Klavierbegleitung f. den Haus- u. Schulgebrauch v. H. M. Schletterer" 3 vols.	MSN
8467	Wilhelm, Karl Friedrich	1815-1873	Vergissmeinnicht an der Quelle "In der klaren stillen Quelle"	No. 60	Unspec.	B. & H.		CHAL (1898)
8468	Wilhelm, Karl Friedrich	1815-1873	Vergissmeinnicht "Freundlich glänzt an stiller Quelle"	No. 47	Unspec.	B. & H.		CHAL (1898)
8469	Wilhelm, Karl Friedrich	1815-1873	Vogels Freude "In dem goldnen Strahl"	No. 27	Unspec.	B. & H.		CHAL (1898)
8470	Wilhelm, Karl Friedrich	1815-1873	Waldhornlied "Wie lieblich schallt durch Busch und Wald"	No. 39	Unspec.	B. & H.		CHAL (1898)
8471	Wilhelm, Karl Friedrich	1815-1873	Waldvögelein "Ich geh' mit Lust durch diesen grünen"	No. 25	Unspec.	B. & H.		CHAL (1898)
8472	Wilhelm, Karl Friedrich	1815-1873	Was fang' ich an "Ach wo ich gerne bin"	No. 29	Unspec.	B. & H.		CHAL (1898)
8473	Wilhelm, Karl Friedrich	1815-1873	Welle und Leben "Auf der Welle leicht"	No. 59	Unspec.	B. & H.		CHAL (1898)
8474	Wilhelm, Karl Friedrich	1815-1873	Wir spielen und hüpfen so munter	No. 23	Unspec.	B. & H.		CHAL (1898)
8475	Wilhelm, Karl Friedrich	1815-1873	Zur Geburtstagsfeier des Kaisers "Heil Kaiser Wilhelm"	No. 62	Unspec.	B. & H.		CHAL (1898)
8476	Willan, Healy	1880-1968	Fairest Lord Jesus		S/S or T/T	Peters	org or pf accomp.	CVMP (1976)
8477	Willan, Healy	1880-1968	Jesu, Good Above All Others		S/S or T/T	Peters	org or pf accomp.	CVMP (1976)
8478	Willan, Healy	1880-1968	King Ascendeth into Heaven, The		S/A	Concordia	May be perf. chorally	CVMP (1976)
8479	Willan, Healy	1880-1968	Rejoice Greatly		high & low v.	Concordia	pf or org accomp.	ASR
8480	Willan, Healy	1880-1968	Rejoice Greatly, O Daughter of Zion		S/A	Concordia	May be perf. chorally	CVMP (1976)
8481	Willan, Healy	1880-1968	When the Herds Were Watching		2 med. v.	Concordia	pf or org accomp.	ASR
8482	Willeby, Charles		Coming home		Unspec.	Boosey	Arr. H. Geehl	BBC (1975)
8483	Williams, R. H.		By the Cross		S/A	Belwin		CVMP (1976)
8484	Williams, W. S. Gwynn		Suo-Gan		S/A	Curwen	Welsh duet	ASR

REC	COMP	DTS	TITLE	OP #	VCG	PUB	COMMENTS	SRC
8485	Wilm, Nicolai von	1834-1911	O kennst du Herz die beiden Schwesterengel	Op. 203 No. 1	S/A	Kahnt		CHAL (1906)
8486	Wilm, Nicolai von	1834-1911	Sterne blitzen am Himmel	Op. 203 No. 2	S/A	Kahnt		CHAL (1906)
8487	Wilm, Nicolai von	1834-1911	Venetianische Nacht "Nun fluhet wie scheidendes Grüssen"	Op. 124 No. 2	Unspec.	Wern-thal		CHAL (1898)
8488	Wilson		At dewy morn		Unspec.	White-Smith	In catalogue page "Vocal Duetts" of White-Smith Music Pub. Co. (no date)	MSN
8489	Wilson		Lonesome Valley, The		S/A	Lorenz		CVMP (1976)
8490	Wilson, Henry Lane	1870-1915	Before You Came		Unspec.	Cramer	Also solo	CVMP (1976)
8491	Wilson, Henry Lane	1870-1915	Carmeña		Unspec.	Reeder & Walsh		BBC (1975)
8492	Wilson, Henry Lane	1870-1915	Carmeña		S/A	Ditson	Also solo, female quartet, pf duet. In anthology "Soprano and Alto Duets" Ed. H. Kiehl. Pub. 1901.	MSN
8493	Wilson, Henry Lane	1870-1915	Carmeña		S/A	Ditson	Also solo, female quartet, pf duet. In anthology "The Ditson Collection of Soprano and Alto Duets" Pub. 1934.	MSN
8494	Wiltberger, August	1850-1928	Missa in honorem St. Margaretha		Unspec.	none listed	org or harm accomp.	CHAL (1898)
8495	Winkhler, Karl Angelus von	1787-1845	Erster Verlust "Ach wer bringt die schönen Tage"		Unspec.	Cranz		CHAL (1898)
8496	Winkhler, Karl Angelus von	1787-1845	Töne "Liebe denkt in süssen Tönen"		Unspec.	Cranz		CHAL (1898)
8497	Winkler, O.		Adolar und Adelina "Eduard liebt Kunigunde"	Op. 70	Unspec.	Glaser		CHAL (1898)
8498	Winkler, O.		Beiden Droschkenkutscher "Wir sind als Droschken-kutscher"	Op. 41	Unspec.	O. Teich		CHAL (1898)
8499	Winkler, O.		Beiden Köche "Nicht umsonst hat aus Paris man"	Op. 12	Unspec.	Fr. Dietrich		CHAL (1898)
8500	Winkler, O.		Fidele Bäckerjungen "Es ruht im besten Schlummer"	Op. 49	Unspec.	O. Teich		CHAL (1898)
8501	Winkler, O.		Hage und Mager "Wo das Haus am höchsten ist"	Op. 25	Unspec.	O. Teich		CHAL (1898)
8502	Winkler, O.		Ich heisse Grete, bin vom Lande	Op. 86	Unspec.	Meiss-ner		CHAL (1901)
8503	Winkler, O.		Musikant und Spekulant "Musicieren, componiren"	Op. 24	Unspec.	O. Teich		CHAL (1898)
8504	Winkler, O.		Schnuppe und Schwuppe, die beiden Sergeanten "Wer irgendwie nur in Stadt"	Op. 28	Unspec.	O. Teich		CHAL (1898)
8505	Winter		Cessario		Unspec.	Lons-dale	Arr. Bishop	BBC (1975)
8506	Winter, E.		Beiden Dienstmänner "Man hört wirklich heutzutage"	Op. 89	Unspec.	O. Dietrich		CHAL (1898)
8507	Winter, E.		Dort am Markte an der Ecke	No. 9	Unspec.	O. Teich		CHAL (1901)
8508	Winter, E.		Menschen alle gross und klein	No. 6	Unspec.	O. Teich		CHAL (1901)

REC	COMP	DTS	TITLE	OP #	VCG	PUB	COMMENTS	SRC
8509	Winter, E.		Ob einer Witz hat	No. 7	Unspec.	O. Teich		CHAL (1901)
8510	Winter, E.		Schnellzug- und Secundär-bahn-Schaffner "Hum. Duoscene"	Op. 150	Unspec.	O. Teich		CHAL (1901)
8511	Winter, E.		Siamesischen Zwillinge "Wer hätte nicht schon längst"		Unspec.	O. Dietrich		CHAL (1898)
8512	Winter, E.		Veretzt man zurück sich so	No. 10	Unspec.	O. Teich		CHAL (1901)
8513	Winter, E.		Was ist nur in den Strassen los	Op. 206	Unspec.	O. Teich		CHAL (1901)
8514	Winter, E.		Wir kennen uns schon viele Jahr	No. 8	Unspec.	O. Teich		CHAL (1901)
8515	Winter, E.		Zwei heirathslustige Damen "Hum. Duoscene"	Op. 242	Unspec.	O. Teich	Arr. Tymian	CHAL (1901)
8516	Winter, E.		Zwei Radsport-Gigerl "Wie sie uns Beide"	Op. 114	Unspec.	O. Dietrich		CHAL (1898)
8517	Winter, Georg	1869-1924	Alte deutsche Volks-Weihnachtslieder (12)	Op. 57	Unspec.	Schwann	Collection of arr. of 12 Christmas folk-songs. Includes duets.	CHAL (1911)
8518	Winter, J.		Rings Abendstille	Op. 4	S/A	Berlin Selbstverl.		CHAL (1906)
8519	Winterberger, Alexander	1834-1914	Abschied "Ach mich hält der Gram befangen"	Op. 59 No. 3	Unspec.	Kahnt		CHAL (1898)
8520	Winterberger, Alexander	1834-1914	Abschied "Horcht, was für ein Dröhnen"	Op. 66 No. 4	2 female v.	Kistner		CHAL (1898)
8521	Winterberger, Alexander	1834-1914	Abschiedsfrage "Es kugelte, es kugelte ein rothes"	Op. 67 No. 4	2 female v.	Fritzsch		CHAL (1898)
8522	Winterberger, Alexander	1834-1914	Adventlied "A, Himmel kommt der Morgenstern"		2 female v.	Fritzsch		CHAL (1898)
8523	Winterberger, Alexander	1834-1914	Ahorn wuchs im Garten	Op. 75 No. 12	2 female v.	B. & H.		CHAL (1898)
8524	Winterberger, Alexander	1834-1914	Als ich hinging über'n Hof	Op. 75 No. 10	2 female v.	B. & H.		CHAL (1898)
8525	Winterberger, Alexander	1834-1914	Armes Kind "Wasser trug das junge Mädchen"	Op. 52 No. 4	Unspec.	Kahnt		CHAL (1898)
8526	Winterberger, Alexander	1834-1914	Barcarole "O Fischer auf den Wogen"	Op. 43 No. 6	Unspec.	Kistner		CHAL (1898)
8527	Winterberger, Alexander	1834-1914	Beim Gänserupfen "Lass dich rupfen liebes Gänschen"	Op. 52 No. 2	Unspec.	Kahnt		CHAL (1898)
8528	Winterberger, Alexander	1834-1914	Bescheid "Wenn ich im Brautgewande"	Op. 30 No. 4	S/A	Kahnt		CHAL (1898)
8529	Winterberger, Alexander	1834-1914	Besser ist besser "Niemals hab' ich noch auf Buchen"	Op. 68 No. 1	2 female v.	R. Forberg		CHAL (1898)
8530	Winterberger, Alexander	1834-1914	Bote der Liebe "Wie viel schon der Boten"	Op. 59 No. 5	Unspec.	Kahnt		CHAL (1898)
8531	Winterberger, Alexander	1834-1914	Bothe Aeugelein "Kömmt'st du meine Aeugelein"	Op. 30 No. 2	S/A	Kahnt		CHAL (1898)
8532	Winterberger, Alexander	1834-1914	Dainos 14 Littauische Volkslieder	Op. 75	2 female v.	B. & H.	14 folk duets	CHAL (1898)
8533	Winterberger, Alexander	1834-1914	Drei Röslein "Ich legte mich nieder"	Op. 59 No. 7	Unspec.	Kahnt		CHAL (1898)
8534	Winterberger, Alexander	1834-1914	Es fiel ein Reif	Op. 59 No. 6	Unspec.	Kahnt		CHAL (1898)
8535	Winterberger, Alexander	1834-1914	Fester Entschluss "An die Quelle rein und klar"	Op. 76 I No. 2	2 female v.	Fritzsch		CHAL (1898)

REC	COMP	DTS	TITLE	OP #	VCG	PUB	COMMENTS	SRC
8536	Winterberger, Alexander	1834-1914	Fischer "Er kam vom See herüber"	Op. 3	S/A	Siegel		CHAL (1898)
8537	Winterberger, Alexander	1834-1914	Frau Maria "Dort hoch auf dem Berge"	Op. 30 No. 1	S/A	Kahnt		CHAL (1898)
8538	Winterberger, Alexander	1834-1914	Freigebigkeit "Fleisst das Wasser gegen'n Wasser"	Op. 59 No. 1	Unspec.	Kahnt		CHAL (1898)
8539	Winterberger, Alexander	1834-1914	Gebrochene Bank "Bank, d'rauf ich so oft"	Op. 59 No. 9	Unspec.	Kahnt		CHAL (1898)
8540	Winterberger, Alexander	1834-1914	Glänzende Treue "Seh' ich's dort nicht glänzen"	Op. 30 No. 10	S/A	Kahnt		CHAL (1898)
8541	Winterberger, Alexander	1834-1914	Glück im Unglück "Im grünen Haine koste"	Op. 30 No. 11	S/A	Kahnt		CHAL (1898)
8542	Winterberger, Alexander	1834-1914	Gold überwiegt die Liebe "Sternchen mit dem trüben Schein"	Op. 30 No. 7	S/A	Kahnt		CHAL (1898)
8543	Winterberger, Alexander	1834-1914	Ich hört ein Sichlein rauschen	Op. 59 No. 2	Unspec.	Kahnt		CHAL (1898)
8544	Winterberger, Alexander	1834-1914	In dem Bächlein fliesset	Op. 75 No. 1	2 female v.	B. & H.		CHAL (1898)
8545	Winterberger, Alexander	1834-1914	In dem bunten Bette liegt	Op. 75 No. 7	2 female v.	B. & H.		CHAL (1898)
8546	Winterberger, Alexander	1834-1914	In der Fremde "Es steht ein Baum im Odenwald"	Op. 30 No. 5	S/A	Kahnt		CHAL (1898)
8547	Winterberger, Alexander	1834-1914	In jenem Walde dort unter Linden	Op. 75 No. 6	2 female v.	B. & H.		CHAL (1898)
8548	Winterberger, Alexander	1834-1914	Jener alte Graukopf hatte	Op. 75 No. 5	2 female v.	B. & H.		CHAL (1898)
8549	Winterberger, Alexander	1834-1914	Keinen Alten "Hab' ich auch nur bleiche Wangen"	Op. 62 No. 3	2 female v.	R. Forberg		CHAL (1898)
8550	Winterberger, Alexander	1834-1914	Komm her o Mädchen	Op. 75 No. 4	2 female v.	B. & H.		CHAL (1898)
8551	Winterberger, Alexander	1834-1914	Kranzwinderin "Smilje pflückt am kühlen Bach"	Op. 53 No. 3	Unspec.	Kahnt		CHAL (1898)
8552	Winterberger, Alexander	1834-1914	Lass ab o Wind, lass ab zu blasen	Op. 75 No. 8	2 female v.	B. & H.		CHAL (1898)
8553	Winterberger, Alexander	1834-1914	Lauter Wunder "Ohnefuss will Krebse fangen"	Op. 68 No. 2	2 female v.	R. Forberg		CHAL (1898)
8554	Winterberger, Alexander	1834-1914	Liebe bis in den Tod "Neblig ist die schöne Sonne"	Op. 66 No. 6	2 female v.	Kistner		CHAL (1898)
8555	Winterberger, Alexander	1834-1914	Liebe "Wie kann ich dich, o Liebe"	Op. 62 No. 5	2 female v.	R. Forberg		CHAL (1898)
8556	Winterberger, Alexander	1834-1914	Liebe "Woher nur nimmt ein Jeder"	Op. 68 No. 4	2 female v.	R. Forberg		CHAL (1898)
8557	Winterberger, Alexander	1834-1914	Liebeswunder "Ich wollt' ich läg und schlief"	Op. 52 No. 1	Unspec.	Kahnt		CHAL (1898)
8558	Winterberger, Alexander	1834-1914	Mädchen am der Donau "Längs der Donau ging sie"	Op. 52 No. 5	Unspec.	Kahnt		CHAL (1898)
8559	Winterberger, Alexander	1834-1914	Mädchens Klage um einen Todten "Eingesunkne alte Burgen"	Op. 43 No. 3	Unspec.	Kistner		CHAL (1898)
8560	Winterberger, Alexander	1834-1914	Mädchens Klage "Wasserholen Abends ging"	Op. 57 No. 7	Unspec.	Kahnt		CHAL (1898)
8561	Winterberger, Alexander	1834-1914	Mädchens Wahl "Ach wie schlief ich sonst so gut"	Op. 82 No. 2	2 female v.	Sch. & Co.		CHAL (1898)
8562	Winterberger, Alexander	1834-1914	Mein wirst du o Liebchen "Fürwahr mein Liebchen"	Op. 76 II No. 3	2 female v.	Fritzsch		CHAL (1898)
8563	Winterberger, Alexander	1834-1914	Neckereien "Wärest du ein Schneider doch"	Op. 76 II No. 5	2 female v.	Fritzsch		CHAL (1898)
8564	Winterberger, Alexander	1834-1914	Nichts "Was wohl die (meine) Leute sagen"	Op. 59 No. 4	Unspec.	Kahnt		CHAL (1898)
8565	Winterberger, Alexander	1834-1914	O schick' mich nicht allein zum Brunnen	Op. 43 No. 5	Unspec.	Kistner		CHAL (1898)

REC	COMP	DTS	TITLE	OP #	VCG	PUB	COMMENTS	SRC
8566	Winterberger, Alexander	1834-1914	Pärchen "Kugelte ein Apfel roth"	Op. 30 No. 12	S/A	Kahnt		CHAL (1898)
8567	Winterberger, Alexander	1834-1914	Ringlein "Auf dem grossen Teiche"	Op. 82 No. 1	2 female v.	Sch. & Co.		CHAL (1898)
8568	Winterberger, Alexander	1834-1914	Sank ein Mädchen	Op. 75 No. 14	2 female v.	B. & H.		CHAL (1898)
8569	Winterberger, Alexander	1834-1914	Scheiden "Ach das Scheiden"	Op. 76 II No. 4	2 female v.	Fritzsch		CHAL (1898)
8570	Winterberger, Alexander	1834-1914	Schlecht verträgliche Gesellschaft "Ei, in einem Haus"	Op. 68 No. 3	2 female v.	Forberg		CHAL (1898)
8571	Winterberger, Alexander	1834-1914	Schnelles Besinnen "Sage mir, mein Sternlein"	Op. 62 No. 4	2 female v.	R. Forberg		CHAL (1898)
8572	Winterberger, Alexander	1834-1914	Schön Maria und das Vöglein "Sitzt Maria in der Hürde"	Op. 71 No. 1	2 female v.	Fritzsch		CHAL (1898)
8573	Winterberger, Alexander	1834-1914	Schöne Djurdja "Djudja, schönes Mädchen"	Op. 52 No. 6	Unspec.	Kahnt		CHAL (1898)
8574	Winterberger, Alexander	1834-1914	Schreiber "O Mütterchen, o sieh doch"	Op. 71 No. 4	2 female v.	Fritzsch		CHAL (1898)
8575	Winterberger, Alexander	1834-1914	Schwarzen Augen "Es wässerte das Mädchen Hanf"	Op. 62 No. 1	2 female v.	R. Forberg		CHAL (1898)
8576	Winterberger, Alexander	1834-1914	Sehnsucht "Hinter jenen dichten Wäldern"	Op. 59 No. 8	Unspec.	Kahnt		CHAL (1898)
8577	Winterberger, Alexander	1834-1914	Seufzer "Wenn zu mir heut Abends"	Op. 66 No. 5	2 female v.	Kistner		CHAL (1898)
8578	Winterberger, Alexander	1834-1914	Slaviches Volkspoesien	Op. 62 and Op. 68	Unspec.	R. Forberg	Collections of duets	CHAL (1898)
8579	Winterberger, Alexander	1834-1914	Slaviches Volkspoesien	Op. 66	Unspec.	Kistner	Collections of duets	CHAL (1898)
8580	Winterberger, Alexander	1834-1914	Slaviches Volkspoesien	Op. 67, 71, 76	Unspec.	Fritzsch	Collections of duets	CHAL (1898)
8581	Winterberger, Alexander	1834-1914	Slaviches Wiegenlied "Schlaf mein Kind in Ruh"	Op. 43 No. 4	Unspec.	Kistner		CHAL (1898)
8582	Winterberger, Alexander	1834-1914	Spinnerin "Spinn, spinn meine liebe Tochter"	Op. 43 No. 2	Unspec.	Kistner		CHAL (1898)
8583	Winterberger, Alexander	1834-1914	Störung in der Andacht "Seh ich dich mein holdes Mädchen"	Op. 67 No. 1	2 female v.	Fritzsch		CHAL (1898)
8584	Winterberger, Alexander	1834-1914	Süssen Schlummer such' ich	Op. 75 No. 3	2 female v.	B. & H.		CHAL (1898)
8585	Winterberger, Alexander	1834-1914	Tanzliedchen "Männlein, Männlein ging einmal"	Op. 30 No. 3	S/A	Kahnt		CHAL (1898)
8586	Winterberger, Alexander	1834-1914	Täubchen "Wo bist du umher geschweift"	Op. 67 No. 2	2 female v.	Fritzsch		CHAL (1898)
8587	Winterberger, Alexander	1834-1914	Traum "Schlief das Mädchen ein"	Op. 62 No. 2	2 female v.	R. Forberg		CHAL (1898)
8588	Winterberger, Alexander	1834-1914	Um den kleinen Weiher wandelt	Op. 75 No. 9	2 female v.	B. & H.		CHAL (1898)
8589	Winterberger, Alexander	1834-1914	Unglücklich Vermählte "Wenn in Frösten"	Op. 71 No. 3	2 female v.	Fritzsch		CHAL (1898)
8590	Winterberger, Alexander	1834-1914	Unter Mutters hellem Fenster	Op. 75 No. 13	2 female v.	B. & H.		CHAL (1898)
8591	Winterberger, Alexander	1834-1914	Verbot "Besuch mich nicht"	Op. 67 No. 3	2 female v.	Fritzsch		CHAL (1898)
8592	Winterberger, Alexander	1834-1914	Verlassene "Neulich schwamm ein flinkes Gänschen"	Op. 30 No. 9	S/A	Kahnt		CHAL (1898)
8593	Winterberger, Alexander	1834-1914	Verlassene "Neulich schwamm ein flinkes Gänschen"	Op. 68 No. 5	2 female v.	R. Forberg		CHAL (1898)
8594	Winterberger, Alexander	1834-1914	Vöglein "Was plaudert dort das Vöglein"	Op. 30 No. 8	S/A	Kahnt		CHAL (1898)
8595	Winterberger, Alexander	1834-1914	Volkspoësien "(10) Deutsche u. slavische f. 2 Frauenst."	Op. 59	2 female v.	Kahnt	Collection of 10 duets	CHAL (1898)

REC	COMP	DTS	TITLE	OP #	VCG	PUB	COMMENTS	SRC
8596	Winterberger, Alexander	1834-1914	Volkspoësien "3 Duette f. 2 Frauenst."	Op. 82	2 female v.	Sch. & Co.	Collection of 3 duets	CHAL (1898)
8597	Winterberger, Alexander	1834-1914	Volkspoësien "6 Duette"	Op. 43	Unspec.	Kistner	Collection of 6 duets	CHAL (1898)
8598	Winterberger, Alexander	1834-1914	Volkspoësien "(7) f. 2 Frauenst."	Op. 52	2 female v.	Kahnt	Collection of 7 duets	CHAL (1898)
8599	Winterberger, Alexander	1834-1914	Volkspoësien "Deutsche u. slavische f. 2 Frauenst." (12)	Op. 30	2 female v.	Kahnt	Collection of 12 duets of Grmn. and Slavic folk poetry	CHAL (1898)
8600	Winterberger, Alexander	1834-1914	Was, o Tochter, was, o Junge	Op. 75 No. 11	2 female v.	B. & H.		CHAL (1898)
8601	Winterberger, Alexander	1834-1914	Wenn ich es wüsste	Op. 75 No. 2	2 female v.	B. & H.		CHAL (1898)
8602	Winterberger, Alexander	1834-1914	Wer theilt am besten "Ruhig mit des Eimers Wucht"	Op. 76 I No. 1	2 female v.	Fritzsch		CHAL (1898)
8603	Winterberger, Alexander	1834-1914	Wiegenlied "Eia popeia, schlief lieber wie du"	Op. 30 No. 6	S/A	Kahnt		CHAL (1898)
8604	Winterberger, Alexander	1834-1914	Wiegenlied "Eia popeia, was raschelt im Stroh"	Op. 82 No. 3	2 female v.	Sch. & Co.		CHAL (1898)
8605	Winterberger, Alexander	1834-1914	Wilde Entchen "Es flog ein wildes Entchen"	Op. 66 No. 1	2 female v.	Kistner		CHAL (1898)
8606	Winterberger, Alexander	1834-1914	Wohlmeinde Gänslein "Flog eine junge Gans"	Op. 66 No. 2	2 female v.	Kistner		CHAL (1898)
8607	Winterberger, Alexander	1834-1914	Zerbrochene Krug "Wollt' 'ne Maid um Wasser"	Op. 66 No. 3	2 female v.	Kistner		CHAL (1898)
8608	Winterberger, Alexander	1834-1914	Zum Stelldichein "Dat du mein Leevsten bist"	Op. 43 No. 1	Unspec.	Kistner		CHAL (1898)
8609	Winterling, W.		Böse Männerwelt sagt von uns immer	Op. 53	2 female v.	Winterling i. L.		CHAL (1901)
8610	Winterling, W.		Den nehmen wir, den nehmen wir nicht "Man sieht's uns an der Nase an"	Op. 21 No. b	2 female v.	Fr. Dietrich		CHAL (1898)
8611	Winterling, W.		Eine Dame, die ich kannte	Op. 54	2 female v.	Winterling i. L.		CHAL (1901)
8612	Winterling, W.		Frau Hutzig und Frau Putzig "Nein, ich kanns nicht mehr ertragen"	Op. 31	2 female v.	Portius		CHAL (1898)
8613	Winterling, W.		Ihr lieben Mägdelein, lasst doch das Freien sein	Op. 41	2 female v.	Winterling		CHAL (1901)
8614	Winterling, W.		Michel und Liese "Michel sagt meine Mutter"	Op. 32	Unspec.	Zimm. i. L.		CHAL (1898)
8615	Winterling, W.		Nein, es ist nicht auszuhalten	Op. 55	2 female v.	Winterling i. L.		CHAL (1901)
8616	Winterling, W.		Ohn' Tanz wär' das Leben	Op. 51	2 female v.	Winterling i. L.		CHAL (1901)
8617	Winterling, W.		Schreiben, Rechnen und Geschichte	Op. 57	2 female v.	Winterling i. L.		CHAL (1906)
8618	Winterling, W.		Trommler von der Schützengilde zu Schilda "Wir stellen uns hier vor"	Op. 23	Unspec.	Fr. Dietrich		CHAL (1898)
8619	Winterling, W.		Wie hat sich alles anders jetzt gestaltet	Op. 58	2 female v.	Winterling i. L.		CHAL (1906)
8620	Wintzer, Elisabeth	1863-1933	Als Grossmama ein Mädchen war	Op. 10	2 med. v.	Simrock	Grmn. woman comp.	CHAL (1911)
8621	Wintzer, Elisabeth	1863-1933	Immer zwei zu zweien	Op. 11	S/A	Simrock	Grmn. woman comp.	CHAL (1911)
8622	Wintzer, Elisabeth	1863-1933	Kommt, wir wollen Blumen binden	Op. 15	S/A	Simrock	Grmn. woman comp.	CHAL (1911)
8623	Wintzer, Elisabeth	1863-1933	Rosen stehn im Mädchengarten	Op. 14	S/A	Simrock	Grmn. woman comp.	CHAL (1911)

REC	COMP	DTS	TITLE	OP #	VCG	PUB	COMMENTS	SRC
8624	Witt, Franz Xaver	1834-1888	Missa Exultet	Op. 9 No. 2	S/A or T/B	Coppen-rath	org accomp.	CHAL (1898)
8625	Witt, Franz Xaver	1834-1888	Missa pro defunctis	Op. 9 No. 1	S/A or T/B	Coppen-rath	org accomp.	CHAL (1898)
8626	Witt, Franz Xaver	1834-1888	Offertorium in Missis St. Pontificum		Unspec.	Coppen-rath	org accomp.	CHAL (1898)
8627	Witt, Julius	1819-1890	Ständchen "Wenn du im Traum wirst fragen"		Unspec.	Bahn		CHAL (1898)
8628	Witt, Julius	1819-1890	Thräne "Wohl was es eine Seligkeit"		Unspec.	Bahn		CHAL (1898)
8629	Witt, Julius	1819-1890	Wunsch "Wie ein Vöglein möcht ich fliegen"		Unspec.	Bahn		CHAL (1898)
8630	Witt, Leopold	1811-1891	Abendlied "Hin ist des Tages rosiger Schein"	Op. 55 No. 2	2 female v.	O. Forberg		CHAL (1898)
8631	Witt, Leopold	1811-1891	Blumen Erwachen "Schnee-glöcken möchte wandern gehn"	Op. 56	2 female v.	O. Forberg		CHAL (1898)
8632	Witt, Leopold	1811-1891	Schlaf in mein Lieb in Frieden	Op. 71	Unspec.	Sch. j.		CHAL (1898)
8633	Witt, Leopold	1811-1891	Überfahrt "Leise klingt des Stromes Woge"	Op. 55 No. 1	2 female v.	O. Forberg		CHAL (1898)
8634	Witt, Theodor de	1823-1855	Rastlose Liebe "Schnee, dem Regen"	Op. 4 No. 1	S/S	Schlesinger		CHAL (1898)
8635	Wittenbecher, Otto	1875-	Altböhmische Weihnachtslieder (2)		Unspec.	G. Richter i. Leipzig	2 Christmas duets	CHAL (1901)
8636	Wittenbecher, Otto	1875-	Freu' dich Erd' und Sternenzelt		Unspec.	G. Richter i. Leipzig		CHAL (1901)
8637	Wittenbecher, Otto	1875-	Kommet ihr Hirten		Unspec.	Richter i. Leipzig		CHAL (1901)
8638	Wittsack, P.		Zu Zwei'n "Hier umher, dort umher"	Op. 2	Unspec.	Kaun		CHAL (1898)
8639	Wolf, E.		Dreissig Tage, welch' Entzücken	No. 2	Unspec.	Rosé		CHAL (1911)
8640	Wolf, E.		Englishmann ist immer smart	No. 5	Unspec.	Rosé		CHAL (1911)
8641	Wolf, L. C.		An Sanct Gertrud's Tag "O Gertrud erste Gärtnerin"	Op. 1 No. 3	S/S	R. & B.		CHAL (1898)
8642	Wolf, L. C.		Hüte dich "Nachtigall hüte dich"	Op. 1 No. 2	S/S	R. & B.		CHAL (1898)
8643	Wolf, L. C.		Kunkelstube "Wie still die Mädchen"	Op. 1 No. 1	S/S	R. & B.		CHAL (1898)
8644	Wolff, C.		Wie der Tag mir schleicht	Op. 2	S/S	Hampe i. Br.		CHAL (1898)
8645	Wolff, Gustav Tyson [also Tyson-Wolff]	1840-1907	Es muss ein Wunderbares sein	Op. 39 No. 5	S/A	Hug		CHAL (1898)
8646	Wolff, Gustav Tyson [also Tyson-Wolff]	1840-1907	Heimliche Liebe "Kein Feuer, keine Kohle"	Op. 39 No. 6	S/A	Hug		CHAL (1898)
8647	Wolff, Gustav Tyson [also Tyson-Wolff]	1840-1907	Im Maien "Im Maien zu Zweien ze gehen"	Op. 35 No. 2	S/A	Hug		CHAL (1898)
8648	Wolff, Gustav Tyson [also Tyson-Wolff]	1840-1907	In dem Dornbusch blüht ein Röslein	Op. 35 No. 1	S/A	Hug		CHAL (1898)
8649	Wolff, Gustav Tyson [also Tyson-Wolff]	1840-1907	Kein Graben so breit	Op. 35 No. 4	S/A	Hug		CHAL (1898)
8650	Wolff, Gustav Tyson [also Tyson-Wolff]	1840-1907	Mond schein am Himmel	Op. 39 No. 4	S/A	Hug		CHAL (1898)

REC	COMP	DTS	TITLE	OP #	VCG	PUB	COMMENTS	SRC
8651	Wolff, Gustav Tyson [also Tyson-Wolff]	1840-1907	Tanzlied "Wie wir zum Tanz"	Op. 39 No. 2	S/A	Hug		CHAL (1898)
8652	Wolff, Gustav Tyson [also Tyson-Wolff]	1840-1907	Und die Rosen, die prangen	Op. 35 No. 3	S/A	Hug		CHAL (1898)
8653	Wolff, Gustav Tyson [also Tyson-Wolff]	1840-1907	Uralt "So bischen Maiensonne"	Op. 39 No. 1	S/A	Hug		CHAL (1898)
8654	Wolff, Gustav Tyson [also Tyson-Wolff]	1840-1907	Wenn die Rosen glühen	Op. 39 No. 3	S/A	Hug		CHAL (1898)
8655	Wolff, Leonhard	1848-1934	Erster Verlust "Ach wer bringt die schönen Tage"	Op. 3 No. 2	S/A	Schlesinger		CHAL (1898)
8656	Wolff, Leonhard	1848-1934	Frühlingslied "Über die Berge wandelt"	Op. 3 No. 1	S/A	Schlesinger		CHAL (1898)
8657	Wolff, Leonhard	1848-1934	Liebesfeier "An ihren bunten Liedern klettert"	Op. 3 No. 5	S/A	Schlesinger		CHAL (1898)
8658	Wolff, Leonhard	1848-1934	Wanderers Nachtlied "Der der von dem Himmel bist"	Op. 3 No. 4	S/A	Schlesinger		CHAL (1898)
8659	Wolff, Leonhard	1848-1934	Weihnachtslied "Es strahlt am Himmelsrande"	Op. 3 No. 6	S/A	Schlesinger		CHAL (1898)
8660	Wolff, Leonhard	1848-1934	Zweigesang "Im Fliederbusch ein Vöglein sass"	Op. 3 No. 3	S/A	Schlesinger		CHAL (1898)
8661	Wolff, W.		August und Adolar, das schneidige Gefreitenpaar "Hurrah nun sind wir da"	Op. 93 No. 1	Unspec.	Danner		CHAL (1898)
8662	Wolff, W.		Blumenmädchen "Kaum dass der holde Lenz"	Op. 36	2 female or 2 male v.	Heinr.		CHAL (1898)
8663	Wolff, W.		Flotte Turner "Zwei flott're Turner"	Op. 99	Unspec.	Danner		CHAL (1898)
8664	Wolff, W.		Im Frack und Chapeau claque "Sie sehen in uns Beid'"	Op. 104	Unspec.	Uhse		CHAL (1898)
8665	Wolff, W.		Jochem Paesels Streiche "Ich bin der Jochem Paesel"	Op. 109	Unspec.	Danner		CHAL (1898)
8666	Wolff, W.		Kellnerpaar vom Grand-Hôtel "Wir kommen an gar schnell"	Op. 95	Unspec.	Danner		CHAL (1898)
8667	Wolff, W.		Radelnde Pärchen "Oft fuhr ich per Rad"	Op. 116	Unspec.	Danner		CHAL (1898)
8668	Wolff, W.		Schuster Sohle und sein Ideal "Ei was kann es Schönres geben"	Op. 2	Unspec.	Fr. Dietrich		CHAL (1898)
8669	Wolff, W.		So ein Wochenmarkt was schöne	Op. 246	2 female v.	Meissner		CHAL (1906)
8670	Wolff, W.		Wenn ich's nur wüsste "Heut sind wir wieder lustig"	Op. 82	Unspec.	Danner		CHAL (1898)
8671	Wolff, W.		Zwei glückliche Tage "Wir sind zwei lustige Gesell'n"	Op. 81 No. 1	Unspec.	Danner		CHAL (1898)
8672	Wolff, W.		Zwei Weibchen froh und heiter	Op. 317	Unspec.	Meissner		CHAL (1906)
8673	Wolff, Wilh.		Polkaschwärmer "Überall in Stadt und Land"		Unspec.	Neumann i. Berl.		CHAL (1898)
8674	Wölfle, Chr.		Friedenshymne "Nun lasst durch's Land"		S/S	Zumsteeg		CHAL (1898)
8675	Wolfrum, Karl	1856-1937	In teifer Nacht	Op. 8	S/A	Coppenrath		CHAL (1906)
8676	Wollanck, Friedrich	1782-1831	Lied der Wasserfee "Auf Wogen gezogen"	No. 3	2 female v.	Bahn		CHAL (1898)
8677	Wollanck, Friedrich	1782-1831	Treulieb "Treulieb ist nimmer weit"	No. 1	2 female v.	Bahn		CHAL (1898)

REC	COMP	DTS	TITLE	OP #	VCG	PUB	COMMENTS	SRC
8678	Wollanck, Friedrich	1782-1831	Wohin "Es wehen die Lüfte wohin"	No. 2	2 female v.	Bahn		CHAL (1898)
8679	Wolzogen, Ernst von	1855-1934	Tanz mit mir, mein schönes Herrl		Unspec.	Harmonie		CHAL (1901)
8680	Wood, Hayden	1882-1959	Beware		Unspec.	A. H. & C.		BBC (1975)
8681	Wood, Hayden	1882-1959	The frog's lament		Unspec.	Boosey		BBC (1975)
8682	Wood, Hayden	1882-1959	When the daisy ope's her eyes		Unspec.	Chappell		BBC (1975)
8683	Wood, Hayden	1882-1959	When the day was young		Unspec.	A. H. & C.		BBC (1975)
8684	Woodforde-Finden Amy	d. 1919	Kashmiri Song		Unspec.	Boosey	Woman comp. Also solo.	CVMP (1976)
8685	Woodforde-Finden Amy	d. 1919	Request, A		Unspec.	Leonard-Eng	Woman comp. Also solo pub. by Cramer.	CVMP (1976)
8686	Wooge, Emma	1857-1935	Fliegt der erste Morgenstrahl	No. 1	high & med. v.	Sulzer	Grmn. woman comp.	CHAL (1901)
8687	Wooge, Emma	1857-1935	Fröhliche, geweihte Nacht	Op. 12 No. 1	Unspec.	Eisoldt & R. Schles.	Grmn. woman comp.	CHAL (1906)
8688	Wooge, Emma	1857-1935	Heiligstes Sakrament, Taufe in Jesu Christ	Op. 10 No. 2	Unspec.	Jonasson-Eckermann	pf or org or harm. Grmn. woman comp.	CHAL (1906)
8689	Wooge, Emma	1857-1935	Hell'ge Nacht mit Engelsschwingen	Op. 10 No. 2	Unspec.	Eisoldt & R. Schles.	Grmn. woman comp.	CHAL (1906)
8690	Wooge, Emma	1857-1935	Ich trat in der Nacht auf die Wies'		high & med. v.	Sulzer	Grmn. woman comp.	CHAL (1901)
8691	Wooge, Emma	1857-1935	Küss mir heute nicht die Hand	No. 3	high & med. v.	Sulzer	Grmn. woman comp.	CHAL (1901)
8692	Wottitz, Th.		Mir echten Weana Vollblutkinder	Op. 104	Unspec.	Blaha		CHAL (1911)
8693	Wottitz, Th.		Winter stimmt jeden gar traurig	Op. 150	Unspec.	Bosworth		CHAL (1911)
8694	Wottitz, Th.		Wo ist die schönste Stadt		Unspec.	Blaha		CHAL (1911)
8695	Wottiz, Th.		I kenn' a schön's Platzerl		Unspec.	Bosworth		CHAL (1906)
8696	Wouters, Adolphe	1849-1924	Source d'Ardenne "O source solitaire"		S/S	Schott i. Br.		CHAL (1898)
8697	Wrangel, Vassily G.	1862-1901	Hor Hur Stilla Vinden Susar		Unspec.	Lundq.	In "Tvastammiga Sanger" Swed. trans. Russ.	CVMP (1976)
8698	Wrangel, Vassily G.	1862-1901	I Skogen		Unspec.	Lundq.	In "Tvastammiga Sanger" Swed. trans. Russ.	CVMP (1976)
8699	Wrede, Ferdinand	1827-1899	Psalm 67 "Gott sei uns gnädig"	Op. 9	S/A	R. & E.		CHAL (1898)
8700	Wüerst, Richard Ferdinand	1824-1881	An den Maienwind "Maienwind, halt, nicht so geschwind"	Op. 58 No. 3	S/A	B. & B.		CHAL (1898)
8701	Wüerst, Richard Ferdinand	1824-1881	Blauen Frühlingsaugen schaun aus	Op. 58 No. 2	S/A	B. & B.		CHAL (1898)
8702	Wüerst, Richard Ferdinand	1824-1881	Da drüben "Da drüben über'm Walde"	Op. 15 No. 2	S/A	Bahn		CHAL (1898)
8703	Wüerst, Richard Ferdinand	1824-1881	Elfenfrühling "Was rauscht vorbei"	Op. 2 No. 3	Unspec.	Chal.		CHAL (1898)
8704	Wüerst, Richard Ferdinand	1824-1881	Es war ein Knabe gezogen	Op. 32 No. 2	S/A	Bahn		CHAL (1898)

REC	COMP	DTS	TITLE	OP #	VCG	PUB	COMMENTS	SRC
8705	Wüerst, Richard Ferdinand	1824-1881	Fröhliche Fahrt "O glücklich, wer zum Liebchen zieht"	Op. 46 No. 4	Unspec.	Bahn		CHAL (1898)
8706	Wüerst, Richard Ferdinand	1824-1881	Frühlingseinzung "Fenster auf, die Herzen auf"	Op. 23 No. 2	S/MS	Schlesinger		CHAL (1898)
8707	Wüerst, Richard Ferdinand	1824-1881	Frühlingsglaube "Linden Lüfte sind erwacht"	Op. 2 No. 2	Unspec.	Chal.		CHAL (1898)
8708	Wüerst, Richard Ferdinand	1824-1881	Gesang der Schifferen "Ich schaue in des Sees Grund"	Op. 2 No. 5	Unspec.	Chal.		CHAL (1898)
8709	Wüerst, Richard Ferdinand	1824-1881	Getrennt sein "Ranken sind verschlungen"	Op. 23 No. 4	S/MS	Schlesinger		CHAL (1898)
8710	Wüerst, Richard Ferdinand	1824-1881	Im Mai "Nun grünt der Berg"	Op. 15 No. 1	S/A	Bahn		CHAL (1898)
8711	Wüerst, Richard Ferdinand	1824-1881	Im Walde singt ein Vogel	Op. 23 No. 1	S/MS	Schlesinger		CHAL (1898)
8712	Wüerst, Richard Ferdinand	1824-1881	Kinderlied "Es lächelt auf's neu"	Op. 2 No. 6	Unspec.	Chal.		CHAL (1898)
8713	Wüerst, Richard Ferdinand	1824-1881	Lied von der Liebsten rothen Mund "Wer gewöhnt was ab das Küssen"	Op. 58 No. 1	S/A	B. & B.		CHAL (1898)
8714	Wüerst, Richard Ferdinand	1824-1881	Liedchen erklinge, schwing' dich	Op. 2 No. 4	Unspec.	Chal.		CHAL (1898)
8715	Wüerst, Richard Ferdinand	1824-1881	Martini Kirchweihe "O seliger Martine"	Op. 23 No. 3	S/MS	Schlesinger		CHAL (1898)
8716	Wüerst, Richard Ferdinand	1824-1881	Morgenlied "Wer schlägt so rasch am die Fenster"	Op. 15 No. 3	S/A	Bahn		CHAL (1898)
8717	Wüerst, Richard Ferdinand	1824-1881	Nach diesen trüben Tagen	Op. 32 No. 1	S/A	Bahn		CHAL (1898)
8718	Wüerst, Richard Ferdinand	1824-1881	Schneeglöcken "Schneeglöcken weiss"	Op. 15 No. 4	S/A	Bahn		CHAL (1898)
8719	Wüerst, Richard Ferdinand	1824-1881	Waldabendschein "Am Waldrand steht ein Tannenbaum"	Op. 58 No. 4	S/A	B. & B.		CHAL (1898)
8720	Wüerst, Richard Ferdinand	1824-1881	Wenn es Frühling wird	Op. 2 No. 1	Unspec.	Chal.		CHAL (1898)
8721	Wüerst, Richard Ferdinand	1824-1881	Wiegenlied "So schlaf in Ruhe"	Op. 2 No. 7	Unspec.	Chal.		CHAL (1898)
8722	Wüerst, Richard Ferdinand	1824-1881	Wisstr ihr, wann es Frühling wird	Op. 2 No. 1	S/A	Chal.		CHAL (1901)
8723	Wuorinen, Charles	1938-	Door in the Wall, The		MS/MS or MS/S	ACA		CVMP (1976)
8724	Wuorinen, Charles	1938-	Door in the Wall, The		MS/MS	ACA		ASR
8725	Wuorinen, Charles	1938-	On the Raft		MS/MS	ACA		CVMP (1976)
8726	Wuorinen, Charles	1938-	On the Raft		MS/MS	ACA		ASR
8727	Wyeth, John		Come, Thou Fount		high & low v.	Beckenhorst	Tune: Nettleton. Arr. C. Courtney. In anth. "Duets for the Master: Sacred Duets for High and Low Voice and Keyboard" Pub. 1989.	MSN
8728	Z'Wyssig, Alberik Johann Josef Maria	1808-1854	Vertraue dich dem Licht der Sterne		S/S	Fries i. Z.		CHAL (1898)
8729	Zangl, Josef Gregor	1821-1897	Missa in honorem St. Dominici	Op. 77	S/A	Böhm & S.	org accomp.	CHAL (1898)
8730	Zapff, Oskar	1862-	Im jungen Grün schon Veilchen blühn	Op. 14 No. 1	Unspec.	vom Ende		CHAL (1898)

REC	COMP	DTS	TITLE	OP #	VCG	PUB	COMMENTS	SRC
8731	Zapff, Oskar	1862-	Mühle im Walde "Im Wald aus kühlem Erlendach"	Op. 14 No. 3	Unspec.	vom Ende		CHAL (1898)
8732	Zapff, Oskar	1862-	Sonnenwende "Blasse, duftende Lenzespracht"	Op. 14 No. 2	Unspec.	vom Ende		CHAL (1898)
8733	Zehrfeld, Oskar	1854-	Brautlied "Wo du nun wandelst"	Op. 19 No. 2	Unspec.	Diller & Sohn		CHAL (1898)
8734	Zehrfeld, Oskar	1854-	Erntefest "Herr, die Erde ist gesegnet"	Op. 26 No. 1	Unspec.	Walde i. Löbau	org or pf accomp.	CHAL (1898)
8735	Zehrfeld, Oskar	1854-	Erntefest "Stimmet mit mir an"	Op. 26 No. 2	Unspec.	Walde i. Löbau	org or pf accomp.	CHAL (1898)
8736	Zehrfeld, Oskar	1854-	Jauchzet dem Hernn	Op. 19 No. 3	Unspec.	Diller & Sohn		CHAL (1898)
8737	Zehrfeld, Oskar	1854-	Ostern "Ostern. Ostern Frühlingswehen"	Op. 19 No. 4	Unspec.	Diller & Sohn		CHAL (1898)
8738	Zehrfeld, Oskar	1854-	Pfingsten "Pfingsten ist kommen"	Op. 19 No. 1	Unspec.	Diller & Sohn		CHAL (1898)
8739	Zehrfeld, Oskar	1854-	Reformationsfest "Wie lieblich ach wie lieblich"	Op. 27 No. 1	Unspec.	Walde i. Löbau	org or pf accomp.	CHAL (1898)
8740	Zehrfeld, Oskar	1854-	Todtenfest "Rust aus im stillen dunklen Haus"	Op. 27 No. 2	Unspec.	Walde i. Löbau	org or pf accomp.	CHAL (1898)
8741	Zeitler, J.		Bächleins Abschied "Es zieht durch duft'gen Wiesen"		S/A	(Friedel) Dresden		CHAL (1898)
8742	Zelter, Carl Friedrich	1758-1832	Der junge Jäger		Unspec.	Goethe-Gesell-schaft	Ed. Friedländer	BBC (1975)
8743	Zelter, Carl Friedrich	1758-1832	Willkommen dem 28 August		Unspec.	Schott	Ed. Landshaff	BBC (1975)
8744	Zenger, Max	1837-1911	Ein Herz in Liebesgedanken	Op. 29 No. 1	S/A	Kistner		CHAL (1898)
8745	Zenger, Max	1837-1911	Frau Jutte "Frau Jutte, liebes Mütterlein"	Op. 29 No. 5	S/A	Kistner		CHAL (1898)
8746	Zenger, Max	1837-1911	Lehre "Mutter zum Bienelein"	Op. 29 No. 3	S/A	Kistner		CHAL (1898)
8747	Zenger, Max	1837-1911	Nach Jahren "Mutter lehnt am schattigen Thor"	Op. 29 No. 4	S/A	Kistner		CHAL (1898)
8748	Zenger, Max	1837-1911	Waldandacht "Frühmorgens, wenn die Hähne kräh'n"	Op. 29 No. 2	S/A	Kistner		CHAL (1898)
8749	Zentner, Wilhelm		Gloria		S/A	Peters	org accomp.	ASR
8750	Zepler, Bogumil	1858-1918	Meine holde Leonore "Scherz-Duett"		Unspec.	Bloch		CHAL (1911)
8751	Zepler, Bogumil	1858-1918	Und dann schieben, schieb-en, schieben "Tanz-Duett"		Unspec.	Harmonie i. B.		CHAL (1911)
8752	Zepler, Bogumil	1858-1918	Wir kamen jüngst von Hamburg her		S/S	Fr. Dietrich		CHAL (1906)
8753	Zerlett, Johann Baptist	1859-1935	Armes Bäumchen dauerst mich	Op. 249 No. 2	Unspec.	R. Forberg		CHAL (1911)
8754	Zerlett, Johann Baptist	1859-1935	Auf jener Felsenhöhe	Op. 151 No. 1	Unspec.	O. Forberg		CHAL (1898)
8755	Zerlett, Johann Baptist	1859-1935	Ein scheckiges Pferd	Op. 249 No. 3	Unspec.	R. Forberg		CHAL (1911)
8756	Zerlett, Johann Baptist	1859-1935	Es ist kein Mäuschen so jung	Op. 235 No. 4	Unspec.	R. & B.		CHAL (1911)
8757	Zerlett, Johann Baptist	1859-1935	Es klingt ein lieblich Läuten	No. 2	Unspec.	Hemme		CHAL (1901)

REC	COMP	DTS	TITLE	OP #	VCG	PUB	COMMENTS	SRC
8758	Zerlett, Johann Baptist	1859-1935	Im Lenz erfreu' ich dich	Op. 235 No. 2	Unspec.	R. & B.		CHAL (1911)
8759	Zerlett, Johann Baptist	1859-1935	In Purpur prangt in Gold der Wald	Op. 198	Unspec.	Bromme i. Wiesb.		CHAL (1901)
8760	Zerlett, Johann Baptist	1859-1935	Kaninchen, Karnickelchen	Op. 235 No. 3	Unspec.	R. & B.		CHAL (1911)
8761	Zerlett, Johann Baptist	1859-1935	Kinderlieder (5)	Op. 249	Unspec.	R. Forberg	Collection of 5 children's duets.	CHAL (1911)
8762	Zerlett, Johann Baptist	1859-1935	Kinderlieder (6)	Op. 235	Unspec.	R. & B.	Collection of 6 children's duets.	CHAL (1911)
8763	Zerlett, Johann Baptist	1859-1935	Lieb' Brüderchen, nun aufgewacht	Op. 249 No. 1	Unspec.	R. Forberg		CHAL (1911)
8764	Zerlett, Johann Baptist	1859-1935	Mein Gott vorüber ist die Nacht	Op. 235 No. 1	Unspec.	R. & B.		CHAL (1911)
8765	Zerlett, Johann Baptist	1859-1935	O stille Nacht "Abendglocken rufen"	Op. 77	Unspec.	Vix i. B.		CHAL (1898)
8766	Zerlett, Johann Baptist	1859-1935	Ringelreihen "Ringel, Ringel, Reihe"		Unspec.	R. Forberg		CHAL (1911)
8767	Zerlett, Johann Baptist	1859-1935	Schnelle Blüthe "Mäd-chen ging im Feld allein"	Op. 25	S/A or T/Br	B. & H.		CHAL (1898)
8768	Zerlett, Johann Baptist	1859-1935	Tannenduft, Kerzenschimmer	No. 1	Unspec.	Hemme		CHAL (1901)
8769	Zerlett, Johann Baptist	1859-1935	Trabe mein Pferdchen nur zu	Op. 198 No. 4	Unspec.	Gries		CHAL (1901)
8770	Zerlett, Johann Baptist	1859-1935	Tröpflein muss zur Erde fallen	Op. 235 No. 5	Unspec.	R. & B.		CHAL (1911)
8771	Zerlett, Johann Baptist	1859-1935	Vorüber "Es eilen die Winde"	Op. 151 No. 2	Unspec.	O. Forberg		CHAL (1898)
8772	Zerlett, Johann Baptist	1859-1935	Walt' Gott "Hast viel gespielt"	Op. 249 No. 5	Unspec.	R. Forberg		CHAL (1911)
8773	Zerlett, Johann Baptist	1859-1935	Wenn die Kinder schlafen ein	Op. 235 No. 6	Unspec.	R. & B.		CHAL (1911)
8774	Zescevich, A.		Amor muto "Allor che il sol"	No. 2	Unspec.	Schmidl		CHAL (1898)
8775	Zescevich, A.		Dormi pur mio dolce amor	No. 1	Unspec.	Schmidl		CHAL (1898)
8776	Ziehrer, Karl Michel	1843-1922	Sei wieder guat "O du mei' liaber Schatz"	Op. 316	Unspec.	Doblinger		CHAL (1898)
8777	Zientarski, Romuald	1831-1874	Rozstanie	Op. 21	Unspec.	K. Schulze i. Leipz.		CHAL (1898)
8778	Zier, E.		Wo du hingehst, da will auch ich hingehn	Op. 4	S/A	Schlim-pert	org or pf	CHAL (1901)
8779	Zierau, Fritz	1865-1931	Weihnachten "Es flammen die Kerzen"		Unspec.	Grüniger		CHAL (1898)
8780	Zimmer, C. [prob. Karl]	1869-1935	Hier unterm blüh'ndem Fliederbaum		Unspec.	Westphal i. Karls-horst		CHAL (1911)
8781	Zimmer, Otto	1822-1896	Sei still	Op. 1	Unspec.	R. & E.		CHAL (1898)
8782	Zimmermann, J.		Kinder-Hausemusik bei frohen Festen "Samm-lung"	Op. 8	Unspec.	Schwann		CHAL (1898)
8783	Zingel, Rudolf Ewald	1876-1944	Fürcht dich nicht, ich habe dich erlöset	Op. 76 No. 2	2 med. v.	Bratfisch	org or harm or pf	CHAL (1911)
8784	Zingel, Rudolf Ewald	1876-1944	O wie so wunderbar ist Herr dein Name	Op. 76	2 med. v.	Bratfisch		CHAL (1911)
8785	Zöllner, Andreas	1804-1862	Alpenrosenlied "Ein Blume blüht verborgen"	No. 7	S/S	Gödsche		CHAL (1898)
8786	Zöllner, Andreas	1804-1862	Aufmunterung "Herz freue dich des Lebens"	No. 10	Unspec.	Gödsche		CHAL (1898)
8787	Zöllner, Andreas	1804-1862	Frühlingszeit "Wie schön ist doch die Frühlingszeit"	No. 4	S/S	Gödsche		CHAL (1898)

REC	COMP	DTS	TITLE	OP #	VCG	PUB	COMMENTS	SRC
8788	Zöllner, Andreas	1804-1862	Heimath und Fremde "Es ist so schön in der Haimath"	No. 8	S/S	Gödsche		CHAL (1898)
8789	Zöllner, Andreas	1804-1862	Herbstwanderlied "Bächlein rauscht so bange"	No. 3	S/S	Gödsche		CHAL (1898)
8790	Zöllner, Andreas	1804-1862	Lenzfrage "Sei willkommen liebe Sonne"	No. 1	S/S	Gödsche		CHAL (1898)
8791	Zöllner, Andreas	1804-1862	Nachtigallenlied "Englein schreiben ihre Lieder"	No. 11	Unspec.	Gödsche		CHAL (1898)
8792	Zöllner, Andreas	1804-1862	Schneeglöcken "Es klingt ein lieblich Läuten"	No. 5	S/S	Gödsche		CHAL (1898)
8793	Zöllner, Andreas	1804-1862	Spinnliedchen "Schnurr' mein Rädchen"	No. 12	Unspec.	Gödsche		CHAL (1898)
8794	Zöllner, Andreas	1804-1862	Und ob der holde Tag vergangen	No. 9	Unspec.	Gödsche		CHAL (1898)
8795	Zöllner, Andreas	1804-1862	Wiegenlied "Schlaf du holdes Bübchen"	No. 6	S/S	Gödsche		CHAL (1898)
8796	Zöllner, Andreas	1804-1862	Winzerlied "Es singet und springet"	No. 2	S/S	Gödsche		CHAL (1898)
8797	Zöllner, Karl Friedrich	1800-1860	Frühlingsahung	Op. 70	S/A	Sch. & Co.		CHAL (1898)
8798	Zöllner, Karl Friedrich	1800-1860	Kennt ihr das Land		S/A	Cranz		CHAL (1898)
8799	Zweifel, B.		So mancher meint, weil wir so klein		Unspec.	Zweifel & Weber		CHAL (1901)

CHAPTER 8

Conclusions and Findings of the Research

SUMMARY OF PURPOSE

Creating a comprehensive reference catalogue of chamber vocal duet literature for female voices composed during the period of 1820-1995 will promote awareness of the literature, and serve as an aid in its procurement.

The study of duet literature is not only valuable in terms of providing aesthetic variety in programming, but also as a tool for enhancing pedagogical techniques for vocal musicians as well as those who study all aspects of music. These advantages include the development and enhancement of intonation, expression, phrasing, psychological support, and the factor of collaboration and enjoyment that comes with performing in ensemble with another singer. In addition, accompanists and coaches who work with singers can benefit from knowledge of this genre for use in their own teaching and performing situations, as well as for use as a means to strengthen collaborative skills between singers and accompanists. Researchers in music history, too, can benefit from the knowledge of a genre that many composers have explored.

The result of conducting this research and compiling a source to provide information has yielded a number of interesting results.

GENERAL FINDINGS

There is clearly no shortage of chamber vocal duet literature, just a shortage of available and accessible resources to aid in the identification and location of this literature. Nearly eighty-eight hundred duets were identified. The problems encountered with existing resources include an emphasis on solo repertoire, and references that contain no separate designation for duet literature. This is detailed in chapter 4: Literature Survey (pages 11-15).

Obtaining information as to composer output and a list of works serves as valuable historical insights into the interests of specific composers. Certain composers have proved to be well known for their output of chamber vocal duet literature. For example, Franz Abt wrote some two hundred duets that meet the requirements of this research. A large number of his other duet compositions were eliminated because they were stipulated for other vocal combinations. Many obscure composers also have a large output, but even so, remain unidentified, such as O. Junghähnel and V. Wienand. They were prolific during an era of many voice teachers, and perhaps they may be included with those who composed for their students or for the custom of the time: family gatherings around the piano and Sunday afternoon musicales.

There are more works of this prescribed traditional complement of performers composed during the nineteenth century than during the twentieth century. However, it is largely because this traditional complement was put aside in favor of exploration of different timbres. Voices were added in varying collaborations, and unusual instrumental juxtapositions favored. Salzman claims that "Western music between about 1600 and 1900 was distinguished by the development of a characteristic kind of musical thinking that has been called 'functional tonality.'"[1] In continuing, he describes what he considers to be the most immense and complex "modes of artistic expression that man has ever developed."[2] It was not so much that twentieth-century vocal composers didn't compose vocal ensemble music, including duets, it is that this prolific traditional nineteenth-century ensemble (voice and piano) has given over to varying vocal timbres with assorted and alternative instrumentation. The focus of this research was to seek out literature suitable for both pedagogical use and accessible performance. JoAnn Padley Hunt compiled a catalogue of the unique literature composed for solo voice with percussion. All of her cited literature has been published or copyrighted since 1950. Her initial research yielded about four hundred works. She states, "New technologies have emerged that not only record the new music but are capable of modifying the voice as well. Composers, who have been actively creating new music since 1950, have inherited a broad musical palette from which to fashion their musical scores."[3] With this exploration and desire to seek out new colors, have come a reduction in the number of works written for a more traditional complement. Unfortunately, complex and colorful ensembles can be costly and difficult to rehearse. This is why the number of duets in the specified parameters of this research falls off as the twentieth century progressed. They are by no means extinct, however.

References specifically naming the pedagogical benefits of vocal chamber duet literature are scarce, but positive, citing confidence building, ear training skills, phrasing, and other techniques. Many inferences can be made by identifying the benefits of cooperative learning and ensemble studies. These have been detailed in chapter 3: Pedagogical Benefits of Studying the Vocal Chamber Duet—Who Can Benefit? (pages 7-9).

Although this substantial number of duets are identified, all may not be widely available. A number are contained within anthologies, and this was addressed as comprehensively as possible. Many of the publishers are now out of business or have been merged into other companies. Having the information may lead the most persevering to locate a specific obscure work in a library by having as complete information as possible. Also, since there is a current interest in publishing obscure works, complete works of composers, and the compositions of women com-

posers, many pieces may become available in time. Requesting specific literature from publishers may encourage their publication, or it may be possible to obtain authorized photocopies of out of print works.

SPECIFIC FINDINGS

Appendixes A through G (pages 389-461) list cross-references that offer information on specific categories of interest. The cross references themselves yield certain implications that are summarized here.

COMPOSERS

Composers totaled two thousand and four (appendix A, pages 389-400), including a category of "unknown composer or arranger" that accounted for eight entries. Identifiable women composers (appendix B, page 401) totaled eighty-one in number, making up an incidence of 4.012%. This number represents the women composers that were able to be identified, as stated. Some of the unidentified composers are possibly women. Several women have historically used pen names probably to enable ease in publication (for example Augusta Holmès published under the name Hermann Zenta, and Elisabetta Oddone was known as Eliodd).

VOICE SPECIFICATIONS

Table 8.1 is a distribution of voice specifications cited (appendix C, pages 403-412). The greatest number of combinations are unspecified, which may be either a decision made by the composer, or by the publisher, enabling any vocal combination to sing the work. These made up 52.404% of the total number of entries, and are not specified even to gender. As stated earlier, it would be up to the performer/teacher to investigate the range/text for appropriateness. In the specified category, the most typical combination is that of soprano/alto, making up 25.753% of the total output. The other combinations drop off markedly, soprano/soprano making up 8.262% and the other combination being less than 7%. Refer below for a complete summary.

Table 8.1: Distribution of
Voice Specifications

VCG	*n*	INCIDENCE %
S/S	727	8.262
S/MS	315	3.560
MS/MS	60	6.682
A/A	15	0.170
S/A	2266	25.753
2 fem v	479	5.444
2 high v	67	0.761
2 med v	105	1.193
2 low v	24	0.273
high/low	141	1.602
high/med	49	0.557
med/low	12	0.136
various	38	0.432
children's	3	0.034
treble	2	0.023
narrators	1	0.011
unspec.	4612	52.415

Total number of entries *n* = 8799,
some entries have more than one choice

Abbreviations include VCG = voicing,
n = number of entries, S = soprano,
MS = mezzo soprano, A = alto, fem = female,
v = voice(s), med = medium, unspec. = unspecified.

PUBLISHED LANGUAGES

Composers may have multiple languages of entries, or entries may be translated into language of publisher. A specific listing of languages and composers appears in appendix D: List of Composers by Published Language (pages 413-425). There is no statistical criterion other than to list composers who are published in specific languages. Table 8.2 represents the distribution by composers representing the twenty-three languages.

Table 8.2: Language Distribution
by Number of Composers

LANG	# of Comp.
Czech	10
Danish	2
Dutch	9
English	371
Finnish	8
French	118
German	1347
German-dialect	61
Hebrew	4
Hungarian	2
Icelandic	3
Italian	89
Japanese	2
Latin	53
Norwegian	5
Polish	2
Polynesian	3
Russian	16
Spanish	15
Spanish-dialect	1
Serbo-Croatian	3
Swedish	19
Welsh	1

Abbreviations: LANG = languages,
Comp. = composers.

The distribution indicates a preference for German-language publications, which stems from the numerous German publishing houses that existed during this period, and probably includes the fact that the Challier Catalogue series was of German origin. German-language and German-dialect publications account for about one thousand four hundred composers represented out of a total of two thousand and four. This does not mean that these composers were not published in other languages. English, French, Italian, and Latin are other languages with a significant representation.

ACCOMPANIMENT OTHER THAN PIANO

Most of the eight thousand seven hundred and ninety-nine entries were composed with piano accompaniment. In fact, only three hundred eighty one were for other accompaniment, or an incidence of 4.330%. The parameter of the accompaniment for this research stipulated practical accompaniment, meaning piano, organ (or harmonium), or a cappella. Table 8.3 below, which summarizes the cross-reference listings of appendix E, (pages 427-428), outlines the alternative instrumental accompaniment (or lack of accompaniment) that occurs in the catalogue.

Table 8.3: Accompaniment
Other than Single Piano

INSTRUMENT	*n*	INCIDENCE %
org or pf	113	1.284
org or harm	25	0.284
org/pf/harm	27	0.307
org only	100	1.136
org w/ opt violin	2	0.023
Total org	267	3.034
harm or org	25	0.284
harm or pf	7	0.080
harm/org/pf	27	0.307
harm only	1	0.011
harm and pf	1	0.011
Total harm	61	0.693
a cappella	42	0.477
pf variants	2	0.023
harp (or pf)	10	0.114
zither (or pf)	1	0.011

Abbreviations: org = organ, pf = piano,
harm = harmonium, opt = optional.

PUBLISHERS

There are six hundred thirty-one publishers listed. They are listed by abbreviation, followed by full name and address, if identifiable. The entire list appears in appendix F: List of Publishers (pages 429-444). Many are no longer in operation or have been absorbed by other companies. The abbreviations of publishers used in the catalogue are listed as they appear in the various sources used in compiling this work (even if variable). Retaining the original abbreviations may serve as an aid in procurement from libraries. Occasionally, the abbreviations were unable to be identified.[4]

NOTES

1. E. Salzman, *Twentieth-Century Music: An Introduction* (Englewood Cliffs, NJ: Prentice-Hall, 1988), 4.

2. E. Salzman, *Twentieth-Century Music: An Introduction,* 4.

3. J. P. Hunt, *Analyses of Music for Solo Voice and Percussion, 1950-1990: An Annotated Catalogue of Representative Repertoire* (Ed.D. diss., Teachers College, Columbia University, 1992), 1.

4. Many of the original publishers no longer exist. Appendix F (pages 429-444) is a listing of publisher abbreviations, their full name (if known), current address, distributor, or history. Much of this information was obtained from Krummel, D. W. and Sadie, S., eds. *Music Printing and Publishing.* New York: W. W. Norton & Company, Inc. 1990. Other helpful sources on the history of music publishing and printing included Krummel, D. W. *The Literature of Music Bibliographies: An Account of the Writings of the History of Music Printers and Publishers.* California: Fallen Leaf Press. 1993. For historical information see also Lenneberg, H., ed. *The Dissemination of Music Studies in the History of Music Publishing.* Lausanne, Switzerland: Gordon and Breach Science Publishers S. A. 1994. It is also possible to contact a number of contemporary publishers on the Internet.

CHAPTER 9

Recommendations for Further Studies

One of the major problems existing with a significant amount of this literature involves procurement. A further study should include location of potential libraries and resources that house copies of the works or manuscripts. As the interest grows in this specific area, there are likely to be more works released for publication.

Additional research can be conducted to complete the task of a resource of this type—one that would include a catalogue compiling the vocal chamber duets for male voices and mixed gender duets. The largest category by voicing that came out of this research is that of unspecified, implying that the other vocal ensembles could potentially address these works. However, there are a number of works that are specifically conceived of for male voices or mixed gender ensembles. This information would be of value to a number of male singers, both professional and students.

In spite of the large number of duets that exist, the use of ensemble literature as a pedagogical tool is frequently restricted to the consideration of choral ensemble works. Little acknowledgment is given to this vast genre. More detail should be paid to its benefits, particularly with regard to balance, ear training, and the development of ensemble skills. This material would be of great value to the studio voice teacher who could promote vocal development and ensemble skills by using this repertoire in situations with a smaller number of students, while still maintaining the integrity of vocal production and skilled listening. The solo voices are still retained as solo voices; they are not buried into a choral sound.

Much emphasis is placed on solo singing in both performance and in pedagogy. It should be the purpose of singers and teachers to explore other venues available to them as an alternative to studying literature for the solo voice and restricting exploration to that repertoire exclusively. The benefits of studying alternatives to solo literature can help to develop the skills that are necessary in any type of ensemble literature, whether it is choral, opera ensemble, or even in the simplest of collaborations: that of the voice with piano accompaniment. By studying chamber vocal duet literature, one can explore all of the periods of music and learn more about blending and collaboration than in any other aspect of study. This is why it is important to investigate this surprisingly large and rich repertoire created by a significantly large number of composers, both well known and obscure. By becoming familiar with this literature, one can discover a genre that provides great benefits to both study and performance. This literature can provide the singer with an enlarged repertoire that includes a wide range of aesthetic expression and that expands interest, creates variety, and enhances the development of ensemble techniques.

It is the writer's opinion that the practice of singing and performing vocal chamber duet literature is not only a means of achieving certain pedagogical and musicianship skills but also has tremendous value as an art form. It has been cited as a favored ensemble in virtually all periods of music. Most likely the reason for its survival as an art form has been the enjoyment in its performance by the singers. Almost in no other collaboration is the intimacy of art song vocal performance retained, while the requirements of partnership are strengthened. Both performers are sharing in the delivery of the poetry, uniting in one idea. Occasionally, they are required to portray individual characters in song. All of this reinforces the importance of collaboration and teamwork, in vocalism, acting, and conveying nuances. A number of reputable solo singers have made this discovery, joining forces in collaboration. These collaborations include Marilyn Horne and Joan Sutherland, Elisabeth Schwarzkopf and Janet Baker. There have also been a number of mixed gender duet partnerships, such as Elisabeth Schwarzkopf and Dietrich Fischer-Dieskau, Evelyn Lear and Thomas Stewart. There is a value in this genre that is known by many fine performing artists, and this knowledge should be passed down to the newest singers.

No singer, even the solo singer, is ever completely alone. There is always another partner, whether it is the conductor or a pianist. Many conservatories and voice teachers appear to neglect that fact. Singing in small ensembles such as duets, trios, quartets, should be part of any vocal pedagogy, much as chamber music is a requirement for string and wind players. The benefits that instrumentalists achieve in small intimate situations are applicable to vocal musicians. The ability to work as a team musician is something that is valued by all musicians, in all situations, and it should be reinforced at all levels of vocal pedagogy. Even a soloist does not work alone.

Bibliography

Abusamra, W. "Small group vs individual instruction in the performance studio." *The NATS Bulletin* (May 1978): 37-38.

Apel, W. *Harvard Dictionary of Music.* Cambridge, MA: Harvard University Press, 1972.

Avey, D. H. "Why can't I get the music?" *The NATS Journal* (September/October 1988): 17-18.

Bailey, L. L. *The Sacred Vocal Duets of Heinrich Schütz and J. S. Bach: An Introduction and Annotated Listing.* Doctoral Dissertation, Southern Baptist Theological Seminary. 1976.

Berry, C. I. *A Study of the Vocal Chamber Duet Through the Nineteenth Century.* Doctoral Dissertation, North Texas State University. 1974.

Berry, C. "Duets for pedagogical use." *The NATS Bulletin* (December 1977): 8-12.

————. "The Italian vocal chamber duets of the Baroque period." *The NATS Bulletin* (September/October 1978): 12-18.

————. "Airs from the British Isles and airs from Moravian duets incorporating diverse folk materials." *The NATS Bulletin* (November/December 1979a): 8-20.

————. "The dialogue duet: 1600-1900." *The Music Review* XL, no. 4: (1979b): 272-284.

————. "Salon duets by operatic composers." *The NATS Bulletin* (September/October 1980): 15-17.

————. *Vocal Chamber Duets An Annotated Bibliography.* Jacksonville, FL: The National Association of Teachers of Singing, Inc. 1981.

Blume, F. ed. *Die Musik in Geschichte und Gegenwart.* Vol. 1-14. Kassel, Germany: Bärenreiter-Verlag. 1949-51.

Boytim, J. F. "Why neglect the sacred solo duet?" *The NATS Bulletin* (February/March 1972): 13-37.

————. "Duet literature for the Christmas season." *The NATS Bulletin* (October 1976): 13-45.

Brusse, C. B. "The relationship between poetic structure and musical structure in selected vocal duets." *The NATS Journal* (March/April 1987): 20-25.

————. *Sacred Vocal Duets An Annotated Bibliography.* Jacksonville, FL: The National Association of Teachers of Singing, Inc. 1987.

Buff, I. M. *The Chamber Duets and Trios of Carissimi.* Doctoral Dissertation, University of Rochester. 1973.

Challier, E. *Grosser Duetten-Katalog.* Giessen: Ernst Challier's Selbstverlag. 1898.

————. *Erster Nachtrag zu Grosser Duetten-Katalog.* Giessen: Ernst Challier's Selbstverlag. 1901.

————. *Zweiter Nachtrag zu Grosser Duetten-Katalog.* Giessen: Ernst Challier's Selbstverlag. 1906.

————. *Dritter Nachtrag zu Grosser Duetten-Katalog.* Giessen: Ernst Challier's Selbstverlag. 1911.

Christy, V. A. *Foundations in Singing.* Dubuque, IA: Wm. C. Brown Company Publishers. 1978.

Chwialkowski, J. *The Da Capo Catalog of Classical Music. Compositions.* New York: Da Capo Press. 1996.

Coffin, B. "Repertoire and the singer." *The Bulletin* (May 15, 1960): 8-9.

————. *Singer's Repertoire. 2nd Ed. Part II: Mezzo Soprano and Contralto.* New York: Scarecrow Press, Inc. 1960.

Cohen, A. I. *International Encyclopedia of Women Composers.* Vols.1-2. New York: Books & Music (USA) Inc. 1987.

Csikszentmihalyi, M. "Singing and the self: choral music as 'active leisure.'" *Choral Journal* (February 1995): 13-19.

Daugherty, F. M. ed. *Classical Vocal Music in Print 1995 Supplement Music-In-Print Series, Vol. 4t.* Philadelphia: Musicdata, Inc. 1995.

Di Natale, J. and Russell, G. S. "Cooperative learning for better performance." *Music Educators Journal* (September 1995): 26-28.

Duets BBC Listing. London, England: The British Broadcasting Corporation. 1975.

Eggebrecht, H. H. ed. *Riemann Musik Lexicon.* Vols. 1-3. Mainz: B. Schott's Söhne. 1972.

Eitner, R. ed. *Biographisch-Bibliographisches Quellen-Lexikon.* Vols. 1-11. Graz, Austria: Akademische Druc-U. Verlagsansalt. 1959.

Emmons, S. and Sonntag, S. *The Art of the Song Recital.* New York: Schirmer Books. 1979.

Eslinger, G. S. and Daugherty, F. M. eds. *Classical Vocal Music in Print 1985 Supplement Music-In-Print Series, Vol. 4s.* Philadelphia: Musicdata, Inc. 1986.

FileMaker Pro. Version 3.0. Claris Corporation. Santa Clara, CA.

Frank, P. *Kurzgefaßtes Tonkünstler-Lexicon für Musik.* Amsterdam: Heinrichshofen's Verlag. 1936.

Fuller, S. *The Pandora Guide to Women Composers Britain and the United States 1629-Present.* London: Pandora, an imprint of HarperCollins Publishers. 1994.

Green, B. with W. T. Gallwey. *The Inner Game of Music.* Garden City, NY: Anchor Press/Doubleday. 1986.

Hinson, M. Senior Professor of Piano, The Southern Baptist Theological Seminary, Louisville, KY. Personal communication. 30 April 1997.

Hunt, J. P. *Analyses of Music for Solo Voice and Percussion, 1950-1990: An Annotated Catalogue of Representative Repertoire.* Doctoral Dissertation, Teachers College, Columbia University. 1992.

Jezic, D. P. *Women Composers The Lost Tradition Found.* New York: The Feminist Press at The City University of New York. 1988.

Johnson, S. O. "Group instruction an alternative for freshman voice students." *The NATS Bulletin* (March/April 1979): 20-21.

Jones, G. Publisher/Dealer, Classical Vocal Reprints, 3253 Cambridge Avenue 2nd Floor, Riverdale NY, personal communication. 17 October 1996.

Kagen, S. *Music for the Voice.* Bloomington, IN: Indiana University Press. 1968.

Kinsey, B. "Voice class structure and purpose." *The NATS Bulletin* (December 1973): 18-22.

Knowles, R. "Basic musicianship for future conductors: hearing and performing two-voice polyphony." *Choral Journal.* (April 1982): 23-25.

Krummel, D. W. *The Literature of Music Bibliography An Account of the Writings on the History of Music Printing & Publishing.* Berkeley, CA: Fallen Leaf Press. 1992.

Krummel, D. W. and Sadie, S. eds. *Music Printing and Publishing.* New York: W. W. Norton & Company, Inc.1990.

Lenneberg, H. ed. *The Dissemination of Music Studies in the History of Music Publishing.* Lausanne, Switzerland: Gordon and Breach Science Publishers S. A. 1994.

Longyear, R. M. *Nineteenth-Century Romanticism in Music.* Englewood Cliffs, NJ: Prentice-Hall, Inc. 1973.

Lust, P. *American Vocal Chamber Music, 1945-1980.* Westport, CT: Greenwood Press. 1985.

Mancini, Giambattista (1774, 1777). Foreman, Edward, ed. *Practical Reflections on Figured Singing.* Champaign, IL: Pro Musica Press. 1967.

Miller, R. "The solo singer in the choral ensemble." *Choral Journal* (March 1995): 31-36.

The Music Buying Guide II. Valley Forge, PA: European American Music Distributors Corporation. 1991.

The Music In Print Series [Brochure]. Philadelphia, PA: Musicdata, Inc. 1997.

Nardone, T. R. ed. *Classical Vocal Music in Print.* Philadelphia: Musicdata, Inc. 1976.

Pougin, M. A. ed. *Biographie universelle des musiciens et Biographie Générale de la musique par F. J. Fétis.* Vols. 1-2. Brussels: Culture et Civilisation. (1878, reprinted 1963).

Radcliffe, P. "Germany and Austria." In *A History of Song,* ed. Denis Stevens. New York: W.W. Norton & Company. 1970.

Raridon, C. W. *Soprano-Tenor Chamber Duets of Steffani.* Doctoral Dissertation, University of Iowa. 1972.

Randel, D. M. ed. *The Harvard Biographical Dictionary of Music.* Cambridge, MA: The Belknap Press of Harvard University Press. 1996.

Rorem, N. *Ariel, Gloria, King Midas.* Phoenix label, PHCD 126. Insert from compact disc. 1995.

———. "The American art song: dead or alive?" *Opera News* (August 1996): 15-30.

———. New York City. Personal communication. 11 July 1996.

Sadie, J. A. and Samuel, R. eds. *The Norton/Grove Dictionary of Women Composers.* New York: W.W. Norton & Company. 1995.

Sadie, S. ed. *The New Grove Dictionary of Music and Musicians.* London: MacMillan. 1980.

Salzman, E. *Twentieth-Century Music: An Introduction.* Englewood Cliffs, NJ: Prentice-Hall. 1988.

Sears, M. E. *Song Index An Index to More Than 12000 Songs in 177 Song Collections Comprising 262 Volumes.* New York: The H.W. Wilson Company. 1926.

———. *Song Index Supplement An Index to More Than 7000 Songs in 104 Song Collections Comprising 124 Volumes.* New York: The H.W. Wilson Company. 1936.

Shafferman, J. A. "Music for the small church choir" *Choral Journal* (November 1990): 19-24. 1990.

Slonimsky, N. ed. *Baker's Biographical Dictionary of Musicians Fifth Edition.* New York: G. Schirmer. 1958.

———. *Baker's Biographical Dictionary of Musicians Eighth Edition.* New York: Schirmer Books. 1992.

———. *The Concise Baker's Biographical Dictionary of Musicians Eighth Edition.* New York: Schirmer Books. 1994.

Stevens, J. Manager, The Foundry Music Company, Audubon Street, New Haven, CT. Personal communication. June, 15, 1996.

Taylor, F. and Gatty, N. C. "Duet." *Grove's Dictionary of Music and Musicians Fifth Edition.* Vol. II. Ed. Eric Blom. London: Macmillan. 1955.

Tilmouth, M. "Duet." *The New Grove Dictionary of Music and Musicians.* Vol. 5. Ed. Stanley Sadie. London: Macmillan. 1980.

Timms, C. "Revisions in Steffani's chamber duets." *Proceedings of the Royal Musical Association* xcvi no. 119. 1969-70.

Timms, C. R. *The Chamber Duets of Agostino Steffani (1654-1728) With Transcriptions and Catalogue.* Doctoral Dissertation, University of London, England. 1976.

Villamil, V. E. *A Singer's Guide to The American Art Song 1870-1980.* Metuchen, NJ: The Scarecrow Press, Inc. 1993.

Whenham, E. J. *Italian Secular Duets and Dialogues c. 1600-1643.* Doctoral Dissertation, Oxford University, Oxford, England. 1979.

Wier, A. E. ed. *The Macmillan Encyclopedia of Music and Musicians in One Volume.* New York: The Macmillan Company. 1938.

Wolverton, V. D. "Repertoire for small vocal ensembles in high schools." *Choral Journal* (October 1990): 33-40.

Wooldridge, W. (1971). "Why not class voice?" *The NATS Bulletin* (December 1971): 20-21.

Appendix A: Complete List of Composers
(2004 total, including unknown)

Aaron, E.
Abbott, Jane
Abramowitz
Abt, Franz
Achenbach, J.
Adam, Adolphe Charles
Adams, Thomas
Adant, L.
Aerts, Felix
Ahnfelt, Oscar
Aiblinger, Johann Kaspar
Alberti, G.
Aletter, Wilhelm
Alexandrov, Anatol
Allitsen, Frances
Altenhofer, C.
Altmann, Gustav
Anderson, Beth
Anderson, Margaret Tweedie
André, Johann Anton
André, Jean Baptiste
André, L. [prob. Christian
    Karl André]
Andrews, Mark
Andriessen, Juriaan
Androzzo, A. Bazel
Anfossi, Pasquale
Angerer, Gottfried
Ansorge, M. [prob. Margarethe]
Apell, Karl
Arditi, Luigi
Arendt, W.
Arensky, Anton
Arnaud, Etienne
Arndts, Maria Vespermann
Ascher
Ascher, E.
Ascher, Joseph
Ashford, E. L.
Attenhofer, Karl
Aue, U.
August, J.
Augustin, F. H.
Ayre, Nat D.
Baader, R.
Babbitt, Milton
Bach, Leonard Emil

Bach, Otto
Bachhofer, R.
Backman, Hjalmar
Bade, Ph.
Bading, P.
Baer, Abel
Bailey
Baker, Richard
Balfe, Michael William
Ball, Ernest
Banck, Karl
Bandhartinger, B.
Bandisch, J.
Bank, G.
Bantock, Granville
Bärmann, W.
Barnby, J.
Bartel, G.
Bartlett, Homer Newton
Bartlett, J. C.
Barwolf, L.
Baschinsky, P.
Baselt, Friedrich Gustav Otto
Bassford, William Kipp
Bastyr, Hans
Bateman, Ronald
Batten, Mrs. George
Battmann, Jacques Louis
Bauckner, Arthur
Bauer, Friedrich
Baum, C.
Baum, W.
Baumann, Alexander
Baumann, Johann
Baumann, Karl Friedrich
Baumfelder, Friedrich
Baumgart, A.
Baumgartner
Baumgartner, Wilhelm
Bazzini, Antonio
Beach, Amy
Beauplan, A. de
Becker, Albert
Becker, Cl.
Becker, Hugo
Becker, Konstantin Julius
Becker, Reinhold

Becker, Valentin Eduard
Beeson, Jack
Beethoven, Ludwig van
Behr, Franz
Bellermann, Heinrich
Belzer, P.
Bemberg, Henri Hermann
Benda, A.
Bendel, Franz
Bender, Jan
Bendl, Karel
Benedict, Jules
Bennet, William Sterndale
Bennewitz, Fritz
Benoy, A. W.
Berger, Francesco
Berger, Jean
Berger, Rodolphe
Berger, Wilhelm
Bergmann, Gustav
Bergmann, Josef
Bergmann, Th.
Bering, Ch.
Berlioz, Hector
Berneker, Constanz
Bernier, René
Berthold, G. [pen name of
    Robert Pearsall]
Berton, F.
Beschnitt, Johannes
Besly, Maurice
Beyer, H.
Beyer, J.
Bial, Rudolph
Bicknese, E.
Bieber, C. [prob. Karl]
Biehl, A. [prob. Albert]
Biehl, Ed.
Bijvanck, Henk
Billert, Karl Friedrich August
Birn, M.
Bischoff, Karl Bernard
Bischoff, Karl Jacob
Bischoff-Ghilionna, Julius
Bishop, Henry Rowley
Bisping, A.
Björnsson, Arni

Blaesing, Felix
Blake
Blangini, G. M. M. Felice
Blaufus, Chr.
Blaufuss, Walter
Bleibtreu, C.
Blobner, Johann Baptist
Blockley, John
Blower, Maurice
Blum, E.
Blum, Karl Ludwig
Blumenthal, Jacob [Jacques]
Blumenthal, Paul
Blumner, Martin
Boch, Fr.
Bögler, B.
Bohm
Bohm, C.
Böhm, Karl
Böhm, R.
Böhm, W.
Bohrer, S.
Böie, Heinrich
Boieldieu, François Adrien
Boissière, F.
Boito, Arrigo
Bond, Carrie Jacobs
Bonheur, Theodore
Bonoldi, Francesco
Bonvin, Ludwig
Borchers, Gustav
Bordèse, Luigi
Born, C.
Börner, Kurt
Bornet, R.
Bornhardt, Johann Heinrich Karl
Bortniantsky, Dimitri
   Stephanovich
Bortolini, G.
Boruttau, Alfred J.
Bosen, Franz
Bosmans, Henriette
Böttcher, E.
Böttger, G.
Bouman, Paul
Boumann, Leonardus Carolus
Bourgault-Ducoudray, Louis
Boyneburgk, Fr. v.
Bracken, Edith A.
Bradsky, Wenzel Theodor
Brah-Müller, Karl
   Friedrich Gustav
Braham, John
Brahe, Mary Hannah
Brahms, Johannes
Brahms-Zilcher
Brambach, Kaspar Joseph
Brämig, Bernard
Brandhurst, Elise
Brandt, August

Brandt, F. [prob. Fritz]
Brandt, Hermann
Brandt, M.
Brandt-Caspari, Alfred
Bratsch, Johann Georg
Brauer, W.
Braun, Albert
Braun, Clemens
Brede, Albrecht
Bredschneider, Willy
Breiderhoff, E.
Breitung, F.
Brenner, Friedrich
Bretschger, H.
Breu, Simon
Briem, W.
Briggs
Briggs, C. S.
Britten, Benjamin
Brixner, J.
Brizzi, S.
Broadwood, Lucy E.
Broadwood, Lucy E. &
   J. A. Fuller Maitland
Brocksch, R.
Browne
Bruch, Max
Brüll, J. [Ignaz]
Brunner, Christian Traugott
Brunner, Ed.
Buchholz, Karl August
Bülow, Charlotte von
Bunakoff, N.
Bünte, August
Bünte, Wilhelm
Buri, E. v.
Burwig, G.
Busch, Carl
Busche, W.
Busoni, Ferrucio Benvenuto
Busser, Henri-Paul
Butté, E. M.
Buydens-Lemoine
Caballero, Manuel Fernandez
Cage, John
Califano, A.
Campana, Fabio
Caracciolo, Luigi
Carafa, Michel Enrico
Carelli, Benjamino A.
Carey, Harry
Carnicer, Ramon
Carse, Roland
Carter, John
Carulli, Gustav
Caryll, Ivan
Cassler, G. Winton
Catenhusen, Ernst
Cattaneo, V.
Cavallini, Ernesto

Chabeaux, P.
Chabrier, Emmanuel
Chaminade, Cecile
Charisius, M.
Charles, Ernest
Chausson, Ernest
Chelard, Hippolyte André
Cherubini, Luigi
Chevallerie, Ernst A. H.
Chisholm, M. A.
Chopin, Frédéric
Christian-Jollet
Christiani, E.
Chwatal, Franz Xaver
Ciccarelli, Angelo
Clapisson, Antoine Louis
Clarke, Emile
Claudius, A.
Claudius, Otto Karl
Clement, M.
Clifton, Harry
Cloos, W.
Coates, Eric
Coccia, Carlo
Coerne, Louis Adolphe
Coëtlosquet, M. du
Colaco Osorio-Swaab, Reine
Coleridge-Taylor, Samuel
Comes
Concone, F.
Concone, Giuseppi
Coombs, C. Whitney
Coquard, Arthur
Coradini, R. & P.
Corliss
Cornelius, Peter
Coupé, H.
Courtney, Craig
Cowen, Frederic Hymen
Cramer, C.
Crampton, Ernest
Crane, Helen
Crelle, August Leopold
Crikeltown, G.
Crosse, Gordon
Cui, César
Curci, Giuseppi
Cursch-Bühren, Franz Theodor
Curschmann, Karl Friedrich
Curti, Franz
Cutler, E.
Cuvillier, Charles
Czerwinsky, Wilhelm
Czibilka, Alphons
Czonka, Paul
d'Anduze, W.
d'Yradier, Chevalier
Dagland, Abbé J.
Dahlgren, Erland
Dahms, M.

Daly
Dammas, Hellmuth Karl
Danysz, K.
Dargomizshky, Alexander
David, Ferdinand
Day, Maude Craske
Debussy, Claude
Decker, Constantine
Decker, H.
Decker, Pauline von
Decker-Schenck, Johann
Degele, Eugen
Degenhardt, E.
DeKoven, Reginald
Delbruck, J.
Delcliseur, F.
Delibes, Léo
Dell' Acqua, Eva
Delmet, Paul
Delson, L.
Denecke, H.
Denefve, J.
Densmore, John H.
Denza, Luigi
Deppen, Jessie L.
Deprosse, Anton
Dessauer, Joseph
Diabelli, Anton
Diack, J. Michael
Dickinson, Clarence
Dickson, Stanley
Diebels, F.
Diebold, Johann
Diemer, Louis-Joseph
Diepenbrock, Alphons
Diercks, H.
Dietler, F.
Dietmann, E.
Dietrich, Amalia
Dijk, Jan van
Dinsmore
Dix, J. Arlie
Doebber, Johannes
Döhler, Theodor
Dolan
Dolmetsch, Arnold
Donaudy, Stefano
Donizetti, Gaetano
Dorel, F.
Döring, August
Döring, Carl Heinrich
Döring, W. [prob. Wilhelm]
Dorn, Alexander Julius Paul
Dorn, Heinrich L. E.
Dorn, Otto
Dougherty, Celius
Doun, Elza
Drath, Theodor
Dregert, Alfred
Dreher, F.

Dressel, R.
Dressler, Friedrich August
Drischner, Max
Drobisch, Karl Ludwig
Dubois, Théodore
Dugge, W.
Dumack, Louis
Dunayevsky, Isaak
Dunhill, Thomas Frederick
Dunlap, Fern Glasgow
Dupré, Claude
Durbec, L.
Dürck, J.
Düringer, Ph. J.
Durra, Hermann
Dussek, Johann Ladislaus
Duval, Edmond
Duvivier, A. D.
Dvorák, Antonín
Dyson, George
Dzerzhinsky, Ivan
Eben, Petr
Eberhard, G.
Eberhardt, Anton
Eberle, Friedrich
Ebner, L.
Edmunds, John
Edwards, Clara
Edwards, George
Egger-Rieser, T.
Eggers, G.
Ehlert, C. F.
Ehret, Walter
Ehrlich, Alfred Heinrich
Ehrlich, Rudolph
Eichberg, Oskar
Eichler, Max
Eichler, O.
Eichmann, J. C.
Einödshofer, Julius
Einödshofer & Schmidt
Eisersdorf, A.
Eisler, Hans
Eissner, E.
Eitner, Robert
Elgar, Edward
Elimar, Herz v. Old.
Ellerton, John Lodge
Elssner, E.
Emge, A.
Emilius, J.
Emmerlich, Robert
Engel, David Hermann
Engelhart, Franz Xaver
Engelsberg, E. S.
Engler, Karl
Erlanger, Gustav
Erlanger, Ludwig
Erler, Hermann
Ernemann, E.

Ernemann, M.
Ernemann, R.
Ernst, A. [prob. Anton]
Ertl, Dominik
Eschmann, Johann Karl
Esser, Heinrich
Esser, R.
Evers, Karl
Exner, O.
Eykens, J.
Eyle, E.
Eyle, W.
Eymieu, Henry
Eyser, Eberhard
Eysler, Edmund S.
Fabiani, D.
Faccio, Franco
Fairfield
Falkner, H.
Fall, Leo
Fanselow, A.
Fauré, Gabriel
Faure, Jean Baptiste
Faust, Karl
Favre, Georges
Fearis, John Sylvester
Fehér, Th. J.
Feist, Alwine
Feldheim, G.
Feldow, D.
Ferber, R.
Ferrari, J. G.
Feyhl, Johann
Fiby, Heinrich
Fidelis, J.
Fiebrich, F. P.
Fielitz, Alexander von
Fink, Christian
Fink, F.
Fink, Ferd.
Fink, R.
Fioravanti, Vincenzo
Fiori, Ettore
Fischer, Anton
Fischer & Blum
Fischer, O. [prob. Oskar]
Fischer, Osw.
Fischer, Rudolf
Fischer & Wacker
Fischof, Robert
Fisher, Howard
Fisher, J.
Fiske, Roger
Fitzenhagen, W. Karl Friedrich
Fleck, Fritz
Fontenailles, H. de
Forman, Edmund
Förster, Alban
Förster, Rudolf
Forsyth, Josephine

Foster, Myles Birket
Foster, Stephen Collins
Fragerolle, George Auguste
Franck, César
Franck, Eduard
Francke, W.
Franco, Johan
Frank, Chr.
Frank, Ernst
Franke, A.
Franke, Hermann
Frankl, A.
Franz, J. H.
Franz, Robert
Franz, W.
Fraser
Freisinger, L.
Freisler, C.
Frenkel, R.
Frenkel-Norden, R.
Freudenberg, Wilhelm
Frey, Martin
Fricke, Richard
Friedland, A.
Friedrich, R.
Friml, Rudolf
Fritzsch, Ernst Wilhelm
Fröhlich, C.
Fröhlich, Ernst
Fromberg, G.
Fromm, Karl Josef
Frommel, Otto
Fuchs, L.
Fuchs, Robert
Fuentes, Laureano
Fuhrmeister, Fritz
Gabriel, Mary Ann Virginia
Gabussi, C. M.
Gabussi, Vincent
Gade, Niels Wilhelm
Gall, Jan Karol
Galland, E.
Gallaty, James M.
Gallois, Marie
Gambini, Carlo Andrea
Ganz, Rudolph
García de la Parra, Benito
Garcia, M. [prob. Mansilla
    Eduardo]
Gastinel, Leon-
    Gustave-Cyprien
Gaston-Murray, Blanche
Gatty, Alfred Scott
Gaul, Alfred Robert
Gebauer, H.
Gebbardt, E.
Geehl, Henry Ernest
Geibel
Gembert, F.
Genée, Richard Franz Friedrich

Georg, Priz zu Sch.-C.
George, C.
Gericke, R. v.
Gerstenberger, A.
Geyer, A.
Ghedini, Giorgio Federico
Giesen, J.
Gifford, Alexander M.
Gilbert
Gilbert, Jean [pen name
    of Max Winterfeld]
Gimeno, P. [prob. Joaquin]
Girschner, Karl Friedrich Julius
Glaeser, Franz
Glaser, J.
Glazunov, Alexander
Gleich, Ferdinand
Glimes, Jean Baptiste Jules de
Glinger, A.
Gliniewski, W.
Glinka, Mikhail Ivanovich
Glover, Charles W.
Glover, Stephen
Glück, August
Goatley, Alma
Gobbaerts, Jean Louis
Godard, Benjamin
Godfrey, Daniel
Goepfart, Karl Eduard
Goepfert, P.
Goës, C.
Goetz, W.
Goetze, Karl [Götze]
Göhler, Karl Georg
Goldberg, William
Goldner, Wilhelm
Goldschmidt, Adalbert von
Göller, A.
Gollmick, Karl
Goltermann, Georg
Gooch
Goodhart, Arthur Murray
Gordigiani, Luigi
Gordon, Stanley [pen name of
    A. W. Rawlings]
Gorzer-Schulz, O. K. F.
Goublier, R.
Gounod, Charles
Grabe, F.
Graben-Hoffmann, Gustav
Grabert, Martin
Grädener, Karl
Georg, Peter
Graham, Robert
Gramman, Karl
Granados, Enrique
Graner, R.
Granier, Jules
Grechaninov, Alexander
Greenhill, Harold

Gregoir, J.
Gregor, Cestmir
Greith, Karl
Grell, Eduard August
Gressler, Franz Albert
Grever, Maria
Grieg, Edvard
Griesbacher, Peter
Grisar, Albert
Groh, A.
Gronau, Ed.
Grøndahl, Agathe Bäcker
Grosheim, Georg Christoph
Groskopf, A.
Grosse, L.
Grossjohann, F.
Grua, Carlo Luigi Pietro
Gruber, L.
Grüel, E.
Grünberger, Ludwig
Grund, Friedrich Wilhelm
Grüner, G.
Grunholzer, K.
Gscheidl, P.
Guastivino, Carlos
Gudmundsson, Björgvin
Guercia, Alfonso
Guglielmo, P. D.
Guiselin, P.
Gülker, August
Gumbert
Gumbert, Ferdinand
Gundlach, jun., L.
Günther, O.
Gurlitt, Cornelius
Gus, M.
Gustav, Prinz v. Schweden
Güth, J. L.
Gutheil, Gustav
Guzmann, Fr.
Haagh, J.
Haan, Willem de [De Haan]
Haas, Joseph
Haase, Rudolf
Hackel, Anton
Hackl, J.
Hacks, G.
Hadeln, E. v.
Haeberlein, H.
Haggbom
Hahn, J. Ch. W.
Haim, F.
Haine, C.
Halle, H.
Hallen, Andreas
Hallstrom, Ivar
Haltnorth, A.
Ham, Charles
Hamblen, Bernard
Hamma, Benjamin

Hammond, William G.
Hanisch, Joseph
Hanscom, E. W.
Hanus, Jan
Hape, Ch. F.
Haring, Ch.
Harker, F. Flaxington
Hart, M. A.
Hartl, Ph.
Hartmann, D. [pen name of David Lundhardt]
Hartmann, Paul Eugen von
Hartog, Edouard de
Häser, C.
Häser, J.
Hasse
Hasse, Gustav
Hasselhoff, A.
Hászlinger, J. v.
Hatton, John L.
Haupt, Karl August
Hauptmann, Moritz
Hauptmann, R.
Hause, C.
Hauser, Moritz H.
Hawley, Charles B.
Hawthorne, Alice [pen name of Septimus Winner]
Hazlehurst, Cecil
Hecht, Gustav
Hefner, Otto
Heidrich, Maximilian
Heidrich, Th.
Heim, A.
Heine, C.
Heinemann, Wilhelm
Heinlein, A.
Heinrich, Anton Philipp
Heinrich, E.
Heins, C. [prob. Karl]
Heins, Karl
Heinz, P.
Heinze, Richard
Heiser, Wilhelm
Heiter, Ernst
Heitmann, M.
Hekking, P. F. R.
Helbig, W.
Hellmesberger, Jr., Joseph
Hellwig, Karl Friedrich Ludwig
Hely-Hutchinson, Victor
Hemberg, Eskil
Hemery, Valentine
Hempel, F. R.
Hennig, C. [prob. Karl Rafael]
Henschel, F.
Henschel, George
Hensel, Fanny Mendelssohn
Henssige, E.

Herbert, Theodor
Herbert, Victor
Hering, C. [prob. Karl Eduard]
Herman, Reinhold Ludwig
Hermann, E. Hans
Hermann, R. L.
Hermann, W.
Hermann, William
Hermany, O.
Hermes, Eduard
Herold, E.
Herrmann, Willy
Hertz, H.
Herzog, Max.
Hess, Karl
Hesselmann, L.
Heuler, Raimund
Heuschkel, Johann Peter
Heuser, Ernst
Heussenstamm, George
Hey, Julius
Hiens, C.
Hildach, Eugen
Hill, Lady Arthur
Hill, Wilhelm
Hiller
Hiller, Ferdinand
Hiller, Paul
Himmel, Fr. G.
Himmel, Friedrich Heinrich
Hinrichs, Friedrich
Hinze, R.
Hirsch, Karl
Hirsch, Rudolf
Hirsche, C.
Hirschfeld, L. v.
Hochberg, Hans Heinrich XIV, B. G. v. [a.k.a. J. H. Franz]
Hochländer, J.
Hodge, Talbot
Hofer, Toni [pen name of Ludwig André]
Hoffmann, Emil Adolf
Hoffmann, L.
Hofmann, Heinrich Karl Johann
Hoft, N.
Hohfeld, C.
Hohnerlein, M.
Hoiby, Lee
Hol, Rijk
Hollaender, Alexis [Holländer]
Hollaender, Gustav
Hollaender, Viktor
Holland, G.
Höller, C.
Holman, Derek
Holmès, Augusta [a.k.a. Hermann Zenta]
Holst, Gustav

Holstein, Franz von
Holstein, Jean-Paul
Hönle, A.
Hope, H. Ashworth
Hopfe, J.
Hoppe, Paul
Horack, C.
Horn, August
Horn, Charles Edward
Horn, E.
Hornig, A.
Hornig, J.
Hornstein, Robert von
Hötzel, C.
Hoven, Johann
Huber, Hans
Hughes
Hughes, Herbert
Hugo, F.
Huhn, Bruno
Hullah, John
Hülle, W.
Hullebroeck, Emiel
Hume, Alexander
Hummel, Ferdinand
Humperdinck, Engelbert
Hutchinson, William Marshall
Huth, Louis
Ibert, Jacques
Iradier, Sebastian [Yradier]
Ireland, John
Isaacson, Michael Neil
Istel, Edgar
Itoh, Hiroyuki
Ivanova, Lidia
Jacke, Ch.
Jäckel, A.
Jacobi, M.
Jacoby, Wilhelm
Jadassohn, Salomon
Jäger, W.
Jahn-Schulze, Hermann
Jähns, Friedrich Wilhelm
Jansen, F. Gustav
Jaques-Dalcroze, Emile
Jehring, Julius
Jensen, Adolf
Jeppesen, Knud
Jirasek, Ivo
Joël, K.
John, F.
Johnson, Noel
Jolas, Betsy
Jones, W. Bradwen
Jordan, Aug.
Jouret, Leon
Junghähnel, O.
Junghans, J.
Jungmann, Albert
Jüngst, Hugo

Jurek, Wilhelm August
Jürisch, E.
Kaatz, F.
Kagerer, M.
Kahle, Th.
Kahn, Robert
Kainer, C.
Kaiser, Karl
Kaleikoa, Malie
Kalla, C.
Kallenbach, Georg E. G.
Kalliwoda, Johann Wenzel
Kammer, R.
Kammerlander, Karl
Kanne, Friedrich August
Kanzler, W.
Kapeller, A.
Karg-Elert, Sigfried [Karg]
Karlsen, Kjell Mork
Kasper, M.
Katzer, Karl August
Kauffmann-Jassoy, Erich
Kauppi, Emil
Kayser, Philipp Christoph
Kean, Edmund
Keel, James Frederick
Kekepuchi
Keller, H.
Keller, Karl
Keller, Ludwig
Kellie, Lawrence
Kennedy
Kent, Edward
Kerle, J. H.
Keue, C.
Keycher, O.
Kienzl, Wilhelm
Kinkel, Johanna [née Mockel]
Kipper, Hermann
Kirchl, Adolf
Kirchner, Hermann
Kirchner, Theodor Fürchtegott
Kirschhof, G. F.
Kittl, Johann Friedrich
Kjerulf, Halfdan
Kleffel, Arno
Kleiber, Karl
Klein, O.
Kleinecke, W.
Kleinmichel, Richard
Klengel, Paul
Klepsch
Klinkmüller, F.
Klose, Oskar
Kloss, H.
Kmoch, A.
Knebel-Döberitz, A. v.
Knebelsberger, L.
Kniese, Julius
Knopf, Martin

Koch, August
Koch, Markus
Kodály, Zoltán
Kohl, A.
Kohl, L.
Kohl, M.
Köhler, Christian Louis Heinrich
Köhler-Wümbach, Wilhelm
Kölling, Ch.
Köllner, Eduard
Kollo, Walter
Könneritz, Nina
    [Georgine, née Eschborn]
Kopelowitz, B.
Korbay, Francis
Korel, H.
Kosch, A.
Koschat, Thomas
Kotsch, H.
Kountz, Richard
Kozeluch, Leopold
Krall, J.
Kratzel, Karl [Kratzl]
Kräulig, L. E.
Krause, C.
Krause, Eduard
Krebs, Karl August
Kreideweiss, R.
Kremling, P. W.
Kremser, Eduard
Krenn, Franz
Kreutzer, Konradin
Kreymann, L.
Krigar, C.
Krigar, Hermann
Krill, Karl
Krinninger, F.
Kromer, Karl
Kron, Louis
Krone, W.
Kronegger, Rudolf
Kronensohn, J.
Krug, Arnold
Krug, Diederich
Krüger, Karl
Kücken, Friedrich Wilhelm
Kügele, Richard
Kuhlau, Friedrich
Kühle, G.
Kühn
Kuhn, C. H.
Kühn, E. [prob. Edmund]
Kühn, Karl
Kühne, C. T.
Kühnhold, Karl
Kuldell, R.
Kulenkampff, Gustav
Kündig, Felix
Künstle, E.
Kuntze, Karl

Küstler, J. H.
Kuusisto, Taneli
Labarre, Théodore
Lachner, Franz
Lachner, Vincenz
Lacome, Paul
Ladendorff, O.
Lafont, Charles-Philippe
Lagoanère, Oscar de
Lalo, Edouard
Lammers, Julius
Lampard
Lamperen, van
Lander, Josef
Lange, C.
Lange, O. H. [prob. Otto]
Lange, R.
Langer, G.
Langert, Johann August Adolf
Lannoy, Eduard
Lansing
Lanz, A.
Laparra, Raoul
Larsen, M.
Laserna, Blas de
Lassel, Rudolf
Lassen, Eduard
Laszky, A. B. [prob. Bela Latsky]
Latour, A. de
Lawson, Malcolm
Lazarus, Gustav
Le Beau, Luise Adolpha
Leal, L.
Lecocq, Charles
Lederer-Prina, Felix
Ledermann, Wilhelm
Lee, Ernest Markham
Legov, M. [pen name of
    Max Vogel]
Lehár, Franz
Lehmann, Johann Traugott
Lehmann, Liza
Lehnard, G.
Lehner, F.
Leicht, Fritz
Leitner, Karl August
Lenz, Leopold
Leo, A.
Leonard, Conrad
Leonard, R.
Leonhard, Julius Emil
Leschetitzky, Theodor
Leser, C.
Leukauf, Richard
Levigne, Peter
Lewalter, Johann
Lewandowski, Louis
Lewerth
Leydecker, A.
Lichner, Heinrich

Liddle, Samuel
Lieb, F. X.
Liebe, Eduard Ludwig
Lier, E.
Limbert, Frank L.
Lincke, Paul
Linderer, Ed.
Lindgren, Olof
Lindner, August
Lindner, E. [prob. Ernst Otto T.]
Lindsay, Miss M. [pen name of
　Mrs.Worthington Bliss]
Lingner, H.
Linnala, Eino
Linné, S.
Lipart, F.
Lipp, Alban
Liszt, Franz
Littmann, H.
Lloyd Webber, Andrew
Lob, Otto
Loes, Harry Dixon &
　George S. Schuler
Loewe, Gilbert
Loewe, Karl Gottfried
Logé, Henri
Löhr, Hermann [Frederic]
Longstaffe, Ernest
Longuet
Lorens, Karl [Lorenz]
Lorenz, Alfred
Lorleberg, F.
Lothar, Mark
Lötti, J.
Lovelace, Austin C.
Lover, Samuel
Lowthian, Caroline [pen name of
　Mrs. Cyril Prescott]
Lubrich, O.
Lucantoni, Giovanni
Lucotte
Lüdecke, L.
Ludwig, August
Ludwig, C. [pen name of
　Julius E. Gottlöber]
Luedecke, Raymond
Lührsz, Karl
Lustig, Gebr.
Lutgen, L.
Lyra, Justus Wilhelm
Maas, Louis
Maase, Wilhelm
MacDowell, Edward
Macfarlane, Elsa
MacFarlane, William Charles
Mächtig, Karl
Mackrot, G. W.
MacLeod, Peter
Mahlberg, C.
Mahnecke, R.

Maier, Amanda [married name
　Rötgen]
Maikowski, M.
Malek, W.
Malibran, Alexander
Malin, Don
Malling, Jorgen
Malotte, Albert Hay
Mangold, Karl Ludwig Armand
Mannfred, Heinrich
Manning, Kathleen Lockhart
Manookin, Robert P.
Mansfeldt, H.
Manziarly, Marcelle de
Marais, Josef
Marchesi de Castrone, Mathilde
　[née Graumann]
Marchesi de Castrone, Salvatore
Marchetti, Filippo
Margot, T.
Mariz, C. J.
Marschner, Adolf Eduard
Marschner, Heinrich August
Marti, E.
Martin, Easthope
Martini, F. v.
Martini, Hugo
Martini, Jean Paul Egide
Martinu, Bohuslav
Marvia, Einari
Marx, Adolf Bernard
Marx, Joseph
Marx, Karl
Marzials, Théodor
Mascheroni, Angelo
Masini, A. [prob. Angelo]
Masini, Francesco
Mason, Gerry
Massenet, Jules
Matthes, J.
Matthiae, E.
Matthias, W.
Matthieux, Johanna [née Mockel,
　later married Kinkel]
Mauri, J.
Mauss, A.
Maxfield, Henry W.
May, Siegfried
Mayer, Joseph Anton
Mayer, Martin
Mayer, William
Mayerhoff, Fritz
McEwen, John
Meienreis, R.
Meier, K.
Meijroos, Hendrik Arnoldus
　[Meyroos]
Meinardus, Ludwig
Meinhold, P.
Meister, Casimir

Melchert, J.
Mellish, Colonel
Mello, Alfred
Melvin, Ernest
Membrée, Edmond
Mendel, Hermann
Mendelssohn, Fanny [see Hensel]
Mendelssohn, Felix
Menzel, J.
Mercadante, Saverio
Mercier, Ch.
Merikanto, Oskar
Merker, R.
Mertens, H. de
Messager, Andre
Messer, F.
Mestozzi, Paul
Metcalf, John W.
Methfessel, Albert Gottlieb
Methfessel, C.
Methfessel, Ernst
Meves, Wilhelm
Meyer, Wilhelm
Meyer-Helmund, Erik
Meyer-Stolzenau, Wilhelm
Meyerbeer, Giacomo
Meysel, E.
Michaelis, Ad. Alfred
Michaelis, Gustav
Michielsen, A.
Migot, Georges
Milhaud, Darius
Mililotti, Leopoldo
Millard, H.
Millard, Harrison
Miller, Henry Colin
Millöcker, Karl
Miltitz, Carl Borromäus von
Minkwitz, Bruno
Mittmann, Paul
Mjöen, J. A.
Moffat, Alfred
Mögling, G. Fr.
Möhring, Ferdinand
Moir, Frank Lewis
Molbe, Heinrich
Molique, Wilhelm Bernhard
Molloy, James Lyman
Monche, L.
Moniuszko, Stanislaw
Moolenaar, S. [prob. Frieso]
Moór, Emanuel
Moore, Dorothy Rudd
Morgan, Robert Orlando
Moritz
Moritz, Franz
Moroni, L.
Morris, C. H.
Morse, Th. F.
Mortari, Virgilio

Moscheles, Ignaz
Mosenthal, Joseph
Mücke, Franz
Mühling, August
Mulder-Fabri, Rich.
Müller, Donat
Müller, Franz
Müller, Heinrich Fidelis
Müller, J. [prob. Johann]
Müller, L. S.
Müller, M.
Müller, Richard
Müller Sr., Adolf
Müller-Hartman, Robert
Munkelt, T.
Münz, C.
Músiol, Robert Paul Johann
Myrberg, August Melcher
Nagiller, Matthäus
Nagler, Franciscus
Nápravník, Eduard
Nater, Johann
Naubert, Friedrich August
Nauwerk, E.
Necke, Hermann
Neckheim, H.
Neibig, G.
Neidhardt, August
Neidlinger, William Harold
Nekes, Franz
Nelson, Rudolph
Nemours, A.
Nesmüller, F.
Nessler, Victor E.
Netzer, Joseph
Neubner, Ottomar
Neugebauer, J.
Neukomm, Sigismund
Neuland, W.
Neumann, Emil
Neumann, H.
Nevin, Ethelbert Woodbridge
Nevin, George Balch
Newton, Ernest
Nicolai, Otto
Nicolai, Wilhelm Frederik Gerard
Niedermayer, Louis
Nieland, H.
Niemann, Gustav
Niese, E.
Niese, Th.
Nikel, Emil
Nikisch, Arthur
Nohé, S.
Noland, Gary
Nolopp, Werner
Norbert, R.
Norman, Fredrick
    Vilhelm Ludvig
Nöroth, J.

North, Michael
Norton, Caroline E. S.
Noskowski, Zygmund
Novaro, Michele
Nuhn, Fr.
Nus, B.
O'Hara, Geoffrey
Oberhoffer, Heinrich
Oberstoetter, H. E.
Oberthür, Karl
Ochs, Siegfried
Oddone, Elisabetta
    [a.k.a. Eliodd]
Odersky, A.
Oehmler, L.
Oelschläger, Friedrich
Offenbach, Jacques
Ogarew, M.
Olson, Daniel
Opel, R.
Operti
Opladen, Adolf
Orr, Buxton
Ortner, A.
Orton, Irv
Otto, A.
Otto, Ernst Julius
Otto, Franz Joseph
Overeem, M. v.
Owen, Anita
Paasch, W.
Pache, Joseph
Pachlov, N. J.
Packenius, J.
Paër, Ferdinando [Paer]
Page, Nathanael Clifford
Paisiello, Giovanni
Palloni, Gaetano
Palme, Rudolf
Panofka, Heinrich
Panseron, Auguste
Pardow, J. H.
Pargolesi, Coronato
Parker, Alice
Parker, Henry
Parlow, Edmund
Pastory, A.
Patat, J.
Pavesi, Stefano
Paxon, Charles W.
Pearsall, Robert Lucas de [a.k.a.
    G. Berthold]
Peellaert, Augustin de
Pelissier, H. G.
Pembauer, Sr., Joseph
Pembaur, Karl
Pentenrieder, Franz Xaver
Perger, Richard von
Perpignan, F.
Persichetti, Vincent

Peter, G.
Peterkin, Norman
Peuschel, Moritz
Pfannschmidt, A.
Pfannschmidt, Heinrich
Pfeil, Heinrich
Pfennig, R. A.
Pflueger
Philipp, A.
Philipp, Bernard Edward
Philipp, J.
Phillips, Montegue Fawcett
Piel, Peter
Pierson, Henry Hugh
Pinkham, Daniel
Pinsuti, Ciro
Pirani, Eugenio
Pircher, J.
Pivoda, F.
Pla, M.
Plag, Johann
Plantade, Charles Henri
Plengorth, Friedrich
Pleskow, Raoul
Pleyel, Ianos [Ignaz Josef]
Pocci, Franz von
Pogge, H.
Pohl, Max
Pommer, Josef
Ponflick, F.
Pontet, Henry
Ponvet, A. M.
Popp, Wilhelm
Por, C.
Porepp, Georg
Pourny, Ch.
Praeger, Heinrich Aloys
Prechtl, Ludwig
Preil, Paul
Preitz, Franz
Pressel, Gustav Adolf
Preyer, Gottfried von
Prior-Lipart, A.
Proch, Heinrich
Procházka, J.
Procházka, Ludwig
Prochazka, Rudolf
Prokofiev, Serge
Proschel, G.
Puchat, Max
Pucitta, Vincenzo
Puget, Louise-Françoise
Queling, Theodor
Quilter, Roger
Quiquerez, Hermann
Rachmaninov, Sergei
Radecke, Robert
Radecke, Rudolph
Raff, Joseph
Raida, Karl Alexander

Raillard, Theodor
Ramann, Bruno
Ramshorst, J. D. von
Randhartinger, Benedict
Raphael, Georg
Raphael, Gunther
Rasbach, Oscar
Rathgeber, Georg
Ray, Lilian
Recli, Giulia
Reger, Max
Reh, H.
Reich, Reinhold
Reichardt, Gustav
Reichardt, Johann Friedrich
Reiche, V.
Reichel, Adolf Heinrich Johann
Reid, Alwyn
Reifner, Vincenz
Reilly, Myles
Reim, Edmund
Reimann, Heinrich
Reinberger, J.
Reinecke, Carl
Reinecke, Karl Ludwig
Reinhardt, F.
Reinhardt, Heinrich
Reinthaler, Karl Martin
Reissiger, Friedrich August
Reissiger, Karl Gottlieb
Reissmann, August
Reissmann, H.
Reiter, Ernst
Renardy, A.
Renaud, Albert
Renker, Felix
Renner, Josef
Renner, M.
Rennes, Catharina van
Reuss, August
Reutter, Hermann
Reutter, Otto
Reynolds, Alfred
Rheinberger, Josef
Rheineck, S.
Ricci, Federico
Ricci, Luigi
Riccius, August Ferdinand
Richard, T.
Richards, Brinley
Richardy, Johann
Richstaetter, M. or W.
Richter, Alfred
Richter, Ernst Friedrich
Riedel, August
Riem, Friedrich Wilhelm
Riemenschneider, Georg
Ries, Ferdinand
Rieter, E.
Rietz, J. August Wilhelm

Riga, Frantz
Righini, Vincenzo
Rijken, Georg
Rilvas, C. de
Rimsky-Korsakov, Nicolai
Rinck, Johann Christian Heinrich
Ringer, A.
Rinnow, P.
Rischbeiter, Wilhelm Albert
Risinger, Karel
Rittau, Bj.
Ritter, Hermann
Roberton, Hugh Stevenson
Robricht, P.
Rocca, Lodovico
Röder, Ewald
Rödger, Emil
Rodhe, Eduard
Rodhe, H.
Roeder, Martin [Röder]
Roes, Carol Lasater
Roessel, J. or L.
Roff, Joseph
Roger, J.
Rogers, James H.
Röhde, A.
Röhricht, Paul
Rolla, Ch.
Romberg, A. [prob. Andreas]
Ronald, Landon
Ronconi [prob. Felice]
Röntgen, Julius
Roose, H.
Rorem, Ned
Roscher, Josef
Rosenberg, Wilhelm [Vilhelm]
Rosenfeld, J.
Rosenfeld, Leopold
Rosenfeld & Thiele
Rosenhain, Jacob
Rosenmeyer, H.
Rosensweig, H.
Rosenthal, Manuel
Rosenzweig, Wilhelm
Rossi, E.
Rossini, Gioacchino
Rössler, Richard
Roth, Bertrand
Roth, Franz
Rothlauf, B.
Rothstein, James
Rotschy, J. B.
Rott, Carl Maria
Rubbra, Edmund
Rubini, Giovanni Battista
Rubinstein, Anton
Rubinstein, Nicolai
Rübner, Cornelius [Rybner]
Ruch, Hannes
Rückauf, Anton

Rücker, August
Rücker, Theodor
Rudnick, Wilhelm
Rudorff, E. [Friedrich Karl]
Rügamer, F.
Rühl, Friedrich Wilhelm
Rühricht, P.
Rungenhagen, Karl Friedrich
Russell, Armand
Russell, Kennedy
Rust, Wilhelm Karl
Ruta, Michele
S. G. P.
Saar, L. V. [Franz]
Sachs, Johann Melchior Ernst
Sacks, Woldemar
Sackur, C.
Saint-Lubin, Léon de
Saint Quentin, Edward
Saint-Saëns, Camille
Salinger, J.
Salis, P.
Sallneuve, C.
Sallneuve, E.
Salvi, Matteo
Samson, L.
Samuel-Rosseau, Marcel
Sanderson, Wilfred
Sans-Souci, Gertrude
Santi, G.
Santner, Karl
Sarjeant, J.
Sarti, Giuseppe
Säuberlich, C.
Sauer, L. & G.
Sauerbrey, J. W. C. C.
Sawyer
Schachner, J. B.
Schäfer, P.
Schäffer, August
Schäffer, Heinrich
Schäffer, Theodor [Schäfer]
Schaper, Gustav
Schaper, O.
Schärf, P.
Schauer, H.
Schenk, A.
Schetana, M.
Schiedel, P.
Schiemer, Georg
Schierbeck, Poul
Schifferl, F.
Schild, Theodor F.
Schilling, Ferdinand
Schindler, J.
Schirmer, A.
Schläger, Hans
Schleidt, Wilhelm
Schleiffarth, G.
Schlesinger

Schletterer, Hans Michel
Schlosser, Paul
Schlottmann, Louis
Schlözer, K. [prob. Karl]
Schmeidler, K. [prob. Karl]
Schmid, Heinrich Kaspar
Schmid, Joseph
Schmid, Th.
Schmidt, A.
Schmidt, Gustav
Schmidt, Hans
Schmidt, M.
Schmidt, M. H.
Schmidt, O.
Schmitt, Aloys
Schmitt, Cornelius
Schmitt, Florent
Schmitt, Georg Aloys
Schmutz & Katzer
Schnabel, Josef Ignaz
Schnabel, Karl
Schnaubelt, Heinrich
Schnaubelt, W.
Schnecker, P. A.
Schneeberger, Ferdinand
Schneider, Bernhard
Schneider, J. [prob. Johann
    Gottlob II]
Schnippering, W.
Schöbe, C.
Schoeck, Othmar
Schofield, Joe
Scholz, Bernard
Schonberg, Stig Gustav
Schorcht, H.
Schorsch, L.
Schotte, Karl
Schouwman, Hans
Schrammel, Johann
Schreck, Gustav
Schröder, M. [prob. Max]
Schroeder, Hermann
Schröter, L.
Schubert, Franz Ludwig
Schubert, Franz Peter
Schubert, Georgine
Schubert, Louis
Schuh, H.
Schuh, J.
Schultz, C.
Schultz, Edwin
Schulz, August
Schulz, Chr.
Schulz, R.
Schumacher, Heinrich Vollrat
Schumacher, Richard
Schumann, Clara Wieck
Schumann, Georg Alfred
Schumann, Robert
Schütky, Franz Josef

Schwartz, Alexander
    [a.k.a. Sascha Landry]
Schwarz, C.
Schwarz, N.
Schwarzlose, Otto
Schweiger, J.
Schwertzell, Wilhelmine von
Schwick, J.
Seestädt, J.
Seidel, O.
Seifert, Uso
Seiffert, Alexander
Seiffert, Karl
Seitz, F. [prob. Friedrich]
Selmer, Johan Peter
Sennes, H.
Sering, Friedrich Wilhelm
Serradell, N.
Sessi, M. [prob. Marianne]
Seyffardt, Ernst Hermann
Sharmann, Cecil
Sharpe, Evelyn
Shaw, Martin
Shelley, Harry Rowe
Shield, William
Shiomi, Mieko
Shostakovich, Dmitri
Sieber, Ferdinand
Siebmann, F.
Silber, Philip
Silcher, Friedrich
Simon, Ernst
Simon, O.
Singer, Jeanne
Sinico, Giuseppe
Sinigaglia, Leone
Sinnhold, R.
Sioly, Johann
Sioly-Weisberg
Sirsch, R.
Sjogren, Emil
Skerjanc, Lucijan Marija
Skop, V. E.
Slunicko, Jan
Smart, Henry
Smit, Leo
Smith, Alice Mary
Smith, H. Arnold
Smith, Lilian
Smith, Seymour
Söchting, Emil
Södermann, Johan August
Solbrück, C.
Soler, Joseph
Söllner, E.
Solomon, John
Somervell, Arthur
Sor, Fernando [Sors]
Sowerby, Leo
Sowinsky, A. Wojcieh [Albert]

Spahn, Adolf
Sparhakel, A.
Speaks, Oley
Speiser, Wilhelm
Spengler, Ludwig
Spielter, Hermann
Spohr, Louis
Sponholtz, Adolf Heinrich
Spontini, Gasparo
Springer, Max
Squire, William Henry
Stacey, Gilbert
Stafford, C. Lloyd
Stainer, John
Stainlein, Louis von
Standke, Otto
Stanford, Charles Villiers
Stange, Max
Stanislas, A.
Starck, L.
Starck, W.
Stark, Ludwig
Starke, Gustav
Starke, H.
Starke, J.
Steffens, Gustav
Stehle, J. Gustav Eduard
Steiber, P.
Steidl, F.
Steidl-Duette
Stein, C. [prob. Karl]
Stein, Josef
Stein, V.
Steinecke, A.
Steinhart, W. W.
Steinitzer, M. [prob. Max]
Steinkühler, Emil
Steizhammer
Stekel, W.
Sterkel, Johann F. X.
Stern, Hermann
Stern, Julius
Stern, S.
Steven, G.
Stieber, P.
Stiegmann, Eduard
Stiehl, Karl
Stöbe, Paul
Stock, Ed.
Stockhausen, Karlheinz
Stöger, A.
Stokhausen, E. v.
Stolberg-Stolberg, L.
Storch, Anton M.
Strand, Tor
Strauch, Fr.
Straus, Oscar
Strauss, Jr., Johann
Streabbog, L.
Strimer, Joseph

Strino, S. A.
Strubel, J.
Stuckenschmidt, H.
Stuckenschmidt, J. H.
Succo, Franz Adolf
Succo, Reinhold
Sugár, Rezsö
Sugiura, Masayoshi
Suhy, K.
Sullivan, Arthur
Sulzbach, Emil
Suppé, Franz von
Sutherland, Margaret
Suzuki, Hideaki
Svara, Danilo
Sveinbjörnsson, Sveinbjörn
Swann, Donald
Szymanowski, Karol Maciej
Talma, Louise
Tancioni, E.
Tate, James W.
Tate, Phyllis
Taubert, Ernst Eduard
Taubert, H.
Taubert, Otto
Taubert, Wilhelm
Tauwitz, Eduard
Taylor, T.
Tchaikovsky, Peter Ilyich
Teich, Otto
Teichmann, A. or O.
Terriss, Ellaline
Teschner, Gustav Wilhelm
Teschner, Wilhelm
Thaler, J. B.
Thamm, P.
Thiel, Carl
Thiele, Eduard
Thiele, Louis
Thiele, Richard
Thiele, Rudolf
Thiele, Th.
Thielen, P. H.
Thierfelder, Albert Wilhelm
Thieriot, Ferdinand
Thiman, Eric Harding
Thoma, Rudolf
Thomas, Arthur Goring
Thomas, N.
Thooft, Willem Frans
Thorn, C.
Thudichum, Gustav
Tichy, Rudolf
Tiehsen, Otto
Tinel, Edgar Pierre Joseph
Tolstoy, Alexei [Tolstoi]
Tomaschek, Johann Wenzel
Topliff, Robert
Toselli, Enrico
Tosti, Francesco Paolo

Tourbié, Richard
Tränkner, M.
Traunfels, H.
Traventi
Triest, Heinrich
Tritto, Giacomo
Troschel, Wilhelm Troszel
Trotere, Henry
Trubel, Gerhard
Truhn, Friedrich Heironymus
Tschiderer, E.
Tschirch, Rudolf
Tschirch, Wilhelm
Tuch, Heinrich Agatius Gottlob
Tuma, A.
Tussenbroek, Hendrika von
Tuuri, Jaako
Uber, Christian Friedrich
  Hermann
Umlauft, Paul
Unger, A.
Unknown composer or
  arranger (8 entries)
Uray, Ernst Ludwig
Urban, Friedrich Julius
Urlaub, A.
Vadtor, Thomas
Van Buskirk, Carl
Van Cromphout, L.
Vangele, V.
Vater, F. A.
Vaughan Williams, Ralph
Veit, Václav Jindrich [also
  Wenzel, Heinrich Veit]
Verbroek, C. J. J.
Verelst, P. F.
Verner, H. C.
Viardot-Garcia, Pauline
Vierling, Georg
Vincent, Heinrich Joseph
Viol, Willy
Visconti, E.
Vogel, Bernhardt
Vogel, Hans
Vogel, M. [prob. Martin]
Voigt, F.
Voigt, Henriette
Voigt, Hermann
Voigt-Kudlik, Th.
Volckmar, Wilhelm
Volkmann, W.
Volle, Bjarne
Vollstedt, Robert
Voullaire, Waldemar
Voutz, H.
Wachsmann, Johann Joachim
Wade, Joseph Augustine
Wagenblass, W.
Wagenbrenner, Josef

Wagener, Paul
Wagner, C. [prob. Karl Jacob]
Wagner, Ernst David
Wagner, Franz
Wagner, Josef Franz
Wagner, Paul Emil
Wakefield, Augusta Mary
Walden, Otto von [pen name of
  Fritz Schindler]
Waldmann, v. d. Aue
Wallace
Wallach Crane, Joelle
Wallbach, Ludwig
Wallnöfer, Adolf
Walter-Kiesel, M.
Wandelt, Amadeus
Wandow, L.
Waniek, Alois
Wanthaler, Gustav
Wany, W. J.
Wappaus, Karl
Wardini, Gebr.
Warren, Betsy
Watelle, Ch.
Weatherly, F. E.
Weber, A. [prob. Berhard
  Anselm]
Weber, Carl Maria von
Weber, Franz
Weber, Gottfried
Weber, Gustav
Weckerlin, Jean Baptiste
Wegeler, C.
Wehner, A.
Weidt, Heinrich
Weigel, H.
Weil, T.
Weinberger, Karl Friedrich
Weinhardt, F.
Weinstabl, Karl
Weinwurm, Rudolf
Weischer, Th.
Weismann, Julius
Weismann, Wilhelm
Weiss, J.
Weiss, Laurenz
Weissbach, M. L.
Wellings, Milton
Wendland, Waldemar
Wendt, Ernst
Wennerburg, Gunnar
Wenzel, Eduard
Wenzel, H.
Wermann, Friedrich Oskar
Werner, Erich
Werner, Otto
Werth, Joseph
Westendorf, T. P.
Westermair, Johann B.

Westmeter, Wilhelm
Weston, R. P. & B. Lee
Weyts, H.
White
White, Maude Valerie
Whitehead, Percy Algernon
Wibergh, Johann Olof
Wichern, Karoline
Wichmann, Hermann
Wickede, Friedrich von
Wickenhauser, Richard
Widmann, Benedikt
Wiedecke, Adolph
Wiedemann, Max
Wiel, Taddeo
Wielhorski, Mikhail
Wienand, V.
Wieniawski, Joseph
Wiesomowiluki, R.
Wilhelm, Karl Friedrich
Willan, Healy
Willeby, Charles
Williams, R. H.
Williams, W. S. Gwynn
Wilm, Nicolai von
Wilson
Wilson, Henry Lane
Wiltberger, August
Winkhler, Karl Angelus von

Winkler, O.
Winter
Winter, E.
Winter, Georg
Winter, J.
Winterberger, Alexander
Winterling, W.
Wintzer, Elisabeth
Witt, Franz Xaver
Witt, Julius
Witt, Leopold
Witt, Theodor de
Wittenbecher, Otto
Wittsack, P.
Wolf, E.
Wolf, L. C.
Wolff, C.
Wolff, Gustav Tyson
Wolff, Leonhard
Wolff, W.
Wolff, Wilh.
Wölfle, Chr.
Wolfrum, Karl
Wollanck, Friedrich
Wolzogen, Ernst von
Wood, Hayden
Woodforde-Finden, Amy
Wooge, Emma

Wottitz, Th.
Wouters, Adolphe
Wrangle, Vassily G.
Wrede, Ferdinand
Wüerst, Richard Ferdinand
Wuorinen, Charles
Wyeth, John
Z'Wyssig, Alberik Johann
    Josef Maria
Zangl, Josef Gregor
Zapff, Oskar
Zehrfeld, Oskar
Zeitler, J.
Zelter, Carl Friedrich
Zenger, Max
Zenter, Wilhelm
Zepler, Bogumil
Zerlett, Johann Baptist
Zescevich, A.
Ziehrer, Karl Michel
Zientarski, Romuald
Zier, E.
Zierau, Fritz
Zimmer, C. [prob. Karl]
Zimmer, Otto
Zimmermann, J.
Zingel, Rudolf Ewald
Zöllner, Andreas
Zöllner, Karl Friedrich
Zweifel, B.

Appendix B: List of Identifiable Women Composers (81 total)

Abbott, Jane
Allitsen, Frances
Anderson, Beth
Anderson, Margaret Tweedie
Ansorge, M.
    [prob. Margarethe]
Arndts, Maria Vespermann
Beach, Amy
Bond, Carrie Jacobs
Bosmans, Henriette
Bracken, Edith A.
Brahe, Mary Hannah
Brandhurst, Elise
Bülow, Charlotte von
Chaminade, Cecile
Crane, Helen
Day, Maude Craske
Decker, Pauline von
Dell'Acqua, Eva
Dietrich, Amalia
Doun, Elza
Dunlap, Fern Glasgow
Edwards, Clara
Feist, Alwine
Forsyth, Josephine
Gabriel, Mary Ann Virginia
Gallois, Marie
Gaston-Murray, Blanche
Goatley, Alma
Grever, Maria

Grøndahl, Agathe Bäcker
Häser, C.
Hensel, Fanny Mendelssohn
Hill, Lady Arthur
Holmès, Augusta
    [a.k.a. Hermann Zenta]
Ivanova, Lidia
Jolas, Betsy
Kinkel, Johanna [née Mockel,
    also Matthieux]
Könneritz, Nina [Georgine, née
    Eschborn]
Le Beau, Luise Adolpha
Lehmann, Liza
Lindsay, Miss M. [pen name of
    Mrs. Worthington Bliss]
Lowthian, Caroline [pen name
    of Mrs. Cyril Prescott]
Macfarlane, Elsa
Maier, Amanda
    [married name Rötgen]
Manning, Kathleen Lockhart
Manziarly, Marcelle de
Marchesi de Castrone, Mathilde
    [née Graumann]
Matthieux, Johanna
    [also Kinkel]
Moore, Dorothy Rudd
Norton, Caroline E. S.
Oddone, Elisabetta
    [pen name Eliodd]

Owen, Anita
Parker, Alice
Puget, Louise-Françoise
Ray, Lilian
Recli, Giulia
Rennes, Catharina van
Roes, Carol Lasater
Sans-Souci, Gertrude
Schubert, Georgine
Schumann, Clara Wieck
Schwertzell, Wilhelmine von
Sessi, M. [prob. Marianne]
Singer, Jeanne
Skerjanc, Lucijan Marija
Smith, Alice Mary
Smith, Lilian
Sutherland, Margaret
Talma, Louise
Tate, Phyllis
Terriss, Ellaline
Tussenbroek, Hendrika von
Viardot-Garcia, Pauline
Voigt, Henriette
Wakefield, Augusta Mary
Wallach Crane, Joelle
White, Maude Valerie
Wichern, Karoline
Wintzer, Elisabeth
Woodforde-Finden, Amy
Wooge, Emma

Appendix C: Index of Entries by Voice Specification

ENTRIES FOR SOPRANO/SOPRANO VOICES (727 TOTAL, 8.262%)

33, 34, 35, 43, 224, 389, 401, 433, 473, 477, 478, 479, 506, 507, 510, 511, 513, 514, 519, 521, 528, 529, 531, 534, 536, 540, 666, 667, 717, 720, 736, 737, 744, 745, 770, 771, 772, 773, 832, 833, 857, 859, 861, 863, 864, 865, 866, 867, 869, 871, 872, 906, 907, 908, 909, 929, 932, 936, 959, 986, 987, 988, 989, 996, 1017, 1021, 1022, 1108, 1109, 1110, 1129, 1137, 1139, 1151, 1154, 1155, 1194, 1195, 1196, 1197, 1240, 1243, 1245, 1268, 1269, 1270, 1271, 1272, 1273, 1314, 1317, 1326, 1334, 1344, 1346, 1357, 1358, 1359, 1360, 1361, 1390, 1391, 1392, 1394, 1396, 1397, 1398, 1401, 1405, 1407, 1434, 1435, 1436, 1437, 1438, 1439, 1460, 1461, 1462, 1464, 1465, 1467, 1471, 1472, 1473, 1474, 1477, 1479, 1483, 1498, 1505, 1506, 1507, 1511, 1512, 1514, 1515, 1521, 1522, 1524, 1528, 1530, 1540, 1546, 1583, 1584, 1585, 1587, 1593, 1598, 1608, 1610, 1611, 1630, 1638, 1639, 1667, 1668, 1669, 1670, 1706, 1711, 1715, 1720, 1721, 1763, 1764, 1781, 1782, 1783, 1784, 1785, 1786, 1799, 1806, 1884, 1885, 1929, 1930, 1931, 1932, 1933, 1934, 1935, 1936, 1940, 2041, 2058, 2059, 2060, 2061, 2062, 2063, 2064, 2065, 2066, 2067, 2114, 2141, 2280, 2301, 2304, 2329, 2367, 2375, 2378, 2380, 2388, 2391, 2392, 2393, 2394, 2396, 2398, 2399, 2400, 2401, 2402, 2403, 2404, 2407, 2409, 2410, 2412, 2413, 2416, 2417, 2418, 2425, 2446, 2448, 2454, 2464, 2477, 2497, 2512, 2598, 2601, 2607, 2615, 2616, 2620, 2623, 2624, 2626, 2628, 2630, 2631, 2632, 2633, 2634, 2635, 2646, 2648, 2665, 2683, 2685, 2701, 2710, 2711, 2716, 2719, 2800, 2847, 2933, 3094, 3097, 3134, 3139, 3141, 3144, 3147, 3150, 3152, 3172, 3173, 3174, 3175, 3314, 3315, 3325, 3382, 3383, 3385, 3432, 3453, 3466, 3546, 3547, 3548, 3549, 3559, 3670, 3697, 3699, 3700, 3701, 3702, 3734, 3735, 3736, 3737, 3738, 3739, 3742, 3743, 3766, 3769, 3770, 3772, 3986, 3988, 3989, 3990, 3991, 3992, 3993, 3994, 3995, 4065, 4070, 4078, 4089, 4092, 4096, 4097, 4135, 4155, 4156, 4157, 4158, 4159, 4161, 4171, 4175, 4179, 4181, 4182, 4184, 4185, 4187, 4191, 4198, 4199, 4200, 4201, 4202, 4204, 4205, 4206, 4207, 4208, 4209, 4210, 4211, 4330, 4331, 4425, 4426, 4436, 4438, 4439, 4476, 4479, 4499, 4501, 4507, 4508, 4511, 4512, 4514, 4515, 4560, 4561, 4565, 4566, 4567,

(Soprano/Soprano—Continued)

4578, 4579, 4603, 4622, 4623, 4624, 4625, 4675, 4676, 4677, 4679, 4683, 4684, 4735, 4737, 4763, 4824, 4825, 4836, 4851, 4864, 4869, 4870, 4898, 4902, 4903, 4904, 4913, 4914, 4923, 4925, 4943, 4944, 4945, 4946, 4948, 4949, 4950, 4984, 5000, 5001, 5049, 5086, 5094, 5095, 5098, 5102, 5111, 5195, 5196, 5197, 5198, 5199, 5200, 5201, 5202, 5203, 5206, 5266, 5267, 5268, 5287, 5288, 5289, 5290, 5308, 5309, 5310, 5351, 5352, 5379, 5381, 5389, 5390, 5392, 5393, 5399, 5401, 5461, 5462, 5464, 5467, 5468, 5586, 5590, 5606, 5671, 5678, 5681, 5682, 5686, 5691, 5721, 5745, 5747, 5764, 5766, 5768, 5771, 5772, 5777, 5779, 5781, 5789, 5792, 5796, 5802, 5803, 5805, 5807, 5808, 5813, 5816, 5819, 5829, 5830, 5833, 5835, 5837, 5846, 5849, 5852, 5853, 5854, 5856, 5860, 5861, 5863, 5865, 5866, 5869, 5872, 5873, 5874, 5878, 5879, 5880, 5882, 5883, 5884, 5886, 5887, 5892, 5897, 5898, 5900, 5901, 5903, 5905, 5909, 5913, 5914, 5915, 5980, 5981, 5982, 6001, 6002, 6005, 6006, 6007, 6008, 6012, 6027, 6159, 6181, 6184, 6185, 6186, 6187, 6188, 6191, 6194, 6322, 6335, 6351, 6352, 6353, 6354, 6355, 6356, 6357, 6358, 6361, 6362, 6363, 6364, 6365, 6367, 6368, 6369, 6402, 6405, 6406, 6444, 6446, 6448, 6449, 6450, 6452, 6512, 6513, 6519, 6658, 6664, 6673, 6677, 6684, 6690, 6701, 6702, 6703, 6716, 6830, 6831, 6832, 6833, 6834, 6837, 6887, 6908, 6909, 6910, 6914, 6962, 6963, 6966, 6976, 6978, 6979, 6983, 6984, 6985, 6995, 6997, 6998, 7000, 7001, 7002, 7008, 7011, 7018, 7020, 7022, 7025, 7039, 7051, 7145, 7220, 7238, 7246, 7267, 7359, 7412, 7413, 7415, 7416, 7421, 7446, 7447, 7449, 7451, 7454, 7455, 7505, 7578, 7579, 7581, 7599, 7616, 7618, 7619, 7636, 7644, 7647, 7648, 7650, 7652, 7653, 7656, 7659, 7661, 7662, 7664, 7672, 7673, 7790, 7799, 7844, 7928, 7932, 7933, 7939, 7984, 7987, 7989, 7990, 7991, 8059, 8103, 8136, 8137, 8140, 8141, 8142, 8144, 8145, 8146, 8148, 8149, 8150, 8179, 8180, 8181, 8182, 8183, 8184, 8185, 8187, 8188, 8189, 8265, 8388, 8389, 8390, 8391, 8392, 8393, 8476, 8477, 8634, 8641, 8642, 8643, 8644, 8674, 8696, 8728, 8752, 8785, 8787, 8788, 8789, 8790, 8792, 8795, 8796.

ENTRIES FOR SOPRANO/MEZZO-SOPRANO VOICES (315 TOTAL, 3.560%)

29, 93, 425, 466, 634, 641, 643, 700, 724, 727, 732, 733, 734, 736, 738, 769, 780, 781, 809, 810, 928, 939, 962, 963, 966, 984, 991, 1059, 1071, 1073, 1108, 1143, 1144, 1146, 1147, 1148, 1149, 1179, 1180, 1183, 1184, 1240, 1245, 1300, 1335, 1342, 1373, 1374, 1377, 1378, 1381, 1384, 1387, 1391, 1393, 1394, 1399, 1401, 1402, 1404, 1405, 1406, 1407, 1411, 1502, 1506, 1514, 1528, 1547, 1548, 1568, 1608, 1630, 1638, 1639, 1837, 1912, 2037, 2047, 2053, 2180, 2182, 2184, 2189, 2193, 2194, 2198, 2200, 2327, 2330, 2337, 2338, 2339, 2391, 2393, 2394, 2396, 2399, 2402, 2407, 2412, 2416, 2418, 2444, 2483, 2549, 2552, 2644, 2650, 2657, 2679, 2680, 2799, 2858, 2870, 2871, 2887, 2888, 2981, 3080, 3081, 3155, 3158, 3161, 3357, 3411, 3732, 3762, 3767, 3771, 3871, 3875, 4162, 4250, 4288, 4289, 4294, 4295, 4296, 4297, 4301, 4305, 4308, 4310, 4313, 4314, 4317, 4320, 4499, 4507, 4511, 4563, 4583, 4728, 4836, 4841, 4855, 4861, 4863, 4891, 4904, 4923, 4986, 4987, 4996, 4997, 4998, 5235, 5338, 5339, 5340, 5343, 5344, 5380, 5670, 5672, 5676, 5680, 5683, 5687, 5692, 5702, 5847, 5851, 5859, 5862, 5864, 5867, 5876, 5877, 5881, 5885, 5890, 5891, 5902, 6016, 6017, 6020, 6033, 6034, 6035, 6036, 6038, 6039, 6040, 6129, 6130, 6131, 6192, 6226, 6228, 6229, 6232, 6239, 6241, 6242, 6244, 6246, 6250, 6253, 6255, 6258, 6259, 6266, 6277, 6284, 6285, 6289, 6292, 6301, 6373, 6374, 6375, 6380, 6395, 6404, 6411, 6539, 6540, 6830, 6831, 6832, 6833, 6834, 6837, 6962, 6966, 6973, 6974, 6984, 6989, 6991, 6997, 6998, 7013, 7020, 7021, 7048, 7150, 7157, 7159, 7384, 7409, 7421, 7446, 7449, 7454, 7601, 7623, 7624, 7637, 7687, 7688, 7689, 7690, 7691, 7692, 7693, 7694, 7695, 7696, 7697, 7700, 7701, 7702, 7703, 7704, 7705, 7706, 7707, 7708, 7709, 7710, 7711, 7712, 7713, 7714, 7715, 7716, 7717, 7718, 7796, 7842, 7885, 7887, 7889, 7896, 8023, 8141, 8145, 8149, 8706, 8709, 8711, 8715.

ENTRIES FOR MEZZO-SOPRANO/MEZZO-SOPRANO VOICES (60 TOTAL, 0.682%)

44, 550, 553, 554, 628, 732, 1475, 1514, 1584, 1634, 1706, 2180, 2182, 2184, 2189, 2193, 2198, 2391, 2393, 2394, 2396, 2399, 2402, 2407, 2412, 2416, 2418, 2800, 3996, 4501, 4836, 4904, 4923, 5108, 5112, 5423, 6199, 6200, 6201, 6917, 6918, 6922, 6925, 6934, 6935, 6936, 6938, 7013, 7223, 7446, 7449, 7454, 7456, 7812, 7813, 7815, 8723, 8724, 8725, 8726.

ENTRIES FOR ALTO/ALTO VOICES (15 TOTAL, 0.170%)

2553, 2554, 2800, 4001, 4002, 4003, 4004, 4005, 4006, 6359, 6360, 6366, 6398, 8275, 8279.

ENTRIES FOR SOPRANO/ALTO VOICES (2266 TOTAL, 25.753%)

12, 17, 33, 35, 92, 93, 98, 112, 117, 118, 129, 141, 142, 144, 151, 153, 157, 159, 160, 165, 167, 174, 178, 182, 186, 188, 190, 196, 202, 208, 212, 216, 236, 237, 241, 246, 254, 255, 258, 259, 266, 271, 279, 280, 286, 287, 288, 293, 296, 298, 303, 307, 308, 311, 315, 316, 323, 324, 325, 328, 362, 369, 370, 371, 372, 373, 374, 375, 376, 377, 378, 379, 380, 381, 382, 383, 385, 386, 387, 388, 390, 395, 416, 418, 419, 420, 421, 422, 423, 424, 425, 426, 427, 428, 429, 430, 431, 436, 438, 444, 445, 450, 453, 454, 456, 461, 464, 469, 473, 475, 483, 486, 487, 488, 490, 492, 493, 494, 495, 518, 523, 527, 533, 542, 543, 544, 545, 546, 558, 559, 560, 561, 573, 589, 590, 591, 592, 593, 598, 599, 602, 605, 606, 607, 608, 620, 631, 632, 647, 655, 656, 658, 659, 660, 661, 662, 664, 665, 668, 669, 670, 671, 672, 673, 674, 675, 676, 677, 678, 679, 680, 681, 687, 690, 711, 727, 728, 731, 733, 734, 735, 738, 743, 769, 801, 802, 804, 811, 850, 862, 868, 870, 873, 877, 878, 879, 880, 881, 882, 883, 884, 888, 889, 890, 891, 893, 895, 923, 924, 925, 933, 955, 956, 958, 961, 962, 964, 965, 967, 971, 981, 995, 1004, 1016, 1020, 1021, 1022, 1028, 1043, 1044, 1045, 1051, 1052, 1055, 1056, 1059, 1060, 1061, 1064, 1065, 1067, 1068, 1070, 1071, 1073, 1074, 1075, 1076, 1079, 1081, 1082, 1083, 1084, 1085, 1086, 1087, 1090, 1094, 1095, 1103, 1104, 1106, 1108, 1112, 1113, 1114, 1116, 1117, 1118, 1119, 1120, 1121, 1122, 1123, 1124, 1125, 1126, 1127, 1128, 1129, 1136, 1138, 1140, 1141, 1142, 1145, 1150, 1152, 1153, 1167, 1168, 1169, 1170, 1171, 1172, 1173, 1174, 1175, 1178, 1185, 1186, 1187, 1188, 1190, 1191, 1192, 1200, 1201, 1202, 1203, 1204, 1205, 1206, 1207, 1208, 1209, 1210, 1211, 1224, 1225, 1226, 1227, 1228, 1229, 1230, 1231, 1232, 1233, 1234, 1235, 1236, 1238, 1242, 1253, 1255, 1258, 1259, 1260, 1261, 1262, 1263, 1264, 1265, 1266, 1267, 1276, 1277, 1280, 1281, 1282, 1283, 1291, 1292, 1293, 1298, 1311, 1312, 1313, 1316, 1319, 1320, 1322, 1323, 1325, 1329, 1330, 1331, 1332, 1336, 1337, 1338, 1340, 1341, 1347, 1348, 1353, 1363, 1364, 1365, 1375, 1376, 1377, 1378, 1380, 1400, 1423, 1440, 1441, 1442, 1450, 1452, 1481, 1486, 1487, 1488, 1489, 1490, 1491, 1495, 1503, 1504, 1509, 1510, 1511, 1513, 1516, 1517, 1518, 1525, 1526, 1532, 1542, 1543, 1550, 1559, 1560, 1561, 1566, 1568, 1570, 1576, 1577, 1578, 1579, 1580, 1588, 1594, 1595, 1596, 1597, 1599, 1600, 1604, 1619, 1623, 1631, 1632, 1637, 1641, 1647, 1651, 1652, 1653, 1654, 1664, 1671, 1672, 1673, 1675, 1676, 1680, 1684, 1691, 1692, 1693, 1694, 1703, 1713, 1733, 1738, 1742, 1755, 1756, 1757, 1758, 1759, 1774, 1787, 1788, 1793, 1794, 1797, 1798, 1801, 1802, 1803, 1808, 1809, 1811, 1814, 1815, 1816, 1817, 1818, 1820, 1821, 1823, 1826, 1827, 1828, 1830, 1836, 1837, 1838, 1839, 1840, 1841, 1843, 1844, 1847, 1848, 1850, 1854, 1855, 1856, 1857, 1858, 1859, 1860, 1862, 1863, 1864, 1866, 1867, 1868, 1870, 1874, 1880, 1881, 1883, 1897, 1898, 1900, 1912, 1944, 1985, 1986, 1987, 1988, 1989, 1991, 1992, 1993, 1995, 1996, 1997, 1998, 1999, 2000, 2001, 2002, 2003,

2004, 2005, 2008, 2011, 2012, 2013, 2014, 2017, 2018, 2019, 2020, 2021, 2022, 2038, 2042, 2048, 2049, 2050, 2051, 2054, 2055, 2056, 2072, 2073, 2075, 2076, 2081, 2084, 2085, 2086, 2092, 2102, 2104, 2105, 2115, 2138, 2145, 2151, 2165, 2170, 2171, 2178, 2179, 2180, 2181, 2182, 2183, 2184, 2185, 2187, 2188, 2189, 2191, 2193, 2195, 2196, 2197, 2198, 2199, 2201, 2202, 2203, 2204, 2205, 2206, 2209, 2212, 2213, 2214, 2215, 2216, 2217, 2219, 2220, 2221, 2222, 2224, 2226, 2227, 2228, 2229, 2230, 2231, 2232, 2233, 2234, 2235, 2236, 2238, 2239, 2241, 2243, 2244, 2246, 2247, 2248, 2249, 2251, 2252, 2258, 2259, 2260, 2261, 2263, 2264, 2295, 2296, 2297, 2298, 2299, 2300, 2303, 2305, 2318, 2319, 2320, 2321, 2322, 2323, 2324, 2325, 2326, 2340, 2341, 2342, 2344, 2348, 2349, 2350, 2353, 2355, 2356, 2357, 2358, 2359, 2360, 2374, 2376, 2377, 2379, 2383, 2390, 2395, 2397, 2405, 2406, 2408, 2414, 2426, 2427, 2443, 2446, 2457, 2458, 2462, 2469, 2470, 2471, 2472, 2483, 2484, 2486, 2511, 2513, 2516, 2519, 2520, 2521, 2522, 2523, 2524, 2533, 2534, 2540, 2541, 2542, 2543, 2544, 2545, 2546, 2548, 2551, 2552, 2557, 2565, 2595, 2600, 2602, 2603, 2604, 2608, 2609, 2613, 2614, 2619, 2621, 2622, 2625, 2641, 2642, 2643, 2647, 2649, 2650, 2652, 2653, 2654, 2656, 2658, 2662, 2663, 2669, 2670, 2671, 2674, 2675, 2676, 2680, 2690, 2691, 2692, 2697, 2698, 2699, 2700, 2702, 2703, 2704, 2705, 2713, 2714, 2718, 2721, 2723, 2727, 2728, 2729, 2730, 2731, 2732, 2733, 2738, 2739, 2741, 2742, 2743, 2745, 2747, 2748, 2752, 2754, 2755, 2756, 2759, 2760, 2761, 2763, 2764, 2765, 2767, 2770, 2771, 2772, 2773, 2775, 2779, 2780, 2781, 2782, 2783, 2784, 2785, 2786, 2788, 2793, 2795, 2797, 2798, 2799, 2802, 2803, 2805, 2807, 2809, 2814, 2834, 2851, 2855, 2858, 2859, 2860, 2861, 2868, 2869, 2875, 2877, 2882, 2886, 2890, 2891, 2898, 2899, 2901, 2905, 2907, 2910, 2911, 2923, 2925, 2927, 2930, 2944, 2945, 2972, 2973, 2975, 2976, 2977, 2978, 2982, 2983, 2990, 2991, 2992, 2993, 2994, 2995, 2997, 2998, 3000, 3004, 3009, 3010, 3011, 3012, 3013, 3014, 3016, 3017, 3018, 3032, 3036, 3038, 3042, 3045, 3057, 3060, 3062, 3063, 3087, 3088, 3089, 3090, 3091, 3117, 3124, 3125, 3126, 3127, 3128, 3130, 3131, 3132, 3133, 3137, 3138, 3140, 3145, 3151, 3162, 3165, 3166, 3169, 3171, 3178, 3179, 3180, 3185, 3186, 3187, 3188, 3189, 3190, 3191, 3198, 3199, 3205, 3206, 3207, 3208, 3209, 3210, 3211, 3214, 3215, 3216, 3229, 3244, 3245, 3246, 3250, 3259, 3269, 3273, 3275, 3283, 3284, 3288, 3289, 3290, 3291, 3292, 3293, 3309, 3312, 3314, 3315, 3321, 3322, 3323, 3339, 3340, 3347, 3349, 3351, 3353, 3354, 3360, 3361, 3362, 3363, 3365, 3367, 3370, 3371, 3372, 3373, 3374, 3375, 3376, 3377, 3378, 3379, 3380, 3381, 3435, 3437, 3440, 3442, 3443, 3445, 3446, 3457, 3458, 3459, 3467, 3487, 3488, 3489, 3490, 3491, 3492, 3493, 3494, 3497, 3503, 3511, 3531, 3533, 3534, 3535, 3536, 3537, 3538, 3539, 3540, 3556, 3561, 3566, 3567, 3568, 3582, 3585, 3587, 3588, 3597, 3598, 3599, 3600, 3606, 3607, 3609, 3623, 3624, 3675, 3676, 3690, 3705, 3708, 3719, 3720, 3730, 3741, 3744, 3748, 3750, 3751, 3767, 3768, 3785, 3786, 3787, 3788,

3789, 3790, 3791, 3792, 3793, 3794, 3795, 3796, 3797, 3798, 3802, 3803, 3804, 3806, 3810, 3811, 3812, 3813, 3815, 3816, 3817, 3819, 3821, 3823, 3824, 3840, 3841, 3842, 3843, 3851, 3870, 3874, 3889, 3890, 3891, 3892, 3893, 3894, 3895, 3896, 3899, 3911, 3912, 3913, 3914, 3915, 3916, 3946, 3960, 3961, 3962, 3966, 3967, 3968, 3969, 3970, 3971, 3974, 3976, 3977, 3978, 3979, 3986, 3988, 3994, 4000, 4007, 4008, 4009, 4010, 4011, 4012, 4013, 4014, 4015, 4016, 4017, 4020, 4022, 4025, 4026, 4027, 4028, 4029, 4030, 4031, 4032, 4033, 4034, 4035, 4036, 4038, 4039, 4040, 4041, 4042, 4043, 4063, 4064, 4066, 4067, 4068, 4072, 4073, 4082, 4084, 4085, 4087, 4093, 4095, 4100, 4101, 4102, 4106, 4107, 4108, 4109, 4110, 4112, 4113, 4115, 4116, 4117, 4118, 4119, 4120, 4121, 4122, 4123, 4172, 4173, 4176, 4177, 4178, 4183, 4188, 4189, 4190, 4193, 4194, 4195, 4196, 4197, 4249, 4262, 4266, 4269, 4270, 4272, 4273, 4274, 4275, 4276, 4277, 4286, 4287, 4288, 4289, 4294, 4295, 4296, 4297, 4298, 4299, 4300, 4301, 4302, 4303, 4305, 4307, 4308, 4309, 4310, 4311, 4312, 4313, 4314, 4315, 4317, 4319, 4320, 4325, 4326, 4327, 4329, 4336, 4337, 4338, 4339, 4341, 4344, 4350, 4352, 4358, 4361, 4363, 4364, 4366, 4367, 4368, 4369, 4370, 4371, 4373, 4375, 4376, 4397, 4415, 4416, 4417, 4418, 4419, 4420, 4428, 4431, 4432, 4434, 4456, 4495, 4496, 4498, 4509, 4513, 4516, 4517, 4518, 4519, 4520, 4521, 4559, 4562, 4563, 4568, 4569, 4572, 4577, 4580, 4604, 4605, 4606, 4620, 4646, 4654, 4656, 4657, 4658, 4659, 4678, 4680, 4682, 4685, 4695, 4698, 4699, 4702, 4704, 4705, 4707, 4709, 4715, 4728, 4744, 4745, 4748, 4750, 4751, 4753, 4757, 4762, 4783, 4788, 4799, 4800, 4801, 4802, 4803, 4804, 4806, 4808, 4816, 4818, 4822, 4823, 4829, 4830, 4842, 4844, 4845, 4846, 4850, 4851, 4852, 4856, 4858, 4866, 4868, 4883, 4887, 4891, 4892, 4893, 4909, 4930, 4937, 4938, 4939, 4942, 4955, 4970, 4980, 4981, 4985, 4986, 4987, 4989, 4990, 4991, 4992, 4995, 5010, 5023, 5026, 5028, 5029, 5030, 5031, 5032, 5033, 5034, 5038, 5039, 5040, 5041, 5042, 5043, 5044, 5045, 5046, 5050, 5065, 5075, 5076, 5077, 5078, 5079, 5087, 5090, 5091, 5092, 5093, 5099, 5102, 5105, 5109, 5110, 5113, 5150, 5151, 5161, 5162, 5167, 5168, 5169, 5170, 5171, 5174, 5175, 5176, 5189, 5194, 5224, 5225, 5226, 5227, 5228, 5231, 5232, 5234, 5235, 5236, 5241, 5244, 5246, 5248, 5256, 5258, 5260, 5262, 5263, 5264, 5265, 5280, 5283, 5299, 5301, 5307, 5311, 5330, 5333, 5334, 5335, 5336, 5337, 5338, 5339, 5340, 5341, 5342, 5343, 5344, 5345, 5346, 5347, 5348, 5354, 5358, 5365, 5369, 5374, 5378, 5396, 5404, 5415, 5416, 5422, 5427, 5428, 5432, 5433, 5434, 5435, 5463, 5466, 5469, 5471, 5474, 5477, 5480, 5485, 5492, 5494, 5498, 5505, 5506, 5509, 5529, 5531, 5532, 5533, 5534, 5535, 5562, 5579, 5583, 5584, 5585, 5591, 5592, 5599, 5600, 5601, 5602, 5603, 5604, 5607, 5623, 5624, 5663, 5664, 5665, 5666, 5669, 5670, 5672, 5673, 5674, 5675, 5676, 5677, 5679, 5680, 5683, 5684, 5685, 5687, 5688, 5689, 5692, 5693, 5694, 5695, 5696, 5697, 5698, 5699, 5700, 5701, 5702, 5703, 5723, 5727, 5728, 5729, 5754, 5756, 5757, 5758, 5767, 5769, 5774, 5778, 5793, 5810,

5815, 5821, 5831, 5839, 5841, 5842, 5843, 5844, 5845,
5848, 5874, 5892, 5900, 5930, 5931, 5932, 5933, 5934,
5942, 5945, 5946, 5948, 5950, 5952, 5955, 5958, 5963,
5964, 5965, 5966, 5971, 5973, 5983, 5984, 5985, 5987,
5988, 5989, 5990, 5991, 5996, 5997, 5999, 6004, 6013,
6021, 6022, 6023, 6024, 6032, 6037, 6055, 6058, 6060,
6062, 6064, 6067, 6069, 6071, 6073, 6074, 6075, 6076,
6078, 6079, 6080, 6082, 6083, 6086, 6087, 6111, 6112,
6113, 6114, 6115, 6118, 6120, 6121, 6126, 6138, 6139,
6140, 6141, 6142, 6145, 6147, 6148, 6149, 6152, 6162,
6163, 6164, 6165, 6166, 6177, 6178, 6179, 6183, 6195,
6197, 6204, 6228, 6235, 6236, 6237, 6238, 6248, 6261,
6276, 6278, 6280, 6281, 6294, 6295, 6297, 6298, 6299,
6300, 6312, 6313, 6314, 6321, 6323, 6324, 6325, 6326,
6327, 6328, 6329, 6330, 6331, 6332, 6334, 6336, 6338,
6347, 6348, 6349, 6350, 6372, 6381, 6382, 6383, 6384,
6385, 6388, 6392, 6397, 6400, 6403, 6404, 6416, 6417,
6418, 6419, 6420, 6421, 6422, 6423, 6456, 6457, 6458,
6459, 6460, 6461, 6462, 6463, 6464, 6465, 6466, 6467,
6468, 6469, 6470, 6471, 6472, 6473, 6474, 6475, 6476,
6477, 6478, 6479, 6480, 6481, 6486, 6489, 6492, 6493,
6496, 6504, 6506, 6520, 6521, 6522, 6523, 6554, 6561,
6562, 6563, 6564, 6566, 6638, 6639, 6642, 6643, 6644,
6645, 6646, 6647, 6648, 6649, 6650, 6651, 6652, 6653,
6654, 6655, 6656, 6657, 6659, 6660, 6661, 6662, 6663,
6665, 6666, 6667, 6668, 6669, 6670, 6671, 6672, 6674,
6675, 6676, 6678, 6679, 6680, 6681, 6682, 6683, 6685,
6686, 6687, 6688, 6689, 6691, 6692, 6693, 6694, 6695,
6696, 6697, 6706, 6707, 6714, 6729, 6730, 6731, 6732,
6733, 6734, 6735, 6736, 6737, 6755, 6756, 6761, 6762,
6763, 6767, 6768, 6769, 6770, 6771, 6772, 6773, 6774,
6775, 6776, 6777, 6791, 6794, 6796, 6797, 6799, 6800,
6802, 6811, 6812, 6813, 6814, 6815, 6816, 6817, 6823,
6824, 6825, 6826, 6827, 6838, 6890, 6891, 6911, 6912,
6913, 6943, 6952, 6953, 6954, 6955, 6958, 6959, 6963,
6964, 6967, 6968, 6971, 6972, 6973, 6974, 6975, 6977,
6980, 6981, 6982, 6986, 6987, 6988, 6989, 6990, 6991,
6992, 6993, 6999, 7000, 7003, 7005, 7006, 7007, 7012,
7013, 7014, 7018, 7021, 7023, 7024, 7025, 7026, 7028,
7029, 7030, 7033, 7034, 7039, 7040, 7045, 7047, 7048,
7049, 7050, 7051, 7056, 7059, 7060, 7062, 7063, 7068,
7069, 7072, 7111, 7112, 7113, 7114, 7115, 7116, 7124,
7125, 7127, 7129, 7154, 7155, 7156, 7157, 7165, 7168,
7169, 7170, 7171, 7172, 7173, 7174, 7175, 7176, 7177,
7178, 7179, 7180, 7181, 7182, 7185, 7186, 7188, 7189,
7190, 7191, 7192, 7193, 7194, 7195, 7196, 7197, 7198,
7199, 7200, 7201, 7202, 7268, 7359, 7362, 7373, 7377,
7378, 7381, 7382, 7383, 7384, 7387, 7388, 7391, 7393,
7394, 7397, 7398, 7399, 7400, 7401, 7419, 7436, 7438,
7439, 7440, 7442, 7443, 7444, 7445, 7453, 7486, 7488,
7493, 7494, 7495, 7496, 7497, 7501, 7502, 7503, 7504,
7506, 7507, 7519, 7521, 7523, 7526, 7529, 7532, 7534,
7535, 7538, 7543, 7545, 7575, 7577, 7598, 7600, 7601,
7621, 7622, 7679, 7682, 7684, 7698, 7797, 7804, 7808,
7809, 7819, 7820, 7821, 7822, 7823, 7824, 7825, 7827,
7828, 7829, 7830, 7832, 7833, 7835, 7839, 7846, 7847,
7852, 7853, 7859, 7861, 7862, 7863, 7868, 7874, 7875,
7876, 7877, 7878, 7915, 7924, 7940, 7941, 7942, 7944,

7945, 7946, 7947, 7948, 7949, 7955, 7956, 7957, 7958,
7959, 7960, 7976, 7983, 7990, 7991, 8001, 8002, 8025,
8032, 8062, 8063, 8064, 8066, 8069, 8070, 8071, 8073,
8099, 8100, 8102, 8105, 8125, 8134, 8135, 8138, 8139,
8147, 8163, 8168, 8169, 8174, 8178, 8186, 8191, 8192,
8217, 8218, 8219, 8220, 8221, 8222, 8223, 8224, 8225,
8226, 8227, 8228, 8229, 8230, 8231, 8232, 8234, 8236,
8237, 8238, 8242, 8244, 8245, 8267, 8268, 8269, 8270,
8271, 8272, 8273, 8274, 8276, 8277, 8278, 8300, 8301,
8302, 8303, 8310, 8311, 8312, 8313, 8314, 8316, 8353,
8355, 8357, 8358, 8359, 8360, 8361, 8362, 8363, 8364,
8365, 8366, 8367, 8368, 8369, 8386, 8466, 8478, 8480,
8483, 8484, 8485, 8486, 8489, 8492, 8493, 8518, 8528,
8531, 8536, 8537, 8540, 8541, 8542, 8546, 8566, 8585,
8592, 8594, 8603, 8621, 8622, 8623, 8624, 8625, 8645,
8646, 8647, 8648, 8649, 8650, 8651, 8652, 8653, 8654,
8655, 8656, 8657, 8658, 8659, 8660, 8675, 8699, 8700,
8701, 8702, 8704, 8710, 8713, 8716, 8717, 8718, 8719,
8722, 8729, 8741, 8744, 8745, 8746, 8747, 8748, 8749,
8767, 8778, 8797, 8798.

ENTRIES FOR TWO FEMALE VOICES
(479 TOTAL, 5.444%)

24, 25, 27, 28, 30, 32, 52, 53, 54, 55, 56, 105, 322, 353,
363, 364, 365, 367, 398, 399, 439, 467, 471, 472, 476, 537,
549, 551, 552, 555, 557, 562, 564, 574, 575, 576, 577, 578,
579, 612, 613, 615, 618, 619, 623, 624, 625, 626, 627, 705,
706, 707, 708, 709, 710, 716, 765, 940, 942, 960, 976, 985,
990, 1254, 1256, 1257, 1274, 1278, 1279, 1301, 1302,
1303, 1417, 1419, 1420, 1466, 1469, 1478, 1484, 1551,
1555, 1609, 1633, 1635, 1636, 1640, 1642, 1644, 1731,
1732, 1736, 1737, 1743, 1744, 1745, 1747, 1753, 1813,
1829, 1834, 1869, 1954, 1955, 1956, 2079, 2094, 2095,
2098, 2099, 2100, 2211, 2223, 2225, 2237, 2250, 2253,
2256, 2257, 2265, 2313, 2316, 2317, 2332, 2334, 2336,
2419, 2460, 2463, 2465, 2466, 2687, 2689, 2712, 2715,
2753, 2762, 2766, 2774, 2777, 2778, 2789, 2819, 2841,
2896, 2906, 2942, 2943, 3082, 3085, 3098, 3103, 3121,
3122, 3167, 3168, 3220, 3223, 3226, 3227, 3236, 3254,
3257, 3263, 3286, 3308, 3317, 3318, 3319, 3320, 3355,
3396, 3397, 3407, 3417, 3423, 3436, 3438, 3439, 3441,
3444, 3447, 3508, 3628, 3629, 3645, 3646, 3651, 3652,
3655, 3657, 3661, 3664, 3667, 3695, 3716, 3717, 3718,
3763, 3845, 3852, 3853, 3854, 3855, 3856, 3857, 3858,
3859, 3863, 3864, 3999, 4019, 4023, 4024, 4037, 4044,
4045, 4051, 4052, 4053, 4055, 4160, 4174, 4180, 4186,
4192, 4236, 4237, 4238, 4340, 4345, 4346, 4347, 4348,
4410, 4427, 4450, 4465, 4506, 4510, 4653, 4673, 4749,
4752, 4754, 5021, 5089, 5107, 5191, 5193, 5284, 5303,
5304, 5305, 5315, 5316, 5317, 5367, 5375, 5452, 5454,
5455, 5457, 5458, 5459, 5484, 5486, 5511, 5565, 5568,
5569, 5570, 5572, 5573, 5574, 5608, 5734, 5735, 5736,
5737, 5738, 5740, 5741, 5744, 5752, 5760, 5762, 5763,
5770, 5773, 5782, 5788, 5795, 5797, 5798, 5800, 5812,
5817, 5823, 5824, 5827, 5836, 5917, 5921, 5926, 5994,
6009, 6010, 6011, 6040, 6110, 6116, 6117, 6132, 6133,

(Two Female Voices—*Continued*)

6134, 6135, 6136, 6137, 6196, 6309, 6340, 6341, 6342, 6343, 6344, 6345, 6346, 6515, 6516, 6534, 6537, 6545, 6548, 6628, 6629, 6630, 6631, 6632, 6633, 6634, 6635, 6636, 6637, 6721, 6724, 6829, 6835, 6950, 7070, 7232, 7269, 7270, 7271, 7428, 7429, 7433, 7441, 7472, 7473, 7474, 7498, 7512, 7515, 7547, 7640, 7641, 7642, 7643, 7719, 7720, 7721, 7722, 7725, 7727, 7729, 7733, 7737, 7739, 7741, 7746, 7752, 7754, 7755, 7756, 7758, 7759, 7760, 7762, 7763, 7767, 7776, 7777, 7778, 7784, 7816, 7817, 7834, 7836, 7837, 7908, 7912, 7913, 8026, 8041, 8042, 8053, 8126, 8251, 8252, 8257, 8260, 8296, 8297, 8298, 8299, 8308, 8520, 8521, 8522, 8523, 8524, 8529, 8532, 8535, 8544, 8545, 8547, 8548, 8549, 8550, 8552, 8553, 8554, 8555, 8556, 8561, 8562, 8563, 8567, 8568, 8569, 8570, 8571, 8572, 8574, 8575, 8577, 8583, 8584, 8586, 8587, 8588, 8589, 8590, 8591, 8593, 8595, 8596, 8598, 8599, 8600, 8601, 8602, 8604, 8605, 8606, 8607, 8609, 8610, 8611, 8612, 8613, 8615, 8616, 8617, 8619, 8630, 8631, 8633, 8662, 8669, 8676, 8677, 8678.

ENTRIES FOR TWO HIGH VOICES
(67 TOTAL, 0.761%)

69, 78, 81, 122, 183, 318, 397, 918, 1496, 1523, 1825, 1833, 1947, 2057, 2068, 2069, 2074, 2294, 2437, 2530, 2645, 2672, 2684, 2693, 2971, 3135, 3136, 3149, 3532, 3579, 3580, 3584, 3586, 3594, 3595, 4147, 4149, 4505, 4655, 4834, 4860, 4872, 4888, 4890, 4897, 4905, 4924, 5052, 5053, 5056, 5059, 5061, 5502, 6401, 6946, 7036, 7099, 7272, 7370, 7379, 7448, 7450, 7470, 7471, 7606, 8031, 8056.

ENTRIES FOR TWO MEDIUM VOICES
(105 TOTAL, 1.193%)

40, 41, 353, 359, 396, 757, 1039, 1162, 1294, 1454, 1457, 1553, 1661, 1723, 1765, 1796, 1891, 1892, 1893, 1894, 1928, 2052, 2148, 2175, 2664, 2724, 2725, 2726, 2751, 2853, 2864, 2872, 2873, 2885, 2889, 2957, 3059, 3092, 3100, 3119, 3120, 3326, 3327, 3328, 3329, 3330, 3331, 3332, 3333, 3334, 3335, 3336, 3337, 3355, 3869, 4335, 4406, 4408, 4412, 4414, 4440, 4502, 4536, 4546, 4552, 4554, 4644, 4687, 4689, 4711, 4738, 4890, 5069, 5481, 5967, 5968, 6370, 6699, 6750, 6835, 6836, 7099, 7213, 7214, 7218, 7221, 7231, 7236, 7240, 7247, 7251, 7253, 7254, 7262, 7263, 7787, 7817, 8110, 8115, 8117, 8122, 8481, 8620, 8783, 8784.

ENTRIES FOR TWO LOW VOICES
(24 TOTAL, 0.273%)

2693, 2694, 3135, 3136, 3149, 3232, 3238, 3242, 3249, 3252, 3256, 3271, 3579, 4505, 6946, 7272, 7977, 7978, 7979, 7980, 8031, 8043, 8044, 8056.

ENTRIES FOR HIGH AND LOW VOICES
(141 TOTAL, 1.602%)

79, 82, 150, 327, 347, 442, 443, 622, 636, 644, 650, 685, 686, 688, 689, 729, 730, 739, 750, 751, 752, 754, 755, 775, 776, 777, 778, 779, 876, 926, 1321, 1328, 1339, 1372, 1485, 1534, 1535, 1536, 1537, 1586, 1589, 1605, 1629, 1882, 2166, 2167, 2168, 2169, 2172, 2173, 2365, 2456, 2539, 2655, 2661, 2666, 2681, 2682, 2696, 2796, 2813, 2897, 2900, 2902, 2979, 2980, 3029, 3056, 3176, 3177, 3313, 3434, 3468, 3509, 3685, 3686, 3687, 3688, 3725, 3799, 3800, 3801, 3805, 3807, 3809, 3814, 3818, 3820, 3822, 3826, 4074, 4318, 4616, 4617, 4837, 4857, 4875, 4896, 4907, 5137, 5138, 5139, 5496, 5503, 5668, 5904, 5906, 5907, 5908, 5910, 5911, 6003, 6088, 6089, 6180, 6234, 6264, 6296, 6396, 6552, 6553, 6700, 6885, 6947, 6948, 6949, 6951, 7146, 7147, 7148, 7149, 7151, 7152, 7153, 7158, 7160, 7161, 7162, 7163, 7164, 7261, 7371, 7372, 7380, 7385, 7386, 7389, 7390, 7392, 7396, 7407, 7425, 7539, 7540, 7542, 7608, 7609, 7610, 7611, 7613, 7614, 7903, 7906, 8101, 8351, 8479, 8727.

ENTRIES FOR HIGH AND MEDIUM VOICES
(49 TOTAL, 0.557%)

20, 26, 361, 548, 663, 1018, 1048, 1053, 1382, 1627, 1662, 1674, 1677, 1678, 1679, 1681, 1682, 1926, 1927, 2152, 2153, 2154, 2192, 2491, 2496, 2678, 2695, 3213, 3510, 3731, 4764, 4765, 4766, 4890, 5233, 5258, 5321, 5567, 6205, 6206, 6746, 6892, 6961, 7630, 7841, 8193, 8686, 8690, 8691.

ENTRIES FOR MEDIUM AND LOW VOICES
(12 TOTAL, 0.136%)

1571, 1572, 2153, 2154, 2155, 2660, 2695, 5244, 8106, 8107, 8108, 8109.

ENTRIES FOR VARIOUS VOICES
(38 TOTAL, 0.432%)

1, 5, 6, 10, 11, 23, 49, 66, 87, 101, 107, 108, 629, 721, 726, 740, 1101, 1499, 1813, 1834, 1869, 2428, 2492, 2637, 2918, 4069, 4086, 4703, 4812, 4828, 4835, 4839, 5581, 6957, 7004, 7010, 7032, 7058.

ENTRIES FOR CHILDREN'S VOICES
(3 TOTAL, 0.034%)

2841, 4406, 6110.

ENTRIES FOR TREBLE VOICES
(2 TOTAL, 0.023%)

695, 1829

ENTRIES INCLUDING NARRATORS
(1 TOTAL, 0.011%)

7167

ENTRIES FOR UNSPECIFIED VOICES
(4612 TOTAL, 52.415%)

4, 7, 8, 9, 13, 14, 15, 16, 18, 19, 21, 22, 31, 36, 37, 38, 39, 42, 45, 46, 47, 48, 50, 51, 57, 58, 59, 60, 61, 62, 63, 64, 65, 67, 68, 70, 71, 72, 73, 74, 75, 76, 77, 80, 83, 84, 85, 86, 88, 89, 90, 91, 94, 95, 96, 97, 99, 100, 101, 102, 103, 104, 106, 109, 110, 111, 113, 114, 115, 116, 119, 120, 121, 123, 124, 125, 127, 128, 130, 131, 132, 133, 134, 135, 137, 138, 139, 140, 143, 145, 146, 147, 148, 149, 152, 154, 155, 156, 158, 161, 163, 164, 166, 168, 169, 170, 171, 172, 173, 175, 176, 177, 179, 180, 181, 184, 185, 187, 189, 191, 192, 193, 194, 197, 198, 199, 200, 201, 203, 204, 205, 206, 207, 209, 210, 211, 213, 214, 215, 217, 218, 219, 220, 221, 222, 223, 225, 226, 227, 228, 229, 230, 231, 232, 233, 234, 235, 238, 239, 240, 243, 244, 245, 247, 248, 249, 250, 251, 252, 253, 256, 257, 261, 262, 263, 264, 265, 267, 268, 269, 270, 272, 273, 274, 275, 276, 277, 278, 281, 282, 283, 284, 285, 289, 290, 291, 292, 294, 295, 297, 299, 300, 301, 302, 304, 305, 306, 309, 310, 312, 313, 314, 317, 319, 320, 321, 323, 326, 329, 330, 331, 332, 333, 334, 335, 336, 337, 338, 339, 340, 341, 342, 343, 344, 345, 346, 348, 349, 350, 351, 352, 354, 355, 356, 357, 358, 360, 366, 368, 384, 391, 392, 393, 394, 400, 402, 403, 404, 405, 406, 407, 408, 409, 410, 411, 412, 413, 414, 415, 417, 432, 434, 435, 437, 440, 441, 446, 447, 448, 449, 451, 452, 455, 457, 458, 459, 460, 462, 463, 465, 468, 470, 474, 480, 481, 482, 484, 485, 489, 491, 496, 497, 498, 499, 500, 501, 502, 503, 504, 505, 508, 509, 512, 515, 516, 517, 520, 522, 524, 525, 526, 530, 532, 535, 538, 539, 541, 547, 556, 563, 565, 566, 567, 568, 569, 570, 571, 572, 580, 581, 582, 583, 584, 585, 586, 587, 588, 594, 595, 596, 597, 600, 601, 603, 604, 609, 610, 611, 614, 616, 617, 621, 630, 633, 635, 637, 638, 639, 640, 642, 645, 646, 648, 649, 651, 652, 653, 654, 657, 682, 683, 684, 691, 692, 693, 694, 696, 697, 698, 699, 701, 702, 703, 704, 712, 713, 714, 715, 722, 723, 725, 741, 742, 746, 747, 748, 749, 753, 756, 758, 759, 760, 761, 762, 763, 764, 766, 767, 768, 774, 782, 783, 784, 785, 786, 787, 788, 789, 790, 791, 792, 793, 794, 795, 796, 797, 798, 799, 800, 803, 805, 806, 807, 808, 812, 813, 814, 815, 816, 817, 818, 819, 820, 821, 822, 823, 824, 825, 826, 827, 828, 830, 831, 834, 835, 836, 837, 838, 839, 840, 841, 842, 843, 844, 845, 846, 847, 848, 849, 851, 852, 853, 854, 855, 856, 858, 860, 874, 875, 885, 886, 887, 892, 894, 896, 897, 898, 899, 900, 901, 902, 903, 904, 905, 910, 911, 912, 913, 914, 915, 916, 917, 920, 921, 922, 927, 930, 931, 934, 951, 952, 953, 954, 957, 968, 969, 970, 972, 973, 974, 975, 977, 978, 979, 980, 982, 983, 992, 993, 994, 997, 998, 999,

(Unspecified—*Continued*)

1000, 1001, 1002, 1003, 1005, 1006, 1007, 1008, 1009, 1010, 1011, 1012, 1013, 1014, 1015, 1019, 1023, 1024, 1025, 1026, 1027, 1029, 1030, 1031, 1032, 1033, 1034, 1035, 1036, 1037, 1038, 1040, 1041, 1042, 1046, 1047, 1049, 1050, 1054, 1057, 1058, 1062, 1066, 1069, 1072, 1077, 1078, 1080, 1088, 1089, 1091, 1092, 1093, 1096, 1097, 1098, 1099, 1100, 1102, 1105, 1107, 1111, 1115, 1130, 1132, 1133, 1134, 1135, 1156, 1157, 1158, 1159, 1160, 1161, 1163, 1164, 1165, 1166, 1176, 1177, 1181, 1182, 1189, 1193, 1198, 1199, 1212, 1213, 1214, 1215, 1216, 1217, 1218, 1219, 1220, 1221, 1222, 1223, 1239, 1241, 1244, 1246, 1247, 1248, 1249, 1250, 1251, 1252, 1275, 1284, 1285, 1286, 1287, 1288, 1289, 1290, 1295, 1296, 1297, 1299, 1304, 1305, 1306, 1307, 1308, 1309, 1310, 1315, 1318, 1324, 1327, 1333, 1343, 1345, 1349, 1350, 1351, 1352, 1354, 1355, 1356, 1366, 1367, 1368, 1369, 1370, 1371, 1379, 1383, 1385, 1386, 1388, 1389, 1393, 1395, 1399, 1402, 1403, 1404, 1406, 1408, 1409, 1410, 1411, 1412, 1413, 1414, 1415, 1416, 1418, 1421, 1422, 1424, 1425, 1427, 1428, 1429, 1430, 1431, 1432, 1433, 1443, 1444, 1445, 1446, 1447, 1451, 1453, 1455, 1456, 1458, 1459, 1463, 1468, 1470, 1476, 1480, 1482, 1492, 1493, 1494, 1497, 1500, 1501, 1508, 1519, 1520, 1527, 1531, 1533, 1538, 1539, 1541, 1544, 1545, 1549, 1552, 1554, 1556, 1557, 1558, 1562, 1563, 1564, 1565, 1567, 1569, 1573, 1574, 1575, 1581, 1582, 1590, 1591, 1592, 1601, 1602, 1603, 1606, 1607, 1612, 1613, 1614, 1615, 1616, 1617, 1618, 1620, 1621, 1622, 1624, 1625, 1626, 1627, 1628, 1643, 1645, 1646, 1648, 1649, 1650, 1655, 1656, 1657, 1658, 1659, 1660, 1663, 1665, 1666, 2267, 2268, 2269, 2270, 2271, 2272, 2273, 2274, 2275, 2276, 2277, 2278, 2279, 2281, 2282, 2283, 2284, 2285, 2286, 2287, 2288, 2289, 2290, 2291, 2292, 2293, 2302, 2306, 2307, 2308, 2309, 2310, 2311, 2312, 2314, 2315, 2331, 2333, 2335, 2343, 2345, 2346, 2347, 2351, 2352, 2354, 2361, 2362, 2363, 2364, 2366, 2368, 2369, 2370, 2371, 2372, 2373, 2381, 2382, 2384, 2385, 2386, 2387, 2389, 2411, 2415, 2420, 2422, 2423, 2424, 2429, 2430, 2431, 2432, 2433, 2434, 2435, 2436, 2438, 2439, 2440, 2441, 2442, 2445, 2447, 2449, 2450, 2451, 2452, 2453, 2455, 2459, 2461, 2467, 2468, 2473, 2474, 2475, 2476, 2481, 2482, 2485, 2487, 2488, 2489, 2490, 2493, 2494, 2495, 2498, 2499, 2500, 2501, 2502, 2503, 2504, 2505, 2506, 2507, 2508, 2509, 2510, 2514, 2515, 2517, 2518, 2525, 2526, 2527, 2528, 2529, 2531, 2532, 2535, 2536, 2537, 2538, 2547, 2550, 2555, 2556, 2558, 2559, 2560, 2561, 2562, 2563, 2564, 2566, 2567, 2568, 2569, 2570, 2571, 2572, 2573, 2574, 2575, 2576, 2577, 2578, 2579, 2580, 2581, 2582, 2583, 2584, 2585, 2586, 2587, 2588, 2589, 2590, 2591, 2592, 2593, 2594, 2596, 2597, 2599, 2605, 2606, 2610, 2611, 2612, 2617, 2618, 2627, 2629, 2636, 2638, 2639, 2640, 2651, 2659, 2667, 2668, 2673, 2677, 2686, 2688, 2706, 2707, 2708, 2709, 2717, 2720, 2722, 2734, 2735, 2736, 2737, 2740, 2744, 2746, 2749, 2750, 2757, 2758, 2776, 2787, 2790, 2791, 2792, 2794, 2801, 2804, 2806, 2808, 2810, 2811, 2812, 2815, 2816, 2817, 2818, 2820, 2821, 2822, 2823, 2824, 2825, 2826, 2827, 2828, 2829, 2830, 2831, 2832, 2833, 2835, 2836,

2837, 2838, 2839, 2840, 2842, 2843, 2844, 2845, 2846,
2848, 2849, 2850, 2852, 2854, 2862, 2863, 2865, 2866,
2867, 2874, 2876, 2878, 2879, 2880, 2881, 2883, 2884,
2892, 2893, 2894, 2895, 2903, 2904, 2908, 2909, 2912,
2913, 2914, 2915, 2916, 2917, 2919, 2920, 2921, 2922,
2928, 2929, 2931, 2932, 2934, 2935, 2936, 2937, 2938,
2939, 2940, 2941, 2946, 2947, 2948, 2949, 2950, 2951,
2952, 2953, 2954, 2955, 2956, 2958, 2959, 2960, 2961,
2962, 2963, 2964, 2965, 2966, 2967, 2968, 2969, 2970,
2974, 2984, 2985, 2986, 2987, 2988, 2989, 2996, 2999,
3001, 3002, 3003, 3005, 3006, 3007, 3008, 3015, 3019,
3020, 3021, 3022, 3023, 3024, 3025, 3026, 3027, 3028,
3030, 3031, 3033, 3034, 3035, 3037, 3039, 3040, 3041,
3043, 3044, 3046, 3047, 3048, 3049, 3050, 3051, 3052,
3053, 3054, 3055, 3058, 3061, 3064, 3065, 3066, 3067,
3068, 3069, 3070, 3071, 3072, 3073, 3074, 3075, 3076,
3077, 3078, 3079, 3083, 3084, 3086, 3093, 3095, 3096,
3099, 3101, 3102, 3104, 3105, 3106, 3107, 3108, 3109,
3110, 3111, 3112, 3113, 3114, 3115, 3116, 3118, 3123,
3129, 3142, 3143, 3146, 3148, 3153, 3154, 3156, 3157,
3159, 3160, 3163, 3164, 3181, 3182, 3183, 3184, 3192,
3193, 3194, 3195, 3196, 3197, 3200, 3201, 3202, 3203,
3204, 3212, 3217, 3218, 3219, 3221, 3222, 3224, 3225,
3228, 3230, 3231, 3233, 3234, 3235, 3237, 3239, 3240,
3241, 3243, 3247, 3248, 3251, 3253, 3255, 3258, 3260,
3261, 3262, 3264, 3265, 3266, 3267, 3268, 3270, 3272,
3274, 3277, 3278, 3279, 3280, 3281, 3282, 3285, 3287,
3294, 3295, 3296, 3297, 3298, 3299, 3300, 3301, 3302,
3303, 3304, 3305, 3306, 3307, 3310, 3311, 3316, 3324,
3338, 3341, 3343, 3344, 3345, 3346, 3348, 3350, 3352,
3356, 3358, 3359, 3364, 3366, 3368, 3369, 3384, 3386,
3387, 3388, 3389, 3390, 3391, 3392, 3393, 3394, 3395,
3398, 3399, 3400, 3401, 3402, 3403, 3404, 3405, 3406,
3408, 3409, 3410, 3412, 3413, 3414, 3415, 3416, 3418,
3419, 3420, 3421, 3422, 3424, 3425, 3426, 3427, 3428,
3429, 3430, 3431, 3433, 3448, 3449, 3450, 3451, 3452,
3454, 3455, 3456, 3460, 3461, 3462, 3463, 3464, 3465,
3470, 3471, 3472, 3473, 3474, 3475, 3476, 3477, 3478,
3479, 3480, 3481, 3482, 3483, 3484, 3485, 3486, 3495,
3496, 3498, 3499, 3500, 3501, 3502, 3504, 3505, 3506,
3507, 3512, 3513, 3514, 3515, 3516, 3517, 3518, 3519,
3520, 3521, 3522, 3523, 3524, 3525, 3526, 3527, 3528,
3529, 3530, 3542, 3543, 3544, 3545, 3550, 3551, 3552,
3553, 3554, 3555, 3557, 3558, 3560, 3562, 3564, 3565,
3569, 3570, 3571, 3572, 3573, 3574, 3575, 3576, 3577,
3578, 3581, 3583, 3589, 3590, 3591, 3592, 3593, 3596,
3601, 3602, 3603, 3605, 3611, 3612, 3613, 3614, 3615,
3616, 3617, 3618, 3619, 3620, 3621, 3622, 3625, 3626,
3627, 3630, 3631, 3632, 3634, 3635, 3636, 3637, 3638,
3639, 3640, 3641, 3642, 3643, 3644, 3647, 3648, 3649,
3650, 3653, 3654, 3656, 3658, 3659, 3660, 3662, 3663,
3665, 3666, 3668, 3669, 3671, 3672, 3673, 3674, 3677,
3678, 3679, 3680, 3681, 3682, 3683, 3684, 3689, 3691,
3692, 3693, 3694, 3696, 3698, 3703, 3704, 3706, 3707,
3709, 3710, 3711, 3712, 3713, 3714, 3715, 3721, 3722,
3723, 3724, 3726, 3727, 3728, 3729, 3733, 3740, 3745,
3746, 3747, 3749, 3752, 3753, 3754, 3755, 3756, 3757,
3758, 3759, 3760, 3761, 3764, 3765, 3773, 3774, 3775,

3776, 3777, 3778, 3779, 3780, 3781, 3782, 3783, 3784,
3808, 3825, 3827, 3828, 3829, 3830, 3831, 3832, 3833,
3834, 3835, 3836, 3837, 3838, 3839, 3844, 3846, 3847,
3848, 3849, 3850, 3860, 3861, 3862, 3865, 3866, 3867,
3868, 3872, 3873, 3876, 3877, 3878, 3879, 3880, 3881,
3882, 3883, 3884, 3885, 3886, 3887, 3888, 3897, 3898,
3900, 3901, 3902, 3903, 3904, 3905, 3906, 3907, 3908,
3909, 3910, 3917, 3918, 3919, 3920, 3921, 3922, 3923,
3924, 3925, 3926, 3927, 3928, 3929, 3930, 3931, 3932,
3933, 3934, 3935, 3936, 3937, 3938, 3939, 3940, 3941,
3942, 3943, 3944, 3945, 3947, 3948, 3949, 3950, 3951,
3952, 3953, 3954, 3955, 3956, 3957, 3958, 3959, 3963,
3964, 3965, 3972, 3973, 3975, 3980, 3983, 3984, 3985,
3987, 3997, 3998, 4018, 4021, 4046, 4047, 4048, 4049,
4050, 4054, 4056, 4057, 4058, 4059, 4060, 4061, 4071,
4075, 4076, 4077, 4080, 4083, 4088, 4090, 4091, 4093,
4094, 4098, 4099, 4103, 4104, 4105, 4111, 4114, 4124,
4125, 4126, 4127, 4128, 4129, 4130, 4131, 4132, 4133,
4134, 4136, 4137, 4138, 4139, 4140, 4141, 4142, 4143,
4144, 4145, 4146, 4148, 4150, 4151, 4152, 4153, 4154,
4163, 4164, 4165, 4166, 4167, 4168, 4169, 4170, 4203,
4212, 4213, 4214, 4215, 4216, 4217, 4218, 4219, 4220,
4221, 4222, 4223, 4224, 4225, 4226, 4227, 4228, 4229,
4230, 4231, 4232, 4233, 4234, 4235, 4239, 4240, 4241,
4242, 4243, 4244, 4245, 4246, 4247, 4248, 4251, 4252,
4253, 4254, 4255, 4256, 4257, 4258, 4259, 4260, 4261,
4263, 4264, 4265, 4267, 4268, 4271, 4278, 4279, 4280,
4281, 4282, 4290, 4291, 4292, 4293, 4304, 4306, 4316,
4321, 4322, 4323, 4324, 4328, 4332, 4333, 4334, 4342,
4343, 4349, 4351, 4353, 4354, 4355, 4356, 4357, 4359,
4360, 4362, 4365, 4372, 4374, 4377, 4378, 4379, 4380,
4381, 4382, 4383, 4384, 4385, 4386, 4387, 4388, 4389,
4390, 4391, 4392, 4393, 4394, 4395, 4396, 4398, 4399,
4400, 4401, 4402, 4403, 4404, 4405, 4407, 4409, 4411,
4413, 4421, 4422, 4423, 4424, 4429, 4430, 4435, 4437,
4441, 4442, 4443, 4444, 4445, 4446, 4447, 4448, 4449,
4451, 4452, 4453, 4454, 4455, 4457, 4458, 4459, 4460,
4461, 4462, 4463, 4464, 4466, 4467, 4468, 4469, 4470,
4471, 4472, 4473, 4474, 4475, 4477, 4478, 4480, 4481,
4482, 4483, 4484, 4485, 4486, 4487, 4488, 4489, 4490,
4491, 4492, 4493, 4494, 4497, 4500, 4503, 4504, 4522,
4523, 4524, 4525, 4526, 4527, 4528, 4529, 4530, 4531,
4532, 4533, 4534, 4535, 4537, 4538, 4539, 4540, 4541,
4542, 4543, 4544, 4545, 4547, 4548, 4549, 4550, 4551,
4553, 4555, 4556, 4557, 4558, 4564, 4570, 4571, 4573,
4574, 4575, 4576, 4581, 4582, 4584, 4585, 4586, 4587,
4588, 4589, 4590, 4591, 4592, 4593, 4594, 4595, 4596,
4597, 4598, 4599, 4600, 4601, 4602, 4607, 4608, 4609,
4610, 4611, 4612, 4613, 4614, 4615, 4618, 4619, 4621,
4626, 4627, 4628, 4629, 4630, 4631, 4632, 4633, 4634,
4635, 4636, 4637, 4638, 4639, 4640, 4641, 4642, 4643,
4645, 4647, 4648, 4649, 4650, 4651, 4652, 4660, 4661,
4662, 4663, 4664, 4665, 4666, 4667, 4668, 4669, 4670,
4671, 4674, 4681, 4686, 4688, 4690, 4691, 4692, 4693,
4694, 4696, 4697, 4700, 4701, 4706, 4708, 4710, 4712,
4713, 4714, 4716, 4717, 4718, 4719, 4720, 4721, 4722,
4723, 4724, 4725, 4726, 4727, 4730, 4731, 4732, 4733,
4734, 4736, 4739, 4740, 4741, 4743, 4746, 4747, 4755,

(Unspecified—*Continued*)

4756, 4758, 4759, 4760, 4761, 4767, 4768, 4769, 4770,
4771, 4772, 4773, 4774, 4775, 4776, 4777, 4778, 4779,
4780, 4781, 4782, 4784, 4785, 4786, 4787, 4789, 4790,
4791, 4792, 4793, 4794, 4795, 4796, 4797, 4798, 4805,
4807, 4809, 4810, 4811, 4813, 4814, 4815, 4817, 4819,
4820, 4821, 4826, 4827, 4831, 4832, 4833, 4838, 4840,
4843, 4847, 4848, 4849, 4853, 4854, 4859, 4862, 4865,
4867, 4871, 4873, 4874, 4876, 4877, 4878, 4879, 4880,
4881, 4882, 4884, 4885, 4886, 4889, 4894, 4895, 4899,
4900, 4901, 4906, 4908, 4910, 4911, 4912, 4915, 4916,
4917, 4918, 4919, 4920, 4921, 4922, 4926, 4927, 4928,
4929, 4931, 4932, 4933, 4934, 4935, 4936, 4940, 4941,
4947, 4951, 4952, 4953, 4954, 4956, 4957, 4958, 4959,
4960, 4961, 4962, 4963, 4964, 4965, 4966, 4967, 4968,
4969, 4971, 4972, 4973, 4974, 4975, 4976, 4977, 4978,
4979, 4982, 4983, 4988, 4993, 4994, 4999, 5002, 5003,
5004, 5005, 5006, 5007, 5008, 5009, 5011, 5012, 5013,
5014, 5015, 5016, 5017, 5018, 5019, 5020, 5024, 5025,
5027, 5035, 5036, 5037, 5047, 5048, 5051, 5054, 5055,
5057, 5058, 5060, 5062, 5063, 5064, 5066, 5067, 5068,
5070, 5071, 5072, 5073, 5074, 5080, 5081, 5082, 5083,
5084, 5085, 5088, 5096, 5097, 5100, 5101, 5103, 5104,
5106, 5114, 5115, 5116, 5117, 5118, 5119, 5120, 5121,
5122, 5123, 5124, 5125, 5126, 5127, 5128, 5129, 5130,
5131, 5132, 5133, 5134, 5135, 5136, 5140, 5141, 5142,
5143, 5144, 5145, 5146, 5147, 5148, 5149, 5152, 5153,
5154, 5155, 5156, 5157, 5158, 5159, 5160, 5163, 5164,
5165, 5166, 5172, 5173, 5177, 5178, 5179, 5180, 5181,
5182, 5183, 5184, 5185, 5186, 5187, 5188, 5192, 5208,
5209, 5210, 5211, 5212, 5213, 5214, 5215, 5216, 5217,
5218, 5219, 5220, 5221, 5222, 5223, 5229, 5230, 5237,
5238, 5239, 5240, 5242, 5243, 5245, 5247, 5249, 5250,
5251, 5252, 5253, 5254, 5255, 5257, 5259, 5261, 5269,
5270, 5271, 5272, 5273, 5274, 5275, 5276, 5277, 5278,
5279, 5281, 5282, 5285, 5286, 5291, 5292, 5293, 5294,
5295, 5296, 5297, 5298, 5300, 5302, 5306, 5312, 5313,
5314, 5318, 5319, 5320, 5322, 5323, 5324, 5325, 5326,
5327, 5328, 5329, 5331, 5332, 5349, 5350, 5353, 5355,
5356, 5357, 5359, 5360, 5361, 5362, 5363, 5364, 5366,
5368, 5370, 5371, 5372, 5373, 5376, 5377, 5382, 5383,
5384, 5385, 5386, 5387, 5388, 5391, 5394, 5395, 5397,
5398, 5400, 5402, 5403, 5405, 5406, 5407, 5408, 5409,
5410, 5411, 5412, 5413, 5414, 5417, 5418, 5419, 5420,
5421, 5424, 5425, 5426, 5429, 5430, 5431, 5436, 5437,
5438, 5439, 5440, 5441, 5442, 5443, 5444, 5445, 5446,
5447, 5448, 5449, 5450, 5451, 5453, 5456, 5460, 5465,
5470, 5472, 5473, 5475, 5476, 5478, 5479, 5482, 5483,
5487, 5488, 5489, 5490, 5491, 5493, 5495, 5497, 5499,
5500, 5501, 5504, 5507, 5508, 5510, 5512, 5513, 5514,
5515, 5516, 5517, 5518, 5519, 5520, 5521, 5522, 5523,
5524, 5525, 5526, 5527, 5528, 5530, 5536, 5537, 5538,
5539, 5540, 5541, 5542, 5543, 5544, 5545, 5546, 5547,
5548, 5549, 5550, 5551, 5552, 5553, 5554, 5555, 5556,
5557, 5558, 5559, 5560, 5561, 5563, 5564, 5566, 5571,
5575, 5576, 5577, 5580, 5582, 5587, 5588, 5589, 5593,
5594, 5595, 5596, 5597, 5598, 5605, 5609, 5610, 5611,
5612, 5613, 5614, 5615, 5616, 5617, 5618, 5619, 5620,
5621, 5622, 5625, 5626, 5627, 5628, 5629, 5630, 5631,

(Unspecified—*Continued*)

5632, 5633, 5634, 5635, 5636, 5637, 5638, 5639, 5640,
5641, 5642, 5643, 5644, 5645, 5646, 5647, 5648, 5649,
5650, 5651, 5652, 5653, 5654, 5655, 5656, 5657, 5658,
5659, 5660, 5661, 5662, 5667, 5690, 5704, 5705, 5706,
5707, 5708, 5709, 5710, 5711, 5712, 5713, 5714, 5715,
5716, 5717, 5718, 5719, 5720, 5722, 5724, 5725, 5726,
5730, 5731, 5732, 5733, 5739, 5742, 5743, 5746, 5748,
5749, 5750, 5751, 5753, 5755, 5759, 5761, 5765, 5775,
5776, 5780, 5783, 5784, 5785, 5786, 5787, 5790, 5791,
5794, 5799, 5801, 5804, 5806, 5809, 5811, 5814, 5818,
5820, 5822, 5825, 5826, 5828, 5832, 5834, 5838, 5840,
5855, 5857, 5858, 5868, 5870, 5871, 5875, 5888, 5889,
5893, 5894, 5896, 5899, 5912, 5916, 5918, 5919, 5920,
5922, 5923, 5924, 5925, 5927, 5928, 5929, 5935, 5936,
5937, 5938, 5939, 5940, 5941, 5943, 5944, 5947, 5949,
5951, 5953, 5954, 5956, 5957, 5959, 5960, 5962, 5969,
5970, 5972, 5974, 5975, 5976, 5977, 5979, 5986, 5992,
5993, 5995, 5998, 6000, 6014, 6015, 6018, 6019, 6025,
6026, 6028, 6029, 6030, 6031, 6041, 6042, 6043, 6044,
6045, 6046, 6047, 6048, 6049, 6050, 6051, 6052, 6053,
6054, 6056, 6057, 6059, 6061, 6063, 6065, 6066, 6068,
6070, 6072, 6077, 6081, 6084, 6085, 6090, 6091, 6092,
6093, 6094, 6095, 6096, 6097, 6098, 6099, 6100, 6101,
6102, 6103, 6104, 6105, 6106, 6107, 6108, 6109, 6119,
6122, 6123, 6124, 6127, 6128, 6143, 6144, 6146, 6150,
6151, 6153, 6154, 6155, 6156, 6157, 6158, 6160, 6161,
6167, 6168, 6169, 6170, 6171, 6172, 6173, 6174, 6175,
6182, 6189, 6190, 6193, 6196, 6198, 6202, 6203, 6207,
6208, 6209, 6210, 6211, 6212, 6213, 6214, 6215, 6216,
6217, 6218, 6219, 6220, 6221, 6222, 6223, 6224, 6225,
6227, 6230, 6231, 6233, 6240, 6241, 6243, 6245, 6247,
6249, 6251, 6252, 6254, 6256, 6257, 6260, 6262, 6263,
6265, 6267, 6268, 6269, 6270, 6271, 6272, 6273, 6274,
6275, 6279, 6282, 6283, 6286, 6287, 6288, 6290, 6291,
6293, 6302, 6303, 6304, 6305, 6306, 6307, 6308, 6310,
6311, 6315, 6316, 6317, 6318, 6319, 6333, 6337, 6339,
6371, 6376, 6377, 6378, 6379, 6386, 6387, 6389, 6390,
6391, 6393, 6394, 6399, 6407, 6408, 6409, 6410, 6412,
6413, 6414, 6415, 6424, 6425, 6426, 6427, 6428, 6429,
6430, 6431, 6432, 6433, 6434, 6435, 6436, 6437, 6438,
6439, 6440, 6441, 6442, 6443, 6445, 6447, 6451, 6453,
6454, 6455, 6482, 6483, 6484, 6485, 6487, 6488, 6490,
6491, 6494, 6495, 6497, 6498, 6499, 6500, 6501, 6502,
6503, 6505, 6507, 6508, 6509, 6510, 6511, 6514, 6517,
6518, 6524, 6525, 6526, 6527, 6528, 6529, 6530, 6531,
6532, 6533, 6535, 6536, 6538, 6541, 6542, 6543, 6544,
6546, 6547, 6549, 6550, 6551, 6555, 6556, 6557, 6558,
6559, 6560, 6565, 6567, 6568, 6569, 6570, 6571, 6572,
6573, 6574, 6575, 6576, 6577, 6578, 6579, 6580, 6581,
6582, 6583, 6584, 6585, 6586, 6587, 6588, 6589, 6590,
6591, 6592, 6593, 6594, 6595, 6596, 6597, 6598, 6599,
6600, 6601, 6602, 6603, 6604, 6605, 6606, 6607, 6608,
6609, 6610, 6611, 6613, 6614, 6615, 6616, 6617, 6619,
6620, 6621, 6622, 6623, 6624, 6625, 6626, 6627, 6640,
6641, 6698, 6704, 6705, 6708, 6709, 6710, 6711, 6712,
6713, 6715, 6722, 6723, 6725, 6726, 6727, 6728, 6738,
6739, 6740, 6741, 6742, 6743, 6744, 6745, 6747, 6748,
6749, 6751, 6752, 6753, 6754, 6757, 6758, 6759, 6760,

6764, 6765, 6766, 6778, 6779, 6780, 6781, 6782, 6783,
6784, 6785, 6786, 6787, 6788, 6789, 6790, 6792, 6793,
6795, 6798, 6801, 6803, 6804, 6805, 6806, 6807, 6808,
6809, 6810, 6818, 6819, 6820, 6821, 6822, 6828, 6839,
6840, 6842, 6843, 6844, 6845, 6846, 6847, 6848, 6849,
6850, 6851, 6852, 6853, 6854, 6855, 6856, 6857, 6858,
6859, 6860, 6861, 6862, 6863, 6864, 6865, 6866, 6867,
6868, 6869, 6870, 6871, 6872, 6873, 6874, 6875, 6876,
6877, 6878, 6879, 6880, 6881, 6882, 6883, 6884, 6886,
6888, 6889, 6893, 6894, 6895, 6896, 6897, 6898, 6899,
6900, 6901, 6902, 6903, 6904, 6905, 6906, 6907, 6915,
6916, 6919, 6920, 6921, 6923, 6924, 6926, 6927, 6928,
6929, 6930, 6931, 6932, 6933, 6937, 6939, 6940, 6941,
6942, 6944, 6945, 6960, 6965, 6969, 6970, 6994, 6996,
7009, 7015, 7016, 7017, 7019, 7027, 7031, 7035, 7037,
7038, 7041, 7042, 7043, 7044, 7046, 7052, 7053, 7054,
7055, 7057, 7061, 7064, 7065, 7066, 7067, 7071, 7073,
7074, 7075, 7076, 7077, 7078, 7079, 7080, 7081, 7082,
7083, 7084, 7085, 7086, 7087, 7088, 7089, 7090, 7091,
7092, 7093, 7094, 7095, 7096, 7097, 7098, 7100, 7101,
7102, 7103, 7104, 7105, 7106, 7107, 7108, 7109, 7110,
7117, 7118, 7119, 7120, 7121, 7122, 7123, 7126, 7128,
7130, 7131, 7132, 7133, 7136, 7137, 7138, 7139, 7140,
7141, 7142, 7143, 7144, 7166, 7167, 7183, 7184, 7187,
7203, 7204, 7205, 7206, 7207, 7208, 7209, 7210, 7211,
7212, 7215, 7216, 7217, 7219, 7222, 7224, 7225, 7226,
7227, 7228, 7229, 7230, 7233, 7234, 7235, 7237, 7239,
7241, 7242, 7243, 7244, 7245, 7248, 7249, 7250, 7252,
7255, 7256, 7257, 7258, 7259, 7260, 7264, 7265, 7266,
7273, 7274, 7275, 7276, 7277, 7278, 7279, 7280, 7281,
7282, 7283, 7284, 7285, 7286, 7287, 7288, 7289, 7290,
7291, 7292, 7293, 7294, 7295, 7296, 7297, 7298, 7299,
7300, 7301, 7302, 7303, 7304, 7305, 7306, 7307, 7308,
7309, 7310, 7311, 7312, 7313, 7314, 7315, 7316, 7317,
7318, 7319, 7320, 7321, 7322, 7323, 7324, 7325, 7326,
7327, 7328, 7329, 7330, 7331, 7332, 7333, 7334, 7335,
7336, 7337, 7338, 7339, 7340, 7341, 7342, 7343, 7344,
7345, 7346, 7347, 7348, 7349, 7350, 7351, 7352, 7353,
7354, 7355, 7356, 7357, 7358, 7360, 7361, 7363, 7364,
7365, 7366, 7367, 7368, 7369, 7374, 7375, 7376, 7395,
7402, 7403, 7404, 7405, 7406, 7408, 7410, 7411, 7414,
7417, 7418, 7420, 7422, 7423, 7424, 7426, 7427, 7430,
7431, 7432, 7434, 7435, 7437, 7452, 7457, 7458, 7459,
7460, 7461, 7462, 7463, 7464, 7465, 7466, 7467, 7468,
7469, 7475, 7476, 7477, 7478, 7479, 7480, 7481, 7482,
7489, 7491, 7492, 7499, 7500, 7508, 7509, 7510, 7511,
7513, 7514, 7516, 7517, 7518, 7520, 7522, 7524, 7525,
7527, 7528, 7530, 7531, 7533, 7536, 7537, 7541, 7546,
7548, 7549, 7550, 7551, 7552, 7553, 7554, 7555, 7556,
7557, 7558, 7559, 7560, 7561, 7562, 7563, 7564, 7565,
7566, 7567, 7568, 7569, 7570, 7571, 7572, 7574, 7576,
7580, 7582, 7583, 7584, 7585, 7586, 7587, 7588, 7589,
7590, 7591, 7592, 7593, 7594, 7595, 7596, 7597, 7602,
7603, 7604, 7605, 7607, 7615, 7617, 7620, 7625, 7626,
7627, 7628, 7629, 7631, 7632, 7633, 7634, 7635, 7638,
7639, 7645, 7646, 7649, 7651, 7654, 7655, 7657, 7658,
7660, 7663, 7665, 7666, 7667, 7668, 7669, 7670, 7671,
7674, 7675, 7676, 7677, 7678, 7680, 7681, 7683, 7685,

7686, 7699, 7723, 7724, 7726, 7728, 7730, 7731, 7732,
7734, 7735, 7736, 7738, 7740, 7742, 7743, 7744, 7745,
7747, 7748, 7749, 7750, 7751, 7753, 7757, 7761, 7764,
7765, 7766, 7768, 7769, 7770, 7771, 7772, 7773, 7774,
7775, 7779, 7780, 7781, 7782, 7783, 7785, 7786, 7788,
7789, 7791, 7792, 7793, 7794, 7795, 7798, 7800, 7801,
7802, 7803, 7805, 7806, 7807, 7810, 7811, 7814, 7818,
7826, 7831, 7838, 7840, 7843, 7845, 7848, 7849, 7850,
7851, 7854, 7855, 7856, 7857, 7858, 7860, 7864, 7865,
7866, 7867, 7869, 7870, 7871, 7872, 7873, 7879, 7880,
7881, 7882, 7883, 7884, 7886, 7888, 7890, 7891, 7892,
7893, 7894, 7895, 7897, 7898, 7899, 7900, 7901, 7902,
7904, 7905, 7907, 7909, 7910, 7911, 7914, 7916, 7917,
7918, 7919, 7920, 7921, 7922, 7923, 7925, 7926, 7927,
7929, 7930, 7931, 7934, 7935, 7936, 7937, 7938, 7943,
7950, 7951, 7952, 7953, 7954, 7961, 7962, 7963, 7964,
7965, 7966, 7967, 7968, 7969, 7970, 7971, 7972, 7973,
7974, 7975, 7981, 7982, 7985, 7986, 7988, 7992, 7993,
7994, 7995, 7996, 7997, 7998, 7999, 8000, 8003, 8004,
8005, 8006, 8007, 8008, 8009, 8010, 8011, 8012, 8013,
8014, 8015, 8016, 8017, 8018, 8019, 8020, 8021, 8022,
8024, 8027, 8028, 8029, 8030, 8033, 8034, 8035, 8036,
8037, 8038, 8039, 8040, 8045, 8046, 8047, 8048, 8049,
8050, 8051, 8052, 8054, 8055, 8058, 8060, 8061, 8065,
8067, 8068, 8072, 8074, 8075, 8076, 8077, 8078, 8079,
8080, 8081, 8082, 8083, 8084, 8085, 8086, 8087, 8088,
8089, 8090, 8091, 8092, 8093, 8094, 8095, 8096, 8097,
8098, 8104, 8111, 8112, 8113, 8114, 8116, 8118, 8119,
8120, 8121, 8123, 8124, 8127, 8128, 8129, 8130, 8131,
8132, 8133, 8143, 8151, 8152, 8153, 8154, 8155, 8156,
8157, 8158, 8159, 8160, 8161, 8162, 8164, 8165, 8166,
8167, 8170, 8171, 8172, 8173, 8175, 8176, 8177, 8194,
8195, 8196, 8198, 8199, 8200, 8201, 8202, 8203, 8204,
8205, 8206, 8207, 8208, 8209, 8210, 8211, 8212, 8213,
8214, 8215, 8216, 8233, 8235, 8239, 8240, 8241, 8243,
8246, 8247, 8248, 8249, 8250, 8253, 8254, 8255, 8256,
8258, 8259, 8261, 8262, 8263, 8264, 8266, 8280, 8281,
8282, 8283, 8284, 8285, 8286, 8287, 8288, 8289, 8290,
8291, 8292, 8293, 8294, 8295, 8304, 8305, 8306, 8307,
8309, 8315, 8317, 8318, 8319, 8320, 8321, 8322, 8323,
8324, 8325, 8326, 8327, 8328, 8329, 8330, 8331, 8332,
8333, 8334, 8335, 8336, 8337, 8338, 8339, 8340, 8341,
8342, 8343, 8344, 8345, 8346, 8347, 8348, 8349, 8350,
8352, 8354, 8356, 8370, 8371, 8372, 8373, 8374, 8375,
8376, 8377, 8378, 8379, 8380, 8381, 8382, 8383, 8384,
8385, 8394, 8395, 8396, 8397, 8398, 8399, 8400, 8401,
8402, 8403, 8404, 8405, 8406, 8407, 8408, 8409, 8410,
8411, 8412, 8413, 8414, 8415, 8416, 8417, 8418, 8419,
8420, 8421, 8422, 8423, 8424, 8425, 8426, 8427, 8428,
8429, 8430, 8431, 8432, 8433, 8434, 8435, 8436, 8437,
8438, 8439, 8440, 8441, 8442, 8443, 8444, 8445, 8446,
8447, 8448, 8449, 8450, 8451, 8452, 8453, 8454, 8455,
8456, 8457, 8458, 8459, 8460, 8461, 8462, 8463, 8464,
8465, 8467, 8468, 8469, 8470, 8471, 8472, 8473, 8474,
8475, 8482, 8487, 8488, 8490, 8491, 8494, 8495, 8496,
8497, 8498, 8499, 8500, 8501, 8502, 8503, 8504, 8505,
8506, 8507, 8508, 8509, 8510, 8511, 8512, 8513, 8514,
8515, 8516, 8517, 8519, 8525, 8526, 8527, 8530, 8533,

8534, 8538, 8539, 8543, 8551, 8557, 8558, 8559, 8560,
8564, 8565, 8573, 8576, 8578, 8579, 8580, 8581, 8582,
8597, 8608, 8614, 8618, 8626, 8627, 8628, 8629, 8632,
8635, 8636, 8637, 8638, 8639, 8640, 8661, 8663, 8664,
8665, 8666, 8667, 8668, 8670, 8671, 8672, 8673, 8679,
8680, 8681, 8682, 8683, 8684, 8685, 8687, 8688, 8689,
8692, 8693, 8694, 8695, 8697, 8698, 8703, 8705, 8707,

8708, 8712, 8714, 8720, 8721, 8730, 8731, 8732, 8733,
8734, 8735, 8736, 8737, 8738, 8739, 8740, 8742, 8743,
8750, 8751, 8753, 8754, 8755, 8756, 8757, 8758, 8759,
8760, 8761, 8762, 8763, 8764, 8765, 8766, 8768, 8769,
8770, 8771, 8772, 8773, 8774, 8775, 8776, 8777, 8779,
8780, 8781, 8782, 8786, 8791, 8793, 8794, 8799.

Appendix D: List of Composers by Published Language (Total Number of Languages Represented: 23)

Czech Language Composers (10 total)

Bendl, Karel
Bergmann, Josef
Butté, E. M.
Dvorák, Antonín
Gregor, Cestmir
Jirasek, Ivo
Martinu, Bohuslav
Pivoda, F.
Procházka, J.
Risinger, Karel

Danish Language Composers (2 total)

Hemberg, Eskil
Schierbeck, Poul

Dutch Language Composers (9 total)

Andriessen, Juriaan
Bijvanck, Henk
Bosmans, Henriette
Colaco Osorio-Swaab, Reine
Dijk, Jan van
Hullebroeck, Emiel
Ramshorst, J. D. von
Schouwman, Hans
Tussenbroek, Hendrika von

English Language Composers (371 total)

Abbott, Jane
Abt, Franz
Ahnfelt, Oscar
Alexandrov, Anatol
Allitsen, Frances
Anderson, Beth
Anderson, Margaret Tweedie

(English—*Continued*)

Andrews, Mark
Androzzo, A. Bazel
Ascher
Ascher, Joseph
Ashford, E. L.
Ayre, Nat D.
Babbitt, Milton
Bailey
Baker, Richard
Balfe, Michael William
Ball, Ernest
Bantock, Granville
Barnby, J.
Bartlett, Homer Newton
Bateman, Ronald
Batten, Mrs. George
Beach, Amy
Beeson, Jack
Beethoven, Ludwig van
Bender, Jan
Benedict, Jules
Bennet, William Sterndale
Benoy, A. W.
Berger, Jean
Besly, Maurice
Bishop, Henry Rowley
Blake
Blaufuss, Walter
Blockley, John
Blower, Maurice
Blumenthal, Jacob [Jacques]
Bohm
Boito, Arrigo
Bond, Carrie Jacobs
Bonheur, Theodore
Bouman, Paul
Bracken, Edith A.
Braham, John
Brahe, Mary Hannah
Bartlett, J. C.
Bassford, Wiliiam Kipp
Brahms, Johannes
Briggs
Britten, Benjamin
Broadwood, Lucy E.

(English—*Continued*)

Broadwood, Lucy E.
  & J. A. Fuller Maitland
Browne
Cage, John
Campana, Fabio
Caracciolo, Luigi
Carey, Harry
Carse, Roland
Carter, John
Caryll, Ivan
Cassler, G. Winton
Charles, Ernest
Chisholm, M. A.
Chopin, Frédéric
Clarke, Emile
Clifton, Harry
Coates, Eric
Coerne, Louis Adolphe
Coleridge-Taylor, Samuel
Comes
Concone, Giuseppi
Coombs, C. Whitney
Corliss
Cornelius, Peter
Courtney, Craig
Cowen, Frederic Hymen
Crampton, Ernest
Crosse, Gordon
Cuvillier, Charles
Dagland, Abbé J.
Daly
Dargomizshky, Alexander
Day, Maude Craske
DeKoven, Reginald
Densmore, John H.
Denza, Luigi
Deppen, Jessie L.
Diack, J. Michael
Dickinson, Clarence
Dickson, Stanley
Dinsmore
Dix, J. Arlie
Dolan
Dolmetsch, Arnold
Dorel, F.

Dougherty, Celius
Doun, Elza
Dunayevsky, Isaak
Dunhill, Thomas Frederick
Dunlap, Fern Glasgow
Dupré, Claude
Dvořák, Antonín
Dyson, George
Dzerzhinsky, Ivan
Edmunds, John
Edwards, Clara
Edwards, George
Ehret, Walter
Elgar, Edward
Fairfield
Fearis, John Sylvester
Ferber, R.
Fiori, Ettore
Fisher, Howard
Fiske, Roger
Forman, Edmund
Forsyth, Josephine
Foster, Myles Birket
Foster, Stephen Collins
Fraser
Friml, Rudolf
Gabriel, Mary Ann Virginia
Gabussi, C. M.
Gabussi, Vincent
Gade, Niels Wilhelm
Gallaty, James M.
Gaston-Murray, Blanche
Gatty, Alfred Scott
Gaul, Alfred Robert
Geehl, Henry Ernest
Geibel
Gifford, Alexander M.
Gilber
Glinka, Mikhail Ivanovich
Glover, Charles W.
Glover, Stephen
Goatley, Alma
Godard, Benjamin
Goetze, Karl [Götze]
Goldberg, William
Gooch
Goodhart, Arthur Murray
Gordigiani, Luigi
Gordon, Stanley [pen name of
    A. W. Rawlings]
Gounod, Charles
Graben-Hoffmann, Gustav
Graham, Robert
Granier, Jules
Greenhill, Harold
Grell, Eduard August
Gumbert
Hackel, Anton
Hamblen, Bernard
Ham, Charles
Hammond, William G.
Hanscom, E. W.
Hanus, Jan
Harker, F. Flaxington

Hart, M. A.
Hatton, John L.
Hawley, Charles B.
Hawthorne, Alice [pen name of
    Septimus Winner]
Hazlehurst, Cecil
Hely-Hutchinson, Victor
Hemery, Valentine
Henschel, George
Herbert, Victor
Hermann, W.
Heussenstamm, George
Hill, Lady Arthur
Hodge, Talbot
Hoiby, Lee
Holman, Derek
Holst, Gustav
Hope, H. Ashworth
Horn, Charles Edward
Hughes
Hughes, Herbert
Huhn, Bruno
Hullah, John
Hume, Alexander
Hutchinson, William Marshall
Ireland, John
Isaacson, Michael Neil
Itoh, Hiroyuki
Johnson, Noel
Jones, W. Bradwen
Kean, Edmund
Keel, James Frederick
Kellie, Lawrence
Kennedy
Kent, Edward
Kjerulf, Halfdan
Korbay, Francis
Kountz, Richard
Kozeluch, Leopold
Kücken, Friedrich Wilhelm
Lachner, Franz
Lampard
Lansing
Lawson, Malcolm
Lecocq, Charles
Lee, Ernest Markham
Lehár, Franz
Leonard, Conrad
Levigne, Peter
Liddle, Samuel
Lindsay, Miss M. [pen name of
    Mrs. Worthington Bliss]
Loes, Harry Dixon & George S. Schuler
Loewe, Gilbert
Logé, Henri
Löhr, Hermann [Frederic]
Longstaffe, Ernest
Lovelace, Austin C.
Lover, Samuel
Lowthian, Caroline
    [pen name of Mrs. Cyril Prescott]
Lucantoni, Giovanni
Luedecke, Raymond
MacDowell, Edward

Macfarlane, Elsa
MacFarlane, William Charles
MacLeod, Peter
Malin, Don
Malotte, Albert Hay
Manning, Kathleen Lockhart
Manookin, Robert P.
Marais, Josef
Martin, Easthope
Marzials, Théodor
Mascheroni, Angelo
Masini, Francesco
Mason, Gerry
Maxfield, Henry W.
Mayer, William
McEwen, John
Mellish, Colonel
Melvin, Ernest
Mendelssohn, Felix
Metcalf, John W.
Millard, Harrison
Miller, Henry Colin
Moffat, Alfred
Moir, Frank Lewis
Molloy, James Lyman
Moore, Dorothy Rudd
Morgan, Robert Orlando
Morris, C. H.
Mosenthal, Joseph
Müller-Hartman, Robert
Neidlinger, William Harold
Nevin, Ethelbert Woodbridge
Newton, Ernest
Noland, Gary
North, Michael
Norton, Caroline E.S.
Oehmler, L.
O'Hara, Geoffrey
Operti
Orr, Buxton
Orton, Irv
Owen, Anita
Page, Nathanael Clifford
Panofka, Heinrich
Parker, Alice
Parker, Henry
Paxon, Charles W.
Pelissier, H. G.
Persichetti, Vincent
Peterkin, Norman
Pflueger
Phillips, Montegue Fawcett
Pinkham, Daniel
Pinsuti, Ciro
Pleskow, Raoul
Pleyel, Ianos [Ignaz Josef]
Pontet, Henry
Quilter, Roger
Rachmaninov, Sergei
Rasbach, Oscar
Ray, Lilian
Reid, Alwyn
Reilly, Myles
Reynolds, Alfred

(English—*Continued*)

Richards, Brinley
Rimsky-Korsakov, Nicolai
Roberton, Hugh Stevenson
Roff, Joseph
Rogers, James H
Ronald, Landon
Rorem, Ned
Rubbra, Edmund
Rubinstein, Anton
Russell, Armand
Russell, Kennedy
S. G. P.
Saint Quentin, Edward
Sanderson, Wilfred
Sans-Souci, Gertrude
Sarjeant, J.
Sawyer
Schnecker, P. A.
Schofield, Joe
Schultz, Edwin
Schumann, Robert
Serradell, N.
Sharmann, Cecil
Sharpe, Evelyn
Shaw, Martin
Shelley, Harry Rowe
Shield, William
Shiomi, Mieko
Shostakovich, Dmitri
Singer, Jeanne
Smart, Henry
Smith, Alice Mary
Smith, H. Arnold
Smith, Lilian
Smith, Seymour
Solomon, John
Somervell, Arthur
Sowerby, Leo
Speaks, Oley
Spohr, Louis
Squire, William Henry
Stacey, Gilbert
Stafford, C. Lloyd
Stainer, John
Stanford, Charles Villiers
Sullivan, Arthur
Sutherland, Margaret
Tate, James W.
Tate, Phyllis
Taylor, T.
Tchaikovsky, Peter Ilyich
Terriss, Ellaline
Thiman, Eric Harding
Thomas, Arthur Goring
Topliff, Robert
Tosti, Francesco Paolo
Trotere, Henry
Unknown composer or arranger
    (8 entries)
Vadtor, Thomas
Van Buskirk, Carl
Vaughan Williams, Ralph
Verner, H. C.
Wade, Joseph Augustine

(English—*Continued*)

Wakefield, Augusta Mary
Wallace
Wallach Crane, Joelle
Warren, Betsy
Weatherly, F. E.
Wellings, Milton
Westendorf, T. P
Weston, R. P. & B. Lee
White
White, Maude Valerie
Whitehead, Percy Algernon
Willan, Healy
Willeby, Charles
Williams, R. H.
Wilson
Wilson, Henry Lane
Wood, Hayden
Woodforde-Finden, Amy
Wuorinen, Charles
Wyeth, John

Finnish Language Composers (8 total)

Backman, Hjalmar
Kauppi, Emil
Kuusisto, Taneli
Linnala, Eino
Marvia, Einari
Merikanto, Oskar
Nieland, H.
Tuuri, Jaako

French Language Composers (118 total)

Adam, Adolphe Charles
Aerts, Felix
Arnaud, Etienne
Barwolf, L.
Battmann, Jacques Louis
Bemberg, Henri Hermann
Berger, Rodolphe
Berlioz, Hector
Berton, F.
Bischoff-Ghilionna, Julius
Boieldieu, François Adrien
Boissière, F.
Bordèse, Luigi
Bourgault-Ducoudray, Louis
Busser, Henri-Paul
Buydens-Lemoine
Carey, Harry
Caryll, Ivan
Chabeaux, P.
Chabrier, Emmanuel
Chaminade, Cecile
Chausson, Ernest
Chelard, Hippolyte André
Chopin, Frédéric
Christian-Jollet

(French—*Continued*)

Clapisson, Antoine Louis
Coquard, Arthur
Coupé, H.
Cuvillier, Charles
Czibilka, Alphons
Debussy, Claude
Delbruck, J.
Delibes, Léo
Dell' Acqua, Eva
Delmet, Paul
Denefve, J.
Denza, Luigi
Diepenbrock, Alphons
Donaudy, Stefano
Donizetti, Gaetano
Durbec, L.
Fauré, Gabriel
Favre, Georges
Fontenailles, H. de
Fragerolle, George Auguste
Franck, César
Galland, E.
Gallois, Marie
Gastinel, Léon-Gustave-Cyprien
Glimes, Jean Baptiste Jules de
Gobbaerts, Jean Louis
Godard, Benjamin
Godfrey, Daniel
Goublier, R.
Gounod, Charles
Gregoir, J.
Guzmann, Fr.
Hartog, Edouard de
Holmès, Augusta
Jaques-Dalcroze, Emile
Jolas, Betsy
Jouret, Leon
Kücken, Friedrich Wilhelm
Lacome, Paul
Lagoanère, Oscar de
Lalo, Edouard
Laparra, Raoul
Latour, A. de
Lecocq, Charles
Lucotte
Lutgen, L.
Malibran, Alexander
Manziarly, Marcelle de
Marti, E.
Martini, Jean Paul Egide
Marx, Adolf Bernard
Masini, Francesco
Massenet, Jules
Membrée, Edmond
Mendelssohn, Felix
Mercier, Ch.
Messager, Andre
Meyerbeer, Giacomo
Migot, Georges
Milhaud, Darius
Moniuszko, Stanislaw
Niedermayer, Louis
Offenbach, Jacques
Overeem, M. v.

(French—*Continued*)

Panseron, Auguste
Peellaert, Augustin de
Perpignan, F.
Pourny, Ch.
Reinecke, Karl Ludwig
Renardy, A.
Renaud, Albert
Rimsky-Korsakov, Nicolai
Roger, J.
Rosenthal, Manuel
Rossi, E.
Rotschy, J. B.
Saint-Saëns, Camille
Sallneuve, E.
Schlosser, Paul
Sinico, Giuseppe
Smit, Leo
Streabbog, L.
Strimer, Joseph
Strino, S. A.
Thomas, Arthur Goring
Unknown composer or arranger
   (8 entries)
Van Cromphout, L.
Vangele, V.
Viardot-Garcia, Pauline
Watelle, Ch.
Weckerlin, Jean Baptiste
Weyts, H.
Wouters, Adolphe

German Language Composers
(1347 total)

Aaron, E.
Abramowitz
Abt, Franz
Achenbach, J.
Adam, Adolphe Charles
Adant, L.
Aiblinger, Johann Kaspar
Alberti, G.
Aletter, Wilhelm
Altenhofer, C.
Altmann, Gustav
André, Jean Baptiste
André, Johann Anton
Ansorge, M. [prob. Margarethe]
Arendt, W.
Arensky, Anton
Arndts, Maria Vespermann
Ascher, E.
Attenhofer, Karl
Aue, U.
August, J.
Baader, R.
Bach, Leonard Emil
Bach, Otto
Bade, Ph.
Bading, P.
Baer, Abel
Balfe, Michael William
Banck, Karl

(German—*Continued*)

Bandhartinger, B.
Bandisch, J.
Bank, G.
Bärmann, W.
Bartel, G.
Baschinsky, P.
Baselt, Friedrich Gustav Otto
Bastyr, Hans
Bauckner, Arthur
Bauer, Friedrich
Baum, C.
Baum, W.
Baumann, Alexander
Baumann, Johann
Baumann, Karl Friedrich
Baumfelder, Friedrich
Baumgart, A.
Baumgartner, Wilhelm
Beauplan, A. de
Becker, Albert
Becker, Cl.
Becker, Hugo
Becker, Konstantin Julius
Becker, Reinhold
Becker, Valentin Eduard
Beethoven, Ludwig van
Behr, Franz
Bellermann, Heinrich
Belzer, P.
Benda, A.
Bendel, Franz
Benedict, Jules
Bennewitz, Fritz,
Benoy, A. W.
Berger, Francesco
Berger, Wilhelm
Bergmann, Gustav
Bering, Ch.
Bergmann, Josef
Bergmann, Th.
Berlioz, Hector
Berneker, Constanz
Bernier, René
Berthold, G. [pen name of
   Robert Pearsall]
Beschnitt, Johannes
Beyer, H.
Beyer, J.
Bicknese, E.
Bieber, C. [prob. Karl]
Biehl, A. [prob. Albert]
Biehl, Ed.
Bijvanck, Henk
Billert, Karl Friedrich August
Birn, M.
Bischoff, Karl Bernard
Bischoff, Karl Jacob
Bisping, A.
Blaesing, Felix
Blangini, G. M. M. Felice
Blaufus, Chr.
Blobner, Johann Baptist
Blum, Karl Ludwig

(German—*Continued*)

Blum, E.
Blumenthal, Jacob [Jacques]
Blumenthal, Paul
Blumner, Martin
Boch, Fr.
Bögler, B.
Bohm, C.
Böhm, Karl
Böhm, R.
Böhm, W.
Bohrer, S.
Böie, Heinrich
Bonvin, Ludwig
Borchers, Gustav
Bordèse, Luigi
Born, C.
Börner, Kurt
Bornet, R.
Bornhardt, Johann Heinrich Karl
Bortniantsky, Dimitri Stephanovich
Boruttau, Alfred J.
Bosen, Franz
Böttcher, E.
Böttger, G.
Boumann, Leonardus Carolus
Boyneburgk, Fr. v.
Bradsky, Wenzel Theodor
Brah-Müller, Karl Friedrich Gustav
Brahms, Johannes
Brahms-Zilcher
Brambach, Kaspar Joseph
Brämig, Bernard
Brandhurst, Elise
Brandt, August
Brandt, F. [prob. Fritz]
Brandt, Hermann
Brandt, M.
Brandt-Caspari, Alfred
Bratsch, Johann Georg
Brauer, W.
Braun, Albert
Braun, Clemens
Brede, Albrecht
Bredschneider, Willy
Breiderhoff, E.
Breitung, F.
Brenner, Friedrich
Breu, Simon
Briem, W.
Briggs, C. S.
Brixner, J.
Brocksch. R.
Bruch, Max
Brüll, J. [Ignaz]
Brunner, Christian Traugott
Brunner, Ed.
Buchholz, Karl August
Bülow, Charlotte von
Bunakoff, N.
Bünte, August
Bünte, Wilhelm
Buri, E. v.
Burwig, G.
Busch, Carl

(German—*Continued*)

Goldschmidt, Adalbert von
Göller, A.
Gollmick, Karl
Goltermann, Georg
Gordigiani, Luigi
Gorzer-Schulz, O. K. F.
Grabe, F.
Graben-Hoffmann, Gustav
Grabert, Martin
Grädener, Karl Georg Peter
Gramman, Karl
Graner, R.
Grechaninov, Alexander
Gregor, Cestmir
Greith, Karl
Grell, Eduard August
Gressler, Franz Albert
Grieg, Edvard
Griesbacher, Peter
Grisar, Albert
Groh, A.
Gronau, Ed.
Grosheim, Georg Christoph
Groskopf, A.
Grosse, L.
Grossjohann, F.
Gruber, L.
Grüel, E.
Grünberger, Ludwig
Grund, Friedrich Wilhelm
Grüner, G.
Grunholzer, K.
Gscheildl, P.
Gülker, August
Gumbert, Ferdinand
Gundlach, jun., L.
Günther, O.
Gurlitt, Cornelius
Gus, M.
Gustav, Prinz v. Schweden
Güth, J. L.
Gutheil, Gustav
Haan, Willem de [De Haan]
Haas, Joseph
Haase, Rudolf
Hackel, Anton
Hackl, J.
Hacks, G.
Hadeln, E. v.
Haeberlein, H.
Hahn, J. Ch. W.
Haim, F.
Haine, C.
Halle, H.
Haltnorth, A.
Hamma, Benjamin
Hanisch, Joseph
Hape, Ch. F.
Haring, Ch.
Hartmann, D. [pen name of
    David Lundhardt]
Hartog, Edouard de
Hasselhoff, A.
Häser, C.

(German—*Continued*)

Häser, J.
Hasse, Gustav
Hászlinger, J. v.
Haupt, Karl August
Hauptmann, Moritz
Hauptmann, R.
Hause, C.
Hauser, Moritz H.
Haydn, Franz Joseph
Hecht, Gustav
Hefner, Otto
Heidrich, Maximilian
Heidrich, Th.
Heim, A.
Heine, C.
Heinemann, Wilhelm
Heinlein, A.
Heinrich, Anton Philipp
Heinrich, E.
Heins, Karl
Heinz, P.
Heinze, Richard
Heiser, Wilhelm
Heiter, Ernst
Heitmann, M.
Helbig, W.
Hellmesberger, Jr., Joseph
Hellwig, Karl Friedrich Ludwig
Hempel, F. R.
Hennig, C. [prob. Karl Rafael]
Henschel, F.
Henschel, George
Hensel, Fanny Mendelssohn
Henssige, E.
Herbert, Theodor
Hering, C. [prob. Karl Eduard]
Herman, Reinhold Ludwig
Hermann, E. Hans
Hermann, R. L.
Hermann, William
Hermany, O.
Hermes, Eduard
Herold, E.
Herrmann, Willy
Hertz, H.
Herzog, Max.
Hess, Karl
Hesselmann, L.
Heuler, Raimund
Heuschkel, Johann Peter
Heuser, Ernst
Hey, Julius
Heins, Karl
Hiens, C. [prob. Karl Heins]
Hildach, Eugen
Hill, Wilhelm
Hiller, Ferdinand
Hiller, Paul
Himmel, Fr. G.
Himmel, Friedrich Heinrich
Hinrichs, Friedrich
Hinze, R.
Hirsch, Karl
Hirsch, Rudolf

(German—*Continued*)

Hirsche, C.
Hirschfeld, L. v.
Hochberg, Hans Heinrich XIV, B. G. v.
    [a.k.a. J. H. Franz]
Hochländer, J.
Hofer, Toni [pen name of Ludwig André]
Hoffmann, Emil Adolf
Hoffmann, L.
Hofmann, Heinrich Karl Johann
Hoft, N.
Hohfeld, C.
Hohnerlein, M.
Hol, Rijk
Hollaender, Alexis [Holländer]
Hollaender, Gustav
Hollaender, Viktor
Holland, G.
Höller, C.
Holstein, Franz von
Holstein, Jean-Paul
Hönle, A.
Hopfe, J.
Hoppe, Paul
Horack, C.
Horn, August
Horn, E.
Hornig, A.
Hornig, J.
Hornstein, Robert von
Hötzel, C.
Hoven, Johann
Huber, Hans
Hugo, F.
Hülle, W.
Hullebroeck, Emiel
Hummel, Ferdinand
Humperdinck, Engelbert
Huth, Louis
Istel, Edgar
Jacke, Ch.
Jäckel, A.
Jacobi, M.
Jacoby, Wilhelm
Jadassohn, Salomon
Jäger, W.
Jahn-Schulze, Hermann
Jähns, Friedrich Wilhelm
Jansen, F. Gustav
Jehring, Julius
Jensen, Adolf
Joël, K.
John, F.
Jordan, Aug.
Junghähnel, O.
Junghans, J.
Jungmann, Albert
Jüngst, Hugo
Jürisch, E.
Kaatz, F.
Kagerer, M.
Kahle, Th.
Kahn, Robert
Kainer, C.
Kaiser, Karl

(German—*Continued*)

Kalla, C.
Kallenbach, Georg E. G.
Kalliwoda, Johann Wenzel
Kammer, R.
Kammerlander, Karl
Kanne, Friedrich August
Kanzler, W.
Kapeller, A.
Karg-Elert, Sigfried [Karg]
Kasper, M.
Kauffmann-Jassoy, Erich
Kayser, Philipp Christoph
Keller, H.
Keller, Karl
Keller, Ludwig
Kerle, J. H.
Keue, C.
Keycher, O.
Kienzl, Wilhelm
Kinkel, Johanna [née Mockel]
Kipper, Hermann
Kirchl, Adolf
Kirchner, Hermann
Kirchner, Theodor Fürchtegott
Kirschhof, G. F.
Kittl, Johann Friedrich
Kleffel, Arno
Kleiber, Karl
Klein, O.
Kleinecke, W.
Kleinmichel, Richard
Klengel, Paul
Klepsch
Klinkmüller, F.
Klose, Oskar
Kloss, H.
Kmoch, A.
Knebel-Döberitz, A. v.
Knebelsberger, L.
Kniese, Julius
Knopf, Martin
Koch, August
Kohl, A.
Kohl, L.
Kohl, M.
Köhler, Christian Louis Heinrich
Köhler-Wümbach, Wilhelm
Kölling, Ch.
Köllner, Eduard
Kollo, Walter
Könneritz, Nina [Georgine née Eschborn]
Kopelowitz, B.
Korel, H.
Kosch, A.
Kotsch, H.
Kratzel, Karl [Kratzl]
Kräulig, L. E.
Krause, C.
Krause, Eduard
Krebs, Karl August
Kreideweiss, R.
Kremling, P. W.
Kremser, Eduard
Krenn, Franz

(German—*Continued*)

Kreutzer, Konradin
Kreymann, L.
Krigar, C.
Krigar, Hermann
Krill, Karl
Krinninger, F.
Kromer, Karl
Kron, Louis
Krone, W.
Kronegger, Rudolf
Kronensohn, J.
Krug, Arnold
Krug, Diederich
Krüger, Karl
Kücken, Friedrich Wilhelm
Kügele, Richard
Kuhlau, Friedrich
Kühle, G.
Kühn
Kuhn, C. H.
Kühn, E. [prob. Edmund]
Kühn, Karl
Kühne, C. T.
Kühnhold, Karl
Kuldell, R.
Kulenkampff, Gustav
Kündig, Felix
Künstle, E.
Kuntze, Karl
Labarre, Théodore
Lachner, Franz
Lachner, Vincenz
Ladendorff, O.
Lafont, Charles-Philippe
Lagoanère, Oscar de
Lammers, Julius
Lamperen, van
Lander, Josef
Lange, C.
Lange, O. H. [prob. Otto]
Lange, R.
Langer, G.
Langert, Johann August Adolf
Lanz, A.
Larsen, M.
Lassel, Rudolf
Lassen, Eduard
Laszky, A. B. [prob. Bela Latsky]
Lazarus, Gustav
Leal, L.
Le Beau, Luise Adolpha
Lederer-Prina, Felix
Ledermann, Wilhelm
Legov, M. [pen name of Max Vogel]
Lehmann, Johann Traugott
Lehmann, Liza
Lehnard, G.
Leicht, Fritz
Leitner, Karl August
Lenz, Leopold
Leo, A.
Leonard, R.
Leonhard, Julius Emil
Leschetitzky, Theodor

(German—*Continued*)

Leser, C.
Lewalter, Johann
Lewandowski, Louis
Leydecker, A.
Lichner, Heinrich
Lieb, F. X.
Liebe, Eduard Ludwig
Lier, E.N
Limbert, Frank L.
Lincke, Paul
Linderer, Ed.
Lindner, August
Lindner, E. [prob. Ernst Otto T.]
Lingner, H.
Linné, S.
Lipart, F.
Lipp, Alban
Liszt, Franz
Littmann, H.
Lob, Otto
Loewe, Karl Gottfried
Longuet
Lorens, Karl [Lorenz]
Lorenz, Alfred
Lorleberg, F.N
Lothar, Mark
Lötti, J.
Lubrich, O.
Lüdecke, L.
Ludwig, August
Ludwig, C. [pen name of
　Julius E. Gottlöber]
Lührsz, Karl
Lustig, Gebr.
Lyra, Justus Wilhelm
Maas, Louis
Maase, Wilhelm
Mächtig, Karl
Mackrot, G. W.
Mahlberg, C.
Mahnecke, R.
Maier, Amanda
　[married name Rötgen]
Maikowski, M.
Malek, W.
Malling, Jorgen
Mangold, Karl Ludwig Armand
Mannfred, Heinrich
Mansfeldt, H.
Marchesi de Castrone, Salvatore
Margot, T.
Mariz, C. J.
Marschner, Adolf Eduard
Marschner, Heinrich August
Martini, F. v.
Martini, Hugo
Marx, Adolf Bernard
Marx, Joseph
Marx, Karl
Masini, A. [prob. Angelo]
Masini, Francesco
Matthes, J.
Matthiae, E.

420

Appendix D

(German—*Continued*)

Matthias, W.
Matthieux, Johanna [née Mockel,
    later married Kinkel]
Mauss, A.
May, Siegfried
Mayer, Joseph Anton
Mayer, Martin
Mayerhoff, Fritz
Meienreis, R.
Meier, K.
Meijroos, Hendrik Arnoldus [Meyroos]
Meinardus, Ludwig
Meinhold, P.
Meister, Casimir
Melchert, J.
Mello, Alfred
Mendel, Hermann
Mendelssohn, Felix
Menzel, J.
Merker, R.
Messer, F.
Mestozzi, Paul
Methfessel, Albert Gottlieb
Methfessel, C.
Methfessel, Ernst
Meves, Wilhelm
Meyer, Wilhelm
Meyer-Helmund, Erik
Meyer-Stolzenau, Wilhelm
Meyerbeer, Giacomo
Meysel, E.
Michaelis, Ad. Alfred
Michaelis, Gustav
Michielsen, A.
Mililotti, Leopoldo
Millöcker, Karl
Minkwitz, Bruno
Mittmann, Paul
Mjöen, J. A.
Mögling, G. Fr.
Möhring, Ferdinand
Molbe, Heinrich
Molique, Wilhelm Bernhard
Monche, L.
Moolenaar, S. [prob. Frieso]
Moór, Emanuel
Moritz
Moritz, Franz
Morse, Th. F.
Moscheles, Ignaz
Mücke, Franz
Mühling, August
Mulder-Fabri, Rich.
Müller, Sr., Adolf
Müller, Donat
Müller, Franz
Müller, Heinrich Fidelis
Müller, L. S.
Müller, M.
Müller, Richard
Munkelt, T.
Münz, C.
Músiol, Robert Paul Johann
Nagiller, Matthäus

(German—*Continued*)

Nagler, Franciscus
Nápravník, Eduard
Nater, Johann
Naubert, Friedrich August
Nauwerk, E.
Necke, Hermann
Neckheim, H.
Neibig, G.
Nekes, Franz
Nelson, Rudolph
Nemours, A.
Nesmüller, F.
Nessler, Victor E.
Netzer, Joseph
Neubner, Ottomar
Neugebauer, J.
Neukomm, Sigismund
Neuland, W.
Neumann, Emil
Neumann, H.
Nicolai, Otto
Nicolai, Wilhelm Frederik Gerard
Niemann, Gustav
Niese, Th.
Niese, E.
Nikisch, Arthur
Nohé, S.
Nolopp, Werner
Norbert, R.
Norman, Fredrick Vilhelm Ludvig
Nöroth, J.
Noskowski, Zygmund
Nuhn, Fr.
Nus, B.
Oberhoffer, Heinrich
Oberstoetter, H. E.
Oberthür, Karl
Ochs, Siegfried
Odersky, A.
Oelschläger, Friedrich
Ogarew, M.
Opel, R.
Opladen, Adolf
Ortner, A.
Otto, A.
Otto, Ernst Julius
Otto, Franz Joseph
Paasch, W.
Pache, Joseph
Pachlov, N. J.
Packenius, J.
Paër, Ferdinando [Paer]
Paisiello, Giovanni
Palme, Rudolf
Panseron, Auguste
Pardow, J. H.
Parlow, Edmund
Pastory, A.
Patat, J.
Pembauer, Sr., Joseph
Pembaur, Karl
Pentenrieder, Franz Xaver
Perger, Richard von
Peter, G.

(German—*Continued*)

Peuschel, Moritz
Pfannschmidt, A.
Pfannschmidt, Heinrich
Pfeil, Heinrich
Pfennig, R. A.
Philipp, A.
Philipp, Bernard Edward
Philipp, J.
Pierson, Henry Hugh
Pirani, Eugenio
Pivoda, F.
Plag, Johann
Plengorth, Friedrich
Pocci, Franz von
Pogge, H.
Pohl, Max
Pommer, Josef
Ponflick, F.
Popp, Wilhelm
Por, C.
Porepp, Georg
Prechtl, Ludwig
Preil, Paul
Preitz, Franz
Pressel, Gustav Adolf
Preyer, Gottfried von
Prior-Lipart, A.
Proch, Heinrich
Procházka, Ludwig
Prochazka, Rudolf
Proschel, G.
Puchat, Max
Puget, Louise-Françoise
Queling, Theodor
Quiquerez, Hermann
Radecke, Robert
Radecke, Rudolph
Raff, Joseph
Raida, Karl Alexander
Raillard, Theodor
Ramann, Bruno
Randhartinger, Benedict
Raphael, Georg
Raphael, Gunther
Reger, Max
Reh, H.
Reich, Reinhold
Reichardt, Johann Friedrich
Reiche, V.
Reichel, Adolf Heinrich Johann
Reifner, Vincenz
Reim, Edmund
Reimann, Heinrich
Reinberger, J.
Reinecke, Carl
Reinhardt, F.
Reinhardt, Heinrich
Reinthaler, Karl Martin
Reissiger, Friedrich August
Reissiger, Karl Gottlieb
Reissmann, August
Reissmann, H.
Reiter, Ernst
Renker, Felix

Renner, M.
Rennes, Catharina van
Reuss, August
Reutter, Hermann
Reutter, Otto
Rheinberger, Josef
Rheineck, S.
Ricci, Luigi
Riccius, August Ferdinand
Richard, T.
Richardy, Johann
Richstaetter, M. or W.
Richter, Alfred
Richter, Ernst Friedrich
Riedel, August
Riem, Friedrich Wilhelm
Riemenschneider, Georg
Ries, Ferdinand
Rieter, E.
Righini, Vincenzo
Rijken, Georg
Rinck, Johann Christian Heinrich
Ringer, A.
Rinnow, P.
Rischbeiter, Wilhelm Albert
Rittau, Bj.
Ritter, Hermann
Robricht, P.
Röder, Ewald
Rödger, Emil
Rodhe, Eduard
Rodhe, H.
Roeder, Martin [Röder]
Roessel, J. or L.
Röhde, A.
Röhricht, Paul
Rolla, Ch.
Romberg, A. [prob. Andreas]
Röntgen, Julius
Roose, H.
Roscher, Josef
Rosenberg, Wilhelm [Vilhelm]
Rosenfeld & Thiele
Rosenfeld, J.
Rosenfeld, Leopold
Rosenhain, Jacob
Rosenmeyer, H.
Rosensweig, H.
Rosenzweig, Wilhelm
Rossini, Gioacchino
Rössler, Richard
Roth, Bertrand
Roth, Franz
Rothlauf, B.
Rothstein, James
Roussel, L.
Rubini, Giovanni Battista
Rubinstein, Anton
Rubinstein, Nicolai
Rübner, Cornelius [Rybner]
Ruch, Hannes
Rückauf, Anton
Rücker, August
Rücker, Theodor

Rudnick, Wilhelm
Rudorff, E. [Friedrich Karl]
Rügamer, F.
Rühl, Friedrich Wilhelm
Rühricht, P.
Rungenhagen, Karl Friedrich
Rust, Wilhelm Karl
Saar, L. V. [Franz]
Sachs, Johann Melchior Ernst
Sacks, Woldemar
Sackur, C.
Saint-Saëns, Camille
Salinger, J.
Salis, P.
Sallneuve, C.
Sallneuve, E.
Samson, L.
Santner, Karl
Sarti, Giuseppe
Sauerbrey, J. W. C. C.
Schachner, J. B.
Schäfer, P.
Schäffer, August
Schäffer, Heinrich
Schäffer, Theodor [Schäfer]
Schaper, Gustav
Schaper, O.
Schärf, P.
Schauer, H.
Schenk, A.
Schetana, M.
Schiedel, P.
Schiemer, Georg
Schifferl, F.
Schild, Theodor F.
Schilling, Ferdinand
Schindler, J.
Schirmer, A.
Schläger, Hans
Schleidt, Wilhelm
Schleiffarth, G.
Schlesinger
Schletterer, Hans Michel
Schlottmann, Louis
Schlözer, K. [prob. Karl]
Schmeidler, K. [prob. Karl]
Schmid, Heinrich Kaspar
Schmid, Th.
Schmidt, A.
Schmidt, Gustav
Schmidt, Hans
Schmidt, M.
Schmidt, M. H.
Schmidt, O.
Schmitt, Aloys
Schmitt, Cornelius
Schmitt, Florent
Schmitt, Georg Aloys
Schnabel, Josef Ignaz
Schnabel, Karl
Schnaubelt, Heinrich
Schnaubelt, W.
Schneeberger, Ferdinand
Schneider, Bernhard

Schneider, J. [prob. Johann Gottlob II]
Schnippering, W.
Schöbe, C.
Schoeck, Othmar
Scholz, Bernard
Schorcht, H.
Schorsch, L.
Schotte, Karl
Schreck, Gustav
Schröder, M. [prob. Max]
Schroeder, Hermann
Schröter, L.
Schubert, Franz Ludwig
Schubert, Franz Peter
Schubert, Georgine
Schubert, Louis
Schuh, H.
Schuh, J.
Schultz, C.
Schultz, Edwin
Schulz, August
Schulz, Chr.
Schulz, R.
Schumacher, Heinrich Vollrat
Schumacher, Richard
Schumann, Clara Wieck
Schumann, Georg Alfred
Schumann, Robert
Schütky, Franz Josef
Schwartz, Alexander
    [a.k.a. Sascha Landry]
Schwarz, C.
Schwarz, N.
Schwarzlose, Otto
Schweiger, J.
Schwertzell, Wilhelmine von
Schwick, J.
Seestädt, J.
Seidel, O.
Seifert, Uso
Seiffert, Alexander
Seiffert, Karl
Seitz, F. [prob. Friedrich]
Selmer, Johan Peter
Sering, Friedrich Wilhelm
Seyffardt, Ernst Hermann
Shostakovich, Dmitri
Sieber, Ferdinand
Siebmann, F.
Silber, Philip
Silcher, Friedrich
Simon, Ernst
Simon, O.
Sinigaglia, Leone
Sinnhold, R.
Sioly, Johann
Sioly-Weisberg
Sirsch, R.
Skop, V. E.
Slunicko, Jan
Söchting, Emil
Södermann, Johan August
Solbrück, C.
Soler, Joseph

(German—*Continued*)

Söllner, E.
Sowinsky, A. Wojcieh [Albert]
Spahn, Adolf
Sparhakel, A.
Speiser, Wilhelm
Spengler, Ludwig
Spielter, Hermann
Spohr, Louis
Sponholtz, Adolf Heinrich
Spontini, Gasparo
Springer, Max
Stainlein, Louis von
Standke, Otto
Stange, Max
Stanislas, A.
Starck, L.
Starck, W.
Stark, Ludwig
Starke, Gustav
Starke, H.
Starke, J.
Steffens, Gustav
Stehle, J. Gustav Eduard
Steiber, P.
Steidl, F.
Steidl-Duette
Stein, C. [prob. Karl]
Stein, V.
Steinecke, A.
Steinhart, W. W.
Steinitzer, M. [prob. Max]
Steinkühler, Emil
Stekel, W.
Sterkel, Johann F. X.
Stern, Hermann
Stern, Julius
Stern, S.
Steven, G.
Stieber, P.
Stiegmann, Eduard
Stiehl, Karl
Stöbe, Paul
Stock, Ed.
Stockhausen, Karlheinz
Stöger, A.
Stokhausen, E. v.
Stolberg-Stolberg, L.
Storch, Anton M.
Strauch, Fr.
Straus, Oscar
Strauss, Jr., Johann
Strubel, J.
Stuckenschmidt, H.
Stuckenschmidt, J. H.
Succo, Franz Adolf
Succo, Reinhold
Suhy, K.
Sulzbach, Emil
Suppé, Franz von
Szymanowski, Karol Maciej
Taubert, Ernst Eduard
Taubert, H.
Taubert, Otto
Taubert, Wilhelm

(German—*Continued*)

Tauwitz, Eduard
Tchaikovsky, Peter Ilyich
Teich, Otto
Teichmann, A. or O.
Teschner, Gustav Wilhelm
Thaler, J. B.
Thamm, P.
Thiel, Carl
Thiele, Eduard
Thiele, Louis
Thiele, Richard
Thiele, Rudolf
Thielen, P. H.
Thierfelder, Albert Wilhelm
Thieriot, Ferdinand
Thoma, Rudolf
Thomas, N.
Thooft, Willem Frans
Thorn, C.
Thudichum, Gustav
Tichy, Rudolf
Tiehsen, Otto
Tinel, Edgar Pierre Joseph
Tolstoy, A.
Tomaschek, Johann Wenzel
Tourbié, Richard
Tränkner, M.
Traunfels, H.
Triest, Heinrich
Troschel, Wilhelm Troszel
Trubel, Gerhard
Truhn, Friedrich Heironymus
Tschiderer, E.
Tschirch, Rudolf
Tschirch, Wilhelm
Tuch, H. G.
Tuma, A.
Uber, Christian Friedrich Hermann
Umlauft, Paul
Unger, A.
Urban, Friedrich Julius
Urlaub, A.
Veit, Václav Jindrich
   [also Wenzel Heinrich Veit]
Verbroek, C. J. J.
Viardot-Garcia, Pauline
Vierling, Georg
Vincent, Heinrich Joseph
Viol, Willy
Vogel, Bernhardt
Vogel, Hans
Vogel, M. [prob. Martin]
Voigt, F.
Voigt, Henriette
Voigt, Hermann
Voigt-Kudlik, Th.
Volckmar, Wilhelm
Volkmann, W.
Vollstedt, Robert
Voullaire, Waldemar
Voutz, H.
Wachsmann, Johann Joachim
Wagenblass, W.
Wagenbrenner, Josef

(German—*Continued*)

Wagener, Paul
Wagner, C. [prob. Karl Jacob]
Wagner, Ernst
Wagner, Franz
Wagner, Josef Franz
Wagner, Paul Emil
Walden, Otto von
   [pen name of Fritz Schindler]
Waldmann, v. d. Aue
Wallbach, Ludwig
Wallnöfer, Adolf
Wandelt, Amadeus
Wandow, L.
Waniek, Alois
Wanthaler, Gustav
Wany, W. J.
Wappaus, Karl
Wardini, Gebr.
Weber, A. [prob. Berhard Anselm]
Weber, Carl Maria von
Weber, Franz
Weber, Gottfried
Weber, Gustav
Wegeler, C.
Wehner, A.
Weidt, Heinrich
Weigel, H.
Weil, T.
Wienand, V.
Weinberger, Karl Friedrich
Weinhardt, F.
Weinstabl, Karl
Weinwurm, Rudolf
Weischer, Th.
Weismann, Julius
Weismann, Wilhelm
Weiss, J.
Weiss, Laurenz
Weissbach, M. L.
Wendland, Waldemar
Wendt, Ernst
Wenzel, Eduard
Wenzel, H.
Wermann, Friedrich Oskar
Werner, Erich
Werner, Otto
Werth, Joseph
Westermair, Johann B.
Westmeter, Wilhelm
Wichern, Karoline
Wichmann, Hermann
Wickede, Friedrich von
Wickenhauser, Richard
Widmann, Benedikt
Wiedecke, Adolph
Wiedemann, Max
Wiel, Taddeo
Wielhorski, Mikhail
Wieniawski, Joseph
Wiesomowiluki, R.
Wilhelm, Karl Friedrich
Wilm, Nicolai von
Winkhler, Karl Angelus von
Winkler, O.

(German—*Continued*)

Winter, E.
Winter, Georg
Winter, J.
Winterberger, Alexander
Winterling, W.
Wintzer, Elisabeth
Witt, Franz Xaver
Witt, Julius
Witt, Leopold
Witt, Theodor de
Wittenbecher, Otto
Wittsack, P.
Wolf, E.
Wolf, L. C.
Wolff, C.
Wolff, Gustav Tyson
Wolff, Leonhard
Wolff, W.
Wolff, Wilh.
Wölfle, Chr.
Wolfrum, Karl
Wollanck, Friedrich
Wolzogen, Ernst von
Wooge, Emma
Wottitz, Th.
Wrede, Ferdinand
Wüerst, Richard Ferdinand
Z'Wyssig, Alberik Johann Josef Maria
Zapff, Oskar
Zehrfeld, Oskar
Zeitler, J.
Zelter, Carl Friedrich
Zenger, Max
Zepler, Bogumil
Zerlett, Johann Baptist
Zientarski, Romuald
Zier, E.
Zierau, Fritz
Zimmer, C. [prob. Karl]
Zimmer, Otto
Zimmermann, J.
Zingel, Rudolf Ewald
Zöllner, Andreas
Zöllner, Karl Friedrich
Zweifel, B.

German-Dialect [Wiener, Tyrolean, Carinthian, etc.] Language Composers (61 total)

Achenbach, J.
Aletter, Wilhelm
André, L. [prob. Christian Karl André]
Angerer, Gottfried
Augustin, F. H.
Bachhofer, R.
Bial, Rudolph
Bleibtreu, C.
Bretschger, H.
Coradini, R. & P.
Crikeltown, G.
Diemer, Louis-Joseph

(German-dialect—*Continued*)

Dreher, F.
Egger-Rieser, T.
Engelhart, Franz Xaver
Ertl, Dominik
Fiby, Heinrich
Fiebrich, F. P.
Fink, F.
Fink, Ferd.
Francke, W.
Frank, Ernst
Frankl, A.
Freisler, C.
Frey, Martin
Fromm, Karl Josef
Gebauer, H.
Hartl, Ph.
Jurek, Wilhelm August
Katzer, Karl August
Kloss, H.
Koch, Markus
Kohl, L.
Koschat, Thomas
Kronegger, Rudolf
Kühle, G.
Lehner, F. L.
Leukauf, Richard
Minkwitz, Bruno
Müller, J. [prob. Johann]
Neckheim, H.
Neidhardt, August
Neumann, H.
Pircher, J. L.
Praeger, Heinrich Aloys
Rosenzweig, Wilhelm
Rott, Carl Maria
Säuberlich, C.
Sauer, L. & G.
Schild, Theodor F.
Schmid, Joseph
Schmutz & Katzer
Schrammel, Johann
Simon, Ernst
Sioly, Johann
Sioly-Weisberg
Steizhammer
Thiele, Th.
Walter-Kiesel, M.
Wottitz, Th.
Ziehrer, Karl Michel

Hebrew Language Composers (4 total)

Rosenfeld & Thiele
Wallach Crane, Joelle
Werner, Erich

Hungarian Language Composers (2 total)

Kodály, Zoltán
Sugár, Rezsö

Icelandic Language Composers (3 total)

Björnsson, Arni
Gudmudsson, Björgvin
Sveinbjörnsson, Sveinbjörn

Italian Language Composers (89 total)

Anfossi, Pasquale
Apell, Karl
Arditi, Luigi
Bazzini, Antonio
Berthold, G. [pen name of
 Robert Pearsall]
Blangini, G. M. M. Felice
Boito, Arrigo
Bonoldi, Francesco
Bortolini, G.
Brahms, Johannes
Brizzi, S.
Busoni, Ferrucio Benvenuto
Campana, Fabio
Carafa, Michel Enrico
Carelli, Benjamino A.
Cattaneo, V.
Cavallini, Ernesto
Cherubini, Luigi
Ciccarelli, Angelo
Coccia, Carlo
Concone, F.
Curci, Giuseppi
d'Yradier, Chevalier
Döhler, Theodor
Donizetti, Gaetano
Fabiani, D.
Faccio, Franco
Franz, Robert
Gabussi, Vincent
Gambini, Carlo Andrea
Ghedini, Giorgio Federico
Gordigiani, Luigi
Grua, Carlo Luigi Pietro
Guercia, Alfonso
Guglielmo, P. D.
Hochberg, Hans Heinrich XIV, B. G. v.
 [a.k.a. J. H. Franz]
Ibert, Jacques
Ivanova, Lidia
Jeppesen, Knud
Kanne, Friedrich August
Küstler, J. H.
Lannoy, Eduard
Latour, A. de
Lucantoni, Giovanni
Marchesi de Castrone, Mathilde
 [née Graumann]
Marchetti, Filippo
Mercadante, Saverio
Millard, H.
Miltitz, Carl Borromäus von
Moroni, L.
Niedermayer, Louis

(Italian—*Continued*)

Novaro, Michele
Oddone, Elisabetta [a.k.a. Eliodd]
Paër, Ferdinando [Paer]
Paisiello, Giovanni
Palloni, Gaetano
Pargolesi, Coronato
Pavesi, Stefano
Pearsall, Robert Lucas de
    [a.k.a. G. Berthold]
Pinsuti, Ciro
Pocci, Franz von
Pucitta, Vincenzo
Recli, Giulia
Reichardt, Gustav
Reichardt, Johann Friedrich
Reissiger, Karl Gottlieb
Ricci, Federico
Righini, Vincenzo
Rilvas, C. de
Rocca, Lodovico
Ronconi, [prob. Felice]
Rossini, Gioacchino
Ruta, Michele
Saint-Lubin, Léon de
Santi, G.
Schubert, Georgine
Serradell, N.
Sessi, M. [prob. Marianne]
Sor, Fernando [Sors]
Tancioni, E.
Teichmann, A. or O.
Teschner, Wilhelm
Toselli, Enrico
Traventi
Tritto, Giacomo
Unknown composer or arranger
    (8 entries)
Visconti, E.
Winter
Zescevich, A.

Japanese Language Composers (2 total)

Sugiura, Masayoshi
Suzuki, Hideaki

Latin Language Composers (53 total)

Adams, Thomas
Bonvin, Ludwig
Curti, Franz
Cutler, E.
Czonka, Paul
Diebold, Johann
Dubois, Théodore
Duval, Edmond
Duvivier, A. D.

(Latin—*Continued*)

Ellerton, John Lodge
Fauré, Gabriel
Faure, Jean Baptiste
Gimeno, P. [prob. Joaquin]
Girschner, Karl Friedrich Julius
Granier, Jules
Grell, Eduard August
Guiselin, P.
Haagh, J.
Hartmann, Paul Eugen von
Hekking, P. F. R.
Krall, J.
Krinninger, F.
Lindner, August
Lloyd Webber, Andrew
Mertens, H. de
Molbe, Heinrich
Mortari, Virgilio
Nekes, Franz
Nevin, George Balch
Nikel, Emil
Panseron, Auguste
Piel, Peter
Plantade, Charles Henri
Rathgeber, Georg
Reger, Max
Renner, Josef
Rheinberger, Josef
Rietz, J. August Wilhelm
Riga, Frantz
Rorem, Ned
Rust, Wilhelm Karl
Saint-Saëns, Camille
Samuel-Rosseau, Marcel
Schubert, Georgine
Sennes, H.
Stein, Josef
Swann, Donald
Talma, Louise
Vater, F. A.
Verelst, P. F.
Wiltberger, August
Zangl, Josef Gregor
Zenter, Wilhelm

Norwegian Language Composers (5 total)

Grøndahl, Agathe Bäcker
Karlsen, Kjell Mork
Kjerulf, Halfdan
Strand, Tor
Volle, Bjarne

Polish Language Composers (2 total)

Moniuszko, Stanislaw
Noskowski, Zygmund

Polynesian Language Composers (3 total)

Kaleikoa, Malie
Kekpuchi
Roes, Carol Lasater

Russian Language Composers (16 total)

Alexandrov, Anatol
Arensky, Anton
Cui, César
Dargomizshky, Alexander
Dunayevsky, Isaak
Dzerzhinsky, Ivan
Glazunov, Alexander
Glinka, Mikhail Ivanovich
Grechaninov, Alexander
Prokofiev, Serge
Rachmaninov, Sergei
Rimsky-Korsakov, Nicolai
Rubinstein, Anton
Shostakovich, Dmitri
Tchaikovsky, Peter Ilyich
Wrangle, Vassily G.

Spanish Language Composers (15 total)

Carnicer, Ramon
Chabrier, Emmanuel
Fuentes, Laureano
García de la Parra, Benito
Garcia, M. [prob. Mansilla Eduardo]
Granados, Enrique
Grever, Maria
Guastivino, Carlos
Iradier, Sebastian [Yradier]
Laserna, Blas de
Mauri, J.
Pla, M.
Ponvet, A. M.
Salvi, Matteo

Spanish-Dialect [Catalonian] Language Composer (1 total)

Caballero, Manuel Fernandez

Serbo-Croatian Language Composers (3 total)

Skerjanc, Lucijan Marija
Svara, Danilo
Uray, Erst Ludwig

Swedish Language Composers
(19 total)

Baumgartner
Dahlgren, Erland
Eyser, Eberhard
Haggbom
Hallen, Andreas
Hallstrom, Ivar
Hasse
Hiller
Lewerth

(Swedish—*Continued*)

Lindgren, Olof
Myrberg, August Melcher
Norman, Fredrick Vilhelm Ludvig
Olson, Daniel
Schonberg, Stig Gustav
Sjogren, Emil
Thierfelder, Albert Wilhelm
Wennerburg, Gunnar
Wibergh, Johann Olof
Wrangle, Vassily G.

Welsh Language Composer
(1 total)

Williams, W. S. Gwynn

Appendix E: Index of Accompaniment Other Than Piano
Total N=383 (4.353%)

ORGAN (267 TOTAL, 3.034%)

Organ or Piano (113 total, 1.284%):

5, 42, 69, 87, 237, 325, 398, 399, 544, 545, 880, 918, 1450, 1485, 1486, 1496, 1523, 1571, 1572, 1779, 1780, 1825, 1833, 1916, 2047, 2049, 2068, 2069, 2071, 2075, 2077, 2078, 2165, 2187, 2294, 2476, 2530, 2649, 2653, 2662, 2675, 2682, 2683, 2739, 2802, 2803, 2923, 2974, 2978, 2979, 3509, 3511, 3532, 4501, 4620, 4872, 4905, 5176, 5369, 5473, 5492, 5523, 5524, 5525, 5526, 5562, 5973, 6082, 6110, 6323, 6334, 6372, 6394, 6395, 6397, 6399, 6400, 6482, 6483, 6561, 6762, 6835, 7124, 7125, 7146, 7147, 7149, 7151, 7152, 7153, 7156, 7160, 7161, 7162, 7163, 7165, 7383, 7439, 7470, 7577, 7606, 8292, 8293, 8294, 8476, 8477, 8479, 8481, 8734, 8735, 8739, 8740, 8778.

Organ or Harmonium (25 total, 0.284%):

924, 1755, 2768, 2815, 2988, 2989, 4011, 4495, 5427, 5667, 6321, 6327, 6328, 6331, 6332, 6338, 6911, 7820, 7821, 7822, 7823, 7824, 7825, 7986, 8494.

Organ or Piano or Harmonium (27 total, 0.307%):

594, 622, 1189, 1560, 1569, 2105, 2944, 3188, 3189, 3191, 3198, 3199, 3587, 4131, 4132, 4133, 4134, 4136, 4137, 4138, 4139, 4154, 6707, 7104, 7442, 8688, 8783.

Organ Only (100 total, 1.136%):

571, 1095, 1281, 1664, 1787, 1788, 1796, 1807, 2194, 2200, 2477, 2534, 2550, 2767, 2791, 2804, 2841, 2862, 2906, 2909, 2972, 3111, 3488, 3955, 4358, 4422, 4423, 4913, 4935, 5050, 5135, 5280, 5390, 5392, 5393, 5399, 5401, 5429, 5483, 5484, 5486, 5487, 5488, 5489, 5519, 5520, 5537, 5664, 5665, 5742, 5840, 5929, 5972, 5974, 5975, 5976, 5977, 6013, 6025, 6027, 6073, 6083, 6084,

(Organ only—*Continued*)

6322, 6333, 6335, 6337, 6339, 6714, 6912, 6913, 7164, 7362, 7523, 7797, 8003, 8004, 8005, 8006, 8007, 8008, 8009, 8010, 8011, 8012, 8013, 8014, 8015, 8016, 8017, 8018, 8073, 8090, 8276, 8277, 8624, 8625, 8626, 8729, 8749.

Organ with Optional Violin (2 total, 0.023%):

5101 (organ or piano or violin),
6805 (organ and optional violin)

HARMONIUM (61 TOTAL, 0.693%):

Harmonium or Organ (25 total, 0.284%):

924, 1755, 2768, 2815, 2988, 2989, 4011, 4495, 5427, 5667, 6321, 6327, 6328, 6331, 6332, 6338, 6911, 7820, 7821, 7822, 7823, 7824, 7825, 7986, 8494.

Harmonium or Piano (7 total, 0.080%):

384, 543, 4359, 4360, 6330, 7462, 8220.

Harmonium or Organ or Piano (27 total, 0.307%):

594, 622, 1189, 1560, 1569, 2105, 2944, 3188, 3189, 3191, 3198, 3199, 3587, 4131, 4132, 4133, 4134, 4136, 4137, 4138, 4139, 4154, 6707, 7104, 7442, 8688, 8783.

Harmonium Only (1 total, 0.011%):

5485

Harmonium and Piano (1 total, 0.011%):

6764

A CAPPELLA PIECES
(42 TOTAL, 0.477%):

40, 366, 367, 633, 1300, 1306, 1307, 1409, 1410, 1509,
1510, 1513, 1516, 1518, 1525, 1546, 1691, 1692, 1693,
1829, 2209, 2958, 3120, 3119, 3562, 3563, 3869, 4468,
4469, 4470, 4471, 4472, 4644, 4734, 4741, 5283, 7425,
7561, 7562, 8100, 8101, 8102.

PIANO VARIANTS
(2 TOTAL, 0.023%):

701 (piano-4 hands accomp.),
4394 (For 1 or 2 piano(s) accomp.)

HARP (OR PIANO)
(10 TOTAL, 0.114%):

724, 1393, 1397, 1398, 1399, 1402, 1404, 1405, 1406,
1411.

ZITHER (OR PIANO)
(1 TOTAL, 0.023%):

8298

Appendix F: List of Publishers (631 Total), Abbreviations, Identification (When Possible) & Known Addresses

Publishers listed within brackets [ ] indicate known distributors. Abbreviations appear as in original source. If no information on address or history was found, then *details unknown* appears in citation. Please note: addresses presented are current at the time of this writing. Some may no longer be correct.

A. H. & C.
Ascherberg, Hopwood & Crew Ltd.
50 New Bond St.
London W1A 2BR England

A. P. Schm. i. Leip.
Arthur Paul Schmidt in Leipzig.
American publisher with operations in Europe. Sold to Summy-Birchard in 1959. Archives in Library of Congress.

ACA
American Composers' Alliance
170 W. 74 St.
New York, NY 10023

Academ
Academia Music Ltd.
16-5, Hongo 3-Chome Bunkyo-ku
Tokyo, 113 Japan [Kalmus,A]

Aderholz i. Br.
Aderholz
details unknown

Aibl
Aibl Munich, Germany publishing firm. Sold to Universal Edition in 1904.

Allans
Allans Music Pty, Ltd.
P. O. Box 4072
Richmond East Victoria 3121
Australia [Presser]

Alsbach
G. Alsbach & Co.
P.O. Box 338
NL-1400 AH Bussum Netherlands
[Peters]

AMC
American Music Center
250 W. 57 St.
New York, NY 10019

AMP
Editions Amphion
26-28 Rue de la Pépinière
Paris, 8e, France [G. Schirmer]

André
[Prob. available through]
Johann André Musikverlag
Frankfurterstraße 28 Postfach 141
D-6050 Offenbach-am-Main,
Germany

Anglo-Continental
details unknown

Annecke
details unknown

APNM
Association for Promotion of
    New Music
2002 Central Ave.
Ship Bottom, NJ 08008

Apollo
Apollo-Verlag Paul Lincke
(formerly in Berlin) Weihergarten 5
6500 Mainz, Germany

Art Masters
Art Masters Studios, Inc.
2614 Nicollet Ave.
Minneapolis, MN 55408

Artia
Artia-Prague
Ve Smeckách 30
Prague 2, Czech Republic

Arts Venture
details unknown

Ashdown
Edwin Ashdown Ltd.
275-281 Cricklewood Broadway,
London NW2 6QR England [Brodt]

Attenkofer
details unknown

Auer
details unknown

Augener
Augener Ltd.
details unknown
[Prob. available through
    E. C. Schirmer]

Augsburg
Augsburg Publishing House
426 S. 5th St.
Minneapolis, MN 55415

Augustin, H.
Hermann Augustin
details unknown

Augustin i. Berl.
Augustin in Berlin
details unknown

Aulagnier
French publisher involved in lawsuit with Troupenas of Paris over the rights to Rossini's *Stabat mater* in 1841.

Ausgb. C. Reinecke
Ausgbabe C. Reinecke.
Edition Carl Reinecke.

B. & B.
Bote & Bock
Hardenbergstraße 9A
D-10623 Berlin Germany
[AMP, Presser]

B. & H.
Breitkopf & Härtel
Walkmühlstraße 52
Postfach 1707 D-6200
Wiesbaden 1 Germany
[Broude A or AMP]

Bachmann
[Prob.] C. Bachmann, publishing firm in Hannover, during the 19th century.

Bahn
Martin Bahn acquired Tragott Trautwein, German publishing firm in 1858. When Bahn died in 1902, the firm was absorbed by Heinrichshofen in Magdeburg.

Bandtlow i. Berl.
Bandtlow in Berlin
details unknown

Banes
details unknown

Banger
details unknown

Bärd & Bruder
details unknown

Bardic
Bardic Edition
6 Fairfax Crescent,
Aylesbury, Buckinghamshire
HP20 SES England [Presser]

Baren
Bärenreiter Verlag
Heinrich Schütz Allee 31-37
Postfach 100329 D-3500
Kassel-Wilhelmshöhe, Germany
or 305 Bloomfield Ave.
Nutley, NJ 07110

Bauderer
details unknown

Bauer
Georg Bauer Musikverlag
Luisenstraße 47-49 Postfach 1467
D-7500 Karlsruhe Germany

Bauer i. Br.
details unknown
[Prob. available through]
Georg Bauer Musikverlag
Luisenstraße 47-49 Postfach 1467
D-7500 Karlsruhe Germany

Bayley & Ferguson
details unknown

Bayrhoffer
details unknown

Becher
details unknown

Beckenhorst
Beckenhorst Press
P.O. Box 14273
3821 North High St.
Columbus, OH 43214 [Presser]

Belwin
Belwin-Mills Publishing Corp.
15800 N.W. 48th Ave. P.O. Box 4340
Miami, FL 33014

Benjamin
Anton J. Benjamin
Werderstraße 44 Postfach 2561
D-2000 Hamburg 13 Germany
[Presser, AMP]

Bennewitz i. L.
details unknown

Berlin Selbstverl.
Berlin Selbst-Verlag
details unknown

Bernard i. Pet.
M. I. Bernard, purchased St. Petersburg, Russian publishing firm of Dalmas in 1828.

Betram i. Br.
details unknown

Beyer i. Düsseld.
Beyer in Düsseldorf
details unknown

Beyer & S.
Beyer & Söhne
details unknown

Biehl i. H.
details unknown

Biol
details unknown

Birchall, R.
Robert Birchall, English publisher. Became Birchall, Lonsdale & Mills (or Birchall & Co., or Mills & Co.) Mills & Son defunct in 1903.

Bisping, Bisping i. M.
details unknown

Blaha
details unknown

Bloch
details unknown

Bloch., Ed.
Ed. Bloch.
details unknown

Blockley
John Blockley. English publishing firm. Amalgamated with Ascherberg, Hopwood & Crew in 1906.

Boesn.
Boessenecker
details unknown

Bohm, Böhm i. A., Böhm & S.
Anton Böhm & Sohn
Postfach 110369 Lange Gasse 26
D-8900 Augsburg 11, Germany

Böhme i. H.
details unknown

Bon i. Konigsb.
Bon in Konigsburg
details unknown

Bongiavani
Casa Musicale Francesco Bongiovani
Via Rizzoli 28 E
I-40125 Bologna, Italy [Belwin]

Boosey
Boosey & Hawkes, Inc.
24 East 21st St.
New York, NY 10010

Bornemann
Editions Bornemann
15 Rue de Rournon F-75006
Paris France [Belwin, Presser]

Bösendorfer
details unknown

Bosse
Gustav Bosse Verlag
Von der Tann Straße 38 Postfach 417
D-8400 Regensburg 1 Germany
[E-A, Magna]

Boston
Boston Music Company
Airport Dr. P. O. Box 131
Hopedale, MA 01747

Bosworth
Bosworth & Company, Ltd.
14-18 Heddon St., Regent St.
London W1R 8DP England

Bote
Bote & Bock
Hardenbergstraße 9A
D-1000 Berlin 12 Germany
[AMP, Presser]

Bowerman
details unknown

Br. & B.
details unknown

Brainard's Sons
American publisher, company
ceased in 1931.

Brandus.
French publishers, mainly in Paris.
Became G. Brandus, Dufour & Cie,
or G. Brandus & S. Dufour. Taken
over by C. Joubert in 1899, company
ceased in 1971.

Bratfisch
Musikverlag Georg Bratfisch
Hans-Herold -Str. 23
D-95326 Kulmbach Germany
[Presser]

Brauer
Editions Musicales Herman Brauer
30, rue Saint Christophe
B-1000 Brussels, Belgium

Braun-Peretti
St. A. Braun-Peretti
Hahnchenpassage
D-53 Bonn Germany

Breitkopf
Breitkopf & Härtel
Karlstraße 10
DDR-7010 Leipzig Germany or
Walkmühlstraße 52 Postfach 1707 D-
6200 Wiesbaden 1 Germany

Bretscher in Karlsruhe
details unknown

Brixner i. W.
details unknown

Brockhaus, M.
Max Brockhaus, Leipzig, Germany
publisher. Reconstruction of the company began in 1949 in Lörrach.

Broekmans
Broekmans & Van Poppel B.V.
van Baerlestraat 92-94
NL-1071 BB
Amsterdam Netherlands [Peters]

Bromme i. Wiesb.
Bromme in Wiesbaden
details unknown

Broude A
Alexander Broude, Inc.
575 8th Ave.
New York, NY 10018

Broude Br
Broude Brothers Ltd.
141 White Oaks Rd.
Williamstown, MA 01267

Bucher i. Würzb.
Bucher in Würzbaden
details unknown

C. E. King
details unknown

C. Fischer
Carl F. Fischer, Inc.
62 Cooper Square
New York, NY 10003

C. Rühle i. L.
details unknown

C. Simon i. B.
Simon in Berlin
details unknown

Callwey
details unknown

Carey, H.
H. Carey
details unknown

Carisch, Carisch & J. i. Mailand
Nuova Carisch s.l.r.
Via M. F. Quintiliano,
40 20138 Milano, Italy [Boosey]

Carus
Carus-Verlag [Hannsler, Foster]

Century
Century Music Publishing Co.
263 Veterans Blvd.
Carlstadt, NJ 07072

Chal.
Ernst Challier & Co. Challier, Berlin
family of publishers. Associated with
Karl Gaillard in Berlin in 1835. Shops
also in Giessen. Taken over by Richard Birnbach in 1919.

Chappell
Chappell & Co.
1210 Avenue of the Americas
New York, NY 10019

**Chemnitz Selbstverl.,
Chemnitz Selbstverlag**
details unknown

Chester
Chester Music
8-9 Frith St.
London W1V 5TZ England
[G. Schirmer]

Choudens
Édition Choudens
38 rue Jean Mermoz
F-75008 Paris France [Presser]

Church
John Church Co. Cincinatti, OH, firm,
partnered with Oliver Ditson in 1890.
Sold to Theodore Presser in 1930.
[Presser]

Cocks
Robert Cocks, English publisher.
Bought by Augener in 1898, name
retained until 1904.

Cohen
details unknown

Colombo
Franco Colombo Publications [Belwin,
Presser]

Concordia
Concordia Publishing House
3558 S. Jefferson Ave.
St. Louis, MO 63118

Coppenrath
Musikverlag Alfred Coppenrath
Postfach 11 58
D-84495 Altotting Germany

Cormorant
Cormorant Press
P.O. Box 169
Hallowell, ME 04347

Cramer
J. B. Cramer & Co., Ltd.
23 Garrick St.
London WC2E 9AX England [Belwin]

Cranz
Édition Cranz
30, rue St.-Christope
B-1000 Brussels Belgium

Crespub
Crescendo Publications, Inc.
6311 North O'Connor Rd. #112
Irving, TX 75039-3112

Curwen
J. Curwen & Sons, bought by Mac-
millan Inc. in 1969.
[G. Schirmer, Leonard-US]

CVR
Classical Vocal Reprints
3252 Cambridge Avenue 2nd Floor
Riverdale, NY 10463-3618

Czech
Czechoslovak Music
   Information Centre
Besedni 3 CS-11800 Prague 1, Czech
Republic [Boosey-rental]

Danner
details unknown

Darvenski
details unknown

Davison
details unknown

De. Dietrich
details unknown

Dean, J.
J. Dean
details unknown

Deneke
details unknown

Deubner
details unknown

Deutscher
Deutscher Verlag für Musik
Walkmühlstr. 52
D-6200 Wiesbaden 1 Germany
[Broude A, Brietkopf]

Dieckmann i. Leipz.
Dieckmann in Leipzig
details unknown

Dienemann i. Potsd.
Dienemann in Potsdam
details unknown

Dietrich
details unknown

Dietrich, De.
De. Dietrich
details unknown

Dietrich, Fr.
Fr. Dietrich
details unknown

Dietrich, Frz.
Frz. Dietrich
details unknown

Dietrich, O.
O. Dietrich
details unknown

Dietrich, Rud.
Rudolf Dietrich
details unknown

Dietrich, Wilh.
Wilhelm Dietrich
details unknown

Diller & Sohn
details unknown

Ditson
Oliver Ditson Co. Absorbed by Theodore Presser in 1931. [Presser]

Doblinger
Ludwig Doblinger Verlag
Dorotheergasse 10
A-1011 Vienna 1 Austria [AMP]

Donemus
Donemus Foundation
Paulus Potterstraat 14
NL-1071 CZ Amsterdam Netherlands
[Presser]

Dörfell
details unknown

Dover
Dover Publications
31 East 2nd St.
Mineola, NY 11501 [Alfred]

Drustva
Drustva Slovenskih Skladatelja
Trg Francoske Revolucije 6
Ljubljana Slovenia

Drzavna [Drustva]
Drzavna Zalozba Slovenije
details unknown

Dümmler i. Löbau
details unknown

Durand
Durand & Cie.
215 rue du Faubourg St. Honoré
F-75008 Paris France [Presser]

Dürre & W.
details unknown

E. Schel. i. W.
E. Schellenberg
details unknown

E-A
European American Music
  Distributing Corp.
P.O. Box 850
Valley Forge, PA 19482

Eberle, Eberle i. W., Eberle i. Wien
Eberle in Vienna. Music engraving
firm, R. v. Waldheim, Josef Eberle &
Co. Became part of Universal Edition
in Vienna in 1901.

Ebling
details unknown

Ebner
details unknown

ECS
E. C. Schirmer Music Co.
138 Ipswich St.
Boston, MA 02115-3534

Ed. Bloch.
details unknown

Ed. Linderer i. Berl.
Ed. Linderer in Berlin

Edm. Stoll
details unknown

Educ
details unknown

Ehrlich in Potsdam
details unknown

Eisoldt & R. Schles.
Eisoldt & R. Schlesinger
details unknown

Elkan & Sch.
Elkan & Schildknecht
Vastmannagatan 95
S-113 43 Stockholm Sweden

Elkan-Vogel
Elkan-Vogel, Inc.
Presser Place
Bryn Mawr, PA 19010

Elkin
William Elkin Music Services
Wood Green Industrial Estate
Norwich, Norfolk NR13 6NY England
[Presser, Novello]

EMB
Edito Musica Budapest
P.O.B. 322
H-1370 Budapest, Hungary
[Boosey, Presser]

Emmermann
details unknown

Enoch
Enoch & Cie., Paris
193 Boulevard Periere
F-75017 Paris France
[Presser, G. Schirmer]

Ensslin & L.
details unknown

Eulenburg
Edition Eulenburg
305 Bloomfield Ave.
Nutley, NJ 07110 [E-A, Peters]

Ewer, J.
J. Ewer. English firm, established in
London in 1823. Merged with Novello
& Co. in 1867, becoming Novello,
Ewer & Co. Name of Ewer dropped in
1898.

F. D. & H.
Francis, Day & Hunter English firm.
Became a subsidiary of EMI Music
Publishing Ltd. in 1972.

F. Hofbauer
details unknown

F. R. Müller i. Leipz.
F. R. Müller in Leipzig
details unknown

**F. Schellenberg,
F. Schellenberg i. W.**
details unknown

F. Whistling
Friedrich Wilhelm Whistling, part of
German publishing family. F. Whistling publisher in Leipzig. Firms dissolved in 1870.

Faber
Faber Music Ltd.
3 Queen St.
London WC1N 3AU England
[Leonard-US, G. Schirmer]

Favorit i. Berl.
Favorit in Berlin
details unknown

Fazer
Musik Fazer
P.O. Box 169
SF-02101 Espoo Finland

Fechner
details unknown

Feldman
B. Feldman & Co., Ltd.
Bought out by EMI. [EMI]

Feuchtinger
Feuchtinger & Gleichauf
Niedermünstergasse 2
D-8400 Regensburg 11 Germany

Firnberg
details unknown

Fischer
Part of the German family of publishers that later came to America.

Fischer, C.
Carl F. Fischer, Inc.
62 Cooper Square
New York, NY 10003

Fischer in Bremen
Part of the German family of publishers that later came to America.

Fischer, P. i. B., Fischer, P. i. Berl.
P. Fischer in Berlin
details unknown

Fischer, P. i. F.
P. Fischer in Frankfurt [?]
details unknown

Foetisch
Foetisch Freres
Rue de Bourg 6
CH-1002 Lausanne Switzerland
[E. C. Schirmer]

FOG III
Dan Fog Musikforlag
Grabrodretrov 7
DK-1154 Copenhagen K Denmark
[Peters]

Forberg, O.
O. Forberg
details unknown

Forberg, R., Forberg, Rob.
Robert Forberg, son of August Robert
Forberg, Leipzig publisher. Robert ran
the company from 1888, which relocated to Bonn and Bad Godesberg
after World War II.

Förster i. Lockw.
details unknown

Foyle
details unknown

Fr. Dietrich
details unknown

Fr. mus. Ver.
[Prob.] Friedrich Wilhelm Fröhlich
Musikverlag
Ansbacher Straße 52
D-1000 Berlin 30 Germany

Frank
Frank Music Corp.
30 West 54th St.
New York, NY 10019

Fredebaeul & K.
details unknown

Freepub
details unknown

Freie mus. Vereinig
details unknown

(Friedel) Dresden
[Prob.] Walter Friedel, who worked
with Theodor Leberecht Steingräber
This publishing house moved to Offenbach am Main in 1956.

Friedländer
Julius Friedländer bought the Carl Peters' firm after the death of Carl G. S.
Böhme in 1860, who had taken it over
in 1828.

Fries i. Z.
Fries in Zurich
details unknown

Fritz Bartels
details unknown

Fritzsche
[Prob.] E. W. Fritzsch. Bought out in
1903 by Linnemann's sons, and later
became part of Kistner & Siegel,
formed in 1923.

Frz. Dietrich
details unknown

Fürstner
Fürstner Ltd. German firm. Many
rights bought by Boosey & Hawkes in
1943, the rest sold to Schott in 1986.

Fürstner Paris
Fürstner in Paris. See preceding entry.

G. Richter i. L.
G. Richter. [Prob.] Gerard Richter.
details unknown

G. Schirm.
G. Schirmer, Inc. (Executive Offices)
257 Park Ave. South, 20th Floor,
New York, NY 10010

Gaertner i. Königsbütte
details unknown

Galaxy
Galaxy Music Corp.
131 West 86th St.
New York, NY 10024 [E.C. Schirmer]

Gallet
details unknown

Gehrmans
Carl Gehrmanns Musikförlag
Odengatan 84 Box 6005
S-102 Stockholm 31 Sweden
[Boosey]

Gerdes i. Cöln
Gerdes in Cologne
details unknown

Gerstenberger
details unknown

GIA
GIA Publications
7404 S. Mason Ave.
Chicago, IL 60638

Giessel jun.
details unknown

Glas, Glas i. Berl.
Glas in Berlin
details unknown

Glaser
American publishing firm acquired by
Famous, another American publishing
firm. Famous became part of Gulf &
Western in 1966.

Gleichauf
Later Feuchtinger and Gleichauf of
Regensburg, Germany.

Gleissenberg
details unknown

GMI
G. & M. International Music Dealers
1225 Candlewood Hill Rd. Box 2089
Northbrook, IL 60062

Gödsche
details unknown

Goethe-Gesellschaft
details unknown

(Goldmark) Schott
details unknown

Goll. i. W.
details unknown

Gray
H. W. Gray & Co., Inc. American
publishing firm, acquired by Belwin-
Mills in 1971. [Belwin, Presser]

Gregg
Gregg International Publishers, Ltd.
1 Westmead, Farnborough, Hants.
GU14 7RU, England

Gries
details unknown

Griesbach i. Gera.
details unknown

Gross i. Insb.
Gross in Innsbruch
details unknown

Grude
details unknown

Grüninger
details unknown

Günther
Unknown which Günther. E. Günther
partner in 1834 of Friedlein publishers
in Leszno, Poland. Carl Wilhelm
Günther joined firm of Hofmeister
publishers in Leipzig in 1905.

Gust. Richter
Gustav Richter
details unknown

Gutheil, Gutheil i. M.
Russian publishing firm, active in
Moscow. Bought out by Koussevitsky
in 1914 and absorbed into Edition
Russes de Musique.

H. Augustin
Hermann Augustin
details unknown

H. Carey
details unknown

Hahn & Lang
details unknown

Hainauer
details unknown

Hal Leonard
Hal Leonard Music
7777 West Bluemound Rd.
Milwaukee, WI 53213

Hamelle
Hamelle & Cie.
175 rue Saint Honoré
F-75040 Paris Cedex 01 France
[Presser, Southern]

Hampe i. Br.
Adolf Hampe Musikverlag
Hohenzollerndamm 54A
D-1000 Berlin 33 Germany [Budde]

Hansen, Hansen-Den
Edition Wilhelm Hansen
Bornholmsgade 1,1 1266
Copenhagen K Denmark
[G. Schirmer, Chester]

Hänssler-Verlag
Hänssler-Verlag
Röntgenstraße 15 Postfach 1230
D-7312 Kirchheim/Teck Germany
[Peters, Antara]

Harmonie i. B.
details unknown

Harms (NY)
T. B. Harms. American publishing
firm. Became part of Warner Brothers
in 1929. [Warner]

Hartmann i. Erberf.
[Prob.] the French publishing firm;
acquired by Heugel in 1891.

**Haushahn, Haushahn i. L.,
Haushahn i. M.**
details unknown

Heckel
German firm of publishers, founded in
Mannheim. Sold some rights to F. Peters in 1908. Independent operation as
of 1986.

Hedler i. Frankf.
Hedler in Frankfurt
details unknown

Hefner i. Obern.-Bu.
Hefner in Obernneudorf-Bucher
details unknown

Hegner i. S.
details unknown

Heinr.
Heinrichshofens Verlag
Liebigstraße 16 Postfach 620
D-2940 Wilhelmshaven Germany
[Peters]

Heins i. B.
details unknown

Hemme
details unknown

Henkel [Henkle?]
[Poss.] Ted Henkle
5415 Reynolds St.
Savannah, GA 31405

Henn
Editions Henn
8 Rue de Hesse
Genève, Switzerland

Herder i. Freiburg
details unknown

Heugel
Heugel & Cie.
175 rue Saint-Honoré
F-75040 Paris Cedex 01 France
[Presser, Southern]

Hey, Hey i. M.
details unknown

Hinds, Hayden & Eldredge
details unknown

Hinrichs i. Leipz.
Hinrichs in Leipzig
details unknown

Hinrichsen
Hinrichsen Edition Ltd.
details unknown
[Peters]

Hinz
Hinz Fabrik Verlag
Lankwinzerstraße 17-18
D-1000 Berlin 42 Germany

Hochstein, Hochstein i. H.
details unknown

Hoenes
details unknown

Hofbauer
[Prob.] Carl Hofbauer. Founded Austrian publishing firm in 1885 with
Josef Weinberger in Vienna. Acquired
by Sikorski -Berlin in 1938

Hofbauer, F.
F. Hofbauer
details unknown

Hoffarth
details unknown

Hoffheinz
details unknown

Hoffmann i. Pr.
Hoffmann in Prague. Jan Hoffmann.
Publishing firm from 1841. Firm sold
to Hofmeister in Leipzig in 1844.

Hoffmann i. Str.
Hoffmann in Streigau
details unknown

Hofmann i. Dresd.
Hofmann in Dresden
details unknown

Hofmeister
VEB Friedrich Hofmeister
   Musikverlag
Karlstraße 10
DDR-701 Leipzig Germany
[Broude A]

Höhr. i. Z.
Höhr. in Zurich
details unknown

Hope
Hope Publishing Co.
380 S. Main Place
Carol Stream, IL 60188

Hug, Hug (Vogel)
Hug & Company. Jakob C. Hug,
Swiss publisher, became associated
with Nägeli's firm in Zurich. from
1802. Since 1973, Hug & Company
name retained. Flughofstraße 61
CH-Glattbrugg Switzerland
[E-A, Peters]

I. Strauch
details unknown

Iceland
Islenzk Tónverkamidstöd
Iceland Music Information Centre,
Sidumuli 34 108
Reykjavik Iceland [Elkan H]

IMC
Indiana Music Center
322 South Swain P. O. Box 582
Bloomington, IN 47401

J. Dean
J. Dean
details unknown

J. Ewer
English firm, established in London in
1823. Merged with Novello & Co. in
1867, becoming Novello, Ewer & Co.
Name Ewer dropped in 1898.

J. Williams
Joseph Williams, English publishing
firm. Taken over by Stainer & Bell in
1962.

Jäckel, Jäckel i. Leipzig
details unknown

Jackman
Jackman Music Corp.
P. O. Box 900
Orem, UT 84057

Jäger i. Berl.
Jäger in Berlin
details unknown

Japan
Japan Federation of Composers
602 Shinanomachi Bldg.
33 Shinanomachi
Shinjuku-ku, Tokyo, Japan

Jessen i. Dorp.
details unknown

Jobert
Editions Jean Jobert
76, rue Quincampoix
F-75003 Paris France [Presser]

Jonasson-Eckermann
details unknown

Junfermann
details unknown

Junne
Otto Junne GmbH
Sendlinger-Tor-Platz 10
D-8000 Munich Germany

Jurgns., Jurgensen i. M.
details unknown

K. & G.
Kühling & Güttner
details unknown

K. Schulze i. Leipz.
K. Schulze in Leipzig
details unknown

Kahnt
C. F. Kahnt Musikverlag
Kennedyallee 101
6000 Frankfurt 70 Germany [Peters]

Kalb
details unknown

Kalmus
Edwin F. Kalmus
P. O. Box 5011
Boca Raton, FL 33431 [Belwin]

Kaun
[Poss.] Hugo Kaun, associated with
Leuckart, a German publishing firm
which resumed activities in Munich in
1948 after World War II.

Keiner i. Stuttg.
Keiner in Stuttgart
details unknown

Kerr
details unknown

King, C. E.
C. E. King
details unknown

Kistner
Fr. Kistner & C. F. W. Siegel & Co.
Adrian-Kiels-Straße 2
D-5000 Cologne 90 Germany
[Concordia]

Klebahn i. Br.
details unknown

Kleine i. P.
Kleine in Paderb
details unknown

Klemm
details unknown

Klinner
details unknown

Klöckner
details unknown

Kober i. B.
J. L. Kober, Czech publisher, in Prague. May refer to a shop in Brno. Affiliated historically with Urbánek.

Kollmann i. Leipz.
Kollmann in Leipzig
details unknown

Körner i. L.
details unknown

Kothe in Loebschütz
details unknown

Kott
details unknown

Krämer, Krämer i. W.
[Poss.] German publisher associated
with Heinrich P. C. Bossler. Firm
sometimes called Krämer & Bossler.

Kramer-Bangert
details unknown

Kratochwill
A. E. Bosworth, founded Bosworth
publishers in Leipzig assisted by Karl
Kratochwill. Bosworth acquired Kratochwill and Chmél in Vienna in
1902. Bosworth publisher remains.

Kreisler i. H.
details unknown

Krompholz
Krompholz & Co.
Spitalgasse 28
CH-3001 Bern Switzerland

Kröner
details unknown

Kunzel
Edition Kunzelmann
Grutstrasse 28
CH-8134 Adliswil Switzerland
or 305 Bloomfield Ave.
Nutley. NJ 07110

Kuprion
details unknown

L. Wright
details unknown

L'Oiseau
Éditions de L'Oiseau-Lyre
Les Ramparts Boite Postale 515
MC-98015 Monaco Cedex

Läutnerer
details unknown

Le Beau
details unknown

Lederer
details unknown

(Leede)
[Prob.] C. F. Leede of Leipzig.
Associated with Cottrau, taken over by
Ricordi in 1884.

Lehmann i. H.
details unknown

Leichseuring or **Leichssenring**
details unknown

Leiner i. L.
details unknown

Lemoine
Henry Lemoine et Cie.
17, rue Pigalle
F-75009 Paris France [Presser]

Lengnick
Alfred Lengnick & Co., Ltd.
Purley Oaks Studios
421a Brighton Rd. South Croydon,
Surrey, CR2 6YR, England

Lentner i. Mün.
Lentner in Munich
details unknown

Leo i. Berl.
Leo in Berlin
details unknown

Leon sen.
details unknown

Leonard, Hal
Hal Leonard Music
7777 West Bluemound Rd.
Milwaukee, WI 53213

Leonard-Eng
Leonard Gould & Bolttler
6-62 Clerkenwell Rd.
London EC1M 5PY England

Lewy i. München
Lewy in Munich, Viennese publisher,
branches in Germany. Associated with
Pazdírek, Czech family of publishers
and musicians.

Libe C
Library of Congress
Music Division
101 Independence Ave. #Lm 113
Washington, D. C. 20540-0002

Lichtb.
Lichtenberger
details unknown
[Donemus]

Lichtenauer
W. F. Lichtenauer
details unknown

Lillenas
Lillenas Publishing Co.
P. O. Box 419527
Kansas City, MO 64141

Linderer, Ed. i. Berl.
Ed. Linderer in Berlin
details unknown

Lindner
details unknown

Linke i. Sorau
details unknown

Litolff
Henry Litolffs Verlag
Kennedy Allee 101 Postfach 700906
D-6000 Frankfurt 70 Germany
[Peters]

Löbel
details unknown

Longman & Broderlip
English firm established in London.
Defunct in the early 19th century.

Lonsdale
Christopher Lonsdale, English publisher associated with Birchall. Company succeeded by Alfred Hayes in
1880.

Lorch
details unknown

Lorenz
Lorenz Corporation
501 East Third St. P.O. Box 802
Dayton, OH 45401-9969

LPME
London Pro Musica Edition,
15 Rock St.
Brighton BN2 1NF England
[Galaxy, Magna]

Lucas
Stanley Lucas, English publisher. Part
of Lucas, Weber, Pitt & Hatzfeld Ltd.
Stanley Lucas & Son emerged; defunct in 1907.

Lucca
Francesco Lucca, Italian publisher.
Acquired by Ricordi in 1888.

Luckhardt
details unknown

Ludwig in Dresden
details unknown

Ludwig i. Lichterf.
details unknown

Lundq.
Abr. Lundquist AB, Musikforlag
Katarina Bangata 17
S-16 25 Stockholm Sweden

Lyra i. Dresd.
Lyra in Dresden. [Poss. available
through] Lyra Music Co.,
133 West 69th St.
New York, NY 10023

M. Brockhaus
Max Brockhaus, German publisher.
From Leipzig, reconstruction of the
company began in 1949 in Lörrach.

Maas i. W.
details unknown

Mackar in Paris
details unknown

Magna
Magnamusic-Baton, Inc.
10370 Page Industrial Blvd.
St. Louis, MO 63132

Maier in Fulda
details unknown

Marks
Edward B. Marks Music Corp.
1619 Broadway
New York, NY 10019
[Leonard-US, Presser]

Marshalls
details unknown

Mauer in Berlin
details unknown

Mayer & Dorn
details unknown

Media
Media Press
P.O. Box 250
Elwyn, PA 19063

Meijroos & K. i. Arnh.
details unknown

Meinhardt i. Br.
details unknown

Meissner
details unknown

Meissonier i. Par.
Meissonier in Paris. Jean Antoine
Meissonnier, French publisher, became
partner of Heugel in 1839.

Mele Loke
Mele Loke Publishing Co.
Box 7142
Honolulu, HI 96821

Melzer in Leipzig
details unknown

Merse.
Merseburger Verlag
Motzstraße 13
D-3500 Kassel Germany

Metzler
English publishing firm, in London.
Acquired by J. B. Cramer in 1931.

Meyer in Erfurt
details unknown

Mez Kniga
Mezhdunarodnaja Kniga
39, Dimitrov St.
Moscow 113095 Russia
[G. Schirmer]

Michaëlis i. N.
Michaëlis in Neu-Ruppin
details unknown

Mignon-Verlag
details unknown

Monopol
details unknown

Morley
details unknown

MS
Music Sales Corporation
225 Park Ave. South
New York, NY 10003

Mück i. W.
details unknown

Müller, F. R. i. Leipz.
F. R. Müller in Leipzig
details unknown

München Selbst-verlag
details unknown

Music Press
details unknown

Musical Million
details unknown

Musick-Woche i. L., Musik-Woche
details unknown

Nagel
Nagels Verlag. German firm of publishers. Began in Hannover, relocated
to Celle after World War II. Acquired
by Vötterle publishing group in 1952.
[AMP, Magna]

Näumann
details unknown

Nauss
details unknown

Neldner
details unknown

**Neumann & Co., Neumann &
Co. i. B., Neumann & Co. i. Berl,
Neumann & Co. i. Magdeb.**
[Prob.] Georg Neumann. Casa Neumann y Breyer in Buenos Aires in
1882. Neumann separate from Breyer
in 1888, continuing until 1960. Affiliated with Ricordi.

Norsk
Norsk Musikforlag AS
Karl Johansgaten 39
P. O. Box 1499 Vika
N-0116 Oslo 1 Norway
[Magna, AMP]

Noton
Kolltjernvn. 11 P. O. Box 1014
N-2301 Hamar Norway

Novello
Novello & Co. Ltd.
Newmarket Rd., Bury St.
Edmunds, Suffolk IP33 3YB England
or 145 Palisades St.
Dobbs Ferry, NY 10522
[Shawnee, Belwin]

NYP Libe
New York Public Library
   for the Performing Arts
40 Lincoln Center Plaza
New York, NY 10023-7498

O. Dietrich
details unknown

O. Forberg
details unknown

O. Schmidt
details unknown

O. Teich
details unknown

Oehmigke
details unknown

Oertel
Johannes Oertel, German publishing
firm who acquired leased rights of
Fürstner firm during World War II.
Fürstner was acquired by Boosey &
Hawkes and Schott-Mainz by 1986.

Offhaus
details unknown

Ongaku
Ongaku-No-Tomo Sha Co. Co. Ltd.
Kagurazaka 6-30 Shinjuko-ku
Tokyo, Japan [Presser]

Oppenheimer
details unknown

Otto in Berlin
details unknown

OUP
Oxford University Press
7-8 Hatherly St.
London SW1P 2QT England
or 200 Madison Ave.
New York, NY 10016

Ouvrieres
Les Editions Ouvrières
12, Avenue Soeur-Rosalie
F-75621 Paris Cedex 13, France
[Galaxy]

**P. Fischer i. B.,
P. Fischer i. Berl.**
P. Fischer in Berlin
details unknown

P. Fischer i. F.
P. Fischer in Frankfurt [?]
details unknown

P. & M., P. & M. (Peuschel)
Praeger & Meier [Poss. available
through] Praeger Publications
383 Madison Ave.
New York, NY 10017

P. Maurice
details unknown

P. & P. Verl.
P. & P. Verlag
details unknown

Pabst i. D., Pabst i. L.
details unknown

Paez
details unknown

Panton
Radlická 99
CS-150 00
Prague 5 Czech Republic
[Artia, General]

Paragon
Paragon Music Publishers
71 Fourth Ave.
New York, NY 10003 [Century]

Paterson
Paterson's Publications Ltd.
8-10 Lower James St.
London W1R 3PL England
[Fischer C]

Pawliska
details unknown

Peer
Peer International Corp.
810 7th Ave.
New York, NY 10019 [Presser]

Peschke
details unknown

Peterling
details unknown

Peters
C. F. Peters Corp.
373 Park Ave. South
New York, NY 10016

Peterson
details unknown

Philharm. Ver. i. B.
Philharmonischer Verlag
[Poss. available through E-A]

Philipp & S.
Philipp & Sohn
details unknown

Pitman Hart
F. Pitman Hart & Co., Ltd.
[Brodt]

Plahn in Jauer
details unknown

Platt
details unknown

Plothrow
details unknown

Pohl-Wohnlich
details unknown

Portius
details unknown

Preiser
details unknown

Presser
Theodore Presser
Presser Place
Bryn Mawr, PA 19010

Preston
English publishing house. Acquired
by Coventry & Hollier in 1834.

Protze
details unknown

Pustet
Verlag Friedrich Pustet
Gutenbergstraße 8 Postfach 339
D-8400 Regensburg 11 Germany

R. & B.
Reiter-Biedermann
details unknown

R. Birchall
Robert Birchall, English publisher.
Became Birchall, Lonsdale & Mills
(or Birchall & Co., or Mills & Co.)
Mills & Son defunct in 1903.

R. D. Row [C. Fischer]
details unknown

R. & E.
Ries & Erler
Charlottenbrunner Straße 42
D-1000 Berlin 33 (Grunewald)
Germany

R. Forberg, Rob. Forberg
Robert Forberg, son of August Robert
Forberg, Leipzig publisher. Robert ran
company from 1888. Relocated to
Bonn and Bad Godesberg after World
War II.

R. & P. Verl.
Raabe & Plothow Verlag
details unknown

R. S. M.
details unknown

Rahter
D. Rahter
Werderstraße 44
D-2000 Hamburg 13 Germany
[AMP, Presser]

Rathke
details unknown

Rau & P.
details unknown

Recital
Recital Publications
Box 1697
Huntsville, TX 77340

Reeder & Walsh
details unknown

Reinecke
Ausgbabe C. Reinecke
Edition Carl Reinecke.

Remick (NY)
Remick Music Corp. Jerome H. Remick, American publisher founded J. H. Remick & Co. in NY. Acquired by Warner Bros. in 1930. [Warner]

Renner i. Dr.
Renner in Dresden
details unknown

Reynolds
details unknown

Rich. Thiele
Richard Thiele
details unknown

Richter, G. i. L.
[Prob.] Gerard Richter.
details unknown

Richter, Gust.
Gustav Richter
details unknown

Ricordi
G. Ricordi & Co. Ltd.
Via Salomone 77
I-20138 Milano, Italy
[Leonard-US, Boosey]

Ricordi BA
Ricordi Americana SA
Cangallo 1558,
1037 Buenos Aires, Argentina
[Leonard-US, Boosey]

Riebe i. Br.
details unknown

Ries
Ries & Erler
Charlottenbrunner Straße 42
D-1000 Berlin 33 (Grunewald)
Germany

Riewe & Th.
details unknown

Roberton
Roberton Publications
The Windmill, Wendover,
Aylesbury, Bucks.
HP22 6JJ England [Presser]

Robitschek
Adolf Robitschek Musikverlag
Graben 14 (Bräunerstraße 2)
Postfach 42
A-1011 Vienna Austria

Robolsky
details unknown

Röhrich
details unknown

Rongwen
Rongwen Music, Inc.
details unknown
[Broude Br]

Roothaan
details unknown

Rörich
details unknown

Rosé
[Prob.] an editor and arranger for Universal Edition, Austrian Publishers in the early 20th century.

Row, R. D.
R. D. Row
details unknown
[C. Fischer]

Roz i. B.
details unknown

Ruckmich
details unknown

Rud. Dietrich
Rudolf Dietrich
details unknown

Rühle, C. i. L.
C. Rühle
details unknown

Rühle & H.
Rühle & Hunger
details unknown

Rühle i. Berl.
Rühle in Berlin
details unknown

Russian State
details unknown

S. & B.
[Poss.] Stainer & Bell?

S. & V.
Sigismund & Volkening
details unknown

Sac. Mus. Pr.
Sacred Music Press of
  Hebrew Union College
One West 4th St.
New York, NY 10012
[Presser, Transcon]

Sackur
details unknown

Salabert
Editions Salabert, Inc.
575 Madison Ave.
New York, NY 10023 or
Francis Salabert Éditions
22 rue Chauchat
F-75009 Paris France [Leonard-US]

Salzer
Viennese publishing firm in the 19th century.

Santis
Edizioni de Santis
Via Cassia 13
00191 Rome, Italy

Sch. & Co.
Schuberth & Co. [Prob. now Edward Schuberth & Co., Inc. of New York City, moved to Carlstadt, NJ in 1971] [Century, Ashley]

Sch. i. L.
Schulbuchhandlung in Langensalza
details unknown

Sch. J.
J. Schuberth & Co., Rothenbaumchaussee 1 D-2000 Hamburg 13 Germany. Julius Schuberth, Leipzig and New York. Bought by F. Siegel in 1891.

Scharff
details unknown

Scharfrichter-Verlag
details unknown

Schauer
Richard Schauer, Music Publishers
67 Belsize Lane, Hampstead,
London NW3 5AX England
[Presser, AMP]

Schauer EE.
Schauer family related to the Benjamin family who acquired Simrock firm (name retained) in 1951.

Schel., E. i. W.
E. Schellenberg
details unknown

Schellenberg, F.,
Schellenberg F., i. W.
F. Schellenberg
details unknown

Schergens
details unknown

Schiefelbein
details unknown

Schirm., G.
G. Schirmer, Inc. (Executive Offices)
257 Park Ave. South, 20th Floor,
New York, NY 10010

Schirmer i. L.
Schirmer (German). German office of
E.C. or G. Schirmer.

Schlesinger
Berlin publishing firm in the 19th
century.

Schlimpert
details unknown

Schm., A. P. i. Leip.
Arthur Paul Schmidt in Leipzig.
American publisher with operations
in Europe. Sold to Summy-Birchard in
1959. Archives in Library of Congress.

**Schmid i. M.,
Schmid i. München**
Schmid in Munich
details unknown

Schmidl
Carlo Schmidl, Italian publisher, acquired by Ricordi in 1902.

Schmidt i. Heilbr
Schmidt in Heilbrunn
details unknown

Schmidt i. Wien
Schmidt in Vienna
details unknown

Schmidt, O.
O. Schmidt
details unknown

Schneeberger i. Biel.
details unknown

Schöningh., Schöningh. i. Pad.
details unknown

Schott
Schott & Co. Ltd.
Brunswick Rd., Ashford,
Kent TN23 1DX England [E-A]

Schott i. Br.
Schott Frères,
30 rue Saint-Jean
B-1000 Brussels Belgium
[E-A, Peters]

Schott i. L.
Schott in Leipzig [?]
details unknown

Schott (Weber)
[Prob.] Gottfried Weber, editor of
periodical *Cäcilia*, published by
Schott 1824-1848.

Schott-Frer
Schott Frères
30 rue Saint-Jean
B-1000 Brussels Belgium
[E-A, Peters]

Schotts
B. Schotts Söhne
Weihergarten 5 Postfach 3640
D-6500 Mainz Germany [E-A]

Schroeder, Walter
Walter Schroeder
details unknown

Schu. i. W.
Schubert in Vienna
details unknown

Schul
Carl L. Schultheiß
Denzenbergstraße 35
D-7400 Tübingen Germany [Peters]

Schulze, K. i. Leipz.
K. Schulze in Leipzig
details unknown

Schwann
Musikverlag Schwann [Peters]
details unknown

Schweers & H.
details unknown

Schwendimann
details unknown

Scien
details unknown

Seeman
Seeman Nachf.
details unknown

Seesaw
Seesaw Music Corp.
2067 Broadway
New York, NY 10023

Seiling
details unknown

Senff
Bartolf Wilhelm Senff, German
publisher. Publishing house sold to
Simrock in 1907.

Sennewald
Warsaw, Poland firm of publishers,
founded by Gustaw Adolf Sennewald.
Defunct after 1905.

Shawnee
Shawnee Press
49 Waring Dr.
Delaware Water Gap, PA 18327-1099

Sheard
details unknown

Siegel
[Prob.] Carl F. W. Siegel, affiliated
with Forberg, German publishers.

Sikorski
Hans Sikorski Verlag
Johnsallee 23 Postfach 132001,
D-2000 Hamburg 13 Germany
[AMP, Leonard-US]

Simon, C. i. B., Simon i. Berl.
Simon in Berlin
details unknown

Simrock
details unknown
[Presser, AMP]

Singspir
Singspirational Music
The Zondervan Corp.
1415 Lake Dr., S. E.
Grand Rapids, MI 49506

Slov. Hud. Fond.
Slovensky Hudobny Fond
Fucikova 29
CS-801 02 Bratislava Slovakia
[Boosey-rental]

Sommermeyer
details unknown

Sonos
Sonos Music Resources, Inc.
P. O. Box 1510
Orem, UT 84057

Spitzner
Spitzner Verlag
details unknown

Staeglich
details unknown

Stahl, Stahl i. B.
details unknown

Stainer & Bell
Stainer & Bell, Ltd.
P. O. Box 110,
Victoria House 23 Gruneisen Rd
London N3 1DZ England
[E. C. Schirmer]

Standke i. Bonn
details unknown

Starcke
details unknown

Starke
details unknown

Starke in Bresl.
details unknown

State Mus. Pub. (Moscow)
State Music Publications (Moscow)
details unknown

Stein i. Potsd.
Stein in Potsdam
details unknown

Steingräber
Edition Steingräber
Auf der Reiswiese 9
D-6050 Offenbach/M Germany

Steinmetz i. Hamb.
Steinmetz in Hamburg
details unknown

Stern
details unknown

Steyl & Th.
details unknown

STIM
STIMs Informationcentral för
  Svensk Musik
(Swedish Information Center)
Sandhamnsgatan 79 Box 27327 S-102
54 Stockholm Sweden

Stockhaus
Stockhausen-Verlag
Kettenberg 15 D-5067
Kürten Germany, or
Stockhausen-Verlag-US
2832 Maple Lane
Fairfax, VA 22030

Stoll, Edm.
Edm. Stoll
details unknown

Strassburger Druckerei
details unknown

Strauch
details unknown

Strauch, I.
I. Strauch
details unknown

Stürtz i. W.
details unknown

Sulzbach i. Berl.
Sulzbach in Berlin
details unknown

Sulzer
[Prob.] R. Sulzer, German publishing
house, absorbed by Ries & Erler in
the early part of the 20th century.

Summy-Birchard Co.
265 Secaucus Rd.
Secaucus, NJ 08540 [Leonard-US]

Supraphon
Edito Supraphon
Pulackeho 1
CS-112 99 Prague Czech Republic
[Artia, Boosey]

Tandler
details unknown

Teich, O.
O. Teich
details unknown

Thalia-Theater-Verlag
details unknown

Thiele, Rich.
Richard Thiele
details unknown

Thiemer
details unknown

Tonger
P. J. Tonger, Musikverlag
Auf dem Brand 3
Postfach 501865
D-5000 Köln-Rodenkirchen 50
Germany [Peters]

Tormann
details unknown

Tourbié
details unknown

Transcon
Transcontinental Music Publications
838 Fifth Ave.
New York, NY 10021

Trnfeld i. Gr.-Licht.
Treuenfeld
details unknown

Uhse
details unknown

Ulbrich i. Berl.
Ulbrich in Berlin
details unknown

Ullrich i. Cöln
Ullrich in Cologne
details unknown

UME
Union Musical Española (Ediciones)
Carrera de San Jeronimo 26
Madrid Spain [G. Schirmer, AMP]

United Mus.
United Music Publishers, Ltd.
42 Riverton St.
London EC2A 3BN England [Presser]

Univ.-Bibliothek
details unknown

Univ. Mus. Ed.
University Music Editions
P. O. Box 192 Fort George Station
New York, NY 10040

Universal
Universal Edition, Ltd.
Bösendorfer Straße 12, Postfach 130
A-1015 Vienna Austria,
or 2/3 Fareham St.
London W1V 4DU England [E-A]

Universe
Universe Publishers
733 East 840 North Circle
Orem, UT 84057 [Presser]

Uppenborn i. Clausthal
details unknown

Urbánek
Mojmír Urbánek, Prague, Czech Republilc publisher. Founded in 1900, firm was nationalized in 1949. Edition M. U. is synonymous name of the firm.

Urse
details unknown

v. Wahlberg
Brix von Wahlberg, Dutch publishing house absorbed in 1898 by Alsbach, another Dutch firm (now Alsbach & Doyer).

Verlag d. Traktahauses
details unknown

Verlag Melodia
details unknown

Verlags-Anst i. Regensburg
details unknown

Vetter
details unknown

Vieweg i. Qu.
Chr. Friedrich Vieweg, Musikverlag
Nibelungenstraße 48
D-8000 Munich 19 Germany
[AMP,Leonard-US]

Virgilius-Verlag
details unknown

Vix i. B.
details unknown

Vix i. Göpp.
details unknown

Volkening i. Minden
details unknown

vom Ende
details unknown

Vormeyer
details unknown

Wagenaar
J. A. H. Wagenaar
Oude Gracht 109
NL-3511 Ag Utrecht Netherlands
[Elkan H]

Wagner i. Dr.
Wagner in Dresden
details unknown

Wagner & Levien
A. Wagner y Levien, Mexico City publishing firm in the mid-19th century. Joint publications with Schirmer in NY, and Hofmeister in Leipzig. Bankrupt in 1936.

Wahlberg, v.
Brix von Wahlberg, Dutch publishing house absorbed in 1898 by Alsbach, another Dutch firm (now Alsbach & Doyer).

Walde i. Löbau
details unknown

Walter Schroeder
details unknown

Walton
Walton Music Corp.
[Hinshaw, Plymouth]

Warner
Warner Brothers Publications, Inc.
265 Secaucus Rd.
Secaucus. NJ 07094 [Belwin]

Waterloo
Waterloo Music Co. Ltd.
3 Regina St. North
Waterloo, Ontario N2J 4A5 Canada
[Boosey, et al]

Wattenbach in Gotha
details unknown

Weber
details unknown

Weber i. Cöln
Weber in Cologne
details unknown

Wehde
details unknown

Weinholtz
Carl Weinholz, German publisher who in 1860 absorbed the firm of Johann P. Spehr. Bauer & Pahlmann took it over in 1872 under name of Bauer only, firm destroyed in 1944.

Weiss Nachf. i. Berl.
Weiss Nachf. in Berlin
details unknown

Weissbach, Weissbach i. B., Weissbach i. Burgst
details unknown

Wenzel
details unknown

Werner i. Münch.
Werner in Munich
details unknown

Wernthal
German publishing firm absorbed by Lienau in 1925. Lienau firm still continues.

Wessel
[Prob.] Christian Rudolph Wessel, London, England publisher of German descent. Wessel & Stodart eventually became Edwin Ashdown Ltd. in 1860 when Wessel retired.

Westermair
details unknown

Westphal i. Karlshorst
[Prob.] Moritz Westphal, Berlin firm. [Branch in Karlshorst?] absorbed by Bote & Bock in 1840.

Wetzler i. Pr.
Wetzler in Prague. Wetzler a German publishing firm. [Branch in Prague?]

Weygand
details unknown

Whistling, F.
Friedrich Wilhelm Whistling, part of German publishing family. F. Whistling publisher in Leipzig. Firms dissolved in 1870.

White-Smith
Boston music publisher, defunct in 1976.

Wiener Musikver.
Wiener Musikverlagshaus
details unknown
[Poss. available through E-A]

Wilh. Dietrich
Wilhelm Dietrich
details unknown

Williams, J.
J. Williams. Joseph Williams, English publishing firm. Eventually taken over by Stainer & Bell in 1962.

Willis
Willis Music Company
7380 Industrial Highway
Florence, KY 41042

Winklmn. i. W.
Winkelmann
details unknown

Winterling, Winterling i. L.
details unknown

Wood
Andrew Wood, Edinburgh, Scotland
publisher. Son John Muir Wood established Glasgow firm called J. Muir
Wood & Co. Defunct in 1899.

Word
Word, Inc.
3319 West End Ave. Suite 200
Nashville, TN 37203

World
World Library Publications, Inc.
3815 Willow Rd. P. O. Box 2701
Schiller Park, IL 60176

Wright, L.
L. Wright
details unknown

Wunderhorn-Verl. i. M.
Wunderhorn-Verlag
details unknown

Year Book Press
details unknown

Zerboni
Edizioni Suvini Zerboni
Via Quintillano 40
I-20138 Milano Italy
[Boosey]

Zierfuss
details unknown

Zimm
Zimmermann
details unknown

Zschocher
details unknown

Zumsteeg
details unknown

Zweifel & Weber
details unknown

Appendix G: Contents of Known Anthologies

A kamaraének mesterei. Edited and compiled by T. Füzesséry. Publisher: EMB. No date.

COMP.	DATES	TITLE	OP. #	VCG	REC
Kodály, Zoltán	1881-1967	Álom	No. 8	Unspec.	3867
———	———	Bánat	No. 3	Unspec.	3868
———	———	Felhö	No. 7	Unspec.	3872
———	———	Gyöngyvirág	No. 4	Unspec.	3873
Saint-Saëns, Camille	1839-1921	Ave Maria		S/MS or T/Br	6395
Sugár, Rezsö	1919-1988	Elmúlt a Vész		S/A or S/MS	7601

Also included in this volume are works by the following composers who are not included in the parameters of this study: Johann Sebastian Bach, Joseph Haydn, Wolfgang Amadeus Mozart, Henry Purcell and Peter Ilyich Tchaikovsky (opera duet).

Album of Sixteen Sacred Duets. Publisher: G. Schirmer. No date, possibly 1880?

COMP.	DATES	TITLE	OP. #	VCG	REC
Abt, Franz	1819-1885	Over the Stars there is rest		S/A	236
Bartlett, Homer Newton	1845-1940	For ever with the Lord		S/A	544
*Bassford, William Kipp	1839-1902	My Faith Looks Up to Thee		S/A	560
Gounod, Charles	1818-1893	For ever with the Lord!		S/A	2652
———		Repentir		S/A	2674
Mendelssohn, Felix	1809-1847	Ich harrete des Herrn		S/MS	4861
Mosenthal, Joseph	1834-1896	I will magnify Thee, O God		S/S/ S/S or S/T	5094/ 5095
Schnecker, P. A.		In his hands are all the corners of the earth		S/A	6761
*Shelley, Harry Rowe	1858-1947	King of Love My Shepherd Is, The		S/MS or S/Br or T/Br	7159
Smart, Henry	1813-1879	Lord is my Shepherd, The		S/A/ S/A or S/MS	7377/ 7384

*These works may be included in later printings; not in original.

Also included in this volume are works with voicings not included in the parameters of this study by the following composers: William Rees (S/T), P. A. Schnecker (A/B), F. A. Sheppard (A/T), Louis Spohr (A/T), and John Stainer (S/T).

Brainard's Collection of Vocal Duets from Popular Modern and Standard Composers. Publisher: Brainard's Sons. Date: 1903.

COMP.	DATES	TITLE	OP. #	VCG	REC
Abt, Franz	1819-1885	When I know That Thou Art Near Me		Unspec.	310
Balfe, Michael William	1808-1870	Trust Her Not		Unspec.	497
Campana, Fabio	1819-1882	Dearest, the Moon Before Us		Unspec.	1315
Chisholm, M. A.		Slumber Sea		Unspec.	1413
Ferber, R.		I Love You Dear		Unspec.	2090
Glover, Stephen	1812-1870	Angels are Watching Us		Unspec.	2499
————	————	Listen, 'Tis the Wood bird's Song		Unspec.	2506
Hackel, Anton	1779-1846	Two Nightingales		Unspec.	2928
Hart, M. A.		Through the Gates of Gold		Unspec.	2984
Kücken, Friedrich Wilhelm	1810-1882	O Swallow, Happy Swallow		Unspec.	4098
Lucantoni, Giovanni	1825-1902	Night in Venice, A		Unspec.	4582
Masini, Francesco	1804-1863	Land of the Swallows		Unspec.	4721
Norton, Caroline E. S.	1808-1877	Juanita		Unspec.	5300
Oehmler, L.		Lord, Hear My Prayer		Unspec.	5327
Owen, Anita		Farewell, Dear Heart		Unspec.	5353
Pinsuti, Ciro	1829-1888	Sunrise		Unspec.	5499
Richards, Brinley	1817-1885	How Beautiful is Night		Unspec.	5993
S. G. P.		Life's Dream is O'er		Unspec.	6379
Smith, Alice Mary	1839-1884	O That We Two Were Maying		Unspec.	7402
Verner, H. C.		Love's Awakening		Unspec.	8019
————		Pride of the Ball		Unspec.	8020

Also included in this volume is a work with style not included in the parameters of this study by the following composer: Giuseppe Verdi (opera duet).

Choice Sacred Duets for All Voices. Publisher: Ditson Date: 1936.

COMP.	DATES	TITLE	OP. #	VCG	REC
Bartlett, J. C.		Day is Ended, The (An Evening Hymn)		S/A	546
Faure, Jean Baptiste	1830-1914	Crucifix		S/A	2073
Gounod, Charles	1818-1893	Forever with the Lord		S/A	2654
Lachner, Franz	1803-1890	My Faith Looks Up to Thee		S/A	4188
Nevin, George Balch	1859-1933	Jesu, Word of God Incarnate		S/A/ S/A or S/MS	5234/ 5235
Schnecker, P. A.		Jesus, the Very Thought of Thee		S/A	6763
Smart, Henry	1813-1879	Lord is My Shepherd, The		S/A	7378

Also included in this volume are works with voicings not included in the parameters of this study by the following composers: Carl Goetz (S/Br), E. S. Hosmer (T/B), Edward Howe (S/Br), A. W. Lansing (S/Br), Felix Mendelssohn (A/Br), George B. Nevin (MS/Br and T/B), Otto Nicolai (S/T), John Stainer (S/T), Alfred Wooler (S/T), and Alfred Whitehead (S/T).

The Ditson Collection of Soprano and Alto Duets. Publisher: Ditson. Date: 1934.

COMP.	DATES	TITLE	OP. #	VCG	REC
Berger, Wilhelm	1861-1911	Du, du liegst mir im Herzen		S/A or MS/A	711
Blumenthal, Jacob [Jacques]	1829-1908	Venetian Boat Song		S/A	878
Böhm, Karl	1844-1920	Still wie die Nacht	Op. 326 No. 27	S/A	895
Brahms, Johannes	1833-1897	Wiegenlied	Op. 49 No. 4	S/A	1116
Caracciolo, Luigi		Nearest and Dearest		S/A	1341
Chaminade, Cecile	1857-1944	L'Angelus	Op. 69	S/A	1376
Henschel, George	1850-1934	Kein Feuer, keine Kohle	Op. 4 No. 1	S/A	3140
Jensen, Adolf	1837-1889	Press Thy Cheek Against Mine Own		S/A	3624
Kjerulf, Halfdan	1815-1868	Last Night		S/A	3798
Logé, Henri		Across the still Lagoon		S/A	4521
Marzials, Théodor	1850-	Friendship		S/A	4709
Mendelssohn, Felix	1809-1847	Auf flügeln des gesanges		S/A	4823
———	———	Gruss	Op. 63 No. 3	S/A	4846
———	———	O sah ich auf der Haide	Op. 63 No. 5	S/A	4893
Page, Nathanael Clifford	1866-	All Through the Night		S/A	5378
Reinecke, Carl	1824-1910	Frühlingsblumen	Op. 26	S/A	5767
Rimsky-Korsakov, Nicolai	1844-1908	A Song of India [Chanson du marchand Hindou]		S/A	6032
Rubinstein, Anton	1829-1894	Der Engel	Op. 48 No. 1	S/A	6238
———	———	Wanderer's Night Song [Wanderers Nachtlied]	Op. 48 No. 5	S/A	6298
Wilson, Henry Lane	1870-1915	Carmeña		S/A	8493

This anthology listing is complete.

Table G.6: *Duettek nöi Hangokra Zongorakísérettel.* Vol. II. Compiled by M. Forai. Publisher: EMB. Date: 1959.

COMP.	DATES	TITLE	OP. #	VCG	REC
Brahms, Johannes	1833-1897	Klänge I		S/A	1082
———	———	Klänge II		S/A	1084
Franck, César	1822-1890	Aux Petits Enfants		S/A	2179
Kodály, Zoltán	1881-1967	Csillagoknak Teremtöje		S/A/ S/MS	3870/ 3871

Continued on next page

(*Duettek nöi—Continued*)

COMP.	DATES	TITLE	OP. #	VCG	REC
Kodály, Zoltán	1881-1967	Kiolvasó		S/A/ S/MS	3874/ 3875
Liszt, Franz	1811-1886	O, Meer im Abendstrahl		S/A	4498
Mendelssohn, Felix	1809-1847	Abschiedslied der Zugvögel		S/A	4816
———	———	Das Ährenfeld		S/A	4830
———	———	Gruss		S/A	4844
———	———	Herbstlied		S/A	4850
———	———	Ich wollt' mein Lieb' ergösse sich		S/A	4866
———	———	Maiglöckchen und die Blümlein		S/A	4883
Rossini, Gioacchino [attr.]	1792-1868	Duetto Buffo di due Gatti		S/A	6197
Schumann, Robert	1810-1856	Das Glück		S/A	6977
———	———	Sommerruh		S/A	7045
———	———	Wenn ich ein Vöglein wär		S/A	7060

This anthology listing is complete.

Duet Album: Selected and Edited by Viola Morris and Victoria Anderson. Publisher: Boosey & Hawkes. Date: 1944.

COMP.	DATES	TITLE	OP. #	VCG	REC
Brahms, Johannes	1833-1897	Die Schwestern	Op. 61 No. 1	high & med. v.	1053
Franck, César	1822-1890	Les Danses de Lormont		high & med. v.	2192
Keel, James Frederick	1871-1954	You Spotted Snakes		high & med. v./ S/MS	3731/ 3732
Schumann, Robert	1810-1856	An den Abendstern	Op. 103 No. 4	high & med. v.	6961
Somervell, Arthur	1863-1937	Under the Greenwood Tree		high & med. v./ S/S or S/MS	7420/ 7421
Thiman, Eric Harding	1900-1975	Spring Wind		high & med. v./ S/MS	7841/ 7842

Also included in this volume are works by the following composers who are not included in the parameters of this study: François Couperin, Claudio Monteverdi, Henry Purcell, and Heinrich Schütz.

Duets for the Master: Sacred Duets for High and Low Voice and Keyboard. Edited and arranged by Craig Courtney. Publisher: Beckenhorst. Date: 1989.

COMP.	DATES	TITLE	OP. #	VCG	REC
Andrews, Mark (arr. C. Courtney)		The radiant Morn hath passed away		2 high v.	397
Courtney, Craig	20th C.	Be Thou My Vision		high & low v.	1534
——	——	Let Us Break Bread Together		high & low v.	1535
——	——	None Other Lamb		high & low v.	1536
——	——	Praise Him!		high & low v.	1537
Holst, Gustav (arr. C. Courtney)	1874-1934	In the Bleak Midwinter		high & low v.	3434
Wyeth, John (arr. C. Courtney)		Come, Thou Fount		high & low v.	8727

This anthology listing is complete.

Forty-Eight Duets Seventeenth Through Nineteenth Centuries. Compiled and arranged for medium voices by V. Prahl. Publisher: ECS. Date: 1941, 1970.

COMP.	DATES	TITLE	OP. #	VCG	REC
Beethoven, Ludwig van	1770-1827	Constancy		Unspec.	630
——	——	Sweet Power of Song		Unspec.	646
——	——	Where flowers were springing		Unspec.	651
Brahms, Johannes	1833-1897	Das Meere	Op. 20 No 3	Unspec.	1047
——	——	Die Schwestern	Op. 61 No. 1	Unspec.	1054
——	——	Phänomen	Op. 61 No. 3	Unspec.	1093
——	——	So lass uns wandern	Op. 75 No. 3	Unspec.	1098
Cornelius, Peter	1810-1874	Come away, death	Op. 16 No 3	Unspec.	1497
——	——	I will lift mine eyes		Unspec.	1500
——	——	Sweet flowers are now blooming	Op. 16 No. 2	Unspec.	1527
Dvorák, Antonín	1841-1904	From the Bough	Op. 38 No. 4	Unspec.	1822
——	——	When the Cuckoo sings	Op. 38 No. 1	Unspec.	1865
Franck, César	1822-1890	La Vierge à la Crèche		Unspec.	2186
Gade, Niels Wilhelm	1817-1890	O, hush thee, my baby (Lullaby)		Unspec.	2411
Gade, Niels Wilhelm	1817-1890	Rose-bud in the heather		Unspec.	2415
Jadassohn, Salomon	1831-1902	As the stars in heav'n are blazing		Unspec.	3570

Continued on next page

(*Forty-Eight Duets—Continued*)

COMP.	DATES	TITLE	OP. #	VCG	REC
Jadassohn, Salomon	1831-1902	Twelve Times		Unspec.	3593
Henschel, George	1850-1934	No fire, nor hot embers		Unspec.	3143
Mendelssohn, Felix	1809-1847	Abendlied		Unspec.	4811
Rubinstein, Anton	1830-1894	Tulerunt Dominum meum		Unspec.	4912
———	———	Huntsman, The		Unspec.	6254
———	———	Lotus-Flower, The		Unspec.	6265
Rubinstein, Anton	1830-1894	O Weary Soul		Unspec.	6271
Saint-Saëns, Camille	1835-1921	Pastorale		Unspec.	6410
Schumann, Robert	1810-1856	Awaken, my Darling		Unspec.	6970
———	———	So wahr die Sonne scheinet		Unspec.	7041
———	———	To an Evening Star		Unspec.	7053
———	———	To the Nightingale		Unspec.	7054
Thomas, Arthur Goring	1851-1892	Contentment		Unspec.	7865

Also included in this volume are works by the following composers who are not included in the parameters of this study: Johann Sebastian Bach, Giovanni Clari, George Frideric Handel, Henry Lawes, Giovanni Legrenzi, Jean-Baptiste Lully, Thomas Morley, Wolfgang Amadeus Mozart, Giovanni Pergolesi, and Henry Purcell.

Izbrannye Duety Russkikh Kompozitorov dlia peniia s fortepiano. (Transliterated title of Russian. Original in Cyrillic). Publisher: GMI. Date: 1948.

COMP.	DATES	TITLE	OP. #	VCG	REC
Arensky, Anton	1861-1906	Fialka		S/A	424
———	———	Minuty schastia [Minutes of Happiness]		S/A	428
———	———	Tikho vse sred Choruiush chei Nochi [Everything is quiet in the Enchanting Evening]		S/A	429
Cui, César	1835-1918	Poslednye tsvety [The Last Flowers]		S/MS	1547
———	———	Tuchki nebesnyie [The Heavenly Little Clouds]		S/MS	1548
Dargomizhsky, Alexander	1813-1869	Deva i Roza [The Maiden and the Rose]		S/S	1585
Glazunov, Alexander	1865-1936	Ekh ty, Pesnia [Oh You Songs]		S/A	2484
Glinka, Mikhail Ivanovich	1804-1857	Vy ne pridete vnov [You Aren't Coming Again]		S/S	2497
Grechaninov, Alexander	1864-1956	Dubravushka [The Little Leafy Grove]		S/A	2743
———	———	Posle grozy [After the Thunderstorm]		S/A	2745

Continued on next page

(Izbrannye Duety—Continued)

COMP.	DATES	TITLE	OP. #	VCG	REC
Rubinstein, Anton	1829-1894	Gornye vershiny [Mountain Heights]		S/MS	6253
Tchaikovsky, Peter Ilyich	1840-1893	Rassved [The Dawn]		S/MS	7701
———	———	V Ogorod vozle Brodu [In the Vegetable Garden by the Ford]		S/MS	7713

Also included in this volume are works with voicings not included in the parameters of this study by the following composers: Mikhail Glinka (A/T and S/T) and Sergei Taneyev (T/B).

The Most Popular Vocal Duets. Edited by Dr. E. J. Biedermann. Publisher: Hinds, Hayden & Eldredge. Date: 1914.

COMP.	DATES	TITLE	OP. #	VCG	REC
Ascher, Joseph	1829-1869	Alice (Life's Dream is O'er)		high & low v.	442
———	———	Life's Dream is O'er (Alice)		high & low v.	443
Benedict, Jules	1804-1885	Moon Has Raised Her Lamp Above, The		high & low v.	685
Blumenthal, Jacob [Jacques]	1829-1908	Venetian Boat Song		high & low v.	876
Campana, Fabio	1819-1882	I Live and Love Thee		high & low v.	1321
———	———	See the Pale Moon		high & low v.	1328
Caracciolo, Luigi		Nearest and Dearest		high & low v.	1339
Chaminade, Cecile	1857-1944	Angelus, The		high & low v.	1372
Gabussi, C. M.		Fisherman, The		high & low v.	2365
Goetz, Karl [Götze]	1836-1887	Calm as the Night		high & low v.	2539
Graben-Hoffmann, Gustav	1820-1900	I Feel Thy Angel Spirit		high & low v.	2696
Grell, Eduard August	1800-1886	Laurel and the Rose, The		high & low v.	2796
Horn, Charles Edward	1786-1849	I Know a Bank Whereon the Wild Thyme Blows		high & low v.	3468
Kücken, Friedrich Wilhelm	1810-1882	Drift, My Bark		high & low v.	4074
Lassen, Eduard	1830-1904	Spring Song		high & low v.	4318
Mendelssohn, Felix	1809-1847	I Would That My Love		high & low v.	4857
———	———	O, Wert Thou in the Cauld Blast		high & low v.	4896
Rubinstein, Anton	1829-1894	Lotosflower, The		high & low v.	6294

Continued on next page

(The Most Popular Vocal Duets—Continued)

COMP.	DATES	TITLE	OP. #	VCG	REC
Rubinstein, Anton	1829-1894	Wanderer's Night Song		high & low v.	6296
Schubert, Franz Peter	1797-1828	Serenade		high & low v.	6885
Smart, Henry	1813-1879	My Boat is Waiting Here for Thee		high & low v.	7385
Tosti, Francesco Paolo	1846-1916	Good-Bye		high & low v.	7906

Also included in this volume is a work with a style not included in the parameters of this study by the following composer: Jacques Offenbach (opera duet).

Romantic Duets—Great Performers Edition. Compiled by E. Lear & T. Stewart. Publisher: G. Schirmer. Date: 1985.

COMP.	DATES	TITLE	OP. #	VCG	REC
Brahms, Johannes	1833-1897	Weg der Liebe	Op. 20 No. 1	Unspec.	1111
Dvorák, Antonín	1841-1904	Moznost	Op. 38	Unspec.	1835
Dvorák, Antonín	1841-1904	Slavíkovsky Polecko Maly	Op. 32 No. 5	Unspec.	1849
Grechaninov, Alexander	1864-1956	Ai-Doo-Doo	Op. 31 No. 7	Unspec.	2740
———	———	Kolibelnaya "Bayoo Bai"	Op. 31 No. 5	Unspec.	2744
Mendelssohn, Felix	1809-1847	Abendlied		Unspec.	4810
———	———	Maiglockchen und die Blümelein	Op. 63 No. 6	Unspec.	4884
Schubert, Franz Peter	1797-1828	Mignon und der Harfner "Nur Wer die Sehnsucht Kennt"	Op. 62 No. 1	Unspec.	6873
Schumann, Robert	1810-1856	Schön Blümelein	Op. 43 No. 3	Unspec.	7031
———	———	So Wahr die Sonne Scheinet	Op. 37 No. 12	Unspec.	7043

Also included in this volume is a work with voicings not included in the parameters of this study by the following composer: Stephen Collins Foster (S/B).

Sacred Duet Masterpieces of the World's Greatest Composers For Two High Voices. Vol. 3. Compiled and edited by C. Fredrickson. Publisher: R. D. Row. Date: 1961.

COMP.	DATES	TITLE	OP. #	VCG	REC
Boito, Arrigo	1842-1918	Give Thanks Unto God		2 high v.	918
Cornelius, Peter	1824-1874	Christ Child, The		2 high v.	1496
———	———	Shepherds, The		2 high v.	1523
Dvorák, Antonín	1841-1904	Hear My Prayer		2 high v.	1825

Continued on next page

(*Sacred Duet Masterpieces—Continued*)

COMP.	DATES	TITLE	OP. #	VCG	REC
Dvořák, Antonín	1841-1904	Lord is My Shepherd, The		2 high v.	1833
Franz, Robert	1815-1892	Let Not Your Heart Be Troubled		2 high v.	2294
Godard, Benjamin	1849-1895	O Thou, Who Madest the Heavens		2 high v.	2530
Hummel, Ferdinand	1855-1928	Alleluia!		2 high v.	3532
Mendelssohn, Felix	1809-1847	King of Love my Shepherd Is, The		2 high v.	4872
————	————	Secret Place, The		2 high v.	4905
Stainer, John	1840-1901	God So Loved the World		2 high v.	7470
Sullivan, Arthur	1842-1900	Lord Has Risen, The		2 high v.	7606

Also included in this volume are works by the following composers who are not included in the parameters of this study: Johann Sebastian Bach, George Frideric Handel, Joseph Haydn, and Henry Purcell.

Sacred Duets A Collection of Two-Part Songs by the Best Composers. Vol. 1 for Two High Voices. Compiled and edited by W. Shakespeare. Publisher: Church. Date: 1907.

COMP.	DATES	TITLE	OP. #	VCG	REC
Abt, Franz	1819-1885	Abendlied	Op. 62 No. 4	2 high v.	122
————	————	Gruss an Maria		2 high v.	183
————	————	Wollt ihr die Engelein hören im Chor		2 high v.	318
Andrews, Mark		The Radiant Morn hath passed away		2 high v.	397
Faure, Jean Baptiste	1830-1914	Crucifix		2 high v.	2074
Gaul, Alfred Robert	1837-1913	They shall hunger no more		2 high v.	2437
Gounod, Charles	1818-1893	Christmas Song		2 high v./ S/S or T/T or S/T	2645/ 2646
————	————	Parce, domine		2 high v.	2672
————	————	What grief can try me, O Lord		2 high v./ S/S or T/T or S/T	2684/ 2685
Hammond, William G.		Far from my Heavenly Home		2 high v.	2971
Mendelssohn, Felix	1809-1847	Denn in seiner (Psalm 95)		2 high v.	4834
————	————	Ich harrete des Herrn		2 high v.	4860
————	————	My song shall be alway		2 high v.	4888
————	————	O wie selig ist das Kind		2 high v.	4897
————	————	Wohin habt ihr ihn getragen		2 high v.	4924
Molique, Wilhelm Bernhard	1802-1869	Die Jahreszeiten		2 high v.	5052
————	————	Du bist, o Gott		2 high v.	5053

Continued on next page

(Sacred Duets A Collection of Two-Part Songs—Continued)

COMP.	DATES	TITLE	OP. #	VCG	REC
Molique, Wilhelm Bernhard	1802-1869	It is of the Lord's great mercies		2 high v.	5056
————	————	Seine Macht ist unerforschlich		2 high v.	5059
————	————	Weint, Kinder von Israel!		2 high v.	5061
Pinsuti, Ciro	1829-1888	There is a Reaper		2 high v.	5502
Saint-Saëns, Camille	1839-1921	Ave Maria		2 high v./ S/S or T/T or S/T	6398/ 6401
Smart, Henry	1813-1879	Evening		2 high v.	7370
————	————	Lord is My Shepherd, The		2 high v.	7379
Spohr, Louis	1784-1859	Children, pray this love to cherish		2 high v.	7448
————	————	Forsake me not		2 high v.	7450
Stainer, John	1840-1901	Love Divine! all love excelling		2 high v.	7471

Also included in this volume are works by the following composers who are not included in the parameters of this study: George Frideric Handel and Benedetto Marcello.

Sacred Duets A Collection of Two-Part Songs by the Best Composers, Vol. 2 for High and Low Voices. Compiled and edited by W. Shakespeare. Publisher: Church. Date: 1907.

COMP.	DATES	TITLE	OP. #	VCG	REC
Abt, Franz	1819-1885	Der Sonntag	Op. 132	high & low v.	150
Adam, Adolphe Charles	1803-1856	Oh, Holy Night!		high & low v.	327
Bennet, William Sterndale	1816-1875	And who is he that will harm you		high & low v./ S/A or A/T or S/Br	686/ 687
————	————	Cast thy bread upon the waters		high & low v.	688
————	————	Let Thy Mind		high & low v./ S/A or A/T or S/Br	689/ 690
David, Ferdinand	1810-1873	Mein Aug' erheb' ich		high & low v./ S/A or A/T or S/Br	1588/ 1589
Foster, Myles Birket	1851-1922	Eye hath not seen, nor ear heard		high & low v.	2166
————	————	If ye then be risen with Christ		high & low v.	2167
————	————	Is it nothing to you?		high & low v.	2168
————	————	Night is far spent, The		high & low v.	2169
————	————	There were Shepherds		high & low v.	2172
————	————	Why seek ye the living among the dead?		high & low v.	2173

Continued on next page

(Sacred Duets A Collection—Continued)

COMP.	DATES	TITLE	OP. #	VCG	REC
Gounod, Charles	1818-1893	Forever with the Lord		high & low v./ S/A or A/T or S/Br	2655/ 2656
————	————	Glory to Thee, my God, this night		high & low v.	2661
————	————	Glory to Thee, my God, this night		S/A or A/T or S/Br	2663
————	————	O, Divine Redeemer		high & low v.	2666
————	————	Until the day breaks		high & low v.	2681
Mendelssohn, Felix	1809-1847	Sonntagsmorgen		high & low v.	4907
Pinsuti, Ciro	1829-1888	Life is passing away		high & low v.	5496
————	————	There is a Reaper		high & low v.	5503
Rubinstein, Anton	1829-1894	Der Engel		high & low v.	6234
Saint-Saëns, Camille	1839-1921	Ave Maria		high & low v./ or A/A	6396/ 6398
Smart, Henry	1813-1879	Evening		high & low v.	7371
————	————	Faint not, fear not, God is near thee		high & low v./ S/A or A/T or S/Br	7372/ 7373
————	————	Lord is My Shepherd, The		high & low v.	7380
————	————	Sabbath Bell, The		high & low v.	7386
————	————	There was joy in Heaven		high & low v.	7389
————	————	Vox Matutina		high & low v./ S/A or A/T or S/Br	7390/ 7391
————	————	When Brighter suns and milder skies		high & low v./ S/A or A/T or S/Br	7392/ 7393
————	————	Where the Weary are at Rest		high & low v.	7396
Topliff, Robert		Consider the Lilies		high & low v.	7903

Also included in this volume are works by the following composers who are not included in the parameters of this study: George Frideric Handel, Wolfgang Amadeus Mozart, Henry Purcell, and Jean-Philippe Rameau.

Schirmer's Favorite Sacred Duets for Various Voices. Publisher: G. Schirmer.
Date: 1955.

COMP.	DATES	TITLE	OP. #	VCG	REC
Adam, Adolphe Charles	1803-1856	Cantique de Noël		S/A	324
Bassford, William Kipp	1839-1902	My Faith Looks Up to Thee		S/A	559
Faure, Jean Baptiste	1830-1914	Crucifix		S/A or T/Br	2072
———	———	Crucifix		S/A or T/B	2076
Granier, Jules		Hosanna!		S/A	2738
Harker, F. Flaxington	1876-1936	How Beautiful Upon the Mountains		high & low v.	2980
Malotte, Albert Hay	1895-1964	Lord's Prayer, The		S/A	4646
Neidlinger, William Harold	1863-1924	Birthday of a King, The		S/A	5175
Shelley, Harry Rowe	1858-1947	Christian, the Morn breaks sweetly O'er thee		high & low v.	7148
———	———	Christian, the Morn breaks sweetly O'er thee		S/MS or S/Br or T/Br	7150
———	———	Hark! hark, my Soul		S/A	7155
———	———	Hark! hark my Soul!		S/A or S/MS	7157
———	———	Christian, the Morn breaks sweetly O'er thee		S/MS or S/Br or T/Br	7150
———	———	Hark! hark, my Soul		S/A	7155
———	———	Hark! hark my Soul!		S/A or S/MS	7157
———	———	King of Love my Shepherd is		high & low v.	7158
Speaks, Oley	1874-1948	Prayer Perfect, The		S/Br or S/A	7438

Also included in this volume are works with voicings not included in the parameters of this study by the following composers: Dudley Buck (A/B), Charles Gounod (MS/B), Bruno Huhn (A/B), Geoffrey O'Hara (A/B).

Soprano and Alto Duets. Edited by H. Kiehl. Publisher: Ditson. Date: 1901.

COMP.	DATES	TITLE	OP. #	VCG	REC
Blumenthal, Jacob [Jacques]	1829-1908	Venetian Boat Song		S/A	877
Bracken, Edith A.		If Thou Wilt Ease Thine Heart		S/A	1028
Brambach, Kaspar Joseph	1833-1902	Frühlingswerden	Op. 2 No. 1	S/A	1138
Caracciolo, Luigi		Nearest and Dearest		S/A	1340
Chaminade, Cecile	1857-1944	L'Angelus	Op. 69	S/A	1375

Continued on next page

(*Soprano and Alto Duets—Continued*)

COMP.	DATES	TITLE	OP. #	VCG	REC
Foster, Myles Birket	1851-1922	Song Should Breath of Scents and Flowers		S/A	2170
Goetze, Karl [Götze)	1836-1887	Still wie die Nacht	Op. 112 No. 1	S/A	2548
Jadassohn, Salomon	1831-1902	Im Volkston	Op. 72 No. 7	S/A	3582
———	———	Mein Herze thut mor gar zu weh!	Op. 72 No. 2	S/A	3585
———	———	Wär' ich ein Vögelein	Op. 72 No. 1	S/A	3597
Kjerulf, Halfdan	1815-1868	Last Night		S/A	3797
Lassen, Eduard	1830-1904	Entfernung		S/A	4300
Logé, Henri		Across the still Lagoon		S/A	4520
Mendelssohn, Felix	1809-1847	Auf flügeln des gesanges		S/A	4822
———	———	Gruss	Op. 63 No. 3	S/A	4845
———	———	Herbstlied	Op. 63 No. 4	S/A or S/S	4851
———	———	O sah ich auf der Haide	Op. 63 No. 5	S/A	4892
Rubinstein, Anton	1829-1894	Beim Scheiden	Op. 48 No. 6	S/A or S/MS	6228
———	———	Der Engel	Op. 48 No. 1	S/A	6237
———	———	Wanderers Nachtlied	Op. 48 No. 5	S/A	6300
Smart, Henry	1813-1879	Sailing Away		S/A	7387
———	———	When the Shadow is Passing		S/A	7394
Stange, Max	1856-1932	Voglein im Walde	Op. 54 No. 3	S/A	7494
Thomas, Arthur Goring	1851-1892	Sunset		S/A	7868
Wilson, Henry Lane	1870-1915	Carmeña		S/A	8492

Also included in this volume is a work with a style not included in the parameters of this study by the following composer: Léo Delibes (opera duet).

Vocal Duets Collection. Vol. 1. Publisher: Allans. Date: 1992.

COMP.	DATES	TITLE	OP. #	VCG	REC
Bond, Carrie Jacobs	1862-1946	Just a Wearyin' for You		Unspec.	920
Foster, Stephen Collins	1826-1864	Beautiful Dreamer		Unspec.	2174
Glover, Charles W.	1806-1863	Rose of Tralee, The		Unspec.	2498
Iradier, Sebastian [Yradier]	1809-1865	La Paloma		Unspec.	3554
Mellish, Colonel (attr.)		Drink to me Only		Unspec.	4805

Continued on next page

(Vocal Duets Collection Vol. 1—*Continued)*

COMP.	DATES	TITLE	OP. #	VCG	REC
Nevin, Ethelbert Woodbridge	1862-1901	Rosary, The		Unspec.	5230
Rimsky-Korsakov, Nicolai	1844-1908	Hindoo Song		S/A	6037
Serradell, N.		La Golondrina		Unspec.	7130
Taylor, T.		Down By the Old Mill Stream		Unspec.	7686
Unknown composer or arranger		All Through the Night		Unspec.	7968
Unknown composer or arranger		Believe Me, If All Those Endearing Young Charms		Unspec.	7969
Unknown composer or arranger		Dark Eyes		Unspec.	7970
Unknown composer or arranger		Lark in the Clear Air, The		Unspec.	7971
Unknown composer or arranger		Londonderry Air		Unspec.	7973
Unknown composer or arranger		Santa Lucia		Unspec.	7974
Unknown composer or arranger		Tiritomba		Unspec.	7975
Westendorf, T. P.		I'll Take You Home Again Kathleen		Unspec.	8304

Also included in this volume are works by the following composers who are not included in the parameters of this study: Thomas Morley, Jacques Offenbach (opera duet), and early English airs.

Vocal Duets Collection. Vol. 2 Publisher: Allans. Date: 1992.

COMP.	DATES	TITLE	OP. #	VCG	REC
Brahms, Johannes	1833-1897	Sandman, The		Unspec.	1096
———	———	Wiegenlied		Unspec.	1115
Chopin, Frederic	1810-1849	Triesse		Unspec.	1415
Gounod, Charles	1818-1893	Serenade		Unspec.	2677
Liszt, Franz	1811-1886	Liebesträume		Unspec.	4497
MacDowell, Edward	1860-1908	To A Wild Rose	Op. 5	Unspec.	4618
Martini, Jean Paul Egide	1741-1816	Plaisie d'Amour		Unspec.	4697
Mendelssohn, Felix	1809-1847	On Wings of Song		Unspec.	4900
Schubert, Franz Peter	1797-1828	Wiegenlied	Op. 98 No. 2	Unspec.	6899

Also included in this volume are works by the following composers who are not included in the parameters of this study: Georges Bizet (opera duet), George Frideric Handel, Edvard Grieg (opera duet), and Wolfgang Amadeus Mozart.

Six Popular Vocal Duets Book I for Soprano & Contralto. Edited and arranged by E. Newton. Publisher: Leonard-Eng. Date: 1906.

COMP.	DATES	TITLE	OP. #	VCG	REC
Barnby, J.		Sweet and Low. A Lullaby		S/A	542
Horn, Charles	1786-1849	I know a bank		S/S	3466
Newton, Ernest	20th C.	Golden Slumbers		S/A	5241
———	———	It was a lover and his lass		S/A	5246
———	———	Now is the Month of Maying		S/A	5248
Rubinstein, Anton (arr. E. Newton)	1829-1894	Wanderer's Evensong, The		S/A	6294

This anthology listing is complete.

Zweistimme Lieder für Sopran und Altstimme mit Klavierbegleitung für den Haus.- und Schulgebrach. 3 volumes (combined in one). Edited by H. M. Schletterer. Publisher: B. & H. No date.

COMP.	DATES	TITLE	OP. #	VCG	REC
Beethoven, Ludwig van	1770-1827	Gesangesmacht "Gesangesmacht du schleichst dich ein" Irisches Lied		S/A	631
———	———	Gute Nacht "Gut Nacht! Gut Nacht!"	Op. 100	S/A	632
———	———	Traum und Wirklichkeit "Mir träumt ich lag, wo Blumen springen" Irisches Lied		S/A	647
Blum, Karl Ludwig	1786-1844	Schwäne kommen gezogen	Op. 13 No. 2	S/A	870
Bosen, Franz		Frühlingsmorgen "Wie reizend, wie wonnig ist Alles umher"		S/A	1016
Brambach, Kaspar Joseph	1833-1902	Frühlingswerden "Welch ein Frühlingsrufen"	Op. 2 No. 1	S/A	1140
———	———	Vöglein im Walde "Lustiges Vöglein im Walde"	Op. 2 No. 4	S/A	1152
Frank, Ernst	1847-1889	Frühlingsahnung "Was ist das für ein reger Drang"	Op. 4 No. 6	S/A	2224
Frank, Ernst	1847-1889	Morgenlied "Noch ahnt man kaum der Sonne Licht"	Op. 4 No. 4	S/A	2241
Gade, Niels Wilhelm	1817-1890	Frühlingsgruss "Leise zieht durch mein Gemüht"	Op. 9 No. 1	S/A	2395/ 2357
———	———	Mein Herz ist im Hochland	Op. 9 No. 3	S/A	2405/ 2406
———	———	Reiselied "Durch Feld und Buchenhallen"	Op. 9 No. 5	S/A	2414
Keller, Karl	1784-1855	Lieblich wie der gold'ne Morgen	Op. 38 No. 2	S/A	3741

Continued on next page

(*Zweistimme Lieder für Sopran und Altstimme—Continued*)

COMP.	DATES	TITLE	OP. #	VCG	REC
Hauptmann, Moritz	1792-1868	Mailied	Op. 46 No. 7	S/A	3032
———	———	Sehnen "In die Lüfte möcht ich steigen"	Op. 46 No. 2	S/A	3036/ 3038
———	———	Waldeslust "Auf dem Rasen im Walde"	Op. 46 No. 4	S/A	3042
———	———	Willkommen uns, o schöner Mai	Op. 46 No. 7	S/A	3045
Hiller, Ferdinand	1811-1885	Wiegenlied "Draussen weht der Abendwind!"	Op. 39 No. 7	S/A	3284
Himmel, Fr. G.		Auferstehn "Auferstehn, aufer- stehn, ja auferstehn wirst du"		S/A	3292
———	———	Der Abend auf dem Wasser "Es tönt das Lied der Nachtigallen"		S/A	3293
Hollaender, Alexis [Holländer]	1840-1824	Frühlingsahnung "O sanfter, süsser Hauch"	Op. 10 No. 3	S/A	3372
———	———	Künftiger Frühling "Wohl blühet jedem Jahr"	Op. 10 No. 6	S/A	3379
Lachner, Franz	1803-1890	Frühlingswonne		S/A	4176/ 4177
———	———	Sonntagsmorgen "Sonntag ist's"		S/A	4189/ 4190
———	———	Wildröschen "O wildes Rothröschen"		S/A	4195
Lachner, Vincenz	1811-1893	April "Gott weiss, wie wohl mir jetzt geschah!"		S/A	4196
———	———	Die Mädchen "Gespielen und Schwestern"		S/A	4197
Meinardus, Ludwig	1827-1896	Lebe Wohl "Wann sich Seelen recht erkennen"	Op. 15 No. 4	S/A	4783
———	———	Nach Canaan "Wie so wunderlich und schmerzlich"	Op. 15 No. 2	S/A	4805
Mendelssohn, Felix	1809-1847	Abschiedslied der Zugvögel "Wie war so schön doch Wald und Feld"	Op. 63 No. 2	S/A	4818
———	———	Das Aehrenfeld "Ein Leben war's im Aehrenfeld"	Op. 77 No. 2	S/A	4829
		Herbstlied "Ach, wie so bald"	Op. 63 No. 4	S/A	4852
———	———	Maiglöcken und due Blümelein "Maiglöcken läutet in dem Thal!"	Op. 63 No. 6	S/A	4887
———	———	Sonntagsmorgen "Das ist der Tag der Herrn"	Op. 77 No. 1	S/A	4909
Methfessel, Albert Gottlieb	1785-1869	Abendlied "Schlaft wohl, ihr Sonnenstrahlen"		S/A	4942
Meves, Wilhelm	1808-1871	Der Vöglein Wiegenlied "Schlafet, schlafet ein"		S/A	4955
———	———	Ruf am Morgen im Walde "Wacht auf, wacht auf, ihr Vögelein"		S/A	4970

Continued on next page

(Zweistimme Lieder für Sopran und Altstimme—Continued)

COMP.	DATES	TITLE	OP. #	VCG	REC
Nicolai, Wilhelm Frederik Gerard	1829-1896	Frühling "Saatengrün, Lerchenwirbel"	Op. 11 No. 3	S/A	5262
Panseron, Auguste	1796-1859	Es tönt der Morgenchor "Die dunklen Scheier fallen"		S/A	5396
Reichardt, Johann Friedrich	1752-1814	Das Veilchen "Ein Veilchen auf der Wiese stand"		S/A	5723
Reinecke, Carl	1824-1910	Das Veilchen "Wie der Himmel klar und blau"	Op. 12 No. 4	S/A	5756
———	———	Die Roggenmohme "Lass stehn die Blume"	Op. 91 No. 5	S/A	5758
———	———	Grüss Gott, du goldengrüner Hain	Op. 109 No. 6	S/A	5774
———	———	Im Wald "Im Wald, im Wald ist Lust unf Fried"	Op. 12 No. 3	S/A	5778
Reinecke, Carl	1824-1910	Wie es der Mühle aussicht "Eins, zwei, drei, bicke backe bei"		S/A	5831
———	———	Frühlingsglaube "Die linden Lüfte sind erwacht"	Op. 35	S/A	6004
Schletterer, Hans Michel	1824-1893	Wie könnt' ich dein vergessen!		S/A	6696
Schulz, Chr.		Die Schwalbe "Es fliegen zwei Schwalben"		S/A	6943
Schumann, Robert	1810-1856	Das Glück "Vöglein vom Zweig lustig solgleich"	Op. 79 No. 16	S/A	6980
———	———	Die Schwalbe "Es fliegen zwei Schwalben"	Op. 79 No. 27	S/A	6982
———	———	Mailied "Komm lieber Mai und mache die Bäume wieder grün"	Op. 79 No. 10	S/A	7023
Spohr, Louis	1784-1859	Mein Heimathland "Wo reiner Liebe gold'ne Strahlen"		S/A	7453
Weber, Carl Maria von	1786-1826	Bald ist der Frühling da!		S/A	8134/ 8135
Wehner, A.		Verlassenheit "Ach wär' ich doch ein Röslein auch"	Op. 3 No. 3	S/A	8186
Wilhelm, Karl Friedrich	1815-1873	Vergissmeinnicht an der Quelle "In der klaren, stillen Quelle"		S/A	8466

Also included in this volume are works by the following composers who are not included in the parameters of this study: George Frideric Handel, Joseph Haydn, Wolfgang Amadeus Mozart, and Giovanni Pergolesi.

Index of Song Titles

TITLE	COMPOSER	REC#
3 Chants de Femmes Berbères	Rosenthal, Manuel	6162
3 Duos, Op. 136	Schmitt, Florent	6746
4 Duetti Sacri	Ghedini, Giorgio Federico	2463
4 Samenzangen	Schouwman, Hans	6811
12 Duos	Saint-Saëns, Camille	6391
12 Duos	Schumann, Robert	6956
20 Mélodies	Gounod, Charles	2637
21 Canti ad ina, due, e tre voci	Ivanova, Lidia	3563
34 Duets	Schumann, Robert	6957
A altes Kindersprüchel "Woa, ir no' klane Fratzen"	Sioly, Johann	7274
A Bisserl Lieb' und a Bisserl Treu' "Was man auch betrachten möge"	Neumann, Emil	5208
A Bleamerl im Mieda	André, L. [prob. Christian Karl André]	391
A Büchsal auf'n Rück'n	Simon, Ernst	7206
A Büchsle zum Schiassen	Koschat, Thomas	3918
A Busserl von Diandlan "Tanzen und singan" [sic]	Koschat, Thomas	3919
A do legst di nieder "Mir zwa haben erst neulich"	Schmutz & Katzer	6752
A,E,I,O,U "Du kennst die fünf Vokale"	Eyle, W.	2026
A Gigerl steigt ein Madel nach	Wanthaler, Gustav	8115
A já ti uplynu [Ich schwimm' dir davon]	Dvořák, Antonín	1809
A Kamaraének Mesterei Duettek, tercett és kvartett zongorakísérettel eredeti és Magyar szöveggel	Anthology	1
A Köchin kauft Aepfeln ein	Roth, Franz	6207
A l'amitié	Aerts, Felix	330
A la Zuecca	Massenet, Jules	4728
A Maderl, so schön wie a Eugel	Schindler, J.	6613
A Musi deriss'g Mann stark	Hornig, A.	3473
A Naïs	Lagoanère, Oscar de	4240
A paar Weana Vorstadt-Kinder "Wir trag'n das gleiche G'wand"	Sioly, Johann	7275
A reveille	Carey, Harry	1349
A une institutrice	Aerts, Felix	331
A Vogerl, a klan's fliagt	Kratzel, Karl [Kratzl]	3956
A-hunting we will go	Newton, Ernest	5237
Abend	Tchaikovsky, Peter Ilyich	7687

TITLE	COMPOSER	REC#
Abend am Meer "O flieh, der Abendhimmel"	Marschner, Heinrich August	4678
Abend am Meer "O Meer im Abendstrahle"	Krill, Karl	4007
Abend am Meer "O Meer im Abendstrahle"	Liszt, Franz	4496
Abend auf der Alm "Alpen glühn im Abendschein"	Abt, Franz	114
Abend auf der Alm "Alpen glühn im Abendschein"	Knebelsberger, L.	3851
Abend auf der Alm "Alpen glühn im Abendschein"	Simon, Ernst	7207
Abend "Dort sinket die Sonne"	Lenz, Leopold	4361
Abend "Es zieht die Liebes Gottes"	Abt, Franz	115
Abend "Glühend sinkt die Sonne"	Banck, Karl	501
Abend "Im Westen ist versunken"	Abt, Franz	116
Abend ist gekommen	Schwarzlose, Otto	7075
Abend kommt so abend kühl	Mayerhoff, Fritz	4764
Abend "Nieder sinkt die Sonne"	Tchaikovsky, Peter Ilyich	7688
Abend "Schweigt furt Menschen laute Lust"	Becker, Reinhold	618
Abend "Sehet es kehret der Abend"	Reissmann, August	5904
Abend so schön	Stange, Max	7481
Abend "Stillen Abend-stunden"	Rinck, Johann Christian Heinrich	6041
Abend thaut herneider	Brambach, Kaspar Joseph	1136
Abend thaut herneider	Dorn, Heinrich L. E.	1743
Abend thaut herneider	Melchert, J.	4800
Abend wölkchen glühen	Schnippering, W.	6778
Abendbild	Kaiser, Karl	3695
Abendbilder "Friedlicher Abend senkt sich"	Limbert, Frank L.	4442
Abenddämmerung "Durch's Gefild weht Lenzluft"	Abt, Franz	117
Abenddämmerung "Im Dunkel schummern die Thäler"	Abt, Franz	118
Abendfeier	Seiffert, Alexander	7100
Abendfeier "Ein Schein der ew'gen Jugend"	Lachner, Franz	4171
Abendfeier "Wie ist der Abend so traulich"	Diercks, H.	1671
Abendfeier "Wie ist der Abend so traulich"	Reissmann, August	5905
Abendfeier "Wie ist der Abend so traulich"	Tuma, A.	7944

TITLE	COMPOSER	REC#
Blauen Frühlingsaugen schaun aus	Wüerst, Richard Ferdinand	8701
Blauen Jung's wed'n wir genannt	Bachhofer, R.	480
Blauer Himmel, klare Lüfte	Attenhofer, Karl	447
Bleamerbrocken "Wia Gott die Welt"	Koschat, Thomas	3924
Bleamerl am Grab "Bleamerin sein schön"	Koschat, Thomas	3925
Bleamerl vom See "Dort beim See da drunt"	André, L. [prob. Christian Karl André]	392
Bleib bei uns "Ach bleib bei uns"	Wienand, V.	8397
Bleibe bei uns, es will Abend werden	Drobisch, Karl Ludwig	1781
Bleibe bei uns Herr, denn es will Abend werden	Nagler, Franziskus	5135
Bleiben möcht' ich immer	Abt, Franz	145
Bleibn nur noch a weng do	Günther, O.	2894
Bleich irrt im Wald Colette	Berlioz, Hector	720
Bless, O Lord, these Rings	Roff, Joseph	6084
Bless this House	Brahe, Mary Hannah	1037
		1038
		1039
Blessed Be the Name of Our God	Manookin, Robert P.	4655
Blick' in den Strom "Sahst du ein Glück vorübergehn"	Scholz, Bernard	6792
Blume Tod "Lieb' Blümlein du blickst so fromm"	Nessler, Victor E.	5182
Blond Gretchen hat Lieschen gebeten	Frank, Ernst	2212
		2213
Blüaht nur anmal "Verstorbene Klesheim"	Sioly, Johann	7285
Blüamli, blamli, alls is derlog'n "Ka Mensch kann's glaub'n"	Brunner, Ed.	1276
Blühende Apfelbaum "Nun seht einmal der Apfelbaum"	Keycher, O.	3753
Blühende Welt "Es schweben die Wälder"	Franke, Hermann	2269
Blühende Welt "Es schweben die Wälder"	Sieber, Ferdinand	7179
Blümchen am Felsen "Wie der Fels auch glühet"	Wilhelm, Karl Friedrich	8440
Blümchen der Freude "Es stürmet so schaurig"	André, Johann Anton	380
Blümchen du holdes, wie prangst du	Abt, Franz	146
Blümchen Geguld	Hellwig, Karl Friedrich Ludwig	3118
Blume der Ergebung "Ich bin die Blum' im Garten"	Deprosse, Anton	1632
Blume prangt am Morgen	Brahms, Johannes (G. F. Handel)	1120
Blumen	Elssner, E.	1918
Blumen Dank "Verschwunden ist die stille Nacht"	Keycher, O.	3754
Blumen Dank "Verschwunden ist die stille Nacht"	Schletterer, Hans Michel	6647
Blumen Erwachen "Schneeglöcken möchte wandern gehn"	Witt, Leopold	8631
Blumen thun die Augen auf	Slunicko, Jan	7363
Blumen und Scmetterlinge 2 Duette f. 2 S	Banck, Karl	506
Blumen "Warum weinst du weisse Rose"	Banck, Karl	507
Blumen wie im Wiesengrund	Abt, Franz	147
Blumenabschied "Ein Mägdelein ging und weinte"	Gurlitt, Cornelius	2896
Blumenandacht "Kommt der Morgen"	Abt, Franz	148
Blumendanken "Blümchen im lieben mag"	Vogel, Bernhardt	8034
Blumenelfen "Wenn es in der Dämmerstunde"	Loewe, Karl Gottfried	4509
Blumengebilde mit farbigem Glanz	Berneker, Constanz	743
Blumengruss "Struass den ich gepflücket"	Kammer, R.	3703
Blumengruss "Struass den ich gepflücket"	Riem, Friedrich Wilhelm	6012
Blumenkampf "Wie ist so stolz"	Concone, Giuseppi	1462
Blumenlied "Ein frisches Blümchen bring' ich dir"	Becker, Hugo	606
Blumenmädchen "Kaum dass der holde Lenz"	Wolff, W.	8662
Blumensegen "Blumen lieb und Blumen traut"	Vogel, Bernhardt	8035
Blümlein Antwort "In unsers Vaters Garten"	Schletterer, Hans Michel	6648
Blümli "Han am em Ort es Blümli g'seh"	Lammers, Julius	4254
Blumzen und die Leberwurscht "In einmen Selcherladen"	Lorens, Karl	4534
Blüthenhauch ist alles Leben	Wegeler, C.	8178
Boating Song of the Yo Eh	Whitehead, Percy Algernon	8318
Bois de pins "Ombre descend de leurs rameaux"	Massenet, Jules	4730
Bon voyage	Bordèse, Luigi	937
Bonheur facile	Bordèse, Luigi	938
Bonne nuit "Terre dort au ciel pur"	Massenet, Jules	4731
bonnie banks of Loch Lomond, The	Miller, Henry Colin	5005
bonnie Earl o' Moray, The	Moffat, Alfred	5023
Borussia, Britannia "Als König Friedrich wollte frein"	Tschirch, Rudolf	7938
Borussia "Wo ist das Volk, das kühn von That"	Spontini, Gasparo	7458
Böse Männerwelt sagt von uns immer	Winterling, W.	8609
Böse Zungen "Kommt da nicht die Karline"	Genée, Richard Franz Friedrich	2446
Bote der Geliebten "Lieblich süsse Wohlgerüche"	Donizetti, Gaetano	1709
Bote der Liebe "Wie viel schon der Boten"	Brahms, Johannes	1045
Bote der Liebe "Wie viel schon der Boten"	Winterberger, Alexander	8530
Bothe Aeugelein "Kömmt'st du meine Aeugelein"	Winterberger, Alexander	8531
Botschaft "Mein Gruss, er kömmt gezogen"	Stern, Julius	7540
Botschaft "Mondenschein, stiller Mondenschein"	Richter, Ernst Friedrich	6002
Botschaft	Schumann, Robert	6974
Botschaft "Nelken wind' ich und Jasmin"	Schumann, Robert	6975
Boulanger et Charbonnier	Boissière, F.	911
Brasilianerinnen "Frisch zu, eilt nur"	Bordèse, Luigi	939

TITLE	COMPOSER	REC#
Cheerfulness	*Gumbert*	2868
Chez Nous	*Christian-Jollet*	1416
Chi dice mal d'amore	*Reichardt, Gustav*	5721
Chi ha ragine	*Gabussi, Vincent*	2368
Chi vuol l'immagine	*Ciccarelli, Angelo*	1425
Children, pray this love to cherish	*Spohr, Louis*	7448
Children's Home, The	*Cowen, Frederic Hymen*	1538
China Mandarin, The	*Bantock, Granville*	539 540
Chineser und a Frauenzopf	*Sioly, Johann*	7287
Choice Sacred Duets	*Anthology*	9, 10, 11
Choice Vocal Duets	*Anthology*	12
Choix et Arrangements pour 2 Voix et Piano de Mélodies Célèbres de Schumann (Scénes Champetres)	*Anthology*	13
Choix et Arrangements pour 2 Voix et Piano de Mélodies Célèbres de Strauss (Gazouillis de Printemps)	*Anthology*	14
Chow Willy	*Marais, Josef*	4663
Christ Child, The	*Cornelius, Peter*	1496
Christ ist erstanden von den Todten	*Rudnick, Wilhelm*	6323
Christ, The	*Shelley, Harry Rowe*	7147
Christabend "Nie vermag zu klingen"	*Santner, Karl*	6491
Christabend "Nie vermag zu klingen"	*Weinberger, Karl Friedrich*	8199
Christbaum am Himmel "Da droben muss Christtag sein"	*Reich, Reinhold*	5707
Christian, the Morn breaks sweetly o'er thee	*Shelley, Harry Rowe*	7148 7149 7150
Christkind "Es weht der Wind und ist so kalt"	*Aiblinger, Johann Kaspar*	348
Christkind kam in den Winterwald	*Porepp, Georg*	5554
Christkindchen "Christ-kindchen kommt vom Himmel geflogen"	*Müller, M.*	5106
Christkindlein kommt 3 kleine Lieder	*Reich, Reinhold*	5708
Christkindlein kommt von Gottes Thron	*Raphael, Georg*	5663
Christmas	*Shelley, Harry Rowe*	7151
Christmas Song	*Gounod, Charles*	2645 2646
Christmas song, A	*Henschel, George*	3130
Christmas Spirit, The	*Loes, Harry Dixon & George S. Schuler*	4503
Christnacht 2 Lieder	*Schaper, Gustav*	6555
Christnacht "Heil'ge Nacht, auf Engelschwingen"	*Köllner, Eduard*	3889
Christnacht "Heil'ge Nacht, auf Engelschwingen"	*Schaper, Gustav*	6556
Christnacht "Heil'ge Nacht, auf Engelschwingen"	*Taubert, Otto*	7645
Christnacht und Weihnachten 6 Weihnachtslieder	*Palme, Rudolf*	5382
Chum Bueb und lueg dis Ländli	*Angerer, Gottfried*	402
Clair de Lune	*Diepenbrock, Alphons*	1667 1668

TITLE	COMPOSER	REC#
Clair de lune "Oh que la nuit est charmante"	*Hartog, Edouard de*	2992
Clayton's Solos and Duets Vol. 2	*Anthology*	15
Cloche du soir	*Aerts, Felix*	335
Cloches de mon village	*Aerts, Felix*	336
Clochettes bleues	*Jouret, Leon*	3636
cloud house, The	*Smith, Lilian*	7404
Coeur sacré	*Panseron, Auguste*	5393
Cohn und der Nachtwächter "Nacht ist rabenschwarz"	*Grabe, F.*	2686
Colinette	*Weckerlin, Jean Baptiste*	8176
Collaboration	*Tate, James W.*	7638
Colomba	*Gabussi, Vincent*	2369
Colonisations-Duett "Heute den Europamüden"	*Thiele, Richard*	7805
Colonisten "Wenn im ersten Morgenstrahl"	*Keller, Karl*	3740
Comala	*Gordigiani, Luigi*	2602
Come away, death	*Cornelius, Peter*	1497
Come Holy Ghost, Creator Blest	*Cassler, G. Winston*	1357
Come il candore	*Reissiger, Karl Gottlieb*	5863
Come join the dance	*White*	8309
Come, merry birds of Spring	*White*	8310
Come sail, my barque is waiting for thee	*Smart, Henry*	7369
Come, Thou Fount	*Wyeth, John*	8727
Come to the Fair	*Martin, Easthope*	4687
Come where the rosebuds sleep	*White*	8311
Coming home	*Sullivan, Arthur*	7604
Coming home	*Willeby, Charles*	8482
Comme ils ont fui	*Mendelssohn, Felix*	4827
Complete Songs of Berlioz, Vol. 1-10	*Berlioz, Hector*	721
Complete Songs, Vol. 1-4	*Mendelssohn, Felix*	4828
Complete Works	*Beethoven, Ludwig van*	629
Come Ye, See the Saviour	*Dagland, Abbé J.*	1571
Complete Works (18 Volumes)	*Glinka, Mikhail Ivanovich*	2492
Complete Works of Hector Berlioz, Vols. 1-10	*Berlioz, Hector*	722
Comtesschen im Pensionat	*Teich, Otto*	7729
Comtesse und Marquis "Comtess'chen ich bitt'"	*Nemours, A.*	5180
Con vanto menzognero	*Sor, Fernando [Sors]*	7423
Concerto spirituale	*Ghedini, Giorgio Federico*	2464
Conquerer (Easter), The	*Coombs, C. Whitney*	1485
convent bells, The	*Dolan*	1703
Consider the Lilies	*Topliff, Robert*	7903
Consiglio	*Gabussi, Vincent*	2370
Constancy	*Beethoven, Ludwig van*	630
Contadini di Siena	*Gabussi, Vincent*	2371
Contentment	*Thomas, Arthur Goring*	7865
Contrabandiere	*Gabussi, Vincent*	2372
Copla	*Bosmans, Henriette*	1018
Cor dulce, cor amabile	*Piel, Peter*	5484
Costanza "Più non si trovano"	*Sieber, Ferdinand*	7180
Couplets giebt es heute verscheiden	*Bornet, R.*	1005

TITLE	COMPOSER	REC#
Die Schwalben "Es fliegen zwei Schwalben"	Schumann, Robert	6985
Die Schwalben sind gekommen	Abt, Franz	151
Die Schwestern	Brahms, Johannes	1053
		1054
Die Schwestern "Wir Schwestern zwei"	Brahms, Johannes	1055
		1056
Die Sonne scheint nicht mehr	Brahms, Johannes	1057
Die Turteltaube und der Wanderer	Rubinstein, Anton	6244
Die Turteltaube und der Wanderer "Sprich, warum sitzest du dort auf dem Zweige"	Rubinstein, Anton	6245
Die Wolke	Rubinstein, Anton	6246
Die Wolke "Vorbei ist der Sturm"	Rubinstein, Anton	6247
Die zwei Zigeunerinnen	Pachkov, N. J.	5373
Diebstahl "Mädel trug des Wegs daher"	Jacobi, M.	3566
Dienstboten "Ja meine liebe Madam Dankelmann"	Schäffer, August	6527
Dienstbotenwechsel "Sie werden wohl entschul'gen"	Dorn, Alexander Julius Paul	1732
Dies ist der Herbst	Pogge, H.	5534
Dies ist der Tag, den Gott gemacht	Wiedemann, Max	8372
Dies und das "Wie traurig sind wir Mädchen d'rau"	Meyer-Helmund, Erik	4980
Dieu bénit des grandes familles	Bordèse, Luigi	947
Digli ch'io don fidele	Reissiger, Karl Gottlieb	5864
Diller-Page Carol Book, The	Anthology	16
Dilly song, The	Marais, Josef	4665
Dina Bla Ogon	Lewerth	4411
Dir "Ich sende diese Blume dir"	Könneritz, Nina [Georgine, neé Eschborn]	3898
Dir muss ich immer singen	Reissiger, Karl Gottlieb	5865
Dir wie mir "Guten Morgen liebe Grete"	Brandhurst, Elise	1155
Dir wird gereicht so manche Dankesblume	Hesselmann, L.	3197
Dirge for Fidele	Vaughan Williams, Ralph	7987
Dirnd'l wie ist mir so wohl "Schaut der Jäger in das Thal"	Simon, Ernst	7216
Distelstöckchen "Alles was ich vorgedeutet"	Wichern, Karoline	8325
Distribution des prix	Bordèse, Luigi	948
Dite Almeno, amiche fronde	Cherubini, Luigi	1394
		1395
Ditson Collection of Soprano and Alto Duets	Anthology	17
Do Not Be Amazed	Bender, Jan	661
Dobrou noc	Procházka, J.	5572
dominic has a doll	Persichetti, Vincent	5440
Donnerwetter, ich bin (Sie sind) schick	Gilbert, Jean	2473
Door in the Wall, The	Wuorinen, Charles	8723
		8724
Doppelleben "Am See am Teich, wie schaukeln"	Taubert, Wilhelm	7650
Doppo il temporale	Gordigiani, Luigi	2604
Dorf und Stadt "Wir sind zum erste Mai"	Kron, Louis	4022

TITLE	COMPOSER	REC#
Dorf-Grete "Grete vom Land"	Kleffel, Arno	3802
Dorflinden "Im Dorfe stehn zwei Linden"	Lassen, Eduard	4298
Doris sprach heute	Blangini, G. M. M. Felice	814
Dorischen "Wia schaut's denn jetzt"	Schifferl, F.	6571
Dormi pur mio dolce amor	Zescevich, A.	8775
Dornen "Dornen mir zur Liebem spriesset"	Blangini, G. M. M. Felice	815
Dornröschen "Schliess' mir schöne Blume"	Weber, Gustav	8161
Dornröschen "Und sie kam zur Hexe"	Taubert, Wilhelm	7651
Dornröschens Herzelied "Dornröschen steht am Waldesrand"	Simon, Ernst	7217
Dort am Markte an der Ecke	Winter, E.	8507
Dort drunten im Tale läufts Wasser so trüb	Frey, Martin	2327
Dort hinter jenem Fensterlein	Abt, Franz	152
Dort in den Weiden steht ein Haus	Brahms, Johannes	1058
Dort oben auf dem Berge	Leydecker, A.	4413
Dort oben auf dem Berge (Blumenhaus)	Heinemann, Wilhelm	3072
Dort oben "Dort oben, dort oben zu der"	Banck, Karl	508
Dort überm Wolkenmeere	Roeder, Martin [Röder]	6077
Dort, wo der Kuckuck schreit "Verliabten Leut' hab'n nie a Freud'"	Sioly, Johann	7293
Dorthin "Ich kann ja hier nicht glücklich sein"	Jacke, Ch.	3564
Dos muass a Weana g'wesen sein "Strassen voll Menschen"	Ertl, Dominik	1972
Dös san lauter altdeutsche Sachen	Schild, Theodor	6582
Doubt Not Thy Father's Care	Elgar, Edward	1912
Douceur	Migot, Georges	4997
Douze Duos	Anthology	18
Dove sei	Guercia, Alfonso	2857
Down By the Old Mill Stream	Taylor, T.	7686
Down in the gardens at Kew	Stacey, Gilbert	7468
Down the Flowing Stream	Newton, Ernest	5239
Draussen blühn die Veigelein	Graben-Hoffmann, Gustav	2693
Dreadful story about Harriet, The	Hughes, Herbert	3504
Dream Faces	Gooch	2595
Dream Faces	Hutchinson, William Marshall	3543
Dream Minuet	Bateman, Ronald	566
Dream of Christmas	Holst, Gustav	3432
Dream of Christmas, A	Holst, Gustav	3433
Dream Seller	Lee, Ernest Markham	4341
Dream Seller, The	Lee, Ernest Markham	4342
Dreams	Hope, H. Ashworth	3450
Dreht sich Feinslieb im Tanz	Brandt-Caspari, Alfred	1168
Drei Blätter "Von theurer Hand ein zartes Blatt"	Lenz, Leopold	4365
Drei Duette Op. 20	Brahms, Johannes	1059
Drei Kinderchen aus dem Fenster sehn	Frank, Ernst	2215
Drei Könige wandern aus Morgenland	Wiedemann, Max	8373

TITLE	COMPOSER	REC#
Ein Sonntag im Mai "Lenz ist da, hinaus"	Korel, H.	3913
Ein stilles Glück kann nimmer walten	Arensky, Anton	422
Ein Strauss aus dem Liedergarten	Köhler-Wümbach, Wilhelm	3887
Ein Stündlein sind sie beisammen gewest	Hirsch, Karl	3310
Ein Stündlein wohl vor Tag "Derweil ich schlafend lag"	Holstein, Franz von	3439
Ein Tag ist wieder hin	Schletterer, Hans Michel	6649
Ein Täubchen flog vom Himmelsrand	Unger, A.	7961
Ein Tauber wollte freien	Simon, Ernst	7222
Ein unangenehmer Gedanke "Ja wenn wir jung noch sind"	Gordigiani, Luigi	2605
Ein Viertelstündchen auf der Liedertafel "Ei seh'n sie doch Frau Muhsten"	Kuntze, Karl	4159
Ein Vogel singt gottlobesam	Rössler, Richard	6203
Ein Vöglein hat gesungen	Prochazka, Rudolf	5578
Ein Vöglein sang im Lindenbaum	Necke, Hermann	5166
Ein Wort "O spricht es aus der Liebe Wort"	Nicolai, Otto	5259
Ein Zeichen der Zeit ist's	Sioly, Johann	7295
Ein Zug, der mich zum Himmel trägt	Grunholzer, K.	2849
Einbildung "Neulich kommt vom Land ein Bauer"	Fischer & Blum	2125
Einbruch bei ein'n Goldarbeiter	Schild, Theodor	6584
Eine Dame, die ich kannte	Winterling, W.	8611
Eine Käferhochzeit "Ich will das Eisenhütlein fragen"	Hiller, Ferdinand	3236
Eine Kochkünstlerin "Duett Prosa"	Legov, M.	4345
Eine lebzeltene Ballade "Bei einem Kirchtag stand"	Schild, Theodor	6585
Eine Liebeserklärung auf dem Lande "Hans und Grethe"	Teich, Otto	7731
Eine moderne Frau "Ein Brief von meiner Adelheid"	Heinze, Richard	3089
Eine Parthie Piquet "A Wittfrau gut erhalten no"	Sioly, Johann	7296
Eine Sonnenblume	Hertz, H.	3192
Eine vergnügte Land-parthie "Vater, die Mutter"	Fischer & Blum	2126
Eine Wassermaus und eine Kröte	Dorn, Alexander Julius Paul	1734
Einen Brief soll ich schreiben	Jadassohn, Salomon	3571
Einer letzten Glocke Klang	Slunicko, Jan	7365
Einien Brief soll ich schreiben	Ramann, Bruno	5632
Einigucken, zucharucken, andrucken "A Bekanntschaft machen"	Sioly, Johann	7297
Einjähriger Nasewitz und sein Putzer "Hum. Duoscene"	Teich, Otto	7732
Einklang "Um Mitternacht entstand dies Leid"	Jadassohn, Salomon	3572
Einladung "Erde orangt als Frühlingsbraut"	Freudenberg, Wilhelm	2319
Einladung "Geehrteste Frau"	Lewandowski, Louis	4409
Einladung "Geehrteste Frau"	Wandow, L.	8112
Einladung "Musst nicht vor dem Tage fliehen"	Taubert, Wilhelm	7652

TITLE	COMPOSER	REC#
Eins, zwei, drei, ei, ei, ei	Peter, G.	5451
Eins, zwei, drei "Ein kleines Kind, wenn's reden lernt"	Fischer, Anton	2116
Einsam durch das Leben gehen	Weissbach, M. L.	8251
Einsame Röslein im Thal "Es liegt ein Weiler fern im Grund"	Hermes, Eduard	3184
Einsamkeit "Hörst du nicht die Quellen gehen"	Haan, Willem de [De Haan]	2910
Einsamkeit "Hörst du nicht die Quellen gehen"	Heuser, Ernst	3201
Einsiedler und die Pilgerin "Pilgerin mit den blassen Wangen"	Gabussi, Vincent	2374
Einst flogen zwei Elfchen spazieren	Jahn-Schulze, Hermann	3601
Eislauf "Zwischen den Tannen im sinnigen Strahl"	Bandisch, J.	536
Ekh tï Pesnya	Glazunov, Alexander	2483
Ekh ty, Pesnia [Oh You, Songs]	Glazunov, Alexander	2484
El Deschidado	Saint-Saëns, Camille	6402 6403 6404 6405
El Desdichado (Bolero)	Saint-Saëns, Camille	6406
El desdichado "Peu m'importe que fleurisse"	Saint-Saëns, Camille	6407
El Majo y la Maja	Garcia, M. [prob. Mansilla Eduardo]	2429
El Musico y el Poeta	Carnicer, Ramon	1351
El Soldado	Pla, M.	5514
El vestido azul	Iradier, Sebastian [Yradier]	3551
Eldenrauten "12 Sammlung Tyroler Alpenlieder"	Hofer, Toni	3331
Eleven Selected Duets	Cornelius, Peter	1499
Elfe "Bleib' bei uns"	Reinecke, Carl	5764
Elfenfrühling "Was rauscht vorbei"	Wüerst, Richard Ferdinand	8703
Elmúlt a Vész	Sugár, Rezsö	7601
Eloge des Chapons	Schmitt, Florent	6748
Emancipirten "Guten Morgen liebe Rath"	Simon, Ernst	7223
Emancipirten "Ja emancipirten sind wir"	Kron, Louis	4026
Emanuel Geibel's Scheidelied "Leb wohl, du grüne Wildniss"	Ogarew, M.	5330
Empor Kalender es hück "Barbier in der Klemme"	Rinck, Johann Christian Heinrich	6043
Endymions Schlaf	Longuet	4531
Engel am Christabend "Über den beschneiten Rüstern"	Reich, Reinhold	5709
Engel kamen	Liebe, Eduard Ludwig	4427
Engel und Hirten "Kommet ihr Hirten"	Palme, Rudolf	5383
Engelküche "Fünf Englein haben gesungen"	Lachner, Vincenz	4198
Englismann ist immer smart	Wolf, E.	8640
Engelküche "Fünf Englein haben gesungen"	Lachner, Vincenz	4198
Englismann ist immer smart	Wolf, E.	8640
Ensemble	Glimes, Jean Baptiste Jules de	2486
Entchen, so geh' doch grade	Ansorge, M. [prob. Margarethe]	407

TITLE	COMPOSER	REC#
Frische Fahrt "Laue Luft kommt blau geflossen"	*Messer, F.*	4937
Frische Madl' im Thal "Bin i nit a frisch's Madel"	*Simon, Ernst*	7224
Frischer, thauiger Sommermorgen	*Hauptmann, Moritz*	3025
Frisches Bächlein	*Widmann, Benedikt*	8360
Friseur et fumeur	*Boissière, F.*	913
Fritz und Rieke "Wie, noch nicht da"	*Lincke, Paul*	4452
Frog's lament, The	*Wood, Hayden*	8681
Froh ertönen Weihnachts-glocken	*Kasper, M.*	3721
Froh und lustig leben wir	*Linderer, Ed.*	4463
Frohe Botschaft "Wenn der Kuckuck wieder schreit"	*Ernemann, E.*	1958
Frohe Lieder willl ich singen	*Möhring, Ferdinand*	5039
Frohe Sinn "Fröhlich und wohlgemuth"	*Keycher, O.*	3755
Froher Sang für Polterabend und Hochzeit "Schmückt das Haus mit frischem Grün"	*Burwig, G.*	1295
Fröhlich soll mein Herz	*Michaelis, Ad. Alfred*	4989
Fröhlich und Wohlgemuth "Sieh' da, mein lieber Wohlgemuth"	*Schäffer, August*	6533
Fröhliche Armuth "So einer hat kein Zweigespann"	*Reinecke, Carl*	5765
Fröhliche Fahrt "O glücklich, wer zum Liebchen zieht"	*Hinrichs, Friedrich*	3298
Fröhliche Fahrt "O glücklich, wer zum Liebchen zieht"	*Wüerst, Richard Ferdinand*	8705
Fröhliche Fink "Fink schlüpft in den Baum"	*Vogel, Bernhardt*	8037
Fröhliche, geweihte Nacht	*Wooge, Emma*	8687
Fröhliche Weihnacht überall	*Palme, Rudolf*	5384
Fröhlichen Schiffer "Schiffer schaukelt hin und wieder"	*Abt, Franz*	162
Frohlocket ihr Völker	*Kühn, Karl*	4133
Frohsinn "Giebt es Schön'res wohl im Leben"	*Abt, Franz*	163
Frohsinn "Giebt es Schön'res wohl im Leben"	*Schubert, Franz Ludwig*	6840
Frohsinn, Walzer-Rondo	*Gumbert, Ferdinand*	2869
Frohsinn "Wenn ich ein Vöglein seh"	*Storch, Anton M.*	7568
From border unto border	*Dzerzhinsky, Ivan*	1873
From the Bough	*Dvořák, Antonín*	1822
Frommer Glaube "Zu heil'gen Kirchenhallen"	*Wienand, V.*	8399
Fronda leggiera e mobile	*Brahms, Johannes (G. F. Handel)*	1121
Frühjahr "Hell ins Fenster scheint die Sonne"	*Altenhofer, C.*	362
Frühling	*Hol, Rijk*	3363
Frühling an das kranke Kind "Nun sind die Wege trocken"	*Weinberger, Karl Friedrich*	8203
Frühling "Erguss der Himmels, Lenzeszeit"	*Hering, C. [prob. Karl Eduard]*	3166
Frühling "Erschliesst unds der Frühling"	*Krebs, Karl August*	3968 3969
Frühling erwacht, Maiglöck-chen lacht	*Reim, Edmund*	5733
Frühling "Frühling klopft mit frischem Strauss"	*Lassen, Eduard*	4303

TITLE	COMPOSER	REC#
Frühling "Frühling kommt"	*Schletterer, Hans Michel*	6653
Frühling "Frühling nun gekommen"	*Kücken, Friedrich Wilhelm*	4081
Frühling "Frühling, wie mit Zauberschwingen"	*Wallnöfer, Adolf*	8107
Frühling "Heraus, heraus ihr Kinder"	*Storch, Anton M.*	7569
Frühling, Herbst "Als der Frühling die Kränze"	*Schultz, Edwin*	6920
Frühling "Hörst du wohl die Glöcklein klingen"	*Grosse, L.*	2827 2828
Frühling "Hört ihr's, das sind"	*Meves, Wilhelm*	4957
Frühling im Alter "Singen die Vögel im grünen Wald"	*Doebber, Johannes*	1697
Frühling im Herbst "Schon ist der letzte Blüthenstern"	*Pierson, Henry Hugh*	5490
Frühling in der Heimath "Es kam der Frühling gezogen"	*Hempel, F. R.*	3124
Frühling ist da	*Abt, Franz*	164
Frühling ist da "Bächlein zum Bache scwoll"	*Abt, Franz*	165
Frühling ist da "Bächlein zum Bache scwoll"	*Kleffel, Arno*	3805
Frühling ist da "Blümlein horch"	*Döring, Carl Heinrich*	1726
Frühling ist es wieder	*Stieber, P.*	7548
Frühling ist kommen	*Widmann, Benedikt*	8361
Frühling ist nah'	*Schletterer, Hans Michel*	6654
Frühling kam [unreadable] über Nacht	*Lewalter, Johann*	4406
Frühling kommt "Thut auch das bange Herz die weh'"	*Nus, B.*	5308
Frühling "Nun werden schon die Bäume grün"	*Hiller, Ferdinand*	3239
Frühling "O gleitet sanft dahin"	*Bordèse, Luigi*	955
Frühling "Saatengrün, Lerchenwirbel"	*Nicolai, Wilhelm Frederik Gerard*	5262
Frühling "Saatengrün, Veilchenduft"	*Nicolai, Wilhelm Frederik Gerard*	5263
Frühling "Seht der Lenz ist wieder da"	*Bordèse, Luigi*	956
Frühling "So wundersam ist doch der Morgen"	*Ponflick, F.*	5539
Frühling und Liebe "Im Rosen-busche die Liebe schlief"	*Baselt, Friedrich Gustav Otto*	552
Frühling und Liebe "Im Rosen-busche die Liebe schlief"	*Esser, Heinrich*	1991
Frühling und Liebe "Im Rosen-busche die Liebe schlief"	*Lassen, Eduard*	4304
Frühling und Liebe "Im Rosen-busche die Liebe schlief"	*Matthieux, Johanna*	4750
Frühling und Liebe "Lass den heitern Frühlingsschein"	*Samson, L.*	6459
Frühling "Und wenn die Lerche hell anstimmt"	*Reinecke, Carl*	5766
Frühling währt nicht immer	*Rischbieter, Wilhelm Albert*	6057
Frühling "Was rauschet, was rieselt"	*Hecht, Gustav*	3062
Frühling "Was rauscht, was rieselt"	*Ansorge, M. [prob. Margarethe]*	408
Frühling "Wer winket uns droben"	*Rennes, Catharina van*	5939

TITLE	COMPOSER	REC#
Frühlingsglaube "Linden Lüfte sind erwacht"	Thoma, Rudolf	7852
Frühlingsglaube "Linden Lüfte sind erwacht"	Wichern, Karoline	8327
Frühlingsglaube "Linden Lüfte sind erwacht"	Wüerst, Richard Ferdinand	8707
Frühlingsglocken	Reinecke, Carl	5769
Frühlingsglocken "Schnee-glöcken thut läuten"	Bach, Otto	477
Frühlingsglocken "Schnee-glöcken thut läuten"	Kücken, Friedrich Wilhelm	4082
Frühlingsglocken "Schnee-glöcken thut läuten"	Scholz, Bernard	6793
Frühlingsglocken "Schnee-glöcken thut läuten"	Schumann, Robert	6994
Frühlingsgruss	Gade, Niels Wilhelm	2395 2396
Frühlingsgruss "Beim murmelnden Bächlein"	Weinberger, Karl Friedrich	8204
Frühlingsgruss "Es blühet der Dorn"	Abt, Franz	170
Frühlingsgruss "Leise zieht durch mein Gemüht"	Gade, Niels Wilhelm	2397
Frühlingsgruss "Nunwehet wieder lind"	Abt, Franz	171
Frühlingsgruss "O Frühlings-zeit, o herrliches Träumen"	Förster, Alban	2160
Frühlingsgruss "O holder Sonnenschein"	Franke, Hermann	2272
Frühlingsjubel "Aus grünen Gezweigen"	Abt, Franz	172
Frühlingsjubel "Frühling, Frühling wonnige Zeit"	Thoma, Rudolf	7853
Frühlingsjubel "Nach des Winters trüben Tagen"	Schletterer, Hans Michel	6656
Frühlingsklage Wölklein ziehen in den Höhen"	Hollaender, Alexis [Holländer]	3375
Frühlingsläuten "Was hör' ich denn da unten läuten"	Drath, Theodor	1766
Frühlingsleben "Funkelnde Felder"	Abt, Franz	173
Frühlingsliebe	Goltermann, Georg	2582
Frühlingsliebe "Wenn der Frühling kommt"	Leonhard, Julius Emil	4385
Frühlingslied	Diabelli, Anton	1655
Frühlingslied	Emmerlich, Robert	1930
Frühlingslied	Lassen, Eduard	4305
Frühlingslied	Schumann, Robert	6995 6996 6997 6998
Frühlingslied "Alle Vögel sind schon da"	Greith, Karl	2760
Frühlingslied "Der du kamst von lichten Höhen"	Reich, Reinhold	5710
Frühlingslied "Der Frühling kehret wieder"	Schumann, Robert	6999
Frühlingslied "Es duftet der Frühling"	Succo, Franz Adolf	7598
Frühlingslied "Es trägt des Windes Schwingen"	Samson, L.	6460
Frühlingslied "Frühling ist gekommen"	Salis, P.	6426
Frühlingslied "Frühling kehret wieder"	Schumann, Robert	7000
Frühlingslied "Frühling naht"	Abt, Franz	174
Frühlingslied "Frühling schwang den Zauberstab"	Sachs, Johann Melchior Ernst	6383
Frühlingslied "Gekommen ist der Mai"	Möhring, Ferdinand	5040
Frühlingslied "Hell strahlt die Frühlingssonne"	Franke, Hermann	2273
Frühlingslied "Himmel lacht"	Lanz, A.	4287
Frühlingslied "Kommt heraus, lasst uns gehn"	Richter, Ernst Friedrich	6005
Frühlingslied "Lämmlein hüpfen auf Rasen grün"	Reissiger, Karl Gottlieb	5868
Frühlingslied "Nun weht gelind der Frühlingswind"	Siebmann, F.	7197
Frühlingslied "Schnee-glöcken klingen wieder"	Schumann, Robert	7001
Frühlingslied "Tief im grünen Frühlingshag"	Esser, Heinrich	1993
Frühlingslied "Tief im grünen Frühlingshag"	Hiller, Ferdinand	3241
Frühlingslied "Tief im grünen Frühlingshag"	Horn, August	3458
Frühlingslied "Tief im grünen Frühlingshag"	Lassen, Eduard	4306
Frühlingslied "Über die Berge wandelt"	Wolff, Leonhard	8656
Frühlingslied "Was regt sich so mächtig"	Rust, Wilhelm Karl	6374
Frühlingslied "Wenn Vöglein ihre Nester bauen"	Wermann, Friedrich Oskar	8283
Frühlingsliedchen "Frühling hat sich eingestellt"	Methfessel, Ernst	4946
Frühlingsliedchen "Frühling hat sich eingestellt"	Wilhelm, Karl Friedrich	8442
Frühlingsliedchen "Vöglein singt im grünen Wald"	Ernemann, M.	1963
Frühlingslüftchen "Muntre Lüftchen, dunkle Lieder"	Concone, Giuseppi	1465
Frühlingslust "Draussen welche Wonne"	Ernemann, M.	1964
Frühlingslust "Es irren und schwirren"	Hempel, F. R.	3125
Frühlingslust "Zweige flüstern"	Abt, Franz	175
Frühlingsmorgen "Glocken-blumen läuten"	Greith, Karl	2761
Frühlingsmorgen "Glocken-blumen läuten"	Schletterer, Hans Michel	6657
Frühlingsmorgen "Heiter lacht vom Himmelsdom"	Krebs, Karl August	3970
Frühlingsmorgen "Morgen ist erstanden"	Rohde, Eduard	6093
Frühlingsmorgen "Wenn die Lämmer wieder springen"	Raff, Joseph	5609
Frühlingsmorgen "Wie reizend, wie wonnig ist Alles umher"	Bosen, Franz	1016
Frühlingsnacht "Überm Garten durch die Lüfte"	Hászlinger, J. v.	3009
Frühlingsnächte sing gefährlich	Emge, A.	1926
Frühlingsregen "Welch' sanfter, milder Regen"	Brambach, Kaspar Joseph	1137
Frühlingsruf "Ein Vogel, ein Vogel, o hört"	Naubert, Friedrich August	5150
Frühlingsruf "Ich hör' 'ne wunderliche Stimme"	Gorzer-Schulz, O. K. F.	2632
Frühlingsruf "Wacht auf, wacht auf, ihr Thäler"	Lachner, Franz	4175

TITLE	COMPOSER	REC#
Gebet "Gott deine Kinder treten"	Meves, Wilhelm	4958
Gebet "Herr gedenk', wie schwach ich bin"	Brambach, Kaspar Joseph	1141
Gebet "O Herr Gott, gesetzt ist mein Hoffen"	Hiller, Ferdinand	3242 3243
Gebet "Vater hör' mein Flehen"	Wienand, V.	8400
Gebrochene Bank "Bank, d'rauf ich so oft"	Winterberger, Alexander	8539
Gebrochene Herz "Ich sah mal a Blümle"	Nessler, Victor E.	5183
Gebrochenes Herz "Rosen und die Nelken und Flieder"	Hauer, Karl	3018
Gebrochenes Herz "Rosen und die Nelken und Flieder"	Kleinmichel, Richard	3828
Gebrochenes Herz "Rosen und die Nelken und Flieder"	Reinecke, Carl	5771
Gebrüder Cohn "Wir sind zwei jüd'sche Handelslait"	Aaron, E.	110
Gebrüder Schulze "Immer charmant, pyramidal"	Halle, H.	2948
Gebrüder Weiss-Marsch "Es sieht wohl jeder gleich"	Weissbach, M. L.	8254
Geburtstags kuchen "Ei sieh da, Frau Mandatar"	Grabe, F.	2687
Geburtstagslied	Elssner, E.	1920
Geburtstagslieder (2)	Standke, Otto	7477
Geburtstagslied "Nimm unsre kleinen Gaben"	Brunner, Christian Traugott	1269
Gedanken an Gott "Denk' ich an dich"	Weiss, Laurenz	8234
Gedankenflug "Wenn Gedanken sichtbar wären"	Rust, Wilhelm Karl	6375
Gedankenleser "Gedanken zu lesen ist jetzt modern"	Sioly, Johann	7302
Gedichte (Drei) als Duette "Sammeltitel"	Mansfeldt, H.	4658
Geduld du kleine Knospe	Freudenberg, Wilhelm	2320
Geduld "Es zieht ein stiller Engel"	Hahn, J. Ch. W.	2938
Gefangene "Ging ein Mädchen Gras zu mähen"	Dvořák, Antonín	1823
Gefangene Sänger "Vöglein einsam in dem Bauer"	Röhde, A.	6088
Geflügelte Amor "Amor kam, wie andere Knaben"	Samson, L.	6461
Gefunden "Ich ging im Walde so für mich hin"	Kittl, Johann Friedrich	3791
Gefunden "Ich ging im Walde so für mich hin"	Klinkmüller, F.	3840
Gegensätze "Eins, zwei drei"	Meves, Wilhelm	4959
Geh' ich im grünen Wald	Thieriot, Ferdinand	7835
Geh', liaba Schatz	Schmid, Joseph	6709
Geh, liaba Schatz, gieb ma an Schmatz	Schmid, Joseph	6710
Geh' mit Gott, vergiss mein nicht	Schletterer, Hans Michel	6658
Geh' nun empfang' die Krone	Sarti, Giuseppe	6512
Geheimniss "Heckenröslein über Nacht"	Neubner, Ottomar	5190
Geheimnisse des Glückes "Lebensglück, Blüthnzier, die so selten"	Concone, Giuseppi	1466
Gehet in seinen Thoren ein	Fröhlich, Ernst	2348

TITLE	COMPOSER	REC#
Geht es dor auch wie mir	Kniese, Julius	3853
Geist der Harmonie "Von fernen Fluren weht ein Geist"	Rungenhagen, Karl Friedrich	6356
Geist des Abends "Geist des Abends ziehet"	Wenzel, Eduard	8268
Geist des Herrn "O lass kein herz dir fremde bleiben"	Lassen, Eduard	4307
Geistliche Sologesange ind Duette, Heft I und Heft II	Anthology	42
Geistliches Duett "Vertrau' dem Herrn in deinem Leide"	Dorn, Otto	1755
Geistliches Lied "In die Höhe führe mich"	Brambach, Kaspar Joseph	1142
Geistliches Lied "So nimm denn meine Hände"	Reinecke, Carl	5772
Gekommen ist der Maie	Müller, L. S.	5105
Gekommen ist der Maie	Solbrück, C.	7413
Gekränkte Mutterherz "Schönsten Gruss, verzeit"	Schäffer, August	6535
Gelobt sie Christus	Schuh, J.	6912
Gelobt sie Jesus Christus	Schuh, J.	6913
Gelungene Antworten "Ein junger Mann mit wenig Bart"	Fischer & Blum	2129
Gemein, fein "Wir wollen es einmal probiren"	Weissbach, M. L.	8255
Gemelli in petto	Coccia, Carlo	1448
Gemischte Gesellschaft aus der Theaterwelt "Hamlet, Prinz von Dänemark"	Sioly-Weisberg	7350
Gemüathlichen "Gemäthlichen seg'ns"	Rosenzweig, Wilhelm	6170
Gemüthliche Ehepaar "Nicht wahr Gustel, so wie wir"	Beyer, H.	759
Gemüthliche Weanerin "'S geht a fesch Maderl"	Schrammel, Johann	6818
Gendamerie von Rummelsberg "Kom. Duoscene"	Maas, Louis	4612
Gendarmes	Offenbach, Jacques	5329
Genfer See "Schiffen wir zwei"	Masini, Francesco	4720
Gensdarm und der Wanderer "Ich komme vom Gebirge her"	Bögler, B.	887
Gentle Holy Saviour	Gounod, Charles	2658
Geputzt, geschmückt, nett und charmant	Werner, Otto	8296
Gesang der Peris "Wiegt ihn hinüber"	Banck, Karl	511
Gesang der Schifferen "Ich schaue in des Sees Grund"	Wüerst, Richard Ferdinand	8708
Gesang der Schwäne "Im Abendschein, in Purpurgluth"	Huth, Louis	3547
Gesang des Vogels über dem Walde "Im goldnen Strahl, über Wald"	Lichner, Heinrich	4417
Gesänge für die Jugend (8)	Weiss, Laurenz	8235
Gesangesmacht "Gesangesmacht du schleichst dich ein" Irisches Lied	Beethoven, Ludwig van	631
Geschichte der Liebe "Wollt ihr wissen, wie die Lieb'"	Kipper, Hermann	3764
Gesellschaftslied für Kinder "Ei seht mir doch die muntre Welt"	Wilhelm, Karl Friedrich	8443
Gespielen "Ihr Lämmer dort am Himmel"	Lachner, Franz	4178
Gestillte Sehnsucht "In goldnen Abendschein getaucht"	Abt, Franz	180

TITLE	COMPOSER	REC#
Godiamo	Campana, Fabio	1318
Gold überwiegt die Liebe "Sternchen mit dem trüben Schein"	Winterberger, Alexander	8542
Golden Slumbers	Newton, Ernest	5241
Goldiger, sonniger Maientag	Kienzl, Wilhelm	3760
Goldkäfer "Goldkäferlein du stolzer Mann"	Schletterer, Hans Michel	6659
Goldne Brücken seien alle Lieder mir	Rudorff, E. [Friedrich Karl]	6343
Goldne Leiter "Wenn die Sonne hoch und heiter"	Doebber, Johannes	1698
Gondelfahrt "Nacht ist so labend"	Gordigiani, Luigi	2609
Gondelfahrt "Rasch hinaus, auf die Wogen"	Panseron, Auguste	5397
Gondellied "Gleite hin, die glänzende Bahn"	Becker, Konstantin Julius	612
Gondellied "Mein Nachen im leichten Scherzen"	Graben-Hoffmann, Gustav	2695
Gondellied "Welle kommt"	Gumbert, Ferdinand	2870
Gondoliera	Henschel, George	3134
Gondoliera "Bello è il cielo"	Rilvas, C. de	6031
Gondoliera "O komm zu mir"	Aue, U.	466
Gondoliera "O komm zu mir"	Baumann, Alexander	582
Gondoliera "O komm zu mir"	Decker, Constantine	1594
Gondoliera "O komm zu mir"	Kücken, Friedrich Wilhelm	4083
Gondoliera "O komm zu mir"	Richter, Ernst Friedrich	6006
Gondolierlied "Abends führt' ich in dem Nachen"	Schlözer, K. [prob. Karl]	6705
Good for Nothing	Berger, Jean	702
Good night, pretty stars	Johnson, Noel	3632
Good-Bye	Tosti, Francesco Paolo	7906
Gornïy Kluch	Rimsky-Korsakov, Nicolai	6035
Gornye vershiny [Mountain Heights]	Rubinstein, Anton	6253
Gornyi Kliuch [Mountain Spring]	Rimsky-Korsakov, Nicolai	6036
Gott der Gnade, schau' hernieder	Güth, J. L.	2906
Gott gab uns	Rinck, Johann Christian Heinrich	6047
Gott grüass't di mei Bua	Egger-Rieser, T.	1886
Gott grüsse dich, kein andrer Gruss	Dorn, Otto	1756
Gott grüsse dich, kein andrer Gruss	Franke, Hermann	2274
Gott grüsse dich, kein andrer Gruss	Mücke, Franz	5096 5097
Gott grüsse dich, kein andrer Gruss	Taubert, Wilhelm	7655
Gott hilft zur rechten Zeit "Was seufzest du im Leben"	Häser, J. [prob. Johann]	2997
Gott ist die Liebe "Vöglein was singst du"	Graner, R.	2736
Gott Rad	Hinrichs, Friedrich	3300
Gott schützt die Kinder "Aus dem Himmel ferne"	Reissiger, Karl Gottlieb	5871
Gott sorgt für Alle "Weisst di wie viel Sterne"	Lenz, Leopold	4369
Gott was for'n Stuss "Wir sind beliebt in alle Welt"	Matthias, W.	4747
Gott willkommen, liebe Sonne	Becker, Valentin Eduard	624
Gott zum Gruss am Weihnachtsfeste	Schmeidler, K. [prob. Karl]	6706
Gottes Rath und Scheiden "Es ist bestimmt in Gottes Rath"	Dorn, Heinrich L. E.	1745
Gottes Vorsehung "Siehe die Lilien auf dem Felde"	Molique, Wilhelm Bernhard	5055
Gottes Zucht "Wenn Alles eben käme"	Lange, R.	4274
Gottesgruss "Gottesgruss rauscht im Walde"	Greith, Karl	2764
Gotteslob "Kein Thierlein ist auf Erden"	Greith, Karl	2765
Grab der Gefallenen des k.k. Jäger-Bat. auf St. Lucia "Schlaft wohl auf St. Lucia Kirchhof"	Herzog, Max.	3194
Grab "Grab ist tief und stille"	André, Johann Anton	383
Grade beim Hôtel zur Eule	Aletter, Wilhelm	353
Grädeste vom Graden "Kommen zu Stellung h'nein"	Sioly, Johann	7303
Graf und die Bäuerin "Komm Dirne mit"	Sterkel, Johann F. X.	7536
Graf und die Tyrolerin "Kom. Wechselgesang"	Tuch, Heinrich Agatius Gottlob	7943
Gräfin und das Mägdlein "Edle Gebieterin"	Concone, Giuseppi	1467
Gräfin und der Hirt "Verschmähter Hirtenjunge"	Sterkel, Johann F. X.	7537
Grain de blé	Bordèse, Luigi	957
Granadas Töchter "Granada geehrt vor allen"	Concone, Giuseppi	1468
Gras ücken "Wenn die Lerchen sich erheben"	Bordèse, Luigi	958
Grasemückchen an dem Brückchen	Attenhofer, Karl	450
Gratulanten "5 Dichtungen"	Plag, Johann	5517
Grauer Vogel über der Haide	Sulzbach, Emil	7610 7611
Grazie a gl'inganni tuo	Cherubini, Luigi	1399
Great Duets From the Masters, Vol. I	Anthology	43
Great Duets From the Masters, Vol. II	Anthology	44
Green Singer, The	Sutherland, Margaret	7622
Gretchen im Walde "Gretchen ist ein Bauermädchen"	Schindler, J.	6620
Gretchen-Gavotte "Gretchen ist so hold"	Wicher, Alb.	8321
Gretchens Beichte "Wieder ist es lange zehn"	Vierling, Georg	8025
Grete, Lene, Franz und Anneliese	Schneider, Bernhard	6768
Grete, liebe Grete	Maas, Louis	4613
Gretelein "Sag' an du liebes Gretchen"	Christiani, E.	1417
Grosse Kinderlieder und Kinderduette (10)	Stekel, W.	7533
Grosse Loch, wie kam es doch	Stekel, W.	7534
Grösseres Glück "O wie glücklich deine Hand"	Vogel, Bernhardt	8038
Grosses Walzer-Duo "Welch ein Glück"	Mulder-Fabri, Rich.	5100

TITLE	COMPOSER	REC#
Guter Rath "Wenn du willst"	*André, Jean Baptiste*	370
Guter Rath "Willst du armer Musikant"	*Reinecke, Carl*	5776
Gyöngyvirág	*Kodály, Zoltán*	3873
Gypsy Love Song	*Herbert, Victor*	3164
Ha, dort kömmt er	*Schubert, Franz Peter*	6861
Ha es klopft, wer mag deas sein	*Millöcker, Karl*	5008
Ha, he, hi, ho, hu	*Gundlach, jun., L.*	2892
Ha, he, hi, ho, hu "Ha, ha, ha, ein Wirtshaus"	*Gundlach, jun., L.*	2893
Ha, was seh' ich, theure Ida	*Wappaus, Karl*	8126
Haar fliegt und wallet	*Wiel, Taddeo*	8386
Hab' als Hahn	*Hollaender, Viktor*	3398
Hab' Erbamen, sieh' meine Leiden	*Gabussi, Vincent*	2376
Hab'n ma erst gestern drahlt, drah'n ma heut a "Mir san zwa Solche"	*Sioly-Weisberg*	7352
Hab'ns im Leben schon Bauern g'sehn	*Minkwitz, Bruno*	5017
Habenera	*Renaud, Albert*	5922
Habt ihr ihn noch nicht vernommen	*Rothlauf, B.*	6211
Habt ihr schon von dem Haus gehört	*Ansorge, M. [prob. Margarethe]*	409
Hage und Mager "Wo das Haus am höchsten ist"	*Winkler, O.*	8501
Haideblume "Haidebleme, niedich kleine"	*Volkmann, W.*	8061
Haideblume niedlich kleine	*Volkmann, W.*	8062
Haidenröslein "Sah ein Knab' ein Röslein stehn"	*Braun, Clemens*	1180
Haidenröslein "Sah ein Knab' ein Röslein stehn"	*Gade, Niels Wilhelm*	2398
Haidenröslein "Sah ein Knab' ein Röslein stehn"	*Hollaender, Alexis [Holländer]*	3377
Haidenröslein "Sah ein Knab' ein Röslein stehn"	*Jadassohn, Salomon*	3578
Haidenröslein "Sah ein Knab' ein Röslein stehn"	*Kleffel, Arno*	3807
Haidenröslein "Sah ein Knab' ein Röslein stehn"	*Köhler, Christian Louis Heinrich*	3886
Hale and Wilder Classic Collection of Sacred Duets	*Anthology*	45
Hallelujah, auferstanden ist der Herr	*Rohde, H.*	6110
Halloh, i hob' an Terno g'macht	*Schild, Theodor*	6589
Halloh, nun sind wir da	*Coradini, R. & P.*	1492
Halt recht im Gemüthe	*Nicolai, Wilhelm Frederik Gerard*	5265
Hamatliab "Bin g'rast umanânder"	*Koschat, Thomas*	3930
Hamkehr "Hâb di amol blos g'segen"	*Koschat, Thomas*	3931
Hand in Hand mit heil'gem Beten	*Spengler, Ludwig*	7442
Hans und Grete "Guckst du mir denn immer nach"	*Kreutzer, Konradin*	3987
Hans und Grete "I bin halt a Madel"	*Hollaender, Viktor*	3399
Hans und Peter, die Don Juans vom Lande "Mein Trine ich beschwör' es"	*Teich, Otto*	7740

TITLE	COMPOSER	REC#
Hänschen ist führwahr (fürwahr) zu dumm	*Frank, Ernst*	2228 2229
Happy policeman, The	*Clifton, Harry*	1443
Harbe Poldi	*Schild, Theodor*	6590
Harbour lights, The	*Squire, William Henry*	7466
Hark! Hark, My Soul	*Shelley, Harry Rowe*	7154 7155 7156 7157
Hark! The goat-bells are ringing	*Smart, Henry*	7374
Hark to the Mandoline	*Parker, Henry*	5405 5406
Harlighetens Morgon	*Dahlgren, Erland*	1573
Harmonie "Ein Engel waltet über alles Leben"	*Oelschläger, Friedrich*	5328
Harmonie-Album	*Anthology*	46
Harre des Herrn "Harre meine Seele"	*Wienand, V.*	8401
Harrenden "Stand ein Bäumlein auf der Höh'"	*Abt, Franz*	190
Hase "Seht mir einer den Hasen an"	*Schöbe, C.*	6779
Hast du Jemand weh' gethau	*Bradsky, Wenzel Theodor*	1029
Hast du Kummer, hast du Sorgen	*Schäfer, P.*	6521
Hat der wilde Sturm	*Kühle, G.*	4110
Hat unser kleiner Stiefelmann	*Heinemann, Wilhelm*	3074
Hatfield bells	*Martin, Easthope*	4688
Hatschi, Prosit "Beim Hindernissrennen haben wir"	*Steidl, F.*	7516
Hausierer und Zeitungsleser "So schau dass d'amal"	*Sioly-Weisberg*	7353
Hausschlüssel "Was, das hat der Hasenfuss gesagt"	*Schäffer, August*	6536
He is My Redeemer	*Schofield, Joe*	6790
Hear My Prayer	*Dvořák, Antonín*	1825
Hebräische Gesänge	*Grädener, Karl Georg Peter*	2712
Heckenröslein über Nacht	*Roscher, Josef*	6133
Hector Berlioz Works	*Berlioz, Hector*	725
Hector Berlioz Works Vol. 1-20	*Berlioz, Hector*	726
Hectors Abschied "Will sich Hector ewig"	*Crelle, August Leopold*	1544
Hectors Abschied "Will sich Hector ewig"	*Grosheim, Georg Christoph*	2822
Hectors Abschied "Will sich Hector ewig"	*Paër, Ferdinando [Paer]*	5376
Hei die Schule ist nun aus	*Einödshofer & Schmidt*	1906
Hei, wir sind die Künstlerschar	*Tourbié, Richard*	7909
Heide, die rote	*Schmitt, Cornelius*	6741
Heidenröslein	*Gade, Niels Wilhelm*	2399
Heil die o Jungfrau	*Greith, Karl*	2766
Heil dir, du junges Paar	*May, Siegfried*	4759
Heil'ge Nacht, auf Engelsschwingen	*Degenhardt, E.*	1604
Heil'ge Nacht auf Engelsschwingen	*Friedrich, R.*	2341
Heil'ge Nacht du sinkest	*Schubert, Franz Peter*	6862
Heilige Nacht "Heilige Nacht des Herrn"	*Mendelssohn, Felix*	4849
Heiliger Abend "Selige Freude so rein"	*Döring, August*	1724

TITLE	COMPOSER	REC#
Heiligstes Sakrament, Taufe in Jesu Christ	*Wooge, Emma*	8688
Heimat, du süsse, du Dörfchen klein	*Voigt, Henriette*	8054
Heimath "Ich weiss ein theuerwethes Land"	*Rudorff, E. [Friedrich Karl]*	6344
Heimath, muss dich nun verlassen	*Hiller, Paul*	3290
Heimath "Muttererde, heilig Land"	*Abt, Franz*	191
Heimath und Fremde "Es ist so schön in der Haimath"	*Zöllner, Andreas*	8788
Heimathlied	*Stein, C. [prob. Karl]*	7519
Heimathrosen	*Opladen, Adolf*	5337
Heimkehr "Entfernte Glocken klangen herauf"	*Kanzler, W.*	3713
Heimkehr "Entfernte Glocken klangen herauf"	*Schultz, Edwin*	6922
Heimkehr "Halt' an, mein munter Rösslein"	*Kücken, Friedrich Wilhelm*	4084
Heimkehr "Holdrio, juchhe"	*Röhricht, Paul*	6113
Heimkehr "In meine Heimath kam ich"	*Salis, P.*	6429
Heimliche Liebe "Kein Feuer, keine Kohle"	*Henschel, George*	3136
Heimliche Liebe "Kein Feuer, keine Kohle"	*Hiller, Ferdinand*	3245
Heimliche Liebe "Kein Feuer, keine Kohle"	*Jadassohn, Salomon*	3579
Heimliche Liebe "Kein Feuer, keine Kohle"	*Sallneuve, E.*	6450
Heimliche Liebe "Kein Feuer, keine Kohle"	*Tiehsen, Otto*	7885
Heimliche Liebe "Kein Feuer, keine Kohle"	*Wolff, Gustav Tyson [also Tyson-Wolff]*	8646
Heimliche Liebe "Mein Schatz, der ist auf den Wanderschaft"	*Hiller, Ferdinand*	3246
Heimlichen Gruss "Mond ist schlafen gangen"	*Thierfelder, Albert Wilhelm*	7827
Heimwärts zieh'n die muntern Sänger	*Gumbert, Ferdinand*	2875
Heimweh "Du sagtest mir einst"	*Vogel, Bernhardt*	8039
Heimweh "Es überkommt ein Sehnen"	*Böie, Heinrich*	906
Heimweh "Nur einmal noch in meinem Leben"	*Simon, Ernst*	7226
Heimweh "Sterne, die ihr niederschaut"	*Brambach, Kaspar Joseph*	1143
Heimweh "Wo auf hohen Tannenspitzen"	*Abt, Franz*	192
Heimweh "Wo auf hohen Tannenspitzen"	*Köllner, Eduard*	3891
Heimweh "Wo auf hohen Tannenspitzen"	*Rohde, Eduard*	6096
Heinze und Janke "Nu was mein'se"	*Ludwig, C.*	4598
Heinzelmännchen, König und Königen	*Goepfart, Karl Eduard*	2533
Heirathsannonce "Hier auf diesem stillen Fleck"	*Kron, Louis*	4030
Heirathslustigen Schwestern "Wir sind ein lustiges Schwesternpaar"	*Kloss, H.*	3846
Heisa, lustig und fidel	*Teich, Otto*	7741
Hélène	*Berlioz, Hector*	727
Hell in's Fenster scheindt die Sonne	*Attenhofer, Karl*	451
Hell in's Fenster scheindt die Sonne	*Hauptmann, Moritz*	3027
Hell ist ein Lied erklungen	*Reinecke, Carl*	5777
Hell'ge Nacht mit Engelsschwingen	*Wooge, Emma*	8689
Helle Kerzenlichter zittern	*Schneider, Bernhard*	6769
Henna	*Lehmann, Liza*	4352
Heraus "Ging unter dichten Zweigen"	*Dorn, Otto*	1757
Heraus "Ging unter dichten Zweigen"	*Hamma, Benjamin*	2961
Heraus "Ging unter dichten Zweigen"	*Krigar, Hermann*	4002
Heraus "Ging unter dichten Zweigen"	*Ries, Ferdinand*	6015
Heraus "Ging unter dichten Zweigen"	*Salis, P.*	6430
Herbst "Bedächt' ger, doch mit frischem Sinn"	*Ponflick, F.*	5540
Herbst "Rothen Blätter fallen"	*Rohde, Eduard*	6097
Herbst "Sommer entschwand"	*Riccius, August Ferdinand*	5985
Herbstabend "Wolken kommen schwarz gezogen"	*Schletterer, Hans Michel*	6662
Herbstgedanken "Vöglein hat sich heiser gesungen"	*Norman, Fredrik Vilhelm Ludwig*	5288
Herbstgefühl "O wär es blos der Wange Pracht"	*Thooft, Willem Frans*	7875
Herbstklage "Holder Lenz du bist dahin"	*Weber, Gustav*	8163
Herbstklang "Schon ist die von dem höchsten Ast"	*Santner, Karl*	6494
Herbstlied	*Mendelssohn, Felix*	4850 4851
Herbstlied	*Schumann, Robert*	7003 7004
Herbstlied "Ach, wie so bald"	*Mendelssohn, Felix*	4852
Herbstlied "Ach, wie so bald verhallet"	*Mendelssohn, Felix*	4853
Herbstlied "Ach wie so bald verhallet der Reigen"	*Mendelssohn, Felix*	4854
Herbstlied "Das Laub fällt von den Bäumen"	*Schumann, Robert*	7005
Herbstlied "Durch die Wälder streif ich munter"	*Salis, P.*	6431
Herbstlied "Es ist nun der Herbst gekommen"	*Bellermann, Heinrich*	655
Herbstlied "Es schleicht um Busch und Halde"	*Tuma, A.*	7946
Herbstlied "Feldenwärts flog ein Vögelein"	*Bach, Otto*	478
Herbstlied "Feldenwärts flog ein Vögelein"	*Brenner, Friedrich*	1203
Herbstlied "Feldenwärts flog ein Vögelein"	*Franke, Hermann*	2275
Herbstlied "Feldenwärts flog ein Vögelein"	*Goltermann, Georg*	2583
Herbstlied "Feldenwärts flog ein Vögelein"	*Liebe, Eduard Ludwig*	4428
Herbstlied "Feldenwärts flog ein Vögelein"	*Neukomm, Sigismund*	5199
Herbstlied "Feldenwärts flog ein Vögelein"	*Reich, Reinhold*	5713

TITLE	COMPOSER	REC#
Hier unterm blüh'ndem Fliederbaum	Zimmer, C. [prob. Karl]	8780
Hier waren grüne Buchen	Brandt-Caspari, Alfred	1169
High in the heavens	Huhn, Bruno	3509
Himmelfahrt "Wie prangt im Frühlingskleide"	Succo, Reinhold	7599
Himmelglanz der Ostertag	Schmeidler, K. [prob. Karl]	6707
Himmelsthräne "Himmel hat ein Thräne geweint"	Nauwerk, E.	5161
Hinan	Böhm, W.	903
Hinauf, hinab "Wie schön recht weit"	Tauwitz, Eduard	7680
Hinaus, hinaus, du junges Blut	Diercks, H.	1676 1677
Hinaus, hinaus zum grünen Wald	Schletterer, Hans Michel	6663
Hinaus, hinaus, zur bunten Flur	Hamma, Benjamin	2962
Hinaus in's Freie "Wie blüht es im Thale"	Abt, Franz	194
Hinaus "Nun hinaus in das freie Feld"	Rohde, Eduard	6098
Hinaus zum Walde, streifte Lisette	Berlioz, Hector	728
Hindoo Song	Rimsky-Korsakov, Nicolai	6037
Hinunter	Böhm, W.	904
Hinunter ist der Sonnen schein	Stern, Hermann	7538
Hipp, hipp hurra, das ist der Gruss	Teich, Otto	7743
Hirondelles	Van Cromphout, L.	7984
Hirsch "Was das nicht des Jagdhorns Ton"	Schöbe, C.	6780
Hirten Wiegenlied "Schlafe, o schlafe lieb Christkindlein"	Nagler, Franziskus	5136
Hirtenknabe "Ich bin vom Berg der Hirtenknab'"	Wilhelm, Karl Friedrich	8444
Hirtenmädchen unbefangen schertz	Gordigiani, Luigi	2610
Hirtenreigen "Was kann schöner sein"	Grünberger, Ludwig	2842
Hirtinnen "Schon sinkt der Abend sanft hernieder"	Concone, Giuseppi	1469
Hoch Deutschland "Ob drohend die Wolken auch"	Dorn, Alexander Julius Paul	1736
Hoch drob'n auf steller Bergeshöh'	Robricht, P.	6071
Hoch vom Himmel droben	Liebe, Eduard Ludwig	4429
Hoch vom Himmel holde Kunde	Döring, W. [prob. Wilhelm]	1729
Hoch wandern die Vögel	Widmann, Benedikt	8362
Hochsommer "Im Föhren-wald wie schwüle"	Rosenfeld, Leopold	6147
Höchste Glück hat keine Lieder	Becker, Reinhold	620
Höchste Leb'n in Grinzing "Mei Weanastadt, mei Vaterstadt"	Schild, Theodor	6591
Hochzeit auf der Alm "Sag' mir du saggrisch Bua"	Simon, Ernst	7227
Hochzeitsgratulanten "Da wäre ich glücklich zur Stadt"	Hollaender, Viktor	3400
Hochzeitslied "Gärtnerin, von allen Vöglein"	Krigar, C.	4000

TITLE	COMPOSER	REC#
Hochzeitslied "Junges Mädchen, komm o Mädchen"	Dressler, Friedrich August	1776
Hoffe nur!	Lassen, Eduard	4308
Hoffe nur "Hoffe nur in stiller Nacht"	Lassen, Eduard	4309
Hoffmann, Hoffman, sei ja kein Hofmann	Beethoven, Ludwig van	633
Hoffnung "Hoffnung endet alle Schmerzen"	Sauerbrey, J. W. C. C.	6517
Hoffnung "Sonne sinkt der Abend blinkt"	Mühling, August	5098
Hoffnung "Und dräut der Winter noch so sehr"	Bergmann, Gustav	712
Hoffnung "Und dräut der Winter noch so sehr"	Salinger, J.	6419
Hoffnung und Gott	Grossjohann, F.	2833
Hoffnung "Wenn die Hoff-nung nicht wär'"	Dorn, Heinrich L. E.	1746
Hoffnung "Wenn die Hoff-nung nicht wär'"	Hiller, Ferdinand	3247
Hoffnung "Wenn die Hoff-nung nicht wär'"	Lange, R.	4275
Hoffnungswalzer lockt und klingt	Nápravník, Eduard	5138
Höhen und Thäler "Mein Mädchen wohnt"	Mangold, Karl Ludwig Armand	4652
Höhen und Thäler "Mein Mädchen wohnt"	Solbrück, C.	7414
Hohes "Hohe Lilie, keine ist so stolz"	Hahn, J. Ch. W.	2939
Hold Thou my Hand	Briggs	1236
Holde Tugend, leite mich in meiner Jugend	Bornhardt, Johann Heinrich Karl	1008
Holden Rosen sind dahin "Nicht klag' ich um den Schmuck"	Salis, P.	6432
Holder Frühling ist's	Brunner, Ed.	1278
Holder Maientag "O wie ist doch"	Abt, Franz	195
Holder Mond jetzt strahlst du	Roscher, Josef	6134
Holderstrauch, der blüthe schön	Kirchner, Hermann	3777
Holdes Fräulein zart und jung	Ludwig, August	4590
Holdseligen sonder Wank	Jadassohn, Salomon	3580
Holdseliges Mädchen, dich hab' ich so gern "Ich sag' es den Sternen"	Tschiderer, E.	7935
Hollunderbaum "Da droben auf jenem Berge"	Bradsky, Wenzel Theodor	1030
Hollunderbaum "Da droben auf jenem Berge"	Schläger, Hans	6631
Holub na javore [Die Taube auf dem Ahorn]	Dvořák, Antonín	1826
Holy Child	Martin, Easthope	4689
Holy Child, The	Graham, Robert	2724
Holy Father, guide	Wallace	8099
Holz und Licht, sowie die Kohl'n	Wanthaler, Gustav	8118
Holzknechtlied "Und die Holzknechtbuama"	André, L. [prob. Christian Karl André]	393
Home, sweet home	Bishop, Henry Rowley	803
Honour, riches, marriage	Sullivan, Arthur	7605
Hope beyond	White	8312

TITLE	COMPOSER	REC#
Ich und mein Bruder Theobald	Teich, Otto	7745
Ich und mein Haus, wir sind bereit	Hauptmann, Moritz	3029
Ich vergonn' es ihm	Henschel, George	3137
Ich vergönn' es ihm "Rosen pflückte ab das Mädchen"	Henschel, George	3138
Ich weiss, dass mich der Himmel liebt	Jadassohn, Salomon	3581
Ich weiss ein fein braun's Mägdelein	Jäger, W.	3599
Ich weiss einen sichern Wanderstab	Bornhardt, Johann Heinrich Karl	1009
Ich weiss, ja nicht, was kommen wird	Klengel, Paul	3837
Ich weiss mein Gott, dass all mein Tun	Herrmann, Willy	3190
Ich weiss nicht, wie mir's ist	Frey, Martin	2330
Ich will dich hegen und pflegen	Schultz, Edwin	6923
Ich will dir's nimmer sagen	Hasselhoff, A.	3007 3008
Ich will meine Seele tauschen	Messer, F.	4938
Ich will Trauern, Trauern schwinden sehn	Umlauft, Paul	7956
Ich wollt' mein Lieb' ergösse sich	Mendelssohn, Felix	4866 4867
Ich wollt' meine Lieb	Mendelssohn, Felix	4868
Ich wollt' meine Lieb' ergösse sich	Mendelssohn, Felix	4869 4870
Ich wollt', meine Liebe	Melchert, J.	4803
Ich wollt', meine Liebe ergösse sich	Mendelssohn, Felix	4871
Ida ind Frieda, die Ball-schwärmerinnen "Wie reizend liebe Frieda"	Kron, Louis	4031
Ideal "Meine liebe Registratorin"	Schäffer, August	6537
Ideal "Taschen Musikalbum"	Simon, Ernst	7229
Idylle	Moniuszko, Stanislaw	5070
Idyllisches Minnelied "Wenn über Wieseen	Noskowski, Zygmund	5303
If ever you're in trouble	Terriss, Ellaline	7793
If I can help somebody	Androzzo, A. Bazel	400
If I were sure	Leonard, Conrad	4379
If Thou, Lord, shouldst number trangressions	Henschel, George	3139
If Thou Wilt Ease Thine Heart	Bracken, Edith A.	1028
If We Marry for Love	Crampton, Ernest	1541
If ye then be risen with Christ	Foster, Myles Birket	2167
If You Ask Anything of the Father	Bender, Jan	672 673
Ihr Damen und Herren merket auf	Peter, G.	5453
Ihr hohen Himmlischen	Schubert, Franz Peter	6866
Ihr Kinderlein kommt	Niemann, Gustav	5272
Ihr Kinderlein kommt	Wagner, Ernst David	8086
Ihr leben Lerchen guten Tag	Bruch, Max	1255
Ihr lieben Mägdelein, lasst doch das Freien sein	Winterling, W.	8613
Ihr lieben Vöglein singt	Lachner, Franz	4182
Ihr seht mich	Blangini, G. M. M. Felice	822
Ihr "Seid meines Herzens stille Vertraute"	Reissiger, Karl Gottlieb	5872

TITLE	COMPOSER	REC#
Ihr Vögelein so zart und fein	Kalliwoda, Johann Wenzel	3699
Il bacio	Arditi, Luigi	417
Il Bacio	Lucantoni, Giovanni	4579
Il Vestito azurro	d'Yradier, Chevalier	1570
Illa se un moto impenetrabile	Teschner, Gustav Wilhelm	7794
Im Abendroth "Wir sind durch Noth und Freude gegangen"	Jansen, F. Gustav	3604
Im April	Stainlein, Louis von	7473
Im Dunkeln Schlummern die Thäler	Abt, Franz	198
Im Eimer das Wasser trieb tanzend	Brandt-Caspari, Alfred	1170
Im feuchten Haar einen funkelnden Kranz	Kremling, P. W.	3981
Im Fliederbusch ein Vöglein sass	Ludwig, August	4592
Im Fliederbusch ein Vöglein sass	Maase, Wilhelm	4615
Im Fluge durch die Welt "Herr von Pumpus hat"	Sioly-Weisberg	7354
Im Frack und Chapeau claque "Sie sehen in uns Beid'"	Wolff, W.	8664
Im Freien 8 Duette f. S. u. A.	Rennes, Catharina van	5945
Im Freien "Bald in dem Busche"	Abt, Franz	199
Im Freien "Kann auch Frühling finster blicken"	Drobisch, Karl Ludwig	1784
Im Freiheitssturm "2- u. 3st. Volkslieder"	Kühnhold, Karl	4141
Im Frühling	Seiffert, Alexander	7101
Im Frühling "12 Kinderlieder"	Tolstoy, Alexei [Tolstoi]	7898
Im Frühling "Blümlein seid gegrüsset"	Bruch, Max	1256
Im Frühling, wenn die Sonn' erweckt	Heinz, P.	3085
Im Frühling "Wie bist du Frühling gut und treu"	Schubert, Louis	6906
Im frühlingsgrünen Eichenhain	Friedland, A.	2337
Im Garten	Tchaikovsky, Peter Ilyich	7691
Im Garten "Ich poch an deiner Thüre"	Gericke, R. v.	2457
Im Gebirge "Auf diesen blauen Bergen"	Krill, Karl	4008
Im Grunde "Mein Herz du musst dich fügen"	Salis, P.	6433
Im Grünen "Im Grün erwacht"	André, Jean Baptiste	371
Im grünen Laub, so dicht	Reissiger, Karl Gottlieb	5873
Im Grünen "Schallt keck von hohen Bäumen"	Brambach, Kaspar Joseph	1145
Im Grünen "Willkommen im Grünen"	Attenhofer, Karl	453
Im Hafen "Als ich an deiner Brust geruht"	Kanzler, W.	3714
Im Hag nah bei des Bächleins Lauf	Slunicko, Jan	7366
Im Haselstrauch "Sag' mir du grüner Haselstrauch"	Erlanger, Gustav	1949

TITLE	COMPOSER	REC#
Im Hause Gottes Kirchliche Festgesänge f. S. u. A.	*Hötzel, C.*	3487
Im heimischen Land	*Rubinstein, Anton*	6255
Im heimischen Land "Im heimlischen Land steht ein friedlicher Hain"	*Rubinstein, Anton*	6256
Im heimlichen Land steht ein friedlicher Hain"	*Rubinstein, Anton*	6257
Im Herbst "Es rauschen die Winde"`	*Marschner, Heinrich August*	4679
Im Herbst "O Waldesluft, wie gehst du bang"	*Schubert, Louis*	6907
Im Herbste "Bald fällt von diesen Zweigen"	*Attenhofer, Karl*	454
Im Herbste "Seid gegrüsst mit Frühlingswonne"	*Rosenfeld, J.*	6143
Im Himmel Wandre Ich...	*Stockhausen, Karlheinz*	7561
Im Himmel wandre ich... (Indianerlieder)	*Stockhausen, Karlheinz*	7562
Im jungen Grün schon Veilchen blühn	*Zapff, Oskar*	8730
Im Land Tyrol "In dem schönen Land Tyrol"	*Simon, Ernst*	7230
Im Lenz erfreu' ich dich	*Zerlett, Johann Baptist*	8758
Im Lenz, im Lenz, wenn Veilchen blühn	*Fielitz, Alexander von*	2099
Im Lenze "Hinaus zum grünen Walde"	*Naubert, Friedrich August*	5151
Im Lenze "Hinaus zum grünen Walde"	*Sachs, Johann Melchior Ernst*	6384
Im Mai, im schönen Mai	*Fink, Christian*	2101
Im Mai "Musst nicht allein im Freien"	*Sieber, Ferdinand*	7186
Im Mai "Musst nicht allein im Freien"	*Thierfelder, Albert Wilhelm*	7828
Im Mai "Nun grünt der Berg"	*Wüerst, Richard Ferdinand*	8710
Im Maien, im Maien ist's lieblich und schön	*Schultz, Edwin*	6924
Im Maien "Im Maien zu Zweien ze gehen"	*Engel, David Hermann*	1939
Im Maien "Im Maien zu Zweien ze gehen"	*Kahn, Robert*	3685
Im Maien "Im Maien zu Zweien ze gehen"	*Ladendorff, O.*	4236
Im Maien "Im Maien zu Zweien ze gehen"	*Wolff, Gustav Tyson [also Tyson-Wolff]*	8647
Im Maien "Nun (Es) bricht aus allen Zweigen"	*Herbert, Theodor*	3163
Im Maien "Nun (Es) bricht aus allen Zweigen"	*Jacoby, Wilhelm*	3568
Im Maien "Nun (Es) bricht aus allen Zweigen"	*Liebe, Eduard Ludwig*	4431
Im Maien "Nun (Es) bricht aus allen Zweigen"	*Plengorth, Friedrich*	5528
Im Maien "Nun (Es) bricht aus allen Zweigen"	*Rohde, Eduard*	6099
Im März "Mit seinen Veilchen kommt der März"	*Schletterer, Hans Michel*	6665
Im Mondenglanze ruht das Meer	*Ochs, Siegfried*	5317
Im Myrthenkranz "Lag einst im Walde auf Gras und Moos"	*Cursch-Bühren, Franz Theodor*	1553
Im Namen Gottes lege ich zur Ruhe	*Nater, Johann*	5142
Im Namen Gottes steh' ich auf	*Nater, Johann*	5143
Im Pfarrhaus "Hallo, mein Pfarrherr"	*Seyffardt, Ernst Hermann*	7134
Im Rosenduft, vom Blüten-hain umfangen	*Gustav, Prinz v. Schweden*	2905
Im Schatten der Linde	*Peuschel, Moritz*	5466
Im schönen Mai "3 Tanzliedchen"	*Martini, F. v.*	4691
Im schönsten Wiesengrunde	*Meyer-Stolzenau, Wilhelm*	4983
Im Sonnengold, im Abendroth	*Peter, G.*	5454
Im Spätherbst "Blätter fallen gelb und matt"	*Abt, Franz*	200
Im Spätherbst "Wie schön willst du dich schmücken"	*Rohde, Eduard*	6100
Im Süden "Ist die Luft so rein gestimmt"	*Horn, E.*	3470
Im Thale "Im Thale der silberne Bach"	*Bisping, A.*	806
Im Theaterbureau "Wenn man nur ein Mittel hätte"	*Simon, Ernst*	7231
Im Thüringer Wald "In dem Thüringer Wald, wo die Erbeeren blühn"	*Popp, Wilhelm*	5549
Im tiefen Wald verborgen	*Hill, Wilhelm*	3224
Im Volkston	*Jadassohn, Salomon*	3582
Im Vorfrühling "Ich steh' auf hohem Berg allein"	*Langert, Johann August Adolf*	4281
Im Wald "Es ist so still"	*Eberhardt, Anton*	1876
Im Wald "Im Wald, im frischen grünen Wald"	*Wilhelm, Karl Friedrich*	8446
Im Wald "Im Wald, im Wald ist Lust und Fried"	*Reinecke, Carl*	5778
Im Wald "Im Wald ist Lust und Fried'"	*Reinecke, Carl*	5779
Im Walde	*Seiffert, Alexander*	7102
Im Walde die Amsel	*Abt, Franz*	201
Im Walde hallt es wunderbar	*Brandt-Caspari, Alfred*	1171
Im Walde "Hinaus, hinaus in's Freie"	*Salis, P.*	6434
Im Walde "Ihr Nixen, Gnomen, Elfen"	*Lachner, Franz*	4183
Im Walde "Ihr Vöglein in den Zweigen"	*André, Jean Baptiste*	372
Im Walde, im grünen (Wald) Walde	*Abt, Franz*	202 203
Im Walde, im grünen (Wald) Walde	*Horn, August*	3459
Im Walde, im hellen Sonnenschein	*Hamma, Benjamin*	2963
Im Walde, im hellen Sonnenschein	*Esser, Heinrich*	1994
Im Walde, im hellen Sonnenschein	*Hiller, Ferdinand*	3250
Im Walde, im hellen Sonnenschein	*Rennes, Catharina van*	5946
Im Walde, im hellen Sonnenschein	*Rijken, Georg*	6030
Im Walde, im hellen Sonnenschein	*Rosenhain, Jacob*	6153
Im Walde, im hellen Sonnenschein	*Schläger, Hans*	6633
Im Walde "Im Wald, im schönen"	*Meves, Wilhelm*	4960
Im Walde "Im Walde, da weht es so linde"	*Möhring, Ferdinand*	5042

TITLE	COMPOSER	REC#
Im Walde "Im Walde, im Walde"	Abt, Franz	204
Im Walde "Im Walde lasst uns weilen"	Ortner, A.	5346
Im Walde möcht' ich leben	Stieber, P.	7549
Im Walde "O Thäler weit, o Höhen"	Hahn, J. Ch. W.	2940
Im Walde "O Thäler weit, o Höhen"	Thiele, Eduard	7801
Im Walde singt ein Vogel	Wüerst, Richard Ferdinand	8711
Im Walde "Tief durch den Wald"	Lachner, Franz	4184
Im Walde "Waldesnacht, du wunderkühle"	Bradsky, Wenzel Theodor	1031
Im Walde "Waldesnacht, du wunderkühle"	Leschetitzky, Theodor	4393
Im Walde "Was flüstern im Walde"	Seyffardt, Ernst Hermann	7135
Im Walde zieh' ich wohlgemuth	Stieber, P.	7550
Im Waldesgrün "Im Waldesgrün ist unsere Lust"	Benedict, Jules	684
Im Weana-Dialekt "Oft da müssen wir Zwa lachen"	Leukauf, Richard	4398
Im Wienerwald draussen	Kronegger, Rudolf	4047
Im wunderschönen Monat Mai	Haeberlein, H.	2934
Im wunderschönen Monat Mai	Hensel, Fanny Mendelssohn	3158
Immer bleibst du Herr	Rinck, Johann Christian Heinrich	6048
Immer leiser wird mein schlummer	Bradsky, Wenzel Theodor	1032
Immer leiser wird mein schlummer	Sachs, Johann Melchior Ernst	6385
Immer lustig, flott und frei	Fischer, Anton	2118
Immer neu fühl ich dies süsse Regen	Carafa, Michel Enrico	1345
Immer wieder muss ich lesen	Legov, M.	4346
Immer wieder schwur ich Liebe	Weber, Carl Maria von	8137
Immer wieder süsses Leben	Weber, Carl Maria von	8138
Immer zwei zu zweien	Wintzer, Elisabeth	8621
Immersa nell aureo vapor	Lannoy, Eduard	4284
Immortalité	Massenet, Jules	4734
Impazienza	Gordigiani, Luigi	2611
Improvisatorinnen "Blumen in das Haar gewunden"	Bordèse, Luigi	959
In a Bower	Nevin, Ethelbert Woodbridge	5227
In auer Tramway sitzt a Köchin	Augustin, F. H.	469
In Berlin fangts Leben an	Hollaender, Viktor	3402
In Bethlehem	Graham, Robert	2725
In Bethlehem Town	Fiske, Roger	2148
In Blumenduft und Blüthenschnee "wenn dich ein Frühlingsgruss ereilt"	Fuchs, L.	2354
In das Bummeln noch so schön	Bredschneider, Willy	1193
In dem Bächlein fliesset	Winterberger, Alexander	8544
In dem bunten Bette liegt	Winterberger, Alexander	8545
In dem Dornbusch blüht ein Röslein	Wolff, Gustav Tyson [also Tyson-Wolff]	8648
In dem Garten am Flusse	Tchaikovsky, Peter Ilyich	7692
In dem grünen Klee sah ich die Holde	Thieriot, Ferdinand	7836
In dem Hotel zur goldnen Gaus	Knopf, Martin	3860
In dem Land Tyrol ist es mir so wohl	Wenzel, H.	8273
In dem stillen Mondenscheine	Reichardt, Johann Friedrich	5724
In dem Walde sah'n wir heut	Reinecke, Carl	5780
In den Beeren "Singe Mädchen hell und klar"	Brahms, Johannes	1077
In den heut'gen Zeiten	Baum, W.	575
In den Sternen stet's geschrieben	Simon, Ernst	7232
In den Thälern laut erschallts	Kücken, Friedrich Wilhelm	4088
In der Christnacht "Kommt ihr Christen fröhlich"	Strubel, J.	7590
In der dunkeln weiten Himmelsferne	Schletterer, Hans Michel	6666
In der Ferne "Heilige Sonntagsstille"	Abt, Franz	205
In der Ferne "Siehst du am Abend die Wolken zieh'n"	Grabert, Martin	2708
In der Ferne "Will ruhen unter den Bäumen hier"	Biehl, A. [prob. Albert]	767
In der Ferne "Will ruhen unter den Bäumen hier"	Franck, Eduard	2203
In der Ferne "Will ruhen unter den Bäumen hier"	Hauser, Moritz H.	3051
In der Ferne "Will ruhen unter den Bäumen hier"	Hollaender, Alexis [Holländer]	3378
In der Ferne "Will ruhen unter den Bäumen hier"	Reissiger, Karl Gottlieb	5874
In der Fremde "Es steht ein Baum im Odenwald"	Möhring, Ferdinand	5043
In der Fremde "Es steht ein Baum im Odenwald"	Winterberger, Alexander	8546
In der Fremde "Hab' ich doch Tag und Nacht"	Abt, Franz	206
In der Fremde "Heil'ge Sonntagsstille"	Stange, Max	7486
In der Fremde "Wind, o lass dein scharfes Weh'n"	Ramann, Bruno	5637
In der Früh' z'Mittag und auf d'Nacht "Es lasst si' wer a Haus"	Sioly, Johann	7305
In der Heimath "Es ist ein tiefes Thal"	Freudenberg, Wilhelm	2322
In der Höhe Gott sei Ehre	Bennewitz, Fritz	692
"In der Mondnacht, in der Frühlingsmondnacht"	Fielitz, Alexander von	2100
"In der Mondnacht, in der Frühlingsmondnacht"	Hirsch, Karl	3311
In der Morgenfrühe "Herr, der du vom schweigenden Himmel"	Reissmann, August	5909
In der Morgenfrühe "Wohl über die Schlucht"	Brambach, Kaspar Joseph	1146
In der Mühle "Rauschet, rauschet Mühlensteine"	Kleffel, Arno	3809
In der nacht	Hol, Rijk	3365
In der Nacht "Alle gingen Herz zur Ruh'"	Schumann, Robert	7007
In der Nacht "Leben ist draussen verrauschet"	Radecke, Robert	5601
In der Nacht "Ungetrübte Ruh' erfühllt mich"	Hiller, Ferdinand	3251

TITLE	COMPOSER	REC#
Le Grillon	Lacome, Paul	4223
Le Montagnard Exilé	Berlioz, Hector	732
Le Noël des Petits Enfants	Lecocq, Charles	4335
Le poète et le fantôme	Massenet, Jules	4738
Le Poète et le Fantôme	Unknown composer or arranger	7972
Le Ranz-des-vaches d'Appenzell	Meyerbeer, Giacomo	4986
Le Renouveau	Coquard, Arthur	1490
Le retour	Mendelssohn, Felix	4876
Le Rhume	Manziarly, Marcelle de	4661
Le Ruisseau	Gastinel, Léon-Gustave-Cyprien	2431
Le retour	Mendelssohn, Felix	4876
Le Rhume	Manziarly, Marcelle de	4661
Le Ruisseau	Gastinel, Léon-Gustave-Cyprien	2431
Le Ruisseau	Lacome, Paul	4224
Le Traineau	Lacome, Paul	4225
Le Trébuchet	Berlioz, Hector	733 734
Le Village	Gastinel, Léon-Gustave-Cyprien	2432
Leb wohl du schöner Wald "So scheiden wir mit Sang"	Esser, Heinrich	1996
Leb wohl du schöner Wald "So scheiden wir mit Sang"	Grosse, L.	2830 2831
Lebe Wohl "Wann sich Seelen recht erkennen"	Meinardus, Ludwig	4783
Leben des Menschen	Rinck, Johann Christian Heinrich	6049
Leben ohne Liebe	Reinecke, Carl	5788
Lebens Mai "Süsser als Abendruh'"	Reissiger, Karl Gottlieb	5876
Lebens Pfeffer ist gewiss	Aletter, Wilhelm	354
Lebensgenuss "Schnell vergeht im Wechsel der Stunden"	Beethoven, Ludwig van	638
Lebensgenuss "Sie rollen schnell, des Menschen Jahre"	André, Johann Anton	386
Lebensglück "Wie glücklich lebt, wer Ruh' und Frieden"	André, Johann Anton	387
Lebenslust	Birn, M.	775
Lebenslust 6 zweist. Kinderlieder	Rennes, Catharina van	5951
Lebenspuls "Wenn hoch am fernen Himmelsbogen"	Santner, Karl	6496
Lebenstrost "Auf den Schnee"	Gorzer-Schulz, O. K. F.	2634
Lebet wohl, es ruft die heil'ge Pflicht	Grunholzer, K.	2850
Lebewohl	Banck, Karl	514
Lebewohl "Ade, es sei geschieden"	Brede, Albrecht	1187
Lebewohl "Lebewohl, lebewohl mein Lieb"	Hauser, Moritz H.	3052
Lebewohl "Lebewohl, lebewohl mein Lieb"	Meinardus, Ludwig	4784
Lebewohl "Lebewohl, lebewohl mein Lieb"	Möhring, Ferdinand	5045
Lebewohl "Lebewohl, lebewohl mein Lieb"	Rennes, Catharina van	5952
Lebewohl "Morgen muss ich fort von hier"	Goldner, Wilhelm	2553
Lebewohl "Morgen muss ich fort von hier"	Thoma, Rudolf	7855
Lebewohl "Wann sich Seelen recht erkennen"	Meinardus, Ludwig	4785
Lecture on Nothing	Itoh, Hiroyuki	3562
Lehn' deine Wang' an meine Wang'	Jensen, Adolf	3623
Lehre "Mutter zum Bienelein"	Zenger, Max	8746
Lehrstunde "Lenz ist, Aedi gekommen"	Romberg, A. [prob. Andreas]	6123
Leichte Fahrt "Lass mich schaukeln"	Eichberg, Oskar	1897
Leichte zweistimmige Weihnachtslieder	Heuler, Raimund	3198
Leichter Scherz "Ma Mutter und ma Vetterlen"	Blum, Karl Ludwig	865
Leichter Sinn "Über Gebirg und Thal"	Brunner, Christian Traugott	1270
Leichter Sinn "Und wie wär es nicht zu tragen"	Gumbert, Ferdinand	2879
Leichtsinnigen "Weil mir g'rad im Sommer"	Sioly, Johann	7315
Leiden einer Modisten "Wie schlimm hat's doch auf Erden"	Kron, Louis	4033
Leise, leise durch die Wipfel	Stange, Max	7487
Leise rauschen die Blätter im Wald	Schletterer, Hans Michel	6670
Leise zieht durch mein Gemüt [sic]	Berneker, Constanz	744
Leise zieht durch mein Gemüth	Alberti, G.	351
Leise zieht durch mein Gemüth	Gade, Niels Wilhelm	2401
Leise zieht durch mein Gemüth	Greith, Karl	2769
Leise zieht durch mein Gemüth	Gumbert, Ferdinand	2880
Leise zieht durch mein Gemüth	Herold, E.	3186
Leise zieht durch mein Gemüth	Schultz, Edwin	6926
Leise zieht durch mein Gemüth	Siebmann, F.	7198
Leise zieht durch mein Gemüth	Tiehsen, Otto	7887
Leise zieht durch mein Gemüth	Wielhorski, Mikhail	8391
Lena ist längst vorüber	Keller, H.	3737
Lenz auf blumigen Fluren lag	Goetze, Karl [Götze]	2545 2546
Lenz fängt an zu Lächeln	Brambach, Kaspar Joseph	1147
Lenz ist angekommen	Ernemann, E.	1959
Lenz ist angekommen	Hill, Wilhelm	3225
Lenz ist angekommen	Hoft, N.	3352
Lenz ist da	Schmitt, Cornelius	6744
Lenz ist da "Es klingt wie Festgeläute"	Pache, Joseph	5362
Lenz ist da "Turih, tarah, der Lenz ist da"	Reinecke, Carl	5789
Lenz, o Lenz, wie soll das enden	Esser, Heinrich	1997
Lenz und Liebe (7 Lieder und 3 Duette)	Lehmann, Liza	4353
Lenz will kommen	Schwarzlose, Otto	7078
Lenzes Sieg "Nun ist er doch gekommen"	Wermann, Friedrich Oskar	8285
Lenzes Wiederkehr "Wenn's wieder Lenz geworden"	Reissiger, Friedrich August	5851
Lenzestraum "Blüthenbaum hegt sel'gen Traum"	Abt, Franz	211
Lenzfrage "Sei willkommen liebe Sonne"	Zöllner, Andreas	8790
Lenzige Nacht	Bohm, C.	890

TITLE	COMPOSER	REC#
Mondnacht "Es war als hätte der Himmel"	Berger, Francesco	696
Mondnacht is', alles ist still	Baschinsky, P.	548
Mondnacht "Mondenschein, still und rein"	Könneritz, Nina [Georgine, neé Eschborn]	3903
Mondnacht "Wie schön bist du"	Abt, Franz	219
Mondscheinbrüder "Für uns gibt's nur a Beleuchtung"	Sioly, Johann	7321
Mondscheinlied "Verstohlen geht der Mond auf"	Hornstein, Robert von	3483
Mondscheinlied "Verstohlen geht der Mond auf"	Reinecke, Carl	5791
Mondscheinlied "Verstohlen geht der Mond auf"	Taubert, Wilhelm	7662
Monk's of Bangor March, The	Beethoven, Ludwig van	641
Monsieur Printemps (Printempts [sic])	Galland, E.	2420 2421
Moon Has Raised Her Lamp Above, The	Benedict, Jules	685
Mord in der Dämmerstunde	Heiter, Ernst	3101
Morgen, auch schon auf den Beiden	Baum, W.	576
Morgen "Ein Morgen-schimmer glüht"	Greith, Karl	2775
Morgen "Fliegt der erste Morgenstrahl"	Baumfelder, Friedrich	591
Morgen i Napoli	Schierbeck, Poul	6569
Morgen kommt mein Männchen wieder	Teich, Otto	7759
Morgen "Schon die trüben Schatten"	Meves, Wilhelm	4965
Morgendämmerung	Tchaikovsky, Peter Ilyich	7696
Morgenfrühe "Vorüber ist die dunkle Nacht"	Schletterer, Hans Michel	6674
Morgengebet "Lieber Vater hoch in Himmel"	Weiss, Laurenz	8239
Morgengebet "Morgen ist erglommen"	Reinecke, Carl	5792
Morgengebet "O wunderbares tiefes Schweigen"	Hahn, J. Ch. W.	2941
Morgenlied	Reissiger, Karl Gottlieb	5882
Morgenlied "Dunklen Schatten fliehen"	Reissiger, Karl Gottlieb	5883
Morgenlied "Erwacht, erwacht, es schwand die Nacht"	Kammerlander, Karl	3706
Morgenlied "Ich bin vom süssen"	Meves, Wilhelm	4966
Morgenlied im Freien "Meeres-fluth mit Purpurgluth"	Taubert, Wilhelm	7663
Morgenlied "Kein Stimmlein noch schallt"	Reinecke, Carl	5793
Morgenlied "Kein Stimmlein noch schallt"	Tuma, A.	7947
Morgenlied "Morgen erwacht"	Meijroos, Heinrich Arnoldus [Meyroos]	4773
Morgenlied "Morgenwinde weh'n frisch"	Weiss, Laurenz	8240
Morgenlied "Noch ahnt man kaum der Sonne Licht"	Franck, Eduard	2204
Morgenlied "Noch ahnt man kaum der Sonne Licht"	Frank, Ernst	2241

TITLE	COMPOSER	REC#
Morgenlied "Noch ahnt man kaum der Sonne Licht"	Könneritz, Nina [Georgine, neé Eschborn]	3904
Morgenlied "Noch ahnt man kaum der Sonne Licht"	Thoma, Rudolf	7858
Morgenlied "Steht auf, ihr lieben Kinderlein"	Eschmann, Johann Karl	1978
Morgenlied "Steht auf, ihr lieben Kinderlein"	Horn, August	3461
Morgenlied "Steht auf, ihr lieben Kinderlein"	Schubert, Franz Ludwig	6845
Morgenlied "Sterne sind erblichen"	Esser, Heinrich	1999
Morgenlied "Vorüber ist die dunkle Nacht"	Wichern, Karoline	8332
Morgenlied "Wer schlägt so rasch am die Fenster"	Wüerst, Richard Ferdinand	8716
Morgenlied "Werde heiter, mein Gemüthe"	Methfessel, C.	4944
Morgenlust "Duftiges Gewölk im Blauen"	Pache, Joseph	5364
Morgenpsalm "Es steigt von blauen Seen"	Franke, Hermann	2279
Morgenroth "Schau', das Morgenroth glüht"	Samson, L.	6469
Morgenroth "Schau', das Morgenroth glüht"	Tchaikovsky, Peter Ilyich	7697
Morgenröthe "Purpur färbt schon"	Donizetti, Gaetano	1716
Morgens im Thaue	Schnaubelt, W.	6760
Morgens in der Frühe	Kücken, Friedrich Wilhelm	4096
Morgenstern "Du blüh'nder Stern"	Reissiger, Friedrich August	5854
Morgenstille "Leiser tönt schon"	Esser, Heinrich	2000
Morgenstille "Leiser tönt schon"	Sering, Friedrich Wilhelm	7128
Morgenwanderung	Stainlein, Louis von	7474
Morgenwanderung im Mondschein	Lassen, Eduard	4314
Morgenwanderung im Mond-schein "Wenn das Mondenlicht"	Lassen, Eduard	4315
Morgenwanderung "Wer recht in Freuden wandern will"	Abt, Franz	220
Morgenwanderung "Wer recht in Freuden wandern will"	Gumbert, Ferdinand	2883
Morgenwanderung "Wer recht in Freuden wandern will"	Lichner, Heinrich	4418
Morgenwanderung "Wer recht in Freuden wandern will"	Seestädt, J.	7095
Morgenwanderung "Wie blitz so hell"	Salis, P.	6436
Morgenwanderung "Wie blitz so hell"	Schletterer, Hans Michel	6675
Morgenwinde, wogt hernieder	Bering, Ch.	718
Morgonsang	Abt, Franz	221
Morning	Berger, Jean	703
Morning	Speaks, Oley	7436
Morning Song	Thiman, Eric Harding	7838 7839
Morremo "Morremo e sciolti di quaggiù"	Marchetti, Filippo	4672
Moselblümchen, Mädchen, Männer "Moselblümchen, o wie duftig"	Nöroth, J.	5292

TITLE	COMPOSER	REC#
Nach Jahren "Mutter lehnt am schattigen Thor"	Zenger, Max	8747
Nachbarin "Mein Stübchen ist mir lieber"	Reissiger, Karl Gottlieb	5884
Nachgefühl "Wenn die Reben wieder blühend"	Thierfelder, Albert Wilhelm	7829
Nacht entfleucht	Weiss, Laurenz	8242
Nacht entfleucht	Wienand, V.	8405
Nacht ist dumpfig und finster	Schubert, Franz Peter	6875
Nacht ist nieder gangen	Roth, Bertrand	6205
Nacht ist schwarz	Reinecke, Carl	5796
Nacht ist wie ein stilles Meer	Bering, Ch.	719
Nacht ist's, die Erde träumet	Clement, M.	1441
Nacht liegt auf fremden Wegen	Wielhorski, Mikhail	8393
Nacht "Nacht ist wie ein stilles Meer"	Eichberg, Oskar	1898
Nacht sank leise hernieder	Denecke, H.	1617
Nacht "Süsse Ahnungs-schauer gleiten"	Rungenhagen, Karl Friedrich	6363
Nacht "Süsse Ahnungs-schauer gleiten"	Tiehsen, Otto	7889
Nacht "Tages letztes Glühten"	Rubinstein, Anton	6269
Nacht "Tiesfes Dunkel ruhet dem Meer"	Banck, Karl	520
Nacht und Träume "Heil'ge Nacht, du sinkest"	Preyer, Gottfried von	5565
Nacht vor dem Gefübde "Morgen ist jener Tag"	Concone, Giuseppi	1474
Nacht "Wie ist der Abend heiter"	Mililotti, Leopoldo	5000
Nacht-Stilte	Dijk, Jan van	1693
Nachtgebet "Nun kommt die Nacht mit leichtem Schritt"	Frank, Ernst	2242
Nachtgesang	Longuet	4532
Nachtgesang "Es feiert die Flur"	Hauptmann, Moritz	3034
Nachtgesang im Walde "Vöglein schlummern"	Pocci, Franz von	5532
Nachtgesang "Leise, leise schallen Lieder"	Banck, Karl	521
Nachtgesang "O gieb vom weichen Pfühle"	Matthieux, Johanna	4752
Nachtgesang "O Mondlicht zart und milde"	Roeder, Martin [Röder]	6079
Nachtgesaug "Bei meinem Saitenspiele"	Hochberg, Hans Heinrich XIV, Bolko Graf v.	3322
Nachtgruss "Mond und goldne Sterne glimmen"	Krill, Karl	4009
Nachtied "Milde dort oben"	Reich, Reinhold	5715
Nachtigall ich hör' dich singen	Reimann, Heinrich	5738
Nachtigall "Kuckuck hat sich zu Tode gefallen"	Scholz, Bernard	6797
Nachtigall "O könnt' ich doch die Nachtigall"	Brunner, Christian Traugott	1271
Nachtigall singt überall	Spielter, Hermann	7445
Nachtigall und Rose "Ach warum sing' ich"	Abt, Franz	224
Nachtigall und Sänger "Nacht-igall singt in den Wald hinein"	Nessler, Victor E.	5186
Nachtigall "Vom fernen Süd' komm' ich"	Gade, Niels Wilhelm	2408
Nachtigall, warum tönt nicht mehr	Schneider, Bernhard	6772
Nachtigallen schwingen lustig ihr Gefleder	Kulenkampff, Gustav	4144
Nachtigallen und Frösche "Ei, wem sollt' es nicht behangen"	Lenz, Leopold	4371
Nachtigallenlied "Englein schreiben ihre Lieder"	Zöllner, Andreas	8791
Nächtlich "Mond umfluthet und umflicht"	Hill, Wilhelm	3226
Nächtlich wandern all Flüsse	Sulzbach, Emil	7612
Nachtlied "Erde ruht, der Himmel wacht"	Sieber, Ferdinand	7191
Nachtlied "Erde ruht, der Himmel wacht"	Weber, Franz	8154
Nachtlied "Mond kommt still gegangen"	Krause, Eduard	3960
Nachtlied "Mond kommt still gegangen"	Knebel-Döberitz, A. v.	3850
Nachtlied "Mond kommt still gegangen"	Weidt, Heinrich	8192
Nachtlied "Vergangen ist der lichte Tag"	Scholz, Bernard	6798
Nachts	Reger, Max	5682 5683
Nachts "Ich wandre durch die stille Nacht"	Hászlinger, J. v.	3011
Nachts "Ich wandre durch die stille Nacht"	Reger, Max	5684
Nachts "Ich wandre durch die stille Nacht"	Taubert, Wilhelm	7664
Nachts "Ich wandre durch die stille, stille Nacht"	Reger, Max	5685
Nachts "Über'm Lande die Sterne"	Holstein, Franz von	3442
Nachts "Wie der Mond so freundlich schaut"	Könneritz, Nina [Georgine, neé Eschborn]	3905
Nachts wir uns küssten	Cornelius, Peter	1519
Nachtwind hat in den Bäumen	Birn, M.	776
Nähe des Geliebten "Ich denke dien, wenn mir der Sonne Schimmer"	Dorn, Heinrich L. E.	1748
Nähe des Herrn	Meijroos, Heinrich Arnoldus [Meyroos]	4774
Nanny und Fanny "Was ich oft im Traume sah"	Müller, Sr., Adolf	5109
Nar Jag Fran Dig Far	Myrberg, August Melcher	5130
Närrisch Liab "I hán di liebá"	Steizhammer	7531
Nascesti alle pene mie	Reissiger, Karl Gottlieb	5885
Naschkätzchen "Ein niedlich, kleines nasch'ges Ding"	Frankl, A.	2290
Nattergalen	Gade, Niels Wilhelm	2409
Nattvandrarens Sang	Rubinstein, Anton	6270
Naturlieder (4)	Esser, Heinrich	2002
Ne, die verdammte Steuer	Linderer, Ed.	4465
Neapel "Seht nun den Lenz erwaschen"	Masini, A. [prob. Angelo]	4717
Neapolitanisches Lied "Gross ist das Königreich"	Rosenhain, Jacob	6154
Nearest and Dearest	Caracciolo, Luigi	1339 1340 1341
Nearest and Dearest, Tuscan folk-song	Caracciolo, Luigi	1342
Nebel "Ich leide, müd und schwer"	Thudichum, Gustav	7881

TITLE	COMPOSER	REC#
Posle grozy [After the Thunderstorm]	Grechaninov, Alexander	2745
Poslednye tsvety [The Last Flowers]	Cui, César	1547
Postillin "Hörst du den lust'gen Postillon"	Abt, Franz	238
Postillon Frühling "Frühling ist ein Postillon"	Santner, Karl	6499
Postillon Frühling "Frühling ist ein Postillon"	Weinberger, Karl Friedrich	8207
Postillon "Postillon ist ein glücklicher Mann"	Storch, Anton M.	7574
Postillon "Postillon ist ein glücklicher Mann"	Wichern, Karoline	8334
Postknecht "Ein Postknecht [unreadable] ich werden"	Wienand, V.	8406
Pour la Fête des Mères	Schlosser, Paul	6700
Pourvoir de l'harmonie	Aerts, Felix	343
Praise Him!	Courtney, Craig	1537
Praise, My Soul, the King of Heaven	Cassler, G. Winston	1360
Praise the Savior	Cassler, G. Winston	1361
Prayer Perfect, The	Speaks, Oley	7437 7438 7439
Predestinazione	Donizetti, Gaetano	1717 1718
Premier Livre de Chansons à Deux Parties, Band 1	Anthology	64
Prênant un corps à la parole	Gounod, Charles	2673
Pres de Toi	Mendelssohn, Felix	4901
Press Thy Cheek Against Mine Own	Jensen, Adolf	3624
Pride of the Ball	Verner, H. C.	8020
Priere	Delbruck, J.	1606
Prière à la Vierge	Peellaert, Augustin de	5424
Prière et voeu	Boieldieu, François Adrien	910
Prílítlo-jaro z daleka	Bendl, Karel	682
Primavera d'Amore	Lucantoni, Giovanni	4583
Primi amori	Gordigiani, Luigi	2618
Primula veris "Liebliche Blume, bist du so früh schon"	Schreck, Gustav	6823
Primula veris "Liebliche Blume, bist du so früh schon"	Triest, Heinrich	7919
Primula veris "Liebliche Blume, Primula veris"	Schreck, Gustav	6824
Primula veris "Liebliche Blume, Primula veris"	Triest, Heinrich	7920
Printemps Breton	Favre, Georges	2080
Prinz Sisi und die Frau Mama	Frank, Ernst	2243
Prinzessin Liesel "Wie klein Liesel vornehm ist"	Weinberger, Karl Friedrich	8208
Priz Sisi und die Frau Mama	Frank, Ernst	2244
Prokoviev Vocal Works Vol II	Prokofiev, Serge	5580
Prsten [Der Ring]	Dvořák, Antonín	1840
Psalm 1 "Wohl dem, der nicht Hoffheinz"	Bischoff, Karl Jacob	794
Psalm 1 "Wohl dem, der nicht Hoffheinz"	Grell, Eduard August	2801
Psalm 13 "Herr, wie lange willst du mein sogar vergessen"	Jadassohn, Salomon	3587
Psalm 18 "Herr, Herr, wie lange willst du mein"	Jadassohn, Salomon	3588

TITLE	COMPOSER	REC#
Psalm 23 "Gott ist mein Hirt"	Reinthaler, Karl Martin	5842
Psalm 23 "Herr ist mein Hirt"	Hollaender, Alexis [Holländer]	3381
Psalm 25 "Herr zeige mir deine Wege"	Bischoff, Karl Bernard	783
Psalm 27 "Herr ist mein Licht"	Bischoff, Karl Bernard	784
Psalm 27 "Herr ist mein Licht"	Grell, Eduard August	2803
Psalm 33 "Danket dem Herrn mit Harfen"	Seyffardt, Ernst Hermann	7139
Psalm 39 "Ich will den Herren loben allezeit"	Bischoff, Karl Bernard	785
Psalm 41 "Wie der Hirsch schreit"	Grüel, E.	2841
Psalm 67 "Gott sei uns gnädig"	Wrede, Ferdinand	8699
Psalm 84 "Wie lieblich sind deine Wohnungen"	Bischoff, Karl Jacob	798
Psalm 84 "Wie lieblich sind deine Wohnungen"	Fink, Christian	2103
Psalm 84 "Wie lieblich sind deine Wohnungen"	Keycher, O.	3756
Psalm 103 "Barmherzig, gnädig ist der Herr"	Bischoff, Karl Bernard	782
Psalm 103 "Barmherzig, gnädig ist der Herr"	Seyffardt, Ernst Hermann	7136
Psalm 133 "Siehe wie fein"	Grell, Eduard August	2802
Psalm 139 "Herr du erforschest mich"	Seyffardt, Ernst Hermann	7138
Psalm "Hebe deine Augen auf zu den Bergen"	Korel, H.	3915
Psalm "Wohl dem der den Herrn fürchtet"	Mauss, A.	4757
Psalmodikon	Olson, Daniel	5332
Pschütt "Es hat nöt nur der Weaner"	Sioly, Johann	7325
Pudel ist ein treues Thier	Wanthaler, Gustav	8122
Puer Natus est Nobis	Dubois, Théodore	1787 1788
Puisqu' ici-bas tout âme	Fauré, Gabriel	2057 2058 2059 2060 2061 2062
Puissance de l'harmonie	Aerts, Felix	344
Pulaski's Banner	Lindsay, Miss M.	4480
Pupille "Pupille tenere del caro"	Banck, Karl	523
Puppe "O allerschönste Puppe mein"	Naubert, Friedrich August	5155
Puppe Wiegenlied "Eia popeia mein Püppchen schlaf ein"	Frank, Ernst	2245
Puppem-Duett "Betrachtet man die Menschengruppen"	Michaelis, Gustav	4994
Puppen Wiegenlied "Schlaf, Püppchen, schlaf"	Kleffel, Arno	3811
Puppenlieder (10)	Breu, Simon	1217
Pussy Cat Duets	Warren, Betsy	8129
Putthühnchen, wo hast du deinen Mann	Kleffel, Arno	3812
Putthühnchen, wo hast du deinen Mann	Naubert, Friedrich August	5156
Pyramidal "Primadonna kommt daher"	Fischer & Blum	2132

TITLE	COMPOSER	REC#
Schifferlied "Hinaus, hinaus in das spielende wühlende Meer"	Huth, Louis	3549
Schifferlied "Kommt herbei, frisch und frei"	Abt, Franz	247
Schifferlied "Schaukle mein Schifflein"	Abt, Franz	248
Schifferliedchen "Hinauf und hinunter"	Abt, Franz	249
Schifferliedchen "Schon hat die Nacht"	Huber, Hans	3500
Schiffers Abendlied "Gleite Kahn, gleite fröhlich"	Krebs, Karl August	3974
Schiffers Abreise	Lagoanère, Oscar de	4246
Schirmer's Favorite Sacred Duets	Anthology	85
Schirmer's Favorite Sacred Duets for Various Voices	Anthology	86
		87
		88
		89
Schlacht du brichst an	Schubert, Franz Peter	6882
Schlaf, Dornröschen , schlaf	Abt, Franz	250
Schlaf ein mein Herz	Radecke, Robert	5603
Schlaf in mein Lieb in Frieden	Witt, Leopold	8632
Schlaf, Jesulein, schlafe und träume	Raillard, Theodor	5625
Schlaf, Kindlein, schlaf	Lachner, Vincenz	4206
Schlaf mir zu verschönen	Blum, Karl Ludwig	869
Schlaf, mmein Kindelein	Wiedemann, Max	8382
Schlaf nun sanft und selig ein	Otto, A.	5349
Schlaf süss "Zu beten bin ich gegangen"	Krug, Diederich	4058
Schlaf wohl	Carulli, Gustav	1354
Schlaf wohl, du Himmelsknabe	Heinrich, Anton Philipp	3080
Schlaf wohl, du Hirtenknabe	Reimann, Heinrich	5739
Schlafe Kindlein hold und weiss	Volkmann, W.	8066
Schlafe mein Liebchen	Beauplan, A. de	601
Schlafe nur Herz	Taubert, Ernst Eduard	7642
Schlafgesang	Elssner, E.	1921
Schlaflied "Schlaf Herzens-kindchen"	Lachner, Vincenz	4207
Schlafliedchen "Horch Kind-chen, was klingst"	Lachner, Vincenz	4208
Schlaget den Reifen	Frank, Ernst	2248
Schlecht verträgliche Gesell-schaft "Ei, in einem Haus"	Winterberger, Alexander	8570
Schlehenblüth und wilde Rose	Bieber, C. [prob. Karl]	765
Schliess die Aeuglein zu	Nater, Johann	5145
Schloss am Meer "Hast du das Schloss gesehen"	Kreutzer, Konradin	3992
Schloss am Meer "Hast du das Schloss gesehen"	Wickede, Friedrich von	8351
Schlummerlied "Alles schläft in süsser Ruh"	Wienand, V.	8408
Schlummerlied der Zwerge an Schneewittchens Bettchen "Schlafe, still ruhn die Bäume"	Weber, Gustav	8171
Schlummerlied "Nacht umhüllt mit wehendem Flügel"	Hasse, Gustav	3002
Schlummerlied "Schlafe, schlaf mein Kindelein"	Pache, Joseph	5367
Schlummerlied "Still ist's im Stübchen"	Sinigaglia, Leone	7271
Schlummerlied "Wie so leis die Blätter"	Tiehsen, Otto	7891
Schlummerliedchen "Ich hauch' es in die weite Ferne"	Deprosse, Anton	1634
Schlummersehnsucht "Stern' am Himmel singen"	Salis, P.	6437
Schlummre auch du [sic]	Abt, Franz	251
Schlummre auch du [sic]	Thoma, Rudolf	7859
Schlummre Liebchen, weil's auf Erden	Häser, C.	2996
Schlummre sacht	Rennes, Catharina van	5954
Schmerz "Als der Apfel reif war"	Dvořák, Antonín	1845
Schmetterling "In den Lüften so lau"	Schletterer, Hans Michel	6681
Schmetterling ist in die Rose verliebt	Altmann, Gustav	364
Schmetterling und Biene "Wie hat mich Gott so schön"	Reinecke, Carl	5803
Schmetterling und das Kind "Mögt gern mit Gott so schön"	Reinecke, Carl	5804
Schmetterlinge "Himmels-bläue, Purpurflügel"	Banck, Karl	529
Schnaberln "O Muater mein i hätt' a Frâg"	Koschat, Thomas	3942
Schnadahüpf'l "Alle Hähne krähen, nur die"	Simon, Ernst	7243
Schnadahüpfeln "Diendl, wie freust mi Du"	Stuckenschmidt, J. H.	7596
Schnadahüpferl "Dass im Wald finsta is"	Taubert, Wilhelm	7665
Schneckenlied "Schneck, Schneck, Mäuschen"	Kleffel, Arno	3813
Schneckenliedchen "Schneck, Schneck, Mäuschen"	Naubert, Friedrich August	5157
Schnee im Märzen, Schmerz im Herzen	Dürck, J.	1803
Schnee kommt eisig geflogen	Rennes, Catharina van	5955
Schnee zerrinnt	Reichel, Adolf Heinrich Johann	5729
Schnee zerrinnt	Renner, M.	5933
Schnee zerrinnt	Schubert, Franz Peter	6883
Schnee zerrinnt, der Mai beginnt	Renner, M.	5934
Schnee zerrinnt, der Mai beginnt	Schubert, Franz Peter	6884
Schneefall "Es fällt aus luft'ger Höh'"	Thudichum, Gustav	7882
Schneeflöckchen "Schnee-flöckchen leicht und leise"	Hofmann, Heinrich Karl Johann	3348
Schneeglöcken "Es klingt ein lieblich Läuten"	Zöllner, Andreas	8792
Schneeglöcken klingen wieder	Esser, Heinrich	2006
Schneeglöcken klingen wieder	Schumann, Robert	7029
Schneeglöcken läutet den Frühling ein	Werth, Joseph	8303
Schneeglöcken "Lenz will kommen, der Winter ist aus"	Buchholz, Karl August	1285
Schneeglöcken "Lenz will kommen, der Winter ist aus"	Ehlert, C. F.	1889
Schneeglöcken "'S was doch wie ein leises"	Dietrich, Amalia	1687
Schneeglöcken "Schnee-glöcken weiss"	Wüerst, Richard Ferdinand	8718
Schneemann "Seht den Mann, o grosse Noth"	Schöbe, C.	6784

TITLE	COMPOSER	REC#
Spannung "Guten Abend mein tausiger Schatz"	*Brahms, Johannes*	1102
Spätherbst "Er kommt durch das bereifte Gras"	*Lenz, Leopold*	4376
Spätsommer "Marienfäden weisse"	*Schletterer, Hans Michel*	6686
Spatzen und die Kinder	*Heitmann, M.*	3109
Spazieren "Schönste Leben ist im Freien"	*Greith, Karl*	2781
Spazieren wollt' ich reiten	*Emmerlich, Robert*	1932
Spaziergang "Ich wollt einmal recht früh aufstehn"	*Taubert, Wilhelm*	7668
Speldewerksterslied	*Hullebroeck, Emiel*	3528
Speranza al cor mi dice	*Blangini, G. M. M. Felice*	839
Sperling "Wer weckt mich aus dem Schlummer"	*Wichern, Karoline*	8339
Sperlinge "Altes Haus mit deinen Löchern"	*Hildach, Eugen*	3215
Spiele aus der Kinderzeit "Betrachtet man das Kinderspiel"	*Eyle, W.*	2034
Spielmann und sein Kind "Sturmwind braust"	*Weidt, Heinrich*	8193
Spiesezettel-Duett "Kleine Mädchen in Pension"	*Meinhold, P.*	4798
Spinn, spinn "Mägdlein heilt Tag und Nacht"	*Feyhl, Johann*	2093
Spinn, spinn "Mägdlein heilt Tag und Nacht"	*Jüngst, Hugo*	3674
Spinnelied	*Schumann, Robert*	7052
Spinnerin "Role liebe Spindel"	*Wieniawski, Joseph*	8425
Spinnerin "Spinn, spinn meine liebe Tochter"	*Scholz, Bernard*	6799
Spinnerin "Spinn, spinn meine liebe Tochter"	*Winterberger, Alexander*	8582
Spinnerlied "Hurtig, wie die Mägdelein"	*Pache, Joseph*	5368
Spinnlied "Rädchen eile, schnurr' immer"	*Krinninger, F.*	4015
Spinnlied "Spinn, (spinn,) Mägdlein, spinn"	*Brenner, Friedrich*	1207
Spinnlied "Spinn, (spinn,) Mägdlein, spinn"	*Hamma, Benjamin*	2970
Spinnlied "Spinn, (spinn,) Mägdlein, spinn"	*Kleffel, Arno*	3816
Spinnlied "Spinn, (spinn,) Mägdlein, spinn"	*Seiffert, Karl*	7107
Spinnliedchen "Schnurr' mein Rädchen"	*Zöllner, Andreas*	8793
Spirit of the Wood	*Parker, Henry*	5413 5414
Sport über Sport ist die Losung der Zeit	*Schild, Theodor*	6603
Sprache der beglückten Liebe "In unseren Herzen wohnt die Liebe"	*Kreutzer, Konradin*	3993
Sprache der Liebe "Das ist der wahren Liebe Macht"	*Dorn, Heinrich L. E.*	1749
Sprich ja zu meinen Taten	*Herrmann, Willy*	3191
Sprichwörter-Duett "Es giebt im deutschen Vaterland"	*Thomas, N.*	7872
Spring	*Keel, James Frederick*	3729
Spring returning, The	*Concone, Giuseppi*	1481
Spring Song	*Lassen, Eduard*	4318
Spring Wind	*Thiman, Eric Harding*	7841 7842

TITLE	COMPOSER	REC#
Spröde "An dem reinsten Frühlingsmorgen"	*Hermann, E. Hans*	3174
Spruch "Dein Herz soll wie dei Quelle sein"	*Lieb, F. X.*	4424
Spruch "Gott mit mir"	*Hiller, Ferdinand*	3270
Spruch "Treue Freunde zu gewinnen"	*Baumfelder, Friedrich*	593
Spurlos "Schneeflocken schweben"	*Sieber, Ferdinand*	7192
Stabat Mater	*Mortari, Virgilio*	5089
Stadt- und Landmädchen "Herrlich ist's am frühen Morgen"	*Junghähnel, O.*	3661
Städterbua und Alnradirn "Es wâr grâd Tânz"	*Koschat, Thomas*	3944
Ständchen	*Becker, Hugo*	608
Ständchen	*Schubert, Franz Peter*	6890
Ständchen "Hüttelein still und klein"	*Beschnitt, Johannes*	754
Ständchen "Hüttelein still und klein"	*Könneritz, Nina [Georgine, neé Eschborn]*	3906
Ständchen "Hüttelein still und klein"	*Rosenhain, Jacob*	6157
Ständchen "Ich halte, Edlitam, am Fenster"	*Decker, H.*	1597
Ständchen "In dem Himmel ruht die Erde"	*Buchholz, Karl August*	1286
Ständchen "In dem Himmel ruht die Erde"	*Neukomm, Sigismund*	5203
Ständchen "In dem Himmel ruht die Erde"	*Raff, Joseph*	5615
Ständchen "In dem Himmel ruht die Erde"	*Vierling, Georg*	8029
Ständchen "Leise flehen"	*Schubert, Franz Peter*	6891
Ständchen "Leise flehen mein Lieder"	*Hoffmann, L. (F. P. Schubert)*	3339
Ständchen "Mond tritt aus der Wolkenwand"	*Hasse, Gustav*	3003
Ständchen "Morgens als Lerche möcht' ich"	*Nauwerk, E.*	5162
Ständchen "Schläfst Liebchen schon"	*Hauptmann, Moritz*	3039
Ständchen "Schliesse deine holden Augen"	*Ries, Ferdinand*	6020
Ständchen "Schummerlos rauschen die Saiten"	*Samson, L.*	6474
Ständchen [Serenade]	*Schubert, Franz Peter*	6892
Ständchen "Sorgenvolle, wetterschwüle Mädchenstirne"	*Gliniewski, W.*	2490
Ständchen "Still, sie schläft! nur leise"	*Gollmick, Karl*	2574
Ständchen "Was wecken aus dem Schlummer mich"	*Matthes, J.*	4745
Ständchen "Wenn du im Traum wirst fragen"	*Witt, Julius*	8627
Star of the East	*Kennedy*	3748
Starry Night	*Densmore, John H.*	1619
Steffel geht zum Dirndl spät	*Schmid, Joseph*	6712
Steh' auf und öffne das Fenster	*Vogel, M. [prob. Martin]*	8048
Steht auf ihr lieben Kinderlein	*Rothlauf, B.*	6215
Steht man in d' Fruah	*Freisler, C.*	2310
Steig (Steige) herauf, Tag des Herrn	*Attenhofer, Karl*	461 462
Stern der Liebe "Es zieht am blauen Himmelsbogen"	*Krebs, Karl August*	3976

TITLE	COMPOSER	REC#
Sterne blitzen am Himmel	Dorn, Otto	1760
Sterne blitzen am Himmel	Wilm, Nicolai von	8486
Sterne "Tausend goldne Sterne winken"	Boumann, Leonardus Carolus	1025
Sterne und Blumen "Sterne machte den Himmel gehn"	Hollaender, Alexis [Holländer]	3383
Sterne und Blumen "Sterne machte den Himmel gehn"	Schnabel, Karl	6756
Sterne "Wenn die Kinder schlafen ein"	Lieb, F. X.	4425
Sterne "Wie freundlich strahlt ihr Sterne"	Rungenhagen, Karl Friedrich	6366
Sternenlied "Wenn dir in's Aug'"	Hiller, Ferdinand	3271
Sternennacht "Es lächeln und nicken in's Dunkel"	Reinthaler, Karl Martin	5843
Sternennacht "Golden winkt die Sonne"	Procházka, Ludwig	5575
Sternennacht, heilige Nacht	Diercks, H.	1680 1681
Sternlein am Himmel	Abt, Franz	269
Sternlein am Himmel	Salis, P.	6439
Sternlein "Uüd die Sonne machte den weiten Ritt"	Bach, Otto	479
Sternlein "Uüd die Sonne machte den weiten Ritt"	Reinecke, Carl	5808
Sternlein "Uüd die Sonne machte den weiten Ritt"	Rennes, Catharina van	5958
Stets inniger sinn' ich dir	Blangini, G. M. M. Felice	840
Steyrer Bua "I bin a Steyrer Bua"	Walter-Kiesel, M.	8110
Steyrisches Lied "Wie tief im Herzen"	Gumbert, Ferdinand	2886
Still as the night	Böhm, Karl	894
Still is the Night	Abt, Franz	270
Still ruht der See	Abt, Franz	271
Still ruht der See	Pfeil, Heinrich	5476
Still ruht der Wald, ein heilig Schweigen	Schäfer, P.	6523
Still, still, wein' nicht so heiss	Limbert, Frank L.	4446
Still, stille, nachtumwoben schläft der Gletscher	Selmer, Johan Peter	7122
Still und friedlich ist die Nacht	Hollaender, Alexis [Holländer]	3384
Still wie die Nacht	Böhm, Karl	895
Still wie die Nacht	Goetze, Karl [Götze]	2548
Still wie die Nacht	Tschirch, Wilhelm	7942
Still wie die Nacht (Still as the Night)	Böhm, Karl	896
Still wie die Nacht, tief wie das Meer	Böhm, Karl	897
Stille	Schmidt, Gustav	6716
Stille Abendroth so weit und breit	Widmann, Benedikt	8367
Stille der Nacht	Girschner, Karl Friedrich Julius	2478
Stille "Es weiss und räth es doch Keiner"	Hauser, Moritz H.	3053
Stille "Es weiss und räth es doch Keiner"	Henschel, George	3149
Stille "Es weiss und räth es doch Keiner"	Leonhard, Julius Emil	4390
Stille "Es weiss und räth es doch Keiner"	Schläger, Hans	6635
Stille Liebe "Meeresrauschen, sonn'ger Himmel"	Fitzenhagen, W. Karl Friedrich	2151
Stille Liebe "Rose sage, warum blühest du"	Christiani, E.	1420
Stille, liebe Seele, stille	Groskopf, A.	2823
Stille Nacht, heilige Nacht	Bank, G.	538
Stille Nacht, heilige Nacht	Breitung, F.	1199
Stille Nacht, heilige Nacht	Lander, Josef	4268
Stille Nacht, heilige Nacht	Leitner, Karl August	4360
Stille Nacht, heilige Nacht	Michaelis, Ad. Alfred	4990
Stille Nacht, heilige Nacht	Niemann, Gustav	5276
Stille Nacht, heilige Nacht	Wagner, Ernst David	8088
Stille Nacht, heilige Nacht	Wiedemann, Max	8383
Stille Stunden "Wo kann der Geist sich heben"	Wienand, V.	8410
Stille Thal "Im schönsten Wiesengrunde"	Franke, Hermann	2283
Stille Thal "Im schönsten Wiesengrunde"	Weiss, Laurenz	8243
Stille Wasserrose steigt aus dem blauen See	Abt, Franz	272
Stille "Wiege mich ein, du Mutter alles Trostes"	Radecke, Robert	5604
Stilles Glück "Unter den Aehren"	Schletterer, Hans Michel	6687
Stimmen aus dem Publikum "Es ist die Gasbeleuchtung"	Sioly, Johann	7333
Stimmen der Elfen "3 Duette"	Loewe, Karl Gottfried	4517
Stimmen der Nacht "Nächtlich wandern alle Flüsse"	Sulzbach, Emil	7614
Stimmen des Trostes "Ihr Alle, die ein hart Geschick"	Concone, Giuseppi	1480
Stockfisch "Grüss Gott, Frau Hein"	Schäffer, August	6545
Stolzer Schwan, wie ziehst du leise	Reinecke, Carl	5809
Störche "Ihr lieben Störche"	Schöbe, C.	6785
Storchs Ankunft "Sieh' der Storch"	Greith, Karl	2782
Stornelli	Oddone, Elisabetta	5324
Störung in der Andacht "Seh ich dich mein holdes Mädchen"	Winterberger, Alexander	8583
Story of cruel Frederick, The	Hughes, Herbert	3505
Story of Fidgety Philip, The	Hughes, Herbert	3506
Strahlend im Schmucke des Lenzes "Passegiata"	Teichmann, A. or O.	7792
Strains from Moravia, Book 1, Op. 32a	Dvořák, Antonín	1852
Strains from Moravia, Book 2, Op. 32b	Dvořák, Antonín	1853
Strampelchen "Still, wie still, 's ist Mitternacht"	Naubert, Friedrich August	5158
Stranger of Galilee, The	Morris, C. H.	5087
Strassenbahn, Strassenbahn	Eisersdorf, A.	1909
Strassenbilder, Ponoroma von Berlin	Thomas, N.	7873
Strauch erzittert	Hornstein, Robert von	3484
Strauss, den ich gepflücket	Curschmann, Karl Friedrich	1556
Streik-Couplet "Täglich hört man nur con Streiken"	Lier, E.	4440
Strickerinnen "Euch zur Arbeit auszuschicken"	Weiss, Laurenz	8244

TITLE	COMPOSER	REC#
Tanzenden Mädchen "O Tanz, du Lieblicher"	Marschner, Heinrich August	4683
Tanzlied der Fliegen "Summ summ summ"	Reinecke, Carl	5810
Tanzlied der Kinder "O Sommerlust bei Finkenschlag"	Lassen, Eduard	4319
Tanzlied der Mücken "Frisch ihr Blumen und Halme"	Fink, Christian	2104
Tanzlied der Mücken "Frisch ihr Blumen und Halme"	Hülle, W.	3522
Tanzlied "Eia, wie flattert der Kranz"	Lachner, Franz	4191
Tanzlied "Es tanzet die helle krystallene Welle"	Reinecke, Carl	5811
Tanzlied im Mai "Zum Reigen herbei"	Riedel, August	6010
Tanzlied im Mai "Zum Reigen herbei"	Wienand, V.	8411
Tanzlied "Schmückt euch, ihr Mädchen"	Reinecke, Carl	5812
Tanzlied "Tanz', Kindlein tanz'"	Lachner, Vincenz	4209
Tanzlied "Wie wir zum Tanz"	Wolff, Gustav Tyson [also Tyson-Wolff]	8651
Tanzliedchen "Lasst uns jetztspringen"	Ernemann, M.	1968
Tanzliedchen "Lasst uns tanzen, lasst uns springen"	Thoma, Rudolf	7861
Tanzliedchen "Männlein, Männlein ging einmal"	Winterberger, Alexander	8585
Tanzliedchen "Ringel, Ringel, Rosenkranz"	Dorn, Heinrich L. E.	1750
Tanzliedchen "Ringel, Ringel, Rosenkranz"	Eschmann, Johann Karl	1980
Tanzlieder "Cyclus"	Hoppe, Paul	3454
Tanzstunden-Erinneringen "Hum. Duoscene"	Simon, Ernst	7246
Tanzweisen in Länderform (5)	Umlauft, Paul	7959
Täppele "Und der Kerschbaum treibt Popezlan"	Koschat, Thomas	3945
Tarentelle	Fauré, Gabriel	2063
		2064
		2065
		2066
		2067
Tarititium "Stets elegant und fein"	Fischer & Blum	2135
Täubchen "Täubchen mein, o Täubchen klein"	Wickenhauser, Richard	8357
Täubchen "Wo bist du umher geschweift"	Winterberger, Alexander	8586
Taube "Pflegt ein artig' schönes Mädchen"	Noskowski, Zygmund	5304
Tauben	Righini, Vincenzo	6028
Taubenflug "Tauben im Flug"	Blaesing, Felix	810
Taubenhaus "Bauer hat ein Taubenhaus"	Abt, Franz	276
Täublein "Dort oben auf dem Berfe, da steht ein hohes Haus"	Schubert, Franz Ludwig	6847
Tausend Grüsse, die wir dir senden	Jadassohn, Salomon	3590
Tausend Sternlein in der Nacht	Roscher, Josef	6136
Te 'l rammenti	Campana, Fabio	1333
		1334
Tears	Tchaikovsky, Peter Ilyich	7710

TITLE	COMPOSER	REC#
Teasing song	Goatley, Alma	2525
Telephon "Wenn man heutzutage"	Schirmer, A.	6627
Tell me, where do fairies dwell?	Glover, Stephen	2511
Tell me, where is beauty found?	Glover, Stephen	2512
Tell us merry birds	White	8316
Tell us, oh tell us	Glover, Stephen	2513
Tell us, Oh Tell us, Where Shall we Find	Glover, Stephen	2514
Temporale	Gordigiani, Luigi	2622
Teneri affetti il cor s'abbandoni	Franz, Robert (G. F. Handel)	2303
Thal ist wintertraurig rings	Brandt-Caspari, Alfred	1174
Thanks be to God	Dickson, Stanley	1662
Thau der Nacht liegt und auf den Wiesen	Horn, E.	3471
Thautropfen "Morgen lächelt in seliger Ruh"	Reinecke, Carl	5813
Theatralischen Hausknechte "Stiefel putzen, Kleider bürsten"	Junghähnel, O.	3662
Theorie und Praxis "Mein lieber Gevatter Bullerich"	Schäffer, August	6547
There is a Reaper	Pinsuti, Ciro	5502
		5503
There was joy in Heaven	Smart, Henry	7389
There were Shepherds	Foster, Myles Birket	2172
There's no one in the world like you	Carse, Roland	1352
Theuren Zeiten "Frau Gevatter, Frau Gevatter"	Kuntze, Karl	4162
They shall hunger no more	Gaul, Alfred Robert	2437
Thirteen Moravian Duets	Dvořák, Antonín	1854
Thirty-Eight Modern Canons	Anthology	101
This is the day	Carey, Harry	1350
Thräne "Aus dem Wald im Schatten"	Dvořák, Antonín	1855
Thräne und Lied "Thräne perlt aus weichem Herzen"	Wilhelm, Karl Friedrich	8462
Thräne "Wohl was es eine Seligkeit"	Witt, Julius	8628
Thränen "Thränen der Menscheit"	Tchaikovsky, Peter Ilyich	7711
Three Canzonets on Love	Carter, John	1353
Three Christmas Carols	Edmunds, John	1882
Three Duets	Brahms, Johannes	1103
Three Duets	Henschel, George	3150
		3151
		3152
Three Duets	Reger, Max	5700
Three Duets Op. 20	Brahms, Johannes	1104
Three Duets Op. 20	Brahms, Johannes	1105
		1106
Three fishers, The	Foster, Myles Birket	2171
Three Hopkinson Songs	Edwards, George	1884
		1885
Through the Gates of Gold	Hart, M. A.	2984
Thrush, The	Sharpe, Evelyn	7142
Thu' nichts Böses, thu' es nicht	Reissiger, Karl Gottlieb	5894
Thurmelfen "Unter Schleier des Geheimen"	Loewe, Karl Gottfried	4518
Thusnelda und Elvira "Wie herrlich, wie fein"	Kipper, Hermann	3770
Thut auch das bange Herz dir weh	Bünte, Wilhelm	1292

TITLE	COMPOSER	REC#
Waldkappele "Wo tief im Tannengründe"	*Schletterer, Hans Michel*	6693
Waldkirche "Wenn zum grünen Waldesgrunde"	*Abt, Franz*	296
Waldkirchlein "Es steht ein Kirchlein im grünen Wald"	*Koch, August*	3865
Waldklänge "3 Duette"	*Liebe, Eduard Ludwig*	4437
Waldleben "Wer recht in Freiheit leben will"	*Salinger, J.*	6423
Waldliebe "Fort, nur fort"	*Randhartinger, Benedict*	5662
Waldlied	*Rubinstein, Anton*	6292
Waldlied "Der Nachtwind hat in den Bäumen"	*Rubinstein, Anton*	6293
Waldlied "Im Walde geh' ich wohlgemuth"	*Krinninger, F.*	4016
Waldlied "Im Walde möcht' ich leben"	*Ernemann, E.*	1960
Waldlied "Im Walde möcht' ich leben"	*Hasse, Gustav*	3005
Waldlied "Im Walde möcht' ich leben"	*Taubert, Wilhelm*	7673
Waldlied "Im Walde möcht' ich leben"	*Wienand, V.*	8417
Waldlied "In den Wald, in den stillen, grünen Wald"	*Reissiger, Karl Gottlieb*	5898
Waldlied "Nachtwind hat in den Bäumen"	*Rosenberg, Wilhelm [Vilhelm]*	6142
Waldlied "Nachtwind hat in den Bäumen"	*Rubinstein, Nicolai*	6308
Waldlied "Waldnacht Jagdlust"	*Lammers, Julius*	4263
Waldlied "Wenn ich geh' im grünen Walde"	*Nessler, Victor E.*	5187
Waldlied "Wo Büsche steh'n und Bäume"	*Pivoda, F.*	5512
Waldlied "Wo das Echo schallt"	*Engel, David Hermann*	1941
Waldlieder (3)	*Dorn, Otto*	1761
Waldlust "Wald, der grüne Wald"	*Höller, C.*	3427
Waldlust "Wie herrlich ist's im Walde"	*Abt, Franz*	297
Waldlust "Wie herrlich ist's im Walde"	*Greith, Karl*	2785
Waldlust "Wie herrlich ist's im Walde"	*Hennig, C. [prob. Karl Rafael]*	3128
Waldmorgen "Es ist so still die Maiennacht"	*Schletterer, Hans Michel*	6694
Waldnacht "Schnurre, schnurre Miesekätzchen"	*Sieber, Ferdinand*	7194
Waldrose "Im Wald bei grünen Bäumen"	*Engel, David Hermann*	1942
Waldsehnsucht "Blauer Himmel, laue Lüfte"	*Liebe, Eduard Ludwig*	4438
Waldvögelein "Ich geh' mit Lust durch diesen grünen"	*Wilhelm, Karl Friedrich*	8471
Waldvögelein "Wie lieblich ist's im Wald"	*Thoma, Rudolf*	7862
Waldvöglein Sang	*Leonhard, Julius Emil*	4391
Waldvöglein Sang "Im grünen Laub so dicht und traut"	*Reissiger, Karl Gottlieb*	5899
Waldvöglein "Vöglein hat ein schönes Loos"	*Rohde, Eduard*	6106
Waldvöglein "Vöglein hat ein schönes Loos"	*Stern, S.*	7543
Waldwünsche "In dem Walde möcht'ich leben"	*Liebe, Eduard Ludwig*	4439
Walk at sunset, The	*Fiori, Ettore*	2115
Wallend geht das Aehrenfeld	*Hummel, Ferdinand*	3538
Wallfahrtslied "Wir wandern über Berg und Thal"	*Esser, Heinrich*	2012
Wallfahrtslied "Wir wandern über Berg und Thal"	*Kleffel, Arno*	3820
Wallfahrtslied "Wir wandern über Berg und Thal"	*Raff, Joseph*	5618
Wallisische Lieder	*Beethoven, Ludwig van*	649
Walpurgisnacht	*Brahms, Johannes*	1109
Walpurgisnacht "Lieb' Mutter heut Nacht"	*Brahms, Johannes*	1110
Walt' Gott "Hast viel gespielt"	*Zerlett, Johann Baptist*	8772
Wälze weiter deine Wogen	*Schmitt, Georg Aloys*	6750
Walzer "Vien m'abbraccia"	*Troschel, Wilhelm Troszel*	7924
Wandeln Glocke "Es war ein Kind, das wollte nicht"	*Wichern, Karoline*	8341
Wanderer in der Sägemühle "Dort unten in der Mühle"	*Wienand, V.*	8418
Wanderer "Mai ist auf dem Wege"	*Kündig, Felix*	4152
Wanderer's Evensong, The	*Rubinstein, Anton*	6294
Wanderers Nachtlied	*Goltermann, Georg*	2591
Wanderers Nachtlied	*Rubinstein, Anton*	6295 6299 6300 6301
Wanderer's Night Song	*Rubinstein, Anton*	6296 6297
Wanderer's Night Song [Wanderers Nachtlied]	*Rubinstein, Anton*	6298
Wanderers Abendlied "Die ihr mit dem Oden"	*Pivoda, F.*	5513
Wanderers Abschiedslied am Abend "Traute Heimath ich muss scheiden"	*Wenzel, H.*	8279
Wanderers Nachtlied "Aller Berge Gipfel ruhn"	*Rubinstein, Anton*	6302 6303
Wanderers Nachtlied "Der der von dem Himmel bist"	*Frank, Ernst*	2256
Wanderers Nachtlied "Der der von dem Himmel bist"	*Nauwerk, E.*	5163
Wanderers Nachtlied "Der der von dem Himmel bist"	*Wolff, Leonhard*	8658
Wanderers Nachtlied "Über allen Gipfeln (Wipfeln) ist Ruh"	*Frank, Ernst*	2257
Wanderers Nachtlied "Über allen Gipfeln (Wipfeln) ist Ruh"	*Glück, August*	2524
Wanderers Nachtlied "Über allen Gipfeln (Wipfeln) ist Ruh"	*Hinrichs, Friedrich*	3307
Wanderers Nachtlied "Über allen Gipfeln (Wipfeln) ist Ruh"	*Jadassohn, Salomon*	3595
Wanderers Nachtlied "Über allen Gipfeln (Wipfeln) ist Ruh"	*Pierson, Henry Hugh*	5491
Wanderers Nachtlied "Über allen Gipfeln (Wipfeln) ist Ruh"	*Reger, Max*	5703
Wanderers Nachtlied "Über allen Gipfeln (Wipfeln) ist Ruh"	*Rungenhagen, Karl Friedrich*	6369
Wanderers Nachtlied "Über allen Gipfeln (Wipfeln) ist Ruh"	*Wieniawski, Joseph*	8428
Wanderlied "Auf schwankem Ast"	*Leonhard, Julius Emil*	4392

TITLE	COMPOSER	REC#
Wanderlied "Ich gehe durch einen grasgrünen Wald"	Brenner, Friedrich	1209
Wanderlied "Ihr lieben Lerchen guten Tag"	Bruch, Max	1260
Wanderlied "Lerche singt ihr Morgenlied"	Reich, Reinhold	5718
Wanderlied "Liebe Sonne strahlt so rein"	Abt, Franz	298
Wanderlied "Vögel singen, Blumen blüh'n"	Esser, Heinrich	2013
Wanderlied "Vögel singen, Blumen blüh'n"	Reinecke, Carl	5821
Wanderlied "Vögel singen, Blumen blüh'n"	Stiehl, Karl	7557
Wanderlied "Vögel singen, Blumen blüh'n"	Tuma, A.	7949
Wanderlied "War lange nun bei euch"	Abt, Franz	299
Wanderlied "Wem Gott will rechte Gunst erweisen"	André, Jean Baptiste	376
Wanderlied "Wie gut der Liebe Gott es meint"	Deprosse, Anton	1637
Wanderlied "Wie scheint mir die Sonne"	Abt, Franz	300
Wanderlied "Wohlauf noch getrunken"	Greith, Karl	2786
Wanderlust "Biene, der Käfer, der Schmetterling"	Schläger, Hans	6637
Wanderlust "Es ziehn nach fernen Landen"	Abt, Franz	301
Wanderlust "Es ziehn nach fernen Landen"	Höller, C.	3428
Wanderlust "Frühling kommt"	Abt, Franz	302
Wanderlust "Heraus, heraus, der Vögel Chor"	Schletterer, Hans Michel	6695
Wanderlust "Heraus, heraus, der Vögel Chor"	Tauwitz, Eduard	7684
Wanderlust "Lenz beginnt"	Köllner, Eduard	3896
Wanderlust "Nun blüh'n die Rosen im Thal"	Brunner, Ed.	1282
Wanderlust "O Wanderglück, O Wanderlust"	Deprosse, Anton	1638
Wanderlust "O Wanderglück, O Wanderlust"	Plengorth, Fr.	5527
Wanderlust "O Wanderlust, o Wanderlust"	Weischer, Th.	8228
Wanderlust "Wanderlust, das ist das höchste Glück"	Abt, Franz	303
Wanderlust "Wanderlust, das ist das höchste Glück"	Mahlberg, C.	4630
Wandern bringt wohl die grösste Freud'	Kühle, G.	4119
Wandern im Frühling "Das ist ein frohes Wandern"	Brede, Albrecht	1191
Wandern, wandern, immer wandern	Frenkel-Norden, R.	2316
Wandernden Lieder "Fallen im Herbst die Blätter"	Ernemann, E.	1961
Wanderrast "Hier ruht sich's gut"	Huber, Hans	3502
Wanderschaft "Wandern ist des Müllers Lust"	Hülle, W.	3523
Wandersmann und Lerche "Lerche, wie früh' schon"	Döring, Carl Heinrich	1728
Wandersmann und Lerche "Lerche, wie früh' schon"	Schöbe, C.	6788
Wandertreue "Wenn Schneeglöckchen läuten"	Nessler, Victor E.	5188
Wandervöglein "Wandervöglein leichtes Blut"	Holstein, Franz von	3446
Wann a and'rer Mensch a Unglück hat, wie kann ma denn da lachen "Es fahrt der magre Bräutigam"	Sioly, Johann	7336
Wann der Auerhahn baltz "Wann der Mondschein schön scheint"	Schild, Theodor	6606
Wann die kleinen Kinder beten	Ansorge, M. [prob. Margarethe]	412
Wann i auf'n Kalenberg steh'	Gruber, L.	2836
Wann i so in der Fruah aufsteh'	Fiebrich, F. P.	2097
Wann ma dö net hätt'n "Wann a Weana stirbt"	Schmitter, C.	6751
Wann ma nach Mitternacht	Lorens, Karl	4553
Wann wir den alten Steffel sehn	Schild, Theodor	6607
Wär' Alles nur ein Traum "Wenn man so sitzt"	Thoma, Rudolf	7863
Wär' ich ein Vögelein	Jadassohn, Salomon	3596 3597
Wär' ich ein Vögelein	Lammers, Julius	4264
Wär' ich. Geliebte, der Blumen Wonne	Nauwerk, E.	5164
Wär' ich nie aus euch gegangen	Birn, M.	777
Waren drei Knäblein zart und fein	Boruttau, Alfred J.	1015
Wärst du mein "So wie die liebe Sonne"	Meinardus, Ludwig	4794
Wart i sag's mein grosser Bruader "Wann die Buam"	Sioly-Weisberg	7357
Wart', ich zeig' dir's, wilder Mann	Fromm, Karl Josef	2352
Wart', Vögelin, wärt'	Unger, A.	7967
Warum duften die Levkojen	Perger, Richard von	5435
Warum "Es verwelken die lieblichsten Kränze"	Jansen, F. Gustav	3609
Warum hat mancher Sänger	Fink, R.	2113
Warum "Himmel ist so leicht und rein"	Düringer, Ph. J.	1804
Warum öffnet du wieder	Schubert, Franz Peter	6896
Warum sinid die Rosen so blass	Wichmann, Hermann	8349
Was an fleissiger Mann an Vormittag alles ausrichten kann "Tischler X, der hat arbeit fast nie"	Sioly, Johann	7337
Was der Frühling ist "Frühling ist ein tapfrer"	Hiller, Ferdinand	3278
Was der Jugend frommt (6)	Nater, Johann	5146
Wâs der Stöfel wer'n will "Geh', Stöfel, geh"	Koschat, Thomas	3948
Was die Thiere alles lernen "Enten lernen schnattern"	Dorn, Heinrich L. E.	1752
Was die Thiere alles lernen "Enten lernen schnattern"	Schubert, Franz Ludwig	6849
Was duftet da für Duft	Nöroth, J.	5294
Was eilst du so	Wagenbrenner, Josef	8082
Was fahlt dir, liab's Schâtzerle	Koschat, Thomas	3949
Was fang' ich an "Ach wo ich gerne bin"	Wilhelm, Karl Friedrich	8472
Was hat er g'sagt, wia hat er g'sagt "'S stenn vor der Lotterie"	Sioly, Johann	7338

TITLE	COMPOSER	REC#
Wie der Lerche "Wie die Lerche möcht ich singen"	Mahlberg, C.	4632
Wie der Tag mir schleicht	Nicolai, Otto	5261
Wie der Tag mir schleicht	Wolff, C.	8644
Wie ein Junker deutsch reden lernte "Kam aus Frankreich jüngst"	Weinberger, Karl Friedrich	8212
Wie ein kleines Spatzenpaar	Knopf, Martin	3861
Wie eine Mutter lieb' ich dich	Selmer, Johan Peter	7123
Wie es in der Mühle aussicht "Eins, zwei, drei, bicke, backe, bei"	Reinecke, Carl	5831
Wie es in der Mühle aussieht "eins, zwei, drei"	Reinecke, Carl	5832
Wie geheimes Flüstern	Fricke, Richard	2336
Wie geschmiert "Es ist ein eignes Ding"	Weissbach, M. L.	8259
Wie Gott mich führt, so will ich geh'n	Riemenschneider, Georg	6013
Wie hat die Nacht	Dietrich, Amalia	1689
Wie hat sich alles anders jetzt gestaltet	Winterling, W.	8619
Wie herrlich ist's im Maien	Schiedel, P.	6566
Wie ist der Abend so traulich	Diercks, H.	1682
Wie ist der Abend so traulich	Stieber, P.	7553
Wie ist der Himmel doch so blau	Stieber, P.	7554
Wie ist die Nacht	Hartog, Edouard de	2995
Wie ist doch die Erde so schön	Abt, Franz	312
Wie ist doch die Erde so schön	Buchholz, Karl August	1287
Wie ist doch die Erde so schön	Doebber, Johannes	1700
Wie ist doch die Erde so schön	Hill, Wilhelm	3227
Wie ist doch die Erde so schön	Hülle, W.	3524
Wie ist doch die Erde so schön	Kleffel, Arno	3822
Wie ist doch die Erde so schön	Reinecke, Carl	5833
Wie ist doch die Erde so schön	Reissiger, Friedrich August	5858
Wie ist doch die Erde so schön	Weber, Franz	8158
Wie ist doch die Erde so schön	Wienand, V.	8420
Wie ist doch die Welt so schön	Rödger, Emil	6075
Wie ist doch hier auf Erden	Wardini, Gebr.	8128
Wie ist so schön "Wohl ist sie schön"	Brambach, Kaspar Joseph	1154
Wie ist so schön "Wohl ist sie schön"	Freudenberg, Wilhelm	2325
Wie ist's auf Bergen doch so schön	Schneeberger, Ferdinand	6765
Wie kann ich froh und lustig sein	Mendelssohn, Felix	4920 4921 4922 4923
Wie klang doch einst naiv und bieder	Hollaender, Viktor	3420
Wie könnt' ich dein vergessen!	Schletterer, Hans Michel	6696
Wie kurz ist doch der Winter	Masini, Francesco	4726
Wie Lerchenjubel und Finkenschlag	Simon, Ernst	7261
Wie lieb du mir im Herzen bist "Ich möchte dir so gerne sagen"	Lenz, Leopold	4377
Wie lieblich o Herr	Sering, Friedrich Wilhelm	7129
Wie lieblich sind deine Wohnungen	Fink, Christian	2105
Wie oft hab' ich durchgangen	Brandt-Caspari, Alfred	1175
Wie plagt der Mensch sich heute doch	Teich, Otto	7779
Wie reizend, wie wonnig	Bosen, Franz	1017
Wie reizend, wie wonnig	Kosch, A.	3917
Wie schön bist du mein Vaterland "Auf die Höhen möcht' ich steigen"	Franke, Hermann	2287
Wie schön, dass ich dich wieder sehe	Kron, Louis	4044 4045
Wie schön geht sich's zu Zweien	Lazarus, Gustav	4328
Wie schön und lieblich	Blangini, G. M. M. Felice	845
Wie schön war's doch in früher'n Jahren	Gruber, L.	2840
Wie singt die Lerche schön	Esser, Heinrich	2014
Wie singt die Lerche so schön	Degele, Eugen	1603
Wie so, ach so, aha, na ja "Jetzt singe ich mal"	Ascher, E.	440
Wie so still, nur der Wipfel sanftes Rauschen	Parlow, Edmund	5416
Wie stolz er geht	Ansorge, M. [prob. Margarethe]	414
Wie Sturmnacht zog unsre Wonne vorbei	Fleck, Fritz	2155
Wie süsse Märchenweisen	Simon, Ernst	7262
Wie tönt an Frühlingstagen	Hummel, Ferdinand	3539
Wie weich die Lüfte wallen	Abt, Franz	313
Wie wird mir denn so weh	Rischbieter, Wilhelm Albert	6063
Wie wundersam "Wie wundersam ist das Verlorengeh'n"	Erlanger, Gustav	1952
Wie's uns Zwa da anschau'n	Schild, Theodor	6610
Wie's uns Zwa seg'n	Hornig, J.	3479
Wiedersehn "Das i gar nix mehr gehört hab"	Reinecke, Carl	5834
Wiedersehn "Gott grüsse dich"	Schneeberger, Ferdinand	6766
Wiedersehn "O weine nicht, wenn aus"	Marschner, Heinrich August	4685
Wiedersehn, Wiederfinden "Wiedersehn, Herzensglaube"	Reissiger, Karl Gottlieb	5901
Wiedersehn "Wiedersehn, du schönes"	Hiller, Ferdinand	3282
Wiedersehn "Wiedersehn, Wort des Trostes"	Drobisch, Karl Ludwig	1786
Wiegenlied	Brahms, Johannes	1115 1116
Wiegenlied	Girschner, Karl Friedrich Julius	2480
Wiegenlied	Haas, Joseph	2921
Wiegenlied	Humperdinck, Engelbert	3542
Wiegenlied	Schubert, Franz Peter	6899
Wiegenlied achte will's dämmern	Tauwitz, Eduard	7685
Wiegenlied "Aeren nur noch nicken"	Bischoff, Karl Jacob	800
Wiegenlied "Aeren nur noch nicken"	Lichner, Heinrich	4420
Wiegenlied "Aeren nur noch nicken"	Nauwerk, E.	5165
Wiegenlied "Aeren nur noch nicken"	Scholz, Bernard	6803

TITLE	COMPOSER	REC#
Zum Glück von zwei Welten	Rinck, Johann Christian Heinrich	6052
Zum Heurig'n fahr'n ma alle	Freisler, C.	2311
Zum Nachtmahl is's uns z'weni, zu der Zausen is's uns z'viel "A recht a keckes Wecken"	Sioly, Johann	7347
Zum neuen Jahr "Wie heimlicher Weise"	Raff, Joseph	5620
Zum Reformationsfest "Ich schäme mich"	Grell, Eduard August	2811
Zum Reien "Es grünet die Haide"	Schmidt, O.	6737
Zum Stelldichein "Dat du mein Leevsten bist"	Winterberger, Alexander	8608
Zum Wald, zum Wald steht nur mein Sinn	Bruch, Max	1261
Zur Ehre Gottes dienen soll	Böttcher, E.	1019
Zur Geburtstagsfeier des Kaisers "Heil Kaiser Wilhelm"	Wilhelm, Karl Friedrich	8475
Zur Hochzeit "Auf, Auf, begrüsst den festlich"	Ledermann, Wilhelm	4340
Zur Kirmes "Horch, wie die Eiche tönt"	Dorn, Heinrich L. E.	1753
Zur Krippe nach Bethlehem	Engelsberg, E. S.	1946
Zur Nacht "Gute Nacht, allen Müden seis gebracht"	Bading, P.	484
Zur Nacht "Gute Nacht, allen Müden seis gebracht"	Vogel, M. [prob. Martin]	8052
Zur Nacht "Lind wallt die Nacht hernieder"	Heuser, Ernst	3204
Zur schönen guten Nacht	Emmerlich, Robert	1935
Zuversicht "Grüne, grüne liebes Gras"	Dvořák, Antonín	1870
Zuversicht "Lerche jubelt mit Gesang"	Kittl, Johann Friedrich	3796
Zuversicht "Wohlauf, es ruft der Sonnenschein"	Thiele, Eduard	7803
Zviretnik	Jirasek, Ivo	3628
Zviretnik "Der Tierkreis"	Jirasek, Ivo	3629
Zwa Lugenschippeln "Du hörst mei lieber Freund"	Rosenzweig, Wilhelm	6175
Zwâ Sterndlan "Zwâ Sterndlan am Himmel"	André, L. [prob. Christian Karl André]	396
Zwâ Sterndlan "Zwâ Sterndlan am Himmel"	Kainer, C.	3694
Zwa Vegetarianer "I bitt, schau'ns uns Zwa nur an"	Leukauf, Richard	4403
Zwa von Nummero vier "I und du von Numme vier"	Neidhardt, August	5173
Zwa Weaner Pflastertreter "Weil für zwa Wiener Kinder"	Sioly, Johann	7348
Zwei alte Jungfern "Was wir vor zwanzig Jahr'n"	Heinlein, A.	3079
Zwei Basen "Ei was seh' ich"	Hinze, R.	3308
Zwei Busserln "Bäurin guckt vom Thorweg aus"	Röhricht, Paul	6121
Zwei Commis "Immer fein nach neu'ster Mode"	Maikowski, M.	4637
	Teich, Otto	7787
Zwei fidele Frösche "Uns Frösche kennt ein jeder Mann"		
Zwei fidele Schützenbrüder "Mensch hast du Geist"	Falkner, H.	2044
Zwei Fleissige Maurer "Na Lehmann, bist du ooch schon hier"	Junghähnel, O.	3668
Zwei Freunde woll'n nach Hause wandern	Francke, W.	2208
Zwei glückliche Tage "Wir sind zwei lustige Gesell'n"	Wolff, W.	8671
Zwei Gräber "Ich bin so schwach"	Gordigiani, Luigi	2627
Zwei Hände wollen heute sich	Haine, C.	2945
Zwei Hausfrauen "Ei schönen guten Morgen"	Genée, Richard Franz Friedrich	2454
Zwei heirathslustige Damen "Hum. Duoscene"	Winter, E.	8515
Zwei kleine Mädchen mit 'nem Hängezopf	Knopf, Martin	3863
Zwei kleine Mädels mit 'nem Hängezopf	Knopf, Martin	3864
Zwei kreuzfidele Leut "Wenn uns einmal der Kummer drückt"	Helbig, W.	3114
Zwei Mädchen und kein Mann "Wir armen, armen Mädchen"	Baselt, Friedrich Gustav Otto	557
Zwei Mägdlein "Algiso, der mich liebt"	Gordigiani, Luigi	2628
Zwei Mode-Fexen "Als wir die Welt erblickten"	Teich, Otto	7788
Zwei Nachtigallen sangen in einem Gartenraum	Hackel, Anton	2929
Zwei ord'ntliche Leut "So zwa wie mir zwa"	Hartl, Ph.	2985
Zwei ord'ntliche Leut "So zwa wie mir zwa"	Säuberlich, C.	6514
Zwei Original-Negel-Gigerl "Zwei elegante Bengel"	Weissbach, M. L.	8261
Zwei Pappelkronen neigen sich	Leydecker, A.	4414
Zwei philosophische Schusterjungen "Ach wie ist das Leben schön"	Teich, Otto	7789
Zwei Radsport-Gigerl "Wie sie uns Beide"	Winter, E.	8516
Zwei Rauscher "Morgens wann ich fröh opstann"	Franz, W.	2307
Zwei Reichsfechtmeister vom reinsten Wasser "Wir Beide sind Fechter"	Ehrlich, Alfred Heinrich	1895
Zwei Reigen "Ein Cherub schritt das Thal empor"	Scholz, Bernard	6804
Zwei Rosen	Lieb, F. X.	4426
Zwei Rosen "Kein Sternlein blinkt am Himmelszelt"	Hiller, Ferdinand	3285
Zwei Rosen "Kein Sternlein blinkt am Himmelszelt"	Hiller, Ferdinand	3286
Zwei steinalte Jungfern	Peter, G.	5459
Zwei Sterne "Edle Musike, ach wie dumm"	Kipper, Hermann	3772
Zwei strenge Wächter des Gesetzes	Spahn, Adolf	7434
Zwei Träume	Proch, Heinrich	5571
Zwei Vöglein fliegen von dem Strauch	Kücken, Friedrich Wilhelm	4102
Zwei von der sel'gen Bürgerwehr "Duett-Scene"	Thiele, Richard	7814
Zwei Wahlmänner "Herr Flink, ich grüsse schön"	Schäffer, August	6551
Zwei Wasser "Ach Elslein lieb'"	Hiller, Ferdinand	3287
Zwei Weibchen froh und heiter	Wolff, W.	8672
Zwei welke Rosen träumen im Sande	Abt, Franz	321

About the Author

Marilyn S. M. Newman is a mezzo soprano who specializes in recital literature and oratorio, performing widely in New England and New York. She is the lower voice in *Duetto Cantabile*, a soprano-mezzo soprano ensemble that performs a variety of vocal music for two voices. Collecting duet literature has been a major part of creating programs for the ensemble for a number of years, and has led to the development of this book.

She is a graduate of Southern Connecticut State University, where she was formerly on the music faculty, the Hartt School (University of Hartford), and received her Doctorate from Teachers College, Columbia University. Prior to committing her life to performing and teaching music, she worked in biological research.

Dr. Newman is a music educator, an elementary school music teacher, choral director, and the coordinator, program developer, and presenter of the *Kids' Concert Connection*, an interactive and presentational educationally based music project for elementary school children sponsored by United Church on the Green, in New Haven, CT.

Dr. Newman and her husband, pianist Norman Hall, reside in Fairfield, CT.